THE BIRTH & EVOLUTION OF SCIENCE

**How *Cooperation and Clash*
Among Civilizations
Determined
Who Gave Birth to It and
How Fair Exchange, Greed, and Creed
Determined Its Evolution**

*Until the lions have their own historians,
the history of the hunt will always glorify the hunter.*

—*African proverb*

THE BIRTH & EVOLUTION OF SCIENCE

How *Cooperation and Clash*
Among Civilizations
Determined
Who Gave Birth to It and
How Fair Exchange, Greed, and Creed
Determined Its Evolution

B. BANSAL, PH.D.

The Birth and Evolution of Science

Copyright © 2014 B. Bansal

All rights reserved.

Editing: Michelle Horn
Layout: Debbi Stocco

All rights reserved. No portion of this publication may be reproduced or utilized in any form or by any means, electronic or mechanical, including photocopying, without permission in writing from the publisher. In all cases, the editors and writers have made efforts to ensure that the text credits are given to appropriate people and organizations. If any infringement has been made, B. Bansal will be glad, upon receiving notification, to make appropriate acknowledgement in future editions of the book. Inquiries should be addressed to storyofsci@gmail.com. Discounts available to educational institutions.

13 ISBN: 978-0-692-35409-4

Library of Congress Control Number: 2014919419

Published by B. Bansal
Printed in the United States of America

*To all those who inspired it
and may never read it,
and
To all those for whom it was written
and hope they will read it.*

TABLE OF CONTENTS

Table of Contents 6
List of Appendices 21
List of Figures 21
List of Tables 22
List of Appendix Figures 23
List of Appendix Tables 23
Abbreviations 24
Author's Note 25
Introduction 26
Book Overview 29

PART 1: Background

Overview of Part I 33

Chapter 1: Nature of Science 34
    1.1 Introduction 34
    1.2 Definition of Science 34
    1.3 Different Classes of Science 34
    1.4 Why Is Science Possible? 34
    1.5 Nature of Scientific Creativity 35
    1.6 Science Is Different from Other Creative Outcomes 36
    1.7 Scientific Method 37
    1.8 Limitations and Power of Science 38
    1.9 Summary 39

Chapter 2: Framing Issues—Civilizations and Science 40
    2.1 Introduction 40
    2.2 Observations Concerning Civilizations 40
    2.3 Issues Concerning Civilizations 40
    2.4 Observations Concerning the History of Science 41
    2.5 Issues Concerning Evolution of Science 41
    2.6 Summary 41

PART II: Emergence of *Homo sapiens* and Civilization

Overview of Part II 42

Chapter 3: Emergence of *Homo sapiens* 43
    3.1 Introduction 43
    3.2 The Four Epochs 43
    3.3 Difficulties in Constructing the Story of *Homo sapiens* 44
    3.4 Instincts and Physical and Mental Attributes 44
    3.5 Evolution of Primates (55M–2.5M BP) 45
    3.6 Evolution up to *Homo sapiens* (2.5M–300,000 BP) 45

    3.7 Emergence of *Homo sapiens* (?–300,000 BP) 46
    3.8 Biological Attributes of *Homo sapiens* 46
    3.9 Summary 47

Chapter 4: Emergence of Civilization 48
    4.1 Introduction 48
    4.2 The Hunting-Gathering Epoch (300,000 BP–11,000 BCE) 48
    4.3 Neolithic Epoch (11,000 to 6500 BCE) 52
    4.4 Early Civilization Epoch (6500 to 3000 BCE) 56
    4.5 Overview of Achievements at the Dawn of Civilization 58
    4.6 Diverse Lifestyles during the Civilization Epoch 59
    4.7 Summary 59

PART III: Development of Theoretical Concepts

Overview of Part III 60

Chapter 5: The Inner Nature of *Homo sapiens* 61
    5.1 Introduction 61
    5.2 The Emergence of New Inner Attributes 61
    5.3 Nature of Beliefs 64
    5.4 Deducing *Homo sapiens* Behaviors from Beliefs 65
    5.5 The Essential Inner Nature of *Homo sapiens* 66
    5.6 Summary 66

Chapter 6: Nature of *Homo sapiens* Creativity 67
    6.1 Introduction 67
    6.2 What Is Creativity? 67
    6.3 Historically Observable Forms of Creativity 67
    6.4 Origin of Creativity 68
    6.5 The Creative Method and Its N&S Conditions 69
    6.6 Forms of Creativity and Unique Mental Attributes 69
    6.7 Evolution of *Homo sapiens* Creativity 70
    6.8 Creative and Productive Processes 70
    6.9 Concept of Internal Creative Balance 71
    6.10 Summary 70

Chapter 7: Temporal Framework 72
    7.1 Introduction 72
    7.2 Significant Milestones in Abstract Systems—Building Capability 72
    7.3 Formal Life Stages of Civilizations 74
    7.4 Formal Life Stages of Science 74
    7.5 The Concept of Logical Sequence in Science 75
    7.6 Eras of Civilization 75
    7.7 Significant Historically Observable Phases of Science 77
    7.8 Temporal Framework of Eras, Stages, and Phases 78
    7.9 Summary 79

Chapter 8: Driving Causes and Outcomes of Social Orders 80

    8.1 Introduction 80
    8.2 Natural Causes 80
    8.3 Intrinsic Causes 80
    8.4 Productive Outcomes 84
    8.5 Creative and Scientific Outcomes 85
    8.6 Constructive Outcomes during Standalone Era 86
    8.7 Constructive Outcomes during Peaceful Interaction Era 86
    8.8 Destructive Outcomes during the Violent Interaction Era 88
    8.9 The Inner Nature of *Homo sapiens* as a Cause 90
    8.10 The Concept of Sustainable Growing Surplus (SGS) 91
    8.11 Summary 93

Chapter 9: The Theory of Interacting Social Order 94

    9.1 Introduction 94
    9.2 Social Orders as an Interacting System of Causes and Outcomes 94

Relating Causes and Outcomes

    9.3 Approaches to Rationalizing Social Order Evolution 96
    9.4 Complex Process of How Causes Lead to Outcomes—Isolated Social Order 98
    9.5 Extending the Analysis to Interacting Social Orders 100

The Concept of the Inner Nature of Social Orders

    9.6 The Hypothesis of the Inner Nature of Interacting Social Orders 106
    9.7 Assessment of the Inner Nature of a Social Order 107
    9.8 The Concept of the External Orientation of a Social Order 111
    9.9 Inner Nature and Ideology of a Social Order 112

Tracking the Evolution of Civilizations

    9.10 Broadest Measures of Inner Nature 112
    9.11 Evolution of Civilizations 112

Inner Nature of Social Orders and Their Scientific Outcomes

    9.12 Rationalizing the Achievements in Science within a Phase 113
    9.13 Rationalizing of Achievements of Science across Phases 114
    9.14 Evolution of Science across Phases 115
    9.15 Summary 115

Chapter 10: The Essential Set of Participants 116

    10.1 Introduction 116
    10.2 Classes of Entities 116
    10.3 The Essential Participants 120
    10.4 Summary 121

PART IV: Birth, Development, and Maturation of Protoscience

Overview of Part IV 122

Chapter 11: Birth, Development, and Maturation of Protoscience (6000–1000 BCE) 123

    11.1 Introduction 123

    Affirmation of Era and Essential Participants

    11.2 Affirming the Era of Civilization 123

    11.3 Essential Participants of the Protoscience Phase 123

    Unique Issues of the Protoscience Phase

    11.4 Diffusion of Creativity and Migrations in the Standalone Era (6000–3000 BCE) 124

    11.5 Assigning Origin of Creative Outcomes 126

    11.6 Significant Achievements in Practical Creativity during the Protoscience Phase 127

    History, Causes, and Outcomes of the Indian Civilization

    11.7 Brief Political History (6000–1000 BCE) 127

    11.8 Natural Causes 129

    11.9 Intrinsic Causes 129

    11.10 Extrinsic Peaceful Causes 133

    11.11 Productive Outcomes 133

    11.12 Creative Outcomes 133

    11.13 Achievements in Science 136

    History, Causes, and Outcomes of the Mesopotamian Civilization

    11.14 Brief Political History (4400–1000 BCE) 140

    11.15 Natural Causes 140

    11.16 Intrinsic Causes 140

    11.17 Extrinsic Peaceful Causes 142

    11.18 Productive Outcomes 143

    11.19 Creative Outcomes 144

    11.20 Achievements in Science 144

    History, Causes, and Outcomes of Egyptian Civilization

    11.21 Brief Political History (3500–800 BCE) 145

    11.22 Natural Causes 145

    11.23 Intrinsic Causes 146

    11.24 Extrinsic Peaceful Causes 147

    11.25 Productive Outcomes 148

    11.26 Creative Outcomes 148

    11.27 Achievements in Science 149

    History, Causes, and Outcomes of the Chinese Civilization

    11.28 Brief Political History (3000–1000 BCE) 149

    11.29 Natural Causes 149

    11.30 Intrinsic Causes 150

    11.31 Extrinsic Peaceful Causes 151

    11.32 Productive Outcomes 151

  11.33 Creative Outcomes 151
  11.34 Achievements in Science 151
Summarizing the State of Civilization and Science
  11.35 State of Civilization at Phase End 152
Assessing the Inner Nature of Participants
  11.36 Inner Nature of Mesopotamian Civilization at Phase End 156
  11.37 Dynamic Inner Nature of Egyptian Civilization at Phase End 156
  11.38 Dynamic Inner Nature of Chinese Civilization at Phase End 157
  11.39 Dynamic Inner Nature of Indian Civilization at Phase End 158
  11.40 Inner Nature of Participants at the End of Protoscience Phases 159
Evolution and Rationalization of Protoscience
  11.41 Evolution of Protoscience during the Phase 161
  11.42 Rationalization of Protoscience 163
  11.43 Life Stage of Science Achieved by Civilizations 165
Looking Ahead
  11.44 Emerging New Participants 165
  11.45 Summary 166

PART V: Birth, Development, and Maturation of Science

Overview of Part V 168

Chapter 12: Birth of Science (1000–550 BCE) 169
  12.1 Introduction 169
Affirmation of Era and Essential Participants
  12.2 Affirming the Era of Civilization 169
  12.3 Essential Participants of the Protoscience Phases 170
Practical Creativity during the Phase—All Civilizations
  12.4 Significant Achievements in Practical Creativity—All Civilizations 170
History, Causes, and Outcomes of the Ancient Greek Civilization
  12.5 Brief Political History (1600–550 BCE) 170
  12.6 Natural Causes 171
  12.7 Intrinsic Causes 171
  12.8 Extrinsic Peaceful Causes or Sum Total of Others' Constructive Outcomes 172
  12.9 Productive and Creative Outcomes 173
History, Causes, and Outcomes of the Mesopotamian Civilization
  12.10 Brief Political History (1000–539 BCE) 173
  12.11 Intrinsic Causes 174
  12.12 Extrinsic Peaceful Causes or Sum Total of Others' Constructive Outcomes 174
  12.13 Productive Outcomes 174
  12.14 Creative Outcomes 174
  12.15 Achievements in Science 175
History, Causes, and Outcomes of the Chinese Civilization
  12.16 Brief Political History (1000–481 BCE) 175

    12.17 Intrinsic Causes 175

    12.18 Extrinsic Peaceful Causes or Sum Total of Others' Constructive Outcomes 176

    12.19 Productive Outcomes 176

    12.20 Creative Outcomes 176

    12.21 Achievements in Science 177

History, Causes, and Outcomes of the Indian Civilization

    12.22 Brief Political History (1000–550 BCE) 177

    12.23 Intrinsic Causes 177

    12.24 Extrinsic Peaceful Causes or Sum Total of Other Constructive Outcomes 179

    12.25 Productive Outcomes 179

    12.26 Creative Outcomes 179

    12.27 Achievements in Science 183

Summarizing the State of Civilization and Science

    12.28 State of Civilization and Science at Phase End 189

Assessing the Dynamic Inner Nature of Participants

    12.29 The Dynamic Inner Nature of the Ancient Greek Civilization 191

    12.30 The Dynamic Inner Nature of the Mesopotamian Civilization 192

    12.31 The Dynamic Inner Nature of the Chinese Civilization 193

    12.32 The Dynamic Inner Nature of the Indian Civilization 193

    12.33 The Dynamic Inner Nature of Participants at the End of Birth Phase 194

Evolution and Rationalization of the Birth of Science

    12.34 Birth of Science during the Phase 195

    12.35 Rationalization of the Birth of Science 196

    12.36 Life Stage of Science Achieved by Civilizations 199

    12.37 An Unfortunate Blunder by Historians 199

Looking Ahead

    12.38 Emerging New Participants 200

    12.39 Summary 201

Chapter 13: First Synthesis of Science (550 BCE–200 CE) 202

    13.1 Introduction 202

Affirmation of Era, Phase, and Essential Participants

    13.2 Affirming the Era of Civilizations 202

    13.3 Major Participants of the Phase 202

Violent End of Two Primary Civilizations

    13.4 End of Mesopotamian Civilization and Ancient Egyptian Civilization 203

History, Causes, and Outcomes of the Persian Empires

    13.5 Brief Political History (539 BCE–224 CE) 204

    13.6 Natural Causes 205

    13.7 Intrinsic Causes 205

    13.8 Extrinsic Peaceful Causes or Sum Total of Others' Constructive Outcomes 207

    13.9 Extrinsic Violent Causes or Sum Total of Others' Destructive Outcomes 207

    13.10 Productive Outcomes 208

  13.11 Creative Outcomes 208
  13.12 Achievements in Science 209
History, Causes, and Outcomes of the Roman Republic
  13.13 Brief Political History 209
  13.14 Natural Causes 210
  13.15 Intrinsic Causes 210
  13.16 Extrinsic Peaceful Causes or Sum Total of Constructive Outcomes 212
  13.17 Extrinsic Violent Causes or Sum Total of Destructive Outcomes 212
  13.18 Productive Outcomes 214
  13.19 Creative Outcomes 214
  13.20 Achievements in Science 215
History, Causes, and Outcomes of the Central Asian Nomads
  13.21 Brief Political History (~150 BCE–200 CE) 215
  13.22 Natural Causes 215
  13.23 Intrinsic Causes 215
  13.24 Extrinsic Peaceful Causes or Sum Total of Constructive Outcomes 216
  13.25 Extrinsic Violent Causes or Sum Total of Destructive Outcomes 216
  13.26 Productive Outcomes 216
  13.27 Creative Outcomes 216
  13.28 Achievements in Science 216
History, Causes, and Outcomes of the Ancient Greek Civilization and Hellenistic States
  13.29 Brief Political History (550 BCE–200 CE) 216
  13.30 Natural Causes 218
  13.31 Intrinsic Causes—Hellenistic States 218
  13.32 Extrinsic Peaceful Causes or Sum Total of Constructive Outcomes 220
  13.33 Extrinsic Violent Causes or Sum Total of Destructive Outcomes 221
  13.34 Productive Outcomes—Ancient Greece 223
  13.35 Creative Outcomes—Ancient Greece 223
  13.36 Achievements in Science—Ancient Greece 225
  13.37 Productive Outcomes—Hellenistic States 226
  13.38 Creative Outcomes—Hellenistic States 226
  13.39 Achievements in Science—Hellenistic States 227
History, Causes, and Outcomes of the Chinese Civilization
  13.40 Brief Political History (481 BCE–220 CE) 228
  13.41 Natural Causes 229
  13.42 Intrinsic Causes 229
  13.43 Extrinsic Peaceful Causes or Sum Total of Constructive Outcomes 231
  13.44 Extrinsic Violent Causes or Sum Total of Destructive Outcomes 231
  13.45 Productive Outcomes 231
  13.46 Creative Outcomes 232
  13.47 Achievements in Science 232
History, Causes, and Outcomes of Indian Civilization
  13.48 Brief Political History (550 BCE–250 CE) 233

    13.49 Natural Causes 235
    13.50 Intrinsic Causes 235
    13.51 Extrinsic Peaceful Causes or Sum Total of Constructive Outcomes.................................. 237
    13.52 Extrinsic Violent Causes or Sum Total of Destructive Outcomes 237
    13.53 Productive Outcomes 239
    13.54 Creative Outcomes 239
    13.55 Achievements in Science 242
Summarizing the State of Civilization and Science
    13.56 State of Civilization and Science at Phase End 245
Assessing the Inner Nature of Participants
    13.57 Inner Nature of the Persian Empires... 249
    13.58 Inner Nature of the Roman Republic.. 250
    13.59 Inner Nature of the Central Asian Nomads 251
    13.60 Inner Nature of the Ancient Greek Civilization (Up to Alexander)................................. 251
    13.61 Inner Nature of the Hellenistic States (Post-Alexander).. 251
    13.62 Inner Nature of the Chinese Civilization 252
    13.63 Inner Nature of the Indian Civilization 253
    13.64 The Inner Nature of Participants at the End of the First Synthesis 253
The Evolution and Rationalization of the First Synthesis of Science
    13.65 First Synthesis in Science.. 255
    13.66 Rationalizing the First Synthesis in Science 257
    13.67 Life Stage of Science Achieved by Civilization.. 261
    13.68 Role of Peaceful and Violent Interaction in Development of Science 261
Looking Ahead
    13.69 Emerging New Participants and Fate of Existing Participants 263
    13.70 A Peek into Coming Chapters 263
    13.71 Summary... 263

Chapter 14: Second Synthesis of Science (200–750 CE).. 265
    14.1 Introduction... 265
Affirmation of Era, Phase, and Essential Participants
    14.2 Affirming Era of Civilization.. 265
    14.3 Major Participants of the Phase 265
History, Causes, and Outcomes of Emerging European Civilization
    14.4 Brief Political History (200–750 CE)... 265
    14.5 Natural Causes 266
    14.6 Intrinsic Causes 266
    14.7 Extrinsic Peaceful Causes or Sum Total of Constructive Outcomes.................................. 269
    14.8 Extrinsic Violent Causes or Sum Total of Destructive Outcomes 269
    14.9 Productive Outcomes 270
    14.10 Creative Outcomes 270
    14.11 Achievements in Science 271

History, Causes, and Outcomes of the Byzantine Empire
 14.12 Brief Political History (293–711 CE) 272
 14.13 Natural Causes 273
 14.14 Intrinsic Causes 273
 14.15 Extrinsic Peaceful Causes 275
 14.16 Extrinsic Violent Causes or Sum Total of Destructive Outcomes 275
 14.17 Productive Outcomes 276
 14.18 Creative Outcomes 276
 14.19 Achievements in Science 277

History, Causes, and Outcomes of the Persian Civilization
 14.20 Brief Political History (224–651 CE) 277
 14.21 Natural Causes 278
 14.22 Intrinsic Causes 278
 14.23 Extrinsic Peaceful Causes or Sum Total of Constructive Outcomes 279
 14.24 Extrinsic Violent Causes or Sum Total of Others' Destructive Outcomes 280
 14.25 Productive Outcomes 281
 14.26 Creative Outcomes 281
 14.27 Achievements in Science 282

History, Causes, and Outcomes of the Chinese Civilization
 14.28 Brief Political History (220–618 CE) 283
 14.29 Natural Causes 283
 14.30 Intrinsic Causes 283
 14.31 Extrinsic Peaceful Causes or Sum Total of Constructive Outcomes 284
 14.32 Extrinsic Violent Causes or Sum Total of Destructive Outcomes 285
 14.33 Productive Outcomes 285
 14.34 Creative Outcomes 285
 14.35 Achievements in Science 287

History, Causes, and Outcomes of the Central Asian Nomads—Second Wave
 14.36 Brief Political History 287
 14.37 Natural Causes 289
 14.38 Intrinsic Causes 289
 14.39 Extrinsic Peaceful Causes or Sum Total of Constructive Outcomes 289
 14.40 Extrinsic Violent Causes or Sum Total of Destructive Outcomes 289
 14.41 Productive Outcomes 290
 14.42 Creative Outcomes 290
 14.43 Achievements in Science 290

History, Causes, and Outcomes of the Indian Civilization
 14.44 Brief Political History (200–750 CE) 290
 14.45 Natural Causes 291
 14.46 Intrinsic Causes 291
 14.47 Extrinsic Peaceful Causes 293
 14.48 Extrinsic Violent Causes 294
 14.49 Productive Outcomes 295

14.50 Creative Outcomes 295
14.51 Achievements in Science 297

Summarizing the State of Civilization and Science
14.52 State of Civilization and Science at Phase End 302

Assessing Changes in the Inner Nature of Participants
14.53 The Inner Nature of the Roman Empire until 476 CE 306
14.54 The Inner Nature of the Byzantine Empire after 476 CE 307
14.55 The Inner Nature of Persian Civilization 308
14.56 The Inner Nature of the Chinese Civilization 309
14.57 The Inner Nature of Central Asian Nomads—Second Wave 309
14.58 The Inner Nature of the Indian Civilization 310
14.59 The Inner Nature of the Participants at the End of the Second Synthesis Phase 310

The Evolution and Rationalization of the Second Synthesis of Science
14.60 The Second Synthesis in Science 311
14.61 Rationalizing the Second Synthesis through Causes 311
14.62 Confirming the Stage of Science for Each Civilization 314

Looking Ahead
14.63 Emerging New Participants and Fate of Existing Participants 315
14.64 A Peek into Coming Chapters 316
14.65 Summary 316

Chapter 15: Third Synthesis of Science (750–1200 CE) 317
15.1 Introduction 317

Affirmation of Era and Essential Participants
15.2 Affirming the Era of Civilization 317
15.3 Essential Participants of the Phase 317

History, Causes, and Outcomes of the European Civilization
15.4 Brief Political History (750–1200 CE) 318
15.5 Natural Causes 319
15.6 Intrinsic Causes 319
15.7 Extrinsic Peaceful Causes 321
15.8 Extrinsic Violent Causes 323
15.9 Productive Outcomes 325
15.10 Creative Outcomes 325
15.11 Achievements in Science 328

History, Causes, and Outcomes of the Chinese Civilization
15.12 Brief Political History (618–1279 CE) 328
15.13 Natural Causes 329
15.14 Intrinsic Causes 329
15.15 Extrinsic Peaceful Causes 331
15.16 Extrinsic Violent Causes 333
15.17 Productive Outcomes 333
15.18 Creative Outcomes 334

15.19 Achievements in Science 335

History, Causes, and Outcomes of the Indian Civilization

15.20 Brief Political History (750–1200 CE) 336
15.21 Natural Causes 337
15.22 Intrinsic Causes 337
15.23 Extrinsic Peaceful Causes 338
15.24 Extrinsic Violent Causes 340
15.25 Productive Outcomes 341
15.26 Creative Outcomes 341
15.27 Achievements in Science 343

History, Causes, and Outcomes of the Central Asian Nomads—The Third Wave

15.28 Brief Political History (800–1206 CE) 345
15.29 Natural Causes 346
15.30 Intrinsic Causes 347
15.31 Productive, Creative, and Scientific Outcomes 348

History, Causes, and Outcomes of the Muslim Civilization

15.32 Brief Political History (750–1200 CE) 348
15.33 Natural Causes 349
15.34 Intrinsic Causes 349
15.35 Extrinsic Peaceful Causes 352
15.36 Extrinsic Violent Causes (651–1200 CE) 353
15.37 Productive Outcomes 357
15.38 Creative Outcomes 359
15.39 Achievements in Science 362

Summarizing the State of Civilization and Science

15.40 The State of Civilization and Science at Phase End 365

Assessing Changes in the Inner Nature of Participants

15.41 Changes in the Inner Nature of European Civilization 366
15.42 Changes in the Inner Nature of the Chinese Civilization 368
15.43 Changes in the Inner Nature of the Indian Civilization 368
15.44 Changes in the Inner Nature of Muslim Civilization 369
15.45 Changes in the Inner Nature of Central Asians 370
15.46 The Inner Nature of Participants at the End of Third Synthesis Phase 371

The Evolution and Rationalization of the Third Synthesis of Science

15.47 Third Synthesis in Science 372
15.48 Rationalizing the Third Synthesis in Science 374
15.49 Confirming the Stage of Science for Each Civilization 380
15.50 Emerging New Participants and Fate of Some Participants 380
15.51 A Peek into Coming Chapters 381
15.52 Summary 382

Chapter 16: Fourth Synthesis of Science (1200–1600 CE) 383

16.1 Introduction 383

Era and Essential Participants
16.2 Affirming the Era of Civilization 383
16.3 Major Participants of the Phase 384

History, Causes, and Outcomes of the Central Asian Nomads—Fourth and Final Wave
16.4 Brief Political History (1200–present CE) 384
16.5 Natural Causes 385
16.6 Intrinsic Causes 385
16.7 Extrinsic Peaceful Causes 386
16.8 Extrinsic Violent Causes—Mongols as Victors 386
16.9 Productive, Creative, and Scientific Outcomes 387

History, Causes, and Outcomes of the Chinese Civilization
16.10 Brief Political History 388
16.11 Natural Causes 389
16.12 Intrinsic Causes 389
16.13 Extrinsic Peaceful Causes 391
16.14 Extrinsic Violent Causes—As Defeated 392
16.15 Productive Outcomes 393
16.16 Creative Outcomes 394
16.17 Achievements in Science 396

History, Causes, and Outcomes of the Indian Civilization
16.18 Brief Political History 397
16.19 Natural Causes 399
16.20 Intrinsic Causes 399
16.21 Extrinsic Peaceful Causes 401
16.22 Extrinsic Violent Causes—As Defeated 401
16.23 Productive Outcomes 404
16.24 Creative Outcomes 404
16.25 Achievements in Science 408

History, Causes, and Outcomes of the Muslim Civilization
16.26 Brief Political History 410
16.27 Natural Causes 411
16.28 Intrinsic Causes—Ottoman Empire 411
16.29 Extrinsic Peaceful Causes 414
16.30 Extrinsic Violent Causes—As Victors and Defeated 414
16.31 Productive Outcomes 416
16.32 Creative Outcomes—Muslim Civilization 416
16.33 Achievements in Science (Muslim Civilization) 419

History, Causes, and Outcomes of the European Civilization
16.34 Brief Political History 422
16.35 Natural Causes 424
16.36 Intrinsic Causes 424
16.37 Extrinsic Peaceful Causes 429
16.38 Extrinsic Violent Causes 429

16.39 Productive Outcomes 433
16.40 Creative Outcomes 434
16.41 Achievements in Science 438

Summarizing the State of Civilization and Science

16.42 State of Civilization and Science at Phase End 443

Assessing the Inner Nature of Participants

16.43 Inner Nature of Central Asian Nomads 446
16.44 Inner Nature of the Chinese Civilization 447
16.45 Inner Nature of the Indian Civilization 448
16.46 Inner Nature of Muslim Civilization 450
16.47 Inner Nature of the European Civilization 451
16.48 Inner Nature of Participants at the End of Third Synthesis Phase 453

The Evolution and Rationalization of the Fourth Synthesis of Science

16.49 Fourth Synthesis in Science 454
16.50 Rationalization of the Fourth Synthesis in Science 455
16.51 Life Stage of Science Achieved by Civilization 461

Looking Ahead

16.52 Emerging New Participants 462
16.53 Summary 462

Chapter 17: Mature Science (1600–1950) 464

17.1 Introduction 464

Era and Essential Participants

17.2 Affirming the Era of Civilization 465
17.3 Essential Participants of the Phase 465

History, Causes, and Outcomes of the European Civilization

17.4 Brief Political History (Europe, the Americas, and Australia) 466
17.5 Natural Causes 472
17.6 Intrinsic Causes 472
17.7 Extrinsic Peaceful Causes 477
17.8 Extrinsic Violent Causes—European States as Victors 477
17.9 Productive Outcomes 482
17.10 Creative Outcomes 483
17.11 Achievements in Science 489

History, Causes, and Outcomes of the Indian Civilization

17.12 Brief Political History 499
17.13 Natural Causes 501
17.14 Intrinsic Causes 501
17.15 Extrinsic Peaceful Causes 503
17.16 Extrinsic Violent Causes 503
17.17 Productive Outcomes 506
17.18 Creative Outcomes 507
17.19 Achievements in Science 510

History, Causes, and Outcomes of the Muslim Civilization

    17.20 Brief Political History 512

    17.21 Natural Causes 513

    17.22 Intrinsic Causes 513

    17.23 Extrinsic Peaceful Causes 516

    17.24 Extrinsic Violent Causes—As Defeated 517

    17.25 Productive Outcomes 519

    17.26 Creative Outcomes 519

    17.27 Achievements in Science 519

History, Causes, and Outcomes of the Chinese Civilization

    17.28 Brief Political History 519

    17.29 Natural Causes 520

    17.30 Intrinsic Causes 520

    17.31 Extrinsic Peaceful Causes 523

    17.32 Extrinsic Violent Causes 523

    17.33 Productive Outcomes 525

    17.34 Creative Outcomes 526

    17.35 Achievements in Science 527

Brief History of Other Key Players

    17.36 Brief Political History of Northeast and Southeast Asia 528

Summarizing the State of Civilization and Science

    17.37 State of Civilization and Science at Phase End 529

Assessing the Inner Nature of Participants

    17.38 Inner Nature of the Chinese Civilization 531

    17.39 Inner Nature of the Indian Civilization 532

    17.40 Inner Nature of Muslim Civilization 533

    17.41 Inner Nature of European Civilization 534

    17.42 Comparative Inner Natures of Participants 537

The Evolution and Rationalization of Mature Science

    17.43 Grand Unifications Leading to Mature Science 539

    17.44 Rationalization of Mature Science 541

    17.45 Life Stage of Science Achieved by Civilization 541

    17.46 Summary 542

Chapter 18: Evolution of Civilizations, Their Science, and Their Inner Natures 543

    18.1 Introduction 543

Evolving Dynamic Inner Nature of Social Orders

    18.2 The Evolving Inner Nature of Social Orders 543

Dynamic Inner Nature and Evolution of Civilizations

    18.3 Evolution of Social Orders through Inner Nature 546

Dynamic Inner Nature and Evolution of Science

    18.4 Evolution of Life Stages of Science across Civilizations 551

    18.5 Summary 552

Chapter 19: Conclusions and Lessons of History 553
19.1 Introduction 553
19.2 Science through Phases and Across Civilizations 553
19.3 Lessons of History 557
19.4 Summary 559

Chapter 20: Glimpses of the Future 560
20.1 Introduction 560

Capitalism, Science, and Religion
20.2 A Brief History of Capitalism 560
20.3 Nature of Capitalism 561

Glimpses of the Future
20.4 Controlling Greed 562
20.5 Controlling Creed 564
20.6 Controlling Aggression and Violence 565
20.7 The Likely Path Forward 565
20.8 Summary 565

Appendices 567
Selected Bibliography 600
Index of Key Concepts 604

LIST OF APPENDICES

Appendix A: Development of Social Conscience 567
Appendix B: The Development of Written Language 571
Appendix C: The Development of Alphabetical Language 573
Appendix D: The Myth of the Indo-Aryan Invasion of India 576
Appendix E: The Roots of the Indian Civilization and Reverse Migration Theory 578
Appendix F: Researching Ancient Civilizations 582
Appendix G: Age of the Universe and Four Yugas in Ancient India 584
Appendix H: Assessment of Western Historiography 586
Appendix I: China and Alphabetical Script 588
Appendix J: Art and the Nava Rasa Theory of Aesthetics 590
Appendix K: The Theory of Vaisheshika School 592
Appendix L: Who Invented Syllogism? 597

LIST OF FIGURES

Figure 5.1: Biosocial Evolution Leads to Inner Psychological Characteristics 63
Figure 6.1: Forms of Creativity 68
Figure 6.2: Creative and Productive Processes 71
Figure 7.1: Concept of the Historically Observable Phases of Science 79
Figure 9.1: Social Orders as a System of Reciprocal Influences 95
Figure 9.2: Relating Causes, Internal Perturbations, Stocks and Outcomes 100
Figure 9.3: Impact of External Peaceful Perturbations and Aggression 106
Figure 9.4: How We Arrived at the Concept of Inner Nature 111
Figure 10.1: Classification of Empires 118
Figure 10.2: The Rise and Fall of World's Empires 118
Figure 15.1: Interaction in the Wake of Violence 373
Figure 16.1: Peaceful Reciprocal Interactions—Sixth Phase 445
Figure 18.1: Evolution of Indian Civilization 547
Figure 18.2: Evolution of Chinese Civilization 548
Figure 18.3: Evolution of Pre-Islam Persian Civilization 549
Figure 18.4: Evolution of Muslim Civilization 549
Figure 18.5: Evolution of European Civilization 550

LIST OF TABLES

Table 3.1: Key Achievements of the genus *Homo* 46
Table 4.1: Key Achievements of Hunting Gathering Period 52
Table 4.2: Selected Achievements of Neolithic Communities 54
Table 4.3: Milestones in Agriculture 57
Table 4.4: Early Timeline of Primary Civilizations 58
Table 4.5: Climate and Social Organization of *Homo sapiens* 59
Table 8.1: Growth of SCS in a Hypothetical World Civilization 92
Table 9.1: Identifying and Assessing the Parameters of Inner Nature 110
Table 9.2: Necessary & Sufficient Conditions of Stages of Science 114
Table 10.1: Empires Created by Nomadic Confederations 119
Table 10.2: Strategic Position of Different Entities at the Dawn of Civilization 120
Table 10.3: Onset of Eras and Stages of Civilization for the Essential Set 121
Table 11.1: Ancient Indian Religious Literature 134
Table 11.2: Philosophy, Religion, and Science in Ancient India 136
Table 11.3: Relative Values of Measurable Parameters of Social Orders—Protoscience Phase 160
Table 11.4: Comparative Inner Nature of Civilizations 160
Table 12.1: Relative Values of Measurable Parameters of Social Orders—Birth Phase 194
Table 12.2: Comparative Inner Nature of Participants 195
Table 12.3: Great Scientists Responsible for the Birth of Science 196
Table 13.1: Relative Values of Measurable Parameters of Social Orders—First Synthesis Phase 254
Table 13.2: Comparative Inner Nature of Civilizations—First Synthesis Phase 254
Table 14.1: Significant Achievements in Practical Creativity—Chinese Civilization 286
Table 14.2: Dinnaga's Truth Table 299
Table 14.3: Relative Values of Measurable Parameters of Social Orders—Second Synthesis Phase 310
Table 14.4: Comparative Inner Nature of Participants—Second Synthesis Phase 311
Table 15.1: Significant Achievements in Practical Creativity 326
Table 15.2: Significant Achievements in Practical Creativity 334
Table 15.3: Significant Achievements in Practical Creativity 342
Table 15.4: Significant Achievements in Practical Creativity 358
Table 15.5: Relative Values of Measurable Parameters of Social Orders—Third Synthesis Phase 371
Table 15.6: Comparative Inner Nature of Participants—Third Synthesis Phase 372
Table 16.1: Significant Achievements in Practical Creativity 395
Table 16.2: Significant Achievements in Practical Creativity 417
Table 16.3: Significant Achievements in Practical Creativity 435
Table 16.4: Relative Values of Measurable Parameters of Social Orders—Fourth Synthesis Phase 454
Table 16.5: Comparative Inner Nature of Civilizations—Fourth Synthesis Phase 455
Table 17.1: Impact of British Colonial Wealth Drain 479
Table 17.2: Relative Values of Measurable Parameters of Social Orders—Mature Phase 537
Table 17.3: Comparative Inner Nature of Civilizations—Mature Phase 539
Table 18.1: Evolution of the Inner Nature of Major Social Orders 544
Table 18.2: Enduring Agression of Social Orders through History 545
Table 18.3: Evolution of Science Across Stages 551

LIST OF APPENDIX FIGURES

Figure A-1: Genesis of Greed and Creed Leading to Aggression 570
Figure B-1: Evolution of Written Language from Spoken Language 572
Figure E-1: Roots of Ancient Indian Civilization and Reverse Migration Theory 580
Figure G-1: Highlights of the Four Yugas of Indian Culture 586

LIST OF APPENDIX TABLES

Table C-1: Comparative Analysis of Language Families 574
Table C-2: Language Capability and Abstract Systems 575
Table F-1: Usefulness of Tools for Comparative Study of Civilizations 583
Table G-1: Highlights of the Four Yugas of Indian Culture 585

ABBREVIATIONS

Sometimes, in order to reduce repetition, we have used abbreviations concepts. Below are the important ones, spelled out for easy reference.

ASBC: abstract systems-building capability
C: capital
EB: empire building
EO: external orientation
EPC: extrinsic peaceful causes
EVC: extrinsic violent causes
FT: fair trade
IC: intrinsic causes
PM: peaceful migrations
ICB: internal creative balance
IOD: instruments of destruction
ISP: institutional structures and processes
L: land
LB: labor
NC: natural causes
O/I: openness/insularity
PRI: practical, religious, and intellectual
P/V: peaceful/violent
SGS: sustainable growing surplus
SPI: sustained political independence
SWD: systematic wealth drainer
VC: violent colonizer or colonization

AUTHOR'S NOTE

I grew up in India and immigrated to Canada at twenty-two. By the time I finished graduate school, I began to sense an inner conflict between a vague feeling of what I thought the history of science really was and how it was taught in schools throughout the world and discussed in the popular media. This feeling remained buried for nearly forty years, raising its uncomfortable head every so often. After I retired, it burst out with full force, and I knew I had to do something about it.

Over the last seven years, my studies led me to conclude that the history of the world's major civilizations has been grossly misrepresented for both political and intellectual reasons. I also concluded that the force behind this misrepresentation by generations of an overwhelming majority of "Western" historians is a belief that the West primarily invented and nurtured science. My studies further led me to conclude that this assertion is simply not true.

The first purpose of this book, therefore, is to discredit this assertion and present an alternative point of view. The second purpose is to highlight the contributions of the rest of civilizations to the birth and development of science, not as a stand-alone narrative but in the context of peaceful and violent conflict among the world's major civilizations. The book necessarily takes a very understanding view of civilizations that could not and did not make significant contributions to science.

I am not a historian by training; I am only one by a perceived necessity. It would indeed be presumptuous to think that a nonprofessional historian can undo the work of literally thousands of historians over last 250 or so years, and there is not, in fact, a need to undo the whole. This narrative needs to be added to and subtracted from in key respects to make it into a whole based on facts and reason, because science is a heritage of humanity, by humanity, and for humanity, to paraphrase Abraham Lincoln. That is why I prefer to think of this book as a work in progress, and I hope that it will encourage like-minded people to challenge, defend, and extend the ideas presented. I believe that historical analysis is ultimately not a question of "facts" and "reason," since both can be twisted. Historical truth largely depends on the quality and transparency of the method employed, and I hope I have outlined a method that is transparent and less amenable to being twisted.

It is true that going against established dogma is difficult. However, science is about challenging the tradition where appropriate and challenging what is falsely claimed as the truth.

It turns out that the group initially developing this version of the history of science has been primarily, but not exclusively, Anglo-Saxon historians, with the French and Germans in a strong supporting role. While it is also true that over the years, a minority of historians from these countries have paid grudging and at times glowing tributes to non-Western civilizations, such as the Indian, Chinese, and Arab civilizations, none has challenged the implicit but central thesis of the Western version of history of civilization and science—and no one should expect them to.

I believe that, over last the four hundred years, the guiding principles of Anglo-Saxon culture—the most successful colonizing and scientific culture of our times—have been nurturing science and glorifying individual self-interest. This has been a winning formula and has been historically responsible for the Industrial Revolution, magnificent leaps in productivity, the systematic drain of the other civilizations' wealth, and developing institutions of democratic capitalism. If laissez-faire capitalism had to take birth, someone had to do it first. Since the Anglo-Saxon form of capitalism is based on the unfettered individual and national self-interest, would not such a form of capitalism have to spring forth from a culture based on the above principles? Now, if such a culture were to describe other civilizations, would not its motives, though couched in rational terms, be questionable? Would historians, philosophers, and other leaders from such a culture not draw a firewall between their objective attitudes toward science and the self-interest-laden attitude of their descriptions of others' achievements when doing so served their purposes? Moreover, would this contradictory attitude not seem natural to them?

However, the principles of mature twenty-first century democratic capitalism assure fundamental freedoms. These freedoms find welcoming soils everywhere as the non-Western and formerly socialist-leaning world realizes that their historical infatuation with socialism and communism over the first four-fifths of the twentieth century was simply an ill-conceived response to Western colonial domination, much like fascism was an extreme response of Germany, Japan, and Italy to unacceptable English and French control, as the Americans waited impatiently in the wings. Therefore, as mature democratic capitalism expands past the lands of its origin and prospers in the formerly colonized and socialist worlds, the storyline for the history of science and civilization is bound to be revisited and subjected to drastic surgery.

This book is, I hope, a small step in that direction.

B. Bansal
Wilmington, Delaware
December 31, 2014

INTRODUCTION

For nearly 250 years now, we have lived in a world dominated by European civilization and the states it spawned in the New World in general and by Anglo-Saxons in particular. The European civilization and the states it spawned in the New World have been termed the Western civilization in a transparent attempt to differentiate from the "Eastern" rest of the world. Two hundred and fifty years of domination by an ethnic group is not an unusually long period by historical standards. However, given that these years span the entire era of mature science and the Industrial and post-Industrial Revolutions of enormous change, it must feel like millennia to those from other civilizations.

Until about the mid-eighteenth century, civilizations did not write comparative histories because of insufficient contact among civilizations; continual political instability caused by a never-ending panorama of empires, scarce skills, and resources; and sheer lack of need. Even after 1750 CE, the effort was grossly insufficient and uneven by all except the European civilization.

European Version of History

Starting in the second half of the eighteenth century, European historians began the arduous and much needed task of constructing a comparative history of civilizations. It was the first time in human history that such a project was undertaken on such a scale. It was a new field, with no one from non-European civilizations to seriously challenge the facts, assumptions, and methods employed. Consequently, the European version of comparative history unabashedly served the worldview of European colonizers and wealth drainers. In candid moments, this was acknowledged, even at a personal level. For example, in *History of English Speaking Peoples,* Mr. Churchill claimed, rather immodestly and tongue-in-cheek, that "history shall be kind to me, for I intend to write it."

This European version of comparative history has systematically underestimated the contributions of other civilizations in enabling the rise of the modern world. These contributions are not marginal or worthy of mere footnotes so that a modern world *could* have arisen without these contributions. Rather, these non-European contributions are *central:* without these contributions, a modern world could not possibly have arisen. It was, if one wanted to be generous, as if the European historians were mesmerized by the substantial accomplishments of their own civilization in the recent past as they strove to construct a comparative history of civilizations. It is true that data about other civilizations was not always readily available to them. Most major civilizations, particularly Indian, did not have a strong tradition of written history. In many instances, historians and archeologists painstakingly worked to literally dig out the data. Nonetheless, it is also true that most of these scholars rushed to make judgments in an unscholarly manner. Therefore, while the task of completing an unbiased comparative history of the world's civilizations lies in the future, the European version has formed the foundation of education in Chinese, Muslim, Indian, and other civilizations for generations now. And since the story must go on, the European history-writing project has been continuous to the present time, albeit with increasing protest from many groups and peoples.

The principal theme of the European version of world history is rather straightforward and runs as follows: Greeks and the ensuing Hellenistic states single-handedly invented critical philosophy and science nearly 2,500 to 2,000 years ago. Romans, while appropriating their practical achievements, foolishly ignored that science as they created the Roman Republic, which was followed by the Roman Empire. By 500 CE, Asian nomadic invaders and European barbarians succeeded in destroying the Roman Empire, in part because of Rome's internal weakness, thus plunging Europe into a thousand years of darkness. After the fall of Rome, Arabs, as their empire expanded into Europe, discovered Greek science and kept it alive as a convenient handoff to Europe half a millennium later, when it woke up from its millennium-long slumber to continue the scientific project through the Italian renaissance, reformation of Christianity, scientific revolution, enlightenment, and the Industrial and post-Industrial revolutions. This version of history glorified Alexander's adventure of "world conquest," the Roman Empire, the Crusades, racism, and colonial conquest. Note how this version of comparative history up to approximately 1750 CE and the domination of the world by a few European states since 1750 CE have fed on each other. As indicated above, the European version of history severely curtailed contributions of other major civilizations *prior* to 1750 CE, while European colonial control prevented proportional contributions from these civilizations *after* 1750 CE. Thus, this version provided the justification for colonial control, and colonial control provided a continuing validity of this version in the eyes of European historians—a wonderfully self-reinforcing circularity.

Principal Foundations of the Western Version

If one examines the vast output of these historians, three themes emerge in the European version of comparative world history to the present time:

- European civilization alone created science and the scientific method.
- European civilization single-handedly created institutions of democratic capitalism.
- European civilization as a whole has always been on the side of good.

Taking the last assertion first, the record is definitely mixed. Certainly, fighting Islamic terrorism and communism and fascism, both illegitimate offspring of the European civilization itself, has been good. It is, however, ludicrous to imagine how the adventures of Alexander, the excesses of the Roman Empire, the Crusades, racism, colonial control, and brutally fighting the resulting anticolonial liberation movements around the world could be considered good.

The second assertion, on the other hand, is definitely valid. However, ultimately, the gradual emergence of the institutions of democratic capitalism in several Western European states beginning in the seventeenth century was a byproduct of science and the scientific method. The resulting acceleration in science-based technological change culminated in the emerging city bourgeoisie overthrowing landed nobility in key European states. Thus began a process lasting nearly three hundred years that ultimately led to a relatively fully developed form of democratic capitalism in the twentieth century. Colonial domination effectively precluded non-European civilizations from participating on the cutting edge of the social and political evolution from 1750 CE forward. The only significant exception, of course, is the island of Japan, which escaped colonization primarily because of its geographical location and the limited pre-industrial attractiveness of its mountainous landmass. Thus, the claim that European civilization single-handedly created science and the scientific method must form the bedrock foundation upon which the European version of comparative history rests. A critique of this assertion is the chief purpose of this work.

Toward a True Version of History

Now if history was an academic, merely past-oriented arena, one could possibly find humor in this self-serving historiography that Western historians painstakingly concocted. However, bad history, through historical consciousness, enters into the present and future and contaminates them. Thus, as non-European civilizations take their rightful place in the world over the next fifty years, they also must recover their own histories (through deconstruction and reconstruction). The two processes of delayed development and the recovery of history will feed on each other. However, during this recovery effort, we must be careful to not repeat the self-serving errors of earlier European historians. The tidal forces of globalization are leading humanity slowly but inexorably toward a world civilization over the next century.

So, although European, West Asian, Muslim, and central Asian aggression largely bears the moral responsibility for destruction, greed, and intolerance in history, European civilization has not hesitated to claim that science as exclusively its invention—a demonstrably preposterous claim. We intend to show that seeds of science were sown in the Indian and Mesopotamian civilizations and nurtured into adolescence by several civilizations. However, these aggressive and violent civilizations transplanted these plantings on their own soil, nurtured them using the wealth of other civilizations, and called the resulting fruits exclusively their own.

From 1750 until the mid-twentieth century, several Western European states perched on the Atlantic Ocean exercised colonial and imperial control over other major civilizations. This control essentially precluded these major civilizations from participating in scientific development during science's most prolific expansion as it attained maturity. This maturity was gained after three millennia of painstaking, interrupted contributions by many civilizations. Consequently, since about 1750, science has in fact been mostly a European activity, something European historians exploited as they strove to construct world history. However, this statement is demonstrably false when extended to the entire three millennia of scientific history.

According to Kenneth Clark, a singularly biased, Anglo Saxon historian, European man created instruments of thought that "separated" him from rest of humanity from 1600 to 1750 CE. He was, of course, referring to Isaac Newton's invention of calculus around 1675 CE and the rise of critical philosophy a century later. Had he done his research, he might have known that calculus was conceived three hundred years earlier in Kerala and was based on the work of the fourteenth-century Indian mathematician, Madhava. Critical philosophy was mostly needed to eradicate the poisonous overgrowth of Christian dogma in particular and monotheism in general. Leaving aside the question of whether Europe was aware of Madhava's work through Portuguese Jesuits who came to Kerala starting in 1498, calculus also appears to have been conceived independently in Japan during Newton's time and a bit later in central Asia by erstwhile nomads.

Fortunately, today we happen to be living in a period when science has begun to end its appearance as an exclusively European/Western affair of last four centuries and has decidedly moved toward becoming a global affair. The book painstakingly and expertly takes the reader through this fascinating story, treating each stage of science on its own merit and not through the backward prism of four centuries of European/Western domination. It explodes the presumption of ancient Greece as the birthplace of science, as many Western historians take careless delight in assuming.

BOOK OVERVIEW

In this brief overview, we highlight unique features of the book, give an overview of how the book is organized, provide a summary of chapter contents, and indicate how the reader may read the book on a fast track.

Unique Features

This work has the following significant unique features:

- The book covers the entire story of *Homo sapiens* through the biological evolution epoch that led to the emergence of *Homo sapiens*, the hunting-gathering epoch, the Neolithic epoch, and civilization epoch as one continuous story. However, it focuses on the civilization epoch, which consists of standalone, peaceful interaction, and violent interaction eras. It further zeroes in on the rationalization of the three-millennia-long history of science, beginning before its birth.
- The book rationalizes the birth and evolution of science primarily on two key concepts: a fixed yet flexible inner nature of *Homo sapiens* as a species and an evolving yet stable inner nature of civilizations in particular and *Homo sapiens* social orders in general.
- The book emphasizes the incompleteness and fallacy in the Marxist analysis of history and its embedded assumptions of the goodness of human nature, the philosophy of atheism, and economic factors as principal drivers of history.
- The book takes an analytical, quantitative, and testable approach to understanding civilizations and the history of science and not merely or even mostly a descriptive approach. It thus uses the scientific method itself to study the history of civilizations and science.
- The book does not focus on a particular civilization; rather, it focuses on dynamic relationships, both peaceful and violent, among all the world's major civilizations and nomadic confederations since the birth of civilization itself.
- The book reaches surprising conclusions and offers a radically new perspective on the history of civilizations and of science and challenges the established, traditional, and biased viewpoint of most European historians.
- The book outlines an approach to analyzing civilizations. While the readers may disagree with some of the facts and conclusions of this work, we hope they find the methodology objective and rigorous.
- The book ties the history of science to not just the intellectual life processes of civilizations, as most analyses of history of science tend to do, but also their practical and religious lives. It argues that reciprocal impact, including the greed some civilizations have exhibited through empire-building, violent colonization, and systematic wealth drain and the intolerant creeds of Christianity and Islam, have determined the evolution of science over last 2,500 years since its birth.
- Finally, the work provides a glimpse of the emerging world civilization over the next century based on:
  - Emergence of genuine, technology-assisted democratic institutions at national and international levels
  - The emergence of *economic constitutions* (to supplement the existing emphasis on political constitutions) that will be required to manage worsening income and wealth inequality and the instability inherent in dynamic capitalism
  - A relative de-emphasis of the politics within democracies
  - The eradication of the millennia-long conflict between science and religion through the rise of agnostic belief systems

Thus, the new world civilization will have integrated institutions based on cooperation among states; will be democratic, agnostic, and strategic in orientation; and will lead to the concept of world citizenship.

Organization of the Book

The purpose of this work, which took seven years to research and write, is to therefore examine the close relationship between civilizations and science. Our ultimate focus is the birth and evolution of science, which is perhaps the most significant form of human creativity. Our basic premise is that the stories of science and civilizations are inseparably intertwined and to date have been told with a bias. This book aims to correct the bias. It has six parts:

>Part I: Background
>Part II: Emergence of *Homo sapiens* and Civilization
>Part III: Development of Theoretical Concepts
>Part IV: Birth, Development, and Maturation of Protoscience
>Part V: Birth, Development, and Maturation of Science
>Part VI: Perspective, Conclusions, Lessons, and Glimpses of the Future

In part I, we focus on defining the nature of science and civilizations. In part II, we briefly describe the long process that led to the emergence of *Homo sapiens* and civilization. This is not central to the main point of the book. However, we have chosen to include this because it sets the stage for the subsequent story of civilizations and science and helps put the story in perspective.

In part III, we develop the concepts and framework employed in this work to analyze civilizations and the history of science. In addition, we identify the key civilizations and nomadic confederations significant in history.

Part IV describes the driving causes and outcomes of four primary civilizations since the first emergence of civilization more than eight millennia ago and rationalizes the course of *protoscience* during standalone and peaceful interaction eras.

Part V discusses the peaceful birth of *science* in one civilization followed by its interrupted development in several civilizations (including the impact of nomadic confederations), followed by its maturation again in a single civilization.

Part VI looks back at the evolution of civilizations, their science, and their inner natures over eight millennia. It summarizes the conclusions and lessons of history and speculates a bit, providing glimpses into the future of civilization (but not science).

Content of the Chapters

In chapter 1, we examine the nature, power, and limitations of science. We look at different categories of science as well as the relationship of science to other forms of creativity and why we especially single out science as the most significant creative activity.

In chapter 2, we make a few commonsense observations concerning civilizations and science and raise thought-provoking questions to be addressed in this work.

In chapter 3, we trace the biological evolution from primates leading to *Homo sapiens* with unique physical and mental attributes and continuing powerful instincts.

In chapter 4, we journey through the long hunting gathering period and relatively short Neolithic period culminating in the birth of civilization around 6,500 BCE and introduce the four ancient primary civilizations.

In chapter 5, we develop the concept of the *fixed yet flexible inner nature* of *Homo sapiens*. A clear understanding of the essential inner nature of the species is the critical foundation upon which any theory of civilization and evolution of science must be constructed. The reader is no doubt is aware how many elegant theories have foundered because of idealistic and utopian assumptions about the essential nature of the species.

In chapter 6, we take up creativity of *Homo sapiens*; its practical, religious, and intellectual forms; and the necessary sufficient conditions.

In chapter 7, we define the eras of civilization and the conditions needed to identify them. We also introduce the concepts of life stages and the logical stages of science. Together with the concept of the eras of civilization, these two concepts lead to the hypothesis of the historical, observable *phases* of science. These phases form the temporal framework employed in the book.

In chapter 8, we define the categories of causes and outcomes in sufficient granularity to organize the sheer quantity of data without being overwhelmed by it and introduce ways to summarize driving causes and resulting outcomes.

In chapter 9, we propose the hypothesis of the *inner nature of a social order* and use the concept to outline a process to rationalize evolution of science. The concept of the inner nature of a social order forms the foundation of historical analysis presented in this book.

In chapter 10, we identify the essential set of civilizations and nomadic confederations that have played the leading role in history of civilizations and birth and evolution of science.

In chapter 11, we analyze the birth, development, and maturation of protoscience or the pregnancy phase of science.

In chapters 12–17, we study the driving causes and significant outcomes, including in science, of major civilizations and for significant nomadic groups. These chapters are organized around the historically observable phases of science beginning with its birth and rationalize the evolution of science in each phase:

Chapter 12: Birth of Science
Chapter 13: First Synthesis of Science
Chapter 14: Second Synthesis of Science
Chapter 15: Third Synthesis of Science
Chapter 16: Fourth Synthesis of Science
Chapter 17: Mature Science

In chapter 18, using actual outcomes of social orders, we show that inner nature of social orders is dynamic yet stable. The outcomes of interacting social orders are simply the result of the reciprocal impact of their dynamic inner natures. We also look back at the evolution of civilization and science across the seven phases. We demonstrate how the shifting center of gravity of science across civilizations since its birth nearly two and a half millennia ago, has been determined by greed and creed of Persian, European, Central Asian, and Muslim civilizations, all of which were either derived from or materially influenced by the two ancient primary civilizations of Mesopotamia and Egypt, both with monotheistic tendencies.

In chapter 19, we present the essential conclusions and lessons of history. Finally, in chapter 20, we speculate a bit and provide glimpses of the future concerning how the species must meet the challenge of controlling the destructive forces of creed and greed while nurturing the creative and productive powers or how civilizations ought to evolve after the long two and half millennia period of intercivilization greed, intolerance and violence.

How to Read the Book

Given its length, there are two fast-track ways to read the book, depending on the interest of the reader:

- The fastest way is to read two relatively brief chapters of part I, followed by the overviews and summary of chapters in parts III, IV, and V, followed by the chapters in part VI. This should inform the reader of the main thrust of story of the civilizations and evolution of science and conclusions in this book.
- A compromise is to read two relatively brief chapters of part I, the overviews and summary of chapters in parts II and III, and chapters in parts IV, V, and VI. This approach enables the reader to delve into data on driving causes and outcomes that form the basis of the conclusions drawn.

For the more theoretically minded reader, there is, of course, no shortcut. However, for those using fast-track approaches, we must note that the six parts of the book are not written as standalone parts. There is continuity from one part to the next.

Summary of Hypotheses and Organizing Concepts

Two hypotheses and four organizing concepts form the foundation of this work.

Two Key Hypotheses

The hypothesis of a fixed yet flexible inner nature of *Homo sapiens*, derived from unique physical and mental attributes and instincts, consists of a fixed part (self-consciousness, free will, and the necessity of beliefs) and a flexible part (creative and productive powers and conscience). The fixed part is shared by all *Homo sapiens* equally at least since late hunting–gathering epoch. The flexible part is behind all social (as distinct from biological and natural) causes driving *Homo sapiens* social orders.

The hypothesis of an inner nature of social orders consists of productive and creative capacities and constructive and destructive orientations. It is not necessarily same as what the social order actually achieves in a given period as its productive, creative, constructive and destructive outcomes.

- Productive capacity refers to its capacity of wealth production through new products and services and internal trade and efficacy in wealth production.

- Creative capacity refers to its capacity of creativity in its practical, religious, and intellectual forms
- Constructive orientation refers to the potential of peacefully engaging with other social orders through fair trade, exchange of creative outcomes, and peaceful migrations.
- Destructive orientation refers to the potential of a social order to engage in aggression and violence against other social orders through empire building, violent colonization, and systematic wealth drain through control of trading routes and territories.

Four Organizing Concepts

- The principal forms of *Homo sapiens* creativity are practical, religious, and intellectual creativity directed at survival, soothing existential anxiety, and satisfying curiosity respectively.
- Consistent with the three eras of civilization (the standalone, peaceful interaction, and violent interaction), there are seven historically observable phases of science: birth, development, and maturation of protoscience, the birth of science, development stage of science (in four synthesis phases), and maturity of science.
- Since the beginning of the peaceful interaction era, to one degree or another, the social orders have collectively constituted a dynamic, interlocking social system of causes (natural, intrinsic, extrinsic peaceful, and extrinsic violent) and outcomes (productive, creative, constructive, and destructive)
- The essential participants in the drama of civilizations and science include eight civilizations and two broad nomadic groups.

The seven chapters of parts IV and V not only rationalize the history of science but also simultaneously demonstrate the validity of the two hypotheses and four organizing principles.

A final word concerning the writing style is in order. A book on this subject matter typically does not contain many figures and tables and has many footnotes and a long list of references with explanatory notes. It is generally written in a style without section notations within the chapters. We have purposefully chosen a style that is mainly analytical, structured, and not merely descriptive; has an abundance of figures and tables for ease of understanding; has section notations within each chapter; has no footnotes; and has relatively few references. The reason for the latter is that the book relies on known data (with all the uncertainties and distortions) and uses a transparent methodology to draw its conclusions. In that sense, the book stands primarily on the analytical method employed. Given the current disagreements concerning the timeline of ancient Indian history for example, some will question the timelines we have asserted. These questions can only be resolved in the future through more research.

Historical conclusions, including those concerning civilizations and their science, must use a transparent method based on scientific method itself and not appear as emerging readymade from the black box of the analyst's mind. This book hopefully meets these important criteria.

Finally, note that we have taken care to avoid unconscious use of the Western or European civilization as a reference point, as many authors tend to do, since its relevance as a unique reference is hardly a given in the evolution of science let alone in the history of civilization.

We hope the reader will enjoy reading the book as much as we have enjoyed researching and writing it.

PART I
BACKGROUND

OVERVIEW OF PART I

This book is based on an examination of the close relationship between civilizations and science. Our ultimate focus is science, which is perhaps the most significant form of human creativity. Our basic premise is that the stories of science and Eurasian civilizations are inseparably intertwined and to date have been told with a bias. In part I, we focus on defining the nature of civilization and science. part I of this book consists of two chapters.

In chapter 1, we examine in detail the nature, power, and limitations of science. We look at different categories of science as well as the relationship of science to other forms of creativity and why we especially single out science as the most significant form of creative outcomes.

In chapter 2, we make broad observations concerning science and civilization and raise some thought-provoking questions that we hope to answer in this work.

Thus, part I introduces civilizations and science through making broad observations and posing thought-provoking questions.

Chapter 1: Nature of Science

1.1 Introduction

Ours has been called the age of science and technology. Over the last hundred plus years, science and technology have come to have an increasingly big presence in everyday life, through a million inventions derived from science and technology and through an understanding of the impact of science on just about every facet of life. As any student of history knows, this was not always the case. Social orders and civilizations throughout history have gone through long periods when something other than science loomed as large or larger in their everyday and intellectual lives. There have been many periods in the history of civilizations when sheer survival, open-ended metaphysical search, revealed faith, empire building, ethical living, or art affected life more than science did. However, today, science appears so fundamental to the modern mind that it seems unreasonable to imagine that some other activity can have the impact of science in our daily and intellectual lives—now or in the foreseeable future. Science, to modern man, appears to be the most effective way for humans to relate to the physical universe on which our species' continued existence depends.

In this chapter, we define science, identify different classes of science, discuss why science is possible, and explore the nature of scientific creativity, its relationship to other major creative outcomes, and its power and limitations. This brief overview of science is intended to provide some of the necessary definitions and background needed in later chapters.

1.2 Definition of Science

Science may be defined as a creative activity that leads to organized and verifiable knowledge about three realms: nature, man, and society. The key word is *verifiable*. This verifiability gives science an objective character and raises it immeasurably above a mere opinion, intuition, or feeling. Conversely, if a subject falls out the realm of verifiability, it ceases to be an appropriate subject for science.

1.3 Different Classes of Science

Not all sciences are created equal. Apart from the subject matter of focus, sciences created by *Homo sapiens* differ in important inherent ways. We may envision, for the sake of convenience, four different classes of science:

- Formal sciences
- Physical sciences
- Biological sciences
- Social sciences

Formal sciences in this study include mathematics, logic, and linguistics. Physical sciences include the precursor of physics or solar astronomy, all later branches of physics, chemistry, and earth sciences (geography, oceanography, atmospheric sciences, soil science, geophysics, etc.) as well as applied sciences, such as engineering and modern science-based technology. Biological sciences include medicine, botany, zoology, and biology. The difference between physical sciences and biological sciences pertains to extent of mathematical reasoning used. Social sciences include politics, economics, history, ethics, psychology, anthropology, and sociology, to name a few, and are characterized by independent free will playing a central role. Hence, these sciences depend on subjective opinions and beliefs to one degree or another. It is important to note that, in addition to its specific concepts and laws, biological or social sciences cannot violate the concepts and laws developed in physical science. This division of science into four classes is crucial to understand both the source of science's limitations and its power. Art and philosophy, together with science, form the great trio of intellectual creativity. But art and philosophy cannot be considered science as they do not pass the criteria of verifiability and falsifiability.

1.4 Why Is Science Possible?

Why science is possible is an interesting question. We discuss part of the answer in chapter 6 since all forms of science are a form of creativity. There are two fundamental reasons why science is possible. First, the observable universe plainly shows regularity and appears lawful and amenable to reason. Second, the observable universe is too vast and complex for any one individual to comprehend all at once. Thus, the process of understanding the universe must necessarily become stepwise (and hence historical) and social. This stepwise and social nature of science makes natural and biological sciences both possible and less than perfect while guaranteeing decreasing imperfection over time. Despite the presence of unpredictable human free will, which makes social sciences less objective than natural and biological sciences in an important way, social phenomenon also shows regularity and appears lawful. Finally, formal sciences are possible intrinsically as they are a product of unique mental powers and require minimal recourse to external reality once the necessary axioms are formulated. Thus, once the desire for absolute knowledge is transcended and progressively less imperfect knowledge is accepted as a goal, science becomes possible. The history of science in all civilizations, as we shall see in the later chapters, is a testimony to this struggle.

In referring to science, Einstein is often quoted as saying that the most incomprehensible thing about the universe is that it is comprehensible. At one level, the statement captures the wonder of why the universe evolved life capable of understanding the universe itself. At a different level, as we indicated above, the seemingly infinite universe is comprehensible because of the implicit pact science makes with the universe that it will only endeavor to provide less than perfect but progressively better answers about the nature of the universe.

Strong and Weak Anthropic Principles: At an emotional level, science becomes possible when the subject matter is approached with a completely open mind. Any unyielding presupposition, irrespective of the source, is likely to injure the course of science. Thus, in our judgment, a true scientific attitude is one of agnosticism that keeps both atheistic and dogmatic religious beliefs at bay because the former cannot be disproved and the latter cannot be proved.

In recent times, as science succeeded in piecing together the evolution of the universe and the evolution of life on our planet that culminated in the emergence of *Homo sapiens*, scientists have wondered why evolution has followed its highly improbable track to intelligent life in the form of *Homo sapiens* capable of understanding the universe. It seems as if the laws of the physical universe were fine-tuned in just the right manner to allow *Homo sapiens* to emerge. This led to the so-called strong anthropic principle (the universe must create its observers) and to the possibility of a creator once the notion of a steady state universe was discarded based on the fact of an expanding universe.

The idea of a creator, however, may be distasteful to some, and that in turn led scientists to formulate the hypothesis of multiple universes (with wormholes connecting them), each with equally improbable laws capable of producing intelligent life. Together, however, an infinite number of such universes, each with infinitesimal probability of producing intelligent life, will allow the emergence of intelligent life in our universe and dispense with the need to postulate a creator. Those who believe in a creator could argue that the joint probability of all possible universes ensuring the evolution of intelligent life also implies a creator! Science, therefore, can neither prove nor disprove the origin of existence. The choice between faith and agnosticism is thus a matter of personal taste. Faith cannot be demonstrated except through faith, and agnosticism has no such limitation. Science thrives best under an agnostic posture (and agnosticism thrives under science) since the belief in a creator may ultimately be injurious to the pursuit of science because it runs the risk of simply accepting that creator instead and doing what He wants us to do. Yet a belief in the nonexistence of a creator is counter to the empirical, open-ended, inquiring spirit of science, all of which in turn leads back to agnosticism. Note, however, that the so-called weak anthropic principle, on the other hand, simply says that if the universe did not create observers, we would not be here, and hence there is no point in asking the question.

1.5 Nature of Scientific Creativity

Science as a creative endeavor is a relatively recent phenomenon compared to the existence of *Homo sapiens*. *Homo sapiens* with a biologically fully developed brain have been around for at least three hundred thousand years and perhaps considerably more. Man has had a spoken language for at least fifty thousand years and some form of written language for at least five thousand years. Thus, for the majority of man's existence, his creativity was expressed through a means other than science and even the written word, because, as we discuss in chapter 3, he was yet to fully develop and be conscious of his unique mental attributes of observation, imagination, and reason. Even after birth, science has obviously been just one of the several significant ways available to man to express his creativity.

While we must withhold a full discussion on the nature of *Homo sapiens* creativity until chapter 6, we want to ask two questions concerning the nature of scientific creativity, anticipating some of the more detailed discussion about this creative nature in subsequent chapters.

Is scientific creativity survival-driven? Science is a form of unique mental powers-driven intellectual creativity of *Homo sapiens*. It should be self-evident that this activity is not needed for the species to survive since science, using even the broadest definition, is not older than civilization.

Why do we think scientific creativity is not survival-driven? It is true that today science, particularly in applied form, appears necessary for survival in a competitive, market-based economy. New understanding of natural or social phenomenon leads to new technologies, and these in turn lead to new ways of exploiting that understanding to satisfy human needs through new products or services. New product introductions allow some market participants to thrive and win and others to wither away, making some level of science necessary for market survival. However, certainly before the rise of market economy, which itself was made possible in part by science, science was not necessary to sustain material life, though practical creativity was. Even today, in a strict sense, scientific progress is not necessary to sustain life. For example, if all humanity could agree to freeze science at current level, man could sustain himself for a long time with his existing scientific knowledge. Considering the thermal and chemical pollution that industrial civilization is responsible for, freezing science at the current level might possibly allow him to sustain himself a little longer than otherwise. Thus, historically, science has been utterly different from survival-driven practical creativity. However, once created, scientific knowledge can have a great impact on human well-being.

Can science address existential anxiety? The answer here is also no, but it is a somewhat qualified no. Existential anxiety, particularity early in *Homo sapiens* social evolution, is a natural state of affairs for a species that knows death but does not want to die. Certainly, to date, science can make no claim concerning existential anxiety. Science only focuses on the "how" and not the "why" of reality. The grandest of scientific theories, the Big Bang, stops at the primeval singularity that the universe was about fourteen billion years ago. It does not know what existed before that singularity and who, if any being, created it and why, though recent theories postulate the existence of multiverses to get around the embarrassment of having to assume the strong anthropic principle as noted above. Science cannot even say if it can ever answer these questions concerning the origin of existence with certainty. The task of addressing the existential anxiety has thus been beyond science so far and has historically fallen on religious theorizing. Of course, religious creativity has been influential in more than just reducing existential creativity. It has also strongly influenced evolution of science and civilizations. We shall frequently return to this subject in subsequent chapters.

On the other hand, if biological science were to make *Homo sapiens* immortal, science then might be in a position to help reduce the existential anxiety but still not eliminate it. The questions of "why universe" and "end of universe" will still remain, although each person alive then would know that he or she will likely be there whenever the answer to the "why" question becomes clear. This unlikely and distant development has the potential to change the nature of existential anxiety since there will be a reduced need to rush to make judgments about the issue of why. While theoretically possible, biological science is not exactly in a position to bestow physical immortality on *Homo sapiens* any time soon. Therefore, we may also conclude that scientific creativity is utterly different from religious creativity, though this does not necessarily mean that science and all forms of religious creativity are opposed to one another. For example, an agnostic doctrine such as Buddhism, which is silent on metaphysics and focuses on ethics alone, need not be in conflict with science.

Thus, historically, science differs from the practical creativity required to sustain material life in that it is not required for survival. It differs from most forms of religious creativity in that it has been unable to address the existential anxiety arising from an awareness of mortality and the issue of why we exist. Science, then, is a form of creativity based on freedom and curiosity that fully uses the entire range of the unique mental powers of observation, reason, and imagination bestowed on *Homo sapiens* by biological evolution. We explore these unique mental powers of the species more fully in chapter 3.

1.6 Science is Different from Other Creative Outcomes

Man uses his biologically gifted and socially developed mental powers of observation, reason, and imagination to express his creative urges in practical, religious, and intellectual (art, philosophy, and science, including science-based practical technology) creativity. In this section, we want to briefly explore the relationship between science and these other forms of creativity. Let us begin by defining practical technology, religion, art, philosophy, science, and science-based technology.

Practical technology may be defined as knowledge, tools, and crafts used by man to control his environment and to satisfy his needs without explicitly using principles of science. The ancient art of practical technology was based on experience throughout. In the last three centuries, science-based technology has fully supplanted practical empirical technology.

Religion consists of metaphysics, ethics, and rituals. Metaphysics is a set of beliefs about the origin of existence or in effect the presumed nature of relationship among God, individual, and the universe. Ethics, when derived from a religious teaching, defines the rules of living, consistent with a particular religion. Rituals are simply a set of repetitive practices derived from the underlying metaphysics as well as the culture and surviving mythology. Broadly speaking, there have been two distinct types of "religions" in human experience: revealed or faith-based and experiential. Both ultimately amount to existential speculation or a frank admission of the futility of speculation. In this context, agnosticism cannot be classified as a religion since it is devoid of metaphysics by definition.

Art may be defined as something that, using an appropriate medium, evokes aesthetic pleasure in man. The aesthetic pleasure might involve appreciating a likeness (representational art), evoking emotions (Expressionist art), creative form (formalistic art), or symbolic art (sublime art or abstract art). This definition would then include all visual arts, such as painting, sculpture, and architecture, and all performing arts, such as dance, music, theater, etc. Art may have functionality.

Philosophy may be defined as rational inquiry into the nature of truth, goodness, and beauty (called Satyam Shivam and Sundram in classical Indian philosophy). It is classified into metaphysics, logic, epistemology, aesthetics, and ethics, in modern terminology. It differs from science in that it does not use controlled observation, and it differs from religion in that it claims no revealed or absolute knowledge. Historically, whenever a science has acquired an experimental basis, it was peeled away from philosophy or religion, as the case may be. The philosopher does not claim absolute results of philosophical inquiry; the results are relative and subject to revision. In this respect, philosophy is similar to science and utterly different from faith-based or experience-based religions.

Science-based technology may be defined as technology developed explicitly using principles of science to satisfy human needs.

Science was defined above as a creative activity that leads to organized and verifiable knowledge about three realms: nature, man, and social order.

Below, we briefly review the relationship of science to these other creative outcomes.

Science and art: A common assumption is that art—in particular, representational art—is a precondition of science. Both the classical Greek and Italian renaissance experiences would seem to support this assertion. Nothing, however, could be farther from the truth, in our opinion. The explosion in representational art before the rise of science in Greece and Italy is a historical fact. However, one must distinguish between historical fact and logical necessity. Art does not teach much about controlled experimentation or logical reasoning. On the other hand, it can certainly sharpen the power to observe. However, so can looking for herbal or medicinal plants in the wilderness. Man first learned about controlled observation by watching the heavens at night and not by sculpting figurines. The rise of science, on the other hand, has had an enormous impact on art. Without the concept of zero, for example, it is hard to see how the idea of a vanishing point could have led to the development of perspective in painting. Many schools in painting, such as cubism, have sprung forth as a direct consequence of breakthroughs in science. Beauty in science is logic-based whereas beauty in art is simply form, proportion, flow, and color. Artistic achievement can help in the rise of science, but it is not a precondition for and does not automatically lead to the rise of science. One only need look at the artistic achievements of ancient Egypt, Persia, the Roman Republic, and the Roman Empire to confirm that.

Science and philosophy: Philosophical inquiry can help science in two ways. In cultures under the sway of a dogmatic, revealed religion that may have an antiscience bias, philosophical inquiry can help restore the creative balance in the favor of science. This has been so in the history of the European civilization. However, the exact opposite has been true in Islamic civilization, where the philosophical working out of the beliefs embedded in the Quran killed Muslim science. Philosophical inquiry in ancient Indian civilization, on the other hand, led to developing the principle of equivalence of lawfulness of the heavenly, terrestrial, and inner or spiritual realms. This latter outcome not only led to esoteric or experience-based religions but also supported science. Secondly, philosophical inquiry is essential in formulating correct laws of logic and epistemology or a theory of knowledge. However, in logic, philosophy probably learns as much, if not more, from science than the other way around. Science does not worry about the discipline of epistemology. From science's perspective, it is irrelevant. A physicist does not conform to the epistemological theory as he goes about his work. Epistemology is simply the philosopher's way of systematizing the method science uses post facto. Thus, we may conclude that philosophical inquiry is a necessary but not sufficient condition for the rise of science but only for a culture steeped in religious dogma.

Science and religion: In theory, dogmatic religions at best may neither encourage nor discourage science. In practice, quite often, dogmatic religions actively hindered science. Thus, we see a conflict between science and dogmatic monotheistic revealed religions in history. The esoteric religions are more proscience but can operate in a subtle way as antiscience. This occurs when the focus on inner spirituality denies the importance of the physical universe and material life—that is, when they tend to become otherworldly and excessively spiritual. On the balance, dogmatic religious traditions are definitely not good for scientific cause, and esoteric religions may, under certain conditions, lead to neglect of science but not intellectually conflict with it.

Science and science-based technology: These are in a close relationship. As mentioned above, science-based technology is simply that subset of technology actively developed through the application of science. Expanding science expands the potential scope of science-based technology. By definition, however, science-based technology can never have a scope greater than that science allows.

Science and practical technology: Before the rise of science, practical technology was not based on science or engineering. Its march was slow but relentless. With the rise of science, technology has tended to be increasingly derived from science and engineering. Thus, science has paid back its historical debt to practical technology. With the rise of science, progress in technology has naturally accelerated enormously.

1.7 Scientific Method

The nature of science is social and stepwise. Each step makes it a little less imperfect. One implication is that theories of science, as we said earlier, can never be proved. They can only be disproved, as Carl Popper (1902–1994) stressed. Thus, while the results of science are uncertain, its method, however, is not. The scientific method may be simply stated as follows:

- Observe a phenomenon in a controlled experimental setting through well-designed experiments.
- Formulate a hypothesis to explain the phenomenon. This is the process of induction.
- Use the hypothesis to predict results quantitatively or entirely new phenomenon. This is the process of deduction.
- Confirm the predictions based on the hypothesis by several observers through more controlled experiments or reject the hypothesis.

As we might expect, the experimental method is the result of a long process of development. The march of science and development of the scientific method went hand-in-hand for a substantial time. This means that early physical science development preceded the full understanding of the experimental method or controlled observations and laws of reason. In fact, we could say one process helped the other to mature. It is, therefore, important to distinguish between science and what we have called protoscience. The latter may be defined as verifiable accumulated knowledge whose development is characterized by a lack of experimental method and use of fully developed laws of reason.

We also note briefly that Thomas Kuhn (1922–1996) added his theory of paradigm shift to the scientific method. This theory stated that often scientists, being human, would hold on to a particular viewpoint rather stubbornly until overwhelming evidence forces them to change their views. This is another way of stating that science goes through a period of evolutionary change followed by a revolutionary reconfiguration.

Finally, Paul Feyerabend (1924–1994) questioned whether one method applied to all sciences and argued that scientists should not adhere to a particular method. After all, scientific method came out of science and not the other way around! In social sciences, the objective falsification of Popper is not always possible. As a result, Popper's and Kuhn's theories are better appreciated in physical sciences while social scientists often prefer Feyerabend's theory.

1.8 Limitations and Power of Science

Limitations of science, to a considerable extent, depend on the class of science because of the fundamental differences among them. The formal sciences are a priori in nature. Their results are obtained from apparently self-evident axioms by using mathematical or formal logic. The results of formal sciences are, thus, as valid as the axioms they are based on. Physical and biological sciences start with verifiable observations about the natural phenomenon and then generalize these observations based on logical reasoning. Social sciences also start with observations about individual human or social phenomenon and use logical reasoning to arrive at conclusions. However, since social sciences always involve human behavior, these sciences have to contend with an independent and fundamentally unpredictable human free will. Thus, formal sciences worry about the truism of their apparently self-evident axioms, natural sciences worry about the objectivity of their observations, and social sciences worry about both the objectivity of their observations and the effect of unpredictable human free will. Consequently, all classes of science have their limitations. These limitations imply that the results of science are neither absolute nor infallible because all scientific theories or results are error-prone, however small, and old theories themselves ought to be and usually are discarded as better theories with less error are developed.

Limitations of formal and natural sciences have come under considerable theoretical study over the last century. In 1931, Kurt Gödel underscored the limitations of formal sciences in the form of his Incompleteness Theorem, which proved that it is impossible to create a system of internally consistent axioms that are the starting point of formal sciences. In the 1930s, limitations of natural sciences also became painfully apparent with development of the Quantum Theory, which eliminated the absolute separation of the observer and the observation. This called into question the objectivity of the data and therefore the results obtained by natural sciences. In response, pioneering work done by Karl Popper, as noted above, persuasively argued for shifting the focus of natural science theories from verification to falsification because verification may be an illusion if the underlying data are uncertain to begin with. Most social sciences, on the other hand, have yet to develop the explanatory and predictive powers granted to natural or formal sciences. Their limitations have been quite apparent. This is why that even the most quantitative social science, economics, has been called a dismal science.

It has been said that relying on reductionism is a more fundamental limitation of science. Reductionism assumes that a higher-level phenomenon can be explained in terms of the next lower level phenomenon. Thus, in theory, an explanation moves from society to individual person, organs, cells, biochemistry, chemistry, and physics, as Steven Weinberg has said. Science correctly assumes that if initial and boundary conditions in a system are known in advance, a study of its independent and dependent variables through controlled experiments at a particular level can determine the quantitative laws that govern the relationship between independent and dependent variables. However, we cannot predict the emergent properties as one goes from one level of complexity to the next higher level. For example, we cannot predict the life-giving properties of common salt from the toxic properties of its constituent elements, sodium and chlorine. We can predict the structure of the sodium chloride molecule from the known structure of its constituents using quantum mechanics but not the new emergent properties of the salt molecule. The universe, thus, is creative, not only in initially creating space/time and matter/energy through the Big Bang but also at each level through the emergence of new miraculous properties. There is no a priori way to predict emergent phenomenon in either direction.

In this sense, science may be defined as a method of simply quantifying the relationship between independent and dependent variables at a particular level of complexity and no more. This is also why we have multiple sciences and not just "one" science and why we can "ignore" laws of physics while formulating laws of economics. Thus, while science may appear to pay lip service to reductionism, it actually operates by assuming that the universe is unpredictably creative in a continuing manner across the multiple, ongoing levels of complexity evolution creates. The universe has ceaseless creativity, and science is simply a way to understand and codify this creativity, one level of complexity at a time. Science, thus, only works if it is applied narrowly one level at a time.

Science thus has limitations; however, its power, social sciences included, is considerable. This power comes from three sources: its ability to explain a phenomenon, whether formal, natural, biological, or social; its ability to predict the phenomenon; and most importantly, its usefulness in satisfying human needs through the application of its results. This first two are primarily of intellectual value; the third, of course has great impact on the daily lives.

1.9 Summary

Science is a verifiable and organized form of knowledge capable of being falsified and may be classified into formal, natural, biological, and social types. Science becomes possible when the illusion of perfect or absolute knowledge is given up. Scientific creativity is utterly different from religious creativity on the one hand and materially different from practical and other forms of intellectual creativity, such as art and philosophy, on the other. It uses the full range of the biologically gifted mental attributes of imagination, observation, and reason. Science may thus be regarded as the most natural and human way through which *Homo sapiens* at a certain stage of social development begin to relate to the universe. However, unlike the unique attributes of observation, reason, and imagination on which science is based, science is not gifted to man. He must discover it through effort. Once science is born and matured, it takes a central position among all other the creative outcomes as if these other forms were destined to lead to science. Historically, art, philosophy, practical technology, and religion have often helped or hindered science by temporarily occupying the driver's seat in the course of history of civilizations. Today, the relationship is reversed, and science has earned the function of keeping a watchful eye over its historic elders.

KEY CONCEPTS

Definition of science
Classes of science
Social and stepwise nature of science
Science and other forms of creativity
Scientific method
Limitations of science

Chapter 2 | Framing Issues—Civilizations and Science

2.1 Introduction

The simple premise of this book is that the intertwined history of civilization and science has determined the evolution of science through travel, trade, exchange of ideas and inventions, and wars among civilizations. It is hard to argue against this premise; however, historians disagree about the specifics and may disproportionately promote the contributions of their own civilizations. In this book, we use facts to systematically untangle this relationship. In this brief chapter, we will make a few observations followed by some thought-provoking questions about civilizations and science from a broader perspective. We want to limit these observations to those most are likely to be considered undisputed. We hope that this simple exercise will point to a thought process that will ultimately help us develop the analytical framework and tools in part III that we use to analyze the relationship between civilizations and science in parts IV and V.

2.2 Observations Concerning Civilizations

- Civilizations have been around for no more than ten millennia, substantially less than 5 percent of the time that *Homo sapiens* have existed.
- Civilizations have come in all sizes, from small city-states to continental behemoths.
- Not all civilizations were independently created. Many were offspring of another civilization, and still others were the result of one or more civilizations merging.
- Civilizations are quite stable, often existing for millennia. Some do perish, however. Like the *Homo sapiens* who create them, civilizations are born, marry, give birth to offspring, divorce at times, and ultimately die.
- Civilizations typically consist of small administrative units called states or city-states that share more than mere geography. They share history and religion and often language, technology, art, philosophy, and culture.
- Civilizations have the capacity to change dramatically over time, though some have a greater capacity to do so than others do. These changes typically occur over long periods. However, the rate of change itself has accelerated over time and is highly variable from one civilization to another and from one period to the next.
- Civilizations, through their administrative units or states, have produced increasingly complex political, military, economic, religious, legal, social, and educational and knowledge-creating structures and decision-making processes designed to meet the needs of its population based upon its knowledge base and its natural environment.
- Civilizations, unlike the hunting-gathering groups and tribes that preceded them, have not been egalitarian. Civilizations create differences in power that originate from the increasingly complex division of labor and the inherently differing ability of the individuals. These differences in power and the different abilities of individuals have naturally led to enormous differences in the wealth, power, and status of the individuals within civilizations.
- Civilizations produce ideas, inventions, and wealth. All civilizations, depending on opportunity, have engaged in fair trade, the exchange of ideas and inventions, and peaceful migrations based on mutual benefit.
- Surprisingly, civilizations rarely go to war; their administrative units or states do.
- States of civilizations have initiated war with states of other civilizations. We can discern an increasing reciprocal influence of these civilizations on one another based on the transfer of ideas and inventions, means of wealth, and wealth itself through control of territory, enslavement of humans, and coerced trade.
- Finally, a civilization is generally—though not always—loved by those born into it. Others from a different civilization may love it, be indifferent to it, or even hate it.

2.3 Issues Concerning Civilizations

The above observations stand the empirical test; they are consistent with the broad factual history of civilization over its entire existence. However, they raise some interesting and, at times, difficult and challenging questions:

- What has been the relationship between civilizations and the peoples who continued to follow hunting-gathering or nomadic lifestyles since the birth of civilization?
- Can we analyze the social evolution of *Homo sapiens* from their emergence some three hundred thousand years (or more) ago to the present into logical periods for greater understanding? Can we further analyze the period since birth of civilizations into eras so

that these eras correspond to different generic types of civilizations?

- What causes civilizations to evolve and change? Is it primarily internal factors, external actors, or some combination of the two? What relative roles do natural, biological, and social causes play?
- Why do civilizations differ from one another? Some civilizations are practical, some seem very religious, some are peaceful, and still others are aggressive and violent. Some are open, and others are insular. Some only fight internally while states of some civilizations invade states of other civilizations. Why is this so?
- As civilizations change, do they retain some of their characteristics? Is there a rather stable core of civilizations that does not change or that changes with great difficulty?
- What are the outcomes of a civilization? Why do civilizations differ in what they create? Some civilizations show a preference for practical inventions; others show it in art, religion, philosophy, or science. Some mostly create wars. And their outcomes change over time, often dramatically. Why is this so?

2.4 Observations Concerning the History of Science

Below, we make observations concerning the birth and evolution of science and present some thought-provoking questions concerning the relationship between civilizations and science, which is the focus of part IV.

- Protoscience, as we define it, has a five millennia-long history, while science proper has a three millennia-long history. That is eight millennia, about the same amount of time that civilizations have existed. Science did not appear magically out of nowhere, and its birth was preceded by long period of pregnancy.
- During its existence, science has achieved remarkable breadth and depth. The breadth of science leaves nothing out: universe, life, *Homo sapiens,* and society. Its depth ranges from the subtleties of a human mind to the very creation of the universe itself. It can handle ordinary numbers and unbelievably subtle mathematical logic.
- A civilization's appreciation and acceptance of science has varied widely over time and across civilizations.
- Science's center of gravity has moved around among civilizations considerably since its birth.
- Science has always depended on the state or administrative units for moral and material support.
- Not all civilizations have participated in or contributed to science equally.

- Science in a civilization has likely been affected by other civilizations, both positively and negatively, directly or indirectly, through peaceful exchange and through war.
- The strong role of the individual is quite apparent in the history of science. We could probably tell its entire story through lives of less than a thousand exceptionally creative individuals.

2.5 Issues Concerning Evolution of Science

The above simple observations concerning of science also raise challenging questions:

- How important has the peaceful transfer of ideas and invention among civilizations been to scientific development?
- If science depends on state support or the wealth allocated to it, does it also depend on fair trade and peaceful migrations among civilizations, which has the potential to greatly affect the wealth of civilizations?
- Since wars and coerced trade can also greatly impact the wealth of civilizations, what is the nature of the relationship among coerced trade, war, and the progress of science?
- If civilizations did not contribute equally to science, which civilizations materially contributed to science?
- What is the relationship between the religious beliefs and the capacity of a civilization to develop science?
- What is the relationship between the political independence the states of a civilization experience and the capacity for a civilization to develop science?
- What is the relationship between openness to others' creativity and the capacity of a civilization to develop science?
- Why have some civilizations contributed more to formal sciences than to natural sciences?

2.6 Summary

In this brief chapter, we made common sense observations and raised broad thought-provoking questions concerning civilizations and science.

KEY CONCEPTS

Observations concerning civilizations
Issues concerning civilizations
Observations concerning science
Issues concerning history of science

PART II
EMERGENCE OF *HOMO SAPIENS* AND CIVILIZATION

OVERVIEW OF PART II

In part II, we briefly describe the long process that led to the emergence of *Homo sapiens* and civilization.

In chapter 3, we begin by briefly tracing the biological evolution from primates leading up to *Homo sapiens*, an evolution giving them unique physical and mental attributes and continuing instincts.

In chapter 4, we outline the long journey through hunting-gathering and Neolithic periods, culminating in the birth of civilization around 6500 BCE. We introduce the reader to the four ancient primary civilizations.

Chapter 3

Emergence of *Homo sapiens*

3.1 Introduction

It is useful to begin at the beginning of the species that created civilizations. We want to glimpse what separates our species from other forms of life from a biological perspective and how these differences impacted the social evolution of the species through hunting-gathering and Neolithic epochs that eventually led to the birth of civilizations.

In this chapter, we begin by defining the four broad epochs in the story of *Homo sapiens* and then briefly sketch the latter period of the biological evolution epoch that led to *Homo sapiens* emerging from the primate some 55 million years ago. We also explore the uniqueness this evolution bestowed upon *Homo sapiens*.

3.2 The Four Epochs

Although a work in progress, the high drama leading to *Homo sapiens* civilizations has four acts:

1. The biological evolution of *Homo sapiens*
2. The rise of countless hunting-gathering cultures as they developed spoken language as well as early practical technologies adapted to diverse geographical and climatic conditions across the globe
3. The emergence of the first agricultural communities as agriculture evolves and nonagricultural technologies are refined
4. The emergence of civilization itself

The first act was tens of millions of years long, beginning with primates; the second was an evolution of cultures lasting about three hundred thousand years; and the third and fourth acts lasted less than ten millennia. Thus, the first act was a biological evolution and the following three were different forms of social evolution. It is indeed an amazing story.

Biological Evolution Epoch

- Evolution leading to *Homo sapiens* started with primates about 55 million years ago and led to the emergence of *Homo habilis*, our most recent matrilineal common ancestor, beginning about 2.5 million years ago in the grasslands of East and South Africa. This biological evolution "ends" with the species *Homo sapiens* about 300,000 years ago in East Africa. This evolution of *Homo habilis* to *Homo sapiens* spanned about 100,000 generations, assuming an average life span of less than twenty-five years.

Hunting-Gathering Epoch

- The migration of *Homo sapiens* from East Africa to all corners of the earth started about 160,000 years ago. The story spans several thousand generations.
- The impact of the dropping of the larynx perhaps more than a hundred thousand years ago enabled spoken language at least fifty thousand years ago.
- The migrating hunter-gatherer human groups created literally thousands of known and forgotten human cultures through successful adaptation to the diverse geographical and climatic conditions. They relied on simple tools made out of stone and bones and used fire.
- The birth of art and, starting with creation myths, the birth of earliest religious impulse and metaphysics began during this period.

Neolithic Epoch

- The invention of agriculture based on domestication of plants and animals started about 10,000 BCE or perhaps significantly earlier based on some theories. It was completed in less than a hundred generations.
- It resulted in the emergence of clusters of villages and rudimentary government.
- The relentless march of practical technology involving discovery or invention of new materials and processes, technologies, and products, including clothing, tools, shelter, and much more occurred during this epoch.

Civilization Epoch

- The birth of cities started before 6500 BCE and continues after more than two hundred generations.
- Great advances in technology, ranging from the plough to computers and space stations, occur during this epoch.
- The division of labor as both the source and the means of exploiting the advances in practical technologies occurred in this epoch.
- The rise of trade initially in the form of barter eventually knitted together disparate communities into civilizations and eventually led to its globalization of trade.
- It entailed wars among civilizations and between civilizations and nomadic social orders.

- It experienced the rise of science as the most significant form of *Homo sapiens* creativity.

3.3 Difficulties in Constructing the Story of *Homo sapiens*

The story of biological evolution of *Homo sapiens* must be constructed with a few teeth, a few bones, and a few pieces of skull found here and there, and if we are lucky, a partial skeleton occasionally. The early social history of *Homo sapiens* also has glaring gaps despite great progress. When facts are missing, the construction of the story requires an overuse of guesswork and deduction, usually to the advantage of the storyteller, a fate we wish to avoid.

The story of the emergence of civilization is also a story of justifiable pride. However, from a different perspective, it is also a story that teaches humility. Did *Homo sapiens* groups migrating out of East Africa 160,000 years ago know that they were even migrating? Or were they just moving, directionless, to where the food supply was good, making migration the result and not the objective? Did human communities migrating and settling in the far northern latitudes know that the climate would give their descendants little chance to invent agriculture and civilization tens of thousands of years later? Or, conversely, did the ancestors of human communities that happened to migrate to favorable conditions for agriculture know that their descendants would be the privileged ones to invent agriculture, the greatest revolution in the history of our species?

Of course, they did not. The human life span is too short compared to the time scale of changes we are talking about. Early human communities were not even faintly aware of the future changes their descendants would bring about; they were simply surviving. Yet some of their actions brought forth monumental changes thousands of years later, and they persevered against all odds. The earliest hunting-gathering human communities even lacked a means of adequately communicating what each member learned individually. Even after spoken language emerged, they still had no way to record their knowledge. All they had at that point was words, and words unfortunately leave no fossils.

It is interesting to note that early human communities not in contact with each other often independently made the same key discoveries or inventions, such as stone and bone tools, the spoken language, and fire, though at vastly different times. As human communities began to contact each other, particularly after the invention of agriculture, they started to learn from each other, thus accelerating the pace of invention and change. The question of who first invented fire is preposterous.

This story also requires humility in telling it. The whole area of anthropology has been compared to a drunk looking for lost car keys where the light is good. Likewise, the book of history begins in the middle despite tremendous effort by archeologists to dig up prehistory. It is the same with constructing the history of the evolution of the genus *Homo* over 2.5 million years. The story of *Homo sapiens*, after all, is more satisfying to tell and easier to sell if it appears complete at every stage of unfolding. However incomplete our knowledge of this story may be, it is, nonetheless, a story that ends in successful invention of sustainable civilizations by no later than 6500 BCE.

3.4 Instincts and Physical and Mental Attributes

We shall employ the concepts of instincts and physical and mental attributes and want to define them upfront.

Instincts: Instincts of a species may be thought of as an inner compulsion for certain actions without any conscious thought or beliefs and without any sense of right and wrong. Instinctual behavior must be automatic, forceful, triggered by an environmental stimulus, unchangeable, requiring no training, and exist in every member of the species. Instincts evolved over extraordinarily long periods based on the adaptation of the organisms to the environment and were driven by natural selection and gene mutation. Thus, instincts are biological in origin. They reside in the unconscious, though not everything unconscious is based on instinct. For our purpose, the most important primate instincts that ensure individual survival are hunger, interspecies aggression (including fight and flight), and curiosity. Those that ensure the survival of the species are sex, dominance-seeking (to allow passing the best genes), parenting, and sociability. Instincts are self-serving for both the individual and the species and generally may be thought to aim at prolonging life in one way or another. Instincts do not recognize ethics or logic, but their fulfillment leads to emotional satisfaction.

Physical attributes: Physical attributes are size, strength, speed, agility, longevity, running, tree climbing, or flying to find safe haven from predators. Physical attributes, in concert with instincts, clearly played a dominant role in primate survival.

Mental attributes: Mental attributes, which also evolved alongside instincts, consist of perception (the senses of sight, sound, touch, taste, and smell), will, memory, emotion, reason, and imagination. It is clear that, with the possible exception of imagination, primates possess all these attributes to one degree or another. Mental attributes differ from instincts in that a subset of these mental attributes is essentially under conscious control. Perception gathers data from the external world, memory stores it for immediate or later use, reason and imagination manipulate it, will is required to execute the needed actions, pleasant emotions aim to reinforce successful actions, and unpleasant emotions discourage unsuccessful actions.

Together, the extremely slowly evolving instincts and mental and physical attributes determined the degree of how well the primates adapted to the environment they shared with other species.

3.5 Evolution of Primates (55M–2.5M BP)

Science teaches that the physical evolution of the universe started with the Big Bang about fourteen billion years ago, and life started to emerge on this planet about four to five billion years ago. Multicellular organisms are believed to have existed for at least a billion years on earth. Since then, natural selection and gene selection (and gene mutation) have produced innumerable species, all with species-specific instincts and physical and mental attributes. Primates, belonging to class Mammalian and order Primates, are thought to have evolved somewhere between eighty-five and fifty-five million years ago.

Primate behavior determined by instincts: Like all life forms preceding them, primate behavior is governed nearly completely by species-specific biological instincts. Successive generations of primates are hardly different from the previous generations. When change occurred, its origin was biological in nature and based on the principle of natural selection and gene mutation in the gene pool of the species. It is true that higher primates shared mental attributes with a species of yet to evolve in the genus *Homo* to one degree or another, particularly perception, rudimentary reasoning, and limited memory. Higher primates also shared some basic emotions, such as anger, fear, and tenderness toward the young with the genus *Homo* as well. However, the behavior is fundamentally guided by biologically fixed instincts since there was no short-term change in behavior from one generation to the next. Primates did not go through a social history over generations. If there is social history, it is limited to the life of an individual member and did not have continuity from one generation to the next. The behavior of individual and social hierarchy within a group was determined by natural variability in mental and physical attributes of the individuals, though it was mostly the latter.

Thus, like all other species, even most evolved primates lived a life driven by instincts and supported by physical attributes and unlike all other species, only very modestly through mental attributes.

All this was about to change for the first time on planet earth, however.

3.6 Evolution up to *Homo sapiens* (2.5M–300,000 BP)

Homo habilis

The evolutionary story of the genus *Homo* is said to begin about 2.5 million years ago with the emergence of several species that may be collectively called *Homo habilis* or *handy man*. These species include Lucy, discovered in 1974, and Ardi, discovered in 1994. This first *Homo habilis* species did not walk erect, though he had the pelvis designed to do so. He had a brain size of about 600 cc, a height of three to four and a half feet, and probably weighed around fifty to seventy-five pounds. *Homo habilis* evolved in East and South Africa in the late Pliocene period. The significant feature of later *Homo habilis* is that he used his hands to craft stone tools, called pebble tools. Pebble tools are choppers made by splitting naturally occurring round pebbles by striking it repeatedly. The use of pebble tools also marked the beginning of what is called the Paleolithic or Old Stone Age. *Homo habilis* was not a big wanderer and was quite content to stay in East and South Africa. *Homo habilis* seems to have died out around 1.4 million years ago after being in existence for a mere million years.

Homo erectus

Nature improved upon *Homo habilis* before he died out, evolving the next important species of the genus *Homo* known as *Homo erectus* more than two million years ago. *Homo erectus*, which may be considered the direct ancestor of modern man, was the first species that walked fully erect, and that feature gave him the name. Erect posture was made possible by locking knees, an improved foot arch, and a different location for the hole in the skull where the spine entered. *Homo erectus* had nearly twice the brain of *Homo habilis*, weighed nearly a hundred pounds, and measured approximately five and a half feet. Upright walking must be hailed as a major milestone because it freed hands from the chores of locomotion and allowed them to do more specialized tasks, making it possible for hand and brain evolutions to reciprocally influence each other. *Homo erectus*, because of his posture, was able to migrate out of Africa into Eurasia as early as two million years ago. Some believe that he may have used fire for cooking, thus considerably reducing time consumed in eating. Some researchers also believe that *Homo erectus* may have built rafts and sailed oceans. Larger brains need more energy, which in turn required consumption of higher energy meats. That in turn required developing better tools to hunt larger animals, and developing better tools needed a larger brain, a wonderful example of the self-reinforcing feedback evident in evolution. *Homo erectus* made large stone hand axes and made more sophisticated tools later, such as scrapers, slicers, and even needles. *Homo erectus* existed for nearly two million years, surviving more than ten glacial periods before dying out about 143,000 years ago.

Homo Neanderthalsis

Natural selection again improved upon *Homo erectus* before he died out and evolved the next significant species known as *Homo Neanderthal sis*. *Homo Neanderthal sis* had a massive brain—nearly the size of *Homo sapiens*—weighed about a hundred pounds, and was about five feet tall. *Homo Neanderthal sis* came into existence only about 250,000 years ago and seems to have migrated primarily into West Asia and Europe. Apart from a larger brain, this species may have had an early form of verbal communication by making alternating high- and low-pitched sounds. *Homo Neanderthal sis* also buried their dead, strongly suggesting that this *Homo* species experienced existential anxiety. The larynx probably had not dropped or fully dropped. By 50, 000 BP, *Homo Neanderthal sis* was making specialized flint and bone tools and, for reasons not well understood, was headed for extinction by about 30,000 BP.

The key achievements of the genus *Homo* up to the emergence of *Homo sapiens* are summarized in table 3.1.

3.7 Emergence of *Homo sapiens* (?–300,000 BP)

Nature's "last" attempt to improve the genus *Homo* again occurred in the East African grasslands at least three hundred thousand years ago, a little before the birth of *Homo Neanderthal sis*. *Homo sapiens* (the self-described wise ones) weighed more than one hundred pounds and measured over five feet, with a brain size of 1,000 to 1,850 cc.

Above, we have briefly sketched the evolutionary history up to species *Homo sapiens*. However, it is important to note that this is an area of active research. Recently, based on new fossil discoveries in East Africa, Frank Spoor has proposed that *Homo habilis* and *Homo erectus* may have shared earth for about five hundred thousand years. This means that *Homo habilis* was a branch that led nowhere. This new evidence has the potential to remove *Homo habilis* from direct ancestral line to modern humans. Similarly, four-hundred-thousand-year-old *Homo sapiens* remains have been discovered recently in the Qesem Cave in Central Israel, pushing back the three-thousand-year date we have used. There is evidence that humans who occupied the site used fire and flint blades. These discoveries have raised the potential to significantly revise the existing theories of the emergence of *Homo sapiens*.

3.8 Biological Attributes of *Homo sapiens*

Unique Physical Attributes

Compared to primates, the unique physical attributes of *Homo sapiens* included an erect walk, with hands free from the chores of locomotion; a physiological ability to make sounds of different frequencies; nearly hair-free skin; sustained physical power equivalent to a fraction of one horsepower; and the nature of its life cycle. The life span was typically less than one hundred years under most favorable circumstances; it had a relatively long childhood and adolescence, potentially even longer years of declining physical and mental powers, and an easy propensity to disease under crowded social conditions.

Unique Mental Attributes

The emergence of *Homo sapiens* resulted in the following differentiated mental attributes compared to those in primates:

- Perception and will perhaps not exceptionally different
- Memory and emotional capabilities significantly superior
- Observation (as distinct from perception), imagination, and reason (with their roles in transforming passive perception to active analytical observation) as unique

With the possible exception of the powers of perception and will, the mental attributes in primates pale in comparison to what *Homo sapiens* have. The unique attributes

Table 3.1: Key Achievements of the Genus *Homo*
2.5 M–250,000 BP

Species	When	Key Achievements
Homo habalis	2.5 M years	Pebble tools
	2.0 M years	Reworked tools
Homo erectus	1.4 M years	Knife
	1.0 M years	Fire
		Cooking
	0.5 M years	Shelter construction
		Clothing
	0.4 M years	Spear
		Pigment for ceremonies
Homo Neanderthal sis	0.25 M years	Verbal communication
		Burial of dead
		Bone tools

of observation, reason, and imagination are biologically gifted; *Homo sapiens* did nothing to earn them! In the beginning, these powers were mere potentialities, and *Homo sapiens* were unconscious of the powers they possessed. These powers were yet to be discovered and developed. It is probable that the individual variability in these powers among *Homo sapiens* is far greater than among the primates for reasons of both nature and nurture.

What is the evidence that the three mental attributes of observation, imagination, and reason are unique? The answer is quite simple: there is an irreconcilable gap between the primates and most primitive humans ever encountered. No primate is known to use a spoken language; no primate uses clothes or weapons, grows plants, or domesticates other animals. It is also true that there is tremendous difference between a savage and civilized man. However, the child of savage brought up by civilized parents would have little difficulty becoming civilized, and the child of civilized parents brought up by savages would grow up to be a savage, provided the child in either case was treated no different from other children. These simple facts lead to three profound conclusions:

1. *Homo sapiens* have biologically gifted, unique mental attributes.
2. These powers can only be actualized through social development.
3. These powers can both progress and regress. Their development depends on the nature of the social environment.

Instincts and Social Conditioning

Homo sapiens share all the key instincts of hunger, survival, sex, parenting, sociability, curiosity, intraspecies dominance, and interspecies violence with primates. However, unique mental attributes of observation, reason, and imagination opened up another avenue of decision making apart from fixed instincts. Using observation, reason, and imagination to make survival decisions created the possibility of relative weakening certain instincts and strengthening others through progressive disuse and social conditioning.

In summary, the biological gifts of *Homo sapiens* are unique mental and physical attributes and a continuing legacy of instincts, with the potential for social conditioning to relatively weaken them.

3.9 Summary

In this chapter, we have briefly traced the evolution of *Homo sapiens* from primates over a period of about 2.5 million years, resulting in the unique mental and physical attributes as a gift of the biological evolution as well as the continuing legacy of instincts with the potential for their relative weakening through social conditioning.

KEY CONCEPTS

Four Epochs
Key instincts of hunger, survival, sex, parenting, sociability, curiosity, intraspecies dominance, and interspecies aggression
Unique physical attributes of erect walking and speech capability
Unique mental attributes of observation, reason, and imagination
Relative weakening of instincts through social conditioning

Chapter 4 | Emergence of Civilization

4.1 Introduction

In this chapter, we review the long social evolution of *Homo sapiens* through the hunting-gathering (including Paleolithic period) and Neolithic epochs. This social evolution involved inventions of key technologies (fire, stone tools, and agriculture) and the emergence of spoken language, culture, creation myths, barter among nearby communities, and even wars by the upper Mesolithic times about fourteen thousand years ago. We then review and summarize the situation at the dawn of the civilization epoch through the achievements of *Homo sapiens* at the end of the Neolithic epoch and the diverse lifestyles in existence at that time.

This social evolution was only possible because *Homo sapiens* concomitantly developed certain inner psychological attributes of self-consciousness, free will, the necessity of beliefs, conscious creative powers, and conscience derived from unique mental attributes. These inner attributes were essential to be creative, form social bonding, and originate conscious purposeful individual and group action. The next chapter deals with the inner attributes and resulting emergence of the *Homo* inner nature. In this chapter, we focus on the outward changes.

It is important to again stress one constant in the story of man, right down to today: the story of man remains a mixture of facts, assumptions, distortion, and fiction. When the story of man's biological evolution is constructed, the genuine lack of facts hinder us. However, as we enter the social evolution of *Homo sapiens*, the lack of facts and the necessity of making assumptions and filling the gaps with fiction hinder us and intentional distortions pick up momentum as we approach the civilization epoch. We will be reminding ourselves constantly of this unfortunate aspect.

4.2 The Hunting-Gathering Epoch (300,000 BP–11,000 BCE)

While the principal drivers during the extremely slow biological evolution of *Homo sapiens* were natural selection and gene selection, principal drivers during the extremely fast-paced social evolution during the hunting-gathering period were natural and social causes. *Homo sapiens* demonstrated some "control" of the natural causes through ceaseless migration during the hunting-gathering stage and by selecting what seemed to be favorable places to settle down during the Neolithic Age.

Migration and Populating the Planet

For the first half of his existence, *Homo sapiens* stayed in Africa. It was probably during this period that the larynx dropped or it dropped fully as early as two hundred thousand years ago, thus creating the possibility of spoken language. Unfortunately, words do not leave fossils. We cannot determine with certainty when *Homo sapiens* first developed a functional spoken language. Most researchers believe it was at least fifty thousand years ago. Since *Homo sapiens* started to migrate out of East Africa around 160,000 BP, this would seem to indicate that language capability would likely have developed after migration started, implying independent language origin by several *Homo sapiens* communities in different parts of the globe. On the other hand, as other researchers believe, spoken language might have developed as early as two hundred thousand years ago, and *Homo sapiens* were already equipped with a spoken language before they started to migrate out of Africa. If the latter happened, it would seem to rule out independent language origin by multiple *Homo sapiens* groups.

Both in Africa and as *Homo sapiens* moved out of Africa, they must have encountered *Homo erectus* and later *Homo Neanderthal sis* species. We know that about a hundred thousand years ago, *Homo sapiens* populated Africa and the Middle East, *Homo erectus* populated Asia, and *Homo Neanderthal sis* was predominant in Europe. By thirty thousand years ago, this diversity had vanished and humans throughout Eurasia and Africa had evolved into anatomically and behaviorally modern form. We know little of the interaction and learning that might have taken place among them with any certainty. *Homo sapiens* likely inherited the stone tool–making technology from *Homo erectus* and *Homo Neanderthal* in Africa and perhaps learned even more during their interactions in Eurasia.

We note that in contrast to this out-of-Africa model of human evolution, the multiregional continuity model asserts that after *Homo erectus* left Africa and populated different parts of Eurasia, the regional populations of *Homo erectus* slowly evolved into different races of *Homo sapiens* that reflected environmental variations. However, the evidence from stone tools and artifacts, the DNA studies, and fossils of modern humanlike remains in Africa all point to the validity of the out-of-Africa model and a common *Homo sapiens* ancestry.

Let us accept the out-of-Africa model and pick up the journey of *Homo sapiens* from back in Africa about 150,000 years ago. For the first 150,000 years, *Homo sapiens* with a fully developed brain, upright walk, and free hands was content to live in and around his birthplace. He most assuredly knew the use of fire and was as good or better in use of stone tools as other species within the genus *Homo*. He no doubt inherited or learned all he needed from members of other *Homo* species who lived in East Africa around that time.

The first questions we must address are why *Homo sapiens* waited for 150,000 years before starting to migrate, and why he decided to migrate then. One answer is that he never really migrated; he was unaware of his full powers and was simply moving in search of food and safety, and perhaps food and safety were good around his birthplace for 150,000 years. But that throws the question right back: What caused food or safety to change near his birthplace about 150,000 years ago?

One *possible* answer is a combination of population growth and climatic changes. Depending on the quality of stone tools, it seems that even in most favorable natural environment, the hunting-gathering mode of existence cannot support a population density of more than one person per square mile. It has been estimated that on average, *Homo sapiens* population doubled every five thousand years during the entire Paleolithic Age, right down to the invention of agriculture. In all likelihood, the rate of doubling of population was lower during the first 150,000 years before he started to migrate out. Let us, therefore, assume the *Homo sapiens* population doubled every ten thousand years during the first 150,000 years of its existence in East Africa. This means that over 150,000 years, the population doubled fifteen times or grew by a factor of 32,768. If the initial group is assumed to consist of just six members, the population would have grown to nearly two hundred thousand, and it would require an area of nearly two hundred thousand square miles to support this population. Thus, even without any climatic pressures, it is easy to see why *Homo sapiens* would be content to stay put near their birthplace for the first 150,000 or so years. It is also equally easy to see why the pressure to migrate out of the birthplace area would be building around that time, give or take a couple of tens of millennia. Do note, however, the population pressure hypothesis does not explain why *Homo erectus* moved out of Africa nearly two million years ago.

It is important to emphasize that the *Homo sapiens'* ability to be successful in diverse environments resulted in a continual increase in population. This in turn required continual migration as long as he remained a hunter-gatherer. This process of populating all five continents took approximately 150,000 years. Significant climatic events at times accelerated, interrupted, or slowed down this journey. At the end of this long process, *Homo sapiens* triumphantly declared his dominion over the entire earth to the animal kingdom.

First migrations: The painstaking gene-tracing research done over the last decade shows that as population pressure built during 160,000 to 145,000 BP, four groups migrated to South Africa, the Congo Basin, the Ivory Coast, and north toward modern Ethiopia respectively. They carried the first generation of mtDNA gene type L1. Over the next twenty thousand years, another group traveled up north through the then-green Sahara, up the Nile into the Levant, thus becoming the first group to migrate out of Africa. It took nearly 35,000 years to get out of Africa. Recent discovery of seventy-thousand-year-old bone tools, which are superior to stone tools, in South African caves has required a significant modification to an earlier theory that *Homo sapiens* required tough climatic conditions of Europe to take stone tool technology to the next stage, thus demolishing an ethnocentric theory by earlier European anthropologists.

Disaster in the Levant: The group that reached the Levant died out by 90,000 BP because of a global freeze caused by last glacial period (110,000–12,000 BP), during which the Levant and the Sahara turned into extreme deserts. Perhaps *Homo sapiens* were not as hardy as *Homo Neanderthal sis*, who occupied the same area later. Or perhaps some other disaster killed them.

Second attempt to migrate: Over the next five thousand years, a second attempt was made to cross into Eurasia, this time through the mouth of the Red Sea, probably using makeshift rafts. This group continued through the Arabian Peninsula toward the Indian subcontinent. Over the next ten thousand years, this group traveled around the Indian coastline through Sri Lanka and reached Western Indonesia, which at that time was a landmass joined to Asia. Ultimately, this group made its way to South China by 75,000 BP.

Mount Toba disaster: Mount Toba in Indonesia erupted in 74,000 BP, depositing fifteen feet of ash on the Indian subcontinent and most of Indonesia, thus killing *Homo sapiens* in the Indian subcontinent and Indonesia during the ensuing thousand-year winter and mini ice age. This catastrophic event is supposed to have reduced worldwide *Homo sapiens* population to fewer than ten thousand adults and may explain the relatively high gene pool homogeneity among *Homo sapiens* today.

Repopulation and crossing into Australia: Over the next ten thousand years, by about 65,000 BP, the Indian subcontinent was repopulated, and *Homo sapiens* moved from Timor to Australia and from Borneo to New Guinea. Most of the area north of India in the Eurasia was too cold during the lower Pleniglacial period for migration and settlement.

The north warms up: By around 52,000 BP, the climate change warms up the north, and *Homo sapiens* move up the Fertile Crescent and return to Levant and by 50,000 BP. They reach Europe after crossing the Bosporus. By

45,000 BP *Homo sapiens* had arrived near modern France, probably near *Homo Neanderthal sis* settlements.

Homo sapiens **arrive in central Asian steppes:** Over the next five thousand years, or by 40,000 BP, several groups from India, South China, and the Fertile Crescent moved into the central Asian Steppes, initiating a long tradition of migrating north.

Populating Northern Eurasia: By 25,000 BP, central Asians had moved into Northern Europe, Russia, and Northeast Eurasia, getting ready to migrate into the New World. This period saw the development of the well-known cave art in France.

Homo sapiens **into the New World:** A new mini ice age began about 25,000 BP. The resulting lowering of the sea level created a land bridge over the Bering Strait, connecting Alaska and Siberia, thus allowing first migration into the first world. This group managed to reach the East Coast of North America before the last glacial maximum around 22,000 BP. Over the next three thousand years, during the last mini ice age, the northern latitude of Eurasia and North America froze, thus closing the land bridge and the ice corridor. This resulted in depopulation of the entire area with isolated, locked-in groups surviving in the north. Over next four thousand years, while the last glacial maximum lasted, some North American groups managed to make their way to South America by 15,000 BP. During the following five thousand years, as the climate continued to warm up, North America was repopulated from Siberia, as well as from the surviving groups already there. Most of coastal South America was populated over next several thousand years.

Development of Speech

Inventing simple stone and bone tools and fire may have been acts of individual creativity or through limited communication among the group members. More sophisticated tools naturally required a complex interaction among the group members and that in turn required a means of communication within the group. This was accomplished through spoken language.

The larynx had dropped as early as two hundred thousand years ago, as we noted above, making speech theoretically possible. The erect posture of *Homo erectus* probably made it possible for the larynx to drop. Next to the stone tools and fire, the spoken word may be considered the most important invention of *Homo sapiens* before established cultures. Spoken word made culture possible, and culture in turn, no doubt, accelerated the march of technology since innovation could now benefit from better communication among group members.

Higher animals show social behavior and cooperation based mostly on biological instincts. Such behavior cannot be characterized as culture in the human sense. For a human culture based on common norms of behavior to originate, it is necessary for the members to be able to communicate relatively complex ideas in a simple manner. However, social behavior based on common norms first requires development of these very norms. Development of shared norms can only occur over a long time through trial and error, taking into account the contingencies of the natural and existing social environments. Such trial and error process in turn cannot occur without some form of communication, and speech was the first significant communication system *Homo sapiens* developed. We of course do not know when and where a reasonably developed spoken language first came into existence. During this period, all human cultures continued independent developing spoken languages, probably at widely different times. It is also likely that some groups may have learned spoken language from other groups.

The descended larynx and hyoid bone (in the absence of the descent of the latter, the tongue remained horizontal, preventing it from shaping the sound) are responsible for pitch and loudness, and in conjunction with various parts of the mouth, make it possible for the human physiology to make sounds with a wide range of frequency patterns. Any fixed combination of these frequency patterns would then by consensus emerge as a recognizable spoken "word." However, it is clear that any agreed-upon combination of sounds to represent a given idea or object was as good as any other combination as long as everybody in the group understood it. The only requirement is that there are enough unique frequency patterns to allow a sufficiently large number of spoken words through unique combinations of these frequency patterns. It turns out this was not a difficult requirement for the human physiology to meet after the larynx and hyoid descended. It is important to note that a parrot too has the substantial physiological capability and is able to mimic the human speech but obviously without understanding since it lacks a human brain. It is also important to understand that a spoken word in a preliterate social order was simply a consistent recognizable sound pattern and no more. The word *tree* was not understood as a combination of the sounds T and R, followed by a shaping sound E. This bit of analysis had not been performed yet. The sound associated with *tree* was yet to be analyzed into its components.

It possible to create unique sounds to represent ideas and objects, and it was also possible to develop a grammar that would simply be an agreed order of words to convey a complex idea and to place that idea in a temporal context through word sounds to represent past, present and future. The development of spoken language, i.e., words and rules of grammar, therefore, required the following:

- The ability to hold an internal idea or an external object as a thought-image in the brain, i.e., the inherent processes of observation and abstraction

- A physiological ability to represent that abstract thought as a fixed, concrete, and distinct sound pattern in order to communicate that image or idea to another human
- An ability to analyze the time element into past, present, and future and create additional sound patterns to represent these time elements
- To agree to an order of words or sound patterns to communicate a complex idea clearly

As an example, the complex idea, "I am thirsty" has three sound patterns, *I* and *thirsty* as basic words, and a sound pattern, "am" to represent the time element. It also has a word order rule that states that "am" will follow "I," followed by "thirsty." Word order rule can vary from one language to another. A spoken language, therefore, at a minimum, has words, syntax, and a tense representation. The underlying infrastructure of mental abstraction, tense analysis, and the physiological ability to produce sound patterns in a spoken language is clearly quite remarkable and clearly dependent on the three unique mental powers that *Homo sapiens* possessed: observation, imagination, and reason.

Are the spoken languages *Homo sapiens* used somehow related? Recent research points to a common origin of all spoken languages as from an African language at least fifty thousand years ago, similar to the common biological ancestry of all *Homo sapiens*. The research is based on number of phonemes analysis of nearly six thousand or so existing spoken languages and a principle known as "the founder effect" borrowed from genetics. The founder effect says that if a very small number of individuals break off from a population, there is a gradual loss of genetic variation. A similar phenomenon shows in the decreasing number of phonemes in languages of people who split off later from the advancing group as *Homo sapiens* populated the planet.

Achievements of Hunting-Gathering Era

We have covered nearly 290,000 years within a few pages. What were the key accomplishments of *Homo sapiens* in this epoch? The last 20,000 to 40,000 years of the hunting-gathering epoch were its golden years, when complex stone tools and a highly developed spoken language produced innumerable human cultures and more complex technologies:

Speech: Speech was the crowning achievement of the hunting-gathering era that made all else possible.

Nonagricultural technologies: During this long period of about 290,000 years, tools evolved from crude stone tools to refined and polished stone and bone tools. He invented the bow and arrow, a vastly superior weapon compared to the spear. He invented rafts to cross the oceans.

Culture and social norms: Culture made it possible for him to invent art and to reduce his existential anxiety through creation myths and burial ceremonies. He improved clothing and shelter. Although at the hunting-gathering stage, *Homo sapiens* creativity was nearly completely practical creativity out of necessity to sustain material life, one can occasionally discern intellectual and religious creativity. No doubt, he also developed norms and codes of social living that suited each culture he invented. The scattered *Homo sapiens* cultures were largely unaware of one another, yet a slow diffusion of learning and sharing among the neighboring cultures occurred.

Animism: Humans in the hunting-gathering epoch also grappled with the problem of explaining the world and his place in it. Clearly, natural phenomenon must have been frightening with *Homo sapiens* having no control. One way, however, to influence these natural forces was to endow them with spirit so that there could be a communication. Thus, the principal religious thought was centered on animism. These spirits of the natural world were nonhierarchical, reflecting the egalitarian nature of the social order.

First domestication of animals: The dog was the first animal to be domesticated as a hunting aide. The earliest known evidence of a domesticated dog is a jawbone found in a cave in Iraq, and it dated to about 12,000 years ago. Domestication of other animals occurred toward the very end of the hunting-gathering stage and was driven by a need for proteins. In many instances, the plant seeds and fruit, in the absence of meat, were unable to provide the full nutritional value required.

Table 4.1 summarizes the key achievements of *Homo sapiens* during this period.

Beyond the Hunting-Gathering Stage

Some *Homo sapiens* communities became isolated on a continent such as in Australia, some settled in very cold climates, and others settled in very hot climates. Some happened to be in plains. Some happened to be in mountainous terrain. Some happened to have little water; others happened to have too much water and hence too much vegetation. Some had just the right amount of water and just the right temperature. Although obvious, this point needs to be emphasized: these human communities were there because of a history of migration, and they had no real memory or record of their migration history. All they had were unreliable myths and stories passed on verbally. Their ancestors had little foresight about how their moves would affect the future generations. But all these communities had one thing in common: they had all tried. They had shown courage born of necessity. As a group, they had accomplished what had never been done on this planet before and to our limited knowledge, anywhere in

Table 4.1: Key Achievements of Hunting-Gathering Period
300,000–11,000 BCE

Species	When	Achievements
Homo sapiens	160K BP	Moving out of Africa
	100K BP	Lithic blade
	77K BP	Bone tools Burial of dead
	60K BP	Raft
	Unknown	Spoken language
	50K BP	Flute, Bow, Mining of flint Mining of hematite for pigment
	37K BP	Tally sticks
	30K BP	Bone needles
	26K BP	Ceramics
	15K BCE	Cave art, Spear thrower, counting
	13K BCE	Bone houses, figurines, trade Dog domesticated,
	11K BCE	First plant domestication

the universe. Collectively and unknown to one another, different groups of a species had walked a million miles to four corners of a planet and succeeded in developing diverse cultures in response to the diverse physical environments it encountered. It was a singularly amazing achievement indeed.

At the end of the hunting-gathering era, *Homo sapiens* had to either invent agriculture and settle down or keep moving as hunter-gatherer bands or cultures. Because of continued migrations, some of these cultural groups were in the right place at the right time to invent agriculture and to usher in the most spectacular jump in *Homo sapiens* development.

Necessary and Sufficient Conditions of the Neolithic Epoch

Clearly, the emergence of speech that led to the birth of cultures, the invention of more sophisticated nonagricultural technologies, and the first domestication of animals may be considered the necessary and sufficient condition of the Neolithic epoch.

4.3 Neolithic Epoch (11,000–6500 BCE)

In this section, we touch on the emerging pastoralist lifestyle and discuss why *Homo sapiens* invented agriculture, where and when it took place, how it diffused across the planet, and where it first established itself on large scale and why. We will also briefly review the development in agricultural and an incredible number of associated technologies and products as well as the reciprocal impact these technologies had on Neolithic communities.

Emerging Nomadic Lifestyle

It is known that sheep were domesticated as early as 9000 BCE near Shania, in what is now northern Iraq. A pastoral way of life depends on herding fully or partially domesticated animals and requires frequent moving in search of new grasslands. Thus, culturally, a pastoral lifestyle has much in common with a hunting and gathering way of life, and both are equally dependent on geographic and climatic conditions. By at least 9000 BCE and likely earlier, coexisting with hunting-gathering communities, we witness the rise of pastoral way of life on the fertile, marginal, or even semiarid lands.

It is indeed difficult to settle the question of what came first, a pastoralist lifestyle or the invention of agriculture, though logically, one may argue that a pastoral lifestyle preceded a settled lifestyle. Perhaps a most reasonable assumption is that in different parts of the globe, the hunting-gathering, pastoralist lifestyle based on the early domestication of animals and a settled lifestyle based on early agriculture were not of equal importance, and there was not a unique sequence. Some locales, depending on ecology, first domesticated animals while others invented or adapted agriculture first.

The Birth of Agriculture

The age of agriculture has also been called the Neolithic age or the New Stone Age revolution. The term is meant to convey that when agriculture was invented, *Homo sapiens* still used stone tools, as metals had not been discovered. Although this change is referred to as a revolution, it was by no means sudden. The birth, diffusion, and establishment of large-scale agriculture were millennia-long processes.

Theories of the birth of agriculture: The hunter-gatherer lifestyle for *Homo sapiens* over nearly 290,000 years had been very successful. Generally, there was plenty of food. *Homo sapiens* lived in small groups of perhaps no more than a few hundred. The lifestyle was healthy and required moving to a new place every so often to allow the old camping sites to recover. Although *Homo sapiens* had migrated to all corners of globe by no later than 10,000 BCE, there was still plenty of space to fill. The population has been estimated to be between five million and ten million around 10,000 BCE. Even with an ice age and resulting glacial ice sheets covering northern latitudes, the planet could have supported several times that population in hunting-gathering mode. So what was the motivation to leave a healthy lifestyle with lots of leisure time and move to essentially a life of drudgery? This question must be tempered by the fact that, depending on location, human communities experimenting with agricultural lifestyles would have gone through a mixed mode combining hunting-gathering, pastoralist, and agriculture lifestyles to hedge the bets.

The question of why agriculture was invented is a difficult one. Three main theories have been proposed. Let us be clear, though: agriculture would have to be invented as the population built up. A hunter-gatherer lifestyle cannot typically support more than one person per square mile, and agriculture, even without the improvements of last several thousand years, could support fifty humans per square mile. The more appropriate question, therefore, is not why was agriculture invented but *when* it was invented.

One of the earliest attempts to explain the invention of agriculture came from Gordon Childe in the 1920s: sudden climatic change around 15,000 BP forced hunter-gatherer communities in the Fertile Crescent to work harder and travel longer distances in search of food. This led them gradually to stay near water and get into farming through invention of agriculture around 7000 BCE, initially through domesticating locally occurring wild wheat known as einkorn in Karacadag in southeastern Turkey. Eurocentric anthropologists enthusiastically subscribed to this theory. Later evidence showing that agriculture was practiced earlier in New Guinea in Melanesia, with the archeological finding of an irrigation system dating back to before 8000 BCE.

This highlighted the need for a better explanation. Carl Sauer provided it in 1952. Still later, in 1972, based on the excavations of Chester Gorman, and W. G. Solheim put forth the unsubstantiated hypothesis of agricultural practice in Thailand's Spirit Caves as early as 20,000 BCE. There is also evidence of wild rye cultivation in Syria as early as 9000 BCE.

Sauer believed that it was not necessarily a switch to agriculture that created a sedentary lifestyle. Rather, it was the other way around: sedentary lifestyle, though not necessarily a pastoral lifestyle, created agriculture. The key elements of his full theory were as follows:

- Agriculture could not have emerged from food shortage, as a shortage of food would not allow the means, time, and slow steps needed over a prolonged time to invent agriculture.

- The invention of agriculture would require plant and animal diversity and therefore a warm climate.

- Early agriculturalists could not establish themselves in river valleys, where agriculture would require drainage and irrigation technologies.

- Agriculture would begin on wooded but not tropical areas with sufficient rainfall.

- Above all, the inventors of agriculture would be sedentary folks such as fishing tribes near fresh water in warm climates.

Despite its convincing nature, not everyone accepts Sauer's theory and the supporting anthropological evidence. Many European anthropologists are enthusiastically support the climate change theory, which is reminiscent of their beliefs that a rough European climate was needed to develop better tools during upper Paleolithic Era until sophisticated bone tools dating back 77,000 BP were discovered in South Africa, as mentioned earlier. Whenever the center of innovation seems to move farther away from the Levant and Europe, there is discomfort among European anthropologists and archeologists. It, unfortunately, is also a recurring theme in European historiography as well.

A third theory has proposed that people who were already settled and trading invented agriculture. However, it appears more likely that invention of agriculture gave impetus to trade between agricultural communities and those still engaged in hunting-gathering or subsisting on pastoral lifestyles. In fact, pastoral lifestyle reached full potential only after agricultural communities domesticated draught animals. Infrequent bartering among hunting-gathering and pastoralist communities no doubt existed. However, it seems improbable that this sort of barter would have led to settled communities, agriculture, and stable trade. Growth in trade was more likely to follow the invention and establishment of agriculture and not the other way around.

Plant domestication: The heart of the invention of agriculture was domestication of plants. It was a difficult problem that required overcoming several difficult challenges:

- Choosing plants that did not shed their seeds at maturity
- Selecting plants that had relatively large seed size and not a bitter taste
- Understanding that some plants, such as lentils, have seeds with a dormancy period, thus requiring extended storage before planting
- Selecting plants with sufficient caloric value

Trial and error thus focused on balancing the taste, caloric value, ease of growing, harvest, and storage of the selected plants. One can envision a process lasting hundreds of years to domesticate naturally occurring plants in a particular locale and how this process required keen observation and the ability to draw appropriate conclusions. In short, through uncontrolled experimentation, agricultural communities were successful in optimizing the genetic makeup of the plants through selective plant breeding techniques.

Impact of Neolithic Revolution

The principle technologies mastered by emerging agricultural communities were plant and animal domestication as well as technologies such as tools and irrigation and techniques to improve the agricultural productivity. The impact of a change from a subsistence economy to a surplus economy was not just limited to sedentary lifestyle and population increase. These were just the beginning. The most significant impact was the emergence of specialization because all members were no longer required to produce and prepare food. Specialization through the slow and steady emergence of skilled nonagricultural technologies established the basis for the products revolution.

Products revolution: Over time, perhaps as many as 5 to 10 percent of adults were freed from the chores of food production. They now shifted their focus entirely to creating nonagricultural products. This required several thousand years and resulted in the invention of different materials, such as ceramics, glass, bronze, and natural fibers, as well as the invention of different processes, such as sintering, melting, churning, weaving, grinding, distilling, spinning, and molding using a potter's wheel. Deepening understanding of these materials and processes over time created a fantastic array of products, such as clothing, shelter, pottery, ornaments, milk products, textiles, and improved means of construction and transportation. Table 4.2 lists some of the selected products invented by these prebirth communities.

Barter: Specialization within a village community or within neighboring villages meant the necessity of barter as the first form of trade. As specialization and the range of agricultural and nonagricultural products grew, trade became increasingly important. This, again over time, led to two changes. First, the rise of protocities with a maximum population of perhaps a few thousand because those engaged in the nonagricultural production needed to be close together to increase their productivity through both competition and shared learning. Second, increased trade underscored the need to invent money. We need not go into the history of money here. Suffice it to say that early communities used just about every imaginable commodity as money before civilizations settled on precious or semiprecious metal as the preferred medium of exchange much later. The principal driver for needing money was the increasing number of products available for exchange. For example, if two communities had one hundred products for bartering, without money, it needed to identify nearly ten thousand (9,900 to be exact) exchange relationships or prices for barter. Using money reduces this to just one hundred relationships expressed in the form of prices. Further, under barter, one party may not need what is available for barter in a particular situation, thus reducing the probability of trade. Thus, the invention of money greatly simplified and accelerated the exchange of products and improved productivity.

To summarize, the Neolithic revolution is by far the greatest revolution in the 300,000-year upward march of *Homo sapiens*. It is the epoch during which several *Homo sapiens* communities independently or through adaptive learning

Table 4.2: Selected Achievements of Neolithic Communities
10,000 BC–6000 BC

Date	Where	Achievement
10,000	Japan	Pottery
	Fertile Crescent	Adobe house, Alcoholic beverage
9,500	Jordan	Granary
8,700	Iraq	Copper
8,000	Near East	Animal Husbandry
7,000	Mehrgarh	Surgery
		Dental surgery
6,200	Catahoyuk	Maps
6,000		Cloths from flax fiber

succeeded in making the transition from a hunting-gathering way to a settled way of life, a condition necessary for emergence of civilization. The settlement and the food surplus brought about through invention of agriculture made all else possible. Through specialization and implied coordination, it allowed man's imagination and reason to create an amazing array of nonagricultural products. Thus, specialization slowly succeeded in creating sociopolitical and economic organisms of increasing complexity until village clusters protocities emerged in several parts of Eurasia in the seventh millennium BCE.

Necessary and Sufficient Conditions of Neolithic Epoch

From the above discussion, it is clear that the necessary and sufficient conditions of the Neolithic period are an invention of agriculture, animal domestication, and developing nonagricultural technologies, and trade based on barter. With the establishment of agriculture, the emergence of civilization was just around the corner.

Diffusion of Agriculture

Thus, it seems reasonable to suppose that invention of agriculture took place in multiple locations independently in New Guinea, Turkey, and perhaps Thailand, and from these and other as yet undiscovered sources it spread to China, the Indian subcontinent, West Asia, and finally Europe. This process of diffusion probably spanned five thousand years, finally reaching the British Isles by about 5000 BCE and still later, Scandinavia. The land that was to later to unleash an industrial revolution had to wait for nearly five thousand years to participate in the greatest *Homo sapiens* revolution, the invention of agriculture.

The situation in Africa, Australia, and the Americas was different. *Homo sapiens* arrived in Australia as early as 65,000 years ago. Although they independently invented agriculture, agricultural lifestyle did not take root in Australia perhaps because of the large virgin continent and sparse population that allowed a longer continuation of the hunting-gathering lifestyle. On the other hand, *Homo sapiens* arrived relatively late in the New World. Again, bountiful and large continents required time to populate and a hunting-gathering life went on a bit longer. Agriculture was eventually invented independently and practiced in the Americas by no later than 5000 BCE. In North Africa and Egypt, the evidence of small-scale agriculture dates back to before 5000 BCE.

Early Development of Agriculture

Agriculture first established itself in the great river valleys of Asia with desert-like or relatively cooler conditions or flat terrains found in the Nile delta, the Tigris–Euphrates delta, Indus–Sarasvati valley, and the Yellow River valley in China. This is because the relatively vegetation-free terrain and the presence of fresh water, including rain or annual flooding, gave them an edge. Thus, the conditions that favored the birth of agriculture were not necessarily those that favored its first serious establishment. By about 7000 BCE, agriculture was firmly established in many parts of Eurasia and coexisted with nearby pastoral and scattered hunter-gatherer communities.

Further animal domestication: The work of tilling the fields was backbreaking and long. Finally, settling down and the consequent reduced spacing of children required that humans keep needed animals close. Animal domestication solved a number of these problems neatly. The protein in milk, meat, and eggs solved the problem of nutrition. The ability of animals to help in plowing and irrigation reduced the work drudgery. Finally, animals also provided hides, wool, and fertilizer. However, animal domestication, coupled with increased population density, sedentary lifestyles, and a lack of sanitation, resulted in sickness and rising death rates. On the balance, though, the animal domestication very effectively complemented the plant domestication. It is probably fair to say that one could not have succeeded without the other. It is interesting to note that while *Homo sapiens* were able to domesticate literally hundreds of plants, the success in animal domestication was limited to perhaps fewer than fifteen animals because of constraints on animal temperament, size, diet, mating habits, and life span. Though success in animal domestication was more limited, it was nonetheless as spectacular in effect, in part because *Homo sapiens* were successful in improving the genetic makeup of domesticated plants and animals through selective breeding. For the first time, *Homo sapiens* as inventor of agriculture were clearly influencing the biological evolution of life on the planet through the domestication technology and selective breeding of plants and animals.

Improved agricultural tools: The third leg (in addition to plant and animal domestication) of the developing agricultural technology was continual improvement in the agricultural tools, starting with digging sticks to break up soil, axes to clear forested areas, and of course the plow and the use of ox and horse to power the plow. In addition, early agriculturists developed methods to store rainwater and use river water for irrigation. These approaches, combined with the techniques of better seed selection, fertilization using animal waste, and weeding resulted in a slow but steady improvement in agricultural productivity as measured by output per acre and per person.

Sustainable food surplus: For our purposes, a sustainable food surplus is conceptually equivalent to the proportion of the population not engaged in producing food. Sustainable food surplus grew over time as agricultural productivity increased. However, expanding the definition of sustenance due to development of key nonagricultural technologies also led to creating new products to satisfy expanding human needs and wants that put a downward pressure on the available surplus for creative endeavors. On balance, however, surplus slowly grew over time. As the early communities settled in, the surplus tended to become more predictable and slowly but steadily growing. Therefore, we may arrive at the concept of a sustainable growing surplus, which was simply the proportion of population *not* engaged in the production of food *and* other nonfood production perceived as required for sustenance. It was generally growing, albeit very slowly, and clearly must have gone through periods of dynamic and volatile changes in a particular community because of changing natural and internal causes specific to that community in a given period.

Emergence of a protocity: The earliest city may be defined as a relatively large collection of people engaged primarily in nonagricultural production and creative endeavors. Sustainable food surplus made the rise of the nonagricultural sector and its new creative endeavors possible. Once the nonagricultural sector grew beyond a certain limit, the rise of a city became the key to increasing the productivity of this sector through increased communication and the exchange of ideas among people engaged in similar activities in a city setting. Those inclined to pursue creative endeavors in a particular city also needed a setting to interact with others engaged in same pursuits. As agricultural communities grew larger with increasing surplus, the emergence of city was a logical step.

4.4 Early Civilization Epoch (6500–3000 BCE)

Th birth of civilizations required continuing improvements in agricultural technologies, sustainable food surplus, and nonagricultural technologies. The birth of civilizations was not an event; it was a process with an endpoint that can only be fixed only when the definition of civilization is stated.

Additional Developments in Agriculture

Large-scale agriculture first established itself in the great river valleys because of the combination of river water and relatively vegetation-free terrain. It was also established in the desert-like climates or with relatively cooler conditions with a river. However, these communities were typically too dependent on one river or were limited to agriculture along the river. If the river dried out or more typically flooded (beyond the annual beneficial flooding that renewed the soil), it would be a disaster. As agricultural technology developed, temperate or subtropical plains with multiple river basins and reasonable rainfall would be more advantageous because rain would allow agriculture to expand to a larger area without dependence on one river. Once again, the conditions that favored the large-scale establishment of agriculture were different from both its birth and its first establishment. It took several thousand years to develop these productivity-enhancing technologies first in single river valleys in desert-like environments in West, South, and Northeast Asia and later in the plains with multiple river basins in South and Northeast Asia from 6000 BCE to about 2000 BCE. As early as 6000 BCE, canals were built in Mesopotamia to divert river water for the purpose of irrigation. By 2000 BCE, Egypt had managed to build a ninety-meter-wide gated canal to divert water from the Nile into a natural depression, in effect creating a lake about six hundred square miles in size.

To summarize the story of agriculture, as table 4.3 shows, the birth of agriculture probably took place in Southeast Asia, with its first establishment in the river valleys and its final large-scale establishment in the temperate and cooler, but not cold, plains of multiple river basins that had moderate rainfall. The overwhelming and changing impact of geographical elements, such as temperature, terrain, rivers, and rainfall, were critical in determining which locations got an edge at a given stage of the birth and gradual expansion of agriculture.

Birth of Primary Civilizations

If we define civilization based on the existence of a sustainable growing surplus; several nonagricultural technologies, such as housing, pottery, clothing, tanning, and stone working; and a city with a population approaching ten thousand, we could then fix the date of birth of civilization around 6500 BCE. The birth of civilization, however, was not a unique, singular event. The birth of the first civilization probably took place around 6500 BCE. Numerous prebirth, settled communities of differing sophistications existed between 10,000 and 6500 BCE. They continued their old ways, transitioned back into a nomadic lifestyle, or developed into civilization after 6500 BCE. We have chosen 6500 BCE as the date of the birth of civilization, and this assumption is not central to the main point of the book. The process of slow and steady improvements in agriculture and nonagricultural technologies, more elaborate division of labor, expanding trade, and more complex societal structures and processes to utilize these technologies continued unabated. The birth of civilization was not an event; it was a rather protracted process lasting millennia, during which different isolated groups gave birth to civilization-like communities depending on their foresight and cooperation of Mother Nature.

Table 4.4 begins with the earliest Indian (before 6500 BCE), the Mesopotamian (before 4500 BCE), and Egyptian (5500 BCE) protocivilizations. A little later, though perhaps as early as 6000 BCE, the Chinese protocivilization appears on the horizon. Of all the earliest four civilizations, only Indian and the Chinese have been continuous to the present. The Egyptian and Mesopotamian civilizations died more than 2,000 years ago and were forgotten until they were dug out of the ground approximately 200

Table 4.3: Milestones in Agriculture
10,000 BCD to 2000 BCE

	Where	Approximate Date	Key Crops
Birth Place	Syria	11, 000 BCE?	Rye
	Melanesia	Pre-10,000 BCE	Tora
	Spirit Caves, Thailand	8000 BCE?	Beans, Peas
	Turkey	7050 BCE	Wheat
First Establishment	Mehrgarh, South Asia	7000 BCE	Wheat, Barley
	Mesopotamia	6000 BCE	Wheat, Barley
	Egypt	5500 BCE	
	China	6000 BCE	Rice, Soy, Taro
	Americas	5300 BCE	
Large Scale Agriculture	Indus Valley	5000 BCE	Wheat
	Ganges Valley	2000 BCE	Wheat
	Yellow River	3000 BCE	Rice

and 150 years ago respectively. Chinese civilization has been conscious of its continuity over at least the past five thousand years. Several major cities of early Indian civilization encountered catastrophic flooding and the eventual drying of the life-giving Sarasvati River. This required an eastward relocation to the plains of the Ganges. Despite this natural calamity, the Indian civilization has retained a memory of nearly 7,000 years of its 8,500-year history through the Rig Veda, which was orally passed on with remarkably faithful preservation. The four civilizations, for all practical purposes, did not know about the existence of other civilizations perhaps until 3000 BCE or a little earlier.

Critical Role of Mother Nature in the Birth of Civilization

It is important to highlight the role of Mother Nature in the birth of civilizations. Civilization is inconceivable without agriculture, the domestication of animals, and the development of rudimentary nonagricultural technologies. Civilizations first arose where natural conditions made extensive agriculture relatively easier. Clearly, early civilizations were unlikely to prosper in frigid, arid, or tropical settings. Environmental factors largely determined the relationship between the level of human effort and sustainable food surplus so necessary for a civilization to survive.

Consider the following list of changes in climate before and after the invention of agriculture:

- At the end of the millennia-long, cooler Younger Dryas period starting at 9500 BCE, the climate turned warm again, with a wet climate returning to the West Asia. This would make Mesopotamia amenable to agricultural development.

- The Himalayan glaciers break up starting around 8000 BCE. This resulted in great river systems of northwest India, including the now extinct Sarasvati River that gave rise to Indian civilization.

- The sea level in the Gulf of Persia around 4000 BCE rose by up to two meters and created a warmer climate more suitable for agriculture in Mesopotamia, giving a boost to the Mesopotamian civilization.

- Rain pattern changes related to shifts in the tilt of the earth's axis of rotation turned North Africa around 6000 BCE into a green and lush place, thus creating positive condition for several protocivilizations to emerge.

- The Baluchistan and adjoining areas were not dry and had considerable rainfall around before 8000 BCE. A later shift in earth's axis of rotation shifted rainfall and began to turn the area into semidesert.

Table 4.4: Early Timeline of Primary Civilizations

BCE	7K	6K	5K	4K	3K	2K	1K	0	1K
South Asian (Indian)	Mehrgarh Phase		Vedic Phase	Harappa Phase		Ganges Phase			
African (Egyptian)			Pre-dynastic Phase			Dynastic Phase			
West Asian (Mesopotamian)	Pre-Pottery	Pottery	Copper Age		Summerian	Babylonian	Assyrian		
East Asian (Chinese)		Peiligang Culture		Yangshao Culture	Longshan	Xias	Shangs	Zhous	

Thus, earliest civilizations after the invention of agriculture emerged primarily where the geographical and climatic conditions were right—i.e., river valleys with abundant water, moderate year-round temperatures, and reasonably plain topology—a testimony to the successful ending of the wandering nature of *Homo sapiens*. Moderate rainfall would make the geographic location even more attractive. These conditions existed around or near the Tropic of Cancer in East Asia, South Asia, West Asia, and North Africa. It is, therefore, hardly surprising that all early civilizations of consequence—Indian, Mesopotamian, Egyptian, and Chinese—flourished not too far from the Tropic of Cancer. Tropical, arid, and frigid conditions were clearly unable to support the birth of civilization, given the level of available technology. Thus, the four primary civilizations emerged independently in vastly separated locations over several millennia.

Necessary and Sufficient Conditions of Birth of Civilizations

Clearly, a developed spoken language is a necessary condition for hunting-gathering cultures, prebirth settlements, and civilizations. The birth of civilization also requires the following three sufficient conditions:

- Sufficiently developed agricultural and nonagricultural technologies
- A growing surplus in food based on a relatively sophisticated division of labor and agricultural and nonagricultural technologies
- A protocity with a population of ten thousand

Above, in a few pages, we have completed the journey from the emergence of *Homo sapiens* to the birth of civilizations. We have included the genesis of cultures through spoken and nonagricultural technologies, the birth of settled communities based on the invention of agriculture that led to a sustainable growing surplus and product revolution, the birth of civilizations through further development of agricultural and nonagricultural technologies, and the creation of cities approaching population of ten thousand. The research underlying this story is far from complete. Hardly a year goes by when new archeological finds does not move the story. However, since our focus is on the period after the birth of civilizations, these new findings probably will not impact us much. A bigger concern for us is the prehistory of civilizations (the period immediately following the birth of primary civilizations and before the invention of writing) or the early "dark period," where a paucity of archeological data—either because of a lack of effort or continuous resettlement—is a stumbling block and a source of debate.

4.5 Overview of Achievements at the Dawn of Civilization

At the dawn of civilization, after more than 290,000 years of social evolution through uncounted cultures, *Homo sapiens* achievements may be summarized as follows:

- Emergence of spoken languages
- Emergence of practical technologies: fire, hunting tools, plant domestication, animal domestication, agricultural tools, and nonagricultural technologies, such as pottery, weaving, shelter-building
- Increasingly sophisticated division of labor and the corresponding societal structures and processes
- Rise of cities

Table 4.5: Climate and Social Organization of *Homo sapiens*
6000 BCE

Life Style	Water Status	Average Temperature	Vegetation Status
Primary Civilizations	moderate	moderate-High	Year round
Secondary Civilizations	moderate	Low	Seasonal
Proto-Civilization-warm	moderate	moderate-High	Year round
Proto-Civilizations-cold	moderate	Low	Seasonal
Nomads - Arid lands	Low	moderate	Low
Nomads - Desert	Little	High	Little
Hunter Gathers - Tropics	Excessive	High	Excessive
Hunter Gatherers - Frigid	Difficult	Very low	Little

- Crude counting ability
- A surplus in agricultural output
- Localized trade based on barter and invention of money
- Creation myths
- Primitive art
- Emerging class distinctions
- Possible conflicts and small-scale wars

With the exception of the last item, these were monumental achievements, with pace accelerating with development of language and agriculture as well as rising concerns. Written language and any progress toward the systematic understanding of natural or social worlds were still in the future.

4.6 Diverse Lifestyles during the Civilization Epoch

If we surveyed *Homo sapiens* populations around the world at the time of birth of civilization, we would find a diversity of lifestyles, some isolated and some in contact. In addition to the four primary civilizations, in Eurasia and North Africa, we find a continued nomadic lifestyle in arid central Asia and the West Asian desert, innumerable hunting-gathering groups stuck in the extreme frigid and tropical climates of North Eurasia, and many proto-civilizations around the globe in both warm and cold geographical areas. The water availability, the average annual temperature and its seasonal variability, and the nature of ecology that determined the existence of these lifestyles is summarized in table 4.5. Even a cursory glance at the table shows a strong relationship between the climate and ecology in various regions and stages of social development during this time.

4.7 Summary

In this chapter, we have briefly traced the long social evolution through hunting-gathering, Neolithic, and the birth portion of civilization epochs. The birth of primary civilizations was not a singular event; it was spread over several millennia. If one defines the birth of civilization based on the emergence of a city with a population of at least ten thousand, we may trace the birth to around 6500 BCE. All early civilizations were born in locations that were relatively benign geographically and climatically. Civilizations could not have arisen in frigid, arid, or tropical locations. However, not all civilizations are traceable to an independent birth. We proposed two sufficient conditions formally required for the birth of civilizations: a sustainable growing food surplus and a city with a population of at least ten thousand.

KEY CONCEPTS

Hunting-gathering epoch
Neolithic epoch
Civilization epoch
Invention of speech
Invention of agriculture
Birth of civilization
Primary civilizations

PART III
DEVELOPMENT OF THEORETICAL CONCEPTS

OVERVIEW OF PART III

In part III, we develop the concepts, methods, and tools used to analyze the intertwined history of civilizations and science in parts IV and V.

In chapter 5, we describe the emergence of the fixed yet flexible *Homo sapiens* inner nature based on its unique biological heritage and long social evolution through the hunting-gathering epoch. Paradoxically, we claim that we need not take into account this inner nature explicitly to explain the differences in the evolution of civilizations and science.

In chapter 6, we examine three forms of *Homo sapiens* creativity, their origins, and necessary and sufficient conditions.

In chapter 7, we first develop a temporal framework based on breaking the civilization epoch into three eras, explore their necessary and sufficient conditions, break the life cycle of civilizations and science into six life stages each, and identify seven distinct historically observable phases of science.

In chapter 8, we identify the causes driving a *Homo sapiens* social order through standalone, peaceful, and violent interaction eras. We also outline categories of the productive, creative, constructive, and destructive outcomes.

In chapter 9, we develop the concept of the inner nature of civilization, which consists of their productive and creative capacities and constructive and destructive orientations from the driving causes. We argue that this inner nature of civilization in a particular period may be assessed by evaluating key measurable parameters. We also show how these concepts will be used to rationalize the broad, varying outcomes of civilization and science in parts IV and V.

Finally, in chapter 10, we identify ten civilizations and nomadic groups that have played a critical role in the intertwined drama of civilizations and science.

Thus, part III summarizes all the necessary concepts and tools needed for parts IV and V to analyze civilizations and the history of science over the last 8,500 years that civilizations have existed.

In brief, part III constitutes the following two hypotheses and four formal assumptions:

- Hypotheses of fixed yet flexible inner nature of *Homo sapiens* and a dynamic yet stable inner nature of social orders founded by the species
- These four assumptions:
    1. Three forms of creativity
    2. The temporal framework of seven phases of science
    3. The social system consisting of interlocking social orders
    4. Ten key participants in the intertwined drama of civilization and science

Chapter 5

The Inner Nature of *Homo sapiens*

5.1 Introduction

In the previous chapter, we discussed the social evolution of *Homo sapiens* through hunting-gathering, the Neolithic and early period of civilization epochs, and the monumental achievements during these epochs These achievements were not accidental. They were rooted in both the unique attributes gifted to *Homo sapiens* by biological evolution as well as the social evolution it went through using these gifts. Mother Nature was both a great resource as well as a constraint on what *Homo sapiens* could achieve. In this chapter, we backtrack a bit and ask that consistent with unique mental and physical attributes and instincts what inner psychological changes occurred in *Homo sapiens* as it moved along the lengthy path from emergence to ultimately inventing civilizations. Or how had *Homo sapiens* become different from its ancestors some three hundred thousand years ago? This is important since it is a truism that this evolution could not have occurred without corresponding inner psychological changes. These achievements in the inner psychological world were no less impressive than those in the outer world; in fact, the latter could not occur without the former. Below we highlight five key attributes to give the reader a feel for the magnitude of the developments that together constitute the fixed yet flexible inner nature of *Homo sapiens* at the dawn of Neolithic age.

5.2 The Emergence of New Inner Attributes

Social existence was critical to realizing the potential inherent in unique mental and physical attributes, despite the continuing existence of a few troublesome instincts. First, it is important to emphasize again the difference between social organization seen in the animal world and *Homo sapiens* social existence. The former is based on instincts alone and hardly leads to changes from one generation to the next. Weakened instincts make the latter possible, but, more importantly, the unique mental and physical attributes allow improvement of the capability of *Homo sapiens* from one generation to the next.

Self-Consciousness

Species-specific *Homo sapiens* self-consciousness may be defined as an awareness of the functioning of mind or a generalized awareness of our unique mental attributes. It is not same as what is commonly defined as individuality. All *Homo sapiens* share a consciousness of self, while individuality differentiates each member of the species. In other words, we fully know we exist. This self-consciousness, as far as we know, is unique on this planet. Primates are clearly conscious but are not self-aware anywhere near the degree humans are. The difference lies in the attributes of imagination and memory or an awareness of future and past as well as the emergence of spoken language made possible by a physiological ability for speech and analytical ability of reasoning power.

Before the emergence of spoken language and ensuing accelerated social development, the neurobiological apparatus responsible for human self-consciousness obviously existed. A pre-language *Homo sapiens* self-consciousness existed but was essentially limited, though it was still far superior to that of primates.

Human self-consciousness no doubt went through many stages. A newborn in a civilized setting clearly possesses consciousness and the potential for self-consciousness. It is not a coincidence that two-year-old children initially begin to refer to themselves in third person, indicating that only after that stage are they becoming aware of their separate identities. With the development of ego, babies realize that the entity they have been referring to in the third person is none other than himself or herself, at which stage the development of biologically possible and culturally accelerated human self-awareness may be said to be essentially complete. A human baby achieves this today in a matter of few years, but the species took tens of thousands of years to achieve it. Thus, *Homo sapiens* slowly became aware of consciousness in the early hunting-gathering epoch. This was indeed a monumental achievement since free will (and ego and superego) is unthinkable without it.

Free Will

Free will is a difficult concept and has determinism as it opposite. Some believe the two are compatible, and others think otherwise. A resolution of this difficulty is that concept of free will at the psychological level does not violate determinism at the physical level. This philosophical debate aside, it is easy to demonstrate that individuals have the freedom to make choices and may thus be held responsible for their actions. Civilizations have always rested on this practical assumption, and it was no different during the early evolution of *Homo sapiens*.

Free will emergence rests on the unique mental powers of imagination, reason, and will. The power of imagination allows a conception of what is possible, reason pretends to sort them, and will makes choice possible. Free will, therefore, may be defined as the internal capacity to make choices that may be different from what others expect. We believe the concept of free will is completely consistent with a lawful universe. In choosing to believe in a true or false proposition or to act in an ethical or unethical manner, no laws of the universe are violated, just as in choosing to sit, stand, or walk no laws of the physics are violated. Since the inner experience of free will arose in a social context, the idea of absolute free will is foolish, as is the idea of strict determinism. It was repeated practical experience, ultimately, that led to the emergence of a conscious free will. Creativity is impossible without free will or free choice on the part of individual in a social context.

Creative, Productive, and Constructive Powers

By creative powers, we mean the ability to create a new idea or invention. Productive power is the ability to turn that idea or invention into a product or service of practical value. Both require the instinct of sociability or constructive powers, since both creativity and productivity are rooted in social existence. These powers are mutually supportive.

Roots of the creative, productive, and constructive powers of *Homo sapiens* are traceable to unique, biologically gifted physical and mental attributes, weakened instincts, and the emergence of speech, which resulted in increasingly sophisticated social organization, though it was simple compared to civilized mode. The instincts of survival, parenting, sociability, and curiosity created needs, and unique mental and physical powers found a creative, productive, and constructive way to satisfy the needs. Even within the context of social existence, the unique physical and mental attributes were mere potentialities in the beginning. They were latent, and *Homo sapiens* were hardly aware of them. It required analyzing the work of supporting physical life into different tasks, allocating these different tasks to different members, and taking note of the resulting creativity and efficiency that made *Homo sapiens* aware of the power of these unique attributes. It was undoubtedly a long process of trial and error, with each success bringing greater confidence and daring.

Perhaps the earliest task specialization was based on gender, with men hunting and women gathering, to exploit the difference in physical strength and child-rearing roles. Task specialization also made it clear that individual members possessed differing abilities and interests, thus reinforcing its importance. Task specialization dramatically improved creativity and productivity while also sowing the seeds of emergence of class, state, and civilization later.

Increasingly sophisticated outcomes through task specialization within a social setting in turn required more sophisticated cooperation. A sense of history, however primitive, made *Homo sapiens* aware of these creative powers and gave confidence that these powers are not accidental or at the whim of spirits or gods, but they are his, at his command, and can be called any time. In other words, repeated, anticipated successful outcomes made humans fully conscious of their increasingly sophisticated creative, productive, and constructive powers.

Conscience

Unique mental and physical attributes and task specialization were not the only elements that made creative, productive, and constructive breakthroughs possible. Right from the beginning, creative advances surprisingly depended on *conscience*. Conscience, for our purpose, may be defined as the awareness of right or wrong or a sense of good and evil. It first crystallized in the hunting-gathering social setting in the absence of wealth or significant surplus. It may be thought of as the long-term guardian of the creative, productive, and constructive powers. With spoken language development, effective social action became possible, which led to heightened conscious creativity and productivity. That in turn required conscience, which in its earliest form was nothing more than the realization that human creativity and productivity is necessarily a stepwise social process and that individual humans cannot amount to much without cooperating with other human beings despite vastly differing abilities and interests.

The conscience, with its social roots, clearly was and has remained in a struggle with instincts that have a narrow focus on individual desires. Self-serving instincts of survival, intraspecies dominance, and interspecies aggression would lead to violence, greed, and intolerance unless the process of socialization nudged the individual toward peaceful coexistence, compassion, and tolerance. The balance of these forces determined whether a resulting conscience for an individual was ethical or unethical and to what degree. Instincts are what one is *compelled* to do through inner biological necessity, and conscience is what one feels one *should* do based on social norms. All social orders of *Homo sapiens* moderate instincts; the question has been to what degree and in what direction.

What is ethical was, of course, hard to define, since it was not necessarily what the witch doctor, social norm, or elders said. Ethics emerged when rights and obligations were seen as two sides of a coin: rights may have slowly evolved to include rights to life, safety, freedom from certain actions, property, and privacy; obligations involve ensuring that same rights for others are not violated. Thus, obligations implied a code of conduct, such as truthfulness, fairness, kindness, humility, and nonaggression, qualities often exhibited in abundance by tribes in hunting-gathering or Neolithic stages. For conscience to be fully effective, it needed to be conscious so that it could affect the choices confronting the individual. This was likely achieved through stories, myths, parental passing on the norms to children, and fear of public humiliation and punishment. In the last analysis, however, conscience and ethics were and have remained a matter of individual choice and required a free will.

We also note how both the fight/flight mechanism and emotions may be activated equally by both instincts and conscience, even when physical survival is *not* at stake. In other words, human social existence, which materially reduced the threats to physical life through a creative manipulation of nature, also created a second social trigger that could activate the biologically inherited fight/flight mechanism and survival instinct even in the absence of the threat to physical survival.

Necessity of Beliefs

Readers may still wonder if self-consciousness, free will, conscience, and creative, productive, and the constructive powers derived from unique mental and physical attributes and weakened instincts are sufficient to complete the picture of the inner nature of *Homo sapiens*. They are incomplete without understanding the concept of the necessity of beliefs, what purpose beliefs serve, and how they fit into a relationship between the universe and a self-conscious life. The following remarks concerning the necessity of beliefs will help clarify these questions.

Lacking the unique physical and mental attributes of *Homo sapiens*, animals are driven by instincts. These instincts provide the *certitude* necessary for purposeful action, which is gained through will (but not free will). With the emergence of unique physical and mental attributes, the certitude instincts provided weakened, relatively speaking. It led to the emergence of self-consciousness; creative, productive, and constructive powers; conscience; and free will as we discussed above. However, these new attributes are an insufficient replacement for the certitude fixed instincts provide for animals. The *Homo sapiens* self-consciousness recognizes its finitude in a seeming infinite universe.

It also recognizes that despite craving perfect and absolute knowledge, such a possibility is denied to the species since creative, productive, and constructive power only promises a stepwise, never-ending process that leads only to relative though progressively better knowledge of the natural and social worlds. *Thus, Homo sapiens require and had to invent beliefs as a precursor to resolute individual action since powerful instincts with certitude no longer sufficed in a complex social setting.* These beliefs do not have to be verifiable; however, they are required by a species with the mental attributes of *Homo sapiens*. These beliefs may pertain to this life or a presumed life after death; they may be either verifiable or unverifiable and may include ethical or unethical attitudes toward fellow human beings. These beliefs ultimately determine the individual action, hence necessity of beliefs for the species.

To summarize, the inner world of *Homo sapiens* at the dawn of civilization not only consisted of biologically gifted mental attributes of observation, reason, imagination, memory, will, emotion, and instincts but also hard-won inner characteristics of self-consciousness; conscious creative, productive, and constructive powers; conscience; free will; and a fundamental necessity of beliefs.

Based on the remarks above, we do not wish the reader to draw the conclusion that these inner attributes emerged sequentially. It is more appropriate to think of these attributes evolving at each stage of social evolution. In figure 5.1, we graphically show the biosocial evolution of *Homo sapiens* up to the dawn of civilization.

Given these fundamental inner characteristics, how do we rationalize or explain the entire range of *Homo sapiens* behaviors? The answer is lies in the fact that beliefs are required for behavior, and *Homo sapiens* have an open-ended capacity to acquire differing beliefs concerning natural and social worlds, a presumed world after death, and fellow human beings. Creative and productive outcomes

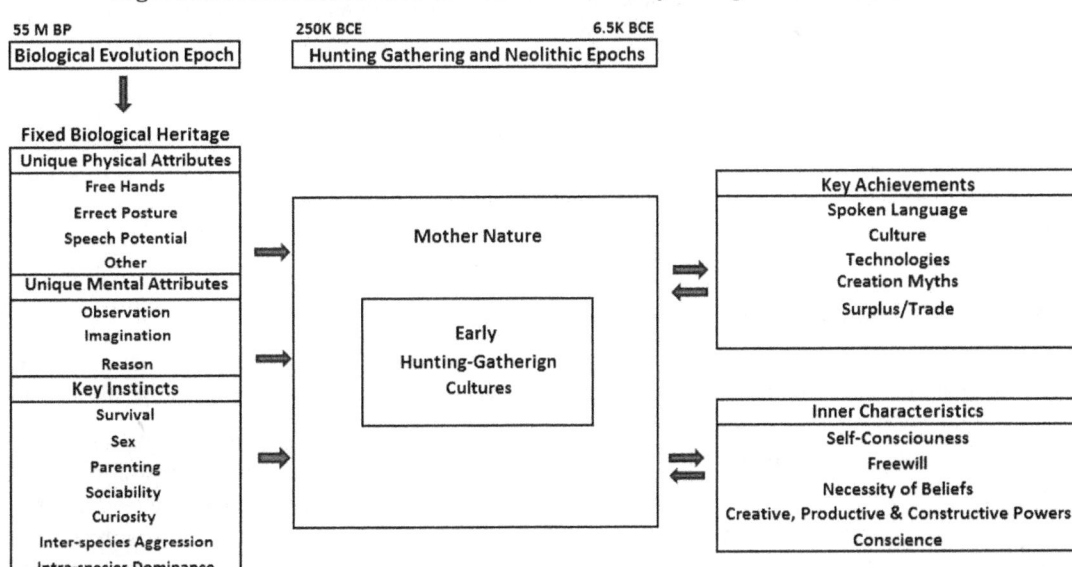

Figure 5.1: Biosocial Evolution Leads to Inner Psychological Characteristics

and range of conscience provide a menu of potential beliefs, and the chosen beliefs govern the entire range of *Homo sapiens*' behavior at individual level.

5.3 Nature of Beliefs

Let us first look at nature of beliefs in more detail since they play a crucial determining role in *Homo sapiens* behavior.

The Belief Formation Process

A belief may be defined as an internal state in which an individual holds something to be true. A belief may be formed after intense reflection or with no reflection but neither guarantees it to be true. Often, a belief may be based on a childhood experience, what an authority figure believed, or indoctrination and repetition. A belief may be about something mundane (I have hair) or something important (the earth is flat). Yet, not all beliefs are equally strong; an individual may have beliefs he considers worth dying for, beliefs that he could be easily dissuaded from, and others somewhere in between. Regardless of how a belief is formed and what it is about, beliefs are central to the existence of *Homo sapiens* as we noted above. Forming beliefs seems to be a crucial feature of a self-conscious finite being such as *Homo sapiens* capable of imagining the infinite since there are always unanswered questions that nudge us toward beliefs, irrespective of information or reason. Even choosing not to have beliefs about some aspect of existence is a form of belief.

The formation of beliefs was likely weak before the emergence of language; however, that did not matter since proportionally, instincts governed behavior. Forming a new belief presumes the existence of free will and a new proposition, or in other words, new creative outcomes (concerning this world or an imagined world or about others) that may be true or false and right or wrong. Creative outcomes may also lead to a changing conscience. For example, creative outcomes could lead to a belief that lightning and thunder meant the wrath of gods, the sun rises in the same direction every day, or it is okay to kill others without reason. All three beliefs may ring true to the believer. *Homo sapiens* during the hunting-gathering epoch were hardly different with respect to the belief formation process than they are today.

Beliefs Concerning this World and the Eternal World (Verifiable and Unverifiable)

Beliefs in this category are simply individual assumptions about the nature of this world or a presumed world beyond death that may or may not be be verifiable, thus creating four possibilities.

Knowledge or ignorance: Creative and productive outcomes classified as knowledge must have two related conditions: it pertains to here and now and must be verifiable. It may pertain to the natural or social worlds or to the *Homo sapiens* themselves. Knowledge, therefore, is nothing other than verifiable practical and intellectual creativity. The former is based on observations, imagination, and unreflective reason. Intellectual creativity, on the other hand, is based on why or how things are. An example of practical creativity is the knowledge that day is followed by night. Intellectual creativity, on the other hand, wants to know why day is followed by night and night by the day and leads to a belief in motion of sun or earth. This necessarily requires controlled observations, unconstrained imagination, and reflective reason. Ignorance, on the other hand, is a creative outcome concerning the natural and social world and *Homo sapiens* and can clearly be shown to be unverifiable but not to the believer.

Agnosticism or faith: Metaphysical speculation or religious creativity is also a form of creativity, but its ostensible focus is not this world. Rather, it is the ultimate reality, the other world, the world after death, or the world beyond this existence. We consider metaphysical speculation to be an understandable part of the creativity of a species that is aware of its finitude and its death. What can be more natural than a finite, self-aware species wondering what is beyond death? Answers to such metaphysical speculation may be believed to be true or false; its conclusions may be held as tentative or as binding faith. We believe that the only valid conclusion the *Homo sapiens* metaphysics can ever reach is to acknowledge that it cannot answer the questions concerning ultimate reality, cannot reach any definitive conclusions about it, and suspects that it may never be able to do so.

Note that verifiable knowledge always seeks to know this world through the unique mental attributes of observation, reason, and imagination, whereas metaphysics pertains to knowing the ultimate reality for which the unique mental attributes may not be a suitable means. In the former, the finite seeks to know the finite, and in the latter, the finite seeks to know the eternal and possibly the infinite. When we realize that our biologically gifted, unique mental attributes are inadequate to address metaphysical speculation, we have two choices: accept that as truth or buy into an unverifiable metaphysics to soothe our existential anxiety. Even the unique mental attributes of *Homo sapiens* prove there is no free lunch, since they give us both verifiable knowledge of this world and the generally socially acceptable unverifiable metaphysics of the possible other world beyond death. Absence of faith is agnosticism, which is a verifiable belief and one true to the spirit of agnosticism.

Faith, thus, is nothing other than religious creativity whose truth is accepted without demonstration and is often too sacrosanct to be questioned. Nearly all religions are a creative outcome that speculates on the possible ultimate reality beyond death. It has taken many forms in the long history of *Homo sapiens*: animism, creation myths, polytheism, monism, monotheism, and atheism, to name a few. We may further divide religious faiths into the tolerant and intolerant variety; typically, most religious faiths except monotheism and at times atheism have been tolerant of other faiths.

We note that historically religion has had two key aspects: a hypothesis concerning the ultimate world and its use in justifying a given social order. Obviously, both are important, but what interests us here is the former not the latter. The fundamental truth about religions is that they are unverifiable and must be accepted on faith (often justified through twisted reason) even though monism and atheism pretend to the contrary. Yet religion, like any other belief, can have a transformative impact on a human being: it can turn a person into a gentle, caring soul on the one hand and a cruel and violent beast on the other.

Beliefs Concerning Human Beings

There is a fundamental difference in beliefs involving the natural and social worlds and the world beyond death and beliefs concerning fellow human beings. Beliefs concerning the former may be true or false, verifiable, or not verifiable. However, when it comes to beliefs concerning other *Homo sapiens*, the issue is not one of truth or verifiability but one of right or wrong. Actions themselves may make either a right or wrong belief about people seem real. These two dimensions of true/false and right/wrong are orthogonal to each other.

Beliefs concerning fellow human beings may range from aggression to peace, from intolerance to tolerance, from greed to generosity, and from equality to inequality. How these beliefs arise in an individual is complex as it involves a struggle among instincts (intraspecies dominance, interspecies aggression, sociability, and curiosity), the generosity of Mother Nature, socialization, and indoctrination. This is discussed in detail in appendix A. The nature of these critical beliefs is responsible for ethical or unethical social conscience, which, it must be emphasized, is not a question of black-and-white but of degree.

We may make a further distinction between beliefs concerning fellow human beings within one's own social order and concerning human beings regarded as outsiders. For reasons of greed and intolerant creeds, there may be a fundamental rupture between the two. For example, beliefs concerning fellow human beings belonging to the same social order may espouse an equality of opportunity, while beliefs concerning human beings as outsiders may espouse intolerance and inequality based on greed or creed and may lead to violent aggression.

Ethical or Unethical Conscience

It is clear from the discussion of the emergence of ethical and unethical social conscience in appendix A that *Homo sapiens* are capable of behavior toward others that includes self-sacrifice, cooperation, healthy competition, unhealthy competition, violence, and cruelty, depending on the outcome of the internal struggle between instincts, history of socialization, and generosity of Mother Nature a social order faced. This is a struggle that occurs at the individual and institutional levels. That humans are capable of both ethical and unethical behavior is an undeniable fact. That is why throughout the ages, humans have described themselves as lying halfway between gods and demons.

We note that given free will, people may choose ignorance over knowledge, faith over agnosticism, and unethical over ethical conscience. It is the noble purpose of the socialization to move these choices in the right direction. However, regrettably, it has not always happened because of a belief in religious and imperialist ideologies.

Reinforcing Role of Emotions

Beliefs in *Homo sapiens* get reinforced by emotions generated by the activation of the fight/flight mechanism even when physical survival is not the issue. Social existence thus created a second social trigger that can also activate the biologically inherited fight/flight mechanism and survival instinct even in the absence of a threat to physical survival.

It is curious that emotions, which originally evolved to respond to and reinforce instincts, could also reinforce behaviors initiated from beliefs. There is no a priori reason why this had to happen. However, emotions do result equally from behavior derived from instincts *and* beliefs. Emotion is not what we choose; it happens to us. There is little free will in emotion since it is an automatic response to behavior or thought-based instincts or beliefs. The broader range of beliefs and behaviors *Homo sapiens* display also led to refined emotional capability over time, consisting of both strongly positive emotions such as joy, love, trust, and wonder and equally strong negative emotions, such as anger, fear, and hate. These refinements in emotions have likely continued to reinforce both instinctual and belief-driven behavior.

5.4 Deducing *Homo sapiens* Behaviors from Beliefs

Given the necessity and central role of beliefs in the inner psychological attributes which in turn are based on unique mental and physical attributes and instincts and its three fundamental categories (knowledge/ignorance, faith/agnosticism, and ethical conscience/unethical conscience), the entire range of *Homo sapiens* behaviors can be deduced from permutations of belief categories through the following simple algorithm:

- Belief in the possibility of knowledge, agnosticism, and ethical conscience lead to the highest creative, productive, and constructive behaviors that *Homo sapiens* are capable of.

- Belief in ignorance, faith, and ethical conscience still can lead to creative, productive, and constructive behaviors but not to the above degree.
- Belief in an unethical conscience will lead to destructive behaviors to one degree or another, regardless of beliefs in knowledge/ignorance and agnosticism/faith, provided the opportunity existed.

Together, these categories of beliefs in *Homo sapiens* form a powerful alternative to behavior determined by instincts alone.

5.5 The Essential Inner Nature of *Homo sapiens*

The above assessment of fundamental psychological attributes based on the biological gift of unique mental and physical attributes, instincts, and a consequent emergence leads us directly to the essential inner nature of *Homo sapiens*. This nature has a fixed aspect and a variable or flexible aspect.

- The fixed aspect is based on the presence of species-specific *Homo sapiens* self-consciousness, free will, and a fundamental necessity of beliefs in equal measure in all individual *Homo sapiens*. Biological gifts and social existence ensure this fixed aspect.
- The flexible aspect consists of the degree to which the creative, productive, and constructive powers and conscience vary in the individual based on biological variability developed and magnified by individual and institutional nurturing.

We call this the fixed-yet-flexible inner nature of *Homo sapiens*. This inner nature is shared in both equal and unequal measures: what makes us equal as individuals is the fixed part and what makes us unequal as individuals is the flexible part. Both are rooted in biological gifts and are developed by socialization. Our inequality as individuals is based on the considerable variability of biological gifts among individuals as well as differences in individual and social nurturing.

The Critical Role of the Individual

We must note that ultimately, regardless of the social setting, all decisions within a social order are made by individuals. Of course, individuals do not act in a vacuum and are influenced by the social order they are part of. However, the role of an individual with free will (we must never forget that) is obviously paramount because biological gifts are not evenly distributed among individuals at birth and do not they have a chance to be nurtured equally.

Thus, genius and talent have played a critical role in creativity, even though they could not exist without the common man. The chance emergence of a powerful individual with daring, vision, and leadership may be particularly influential, though such a leader also had to act within the natural and social environment of which he himself was a product. Thus while a Buddha, Christ, Mohammed, and Genghis Khan each had a unique personality derived from unique biological and social factors, we also believe such powerful personalities were not inevitable or fated but depended on unique confluence of biological and social factors within a given cultural setting. This notion leaves open the possibility of unique individuals influencing history disproportionately, often followed by a disproportionate reaction as well. This observation does not require subscribing to the great man theory of history.

5.6 Summary

In this chapter, we have identified the elements of the inner nature of *Homo sapiens*: a fixed component consisting of self-consciousness, free will, and necessity of beliefs shared with little individual variation and a flexible component. The flexible component consists of creative, productive, and constructive powers and conscience with significant individual variation. Both components crystallized during the long hunting-gathering epoch and are founded on the unique *Homo sapiens* mental gifts of observation, reason, and imagination; unique physical attributes of speech and erect walking; and instincts of hunger, survival, sex, parenting, sociability, curiosity, intraspecies dominance, and interspecies violence. These gifts enabled the emergence of spoken language and culture, which in turn played a decisive role in the formation of a uniquely *Homo sapiens* inner nature. These five characteristics fully explain the entire range of creative, productive, constructive, and destructive behaviors the *Homo sapiens* are capable of.

However, before further understanding their significance, we must pause and bring together remarks concerning the creativity of *Homo sapiens*.

KEY CONCEPTS

Self-consciousness; conscious creative, productive, and constructive powers; conscience; free will; necessity of beliefs
Knowledge/ignorance (true, false)
Faith/agnosticism (verifiable, unverifiable)
Conscience (ethical, unethical)

Chapter 6

Nature of *Homo sapiens* Creativity

6.1 Introduction

It is clear the ascent of *Homo sapiens* from being the most evolved mammal to the inventor of civilization would be unthinkable without a display of extraordinary creativity. Thus, creativity must be an essential aspect of his fundamental nature and be rooted in his biosocial nature. We might even say that humans cannot help but be creative. In this chapter, we explore the creative nature of *Homo sapiens* in detail: its origin, significant forms of creativity, potential conflicts among these forms, its broad evolution since the emergence of the species, the necessary and sufficient conditions of its existence, the dramatic variability of creativity among individuals, and the distinction between creativity and wealth production process or productivity.

6.2 What Is Creativity?

Like *Homo sapiens*, the Universe also shows amazing creativity in its evolution. We could reasonably (and self-righteously) argue that, as far as we know, *Homo sapiens* are the highest expression of this creativity. Thus, it should not be too surprising that as conscious beings and as most evolved children of the universe, we share this propensity for creativity with the universe. Creativity, for our purposes, may simply be defined as something new emerging as a direct result of human thought or action. Creativity so defined could take the form of something immaterial, like an idea, or something more substantial, like an invention. A spear, a spoken language, a quantum theory, a work of art, or a creation myth to explain the origin of the universe all qualify as examples of human creativity. Science clearly is a creative endeavor, but it is only one of the many forms of human creativity. Art is often associated with creativity, but not all art is creative. One could argue, for example, that, after the initial impulse, the art of ancient Greece was not creative as it was rule-bound and focused on repetitive production. On the other hand, the poetry of ancient Greece could be considered a continuing creative activity. Thus, merely reproducing things to support the life of the species is not creativity since it is not creating something new.

6.3 Historically Observable Forms of Creativity

When we look at the more than fifty thousand–year history of *Homo sapiens* creativity or since the invention of spoken language, three separate but connected areas of focus for the creative powers of our species jump out:

- Practical creativity: physical survival or necessity-driven
- Religious creativity: existential anxiety-driven
- Intellectual creativity: curiosity-driven

The first form of creativity exists because it *must*, since as physical beings we need nourishment, shelter, and safety to survive. The second form exists because we *wish*, as mortal beings, to live beyond death. The third form exists because we *want* to create for the sheer joy of it.

Physical Survival-Driven or Practical Creativity

Survival-driven creativity is most evident and is the earliest creative form *Homo sapiens* exhibited. *Homo sapiens* are physical beings and need material sustenance to exist. Our physical survival is constantly at risk due to threats from the heavens; changes in the earth's geology and climate; challenges from other life forms, including our own; old age; and disease. *Homo sapiens* have met these challenges by inventing hunting tools, domesticating animals and plants, building better shelters and modes of transportation, improving clothing and tools of warfare, discovering medical cures, and much more. This slow but relentless march of practical creativity through the invention of new materials, processes, and products generally occurred without support from science until recent times. We could safely assert that, without this survival-driven technology, even the rise of science itself would be inconceivable. However, this practical creativity is only as effective as the social structure and division of labor through which it arises and through which it is transformed into useful products. Thus, the refinements in societal structures and processes that are most conducive to creativity are a second more suble form of practical creativity. Most attention on the *Homo sapiens* throughout the ages has been focused on this necessity-based form of creativity. It has been and continues to be the most fundamental driver of creativity. A purist might even be tempted to say the other two forms simply exist to support this form of creativity.

Existential Anxiety-Driven or Religious Creativity

Homo sapiens do pay a price for the unique gifts of biological evolution since these powers relatively freed *Homo sapiens* from the shackles of instincts and freed them to imagine, think, believe, and act freely. At some point, certainly after the emergence of spoken language, the unique mental attributes of observation, reason, and imagination made the species acutely aware of mortality, thus creating an existential anxiety and forcing the species into metaphysical speculation. It is probable that even chimps, our closest living relatives, are not aware of their mortality. Man, and perhaps a few other species of the genus *Homo*, are the only life forms on earth that ever wondered where they came from and where they will go after they die. Man foresees his own death and is often unwilling to fully accept it. In our opinion, the desire to reduce existential anxiety, coupled with early intellectual confusion, has historically driven the species to invent creation myths, spirituality, and religious dogma. Metaphysical assertions cannot be proved; they are real only to the believer. In this work, we take as self-evident the fact that all metaphysical statements are foremost psychological in origin and cannot be proved or disproved.

Freedom-Driven or Intellectual Creativity

Human actions are not just driven by necessity or existential anxiety. They are also free, that is, the actions are based not on a need for survival or desire for immortality but out of free will and a mere curiosity or even mood or whim. This freedom and curiosity is derived from our unique mental powers, and instincts allow humans the possibility to create for no apparent reason or necessity. It drove *Homo sapiens* to create art, philosophy, and science.

Thus, we may say that man creates because of *physical survival* to sustain material life and is driven only in part by instincts. However, in addition, man also creates to reduce his *existential anxiety* because he wants to live beyond death and out of *curiosity* simply because he wants to. Figure 6.1 summarizes the three forms of creativity.

6.4 Origin of Creativity

Although creativity and intelligence are positively correlated, they are not necessarily the same. Intelligence is associated with analytical, left-brain thinking and creativity is associated with right-brain thinking. Intelligence may be thought of as necessary, but it is not a sufficient condition of creativity. The divergent/convergent model of creativity is based on this differentiation. The analytical, intelligence-driven portion is the divergent part, and the lateral thinking or the insight part is the convergent part. Unlike intelligence, however, emotions are not necessarily positively related to creativity. Both emotionally healthy and unstable personalities have been known to be highly creative.

From a neurobiological point of view, creativity has been shown to be a result of an interaction between the frontal lobe and the temporal lobe, mediated by the limbic regions of the brain. The creative process has also been analyzed into the sequential steps of preparation, incubation, intimation, illumination, and verification. Another attempt to explain creativity looks at various types of creative personalities, such as that of an artist, a sage, and a humorist. However, such a view reflects the bias that scientific and practical creativity is not on par with artistic and religious creativity.

In our view, ultimately all attempts to explain creativity suffer from a fundamental problem: the apparent mystery of something new coming out of something existing, a phenomenon that scientific inquiry takes for granted and that philosophers explain as quantitative change leading to qualitative change. The latter is hardly an explanation; it is simply a statement of what is. This is not too different from the current problem cosmology and astrophysics face in explaining the origin of the universe from a singularity. We shall, of course, not dwell on this issue now but simply observe that creativity or the emergence of something new simply is and varies dramatically among individuals and civilizations. One only has to observe the individual mathematical or musical genius or a particular civilization in different historical periods to appreciate this simple fact. Creativity thus is both biological and social. Bottom line: creativity is highly satisfying and indeed perplexing, but perhaps it is no more so than existence itself, because existence itself is an act of profound creativity on the part of the universe.

Figure 6.1: Forms of Creativity

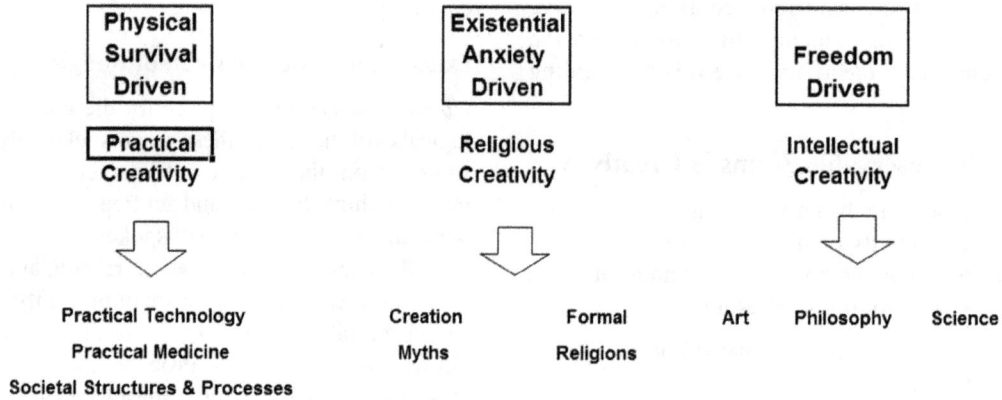

6.5 The Creative Method and Its N&S Conditions

Nature of the Creative Method

A little reflection shows that the creative method, distinct from the method of science, is qualitative in nature and not based on controlled observations and therefore lacks the precision of science. In a sense, it was *the* scientific method before the rise of the scientific method. Throughout most of civilization's existence, the creative method has been used to extend the frontiers of knowledge and productivity.

Necessary and Sufficient Conditions of Creativity

The unique mental attributes are the foundation of creativity. Creativity, however, is not just passively derived from the mental attributes of observation, imagination, and reason; it also requires a *creative environment* to flower, which in effect requires economic and political support to pursue creativity, a culture of openness based on sharing and receiving new ideas, and an appreciation of the individual's role. Only under these conditions does the mind progress through existing knowledge to a state of doubt to formulation of contradiction to a new idea or invention.

Existence of Economic and Political Support: Existence of economic and political support implies an appropriate division of labor within a social order and the availability of necessary physical and human resources for creative endeavors.

Role of Individual: Creativity in one aspect is rather unique. Creativity clearly needs the material and psychological support of the group, as we noted above. However, creativity in the last analysis is an individual affair, and its strength varies dramatically among individuals. The more an individual is valued, the more conducive the culture is to creativity.

Openness to New Ideas: A culture of sharing and receiving of new ideas is the third necessary and sufficient condition. It follows from the simple fact that new ideas are fragile, can be easily ridiculed or ignored, and need other ideas to make them worthwhile. It will, however, be important to distinguish between this internal sharing from openness to the creativity of other civilizations.

Mastery of Conscious Creative Process

The creative method was the scientific method before the birth of science proper and developed out of the social, stepwise, and historical nature of the creative process.

Given the above models purporting to explain creativity, how did early social orders of *Homo sapiens*, including civilizations and nomadic tribes, discover and understand the creative method? Again, the short answer is applying the inherent powers of observation, reason, and imagination to the relevant practical, social, and natural problems. For example, consider discovery of gold on the Indian subcontinent. One might hypothesize the chance presence of gold or ore on earth's surface. In the latter case, cooking fires may have converted the ore to gold, which has a relatively low melting point of 1064 Centigrade. Gold nuggets near fire were discovered, and through socially interactive and repeated observations, imagination, and reasoning, gold was traced to the ore and its conversion by fire. A useful metal was discovered, and *Homo sapiens* learned that it was possible to create something totally new by using what was known, combining A and B to create C, or creating gold through ore, fire, and air. Thus, it was possible to understand creativity and be creative without controlled experimentation; the latter simply adds efficiency and a greater effectiveness to the discovery process and makes it more precise, quantitative, and broader. The social orders naturally began to consciously understand and master the nature of the creative method without understanding controlled experimentation and scientific methodology.

Let us be clear: a group, tribe, civilization, or social order can only be creative through creative individuals effectively using and understanding the creative process based on unique mental powers of the species and the societal structures and processes of the social order. A social order can provide an environment for creativity: it could do so by valuing creativity, providing structures and processes that allow creative freedom, balancing creative orientation, and encouraging openness to new ideas internally or from other social orders. Thus, social orders create the conditions necessary for creativity, and individuals are creative based on their individual biological heritage of unique mental and physical attributes to make creativity possible.

The differences in individual creativity are most definitely traceable to the differences based on genetic and environmental influences as well as learned work habits. Creative achievement, however, ultimately depends on the joint, seamless efforts of the continuum from genius to the talented to the common man. All three types are the product of social existence, and one could hardly exist without the other.

6.6 Forms of Creativity and Unique Mental Attributes

Not all forms of creativity depend equally on the unique mental attributes of observation, reason, and imagination. While capacity for observation seems more or less given, ability to imagine and reason show remarkable potential to get better over time. How do the three forms of creativity or practical, intellectual, and religious creativity employ these unique mental powers? Does each form of creativity employ these powers equally? Do they all employ all three of these powers? For example:

- Imagination is required everywhere but particularly in artistic, scientific, and religious creativity.

- Philosophy and sciences require a high use of reason and imagination.
- Art, science, and science-based technology require high use of observation.
- Practical technology relies on observation, imagination, and reason, though in a considerably less rigorous manner than science and science-based technology.

Taken together, the three forms of creativity and their outcomes utilize the full range of human powers. However, only in science do these powers find their full expression.

We want to note that the unique mental powers of observation, imagination, and reason are not without pitfalls. Observation, or more accurately, perceptual power, is famously known for succumbing to optical illusions. Our imaginations have limitations: when it imagines the future, it can leave what is important out and bring it what is not relevant or may simply project the present into the future. Reason is famous for not only logical errors but also psychological rationalization. In science, many examples of these limitations produce bad science. However, when a group of independent scientists use these powers, providing checks on one another, it is much more liable to produce the scientific "truth."

6.7 Evolution of *Homo sapiens* Creativity

For the more than three hundred thousand years that *Homo sapiens* have existed, practical creativity was essentially the only form of creativity for close to 250,000 years. Following this, artistic and religious forms of creativity slowly emerged, coexisting with practical creativity through the later hunting-gathering, Neolithic, and early civilization epochs. Only about five to six millennia ago, philosophical and scientific creativity slowly began to challenge religious creativity and began to put practical creativity on a firmer scientific footing.

6.8 Creative and Productive Processes

It is also important to make a distinction between creativity and the productive or wealth production process. The wealth production process includes not only wealth production using relevant creative outcomes but also nurturing the factors that create wealth: land, capital, and labor. By contrast, creativity is a conscious or unconscious insight that creates something new. This distinction does not preclude the possibility of "creativity" in the wealth production process. It is, however, of a qualitatively different nature. "Creativity" in wealth production is driven by a desire to be efficient in using resources, including creating new products and services and using trade. We note that every human social organization faces how wealth may be allocated to consumption, luxuries for the elite, and military capability on the one hand and capital formation, labor productivity, land productivity, and creative endeavors on the other. Figure 6.2 shows the process behind these decisions. We will revisit the all-important wealth allocation process in more detail in subsequent chapters.

6.9 Concept of Internal Creative Balance

We define the internal creative balance of a *Homo sapiens* social order simply as relative predominance of practical, religious, and intellectual forms of creativity during a particular period. The concept of internal creative balance may be applied to all social orders of *Homo sapiens*: states, city-states, empires, and civilizations as well as nomadic formations. However, the application to civilization as a whole is of most interest to us since civilizations by far are the most enduring of these four entities. Throughout early history, states, city-states or empires typically tended to exist within a single civilization (and a civilization developed out of them) and were clearly less enduring than the civilization itself. By 500 BCE, it became possible for empires to extend across established civilizations and nomadic federations in a significant way.

Purposeful allocation of sustainable surplus to the three forms of creativity has many possible outcomes. Historically, three solutions are notable:

- Sustained allocation of the surplus supporting practical creativity is dominant. This means that creativity is directed primarily at practical nonmilitary technology and offensive and defensive military technology. Intellectual and religious creativity are not valued or are valued very little. We call this type A, internal creative balance.
- Sustained surplus allocation that supports practical creativity is important but not to the same degree as the first type, and religious creativity is valued much more than intellectual creativity. We call this type B, internal creative balance. It has two sub forms, one without science–religion conflict (type B1) and one with science–religion conflict (type B2). The latter has typically been mostly associated with monotheism.
- Sustained allocation of the surplus is balanced, and all three forms of creativity are valued, though not necessarily equally. Numerically, allocation to practical creativity may continue to be the largest component but not to the suffocation of either of the other two. We call this type C or favorable internal creative balance. A favorable internal creative balance implies the existence of internal creative freedom.

Historically, we do not find examples of civilizations where practical and intellectual creativity dominates to the near exclusion of religious creativity until the rise of

Figure 6.2: Creative and Productive Processes

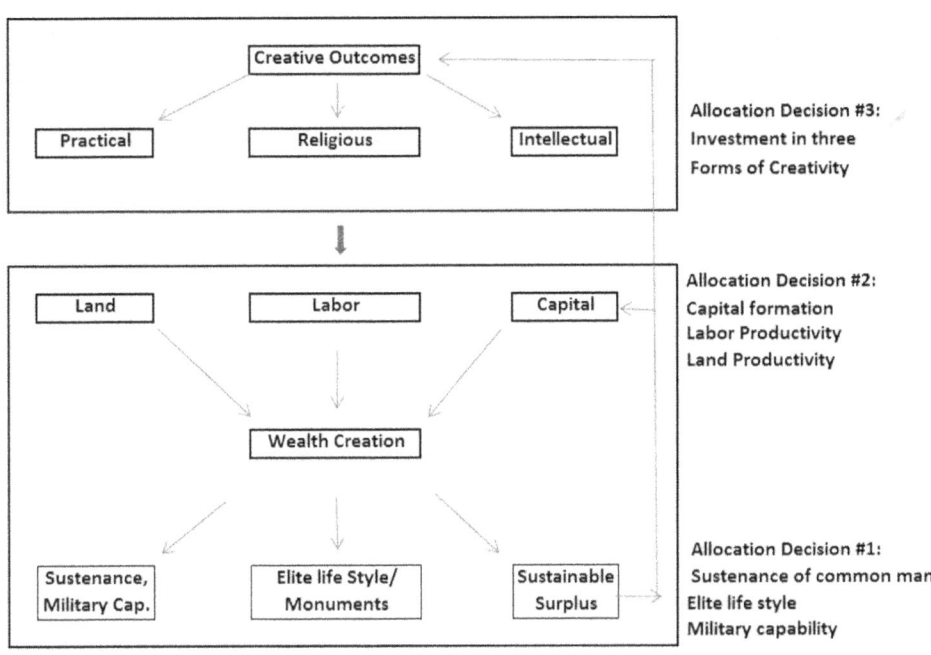

communist states in the twentieth century. It is as though *Homo sapiens* could only move from primarily practical to exclusively practical and intellectual creativity by believing they had conquered their religious or existential anxiety. Thus, the focus of allocation seems to gradually shift from practical to religious to intellectual creativity for civilizations as a whole in the long sweep of history.

Internal creative balance assessment: How do we assess the internal creative balance of a social order, particularly an ancient one? One approach may be to look at practical inventions, temples, churches and mosques, and places of learning, as well as the nature of its art, protoscience, religion, and philosophy. These buildings, inventions, and intellectual outcomes can indicate the relative importance of practical, religious, and intellectual creativity in a particular social order. However, this approach is far from being certain as it depends on the absence of resettlement and climatic cooperation in preserving the ancient physical structures. Still, our experience, though, is that in studying most civilizations from different perspectives, the internal creative balance type is quite clear and little doubt left in the mind.

6.10 Summary

We identified three forms of creativity, practical, religious, and intellectual, and underscored the possibility of imbalance and conflict among these forms of creativity in a social order. The major creative outcomes, such as inventions, religious doctrines, art, philosophy, science, and technology do not use the unique mental attributes equally. A gentle shifting of emphasis from practical to religious to intellectual creativity is plainly visible in the long social evolution of *Homo sapiens*. We also defined the necessary and sufficient conditions of the creative method and differentiated it from the scientific method. We distinguished between creativity and the wealth production process, which has its own "creative" outcomes. Creativity, though a social phenomenon, is highly dependent on the individual, and there is wide variability among both individuals and social orders.

KEY CONCEPTS

Homo sapiens creativity
Three forms of creativity
Internal creative balance of a social order
Creative method
Variability in individual creativity
Creativity and the wealth creation process

Chapter 7 | Temporal Framework

7.1 Introduction

In the opening chapter, we defined science as organized, verifiable knowledge of natural, biological, and social worlds. Thus, science is verifiable, has relative knowledge, and has a stepwise social character. In chapter 3, we witnessed the emergence of *Homo sapiens* with unique physical attributes of erect walking, free hands, the potential for speech, unique mental attributes of observation, imagination, and reason and heightened mental powers, such as memory and emotions. In chapter 4, we witnessed the birth of hunting-gathering cultures through the invention of spoken word and the birth of four primary civilizations through the invention of agriculture. In chapter 5, we outlined the hypothesis of the fixed yet flexible inner nature of *Homo sapiens*, which consists of self-consciousness, free will, the necessity of beliefs and conscience, and productive, creative and constructive powers as flexible psychological aspects. Finally, in chapter 6, we studied the nature of *Homo sapiens* creativity.

In this chapter, we want to start by identifying ten key milestones in the creative and scientific breakthroughs that together may be termed abstract systems-building capability *Homo sapiens* painstakingly developed since emergence. The long arc of practical, religious and intellectual creativity is intimately tied to these milestones since it is the power of the methods employed that determined the outcomes. Following that, we shall present formal definitions of stages of civilization, stages of science, and the eras of civilization. The first two aim at identifying the key milestones in the evolution of civilization and science while the third captures the changing relationship among major civilizations and among civilizations and nomads since the birth of civilizations. From these formal definitions, we shall arrive at the historically observable "phases" of science that take into account both the upward arc of science and the changing relationship among the significant participants in history.

7.2 Significant Milestones in Abstract Systems-Building Capability

Practical, religious and intellectual creativity for a *Homo sapiens*-like species is not possible without a *method* and the five inner psychological attributes outlined in chapter 5. Unlike the mental attributes of observation, imagination, and reasoning, knowledge is not given to *Homo sapiens* spontaneously. *Homo sapiens* are not gods, though we definitely have a propensity to invent and worship them. There are potential pitfalls in the power of observation, in particular its incomplete and uncontrolled character. There are pitfalls of faulty reasoning for which the species has a natural propensity and imagination, though indispensable for creativity, it hardly guarantees it. Our gifts are not flawless. The method by which *Homo sapiens* acquire knowledge is nothing but an incredible, long effort to minimize these shortcomings in mental attributes while using and developing these very attributes. Thus, both the method and the five inner psychological attributes are derived from the unique mental attributes.

We propose the following ten key milestones, in rough chronological order, in the development of the creative and scientific *method*, with their significance briefly noted.

The emergence of spoken language (200,000–50,000 BP): Inventing spoken language allowed *Homo sapiens* to develop culture and communicate with one another, allowing the process of creativity to transition from primarily an individual affair to a social project based on sharing and the interchange of ideas through spoken words. The invention of the spoken word happened so long ago and has so permeated every known human culture that it is well to emphasize that it is a specifically human invention embodying exceptional creativity.

Mastery of creative method (50,000 BP–3000 BCE): Conscious creative method was defined as the scientific method before the invention of the scientific method. It allowed nonagricultural and agricultural technologies (15,000–10,000 BCE) to develop and led to the birth of civilization around 8500 BCE.

The vast array of practical inventions is proof that *Homo sapiens* had mastered the creative method by about 1000 BCE. The mastery of the creative method involved understanding and applying the idea that it is possible to create something new from old elements without attributing the change to an external agency. It involves a clear understanding that the causes of changes reside in the object itself or other objects around it. In short, it requires understanding and an unconscious or conscious application of laws of logic or rationality to social and natural phenomenon based on observation and imagination.

The emergence of cities was an important step in developing the creative method. Those inclined to pursue creative endeavors needed a setting to interact with others engaged in same pursuits. Creativity is hardly a result of the effort of isolated individuals, even geniuses. Creative outcomes are a result of a stepwise social process that requires a free interplay of ideas. Only through such interplay can useful and relatively correct ideas emerge.

Buddha formally enunciated the creative method in his concept of dependent co-origination. What this mastery still lacked was an understanding of the process of controlled experimentation and quantification.

Written script (3000 BCE or earlier): Written script made it possible to preserve and faithfully though not perfectly transmit knowledge across generations and across distance, thus allowing interactive and cumulative effects to occur. The invention of writing was a long process, perhaps beginning as early as 4000 BCE and lasting nearly two millennia. It culminated in the invention of sublime alphabetical script. In appendix B, we briefly trace this fascinating journey. Thus, without a written script, knowledge accumulation will be slow and limited and will eventually hit a wall because successive generations have to recreate knowledge that was not retained by memory. The limitations of memory will generally define the limits of intellectual creativity in the absence of a written script.

As important as written script may be to knowledge transmission, the need to record commercial transactions also drove the invention of the written script. Once invented however, written script could be used to preserve knowledge, thus vastly improving the effectiveness of communication over distance and transmitting knowledge to the future generation of thinkers without limits of memory.

Alphabetical script (3000 to 1500 BCE): Clearly, creativity would be nearly impossible without a *spoken* language and would be rather limited without a written script. It is obviously possible to develop and transmit limited practical knowledge effectively by using a written script. However, without an alphabet, it is difficult, though not impossible, to effectively develop and communicate complex knowledge across generations and over distance well. This is because alphabetical script allowed a potentially infinite number of words to be created using a handful of symbols, each with a specific meaning and thus neatly bypassing the issue of memory in using nonalphabetical logographs.

Religious and intellectual creativity necessarily requires developing complex abstract systems. A written script based on the concept of an alphabet fulfills that requirement. The evolution of alphabetical script and why such a script is critical for the birth of science is presented in appendix C. Since China is the only major existing civilization that failed to develop or adopt the alphabetical script, in appendix I we briefly discuss why China did not develop or adopt an alphabetical script and the impact of this important fact on science in the Chinese civilization.

Logic and epistemology (1000 BCE–500 CE): Once alphabetical script made precision in the written word possible, developing the laws of logic and codification of the existing method of knowledge became possible. Epistemology refers to the theory of how knowledge comes about. It is nothing other than the integration of theories of logic, creative method, and scientific method. Scientists do not explicitly worry about it; only philosophers do. Nevertheless, a sound epistemological theory carries the potential to guide scientists.

Method of controlled experiments in the heavens (500 BCE–1500 CE): Natural observations in general only allow broad logical inferences because either the observations are insufficient or the observations need to be made in measuring invented concepts. Fortunately, there was one exception: solar astronomy, where naturally occurring, controlled experiments could be observed and learned from before controlled experiments on earth could be devised.

Decimal system of counting (500 BCE–500 CE): By decimal system of counting, we mean the system of counting based on ten digits and the concept of zero. Quantitative measurements, so essential for recording observations, required a counting system and one that had to have the ability to handle large numbers and negative numbers as well as allow rapid arithmetical operations of adding, subtracting, dividing, and multiplying.

Method of controlled experiments on earth (1000 BCE–1600 CE): Bringing the idea of controlled experiments from the heavens to earth allowed its initial application to terrestrial motion, optical phenomena, and physical chemistry.

Calculus (500–1675 CE): Physical nature exhibits phenomena with continuous change, such as uniform velocity or a change of position with time, and they are practically infinitely divisible. Thus, to understand such phenomenon, a methodology to determine a ratio of two small dependent quantities as the denominator approached zero is required. The science of calculus provided such a methodology to measure continuous change. Thus, a method was needed to not just quantify controlled observations but also be able to handing continuous change mathematically. The science of calculus made this possible.

Scientific method (1000–1750 CE): By scientific method, we mean a union of observations from controlled experiments, with logical reasoning based on free use of imagination. A combination of controlled experimentation, a decimal counting system, calculus, and a sophisticated epistemology finally converged to produce the scientific method. Without the scientific method, it is clearly possible to be creative; however, the outcomes are left to chance through a hit-and-miss process. Controlled experimentation adds rigor and efficiency to the process. The ultimate proof that science has matured was the emergence of the mature scientific methodology and a corresponding theory of knowledge. Scientific methodology includes and supersedes the creative method.

Collectively, we have called these ten milestones *Homo sapiens'* evolving abstract systems-building capability. These milestones in the methods of knowledge will serve as backdrop in identifying the stages of civilization and science. These milestones are achievements of formal sciences, philosophy and natural sciences.

7.3 Formal Life Stages of Civilizations

After birth, beginning at about 6500 BCE, we propose the following six formal life stages of civilizations:

1. **Preliterate:** All civilizations from 6500 to 3000 BCE. These civilizations are without a written script but have an understanding of the creative method.
2. **Literate:** Civilizations from 3000 BCE to present; they have at least a rudimentary logograph.
3. **Mature literate:** Civilizations from 1500 BCE to present; they have a fully developed alphabetic script.
4. **Rational:** Civilizations from 900 BCE to present. They have alphabetical script and at least a modest beginning in logic and epistemology.
5. **Prescientific:** Civilizations from 550 BCE to present. They have an early experimental method with respectable progress in logic and epistemology.
6. **Scientific:** Civilizations from 1600 CE to present. These civilizations have a mature scientific method, including a fully developed controlled experimentation methodology and a sound epistemology.

Clearly, civilizations stuck at the earlier stages of civilization continue to coexist in latter periods.

Using some of the milestones in the method of knowledge, we have divided the civilization epoch into six formal stages reflecting its evolving internal maturity. However, it is important to note that this division is only a tool that must not be used mechanically, because if one tried, one could find exceptions. In reality, we have an overlapping continuity from one stage to the next. There are no breaks, and those living during the periods of great transitions may hardly perceive as much since the time scale of these transitions was typically longer than the time scale of one human life. Yet one cannot deny the importance of the key achievements in abstract systems-building capability that modified the ability of a social order to be creative. The old often continued to exist with the new for a long time.

7.4 Formal Life Stages of Science

Not surprisingly, we can also formulate formal life stages of science, namely the birth, development, and maturation stages of protoscience and science. Life stages of science run parallel to the life stages of civilization, for the leading edge civilization are nothing more than defining certain guideposts of progression of science. The stages of the birth, development, and maturity of protoscience are defined as stages before birth of science proper. The birth of protoscience may be said to begin shortly after the birth of civilization.

Definition of Protoscience

We define protoscience as a form of intellectual creativity consisting of the first tentative steps generally in response to the practical needs of ancient civilizations, such as marking the seasons, the skills in counting and measuring, writing, and practical medicine based on an increasing understanding of the creative process. Civilizations were clearly a long way from understanding the scientific method; however, understanding the creative process was sufficient to pursue protoscience. The protoscience stage may itself be broken into birth, development, and maturation stages.

The Birth Stage of Protoscience

Fixing the formal birth date of protoscience, much like the formal birth date of civilization, is somewhat arbitrary, but the date itself is very not important and roots of protoscience probably go back farther than any formal date chosen. For example, we do not know when the first counting system was conceived. The birth of protoscience may be considered running parallel to the preliterate stage of civilization, starting with birth of civilization around 6500 BCE.

The Development Stage of Protoscience

The development stage of protoscience may be said to begin with the emergence of written script (~3000 BCE or a little earlier), thus coinciding with the beginning of the literate stage of civilization. Significant breakthroughs in practical and religious creativity, such as the invention of the wheel and ideas of monism and monotheism, also occurred during development stage of protoscience. All primary civilizations participated in developing protoscience.

The Maturity Stage of Protoscience

Finally, the mature stage of protoscience may be said to begin with the full development of alphabetical script (1500 BCE) and end with the birth stage of science beginning around 1000 BCE.

The Birth Stage of Science

The process of the birth of science was completed by around 550 BCE, coinciding with the beginning of violent interaction among civilizations. The birth of science, like the birth of civilization itself, is clearly a matter of definition and depends on assessing when the practical creativity and formal and astronomical sciences have developed sufficiently to claim the birth of science.

The Development Stage of Science

Science proper remained in the development stage from about 550 BCE until around 1600 CE when, building on Indian, Greek, and Muslim achievements efforts, Copernicus and Galileo succeeded in formulating laws of heavenly and terrestrial motion and the methodology of science.

Mature Stage of Science

Science may be said to have entered the mature stage around 1600 CE, which has continued to the present. This effectively ended the more than two millennia–long development stage of science (550 BCE–1600 CE). By the time science reached the stage of maturity, the world had begun to fall under the domination of one civilization.

7.5 The Concept of Logical Sequence in Science

The concept of logical sequence of science may be understood by considering a standalone civilization. By definition, the civilization will not experience peaceful interaction or military conflicts with other civilizations and will not be subjected to another civilization controlling its surplus, grabbing its land, or draining its wealth. It will remain free to actualize its inner values. Not all rising and falling states within the civilization may experience uninterrupted freedom; however, that will not be fundamentally important since this type of intracivilization conflict will simply shift the center of gravity of science to another state with comparable social ethics and belief systems. To reemphasize, in such a civilization has the following attributes:

- Other civilizations will not impact development during the birth, development, and maturity of protoscience and science will not be impacted by other civilizations and will therefore follow its own inner logic.
- Different sciences will pass through a logical sequence according to the interdependencies among them. In other words, they proceed from formal to natural to biological to social science.

Formal, natural, biological, and social sciences will pass through their individual periods of birth, development, and maturation. We do not mean to suggest that these sciences would be sharply divided from one another. More appropriately, these sciences may be thought of as successive, overlapping waves. Significant development of a new class of science would be unlikely before the birth of all earlier classes of science in the above general sequence, and the degree of achievement in a science would depend on the degree of development of all previous sciences. The same is true for a sequence within a broad class of science. For example, within exact natural sciences, it would be foolish to expect an emergence of nuclear science before chemical and electrical sciences, just as it would be unreasonable to expect biochemistry to emerge before botany. These interconnections and dependencies among sciences would have an internal logic to them.

The suggested logical sequence of sciences simply means that formal sciences will develop first as they are a creation of logic alone and are critically required for the birth of other sciences. However, at this stage, without a thorough understanding of the experimental method, attempts at exact and other natural sciences are no better than progressively improving speculations. Observations of the motion planets and gravity induce on earth would first teach humans about the laws of motion since solar system and motion under gravity here on earth are the grand, naturally occurring "controlled experiments" that are observable without sophisticated instruments. Solar and terrestrial mechanics, starting with the laws of gravitation and motion, would then become possible through a synthesis of quantitative methods from formal sciences and lead to the birth, development, and maturation of first natural science, astronomy, and terrestrial physics followed by chemistry and earth science. The biological sciences, such as botany, geology, zoology, etc., then begin to come into existence. Social sciences having the additional complexity of independent human free will necessarily come last. These sequential sciences therefore may be thought of as the necessary, logical, and sequential waves that science must pass through to achieve maturity.

The logical sequence of science is nothing more than the statement that science moves from the simple to the complex, from logical to real, and from natural to social realms. Thus, rules of arithmetic must precede algebra and trigonometry, understanding laws of motion must precede understanding laws of energy conservation, botany and chemistry must precede biochemistry, etc.

If science had achieved maturity because of a single civilization's effort, we would expect to see such a logical sequence throughout in scientific development within that civilization. The birth of formal sciences would be followed by a lagging yet overlapping sequential development of formal, solar astronomy, exact natural, other natural, and social sciences. Of these, the birth of science and basic solar astronomy would come to a formal end while other exact, natural, and social sciences would have continued ad infinitum within that civilization.

7.6 Eras of Civilization

The path from the earliest Neolithic communities to four primary civilizations likely entailed considerable force. However, history shows that once primary civilizations were established and situated in the river valleys, they did not engage in military conflicts or even trade with other civilizations for a significant period. This was not necessarily due to a peaceful orientation; rather, in most cases, it reflected the primitive state of weapon development and transportation relative to the spatial distance separating them. The wars among states or city-states within an early civilization were common. Thus, after birth, civilizations went through a standalone or noninteractive era followed by an era of peaceful interaction. Advances in practical technology that made travel, migrations, and limited trade significantly less burdensome made this change possible. The era of extended military conflicts followed, which was made more intense and deadly through extending weapon range and transport technologies among civilizations, starting with the emergence of the Persian Achaemenid Empire. This has continued unabated to the present day, though its form has evolved considerably.

But how do we delineate these eras precisely? We know the era of violent interaction started around 550 BCE with the Achaemenid Empire, which came into existence through the consolidation of Persian and Mede tribes followed by the absorption of the Lydian Empire in 547 BCE and the neo-Babylonian state in 539 BC, thus creating the first, though physically circumscribed, multiethnic empire by an erstwhile nomadic people. From chapter 4, we may also assume that the earliest civilization emerged around 6500 BCE. Less clear is the period when, after settling down, primary civilizations began to interact with one another in a significant way but without any military conflicts. This interaction took place through the diffusion of ideas and inventions by the individual traveler, relatively peaceful group migration, and barter based on fair exchange principles. Such interaction among the four primary civilizations has been reasonably well documented through academic research, and significant interaction does *not* go back more than about five millennia or perhaps a few centuries earlier.

It is, therefore, reasonable to assume that after birth, there was a period when civilizations were in a standalone era, when primary civilizations, on the whole, evolved essentially independently of one another.

Only after the standalone era ended did civilization begin to influence one another indirectly but still peacefully. The initiation of such interaction obviously varied with civilizations, perhaps beginning in a significant manner around five thousand years ago or about 3000 BCE. It may be said to have formally ended by about 550 BCE with the emergence of Achaemenid Empire. Again, this is not to suggest the lack of conflict *within* early civilizations before the violent interaction began or the absence of peaceful migrations and fair trade after the violent interaction era began. To emphasize, there always has been varying degrees of conflict among states within civilizations and often between the bordering states of a civilization and the nearby nomads. However, as we shall repeatedly emphasize throughout the book, conflicts among states once a civilization was established simply moved the center of control from one state or city-state to another without fundamentally and permanently affecting the direction and evolution of the civilization. And the limited conflicts among civilizations and nomads until rise of Islam generally favored civilizations in that civilizations eventually successfully absorbed them. Thus, starting at about 6500 BCE, we may identify three broad and distinct eras: standalone, peaceful interaction, and violent interaction.

Not all civilizations existing today went through a standalone or peaceful interaction eras as distinct civilizations. Some civilizations were born in the peaceful or violent interaction eras. For example, the European civilization was born toward the end of the era of peaceful interaction, Persian civilization at the beginning of violent interaction era, and the Muslim civilization was born at the high noon of the violent interaction era. In fact, a dramatic and broad-based increase in extended military conflicts coincided with the birth of European, Persian, and particularly Muslim civilization, with the latter two embodying significant nomadic features. These three civilizations did not experience the first two eras as distinct civilizations.

It is also interesting to note how the balance among the practical, religious, and intellectual forms of creativity changed over the three eras. The standalone era was dominated by practical creativity. Civilizations had given up the hunting-gathering lifestyle long ago, and the need of the day was to negotiate a new contract with nature by continually developing practical technology in general and continued domestication of animals and plants in particular. In the latter part of the standalone era, though practical creativity continued to be the dominant form of creativity, religious creativity, followed by intellectual creativity, began to become more important. The violent interaction era, on the other hand, has been dominated by the struggle between the religious and intellectual forms of creativity and the eventual triumph of the latter.

Note that the concept of civilization eras does not preclude civilizations at different life stages to coexist. It is possible for civilizations at all six stages to coexist in a violent interaction era. The twentieth century has supported preliterate, literate, mature literate, rational, prescientific, and scientific civilizations.

Necessary and Sufficient Conditions of the Transition of Eras

Below, we state the rather obvious necessary and sufficient conditions that must be met for these eras to emerge. The necessary and sufficient condition of the standalone era is:

- The range of transportation technologies must be less than the spatial distance between the nearest two civilizations.

The necessary and sufficient conditions of the peaceful interaction era are:

- The range of transportation technologies must be greater than the spatial distance between the nearest two civilizations.
- The range of weapons technologies must be less than the spatial distance between the nearest two civilizations.
- Openness to trade and creativity of other civilizations.

The necessary and sufficient conditions of the violent interaction era are:

- The range of transportation technologies must be greater than the spatial distance between the nearest two civilizations.
- The range of weapons technologies must be greater than the spatial distance between the nearest two civilizations.
- Aggressive orientation based on intolerant creed or greed by at least one civilization.

Let us review these conditions in some detail.

Range of transportation technologies: Transportation technologies include both land and sea travel. The invention of the wheel took place toward the end of standalone phase, about 3500 BCE, and the use of a horse as a long-distance instrument occurred toward the end of the peaceful interaction era. The shipbuilding technologies go farther back. The Egyptians built ships as early as 3000 BCE. Recent excavation at Dwarka in western India has established significant maritime activity as early late 3100 BCE. Given this rough chronology of the development of different transportation technologies, clearly during the majority of the standalone era, the range of transportation technologies was smaller than the distance between the Indian, Egyptian, Mesopotamian, and Chinese civilizations. During the peaceful interaction, trade became possible by sea travel and land through a relay system. At the start of the extended military conflict era, using a horse with harness for long-distance transport became possible.

Range of weapons technologies: Similarly, the range of weapons technologies was continually extended as horse riding and breeding was perfected and by iron discovery in the second millennium BCE. During the standalone and peaceful interaction eras, war among primary civilization was literally impossible, but that changed by 500 BCE.

Openness to the creativity of other civilizations: Transport technologies were indeed required for peaceful interaction among civilizations. However, the second required element was the openness of civilizations to engage in creative exchange, peaceful migrations, and fair trade. Civilizations have a natural openness provided this openness is not impacted by geographical or linguistic isolation, a sense of superiority, or a sense of apprehension possibly resulting from experiencing the aggression of others. The following types of openness are historically relevant.

Aggressive orientation: The roots of aggression have been discussed in appendix A. Here we simply note that aggression may be internally or externally directed. Weapons technologies with appropriate range and greed or creed are necessary for an aggressive posture among civilizations; however, for war to occur, the aggressor must perceive himself as having superior military strength and intelligence-gathering capability.

The necessary and sufficient conditions of the eras defined above are nothing but specific outcomes achieved by one or more civilizations required for the onset of a particular era. Note that the onset of an era must necessarily be defined by the "leading" civilization.

7.7 Significant Historically Observable Phases of Science

The proposed life stages of civilization and science are six each as noted in 7.4 and 7.6, and their starting and ending dates run parallel. The formal life stages of science describe the natural life cycle of science. However, they are not exactly suitable for our purpose of understanding the intertwined relationship between civilizations and science.

Birth, Development, and Maturity Stages of Protoscience

During the long protoscience phase, when the pace of scientific development was slow and civilizations were standalone or interacting peacefully, it is unnecessary to focus on the birth, development, and maturity of protoscience separately for our purpose. We can combine the three stages of protoscience because of the slow pace of development and essentially the scientific development based on its inner logic within each civilization.

Birth Stage of Science

Because the birth of science took place in one civilization under peaceful and subdued interaction, a single stage to study the birth of science is appropriate as well.

Development Stage of Science

During the development stage of science when the pace of development picked up and when civilizations began interacting violently through coerced trade, conquest played a dramatic role; a single stage is too broad and fails to capture all the drama.

Extended military conflicts during the violent interaction era had the power to disrupt the logical development of science within a particular civilization. The development life stage within a civilization was now capable of being stretched, accelerated, slowed down, put on hold, or even aborted within a particular civilization. Thus, given the differing military capability, openness, insularity, and the internal creative balance of civilizations engaged in these extended conflicts, we would expect to see the center of gravity of science during the development stage continue to shift from one civilization to another. This, in fact, happened. The development stage of science, therefore, may be viewed as split into a number of seemingly irrational, violence-driven, distorted, and battered substages, when the scientific leadership passed from one civilization to another. We might correctly expect these substages when added together to be longer than an uninterrupted development life stage in the leading civilization although, the reverse, though highly unlikely, is conceivable.

We may ask how many substages of science we actually observe during the development stage. We postulate that development stage of science after the birth of science scattered across the civilizations went through four substages that correspond to the following four specific cross-civilization syntheses in science:

- The Greek-Hellenistic-Indian Synthesis (550 BCE–200 CE)
- The Indian Synthesis (200–750 CE)
- The Arab Synthesis (750–1200 CE)
- The Italian Synthesis and the Western European Synthesis (1200–1600 CE)

Each of these substages consists of a higher synthesis in science achieved by a civilization based the previous achievements of other civilizations. We wish to emphasize that the number, location, and duration of these substages of development essentially depended on the historical causes, and there was little inner logic or inevitability about them. Many other sequences could have easily have occurred, depending on the contingencies of history.

The four substages of the development stage described above are based on a different civilization synthesizing the achievements of other civilizations while making its own contributions during the violent interaction era. These substages were scattered across several civilizations; no civilization was dominant. The inner logic of the development within a particular civilization was disrupted, often for centuries. We believe that the concept of science substages during the life stage development is supported by the observable intertwined history of civilizations and science.

Mature Stage of Science

The development stage was characterized by sequential development in multiple civilizations, with disrupted inner sequences within a civilization. The mature stage was its opposite: maturity within a single civilization was based on the inner logical sequence of science. However, because science had achieved maturity, its pace increased dramatically. The mature stage may be understood by the following five grand unifications that correspond to its five significant substages:

- Unification of gravity and terrestrial motion (1600–1675 CE)
- Unification of electricity and magnetism (1750–1875 CE)
- Unification of gravity and electricity/magnetism (1875–1915 CE)
- Unification of electric/magnetism and weak nuclear force (1950–1975 CE)
- Unification of electricity, magnetism, and weak and strong nuclear forces (1975–present)

Thus, during the mature stage, science returned to its protected, logical development after a gap of nearly two millennia. Even though the pace of development jumped by perhaps an order of magnitude because the developments in science took place in just one civilization during the mature stage, there is little need to divide the stage further for our purpose.

Historically Observable Phases of Science

Thus, we postulate seven historically observable phases or distinct periods:

- Protoscience phase (6000–1000 BCE)
- Birth phase (1000–550 BCE)
- Four development phases (550 BCE–1600 CE)
- Maturity phase (1600–2000 CE)

We must end by noting that nothing is fixed or predetermined about the number of phases one may divide the life stages. As noted above, the mature stage could be further divided in more phases, depending on the objective of the study. The number of phases should be as low as possible to keep analysis simple but as high as necessary to ensure it is not simplistic and to make sure it lays bare the intertwined nature of civilizations and science, which is our objective in this work. There may be multiple ways to break the life stages of science, depending on one's objective; we have chosen seven phases organized in seven chapters.

7.8 Temporal Framework of Eras, Stages, and Phases

The relationships of the life stages of civilization, life stages of science, and eras of science are shown in figure 7.1. Note that the average duration of the phases after protoscience maturation is about three hundred years or about ten generations.

We may envision this framework of eras, stages of civilization, and life stages as comparable to the scaffolding needed to construct a building. Using this framework will ease the study of reciprocal relationship between civilizations and the history of science. We readily acknowledge upfront both its a priori nature and that the framework may not strictly be rigorous and perhaps cannot be. Just as the scaffolding is not the building under construction, the framework is not the truth but a means to the truth. Once the building is constructed, the scaffolding can be discarded, for it would have served its entire purpose.

7.9 Summary

In this short chapter, we have proposed the formal life stages of civilizations and science, the inner logical sequence of science, and three broad eras of civilization. Using these concepts, we presented the empirically testable framework of the seven historically observable phases of science that define our temporal framework. We do not claim the definitions of eras and stages are strictly rigorous, for they may be different for someone with a different perspective. They are not necessarily the truth but only a means to the truth.

> **KEY CONCEPTS**
>
> Preliterate, literate, mature–literate, rational, prescientific and scientific stages of civilization
> Life stages of protoscience and science
> Logical sequence in science
> Standalone, peaceful interaction, and violent interaction eras
> Necessary and sufficient conditions of eras
> Seven phases of science

Figure 7.1: Concept of the Historically Observable Phases of Science
(Timeline not to scale)

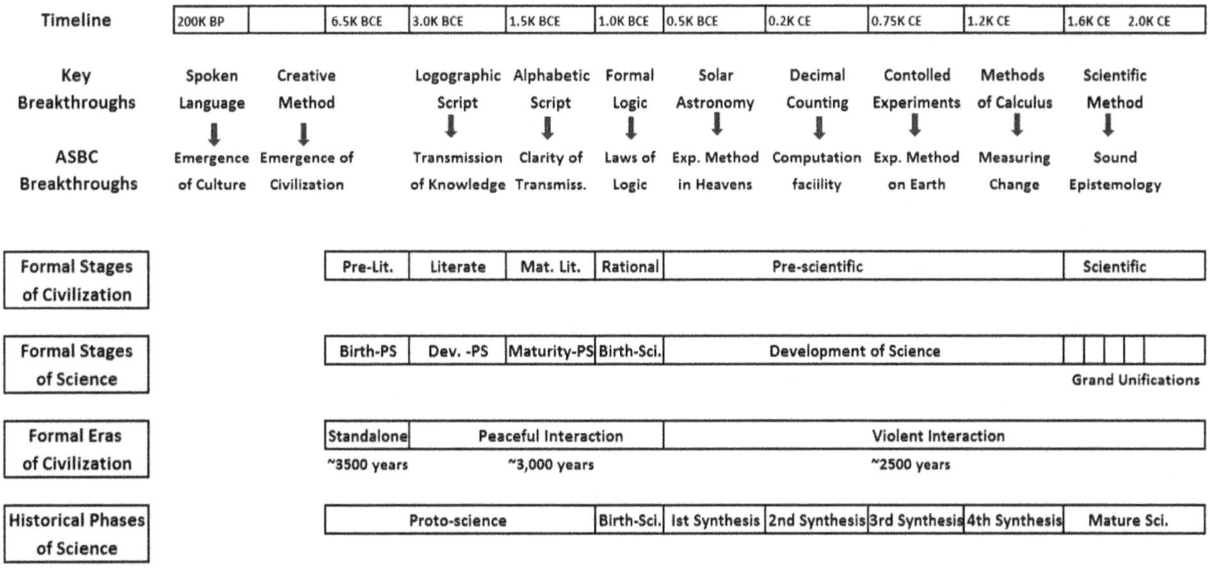

Timeline	200K BP		6.5K BCE	3.0K BCE	1.5K BCE	1.0K BCE	0.5K BCE	0.2K CE	0.75K CE	1.2K CE	1.6K CE 2.0K CE
Key Breakthroughs	Spoken Language ↓	Creative Method ↓	Logographic Script ↓	Alphabetic Script ↓	Formal Logic ↓	Solar Astronomy ↓	Decimal Counting ↓	Controlled Experiments ↓	Methods of Calculus ↓	Scientific Method ↓	
ASBC Breakthroughs	Emergence of Culture	Emergence of Civilization	Transmission of Knowledge	Clarity of Transmiss.	Laws of Logic	Exp. Method in Heavens	Computation facility	Exp. Method on Earth	Measuring Change	Sound Epistemology	

Formal Stages of Civilization	Pre-Lit.	Literate	Mat. Lit.	Rational	Pre-scientific	Scientific

Formal Stages of Science	Birth-PS	Dev. -PS	Maturity-PS	Birth-Sci.	Development of Science	Grand Unifications

Formal Eras of Civilization	Standalone	Peaceful Interaction	Violent Interaction
	~3500 years	~3,000 years	~2500 years

Historical Phases of Science	Proto-science	Birth-Sci.	1st Synthesis	2nd Synthesis	3rd Synthesis	4th Synthesis	Mature Sci.

Chapter 8: Driving Causes and Outcomes of Social Orders

8.1 Introduction

In this chapter, we describe the general categories of causes that determine the evolution of *Homo sapiens* social orders (natural, intrinsic, extrinsic peaceful, and extrinsic violent) and general categories of outcomes (creative, productive, scientific, constructive, and destructive). We shall present these causes and outcomes in their rough historical order of appearance and in sufficient granularity to allow us to be able to use these categories to organize the overwhelming amount of data concerning causes and outcomes. The categories of causes and outcomes must be comprehensive and must apply to any *Homo sapiens* social organization of interest to us, including city-states, states, empires, civilizations, and nomadic confederations. Thus, in the discussion below, any of these terms may be used, depending on the context and appropriateness.

8.2 Natural Causes

Natural causes are the physical and ecological environments in a given locality. These were the challenges, the constraints, and, at times, the advantage for a budding civilization. They were the natural givens. However, that does not mean these factors did not or could not change during a given historical phase of interest to us. The climate, ecology, and even geography can change over longer periods or even abruptly through the geological and astronomical variables working behind the scenes. Thus, natural causes may be grouped into the following categories:

- **Geographical** factors, including the location and topology and the richness of soil of the area as well as the surface water, including the river systems it supports.
- **Climatic** factors, including the average annual precipitation and temperature as well as seasonal variations.
- **Geological** factors, consisting of the natural causes that may impact the geographical and climatic variables through gradual changes in earth's crust and atmosphere through erosion, tectonic plate movements, and sudden changes, including earthquakes and volcanic eruptions. It also includes mineral deposits.
- **Ecological** factors that underscore the relationship between the physical environment, as defined by the geographical and climatic factors, the form of plant and animal life it is capable of supporting, and even how the environment may be responsible for affecting the evolution of life over geological time spans.
- **Astronomical** factors that include changes in solar activity, shifts in earth's axis of rotation, and meteor activity potentially affecting earth and its climate.

All these factors were capable of strongly influencing or even determining the birth of civilizations and impacting evolution gradually or abruptly. From a practical point of view, it is useful to group the natural causes into two groups: those that determine the degree of the natural bounty of a location and those that can gradually or abruptly change this basic natural bounty.

- Natural bounty depends on geographical, climatic, and ecological factors. These factors determine the ease with which a settled mode of life may be established.
- Natural disasters can result from climate change caused by astronomical and geological factors. These activities, though they can occur any time, have a time scale considerably longer than a historical time scale of about ten millennia we are dealing with.

Natural bounty may be characterized as relatively stable but amenable to gradual changes and natural disasters as essentially unpredictable.

While it is true that historically, human civilizations have only modestly affected the course of biological evolution on the planet through plant and animal domestication, they so do lately through pollution. It is also true that the impact of some of the natural causes could be mitigated—for example, the impact of soil erosion due to excessive rain can be mitigated by planting trees. However, significant natural events, such as earthquakes, climate change, and the shifting course of a river, for example, were not predictable, let alone controllable. They are not controllable even with current technological know-how. Even a modest control of natural forces has been clearly impossible for civilizations throughout history. The response to these slow or abrupt natural causes and events determined the fate of civilizations.

8.3 Intrinsic Causes

One would expect the intrinsic causes to consist of the evolving institutional systems, structures, and processes of a social order. In addition, we need to consider beliefs and attitudes concerning existential anxiety, fellow citizens, and other social orders.

Institutional structures may be further broken into political system, military capability, economic organization, systems of religious faith, legal systems, social structure, and educational and knowledge creating institutions.

Institutional processes are perhaps too numerous to list. However, the most significant from our perspective are wealth allocation decisions since they have a major impact on creative outcomes and the disruptive process of internal wars and degree of social cohesion, which have a significant impact on state formation and productive outcomes. These structures and processes naturally became increasingly more sophisticated, particularly within cutting-edge civilizations.

Key Institutional Structures and Processes

A political system refers to the type of political system the social order has. It includes origin, distribution, use, and transfer of power (tribal traditions, monarchy, dictatorship, and democracy); legislative structures to create laws; an executive hierarchy to ensure they are obeyed; and a judicial structure capable of punishing the transgressors. To what extent are these three branches independent and coordinated? The political system also defines the power and role of bureaucracy in developing economic policy and the political freedom the system allows its citizens: how responsive the system is to the evolving needs of the social order. Finally, is the political system compatible with economic freedom of its citizens, or does it merely regulate the economy lightly or strongly?

Military capability includes the quality of infantry, cavalry, and naval units of the military, and more recently, the air force; the structure of units and formations; the command structure; the stage of weapons (range and extent of destructive power) and transportation technologies embedded in the various units; the sophistication of military strategy and tactics at its disposal; intelligence gathering; conscripted versus professional army; and the quality of training and morale the units and soldiers possess. Differentiation between defensive and offensive capability is critical: Is the war department misnamed as the defense department?

The economic organization includes the state of agriculture, manufacturing, services, financial, commerce, infrastructure, and trade sectors and technologies imbedded in these sectors as well as the granularity of the existing division of labor. It is important to understand the extent of public versus private ownership of these sectors and the nature of relationship between cities and villages. Also important to understand is whether it is barter or a money-based economy and the state of labor, money, capital, and product markets, however underdeveloped. Similarly, taxation policy and the state of contract law development are important. It is also important to understand how the state helps the various sectors of the economy, for example, through irrigation projects and developing infrastructure, funding manufacturing enterprises, managing money supply, and ensuring commerce and trade risks. These elements not only define the economic organization and the rate of productivity improvements but also the state of economic freedom.

In systems of religious faith, we will need to examine the nature of metaphysics its religions espouse: whether it is animism, polytheism, monism, monotheism, agnosticism, or even atheism since the nature of religious organization in the state is impacted by the nature of underlying faith. How ritualistic and superstitious is the religion? The nature of clergy is important: is it a necessary middleman, is the role hereditary, and is the clergy required to be celibate? What is the purpose of religion: How worldly or otherworldly is the religion, how does it impact attitude concerning creativity in general and science in particular as well as its position on conversions? How tolerant it is toward other faiths? How explicit is the moral code it espouses? Is the code written down? Do the religious institutions have the power to punish the violators, thus effectively creating a parallel judiciary? Does the religion harbor excessive spirituality or a conflict between science and religion?

Legal systems, as distinct from a judicial structure, include whether a formal written code exists or whether it is informal and customary or even of religious origin. Are the criminal and civil sides well developed? What is the relative importance of executive law, social custom, common law, and legislative law? How independent is the judiciary? Is the law lenient or strict? Is the legal process relatively fast or slow? What role does the chief executive play in appointing judges and executing the law? Are all citizens equal in the eyes of the law? What are the degree of development of legal code and the quality of judiciary that together ensure the equality and justice to all citizens in all arenas. Does the legal code ensure the fundamental right of property, freedom of speech, and freedom of religion?

Social structure defines the degree of wealth and power polarization. Do slavery, racism, and caste systems exist? What is the position of women in the social hierarchy and their economic participation? How significant is the possibility of upward mobility? Are people differentiated on the basis of ethnic origin and religious beliefs? What is the relative importance of economic class, caste, and race, religion, and ethnicity in determining social structure within a state or civilization? Does social structure exhibit excessive inequality?

Knowledge-creating institutions consist of formal institutions as places of creating new knowledge. The relevant questions are: Are the institutions formal or informal? What is the focus? What is the nature of creative freedom and the role played by religion? What is the level of support for these institutions?

Note that formal institutions focusing on practical, religious, and intellectual creativity came rather late. There were no practical knowledge-creating institutions until modern times as development of practical technology had not yet separated from the wealth production process. Improvements in the tools and technology were mostly part of the wealth production process, and an individual inventor was responsible for practical creativity. To what extent did the priest class monopolize religious and philosophical creativity? When did the rise of formal universities begin to change this state of affairs?

Educational institutions consist of formal institutions educating citizens. The relevant questions are about the level of support by the state and whether the education was confined to the elite or more widespread. When did a social order establish formal universities with an educational component?

Key Institutional Processes

Wealth allocation process: Sustainable growing surplus (SGS) in the earliest civilizations may be defined simply as the wealth created in a given period left over after sustenance and for our purposes was equivalent to the proportion of the population not engaged in the food production. From the concept of SGS, we may arrive at the concept of net SGS after subtracting the wealth consumed by opulence, luxuries, and monuments desired by the elites for physical, egotistical, and existential reasons. From the concept of net SGS, we may proceed to the concept of net-net SGS after subtracting the wealth needed to replace the tools, equipment, and other resources used in agricultural and nonagricultural production, however primitive. This net-net SGS was available for military capability and creative endeavors. To take the matters one step further, the net-net SGS was typically preferentially available for practical creativity directed at military capability for defensive and offensive needs and religious creativity and only what remained as net-net-net SGS was available for intellectual creativity, if it supported the ego or political needs of elite through association with intellectual creation.

Thus, significant SGS needed to exist before one could expect the elite to allocate even a small amount to intellectual creativity. Fortunately, the surplus needed for initiating and sustaining intellectual activities was quite small. A tiny percentage of population, as little as one tenth of a percent or even less, if engaged in intellectual creativity in a sustained manner over generations at the right stage, could do wonders. We think it was because intellectual creativity by definition always attracted the talented and the genius of the civilization, and therefore it was possible to make revolutionary progress in the relatively short period of a few generations in certain social orders. Typically, the genius everywhere did not care for a luxurious lifestyle. It needed minimal support but needed the state or elite to value what it accomplished in a sustained manner because intellectual creation is a stepwise and social process. Thus, the situation may be summarized as follows:

the SGS available for intellectual creativity was highly dependent on use by other higher priority activities, but intellectual creativity required very little of the surplus. It needed sustained support and appreciation in greater abundance. Still, it was the lifeblood required in the birth and development of science.

The key questions are: Who made the allocation decisions, how wise were they, what were its outcomes, and how formal and conscious was the process? Thus, a particular state within the civilization at any stage of development, consciously or not, faced five distinct decisions with respect to wealth allocation:

1. How much of the wealth produced will be allocated to sustenance of ordinary citizens?

2. How much SGS will be set aside to support opulence of the elite?

3. How much of the wealth created will be reinvested back into the wealth production process itself to make it more robust and less dependent on natural calamities?

4. How much of the wealth will be allocated to military needs, and how will this military allocation be split into offensive and defensive capabilities?

5. How much of the wealth will be allocated to creative endeavors across practical, intellectual, and religious creativity?

Are the decisions made by the elite political, military, or economic elite? What is the degree of input from religious organization in ancient times or more recently from markets? How explicit and conscious were the decisions, particularly those related to creative endeavors?

Historically relevant forms of wealth allocation may be summarized as favoring elite decadence, military spending, practical creativity, religious creativity, intellectual creativity, and balanced allocation.

Internal wars: How frequent and vicious were the wars among the states of a civilization? These wars channeled a greater proportion of surplus into military capability, destroying the accumulated wealth and life and causing a shift in the control of surplus. These clearly have implications for the focus on creative and productive endeavors, such as undertaking public works projects and supporting knowledge creation institutions.

Social cohesion process: The structures and processes responsible for knowledge creation, wealth production, and wealth allocation based on division of labor and military capability also create differences in the power and wealth individuals enjoy. These differences create centrifugal forces that carry the potential to tear the social fabric of the state of a civilization and therefore create a need for centripetal forces to contain the potential damage. The centrifugal tendencies of excessive wealth polarization and wars among states of a civilization are ultimately driven by religious differences and greed nurtured by economic institutions, a state, or a civilization and is supported by wealth allocation to military capability and luxuries for the elite. What is the weight of the needed centripetal forces, including wise state policies, tolerant religious doctrine, nationalism, and the internal police force in promoting social cohesion?

Categories of Beliefs Revisited

In chapter 5, we discussed the necessity of beliefs for a species like *Homo sapiens*. We also stressed the following three fundamental categories of beliefs:

- The possibility of knowledge of this world and the world beyond death
- The possibility of knowledge of the world beyond death
- Fellow human beings considered belonging to the same group, tribe, or social order

It should come as no surprise that the systems of religious faith played a critical role in all categories.

Beliefs concerning the possibility of knowledge of this world: Early in the history of civilization, these beliefs sprang from both religious convictions driven by existential anxiety as well as intellectual confusion. For example, a religious belief might assert the existence of gods controlling the world at their whims, thus making the world no longer objectively lawful. Likewise, a religious belief might assert that true knowledge is only possible through intuition and not a union of data and reason or the knowledge already contained in a book ordained by God. Similarly, intellectual confusion might be a great impediment to the possibility of knowledge of this world and be in collusion with religious beliefs.

Beliefs concerning the possibility of world beyond death: Belief concerning the possibility of the knowledge of a possible world beyond death is what religion is all about, apart from its role in supporting ethics. In this work, we take an understandably sympathetic view toward the necessary historic role of religion in the rise of civilizations. However, it is also clear that monistic religions have often fallen victim to the phenomena of excessive spirituality while the monotheistic religions carry the greater risk of science–religion conflict. Thus, the role religion played with respect to the possibility of the knowledge of this world is critical. Situated in the middle of these polar opposite religious systems are the doctrines of atheism, polytheism, and agnosticism. Of the three, atheism and polytheism, though far better than monism and monotheism, assume what cannot be definitively demonstrated. Only agnosticism and atheism consistently support the possibility of knowledge of this world.

Beliefs about fellow human beings: In a given social order, religious beliefs might support or discourage equality, just as religious beliefs stake widely differing claims concerning the possibility of knowledge. Likewise, secular beliefs may entertain a wide range of notions about political, social, and economic equality. The historic significance of religious beliefs is like the secular beliefs. It has supported a wide range of beliefs concerning equality and freedom here on earth. Irrespective of the religious and secular source of the beliefs, all social orders have rather well-defined notions of political and religious freedom as well as economic equality and equality of opportunity. To the extent these beliefs are important, they are supported by the resultant institutional systems and structures.

Formation of attitudes toward other social orders: History or memory of the past plays a critical role in two distinct ways, one internal and other external. The evolution of internal institutional structures and process are history-dependent. This means that there is inertia in these processes, either because of personal emotional investment or because of more objective, vested interests. The net effect is that the rate of changes of the institutional structures and processes is typically slowed down except during revolutionary times, when the old is swept aside rather quickly.

Second, and even more important, the attitudes toward other social orders are strongly dependent on the early history of a social order. There are two possible scenarios here: the attitudes of a social order toward others were formed during its own relatively unknown prehistory and reinforced continually or were inherited from other primary social orders. We wish to focus on the former since the latter is derived from the former.

Early in their histories, all primary complex social orders underwent processes that largely determined their relative attitudes of:

- Violent greed (using violence to get what other social orders possessed) or peacefulness
- Intolerance of others' creed
- Openness/insularity (degree of interest in other social orders)

In appendix A, we have argued that the *degree* of greed, violence, intolerance, and openness toward other social order exhibited by a social order strongly depended on:

- Differing natural bounty
- The emergence of imperial ideologies
- The emergence of intolerant creeds
- Unique early experience with nearby nomads during the standalone era

Harsh natural bounty (dry, arid, and cold) was more likely to create an attitude of violent greed, while a bountiful environment (warm and moist) is more likely to produce an attitude of peacefulness. Most of the aggression against other social orders in history has originated in central Asia, West Asia, and Europe, and they all have a harsher natural environment compared to South and East Asia, which have borne the brunt of aggression from these three geographical areas. However, natural bounty was not all that determined the degree of violent greed a social order developed. The emergence of an imperial ideology and the nature of its religious faith played a critical role. Without these, greed, intolerance, and aggression might have simply remained at an individual level of little consequence to us.

Violent greed is not an absolute; it is a relative quality, and institutional structures and processes must support it to be effective. Intolerance may either be of religious origin or result from violent greed. A religion that proclaims it is the only true faith is sure to develop religious intolerance. Likewise, if a social order defeats another, its imperial ideology will likely lead to an attitude of superiority and implied intolerance.

What about openness and insularity of social orders? *Homo sapiens* have instincts of sharing and parenting and thus a predisposition to openness. During the standalone era, (when conflict among primary civilizations was not possible because of the state of transport and weapons technologies), for Chinese and Mesopotamian civilizations, there were no significant natural barriers between civilization and nearby nomads. Others, like Indian and Egyptian, were more fortunate in having natural barriers, such as the Himalayas and desert respectively. Thus, the Chinese and Mesopotamian civilizations had to deal with nomads during their formative years. The Chinese were generally successful in keeping the nomads out, and the Mesopotamians were more successful in absorbing them, often after being defeated by them. Thus, the former tended to develop an attitude of superiority and insularity while the latter an attitude of openness with respect for outsiders. Such early experiences remained reinforced for both during their subsequent early histories. Thus, early experience with nomads was a significant factor in forming the attitude of openness/insularity.

The attitudes toward others may, therefore, be defined by the degree of violent greed/peacefulness, tolerance/intolerance and openness/insularity.

The attitudes of violent greed, intolerance, and insularity, though first crystalized in the standalone era for the four primary civilizations, became particularly relevant in the peaceful and violent interaction eras. During the standalone era, these attitudes merely shaped the nature of wars and social inequality among the states within a social order. In the later eras, these attitudes shaped the relationship both among states within a social order as well as among different social orders. In social orders derived from earlier social orders, these attitudes were naturally transmitted.

It is important to emphasize again that these attitudes are not black and white; it has shades of gray since the inner nature of *Homo sapiens* allows for these attitudes in all *Homo sapiens*. The only questions are to what degree the natural causes required them, social causes nurtured them, and wars with nomads fostered them.

Together, these attitudes define the external social conscience of a social order to toward other social orders.

We may note that a social order that displays low social conscience externally may possess a high internal social cohesion. This internal social cohesion, otherwise known as nationalism, is often a strategy employed by a clever dominant class within a state to create a consensus to indulge in violence in the pursuit of greed and creed against other social orders. Thus, an aggression against other social orders in the name of a state or nation may be glorified and rewarded.

Though these attitudes about other social orders emerge from intrinsic causes, these attitudes are also the basis of the constructive and destructive outcomes of a particular social order (sections 8.8 and 8.9) and when added or integrated across all relevant social orders, become the extrinsic peaceful and extrinsic violent causes for a particular social order respectively.

History-Dependent Nature of Intrinsic Causes

It is important to emphasize that all elements of the intrinsic causes or the institutional structures and processes, and beliefs about the world, ultimate reality, fellow human beings (internal social conscience), and beliefs about other social orders (external social conscience) are strongly history-dependent. In a sense, social order hands these down to the members of the social order, who, while feeling bound by them, can change them as they see fit. Thus, an ongoing vigorous debate between "conservatism" and "liberalism" has been a feature of any dynamic social order.

8.4 Productive Outcomes

In a fundamental sense, for a standalone social order, the productive outcomes are simply a function of natural and intrinsic causes or its institutional structures and processes.

Wealth Production

For our purpose, wealth is producing something through land use, exertion of labor, and capital. Production of wealth has always been a function of labor, land, *and* capital ever since *Homo sapiens* learned to make tools. An increase in wealth production can only be accomplished through improvements in bringing more land under cultivation (quality and quantity of land at a civilization's disposal was, however, fixed in the short run) and quantity and quality of labor force that could be impacted by worker skills and migration patterns. Until modern times, these were hardly under any form of sophisticated control and rate of formation of capital to assist labor. In nearly all complex social orders, wealth production has been a shared responsibility of public and private sectors consisting of large and small enterprises but with widely differing private property rights. Similarly, trade, product, labor, and credit markets have always existed—however primitive, dysfunctional, and opaque—in complex social orders. Wealth production in all social orders has also been a strong function of the degree of social, political, and economic inequality and even religious belief systems or in short, the degree of economic, political, and religious freedom enjoyed by individuals.

New products and services: Quality of life improvements and increasing wealth have necessarily required developing new products and services throughout the entire history of *Homo sapiens*. These words have a modern ring to them, but the underlying processes are not modern.

Internal trade: Internal trade plays a key role in wealth creation through increased efficiency and by creating demand for new products. It is highly dependent on infrastructure, transport, and communication technologies as well as the existence of markets for goods. Division of labor necessitates a nominal level of internal trade and could grow beyond that by presence of a market and transport, storage, and infrastructure technologies.

Improving Stock of Factors of Wealth Production

As we discuss in chapter 9, it is not possible to deduce the productive, creative, and scientific outcomes (the last two are discussed in next section) directly from intrinsic causes. The "intermediate variables" determined by the natural and intrinsic causes but more directly relatable to productive, creative and scientific outcomes are required.

The existing stocks of *factors of wealth production* and *knowledge* may be defined respectively as:

- Existing state of factors of wealth production or capital, land, and labor
- Existing knowledge stock of past practical, religious, and intellectual outcomes; its store of abstract systems-building capability; and the institutional structures and processes to support knowledge creation

Productive outcomes consist of wealth production as well as changes in the stock of land, labor, and capital at the disposal of the social order through adding new arable land, improving existing land, improving labor productivity through education, and capital formation through new investment in production equipment.

8.5 Creative and Scientific Outcomes

The creative outcomes of a civilization are simply its practical, religious, and intellectual creativity defined in chapter 6 and the state of its abstract systems-building capability essential to religious and intellectual creativity and helpful to practical creativity. Creative outcomes always result from wise and sustained allocation of the surplus to creative endeavors and resisting squandering the surplus on luxuries and monuments and, though at times justifiably necessary, on military capability.

- Practical creativity may be classified into *new* materials, processes, energy sources and tools, agricultural technologies, nonagricultural products, building construction techniques, transport technologies, weapons technologies, infrastructure, communication technologies, and breakthroughs in practical medicine.

- Religious creativity includes creation myths, new religious doctrines, and synthesis of existing ones.

- Intellectual creativity includes art, philosophy, and science. Art comprises of all visual arts, such as painting, sculpture, architecture, etc. and all performing arts, such as dance, music, theater, and literature that includes fiction (stories, novel) and nonfiction (poetry, essays, books, etc.). Philosophy includes metaphysics, epistemology, aesthetics, and ethics. Science comprises of formal sciences (mathematics, logic, and linguistics), natural sciences (astronomy, physics, earth science, and chemistry), biological sciences (biology, zoology, and medicine), and social sciences (history, political science, economics, social science, psychology, anthropology, and law). These sciences, particularly physics, will need to be further divided into solar astronomy, branches of classical physics (mechanics, electromagnetism, and thermodynamics), nuclear physics, quantum mechanics, and cosmology to fully understand the relevance of their historical development.

- Abstract systems-building capability (ASBC) consists of nine breakthroughs, excluding the spoken language noted in chapter 7: written script, conscious creative method, alphabetical script, logic and epistemology, experimental method in the heavens, a decimal counting system, an experimental method here on earth, calculus, and the scientific method. Thus, ASBC may be thought of as intellectual infrastructure consisting of breakthroughs mostly in formal sciences and philosophy that makes other more substantive practical, religious, and intellectual creative outcomes possible.

- Innovation in institutional structures and processes, (though part of intellectual creativity and social sciences) needs to be singled out because of its importance and refers to changes in societal structures and processes that constitute the intrinsic causes. Innovation is not just confined to breakthrough in practical, religious, and intellectual creativity and abstract systems-building capability. It also refers to the very structures and processes responsible for them.

Thus, creative outcomes consist of not only breakthroughs in practical, religious, and intellectual creativity but also the rare but critical breakthrough in abstract systems-building capability.

8.6 Constructive Outcomes during Standalone Era

We have implied above that there was little interaction among participants during the standalone era. Strictly speaking, that is not quite accurate. While it is true that purposeful interaction was absent, there was indeed slow, mediated "leakage" or diffusion from one social order to another. Let us briefly note how.

Elements of Diffusion

We may begin by asking what one social order could get from another social order in the absence of a developed means of transport and writing systems. The answer is that it could mostly be a diffusion of practical technology and an infusion of new blood and perhaps ideas during the standalone era. However, in the absence of writing systems, it was indeed difficult to transmit ideas. In addition, there was little interest in the religious creativity of other civilizations. Consequently, the diffusion of practical creativity or inventions were accepted most frequently in the creativity arena.

Diffusion Channels

Though few verifiable records of individual travel exist during the standalone era, we must assume that in the absence of trade, individual travel and mass migrations were the only sources of the diffusion.

Individual travel: The diffusion of practical creativity to other civilizations was a natural extension of what occurred within a civilization. Diffusion occurred across the frontier state and oozed into neighboring minor civilizations or nomads who acted as intermediaries. The adjoining frontier states of two neighboring social orders often shared language and culture, making it easier for diffusion to occur. Individual travel was mostly a matter of individual choice, and therefore it would appear wholly as a chance phenomenon. However, over centuries, sufficient individuals with wanderlust and perhaps circumstances requiring them to travel made this channel not only a dependable mode of diffusion but also a significant one. Individual travel can take two forms: one that involved a series of short distance travels, like a relay race, but with substantial built-in time gaps or a one-scoop long-distance travel. Clearly, the former was slower but was probably more frequent in the standalone era. The latter occurred less frequently but with a greater speed and reach. The diffusion could occur through word-of-mouth or through an actual artifact as appropriate.

Mass migrations: Although an individual traveler was a source of great ideas and inventions capable of affecting a civilization, we also want to recognize *mass migrations* as an independent category. However, migrations during the standalone era and before were hardly purposeful, unlike migration during peaceful and violent interaction eras. Migrations were driven by tribal wars and natural disasters and likely consisted of several incremental steps. Mass migrations were a natural vehicle to transmit intellectual and religious creativity during the standalone era when writing systems did not exist.

General Nature of Channels

These early primitive channels were peaceful, and there was little question of one civilization controlling another.

8.7 Constructive Outcomes during Peaceful Interaction Era

Constructive outcomes that initiated during peaceful interaction era may be defined simply as those that required *purposeful cooperation* with another civilization. Thus, they are fundamentally different from natural and intrinsic causes of the civilization since they resulted from causes driving *other* civilizations, and they are different from diffusion during the standalone era in that they are planned and purposeful and not accidental.

Note that summation of all relevant constructive outcomes impacting a particular social order is simply the extrinsic peaceful causes for that social order. There is little need to discuss extrinsic peaceful causes apart from the summation of all relevant constructive outcomes.

Elements of Constructive Outcomes

The following categories from productive and creative outcomes are relevant as constructive outcomes:

- Practical, religious, and intellectual creativity
- Abstract systems-building capability
- Fair trade
- Peaceful migrations
- Knowledge of institutional structures and processes

These are nothing other than the *creative* and *productive* outcomes of one civilization available to another civilization under conditions of peace *and* openness on the part of both civilizations.

Practical, religious, and intellectual creativity: When both social orders are open to exchange, diffusion of practical, religious, and intellectual creativity may occur with each social order free to accept and internalize them or ignore them.

Abstract systems-building capability: In addition to specific creative outcomes, a social order may also be open to the abstract systems-building capability of another social order. As noted before, abstract systems-building capability consists of writing systems, including alphabetical script and understanding the creative method, logic, epistemology, and scientific method, including the experimental method. In short, the creative tools make creative outcomes possible.

Fair trade: Trade occurs through two scenarios. Either social order X has an excess supply of product A and an unmet demand for product B, and social order Y has an excess supply for product B and an unmet demand for product A, or location X is able to produce product A more efficiently (after netting the cost of transportation), and location Y is able to do the same for product B. In the first case, both sides get a product they did not have. In the latter case, both sides gain economic efficiency through trading. There is great incentive behind trade since identifying an opportunity (new commodity or a price differential) and filling it could be lucrative.

Peaceful migrations: Migrations occur through peaceful mass exploration and may be required by trade. The expulsion and migration of Jews from Egypt to Palestine to escape conditions of near slavery is a well-known example. Records of most migration during both standalone and peaceful eras, however, exist mostly in the mythical accounts of civilizations, with rather limited substantiation and excessive theorizing. Peaceful migrations have also occurred because of natural disasters. Peaceful migrations in or out can have a significant impact on the productive outs from the transfer of ideas and inventions. The course of history has been altered by many known mass relocation of groups.

Knowledge of institutional structures and processes: Exchange of creative outcomes, abstract systems-building capability, trade, and peaceful migrations were not the only things that took place during the peaceful interaction era. Social orders also began to glimpse at the political systems, military capability, economic organization, legal systems, knowledge-creating and educational institutions, and wealth-allocation processes of other social orders. However, these glimpses during this era were just that: glimpses that aroused mild curiosity. In general, the desire and need to examine how other social orders operated was not strong. The productive and creative outcomes and abstract systems capability of other social orders were of prime interest.

Transmission Channels

The lone traveler, peaceful migrations, and fair trade were the principal channels used for peaceful interaction among civilizations. Each of these channels was in principle capable of transmitting ideas and inventions, goods and people, though not with same degree of ease and efficiency. For example, a lone traveler could transmit an idea or an invention, transport goods, and migrate himself. Peaceful migration, though generally aimed at the movement of large groups of people, must necessarily involve transmission of ideas and inventions but not tradable goods. Similarly, trade, though primarily aimed at transporting physical goods, involved people at either end and often in between. Thus, people conducting long-distance trade in ancient times essentially formed a human chain that was also capable of transmitting ideas and inventions. Further, those conducting trade could also choose to permanently relocate to the civilization at the other end if opportunity and circumstances warranted. Therefore, there was considerable overlap among the three channels, and this overlap among the channels was good since they ensured efficient transmission, movement, and the diffusion of creativity, transfer of people, and transport of physical goods respectively.

These peaceful channels are fundamentally positive by nature. They are based on freedom and equality among civilizations, and as such, were unlikely to consciously dilute the state of equality and individual striving within a receiving civilization. Calling these channels peaceful is appropriate because they generally involved no destruction of life and property, cruelty, savagery, looting, exploitation, or imposition of one civilization's views on others.

In the final analysis, all peaceful channels, indeed all channels, ultimately worked through people.

Diffusion through individual travel: During the peaceful interaction era, transmission of creativity (ideas and inventions) to other civilizations continued though its relative importance naturally declined. In the era of extended military conflicts, there were indeed many documented examples of adventurous famous travelers, such as Indian Buddhist monks to Southeast Asia; the Italian trader Marco Polo, who went to China; Chinese monk Fie Han, who traveled to India; and the Persian Alburani, who came to India.

Peaceful migrations: Peaceful migrations were an incidental channel for transmitting ideas and inventions. The transmission of ideas and inventions were unintended consequences of the peaceful migrations.

Fair trade: The choice of fair trade as a separate channel is justified not only because of its potential economic impact but also because it carried people, ideas, and inventions. Trade mediated through a chain of trading posts is, in principle, considerably easier than long-distance individual travel because it can mitigate the need for long-distance travel. As land and sea travel improved slowly, direct trade between widely separated civilizations also became possible. Several important trade routes linking India and West Asia were developed.

Historically, all three channels have been important; however, if one were to rank them, they would be in the order of fair trade, migrations, and individual travel.

Effectiveness of Channels of Transmission

The effectiveness and speed of the peaceful channels of transmission in the last analysis depends on the degree of insularity of the originator and receiver acting as gatekeepers. This attitude was particularly important in the case of religious and intellectual creativity diffusion and mass migrations since practical creativity and fair trade were likely to find acceptance by most social orders because of the obvious benefits. History shows that creativity is not a monopoly of any particular group, culture, race, or civilization. Each major existing civilization has gone through periods when it was the most creative civilization in the world. All major civilizations have made contributions without which we would not be where we are today. Given that, the attitudes of openness relative to creativity can become critical so that a civilization that is not necessarily very creative in a particular period may at least be *receptive* to the creativity of other civilizations.

The notions of openness/insularity and the physical speed of transmission may be integrated using a three-factor rate of diffusion model. The first factor is the degree of insularity of the civilization responsible for the creative act. The insularity may range from fully willing to fully unwilling to share the fruits of its creativity; in the latter case, the ability to keep the creative outcome a trade or state secret becomes paramount. The sharing may be free or have a cost associated with it. The sharing may be immediate or have a built-in time delay to give the originator an advantage. The second factor is the physical rate at which the creative invention or discovery may be able to travel from its place of creation. This transmission during the peaceful era, as discussed above, was made possible through travel, peaceful migrations, and fair trade. The third factor affecting diffusion of creativity is the degree of insularity of the receiving civilization. This may also range from aggressively seeking to a passive lack of interest. The three-factor model shows that the rate of transmission cannot exceed the physical speed of the channel. This occurs when there is substantial openness on the part of the originator and the receiving civilization.

It is interesting to note that these three factors have played very different roles in different eras relative to the practical, religious, and intellectual forms of creativity, migrations, and trade. The receptivity to practical creativity and fair trade has been universally high simply because it is immediately beneficial, nonthreatening, and easier to comprehend, as noted earlier. However, the resistance to religious and intellectual creativity and migrations has been high in certain eras for some civilizations for political, social, economic, and religious reasons. The relative importance of these factors has also changed dramatically from ancient times to modern times.

General Nature of the Channels

Again, these channels were essentially peaceful with no one social order controlling another. The impact of constructive outcomes is typically slow (though faster than diffusion during standalone era), not necessarily reciprocal or symmetrical, and will typically be direct in specific trade and creative exchange. Then it will work slowly through institutional structures and processes over a longer time. The key to peaceful interaction among civilizations is the degree of openness to the influence of others.

8.8 Destructive Outcomes during the Violent Interaction Era

The last of category of outcomes are the destructive outcomes that by definition came into existence during the violent interaction era. These may be defined as those that require violent aggression toward another social order. Thus, they are fundamentally different from not only natural and intrinsic causes but also constructive outcomes in that they seek not purposeful cooperation but purposeful destruction of another social order.

Note that summation of all relevant destructive outcomes impacting a particular social order is simply the extrinsic violent causes for that social order. There is little need to discuss extrinsic violent causes apart from the summation of all relevant destructive outcomes.

Three Instruments of Destruction

Three instruments of destruction (IOD) have been used by civilizations to control another civilization through violent means: the empire builders, the violent colonizers, and the systematic wealth drainers.

The era of violent interaction among civilizations has not been uniform with respect to the speed and nature of changes brought about by these instruments of destruction during their 2,500-year existence. We can actually discern three distinct periods that correspond to the changing nature of the instruments of control.

The first period was the longest and was dominated by empire builders who generally relocated to the conquered territory and began about 550 BCE. The second period was initiated by Europeans and resulted in a violent colonization of the New World based on the control of sea routes and new territories and a coerced mercantile trading pattern with the Old World, constituting a global, triangular relationship. Mercantile trade with the Old World was a less brutal form of systematic wealth drain based on control of sea routes and worked in parallel with violent colonization of the New World. It began about 1500 CE and lasted until about 1750. This was followed by a more horrible form of systematic wealth drain based on controlling territories in the Old World, continuing control of sea routes, and the rise of capitalism in parts of Western Europe.

Elements of Destructive Outcomes

Each IOD had its own unique element, but each resulted in loss of sustained political independence of the invaded social order.

Empire builders: The empire builder may be a "loot and withdraw" conquer and control long-distance or a "conquer and stay" variety. The impact of the first may be devastating in the short term because of looting and the destruction of life and property; however, civilization would recover rather quickly. The "conquer and stay" empire builder intends to control the SGS of the defeated civilization after it lost its sustained political independence, and we focus on this type of empire builder.

Violent colonizers: The violent colonizers excelled in displacing and exterminating indigenous populations in the New World, resulting in land usurpation. It also created the institutions of slavery and indentured labor required to produce wealth from the usurped land. In parallel, the mercantile traders replaced the millennia-long tradition of fair trade among social orders in the old world by coerced trade based on controlling sea routes.

Systematic wealth drainers: Finally, systematic wealth drainers, controlling sea routes and territories in the Old World, engaged in the most horrible form of wealth drain from larger, established, and highly productive civilizations in the Old World to a few small European states perched on the Atlantic Ocean.

An early form of wealth drain existed through long-distance control of the territory through a loyal governor backed by military presence or more likely by physical relocation to the conquered territory in sufficient numbers. This occurred when the conquered civilization was densely populated, produced significant wealth, the aggressor was small in numbers with limited transportation back and forth to original home base, and there is insufficient opportunity for trade or when the aggressor is unable to transplant the superior wealth production capabilities to his home base for geographic, climatic, or technological reasons. Under these conditions, land could not be expropriated; people could not be employed to produce wealth elsewhere, wealth could not be controlled through trade, and the conquered population was too large and advanced to be displaced or killed.

Therefore, the strategy of the aggressor was to transfer the wealth the conquered population produced. The early examples of this form of wealth drain are ancient Egypt and the Roman Empire. Thus, wealth drain evolved from ancient Egypt to the Roman Empire to modern western European states. Only the latter, with its sophisticated control of territory and trade routes and pretensions to the contrary, deserves the questionable title of systematic wealth drain.

In parallel with these new elements of SGS control, land usurpation, slavery and indentured labor, coerced trade, and a systematic wealth drain, the old elements of creativity exchange, abstract systems-building capability and knowledge of the institutional structures and processes not only continued but also accelerated. Of course, there was little room for fair trade and peaceful migrations as the world came increasingly under the domination of violent colonizers and systematic wealth drainers.

Essential Nature of Instruments of Destruction

Violence as the common thread in all instruments of destruction: All three instruments of control thrive on aggressive, violent attitude toward others and aim to control the empire builder's sustainable growing surplus, violent colonizer's control of land, or systematic wealth drainer's wealth drain. We note that all three instruments are in essence a different form of "empire." The difference is whether they are after control of surplus, land ownership, or wealth transfer, whether they do it by relocating to the conquered territory or through long-distance control, and whether they work with the conquered population or displace/exterminate it.

Instruments of destruction as channels of transmission: It is clear that during the standalone era, the slow diffusion of ideas and inventions through individual travel and mass migrations were important channels. During the peaceful interaction era, fair trade, at least among the leading civilizations, became the principal channel. What about the violent interaction era? Was there a place for peaceful interaction during the violent era?

- First, the channels of individual travel, mass migrations, and fair trade often remained active to one degree or another and among civilizations not involved in violent conflict.

- Second, in social orders engaged in conflict, these channels, after an initial period of naked violence, became less so in some regards while continuing to depend on IOD for their effectiveness or even existence.

How one characterizes these apparently peaceful channels during the violent interaction era depends on how what constitutes peaceful interaction is defined. Operationally, these channels may clearly constitute peaceful interaction provided there is freedom to travel and trade. However, strategically, they may owe their existence to a violent IOD. It is perhaps appropriate to call these channels as peaceful channels originating in the wake of war and violence.

Thus, IODs have a *dual* purpose: as a means of control and as a channel for controlled transfer of ideas and inventions, migrations, and trade. To distinguish between these from peaceful transmission channels, these channels practiced *forced transfer* in place of diffusion, *violent colonization* in place of peaceful migrations, and *coerced trade* and systematic wealth transfer backed up by political and military control of territories and/or trade routes in place of fair trade. Both peaceful and violent channels have continued to coexist. The chief characteristics of the violent channels are their high speeds and dramatic, nonsymmetric and nonreciprocal impacts on the aggressor and victims.

8.9 The Inner Nature of *Homo sapiens* as a Cause

Fixed Yet Flexible Nature as an Independent Cause in Social Evolution

We have outlined the nature of significant causes and outcomes except one conspicuous by its absence: the inner nature of the species. Thus, the remaining question is: What about the role played by the fixed yet flexible inner nature of *Homo sapiens* (self-consciousness; free will; necessity of beliefs; creative, productive, and constructive powers; and conscience) in determining the substantial differences observed in the evolution of social orders?

Imagine a planet with two different species, each capable of creating a civilized, settled mode of life. If the two life forms were endowed differently (mentally, instinctually, and physically), the significance of a relationship between productive, creative, and scientific outcomes and the inner nature would hardly be lost on an observer. That the *absolute* magnitude of the outcomes for a *Homo sapiens* social order should depend on of the biological gifts of the species is clear as well. If *Homo sapiens* were better endowed in mental and physical attributes or if instincts were weaker or stronger, it would clearly affect the absolute speed and perhaps the direction of evolution of social orders founded by the species. However, *Homo sapiens* are the only life form capable of creating social orders on this planet, so the role of biological gifts in explaining *differences* among social orders is often confused since what is true for the individuals is assumed true for the social order. The following two errors are made in drawing that conclusion.

Individual creative, productive, constructive, and destructive behaviors translate into observable creative, productive, constructive, and constructive behavior at the group level. However, what is true for the individual may not necessarily be true for social order levels since the character of a social order is not simply the algebraic sum of the characters of individuals it is comprised of. It must be normalized by the relative power of individuals within the group, which can vary dramatically among individuals.

Secondly, since the fixed aspect of the inner nature is by definition the same for *Homo sapiens* in all social orders, *differences* in creative, productive, constructive, and destructive behaviors leading to outcomes can only be attributed to the flexible part of the inner nature. However, the law of large numbers assures us of that. Although these unique mental and physical attributes and conscience vary dramatically among individuals, they cannot vary among groups of substantial size. Therefore:

- The differences in creative and productive outcomes must be explained by the *differences in natural and social causes* of the two social orders being compared and not the differences in unique mental and physical attributes of individuals within the social order. Only if we were to compare social orders founded by two *different* species, the differences in *their* creative, productive, constructive, and destructive outcomes may be explained partially by differing biological heritage of the two species.

- The differences in constructive outcomes (openness to outcomes of other social orders), which play an important role in creative and productive outcomes is similar. There is a struggle among instincts of sociability and curiosity, the natural bounty, and ideology early in the history of a social order that creates differing propensity toward constructive outcomes. However, the instincts are shared equally. Therefore *differences in social and natural causes* must explain the differing constructive outcomes.

- Similarly, the interaction between the instincts of intraspecies dominance and interspecies aggression and the natural bounty early in the history of a social order can result in a wide range of destructive outcomes, ranging from peaceful to violent and everything in between. Again, the instincts are shared equally across all social orders (the law of large numbers assures that); hence, the differing destructive outcomes must result from *differences in social and natural causes*.

When the above paradigm is questioned, as it often has been, it leads inevitably to the hypotheses of racism or caste.

The reader may still raise the issue of the unusual confluence of genetic and environmental factors in a leader of exceptional talent and his seemingly enormous impact on the course of history. This point of view is expressed formally in the Great Man Theory of history we referred to earlier. However, once we note that a Gandhi could not have emerged in European civilization, a Hitler or Napoleon could not have emerged in Indian civilization, and a Mohammed could not have emerged in the Chinese or Indian civilizations, the seemingly substantial impact of these individuals does not seem all that substantial anymore since it is the civilizations that created these extraordinary individuals. Had a Gandhi, Hitler, Napoleon, or Mohammed not arisen, their roles would likely have been filled by of collection of other, lesser or greater leaders. To the extent the latter cannot be demonstrated, it is beyond the analytical process employed in this work.

The points below emphasize the influence of a fixed yet flexible inner nature as an independent cause:

- The fixed inner nature is irrelevant in explaining *differences* in the evolution of social orders since it is shred equally among all individuals, for that is what makes us human.
- The flexible inner nature is responsible for differences in creative, productive, constructive, and destructive outcomes. These outcomes can be fully explained by difference in natural and social causes since the intrinsic and extrinsic social causes fully reflect this flexible inner nature of the species.

Thus, the surprising and simplifying conclusion is that we need not take the inner nature of the species into account as an explicit additional cause in explaining differences in the evolution of social orders since it is already expressed through natural and social causes! These remarks amount to nothing more than rejecting the theories of racism and caste/reincarnation while accepting the self-evident variability in the biological gifts among individuals and absence of such variability among large *Homo sapiens* groups based on the law of large numbers.

8.10 The Concept of Sustainable Growing Surplus (SGS)

Before leaving the chapter, we need to formally define the concept of sustainable growing surplus and methodology of its assessment. For our purposes, the existence of the net internal sustainable SGS is more important than the level of wealth produced. SGS is simply the wealth left after ordinary consumption and supporting the luxurious lifestyle of the elite in a social order and is available for military capability, replenishing the factors of wealth production, and creative endeavors. Social orders with high wealth production and little net SGS will not only lack the growth potential but also quickly wither away.

Internal SGS is simply the internal capacity of a social order to produce wealth less ordinary consumption and the luxurious lifestyles of the elite. On the other hand, *total* net SGS must include the impact of peaceful and violent interaction with other social orders. SGS during the peaceful and violent interaction eras depended not only on internal SGS but also on its augmentation or loss through interaction with other social orders. During these eras, it was possible to attain high SGS through purely internal activity or a combination of internal creation and external interaction. Thus, total SGS results from three processes:

- The portion of wealth a social order produces internally that ordinary citizens and the elite do not consume. Economic freedom, natural bounty, technological sophistication, internal inequality, and internal wars affect the magnitude of this surplus. During the standalone era, only this form of SGS was possible.
- The portion produced through peaceful interaction with other social orders was based on mutual benefit through exchange of creative outcomes, trade, and migration and had potential to augment internal SGS considerably. This originated during the peaceful interaction era and remained possible during the violent interaction era as well.
- The portion of wealth acquired through aggression and violent interaction for the sole benefit of aggressor. This began with the advent of violent interaction era and once it began, it had the potential to overwhelm the first two forms under certain conditions.

Measure of SGS: In the short run, internal SGS of a social order was simply the proportion of wealth not consumed by common man and elite. However, its growth and sustainability depended on population growth and productivity growth, with the latter defined as resulting from desirable changes in labor, land, and capital. Thus, SGS may be thought of as dependent on population growth and changes in rate of savings or capital accumulation and growth in labor productivity if changes in quality of land are assumed negligible.

In table 8.1, the growth of these three components is shown for a hypothetical social order beginning 6000 BCE and achieving the status of planet-wide civilization comparable to an advanced modern state at the end of the twentieth century. The change in savings as a proportion of wealth produced is assumed to vary from 5 percent in the standalone era to 25 percent today. The population growth data are based on several studies that estimate the population of *Homo sapiens* to have grown from about 13 million in 6000 BCE to over 6 billion by 2000 CE. The growth factor in productivity during the entire civilization epoch is estimated to be 256. This is based on wealth production estimates of about $200 per person per year in 6000 BCE

Table 8.1: Growth of SCS in a Hypothetical World Civilization

Civilization Era	Total Years	Savings Rate	% Savings Growth Factor	Productivity Growth Factor	Population Growth Factor	SGS Growth Factor	Productivity Growth per century	Population Growth per Century	SGS Growth per Century	SGS Annual Growth
Standalone	3000	5%		2	3.57	14.28	2.30%	4.40%	0.48	0.10%
Peaceful Interaction	2550	~20%	4	2	3.26	16.3	2.70%	4.90%	0.64	0.11%
Violent Interaction										
EB	1950	~25%		2	3	15	3.60%	5.80%	0.77	0.14%
VC	300	~25%	~1.25	2	1.89	3.78	26%	23.70%	1.26	0.44%
SWD	200	~25%		16	6.39	127.8	300%	157%	63.9	2.45%
	8,000		5x	256x	450x	equals 576,000				

EB: Empire building
VC: Violent colonization
SWD: Systematic Wealth Drainer

and growing to $51,200 per person per year in 2000 dollars for a modern state. The population and productivity growth factors are then distributed among the differing eras based on expected and known acceleration in productivity and population levels in each era. Surprisingly, the data in table 8.1 shows that for such a hypothetical social order a greater contribution in SGS growth would come from population growth, followed by productivity growth, followed by the saving rate.

The real significance of table 8.1 is how small SGS growth per century for this hypothetical planet-wide social order was until recent times. The growth in SGS per year is even less dramatic, varying from about 0.1 percent in the standalone and peaceful interaction eras to 0.15 percent during the empire-building period, followed by 0.44 percent during the violent colonization period and 2.45 percent during the systematic wealth drain period. Thus, on the average, annual growth rate of SGS has varied by a factor of about 25 (2.45 percent divided by 0.1 percent) over the entire history of this imaginary *Homo sapiens* social order. The variation in SGS growth across historical civilizations combined with long periods for compounding resulted in widely varying SGS across civilizations in a particular era and across eras despite low annual growth rates.

This bit of analysis means that any comparison of SGS across social orders in a particular period must be relative and not absolute since a comparison of the absolute magnitudes across long time spans would be essentially meaningless for our purpose.

Difficulty in Assessing SGS: It is indeed difficult to assess the relative magnitude of SGS of ancient civilizations because of the lack of specific data concerning productivity and consumption. Its assessment in later chapters will be by necessity indirect and based on guestimates. In particular, we note that:

- No estimates of wealth produced by civilizations prior to the Common Era are available.

- A 1999 study by Angus Maddison essentially claimed comparable GDP per capita for all major civilizations (Europe, China, India, and Muslim) until about 1500 CE and since 1500 CE to the present, the European civilization (and its various offshoots) has pulled ahead by one to two orders of magnitude in per capita GDP compared to other civilizations.

- SGS is determined by not only internal wealth production but also the impact of constructive and destructive causes (discussed later in the chapter), including coerced trade and territorial control.

- Our concern is not the relative size of the economies since they are directly proportional to population for fixed productivity. Lately, there has been a lot of noise in the press about how large the Indian and Chinese economies were prior to 1750 CE. How could they not have been, given their populations and higher productivity of land in a preindustrial period?

- From our perspective, it is difficult to justify the Angus Maddison claim that productivity in Europe before 1500 CE was comparable to that in India and China, since productivity was a far stronger function of natural bounty (soil productivity and number of growing seasons each year) than quality of capital and technology employed in productive endeavors. India and China are clearly more endowed in natural bounty than Europe and West Asia are, and up to

1000 CE, they probably beat both Europe and West Asia in productivity and continued to beat Europe until 1500 CE. Thus, the Maddison study is likely flawed and seems like a transparent attempt to prove that European civilization was never behind Asia in productivity since its birth.

The bottom line is that SGS comparison is indeed difficult to quantify by civilization, particularly before modern times. And until further research, we must remain satisfied with its relative assessment through its characterization as high, moderate, and low.

8.11 Summary

In this chapter, we outlined in detail the four categories of causes (natural, intrinsic, peaceful extrinsic, and extrinsic violent causes) and three categories of outcomes (productive, creative, and scientific). Constructive outcomes, when summed over all relevant social orders, are none other than the extrinsic peaceful causes, and destructive outcomes, when summed over all relevant social orders, are none other than the extrinsic violent causes. We have defined these categories in sufficient granularity to handle the overwhelming amount of data on causes and outcomes of social orders.

Surprisingly, we concluded that both the fixed and flexible parts of the inner nature of *Homo sapiens* need not be taken into account explicitly in explaining the *differences* in the evolutions of different social orders. This is because all social orders are founded by the same species, all individual members share the fixed aspect of the inner nature equally, and the flexible part, while it varies dramatically among individuals due to differing genetic endowments and environmental impacts, the law of large numbers assures us of its invariability at the level of social order. Thus, natural causes and social causes (intrinsic and extrinsic) alone need to be taken into account in explaining the differences in the evolution of social orders founded by a single species on this planet since social causes already reflect the inner nature.

KEY CONCEPTS

Natural causes
Intrinsic causes
Productive outcomes
Creative and scientific outcomes
Constructive outcomes
Destructive outcomes
Extrinsic peaceful causes
Extrinsic violent causes
Instruments of destruction
The inner nature of *Homo sapiens* as an independent cause

Chapter 9: The Theory of Interacting Social Orders

9.1 Introduction

In chapter 4, we defined the birth of civilizations based on a modest but sustainable growing surplus derived from development or adoption of key agricultural technologies, including animal domestication and nonagricultural technologies, such as building shelter, pottery, clothing, tanning, and stone work with a city of at least ten thousand. It also included simple division of labor and trade based on barter.

In this chapter, we are going to treat civilizations and nomadic confederations as components of a complex and reciprocally conditioned system connected through causes and outcomes. Therefore, it is appropriate that we develop a systems approach. Just as a species appears unchanging even though the theory of evolution teaches us to the contrary, civilizations, particularly ancient civilizations, may appear static but were hardly ever so. The outcomes constantly changed under dynamic natural, intrinsic, and extrinsic causes.

The concept of the historically observable phases of science and the categories of causes and significant outcomes discussed in chapters 7 and 8 are quite sufficient to organize the data. In this chapter, however, we want to develop a methodology to rationalize the evolution of civilizations and their productive, creative, and scientific outcomes by relating causes and outcomes. The methodology we want to develop must apply to both civilizations and nomadic confederations since the latter have had a substantial, disproportionate, and direct impact on civilizations and an equally substantial, though indirect, impact on the development of science.

Our approach in this chapter will be as follows:

- Define a reciprocally conditioned social system consisting of social orders with interlocking causes and outcomes, particularly during the peaceful and violent interaction eras.
- Assess possible approaches to developing a theory of interacting social orders to relate outcomes to reciprocal driving causes.
- Develop an appreciation of the complex process through which causes lead to outcomes in this system of reciprocally conditioned social orders.
- Propose the concept of inner nature of social orders and a method to assess it.
- Utilize the concept of inner nature to rationalize the evolution of civilizations and science both within and across phases.

9.2 Social Orders as an Interacting System of Causes and Outcomes

In chapter 5, we discussed that *Homo sapiens* social orders have been created and developed by a species that is capable of creative, productive, constructive, and destructive behaviors founded on its fixed yet flexible inner nature. Second, we noted in chapter 6 that the social order itself has been essential to realize the full, biologically based creative potential of the species. We could say that the social order and the creative potential of the species have been in a symbiotic relationship. Third, we have defined civilization as a social order with identifiable causes and observable outcomes. Fourth, chapter 8 discussed how the social orders are highly responsive to the influence and control of other social orders through diffusional, peaceful, or violent interaction. Therefore, a *Homo sapiens* social order has been, in general, part of a dynamic, history-dependent, reciprocally conditioned *social system,* which, though founded by a species that needs both the physical and biological worlds to exist, is nevertheless readily distinguishable from both worlds as it essentially lives a self-conscious social existence. The latter means that the power and position of the species on the planet is nearly completely dependent on the quality of social relationships among individual members within a social order and the relationships with other social orders.

The four categories of causes and four categories of outcomes depicting social orders as a system of reciprocal influences are shown in figure 9.1. Note, in particular, that:

- The sum of constructive *outcomes* of relevant social orders are nothing other than the *extrinsic peaceful causes* for the receiving social order, which may be expected to be more or less symmetric and positive in impact because they are based on free choice for both sides.

- Likewise, the sum of the destructive *outcomes* of relevant social orders is nothing other than the *extrinsic violent causes* for the invaded social order. However, their impact must be necessarily asymmetric and likely negative on the defeated and positive on the victors because they are based on a victor controlling the defeated.

For the sake of completeness, we have also included the fixed yet flexible inner nature of the species as a cause. However, as we have argued in chapters 5 and 8, we need not consider this inner nature as an independent cause in explaining the *differences* in the evolution of social orders. This is because all *Homo sapiens* share the fixed part of inner nature equally, and the flexible part, despite dramatic variability among individual members, is fully reflected in intrinsic and extrinsic causes. The law of large numbers assures us that in a large enough gene pool, the individual genetic variability will cancel. The flexible nature is indeed responsible for the variability in intrinsic and extrinsic social causes. We would have to take into account the inner nature of the species if civilizations on the planet were founded by two different species.

The true significance of figure 9.1 is that outputs of one social order (through processes of exchange of creative outcomes, abstract systems-building capability and institutional structures and processes, fair trade, peaceful migrations, empire building, violent colonization, coerced trade, and systematic wealth drain) act as desired or undesired causes for another social order. These processes have made and continue to make social orders an increasingly reciprocally conditioned, interacting, and dynamic system. As noted in chapter 8, one need not worry about the extrinsic causes during the standalone era except the extremely slow passive diffusion of ideas and inventions.

Victorious and Defeated as a System

The key element of treating the social orders as part of a system of reciprocal influences is to treat the defeated and victorious as a system particularly during the era of military conflicts. As we move from extrinsic peaceful causes to extrinsic violent causes, we move from a world of gradual and modest reciprocal influences to a world of faster, dramatic, and nonsymmetrical impact primarily because of aggressive and greedy civilizations or those with intolerant religious beliefs (or both) acquiring and developing weapons and transportation technologies. These two reasons fed on each other, leading to an increasingly dramatic impact on both defeated and conquering civilizations. Thus, as we shall demonstrate, the three instruments of destruction in particular, acting simultaneously as channels of transmission *and* a means of control, discouraged individual striving, creativity, and equality when *both* the victorious and defeated civilizations are considered as a *reciprocally conditioned system*. However, the effect is not uniform for all instruments of control. The empire builder that relocates to the conquered territory typically had little contact with the home territory after an initial period, and since the wealth did not drain out, there is little need to consider the conquered and conquering territories as a system as far

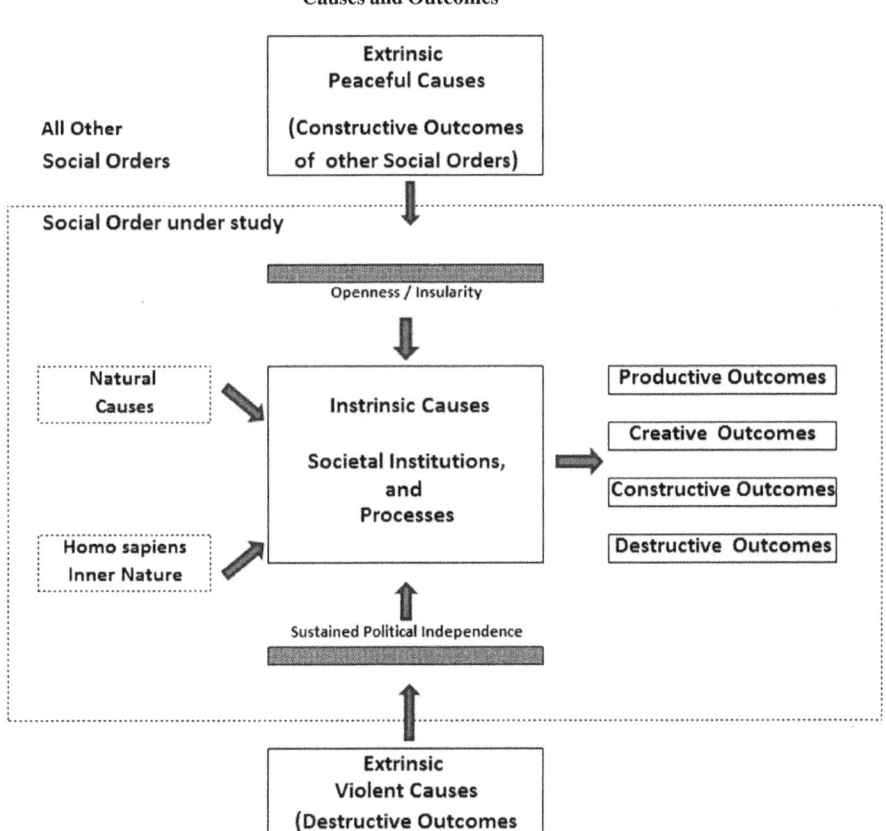

Figure 9.1: Social Orders as a System of Reciprocal Influences
Causes and Outcomes

as wealth is concerned. The impact on creative endeavors, however, may be a totally different matter in this case.

Similarly, the violent colonizers exterminated, dislocated, or absorbed the original civilization, and there is little need to consider the two as a system as well since one of them ceased to exist. The relationship between a violent colony and the mother country, however, must be considered as a system (how else does one explain the wars of independence in both North America and South America in the eighteenth and nineteenth centuries respectively?). The case of systematic wealth drain, whether the mother country from a new colony or a civilization drains the wealth, however, clearly calls for a systems approach. This is why we shall examine the violent colonizer and the systematic wealth drainer locked into extended military conflicts with New World colonies or Old World civilizations *as a system*.

Relating Causes and Outcomes

9.3 Approaches to Rationalizing Social Order Evolution

Developing a complete theory to rationalize the evolution and outcomes of a social order including its sciences is difficult since social orders, like an individual life, have had a unique history and personality right up to the present. Given this, rationalizing the evolution of a social order must necessarily have a relatively modest aim, as there are significant fundamental limitations that we must place on any theory hoping to rationalize the evolution and outcomes of complex, interacting social orders. In principle, there are only three possible approaches:

- A cause-based approach that rationalizes outcomes directly based on specific causes
- A concept-based approach that develops *intermediate parameters* derived from underlying causes to rationalize the outcomes
- An outcomes-based approach, where a subset of outcomes is used to rationalize other outcomes

Cause-Based Approach

The cause-based approach essentially suffers from the following significant limitations:

- The list of specific causes is typically too numerous.
- We must deal with three forms of relationship between causes and outcomes: causes leading to outcomes, causes leading to other causes, and outcomes in turn acting as causes.
- Cross-relationships among causes and outcomes at multiple levels of interaction inevitably introduce great complexity in analysis.
- Social orders, like *Homo sapiens* themselves, have freedom to respond differently to the same cause because individuals who have free will and can entertain vastly differing beliefs ultimately make the decisions.

The approach based on causes appears to have its limitations, as will become clearer in the next section.

Approach-Based Use of Intermediate Concepts

Suppose we were to focus on all causes of a social order during a particular period, abstract a number of intermediate concepts that represent all causes, and show that we can successfully use *these* intermediate concepts to rationalize the outcomes. If the same intermediate concepts in principle hold for all social orders during all phases, though they may take on different *values* in different phases, we may then be on to something.

Such an approach is fundamental to natural sciences and has been used very successfully in many fields, including, for example, in analyzing thermodynamic systems constituting an ideal gas, where a few simple variables at the macroscopic level (system parameters) can successfully describe the state of a system with very large number of molecules having different energies and motions at a microscopic level (causes). What is gained in simplicity far outweighs what is lost in specificity of information, particularly since the system was too complex to be analyzed at the microscopic level, and the parameters at the macroscopic level are highly successful in characterizing the system. Their ability to predict the behavior of the system at macro level gives credence to these few parameters. Fortunately for thermodynamics, molecules have no free will, and controlled experiments are possible. We can thus predict the future behavior of a thermodynamic system. The approach of natural science correctly assumes that an identity is between underlying causes at one level and observable outcomes at a different level, which simply means natural world is lawful and knowable.

Since we are dealing with social and not natural systems, we may wish to settle not for predicting the outcomes and perhaps not even a complete explanation of the past, but rather, an ability to more or less rationalize the past and possibly ascertain key future trends. Thus, the approach of classical sciences may succeed in social sciences as well if we are willing to moderate our expectations in that a prediction of the future cannot be the objective because of free will in *Homo sapiens* and the impracticality of controlled experiments. Thus, we would be willing to use thought experiments as next best alternative.

How does one assign values to the parameters abstracted from underlying causes? In natural science, a quantitative relationship is developed between the directly observable parameters of the system, which are then assigned values based on the actual measurements. By knowing some parameters, others may be predicted. Again, we do not expect to predict the future in analyzing social systems since controlled experiments to develop quantitative relationships are hardly possible. However, it is certainly possible to develop a qualitative or semiquantitative relationships among the parameters based on reasonable historical data supplemented by thought experiments.

We note that Marxian analysis of a laissez-faire capitalist society resulted in three such parameters: forces of production (or state of practical technology in our terminology), social relations of production and superstructure (or societal structures and processes in our terminology), and class struggle (or the antithesis of social cohesion in our terminology) that determine its dynamics. Marx claimed that for all social orders, including precapitalist societies, class struggle alone was the motive engine of history. He did not fully consider external peaceful and violent causes impacting social orders. Marx, of course, dealt with religion extensively in his writings, calling it the opium of the people, thus focusing on its role in reinforcing internal inequality but not in existential anxiety. Being an atheist, he rebuffed existential anxiety as defined in this book as a weakness. However, in all fairness, his primary focus was on the workings of laissez-faire capitalist economy and not a theory of interacting social orders in general or a theory of history of science in particular.

The real shortcoming of a Marxian analysis of a laissez-faire capitalist economy, however, was neglecting the role of competition in further development of forces of production and new products through new scientific and technological breakthroughs. (That omission forced him to assume an equal rate of return in all sectors of the economy since all sectors sold undifferentiated commodities in his system.) Marx also had an overly optimistic estimate of human nature rather than a fixed yet flexible human nature comprised of creative, productive, constructive, and destructive aspects as we have proposed. Marx, in his own words, strongly believed in the "original goodness and equal intellectual endowment of men (Did he believe he was not intellectually superior to an ordinary person?), the omnipotence of experience, habit, and education," a statement that can be demonstrably proven to be false.

Further, capitalism since Marx has proved capable of producing more than just commodities that competed merely on price. It has prospered through producing new products based on new scientific breakthroughs in highly organized industrial labs, government funding for basic R&D, macroeconomic management through fiscal and monetary policies, the rise of a welfare state that acts as a stabilizing influence in the economy by providing a spending floor, and initiating wars among states and civilizations. Marxian analysis amounts to a truism that if capitalism has static forces of production and thus is a system of production and exchange of commodities alone, it will be highly unstable through competition based solely on price and will self-destruct by precipitating the rise of a working class tired of economic instability. Experience in the nineteenth and early twentieth centuries seemed to prove the truth of his conclusions for a while, proving the value and the pitfalls of the second approach.

One could reasonably argue that any comprehensive analysis of a history of social orders, given its complexity, must be based on an approach that is based on intermediate concepts abstracted from driving causes.

Approach Based on Outcomes

Consider the definition of eras in chapter 7 as an example of this approach: the absence of transportation and weapons technologies with a range greater than the distance to a nearest civilization and able to overcome natural barriers confirms existence of the standalone era. The presence of transportation technologies with a range greater than the nearest civilization and the absence of weapons technologies with a range greater than a spatial distance to the nearest civilization confirms the existence of the peaceful interaction era. However, this is clearly akin to using one outcome to explain another outcome—a bit of circular logic. Nevertheless, if one finds this definition useful, this approach has value. If this approach were used in rationalizing all outcomes directly, the use of circular logic would border on absurd. We suggest that a judicious combination of the three approaches will prove to be most helpful for the task.

Before leaving this section, let us emphasize the obvious point: no theory to rationalize a social order evolution and its science can aim to predict the future or even fully rationalize the past outcomes. In constructing such a theory, we cannot hope to go beyond this important caveat. The history of social orders can be rationalized, more or less, but it is hardly logical and objective like the natural sciences. Outcomes are by their very nature are full of creative surprises, with outcomes acting as causes in turn. Only the past outcomes of a social order can therefore be understood and rationalized using data from causes and outcomes. We may conjecture about the future; however, the future is hardly predictable. We may ascertain trends through analysis but cannot claim to possess a crystal ball. Thus, social sciences, of which social order evolution and science are a part, are fundamentally different in outcomes from natural sciences despite sharing common methodology.

To summarize, if all social orders founded by the same species have natural, intrinsic, and extrinsic causes (the latter during peaceful and violent interaction eras), why did the social orders not evolve along similar lines and have similar outcomes? The reason is that causes have different force because of the differing *flexible inner nature* of the individuals in different social orders, and individuals have differing power within the social order. The abstracted intermediate concepts, whatever they may be, all aim at assessing the total of the flexible inner nature of individuals normalized by their power in the social order. This is why the approach based on intermediate concepts, supplemented selectively by causes and outcomes-based approaches, is the only approach that works.

We first use the above approach for a standalone, isolated social order, since that is the simplest possible scenario. We will then extend it to cases involving peaceful and violent interaction scenarios.

9.4 Complex Process of How Causes Lead to Outcomes—Isolated Social Order

Let us start by considering a completely isolated social order at equilibrium and at internal peace. In the standalone era or an isolated civilization in any era, the exchange of creativity, fair trade, and peaceful migrations and the possibility of control and violence are absent.

In chapter 8, we defined natural and intrinsic causes and productive, creative, constructive, and destructive outcomes. Fortunately, for the case of an isolated social order, we only need to worry about natural and intrinsic causes and productive, creative, and scientific outcomes. The problem of relating the natural and intrinsic causes and the productive, creative, and scientific outcomes for such a social order may be conceptualized as follows:

- The social order has a given natural bounty, land fertility, and ecology. No doubt, Mother Nature can stage gradual and abrupt changes at its whim, but let us assume that in the short run Mother Nature has no surprises in store for the social order.
- The social order has its institutional structures and processes. That it barters or has a money-based economy is not relevant.
- The social order has its beliefs concerning fellow citizens: equality, equality of opportunity, and political, social, and economic freedom.
- The social order also has an existing stock of factors of wealth production at its disposal in the form of capital (C), land with specified productivity (L), and labor with given productivity (LB).
- The social order also has a stock of knowledge base that consists of its accumulated practical, religious, and intellectual creativity (PRI), abstract systems–building capability (ASBC), and ideas to improve institutional structures and processes (ISP). The significance of ASBC is that it imposes an upper limit on the possible creative outcomes.
- The stocks of factors of wealth production and knowledge have resulted from its own, unique past history. They are the inheritance, the family jewels, of the social order. Thus, outcomes are not just a function of driving causes but also depend on past outcomes consisting of stocks of knowledge base and factors of wealth production. This statement captures the history-dependent nature of outcomes and makes the analysis significantly more complex.
- The wealth allocation process is at the very heart of this process of producing productive, creative, and scientific outcomes. The population consumes the majority of wealth produced. The balance or SGS ranges from a low 5 percent to a high 50 percent. It is appropriated by the state or saved by individuals and supports the elite lifestyle, military capability, replenishment of the stock of factors of wealth production (capital, land, and labor), and knowledge creation. The portion allocated to knowledge is divided into practical, religious, and intellectual endeavors. The latter may be further apportioned into art, science, and philosophy.

The critical question then is how the given natural bounty; the institutional structures and processes, including beliefs concerning the possibility of knowledge and fellow human beings; the existing stock of the factors of wealth production; *and* existing stock of knowledge interact to produce changes in wealth produced and knowledge accumulated for the next round. These changes in wealth and knowledge are strongly dependent on the wealth allocation process. Depending on the wisdom of this allocation, the stocks of factors of wealth production and knowledge are either added or subtracted for the next round.

In essence, a creative outcome in practical, religious, or intellectual creativity initiates an internal perturbation wave whose end is impossible to predict. Likewise, an increase in productive outcomes carries the potential for greater allocation to and support of creative endeavors.

Internal Perturbations

Perhaps the most visual way to understand how natural and intrinsic causes lead to changes in wealth production and knowledge creation within an isolated standalone social order is to envision two forms of internal perturbations: creative and productive. They are both rooted in the creative and productive powers of the species in social existence. The former includes practical, religious, and intellectual creative breakthroughs; rare innovations in the abstract systems-building capability; and changes in societal structures, processes, and beliefs.

The latter includes perturbations that replenish or upgrades the wealth production factors through increase in the quantity or quality of these factors. It is, however, literally impossible to predict the end of these perturbations. Old structures, processes, and beliefs slowly and often reluctantly melt away and give way to new structures, processes, and beliefs. Resulting changes in wealth production carry the potential for differing allocation to and support of creative endeavors. The following examples should help clarify this process.

Breakthrough in practical creativity: Consider the discovery of iron, which carried the potential to leave behind the Bronze Age and usher in the Iron Age. Iron is much harder and has great potential in agriculture through tools, such as a plough and an ax. If its revolutionary potential is understood and implemented, it would launch a great number of changes in institutional structures and processes, including the manufacture of iron tools and an increased grain production that might lead to greater internal trade and to needing better roads. Greater trade may require money invention. Greater productivity will spawn new nonagricultural industries since fewer people will be devoted to agriculture. It may give rise to increased power to grain traders, and the government might pass laws to curb or harness this power. Increased productivity will lead to increased wealth production and may result in greater allocation to creative endeavors. Thus a seemingly "minor" discovery that itself was likely perfected over centuries sets in motion changes in economic organization and wealth production, legal system, social structure, and even political system. It is amazing how exquisitely sensitive the seemingly inert ancient societal structures and processes were to a breakthrough in practical creativity if the leadership of the social order was wise and daring. Thus, a breakthrough in practical creativity creates a *reciprocal feedback* between driving causes and outcomes mediated by the stocks of factors of wealth production and knowledge. It results eventually in a new equilibrium for institutional structures and processes and beliefs and the stocks of knowledge and wealth production factors.

A breakthrough in religious creativity: Similarly, the impact of a breakthrough in religious creativity can be profound. Consider the idea of reincarnation and the law of karma. Such an idea, once it takes hold, may have a profound impact on a people's conscience, which in turn may reduce a need for a formal legal code. The idea could be used to explain wealth polarization and thus discourage outrage against a possibly unjust structure, which could have profound impact on its political system. It may also turn some people more fatalistic and reduce motivation to work hard while turning others more stoic and devoted to work without expectation of results. Thus, it is easy to see how a religious innovation could stagnate or dramatically alter the societal structures and processes over time and thus change creative and productive outcomes. Similarly, the rise of an intolerant creed could lead to wars and oppression and create conflict with science. Again, a breakthrough in religion leads to a *reciprocal feedback* between driving causes and outcomes mediated by stocks of knowledge and wealth production factors resulting in a new equilibrium for institutional structures and processes and the stocks of knowledge and wealth production factors.

A breakthrough in intellectual creativity: Consider a breakthrough in chemical science, the ability to produce dyes from coal and oil, supplanting the use of vegetable dyes in the nineteenth century. The new process was cheaper and sprouted the German chemical dye industry, destroying the traditional dye industry in India. Thus, it led to capital formation in the German chemical dye industry, removed it from the Indian dye industry, and added quickly to the knowledge stock in Germany as it contributed to its slow destruction in India. Here the feedback between a scientific outcome and one of the production factors and knowledge stock changed all three.

A breakthrough in abstract systems-building capability: Next consider a breakthrough in abstract systems-building capability: the invention of writing. Writing made it possible to keep better records; made written, enforceable contracts possible; and encouraged trade. Writing made it possible to systematize religious and legal ideas. Writing created the need for writers, which in turn required schools. An ability to write created a class of people who could use their skills for political gain. Writing allowed production methods to be written down and communicated over long distances, leading to much faster transmission of innovations. Again, it is easy to see how writing would impact structures and processes within a social order. Once again, a breakthrough in intellectual creativity carried the potential to lead to a *reciprocal feedback* between driving causes and outcomes, resulting in a new equilibrium for the knowledge base and the wealth production factors.

A breakthrough in institutional structures and processes: History is replete with examples of breakthroughs in institutional structures and processes at both grand and not-so-grand levels that have changed the course of history. Some of obvious examples include the ideas of monarchy, feudalism, the divine right of kings, middle kingdom, democracy, and socialism. Less obvious examples include creating a fighting unit to supplant individual fighters and, more recently, the rise of industrial labs aimed at creating new products and processes and reserve banks to manage the money supply in an economy. In these examples, a change in the institutional structures and processes directly or indirectly impact both the outcomes and the stock of production factors and through that, a change in the knowledge stock mediated by a reciprocal feedback process.

Thus, we envision six different forms of internal perturbations for an isolated social order:

- Practical, religious, and intellectual creative outcomes
- A change in abstract systems-building capability
- A change in institutional structure and processes and beliefs
- A change in capital stock
- An improvement or degradation of land quality
- An improvement or decline in labor quality

Summary

Based on the above analysis, the progressive or regressive productive, creative, and scientific outcomes of an isolated social order in any era are a function of the reciprocal feedback process among:

- Natural bounty, which may be thought of as an independent gradual or abrupt forcing function
- Existing stock of knowledge and factors of wealth production
- The six internal perturbations arising from the institutional structures and process and in turn impacting them

At this stage in the analysis, the six internal perturbations and knowledge and wealth stocks are intermediate concepts. The reciprocal feedback process for an isolated social system is shown schematically in figure 9.2.

9.5 Extending the Analysis to Interacting Social Orders

What about the relationship between causes and outcomes of social orders interacting peacefully or violently with other social orders? For the case of a peacefully interacting social order, this will depend not only depend on natural and intrinsic causes but also on the impact of the sum total of constructive outcomes of all relevant social orders. Similarly, for a violently interacting social order, this will depend on not only natural and intrinsic causes but also the sum total of destructive outcomes of all relevant social orders. Below we extend the analysis to peaceful and violently interacting social orders.

Peacefully Interacting Social Orders

Fortunately, the constructive outcomes impacting an erstwhile isolated social order are, from an analytical perspective, no different from internal perturbations. A practical invention originating outside the social order may face more resistance. However, to the extent it is accepted, the ultimate results would hardly be distinguishable from a similar internal perturbation, though the process may be

Figure 9.2: Relating Causes, Internal Perturbations, Stocks, and Outcomes
Standalone Social Orders

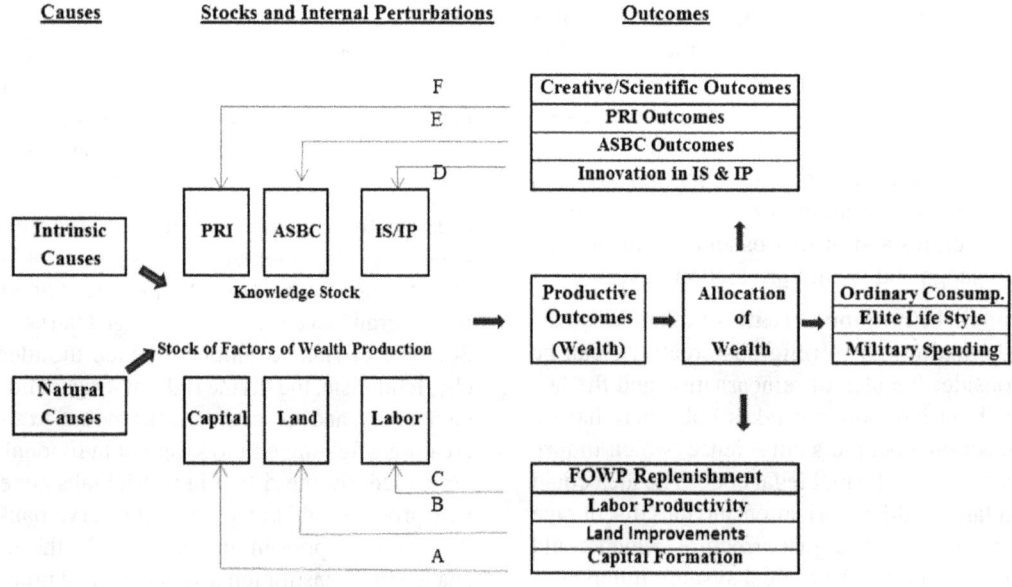

Key Internal Perturbations (6)
A: Increase in Capital Formation
B: Increase in Labor Productivity
C: Land Improvements
D/E/F: Additions to Knowledge Stock

PRI: Practical Religious, Intellecual Creativity
ASBC: Abstract System Building Capability
IS/IP: Institutional Structures and Processes
FOWP: Factors of Wealth Production

different. Peacefully interacting social orders can exchange the following classes of external perturbations:

- Practical, religious, and intellectual creative outcomes
- Abstract systems-building capability
- Institutional structures, and processes
- Fair trade or exchange of goods
- Exchange of capital (rather limited until modern times)
- Peaceful migration or transfer of people

Note that the first three are the same as the internal perturbations for an isolated social order while the last two impact factors of wealth production through changes in capital and labor.

Each of these external peaceful perturbations acts in a manner similar to an internal wave, provided the social order is completely open to these perturbations, which, of course, no social order is. These peaceful external perturbations are able to impact the productive and creative outcomes, abstract systems-building capability, the institutional structures and processes, and the outcomes of the social order to the extent the social order is open to this voluntary influence. Thus, the *openness and insularity of the social order* becomes the controlling factor as far as the impact of the peaceful interaction is concerned.

The peaceful interaction among civilizations consists of three steps as noted in chapter 7:

1. **Arrival:** Random waves of practical, religious, and intellectual creativity, new institutional structures and processes, the possibility of fair trade, and peaceful migration from another civilization arrive. This in turn depended on the openness of originating civilization.

2. **Acceptance:** Acceptance of these waves, depending on the openness/insularity of the receiving civilization and the efficacy of the transmission channels.

3. **Internalization:** A civilization's ability to internalize these waves. That process is no different from the one described for a standalone civilization since it is a similar to an inner stimulus for required changes in internal structures and processes. Over time, peaceful, extrinsic causes are as capable of impacting the outcomes as an "internal" breakthrough, provided there is openness.

Civilizations have often been resistant to the religious and intellectual creativity of others. Readers may rightly ask if there have not been civilizations insular to practical creativity and offer of fair trade from other civilizations. While it is possible for a civilization to initially resist practical technology or fair trade particularly if it carries the potential to upset the internal power balance, history shows that is rarely the case after an initial period. As noted before, there is a very good reason for not resisting practical creativity and fair trade while resisting religious or intellectual creativity. The connection between practical creativity, fair trade, and wealth was always eminently clear while the connection between religious and intellectual creativity and wealth creation was often unclear and often resisted (until modern times when it became obvious). It was resisted because breakthroughs in religious and intellectual creativity often contradicted established beliefs to soothe existential anxiety and beliefs concerning possibility of knowledge of the real world.

Thus, during the peaceful interaction era, the reciprocal feedback process is impacted by the sum total of constructive peaceful interaction. This impact is nearly always positive; the only question is that of degree.

Violently Interacting Social Orders

Standalone social orders lack access to other social order's creative outcomes, migrations, and fair trade, and the peacefully interacting social orders had access to creative outcomes, migrations, and fair trade without control. However, the violently interacting social orders necessarily have access to others' creative outcomes and could displace and compel others into coerced trade and forced migrations (slavery and indentured labor), resulting in wealth drain.

External peaceful perturbations are by nature mild and without any external control. This completely changes with violent interaction. Violent interaction has two possibilities: the aggression is unsuccessful, and the invaded social order retains its sustained political independence. In this case, the external perturbations are checked, and only those aspects the invaded social order desires are adopted, thus reverting back to the situation of a perturbation arriving with the receiving social order in control. The other possibility is that the invaded social order is defeated on the battlefields in a sustained manner, thus losing its sustained political independence. The defeated social order may experience three scenarios depending on the nature and objective of the instrument of destruction. Thus, the impact of empire builders, violent colonizers, and systematic wealth drainers on the reciprocal feedback process between causes and outcomes may be analyzed in three steps:

- Loss of sustained political independence (military aspect)
- Loss of control of sustainable growing surplus, land, or wealth itself (economic/political aspect)
- Impact of the external destructive perturbations on institutional structures and processes, followed by impact on the productive, creative, and scientific

outcomes for both the victor and the defeated social orders considered as a system

The first step is a common feature of all forms instruments of destruction, but the second and third steps strongly depend on their specific natures. The empire builder seeks to control the surplus by replacing the indigenous elite, and the violent colonizers seek to expropriate the land and displace or exterminate the indigenous elite and population while resisting the demand of wealth transfer to "mother country." The systematic wealth drainer seeks to drain the wealth while keeping the obedient among the sold-out elites in place as allies.

Loss of sustained political independence: The first step naturally involves military conflict between social orders fought through frontline states. If, over time, military conquest is lasting and substantial, it results in the defeated social order losing sustained political independence. We use the word "sustained" because it is not loss on one battlefield or loss of political independence for a decade that can bring down a civilization for civilizations are far more resilient than that; the loss must be sustained and can only be achieved through extended military victories one domino at a time. The aggressor puts together a superior military capability often through superior military technology, generalship, and well-trained soldiers imbued with greed, religious zeal, or occasionally with the personal ambition of a leader. The aggressor may be either a state, empire, or a nomadic federation.

It is critical to note is how relatively unimportant the size of the invading force has been in history or even the population of the state or nomadic federation from which this invading force originated. For example, Babur attacked India with a force of twelve thousand. Clive won a decisive battle with less than ten thousand soldiers.

Most nomadic federations probably had a population of few hundred thousand, with a sizable proportion of all able-bodied men constituting the fighting force of up to a few tens of thousands. Also needed was a strong intelligence-gathering system. At the other extreme was the Roman Empire, with a strong territorial and population base that had an ability to marshal a strong fighting force to overwhelm the enemy. Once the aggressor decided that the opportunity was ripe, it initiated an extended military campaign that typically lasted for decades or at times longer. In the beginning, the conflict would be between the aggressor and a frontline state. With successive victories over time, the frontier was pushed back, and at some point, if the aggressor continued to win on the battlefield, the military defenses of the attacked civilization collapsed, resulting in the loss of sustained political independence.

Loss of control of surplus, means of wealth, or wealth drain: The second step occurs when the control of surplus, means of wealth, or wealth itself passes decisively into the hands of the victor. The empire builder is after control of sustainable growing surplus; the violent colonizer is after control of land through displacement or extermination of the indigenous population; and the systematic wealth drainer is after not just the control of the sustainable growing surplus but also the indiscriminate drain of the surplus and wealth out of the civilization. The worst affected are the victims of violent colonization, followed by victims of systematic wealth transfer, followed by the victims of "conquer and stay" empire builders. All three aim to control; they only differ in whether it is the surplus, land, or the wealth they are after.

Let us look at each.

Empire Builder

The invader may be the "loot and withdraw" or "conquer and stay" variety. The impact of the former may be devastating in the short term because of looting and destruction of life and property; however, civilization would recover rather quickly because accumulated wealth was hardly ever more than ten years' worth of wealth produced, and the looters could not haul away all of it. We focus on the "conquer and stay" empire builder below.

Impact on the productive outcomes within the defeated civilization: The sustainable growing surplus naturally stayed in the conquered civilization but was now at the disposal and mercy of the empire builder. This type of empire building (without wealth drain and population displacement) simply replaced the indigenous elite with the foreign elite. By definition, there was no material change in the surplus available to the civilization, assuming that the conquerors did not mismanage the wealth production process in the defeated civilization and did not institute a material change in taxation policy to fund personal luxuries or other projects. In such a situation, the impact on sustainable growing surplus will be modest but change in its control relatively fast and impact on productive outcomes relatively small. It may even be positive, depending on the access to new practical technologies and trade made possible by the conqueror. Thus, the long-term impact on wealth creation may be positive or negative, depending principally on changes brought about by the victor in wealth allocation and new technology adoption and his impact on economic freedom, social cohesion, and internal wars. It is a question of policy changes dictated by a victor's inner nature and priorities.

Impact on the creative and scientific outcomes within the defeated civilization However, an empire builder, now in control, will have different priorities toward wealth allocation in particular. Based on control of sustainable growing surplus, the impact of an empire builder on creative and scientific outcomes will be driven by his own internal creative balance and his openness to the creativity of the defeated civilization. Not all empire builders, however, are created equal. There can be dramatic differences among them, depending on their creative orientations and whether they have open or insular natures. That they have an aggressive and warlike orientation aimed at controlling the surplus is a given. However, one empire builder may have a practical internal creative balance and insular nature, another may have a favorable internal creative balance and an open orientation, and a third may have a religious internal creative balance with selective openness. The same applies to the defeated civilization with respect to these dimensions; however, the defeated civilization does not matter much since it is not in control. The impact of an empire builder on creative and scientific outcomes in general may be studied through three basic scenarios:

1. The defeated civilization has greater strength in a particular creative area.
2. The victor has greater strength in a particular creative area.
3. Both have comparable strength in a particular creative area.

Consider first the case, when both the victor and the defeated have comparable strength. Since the empire builder permanently settles in the conquered territory, it will likely result in cross-fertilization and synthesis, provided the victor has openness in that particular area. Now consider the case when a victor has greater strength in a particular creative arena. When the empire builder permanently settles in the conquered territory, it will likely result in transplanting the superior strength irrespective of the insularity of the defeated. Finally, consider the case when only the loser has superior strength in a particular arena. When the empire builder is a settler, superior creative outcomes may be adopted by the victor if he has openness in that particular area.

- The strategy of the victor with respect to creativity may be captured in following generic responses:
- Rejection
- Adoption
- Synthesis
- Transplantation

Thus, in the case of the relocating empire builder, the creative and scientific outcomes of the defeated will be determined by its creative orientation and the openness and may be positive or negative. The impact on the conqueror's home territory is not relevant, as he has relocated to the conquered territory.

Violent Colonizer

Violent colonization was driven by a greed for land coupled at times with intolerant creed and is uniquely a European phenomenon. Violent colonization is a triangular process involving the colonized, the emerging state of the colonizers, and the mother country supporting the colonizers. In reality, only the colonizers and the mother country need to be considered. Violent colonization is based on complete control of land and substantial displacement or extermination of the original, often sparse population. Because the victor was far superior in most arenas and because the old social order of the defeated eventually ceased to exist, impact on productive, creative, and scientific outcomes of the colonized becomes essentially irrelevant. The defeated people in the colonies had little option except adapt completely or wither away.

Impact on productive outcomes of the colonizers and mother country: Modern violent colonization began in the Americas in sixteenth century, continents that were at an earlier stage of development compared to Eurasia and North Africa. Violent colonization impacted the wealth creation in not only the colonized land but also the mother country. Consider the English colonization of North America. Colonization made available the virgin land to the newcomers. When a newly established colony is not politically free, depends on a mother country for survival, and exists in part for the benefit of the mother country, it can materially increase the surplus available to the mother country. Wealth production in the new territory may be supplemented through slave or indentured labor, thus allowing the colonizers and the mother country to benefit at the expense of both the slave labor and displaced indigenous population. The actual surplus available to the colonizing state will depend on specific factors of population transferred from the colonizing country, level of slave labor, and the proportion of the new surplus appropriated by the mother country.

However, not all violent colonizers are created equal. The English colonizers displaced or destroyed the indigenous populations in Australia and North America with little inclination to intermarry or make religious conversion. The Maori people of New Zealand are a minor exception to this since New Zealand was of little strategic value to the British, and the number of people who migrated to New Zealand from Britain relative to local population was not overwhelming and included only a minority of the English strain. They were mostly Scottish and Irish with a different attitude. The Spanish and the Portuguese colonizers in Central and South America, on the other hand, were more interested in gold and converting the indigenous people to Christianity, having witnessed inquisition and having bypassed the religious reformation at home. They were also more prone to intermarry. These differences were driven by the fact that English colonization peaked after the reformation of Christianity in Europe and the death of feudalism in the context of a growing mercantilism and a nascent capitalism struggling to take birth. Yet, the essential motivation of both English and Spanish colonization was land acquisition and through it the acquisition of the surplus (augmented through slave and indentured labor) and commerce with the mother country.

Wealth creation in the newly established colonies depended on the transfer of technology and resources from the mother country and the transfer of wealth back to the mother country. This process is fundamentally different from what occurred between systematic wealth drainers and defeated civilizations in Asia and Africa in a later historical period because of the magnitudes involved. The mother country initially retained the political and military control of the territory as well as control of trade routes. Only this control did not last as long. Over a seventy-five year period beginning with the last quarter of the eighteenth century, most of the colonies in the New World rebelled and became free to one degree or another. About the same time, most civilizations in Asia and Africa began losing their political independence to European systematic wealth drainers (discussed below).

Assume that the colonizing mother country has a population base of ten million and has a base sustainable growing surplus at 10 percent of its wealth creation capacity. Assume further that one million of its population is transferred to the colony supplemented with two million slaves kept at one-fourth the standard of living of the owners. If the colony is as productive as the mother country and half of the surplus produced by the colonizers and slaves is expropriated by the mother country, it surplus will jump by 150 percent and will be two and half times bigger. The transfer to the mother country will adversely impact the pace of development of the colonizing state. Clearly, wealth transfer would impact the productive outcomes of the mother country positively if used wisely while slowing down the development of the colony. In the long run however, it would lead the colony to revolt for independence.

Impact on creative and scientific outcomes of the colonizers and mother country: If the productive outcomes of the colonizers took time to become free from the claws of the mother country, the process was even longer for the creative and scientific outcomes. It depended on the creative orientation of the mother country (from where colonizers came) and the openness of the mother country. In this respect, even violent colonization is similar to the case of an empire builder except for the displacement and extermination of the indigenous population and the impact on the mother country through wealth transfer from the colony to the mother country.

Thus, in the case of the violent colonizer, the creative and scientific outcomes of the colonizer are determined by its creative orientation and the openness of the mother country and thus may be positive or negative. The impact on the productive, creative, and scientific outcomes of the mother country will be determined by the degree of wealth transferred and its allocation. The impact on the outcomes of colonized is essentially irrelevant since it ceases to exist.

The Systematic Wealth Drainer

Modern systematic wealth drainers are also a uniquely European phenomenon. Systematic wealth drain may be said to occur when the victor cannot or does not wish to displace the indigenous population and does not wish to settle down permanently in the conquered land. Rather, it sees the economic and political control as the most appropriate way to achieve his objective of wealth drain. Colonies in the New World and Australia were directly responsible for the lack of desire on the part of European wealth drainers to settle in conquered territories in Asia.

Impact on reciprocal productive outcomes of the defeated and victor: Historically, systematic wealth drainers come in three increasingly destructive forms involving control of the sea trade routes, the territory, and both. Like violent colonization, systematic wealth drain is essentially the brainchild of European civilization.

When trade routes are controlled, the impact of systematic wealth drain will be to reduce the surplus available to the producing civilization through coerced trade. On the other hand, if territorial control is involved, the impact can be much more devastating. The agriculture of the controlled territory could be reconfigured to feed the manufacturing needs in the home country. If its industry is seen as a competition, it could be subject to destruction through import and export duties. Its education system could be redesigned to indoctrinate its people. Its infrastructure would only be developed up to the point that allows the movement of the raw materials and manufactured product in and out of the country. When territory and trade routes are controlled, the situation gets infinitely worse for the defeated civilization and equally rewarding for the victorious.

Let us consider the historically significant case of systematic wealth drain from a civilization with a significantly greater population than the wealth drainer. This scenario is not far from reality, given the control of much larger civilizations by several European states for nearly two hundred years beginning about 1750 CE. If a civilization is densely populated and has land more productive than that of the conqueror, it makes no sense to displace or destroy the population, and it is not possible to do so. It is more profitable in this case to impose unfair trade conditions to extract as much surplus as possible.

Let us assume a pre-industrial world with systematic wealth drainer state A and civilization B. Assume that state A has a population base of ten million and has an internal sustainable surplus at 10 percent of the wealth created. Let us further assume that civilization B has a population base of hundred million and has an internal sustainable surplus at 10 percent. Assuming the same level of productivity for both, if state A is able to expropriate all the sustainable surplus of civilization B, its surplus will jump to ten times its base sustainable surplus or 110 percent of its total wealth because of the population multiplier effect. *In other words, the SGS will be greater than its internal wealth production!* If the wealth drainer controls the territory and through tax or tariff policy is able to reduce the standard of living in civilization B by just 10 percent, SGS will jump to 210 percent of wealth created or twenty-one times its base SGS. This analysis does not even take into account that civilization B may have a higher pre-industrial productivity because it is able to produce three crops per year versus just one for the wealth drainer. It also does not take into account the resources spent to maintain control. It might have taken state A several centuries to achieve that level of SGS in absolute terms without controlling a much bigger civilization. Thus, a strategy of systematic wealth drain can phenomenally and quickly increase the sustainable surplus available to the victorious state if it drains wealth from a much larger civilization.

The impact of systematic wealth drain from a much larger civilization is significantly greater than from a small colony discussed above. That a colony may kick out the mother country sooner than an established civilization that has fallen prey to designs of a systematic wealth drainer further enhances this fact. Thus, there is more time to squeeze the conquered civilization than a new colony. In both cases, however, the impact on the surplus of the conqueror will be typically dramatic and can occur rather swiftly. By contrast, the reader will recall, in the case of empire building, the surplus continues to reside in the civilization being controlled, and any changes in it will be generally modest and occur gradually.

Why the recent European aggression took the route of violent colonization and systematic wealth drain while the earlier European, Muslim, and Nomadic aggression took the route of empire building is an interesting question. The answer is that Europe is not arid. Its natural environment could support a larger population, and it was geographically farther away from the large established civilization in East and South Asia. However, as technologies made the distances shrink, Europeans outdid the Muslims and central Asians by a wide margin. The Muslim populations, though much smaller, needed to leave their arid homelands to manage the relatively faraway conquered territories in order to enjoy their surplus. The Americas, which were discovered by Europeans accidentally while attempting to find a way around the Muslim control of the land trade routes to Asia, happened to be lightly populated and at an earlier stage of development and thus ripe for violent colonization. And a strategy of wealth drain first through mercantilism and later through manufacturing at home was ideal to drain wealth from established civilizations as control of trade route eventually led to control of territories.

Impact on reciprocal creative and scientific outcomes of the defeated and victor: The impact of a systematic wealth drainer on the creative outcomes of the controlled civilization was driven by the degree of wealth drain since the systematic wealth drainer was focused on not just draining the SGS but draining as much wealth as possible. Not all systematic wealth drainers are created equal. There can be dramatic differences among them, depending on their creative orientation and whether they have an open or insular nature. That they have an aggressive and warlike orientation aimed at controlling wealth is a given. However, one systematic wealth drainer may have a practical creative orientation and be insular, another may have a balanced creative orientation and an open orientation, and a third may have a religious orientation with selective openness. Yet all three are systematic wealth drainers. The same applies to the defeated civilization with respect to these dimensions.

The scenarios that govern the impact of empire builders on creative outcomes also govern the impact of systematic wealth drainers, but now the two must be considered as a reciprocally conditioned pair, and the degree of wealth drain trumps creation orientation and openness. That drain of wealth has a dramatic asymmetric impact on the creativity of both civilizations should be self-evident. The surplus available for creative endeavors will decline or even be negative, depending on the degree of wealth drain for the conquered civilization, and the surplus available to the victor may increase by an order of magnitude or more as we saw above. This allows the victors over time to fancy that the conquered are not a creative bunch or that the victors are significantly more creative than the conquered. It hardly occurs to the conquerors that they may actually be the cause for it. Quite the contrary. Eventually, they also begin to fancy that it as their historic mission to remake the conquered in their own image. It is equally true that, over time, sustained systematic wealth drain will lead to a dramatic change in the conquered civilization's creative attitudes, resulting in a dramatic change in the very soul of the civilization, thus inadvertently reinforcing the self-importance of the conqueror.

Thus in the case of systematic wealth drainer, the impact on the creative and scientific outcomes of the defeated civilization will be dramatic and negative, and its magnitude will initially be determined by the degree of wealth drain to the victor and over time by the openness of the conquered civilization if the aggressor is a creative entity. The impact on the victor will be determined by the degree of wealth drain to the victor, wealth allocation, and the creativity of the defeated, which the victor will access. Thus, we must consider the victor and defeated as a system.

Each of the above forms of control will forcibly impact the productive, creative, and scientific outcomes and the institutional structures and processes of the conquered and conquering social order. This is fundamentally different from the impact of degree of openness-insularity in the case of peaceful interaction above.

The impact the five peaceful external perturbations and three violent and destructive perturbations on the productive, creative, and scientific outcomes is summarized in figure 9.3.

In the last two sections, we have identified stocks of factors of wealth production and knowledge as the base and perturbations as the intermediaries that together determine the outcomes. We have identified six internal, five peaceful, and three violent destructive perturbations within standalone, peacefully interacting, and violently interacting social orders respectively that originate from intrinsic and extrinsic causes and how determine the productive, creative, and scientific outcomes.

The Concept of the Inner Nature of Social Orders

Clearly, internal and external perturbations, while highly useful in visualizing how causes lead to outcomes, are not readily measurable. Yet, the internal and external perturbations, which result from intrinsic and extrinsic causes, are hinting at the differing nature of social orders. Internal perturbations point to the intrinsic productive and creative capacity of a social order while external perturbations point to the positive or negative impact of other social orders on this productive and creative capacity. Using these concepts, below we first propose the existence of an inner nature of interacting social orders. We will then propose methodology to assess it based on measurable parameters that reflect not only the internal perturbations and knowledge and wealth stocks of an isolated social order, the peaceful and violent external perturbations but also the natural causes affecting the social orders. It is the inner natures of the interacting social orders that will help us achieve the objective of rationalizing the differing productive, creative and scientific outcomes of social orders.

9.6 The Hypothesis of the Inner Nature of Interacting Social Orders

If there is an" inner nature" of a social order, it must be a reflection of all the driving causes as well as its history since social orders are historical entities whose present behavior is determined both by current driving causes *and* their history. To deny this amounts to rejecting both the consistency, and at times, the apparent irrationality in the behaviors of the social orders. The more traditional or conservative a social order is, the more its present behavior is determined by its past. The question is how we may determine the inner nature of a social order from the causes driving it and its past conscious or unconscious history.

At the outset, we must allow the inner nature of this social order to exhibit both malleable and potentially stable aspects. This is because if the outcomes are both dynamic and resist change and if outcomes are to be rationalized

Figure 9.3: Impact of External Peaceful Perturbations and Aggression

	Impact on Productive Outcomes	Impact on Creative & Scientific Outcomes	
Peaceful Transmission of PRI Creativity; Abstract Sys. Building Cap.; ISP Creativity; Fair Trade; Peaceful Migrations →	Positive Impact *Determined by Degree of Openness*	Positive Impact *Determined by Degree of Openness*	
	Minor Impact on Defeated *Determined by Economic policies of the Victor*	Significant Impact on Defeated *Determined by Creative Orientation & Openness of the Victor*	← Empire Builders
Legend: ISP: Institutional Structures & Processes; PRI: Practical, Religious, Intellectual	Drastic Impact on Defeated Major Impact on Colonizer & Mother Country *Determined by degree of Wealth Transfer*	Drastic Impact on Defeated Major Impact on Colonizer & Mother Country *Determined by degree of Wealth Transfer*	← Violent Colonizers
	Drastic Impact on Defeated Major Impact Systematic Wealth Drainer *Determined by degree of Wealth Transfer*	Drastic Impact on Defeated Drastic Impact on Systematic Wealth Drainer *Determined by degree of Wealth Transfer*	← Systematic Wealth Drainers

Aggression by

by this inner nature, then the inner nature too must be both malleable and stable reflecting the changing nature of natural, intrinsic, and extrinsic causes and resisting to this change.

The Concept of the Inner Nature of a Social Order

The concept of the inner nature of social orders is central to the analysis of civilizations and history of science in this work. It allows us to grasp the essence of a social order's soul and place it in the proper historical, intellectual, and moral context more simply and readily without constantly referring back to unbelievably complex and interrelated causes.

It helps to visualize the inner nature of a social order as comparable to an individual's character (formed by his genetic makeup and the environmental causes affecting his life and its significance in rationalizing behaviors). Individuals do not just produce behavior; they also develop a character or firmly held beliefs, attitudes, and values that drive their actions. Likewise, complex social orders also do not just have driving causes and productive, creative, constructive, and destructive behaviors; the causes and outcomes help mold the character of social orders that, much like the character of an individual, may even be unchanging in certain aspects. The inner nature of a complex social order ultimately reflects its creative, productive, constructive, and destructive tendencies, which are expressed as its broadest ideology in action. Inner nature is, thus, akin to an individual personality in that both resist change in some aspects but are capable of change and evolution in other aspects—occasionally even a dramatic change.

As a simple analogy to an individual in a social environment, the natural causes are equivalent to the surrounding physical environment including food and oxygen. Intrinsic causes may be said to constitute the anatomy and physiological and neurological processes. The influence of friends may be said to be equivalent to extrinsic peaceful causes or constructive outcomes of others, and the demands of the bullies and enemies may be said to be the extrinsic violent causes or destructive outcomes of others. The productive and creative power is equivalent to physical and mental powers of the individual.

We shall present inner nature and its assessment in three steps:

1. We postulate its four components abstracted from the underlying natural and intrinsic causes.
2. We ask what parameters can be used to determine these components.
3. We ask what range of values these parameters are allowed to assume to assess the inner nature of a social order.

We propose that the inner nature of a social order at a point in history consists of the following two capacities and two orientations, reflecting all natural, intrinsic, and extrinsic causes driving it.

- **Productive capacity:** The productive capacity of a social order is simply the intrinsic ability it possesses in wealth production and related activities of internal trade, creation of new products and services, and improving its stock of factors of wealth production at a given point in history.

- **Creative capacity:** The creative capacity is simply the ability a social order possesses in practical, religious, and intellectual creativity (the latter including art, philosophy, and science), abstract systems-building capability, and changes in institutional structures and processes, thus improving its knowledge stock at a given point in history.

- **Constructive orientation:** The constructive orientation is the ability and disposition of a social order to engage in a *mutually beneficial* peaceful interaction with other social orders at a given point in history. This is not relevant for the isolated system but will be for peacefully interacting social orders.

- **Destructive orientation:** The destructive orientation is the ability and disposition that a social order possesses to engage in violent, destructive control of other social orders solely for *its own benefit*.

Thus the inner nature of a social order in different eras may be simply envisioned as:

- Its evolving character expressed as its productive and creative capacity for a standalone isolated social order
- By its productive and creative capacity and constructive orientation for a peacefully interacting social order
- By its productive and creative capacity and constructive and destructive orientation for violently interacting social orders

9.7 Assessment of the Inner Nature of a Social Order

What parameters may be used to assess the productive and creative capacity and the constructive and destructive orientation of a social order at a given point in its history?

We shall approach this problem from the perspective of perturbations and knowledge and wealth stocks. It is important to recognize that attempts to identify the relevant parameters from the intrinsic and extrinsic causes directly will be an exercise in futility, and identifying them from the outcomes borders on using circular logic as noted above. The concept of stocks and perturbations allows us to focus on what is truly significant without worrying about every detail. This approach is similar to the concept of dynamic programming in mathematics, where proceeding from a presumed solution makes the problem a lot easier to solve than proceeding from the causes toward the solution. The former leads to simple (but not simplistic) convergence while the latter leads to unmanageable divergent complexity.

When a question is posed in this manner, one is able to consolidate the intimidating complexity of the natural, intrinsic, and extrinsic causes *and* relevant history into a limited number of readily measurable parameters. We propose the following twelve parameters as reasonably sufficient to determine the capacities and orientations of a social order in a particular period, with several parameters appearing in more than one component of the inner nature.

Productive Capacity

Natural bounty: Natural bounty is based on natural causes, such as soil, climate, and ecology for a particular social order. It was not only responsible for greater land productivity but also indirectly for developing institutional greed as noted below. We may assess it as low, medium, or high.

New technology adoption: It is one thing to have developed new technologies or to have new technologies available from other social orders and quite another to actually aggressively adopt them and use them in wealth production. Thus, wealth production is a strong function of the rate of new technology adoption, whether of foreign or domestic origin. Technology adoption in social orders, particularly in the past two thousand years, are relatively well documented and can be used to assess the rate of new technology adoption as low, medium, or high.

Relative economic freedom: The degree to which the economic organization allows individual entrepreneurial behavior depends on the state of labor, product, and credit markets (however underdeveloped) and the degree of freedom they enjoy. Internal economic freedom will also foster the skill and ability level of workforce, from the lowest to the highest, depending on the quality and openness educational institutions at different levels. Given the long history of despotic rule in most social orders, it is the relative not absolute degree of economic freedom that is critical. It must be noted that the economic freedom a social system enjoys internally has no necessary correlation with what it espouses externally. Relative economic freedom too may be assessed as low, medium, or high.

Social cohesion: Every known social order except in mythical accounts has been fractured along ethnic, linguistics, class, religious, caste, racial, and cultural lines to one degree or another. Diversity, not uniformity, is a normal state of affairs for *Homo sapiens*. However, for a social order to function and certainly achieve greatness, a common ground must be found to create unity and a workable state out of this diversity. The social cohesion process, consisting of force, greed, custom, religion, and indoctrination, is aimed at creating the necessary social cohesion using some combination of acceptable religious, racial caste, or nationalistic ideologies. Often, these have been quite successful, particularly if such an ideology is in the self-interest of the social order at the expense of other social orders. Thus, these ideologies naturally accompany propaganda to hide the self-interest. The motive force of history is not only the diversity that divides but also, more important, the ideologies that unite to create a nation or a state worthy of dying for. Social cohesion for a social order may also be assessed as low, medium, or high at a given point in its history. Social cohesion has shown itself to be a highly variable phenomenon.

Wealth allocation: By wealth allocation we simply mean how wealth is allocated to support the common man; the lifestyle of the elite; military capability, particularly offensive capability; and replenishing the factors of wealth production and creative endeavors. It is difficult to quantify wealth allocation. We will only be able to guestimate whether allocation favored elite lifestyles, military spending, or productive or creative endeavors and that should be sufficient for our purpose.

Creative Capacity

Wealth allocation: A further division reflected in the internal creative balance of a social order is how the allocation to creative endeavors is further subdivided into allocation to practical, religious, and intellectual activities. Obviously, direct, hard reliable data are only available at most over last couple of centuries for a handful of states. It is difficult to quantify wealth allocation. We will only be able to guestimate whether allocation favored practical, religious, intellectual, or balanced allocation.

Abstract systems-building capability: To what degree does the social order possess the last nine breakthroughs described in section 7.2 as the infrastructure and the backbone of creative capacity: written script, conscious creative method, alphabetical script, epistemology and logic, decimal system, experimental method in heavens, calculus, experimental method here on earth, and scientific method? As noted before, it is very difficult indeed to develop the last six elements of abstract systems-building capability without alphabetical script. Abstract systems-building capability may simply be characterized as weak, moderate, and strong with alphabetical script as the first dividing line and the decimal system of counting as the second dividing line.

Creed: Religious creeds within a social order may be naive polytheism, structured polytheism (Hinduism, as an example), monism (Vedanta, Taoism), agnosticism (Buddhism), intolerant monotheism (classical Christianity,

Islam), and relatively tolerant monotheism (contemporary Christianity), leading at times in excessive spirituality and science–religion conflict.

Science aims at understanding the world through observation, reason, and imagination without reference to a non-material, spiritual being. Most religions, however, reflect existential anxiety and intellectual confusion, and assume either the creation or operation of the world or both to be controlled by a deity. Thus, the struggle between the two is fundamental and unavoidable simply because religion could be and needed to be conceived before science could develop. This struggle appears when science attempts to demonstrate that it can explain the operation of the world through natural laws without reference to a deity or when science prefers science in matters of origin. In the case of monotheism, often this struggle appears when science demonstrates that the specifics and timeline of the metaphysics are assumptions without proof. In the case of monism, it appears as a question of scientific method versus a spiritual method based on power of intuition for God-realization and ultimate knowledge. It ends when one begins to see religious assertions as nothing more than a mental phenomenon resulting from a desire for immortality or from intellectual confusion. Thus, historically this struggle has been a necessity, and civilizations had to go through it. It must be seen as unavoidable. We may term this struggle as a more *direct science-religion conflict* for monotheism and a softer *excessive spirituality* for polytheism and monism. Measuring the nature of creed will be thus rather straightforward: Is the creed excessively spiritual, does it harbor science-religion conflict, or is it balanced while allowing religious freedom?

Constructive Orientation

Since history shows creativity is not the monopoly of any one civilization, it follows that openness to creativity of other civilizations is an important condition determining the outcomes of peacefully interacting civilizations. Civilizations have a natural openness, provided this openness is not impacted by geographical or linguistic isolation, a sense of superiority, or a sense of apprehension possibly resulting from experiencing the aggression of others. Constructive orientation or degree of openness may be measured by assessing the following.

Geographical isolation: This refers to how isolated a civilization is from other civilization because the means of transportation are unable to bridge the spatial distance or natural barriers.

Linguistic isolation: This has little to do with an inability to understand a foreign language since nearly all civilizations have had that issue and easily overcame it. By linguistic isolation, we mean difficulty in accurately translating the religious and intellectual abstract systems from an alphabetical script to a logograph. This carries the potential to become a significant barrier in diffusion of religious and intellectual creativity.

Creed: The intolerance exhibited by a creed clearly played a role in the constructive orientation. It stands to reason that social orders with intolerant creed would be less open and more insular.

Early success with nomads: Early nomadic wars are important since primary civilizations did not engage in wars with one another early in their history. Hence, wars with nomads played a disproportionate role in the history of some civilizations. If a civilization failed to defend itself against nomads during the standalone or peaceful interaction eras and successfully absorbed them, it would reinforce an open attitude toward other social orders. On the other hand, if a civilization was successful against a nomadic threat through strong defensive military capability early in its history and is geographically isolated, it would run the risk of developing a superior and insular attitude to civilizations as well.

The following types of openness are historically relevant:

- Type 1: Open only to fair trade and practical creativity
- Type 2: Open to fair trade and practical and religious creativity but insular to the intellectual creativity of other civilizations
- Type 3: Open to fair trade and practical and intellectual creativity but insular to the religious creativity of other civilizations
- Type 4: Open to fair trade and all three forms of creativity of other civilizations

The importance of openness is no more than an assumption than it is highly unlikely for creative outcomes to confine themselves within one civilization over millennia.

Destructive Orientation

By destructive orientation, we mean whether a social order has been peaceful or has engaged in empire building, violent colonization, and systematic wealth drain with respect to other social orders. It does not include internal wars, which can be equally terrible since internal wars result in the control of internal sustainable growing surplus to a new dynasty with similar values and does not result in controlling wealth production factors or wealth usurpation itself by an instrument of destruction with different values. The attitude of aggression and violence that developed early in the history of a social order depends on complex interaction among instincts of interspecies dominance and interspecies violence, natural bounty, and ideologies of creed and greed.

Natural bounty: Natural bounty, as noted above, is based on natural causes, such as soil, climate, and ecology, for a particular social order as noted above. Its presence ensured greater productivity, and its absence fostered institutional greed as noted below.

Intolerant creed: This refers mostly to the role played mostly by monotheism in promoting religious intolerance and initiating wars and conflict, not because of greed but because of religious intolerance. Often this has played a secondary contributory role in generating violent and destructive orientation.

Institutional greed: Institutional greed may develop from the economic system (need for greater profit), land shortage (because of population pressures), raw materials (because of a lack of natural bounty), or a need for external markets (because of an imbalance between internal production and demand resulting from income polarization). Institutional greed emerges typically as a direct result of some form of external economic dependence and does not refer to individual greed. It thus depends on the nature of natural bounty and economic system of the social order.

Destructive orientation is measured by the presence of violence in the aggressor and its absence by the existence of sustained political independence in the invaded social order.

It is important to note that the number of parameters chosen to assess inner nature is a practical matter. It is not a constraint. For example, we feel it sufficient to use new technology adoption, economic freedom, wealth allocation, and social cohesion as sufficient to assess productive capacity. One can argue that the state of educational institutions is also important. However, its addition is not critical since technology adoption, economic freedom, and social cohesion already reflect that in sufficient manner. It is a balance between keeping it simple and aiming for perfection.

The process outlined above to assess the inner nature is clearly not without pitfalls. The list of suggested parameters may be incomplete, their assessment from the causes may be subjective, and the consolidation of the characteristics into capacities and orientation may not be sufficiently accurate. In its defense, however, we argue that any process that attempts to rationalize outcomes of social orders must go through a similar process. The only question is whether such a process is accurate and transparent or occurs in the black box of the researchers' mind. The suggested process can certainly claim it is both. It is out there, hung like the proverbial dirty laundry for the reader to see and evaluate.

Table 9.1: Identifying and Assessing the Parameters of Inner Nature

Category of Causes	Specific Causes	Dimensions of Inner Nature	Measuring Parameters	Allowed Values	Broad Measures of Inner Nature
Natural	Geo, Clime, Ecology		Natural Bounty	L, M, H	
Intrinsic Causes	Institutional Structures, Institutional Processes, Formative Beliefs	Productive Capacity	NTA	L, M, H	Internal SGS
			Relative EF	L, M, H	
			Social Cohesion	L, M, H	
			Wealth Allocation	Cons., ED, MS, CE	
		Creative Capacity	ASBC	W, M, S	ICB
			Wealth Allocation	CS., ED, MS, CE	
			Creed	ES, SRC, Balanced	
Extrinsic Causes	Others' Constructive Outcomes, Destructive outcomes	Constructive Orientation	GI/LI	Type 1, 2, 3, 4	O/I
			Creed		
			ENW		
		Constructive Orientation	Institutional Greed	L, M, H	Violent Greed/ SPI
			Intolerant Creed	L, M, H	
			Natural Bounty	L, M, H	

Legend

NB: Natural Bounty
NTA: New Technology Adoption
EF: Economic Freedom
EF: Economic Freedom
ASBC: Abstract Sys Building Cap.
GI: Geographic Isolation
LI: Linguistic Isolation
ENW: Early Nomadic Wars

CS: Consumption by labor
ED: favors Elite Decadence
MS: Favors Military Spending
CE: Supports Creaive Endeavors
ES: Excessively Spiritual
SRC: Science Religion Conflict
SPI: Sustained Political Independence
TT/WT: Transport/Weapons Technologies

SGS: Sustainable Growing Surplus
ICB: Internal Creative Balance
O/I: Openness/Insularity
SPI: Sustained Political Undependence
P/V: Peaceful or Violent
W: Weak
M: Moderate
S: Strong

To summarize, we may assess the inner nature of a social order by parameters listed in table 9.1 to a level of sufficient accuracy for our purpose.

A Look Back: How We Arrived at the Concept of Inner Nature

Before we leave this section, it is useful to look back and summarize how we arrived at the concept of the inner nature of a social order and the methodology of its assessment. Figure 9.4 summarizes this process. We started with the causes and analyzed the stock of factors of wealth production and knowledge and internal and external perturbations to understand the process qualitatively that creates productive, creative, and scientific outcomes. We put forward the hypothesis of inner nature and proposed measurable parameters to assess this inner nature quantitatively.

9.8 The Concept of the External Orientation of a Social Order

The external orientation of a social order simply combines its constructive and destructive orientations at a given point in its history. External orientation may be an essentially peaceful orientation toward other social orders or express itself as empire building, violent colonization, and systematic wealth drain. It may entertain an open or an insular attitude toward other social orders. As noted above, openness/insularity to creativity pertains mostly to openness or insularity to religious or intellectual forms of creativity since most social orders have shown openness to practical creativity, which has no overt ideological implication and to fair trade since it is manifestly beneficial to both sides by definition or it will not occur. It may be types one to four as noted above.

We need not remind the reader that aggression and violence is not limited toward other social orders. All civilizations have witnessed terrible internal wars. However, such internal wars among the states of a civilization at most shift the control of sustainable surplus to a different state with more or less similar values and beliefs. Thus, the far less corrosive and substantive impact of internal wars must also be looked at in assessing a civilization's creative and productive orientation.

Below we list the eight historically relevant forms of external orientation out of a possible maximum of sixteen (four destructive orientations times four construction orientations).

1. **Type I: Peaceful with Type 4 Openness:** Characterized principally by peaceful orientation with respect to other civilizations and an attitude of openness with respect to all forms of creativity and fair trade.

2. **Type II: Peaceful with Type 2 Intellectual Insularity:** Characterized principally by peaceful orientation with respect to other civilizations and an attitude of openness with respect to practical creativity and fair trade only and insularity with respect to intellectual or creativity.

3. **Type III: Empire Builders with Type 4 Openness:** Characterized by violent aggression with respect to other civilizations but open with respect to all forms of creativity but with a propensity for coerced trade.

4. **Type IV: Empire Builders with Type 1 Religious and Intellectual Insularity:** Characterized by violent aggression with respect to other civilizations and open only with respect to practical creativity with a propensity for coerced trade.

5. **Type V: Violent Colonizers with Type 3 Religious Insularity:** Characterized principally by violent

Figure 9.4: How We Arrived at the Concept of Inner Nature

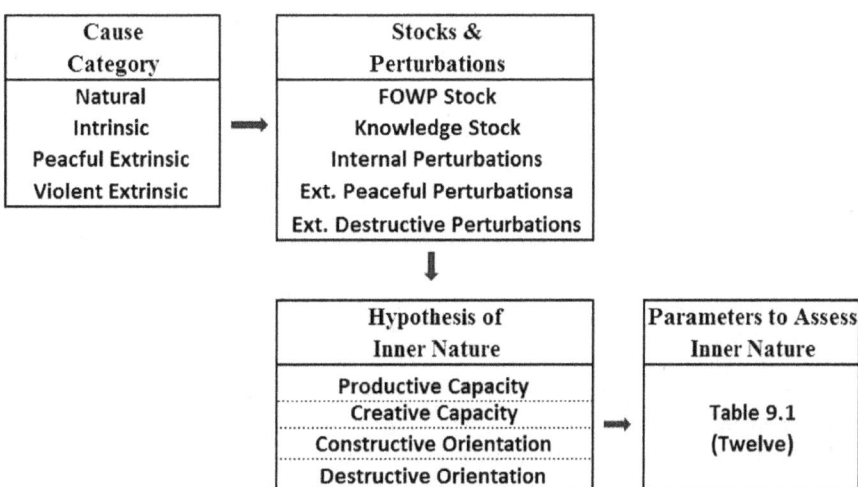

orientation with respect to other civilizations and open only with respect to practical creativity and with a propensity for coerced trade.

6. **Type VI: Violent Colonizers with Type 4 Openness:** Characterized principally by violent orientation with respect to other civilizations and an attitude of openness with respect to all forms of creativity but with strong propensity for coerced trade.

7. **Type VII: Systematic Wealth Drainers with Type 1 Religious and Intellectual Insularity:** Characterized by violent orientation, with strong propensity for wealth drain and intellectual insularity.

8. **Type VIII: Systematic Wealth Drainers with Type 4 Openness:** Characterized by violent orientation and an openness with respect to all forms of creativity but with strong propensity for wealth drain.

It is easy to see that these historically observable external orientations lead to 64 types of interacting pairs (8x8). However, without getting into details, only about a dozen such pairs are historically relevant.

9.9 Inner Nature and Ideology of a Social Order

In chapter 8, we emphasized the importance of beliefs and ideologies as an integral part of the intrinsic causes have the appearance of an independent cause. Social orders not only possess institutional structures and processes, but also develop beliefs or ideology embedded in *and* energizing these structures and processes. These beliefs pertain to the possibilities of knowledge of this world (science) and world beyond death (religion), attitudes concerning fellow citizens, and attitudes toward other social orders (conscience). It is easy to see how these beliefs parallel the concept of inner nature. Beliefs concerning the possibility of knowledge of this world and attitude toward fellow citizens strongly parallel the productive capacity. Beliefs concerning the possibility of knowledge of this world and concerning the world beyond death (religious beliefs) strongly impact creative capacity and beliefs concerning other social orders parallel the constructive and destruction orientation of the social order. The concept of inner nature may be thought of as a way to assess these beliefs and have put them on a more firm theoretical foundation. The inner nature and the beliefs and attitudes are two sides of the same coin since both are derived from causes.

Tracking the Evolution of Civilizations

In this final section, we briefly describe on how we will use the hypothesis of the inner nature of social orders to rationalize the state of science within a particular social order and its evolution across the stages. The concept of inner nature may also be used to rationalize the productive and creative outcomes in general. However, we focus on scientific outcomes for two reasons: scientific outcomes are the focus of this work and rationalizing scientific outcomes is hardly possible without rationalization of productive and creative outcomes.

9.10 Broadest Measures of Inner Nature

It is noteworthy that in the absence of changes in natural bounty, internal SGS is a simple, inclusive, high-level measure of productive capacity, at least in the short run. Similarly, internal creative balance (ICB) is good measure of the creative capacity since a lopsided ICB will affect both the creative output and its distribution among practical, religious, and intellectual aspects. The simple measure of constructive orientation is an openness/insularity scale. Finally, the simplest measure of destructive orientation is the initiation of offensive violence, which is effective only with the loss of sustained political independence (SPI) of the invaded; in the presence of SPI, destruction orientation of others is at most a destructive nuisance. Thus, it is appropriate to measure the destructive orientation of an aggressive social order by its violence and by the ability of the other social orders to push it back or their ability to hang on to their SPI.

Below, we formally define sustained political independence (SPI) since SGS, ICB and O/I have already been defined in sections 8.5, 6.8 and 9.6 respectively.

Sustained Political Independence (SPI)

SPI is defined as political freedom experienced by a civilization (though not necessarily by every state within that civilization) over an extended time, interrupted at most by relatively short, reversible periods, thereby ensuring that civilization's core values not only remain intact but also are actualized in its productive, creative, and scientific outcomes. SPI may be thought of as a shield by which a civilization defends its conscience and beliefs, its SGS, and ICB. The SPI of a standalone and peacefully interacting civilizations is a given and did not have to be earned. When civilizations entered the era of extended military conflicts, it had to be earned and defended. SPI is a critical condition needed for the birth, development, and maturation of science. SPI is only relevant to science by its absence. Its presence by itself does not mean a whole lot. The measure of SPI is simply yes and no.

9.11 Evolution of Civilizations

The most telling measures of the state of a social order are SGS, ICB, openness/insularity, peacefulness/violence, and implied SPI. The concept of external orientation combines the last two. Of the SGS and ICB, ICB is significantly more important strategically since as a measure of the balance in creative capacity, it determines both the present and future SGS levels. Thus, broad evolution of civilizations across the historically observable phases of science may be accomplished relatively easily by tracking its changing *external orientation* and *ICB*.

Inner Nature of Social Orders and Their Scientific Outcomes

In this final section, we outline how we shall use the concept and assessment of the inner nature of social orders to track the evolution and to rationalize the scientific achievement of social orders within a phase and across phases. This has been our ultimate objective in part III. In the following sections, we discuss how we can evaluate the evolution of science and rationalize scientific achievements of a social order *within* a phase and *across* phases.

9.12 Rationalizing the Achievements in Science within a Phase

Once the inner nature of a social order during a phase has been assessed, the scientific achievements of a social order may be rationalized through appropriate parameters, depending on the nature of its interaction with other social orders parameters. However, the parameters required to assess the inner nature of social orders are not of equal importance in every phase for every social order in every era. For example, high internal SGS depends on natural bounty, economic freedom, and wise allocation. Social cohesion, though highly desirable, is not critical since science typically did not make excessive demands on SGS, though consistent allocation was most definitely critical. Most significantly, it was possible to compensate for low internal SGS through fair trade, coerced trade, or systematic wealth drain. On the other hand, the nature of creed is highly significant but not determining either since it can be slowly overcome by scientific outcomes themselves if other elements are favorable.

Likewise, the nature of openness is important as its absence will slow down, but it too will not necessarily prevent scientific achievements. Scientific outcomes themselves have the potential to make the social order less insular in the long run. It is, however, impossible for scientific achievements to go beyond that permitted by the state of abstract systems-building capability a social order possesses. Similarly, in the absence of sustained political independence, science will remain in a state of suspended animation in the social order, or worse, it will regress.

Yet the sheer presence of SPI will hardly guarantee achievements in science. We may summarize these critical observations as follows:

- Favorable natural bounty, economic freedom, wise allocation, and social cohesion are important but not critical since a low internal SGS can be augmented by other means.

- A balanced creed, (or agnosticism and atheism), wise allocation of SGS, and openness to the creativity of other social orders will help the cause of science enormously.

- Achievements in science by a social order cannot go beyond the limits imposed by its abstract systems-building capability.

- Absence of sustained political independence will always arrest state of science.

These observations lead to the following simplified rules to rationalize the scientific achievements of a social order.

The standalone social order: The achievements in science depend critically on internal SGS and its wise allocation since there is little opportunity to augment it through fair trade or violent greed. The determining parameters are the state of its abstract systems-building capability (ASBC) and the nature of its creed and therefore may be rationalized through the following:

- Relative internal SGS
- Allocation of SGS (as a subset of wealth allocation)
- Nature of its creed
- State of its ASBC

The peacefully interacting social order: The achievements in science are a little less dependent on high internal SGS since there is opportunity to augment it through fair trade. The determining parameters are still the state of its abstract systems-building capability and the nature of its creed. In addition, the openness of the social order to the creativity of other social orders will nearly always accelerate the progress in science and occasionally even determine it. Therefore, its science may be rationalized through these elements:

- Relative internal SGS
- Allocation of SGS (as a subset of wealth allocation)
- Nature of its creed
- State of its ASBC
- Openness/insularity

The case of the violently interacting social orders merits differing treatment for the invaded, victorious, and defeated social orders treatment because of external control and the impact on productive and creative outcomes.

The violently interacting social orders—invaded social order: Internal SGS continues to be important, as are ASBC, nature of creed and openness to constructive outcomes of others. However, the presence of sustained political independence is critical now. Therefore, its science may be rationalized through the following:

- Relative internal SGS
- Allocation of SGS (as a subset of wealth allocation)
- Nature of its creed
- State of its ASBC
- Openness/insularity
- SPI

The violently interacting social orders—victorious social order: Internal SGS is not nearly as important since it may be increased by an order of magnitude in the historically important case of small states controlling much larger civilizations. Of course, mere wealth does not guarantee scientific outcomes. Thus, ASBC, creed, and openness remain the key factors. Its science may be rationalized through these elements:

- Relative internal SGS
- Allocation of SGS (as a subset of wealth allocation)
- Nature of its creed
- State of its ASBC
- Openness/insularity
- Nature of violent greed

The violently interacting social orders—defeated social order: All that is relevant after the loss of sustained political independence is the violent greed and the creed of the victor until its overthrow.

- Nature of creed of the victor
- Nature of violent greed of the victor

9.13 Rationalizing of Achievements of Science across Phases

The reader will recall the six life stages of science identified in chapter 7, figure 7.1: birth; development and maturation of protoscience; and birth, development, and maturation of science proper. Figure 7.1 also showed the relationship between life stages and the seven phases of science: birth, development, and maturation of protoscience corresponding to phase I; birth of science to phase II; the development stage to phases III, IV, V, and VI; and mature life stage of science to phase VII. In table 9.2, we identify the necessary and sufficient conditions of each stage of science expressed as minimum required values of key of the parameters of the inner nature. Thus, the state of a social order's inner nature may be used to define the stage of science achieved by a social order during a given phase. Determining the stage of science will also identify the leading and lagging social orders as far as achievements in science are concerned.

Table 9.2: Necessary and Sufficient Conditions of Stages of Science Achieved by the Leading Social Order

Life Stage of Science	Rel. Int. SGS (1)	Wealth Alloc.	ASBC (*)	Nat. of Creed	Openness Insularity	SPI	Violent Greed Victor	Violent Greed Defeated
Birth-PS	H	PC	1	N/R	N/R	N/R	N/R	N/R
Dev.-PS	H	PC	2	N/R	Types 3, 4	N/R	N/R	N/R
Maturity-PS	H	IC-S	3, 4	Bal.	Types 3, 4	N/R	N/R	N/R
Birth-Science	H	IC-S	5	Bal.	Types 3, 4	N/R	N/R	N/R
Dev.-Science	H	IC-S	6, 7, 8	Bal.	Types 3, 4	Reqd.	Helps	None
Maturity-Science	H	IC-S	9, 10	Bval.	Types 3, 4	Reqd.	Helps	None

Legend:
SGS: Sustaibale Growing Surplus
ASBC: Abs. Sys Building Cap
O/I: Openness/Insularity
SPI: Sustained Political Independence
(1) Total
(*): Numbers Refer to State of ASBC
PC: Favors Allocation to PC
IC-S: Allocation to IC favors science
Types 3, 4 refer to Openness/Insularity scale
PC: Practical Creativity
IC: Intellectual Creativity

9.14 Evolution of Science across Phases

Shifting CG of Science

It will also be helpful to ask the question if the center of gravity of science has shifted during the phase and why. By center of gravity of science, we mean the leading civilization or civilizations that contributed to the developments in science during the phase. Clearly, the center of science will move with the leader of science in a particular phase, which, as we noted above, is determined by which social order achieved the highest stage of science in the phase. By mapping the actual stage of science in each historically observable phase, we would be able to show the evolution of science in each social order over its entire historical period.

9.15 Summary

In this chapter, we have developed the concept of a social *system* consisting of interlocking social orders. We outlined a different approach to rationalize the outcomes of a social order in such an interconnected system and showed that the direct approach to rationalize outcomes from driving causes is unmanageably complex. Thus, we developed the concept of an inner nature. We proposed how we could assess the inner nature of social orders at a particular time in history. Finally, we discussed the approach to use inner nature of social orders to track their evolution and to rationalize their science within and across phases.

KEY CONCEPTS

Productive and creative capacity
Constructive and destructive orientation
Inner nature of social orders
External orientation of social orders
Broadest measures of outcomes
Rationalization of the science
Evolution of science and civilization

Chapter 10 | The Essential Set of Participants

10.1 Introduction

In chapter 4, we identified four epochs: the biological evolution of *Homo sapiens* from primates, birth, and development of hunting-gathering cultures through spoken language development and non-agricultural technologies; birth of early settled communities in the Neolithic epoch; and invention of agriculture followed by emergence of civilizations in the civilization epoch. The process ultimately led to the birth of civilizations (and innumerable secondary civilizations and other entities) starting before 6500 BCE.

In this chapter, we formally define significant social orders, and we ask and answer the question if we can identify an essential set of participants that have been critical to the birth, development, and maturation of science either *directly or indirectly*. If we can achieve that, we would have succeeded in limiting the number of civilizations and other entities we must deal with. Fortunately, the answer question is in the affirmative.

10.2 Classes of Entities

Since the birth of civilizations, five principal classes of entities have been in existence: the hunting-gathering cultures, the prebirth settled communities, the nomadic confederations, civilizations comprised of city-states, and states and empires. Below we summarize key characteristics each of these social orders.

Hunting-Gathering Cultures

Most hunting-gathering cultures including Eskimo, Australian, some Native American Indian, Polynesian, and African, never experienced a full-blown Neolithic stage. These social orders lacked a sustainable food surplus because they did not have fully developed agriculture. A significant majority of the food was obtained through gathering which requires frequent relocation to allow the old sites to recover. Because of mobility, these groups had to minimize material possessions and were thus egalitarian with transparent division of labor. These communities had populations ranging from a hundred to several thousand and showed considerable variation depending on climate and available hunting and storage technologies since not all groups consumed what they gathered or hunted in a typical day. If these hunting-gathering cultures encountered civilization, they slowly tended to change their ways but posed little threat to civilizations. On the contrary, civilization likely posed a threat to them.

Nomadic Confederations

The nomadic social order is a different lifestyle existing typically in arid or desert environments. While the hunting-gathering cultures lacked the technology of animal and plant domestication and relied more on foraging than hunting, the nomads typically had domesticated the animals and knew of agriculture but were unable to practice it on a sufficient scale due to climate constraints. Similarly, they relied more on hunting than gathering. They did not move as frequently and engaged in more extensive trade with civilizations. For that reason, they typically flourished closer to civilizations. Nomads existing in deserts depended on trade to a greater extent. The fact that nomads have only existed in arid or desert-like conditions is hardly surprising because that is what makes them nomads in search of food, water, and pastures.

A nomadic confederation as a collection of nomadic tribes often came together to attack a civilization though not always. These confederations did not hold together for more than a few hundred years but often came to pose a great threat to civilizations; however, after conquest, they usually adopted the ways of civilization, though only after a period of resisting the settled lifestyle.

Neolithic Communities

Early settled communities were comprised of humans engaged in agricultural and nonagricultural pursuits and consisted of clusters of villages scattered over an area measured at most in hundreds of acres in favorable natural locations. These early communities were essential to the ultimate emergence of civilizations. Often nearby emerging civilizations absorbed or conquered these communities. There is no fundamental distinction between these communities and civilization except for scale and complexity. Their modest size prevented them from being a threat to civilizations.

Civilizations

If a civilization is defined as a social ordering of *Homo sapiens* with a sustainable food surplus, agricultural and nonagricultural technologies with sophisticated division of labor, both village and city settings, and sufficiently developed spoken language to transmit knowledge to the next generation, it leaves lots of room for what constitutes a civilization. Somewhat arbitrarily, we proposed the emergence of a city with a population of ten thousand or more to constitute the birth of civilization. The essential constituent units of a civilization are city-states and states that differ only in size.

City-States: Early city-states comprised of humans engaged in agriculture and nonagricultural professions comprising of a city and perhaps hundreds of surrounding villages. They were usually small (a few thousand square miles) and came into existence where natural barriers existed within a defined geographical area. The city-state model was too small geographically to survive as a civilization after the fall of ancient Greece about 200 BCE.

States: States are usually bigger in size (~25,000–100,000 square miles) than city-states. States typically develop a more lasting ethnic identity based on a common language. In recent history, they formed the basis for the rise of modern nations. States within a civilization typically fought with one another, and any particular ruling dynasty did not last for more than a few hundred years. A state typically had multiple cities and thousands of villages.

A **civilization,** then, is a collection of city-states or states that nearly always share a defined geographical area, have similar values and a common history and culture. Civilizations have varied in size from a city-state to a subcontinental geography (one million square miles or more). They have proven to be more enduring than all other entities, typically lasting millennia. Civilizations do not fight one-on-one. They usually fought through a defending "frontline" state and an aggressor state from another civilization, empire, or nomadic confederation. If the invader won, it attempted to gradually extend its control over other states within the civilization. Thus, the states of a civilization carried the potential to pose a threat to the states of another civilization.

Classification of civilizations based on origin: History is littered with civilizations. Below, we distinguish between civilizations based on origin and ultimate fate.

- Primary civilizations have an origin traceable to their own unknown prehistory. There are only four primary civilizations: Indian, Chinese, Mesopotamian, and ancient Egypt.
- Secondary civilizations are heirs to a previous civilization or are offshoots of another civilization, such as ancient Greece, ancient Persia, European, Korean, Japanese, Russia, and the United States as well as those that have remained small yet influential, such as the Jewish Diaspora, including the state of Israel.
- Fusion civilizations are a result of a synthesis of two or more civilizations: Muslim Indonesian, Vietnamese, Thai, and Central and Latin American.
- Dead civilizations shined brightly once but did not survive to the present because they were conquered or absorbed into other civilizations. Examples include Mesopotamian, ancient Egyptian, ancient Greek, and Hellenistic states.

It is worth noting that until the modern era, primary and significant secondary and fusion civilizations existed only in the Eurasian and North African theaters and not in Australia, Americas, and sub-Saharan Africa. Why this is so is a complex question that we will have ample opportunity to explore in part IV.

Today, the land mass of the planet is disproportionally under the control of European (and its derivative states) and the Muslim civilizations.

- European civilization, with roughly 20 percent of the world population, controls one-half of the total land mass, and Muslim civilizations, with roughly 20 percent of the world population, controls nearly 40 percent of the land mass.
- By comparison, Chinese and Indian civilizations have roughly 20 percent and 17 percent of the world population and control roughly 5 percent and 2 percent of the total land mass.

Empires

An empire is a temporary collection of city-states, states with or without a nomadic confederation across a single civilization or multiple civilizations. Empires rose and fell, and at their heights have been more powerful than states and civilizations they contained, but they do not last as long as civilizations. It is unusual to find an empire lasting more than a few hundred years with continuing vitality. Empires may be created solely within a civilization, across civilizations, or across a nomadic federation and a civilization. Thus, empires may be intracivilizations, intercivilization, created by nomadic confederation, or a civilization as shown in figure 10.1.

Eurasian political history over the last two and half millennia or during the era of violent interaction has resulted from the conflict among civilizations (comprising of competing states with intracivilization empires), multicivilization empires originated by states of another civilization, and multicivilization empires originated by a nomadic confederation.

Whatever else one may say about the empires; one incontestable fact throughout history is that empires always fancy they will last for a thousand more years, as Churchill hopelessly wished for the British Empire in the midst of its destruction. Another aspect of empires is that early in history, the need to hide the sinister motives behind building the empires was not as compelling. In recent history, however, empires have felt an increasing need to hide their true motives in a religious, racial, altruistic, or ideological cloak because of the increasing sophistication of the conquered and because the professed values of the recent empires have always been in contradiction with their actions.

It is instructive to compare intra- and intercivilization empires in history to see how they differ with respect to time they take to achieve their peaks, how long they stay there, and how fast they disintegrate. In figure 10.2, we show this dynamic for major empires the world has seen over last two and half millennia. We may draw the following broad conclusions:

- Empires rarely have vitality that lasts longer than few hundred years. The Ottoman Empire lasted for six hundred years; however, it was practically

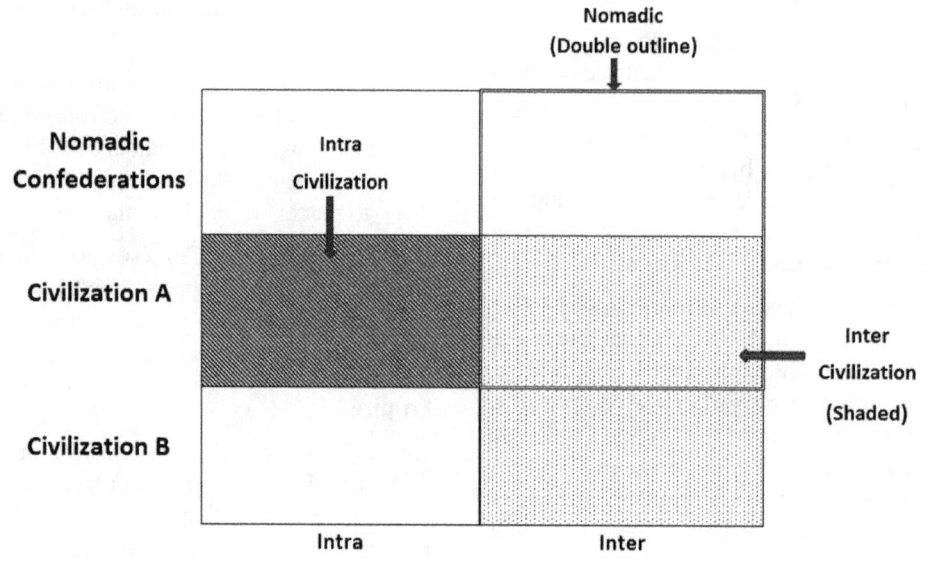

Figure 10.1: Classification of Empires

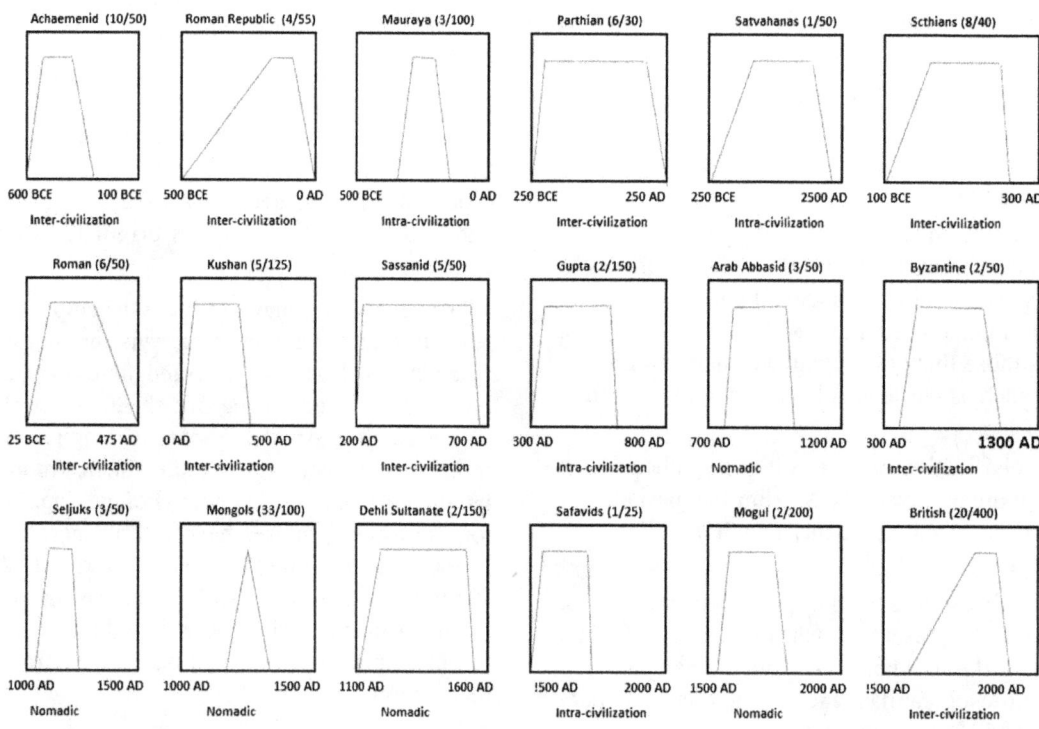

Figure 10.2: The Rise and Fall of the World's Empires
Empire Name (Max Area in Sq Km/Max Population in Millions)

nonexistent for the last couple of hundred years and lasted only because the new empires had a bigger fish to fry and defeating Ottoman Empire was not at the top of their list. More typically, the empires remain at peak for less than a couple of hundred years.

- It takes about fifty to a hundred years to put together an empire and about the same time to decline.
- The empires within a single civilization took less time to rise as the would-be victor had more knowledge than the enemies to be conquered and would find greater acceptance by the defeated states. The Mongol Empire is a glaring exception to that observation but only if one does not take into account their extensive, sophisticated pre-attack intelligence gathering system.
- Empires across civilizations typically took much longer to put together for obvious reasons. The apparent exceptions, like the Roman and the Mogul empires, can be explained since they were in a sense continuation of the Roman Republic and Delhi Sultanate respectively.

The British Empire is a specific example of empire dynamics. It had a very slow rise of nearly 250 years, a peak dwell time of less than fifty years, and a rapid decline within fifty years. It had a slow rise because the empire began as a commercial enterprise and was based on a policy of "divide and rule." It needed the conquered civilizations' own resources to control it, and its interests remained primarily commercial. Its peak dwell time was one of the shortest of major empires, and it declined fast not because it was unjust or because it was based on control, since all empires are similar in these respects, but because it was based on systematic wealth drain on a massive scale. Its success necessarily created powerful enemies in European civilization about the time it reached its peak. These enemies desperately wanted to do the same since they also needed markets and raw materials for their industries. The resulting two worldwide military confrontations between entrenched and would-be imperial powers of European states, the national independence movements, and the dictates of a rising United States after World War II quickly put it out of its misery.

A focus on nomadic empires: On the surface, it appears surprising that a nomadic confederation could overwhelm a civilization that may be hundred to thousand times as populous and far wealthier. However, four conditions have been critical to nomadic confederations creating empires:

- The military and political weakness of the civilization to be conquered
- The diffusion of weapons technology and domestication of horses as a long-distance carrier of fighting force and bred on vast grasslands from civilizations to nomads
- A sophisticated intelligence-gathering system
- The rise of a charismatic leader capable of uniting the disparate nomadic tribes

A fifth condition, though not necessary, if present, has been of great value in increasing the longevity of the empire created. That condition is the existence of an ideology that espoused violence in the name of an uncompromising monotheistic faith. Table 9.1 summarizes the major empires created by people of relatively recent nomadic origin. Several of these empires may virtually be considered intracivilization (Mongol Kublai Khan in China, Mughal, and Manchu) or intercivilization (Arab, Seljuk, and Ottoman). In table 10.1, the empires created by nomadic peoples have also been delineated.

Civilizations and empires contrasted: It is easy to see how similar and different civilizations, intracivilization and intercivilization empires, and empires originated by a nomadic confederation are. Empires have a shorter life span and are based on force. Civilizations have a much longer life span and are not based on force. They have an organic unity based on geography, culture, religion, language, and shared history. Empires are relevant to only those who have control *over* them. Civilizations are loved by those *in* them. Civilizations resemble parents who give birth and lovingly raise their offspring; empires, particularly the intercivilization and nomadic, resemble street bullies who want to control.

Table 10.1: Empires Created by Nomadic Confederations

Name of Empire	Name of Confederation	Place of Origin	Empire Location	Time Period	Religious Affiliation
Kushan Empire	Yuezi	Central	North India	1st-3rd century	Buddhism
Hun Empire	White Huns	Central	West Asia	4th-6th century	None
	Golden Horde	Asia	Europe, India		
Gokturk Empire	Gokturks	Central	West Asia	6th-8th century	None
Arab Empire	Muslims	Arabian	West Asia	7th-10th century	Islam
Seljuqs Empire	Seljuqs	West Asia	West Asia	11th-12th century	Islam
Mongol Empire	Mongols	Central	West Asia	13th-14th century	None
Ottoman Empire	Osmani	West Asia	West Asia	14-20th century	Islam
Moghul Empire	Mughul	Central Asia	India	13th-19th century	Islam
Manchu	Manchu	Central Asia	China	17th-20th century	None

Table 10.2: Strategic Position of Different Entities at the Dawn of Civilization

Type of Entity	Creativity in Ideas/Inventions	Level of External Trade	Diffusion of Creativity	Threat to Civilizations
Hunting gathering	Modest	minimum	minimum	none
Pre-birth settlements	Modest	inconsequential	inconsequential	inconsequential
Nomadic Confederations	limited	limited	limited	extensive
Civilizations	significant	extensive	significant	extensive

10.3 The Essential Participants

In judging which entities are essential to our purpose, we use the following criteria:

- Creativity in ideas and inventions
- Volume and significance of external trade
- Extent of peaceful exchange of ideas and inventions
- Originators and recipients of significant military conflicts
- Impacted by significant land usurpation and wealth transfer

The results of mapping these elements for all entities are shown in table 10.2. It is clear that the hunting-gathering group and prebirth settlements are not of consequence when studying the relationship among and between civilizations and the birth and evolution of science. Civilizations and nomadic confederations alone are. But not all civilizations or nomadic groups are relevant either. Some were too small and isolated and never showed any interest in science. This is an important question perhaps suggesting that interaction and exchange of ideas, no matter how slow and indirect, are critical to science. Yet other civilizations that no longer exist made monumental contributions to science and were later absorbed into other civilizations.

Science development appears to be primarily a Eurasian (and North African) affair. A little reflection shows that western Eurasia is the home of Mesopotamia, Arab desert lands, ancient Persia, and by extension, Egypt. Northern Eurasia is Ancient Greece and Europe, eastern Eurasia is China, southern Eurasia is India, and central Eurasia is the homeland of central Asian nomads. The Muslim civilization prospered in all part of Eurasia at one time or another, except in China. It seems to us that nomadic confederations periodically disturbed the great settled civilizations in the west, east, north, and south of Eurasia and learned from these civilizations, sometimes moving science forward and eventually getting absorbed into civilizations. They brought unimaginable destruction and kept the pot stirred. The history of science until last few centuries, we believe, is intimately connected to this process. We do not want to leave the impression that only the nomads stirred the pots. Certainly, the misadventure of Alexander and European Crusades stirred the pot rather effectively in premodern times.

From the above considerations, we postulate that the essential set of participants important to understanding the intertwined relationship between civilizations, and the birth and evolution of science consists of the following eight civilizations and two nomadic groupings:

Primary civilizations (4): Indian, Mesopotamian, Egyptian, and Chinese

Derived civilizations (3): Ancient Greece and Hellenistic states, European (Roman Republic, Roman Empire, European proper, and Western civilization), and Persian

Fusion civilizations (1): Muslim (Arab, Persian, and Turkish incarnations)

Nomadic groupings (2): Central Asian and Arab

Our focus will be limited to these ten entities. We will, however, bring in other secondary civilizations as necessary. While this essential set is only an assumption at this stage whose validity we shall need to demonstrate, it will allow us to focus on a limited number of players as we embark on our quest.

The four primary civilizations were born in the four river valleys with favorable natural settings. The two that had the desert-circumscribed small footprint, Mesopotamian and Egyptian, perished or were absorbed into other civilizations about 2,500 years ago and were rediscovered only during last two hundred years. Ancient Greece was derived mostly from Mesopotamian, Egyptian, and Phoenician civilizations with some influence from the Indian civilization. Ancient Persia was derived from the Mesopotamian civilization and was influenced by ancient Indian civilization. The European civilization was derived from Mesopotamian, Egyptian, and ancient Greek civilizations. Arab and Turkish nomads and Persian civilization fused into the Muslim civilization and expanded further.

Our premise is that the intertwined relationship between the history of science and civilizations can be explained by the evolution and reciprocal impact of these eight civilizations and two nomadic confederations originating from central Asia and Arabia. On this premise, we will move forward.

Table 10.3: Onset of Eras and Stages of Civilization for the Essential Set

Stage of Civilization →	Era		
	Standalone/ Pre-literate	Peaceful Interaction/ Literate, Mature Literate Rational	Violent Interaction/ Pre-scientific Scientific
Indian Civilization	6500–3000 BCE	3000–321 BCE	321 BCE–present (1)
Mesopot. Civilization	4500–3000 BCE	3000–539 BCE (2)	
Egyptian Civilization	3150–2000 BCE	2000–525 BCE (2)	
Chinese Civilization	3500–500 BCE	500 BCE–1279 CE (3)	1279 CE–present
Greek / Hellenistic	2000–750 BCE	750–334 BCE	334 BCE–30 BCE (4)
Persian Civilization		1000–539 BCE	539 BCE–656 CE (5)
European Civilization		750 BCE–500 BCE	500 BCE–present
Central Asian Nomads	2000–200 BCE		200 BCE–1500s CE
Arab Nomads		2000 BCE–660 CE	660 CE–1071 CE
Muslim Civilization			660 CE–present

Beginning and End on an Era defined by leading edge civilization

Era Begins	6500 BCE	3000 BCE	500 BCE
Era Ends	3000 BCE	500 BCE	continuing

(1) Alexander's Failed Invasion (3) Conquered by Mongols (5) Ended by Arabs
(2) Conquered by Persians (4) Ended by Roman Empire

In table 10.3, the onset of standalone, peaceful, and violent eras for each of the ten essential players are delineated. The reader may recall that the onset of these eras for an individual civilization, as a practical matter, may be different from the onset for civilizations as a whole.

10.4 Summary

In this short chapter, we have postulated an essential set of players consisting of eight civilizations and two nomadic confederations whose independent development and reciprocal interactions must be studied to understand the intertwined relationship between civilizations and their science. We also identified three different types of empires: intracivilization, intercivilization, and nomadic; outlined the basic characteristics of empires in general; and showed how they differ from civilizations.

> **KEY CONCEPTS**
>
> Entities
> Life cycle of significant empires in history
> Essential set of participants

PART IV
BIRTH, DEVELOPMENT, AND MATURATION OF PROTOSCIENCE

OVERVIEW OF PART IV

In part IV, consisting of a single chapter, we tell the story of protoscience. Our approach to chapter 11 and each of the six chapter of part V will be essentially the same:

- We affirm the era and the key participants of the phase first.
- We then discuss political history, natural and intrinsic and extrinsic causes (which are nothing other than the summation of the constructive and destructive outcomes of all relevant social orders respectively) and significant productive, creative and scientific outcomes of each social order.
- We then assess the inner nature or productive and creative capacity and constructive and destructive orientation of each social order.
- Next, we summarize the state of civilizations and science for the phase as a whole.
- We then summarize the broad evolution of science during the phase and rationalize the state of science achieved by each social order during the phase through the inner natures of interacting social orders.
- Finally, we end the chapter by reviewing the new participants on the horizon and providing a chapter summary.

In chapter 11, we focus on the birth, development, and maturation of protoscience in four primary civilizations: Indian, Mesopotamian, Egyptian, and Chinese civilizations.

Let us begin our story.

Chapter 11

Standalone and Peaceful Interaction Eras—First Phase: Protoscience

Birth, Development, and Maturation of Protoscience (6000–1000 BCE)

11.1 Introduction

Establishing the beginning of the protoscience phase, like the birth of civilization itself, is necessarily an arbitrary date that depends on how one defines protoscience and on an ability to accurately estimate the dates of key creative outcomes scattered across the multiple noninteracting civilizations that existed more than eight millennia ago. Both tasks are not easy to accomplish. Still, in principle, the birth of protoscience may be said to begin with a significant jump in the rate of knowledge accumulation in several related areas, such as arithmetic, astronomy, medicine, and astrology, with the latter constituting one of the earliest uses of astronomy. Protoscience clearly began in the absence of writing, fully developed rationality, and the experimental method.

It is not difficult to imagine that the roots of protoscience activity lie in the Neolithic epoch. However, we believe that the protoscience phase began in earnest sometime after the birth of civilization. Based on evidence from Anatolian, Indian, Mesopotamian, and Egyptian civilizations, we believe it is doubtful that protoscience could have begun in earnest any earlier than 6000 BCE. Thereafter, it went through a long period of development and maturation and ended around 1000 BCE, when the process of the birth of science proper began. The three phases of protoscience spanned the standalone era (6500–3000 BCE) and nearly all of the peaceful interaction era (3000–550 BCE). The beginning of protoscience thus began nearly three millennia before the emergence of written language and ended about a millennium after the earliest full development of alphabetical script.

The protoscience phase is long by comparison to subsequent phases—lasting five millennia. By contrast, the next six phases together have been a little more than half as long. The birth of science was understandably preceded by a long gestation period. However, this gestation period appears long only from our current perspective. Considering the length of the hunting-gathering stage or how long it took to develop spoken language, invent agriculture, or even to diffuse agriculture across the globe, the length of the gestation period of science hardly appears surprising.

Note that we use "participants" and "social order" to refer to any combination of a civilization, city-state, empire, or nomadic confederation.

Affirmation of Era and Essential Participants

11.2 Affirming the Era of Civilization

Archeological findings show that at the dawn of civilization, the four primary civilizations were standalone noninteracting civilizations because the transport technologies relative to the spatial distance were insufficiently developed. By 3000 BCE or perhaps a little earlier, transport technologies, including ships, wheeled wagons, and roads, had developed sufficiently to bridge the distance among some neighboring civilizations. The same, however, could not be said about long-distance weapons technologies. These still awaited the invention of the horse collar, saddle, reins, and stirrup as well as high-quality iron weapons. As a whole, these inventions did not come into existence until the middle of the last millennium before the beginning of the Common Era. However, depending on the nature of geographical barriers separating a civilization and the nearby nomadic tribes, conflicts between a civilization and outlying nomads did occur during the protoscience phase. Thus, the protoscience phase, which may be said to begin roughly half a millennium after the beginning of the standalone era and ended about half a millennium before the end of the peaceful interaction era, essentially covered most of the standalone and peaceful interaction eras.

Three protoscience phases and the birth phase of science covered in the next chapter are the only phases characterized by an absence of war among major civilizations. In saying so, we are not suggesting an absence of destructive character in primary civilizations during the standalone and peaceful interaction eras; destructiveness was there but remained localized. Conflict requires both a means to wage conflict and the motivation to do so. And existence of the means to wage war in the absence of motivation can also be the basis of peaceful interaction among civilizations. Wars among states of a civilization and among civilizations and nearby nomads (mostly initiated by nomads) did take place using infantry and crude, short-distance chariots. These destructive events fall within our definition of the peaceful interaction era.

11.3 Essential Participants of the Protoscience Phase

If the reader requires writing to exist as a pre-condition for civilization, then protoscience began before the rise of civilization and possibly before large-scale agriculture was established. However, we have termed civilizations without a written language as preliterate civilizations, those with a written language as literate civilizations, and those with alphabetical script as mature literate civilizations. Writing is not a prerequisite for civilization as defined in this work. All major river valley civilizations that prospered on the Indian subcontinent (~6500 BCE), in Mesopotamia in West Asia (~4500 BCE), in Egypt in North Africa (~3500 BCE), and in China in East Asia (~4000 BCE) naturally entered the first protoscience phase as preliterate civilizations without a written language, albeit at significantly different times. Each civilization went through a long evolutionary period before inventing or adopting written language.

There were only four major civilizations during the protoscience phase: Indian, Mesopotamian, Egyptian, and Chinese. They were situated by necessity near significant river systems within a narrow geographical band around the Tropic of Cancer. It was as if the earliest civilizations were mortally afraid of being shriveled up in colder climates, being dried up in desert, and being smothered by vegetation overgrowth in tropical settings. There is hardly a more convincing argument for the strong relationship between the emergence of civilization and geography, climate, and ecology.

Nomadic tribes not fortunate enough to possess valuable lands (valuable relative to climate and the technology of the day) existed on the edge of these civilizations. These tribes existed to the east, west, and north of the Mesopotamian civilization; to the east, west, and south of the ancient Egyptian civilization; and to the north and west of the Chinese civilization. The Indian civilization was different. It did not face any known significant threat from the nomads during the protoscience phase because of the formidable Himalayan barrier. Quite the contrary, recent research has pointed to the tantalizing possibility of an exodus of several groups out of the Indian subcontinent, settling as far west as Ireland. The now-discredited hypothesis of the Indo-Aryan invasion of India and emigration *from* the Indian subcontinent poses an uncomfortable challenge to the much-loved hypothesis of a north-to-south migration pattern since the birth of civilizations. This is discussed in appendices D and E.

The conflict with nomads did have a modest to significant impact on Mesopotamian, Egyptian, and Chinese civilizations (of the three, the Chinese civilization generally had an upper hand with respect to nomads). The Indian civilization remained outside the crosshairs of nomads during the protoscience phase. Thus, right at the outset of history, primary civilizations had a very diverse experience with respect to nomads, and this, as we shall see, was to have a profound effect on their evolution. Successive states in Mesopotamia coalesced through the integration of the settled Mesopotamians and the often victorious nomadic stocks from east and north. This violent mingling of settled and nomadic tribes is easily explained by limited fertile land, the nature of geographical terrain, and the resulting relative proximity of the civilization and nomads. Ancient Egypt fell to the nomadic invasion once when Hyksos conquered Egypt in the middle of second millennium BCE. Two centuries later, when Egypt overthrew their rule, Egyptians themselves turned imperialistic toward some of the minor civilizations and nomads in West Asia.

Unique Issues of the Protoscience Phase

In this section, we discuss important issues unique to the protoscience phase because of a lack of reliable or because of one-sided historical data. In essence, these issues constitute the bulk of ongoing and incomplete archeological research pertaining to the standalone and peaceful interaction eras.

11.4 Diffusion of Creativity and Migrations in the Standalone Era (6000–3000 BCE)

The reader will recall that the protoscience phase spanned the three millennia of the standalone era and the first two millennia of the peaceful interaction era. However, it would be inaccurate to presume that civilizations only began to impact other civilizations during the peaceful interaction phase. Ideas and inventions never respected geographical boundaries, even in the absence of trade and military conflicts. During the standalone phase, ideas and inventions diffused from their birthplaces, albeit significantly slowly, through isolated, infrequent individual travel; through mediation through nomads; and from infusions of people through mass migrations, which were generally peaceful since most of planet was relatively unpopulated.

In this section and the next, we touch on how civilizations reciprocally and unconsciously influenced other civilizations during the standalone era based on a mix of "what is known" and "what must have occurred." The diffusion of inventions and migrations during the standalone era were often mediated, not direct, exceedingly slow, necessarily asymmetric, and fortuitous. In general, it is not possible to talk about specific pairs involved in the diffusion of ideas and inventions with reasonable certainty given the state of archeological research. All we can say is that diffusion certainly occurred and probably involved most major and minor civilizations and several nomadic groups.

It is difficult as well to establish the general or specific direction of the diffusion of ideas and inventions because of uncertain research and bias. For example, if one believes the strong oral tradition of the Indian civilization and believes in the recent research concerning the timing of epic of Mahabharata, one must conclude that wheel existed in the Indian civilization significantly before 3000

BCE. Western historians commonly assign its invention to Mesopotamia around 3000 BCE. The gaps and disagreements in these assessments are so broad and recent that it is difficult to draw any conclusions except that Western historians over the last couple of centuries drew premature conclusions while archeologists from other civilizations were hardly in a position to challenge them.

It is worth emphasizing that such diffusion initiated in the absence of formal trade among civilizations and was mediated through travel, mass migrations across civilizations, and for some civilizations, peaceful or violent interaction with the nomads. Even in the absence of trade, the generally peaceful movement of several groups out of India and the violent migration of nomadic tribes into Mesopotamian and Chinese civilizations occurred during the standalone era. There is, however, considerable uncertainty regarding these migrations and their impacts.

Diffusion of Practical Creativity

One might naively assume that there was a modest diffusion of practical creativity during the standalone era. Indeed, the diffusion was no doubt extremely slow by modern standards due to the distance among major civilizations and the state of infrastructure, communication, and transportation technologies. However, we are talking about three millennia and, unlike modern times, there was essentially no formal, enforceable restriction on leaking technology and knowhow, with a few notable exceptions, such as silk harvesting (and that was in the peaceful interaction era). It was certainly possible for practical technology to diffuse during the standalone era even in the absence of significant long-distance intercivilization trade. Although the diffusion of practical inventions was a very slow process that is difficult to trace, its cumulative significance is undeniable during the standalone era. Let us consider the following examples.

Water well: We do not know how old the invention of well is. The earliest known well, dating back to ~5000 BCE, is constructed out of wood and was located in Kuckhoven, Germany, of all places. Wells constructed using bricks are known to have existed in several ancient civilizations, and were possibly invented independently. It is nearly impossible to trace the diffusion of this invention across civilizations and continents. The earliest transmission of water wells likely occurred through individual travel. A small civilization confined to the banks of a river for drinking water, but not necessarily for agriculture because crops have sufficient rain, could now move farther away from the river and bring more area under cultivation by utilizing rain. The diffusion of water well technology would play a significant role in the expansion of agriculture in such a civilization by creating a source of drinking water initially as well as water for irrigation later.

Horse: Horse domestication is said to have occurred in the Ukraine around 4500 BCE. Originators or receivers in various cultures and civilizations that became aware of the usefulness of the horse did not appear to resist diffusion. The diffusion simply depended on the rate of transmission. Originally, a horse was domesticated as a source of meat, then as a work animal on the farm, followed by use in riding and chariots, and eventually for military purposes. The full benefit of the horse also required the invention of harness, collar, and reins and, of course, the lighter wheel with spokes and axle that occurred in the later phases.

Bronze: Prior to the accidental discovery of bronze, probably before 3500 BCE in the standalone era, and its diffusion during both the standalone and peaceful interaction eras, the principal metals used were gold, silver, and copper. Bronze is an alloy of copper and tin and is harder than either of them. Thus, between 3500 BCE and 1000 BCE, until the discovery and fully widespread use of iron, is called the Bronze Age. The discovery of bronze is said to have taken place in Mesopotamia and reached Persia and China by about 2000 BCE. The originators and receivers do not appear to have resisted diffusion, and travel determined its rate of diffusion. The invention travelled several thousand miles in less than two thousand years. Even after the discovery of iron, bronze was used primarily in artistic castings since it contracts slightly on cooling and is thus easily separated from intricate molds.

Mass Migrations during the Standalone Era

Indo-Aryan Migration: Peaceful migrations are as old as *Homo sapiens*. In chapter 3, we traced the story of populating the planet, which involved both global and localized movement. The invention of agriculture initiated another migration to river valleys suitable for agriculture. However, at the beginning of the standalone era, migrations had slowed down, occurring generally under conditions of expulsion or localized wars. The bold new hypothesis of the migration of well-established Indo-Aryans out of India about 4600 BCE calls into question the very foundation of Eurasian prehistory as it exists today. It was likely one of the early causes that eventually succeeded in civilizing southern Europe by 1000 BCE. Overall, with the exception of Indo-Aryans, known migrations during the protoscience phase must be judged only modestly important. We also note that unlike during the peaceful era, migrations during the standalone era were not necessarily peaceful, given the relatively weak nature of civilizations. Undoubtedly, there were countless other migrations—local, regional, and global.

The greatest impact of the diffusion of practical creativity during the standalone era occurred on productive outcomes. Certainly, religious and intellectual creativity diffused during the standalone phase. However, it is difficult, if not impossible, to be specific about it. Migration patterns deduced from linguistic analysis is one of the few tools but is hardly reliable and does not open the door for reliably assessing the diffusion of religious and intellectual creativity.

11.5 Assigning Origin of Creative Outcomes

The truth is that our knowledge of the origin and timing of creative outcomes even in the peaceful interaction era is far from perfect and is evolving. This is why we have chosen not break the outcomes in practical creativity by civilization and summarize these achievements for civilizations as a whole in the following section. Thus, any description of diffusion during the standalone era must be a combination of "this is what happened" and "this is what must have happened" or "this is what most likely happened." This problem gets progressively less important as we leave the standalone era.

In chapter 8, creative outcomes are classified into practical, religious, and intellectual types, with the latter further broken into art, philosophy, and science. The question is how archeologists have determined the contributions of different civilizations and assigned priority of origin to creative outcomes during the protoscience phase. The protoscience phase began eight millennia ago, before the advent of writing, and ended around 1000 BCE or about two thousand years after the invention of the earliest form of writing. Fundamentally, there are three ways we can do this: archeological remains, using tools such as carbon dating, DNA, and hydrological, linguistic, and astronomical studies; oral traditions; and analyzing written records. However, the protoscience period began before written language was invented and overlapped with nearly the entire standalone and peaceful interaction eras. Therefore, during the first three millennia of the protoscience phase, archeological remains and oral tradition are the only sources available. Oral tradition, with the notable exception of the Indian Vedic tradition, which was focused on religious and intellectual creativity only, is often unreliable. During the peaceful interaction era, written records are increasingly available. Though analysis of archeological remains with modern tools is increasingly reliable, there are issues with archeological research, and some of them are fundamental in nature:

- The scope of archeological research relative to different civilizations to date has been uneven. The ancient Egyptian civilization was discovered over 200 years ago and the Mesopotamian about 160 years ago. By comparison, the Indus ruins were discovered about eighty years ago and Mehrgarh less than forty years ago. It is true that the majority of archeological research money to date has been funneled to Egypt and Mesopotamia because Western civilization, as the chief sponsor of this research, has chosen to link its cultural and religious roots *exclusively* to West Asia and North Africa in part because these two civilizations are no longer living and thus unable to play the role of living elders. This imbalance becomes more pronounced when one factors in the larger area covered by over 1,200 Harappa settlements that have been discovered to date over an area of 150,000 square miles, for example.

- The likely destruction of archeological evidence through *continuous resettlements* over millennia. In the case of Indian civilization, the large population exacerbates this, though the population was supported by its exceptional endowment of fertile plains and favorable climate, enabling multiple crops each year.

- The Indian civilization's greater reliance on oral tradition even after writing was invented in the protoscience phase makes developing an unambiguous timeline difficult.

- The drier climate and stone construction in Egypt and West Asia led to better archeological site preservation.

- The potential bias in Western research and its rather unscholarly rush to ascribe inventions and ideas to dead civilizations of West Asia and North Africa. We suppose dead parents are easier to glorify than living ones.

Further, there is a basic difference with respect to the practical, religious, and intellectual creativity when tracing their origins during the early protoscience phases. To the extent that a creative outcome could take a physical form and was preserved through the ages or that its physical form remained *unique* to a particular civilization, its origin can be determined with relative certainty. Thus, the art, architecture, and religious creativity of the protoscience phase are more easily traceable than philosophical, protoscientific speculations, and practical inventions. Because of this fundamental asymmetry, we know without doubt that the goddess Isis was a product of Egyptian religious creativity. This asymmetry also gives us the ability to recognize ancient Egyptian art without hesitation. On the other hand, we can only guess and can never be sure where the first potter's wheel was invented or identify the likely long genealogy of the invention. It is best to view the question of origin of practical inventions during protoscience phases as work in progress and understand that the current assignment of the priority of inventions during the protoscience phase is not necessarily the final word. During the latter part of the protoscience phase, when intellectual creativity picked up speed, assigning priority becomes easier but is still not definitive because of written records or, in the case of Indian civilization, because of a reliable oral tradition. In many cases, this assignment pertains to improvements and not original inventions. This is a big problem only in the earlier protoscience phase, since with the end of the standalone era, we enter the historical period when written records begin to increasingly dominate our assessment of civilizations. The key issues concerning researching ancient civilizations are summarized in appendix F.

Because of these difficulties, we have chosen not to present civilization's achievements in practical creativity of protoscience phases even though mountains of questionable data are available.

11.6 Significant Achievements in Practical Creativity during the Protoscience Phase

We will summarize the achievements in practical creativity for materials; processes; energy; tools; agricultural technologies, consisting of tools, plant and animal domestication, and irrigation technologies; nonagricultural products; building construction techniques; transport technologies; weapon technologies; infrastructure technologies; communication; and practical medicine.

Materials: Before the beginning of the protoscience phase, it is probably safe to say that the primary materials known to civilizations were stone, wood, bones, plant fibers, and clay. The materials mastered during the protoscience phase included copper, bronze, silver, gold, tin, iron, glass, silk, concrete, perfumes, and bitumen.

Processes: Civilizations mastered weaving, soldering, sintering, grinding, bag pressing, distillation, lost wax and conventional casting, incubation, and cooking processes, such as churning, boiling, baking, and frying.

Energy: In addition to using animals to augment muscle power primarily through horse, elephant ox, donkey, and camel, civilizations also learned the use of oils, natural gas (transported through bamboo in China), and coal as sources of heat and light energy.

Tools: The significant tools invented during the protoscience phase include the bow and arrow, sword, plow, axe, wheel, potter's wheel, wheeled ladder, plumb line, angle, measuring stick, drill, the screw pump (later called the Archimedes' screw), loom, balance, bellows, rotary hand mill, compass, crank, and weighing balance.

Domestication of plants and animals and irrigation technologies: Civilizations learned to domesticate chickens, pigs, cows, water buffaloes, goats, sheep, ducks, and honeybees. Civilizations also learned to better domesticate wheat, rice, tobacco, peanuts, cotton, sweet potato, and yams, among others, and various spices. In addition, civilizations also learned irrigation techniques, including wells, canals, and dikes.

Nonagricultural products: Among the products invented were cotton clothing, sandals, lamps, candles, water clocks, sundials, mirrors, wooden and brick water wells, beer, liquor, decorative pottery, furniture, yogurt, and butter, to mention a few. Business products include contracts, insurance, seals, open markets, overland and sea trade, and grain storage systems.

Building construction techniques: Key innovations here included rectilinear buildings, reed houses, stone buildings, sea walls, columns, arches, bridges, dams, canals, multistory and large buildings, pyramids, Stonehenge, planned cities, gardens, public baths, underground drainage, and central heating.

Transportation and infrastructure technologies: During this phase, civilizations learned to make boats (not just dugout canoes), skis, sailing ships, wheeled vehicles, chariots, paved roads, and spoked wheels.

Communication technologies: Civilizations also invented a rudimentary postal system.

Weapon technologies: Key actual and potential weapon technologies included bow and arrow, iron swords, the domestication of horses, body armor, and chariots.

Practical medicine: Practical medicine naturally remained stuck in herbal treatments and shamanism. Disease diagnosis and the theory of illnesses were still in the future. Dental surgery in the Mehrgarh period of Indian civilization was an exception.

History, Causes, and Outcomes of the Indian Civilization

11.7 Brief Political History (6000–1000 BCE)

Establishing the timeline of the ancient Indian civilization is a daunting task and is truly a work in progress (see appendix E). The very ancient nature of civilization, a weak tradition of writing until historical times, a strong oral tradition, and a relative lack of archeological evidence due to continuous resettlement of the same highly fertile area over millennia makes it not only difficult to establish a consistent timeline but also easier for those with a vested interest to distort it. But it is not as hopeless as it may seem. Consider the following key elements of the accumulating linguistic, archeological, astronomical, and literary evidence during the twentieth century:

- The discovery of the Indus ruins in 1922 CE pushed back the timeline to 3300 BCE.
- The hypothesis of the Indo-Aryan invasion of India in 1500 BCE put forward by Max Mueller in the mid-nineteenth century and funded by British imperialists has been exposed to be a complete farce by several researchers, such as N. S. Rajaram, Subhash Kak, and David Frawley, over the last twenty-five years, even though a guilt-ridden Max Mueller retracted it much earlier while on his death bed.

- The astronomical modeling based on eclipses and mentioned in *Mahabharata* has strongly suggested the date of Mahabharata civil war was 3170 BCE.
- A metal bust discovered in 1958 near Delhi has been dated to 3700–3800 BCE.
- The Rigveda records the vernal equinox in the constellation Orion, and the Brahmanas record it in the Pleiades constellation. We may thus assign roughly 1,500 years between the composition of Rig Veda and the Brahmanas. In the early twentieth century, venerable Indian scholar and patriot Bal Gangadhar Tilak based his extensive research on Rig Veda, dating it back to at least 4000 BCE.
- Based on linguistic and cultural analysis, in 2000 CE Shrikant Talageri concluded that a people known as Druhyus emigrated from India around 4600 BCE. this reverse migration, in addition to the migration from their central Asian home around 7000 BCE, as proposed by Colin Renfrew in 1984, may explain the similarity between Sanskrit and European languages.
- The initial discovery of Mehrgarh in 1974, spread on 168 acres with an estimated population of twenty thousand, pushed back the roots of civilization to 7000 BCE.

Based on the above data, we believe that the roots of Indian civilization go back to 7000 BCE. Driven by natural calamities, ancient Indian civilization went through four distinct periods:

- Mehrgarh period (6500–2600 BCE), with four subperiods
- Vedic period (4600–3750 BCE)
- Harappa period (3750–2000 BCE)
- Early Ganges period (2000–1000 BCE)

Let us look at each period.

The Mehrgarh archeological site ultimately covers an area of five hundred acres, It is located near the Bolan Pass in Pakistan and dates back to 7000 BCE. It was discovered only in 1974, as mentioned above. The site is an assemblage of villages from different periods. By the sixth millennium BCE, the Mehrgarh city was about 168 acres and was undoubtedly the largest city of its time in the world, with a population in excess of twenty thousand. By comparison, the contemporary "city" of Catal Huyuk in Anatolia had a population of about four thousand and covered about thirty acres. Because of its recent discovery, comparatively little is known of the Mehrgarh period. The continuity between the Mehrgarh and Vedic periods is corroborated by the presence of terracotta artifacts, such as bison carts. The significance of the Mehrgarh discovery is that it has established beyond doubt the continuous roots of civilization on the subcontinent beginning around 7000 BCE and has connected civilization on the subcontinent to the Neolithic epoch. It also shows that the Indus alley civilization was simply a more advanced urbanized stage of civilization in India. The discovery marks Mehrgarh as the oldest archeological ruin of its size discovered to date.

Oral tradition and recent research has shown that a Vedic King named Mandhata conducted war against a people known as Druyhus. The Druyhus were defeated and forced to emigrate out of India around 4600 BCE. A branch of Druyhus migrated to Europe and came to be known as Druids or Celtic priests, and they believed in the immortality of the soul and reincarnation. Nearly a thousand years later, the Vedic king, Sudas, fought a second war against a federation of ten kings, including the remaining Druyhus still in Northwest India. Seer Vasistha recorded this battle in Rig Veda. The battle resulted in the emigration of Partha, Balahanas, and Pakhtas, known today as Parthians, Baluchis, and Pathans, out of India. This recent research amounts to a new theory of the reverse migration of Aryans mentioned above and potentially explains the presence of so-called Indo-European language throughout western Asia, central Asia, and Europe. It is noteworthy that there is no record of conflict with nomads from either the west or the north of Indian subcontinent during the Vedic period of Indian civilization. The Sarasvati River drying due to tectonic plate shifting signaled the end of the Vedic period.

Early in the Harappa phase, two powerful states arose through the consolidation of different tribes: the Kurus in the northern end of the Sarasvati River and the Yadavs in the southern end. The great civil war of Mahabharata was, we believe, fought among the Kurus during this phase in 3067 BCE, based on astronomical modeling of the lunar eclipses mentioned in *Mahabharata*. The Harappa phase began its decline sometime in the third millennium due to the lingering effect of the civil war but was mostly due to the change in climate pattern. A few centuries later, floods ended the great cities that had been founded on the banks of Indus. Encroaching aridity precipitated an exodus to the east, thus initiating the Ganges period. Over 1,200 sites containing ruins of the Harappa phase are scattered along Indus and as far as Roper City in North India. Thus, the Harappa phase covered an area of about 150,000 square miles, with an estimated population of around five million! Again, there is no record of conflict with nomads from either the west or the north during the Harappa period of Indian civilization.

During the established Ganges period around 1500 BCE, northern India was a patchwork of monarchies or republican monarchies—such as Kosala, Videh, and Audhoya—that were comparable in size to the modern nation states of Europe when the conjectured invasion of horse-riding, tall blondes from possibly as far away as Norway took place! Although the records are unreliable, it is clear that during the Ganges period, Indian civilization was peacefully migrating eastward and establishing itself in the fertile plains of the Ganges River as a second mingling of populations occurred. Therefore, we would hypothesize that it was an era of peace and expansion and essentially without excessive internal warfare. The focus was not on grabbing what belonged to someone else; it was to gain control of what nature had made possible.

11.8 Natural Causes

Readers may recall that natural causes consist of geographical, climatic, ecological, geological, and astronomical components and may be consolidated into a base natural bounty and the gradual and abrupt changes that a social order must respond to in order to survive and prosper.

Undoubtedly, natural causes played a determining role in the birth and decline of Mehrgarh as its birth took place toward the end of the Dryas period, starting 9500 BCE, when a strong warming trend brought warmer climate, rain, and great river systems fed by melting Himalayan glaciers. This trend seems to have lasted about three millennia, when another mini cooling trend and a major change in the weather pattern related to changes in earth's orbit and tilt had occurred around 7000–8000 BCE. This initiated the slow desertification of not only northwest India but also Sahara and Nubia, forcing a slow eastward migration from Mehrgarh. As a result, the population and the center of civilization moved east probably around 5000 BCE, and over time, Mehrgarh lost its once-prominent position. The birth of civilization in Mehrgarh took place at the intersection of water and desert: enough water but not too much; enough warmth but not too much. Otherwise, we run into frigid, desert-like, or tropical conditions, and nature had upper hand.

Let us acknowledge that we do not know when the people of Mehrgarh moved east toward the Indus and Sarasvati Rivers, pushed by approaching aridity and the discovery of the smaller Indus River and the then-mighty Sarasvati River, with the potential to expand agriculture in the fertile plains.

The Vedic period was ended by yet another natural event: the tectonic plate shifts that occurred throughout its existence. These shifts resulted in the Sarasvati River eventually drying, thus shifting the civilization a little to the west since these same tectonic shifts had made the Indus River mightier through the capture of the Sutlej River and other tributaries of the once-mighty Sarasvati River. It is important to note that the two cities from the Harappa period have survived because they were buried underground. Many other cities undoubtedly have not survived because of continuous resettlement of the area over the succeeding millennia. It is therefore wrong to conclude that these two cities were the oldest or the only cities of the Harappa period.

The Harappa phase, weakened by the civil war of Mahabharata, ended in yet a third ecological disaster with increasing aridity and encroaching desert by later centuries of the third millennium. This resulted in a gradual move farther east, beyond the now-dry Sarasvati River to the plains of the Ganges River, thus initiating the Ganges phase. Helped by the tectonic shifts, the Ganges River had earlier captured the upper tributaries of Sarasvati and the Yamuna Rivers and had become mightier.

Thus, there was a continual general movement from west to east and later from north to south during the phase. It is clear that in addition to population growth and natural expansion of the civilization, the determining drivers of this movement have been adverse astronomical and geological changes. Early Indian history remained at the mercy of natural forces until it found its greater home east of the Indus in the plains of Ganges by about 2000 BCE. However, these natural changes were spread over millennia, making it possible for distinct periods of early Indian civilization and giving it time to respond to the wrath of Mother Nature.

The base natural bounty of the early Indian civilization may, therefore, be judged to be high, but it experienced terrible gradual and abrupt changes during the four or five millennia of its existence.

11.9 Intrinsic Causes

The reader will recall that intrinsic causes can be effectively captured through the key institutional structures and processes noted in chapter 8. Since the protoscience phase spanned five millennia, and all four civilizations went through lengthy, distinct periods. Where appropriate and possible, we will point out the changes in natural and intrinsic causes as civilizations went through these substantially differing periods.

Mehrgarh Period: Institutional Systems, Structures, and Processes and Beliefs

The significance of the Mehrgarh discovery is that it provides continuity to the discoveries in the Indus valley and supports the theory of the continuity of Indian civilization from 7000 BCE on. It thus strikes another blow at the Aryan migration theory. Undoubtedly, we will learn more about Mehrgarh as the research continues. The evolving, complex, and related issues of the discredited Aryan invasion hypothesis, the origin of Indo-Aryan languages, the reverse migration out of India, and the true roots of Indian civilization are discussed in more detail in appendices E and F, respectively, as noted earlier. In this book, we subscribe to the Indo-Aryan migration into the Indian subcontinent around 7000 BCE and several reverse migrations out of India from 4600 to 1600 BCE as the most reasonable explanation of similarity in the Indo-European languages.

We know little about the political organization of the Mehrgarh settlement. It is not known if Mehrgarh had any offensive or defensive military capability. There is little evidence of any weapons. Mehrgarh was an agricultural civilization that cultivated barley, wheat, dates, and cotton. It also had domesticated animals, such as goats, sheep, and cattle. It had a significant nonagricultural sector, including flint knapping, bead making, tanning, metalworking, basket weaving, pottery, and cotton weaving. It had relatively sophisticated tools, such as potter's wheels and bow drills, more than six thousand years ago, thus indicating an ability to develop or adopt new technology. It seems it exported pottery to eastern Iran by the third millennium. Even the earliest Mehrgarh houses were made of mud bricks and had four to six rooms. They were rectangular, unlike the round houses at Catal Huyuk, for example. The settlement also had workrooms and grain storage rooms. It is estimated that population of Mehrgarh civilization during the sixth millennium was around 250,000. We may state with confidence that the Mehrgarh period had a sustainable food surplus, since it had a rather large city population. Not much is known about the role of government, if any, in the economy.

There appears to be no organized religion in Mehrgarh as there is little evidence of places of worship. It appears as if Mehrgarh worshipped a female goddess resembling Indriya, the oldest reference to later Vedic gods. There was little science or religion, so there must have been little science-religion conflict and little excessive spirituality. We know little about its laws, customs, or justice system. Given its egalitarian social structure, one may presume it was a just society with little wealth polarization as there is little evidence of palatial structures. This is, however, something to be expected at such an early period in history. The presence of a female goddess without any male counterparts points to a matriarchal social structure. We may conclude that wealth allocation favored practical creativity in allocating the meager surplus, as there is little evidence of places of worship or wealth polarization. Given the egalitarian social structure, absence of organized religion, and absence of military capability, we may assume that Mehrgarh possessed high social cohesion. There is no evidence to date of any internal wars or weapons in Mehrgarh.

Vedic Period: Institutional Systems, Structures, and Processes

Politically, the Vedic phase was organized into small monarchies reflecting lingering tribal loyalties. We know little about the structure and capability of military in Vedic period, except that internal wars were fought and organized armies existed. Nearly self-sufficient agricultural villages were the basic unit of the social and economic structure of the Vedic society, with technologies comparable to the later Mehrgarh period. Vedic religion was definitely polytheistic, with the male and female gods representing the forces of nature endowed with human emotions and the power to grant wishes. It appears that in parallel with this polytheism, the seeds of panentheism (God interpenetrates nature), pantheism (the universe is God), and even agnosticism (impossible to prove or disprove existence of God) were present. The ritual of symbolic sacrifice at the fire altar, designed to reflect the state of cosmological knowledge linking the heavens to the inner psychological realm, required chanting sacred words. This ritual, though based on polytheism, seemed to hint at a nascent monism. The desire for perfect chanting created an aching need for a more perfect spoken language. It was as if the words literally carried upward by the fire were the means of communication with the divine. This partly explains the later emphasis on the development of perfect spoken and written language during the next phase. Though fundamentally different in concept, from a narrow metaphysical perspective, the Vedic fire altar served a function similar to those of the Mesopotamian Ziggurats, Egyptian pyramids, and the Chinese ancestor worship, which is that of linking with the power in the heavens. Although the Indian civilization was fundamentally spiritual during the period, there were no temples or great monuments constructed since religion was centered on symbolic fire-based sacrifice (of the self) and communication with the divine based on chanting. Although there was little science-religion conflict, the danger of excessive spirituality lurked in the background.

The concept of dharma, or righteousness, performed the function of a more formal legal framework in Vedic India. The Vedic period did not a have slave system, and the emergence of caste system was still in the future. It seems that the main distinction was between the four varnas and the avarnas: those who lived within an established social order and those outside the law. The four varnas were considered equal, with intermarriage permissible, and there was movement among the four varnas depending on an individual's interest and ability. The ideal of the social order was pursuit of social good: nothing for individual, all for society. The status of women, though confined to the household, was high.

During the Vedic period, class distinctions were small and in part because of its spiritual and esoteric orientation probably did not have excessive inequality. Like most social orders of the day, specialized knowledge-creating institutions were yet to emerge. Generally, Brahmins focused on intellectual and religious knowledge, and the Vaishyas and others focused on practical knowledge. The wealth allocation favored religious or practical creativity. The concept of dharma and the social customs were used to ensure social cohesion. Significant internal wars resulted in an exodus of certain groups as noted above.

Harappa Period: Institutional Systems, Structures, and Processes

Political System: Politically, the Harappa period was organized around two strong states, Kurus and Yadavs, and was based on continuing tribal affiliations.

Military capability: Military in the Harappa period probably consisted of soldiers on foot, known as pattis, and on chariots, known as rathins. The chief weapons included chakras, body armor, mace (a heavy club with a head), and bow and arrow. The army was commanded by Senani, who reported to the king. It appears that the army consisted of professional soldiers drawn predominantly based on caste affiliations.

Economic system: If the Vedic period was spiritual in orientation, the Harappa phase was definitely more practical but without rebelling against the Vedic spirituality. Consequently, we see large cities form (such as surviving Harappa and Mohenjo-Daro) and ports with strong maritime trade. During the Harappa phase, the balance of power seems to have shifted to the cities. The development of trade with Mesopotamia and the port ruins in Gujarat (Lotham) indicate significant economic development in agricultural and nonagricultural sectors. Numerous seals from Harappa have been discovered in Mesopotamia.

Systems of religious faith: Compared to the Vedic phase, it appears that the religious impulse had turned more ritualistic, with beliefs in spells and sorcery, as evidenced by the composition of Yajur and Atharva Vedas. There was little overt science-religion conflict.

Legal system: The concept of dharma or righteousness continued to perform the function of a more formal legal framework as in the Harappa period as well.

Social structure: There was no slavery system, and wealth polarization increased compared to the Vedic period. A rigid caste system was still in the future despite its mention in Gita, probably because *Gita* and *Mahabharata* were put in writing much later, based on oral transmission. It is noteworthy that the Yadav clan was in power, and Yadavs would not be considered as part of the three upper castes later in the Ganges period.

The Harappa ruins show the power of the state increased and though the class distinctions increased, pointing they point to a relatively egalitarian society. Oral tradition describes palaces being built. Yet, there was absence of royal monuments and elaborate temples. Military expenditures were definitely increasing compared to the Vedic phase. The wealth polarization during the Harappa period probably became a little more pronounced as civilization turned practical; however, the underlying spirituality and concept of dharma kept the excessive inequality in check. Thus, class conflict in the absence of significant wealth polarization and slavery and the presence of spiritual orientation was minimal. The caste system had begun to emerge but was still flexible enough to accommodate meritocracy.

Knowledge-creating and educational institutions: There were no formal knowledge-creating institutions; however, dedicated individuals ran academies to educate the royal class and commoners. These academies focused on both spiritual and practical matters. New knowledge creation was left to individual effort and these academies.

Wealth allocation: Harappa civilization was highly advanced technically for its time, as evidenced from the state of ruins at Harappa and Mohenjo-Daro. Therefore, the surplus had increased. Even though the civilization was more practically oriented, there was considerable effort aimed at understanding the nature of the world and God through meditation alone. Thus, wealth allocation was directed toward practical needs and understanding nature through a naive but admirable spiritual focus.

Social cohesion: Social cohesion remained high due to developing caste norms and the concept of righteousness despite the absence of a formal, written legal code and an increasingly rigid caste structure. The concept of dharma and customs continued to ensure social cohesion.

Internal wars: The Harappa period witnessed the terrible Mahabharata war fought between two powerful kingdoms. The war lasted a mere eighteen days and was fought in a righteous manner.

Ganges Period: Institutional Systems, Structures, and Processes

Political system: The political structures continued to evolve, and toward the end of Ganges period, northern India consisted of several large republics with the power of a king circumscribed by councils. We see the emergence of great cities, such as Kashi, Ujjain, and Ayodhaya in the Ganges plain. The village continued to remain nearly self-sufficient and democratic in nature through a village-centered democracy known as the Panchayat system. The Panchayat system consisted of a council of five elders that had the power to make local laws, enforce them, and punish the transgressors. The idea of separation of powers did not exist, and the village democracy relied on the high moral standard of the elders and public opinion.

Military capability: There was increasing emphasis on the science of war, including the use of iron weapons and elephants. However, the wars were fought based on principles and not deception. The Ashvamedha ritual employed a wandering horse and involved an open challenge to either submit or fight based on where the horse travelled. It was a common ritual and was based on minimizing unnecessary bloodshed and destruction while allowing the stronger kingdoms to expand. This unique concept in the history of war conferred a sort of objectivity in territorial expansion and ensured that the threat of war was initiated only when overwhelming strength was attained, thus minimizing killing.

Economic system: It was an era of expansion of agriculture. There is strong evidence that *Homo sapiens* in the hunting-gathering stage inhabited the subcontinent as far back as 74,000 BCE. The fusion between the "original" population in the subcontinent and the eastwardly expanding Indo–Aryan people with agricultural technology after 2000 BCE was mediated through the more formalized institution of Chaturvarna, which slowly became ossified into caste system. As the populations comingled, a broad-based and distinctly Indian racial type reflecting division of labor through the caste system, the metaphysics of karma and reincarnation, and a lingering memory of possible different origins of the two peoples developed. The challenge of integrating the original inhabitants of the Ganges plain, unlike the more recent process of colonization in North America for example, into an agricultural social order was accomplished without wholesale dispersion, extermination, relocation, and violence. A caste system was useful in directing specific castes into productivity improvements, and the pursuit of knowledge through a fixed division of labor, despite all its evils, began in this period. This process of fusing racial stock was hardly unique; what was unique and regressive was the religious sanction of the classes, thus converting the class system into caste system. If one delves far enough back in time, nearly every civilization in history is a composite of different peoples.

Systems of religious faith: The discovery of iron in the middle of the second millennium eased the ecological shock and painful eastward migration, Comfortable settlement in the Ganges plain turned the civilization once again toward spirituality, as evidenced by the metaphysical speculations in earliest Upanishads in Rig Veda. These speculations date back to 1000 BCE after a ritualistic period when the Aranyakas were composed. With Upanishads, the evolution of Indian spirituality from polytheism to monism with its key concepts of Atman and Brahman may be said to have been be completed. Throughout this period, Indian civilization did not experience overt conflict between religion and science.

Legal system: A formal religious code (that is, the Manu code), let alone a legal code, were still yet to emerge, in part because the caste system and religious education provided the framework to mold behavior into socially acceptable forms.

Social structure: Social structure was increasingly governed by a caste system with overlaid class distinctions. The wealth increasingly came into the hands of commercial caste. There was little opportunity for the lowest castes to break out. The metaphysical speculation, with concepts of reincarnation and karma, led to the caste structure and laid the foundation of an entrenched social inequality based on birth that has only recently begun to break down. Thus, a caste system was hardening during the Ganges period, even though monism never sanctioned it explicitly, as is evident in early Upanishads.

Knowledge-creating and educational institutions: Knowledge creation continued to be based on individual motivation and interest. Academies run by gifted teachers multiplied, particularly toward the end of the period. These academies functioned as both educational and knowledge-creating institutions in spiritual and practical matters, such as military technology. However, astronomical sciences in particular seemed to have been the monopoly of the Brahmins who were in the royal service.

Wealth allocation process: The spiritual orientation of tolerant monism prevented excessive allocation of sustainable surplus to personal luxuries. The royalty carried on a tradition of renunciation of power and wealth in favor of a spiritual life. There was little danger of external attack, so military expenditures were also small. Wealth allocation remained focused on practical creativity and religious matters.

Social cohesion process: The concept of dharma, social custom, epics of *Ramayana* and *Mahabharata*, religious doctrines of karma and reincarnation, and the resulting caste system provided social cohesion. There was no slavery or excessive use of physical force to ensure social cohesion.

Internal wars: The internal wars among the various states were modest during this period, and wars were fought based on accepted rules and did not involving looting or extortion from the population.

Formative Beliefs and Ideology at the End of the Protoscience Phase

As we discussed in the theory chapters, the attitudes of a civilization toward knowledge are shaped largely by its religious beliefs and state of abstract systems capability. Its social conscience or attitudes toward fellow citizens and other social orders are determined by a struggle between instincts on the one hand and its natural bounty, religious beliefs, early experience with nomads, and the nature of greed its institutions harbor on the other.

As we examine the evolution of Indian religious thought from crude polytheism to sophisticated monism that resulted in concepts of reincarnation and karma, significant evolution of abstract systems-building capability, and limited, peaceful experience with other social orders, it is relatively easy to rationalize the following formative beliefs and attitudes the Indian civilization developed through the long protoscience phase:

- The possibility of practical knowledge, tempered by emergence of excessive spirituality derived from monism; spirituality that claimed supernatural powers based on meditative concentration.
- The caste system sanctioned by concepts of reincarnation and moral law of karma; a belief that impacted the emergence of the concept of political, social, and economic equality.
- Openness toward other social orders based on fair trade and creative exchange.
- Nonviolent interaction with other social orders derived from its abundant natural bounty and tolerant religiosity.

We will discuss these remarks later in the chapter when we discuss the inner nature of civilizations at the end of the protoscience phases.

11.10 Extrinsic Peaceful Causes

Readers will recall from chapters 8 and 9 that the constructive causes impacting a social order are simply the sum of all relevant constructive outcomes of all **other** relevant social orders. Readers will also recall that constructive causes consist of the exchange of creative outcomes, abstract systems-building capability, innovations in institutional systems, structures and processes, fair trade, and peaceful migrations.

There was little contact between the Chinese and Indian civilizations during the protoscience phase. Only Mesopotamian civilizations modestly impacted the Indian civilization.

Impact of Mesopotamian Civilization

Fair trade: About all that is certain is the impact of trade between Indian and Mesopotamian civilizations. It seems that peaceful migrations and the transmission of creativity occurred out of India to western Asia and not the other way around. The impact of trade, its magnitude, and its composition are not known with any confidence.

Impact on productive outcomes: In the absence of better data, all we can conclude is that fair trade likely had a positive impact on the productive outcomes of the Indian civilization through normal reciprocal fair trade efficiencies.

11.11 Productive Outcomes

Wealth production: During the protoscience phases, one can discern a strong trend in the Indian civilization of increasing the sustainable growing surplus (SGS) despite several significant natural setbacks. The fertile plains; river systems fed by Himalayan snow; gentle, flat terrain; discovery of iron; moderate climate; and rain coupled with eastward expansion drove this growth in surplus. The emergence of great cities and republics as well as an increasing population during this phase is a testimony to this trend. It does not appear that state power either controlled or helped the economic activity through irrigation projects during this period. There was little need for it, in contrast to Egypt, with its single, mighty, unruly river, or Mesopotamia, where geography was constrained by two moderate size rivers.

New products and services: The likely products and services that originated in the Indian civilization during the phase included gold, cotton, sugar, iron, drainage systems, docks, wheels, and cartography, to name a few.

Internal trade: Trade continued to expend as the economic output expanded. India traded extensively with Mesopotamia and to a lesser, uncertain extent with Egypt. International trade even on this scale was hardly possible without an internal network of roads and markets, traders, regulations, and weights and measures. Large cities in the Ganges plains corroborate strong internal trade. Internal trade before 1000 BCE was likely conducted through barter and a reciprocal exchange of goods and likely consisted largely of grain, cloth, and metal artifacts.

11.12 Creative Outcomes

Before we delve into the specific achievements of Indian civilization during the protoscience phases, we want to make a few comments on the Indian oral tradition that became the bedrock of knowledge preservation during the Vedic and later periods. We will then get into the specific creative achievements of the Indian civilization during the phase.

Indian Oral Tradition

We know with reasonable certainty that the Indian civilization did not possess a written script at the time the composition of the Rig Veda (as early as 4500 BCE) began. However, a written script is certainly known to exist in the Harappa phase (starting 3750 BCE), as we have noted above. Thus, right at the outset, inquisitive people of the Vedic period faced the problem of how to preserve and transmit their findings concerning metaphysics, astronomy, mathematics, and philosophical speculations without a written script. They devised a brilliant two-part solution to this dilemma:

- Compress the findings into as few words as possible
- Use the verse form, as it is a very effective aide to memorization

While this solution was effective in preserving their findings in the absence of a written script, it is easy to see how the lack of written script would have made knowledge accumulation slower. However, considering writing had not been invented anywhere yet, there was little choice.

Although the Harappa phase had a developed protoalphabetical script probably before 3000 BCE, the use of oral transmission had acquired a life of its own and continued in part because Indians did not want to entrust their scared books to perishable materials. Further, material accumulated from the millennia-long effort was too vast to inscribe on the stone or clay tablets (in the absence of paper or equivalent material) since their dissemination requiring transport of bulky stone tablets within a 500,000-square-mile area would be impractical. Assigning specific Brahmin families to faithfully commit different sections of the scared books to memory and pass on to the next generation was a practical choice to preserve knowledge at the time; it was also unique and brilliant. It could only have been needed by a civilization with a millennia-long history predating the emergence of writing.

Below, we review the creative outcomes in religious, philosophical, scientific, and artistic arenas and productive outcomes of the Indian civilization without explicitly distinguishing between the Vedic, Harappa, and Ganges periods. Within the scientific arena, our focus will be on three categories of formal sciences (counting and measuring, arithmetic, and alphabetical script), natural sciences (astronomy), biological sciences (medicine), and social sciences (practical ethics, psychology, and astrology).

Achievements in Religious Creativity

Table 11.1 summarizes the religious literature of ancient India. Rig Veda, almost certainly the oldest known record of man's search for knowledge, contains hymns of praise of the gods and metaphysical speculation. It has been called the intellectual counterpart of the colossal Egyptian pyramids that have come down to us from antiquity. Sama Veda includes the hymns selected for singing. Because the Vedic people did not possess a notation to write music, it gives us no clues about the melodies associated with each hymn as they were passed down orally. The transition from the Rig and Sama Vedas to the Yajur and Atharva Vedas probably marked the end of the Vedic period. The simplicity and freshness of the Rig Veda gives way to rituals, spells, and even sorcery and signifies the increasing importance of priests. Brahmanas and Aranyakas continue the same tradition, though to a lesser extent. The former includes rituals for the householder and the latter for the forest dweller, keen on awakening presumed spiritual powers. Brahmanas may mark the transition to Ganges period. Finally, the Upanishads represent a mature reaction to the rituals and mark a transition from polytheism to monism. Thus, one sees a fluid transition from naive polytheism to a ritualistic polytheism to a tolerant monism, with shades of agnosticism, a movement thankfully distinct from the

Table 11.1: Ancient Indian Religious Literature

Book	Composition Date, BCE	Number of Verses	Number of Unique Verses	Equivalent ~Pages(*)	Subject Matter
Rg Veda	4500	10,859	10,859	1,000	Praise Hyms to gods
Sama Veda	4000?	1875	75	< 10	Hyms selected for singing
Yajur Veda	3000 ?	1975	~1,200	120	Scarificial hyms
Artharva Veda	2000?	5977	4,000+	400	Spells, Sorcery, Incantation
Brahamanas	1500?	There are 12 Brahamanas			Ritual text for householder
Arranyakas	1200 ?	There are ~10 Aranyakas			Rtual texts for forrest dweller
Upanishads	900	There are 108 Upanishads			Metaphysical speculation
Brahma Sutras	500 BCE?	555	555	35	Systematised Vedanta
MahaPuranas	500 CE?	440,000	440,000	44,000	History of Creation Political geneologies Phiolosopy/Geography

(*) Assuming 10 versus per page

polytheism to intolerant monotheism developed by West Asian civilizations. The rise of monism and agnosticism in fact provides the philosophical backdrop for the coming birth of science in the Indian civilization that we discuss in the next chapter.

Achievements in Philosophical Creativity

The foundation and perhaps the curse of mature Indian protoscience was the principle of equivalence, that is, unbroken lawfulness of heavenly, terrestrial, and inner psychological worlds on the one hand and its insistence on one fundamental cosmic spiritual reality on the other. Spirit was more fundamental than matter. This apparent conflict manifested itself in several expected forms:

- An early focus on astronomy mixed with metaphysical speculation. The heavenly bodies were treated as gods.
- A ritual of sacrifice, psychological in essence, to access the heavenly gods. This elaborate ritual required an altar whose design, as we noted earlier, reflected their astronomical understanding of the heavens and required invoking sacred verses from Rig Veda, whose structure and organization itself imbedded a hidden code. This again reflected their knowledge of the heavens.
- A system of medicine that was at once holistic and experience-based, completely devoid of shamanism yet considered divine in origin.
- An insight that claimed that a higher inner self was not different from the ultimate external reality. This inner self, which sits higher than the thinking mind, in the absence of strong societal institutions, formed the unshakable foundation of Vedic and subsequent humanism, compassion, and ethics of Indian civilization.
- Development of the pseudoscience of astrology to fill the gap between the heavenly macrocosm and the earthly microcosm. Since the terrestrial middle realm could not be explained by the contemporary social and natural sciences, it was therefore explained by metaphysics of karma and reincarnation and the pseudoscience of astrology.
- Development of a system of meditation to awaken the inherent spiritual powers assumed to exist in man.

Thus, Indian civilization during the protoscience phase marched along two parallel paths: a spiritual path that led to tolerant monism to awaken the presumed inherent spiritual powers and an intellectual path that focused on understanding the natural world through intellectual creativity. The former path at times made exaggerated claims about its possibilities, and the latter was naturally limited by the lack of experimental method during the current phase. The two paths, however, agreed with the principle of equivalence. As a result, Indian civilization never persecuted its religious or intellectual genius. The idea of executing a Plato, a Jesus, or a Galileo would be both unthinkable and laughable in the context of ancient Indian civilization.

Achievements in Art

Apart from pieces of art excavated from the Indus Valley civilization dating back to before 3000 BCE (the famous dancing girl and the proud priest–king are among the earliest known sculptures), not much in Indian art seems to have survived until the Mauryan period, a time span of more than two thousand years. One may draw two possible conclusions from this: Indian civilization did not produce much art or the art it produced did not survive. The former conclusion seems unlikely for a number of reasons: (1) the Indus valley cities survived fortuitously because they were buried underground, (2) art from other millennia also did not survive, and (3) surviving pieces of art and the description of Mauryan architecture by foreigners show considerable sophistication that would be unlikely in the absence of ongoing development or fairly rapid adoption of a foreign artistic tradition, possibly Persian.

It is also likely that after the Sarasvati River dried up and the Indian civilization moved east, it had to reestablish itself and as a result became more rural-based and thus art took a back seat. The balance between performing arts and visual arts has also been different in Indian civilization. Similarly, the role of individual ego on the part of the elite and artists was very different, resulting in the elite not being interested in creating art as a means of promoting self or projecting power and the artists not bothering to sign their works of art. The driving forces of art in most cultures have been either religious, the lifestyle of the elite, or a strong interest in nature or contemporary social life. The main evolution of Indian religiosity during these two millennia was toward tolerant monism focused on attaining self–God union here on earth. It had little need yet to create neither images of gods etched in stone or temple-based architecture.

The spiritually minded Spartan elites were not interested in creating tombs, temples, and palaces during this period. Finally, soil fertility and climate were capable of supporting a large growing population, and it seems that continuous dense resettlements destroyed all old structures, including art objects. That the principal medium of art was wood and not stone until the time of Ashoka, centuries after the current phase, further corroborates this. Wood was abundant on the Ganges plains during this period.

This broad picture of factors affecting Indian art is also consistent with Indian civilization evolving from rural to urban in the Harappa period and back to rural in the early Ganges phase despite many grand cities. Only toward the end of the current phase did urbanization speed up again. It is, however, clear that Indian art during this phase does not reach the heights achieved by the sublime ancient Egyptian art. Egyptian art was driven by religion and the elite lifestyle in an urban setting along the mighty Nile. The Indian mind, on the contrary, was focused on understanding the inner world and was beginning to focus its energies on intellectual understanding the external world only toward the end of this phase.

11.13 Achievements in Science

Sources of Ancient Indian Protoscience

Afghani and Turkish invaders after 1200 CE destroyed most of the libraries and temples that were repositories of ancient books, and in the nineteenth century the British excelled in purposeful distortion of Indian history. Indian civilization has a long tradition of oral transmission dating back to the Vedic period, so its history and traditions have been preserved both through both oral and written means, albeit with an uncertain timeline. This means the chronology, analysis, and interpretation of ancient Indian achievements is a work in process and makes it easier for historians to arbitrarily assign later dates to Indian achievements, thus claiming Greek priority in certain achievements. From a Western perspective, there is a tendency on the part of Indians to assign earlier dates without evidence. The counterargument is that Greek achievements have been analyzed and interpreted to the *n*th degree and made part of a modern mythology over the last two hundred years. These reasons make the study of ancient Indian science more difficult until Indians undertake considerably more research.

The knowledge of a particular field, say astronomy, from ancient India was in the Vedas and the Brahmana or occasionally in a specific treatise devoted to astronomy. There are several reasons for this apparent lack of organization. Perhaps the most important is that modern scholars have not organized the material, long time periods are involved, and uncounted authors contributed to a particular branch of knowledge over millennia. It is difficult to organize material in a rational manner when it is not written down. Table 11.2 cross-references the important source books or systems and the area of intellectual creativity in ancient India.

Commentators tend to view each achievement of ancient Indian science in isolation and without understanding how Indian science would have evolved had its march not been truncated by the Muslim empire builders after 1200 CE and British systematic wealth drainers after 1750 CE and how the ancient Indian achievements would have appeared had they led to modern science. The advance of science changes the meaning of words within a language. As an example, the word *physics* has a precise meaning when used today. Therefore, if the word is used to convey Aristotle's philosophy concerning understanding nature through contemplation *without* experiments and not through contemplation after experiments, then he will

Table 11.2: Philosophy, Religion, and Science in Ancient India
Source Books or Schools of Thought

Area of Knowledge	Vedas (*)	Upanishadic Literarature	Puranic Literature	Jain Literature	Buddhist Literature	Natya Shastra	MahaBharata Ramayana	Ashtadhyai/ MahaBhasya	Nyaya School	Visheshka School	Samkhaya School	Ayur Veda (**)	Yoga School	Artha Shastra
Earliest Date (BCE)	4500	900	1000	500	500	600	2000	700	600	600	600	900	300	300
History	X		X				X							X
Philosophy														
Metaphysics/ Religion	X	X	X	X	X									
Epistemology		X		X	X				X	X				
Aesthetics						X								
Ethics				X	X		X						X	
Formal Sciences														
Mathematics	X		X											
Linguistics	X							X						
Logic			X	X					X	X				
Natural Sciences														
Astronomy	X													
Atomic Theory											x			
Physics											X			
Chemistry											X			
Cosmology/Evolution	X		X								X			
Social Sciences														
Medicine												X		
Psychology													X	
Political theory														X

(*) Four Vedas including Samhitas, Brahamanas, Aranyakas and Vedangas   (**) Including Charaka and Sushrita Samhitas

appear to the reader a larger figure than he really was. The reverse is true for achievements of most ancient civilizations because the words used still have a primarily nonscientific use, and therefore, Aristotle's counterparts will appear diminished by comparison. It is important to keep this distinction in mind.

Achievements in Formal Sciences

We now summarize the achievements of Indian protoscience in the areas of counting and measuring, arithmetic, writing, astronomy, medicine, psychology, practical ethics, and astrology.

Mathematics: The origin of counting and measuring obviously predates the protoscience phases. Separating the number from a collection of similar, real objects was an act of sublime abstraction that probably occurred tens of thousands of years ago, and as most other firsts, it probably occurred in multiple places independently. Counting objects requires integers alone. However, length, area, mass, or time requires a second level of abstraction as these quantities can be subdivided infinitely. One therefore needed to go beyond mere integers to fractions and irrational numbers, thereby successfully reducing the problem of measuring to counting and problem of geometry to arithmetic.

People of Vedic and later periods developed an unmatched ability to perform arithmetic operations such as addition, subtraction, multiplication, and division. Arithmetic, summarized in the Sulbha Sutra, of this period provides wonderful shortcut rules for multiplication. These rules clearly show that Indian civilization had already initiated the development of the place value notational system to represent numbers.

- **Large numbers:** Developed an ability to be comfortable with large numbers. A vocabulary represented extremely large numbers. For example *mahashankh* stood for ten quintillion or ten raised to a power of nineteen!
- **Decimal weights:** The Harappa people used weights and measures based on the decimal system, adding further support to the idea that the decimal number system has ancient roots.
- **Measurement of length:** Harappa people also made strides in accurate length measurement. A ruler with the smallest division measuring just 1.7 mm has been found at a Harappa site.
- **Measurement of time:** Recent discoveries at Harappa also include a pot with a hole at the bottom. The shape and size of the pot imply that the pot may have been used as a simple water clock to measure time.

- **Geometry:** One also finds the beginning of geometry in this period. The Vedic and Indus–Sarasvati protoscientists knew how to calculate areas of square, rectangle, and circle as evidenced by the planned cities they built. They knew properties of the right triangle and pyramid and the formula for the square root of two using the method of continued fraction.

Alphabetical script: The history of alphabetical script as taught in schools today starts with ancient Egyptian hieroglyphs. A writing system consisting of twenty-two hieroglyphs was invented by about 2700 BCE and was followed by a protoalphabet called Canaanite by 1700 BCE. This evolved into Phoenician alphabet by no earlier than the fourteenth century BCE. The Phoenician alphabet is supposed to have formed the basis of the Greek *and* Indian alphabet.

In stark contrast to this bit of linguistic mythology, seals from Harappa dated to 3500 BCE show a protoalphabetical script. These seals, incidentally, also show a reference to Rig Veda. The Harappa script is based on a generic vowel used for words that begin with a vowel. There is an abundance of such words in Sanskrit. This vowel was not used within a word. The inner vowels were still supplied by the reader. We may thus claim that Harappa invented the first protoalphabetical script before the Mesopotamian alphabetical script. Given the trade between Sumer and Harappa and the close contacts between Sumerian and Egypt, new research without any preconceived notions is needed to understand the flow of inventions concerning alphabetical script.

Achievements in Natural Sciences

Astronomy: Astronomical observations and speculations were driven by the twin objectives of the need to mark seasons and to determine the auspicious timing for the ritual of sacrifice (of self).

- The *Vedanga Jyotisha:* This earliest known astronomical work likely dates back prior to 1000 BCE. It provides rules for predicting positions of the planets, sun, and moon and established rules for observing these heavenly bodies. Recent research shows that astronomers at that time knew the twelve signs of the zodiac, seven planets, twenty-seven constellations, and predicting eclipses. The chief purpose of the *Vedanga Jyotisha* was to ascertain auspicious times for important events based on the position of heavenly bodies. This was hardly surprising for the times. However, it is important to note that this was the first time the human mind had actually used mathematics to predict a natural phenomenon. That there were many errors in their computations is not important. What is important is their discovery that observation and quantitative logic was combined to predict a natural phenomenon.

- **Stars as suns:** An old Sanskrit verse in Rig Veda states, "Sarva Dishanaam, Suryaha, Suryaha, Suryaha," which means that there are suns in all directions. This verse, which describes the night sky as full of suns, indicates that in ancient times Vedic astronomers had arrived at the important discovery that the stars visible at night are similar to the sun visible during daytime. In other words, it was recognized that the sun is also a star, though the nearest one. This understanding is demonstrated in another verse, which says that when one sun sinks below the horizon, a thousand suns take its place.

- **Zodiac:** As mentioned above, the background stars or the celestial sphere was divided in two ways. One was based on the apparent motion of the sun from south to north and back into twelve zones, and the second was based on the motion of moon into twenty-seven Nakshatras as the moon takes about twenty-seven days to complete a rotation around earth.

- **Precession of the equinox:** During the time of the Vedas around 4000 BCE, the vernal equinox was observed and recorded in the constellation Mrigasari (Orion) and during the time of Brahmanas around 1900 BCE in the constellation Krtttika (Pleiades). These observations show an awareness of the precession of the equinox.

- **Heliocentric model:** The earliest known concept of a heliocentric model of the solar system in which the sun is at the center of the solar system and the earth orbits around it is found in several texts. Yajnavalkyaa (1000 BCE) in Shatapatha Brahmana recognized that the earth was round and believed that the sun was "the center of the spheres," as described in the Vedas at the time. His astronomical text in Shatapatha Brahmana (8.7.3.10) stated: "The sun strings these worlds—the earth, the planets, and the atmosphere—to himself on a thread." He recognized that the sun was much larger than the earth, which would have influenced this early heliocentric concept. He also estimated the relative distances of the moon from the earth as 108 times the diameter of the moon and the diameter of sun as 108 times the diameter of earth, based, no doubt, on data from total solar eclipses. The Aitareya Brahmana (ninth to eighth century BCE) states: "The sun never sets nor rises. When people think the sun is setting, it is not so; they are mistaken." This indicates their knowledge that the sun is stationary and the earth is moving around it.

- **Age of the universe:** Ancient Indian civilization was perhaps the only civilization that deeply reflected on the cyclical nature of the universe. They estimated the length of this cycle to be billions of years by a fortuitous coincidence, as explained in appendix G. It happens to be close to the modern estimate. Multiple models for the solar system with unresolved viewpoints were proposed: one view stated that the sun never rises or sets, which meant that the earth rotated though it was not specified whether earth rotated on an axis or around the sun or both. One presumes that the former was implied and was interpreting the phenomenon of a precession of the equinox as sun's apparent slow rotation with respect to fixed stars. Using this mixture of fact and fiction, ancient Indians computed the age of the universe to be 4.32 billion years versus the modern estimate of 14 billion years. The contrast to 4004 BCE as the birth of universe in the bible two millennia ago is telling.

- **Calendar:** A lunar calendar was developed with thirteen months. Based on his heliocentric model, Yajnavalkya proposed a ninety-five-year cycle to synchronize the motions of the sun and the moon, which gives the average length of the tropical year as 365.24675 days, which is only six minutes longer than the modern value of 365.24220 days. This estimate for the length of the tropical year remained the most accurate anywhere in the world for over a thousand years. The calendar in ancient India was based on the 2,700-year Ursa Major or the Saptarsi cycle with a beginning date of 6776 BCE, a date whose use was confirmed by Greek historians (Pliny and Arrian) during Mauryan times. (Aryabhata reset the beginning date in the fifth century CE to 3076 BCE based on a redefinition of the starting constellation from Aswini to Magha, or 900 years, and subtracting one full 2,700-year cycle. Aryabhata did so to coincide the beginning of the calendar with his estimate of the Mahabharata civil war, an event of great political and religious significance marking the beginning of the so-called kali Yuga. The Saptarsi calendar with this beginning date of 3076 BCE is still used in parts of India.)

Achievements in Biological Sciences

Medicine: The Indian system of protomedicine codified in Yajurveda was divided into eight branches:

1. Internal medicine: Kayachikitsa Tantra
2. Surgery: Shalya Tantra,
3. Ears, eyes, nose, and throat: Shalakya Tantra
4. Pediatrics: Kaumarabhritya Tantra,
5. Toxicology: Agada Tantra
6. Reproductive medicine: Bajikarana (or Vajikarana) Tantra

7. Health and longevity: Rasayana Tantra
8. Spiritual healing/psychiatry: Bhuta Vidya

- Physical health was perceived to be a result of the balance between three humors called vatta (wind), pitta (bile), and kapha (phlegm). Similarly, mental health was a result of a balance between sattva (ethics), rajas (actions), and tamsic (base desires) mental elements. These mental elements may be considered to parallel superego, ego, and id respectively. Patient evaluation was based on what is pratyasha (observation) and anuman (inference).

- The approach was holistic and employed a wide range of techniques, including dietary recommendations, herbal medicine, surgery, massage, and purgatives to cleanse the body.

- There was a Guru Kulum system to train doctors based on a one-on-one teacher–pupil training and the exchange of information among doctors. There was also a constant effort to bring the domestic and tribal remedies into the mainstream through the vaidyas or physicians. Finally, for mental health and physical health, the science of yoga was conceived, which progressively led the person from physical to mental health and onwards to spiritual health.

- The herbal medicine of Ayurveda required a thorough knowledge of plants and their classifications. For example, the Atharvaveda divides plants into eight classes, Visakha (spreading branches), Manjari (leaves with long clusters), Sthambini (bushy plants), Prastanavati (which expands), Ekasrnga (those with monopodial growth), Pratanavati (creeping plants), Amsumati (with many stalks), and Kandini (plants with knotty joints).

Biology: A classification of the plant kingdom, probably a first, was also summarized in Taittiriya Samhita and classifies species into vrksa, vana, and druma (trees), visakha (shrubs with spreading branches), sasa (herbs), amsumali (a spreading or deliquescent plant), vratati (climber), stambini (bushy plant), pratanavati (creeper), and alasala (those spreading on the ground).

Though experience-based, the hallmarks of the protoscience of Vedic and later medicine was a lack of controlled experimentation, combination of the natural and the spiritual treatment, and a unity of the three realms of body, mind, and spirit.

Achievements in Social Sciences

Psychology: In ancient Indian psychology, consciousness was the subtlest and deepest part of our being: more subtle than the body, brain, emotions, and thoughts. This center of our being never sleeps: it is always present. How do we know this? The sages observed that we have at least three empirically observable states of consciousness: waking, dreaming, and dreamless states. The waking state is dominated by the presence of senses, the dreaming state by the absence of senses, and the dreamless state by absence of thought, emotions, and will, or a complete absence of mental activity. We know the third state in retrospect, after waking from dreamless state. Earliest Upanishads teach that this third state is close to a state of bliss of a negative sort: a complete absence of the pair of opposites. Upanishads further asserted that behind the drama of these three states is the ever-present, unbroken witness or eternal self that makes the three states possible. This eternal self gives us a sense of being and is capable of infinite being, joy, and knowledge. Realization of this higher self became the highest goal of life of these oldest *Homo sapiens* psychologists.

Practical ethics: The rising complexity of social relationships due to an increasing division of labor during the protoscience phase on the one hand and a relatively immature state of social and political institutions on the other required a more sophisticated formulation of both personal and business ethics, with religious sanction to encourage voluntary compliance. The alternative modern approach based on rational self-interest and punishment requires a rational understanding of the social processes and stronger institutions that simply did not exist during the protoscience phase. Thus, on the personal level, we see the formulation of the concept of dharma or righteousness. Since the wall separating the personal and business lives was weak, in general, business ethics were nearly indistinguishable from the demands of personal ethics. Dharma thus codified the social norms and ideals with a religious sanction and did not rely on a legal code or judicial system.

Astrology: The phase of protoscience in Indian civilization also saw astrology and associated pseudo-sciences like palmistry and numerology emerge. As indicated above, astrology filled an important gap between an increasing understanding of a lawful heaven through astronomical observations and a mind capable of reason on the one hand and a near total absence of social sciences to explain the "fate" of the individual on the other. Using concepts of karma and rebirth as the basis, the pseudoscience of astrology was developed to explain the material human condition here on earth. The basic architecture of the pseudoscience of astrology in all civilizations, including Indian, was essentially the same: using astronomy, the position of selected planets, moon, and sun in the zodiacs (sun- or moon-based) at the time of an individual's birth or at the time of an important life event was calculated. The planets, moon, and sun were given both positive and negative psychological, social, and familial attributes as well as relative powers. Depending on the lineup of these heavenly bodies at the time of birth or an important life event, the outcomes were predicted. In the Indian version of astrology, a distinction was made between accumulated karma and action karma, which provide the astrologer a failsafe cover in case his predictions did not come true. This leeway was made possible since the positive fruits of karma in this life may be sufficient to compensate the negative fruits of accumulated karma over previous lives.

Summarizing Achievements in Abstract Systems-Building Capability (ASBC)

As noted in chapter 7, the breakthroughs in ASBC mostly reside in formal and natural sciences and philosophy. Clearly, by the end of the phase, the ASBC of the Indian civilization was highly advanced as it included alphabetical script and a mastery of the creative method.

History, Causes, and Outcomes of the Mesopotamian Civilization

11.14 Brief Political History (4400–1000 BCE)

Preliterate civilization, by our definition, may be said to have taken birth in Mesopotamia in the Uruk period starting around 4400 BCE. Following this, there was a long period that resulted in the emergence of the powerful Sumerian city-states by 2900 BCE at the start of Bronze Age. The wheel was in use at the beginning of this period and Cuneiform toward the end. The Sumerian power lasted until about twenty-fourth century BCE, followed by the short-lived Akkadian Empire (twenty-fourth to twentieth century BCE), followed by an equally short period of Sumerian resurgence (twenty-second to twentieth century BCE). Sumerians then yielded to the Assyrians (twentieth to eighteenth century BCE) and Babylonians (eighteenth to seventeenth century) who in turn yielded to a relatively long Kassite rule from the sixteenth to the twelfth century BCE. Mesopotamia now entered the Iron Age probably based on discovery of iron in India and was ruled by Hittite dynasties (eleventh to seventh century BCE) and again by Assyrians (tenth to seventh century BCE).

The three significant states of Sumer, Babylonia, and Assyria and the corresponding periods may be said to constitute the successive incarnations of the Mesopotamian civilization, just as Mehrgarh, Vedic, Harappa, and Ganges periods constitute the four periods of ancient Indian civilization. Although they were materially different from one another in some respects, one can see continuity in all three. Mesopotamia was home to many cities, such as Ur, Lagash, Nippur, Babylon, and Ashur. Throughout its long history, Mesopotamia oscillated between centralized modest-size empires and small independent city-states constantly at war with one another.

There is uncertainty regarding where Sumerians came from. They were likely people of the east, entering Mesopotamia from the north and slowly making their way south along the Tigris and Euphrates Rivers, establishing themselves on the land between the two rivers. Babylonians were a melding of Sumerians and Akkadians, a Semitic tribe. The Assyrians, however, included Babylonian, Akkadian, Mitanni, and Hittite stocks and thus carried a greater proportion of nomad and foreign blood. The south, home of Babylon, was more fertile because of the rich soil brought by the rivers during the rainy winters. Mesopotamia as a whole covered an area of less than fifty thousand square miles and probably had a peak urban population of a few hundred thousand, counting all cities. In physical scale, Mesopotamia even at its height resembled more a state than a civilization.

11.15 Natural Causes

In our judgment, natural causes played a significant role in the long evolution of Mesopotamian civilization. Climate change, while instrumental in giving birth to the Mesopotamian civilization (rising sea level by up to two meters around 4000 BCE created a warmer climate more suitable to the development of agriculture) was relatively unchanged after that. Of all the ancient standalone river valley civilizations, the geography of Mesopotamia was unique in certain important aspects. It did not have the protection of the high mountains (Indus) or extreme desert (Egypt) or mostly mountainous terrain (Yellow River). In addition, the fertile plains of Mesopotamia were relatively smaller. These geographical features profoundly affected the relationship between the settled people and nomads around Mesopotamia a lot earlier than in the case of other civilizations. The area was the meeting ground of Semitic nomads from the west, central Asians from the north, and Indo-Aryans groups from the east. The continuing geographical proximity of nomadic threat never quite allowed the civilization to settle down militarily. In other words, the nomads were never too far from the civilized states or city-states in Mesopotamia, particularly after the Sumerian phase. Nomads have, of course, always existed just around the corner from civilizations, patiently waiting for the opportunity to pounce on civilizations. Only this was more so in ancient Mesopotamia, and it happened earlier and more frequently.

11.16 Intrinsic Causes

Institutional Systems Structures and Processes

Political system: Early on, each city was ruled by a priest-king. Later, powerful kings knitted the city-states into centralized states numerous times. The city-states were typically independent, self-sufficient, and resisted unification, a model the Greeks later followed. At least twelve major city-states have been identified during its long history. The significant unified states of Sumer, Babylonia, and Assyria were all ruled by strong absolute monarchs who believed in the divine right of kings. In the concept of the divine right of kings, we see an early instance of political and religious elements merging. One finds the towering figures like those of Hammurabi, Gilgamesh, and Ashurbanipal, who would tolerate no dissent and no shades of gray.

Military capability: Given the constant warfare among city-states, it is not surprising that Mesopotamia excelled in military technology and techniques. During the latter part of the peaceful interaction era, the armies were typically foot soldiers with metal helmets and wicker shields. They carried spears and axes. They also used an early version of two- or four-wheeled chariots and used wild donkeys. Mesopotamians were familiar with laying siege, phalanx formation, and defensive mud brick walls, but these were usually ineffective in protecting the cities under attack.

Economic system: Priests, who were also by far the biggest merchants and financiers, controlled the Mesopotamian economy. As trade expanded, Sumerians started using different tokens to represent different economic goods being traded in an effort to quantify the goods; later they began to draw the token shape on clay balls. Over time this led to the so-called cuneiform script, which helped expand the commerce even more. The taxation was heavy, uneven, and in the name of gods. The Babylonian state knew how to mine and process gold, silver, iron, copper, lead, and oil. (In the fourth century BCE, Alexander was incredulous on hearing about a liquid that burns. He did not hesitate to cover a young boy with the liquid and ignited him by torch.) Unfortunately, we do not know the specifics of trade with Egyptian and Indian civilizations and the extent of its impact on Mesopotamian economy. Mesopotamia lacked stone and timber; as a result, the houses were built from sun-dried mud bricks.

The basis of wealth creation was broad and centered on small cities with surrounding farmland both near and far from the Tigris and Euphrates. Cities farther from the rivers required an irrigation system consisting of canals, ditches, and dikes, which required significant annual maintenance typically achieved through forced labor.

Agriculture was supplemented with cattle, fishing, and hunting. Fertile soil quickly led to a food surplus, which in turn led to a flourishing nonagricultural sector. Both sectors in turn led to internal and external trade. Interestingly, Mesopotamian civilization was essentially urban because of the size and terrain of the area and the existence of many small independent cities with surrounding farmland. By one estimate, 89 percent of the population lived in the cities, making it the first urban civilization.

Systems of religious faith: The Mesopotamian states were theocratic in nature, with state and religion in collusion. The religion was polytheistic, with one count of gods supposedly numbering sixty-five thousand. The temples, and not the palace, were the center of the cities and center of both learning and worship. Around 2000 BCE, Mesopotamians began building temples on Ziggurats to link heaven and earth. Ziggurats were pyramid structures that supported the temples. Mesopotamian gods behaved much like people, with similar emotions. Mesopotamians wanted to treat the gods and goddesses right because they provided everything. Each city had a main god and many lesser gods. The belief in the afterlife in Mesopotamian civilization existed, and everybody went to the "Great Below" after death regardless of his or her social status or actions during life. There was considerable emphasis on omens and divinations. For instance, one text states that if a man has a flushed face and his right eye is sticking out, he would be devoured by dogs far from his house!

During the early part of the phase, the emphasis was on practical creativity, and there was little conflict between religion and protoscience. However, later in the phase, intolerant religious practices tending toward monotheism took hold, partly to maintain social cohesion, and the possibility of science-religion conflict raised its ugly head. This set the stage for such conflict to become a central fact of later West Asian and European civilizations.

Legal system: Hammurabi gave the first formal legal code to the world and claimed it descended from the gods as Moses was to do a nearly half a millennia later. The code covered commercial law, family law, and even sexual conduct in detail. It allowed men to indulge in sex outside of marriage but not women and severely punished incest, for example.

Social structure: Socially, the Mesopotamian society allowed slavery, and women definitely held a lower status, often secluded in their own homes. There appears to have been considerable wealth polarization in Mesopotamian states. The class conflicts in the Mesopotamian states resulted from the feudal system of ownership of limited land and control of commerce by priests. The principal classes were the political-religious elite; the middle class, consisting of small businessman, physicians, and scribes; the lower-class farmers; and a significant slave population. There was excessive inequality the feudal system, and the priest-kings created and amplified wealth polarization with the state and religion, providing the legal, physical, and moral power to enforce the wealth disparity.

Knowledge-Creation and education institutions: Knowledge creation was the implicit domain of priests and craftsmen. The former focused on religion, astronomy, and writing and the latter on practical technology. Mesopotamia may have been the first civilization to have formal schools in cities, called Edubbas, where scribes learned how to use the cuneiform script. Contrary to common perception, these schools, however, cannot be characterized as either knowledge-creating or even knowledge-disseminating educational structures. They were in realty accounting schools serving mainly the needs of commerce.

Wealth allocation process: There was considerable spending on the military as well as on monuments, temples, and luxuries, such as the famous hanging gardens of Babylon, where a screw pump was used to transport the needed water; the famous tower of Babel is supposed to have been 650 feet tall and had seven stages. Military spending was necessitated by the nomadic threat and the desire to expand and consolidate the city-states. Babylonians, particularly toward the end under Chaldeans dynasty began to shift surplus toward the intellectual creativity, which was driven by religious/astrological motives, as we shall discuss in the next chapter. Thus, wealth allocation went through several phases.

Social cohesion process: Social cohesion was maintained through formal legal code, religion, and physical force in the later periods. The superior military strength of the victorious state generally tamed the centrifugal force of both internal fighting and nomadic invasions.

Internal wars: Internal wars were fought unabashedly for commercial reasons to control silver mining, for example. States fought very destructive wars to the bitter end and typically with considerable destruction. This type of conflict meant that it took longer for civilization to recover from internal wars and made it nearly impossible to reduce military spending.

Formative Beliefs and Ideology at the End of Protoscience Phase

As we examine the relatively stagnant religious thought, significant evolution of abstract systems-building capability, and substantial, continual wars with nomads, it is relatively easy to rationalize the following entrenched beliefs and attitudes the Mesopotamian civilization developed at the end of the long protoscience phase:

- A belief in the possibility of real knowledge through a union of data and reason, tempered by polytheism that bordered on superstition
- An entrenched class system that priests and merchants dominated
- A belief in the open interaction with other social orders
- A belief in violent interaction derived from its limited geography, lack of religious tolerance, and greed of its institutions controlled by priest-financiers

We will pick up on these remarks later in the chapter when we discuss the inner nature of Mesopotamian civilization. Even though the Mesopotamian civilization ceased to exist after 550 BCE, these formative attitudes and beliefs are significant in the broad evolution of civilization since they were passed on to derivative civilizations in West Asia and Europe.

11.17 Extrinsic Peaceful Causes

Mesopotamian civilization was strongly impacted by the Indian and Egyptian civilizations during the protoscience phase.

Impact of Indian Civilization

Channels of transmission: It is likely that migrations from India to west Asia occurred in the wake of natural disasters during the Indus period around 2000 BCE. These migrations are referred in the Hittite-Mitanni treaty dating from the middle of the second millennium. These migrations and the already established Indian-Mesopotamian trade likely resulted in transmission of knowledge from India to West Asia.

Transmission of creativity: This occurred mostly in mathematics and astronomy.

- **Mathematics:** Recent research has shown that Babylonian mathematics originated in the Indian Sulbha Sutra (literally, mathematical shortcuts) and was transmitted to Babylon. Siedenburg (1978) concluded that either Babylonians learned rules of arithmetic and early geometry from Indians, or they both learned geometry from a third source before 1700 BCE. In his day, Vedic civilization was generally thought to not exist before 1500 BCE; however, with the Aryan invasion theory essentially dead, one must draw the inevitable conclusion that that Babylonians learned early arithmetic and geometry from Indians, and later, the Greeks learned from Babylonians. Certainly, the existence of the Mesopotamian-Indian trade discussed below would make it a probable phenomenon. Seidenberg found that the theorem of Pythagoras was used in the construction of the altars. He concluded that Vedic altar construction techniques were the basis of the first breakthroughs in geometry and algebra, noting the religious impetus behind the rise of mathematics. This is not an extreme view, since the later breakthroughs in algebra and mathematics too resulted from an unusual source—Panini's grammar, as we shall discuss in the next chapter.

- **Astronomy:** Several ideas support the hypothesis of the flow of astronomical knowledge from India to Mesopotamia in the second millennium: the ratio of the longest to shortest daylight period in Mesopotamian texts is equal to 1.5, which corresponds to that in the Indian texts (even though Mesopotamian local value is closer to 2). The use of the lunar day or the notion of tithi and linear zigzag function in determining the length of daylight for the in-between months appear to be of Indian origin.

Fair trade: One of the earliest examples of significant trade between civilizations was between Mesopotamia and the Indus valley as early as 3500 BCE. This sea-based trade occurred through Lotham, in Gujarat, India, as recent excavations demonstrate. We do not fully know what was traded or the specific impact of this trade. The trade between India and Mesopotamia, which involved travel of sailors and merchants, was probably a significant conduit for diffusion of ideas and inventions.

Peaceful migrations: The Mitanni Kingdom that existed in Mesopotamia during 1500 to 1300BCE had a distinct Vedic religion, including Vedic gods such as Mitra, Varuna, and Indra, as well as language with strikingly common words. This is believed to be of direct Indian rather than Iranian influence. In all likelihood, it was not just the language that the Indo-Aryans, such as Mitanni, took with them to Mesopotamia!

Impact on productive outcomes: Impact of trade can occur through two channels. First, trade can create economic efficiencies through the principle of comparative advantage, and the introduction of new products and fair trade usually works out to the benefit of both trading partners. Second, trade never comes alone. Trade is mediated through people at either end and in between. This sets up a super channel for transfer of more than just goods and is far more effective than possible through diffusion unaided by trade. However, there is no record of trade followed by of technology that would impact productive outcomes at both ends, though we believe it must have occurred.

Impact on creative outcomes: There is little known creativity in mathematics and astronomy in Mesopotamia before 1700 BCE. Thus, if the Seidenberg hypothesis is correct, Indian civilization may have been responsible for instigating advances in mathematics and astronomy to Mesopotamia. It is reasonable to hypothesize that trade spurred economic activity on both sides, which in turn increased the likelihood of increased allocation to intellectual creativity.

From Egyptian Civilization

Channels of transmission: It has been proposed that the Egyptian civilization was an offshoot of the Sumer civilization or was at least strongly influenced by Sumer in its birth. However, about a millennium later, after the age of great pyramids, Egypt influenced Mesopotamia in significant ways. This interaction also occurred primarily through trade.

Transmission of intellectual creativity: We do not know with certainty when alphabetical script was invented. We know that Egyptian civilization had invented hieroglyph writing, which combined elements of logograph and alphabetical writing as early as 4000 BCE. Indian civilization during its Harappa phase had a proto alphabetical script around 3200 BCE or earlier. Mesopotamian civilization had invented a logograph known as cuneiform for commercial purposes by 3400 BCE. Scholars cannot definitively trace the diffusion of writing systems across civilizations, and some believe that the roots of cuneiform are in Egypt, though other scholars dispute that and believe the reverse happened.

Transmission of religious creativity: The Semitic tribes first emerged in history in Egypt as slaves that were rescued by Moses in an exodus across the Red Sea that landed them in the land between the Egyptian and Mesopotamian civilizations by about 1300 BCE. For over a millennium, these tribes stayed in the modern Palestine area building the city-states of Judah in the north and Israel in the south. The Kingdom of Israel was destroyed by Assyria in the eighth century BCE, and Babylonians destroyed the kingdom of Judah a little later. For over two millennia, until the founding of Israel in 1948, Jewish people have existed as a diaspora in the interstices of European and Muslim civilizations. The essential significance of Jewish tribes in the protoscience phase was the introduction of monotheism in the Mesopotamian region. Jewish slaves were probably first exposed to the idea of monotheism as originated by Ikhnaton in the sixteenth century BCE.

Fair trade and migrations: Significant trade is said to have occurred between Egypt and Sumer, impacting the economies of both.

Impact on productive outcomes: There was little impact of Egyptian civilization on Mesopotamia except possibly in irrigation techniques.

Impact on creative outcomes: As noted above, in both linguistic and religious creativity, Mesopotamia was strongly influenced by Egypt, just as it was influenced by Indian civilization in mathematics and astronomy.

11.18 Productive Outcomes

Wealth Production

Mesopotamian geography required irrigation using canals, dams, and aqueducts and drainage for agriculture near the rivers where land was fertile. Farther away from rivers, the land was dry, uninhabitable, and not good for agriculture. Thus, agriculture required skill, and cities were built on the river banks. Rainfall was unpredictable, and there was an increasing threat of salinity. This increased the importance of domesticated animals as a backup to food shortages and making beer and wine. There was significant variation in the wealth of farmers since land near the rovers was more fertile, and priests who acted as bankers owned a significant portion of land. These conditions, while creating a healthy surplus, kept the population and size of the civilization small and fragmented.

New Products and Services

However, as Mesopotamians mastered the irrigation technology, the surplus increased and stabilized, which led to a significant nonagricultural sector that focused on building temples, working copper, casting bronze, textiles, making glass, and weapons made from metals.

Internal Trade

Internal trade was vigorous, helped by the river-centered nature of the civilization. There is evidence of significant trade with Indian and Egyptian civilizations.

11.19 Creative Outcomes

Practical Creativity

If we are to judge by the opinion of the archeological research establishment, Mesopotamian civilization was a chief source of practical creativity at the dawn of human civilization as summarized in section 11.6.

Achievements in Religious Creativity

Religious creativity in Mesopotamia never went beyond crude polytheism and did not venture into monism, monotheism, atheism, or agnosticism. Religious creativity was fully in service of the state and lacked a direct focus on the existential anxiety. Thus, we do not see a philosophical discourse or a critique of polytheism in Mesopotamian civilization.

Achievements in Philosophy

Achievements in philosophy were not significant. A Babylonian composition known as *Dialogue of Pessimism,* which is a conversation between a slave and master, is considered by some a forerunner of philosophical thought of Heraclitus, Plato, Socrates, and later Greek sophists. However, the dialogue focuses on life's absurdity and is more akin to a social satire and not a philosophical discourse.

Achievements in Art

Much like the three key periods of Mesopotamian civilization, art may be divided in Sumer and Akkadian, Assyrian, and Neo-Babylonian periods.

Sumer and Akkadian art: Painted stone objects dating as far back as five thousand years consisted of exquisite animal and human figurines, both stylistic and representational, as well as cylinders and seals with inscriptions that were carved, molded, or inlaid. The quality and workmanship must be considered comparable to Egyptian art. The relief known as Queen of Night from 1800 BCE must have been an inspiration for Greeks a thousand years later as it appears very "Greek."

Assyrian art: If Sumer and Akkadian art objects were modest in size and refined with deep relief, the Assyrian art was massive and royal in orientation. It consisted of winged animals (typically horses and lions) with stylized, bearded human heads meant for protecting the palaces or wall panels in low relief meant to serve as paintings in a palace. Many wall reliefs depicted combat scenes.

Neo-Babylonian art: The Neo-Babylonian city-state focused more on decorative architecture, such as the famed Ishtar gate with animals in low relief on the walls in glazed colors, though it continued the earlier traditions.

Mesopotamian art not only influenced the Greek art immensely but also the art of the Persians, who conquered Mesopotamia, as we shall note in chapter 12. It is no exaggeration to state that based on archeological findings to date Mesopotamian was one of the earliest birthplaces of sculpture.

11.20 Achievements in Science

Below we summarize the achievements in protoscience. Sumer, Babylonian, and Assyrian contributions during the protoscience phase, as might be expected, were in formal sciences (linguistics and arithmetic) and natural sciences (astronomy, calendar and medicine). Below, we briefly summarize the significant achievements in each of these areas.

Linguistics: Mesopotamia developed a syllabic language written in cuneiform as early as 3300 BCE to serve commercial interests, and it went through a long process of development in parallel with the development of Hieroglyphs in Egypt. Cuneiform required thousands of characters each needed to represent a different object or idea and proved to be an effective means to keep track of the commercial transactions.

Mathematics: Babylonians developed a system of arithmetic calculation based on the number sixty.

Babylonians developed the methods for multiplying numbers using precalculated tables of squares and expressing multiplication as combination of squares of numbers. They did not develop an algorithm for division and were forced to resort to tables of reciprocals. Babylonians knew how to solve the quadratic equation because of their roundabout method of multiplication. Babylonians also knew rules to compute areas and volumes of simple geometric figures. The initial approximation of pi was 3.0 was later revised to $3^{1/8}$.

Astronomy: Babylonian astronomers kept records of eclipses and the rising and setting of stars, planets, and the moon. Thus, they recognized recurring events and were able to develop an approximate relationship between the tropical year and synodic month. They developed a calendar of twelve months and 354 days, adding a thirteenth month as needed to harmonize the calendar with seasons. As we shall discuss in the next chapter, the civilization produced great strides in astronomy under the Neo-Babylonian state; however, the civilization was suddenly absorbed into the rising Persian Empire and came to an abrupt end.

Medicine: There was limited development in medicine, though it was still under strong religious influence. Babylonian physicians successfully convinced the state to divorce medicine from superstition and shamanism. However, it was a different matter to convince the common people, resulting in the continuation of many irrational methods of treatment.

Thus, the creative and productive energies of the Mesopotamian civilization were mostly directed toward commerce and innovations in linguistics, mathematics, astronomy, and art. Not surprisingly, one does not yet detect a mind focused on a critical analysis of religion and philosophy in Mesopotamian civilization.

Summarizing Achievements in Abstract Systems-Building Capability (ASBC)

Clearly, by the end of the phase, the ASBC of the Mesopotamian civilization was highly advanced as it included alphabetical script and a mastery of creative method.

History, Causes, and Outcomes of Egyptian Civilization

11.21 Brief Political History (3500–800 BCE)

Egyptian civilization has roots going back to 3500 BCE and was likely a result of a fusion of West Asian, African, and possibly Indian stock. They probably learned from the Sumerian civilization. Around 3150 BCE, ancient Egypt got a boost from the genius of Imhotep, who was Egypt's first protoscientist, artist, physician, chief adviser to the king, and architect. The next five hundred years were the age of the great pyramids in Egypt. This age of pyramids ended with Pharaoh Pepi II, who ruled from 2738 to 2644 BCE, and four centuries of chaos followed. That led to the rise of Amenemhet in 2212 BCE. All arts except pyramid building excelled during this period. A canal linking the Nile to the Red Sea and other irrigation systems were built. The wealth of Egypt increased, as did the attacks from nomads. Ultimately, Asian nomads called Hyksos took advantage of a period of disunity and conquered Egypt in 1800 BCE. They ruled for two hundred years.

In 1600 BCE, the Hyksos were driven out in a war of liberation, and Egypt entered its own age of imperialism with a thousand-year war with West Asia and other neighbors. Thutmose III, through a series of fifteen campaigns, made Egypt reign supreme in the Mediterranean world and West Asia in the fifteenth century BCE. The tributes poured into the treasury from all over, and money was directed toward a good life for the elite. A philosopher-king, Ikhnaton, ruled Egypt in the fourteenth century BCE. The empire suffered when this philosopher-king hesitated to use force against rebellious Syrians. He, therefore, did not succeed at holding the empire together. He was followed by the Ramses dynasty for about two centuries and then by a Libyan dynasty for another two centuries. Thus, during its history of three millennia, Egyptian civilization went through five key periods: the pyramid period, the chaotic period, the peaceful and prosperous period, the Hyksos period, and the imperial period. These periods were followed by decline.

11.22 Natural Causes

The origins of ancient Egypt are also uncertain; however, the Sumerian influence on early Egyptian language, architecture, sculpture, and pottery points to possible Sumerian origin or influence. The earliest kingdom rose out of the waters of Nile and the sands of the Sahara around 3500 BCE, through a union of the southern and northern settlements along the Nile by Menes. The result was a fusion of African and Asian racial stocks.

Natural causes played a significant role in the birth and evolution of Egyptian civilization primarily through the mighty Nile. The intersection of the Nile River and the desert conditions it encountered in Northeast Africa defined the unique character of ancient Egypt. For starters, civilization grew in Egypt because the extreme dry conditions meant there was little need to clear the ground for agriculture, and the abundant yet gentle river ensured the possibility of agriculture without dependence on scarce rain on the banks of Nile. It also brought fertile soil each year. However, more important, the surrounding desert required the civilization be confined along the river, and it was dependent on large irrigation projects that could only be undertaken by the state. The river greatly facilitated internal trade. The natural setting also meant depending on foreign sources for certain materials, such as wood. The result of these unique natural factors was a civilization with a highly centralized state along a mighty river providing peace and prosperity, and the civilization was greatly interested in foreign trade very early in human history.

We may judge the natural bounty of Northeast Africa to be low and confined, and it experienced little gradual or abrupt natural changes during the current period.

11.23 Intrinsic Causes

Institutional Systems, Structures, and Processes

Political system: At the top of the political structure was a god–king, followed by a prime minister, who was also the chief justice and finance minister. Next, there was a priest class, which encouraged superstition and corruption and was steeped in ritual. Ancient Egypt was a tightly controlled state made possible not by a strong military but by geography and religion; Egyptians were bound both to the banks of the Nile because of the unforgiving desert and to the rituals because of the priests and superstition. Politically, during long periods of centralized power, pharaohs stood as a godlike colossal, much like the pyramids they commissioned.

Military capability: The Egyptian army was responsible for defense, aggression, and protection of overseas mining operations and trade routes. The army consisted of professional soldiers and mercenaries. The soldiers used bow and arrow, spears, and a sickle-shaped sword. The Hyksos introduced chariots. Often the pharaoh led the army. There were considerable improvements in weapons as Egypt went through the Bronze and Iron Ages.

Economic system: Economy centered on the Nile, with far-flung mining operations run as government monopolies since Egypt lacked a mineral wealth of its own. The pharaoh or landlords owned the land. Farmers paid a tax of up to twenty percent. It has been estimated that most people died in their thirties, and the infant mortality rate was nearly 33 percent. Egyptian workers excelled at many trades, which were passed from father to son. It was an economy under tight government regulation. Ancient Egypt undoubtedly invented the concept of a centrally controlled economy. The scribes in the royal service were an ancient version of bureaucracy that kept track of a highly regulated economy. One could also hire scribes to write contracts or even personal letters. There was a postal system. Chief transport was through the Nile and because of that, roads were not developed, and there was no need to do so. External trade was more developed than the internal trade. It seems that the local population worked the fields and paid taxes, and the state imported raw materials and exported the finished products to maintain a luxurious lifestyle.

Thus, ancient Egypt had two principal means of wealth creation: internal wealth creation based on harnessing the waters of the Nile through dikes and canals and external wealth creation based on importing raw materials and exporting finished goods by the highly centralized manufacturing sector, with commerce controlled by the government. The government did not merely pave the way for the private sector; it was the importer, manufacturer, exporter, and the sole benefactor. Relative to external wealth creation, ancient Egypt went through two stages: until about the middle of the second millennium BCE, the sector could be characterized as based on the fair trade principle. However, after the Hyksos were defeated, Egypt turned imperialistic, and for the next millennium, trade must be characterized as coerced trade. It was not necessarily based on formal control of trade routes and territories; however, Egyptian state power was so dominant relative to the states it traded with that for all practical purposes, the relationship after the middle of second millennium BCE must be characterized as based on coerced trade.

Systems of religious faith: The religious impulse was strong. It was polytheistic, based on a belief in immortality of *both* body and soul. The temples were not generally open to the public. The public worshipped gods at home. Early in Egyptian history, a pharaoh's power was derived from the divine right of kings; however, the role of the pharaoh was later deemphasized, and the priests established a direct relationship to control the masses through oracles, signifying a shift of power from the pharaoh to the priests. The pharaoh continued to remain both the king and religious head throughout Egyptian history despite his changing role.

Thus, religion in ancient Egypt was derived from the god–king pharaoh. It was more directed to fulfill the royal needs and not for satisfying a metaphysical doctrine. As a result, the science–religion conflict was not severe. In Egypt, it was a question of supporting the royalty through practical and religious creativity versus intellectual creativity.

Legal system: The legal system, both criminal and civil, was well developed with local courts, the office of prime minister, and the pharaoh himself as the supreme court. Punishment for crimes was clearly indicated, with the harshest being embalmed alive. Law enforcement depended almost exclusively on the godlike authority of the pharaoh, with the police and army playing little role. Law recognized all citizens as equal before law.

Social structure: Ancient Egyptian society was highly stratified and had a castelike structure. It consisted of slaves, farmers, artists and craftsmen, officials and scribes, priests, noble families, and the pharaoh. Women enjoyed far greater freedom in their personal lives in ancient Egypt than in Mesopotamia. They, however, were not allowed to become part of the administrative class. The society was stratified. Feudal lords and priests formed upper class, the artisans and scribes the middle class, the farmers were lower class, and the captives from wars were the slaves. These slaves provided the labor for building pyramids. The social structure derived its remarkable stability from the authority and godlike status of the pharaoh and a hereditary caste system based social structure. Ancient Egypt practiced slavery only with war captives and not with its own citizens. Overall, ancient Egypt must be judged to have *excessive inequality* given the role of the pharaoh, the castelike social structure, the priests played, and the treatment of noncitizens as slaves. The slaves revolted several times.

Knowledge-creating institutions: Egypt had a thriving class of scribes. However, very much like Mesopotamian civilization, it did not have formal knowledge-creating institutions. It was left to craftsmen, priests, and medicine men to develop new knowledge based on individual effort. One does not detect academies founded by wise teachers in ancient Egypt.

Wealth allocation process: The surplus, made possible by abundant bounty of the Nile and exports, was channeled into the pyramids to ensure an eternal life of comfort for the mighty pharaoh during the pyramid period. Here at the outset of history, we see waste of the precious surplus on a scale as colossal as the pyramids it was used to build. In later periods, the surplus was spent on public works and luxuries for the elites.

Social cohesion process: Social cohesion was made easier by the natural terrain, which allowed a highly centralized state. The godlike status of the pharaoh, the stronghold of religion, the rigid social structure, a written legal code, and the strong role of government in the economy all contributed to social cohesion. There was internal peace, mostly because of the centralized, river-bound longitudinal state made possible by the Nile.

Internal wars: Ancient Egypt was a highly centralized civilization protected by desert, the Nile, and the Mediterranean, and it rarely had internal wars, in part because of its river-entered geography.

Formative Beliefs and Ideology at the End of the Protoscience Phase

As we examine Egyptian religious thought with the concept of the divine right of the pharaoh and a population controlled by superstition, its relatively modest evolution of abstract systems-building capability, and its near complete cultural isolation, it is relatively easy to rationalize the following entrenched beliefs and attitudes the Egyptian civilization developed at the end of the long protoscience phase:

- A weak belief in the possibility of real knowledge through a union of sense data and reason, tempered by a polytheism that often bordered on superstition
- An entrenched caste-like class system dominated by the priest class that sanctioned slavery
- A belief in little interaction with other social orders except to obtain needed raw materials
- A relatively modest belief in violent interaction acquired from nomads who conquered Egypt in the middle of the second millennium BCE that became the basis of Egypt's interaction with minor civilizations for nearly a millennium

We will pick up on these remarks later in the chapter when we discuss the inner nature of Egyptian civilization. Similar to the Mesopotamian civilization, these formative attitudes and beliefs are significant in the broad evolution of civilization since they were passed on to derivative civilizations in West Asia and Europe.

11.24 Extrinsic Peaceful Causes

From the Indian Civilization

Channels of transmission: We have noted earlier that the Egyptian civilization arose by consolidating the Neolithic cultures of Upper and Lower Egypt that had existed since 7000 BCE. It is generally believed that the racial stock of ancient Egypt was African with local variation resulting from gene flow, gene mutation, and natural selection based on geographical and cultural factors. It has also been asserted that the Punt region to which ancient Egypt traced its origin is present day Ethiopia, and the Indus valley people colonized it. That physical characteristics of present-day Ethiopians and Somalis resemble those of Indians is significant. True or not, we cannot describe the impact of the Indian civilization on ancient Egypt with any certainty.

Transmission of creativity: Egypt may have learned about cotton from India. There is considerable similarity between the Indian caste system and the Egyptian social structure, which places priests in the first rank, followed by kings, traders, artisans, and menial workers with a slave-like status. It has been suggested that Egyptian mummies were wrapped in Indian muslin. Terracotta mummies have been excavated in Lotham and Mohenjo-daro, and Indus seal characters have been found on tablets excavated from Easter Island.

From the Mesopotamian Civilization

Channels of transmission: Setting aside the hypothesis that the Egyptian civilization may have roots going back to both Indian and Mesopotamian civilizations, trade was the principal transmission channel after 3000 BCE. Egypt had limited natural resources and thus had great need for trade, and Mesopotamia was richer in natural resources and had a commercial orientation.

Transmission of practical creativity: It would seem that such practical inventions as the wheel originated in Mesopotamia and were transmitted to Egypt but it is difficult to be certain.

Transmission of intellectual creativity: Many scholars believe that the idea of expressing words through written symbols was brought to Egypt from Mesopotamia since

Sumerian script predates Egyptian hieroglyphs according to some scholars. However, recent evidence suggests that the reverse may be true as hieroglyphs may date as far back as 4000 BCE.

Fair trade with Mesopotamia and other regions: Perhaps the most noncontroversial way other civilizations impacted ancient Egypt was through trade, going back to the predynastic period or before 3100 BCE. Trade with Nubia in the south consisted of gold and incense. Pottery was imported from Palestine as early as 3000 BCE. Timber was imported from Phoenicia in the east, and ebony, ivory, and wild animals came from Punt, near present-day Somalia. Anatolia in the north provided tin and copper, while Afghanistan in the far south provided blue stone. Olive oil came from Crete. These imports were paid through grain, textiles, glass and stone objects, and papyrus. This extensive trade must have been accompanied by diffusion of technology, ideas, and inventions. Unfortunately, there is little definitive evidence for it.

Migrations: Trade for key materials and later conquests necessarily meant an influx of different peoples as traders or captured slaves, with the latter providing the labor to build the pyramids.

Impact on productive outcomes: Clearly, cotton, the wheel, and extensive trade had a significant influence on productive outcomes.

Impact on creative outcomes: The outcomes on creative impact depends on which theory one subscribes to regarding the invention of written script. In general, ancient Egypt, despite extensive trade, maintained an insular nature in part because of its geography. In art, architecture, religion, social structure, agriculture, and science, ancient Egypt was both a leader and was insular to others' creativity.

We note that the peaceful though limited interaction among the Indian Egyptian and Mesopotamian civilizations truly formed the Afro-Eurasian old world system for nearly three millennia, with a variable flow of goods, people, ideas, and inventions. The research to date is both incomplete and biased. *This old world interacted without wars among civilizations that essentially lacked ideologies of greed with respect to other civilizations.* All civilizations developed around mighty rivers and interacted through coastal sea trade. This old world served as the springboard for all civilizations in North Africa, Europe, West, North Asia, and South Asia, just as Chinese civilization served as the springboard for all civilizations in East Asia. Had it not been for the Himalayan barrier, all *Homo sapiens* civilizations today might have a single Afro-Asian heritage.

11.25 Productive Outcomes

Wealth production

Like Mesopotamia, Egyptian land was fertile because of new soil brought annually by the Nile. The compliant population was, unlike Mesopotamia, mostly at peace with itself. A strong centralized governance exerted a forceful presence in the economic activity through irrigation projects and fair or coerced foreign trade. Thus, we may assume that Egypt had a growing surplus and increasing wealth.

Internal Trade

Speaking relatively, internal trade was constrained as in other civilizations in part because the state controlled the economy and external trade through duties. Internal trade consisted of grain, fish, beer, oil, vegetables, and textiles. In an earlier part of the phase, trade was in barter form, with grain and oil serving as money. This continued after the introduction of coins in the second half of first millennium BCE.

11.26 Creative Outcomes

Ancient Egypt excelled in art, architecture, technology, and medicine. In addition, it made early contributions to written language and mathematics.

Achievements in practical creativity

Several of the achievements in practical creativity listed in section 11.6 may be attributed to ancient Egypt, including paper made from beaten strips of the papyrus plant. For a while, this was the only writing material until parchment from animal skin was invented.

Achievements in Religious Creativity

The basic religious impulse in Egypt remained polytheistic, and over millennia, the ongoing production of creation myths and the shifting power of gods resulted in an immense, confusing literature. The priests made little attempt to harmonize it.

Ikhnaton, in the fourteenth century BCE, commanded his people to reject polytheism and rituals and embrace monotheism. However, he failed in this attempt. One curious aspect of Egyptian polytheism was its belief that spirit after death still needed body as a physical home to return to. It must be said that with the exception of Ikhnaton, Egyptian religiosity remained trapped in narrow and crude polytheism throughout its history.

Achievements in Art

Egyptian painting embodied simple shapes and lines with little depth perception. However, sculpture was sublimely beautiful and reflected an exacting realism. Undoubtedly, this was the foundation of later Greek art. Egyptian sculpture, like the later Greek sculpture, was painted in vivid colors.

Ancient Egypt was richly endowed with stone. Egyptians were skilled builders of large stone structures, such as pyramids, and effectively used heavy columns and beams to create large temples. The golden ratio was reflected in Egyptian architecture.

Egyptians developed glass material into an art form. A slave who had the misfortune to break a royal glass object could be sentenced to death. They also invented cement and "plaster of Paris." They knew how to mine gold, silver, and tin, among other metals. They also developed the embalming process to an art form.

11.27 Achievements in Science

Linguistics: Egyptians invented a hieroglyphic writing about four thousand years ago that, unlike in Mesopotamia, never fully evolved into the alphabetical script on its own. This phonetic writing system formed the basis of the latter Phoenician alphabet.

Mathematics: Incredibly, ancient Egyptians used a decimal system and were aware of fractions. They had hieroglyphic symbols for some simple fractions. They could multiply and divide by two. Their number notation, however, was cumbersome.

Egyptians excelled in geometry. They were familiar with the Pythagorean theorem and knew how to approximate the area of a circle by squaring seven-eighths of its diameter. They could calculate the volume of a square pyramid. They could solve equation with one or two unknowns and find square roots, thus anticipating an early form of algebra.

Medicine: Medicine was specialized among physicians, who were formally trained in a "house of life" or a medical university. They had a better understanding of anatomy than their Mesopotamian counterparts did. They could set the bones and perform stitches. Dentistry was emphasized since the dental health of the population was poor because the stone-ground flour in their food abraded their teeth.

Summarizing Achievements in Abstract Systems-Building Capability (ASBC)

The ASBC of the ancient Egyptian civilization, after an early leadership, stalled; it clearly mastered the creative method but failed to invent or adopt alphabetical script.

History, Causes, and Outcomes of the Chinese Civilization

11.28 Brief Political History (3000–1000 BCE)

In the Yellow River valley, the earliest Chinese civilization can be traced at least as far back as 3000 BCE, with roots going back several millennia. The three sovereigns and five emperors from 2852 to 2205 BCE were the mythological rulers of China with no written records. There are written bone records on oracle bones starting from about 2200 BCE. They describe the Chinese dynasties beginning with the Xian (2205–1750 BCE) followed by Shang (1716–1122 BCE) and Zhou (1122–256 BCE). Major known cities in ancient China were Eliot, Anyang, Zhengzhou, and Lingjiatan. Adopting the language and culture of the Shang, the early Zhou rulers, through conquest and colonization, gradually extended the Shang culture through much of China north of the Yangtze River. Thus, the Chinese state under Shang and even early Zhou was a result of nomadic and Chinese stock and was about a tenth of the size of present-day China, excluding Tibet. The wars among states in China belong to later periods of Chinese history. Shang troops fought frequent wars with neighboring settlements and nomadic herdsmen from the inner Asian steppes. The last Shang ruler, a despot according to traditional Chinese accounts, was overthrown by a chieftain of a frontier tribe called Zhou, which had settled in the Wei area.

11.29 Natural Causes

Chinese civilization is the oldest living civilization that with a continuous, unbroken, and written memory of its past going back more than four thousand years, with roots in several Neolithic cultures dating back several thousand years. Natural causes played an important role in the birth and early development of Chinese civilization in the Yellow River valley in northern China. The terrain was mountainous, which resulted in producing a hardy people. About 5,500 years ago, a global climate change occurred, and the average temperature dropped by two to three degrees centigrade due to solar activity and changes in the earth's orbit. As a result, the ancient Chinese migrated from the outer areas to the center regions, from highlands to low altitude places that were more comfortable to live in. The base natural bounty in East Asia was high but required greater industry to unlock it, and it experienced continual abrupt changes from severe flooding.

11.30 Intrinsic Causes

Institutional Systems, Structures, and Processes

Political system: The political structure typically consisted of a ruler supported by aristocratic clans that had marriage and personal relationships with the ruling family.

Military capability: Chinese military during this phase consisted of conscripted peasants, who were often ill-trained, and the chariot-riding noblemen. Each was equipped with bronze spears and swords. The army was not suitable for long campaigns, yet it was successful against the settled people called the Donghu in the south and east as well as the nomadic threat from the north and west. China developed professional armies only after the warring states period of the next phase (fifth century to third century BCE).

Economic system: Chinese civilization during the protoscience period was focused on expanding the Chinese state and bringing more land under agriculture, which was difficult because the terrain around the Yellow River was mountainous and frequently flooded. The economy was based on cultivating millet. Ancient China under the Shang supported slavery and coercive labor. However, the extent of slavery was markedly less than in either Mesopotamia or Egypt.

The creation of surplus in ancient China was harder because more of the terrain was difficult to bring under agriculture. China was also under constant attack from the nomads as there was no natural protective barrier in the north and the west. Thus, the Chinese state had to invest considerable resources for defensive purposes. The kings were buried underground in large pits with many of the comforts for the afterlife, though not on the scale of the aboveground pyramids in Egypt.

Systems of religious faith: The religious impulse was ancestral worship coupled with polytheism with a single deity, Di, sitting atop the polytheistic gods and the ancestors. There was no science–religion conflict or excessive spirituality in ancient China.

Legal system: Instead of using law and punishment to control behavior, there was greater emphasis on ethics and custom. There was little attempt to base the origin of law on divine sources. The leaders were expected to set a moral standard and lead by example.

Social structure: Ancient Chinese society was stratified but not completely based on wealth. The nobility were at the top, followed by gentlemen scholars, the peasant, the craftsman, and the merchant–traders. The peasants were held in high esteem but not the merchant–traders. Under Shang, there was slavery, but it seems to have been abolished after that. The position of women was definitely second class. They were considered not worthy of literary education and could not hold any official positions.

With the exception of slavery during the Shang dynasty, excessive inequality did not exist in the ancient Chinese civilization. The roles of customs and tradition appear to have been sufficient to ensure social cohesion. Thus, religion, law, and physical force were markedly less important in managing class conflicts in ancient China. Tradition, reinforced by ancestor worship, ethical rules of behavior, and belief in a heavenly mandate to rule were more important. Periodically, when the excesses of the state and ruling classes crossed the limit, the Chinese civilization underwent an upheaval and succeeded in creating a new political order, as we shall note in the later chapters.

Knowledge-Creating and educational institutions: There were no formal knowledge-creating institutions in China during this phase. Toward the end of this phase, formal school focused on providing ethical and other education.

Wealth allocation process: Overall, the Chinese civilization showed greater wisdom in wealth allocation despite the fact that wealth allocation process was centralized. However, the tax burden was not excessive. The available surplus was directed mainly toward practical creativity and military capability. The absence of extensive monuments from the phase as a whole indicates relatively a rather modest elite lifestyle.

Social cohesion process: The chief means of social cohesion in ancient China were neither religion nor physical force; it was the social values of the importance of family, ancestral worship, and the unwritten ethical contract between the common man and the rulers. Focus on family, ancestors and ethical living ensured a high degree of social cohesion in ancient China.

Internal wars: China enjoyed strong centralized state, and internal wars were not very frequent. Immediately after the current phase ended, China entered the so-called warring states period that we cover in the next chapter.

Formative Beliefs and Ideology at the End of Protoscience Phase

As we examine the simple family-oriented Chinese polytheism; its relatively weak evolution of abstract systems-building capability; its near complete cultural, linguistic, and geographical isolation from other civilizations; and its considerable success in dealing with local nomads, it is relatively easy to rationalize the following entrenched beliefs and attitudes that the Chinese civilization developed at the end of the long protoscience phase:

- A weak belief in the possibility of real knowledge through union of sense data, reflecting its weak abstract systems-building capability

- A relatively modest class system that did not develop either a slavery or caste system
- A belief in insularity bordering on a superiority complex with respect to other social orders
- A strong belief in peaceful orientation toward other social orders unless attacked

We will pick up on these remarks later in the chapter when we discuss the inner nature of Egyptian civilization.

11.31 Extrinsic Peaceful Causes

The Chinese civilization was essentially isolated from the Indian, Mesopotamian, and Egyptian civilizations during the protoscience phases. It thus had no significant constructive causes affecting it.

11.32 Productive Outcomes

Wealth Production

The case of ancient China was a bit different. The center of civilization was the northeast area with its cooler climate, mountainous terrain, and devastating annual floods. Thus, Chinese civilization probably had a greater need for improvements in practical technology before it could harness its natural bounty. This not only explains, in part, the focus on practical creativity and insufficient trade with other civilizations in China, but also suggests a relatively slower increase in sustainable surplus during the current phase. Toward the latter part of the phase when civilization moved south to a warmer climate, the situation eased a little.

Internal Trade

It is difficult to assess the internal trade in ancient China except that it involved cattle, grain, salt, fish, iron, and silk. Rich merchants conducted the trade, despite a lack of good transport facilities. It does appear that earliest form of money used in China were shells and coins made from jade, copper, bones, stone, and pottery. Neither coins nor paper money were used during the current phase.

11.33 Creative Outcomes

Achievements in practical creativity: The unique and outstanding Chinese contribution in practical creativity during the era includes silk, abacus, early forms of sundials, acupuncture, early forms of differential gear as part of a south-pointing magnetic chariot, and herbal medicine. Finally, as if a preview of the Chinese genius of practical creativity to come, the invention of a kite also dates back to the protoscience phase.

Achievements in religious creativity: Most scholars regard Di as a collection of polytheistic gods and not as a monist god. Thus, it appears that Chinese religious impulse did not go beyond a curious mixture of polytheism tending toward monism and ancestor worship.

11.34 Achievements in Science

The scientific achievements of Chinese civilization during the protoscience phase were in the area of linguistics, observational astronomy, practical medicine, and practical arithmetic.

Linguistics: Chinese logo-syllabic script was invented by at least 2500 BCE. A logo-syllabic script is a logograph combined with syllabic signs and determinatives. It would thus be considered a more archaic form of writing compared to hieroglyphics, which included some alphabetical elements.

Observational astronomy: In astronomy, the Chinese astronomers were among the first to record eclipses, cyclical sunspots, and meteoric showers. The relative absence of a belief in the perfection of heavenly bodies as Plato later stated and the absence of a strong belief in these heavenly objects as gods probably played a role in these remarkable achievements in observational astronomy.

Mathematics: The Chinese also invented the abacus, the world's first computer, probably before 750 BCE.

Medicine: Practical medicine also made excellent progress. The invention of acupuncture dates back to the protoscience phase. The Chinese also made significant advances in herbal medicine during this phase.

Summarizing Achievements in Abstract Systems-Building Capability (ASBC)

The ASBC of the Chinese civilization at phase end was not as advanced as Indian and Mesopotamian civilizations. It was more in the Egyptian league as it too mastered the creative method but failed to invent or adopt alphabetical script. The difference, as we shall note in the following chapters, is that while Egypt rectified this shortcoming eventually, China has failed to do so until the present time. It has, however, tried to reduce the impact through conceptual framework developed in other civilizations in areas such as religion and science while historically concentrating its creative impulse on practical technologies.

Summarizing the State of Civilization and Science

It is useful summarize the state of civilizations as a whole at the end of the long protoscience phase before going further. The state of civilization as a whole may be effectively summarized through an overview of political history, creative (practical, religious, philosophical, artistic, and scientific), productive (wealth creation, internal trade), and constructive (exchange of creativity and abstract systems-building capability, fair trade, and peaceful migrations) outcomes. The destructive outcomes in the protoscience phase are not relevant, as the destructive tendencies primarily remained local in nature.

11.35 State of Civilization at Phase End

Overview of the Political History of the Phase

We may note several important aspects of the first phase political history. First, this history mostly is not a written history handed down to us; it is a history constructed in the last two centuries through painstaking research almost exclusively by European scholars (with a clear vested interest) who felt safe promoting dead civilizations and demoting the non-European living civilizations that a few Western European states controlled. Second, all these civilizations were situated in the river valleys. Third, these civilizations remained in relative isolation until about 3000 BCE, and the political interaction after 3000 BCE was both modest and peaceful. However, after 3000 BCE these civilizations had developed a written script, and two of them, Indian and Mesopotamian, completed the development of alphabetical script. All civilizations were ruled by successive monarchies and had a different degree of centralization and the power of the state. Egyptian civilization, due to its geographical setting, was perhaps least fragmented, and Indian civilization, because of its geography and religiosity, was the largest and least centralized.

State of Productive Outcomes

All four major civilizations demonstrated the capability to generate a sustainable growing surplus based on development and absorption of agricultural technologies suited to the differing geographical conditions. There was modest to significant interaction among Indian, Mesopotamian, and Egyptian civilizations through trade and migrations as noted above.

State of Practical Creativity

Undoubtedly, practical creativity made greatest strides during the protoscience phase. Civilization laid the foundations of religious and intellectual creativity; however, achievements in practical creativity reached soaring heights during the phase, as summarized in section 11.6. Perhaps the most significant and earliest invention of this phase was the potter's wheel, which allowed humans to understand the benefits of rotary motion and led to the development of the wheel and more complex tools such as the pulley, drill, and lathe later on. Clearly, the bow and arrow, swords, axe, domestication of horse and elephant, sailing ships, iron, and chariots had critical military significance. There was substantial development in building construction, weaving, pottery, metallurgy and ship-building, and irrigation technologies.

State of Religious Creativity

Practical creativity not only produced the productivity gains needed for the manifold increase in sustainable surplus but also helped sharpen intellectual powers through invention of complex products, processes, and tools. Simultaneously, religious creativity also went into high gear during the protoscience phase to address the issue of existential anxiety. There were two drivers for this new development: growing surplus could support a priestly class focused on this task and the increasing ability of abstract reasoning on the one hand and total lack of scientific explanation of the social and natural phenomenon, including the origin of the world, on the other. Both opened the doors for speculative explanations concerning origin and existence of the world.

Natural polytheism: The first product of this speculative activity was natural polytheism. Essentially, polytheism is a substitution of a god for a social or natural phenomenon that man was unable to explain, such as a fire or thunder, the sun, the planets, and the stars. Thus, these gods were given attributes that would "explain" the phenomenon in question. These lesser gods, however, could not explain the issues about the origin of the universe and, of course, the origin of these lesser gods themselves. Several possible answers to this problem were formulated during the protoscience phase. However, not all were assimilated into major civilizations equally.

God-centered solutions: The first answer is the human soul survives death, and a higher being existed before the universe, lesser gods, and human beings came into existence. This god has existed forever and is responsible for the origin of the universe and any possible lesser gods. This line of thinking took three essential forms or variations:

- **Structured polytheism:** God is greater than the world and is both imminent and transcendent. God may be conceived in multiple, structured forms, such as a trinity (with a division of labor amounting to creation, sustenance, and destruction of the universe) and other lesser gods with specific powers and responsibilities. It was possible for these gods to intervene if the world needed such intervention. Tolerance was shown toward differing conceptions since it was realized that our limited intellects might be unable to definitively describe such a being. The world functioned based on a moral law set by God, and souls reincarnated until they achieved oneness with God. The world also went through cycles of creation, existence, and destruction.

- **Monotheism:** God is greater than the world and is perceived as a transcendent god that could not be conceived in any physical form. This god sent his messengers to earth to lay down the law and judged human beings after death on judgment day based on their behavior on earth.

- **Monism:** God and the world are identical, and it is the purpose of the self to realize it too is no different from the god–world identity. This god–world identity is eternal consciousness and not the matter–energy complex of science.

Thus, two extreme variations of the first answer were monism and monotheism. The former shows in the deliberations of Indian and Chinese civilizations as Brahman and Tao toward the end of the period, and the latter shows up in the religious formulation of the Egyptian civilization and Jewish people, also during the latter part of protoscience phase. Most civilizations were perhaps too preoccupied with practical life to notice that this path from natural polytheism to monism or monotheism simply removed the basic questions of existential anxiety and origin of the world one notch higher, that is, to a question of who created this one god. Monotheism required this belief in one god without proof, and monism claimed that personal experience during higher states of consciousness provided the needed proof of the principle of monism. The value of this religious innovation, however, was perhaps that it gave humans the psychological strength and necessary pause to pursue practical creativity during this phase, though it also allowed religion to often justify excessive class and caste distinctions.

Atheism: The second answer is to deny the existence of any being that humans could not observe, feel, or touch. This approach assumed that the universe either had always existed or came into being on its own. Logically, this position is no different from that of monism or monotheism in that all three are based on a belief without proof. Atheism had the potential to deal successfully with the explanation of the social and natural phenomenon but not the issue of the origin of the world. Indian thinkers speculated about atheism, but it remained of marginal consequence until after the protoscience phase.

Agnosticism: The third answer, of course, is that we do not know and *perhaps* can never know the answer to the question of ultimate origin. This is agnosticism and has the merit of intellectual honesty but may be psychologically and existentially unsatisfactory to some. It does, however, sidestep the overworked dichotomy between faith and reason and between science and religion. We can glimpse agnosticism in the philosophical musings buried in the Rig Veda and later in the early Upanishads within the Indian civilization. Buddha was to enunciate a mature agnosticism as a system a few hundred years after the end of the protoscience phase.

Civilizations, therefore, discovered all the fundamental approaches to the existential anxiety the species felt, with many variations during the protoscience phase.

State of Philosophical Creativity

Philosophy had not yet separated from religion. However, we can detect basic metaphysical, epistemological, and ethical issues being raised in religious systems: origin of existence, origin of knowledge, and ethical rules to live by. Rules of logic were beginning to be understood through early developments in linguistics and mathematics. Similarly, civilizations had begun to understand the necessary and sufficient conditions of the creative process.

State of Artistic Creativity

Most progress was made in the area of sculpture and representational art carved in stone as paper or other media were still to be invented. The concept of perspective was still in the future for most civilizations, as was understanding musical scales. The performing arts, such as drama and dance, no doubt existed in several civilizations.

State of Science

The five-millennia protoscience phase produced remarkable achievements and laid a firm foundation for the coming birth of science. Below, we summarize significant achievements in specific sciences for civilizations as a whole.

Mathematics: The basics of counting and measuring were established. Rules for adding subtracting, multiplying, and dividing were formulated based on a protodecimal system. Extremely large numbers were conceived. The beginnings of geometry and algebra were established, resulting in the ability to calculate the areas of simple figures, such as a circle, square, and rectangle. Unique properties of right-angled triangles were understood.

Logic: Formal logic was yet to be developed and applied to mathematics.

Linguistics: The writing systems progressed from ideographs to logographs to protoalphabetical and true alphabetical scripts over a period of about two millennia. Alphabetical script may be regarded as the greatest intellectual achievement of the protoscience phase.

All major civilizations independently developed writing systems based on ideograph or logographs. The writing systems progressed from ideographs to logographs to protoalphabetical and true alphabetical scripts over a period of more than a millennium starting before 3000 BCE. The sublime invention and subsequent diffusion and adoption of alphabetical script took place in all major civilizations except the Chinese civilization.

Natural sciences: Achievements in astronomy may be classified in terms of *observations* concerning the motions of the planets, moon, sun, and distant stars and using these observations to empirically develop *rules* to predict eclipses and define solar and lunar years. These empirical rules, however, were yet to be based on an all-encompassing theory. There was an awareness of the precession of the equinox based on observations recorded over millennia. The sun was conceived as just another star. The solar system was conceived as heliocentric in one formulation. The fixed nature of distant stars of what we know today as Milky Way galaxy through mapping of zodiacs occurred. Using these observations, several different calendars with differing accuracy were established.

Medicine: In contrast to the distinction between science and practical technology, the distinction between practical medicine and medicine as science can only be drawn arbitrarily in the ancient world. In large measure, medicine remained a practical art essentially down to the nineteenth century. Nevertheless, we may assume that medicine took its first step as a science when the process of disease identification or differential diagnosis started to become rational and organized. Using this definition, although medicine remained a practical art through the protoscience phase, it made significant progress in many civilizations, including such procedures as in vivo dental drilling and dental bridges; acupuncture; limited surgery; wound care, including external poultice recipes; setting broken bones; and mummification. In addition, medicine also evolved herbal treatment, use of shamanism as a cure, the importance of diet in treatment, and the physician as a specialist.

The entire field of medicine was organized into eight branches by physicians of Indian civilization. The three-humor theory of health was proposed long before the Greeks got wind of it. Similarly, psychological health was conceived as a balance between Sattva (superego), Rajas (ego), and Tamas (instincts). Herbal medicine was developed in several civilizations. Medicine took a first step as a science through disease identification or differential diagnosis and started to become rational and organized. Medical procedures, herbal treatments, shamanism as a cure for psychological illness, the importance of diet in treatment, and the emergence of physician as a specialist all developed during this phase. There was an early attempt to classify the plant kingdom.

Astrology: The regularity in astronomical observations, intellectual confusion, and poorly developed natural and social sciences gave rise to the pseudoscience of astrology. Astrology functioned as a method of prediction as well as a way to control the future. The latter was done through pinpointing the auspicious times to execute important events.

Social sciences: The progress in social science was naturally minimal as evidenced by the prominence given to astrology in nearly all civilizations during the phase. A start was made in psychology through attempts to understand consciousness. Three states of consciousness—waking, sleeping, and dreamless sleep—and an ever-present eternal self behind these states were postulated, showing that the science of psychology was fully capable of lapsing into metaphysics. All civilizations made significant contributions toward developing practical ethics, though none was able to shed religious and metaphysical associations.

In summary, protoscience made an excellent start in formal, natural, and medical sciences. One cannot claim or expect the protoscience phase to lay the theoretical foundation for these sciences because even a modest step toward that would constitute the birth and not pregnancy stage of science. The same could not be said of social sciences, as evidenced by the focus on astrology masquerading as social science in all major civilizations.

All four primary civilizations made great but varying contributions to protoscience, even though the archeological research to date is uneven. These four civilizations produced a different mix of art, mathematics, astronomy, medicine, and religion to address existential anxiety. Their contributions prove that all *Homo sapiens* groups that made an early successful jump to a settled way of life in favorable natural conditions displayed uninterrupted but uneven incredible creativity throughout the protoscience phase.

Extrinsic Peaceful Causes or Total of Constructive Outcomes

Exchange of practical creativity: The direct cumulative impact of the transmission of practical technology across civilizations on the sustainable growing surplus was significant, even if it was excruciatingly slow and materialized over millennia. The impact occurred directly through trade or indirectly through individual travel. Most major civilizations by 1000 BCE had picked up many key practical inventions that occurred through a slow diffusion during the standalone era and more conscious and direct transfer during the peaceful interaction eras. Sustainable surplus in major civilizations experienced a steady growth with the diffusion of agricultural innovations and technologies during the phase. An increase in sustainable surplus was indeed the foundation of other forms of creativity, which in turn impacted the surplus.

Exchange of religious creativity: The impact through diffusion of religious creativity on civilizations must be judged relatively minor. It remained localized during the peaceful interaction era mainly because the major evangelizing dogmatic religions in general and monotheism in particular were yet to be fully developed, and the era of extended military conflicts among civilizations was still in the future, though around the corner. Transmission of religious creativity was primarily confined to within the originating civilization during this phase.

Exchange of intellectual creativity and abstract systems-building capability: Diffusion of writing systems, counting and measuring systems, mathematics, astronomical observations, medicine, and astrology across most major civilizations occurred during the peaceful interaction era. It stretches imagination to think that writing systems could diffuse from one civilization to another without diffusion of the ideas these same writing systems were used to convey. The writing systems in general and the alphabetical scripts (3000–1000 BCE) in particular set the stage for potentially dramatic changes in intellectual creativity. However, nearly all major civilizations adopted or developed alphabetical script during the phase, with the Chinese civilization being a notable exception. Much like religious creativity, philosophical creativity did not diffuse outside the orbit of the civilization producing it during the phase to an appreciable extent. On the other hand, the diffusion of art was broader but still remained confined to emerging civilizations derived from Egyptian, Mesopotamian, or Greek civilizations.

Fair trade: As noted above, migrations and trade not only spurred economic activity directly but also were the most important conduits for exchange of ideas and inventions. The trade between Indian and Mesopotamian civilizations was clearly the first well-established, large-scale international trade. Mesopotamians traded extensively with Indian and Egyptian civilizations. Some scholars believe that the Egyptian civilization was an offshoot of the Sumerian state. Egypt had plenty of building stone, copper, lead, and gold but lacked timber and other exotic materials. It imported aromatic resins, ebony, ivory, blue stone, and tin from many places, including Palestine, Anatolia, Greece, and Afghanistan. It primarily exported grain, gold, linen, papyrus, and finished products of glass and stone.

Peaceful migrations: We have mentioned how various groups either voluntarily or under compulsion migrated out of India to West Asia and Europe, carrying their religion and language with them. Thus, the exact opposite of the well-known pattern of migrations from north to south in Eurasia over the last two millennia existed during the previous two prior millennia. This calls into question the often repeated assumption of exclusivity of the north to south peaceful migrations and attacks in history.

The constant wars and intermarriage with nomads from far and near, including Akkadians, Mitanni, and Hittites, created many new racial stocks throughout its long history. Mostly, violent migrations into the civilization resulted in continual racial renewal.

With the exception of a few trading colonies that ancient Egypt established, migrations in ancient Egypt were always into Egypt, either through conquered slaves or the Hyksos and later other neighbors who conquered Egypt. Migrations were not a significant factor in setting the direction of Egyptian civilization.

The migration patterns in early China seem confined to and based on war with the northern and western nomadic tribes. Similarly, trade with other civilizations was not developed. However, internal trade expanded as the Chinese state grew.

In summary, the peaceful reciprocal influence on civilizations was mostly confined to practical technology, mathematics, and writing systems because of their practical significance.

State of Extrinsic Violent Causes or Total of Destructive Outcomes

Except for Egyptian imperialism, wars among civilizations were still in the future. During the long protoscience phase, we witness four major civilizations with few military conflicts among them. For the first time in history, a visible struggle was set up among the three forms of creativity: practical, religious, and intellectual toward the end of the protoscience phase. At the same time, wealth polarization had begun to increase class distinctions within the civilizations. Improving military technology intensified internal wars that held the potential to initiate the era of extended military conflicts among civilizations. Civilizations were thus beginning to develop the potential to use the creativity to not only build a better life but also, by the end of current phase, control, dominate, and exploit other civilizations. A contradiction thus developed among not only the three forms of creativity but also between creativity on the one hand and the three fundamental forms of conflict among *Homo sapiens* on the other: those of class and caste, internal wars among states, and the coming extended military conflicts among civilizations.

Assessing the Inner Nature of Participants

It would be inaccurate to suggest that the inner nature of civilizations did not evolve considerably during the long protoscience phase. It did indeed. However, we have chosen to assess the inner nature of the four primary civilizations at the end of the long protoscience phase. There are two reasons for this:

- Because of uncertain time lines, evolving causes and outcomes are difficult to analyze into segments to enable us to assess the evolving inner nature.
- There is comparatively less need to do so because our objective is to focus on the intertwined relationship between civilizations and science, and civilizations during the protoscience phase either were in relative isolation from one another or interacted peacefully.

It would also be inappropriate to think in terms of an "average" inner nature of civilization during the phase because of its length despite the slow pace of change. All other phases are an order of magnitude smaller than the protoscience phase, and it makes more sense to assess the "average" inner nature of these phases, though with some caution and allowing some appreciation of its evolution within the phase. Excessive discomfort with an "average" inner nature of a phase simply means the phase needed to be subdivided. Balancing need to keep it simple but not simplistic, we have chosen to assess the inner in the first phase at phase end and all subsequent phases as "average" for the phase.

11.36 Inner Nature of Mesopotamian Civilization at Phase End

Productive Capacity

Though lush and green during the early part of the protoscience phase (modern research suggests it was the inspiration for the home of the Garden of Eden in the bible), Mesopotamia was relatively confined geographically with moderate natural bounty. The government involvement in the economy, though strong, was not excessive. Its role appears to have been one of enabler than a controller. Thus, Mesopotamian civilization through the Sumer, Babylon, and Assyrian periods was a vibrant economy with a relatively high degree of internal economic freedom but with a low equality of opportunity because of excessive wealth polarization and class conflicts as evidenced by slavery, the status of women, and commerce controlled by the priests and the aristocratic class. The civilization displayed high new technology adoption, ever ready to develop and apply new technologies and methods. Its wealth allocation had traditionally favored the luxurious lifestyle of the elite, military spending and temples, but toward the end of the phase it began to favor creative endeavors. Its social cohesion was low: it lacked a shared religion, needed strong monarchs and a legalistic orientation to maintain internal peace, and needed to absorb the conquering nomads that renewed the racial stock. Their looting of each other through extremely aggressive internal wars driven by greed and fought to bitter end never really let the civilization settle down resulting in shifting control of SGS.

Creative Capacity

Although Mesopotamia had a strong dogmatic, polytheistic, and splintered religious orientation with a theocratic state, the religion played a second fiddle to commerce. Thankfully, it did not possess missionary zeal and tolerated limited diversity with excessive spirituality. We would assess its creed as balanced. Still, the seeds of science–religion conflict existed. Its astronomy was driven more by fear of the gods and not curiosity but had a measure of creative freedom driven by commercial interests. The creative environment varied considerably and creative orientation steadily progressed from low to high and narrow to broad with a strong abstract systems-building capability, including alphabetical script and a conscious creative method toward the end of phase. The creative capacity of Mesopotamian civilization was broad and high at phase end.

Constructive Orientation

Mesopotamian civilization faced no significant geographic or linguistic isolation. It was open to the creativity of other civilizations as evidenced by its trade and creative exchanges with Egyptian and Indian civilizations and possible adoption of Indian mathematics as recent research has suggested. It, however, showed little interest in the religious creativity of other civilizations, and its own polytheistic creed, which harbored superstition, never matured to monism, monotheism, or agnosticism. Its defensive military capability was often bested by early nomadic wars. Nomads often succeeded because of a smaller, flatter, and indefensible geographical setting, thus creating new hybrid racial stocks. It had a mixed record against nomadic invasions but was successful in absorbing the nomads. This contributed to its openness.

Destructive Orientation

The natural bounty was moderate because of geographical constraints as noted above. Though there were no wars with other primary civilizations, Mesopotamian civilization acquired an attitude of aggression toward outsiders. The internal wars among the cities were often vicious. In addition, though Mesopotamia did not develop a formal systematic intolerant creed, it exhibited early signs of intolerance. The desire to conquer other civilizations, driven by institutional greed (economy controlled by priests and a strong trade orientation), was undoubtedly there, but it lacked offensive military capability. The orientation of Mesopotamian civilizations during the formative period must, therefore, be characterized as violent with strong empire-building motive, though it did not manifest itself in conflicts with other civilizations because of the limited range of its military technology. In this respect, it succeeded in establishing an early template for derivative civilizations of West Asia and Europe. And of course, the civilization itself was conquered by and absorbed into the Persian Empire after the protoscience phase ended, as we shall discuss in the next chapter. Thus, despite the absence of invasion from other civilizations, we would characterize the destructive orientation of Mesopotamian civilizations toward other civilizations as having developed a latent violent orientation.

11.37 Dynamic Inner Nature of Egyptian Civilization at Phase End

Productive Capacity

The natural bounty was moderate despite the great Nile because it was surrounded by desert with little rain and because the Nile flooded annually and was difficult to irrigate. Productive capacity was supplemented through coerced trade in the imperial period. Ancient Egypt must be characterized with a low degree of internal economic freedom because of the highly regulated Nile-centered nature of its economy. The new technology adoption must be judged high. Egyptian civilization developed new technology in irrigation, building construction, and several manufacturing technologies, such as glassmaking. Its wealth allocation favored building monuments and large agricultural projects. Its otherworldly religiosity and the god–king status of the pharaoh meant channeling resources toward monuments and ritual often at the neglect of creativity. Ancient Egypt, we believe, had a low equality of opportunity. It allowed the conquered to be used as slaves and developed a castelike structure, Government bureaucracy and priests controlled the wealth. Its social cohesion was based on the godlike status of the pharaoh and its unique geography, which tightly bound its citizens to the state, despite a castelike structure. Because of its unique geography, the internal wars in ancient Egypt were nonexistent. As a result, it maintained a centralized state with no internal shifting of the SGS.

Creative Capacity

After the age of the pyramids, Egyptian civilization turned increasingly practical, as it was tired of chaos and an excessive focus on wasteful monuments. Still despite its monumental achievements in practical technology, Egyptian civilization failed to raise itself above its ritual-soaked religiosity; practical, artistic orientation; and good life (and afterlife) for the elite. Thus, although Egypt showed remarkable practical and artistic creativity, it never made the leap toward philosophical and scientific creativity. One does not see a great effort at linguistics (beyond hieroglyphics), logic, arithmetic, or abstract systems-building capability beyond what was needed for practical purposes. Its achievements in astronomy lagged behind those of Mesopotamia. Its creative freedom must be judged to be high but narrow because of the godlike pharaohs. We may hold Egypt responsible for the idea of monotheism and the divine right of kings. Egypt wasted its own surplus and that of the territories on monuments and luxuries and, with hindsight, on foolish metaphysics. Ancient Egypt displayed a strong tendency toward science–religion conflict. We must characterize the creative capacity as high but narrow with a greater worldly expression of otherworldly religiosity and a high early artistic impulse than found in any other ancient civilization. Thus, the creative capacity of Egyptian civilization was narrow but high during the phase.

Constructive Orientation

Ancient Egypt may be rightly regarded as isolated, and it did not mostly face the nomadic threat because of its geography. The combination of the mighty Nile River and the absence of natural bounty away from its banks required Egypt to trade with neighboring minor civilizations, yet the resulting highly centralized state inculcated a sense of insularity. In the early stages, Egyptian civilization mostly engaged in essential fair trade only. Ancient Egyptian civilization must be characterized as open with respect to practical technology and trade with other civilizations and insular with respect to migrations and religious and intellectual creativity.

Destructive Orientation

Later in the phase, possibly because of the influence of foreign conquerors, it actually engaged in aggression and coerced trade with surrounding minor civilizations. Thus, its aggressive tendencies must be judged high toward the end of the phase. Thus, the external orientation of ancient Egypt started out as peaceful but turned into that of empire builders interested in a systematic wealth drain by about 1600 BCE. Unlike the Mesopotamian civilization, one notices fluidity in the external orientation of ancient Egypt during three millennia of its existence. During the first three periods, the orientation was primarily inward, if not peaceful. In the fourth period, it lost its political independence and after regaining it, civilization turned violent with an offensive military capability directed toward minor civilizations. Its limited ecology and natural resources forced it into picking on little guys in its backyard. Ancient Egypt nurtured institutional greed and indulged in coerced trade necessitated by its lack of resources. It possessed defensive and later offensive military capability, but its Nile-centered geography meant that it did not always need the former.

11.38 Dynamic Inner Nature of Chinese Civilization at Phase End

Productive Capacity

Like the Mesopotamians, the ancient Chinese also were practical and fully engaged in agriculture. Notwithstanding a harsher natural environment, the Chinese demonstrated exceptional hard work and focus and relative freedom from the state. Thus, we would characterize it with high economic freedom. The new technology adoption for the practical-minded Chinese was probably medium, possibly high, in this phase. Wealth allocation in ancient China was balanced, with no evidence of excessive wasteful monuments. Absence of a religion-sanctioned inequality and a lack of both slavery and caste structure ensured high equality of opportunity. The social cohesion was also very high, given the essential lack of slavery, a caste system, a strong state, strong family and ancestral ties, and an internal unity derived from a constant nomadic threat. Internal wars in ancient China during the current phase were not excessive, with dynasties lasting multiple centuries, thus resulting in a stable SGS control.

Creative Capacity

Creative freedom in China was not hampered by religion or state; however, creative outcomes were limited practically because of the absence of alphabetical script without which intellectual and sophisticated religious creativity was difficult indeed. We would therefore characterize it as medium, perhaps even low. However, unlike the Mesopotamians and Egyptians, the religious impulse in Chinese civilization was markedly weaker. The central focus of the ancient Chinese civilization was family and ancestors and not some far-off gods. There was little science religion conflict mainly because of the absence of an organized religion. Although China had developed a logographic script by 2200 BCE, one does not observe significant developments in abstract systems-building capability in China during this period. Exceptionally well-made bronze vessels have been discovered, going back to the Shang period, attesting to a highly developed state of metallurgy. The Chinese civilization's focus on practical creativity and a family-centered life unencumbered by both religious overgrowth and intellectual refection (apart from how to live ethically) was evident at this early stage. We would, therefore characterize the creative capacity as low and narrow despite creative freedom.

Constructive Orientation

A unique characteristic of the Chinese civilization during the formative period was its insularity with respect to other civilizations. Geographical and linguistic isolation and early continual and successful experience in keeping nomads out were the contributing factors. Chinese civilization developed insularity with a type 1 openness and was not open to other civilizations except in fair trade and practical creativity, principally because of its continuing terrible but generally successful experience with nomads. In other words, early Chinese experience with invading nomads was difficult and largely successful, and it led to a sense of cultural superiority and isolation. Nonstop violent interaction with the nomads and a lack of interaction with other civilizations contributed toward making the Chinese civilization the most insular of all primary civilizations. Lacking a Himalayan barrier, China was forced to develop defensive military capability early in its history, including the construction of the Great Wall.

Destructive Orientation

China was blessed with natural bounty, though it required more industry because of its terrain topology in the north. However, it constantly faced the nomadic aggression and was spatially isolated from other civilizations. Chinese civilization did not develop an intolerant creed. Given these considerations, it is not surprising that China developed a peaceful but a strong defensive posture. Thus, we would judge China as having a peaceful external orientation with strong defensive capability with respect to the constant threat of northern nomadic tribes to keep nomads away. Ancient China did not develop institutional greed since it did not need land, raw materials, or markets from other civilizations.

As we shall see in the following chapters, the peacefulness and insularity with respect to other civilizations have remained essential features of the Chinese civilization.

11.39 Dynamic Inner Nature of Indian Civilization at Phase End

As noted above, during this lengthy phase of five millennia, Indian civilization faced and met three profound challenges from Mother Nature: the desertification of Mehrgarh, the drying of the Sarasvati River, and flooding of the mighty Indus River. These events respectively marked the transitions to Vedic, Harappa, and Ganges periods with evolving productive and creative capacity.

Productive Capacity

During the Mehrgarh period, an embryonic or nonexistent state interfered little, thus internal economic freedom was high even though the state of product markets and money were undoubtedly embryonic or even nonexistent. They used all the technological know how in their possession, and it may be safely assumed that new technology adoption was high, but the rate of technological innovation to be naturally low. We know little of their wealth allocation balance except that equality of opportunity appears high, resulting in high social cohesion. Internal wars did not exist in the Mehrgarh period, so its SGS stability may be presumed to be high.

The Vedic society was built around the Sarasvati River and was perhaps not too different from Mehrgarh in productive aspects. The key differences were expanded agriculture with domesticated cattle playing a greater role. Wealth allocation probably favored religious creativity. The Vedic period was egalitarian with a high equality of opportunity, though there was perhaps a greater polarization in wealth and power, but still, it was not excessive. Thus, social cohesion remained high despite a rise in the status of priests and fighters. There were infrequent internal wars in the Vedic period, resulting in continuing high SGS stability.

By the Harappa period, the state of practical technology had improved dramatically, as evidenced by its underground sanitary system, its trade with Mesopotamia, and the grid-like layout of its cities. State interference remained low, resulting in continuing high economic freedom. The new technology adoption was high and wealth allocation perhaps more balanced. Social cohesion remained high while caste differences had begun to appear. The social order of Harappa was still relatively egalitarian with a high equality of opportunity. A devastating but short Mahabharata war in the Harappa period left a permanent mark on the Indian psyche. However, apart from that, SGS stability was likely high.

During the Ganges period, states were better organized, and there were improvements in agricultural and nonagricultural technologies, including the discovery of iron. Given the natural bounty of the land in the east, the discovery of iron around 1500 BCE and the low level of state interference in the economy (compared to Egyptian civilization, for example) resulted in continuing high economic freedom. Thus new technology adoption remained high with the wealth allocation balance swinging back to favoring religious creativity. The social order in the Ganges period was structured around a flexible caste system with decreasing equality. Order was maintained through the concept of dharma and not an internal police force, thus still promoting social cohesion. During the Ganges period, the emergence of a more critically examined and tolerant monism increasingly supported the creeping social inequality. There were only modest internal wars in the Ganges periods with high SGS stability

Creative Capacity

Right from its birth, the issue in the Indian civilization was not a lack of creative freedom, science–religion conflict, or openness. Rather, it was how important knowledge of this world was in comparison to a focus on the eternal world. In this respect, Indian civilization changed dramatically from one period to next during the protoscience phase. The Mehrgarh period was practical, followed by a polytheistic religious orientation during the Vedic period, followed by a return to a relatively more practical orientation, and followed once again by a religious orientation, this time in the form of mature monism with a strong philosophical bent. These attributes were assured by tolerance, a spiritual orientation that was unafraid of freedom of thought, the absence of a monotheistic streak, and an underlying agnostic streak going as far back as Rig Veda. The creative capacity continued to broaden and deepen from one period to next, with substantial improvements in abstract systems-building capability, including writing, alphabetical script, conscious creative method, and a developing rational outlook. The creative capacity must be judged broad and high at phase end.

Constructive Orientation

Indian civilization was essentially geographically isolated as far as land routes were concerned despite occasional migrations out but remained in substantial contact with Mesopotamian and Egyptian civilizations via the sea. The Indian civilization did not need to face the nomadic threat and remained oblivious to the need for defensive military capability against nomads, who were secure in their native Himalayan protection. Defensive military capability, essential for peaceful interaction, did not matter in this phase. Indian civilization remained open to trade, exchange of creativity, and migrations during the peaceful interaction era of the phase despite the absence of defensive military capability. It therefore exhibited openness, remaining open to others' creativity; freely shared its own creative outcomes; engaged in fair trade; and entertained peaceful migrations.

Destructive Orientation

Indian civilization did not develop a belief in violence directed at other civilizations and it was not at the receiving end of nomadic invasions during the phase. It lacked institutional greed mainly because of its high natural bounty despite experiencing terrible gradual and abrupt environmental shocks. It did not develop intolerant creeds or belief systems. Its high natural bounty meant it did not need to attack other civilizations and thus never developed an imperial orientation and offensive military capability and could afford the luxury of developing an excessive spiritual orientation instead. It is indeed difficult to think of another instance in history when a major civilization enjoyed the absence of external invasions and fair internal peace for five millennia. What this did to the psyche of Indian civilization is an interesting question to ponder.

The key parameters measuring the inner nature of these four civilizations during each significant period of the protoscience phase are summarized in table 11.3.

This completes the assessment of the parameters that define the inner nature of each significant participant during the protoscience phase. We have employed the concept of measurable characteristics to assess the evolving productive and creative capacity and constructive and destructive orientation of each participant during the phase.

11.40 Inner Nature of Participants at the End of Protoscience Phases

In chapter 9, we suggested that the broadest practical measures of a social order's inner nature are its internal SGS (sustainable growing surplus), ICB (internal creative balance), O/I (position on the openness/insularity scale), violence/peacefulness, and its SPI (sustained political independence). The last measure is a practical way to

Table 11.3: Relative Values of Measurable Parameters of Social Orders
At the End of Protoscience Phase (1000 BCE)

Measurable Parameters	Productive Capacity					Creative Orientation			Constructive Orientation				Destructive Orientation		
	NB	EF	NTA	WAB	SC	Creed	ASBC	WAB	GI	LI	ENW	Creed	NB	IG	IC
Mesopotamian	Mod	High	High	CE	Low	Bal.	Strong	CE	Low	Low	Defeat	Bal.	Mod	Med	Low
Egyptian	Mod	Low	High	ED	High	ES	Med	MS	High	Med	Victory	ES	Mod	High	High
Chinese	High	High	Med	PE	High	Bal.	Weak	PE	High	High	Victory	Bal.	High	Low	None
Indian	High	High	High	CE	High	ES	Strong	CE	High	Low	N/A	ES	High	Low	None

NB: Natural Bounty
EF: Economic Freedom
NTA: New Technology
WAB: Wealth Allocation
SC: Social Cohesion

ASBC: Abstract Systems Building Capability
GI: Geographic Isolation
ENW: Early Nomadic Wars
LI: Linguistic Isolation
IG: Institutional Greed
IC: Intolerant Creed

Wealth Allocation:
ED: favors Elite Decadence
MS: Favors Military Spending
PE: Favors Productive endeavors
CE: Supports Creative Endeavors

assess the impact of the violent orientation of others on a social order.

Indian Civilization

The inner nature of the Indian civilization at the end of the protoscience phase consisted of a high internal SGS, a creative capacity tending toward type C ICB, type 4 openness or constructive orientation, and a peaceful orientation toward other civilizations. It thus had a type I external orientation.

Mesopotamian Civilization

The inner nature of Mesopotamian civilization at the end of the protoscience period consisted of high but fluctuating internal SGS or productive capacity, a creative capacity tending toward type C ICB, a type 3 openness or constructive orientation, and a latent destructive orientation that did not materialize in violence against other civilizations. It thus had a type I external orientation.

Egyptian Civilization

The inner nature of ancient Egyptian civilization during the protoscience period consisted of a moderate internal SGS or productive capacity, a type B2 ICB creative capacity, a type 1 openness or constructive orientation, and a violent destructive orientation. It thus exhibited an insular and violent empire building or a type IV external orientation.

Chinese Civilization

The inner nature of the ancient Chinese civilization at the end of the protoscience phase consisted of a high internal SGS or productive capacity, a type A ICB or creative capacity, type 1 openness or constructive orientation, and a peaceful orientation toward other social orders. It thus had an insular and peaceful or a type II external orientation.

The comparative inner nature of the four primary civilizations at the end of protoscience phase is shown in table 11.4.

Table 11.4: Comparative Inner Nature of Civilizations
At the End of Protoscience Phase (1000 BCE)

Civilization	Productive Capacity	Creative Capacity	Constructive Orientation	Destructive Orientation	
	Internal SGS	ICB	O/I	P/V	SPI
Mesopotamian	H	⇒ Type C	Type 3	Peaceful	Yes
Egyptian	M	Type B	Type 1	Violent	Yes
Chinese	H	Type A	Type 1	Peaceful	Yes
Indian	H	⇒ Type C	Type 4	Peaceful	Yes

SGS: Sustainable Growing Surplus
ICB: Internal Creative Balance
O/I: Openness/Insularity
P/V: Peaceful/Violent
SPI: Sustained Political Independence

H: High
M: Moderate
L: Low

Evolution and Rationalization of Protoscience

In this section, we discuss the evolution of protoscience during the phase, including the nature of participation by the four primary civilizations. We also rationalize the protoscientific outcomes in each civilization using their inner natures.

11.41 Evolution of Protoscience during the Phase

Significance of Protoscience Phase

Conventional Western historiography of science of the last two centuries has consistently underestimated the importance of protoscience that was critical to birth of science. This is eminently understandable because European civilization was yet to take birth during the protoscience phase and therefore did not participate in the development of protoscience. It has persistently insisted in ascribing the birth of science solely to a standalone ancient Greek civilization as a nearly magical event. This issue of this bias in Western historiography and its psychological basis are briefly discussed in appendix H.

The long protoscience phase may also be rightly regarded as the pregnancy phase of science to which all major civilizations of the phase contributed, a list that poignantly does not include either European or Muslim civilizations. Despite this, one cannot ignore developments, such as the crude observatory at Stonehenge in England, as testaments to protoscience and to human curiosity and ingenuity. There are, of course, historians, who continue to insist or who want to believe that scientific creativity by definition has been limited to European civilization, with a limited role assigned to the Muslim civilization as Western civilization slumbered in the dark middle ages. Thus, the critical role of protoscience is mostly swept under the rug.

Drivers of Protoscience

Ever since the invention of agriculture, major civilizations continually endeavored to develop practical agricultural and nonagricultural technologies in materials, processes, products, construction, transportation, communication, and infrastructure as we discussed in section 11.6. This accumulated practical innovation was essential for protoscience to take birth. The critically important slow and steady progress in practical technology is of course not what we mean by protoscience. While the birth of protoscience could hardly have happened without developments in practical technology, progress in practical technology could hardly guarantee the birth of protoscience; civilizations had to go beyond that.

Practical impetus: Practical necessities of the day clearly gave great impetus to protoscience; these necessities were agriculture, medicine, and emerging internal commerce. By the needs of agriculture, we mean primarily marking the seasons needed for planting crops. Agriculture and settling down had brought forth unhealthy crowding, resulting in increased incidences of disease. Unhealthy living conditions brought about by the settled lifestyle and drudgery of agriculture meant practical medicine was essential to bring unhealthy humans back to health expeditiously. Finally, as the surplus grew in size and transportation technologies advanced, internal trade grew. Needs of commerce, therefore, created a need to keep track of the increasingly complicated transactions, and thus necessitated developing new skills in counting, measuring, and recording commercial transactions. This could only be met fully through a writing system, though it occurred after the birth of science. Memory and honesty alone could hardly be used as a foundation for commerce.

Early in the standalone era, the sustainable food surplus not only helped create the practical nonagricultural technologies but also made it possible for a small group of talented individuals to ponder answers to the important needs mentioned above. These questions required the full use of the unique mental powers of the species. It is not surprising that all civilizations found essentially accurate, usable answers to these questions when they focused a small portion of their surplus to these questions in a sustained manner. The seasons could be predicted, objects could be counted and measured, measurements could be put in rudimentary writing, and sick individuals could be treated through a combination of practical medical knowledge and shamanism. All this was possible because civilizations were consciously beginning to understand the basics of the creative process: its social, stepwise, and historical nature.

Religious–intellectual confusion: However, finding practical solutions to important questions was insufficient too. Religious and intellectual stirrings, often in contradiction and driven respectively by existential anxiety and uncomfortable, conscious intellectual confusion, wondered how the natural and social worlds functioned. This period, therefore, represents a stage when the human mind, while intuitively sensing the regularity in the natural world, was utterly unable to free itself from the power of polytheistic gods it had created. Different civilizations developed different attitudes toward gods: some feared them, others praised them, some remained aloof, some "mingled" with their gods, and still others loved them. Some believed that while the gods—and through them, nature and society—were generally lawful, they reserved the right to behave on whim, much as how the social and natural forces appeared to human mind.

Astronomy–astrology conundrum: Thus, the unexplained forces of nature were conceived as gods, though with very human emotions of anger, jealousy, whim, and a need for praise. These products of human imagination created fear in the hearts of both the elites and the common man because of their perceived power and presumed control over the fates of men. Thus, a need arose to pacify them in two entirely different ways: praise and control. One possible approach to the latter strategy was to determine the time when these gods were in a weakened state because of their internal strife or conversely, when they were in a good mood. These forces of nature conceived as gods included, but were not limited to, the sun, moon, and five planets whose peculiar, repeating motions against the relatively fixed stars had aroused curiosity. Thus, the idea arose that certain configurations of these heavenly gods either corresponded to their good moods or weakened states, and important activities initiated during those periods had a greater probability of success. Predicting the position of these heavenly gods, therefore, was critical so that important events such as coronation, aggression, or a royal marriage could be initiated at such a time or so the fate of a royal baby could be predicted from the time of his birth. Understanding the motions of these heavenly bodies was, therefore, supported by the political classes of the time in all major civilizations.

Early observational astronomy thus got its impetus from both the farmer and the king, and the resulting pseudoscience of astrology supported both. The farmer needed information about the onset of seasons, and the royalty needed the auspicious time for key events or a prediction of future. It was not just the fear or self-interest and desire for successful outcomes that created a need to understand the heavenly bodies, for such a viewpoint would be based on a narrow view of human nature. It was also possible to love these gods without an ulterior motive because in some civilizations, these gods were conceived as the essence of the universe, and the purpose of life was to be one with these gods based on an understanding on these gods. However, even these civilizations wanted to know the auspicious time and manner to pay homage to these gods, and for that, they desired astronomical knowledge. Thus, primitive astronomy and the rising pseudoscience of astrology would help explain changes in the natural and social worlds that mind could not or would not explain.

Religion as ally: It is important to note that during the birth process, religious beliefs were not an impediment; religion was an ally pushing for birth of protoscience as it encouraged both astronomy and astrology. It was not the only ally since practical needs and intellectual confusion needed answers to same questions.

To summarize, practical needs, existential anxiety, and uncomfortable intellectual confusion gave birth to protoscience in different civilizations at different times during the standalone era. Religious impulse during the standalone era was paradoxically a boost to protoscience. It was too weak to oppose science precisely because monism and monotheism were yet to be conceived. Clearly independent birth of protoscience in different civilizations at different times was a protracted process and not an event. All four primary civilizations satisfied the requirements of the birth of protoscience (relatively high SGS, little science–religion conflict, and allocation to creative endeavors) during the protoscience phase.

Critical Questions Concerning the Evolution of Science

The critical questions concerning the evolution of science in any phase are:

- Did the progress of protoscience take place in one, several, or all major civilizations?
- Did this development take place in a linked matter or an independent manner?
- Was the linkage explicit and conscious, or was the linkage unconscious and mediated?
- Were the linkages peaceful through free exchange of creativity, fair trade, and peaceful migrations, or did they occur in the wake of one-time looting, empire building, violent colonization, and systematic wealth drain?

Differing Evolution of Protoscience across Civilizations

It is clear from the scientific outcomes and our definition of protoscience that all civilizations participated in the development of protoscience to one degree or another, either independently or in modest, peaceful cooperation during the current phase.

- The birth and early development of protoscience occurred in a parallel and largely independent fashion across all four major civilizations during the standalone era.
- Continuing development and maturation of protoscience also occurred in a parallel but in a modestly interdependent manner, primarily across two of the four civilizations during the peaceful interaction era.

In particular:

- Egyptian civilization focused primarily on art and architecture, displayed relatively less interest in astronomy and mathematics, and never fully transitioned from hieroglyphs to alphabetical script.
- Indian civilization focused on observational and computational astronomy, mathematics, simple geometry, and alphabetical script.
- Mesopotamian civilization focused on observational and computational astronomy, arithmetic and simple geometry, and developing alphabetical script.

- Chinese civilization did not move beyond logographic script and focused primarily on practical technology, practical medicine, and observational astronomy.

Of the four civilizations, Indian and Mesopotamian civilizations were in a leadership role during the protoscience phase, while the Egyptian and Chinese civilizations lagged. Thus, development of protoscience in the standalone era continued in each civilization along its own unique path. The struggle between science and religion was yet to evolve as a major factor, except in the case of Egyptian civilization. Abstract systems-building capability, through writing and conscious understanding of the creative method and constructive orientation, drove the differing developments in protoscience.

11.42 Rationalization of Protoscience

As we argued in chapter 9, the scientific achievements of a social order in any phase and any era may be rationalized through the inner nature of all relevant social orders. For the standalone era, this meant looking at the internal SGS, its allocation, the nature of its creed, and the state of its ASBC or abstract systems-building capability. For social orders interacting peacefully, we included the above plus the nature of its openness/insularity to the constructive outcomes of other social orders.

Since we assessed the inner nature of the civilizations at the end of the phase and acknowledged that the protoscience phase is too long to justify the concept of an "average" inner nature across the phase, the following assumes that the achievement in science for a civilization during the protoscience phase. It can be rationalized using the inner nature at the phase end. But this is only true as a first approximation. This is an assumption that be relaxed but we believe it will not change the conclusions.

Rationalization of Chinese Protoscience

Internal SGS: There was little constraint from the state of relative internal SGS, which was high and sufficient to support science if the civilization chose to do so.

Allocation of SGS: The SGS was not excessively squandered on elite decadence or monuments. However, a considerable fraction of SGS was allocated to military spending to contain the nomadic threat. In essence, Chinese civilization had to do this very early in its history since it lacked a Himalayan barrier between it and the nomads.

Nature of creed: Chinese religion remained simplistic and polytheistic without any potential conflict with science, either in the form of excessive spirituality or overt science–religion conflict. There was none of the divine right of kings, a complex mythology, or world-denying metaphysics.

Abstract Systems-Building Capability: China demonstrated excellent appreciation of creative method and invented writing by at least 2000 BCE. However, it failed to move in the direction of alphabetical script. As a consequence, it never reached the stage of mature protoscience. The issue of the relationship between alphabetical script and science is a complex one and is discussed in appendix I.

Openness/Insularity: China was insular during the phase and remained focused on a successful effort to contain the nomadic threat.

Thus, SGS, its allocation, the nature of creed, and sustained political independence all favored achievements in science. However, these positives were opposed by its state of abstract systems-building capability and its insularity to the creativity of other civilizations. China thus did not progress to mature protoscience during this period. The lack of religious motivation and continued absence of movement away from logograph to alphabetical script kept development of Chinese protoscience down.

Rationalization of Egyptian Protoscience

Total SGS: The internal SGS was moderate because of the constraint of geography, a need to develop irrigation, and a relatively small population. However, it was supplemented through both trade and slaves from surrounding minor civilizations. Thus, SGS was not a limitation for the Egyptian civilization

Allocation of SGS: This was indeed a significant negative factor initially because of the resources needed to build pyramids and later because of an excessive focus on art and architecture and the lifestyle of the pharaoh and ruling priest class.

Nature of creed: The case of Egyptian civilization was different. Religion, controlled by the state, was polytheistic but had a strong dose of the divine right of kings and a belief in the survival of both body and soul after death. Thus, the pharaohs were hardly interested in any scientific explanation of natural phenomenon that might dilute their power.

Abstract systems-building capability: Ancient Egyptians clearly excelled in their understanding of the creative method. This is clear when one examines the majesty of the pyramids and their art. After an early invention of logograph, Egyptian civilization never quite adopted the alphabetical script, thus holding back its ability to move forward to mature protoscience.

Openness/Insularity: The focus of constructive engagement with other civilizations was to access the raw materials Egypt lacked. Ancient Egypt was hardly interested in the intellectual achievements of other civilizations.

Sustained political independence: Egyptian civilization retained SPI during most of the phase except when it was conquered by nomads, who were driven out two centuries later.

Limited abstract systems-building capability, an insular nature, and a priesthood consumed by religion meant a limited contribution by the Egyptian civilization to mature protoscience. The focus remained on art and practical creativity.

Rationalization of Mesopotamian Protoscience

Internal SGS: The internal SGS of the Mesopotamian civilization must be characterized as moderate high or somewhere between the Egyptian and the Chinese civilizations. The SGS did not hold back the march of protoscience in Mesopotamia.

Allocation of SGS: Allocation of SGS was a factor that probably held back science in Mesopotamia during the phase. The vicious internal fighting and the lifestyle of the elite consumed the SGS. The focus on astronomy came not from religious beliefs or curiosity but from the superstition of the royalty, who wanted to know the auspicious times for major life events.

Nature of creed: Fortunately, monotheism continued to elude Mesopotamia during the last part of the phase, despite being next door to the recently arrived Jewish slaves from Egypt. Still, a very weak monotheistic religious streak had the potential to stop the advance of protoscience dead in its tracks. Fortunately, this did not occur, and relatively tolerant polytheism bordering on superstition, with an ill-defined cosmology and with gods who did not judge humans after death came into existence instead. Though it was full of superstition, it did not slow down the protoscience. Quite to the contrary—superstition was the driving factor.

Abstract Systems-Building Capability: The abstract systems-building capability expanded through the invention/adoption of alphabetical script, as did the understanding of the creative method. However, there seems to have been little formal understanding of the theory of knowledge or epistemology because of a lack of critical philosophy in the highly commercial and political culture of Mesopotamia. Mesopotamia was in an excellent position to make world-class contributions to mature protoscience.

Openness/Insularity: Constructive orientation expanded, not necessarily through trade or creative exchange, but in exchange and a mingling of area populations because of wars and increasing commercial opportunities. Mesopotamian civilization was very open to the practical and intellectual creativity of other civilization. It absorbed all it could from the Indian civilization in mathematics and astronomy, thus moving forward its protoscience.

In short, the absence of religious constraints, an excellent abstract systems-building capability, and openness to the constructive outcomes of others readily explain the achievements of Mesopotamian protoscience.

Rationalization of Indian Protoscience

Differing achievements in creative capacity (principally evolving the role of religion and abstract systems-building capability) and constructive orientation (openness to exchange of creativity) drove protoscience development. During this part of the phase, the nature of the relationship between religion and protoscience began to diverge a little.

Internal SGS: Indian civilization, despite horrible natural disasters (desertification and drying, flooding, and salination of rivers), retained the ability to create high SGS through natural bounty and a large population—more than enough to support science if the civilization chose to do so.

Nature of creed: During the peaceful interaction era, the struggle between the religious and intellectual impulses or the struggle between the principle of equivalence of the heavenly, terrestrial, and inner realms on the one hand and the entrenched polytheism of the Vedic civilization on the other surfaced. The former is a statement of the potential of natural and social sciences to understand the world, and the latter is the brakes that conservative religious impulse wished to apply to real knowledge moving forward. Fortunately, this struggle was mostly benign, and it did not hold back the development of monism or protoscience. Polytheism, nascent monism, and agnosticism lurking beneath the surface encouraged religious pluralism and meant Indian civilization did not send any of its great agnostic thinkers to the gallows.

Abstract systems-building capability: The abstract systems-building capability of the Indian civilization was world-class in the period. Indian civilization possessed a protoalphabetical script during the Harappa period around 3000 BCE. Based on the shape of the letters, some claimed that Brahmi script in India was derived from Aramaic script in the seventh century BCE. However, Mitanni migrated from India around 1500 BCE to West Asia, making the reverse hypothesis plausible as well. Indian civilization during the early peaceful interaction era understood the creative method well. There are indications that the roots of decimal counting go to the Harappa period. The Sulbha Sutras contained highly developed arithmetic and the beginning of geometry. Religious pluralism led to speculative philosophy and reflections on the possibility of knowledge through the union of sense data and reason. This substantially strengthened the abstract systems-building capability.

Openness/Insularity: Indian civilization remained open to the creativity of other civilization; however, it seems that for trade, ideas and people flowed out of the subcontinent and not into it.

The noninterfering role of religion and a strong abstract systems-building capability are consistent with Indian achievements in protoscience during the period and resulted in a tolerant reflective orientation within the Indian civilization during this last period of the phase.

Comparing Development and Maturation of Protoscience in the Four Civilizations

It has been observed that during the peaceful interaction era, mathematics, astronomy, practical medicine, and astrology remained mostly confined to within civilizations while trade and migrations were more predominant. However, we must note the substantial diffusion of mathematics, astronomy, medicine, and astrology from one civilization to another was more likely as the diffusions of writing systems than what is commonly believed. The difference is that the diffusion of writing systems can be traced more easily by comparing the writing systems themselves. It is more difficult to do so for other forms of intellectual creativity during the peaceful interaction era. As noted before, recent research has raised the probability that Mesopotamian mathematics may be traced to India, and ancient Egypt is known to have trade links with Babylonia. In our judgment, given the gaps in research, it is safer to assume that Indian, Mesopotamian, and Egyptian civilizations had more communication than currently envisioned. The hypothesis of the Aryan migration out of India and the similarities between the Indo–Aryan Vedic religion and the religion of Mitanni people tend to support this assertion.

Indian civilization displayed both openness and a tolerant mature attitude toward religious beliefs, though it flirted with excess spirituality. The Mesopotamian civilization displayed an admirable openness and a religious impulse that bordered on intolerance and one that supported divine right of kings. The Egyptian civilization had an insular nature, had an intolerant religious orientation, and originated the concept of the divine right of the kings. Finally, the Chinese civilization, though insular, did not develop religious impulse that was either intolerant or excessively spiritual and was more practical.

The entire process occurred at glacial speed over a period of more than five millennia, hindered as it was by the intellectual confusion that both helped and hindered the emergence of religious explanations of the natural and social phenomena. As we compare how the four civilizations differed in their abilities to develop mature protoscience, we conclude that the differing outcomes were driven primarily by differences in ASBC (abstract systems-building capability) and only secondarily by creed and openness. The impact of a destructive orientation or greed was fortunately absent during the phase.

11.43 Life Stage of Science Achieved by Civilizations

In chapter 9, we outlined the necessary and sufficient conditions of the stages of science. At the end of the protoscience phases, based on the inner nature and the underlying parameters in table 11.2, the four primary civilizations achieved the following life stage in science by phase end:

- Indian Civilization: Mature Protoscience
- Mesopotamian Civilization: Mature Protoscience
- Egyptian Civilization: Development stage of Protoscience
- Chinese Civilization: Development stage of Protoscience

Already, two out of the four primary civilizations were falling behind in science principally because of intrinsic causes, and both lagged in development or adoption of abstract systems-building capability because of their insular natures.

Looking Ahead

11.44 Emerging New Participants

Major civilizations did not just influence one another during the phase; they were, together with several minor civilizations, also responsible for the emergence of significant new civilizations.

Ancient Greek Civilization (2000–900 BCE)

The supposed roots of Greek civilization go back to the Indo–Aryan migration into the area in about 2000 BCE. Borrowing bronze technology from the Balkans, the Cretans built the first significant settlement on the island of Crete by about 2000 BCE. At the time, Indian civilization was beginning to relocate to the Ganges plain in response to natural disasters and was using iron technology. Cretan civilization, also due to natural calamities, withered and was followed by Mycenaean civilization on the Greek mainland by about 1500 BCE. Egyptian records indicate a complete destruction of the Mycenaean civilization at the hands of foreign invaders by about 1000 BCE. However, by 750 BCE, a new, vibrant civilization arose from the ashes of the Mycenaean civilization arose. This revival is celebrated in Homeric poetry, after Greeks learned to write again using a modified form the alphabet they borrowed from the Phoenicians. This Greek civilization, as we shall discuss in chapter 12, prospered for nearly a thousand years before declining.

In birth, the ancient Greek civilization is indebted to the Mesopotamian, Phoenician, and ancient Egyptian civilizations. The early migration of Indo–Aryans probably provided the racial stock and spoken language out of which ancient Greece was eventually born. Phoenicians, who had created a true alphabetical script, transmitted it to the Greeks about 1100 BCE. Greek civilization would not have been able to produce a Homer, and later, a Plato or an Aristotle without this alphabetical script from Asia. The Greeks did not invent it; they simply borrowed and improved it. Similarly, Greek art owes a great deal to Egyptian art. Sculpture and painting in both civilizations were representational forms of art. Painting in both civilizations lacked the concept of perspective. That early Greek civilization owes a debt to Indian civilization is something we take up in coming chapters.

Jewish Tribes (2000–750 BCE)

Like the origin of most peoples, Jewish origin is also shrouded in controversy. If one accepts the biblical story, Jewish tribes lived in Canaan after 2000 BCE with the well-known burial site in Hebron. The twelve Jewish tribes trace their origins to twelve sons of Jacob. However, famine led to an exodus to Egypt, followed by four centuries of slavery in north Egypt, followed by an exodus from Egypt under Moses and Joshua. The Jews settled in modern-day Palestine after wandering in the Sinai desert for forty years. Joshua conquered Canaan in 1400 BCE, and Moses received the Ten Commandments around that time. There is little archeological evidence of the exodus to and from Egypt. This was followed by a confederation of twelve Jewish tribes ruled by judges that lasted for several centuries.

Around 1000 BCE, the political organization transitioned to a monarchy under Saul, followed by his son David and grandson Solomon. A civil war led to the kingdom of Israel in the north and kingdom of Judea in the south being dominated by two tribes. The kingdom of Israel was conquered by the Assyrians in the eighth century BCE. There is little doubt that Mesopotamian and Egyptian religious thought strongly influenced the development of Jewish thought since Jewish settlements in Palestine were sandwiched between these two civilizations. In this book, our interest in Jewish people will be limited to their impacts on the development of monotheism and the significant role played by Jewish diaspora in European history.

The above short list only hints at the influence the major civilizations of the phase had on two emerging significant civilizations. A complete list of minor civilizations of the period is beyond the scope of this book and is not essential to our purpose.

11.45 Summary

The phase of protoscience is the most misunderstood and least appreciated and constitutes the longest phase in the story of science. All four major civilizations of the phase passed the test of the necessary condition of its birth and development, while only Indian and Mesopotamian civilizations led protoscience to its maturity after successfully inventing or adopting alphabetical script. This phase links the precivilization world of the Neolithic epoch to the coming birth of science. Our full understanding of this phase is limited and colored by the imbalance and hasty interpretation of the substantial archeological data from West Asia and North Africa on the one hand and its relative paucity from South and East Asia on the other. For more than a century now, the knee jerk reaction of the receivers of archeological research grants at major universities in the United States and Europe has been to make a beeline to West Asia. As we delve into the story of science in chapter 12, we will continue to be vigilant in approaching the issue of who first discovered or invented what for several reasons:

1. Archeology and its associated sciences are relatively young.

2. Newer tools like DNA studies and constantly improving techniques like carbon dating are resulting in new facts and new interpretations.

3. There is a long and unfortunate history of unintentional or deliberate misinterpretation of the facts due to cultural and ideological bias.

4. Fourth, as noted above, archeological research has been uneven to date, focusing primarily on the dead civilizations of West Asia.

In this chapter, we reviewed the protoscientific achievements of all major civilizations of the phase: Indian, Egyptian, Mesopotamian, and Chinese. Magnificent achievements of many other smaller ancient civilizations, such as the Phoenicians and Jews, are also on record, and we did not discuss them in detail. The protoscience phase made great strides in practical creativity while anticipating, though not fully developing, the religious solutions to the existential anxiety experienced by the species. We positively glimpse the beginning of rational knowledge and intellectual creativity during this phase. With rising surplus due to significant productivity gains resulting from practical inventions and their slow diffusion across civilizations, we also begin to witness the choices civilizations made to pursue different forms of creativity.

The stage also crystallized the differing external orientation of civilizations toward other differing social orders of not only the major civilizations but also, by proxy, indeed, the entire set of essential players, since the later civilizations were either materially influenced or were derived from the four primary civilizations of this phase. The destructive orientation, though latent, also crystallized during the phase. The achievements of the future phases indeed stand on the shoulders of the mostly underappreciated giants of the protoscience phase.

Chapter 11 · Birth, Development, and Maturation of Protoscience (6000–1000 BCE)

Hopefully, defining the era and its key participants; reviewing the brief political history and natural, intrinsic and extrinsic causes; a review of productive, creative, and scientific outcomes; deducing the inner nature; a summary of the state of civilization and science at phase end; and rationalization of science for each participant has given the reader an appreciation of the analytical method. We will continue this approach in the following chapters.

Toward the end of this stage, improvements in military capability were intensifying the military conflicts among nomads, civilizations, and states within a civilization. It also set the stage for the coming military conflict among spatially separated civilizations. We shall get into this unfortunate aspect of civilization, but first, we must witness the glorious, peaceful birth of science proper.

PART V
BIRTH, DEVELOPMENT, AND MATURATION OF SCIENCE

OVERVIEW OF PART V

Looking ahead, in part V, we tell the story of the birth, development, and maturation of science. However, the story of science cannot be told without the story of civilizations and nomads engaged in exchanging ideas and inventions, with peaceful migrations and fair trade among civilizations on the one hand and the deadly extended military conflicts initiated by empire builders, violent colonizers, and systematic wealth drainers on the other. It is thus a double story: a glorious part and a not-so-glorious part. It is a story of humans discovering, developing, and actualizing the full range of unique mental gifts that biological evolution bestowed on them and a story of the insularity, greed, and irrational faith humans are capable of. It is simultaneously a story of pride and reflection.

Part V consists of seven chapters, each corresponding to one or more phases of science. Our approach to each of the following six chapters will be essentially the same:

- We affirm the era and the key participants of the phase.
- We then discuss political history; natural, intrinsic, and extrinsic causes (which are nothing other than the summation of the constructive and destructive outcomes of all relevant social orders respectively) and significant productive, creative, and scientific outcomes of each social order.
- We then assess the inner nature or productive and creative capacity and constructive and destructive orientation of each social order.
- Next, we summarize the state of civilizations and science for the phase as a whole.
- We then summarize the broad evolution of science during the phase and rationalize the state of science achieved by each social order during the phase through the inner natures of interacting social orders.
- Finally, we end the chapter by reviewing the new participants on the horizon and providing a chapter summary.

We focus on Indian, Mesopotamian, Egyptian, Chinese, Greek, Hellenistic, Persian, Roman, and Muslim Civilizations and central Asian and Arab nomads in the first seven phases, with the focus shifting to the European civilization in the last two phases. Greek and Hellenistic science had died by the end of the second century CE and Muslim and Indian science by the sixteenth century. The latter did not come to life until the later part of the nineteenth century under the influence of European science.

In history, science appears now exclusively as an Indian affair, now a Greek affair, now an Arab-Persian affair, now an Italian affair, and now a Northwest European affair. Today, we happen to be living in a period when science has beginning to end its appearance as an exclusively European/Western affair of last four centuries and has decidedly moved toward becoming a global affair.

Let us continue our story.

Chapter 12

Peaceful Interaction Era—Second Phase: Birth of Science

Birth of Science (1000–550 BCE)

12.1 Introduction

In the last chapter, we reviewed the achievements of the protoscience phase in Indian, Mesopotamian, Egyptian, and Chinese civilizations. The protoscience phase, as we saw, was an exceptionally long phase, starting some three millennia before the development of written language and culminating about a millennium after the fundamental development of alphabetical script was more or less complete. Its achievements in practical, intellectual, and religious creativity were indeed impressive, if necessarily slow. In leaving the protoscience or the pregnancy phase of science, we are about to leave a time when all civilizations could develop in relative isolation or in peaceful interaction with one another, though they were not necessarily safe from nomadic invasions or immune from local empire building through internal wars. However, with the end of the birth phase discussed in this chapter, we also coincidently and fortuitously arrive at the end of the two-and-a-half millennia of peaceful interaction among civilizations. Thus, right after the birth, the story of science began to be affected by not only the inner dynamics of civilizations, the inner logic of science itself, and beneficial peaceful interaction among civilizations but also extended military conflict among civilizations. This coexistence of violent intercivilization conflicts and the checkered development of science has continued right up to the present time.

Another way to look at this phenomenon is that military conflicts broadened their ranges from within and between a civilization and the *nearby* outlaying nomads to include wars among spatially separated civilizations and civilizations and *distant* nomads due to the continuing development of military technology and tactics. This meant that the evolution of civilizations and progress in science were not only dependent on natural, intrinsic, and peaceful extrinsic causes but also potentially determined by civilizations or nomads dominating other civilizations. In addition, the sheer diffusion of ideas now began to take on a bigger role through the increased frequency of invasions and increased trade and travel. The plot of civilizations and science, therefore, can be expected to thicken right after its birth.

In this chapter, however, we focus on a narrower slice of history sandwiched between the last centuries of the peaceful interaction era and the beginning of a violent era, during which the birth of science began in approximately 1000 BCE, when Baudhayana updated Sulbha Sutras and when the Upanishads were composed. It ended around 550 BCE when Sushruta probably finished compiling his encyclopedia of medicine.

The organization of the chapter follows closely the organization of the last chapter.

A word concerning the headline dates of phases as they relate to the actual description of events in a particular chapter is in order. Going forward, the story of civilizations within a chapter may not always exactly coincide with the dates of the phase. If it makes more sense to delay or continue the story of a particular civilization relative to the phase end date, we will take that approach, even though it may not be consistent with the headline period of that chapter. However, in the following chapter, we will always pick up the story from where we left it off in the previous chapter or before, if needed.

Affirmation of Era and Essential Participants

12.2 Affirming the Era of Civilization

Major civilizations of the second phase continued to be in the peaceful interaction or standalone mode, depending on the existence of reciprocal trade, migrations, and the exchange of ideas and inventions. Specifically, the Chinese civilization and the emerging Roman state could be characterized as being in the standalone era. More important, immediately after the end of this phase, civilizations first entered the era of extended military conflicts. The march of practical technology, including transport and weapons technology, until recent times, did not depend on the state of science. This implies the possibility of military capability to decouple from the state of science within a particular civilization. Thus, a civilization with a favorable internal creative balance could lag in military capability, a civilization or a state lacking a favorable internal creative balance could be stronger militarily, or a civilization could have both favorable internal creative balance and military strength. In today's world, it is harder to conceive of this scenario, given the strong linkage between science-based technology and military strength. We need to reemphasize that by extended military conflicts between civilizations, we do not necessarily mean an alliance of all states within a civilization to engage all states of another civilization militarily. These engagements typically occurred between two "front line" states from different civilization since civilizations were never administrative units. The "front line" moved depending on military outcomes. With the current phase, the peaceful interaction era ends.

12.3 Essential Participants of the Protoscience Phases

The birth phase is the shortest of all phases and was not only the phase that gave birth to science but also the most prolific phase relative to the birth and death of significant civilizations. During this phase, two major civilizations, those of Persia and Rome, were born and were becoming a force to reckon with by the end of the phase. Two primary civilizations, those of Egypt and Mesopotamia, declined irreversibly and died shortly after this phase ended. Indeed, it is hard to think of another comparable phase of history in this respect.

Thus, we focus on Indian, Mesopotamian, Chinese, and ancient Greek civilizations during this phase. We say good-bye to ancient Egypt while appropriately delaying the discussion of the Roman Republic and Persian civilization until the next chapter.

Practical Creativity during the Phase—All Civilizations

During the birth phase, there was significant progress on the practical creativity front, particularly considering that the birth phase was less than 5 percent as long as the protoscience phase. The practical ideas diffused primarily through declining travel and trade. As in chapter 10, we will detail these achievements in the basic categories of materials, processes, tools, and energy and the "product" categories of agricultural, nonagricultural products and construction, communications, transportation, and infrastructure. We will not break these practical inventions by civilization for two reasons. First, given the uneven state of archeological research, it is difficult to do that with reasonable confidence; second, for the same reason, it is nearly impossible to determine the dates of origin of some of these inventions. Thus, all we can say is that these inventions occurred approximately in the current phase, give or take a few centuries on either side! Another way of saying the same would be to acknowledge that the specific list of achievements in practical creativity in the following section could easily have appeared in the previous or following phase. Given the absence of resistance in adopting these inventions, it is more than likely that multiple civilizations contributed to the final form of many of these inventions. The genealogy of specific contributions to key inventions is impossible to determine at the current state of knowledge and perhaps can never be determined accurately.

12.4 Significant Achievements in Practical Creativity—All Civilizations

Materials: During this period, the key new materials invented were cast iron and steel.

Processes: Key new processes included incubation, liquid extraction, and fumigation.

Tools: Humans during this period developed a continuous-motion potter's wheel, lever, bellows or an air pump, the abacas, a battery for "electroplating," oil lamps, sundials, and maps.

Energy: Key inventions or discoveries of the period were the water wheel, whale oil, and petroleum.

Agricultural products and technologies: Use of manure as fertilizer to increase crop yield was developed.

Nonagricultural product and technologies: Aqueducts were a significant invention and allowed large cities to develop farther from sources of water.

Construction: Key practical innovation in this category included glass windows, very long earthen dams, amphitheaters, improved arches and domes, and large buildings, such as the Horyuji pagoda.

Transport: Naval ships, including biremes and triremes; stone bridges; anchors; floating pontoons; underwater tunnels; land tunnels; lighthouses for navigation; and pontoon bridges.

Infrastructure: The inventions here included faster ships with multitier and multifile rowers, the compass, the horse harness, optical signaling, and canals.

It is clear that this period witnessed a number of inventions of great military significance, including the faster ships, steel, harness, pontoon bridges, maps, phalanx formation, and optical signaling. Thus, we see a greater allocation of the surplus on inventions of military significance, accelerating the frequency and scope of military conflicts and enhancing the possibility of wars among civilization.

History, Causes, and Outcomes of the Ancient Greek Civilization

In discussing the natural and intrinsic causes in this chapter and the following chapters, we shall use the following criteria in the interest of brevity:

- When a participant was discussed in the previous chapter, we shall only focus on significant changes in these causes.
- When a participant is new, we shall discuss the causes in the level of detail warranted.

12.5 Brief Political History (1600–550 BCE)

The Mycenaean civilization (1600–1100 BCE) was divided into petty kingdoms ruled by monarchs based on the idea of the divine right of kings borrowed from Egypt. Ancient Greece emerged from the ruins of the Mycenaean civilization by adopting the Phoenician alphabet. Geography, climate, and a growing population (by some estimates, 4 percent per year) played a determining role in the emergence of ancient Greece because of limited fertile land and internal commerce, which was made difficult by terrain and dry, unnavigable rivers for several months in a year. These factors drove the Greeks to establish overseas colonies—it was not a sense of adventure as is sometimes implied. Thus, the period initially witnessed the emergence of city-states often at war with one another: Sparta and Massena fought a war during 730–710 BCE and a second war during 640–630 BCE; city-states of Chalcis and Eretria fought a long war during 710–650 CE to control the fertile Lelantine plain of Euboea, weakening both cities; and the city-states of Chalcis and Athens fought in the early sixth century, with Eretria joining forces with Athens. Two other forces were at work during the archaic period: colonization in Italy and Anatolia and differing political evolution in different city-states within Greece. Colonization in Italy, including Sicily and Anatolia, was driven by a land shortage and excessive population growth. It is important to note that the mother city-states did not control these colonies politically; they were independent, with the mother city-state providing cultural, linguistic, and religious infrastructure. On the Italian Peninsula, these colonies came to be known as Magna Grecia. These overseas colonies were to come in conflict with the Roman Republic and Persian Empire centuries later.

By far, the most interesting was the different political evolution of the city-states. For example, Sparta preferred oligarchy or control by a privileged few, the city-states of Corinth preferred tyranny or the control of the city-state by an illegitimate ruler, and Athens fluctuated between periods of tyrannies (including infamous Draco) and finally settled on elitist democracy. If one were to ask the question why these political differences arose, the answer must be a combination of the coincidental emergence of personalities, the differences in the relative power of the aristocratic class, and the rise of wealthy merchants through foreign trade.

12.6 Natural Causes

As indicated above, the geographical setting of the ancient Greek civilization had two significant features: rough terrain and rivers that slowed down to a trickle in summer. This had two consequences: the city-states could hardly grow to a normal size, with the resulting political landscape of stunted city-states separated by natural barriers, and developing sea travel for trade and communication were necessary for survival.

12.7 Intrinsic Causes

Institutional Systems, Structures, and Processes

Political system: The political structure of ancient Greece varied highly from one city-state to another and evolved over time. Oligarchy, tyranny, and democracy (for free male citizens only and coupled with slavery for other males and a second-class status for woman) all had their time in ancient Greece. Oligarchy or the rule of few aristocrats in Sparta was highly militarized and disciplined. Tyranny in Corinth probably resulted from the rising power of the merchants, who rebelled against the aristocrats. Under eventual "democratic" form in Athens, only the elite could hold offices, thus making it a democracy for the chosen few. It seems to us that Greeks were forced into a limited form of democracy during certain periods precisely because of extensive slavery. With three-fourths of the population as slaves and women excluded, educating the young men of aristocratic origin and providing equal opportunity for political advancement was an effective way to distinguish them from the remaining free citizens. The number of free adult males in ancient Greece was probably no more than 50,000 to 75,000 during the current phase.

Military capability: The early Greek city-states were too small to entertain the idea of a professional army, opting instead for an army consisted of mostly farmers during the summer months. Evidently, these early armies were very lightly armed since wars resulted in a small loss for both sides, though they often proved deadly for the commanders who led the charge.

Economic organization: The economy was based on agriculture and domestication of animals. Slaves provided agricultural labor. The key drivers of the economy, as noted earlier, were land shortage, overseas colonization (which ceased by the end of current period), and foreign trade. Colonization drove developments in manufacturing and commerce. It has been estimated that Greek economy grew severalfold during the period. Colonization and commerce increased the size of effective Greek world so it was greater than present-day Greece.

Systems of religious faith: The Greek religion was polytheistic and ritual-based, offering animal sacrifice to the twelve Olympian deities. The priest class performed rituals but, unlike the Brahmins in Indian civilization, it was not a hereditary orthodoxy. Thus, religion was an individual affair, and there were no organized religious institutions, resulting in a nearly complete separation of state and religion. Polytheistic ancient Greece was beginning to show interest in philosophy toward the end of this phase. Because the religion was polytheistic with little movement toward either monism or monotheism, science-religion conflict and excessive spirituality were essentially nonexistent, though this does not imply that Greek civilization had achieved favorable internal creative balance during the current phase.

Legal systems: Greeks, unlike the later Romans, had no formal codified law. However, the laws of inheritance, commerce, and contracts seem to be well established and practiced. There are references to the existence of courts and judicial officials.

Social structure: The social structure strongly supported slavery, with three-fourths of the population being slaves. Right at its birth, more than the Egyptian, Mesopotamian, Chinese, Indian, and Persian civilizations, civilization on the European continent permitted slavery on a massive scale. The social rank of slaves was at the bottom followed by women, free male citizens, and the elite. The women and slaves, however, seem to have accepted their inferior social position, as there were few known rebellions staged by the slaves. Though there was excessive inequality, the class antagonisms were well managed through strong military, common city deity, and commercial law, providing an excellent measure of social cohesion within a city-state.

Knowledge-Creating and educational institutions: One of the consequences of restricting the political offices to the elite was the need to educate wealthy young men. This resulted in establishing many academies with gifted teachers beginning to come forth. These great teachers and academies (and not exclusively a tradition of love of knowledge) were supported by the policy that initiated intellectual creativity in Greece.

Wealth allocation: Constant internal wars required considerable wealth allocation to the military, as evidenced by naval inventions of larger ships and the later development of the phalanx, a highly effective form of human tank. On the religious side, the surplus allocated to temples and other religious activity was modest by the standards of the day.

Social cohesion: Despite widespread slavery and excessive wealth polarization, from the very beginning, ancient Greece demonstrated surprisingly high social cohesion because of cultural, linguistic, and religious unity; geographical compactness; the high value placed on education and wisdom; acceptance of slavery as natural by slaves; and interclass mobility for nonslaves based on wealth accumulation. In other words, slaves accepted their lots, and free citizens could transcend their class through hard work and success.

Internal wars: There were endless internal wars among the city-states, but they usually cooperated in the face of external aggression and were, therefore, able to maintain political independence.

Formative Beliefs and Ideology at the End of Birth Phase

The relatively benign polytheism of ancient Greeks; their earnest desire for knowledge, as evidenced by the speed with which they learned to write from Phoenicians and to sculpt from Egyptians; a social order based on slavery; their vicious, prolonged internal wars; the value they placed on the strength and beauty of the physical body; their need for trade because of limited natural bounty; and their need to found new colonies in Italy and Anatolia under population pressures all point to a belief system that may be summarized as follows:

- A belief in knowledge based on speculation and driven by philosophical idealism but unencumbered by religious dogma
- A belief in the fundamental inequality among men demonstrated by a majority of population under slavery
- A belief in openness toward the creativity of others
- A belief in aggression toward other social orders

These beliefs, though derived in part from Mesopotamian and Egyptian civilizations, are important since as the first civilization of any consequence on the European landmass, these beliefs strongly impacted the beliefs of other European civilizations that followed the ancient Greeks.

12.8 Extrinsic Peaceful Causes or Sum Total of Others' Constructive Outcomes

Impact of Egyptian Civilization and Phoenicians

During its formative period, Phoenicians, Egyptians, and several minor cultures in eastern Europe strongly influenced Greek civilization.

Channels of transmission: Trade, individual travel, and Greek colonization activity in Asia Minor were the principal channels.

Transmission of intellectual creativity: Ancient Greece acquired its alphabet from Phoenicians.

Before Greek art influenced Achaemenid art, it went through a period of "Orientalization" in art during 720 to 600 BCE. It was indeed a revolution in both materials and motifs. Use of stone, metal, and ivory increased dramatically in comparison to wood, and the style moved away from simple geometric style to a more elaborate style with different sensibilities, such as the use of birds and plants on vases. The Egyptian influence moved the Greek statues from abstract figures in geometric style to a representational form of art. The statues from this period show the idealization, stiffness, and at times gracefulness of Egyptian art. It took a couple of centuries for Greek artists to arrive at a natural representation in sculpture.

Fair trade: Trade between Phoenicians and Greeks was vigorous in the early centuries of this phase. In fact, if Egypt influenced Greece in art and Indian civilization influenced philosophy and science, the Phoenicians taught the Greeks the art of seafaring and virtues of trade (unfortunately, including slave trade) and colonization. Since Phoenicians, who were the chief naval and trading power, mostly controlled the southern shores of Mediterranean, the Greeks over time came to control its northern shores, with Sicily emerging as region of shared influence. Greece imported glass, timber, slaves, hunting dogs, and a purple dye known as Tyrian purple, which was derived from a sea snail. The word *phoinios*, from which *Phoenician* is derived, means *purple* in Greek and shows how important trade with the Phoenicians was. Since the Phoenicians also traded with Egypt, Iberia, Britain, Cyprus, Carthage, and Atlantic coastal Africa, they clearly must have broadened the Greek trade horizons considerably.

Impact on productive outcomes: The impact on productive outcomes was considerable through both colonization and trade. It is no perhaps exaggeration to say that with trade and colonization patterned after Phoenicians, ancient Greece would have remained a minor culture barely remembered by history. Thus, the Greek debt to Phoenicians is greater than their debts to Egypt and India, since without the former, the latter would not have happened.

Impact on creative outcomes: The roots of Greek art can be traced to Egypt, which was truly the first form of significant intellectual creativity in Greece. It has been suggested that early Greek interest in philosophy and mathematics is traceable to art.

Impact of Mesopotamia and India

Channels of transmission: Individual travels to Mesopotamia and Asia Minor were the principal channels.

Transmission of intellectual creativity: Greek civilization was rapidly developing during this phase. Greek travelers are said to have begun visiting Babylon and India in search of "knowledge" and were most assuredly influenced by their achievements. We shall discuss this in more detail in the next chapter. Recent research has suggested that Greek adventurers and knowledge-seekers traveled to India as early as the sixth century BCE. These early Greek travels to Asia may form the knowledge base for Alexander's campaign two centuries later.

12.9 Productive and Creative Outcomes

The teachers in the earliest academies had begun to speculate about the nature of the universe, the nature of the human mind, and the possibility of knowledge toward the end of the current phase. Because the small city-states constantly fought with each other, the academies also got into recording events or history. The polity also supported the cause of theater and drama, strangely of a tragic storyline. Thus, there was strong, though indirect, support for the intellectual creativity. Constant wars also demanded practical innovation in weapons and in organization of the military. On the left, practical creativity was valued, on the right, the impulse for religious creativity was not overwhelming, and in the middle, intellectual creation was beginning to be sponsored by the state for its own purpose. Even a cursory study of the economic, political, and social structures of ancient Greece clearly demonstrates that by 500 BCE, it had not yet achieved a favorable internal creative balance but was getting close.

Thus, by the end of the current phase, ancient Greece was on its way to achieving a favorable internal creative balance, as evidenced by the rise of Pythagoras (582–507 BCE), who was likely influenced by Indian learning in general and Jain philosophy in particular. The decisive change occurred in the next phase, when Greeks became acquainted with Mesopotamian astronomy and Indian achievements in science. We cover the brilliant creative achievements of the Greek civilization and Hellenistic states more fully in the next chapter.

Summarizing Achievements in Abstract Systems-Building Capability (ASBC)

As noted in chapter 7, the breakthroughs in ASBC mostly reside in formal sciences and philosophy. Clearly, by the end of the phase, the ASBC of ancient Greece must be characterized as moderate: it had adopted alphabetical script and mastered the creative method but had relatively weakly developed epistemology.

History, Causes, and Outcomes of the Mesopotamian Civilization

12.10 Brief Political History (1000–539 BCE)

The neo-Assyrian state founded in 911 BCE flourished, with Babylon occupying a pivotal place in Assyrian state. Taking advantage of a civil war, Nabonassar expanded the power of Babylon in 747 BCE, though nominally continuing to be a vassal of the Assyrian king Tiglath-Pileser. The year 747 BCE may thus be regarded as the founding of the neo-Babylonian state. Fourteen years after the death of the powerful Assyrian king, Ashurbanipal, in 612 BCE, Babylonians under Nabopolassar, a Chaldean, in alliance with Persians, captured the capital city of Nineveh and reduced it to ruins to expand the neo-Babylonian state. However, in 539 BCE, in its moment of weakness, Mesopotamia itself was absorbed into a rising Persian Empire, never to exist again. For over two millennia, neither the Mesopotamians nor the world had any memory of ancient Mesopotamia until its ruins were discovered in the mid-nineteenth century. The neo-Babylonian state lasted two hundred years and was, therefore, the last hurrah of the Mesopotamian civilization.

12.11 Intrinsic Causes

Significant Changes in Institutional Structures and Processes

The fundamental distinction between the Assyrian state in the north and the new Babylonian state in the south was that a military dynasty ruled the former and priests-turned-kings ruled the latter. While the soldier reigned supreme in Assyria, the priests, farmers, and traders mattered in Babylonia. There were other few fundamental changes in political, economic, religious, social, and military structures. Slavery was still pervasive. Women were still auctioned for marriage. Religious ceremonies included animal sacrifice, and people remained superstitious; men held a yearly festival called Mushtkaru Buylshu to ward off evil spirits. The religion remained polytheistic, unaffected by Zoroastrianism on the eastern flank and monotheistic Judaism on the western flank.

The upper classes lived in greater luxury and displayed arrogance, with significant spending on monuments and palaces as evidenced by the tower of Babel and the Hanging Gardens. The class conflicts were worse in the Assyrian north compared to the Babylonian south. However, Mesopotamia as a whole remained a highly stratified society. Internal wars were fought with high frequency and undiminished viciousness. Their internal divisions created an opening for Darius to conquer Mesopotamia. Probably the science-religion conflict in Babylon was modest at worst because the ruling elite were more business-friendly and because the city was very cosmopolitan with many religious and ethnic strains constituting its makeup.

Changes in Beliefs and Ideology at the End of Birth Phase

Perhaps the only significant change was greater social equality and equality of opportunity in the neo-Babylonian state that emerged during the phase because it was a seething mixture of different ethnic strains all competing in a relatively open manner.

The belief in the possibility of knowledge and attitudes of openness and aggression toward others continued unchanged.

12.12 Extrinsic Peaceful Causes or Sum Total of Others' Constructive Outcomes

Impact of Indian Civilization

Channels of transmission: Trade remained the principal channel of transmission; however, its importance was relatively declining.

Transmission of creativity: It is known that Ashurbanipal (668–626 BCE)—a very Indian-sounding name—cultivated Indian plants that included cotton or "wool-bearing trees" of India. Little else is known of any creative exchange during the phase.

Fair trade: The trade between India and Mesopotamia declined but likely continued during the current period. Knobbed pottery in Sumer has been traced to India. Trade with others was generally in decline because of changes in Mesopotamian and Egyptian civilizations and because Greece, Persia, and the Roman Republic were still being established. Thus, Indian civilization was, despite its openness to the creativity of other civilizations, in a stagnant period with respect to interaction with the rest of the world.

Peaceful migrations: There were no significant migrations in or out of India during this period in part because most other civilizations were in decline, in early phases of birth, or were insular in nature.

Impact on productive outcomes: Impact on productive outcomes must be considered as modest at best.

Impact on creative outcomes: There was little impact on the creative outcomes.

Impact of Egyptian Civilization

During this phase, Egyptian and Mesopotamian civilizations were in a long-term decline and did not directly or materially influence one another.

12.13 Productive Outcomes

Productive Outcomes

The neo-Babylonian state was truly a melting pot, attracting Chaldeans, Persians, and many other groups. It seems that the newcomers had opportunities commensurate with their talent, resulting in increased wealth production. We also believe that while external trade likely suffered because of the political instability resulting from civil strife and the pressures exerted by Persian Empire on the eastern flank, internal trade in the neo-Babylonian state probably got a boost because of the power enjoyed by the business class.

12.14 Creative Outcomes

The significant creative outcomes of Mesopotamian civilization occurred in practical technology, mathematics, astronomy, and medicine. We have already dealt with achievements in practical creativity for civilizations as a whole above. There was little in religious and philosophical creativity in Mesopotamia that deserves special mention. Thus, below we summarize achievements in formal, natural, and biological sciences.

12.15 Achievements in Science

Achievements in Formal Sciences

Mathematics: It is interesting to compare the achievements of the Old Babylonian period of 1800–1500 BCE and the Babylonian mathematics transmitted to us from the Seleucid empire in the post-Alexander period. One finds little progress from one period to the next, and we must conclude that Babylonian mathematics remained in a state of suspended animation for over a millennia. This observation has several implications: it strengthens the notion that mathematics from the older period was transmitted from India and that the Mesopotamian civilization was not particularly strong in formal sciences. One does not find related breakthroughs in linguistics and logic either. Finally, it also strengthens the argument that the greater ability to predict eclipses was really driven by the needs of astrology and not a real scientific orientation. The hallmark of the scientific orientation is typically genuine breakthroughs in several areas of knowledge, not just one.

Achievements in Natural Sciences

Astronomy: Babylonian astronomers recognized that the motion of astronomical bodies is periodic. Astronomer Ammisagugga's Table 63 recorded the period between first and last visible risings of Venus as twenty-one years. Babylonian astronomers did not believe in geocentric theories because there was little evidence of that; that unique honor must be reserved for Aristotle's speculations several centuries later.

Babylonian astronomers had a greater interest in establishing the position of heavenly bodies than in establishing their motion. The observations, which were indeed extensive, were strictly empirical and lacking, unlike later astronomers of Hellenistic states, geometry, or philosophical speculation. There is reason to believe that Babylonians subscribed to a heliocentric solar system based on the writings of several Chaldean astronomers, such as Kidinnu, Sudines, and Naburimannu. It is not clear whether the idea originated within Babylon.

Achievements in Biological Sciences

Medicine: The *Diagnostic Handbook* written almost half a millennium earlier was still the main reference book physicians used. One may therefore conclude that significant progress in the medical field did not occur during the current phase.

Summarizing Achievements in Abstract System-Building Capability (ASBC)

Clearly, by the end of the phase, the ASBC of Mesopotamian civilization must be characterized as advanced: it had developed alphabetical script, mastered the creative method, and despite lacking formal epistemology, showed skill in uniting observation and reason in astronomy.

History, Causes, and Outcomes of the Chinese Civilization

12.16 Brief Political History (1000–481 BCE)

Chinese civilization continued its peaceful and insular evolution during the current phase. The nomadic attacks destroyed its capital and forced the western Zhou (1122–771 BCE) to move east and initiate the eastern Zhou period starting in 771 BCE. Following this, the Chinese civilization went through the so-called Spring and Autumn Period (771–481 BCE), during which Zhou powers weakened considerably and most states professed only a symbolic allegiance to the central authority, It was a period of constant strife. During the Spring and Autumn Period, there were over 480 internal wars, fifty-two vassal states vanquished, and thirty-six kings killed.

12.17 Intrinsic Causes

Significant Changes in Institutional Structures and Processes

We will not delve into a detailed description of the changes in internal structures and processes of the Chinese civilization during the current phase, as there was little change of significance from the end of the first phase. We limit ourselves to noting that Chinese political authority was fragmented, with a highly decentralized political structure, a very weak monarch, and actual power residing in the hands of the provinces and feudal lords. However, this Chinese feudalism must not be confused with European feudalism of the Middle Ages. The Chinese version was on a much bigger scale, with each fiefdom two to three orders of magnitude larger than that of European feudal lords in the Middle Ages. In a later section, we focus on the emerging uniqueness of the Chinese civilization since this uniqueness is most relevant to us in terms of the history of science. Slavery in China was either nonexistent or was minimal. China did not develop a caste system. Wealth polarization was moderate, and thus China experienced relatively moderate class stratification. The current period was a period of constant internal wars, though externally, true to its nature, China was peaceful unless attacked. There was little science-religion conflict since both science and organized religion did not exist.

Changes in Beliefs and Ideology at the End of the Birth Phase

There was little significant change in the belief system of the Chinese civilization during the current phase. The civilization remained weak in abstract systems-building capability and thus entertained only a modest belief in the possibility of real knowledge through reason and observation, commendably continued to lack slavery and caste system, remained insular while developing a natural sense of cultural superiority, and remained peaceful toward other social orders unless attacked.

12.18 Extrinsic Peaceful Causes or Sum Total of Others' Constructive Outcomes

China was relatively insular to outside influences because of geographical barriers and distance, and there was little influence in either direction.

12.19 Productive Outcomes

Steady improvements in wealth creation probably continued, interrupted by plentiful internal wars during the phase. There was considerable internal trade, and the Chinese civilization generally resisted any peaceful migrations to other parts of the world.

12.20 Creative Outcomes

Uniqueness of Chinese Civilization

Chinese civilization is perhaps the most unique major long-living civilization in history. This uniqueness has a direct bearing on China's ability to excel in practical creativity, an inability to match that excellence in religious and intellectual creativity, and an ability to maintain unequaled continuity and sustained political independence relative to other civilizations and nomads over a nearly five-millennia recorded history with only a couple of exceptions. From the perspective of the rest of the world, China stands out as the great continuous contributor of the practical inventions until the end of first millennium CE. Consider the following:

- The terrain in North China is not generally flat, unlike other ancient centers of civilization in India, Egypt, and West Asia. However, it was definitely not like a desert either. It did not lack water—one might say that often it had too much of it. This made agriculture more difficult, and the people hardy and hardworking.
- Politically, during this period, as in any significant period in China's long history, China moved between centralized authority and a period of chaos from infighting or nomadic invasions. However, central authority always had the last word in China.
- China's external orientation was that of nonaggression. No doubt, part of this has to do with the values of Chinese civilization. However, it was also because China needed its military strength to maintain a Chinese state that had the natural potential to be as big as most empires. Bound by desert and Siberia in the north and west, Himalayas and the Tibetan Plateau in the south, and a sea in the east, the Chinese state always wanted to fill the available landmass early in its history.
- China also remained insular in many ways. It invented a logograph and became heavily invested in this form of writing early on. This logographic script provided China with a linguistic unity because logographs do not evolve into different written scripts. This linguistic unity and relative geographical isolation from the rest of the world provided China with an unusual cultural identity internally and insularity externally.
- The focus of social life was decidedly family and ethical living. China only had limited slavery in its early history.
- The surplus in China was thus was hardly wasted on monuments to the extent it was in ancient Egypt. The Chinese state instead invested in projects such as the Great Wall, which helped protect China from invasions and helped create a cultural and political unity as well as create great irrigation projects time and again.

All the above comments apply to current phase and more or less to later phases.

Achievements in Religious Creativity

Until the arrival of Buddhism more than half a millennium after the current period ended, religion in China never went beyond open-ended polytheism, ancestor worship, and Taoism. China never experienced the rise of a priest class with economic power. Religion never played a controlling role in Chinese culture for long.

Achievements in Philosophical Creativity

About 600 BCE, the philosophy of Taoism, originated by Lao Tze during the Warring States period, was based on an intuitive understanding of natural law and how man should accept it and not fight it. It preached harmony with nature, personal development based on freedom, and search for immortality. The Taoist concept of yin and yang is actually a general theory of evolution and change based on two opposing aspects in a natural or social phenomenon. The origins of Taoism go back to Chinese polytheism, as evidenced by the Tao deities such as the Jade emperor or supreme deity, the god of prosperity (Cai Shen), the god of war (Guan Di), and the gods of good luck (the so-called eight immortals that actually appeared much later during the Tang dynasty). It is interesting to note that this version of Chinese polytheism is not rooted in forces of nature that were feared or loved; rather, it was rooted in perceived social forces, such as good luck and war. This of course follows the basic premise that man must necessarily live in harmony with nature, so the control of events shifts to social forces, an essentially accurate description of the human condition. Taoism did not truly flourish in China until about five hundred years later.

Achievements in Art

During the phase, Chinese art continued to focus on jade, bronze castings, wooden sculptures, glass beads, and lacquerware. Excavations going back to the state of Chu in the Yangtze River valley during the Warring States period have uncovered many art objects. The highly expressive Taoist symbol of yin and yang, though its date of origin is difficult to determine accurately, is believed to have been developed during the current phase. The state of Chu was a rich source of art in early China and developed in the Yangtze River valley. Excavations of Chu tombs have found painted wooden sculptures, jade disks, glass beads, musical instruments, and an assortment of lacquerware.

12.21 Achievements in Science

Formal Science

Chinese civilization did not adopt or invent alphabetical script and therefore and did not fulfill all the necessary and sufficient conditions of mature protoscience and the birth of science. One does not witness any significant advances in mathematics and formal logic either.

Natural Science

However, the strong practical bent of the civilization did not entirely prevent Chinese thinkers from making accurate observations of heavenly bodies and developing a less sophisticated version of the principle of equivalence during this phase. Chinese observations about the astronomical phenomenon of solar eclipses, exploding supernovas, and shooting stars were recorded around this period and earlier.

Summarizing Achievements in Abstract System-Building Capability (ASBC)

By the end of the phase, the ASBC of the Chinese civilization must be characterized as low: it had mastered the creative method but had failed to adopt or develop both alphabetical script and epistemology.

History, Causes, and Outcomes of the Indian Civilization

12.22 Brief Political History (1000–550 BCE)

In India, the Aryans had spread themselves to the east along the Ganges as well as to the south by 1500 BCE through expansion of agriculture and cultural diffusion. Under the stable social structure of a caste system and enlightened spirituality, the civilization prospered. It sprung forth sixteen states comparable in size to the nation-states of modern Europe, including Kosala, Magdha, Kur, Panchala, Kashi, and Kamboja, which were known collectively as Mahajanapadas or the People's Great Republics. In addition, a number of small states existed. These states had either hereditary or elected rulers. By the end of the current phase, these states were beginning to coalesce into four regional empires of Kosal, Magdha, Vatsa, and Avanti.

12.23 Intrinsic Causes

Changes in Intrinsic Causes—Institutional Systems, Structures, and Processes

Political system: The political structure of states within the Indian civilization had three levels; the smallest unit was of course the village. The village was a nearly self-contained democracy with an elected *panchayat* to run village affairs. Each village would have the critical non-agricultural skills, such as a carpenter, ironsmith, and tanner, to address local needs. The next structure was the city government, headed by the city assembly. The last structure was the monarch and his council of ministers that managed the affairs of the state, either with monarch as the head of the state or at times as a republican form. A council of appointed elders called *samiti* or a senate limited the king's powers and assisted him in the administration of the state. In addition, there was also a *sabha* that fulfilled the role of judiciary. Thus, the power of monarchy was far from absolute and never divine. Both political structures and religious and ethical codes limited his powers. Ancient literature mentions at least sixteen such states in northern India alone. As we shall point out in the next chapter, by the fifth century BCE, however, North India was ruled by the unpopular Nanda dynasty. It covered an area of about three million square kilometers and had a population of around fifty million.

Military capability: Rules of military engagement protected the villages. The armies did not overrun villages and were not allowed to coerce food and shelter from the villagers. The war among states was fought in open fields and was based on clearly defined ethical rules of warfare. The development in weapons was unimpressive, with this civilization relying on swords, axes, mace, bow and arrow, and javelins. The war tactics, on the other hand, continued to evolve and included overly complex formations known as the wheel, lotus, eagle, and needle and fish. The eagle formation, based on copying the toughness of an eagle to a fighting force, was particularly interesting: the beak consisted of elite troops and mounted elephants, the wings were the swiftest troops, and the body consisted of the rest. The military retained the four-part structure: infantry, elephants, chariots, and archers.

Economic organization: The people owned the land and both farming and raising cattle were practiced. The crafts and industry were highly developed and organized into guilds, such as stoneworkers, woodworkers, metalworkers, leatherworkers, ivory-workers, painters, decorators, potters, dyers, fisherman, sailors, trappers, hunters, butchers, confectioners, barbers, florists, cooks, and basket makers, to name a few. The existence of guilds and the absence of slavery and landlords points to a relatively egalitarian society with "no landlords, no paupers, no millionaires, and no slums." The defining principle of the economic structure was the concept of *chaturvarna*, which divided people into four categories depending on their ability and temperament: the intellectuals and priests, soldiers, merchant class, and workers. It was not precisely the class system that we find in other civilizations, although it obviously met the need for division of labor and social stability. The real significance of the concept was that ideally it allowed an individual to achieve what he was capable of achieving. In practice, though, birth had become an increasingly significant determinant of the varna. But there were also many famous examples of people changing their varnas from what was defined by birth. The guidance on taxation was one tenth of the produce in kind. The village unit was primarily a barter system. However, a cash economy typically developed in the cities. There was limited trade between the cities and villages when the power of the state shrank, and this trade expanded during periods of expansion of the power of the state.

Religious systems of faith: Perhaps the most dominant aspect of Indian life during this period was thoughtful spirituality. Early Indian thinkers thought deeply about existential anxiety and faced it intelligently and courageously and not based on faith or revelation. Their reflections ultimately led them to the notion of consciousness or being as the unchanging, limitless, eternal, and a self-evident reality. They further saw this individual consciousness as equivalent to the ultimate reality of the universe. To achieve this goal, they perfected the techniques of yoga and meditation. Indian thinkers did not stop there. They used this spiritual insight to order social, economic, and political life. However, this was not accomplished through a dogma with a judging god upon death. They wanted to experience the ultimate reality here on earth. The point was to live a full life, including sensual pleasure, worldly success, duty to others, and ultimate liberation. Their approach to spirituality was as experimental as realistically possible and therefore could not be easily threatened by potential new spiritual, psychological, or scientific discovery. Thus, their religiosity was not rigidly structured; it was an organic part of social structure. It tolerated a wide range of beliefs, including atheism, surviving Vedic polytheism, emerging pantheistic Hinduism, and agnosticism, thus ensuring religious and intellectual freedom. But the caste system continued to become increasingly rigid during this phase, resulting in the formidable protestant reactions of Buddhism and Jainism in the next phase. The emerging strength of monism was balanced by a strong streak of polytheism and agnosticism lurking in the background. The key was a tolerance of diverse religious viewpoints. Thus, Indian civilization remained incapable of producing an intolerant monotheistic doctrine.

There was little science-religion conflict during this phase, and the role of spirituality was counterbalanced by both an agnostic belief system and the emergence of rational thinking. The world had never witnessed such religious creativity and amazingly, these irreconcilable systems existed side by side. No saints or thinkers were executed.

Legal system: A formally codified law or even canonical law was still to emerge. The concept of dharma or righteous conduct, the panchayats in the villages, and the sabha in the cities formed the backbone of the legal system. The circumscribed power of the kings, the absence an elite class addicted to the good life because of a spiritual orientation, and the relative absence of extreme wealth polarization all tended to reduce the need for formal law. The customs, ethics, and concept of dharma seemed to suffice.

Social structures: Within the higher castes, social structure was derived from the Harappa and Ganges phases of the civilization. The basic unit was the extended family or *kula* and was headed by a *kulapati*. A collection of kulas was called a *vas* and was headed by a *vaspati*. Multiple vas units constituted a *gana* and were headed by a *ganapati*. Finally, several ganas constituted a *rashtra* or a state or nation. Increasing rigidity in the caste system Hinduism sanctioned meant that the caste system was effective in both intensifying class conflicts and providing social cohesion since all classes universally accepted the law of karma and rebirth.

Knowledge-creating and educational structures: Knowledge-creating institutions in Indian civilization during the phase consisted of academies run by great teachers and were focused on religious, ethical, philosophical, and scientific research and were supported by the ruling dynasties. Knowledge in practical creativity was left to the individual engaged in the economic activity. The academies also served as educational institutions for the children of wealthy families—a model that similar to one that evolved in ancient Greece as well.

Wealth allocation: External wars were unknown and interstate wars were infrequent. When these wars occurred, the rules of engagement were well defined. Thus, military expenditures were not high. The absence of an elite focused on the good life and the relatively egalitarian nature and spiritual orientation of society meant that the surplus was not wasted on luxuries. Similarly, the rising tide of monism, with its focus on the identity of Atman and Brahman within meant that temple-building simply did not exist. Spiritual inquiry attracted some of the best minds. However, spiritual inquiry was dramatically different from a dogmatic religious inquiry as it also included studies in physical body philosophy, psychology, and logic. Therefore, it is more appropriately classified as an intellectual endeavor. Thus, the wealth-allocation process ensured that a respectable portion of the surplus went into practical and intellectual creativity.

Social cohesion: Given the lack of slavery and excessive economic disparity, the self-enforcing concept of dharma under the law of karma and reincarnation was sufficient to provide social cohesion. More than any other civilization, Indian civilization did not rely on political, religious, or economic institutions to ensure social cohesion; it employed concept of individual dharma.

Internal wars: The current phase was a continuation of the age of republics and the coming age of empires. As a result, the internal wars were still rather circumscribed.

Formative Beliefs and Ideology at the End of Birth Phase

Because of breakthroughs in epistemology and logic, Indian civilization further strengthened its belief in the possibility of real knowledge based on union of sense data and reason. However, rising monism not only created the potential for excessive spirituality as a route to knowledge based on contemplation alone but also strengthened belief in reincarnation and karma, which strengthened the caste system. The civilization remained opened to the creativity of others and remained peaceful toward other social orders.

12.24 Extrinsic Peaceful Causes or Sum Total of Others' Constructive Outcomes

Because of instability in West Asia, the emerging nature of the ancient Greece and Roman worlds, and the insularity of the Chinese civilization, there was little interaction between India and other civilizations.

Mesopotamia and India

The Indian civilization's trade with Mesopotamia had begun its decline after the center of gravity of Indian civilization began moving east due to the Indus River flooding in the early second millennium BCE.

12.25 Productive Outcomes

There is no record of significant changes in wealth creation. The slow and steady invention and adoption of practical technology no doubt continued.

12.26 Creative Outcomes

In discussing the creative achievements during the phase, we will focus on specific disciplines as well as the underlying philosophical systems or schools of philosophy, which are typically multidisciplinary and include religion, philosophy, and sciences. The advantage of this two-prong approach will be to get a fuller appreciation of the achievements without unnecessary repetition. We start with achievements in religion followed by philosophy and then move through formal, natural, and social sciences. In detailing ancient Indian achievements during this and subsequent phases, one does, however, face a daunting task: the sources are vast; the achievements are spread in literature on science, religion, and metaphysics; dating the material is at times uncertain; much material has been lost or not fully deciphered or understood; and one needs to separate the truth from intentional and unintentional distortion by foreign and domestic vested interests. It is a task whose completion will require decades of objective scholarship. We base our story in this book almost exclusively on the existing secondary and tertiary sources with a commonsense selection. Our focus is on providing a fairer interpretation of the evolving "facts" as understood today. Significant sources of ancient Indian philosophy, religion, and science, as we mentioned in chapter 9, have been briefly summarized in appendix H.

Ancient Indian civilization from about 1000 BCE on was a culture where social, economic, political, and religious structures embodied freedom in an environment of sustained political independence and an internal creative balance favorable to intellectual creativity. From 900 to 550 BCE was a period of extraordinary intellectual and spiritual creativity. Indian civilization covered an area more than order of magnitude greater than that of Greek city-states at their height, and the period under consideration in this chapter is nearly as long as the entire period of the existence of the organized Greek city-states at their peak or from about 500 to 250 BCE. In addition, Indian spirituality was of a deeper, freer, and abiding character than that of the Greeks and was, therefore, more intertwined with science because it had less need for separation.

Individual life was not without firm yet flexible guidance. The concept of four stages of life was well established and corresponded to four great goals of life: pleasure, success (with its three aspects of wealth, fame, and power), duty to others, and spiritual liberation. The first two formed the path of desire and the latter two the path of renunciation. These goals were not exclusive assigned to a particular stage; rather a goal peaked in one stage and then gently gave way to the next goal in the following stage. In other words, they overlapped to an extent, depending on individual inclination. There was, thus, balance, dynamics, and freedom in the way an ideal individual life evolved.

In short, it appears to us that religious and intellectual creativity in Indian civilization during this period was the gentle outpouring of a tolerant, philosophical, spiritually inclined, and curious people not burdened by religious dogma, practical demands of empires, or internal wars and blessed with natural bounty. As we shall see in the following chapters, this outpouring materially slowed down only when the civilization lost its sustained political independence to creed-mad invaders (Turks and Moguls) and dried out altogether when greed-mad invaders (Portuguese, French, and British) systematically drained its wealth on a sustained basis.

Thus, Indian civilization during this phase embodied both structure and freedom and allowed the individual the space needed to be creative. It was certainly an amazing achievement for its age and perhaps for any age. As we review the religious and intellectual achievements of Indian civilization during this period, we must keep in mind this nondogmatic spiritual otherworldliness coupled with a worldliness embodying individual freedom. The Western assessment of ancient Indian civilization is burdened with a near exclusive emphasis on the former at the expense of the latter since that served the needs of Western imperialism since 1750 CE. Below we cover the achievements of Indian civilization in religion, philosophy, and formal, natural, social, and biological sciences during the current phase.

Achievements in Religious Creativity

It is indeed difficult to separate developments in religion and philosophy during the phase, or most other periods of Indian history for that matter, since there is considerable overlap. Development of monism and Buddhism has both religious and philosophical implications, particularly in metaphysics and ethics. Complicating matters further, often developments in epistemology and logic also took place under the guiding hand of a religious/philosophical system. Nevertheless, we have chosen to treat Hinduism and Jainism as religions and most other religious doctrines, including monism and Buddhism, as philosophical systems.

Hinduism: In Brihadaranyaka Upanishad, Yajnavalkya elaborates on the metaphysics of rebirth and transmigration of soul from one body to another and the law of karma without attempting to demonstrate it. By becoming free of desire, the soul can revert to the Brahman and put an end to the transmigration process. The law of karma that controls the reincarnation cycle is postulated as a moral law of action and reaction.

Jainism: Jainism is dualistic—that is, matter and souls are entirely different types of substances. It borders on atheism since a creator god is denied. The universe is eternal, matter and souls being equally uncreated. The universe contains gods or greater souls who may be worshipped for various reasons, but there is no being outside it exercising control over it. Thus, both the imminent and transcendent nature is denied to the god. The belief in transmigration is retained; however, the concept of karma in Jainism is fundamentally different: it represents a natural law and not a moral law as in Hinduism. Thus Jainism, while denying even an imminent or transcendent god, accommodates the multiple gods of the majority polytheistic Hindu population and the idea of transmigration. In this respect, to accommodate Hinduism, it resembles historical Buddhism.

Achievements in Philosophical Creativity

We will discuss the achievements in philosophy under metaphysics, epistemology, ethics, and aesthetics since logic will be discussed under Formal Sciences. The ancient literature here is so extensive that we must be necessarily very selective. We hope to cover a reasonably broad spectrum pertaining to this period.

Metaphysics: Metaphysics is by definition speculative unless it metamorphoses into a faith, in which case it no longer remains speculative for the believer but will continue to be so for nonbelievers. Ancient India during this phase produced just about every conceivable kind of metaphysics. This is hardly surprising, given the free and intellectually charged atmosphere, absence of established science, and the tradition of speculative metaphysics we find beginning with Rig Veda dating back to 4000 BCE. This tradition talks about the existence of a nonbeing originally and how the being evolved out of it or how life evolved out of matter. Another theory in Rig Veda argues that in the beginning there was neither being or nonbeing and then struggles with how the world or God might have arisen out of it, thus taking a nascent agnostic or a skeptical position. Below, we summarize the key metaphysical doctrines that emerged during the current phase.

Vedantic monism: The approach of monism was systematized by Indians as recorded in the Upanishads. It was immortalized by "Ahm Brahma ashmi" or God and self are identical. This uttering would, of course, be considered a blasphemy in any monotheistic religion! In Chandogya Upanishad, Sandliya establishes the doctrine of the equivalence of Atman and Brahman. Atman is the individual consciousness, belonging to a different order of existence than body and mind, and Brahman is the ultimate reality of the universe. The identity may be realized through meditation when a higher mental state is reached. Monism may be seen as an attempt by human mind to explain the world without a transcendent but through an imminent God while retaining the immortality of human spirit.

- **Earliest agnosticism:** Sanjaya Belatthiputta, a contemporary of Buddha, and Mahavira were the leaders of the agnostics (*ajnanavada*). Sanjaya rejected all the theories of transmigration, rebirth, and the equivalence of self and Brahman. Here is a sample of what he preached:

  If you ask me if there exists another world after death, if I thought that there exists another world, would I declare that to you? I don't think so. I don't think in that way. I don't think otherwise. I don't think not. I don't think not not. If you asked me if there isn't another world...both is and isn't...neither is nor isn't...if there are beings who transmigrate...if there aren't...both are and aren't...neither are nor aren't...if the Tathagata exists after death...doesn't...both...neither exists nor exists after death, would I declare that to you? I don't think so. I don't think in that way. I don't think otherwise. I don't think not. I don't think not not.

  Sanjay's agnosticism has been called dialectical existentialism because he did not lay out a path to nirvana.

- **Buddhism:** There is no god or immortality of soul in original Buddhist teaching. The original teaching of Buddha was purely agnostic and insisted on the nonexistence of the soul, the impermanence of all existence, and suffering all "conditioned" life experiences. The evolution and impermanence of the world was explained through the concept of dependent co-origination, which stated that change occurs through reciprocal impact of one part of the universe on another. The focus was on achieving nirvana or elimination of suffering through right knowledge, right actions, right beliefs, and meditation. When nirvana is attained, conditioned existence or suffering stops, and only the state of nirvana exists. The concept of transmigration was incorporated later, thus subordinating natural law to moral law and thereby negating the central doctrine of Buddhist agnosticism. Buddha himself refused to speculate about the ultimate nature of the universe. His primary concern was suffering humanity. His message embodied compassion and avoiding the extremes in life. What distinguishes Buddhist agnosticism from modern existentialism is absence of despair in the former.

- **Dualism:** In the Vaisheshika system, God is the efficient cause of the world, while the atoms are the material cause. Atoms and souls are eternal, uncreated, and finite in space and time. There is only one God who is omniscient and omnipotent; grace and intelligence are eternal. Though God established the laws of the universe and governs it, he is never entangled in the cycle of existence. Souls may achieve liberation through ethical living and doing duty.

- **Fatalism:** While the Hindus, Buddhists, and Jains believed that karma could be altered by the deeds in this life, Ajivikas believed that karma was entirely predestined (*niyati*) and could not be altered at all. This doctrine remained a minor school at best and is of historical interest only.

- **Materialism:** The school of materialism called *lokayata* did not believe in the cycle of rebirth and transmigration. The frugal virtues of Buddhism and Jainism were rejected and followers were encouraged to reject all religious observances and make the most of life's pleasures, thus risking falling into hedonism. The original writings of the lokayata are lost to us, though Brhaspati is said to be its author. The lokayata was radically antitradition and regarded the Vedas as false.

The breadth of speculation by Indian philosophers and metaphysicians during this period is remarkable and is the unshakable proof of the prevalent creative freedom. It is fair to state that mainstream metaphysical position in ancient India during this phase refused to choose between materialism and spiritualism, believing it to be a false choice. It stuck to the notion that both are real, and the spirit cannot be derived from matter alone. In creative evolution, they need each other. One can open one's eyes and affirm matter, and at the same time, one can close one's eyes and affirm the existence of spirit.

One can see the evolution of natural polytheism from the previous phase to monism, agnosticism, and atheism. Significantly, structured polytheism with the Hindu trinity was to emerge nearly a millennium later.

Epistemology: Many thinkers contributed to the development of epistemology during this period. We shall focus our attention on just two: Uddalaka and Kannada. The former was among the first, and the latter was the most significant.

Uddalaka: Uddalaka may be considered the true founder of epistemology. He is first mentioned in Satapathabrahmana, but actually laid out his theory of knowledge in Chandogya Upanishad (eighth to seventh centuries BCE) in the form of a dialogue with his son. Uddalaka begins by doubting the received traditions, including Vedanta, in favor of the careful observation of nature and using induction in drawing conclusions from the observations. He stressed the idea of universal natural laws, universal natural elements, mental elements (logical categories), and understanding causal relationship through experimentation and induction. He believed that it was possible to generalize about the nature of things by disregarding the surface differences. He stressed that there had to be an original matter and energy for the universe to evolve and that upon death, life goes back to the ultimate elements without attainment of a higher mental state. Thus, for the first time in human history, the law of gods gave way to natural law based on observation and reason. It is noteworthy that he was given a place of honor in the same Upanishad that also honored the metaphysics he was arguing against!

Kannada: If Uddalaka was the genius to first formulate a relatively basic but essentially accurate theory of knowledge, Kannada systematized it and gave it full expression. His work, called the Vaisheshika (*particularity*) school, may be regarded as both a theory of knowledge as well as its application to several fields in the arena of natural science. Here we limit ourselves to briefly summarizing his epistemology while covering his achievements in specific sciences below under natural sciences. Kannada asserted that there are two means of knowledge: sensation (*pratyaksha*) and inference (*anuman*) through the middle term (*laingika*). He defined his theory of inference as consisting of the processes of induction and deduction. Kannada also defined two laws of casualty, four invalid means of knowledge, possible errors in the process of induction, and his method of exhaustion to supplement his theory of inference. A more detailed discussion of his brilliant epistemology is included in appendix K.

Ethics: Any discussion of ancient Indian ethics must begin with an understanding of the concept of dharma and its interpretation in the Vedas and Upanishads, Buddhism, and the two great epics of *Mahabharata* and *Ramayana*. There is uncertainty as to when these works were first compiled in the form known to us. It is therefore difficult to develop an accurate timeline of the development of ancient Indian ethical theory. In what follows, we summarize the main threads of the Indian ethical theory without worrying too much about its timeline. It is probably safe to assume, however, that these major works were conceived no later than about 2,500 years ago and for that reason are included in the current phase.

The concept of dharma first finds expression in Rig Veda. It is definitely unlike a simplistic rule-based ethics, such as the Ten Commandments. Indian thinkers were concerned that a rule-based ethics is difficult to apply in specific instances since sometimes the best rules must be violated in order to be ethical. Instead, emphasis was placed on internal freedom and character development. The notion of internal freedom is enshrined in the concept of swadharma or one's own dharma. The point is repeatedly made in the Vedas and Upanishads that one's own dharma, However, imperfect, is better than the dharma of another. Clearly, this internal freedom could easily lapse into unethical behavior. Therefore, a lot of attention was devoted to ensuring that this tendency was minimized. The Indian approach to this problem was three fold:

1. **Concept of karma:** The concept of karma was introduced to solve the problem of evil. It is compatible with individual responsibility and reason, and it supports the idea of internal freedom. It degenerates into fate only if one is ignorant of the causal connections in the world. The unfortunate marriage between the concept of karma on the one hand and the concepts of reincarnation and a caste system resulted when the unholy alliance of metaphysics and vested social interests hijacked the concept of karma. Perhaps it is best to think of karma as a psychological law as far as the ethical theory is concerned. The significance of the law of karma, if viewed in this manner, is that it acts as a check on the internal freedom granted to the individual in his conduct. It was indeed a powerful force, constantly reminding the individual that there was indeed no free lunch.

2. **Dharma embodying both duty and virtue:** The two contradictory yet compatible aspects of duty and virtue find expression in the elaboration of the concept of dharma. On the one hand, the concept of dharma appears to resemble the concept of duty with limited reliance on the internal rule-based ethics. Rama, the hero of the epic *Ramayana*, displays a strong sense of rigid adherence to duty. This approach is similar to the inflexible Kantian moral imperative. On the other hand, the concept of dharma also embodies the concept of virtue. This is stated in the formulation "for the sake of happiness of many and for the sake of good of many." Krishna, the hero of the *Mahabharata* epic, displays an ethic based on virtue. This approach is similar to the utilitarian theory of ethics, which states that moral rules must be abstractions from what is socially virtuous. Both of these formulations in ancient India operated within the context of character development that emphasized truthfulness, generosity, forgiveness, goodness, kindness, and self-control. The teachers placed the idea of self-control at the center of character development since they felt character development was impossible without self-control. The much celebrated approach to developing self-control was enshrined in the science of yoga. The contradiction between concepts of duty and virtue within dharma was left unresolved on purpose as it was felt that both have a role to play in the ethical behavior.

3. **The golden mean:** Buddhists pioneered the concept of a middle path between the extremes and is well known. However, a mechanical adherence to the middle path can easily become sterile. The individual must be granted the freedom to choose behavior given the situation he finds himself in. Therefore, if the middle can take any position between the extremes, barring the extremes themselves, the golden mean can only be a crude first approximation and not the answer by itself in situations requiring ethical choices. Thus, the concept of golden mean as an ethical device can

only work within a broader framework of character development that Buddhist thought also so carefully emphasized.

Thus, we may surmise that the Indian theory of ethics embodied a character-based approach and not a rule-based approach to the problem of ethics. It granted the individual the internal freedom and developed successful approaches that prevented the misuse of this internal freedom. The Kantian moral imperative, the golden mean of Aristotle, and the more recent utilitarian theory of ethics find expression in the classical Indian theory of ethics. These approaches were given not just theoretical a formulation; they were given real-life meaning through the life experiences of great heroes like Krishna, Rama, and Buddha. This trio counts among the greatest personalities of history.

Aesthetics: Bharata proposed a theory of art, called the Rasa theory or theory of aesthetic pleasure, toward the end of the current phase. The Rasa theory viewed the artist as first subjectively experiencing the object of art being created and then objectifying that experience through a medium, such as theater, sculpture, or painting, thus a giving physical form to his subjective experience. The viewer then experiences similar or somewhat different emotions, depending on his own mood. Thus, art is a vehicle of self-expression for the artist, capturing that experience in the object of art, a medium to communicate that experience to the viewer and a way of reflecting on what is virtuous or meaningful in life on the part of the viewer. The Rasa theory does not dwell on the form of the object of art; it focused on the subjective state that a work of art evokes. Thus, the Rasa theory did not emphasize the need to understand the perceptual or intellectual aspect of the art from a theoretical point of view. Bharata started with an analysis of the psyche (*bhava–jagat*) identifying eight inherent emotions (*sthayi bhavas*), thirty-three transient emotions (*sanchari bhavas*), and a number of secondary emotions (*vibhavas* or *anubhavas*). The eight inherent emotions Bharata enumerated are love (*rati*), comedy (*hasya*), tragedy (*shoka*), anger (*krodha*), valor (*utsah*), fear (*bhaya*), horror (*jugupsa*), and surprise (*vismaya*). Bharata theorized that an emotion etched into a medium and conveyed to the viewer through senses transpired into Rasa and delighted the viewer. Bharata viewed Rasa as a unitary aesthetic channel through which the eight emotions express themselves through a work of art. Typically, one of these eight sentiments dominates in a particular piece of art. A more detailed discussion on art and Bharata's Nava Rasa theory of art is included in appendix J. The Nava Rasa theory most definitely was the first formal theory of art in the history of the world.

12.27 Achievements in Science

Formal Sciences

Under formal sciences, we discuss the key Indian achievements in mathematics, linguistics, and logic during the birth phase of science.

Mathematics: In mathematics, the earliest achievements of Indian civilization come from the Sulbha Sutras attached to Rig Veda at later dates. These ideas were further developed and tackle arithmetic and geometry and touch on algebra:

- A fully developed decimal place value system, with roots going back to Indus-Sarasvati era. The concept of zero was used in a text called *Lokavibhaga* dating back to 458 BCE, but there was no explicit symbol for it yet.
- Several beautiful shortcuts for multiplication of large numbers, indicating an excellent faculty for manipulating numbers.
- Full comfort with numbers as large as ten to the nineteenth power. Words for each large number are mentioned. By contrast, the largest number visualized by the Greeks several hundred years later was ten thousand.
- The concept of infinity was developed. Rig Veda states if infinity is subtracted from infinity, infinity remains.
- The concept of fractions and irrational numbers existed as evidenced by the formula for the square root of two.
- The so-called Pythagorean theorem is stated with an implied proof and several examples of triples.
- An approximate method for squaring circles and an exact method turning squares into rectangles is described.
- There is evidence of use of letters for numbers in later Sulbhasutra, a small initial step toward algebra.

The great mathematicians during the current phase associated with Rig Veda mathematics are Baudhayana (800–740 BCE), Manava (750 BCE), and Apastambha (650 BCE).

Linguistics: Sometime between the eighth and sixth centuries arose a man of extraordinary genius in Northwest India in the town of Shalatula, near present-day Attock in Pakistan. His name was Panini. He was a grammarian who developed a thoroughly scientific theory of phonetics, phonology, and morphology. He began by classifying about 1,800 basic elements like nouns, verbs, vowels, and consonants and created rules to logically create words and sentences from these elements. Using his rules, the constructs, at the word level, have unambiguous spelling and pronunciation, and at the sentence level, they have a valid meaning. In other words, he created the world's first and perhaps the only context-free grammar more than 2,600 years ago. Panini is considered a forerunner of formal language theory and the first person to conceive the normal form essential to formulating computer languages. Recent research has shown that Panini's groundbreaking work set the stage for the science of algebra and mathematical analysis to emerge. His approach to grammar has also been assessed as similar to a mathematical function and Boolean algebra. Panini's work may be truly regarded as one of the greatest monuments to human intelligence. He may rightly be considered as the first scientist, in the strictest sense of the word, produced by any civilization.

It is important to note that while the geometry in Sulbha Sutras may rightly be regarded as arising out of religious imperative (needed to construct altars), the same cannot be said for arithmetic and Panini's grammar. There was no pressing religious requirement at work here. Therefore, these developments must be regarded as arising out of freedom driven by creativity. It is not known how many later Greek achievements were influenced by these breakthroughs. There was contact among the ancient Greeks and Indians, certainly after Alexander and more than likely before Alexander. For example, there are references to Democritus visiting India and the amazing similarity between Kannada and Democritus atomic doctrines and the Jain and Pythagorean doctrines. While more research is clearly needed to settle these questions, we take up this issue in greater detail in the next chapter.

Logic: The roots of logic as a discipline dates back to around 1000 BCE or earlier in developing effective ways to debate and solving puzzles. The earliest name in this regard is that of Astavakra, about whom not much is known with certainty. In the sixth century BCE, Medhatithi Gautama founded the Anviksiki school. Anviksiki literally means science that is preceded by observation or the science of how to draw conclusions based on facts. Gautama defined what he called the *yantra yukti* or terms of scientific argument. Medhatithi also established a council or *parishad* for debate and established what he called *vada-vidhi* or methods of debate. He established the standard of examination of the truth of a statement or *pariksha*, and his interests went beyond the laws of debate since he went on to define the science of *Karyabhinirvrtti* or the science of project management, including planning and resources required to accomplish an objective.

Achievements in Natural Sciences

As mentioned before, at this stage of development, one cannot expect any breakthroughs in terrestrial natural sciences. The path to terrestrial natural sciences does not necessarily come through art to critical philosophy to solar astronomy to natural science; it must come through a pathway that moves from solar astronomy to the development of the experimental method to terrestrial natural sciences. The former path may be true for a particular civilization; the latter must be true for any civilization. This is because motions of heavenly bodies first taught humans about controlled experimentation. Consequently, at this stage in the development of science, as civilizations were beginning to engage in intellectual creativity, one finds much insightful speculation concerning astronomy, physics, and the origin of the world. The gods in the heavens and the cultural creation of myths began to give way to the naturalistic speculations consistent with emerging epistemology. We find this in Indian and later in Greek civilizations. We would argue that the breakthroughs in the formal sciences gave man the confidence needed to begin to move away from superstition to the rational approach. The ability to predict the hypotenuse of a right-angle triangle from the two other sides must have seemed mind-blowing and empowering; the human mind must have wondered what else could be predicted.

Let us briefly review what the Indian scientists speculated on during this period in the realm of natural science.

Vishesheika: The Vaisheshika school concerning the atomic structure of matter was founded by Kannada in the sixth century BCE, almost two hundred years before Democritus (460–370 BCE) in Greece. *Vaisheshika* means *particularity,* and his system clearly stated the ultimate reality consisted of atoms and void (in addition to souls that formed part of his metaphysics, already covered). He further stated that atoms moved and combined with one another not because of a spiritual force but an invisible impersonal force and postulated the existence of *dvyanuka* (biatomic molecule) and *tryanuka* (triatomic molecules). He theorized *gurutva* (gravitation) to explain why objects fall to earth.

The most interesting and startling aspect of the Vaisheshika school is Kannada's physics. It is absolutely incredible that his physics has not been accorded its proper place in the history of science. Kannada basically sees two types of actions: those that occur at the aggregate level and those that occur at the molecular level. The former are generally visible while the latter are not. In the aggregate category, Kannada identifies five actions: dropping (*avaksepana*), lifting (*utksepana*), contraction (*akuncana*), expansion (*prasarna*), and movement (*gamana*). In modern language, we can identify the first action as the effect of gravity (vertical force), the next three as the effects of heat or energy, and the last as the effect of a terrestrial, nongravitational force. Through these actions, ordinary matter may retain its identity. In the second category, the actions are invisible. Therefore, Kannada postulates the existence of certain generic invisible processes to explain the change of the state of matter. He identifies the processes of conjunction (*samayoga*), disjunction (*vibhaga*), inherence (*samavaya*), and co-combination (*ekarthasamavaya*). In modern language, we may identify the first two as akin to reversible physical changes such as evaporation and condensation and the latter two as akin to irreversible chemical changes. Kannada also uses these generic processes to explain some of the actions at the macro level. In other words, the actions at the macro level have processes as their counterpart at the molecular level.

- Kinematics or horizontal motion: Kannada describes horizontal motion correctly by stating that action produces motion, the relationship of the motion to the object being that of Samavaya or inherence, meaning they cannot be separated. The motion (vega) continues until checked by an obstacle or gravity. In modern language, this may be stated as "a body in motion stays in the state of motion until it is acted by a force." The property of inertia is associated with horizontal movement of solids and those of fluidity and viscosity to the fluid state.
- Heat: Kannada identifies the effects of heat as expansion/contraction and lifting with solids and fluids respectively.
- Gravity: The property gurutva is inherent in matter and causes objects to fall.
- Physical change: The processes of conjunction and disjunction are invoked to explain physical changes, such as melting.
- Chemical change: The processes of combination and cocombination are used to explain irreversible and invisible chemical change. Kannada does not mention the reversible chemical change.

In summary, the natural science embedded in the Vaisheshika school sees a lawful universe with a Newtonian space and time pervading it. The atoms, which are indestructible, combine to create molecules and then gross matter.

Forces and energy act on gross matter and change its properties. One can see the beginnings of theories of gravity, thermal changes, kinematics, physical chemistry, and chemical reactions in Kannada's brilliant observation/reflection but not experiment-based science. In Vaisheshika, for the first time, the human mind attempted to understand physical reality on a rational basis. The theory of the Vaisheshika school is discussed in greater detail in appendix K.

Astronomy: The roots of astronomy in ancient India go back to several thousand BCE, as discussed in chapter 10. The ninety-five-year cycle coordinating the motions of moon and sun continued to be used. An astronomer named Laghda systematized earlier knowledge into *Vedanga Jyotisha*, probably toward the end of the current phase. Astronomy continued to be based on sidereal calculations.

Samkhya school or theory of evolution: Ancient Indian thinkers were not only concerned about laws of the heavens (astronomy) and the inanimate world here on earth (matter, properties, actions, space, and time in the Vaisheshika school, for example) but also the origin of life here on earth. The Vaisheshika school assumes the eternal, uncreated individual souls; Samkhya philosophy sought to answer the question of origin of life. The Samkhya school is fundamentally materialistic. It starts by assuming the self-existent nature (*prakriti*). Prakriti consists of the five great elements—*Panch mahabhutas*—of earth, fire, water, air, and ether and three creative qualities or energies known as *satvic, rajas*, and *tamsik*. It has the potential to evolve. But what is the mechanism involved in the evolution? Kapila begins the process of evolution by first evolving *mahat*, which is pure potentiality. Mahat in turn led to the evolution of *buddhi* (intelligence) and *ahankara* (ego). Kapila then postulates that the existence of a *lamarckian* "need" within Mahat to generate the five functions (sight, taste, hearing, touching, and smell) and functions, in turn, lead to the five organs of sense (eye, tongue, ear, skin, and nose), which in turn lead to five organs of action (larynx, feet, hands, excretory, and generative organs) The process of evolution in Kapila proceeds from higher to the lower, from subtle to gross and from psychological to the physical.

It is important to note that the Samkhya school explicitly denies the existence of a personal creator, boldly stating that creation and creator are one. For Kapila, all existence is either free or bound, and God can be neither; for if God was bound, he cannot be God, and if he were free, he would not have created an imperfect world. Nevertheless, he felt compelled to postulate the existence of another reality, the *purusha* or universal soul, since he could not see how consciousness could arise out of Prikriti or how matter could evolve to think and feel and see, thus upsetting his materialism. Purusha is incapable of evolving by itself; it is, however, indispensable to initiate the evolutionary process. Purusha is, therefore, the eternal universal psychical entity necessary to explain the beginning of evolution and the existence of spirit. Therefore, while Kapila saw no need for a vital force to bridge the inorganic and organic worlds, he did see the need to bridge the physical and mental worlds and felt compelled to introduce the concept of prusha. Thus, we may call him a reluctant materialist. Once his evolution gets going, it needs no other force. Kapila also saw purusha as a universal spirit that is not the source of individuality or personality, both of which lie within the evolutes of prakriti.

Thus, Kapila enumerates his twenty-five *tattwasa* or categories as purusha, prakriti, mahat, buddhi, and ahankara, five basic elements, functions, senses, and organs of action. The word *Samkhya* means *enumeration*.

Kapila's concept of an initial impulse imparted by purushas to prakriti is both similar to and different from the concept of the "form" within substances as postulated by Aristotle some centuries later. As Aristotle stated, form is distinct from substance. It is not same as substance, but it is in every substance, and every substance has its own form that it strives to achieve. Thus, Aristotle allows growth through the presence of a specific form within each substance. His idea of growth is a prisoner of the idea of teleology or predetermination for each substance. Kapila's theory may be thought of in a much broader manner since it provides for the genesis of the object and not just its predetermined growth. And there is no predetermination imposed by Kapila's Purusha on evolution.

Kapila clearly anticipates several later thinkers, such as Aristotle, Lamarck, and Kant. Kapila's theory of evolution, however, like all pre-experimental "speculative" theories, is wrong in nearly every detail. Evolution proceeds from inorganic to organic to mental. His order is exactly the reverse. Evolution does not proceed based on an inner need and is not blindly imposed by environmental forces. It is a result of the creative interplay of the inner and outer in an open-ended manner based on chance gene mutations. Kapila, in the absence of painstakingly accumulated physical evidence, could not see any of that, and we could not expect him to. His theory must be judged by comparison to his contemporaries and not contemporary ideas concerning evolution. On that count, he comes out on top indeed. He may be rightly regarded as the father of all evolutionary theories to explain origin of life.

Achievements in Biological Sciences

We have chosen to group medicine as a natural science. It combines aspects of both natural and social sciences. The science of medicine was indeed given a high priority during the current phase in India. The earliest beginnings of medical science occurred in the Vedic period and were recorded in the Ayurveda. We discussed this in some detail in chapter 11. Here, we pick up that development from about 900 BCE onward.

Medicine: Punarvasu Atreya was the first great physician to systematize the current knowledge of medicine in the eighth century BCE, organizing the entire knowledge into eight branches. Prior to that, only individual monograms summarizing knowledge on specific topics, called *kalapas*, circulated. Tradition has it that Atreya asked his six best students (Agnivesha, Bhela, Jatukarna, Parashara, Harita, and Ksharapani) to compose a medical encyclopedia containing all medical knowledge. The one Agnivesha assembled was judged to be the best. Charaka later revised the Agnivesha Samhita in the sixth century BCE and came to be known as Charaka's Samhita. It remained the premier source for medical knowledge for nearly two thousand years all over the world.

Charaka may be rightly regarded as the father of medicine. His encyclopedia consisted of eight parts containing 120 chapters with 8,400 verses in all. Charaka, following Atreya, also divided his Samhita into eight parts:

> *Sutra Sthana* or general principles
>
> *Nidana Sthana* or pathology
>
> *Vimana Sthana* or diagnosis
>
> *Sarira Sthana* or anatomy and physiology
>
> *Indriya Sthana* or prognosis
>
> *Kalpa Sthana* or pharmacology
>
> *Sidhi Sthana* or treatment strategies

The classification has a very modern feel to it.

The key concept of the Ayurveda system, of which the Charaka Samhita is the best example, are the three doshas: *vatta*, *pitta*, and *kapha*, which govern the principles of movement, food transformation, and growth, and protection. In modern language, these concepts correspond to the neuromuscular system, the metabolic system, and the intracellular processes responsible for growth and protection. Each individual is made of a unique combination of vatta, pitta, and kapha and thus Ayurveda sees each person as unique. In addition, the mind-body connection was fully recognized since the relationship between disease and emotion was understood. The concept of three doshas enabled the physicians to provide an individual diagnosis based on the individual's constitution. The treatment plan developed based on diagnosis was not passive. It included herbal medicine, diet recommendation, and spiritual (psychological) guidance.

The state of specific medical knowledge in the Samhita was outstanding for its time. It was definitely devoid of any reliance on magical elements and was thoroughly experience-based and rational. Charaka lists 360 bones in the body, including teeth and nails. He believed the heart was a controlling organ with a single chamber that had thirteen main channels to carry blood. He also believed that smaller vessels took nutrients to other parts of the body. This may be regarded as the first rudimentary description of the human circulatory system. Charaka possessed a sophisticated knowledge of metabolism, believing that the three *dhatus*—blood, flesh, and marrow—interacted with food to produce dosha, which enabled the body to function. For the same food, the dosha produced is different in different bodies, and this accounted for both the differences in people and the presence of disease. In addition, Charaka also understood genetics as a potential source of disease, stating that both gender and birth defects like lameness and blindness are not due to defects in the parents but in the ovum or sperm. Charaka appears to have appreciated the presence of "germs" in the body but was not sure of their importance. Finally, Charaka believed that an obstruction of the channels carrying blood in the body led to disease and deformity, thus anticipating atherosclerotic diseases.

This glimpse of the medical knowledge compiled in the Samhita is not intended to be complete. It is meant to convey the idea that Charaka's system and Agnivesha's system, from which it was derived, were experience-based, had an experimental basis, were completely rational, and may be rightly considered the first formulation of the science of medicine in the world.

Just as Atreya may be considered the father of medicine, Dhanvantri, probably his contemporary, may be considered the father of surgery. His most illustrious disciple, Sushruta, wrote the most enduring encyclopedia on the science of surgery probably in the sixth century BCE. Sushruta insisted that it is not possible to be a good surgeon without a thorough knowledge of medicine. As a result, barbers and the like were kept out of the profession of surgery in ancient India. It is worth recalling that barbers were considered surgeons in the Western world until as late as the eighteenth century.

Sushruta Samhita is thus a book that has the objective to teach the principles of surgery and plastic surgery while ensuring the prospective students are thoroughly grounded in principles of medicine. The book itself is divided into two parts: Purva-tantra and Uttara-tantra. The Purva-tantra is divided into five sections: general principles, pathology, anatomy, pharmacology, and principles of treatment. The Uttara-tantra contains the remaining four specialties of ENT, pediatrics, treatment strategies. and treatment strategies.

Sushruta identified 1,120 diseases, classifying them into four categories: traumatic, bodily, mental, and natural. The *Samhita* contains excellent descriptions of leprosy, pulmonary tuberculosis, skin diseases, epilepsy, diabetes, goiter, venereal diseases, and urinary diseases. He described the four classical stages of healing of a wound. He also classified bones and their reaction to injuries. Twelve types of joint dislocation (*sandimukta*) and fractures of the shaft (*kanda-bhanga*) were systematically described. He also identified various treatments of the fractures, such as traction, manipulation, and stabilization. He clearly believed that burns, heatstroke, sunstroke, and frostbite produce very similar damage and must be managed as thermogenic damage. He described the cause of hay fever very accurately.

Sushruta insisted on training his pupils through dissecting dead bodies and testing surgical techniques on vegetables and clay-filled leather bags. He was probably the first one to use dummies to teach his students fourteen different types of bandages on different parts of the body.

Sushruta was proficient in over three hundred surgical procedures. He classified surgical procedures into eight classes: *chedna* (excision), *bhedna* (incision), *lekhna* (scrapping), *vyadhana* (puncturing/draining), *esana* (probing), *sravana* (bloodletting), *svana* (stitching), and *vsraya* (evacuation). He practiced cauterization and used wine and the fumes of cannabis as anesthesia. Sushruta performed a variety of operations including cataracts, prostate, hemorrhoids, and plastic surgery, including nose repair. His technique of using flaps in rhinoplasty reads like a description out of a modern textbook. Sushruta classified all instruments used in his surgical practice. He had 101 blunt instruments and 20 sharp instruments. He encouraged surgeons to invent new instruments, recognizing that new procedures would require new instruments. Finally, Sushruta described the use of prosthetics for amputees.

There is little doubt that there was a long process of development of medical science before even a genius of Sushruta's caliber could have written his encyclopedia. Equally, there can be no doubt that these physicians of ancient India laid the foundations of an experimental and rational science. His encyclopedia had a worldwide appeal for over two thousand years. China, the Middle East, and Europe all benefited from this encyclopedia and his genius for over two millennia.

Botany: Botany continued to be considered a part of medical sciences with interest in plant classification. Charaka Samhitā, Sushruta Samhita, and the Vaisesikas all include elaborate plant taxonomy.

It is too tempting to not say a few words of comparison between the medical science evident in these two encyclopedias from ancient India and the later Greek medicine. Hippocrates, the greatest physician of ancient Greece, taught medicine in the fourth century BCE, two hundred to three hundred years later than Sushruta. We do not know the extent to which Greek medicine benefited from ancient Indian medical knowledge. There clearly were contacts through travels. The Indian concept of three doshas parallels the concept of the three humors ascribed to Hippocrates. Similarly, the Hippocratic Oath closely resembles its Indian version. It is interesting to note that Greek medicine did not know much about human anatomy because of the Greek taboo forbidding the dissection of human bodies. As a result, Hippocratic medicine could only provide a general diagnosis, and its focus was passive treatment and prognosis. Finally, we note that the image of Hippocrates shown in Western writings was created in the nineteenth century and serves to reinforce the idea that ancient Greece took him as seriously as he is depicted today. The revival of Hippocratic treatment in the nineteenth century prompted one French physician of the day to comment that this revival amounted to "meditation upon death" and "making up the whole history of medicine."

Clearly, the later Greek scientific attitude did not extend to medicine.

The above discussion is not intended to be a comprehensive exposé of ancient India's achievement in natural science. The objective was to focus on what we consider significant achievements in the key areas of astronomy, physical sciences, the theory of evolution, and medicine.

Achievements in Social Sciences

Psychology: Perhaps only secondary to a focus on formal sciences and metaphysical speculation, the human psyche was explored more fully in ancient India than perhaps any other area of knowledge. This focus resulted from the ontological assumptions about the nature of reality or metaphysics. As we discussed earlier, mainstream Indian metaphysics did not deny the reality of matter and commits the error of falling into the idealist camp. No Indian philosophers postulated the existence of preexisting forms as Plato proposed and as Hegel proposed two thousand years later in the guise of an eternal absolute idea, about which he had absolutely nothing specific to say. However, with few exceptions, such as Buddha, Indian philosophers also did not believe that the psychological world could be derived from the material world. Thus, the Vaisheshika school postulated the existence of eternal souls, though without God as a controller. Mainstream ancient Indian thought comfortably straddled the twin worlds of matter and psyche, though in many latter periods, Indian religious thought tended to degenerate, focusing exclusively on the inner world and denying the reality of matter. The unfortunate net result of this interesting position was that more than any other ancient civilization, a majority of Indian thinkers in the later periods placed a greater focus on the inner world of psyche.

Below, we will attempt to capture key findings in the field of psychology by the ancient Indian philosophers and sages and note the points of similarity with modern psychology.

- **Achieving higher consciousness:** Achievement of this higher consciousness was thought possible through meditation and yoga based on inner concentration and detachment. Four paths, each known as a particular yoga, were developed to achieve this state.

  Karma yoga was conceived for an active person and is based on the distinction between sakama karma (desire-driven actions) and nishkama karma (duty-driven action). A karma yogi engages in action but with a dispassionate attitude.

  Bhakti yoga was conceived for emotionally sensitive persons and aims at God-realization through devotion and love. It attempts to replace the emotions of fear, hate, and anger with love.

  Raj yoga: The third yoga is called the Raja yoga and was developed for a strong-willed person. It was based on a progressively deeper understanding and control of mental processes as they occurred.

  Jnana yoga: The fourth and final type of yoga was called the Jnana (intellect) yoga, appropriate when a person seeks answers to existential questions intellectually. It is through intellect and reasoning coupled with meditation based on inner concentration and detachment that such a yogi achieves higher states of mind and higher states of consciousness.

All four paths are supposed to lead to a transformation of the personality through the destruction of ego and false desires, leading to infinite joy, being, and essential knowledge of reality. Some believed that the first three forms of yoga are simply preparatory stages for Jnana yoga. However, there was no consensus on that since the highest stage was reachable in principle through all four forms.

- **Body, mind, and consciousness:** The theory of five sheaths (koshas) enclosing the self or consciousness described this relationship as follows: the outermost sheath is the physical environment through which the gross body partakes physical nourishment or food (*annamaya kosha*). The second sheath is the sheath in which physical food is converted into energy (*pranamaya kosha*) needed to operate the body. It may also be thought of as the physiological processes that power the senses and organs of action. The next sheath is the emotion (*manomaya kosha*), which is the sheath where thought and emotions are processed. The fourth sheath is the sheath of knowing (*vijananmaya kosha*). It is also the level of ego consciousness and reason. The innermost sheath is the sheath of being (*anandamaya kosha*). This sheath is supposedly able to experience bliss, which is different from the motions and thought the mind is capable of. In the center of these five sheaths is the self, the changeless observer. The sages explicitly said that this self is best described as indescribable. It is to be experienced to be known.

- **Structure of the mind:** The mind may be thought of as the third and fourth sheaths described above and taken together. From a different perspective, these two sheaths (or the mind) was thought to possess the three qualities (*gunas*) of *tamas, rajas,* and *sattva* and may be roughly translated as desiring-impulsive, rationalizing-deciding and normative-judging aspects of the mind or id, ego, and superego.

- **Behavioral tools:** The study of psychology was not undertaken for purely academic purposes—quite the contrary. The study of psychology was undertaken for two reasons: to help the majority of people live happier lives and to help an insignificant minority experience higher states of consciousness. We have already discussed the principal means of achieving the latter: yoga. The ancient Indian thinkers devised four main tools to help the majority of ordinary people lead happier and more fulfilling lives. The first of these tools was the concept of the four great stages, called *asharmas*. They were discussed earlier in this chapter: learning, pursuit of wealth, fame and power, the stage of duty to others, and the stage of self-realization. The first three stages legitimized and valued an ordinary worldly life. The concept of karma, which ensured that good deeds were rewarded and, in a similar vein, that bad deeds did not go unpunished, was the second great tool. The third great tool was the development of dharma, which emphasized tolerance of different points of view, compassion toward the needy and weak, and nonviolence toward other forms of life. Finally, the last tool was a flexible caste system that in theory allowed members of all castes to rise to the level of their abilities. The caste system in ancient India must be viewed against a background of slavery and a highly polarized and static class system prevalent in most ancient societies and not by its degenerated and outmoded nature today. And indeed, it comes out rather well on that count.

There are indeed many points of similarity between psychology as developed by ancient Indian thinkers and the modern science of psychology. We mention a few briefly. The concept of a tripartite division of psyche into id, ego, and superego by Freud is similar to the qualities of tamas, rajas, and satva. The concept of Maslow's hierarchy of needs closely parallels the concept of ashramas or stages of life. Similarly, Maslow's concept of metamotivation is similar to the concept of the nishkama karma in karma yoga. The whole arena of relaxation response through meditation, including slowing down the heart rate, has been demonstrated in countless studies. The study of paranormal powers including hypnosis was learned by Europeans after they came to India. Freud's concept of ordinary consciousness, subconscious, and the unconsciousness parallels the waking, dreaming, and dreamless states. Jung's concept of archetypes also parallels the ancient Indian concept of samaskaras. Finally, the psychosomatic phenomenon is explicitly recognized in Ayurveda, which states that an emotional state can lead to disease. These are a few of the similarities that even a casual study of ancient Indian texts can reveal.

It is also important to discuss the method ancient Indian researchers used in psychology. The epistemology or method to create knowledge must follow an assumed ontology (our assumptions about ultimate reality, matter, consciousness and will define what is an acceptable method and proof of valid knowledge. If one believes that the inner world is not derived from matter, the tools employed in exploring this inner world may not be those employed in the study of matter. Thus, it was not the experimental method of physical sciences but the method of inner observation based on concentration and detachment coupled with reason that ancient Indian psychologists used. Since observations of the psyche resist quantification, their method may be characterized as qualitative and objective since these sages or psychologist/scientists had no agenda The psychological findings of these ancient psychologists did not pertain primarily to the behavioral sciences or man's outward behavior but primarily to the science of the consciousness itself or the inner workings of the psyche and its relationship to the stages of consciousness. It should be mentioned that though many sages claimed their knowledge as direct or revealed, it was by necessity based on inner detached observations and use of reason. We must reject their claim of revelation in much the same manner as we ignore the assertion of a physicist like Newton that God ensures the operation of the laws of physics and just focuses on his physics.

Summarizing Achievements in Abstract Systems-Building Capability (ASBC)

By the end of the phase, the ASBC of the Indian civilization must be characterized as the most advanced in the world: it had developed alphabetical script, mastered the creative method, and could boast of the most highly developed epistemology.

Summarizing the State of Civilization and Science

12.28 State of Civilization and Science at Phase End

Overview of the Political History of the Phase

During the phase, the Indian and Chinese civilizations were strong and because of turmoil in West Asia evolved solely based on their long-established inner dynamics. The center of military action and violence was West Asia, southern Europe, and North Africa. In this region, two proud civilizations, Mesopotamia and Egypt, went into irreversible decline; Persians developed sufficient military power capable of creating the first global empire; the Greeks acquired all the elements to become a civilization; and the Roman Republic (though we discuss the Roman Republic in next chapter) was to become a broader form of democracy of the elite by transitioning from electing a lifetime monarch to a chief executive with a one-year term.

State of Productive Outcomes

Wealth creation continued its slow and steady progress in civilizations that were spared invasions. However, fair trade declined precipitously during the phase because of the uncertainty caused by the demise of two major civilizations and the emergence of several significant civilizations.

State of Practical Creativity

The most significant and alarming development were the practical inventions of great military importance, including faster ships, steel, the harness, pontoon bridges, maps, phalanx formation, and optical signaling. With the exception of steel, several inventions mostly took place outside the Indian civilization.

State of Religious Creativity

The three fundamental solutions to existential anxiety—monism/monotheism, agnosticism, and atheism—went beyond the natural polytheism based on the fear of seemingly alien natural forces identified in the previous chapter and were further developed. The Jewish states in West Asia and the Persian civilization took the lead in developing monotheism while the Indian civilization developed the remaining solutions. The real breakthrough was the emergence of Indian agnosticism, since through it for the first time in history the human mind honestly and rationally confronted its objective condition in the universe. It was indeed a phenomenal achievement still unequaled in the sphere of religious creativity.

State of Philosophical Creativity

The birth phase can rightly lay claim to inventing the discipline of formal logic, the first formal art theory, and the essentials of a sophisticated epistemology based on unique mental attributes of observation, imagination, and reason.

State of Artistic Creativity

The state of artistic activity got a boost from the emerging Persian civilization. The great age of Egyptian art was behind us and that of ancient Greece was still ahead. Based on current findings in archeology, it is perhaps fair to say that both Indian and Chinese civilization were yet to show a significant interest in art; the former was knee-deep in religious, philosophical, and scientific pursuits, and the latter nurtured a practical orientation in essential isolation from other civilizations.

State of Science

As noted above, the state of science went through a phenomenal expansion as achievements in linguistics, mathematics, astronomy, medicine, speculative physics, chemistry, and the theory of evolution demonstrate. What was achieved in specific sciences during this short phase is indeed remarkable

Linguistics: Panini grammar is rightly considered one of the greatest accomplishments of the human mind, and it is believed that it indirectly laid foundations of later Indian mathematics. As we shall note in the following chapters, one can trace an unbroken greatness of Indian mathematics from Panini to Madhva in the fourteenth century.

Epistemology: Kannada and Uddalaka laid the foundations of a theory of knowledge based on perception and quantitative reason. The Indian, Muslim, and European epistemologies that followed over the next two millennia were simply an elaboration of the principles laid out by these thinkers.

Logic: Gautama established the foundations of both abstract and practical reason.

Astronomy: In Babylon, a school of astronomy flourished that developed precise rules to predict the positions of the planets, sun, and moon. In India, the Jyotisha Vedanga did the same for motions of the sun and moon.

Physics and chemistry: Kannada outlined the atomic theory of matter, the concept of gravitation, different types of motions, and the reversible and irreversible physical-chemical process of change of state of matter.

Medicine: Charaka and Sushruta put diagnosis and surgical intervention respectively on a firm factual basis.

Psychology: Indian civilization developed the concept of states of consciousness and developed theories to elaborate the relationship between body, mind, and consciousness.

Evolution: Kapilla's theory of evolution, though essentially wrong in that it proceeded from general to specific, was the first systematic attempt at explaining the existence of life and consciousness. It did not limit itself to the development growth of specific life forms; rather, it focused on its general evolution.

Although the current phase was rather short compared to the protoscience phase, the birth phase in a sense is most important, since during this phase, for the first time, the human mind experienced the possibility of rational knowledge, particularly in linguistics, epistemology, logic, astronomy, physics, and medicine. In religious creativity, the human mind laid foundations of agnosticism and monism. In fact, in our judgment, until modern times, it is difficult to point out another period comparable creativity. The phase also exposes the feeble attempt of Western historians to console themselves through their assertion of ancient Greece as the birth place of science. As we shall see in next chapter, Greek representational art, derived as it was from Egyptian art, made astounding progress; however, its contributions in geometry and astronomy occurred after Greeks had absorbed the Indian and Mesopotamian knowledge in the post-Alexander period in lands far away from Greece.

Chapter 12 · Birth of Science (1000–550 BCE)

State of Constructive Outcomes

During this brief phase, as we have emphasized before, the peaceful interaction among civilizations was at a low point since Egyptian civilization was in an irreversible decline throughout the phase, and Mesopotamian civilization suddenly collapsed toward the end of the phase. Chinese civilization continued its geographical isolation, and Persian, Greek, and Roman states were too new to have a significant impact, as if to underscore the calm before the storm. Below, we summarize the impact of practical, religious, and intellectual creativity as well as migrations and trade on civilizations during the phase. How Egyptians and Phoenicians impacted ancient Greece was the most significant impact of peaceful interaction.

Exchange of practical creativity: As in the protoscience phase, the slow diffusion of practical inventions likely continued to impact the productivity and surplus of the civilizations provided a civilization welcomed these inventions. Perhaps of greater significance were the inventions of military significance, though their impact was mostly to occur after the current phase. It is, however, difficult to trace the specific genealogy of the diffusion of these inventions in this short phase at the current stage of research.

Exchange of religious creativity: As in the previous phase, the reciprocal impact of the diffusion of religious creativity was negligible and mostly confined to local regions or within a civilization. As we shall see in the next several chapters, the reciprocal impact of religion on civilizations was about to change dramatically. However, for now, the role of a particular religion, while becoming stronger within the originating civilization, did not extend beyond its own borders. Missionary zeal with or without the support of military force was still in the future.

Exchange of intellectual creativity: There was little discernible interchange in philosophy and science during the phase. There was likely continuing diffusion of writing systems. In intellectual creativity, the greatest impact was in the artistic arena among Greece, Egypt, Mesopotamia, and the Achaemenid Empire.

Migrations and fair trade: Peaceful migrations during the period, though not as dramatic in impact as the Indo-Aryan migration out of India or the Jewish migration out of Egypt during the protoscience phase, probably existed given that population density was small, and much unoccupied land was available. There was significant colonization around the Mediterranean, particularly by the Greeks and Phoenicians, and colonization was generally peaceful, though not always. Similarly, the Indian civilization continued an eastwardly advance in the Ganges plain and the south. It was mostly peaceful, and by the end of the period, it had spread as far east as Assam. Again, these migrations were local in scope and increasing the sphere of influence of a civilization; the influence was not across civilizations.

With the decline of Egyptian and Mesopotamian civilizations, isolation of Chinese civilization, and the infancy of Greek and Roman civilizations, the world trade declined precipitously during the current period. However, its role as a proportion of the economic output was small anyway, and therefore the economic adjustment was probably not too painful. Decline in trade probably had a greater impact on the diffusion of practical technology and migrations; however, its direct impact was not as significant or sudden. The current phase remained busy with the demise and emergence of civilizations.

State of Destructive Outcomes

The second phase is not only distinguished by the birth of science as we discuss below but also by the emergence of the era of violent interaction among civilizations toward the end of the phase. There was an increased allocation of the surplus to inventions of military significance in some civilizations. Likewise, the Mesopotamian and Egyptian civilization showed internal fissures that contributed to their decline. However, the confined though fertile geographical setting of these civilizations also likely contributed to their demise. Their choice was to expand or wither in the face of the expanding minor civilizations around them.

Assessing the Dynamic Inner Nature of Participants

In this section, we assess the changes in the inner nature of participants from the changes in natural causes and institutional structures and processes driving the civilizations. Naturally, when we encounter a new civilization, such as Greek civilization in this chapter, we will assess its inner nature in more detail, including the impact of its basic natural bounty and early historical experience.

12.29 The Dynamic Inner Nature of the Ancient Greek Civilization

Productive capacity: The economic freedom in the Greek city-states was highly selective and at best moderate, given that as many as three-fourths of the population were slaves, despite low government role in the economy and low taxation. (Even in the city of Athens at its height in the fifth century BCE, slaves constituted over one-third of the population.) Women had a second-class status. New technology adoption was probably low as well since economic activity had low status in general. Similarly, non-agricultural production was subordinated to participation in political and social activities, though ceramic, bronze casting, excellent stonework, and wrought iron technologies were practiced. These facts follow from the high proportion of slaves and a very elitist social structure that lived off the countryside produce without participating in it, though they controlled it. Its wealth allocation favored the elite and military. Given the existence of different gods, political unity in the face of attack by a foreign aggressor, absence of a caste system, and an extensive slavery system without revolts among slaves, social cohesion must be judged to be moderate despite a highly stratified society with low equality of opportunity.

In their zeal to ascribe everything modern to ancient Greece, many Western historians have attempted to argue that ancient Greece had a market economy. Nothing could be farther from truth in this slave-owning civilization. Internal trade was modest, but overseas trade was controlled by city-states to ensure grain and timber to the cities and was paid for in silver. The economy was thoroughly monetized with a wide circulation of coins and was structured around the profitable foreign trade needed to create revenue to fight wars with other cities. Constant wars among the city-states meant that it had low SGS stability.

Greeks established colonies on the Italian Peninsula and were in the process of becoming a Mediterranean sea power. But for its colonies, it would be difficult to characterize the Greek states as prosperous during the current phase. The terrain was difficult, and internal wars, prevalence of slavery, and limited internal trade continually hampered productive effort. Thus, internal creative capacity was modest. Right at its birth, European civilization was learning an important lesson: foreign lands and foreign trade were the keys to its survival and prosperity.

Creative capacity: The economic structure provided a small minority of males the needed time and money to engage or encourage creative endeavors, such as sculpture, architecture, and philosophical debates, when not fighting another state. Creative freedom for this group must be judged to be at least moderate (despite the fact ancient Greeks would not think twice about executing a Socrates in the next phase) but low for the rest. Science-religion conflict was low because Greek religion never went beyond naive polytheism. Greek civilization naturally started out with a practical orientation that over time achieved an intellectual bent toward the end of current phase. However, during the current phase, the internal creative balance of the Greek civilization must be characterized as mostly practical. It was showing signs of an intellectual orientation, as Pythagorean philosophy shows (soon after the current phase ended). That philosophy may be considered a modest Greek version of the principle of equivalence that Indian thinkers had discovered India in the Vedic Age but was tarnished by numerology. The role of religion was balanced with neither excessive spirituality nor science-religion conflict. The entrenched polytheism of ancient Greece was reminiscent of Vedic polytheism. Ancient Greek city-states were rapidly acquiring a world-class abstract systems-building capacity. The creative capacity of ancient Greece by the phase end was indeed broad and deep.

Constructive orientation: Ancient Greece was forced into foreign trade and colonization because of its modest natural bounty, which ended its geographical isolation. The geographical location also protected ancient Greece from early experience with nomads. Greeks were open to influence from Phoenicians in language; from Indians in religion, science, and philosophy; from Mesopotamians in astronomy; and from Egyptians in and art throughout the existence of both ancient Greece and its literally distant progeny, the Hellenistic states that we take up in the next phase. Ancient Greek city-states possessed sufficient defensive military capability as they came together in the face of external attack. Thus, the constructive orientation of ancient Greece must be characterized as at least type 3 and perhaps type 4 openness.

Destructive orientation: The prosperity of ancient Greece during the current phase depended on regional foreign trade and colonization. Thus, because of a modest natural bounty, institutional greed was built early into Greek society, though to a lesser degree than in the Roman Republic, and was projected beyond its borders to the extent possible militarily. Fortunately, it never developed an intolerant creed. The internal orientation was aggressive infighting with a strong element of cooperation in the face of an external threat. The external orientation of the emerging Greek civilization was determined by the peculiarities of the Greek geography and early history. The aggressive impulse shown in internal wars, propensity for trade, need to colonize around the Mediterranean and in Anatolia, and an openness to outsiders resulted substantially from the Greek terrain with little flat land and rather modest rivers. Though the external orientation was aggressive, it was not imperialistic yet; it couldn't be, given the presence of the strong Persian Empire on its eastern flank and a barren, nomadic, and cold land to the north. Ancient Greece during this phase enjoyed sustained political independence and was focused on practical creativity that tended toward intellectual and relatively peaceful expansion through small colonies.

12.30 The Dynamic Inner Nature of the Mesopotamian Civilization

Productive capacity: There was positive change in the productive capacity because of the highly entrepreneurial culture of the melting pot that neo-Babylon state had become, despite the fact that the neo-Babylonian state witnessed diminished social cohesion and internal dissension fomented in part by the rising Persian Empire.

Creative capacity: The creative capacity also improved significantly. During this short phase, the creative freedom in the neo-Babylonian state was high. Yet the fear of gods in the sky drove Mesopotamian astronomy. No equivalence principle claiming the lawfulness of heavenly, earthly, and psychological realms was enunciated. Still, its creative capacity must be judged to be deep and broad, in part because of high abstract systems-building capability. Unfortunately, Persian conquest prevented it from fulfilling its potential and taking it to next stage.

Constructive orientation: Until the end, Mesopotamian civilization remained strong, open, independent, and engaged in trade with Indian and Egyptian civilizations. The extent of creative exchange that may have occurred is unknown except in specific instances, such as the import of Indian cotton plant mentioned earlier. Civilization, as in the past, remained open to the practical and intellectual creativity of other civilizations and the migration of outsiders, such as Chaldeans and Persian Medes, who played a strong role in the neo-Babylonian state, thus displaying a type 4 openness. Its defensive military capability and loss of social cohesion was insufficient to hold back the Persians.

Destructive orientation: Internally, the civilization remained highly stratified with increasing wealth polarization. Since it was a melting pot of different ethnic groups thrown together through their opposition to the strong Assyrian state to the north, it managed to create internal peace for the Babylonian state. There was little change in its institutional greed and or emergence of a formal intolerant creed and only a marginal increase in its offensive military capability. Its destructive orientation remained as aggressive and violent as it allied itself with the Persian civilization to defeat Assyria in the north and in turn was defeated by and absorbed into the Persian Empire in its moment of weakness.

12.31 The Dynamic Inner Nature of the Chinese Civilization

Productive capacity: Through practical inventiveness and hard work, Chinese civilization overcame the geographical challenges, and its surplus continued its upward trend. The Chinese peasantry enjoyed relative economic freedom, as, unlike ancient Greece, there was no slavery. The practical nature of the civilization probably meant a high degree of new technology adoption. Its social cohesion was unusually high, given the absence of slavery and caste systems, a strong family ethic, success against nomadic pressures, the absence of religious divisions, and cultural unity based on its unifying logographic script and its values of peaceful and ethical living. The wealth allocation likely favored defensive military capability and public works, and equality of opportunity was relatively high. However, the Chinese civilization during the current phase went through its periodic internal instability, resulting in instability in SGS control. The productive capacity that remained was high.

Creative capacity: The creative focus was intensely practical, and creative freedom was not restricted by science-religion conflict; however, the absence of alphabetical script and epistemological reflection meant a low abstract systems-building capability. The creative capacity remained narrow and at best modest during the phase.

Constructive orientation: Continuing geographical and linguistic isolation and success against nomads reinforced the strong insularity. China maintained a strong defensive military capability in part through initiating the construction of pieces of the Great Wall during the current phase. Thus, China began to move toward a type 2 openness toward the intellectual creativity of others, and it was indeed damaging to philosophical and scientific development.

Destructive orientation: China lacked both institutional greed and intolerant creed. China neither was an imperialist power nor attacked by an empire builder such as the Persian Empire. It did not experience conquering civilizations during the phase. It did not believe in violence or possess offensive military capability. Though fractured internally during the current phase, the civilization was largely able to maintain its sustained political independence. During the current phase, China remained peaceful with respect to rest of the world.

12.32 The Dynamic Inner Nature of the Indian Civilization

Productive capacity: The sustainable growing surplus probably continued its slow and steady improvement with the system allowing high economic freedom since a highly centralized state such as the Maurya Empire was yet to emerge. Unlike most other civilizations of the phase, states within the Indian civilization were not as tightly controlled or centralized, and monism was ascendant. As a consequence, new technology adoption would at best get a medium rating since the state did not push to adopt new technology through known significant state projects. The social cohesion, in part ensured by the caste system and cultural and religious unity, must be judged to be high. However, the condition of equality of opportunity was worsening because of the hardening caste system despite the absence of slavery and a significant wealth polarization. Fortunately, this was not yet a major divisive factor since extremism in religion in the form of monotheism did not find fertile ground, and relatively tolerant polytheism or monism or budding agnosticism reigned supreme. The internal wars may be characterized as moderate because of relative internal peace and because of an absence of a desire to consolidate the states and republics into an empire. SGS retained its stability for most part. The productive capacity remained high.

Creative capacity: The internal creative balance of the Indian civilization during this phase was undoubtedly type C with unprecedented creative freedom for the age—and perhaps any age. As a consequence, substantial progress was made in intellectual creativity in the midst of enlightened spirituality. Science-religion conflict was low because of the religious diversity civilization encouraged. During the last five hundred years of the peaceful interaction era including the current phase, this conflict on the one hand led to the Upanishads, confirming the hypothesis of the equivalence between the inner essence of man and the outer essence of the universe. On the other hand, it led to several schools of philosophy and emerging science that stressed the possibility of knowledge through union of sense data and reason. Fortunately, this struggle was benign, and Indian civilization remained true to its values and did not send any of its great agnostic thinkers to the gallows. The struggle between the religious and intellectual impulses had the potential to stop or slow the advance of science dead in its tracks. Fortunately, it did not, unlike in the future phases when it unfortunately did. Indian civilization developed alphabetical script, rational thinking, and sound epistemology and thus possessed high abstract systems-building capability better than any other civilization of the phase. The creative capacity remained broad and deep.

Constructive orientation: The civilization retained its type 4 openness to diverse viewpoints within and without for it had nothing to fear from such creativity. It did not possess the defensive military capability to any substantial degree and was not aware of such need.

Destructive orientation: Indian civilization lacked institutional greed because of its core values, geographical location, and natural bounty. It also did not develop an intolerant creed as its beliefs systems including polytheism, monism, agnosticism, and atheism were openly debated. Indian civilization enjoyed freedom from nomadic invasions since the Chinese had yet to deflect central Asian nomadic pressure toward the Indian subcontinent. The destructive orientation remained peaceful, and the civilization lacked offensive military capability.

The changing parameters that define the inner nature of civilizations consisting of capacity and orientation during the phase are summarized in table 12.1.

12.33 The Dynamic Inner Nature of Participants at the End of Birth Phase

Ancient Greek Civilization

Thus, we may summarize the inner nature of the emerging ancient Greek civilization during the birth phase as comprising of modest internal SGS, a creative capacity approaching type C, and a type 4 constructive orientation. It developed a destructive orientation that, consistent with its improving military capability, was projected against surrounding minor civilizations during the phase. The external orientation of ancient Greece during the phase was type III.

Mesopotamian Civilization

The inner nature of Mesopotamian civilization during the birth phase consisted of a high productive capacity as represented by its high internal SGS, a type C creative capacity, a type 3 constructive orientation, and a latent destructive orientation with respect to other civilizations. The ostensible external orientation remained open and peaceful or type I.

Table 12.1: Relative Values of Measurable Parameters of Social Orders
Birth Phase, 1000–550 BCE

Measurable Characteristic	Productive Capacity					Creative Capacity			Constructive Orientation				Destructive Orientation		
	NB	EF	NTA	WAB	SC	Creed	ASBC	WAB	GI	ESAN	LI	Creed	NB	IG	IC
Ancient Greece	Low	High	Low	MS	High	Bal.	Strong	MS	High	N/A	Low	Bal.	Med	High	Low
Mesopotamian	High	High	High	CE	Low	Bal.	Strong	CE	Low	Low	Low	Bal.	Med	High	High
Chinese	High	Med	Med	PE	High	Bal.	Weak	PE	Low*	High	High	Bal.	High	None	None
Indian	High	Med	Med	CE	High	ES	Strong	CE	High	N/A	Low	ES	High	Low	None

NB: Degree of Natural Bounty
EF: Economic Freedom
NTA: New Tech. Adoption
WAB: Wealth Allocation Bal.
SC: Social Cohesion
ASBC: Abstract Sys. Building Capability
GI: Geographic Isolation
ESAN: Early Success against Nomads
LI: Linguistic Isolation
IG: Institutional Greed
IC: Intolerant Creed
ED: Favors Elite Decadence
MS: Favors Military Spending
PE: Favors Productive Endeavors
CE: Supports Creative Endeavors
ES: Excessively Spiritual
SRC: Sci. Religion Conflict
Bal: Balanced

Chinese Civilization

Thus, we may summarize the inner nature of Chinese civilization during the birth phase as high productive capacity as evident from its high internal SGS, a type A creative capacity, and a type 1 constructive orientation. Its destructive orientation remained peaceful and defensive during the phase. The external orientation of the Chinese civilization remained type II.

Indian Civilization

We may summarize the inner nature of Indian civilization during the birth phase as high productive capacity as represented by its high internal SGS, a type C creative capacity, and a type 4 constructive orientation. It remained peaceful toward other civilizations during the phase. The external orientation of the Indian civilization in the current phase remained type 1. The comparative inner nature of the four civilizations is summarized in table 12.2.

Evolution and Rationalization of the Birth of Science

12.34 Birth of Science during the Phase

Nature of Participation by Civilizations

As in the previous chapter, the key questions are:
- Did the progress of science take place in one, several, or all major civilizations?
- Did this development take place in a linked matter or an independent manner? Was the linkage explicit and conscious, or was the linkage unconscious and mediated?
- Were the linkages peaceful through fair trade and peaceful migrations, or were they violent based on empire building, violent colonization, and systematic wealth drain?

Progress in science during the phase took place primarily in Indian and Mesopotamian civilizations. Because of declining trade activity and turmoil in West Asia and North Africa, the interaction among civilizations went into low gear. Consequently, the development of science took place in an essentially independent manner for all practical purposes, though we must remain mindful of the standalone diffusion and peaceful interaction in the last phase.

What Constitutes the Birth of Science?

In chapter 1, we defined science as consisting of formal, natural, biological, and social categories; each of these categories in turn includes many subfields. We may ask which science constitutes the birth of science: formal, natural, biological, or social or some combination of these or all four. Still further, we may ask how far the scientific methodology would need to have developed before we can claim the birth of science. Would we need to demonstrate complete development of epistemology and the experimental method? Or can we claim the birth of science before all four categories of science and scientific methodology have shown relative but not mature development? Thus, there can be clearly considerable arbitrariness in defining what constitutes the birth of science. However, the situation is not nearly as arbitrary as it might seem for a number of reasons. The inner logic in the development of natural science can be a big help here. Clearly, a relatively complete understanding of solar astronomy was essential before the experimental method could be fully developed since the solar system constitutes the first, grand, obvious, and naturally occurring controlled experiment available to man from which he first learned about controlled experiments. Thus, if we were to say that complete development of the experimental method and an understanding of solar astronomy and hence gravity-driven terrestrial motion are essential before birth of science can be claimed, we would

Table 12.2: Comparative Inner Nature of Participants
Birth Phase, 1000–550 BCE

Civilization	Productive Capacity	Creative Capacity	Constructive Orientation	Destructive Orientation	
	Internal SGS	ICB	O/I	P/V	SPI
Mesopotamian	High	⇒ Type C	Type 3	Violent	Yes
Ancient Greece	Moderate	Type A ⇒ C	Type 4	Violent	Yes
Chinese	High	Type A	Type 1	Peaceful	Yes
Indian	High	Type C	Type 4	Peaceful	Yes

Legend
SGS: Sustainable Growing Surplus
ICB: Internal Creative Balance
O/I: Openness/Insularity
P/V: Peaceful/Violent
SPI: Sustained Political Independence

have to wait until the time of Newton to claim birth of science. After early developments in formal sciences, natural science first rationalized solar astronomy immediately, followed by terrestrial mechanics. Other sciences could develop on a firm basis only after the scientific methodology was firmly established. Given these considerations, we conclude that birth of science can be claimed when the human mind achieves rationality through sufficient development of one or more sciences and begins its qualitative, though speculative, understanding of the universe, society, or the inner psychological world without recourse to gods. It is also when man begins to realize that his world, be it natural, social, or psychological, can be understood based on facts and reason alone and has taken a few early but substantial steps to demonstrate that belief.

Perhaps a more reasonable set of achievements to claim birth of science would then be as follows:

- In parallel to a belief in the power of gods, a contradictory belief in the lawfulness of the natural world without any interference from gods emerges in the civilization.
- A belief in the method of observation and reason to understand the natural, social, and inner psychological phenomenon.
- Application of reason and observation to a natural phenomenon to yield knowledge that may be experimentally verifiable, leading to significant development in more than one category of science.

We note that the criteria we propose is more restrictive than what Western historians use in claiming that ancient Greece gave birth to science.

Birth of Science in Indian Civilization

Using the criteria outlined above, the collective achievements in astronomy by Yajnavalkaya from the previous phase; in epistemology by Uddalka and Kannada; the mathematics of Baudhayana, Manava, and Apastambha; the physics and chemistry of Kannada; the evolutionary theory of Kapila; the grammar of Panini; the medicine of Charaka and Sushrita; and science of consciousness developed by many thinkers in India during this phase easily constitute the birth of science. And using the same criteria, no other civilization could claim the birth of science during the current phase or before this phase. Though at present relatively unknown, we list these great names associated with the birth of science listed in table 12.3.

Differences in Science across Civilizations

Only the Indian and Mesopotamian civilizations pushed the frontiers of science during the phase. And the scope of science in Mesopotamian civilization was confined to astronomy, while the scope in the Indian civilization was much broader as the list of scientific outcomes clearly demonstrates. Both Chinese and Egyptian civilizations remained mired in the development stage of protoscience principally because they refused to adopt alphabetical script. Ancient Greece, as an eager student, showed considerable promise and potential. It is indeed hard to point out scientific achievement in ancient Greece and its progeny, the Hellenistic states, much before Alexander. Greek thought during the phase and a couple of centuries after the current phase ended remained mired in philosophical idealism and remained focused on ethics.

12.35 Rationalization of the Birth of Science

As noted in chapter 9, the scientific achievements during the peaceful interaction era may be accomplished through the following parameters used to assess the inner nature:

- Internal SGS
- Allocation of SGS
- Nature of Creed
- State of ASBC
- Openness/Insularity

Why the Chinese Civilization Could Not Give Birth to Science

The level of internal SGS, its allocation, and the nature of its creed did not prevent China from achieving a mature protoscience stage and giving birth to science; it was the state of its ASBC and its insularity.

Table 12.3: Great Scientists Responsible for the Birth of Science
Birth Phase, 1000–550 BCE

Area	Scientists
Mathematics	Baudhayana, Manva, Apastamba
Astronomy	Yajnavalkya, Atreya
Grammar	Panini
Epistemology	Uddalka, Kanada
Medicine	Atreya, Charaka, Sushruta
Evolution	Kapila
Physics/Chem.	Kanada
Psychology	Several

Abstract systems-building capability: Despite the absence of science-religion conflict, a remarkable practical orientation, and natural bounty, Chinese civilization did not move beyond the development stage of protoscience during the current phase. This must be attributed to its refusal to adopt alphabetical script, which is essential to developing abstract systems-building capability. Historically, religious creativity has been one of the first arenas to use abstract systems-building capability. In the absence of science-based explanations of social and natural worlds and the existence of existential anxiety, religious impulse nearly always rushed to fill the vacuum, and China, pointedly, never developed a sophisticated religion. A lapse into excessive spirituality is the Achilles heel of Indian civilization, the science-religion conflict is the Achilles heel of European and West Asian civilizations, and the absence of abstract systems-building capability is the Achilles heel of the Chinese civilization. There is indeed no free lunch.

Openness/Insularity: That China never developed complex abstract systems-building capability in turn must be attributed to its insular nature, which in turn must be attributed to success against nomads early in its history and a resulting sense of cultural superiority.

Why Ancient Greek Civilization Did not Give Birth to Science in Current Phase

Greek civilization during the phase allowed the possibility of birth of science; it simply did not meet all sufficient conditions of political support and sustained allocation yet. Its science remained in the stage of mature protoscience.

Internal SGS: Internal SGS of ancient Greece during the phase was moderate given its population size and geography. It was, However, augmented by fair amount of Mediterranean-based trade. The internal SGS did not hold back the birth of science in ancient Greece during the phase

Allocation of SGS: We believe that Greek civilization lacked this political support during the current phase since the teaching academies, the chief source of Greek philosophical speculations, were still largely in the future because the city-states were still small and did not require extensive training of the elite youth to prepare them for high positions. Access to Mesopotamian astronomical data and geometry through Alexander's invasion too were centuries into the future as was development of geometry implied in Mesopotamian astronomy.

Nature of creed: Ancient Greece during the phase had a polytheistic creed resembling the Indo-Aryans in the subcontinent millennia earlier. It never suspected monotheism or monism. Thus, both science-religion conflict and excessive spirituality were foreign to it.

State of ASBC: It would be improper to characterize the ASBC of ancient Greece during the phase as world-class. It had mastered the creative method and had adopted alphabetical script from the Phoenicians, but it still lacked world-class sophistication in logic and epistemology

Openness/Insularity: Ancient Greece during the phase was an open civilization ready to learn from others constructive outcomes, as evidenced by its debt to Egypt in art, to Phoenicians in linguistics, and its developing trade with several minor civilizations.

One would strain to discover significant original Greek contributions in mathematics, epistemology, medicine, and astronomy before 550 BCE. Pythagoras was a twenty-year-old youth in 550 BCE. Pre-Pythagoras Greece could not possibly have given birth to science. It would be a stretch even for post-Pythagoras and pre-Alexander Greece as evidenced by the focus and achievement of Plato's idealist philosophy consisting of preexisting forms and Pythagoras' numerology. With Democritus through Indian influence followed by Aristotle's speculative science, corrective influence of well-grounded Mesopotamian astronomy and high SGS through Alexander's empire we begin to see the seeds of the change that came to brilliant fruition in the post-Alexandrian Hellenistic world, as we discuss in the next chapter.

Why the Mesopotamian Civilization Came Close to Giving Birth to Science

Internal SGS: The neo-Babylonian state in Mesopotamian enjoyed high SGS because of its business-friendly cosmopolitan nature.

Allocation of SGS: During the neo-Babylonian state, astronomy was highly valued. As a measure of their prowess, classical European sources frequently equated the term Chaldeans with astronomers of Mesopotamia.

Nature of creed: Religious creed, though superstitious, took a back seat to commercial and business interests. Though Mesopotamian civilization never fell in the monotheistic trap, it was surrounded by would-be creators of monotheism: Jewish kingdoms, Persians, and Egyptian monotheistic tendencies that impressed it. Its religious impulse therefore had elements of intolerance and violence. However, despite this modest science-religion conflict, its political class was able to provide sustained allocation and support to astronomy as it was deemed helpful in business and politics.

State of ASBC: The state of ASBC was high despite an apparent lack of locus on logic and epistemology. Its astronomy understood laws of reason and essence of the theory of knowledge even though they did not formalize these disciplines.

Openness/Insularity: In the absence of either monism or developed monotheism and a successful tradition of absorbing nomads, Mesopotamian civilization was open to the constructive outcomes of other civilizations.

There are two schools of thought concerning the contributions of the neo-Babylonian state to astronomy: one generous and the other perhaps a bit harsh. The generous view is that during the two last centuries of the phase, neo-Babylonian astronomers developed a new approach to astronomy. They began to speculate about nature of how the universe evolved and began to use rational methodology to predict the position of eclipses and planets. This was an important contribution to astronomy and has been generously called the first scientific revolution by some. A crystal rock shaped like a lens was discovered near Nimrud, and this find, coupled with a description of Saturn surrounded by snakes, has formed the basis of speculation concerning the existence of an early telescope in Mesopotamia. This speculation is difficult to assess since snakes occur commonly in Mesopotamian mythology, and Saturn was considered an evil planet. This new approach to astronomy was transmitted to the Greeks through Alexander and formed the foundation of Greek astronomy.

The less generous view is that the priest-astronomers over decades collected considerable data on eclipses and understood their cyclical, periodic nature. The motivation of these priest-astronomers was not science or curiosity; rather it was religion. They did not observe planets; they observed powerful gods capable of anger and of marching across the night sky. They never developed any geometric models or theories of the universe. They did not use the scientific method to test hypotheses concerning the heavens. They did, however, work hard to improve their predictions of eclipses because they wanted to understand the gods in the sky and gain influence with the political elite. In this they were successful, particularly during dangerous times when royalty paid more attention to their predictions. In short, their orientation was religious, and their astrology-astronomy was directed to sustain the elites and themselves. They had not yet discovered the principle of equivalence or lawfulness both here on earth and in the skies. By the time the Assyrians came to dominate Mesopotamia and beyond, the practice of judicial astrology—relating the motions of the gods to kings and empires—was the crux of astronomy as a whole.

It is not surprising the astronomers of ancient Mesopotamia wielded a considerable amount of power when one considers that they were able to predict eclipses. They learned this skill through decades of observation and careful record keeping. They commanded hundreds of tablets beyond the reach of the uneducated, much like the Brahmins in India. All this information was vital to their power of prediction and royal influence. It is not as if their advice was always taken. However, in times of uncertainty and danger, their council was frequently sought.

It is interesting to ponder how the neo-Babylonian under the Chaldeans would have evolved had it maintained its political independence and not gotten absorbed into the Persian Empire in the next phase. As a consolation as we noted above, Babylonian data and insights into astronomy were not lost as they were transmitted to the Greeks, who benefited from it enormously. The Persian Empire, however, failed to recognize the value of this nascent protoscience, and over time, it withered away. In chapter 13, we will explore how the relationship between early Indian, Greek, and Babylonian astronomy played out in the centuries that followed. Finally and most importantly, Mesopotamian achievements in astronomy are without corresponding achievements in mathematics, medicine, logic, epistemology, and ethics.

Clearly, the Mesopotamian civilization had political independence, a high state of abstract systems-building capability, and openness to the creativity of other social orders, though its creed, bordering on intolerance, was devoid of excessive spirituality and science-religion conflict. Thus, it met all the necessary and sufficient conditions of science. In our view, it also came close to meeting the criteria outlined above in what constitutes the birth of science. It was destined to surpass it had it not been conquered by Persians a decade after the end of the current phase.

Why the Birth of Science Took Place in the Indian Civilization

Internal SGS: Indian civilization continued to have a high internal SGS even though trade with other civilizations had declined significantly.

Allocation of SGS: The sustained allocation of resources through the Ashram system (independent academies) and low science-religion conflict made it possible for the Indian civilization to nurture scientific creativity.

Nature of creed: The religious impulse of Indian civilization during the current phase was very interesting, contradictory, and worth emphasizing. It did believe that planets and sun were indeed gods; however, the gods could be helpful if their forces were not allowed to be additive through picking correct times for key events through astronomical calculations. In other words, these planetary gods were lawful and did not behave on whim. This naturally followed the principle of equivalence. Furthermore, elemental gods such as fire and wind were thought to be amenable to reason, predictability, and control, as Vaisheshika theorized. The strategy with respect gods in the sky was both praise and understanding their lawfulness. Thus, similar to Mesopotamia, the driving force behind the ancient science of Jyotisha (light from heavens) or astronomy was also the need to determine the auspicious time for important events. The contradictory religious impulse was evident in the attitude that treated the gods in the sky and elemental (fire, wind, earth, etc.) gods on earth as lawful while using praise to improve odds of success.

State of ASBC: The Indian civilization could boast of world-class abstract systems-building capability at the end of the phase.

Openness/Insularity: It is also worth noting that Indian civilization remained safe from external invasions while being open to the creativity of others.

Sustained political independence: Indian civilization remained free from nomadic and other invasions. During each of the following five phases, Indian civilization joined several other civilizations in facing wave after wave of foreign attacks. However, it also seems safe to assume there was little impact of other civilizations on the course of scientific activity in the Indian civilization during the current phase: one of the civilizations, Egypt, in a state of irreversible decline, another, Mesopotamia, was preoccupied with internal turmoil; China remained essentially in standalone mode; and Greece was merely a promising upstart. Thus, the last push leading to the birth to science was due to the internal efforts of one civilization. The birth of science was the culmination of the long period of protoscience growth to which all major and many minor civilizations contributed.

Shifting Center of Gravity of Science

There was no shifting of the center of gravity of science. The center in Mesopotamia died, and the Indian civilization emerged as the only significant center of gravity of science at the end of the phase, with ancient Greece waiting impatiently in the wings.

12.36 Life Stage of Science Achieved by Civilizations

Based on the inner nature of civilizations and the underlying parameters summarized in table 12.1, the five key civilizations achieved the following life stages in science:

1. Indian Civilization: Birth of science
2. Mesopotamian Civilization: Close to birth of science
3. Egyptian Civilization: Development stage of protoscience
4. Chinese Civilization: Development stage of protoscience
5. Greek Civilization: Mature protoscience

12.37 An Unfortunate Blunder by Historians

The reader will no doubt ask the question why most historians have not even considered the Indian civilization a serious contributor to birth of science, let alone being primarily responsible for it. How could such a monumental error come about? The reasons for this in our judgment fall into four broad categories: the oral nature of Indian intellectual and spiritual tradition, the seven-century dark age of Indian science under Muslim and British rule, Indian civilization being at lowest point of its 8,500-year history in the nineteenth and twentieth centuries, and the ethnocentrism of European/Western historians who are, by and large, the chief writers of history of science as it exists today. Let us consider each briefly:

- The roots of Indian intellectual and spiritual creativity go back to before the invention of written language and therefore, by necessity, its capture had to begin as oral tradition. This critical point is so often overlooked. It is indeed one of the wonders of human civilization that subtle thought in Rig Veda came into existence before writing was invented. The oral tradition unfortunately continued even after written alphabetical script and paper were invented because of the desire of the Brahmin caste to continue control. In addition, the strong spiritual tradition, with its untiring focus on spiritual liberation, resulted in a weak focus on writing history. This condition was common until the rise of the Greeks. This combination has resulted in a fuzzy timeline of ancient events in Indian history, leaving the timing of the key events open to honest misinterpretation and intentional distortion. Only the most ancient continuous civilization on the planet could have the potential to face this problem to this degree.

- The last seven centuries of Indian civilization have been the worst in its eight-millennia-plus history from the standpoint of intellectual creativity. No doubt, the Indian civilization in these centuries has produced great architecture and music under Muslim rule and great mathematics away from Muslim rule (and produced great poverty under the British rule). But given the natural bounty and large population, this great architecture is hardly surprising. However, Indian civilization, with a few notable exceptions in mathematics, has produced little comparable in intellectual creativity over the last seven centuries. This is also understandable given that Muslim rule was practical and religious in orientation, and British rule simply focused on wealth drain and a justification of the empire by hook or crook (as in James Stuart Mill's *History of British India*) through a civilizing mission. The upshot of these disastrous seven centuries is that Indian intellectuals in the twentieth century have not had the facts, resources, and psychological independence to reconstruct their own past. It has been done for them. In fact, existing history of several civilizations is biased and parochial and has only been written for them. And history of science cannot be written independent of history in general.

- The Eurocentrism of the Western historians, though understandable, both for reasons of parochialism and serving the needs of political control of other civilizations over last three centuries, has resulted in creating a version of history in which Europe has been the top dog and just about the only dog in intellectual creativity from start to finish. The Muslim civilization is given a minor concession in keeping the Greek flame alive while the West slept for a mere thousand years, which is nearly half of the entire existence of European civilization! It was a long slumber indeed. It is conveniently forgotten that Western Europe, the cradle of science since 1500 CE, had been sleeping for its entire existence until the Muslims rudely woke it. The Chinese are granted their due in practical creativity since that does not threaten the notion of Western monopoly in intellectual creativity. Eurocentrism, a creation of West Europeans, conveniently forgets that Western Europe did not even exist on the intellectual map of the world a mere thousand years ago. Thus, the Western concept of its recent greatness and its counterpart, the Indian lack of awareness of its past greatness, are examples of polar opposites through which historical truth is distorted.

Western historians are only comfortable acknowledging their intellectual debt to civilizations that:

- No longer exist, such as Mesopotamian and Egyptian civilizations
- Existed on continental Europe, even though ancient Greece was closer to Asia than to northern Europe
- Are Greek-inspired Hellenistic states

They are uncomfortable acknowledging the intellectual debt to civilizations they have controlled to varying degrees in the recent past: Indian, Chinese, and Muslim. The Chinese case is easier since their creativity was primarily practical in nature. In the Muslim case, the importance of their Greek connection is exaggerated and Muslim contributions reduced. In the Indian case, that objective is achieved through a bullheaded insistence on the Aryan invasion of India in 1500 BCE and by exploiting and distorting the oral nature of ancient Indian tradition. All this is wrapped up and backed up by "scholarship" at leading universities in United Kingdom and United States. We may look at the western European version of history and the history of science as a valiant attempt at self-consolation since West Europeans are historically the last major sub-civilization to show an interest or skill in science acquired through Scholasticism in the wake of the Arab synthesis in the Iberian Peninsula. This is ultimately going to be a failed attempt and is in the process of being exposed as a farce.

It needs to be acknowledged that the birth of science could have taken place largely independently in more than one civilization since there was only modest communication between the civilizations during the phase. The possibility of a standalone civilization in the peaceful interaction or even in the extended military conflicts era giving birth to science independently cannot be ruled out a priori. Historically, however, the crowning achievement of the era of peacefully interacting civilizations was the birth of science by Indian civilization.

Bottom line: the birth of science took place in one civilization essentially independent of interaction with other civilizations during the phase: geographical isolation (Chinese civilization), precipitous decline in trade (Mesopotamian civilization), and early stages of other civilizations (decline of Egyptian and birth of Persian and Greek civilizations).

Looking Ahead

12.38 Emerging New Participants

During the phase, we witness three new centers of power gradually emerge: the Achaemenid Empire, which was precursor to the Persian civilization; the Roman Republic; and emerging confederations of central Asian nomads that were to become the first of the four waves of attacks on civilizations during the violent interaction era.

Origin of the Achaemenid Empire (Eighth century–550 BCE)

The area east of Mesopotamia had been home to the Elamite civilization since the copper age. By 1000 BCE, the area further north of Elamite region witnessed the arrival of Medes (into the northern Zagros Mountains), Mannaeans, and Parsu or Amadai people from Kurdistan in the ninth century BCE to the region south of Elamite civilization. These groups had been under the de facto control of Assyrian state in northern Mesopotamia and resented it. The Persian Empire was the successor to the Mesopotamian civilization in West Asia, and it that stretched from Egypt to Baluchistan at its zenith in the sixth century BCE. The empire can trace its origin to the Amadai people. The first ruler of significance produced by the Amadia was Deioces in the late eighth century BCE. The famous Magi priest-scholars were the sixth tribe of Medes, according to the Greek historian Herodotus. In 646 BCE, the Assyrian king Ashurbanipal ended the Elamite supremacy, creating an opening for the Medes and Parsu. The defeat forced the tribes surrounding Elamite to coalesce into more centralized state to defend themselves against Assyrian power. In 612 BCE, Deioces's grandson, Cyaxares, and the Babylon king Nabopoassar attacked Assyria, which was preoccupied with a civil war, destroying its capital, Nineveh. Assyria thus came under Babylon control. The Persians expanded into the Elamite area. This early empire did not last as the upper classes degenerated into a luxurious lifestyle, and less than thirty years after the death of Cyaxares, his son Asyages was overthrown by Cyrus the Great in 555 BCE.

There was obviously significant ongoing contact between Mesopotamian and Elam people living in the Persian lowlands that went back millennia before the current phase began. However, until the current phase, Persia remained subordinate to Mesopotamian in practical and intellectual creativity, as evidenced by "Persian" adoption of the Akkadian language before the current phase began. The rise and amalgamation of Persian tribes was indeed a long process. The transmission of ideas occurred through proximity or diffusion, travel, and in the wake of military conflicts.

The Origin of the Roman Republic (753–509 BCE)

The origin of the Roman Republic may be traced to several earlier civilizations on the Italian Peninsula: the Etruscan civilization with its possible Asian origin that flourished in northern Italy beginning around the eighth century BCE, Villanovan culture in northern Italy from the ninth century BCE, Magna Graecia founded by Greek colonizers in southern Italy, and a smattering of Indo-European-speaking settlements in different parts of the peninsula. The city of Rome was founded in 753 BCE. Until 509 BCE, Rome was ruled by a series of seven "kings."

Central Asian Nomads—First Wave

Central Asian nomads is a very broad term meant to signify pastoral people living north and west of China and east of the Iranian plateau. The land is arid and the climate cool and suited for a pastoral social order. From the central Asian nomad's perspective, civilizations with wealth grew all around them, and it appeared natural to them to attack them. From this phase until the beginning of the last phase, when European sea power controlled all civilizations, central Asians have ventured out time and again and conquered or looted civilizations while learning from them. The first wave consisted of Xiongnu and Yeuzhi. Xiongnu came from north of China. No one knows their origin for sure, but their activities can be traced as far back as ninth century BCE. The home of Yeuzhi tribe was to the west of China and south of Xiongnu stronghold in the Qillan Mountains.

12.39 Summary

The birth of science first took place in ancient India over the period 900–550 BCE. It progressed from firm steps in formal sciences to tentative steps in the natural, biological, and social sciences. We ought to expect this natural sequence. Both ancient Indian and Babylonian civilizations fully met all the conditions for the birth of science we outlined in chapter 7, though the Babylonian civilization did not survive Persian aggression. It is most certainly an exaggeration to state that it came close to giving birth to the science of astronomy if birth of astronomy means beginning of its theoretical underpinnings and not just observational and accurate computation of positions of heavenly bodies.

We concluded that the birth of science took place through substantially independent efforts in ancient India because major civilizations either disappeared (Mesopotamian, Egyptian), were still emerging (Greek, Persian, and Roman), or were isolated (Chinese). However, it clearly owed a great debt to the shared foundation of protoscience developed during the preceding four millennia. As we shall note in chapter 16, this situation, however, was very different from the last phase of science when one civilization monopolized science by effectively preventing others from contributing to it through systematic wealth drain based on military and political control.

Coincident with the birth of science, civilizations, starting with the Persian conquest of Mesopotamia and Egypt and continuing with the Persian-Greek wars and Alexander's invasion of Asia, the Roman Republic, the Roman Empire. and still later, the Arabs, central Asian tribes, and Europeans, fully entered and have remained in the era of violent interaction through extended military conflicts. From here on, the progress in science and its center of gravity would be determined not just by the inner impulse of civilizations or by peaceful interaction among civilizations but also by the outcome of terrible, extended military conflicts driven by both creed and greed. The former was fully capable of killing science internally through faith and the latter externally through poverty, resource squeeze, and starvation.

Thus, unlike a human birth, the birth of science was a nearly bloodless event. However, since its birth, as we shall see, it has lived a mostly blood-drenched life as a foster child being shunted from one foster home to another, ultimately finding a safe haven in a bullying, greedy, and monotheistic European civilization. However, now that the child has grown into a successful adult, many foster parents wish to claim science as their forever beloved child. Yet, nobody is asking the foster child what she thinks of the string of foster parents she has had to endure. This, in fact, is what we intend to do in the next four chapters, which together constitute the development stage of science.

Chapter 13

Violent Interaction Era—Third Phase: Development Stage

First Synthesis of Science (550 BCE–200 CE)

13.1 Introduction

In proposing the life stages of science in chapter 7, we called the period after birth the development stage of science, a period of infancy and childhood that led to the stage of mature science about two millennia later. However, as mentioned in the previous chapter, the birth of science was followed by the emergence of heightened conflict among civilizations and between civilizations and nomads that has continued into the twenty-first century. This has not been a continuous conflict of all against all. Rather, this a conflict was punctuated by long periods of peace among some civilizations because wars had the potential to exhaust the meager surplus of civilizations, civilizations in conflict continually played musical chairs, and not all civilizations played the role of the aggressor. However, despite the terrible cost of such conflicts, each of the four phases constituting the development stage of science was a step forward for science. This is because military might often supported war and trade and resulted in increased transfer of wealth and knowledge among civilizations. This heightened transfer of knowledge and wealth always resulted in a new synthesis of science.

A significant feature of the current phase was the rise of the central Asian nomads and their nearly two-millennia-long unmitigated ability to repeatedly overwhelm civilizations, primarily in India, West Asia, and Europe. China often, but not always, was able to deflect this nomad pressure toward South and West Asia and Europe, allowing her to focus her energies on practical creativity of immense global value.

Another interesting feature of the phase was the birth of European civilization through the empire building efforts of the Roman Republic and the Roman Empire. Before the rise of Rome, the ancient Greek civilization was more inclined toward Asia, with modest links to European mainland. However, the demise of ancient Greece at the hands of the Roman Republic and a relatively quick resurgence of the Persian Empire after its defeat at the hands of Alexander forced Rome to confine its imperial designs to continental Europe and North Africa, laying the groundwork for the European civilization to emerge. European civilization was initially confined to a narrow band around the Mediterranean Sea.

The organization of this chapter closely follows the organization of the last two chapters.

Affirmation of Era, Phase, and Essential Participants

13.2 Affirming the Era of Civilizations

We noted the emergence of violent interaction among civilizations toward the end of the birth phase above. The rise of central Asian nomads, who had learned from the Chinese to master the horse as a war weapon, combined with empire building by Greeks, Romans, and Persians, truly made this phase as the first full-blown phase with extended military conflicts among several major civilizations and civilizations and nomads a norm. It was still possible for a civilization to not experience conflict and war for extended time. The threat of war was, however, always there, like Damocles's sword, though civilizations were not always aware of this threat. And it was only a matter of time a civilization or a nomadic confederation acquired the military strength, produced an ambitious and charismatic leader, and trouble started again. Yet, some civilizations showed relatively little ability to learn from this repeating pattern.

13.3 Major Participants of the Phase

Indian and Chinese civilizations and ancient Greece from the previous phase continued to be major players during this phase. They were joined by the Achaemenid Empire; the Roman Republic and its successor, the Roman Empire; and, of course, the successor of ancient Greece, the Hellenistic states. In addition, we see the rise of several central Asian nomads, including Xiongnu and Yuezhi (later called Kushans) as well as a number of other states that sprouted in the wake of Alexander's invasion of Asia. Of the major players of the last phase, ancient Egypt and Mesopotamia did not survive the current phase, and three—namely, ancient Greece, the Roman Republic, and the Hellenistic world—were successively absorbed into the Roman Empire before the phase ended.

Violent End of Two Primary Civilizations

Before we delve into the key players of the phase, we would like to discuss the violent end of two of the four primary civilizations at the hands of the Persians and the Roman Republic. Of the two, Mesopotamia collapsed rather quickly, while the Egyptian civilization, despite being weakened by neighbors during the previous phase, still took centuries to cease to exist.

13.4 End of Mesopotamian Civilization and Ancient Egyptian Civilization

Loss of sustained political independence (SPI): Cyrus conquered Mesopotamia in 539 BCE and, like all empire builders, projected himself as a proud liberator of Babylon, for he did provide a measure of religious and cultural freedom to the Babylonians. Because of proximity and the considerable similarity of cultures, the Mesopotamian civilization quickly ceased to exist as a separate identity after Persian conquest.

Loss of control of wealth or means of wealth creation: Loss of SPI led to replacing the indigenous elite with foreign elite, without significant or sustained drain of wealth or the imposition of a new creed. The pattern of land ownership or enslavement of the population did not materially change except, of course, for control of the sustainable growing surplus.

Impact on productive outcomes: Overall, Achaemenids probably had a positive impact on the productive outcomes of the Mesopotamian territory. At the very least, they provided political stability and encouraged internal trade through better roads and security. All empire builder-settlers naturally have a vested interest in supporting wealth creation in the conquered civilization.

Transmission of creativity: Mesopotamian civilization was superior to the Achaemenid Empire in most creative arenas, and since the conquest put an end to the divided Mesopotamian civilization, the issue of transmission of creativity to Mesopotamia is moot. It was more a question of whether the conquerors would value what Mesopotamia had achieved in astronomy and art.

Impact on institutional structures and processes: Since Mesopotamian city-states ceased to exist, the question of impact on its societal structures and processes is also moot. The relevant question is precisely the opposite: How did Mesopotamian civilization impact the structures and processes of the conquering Persians?

Net impact: On balance, the conquest of Mesopotamian civilization (apart from its destruction) was a backward step for science because Achaemenids did not value Mesopotamian astronomy and simply used its artistic achievements as a glue in their diverse empire and as a display of its power and glory of the world's first inter-civilization empire.

Ancient Egyptian Civilization

Loss of sustained political independence (SPI): Cyrus conquered Mesopotamia in 539 BCE, and his son conquered Egypt in 526 BCE. Egyptian civilization had been in a long-term decline, and the Persian conquest simply accelerated the trend. Because of distance and the unique nature of Egyptian civilization, it did continue to maintain its weakened identity after it lost its sustained political independence again, this time to Persians. It was, unfortunately, not the last time. Two hundred years later, Alexander conquered Egypt without a real fight, followed by the Roman Empire three centuries later. Another three centuries would pass under Byzantine control before Persians would again conquer Egypt, followed shortly by the Arabs and Ottomans.

Loss of control of wealth or means of wealth creation: Achaemenid conquest simply meant replacing the indigenous elite with Persians, without significant or sustained drain of wealth or imposition of a new creed. Both the Achaemenids and Greeks were settler-conqueror types to one degree or another. The Persian Empire saw Egypt as a dependable source of food grain and wanted to do nothing to change that. Similarly, Alexander saw Egypt as an easy target and a source of replenishing his war efforts against Achaemenids, and thus did not disturb the Egyptian economy beyond using its sustainable growing surplus to oil his war machine. The Ptolemy dynasty became essentially Egyptian in outlook, much like the Indo-Greeks became Indian. The Roman Empire was more distant and saw Egypt as a distant colony whose wealth it felt it had the natural right to drain.

Impact on productive outcomes: It is doubtful that the Persians impacted the productive outcomes of ancient Egypt significantly, except temporarily in a negative way because of wars of conquest. After that, the positive impact was through providing political stability. There is also evidence that the Achaemenid Empire adapted Egyptian irrigation technologies. Following the Persians, Alexander conquered Egypt and founded the city of Alexandria. Productive outcomes of ancient Egypt under the Ptolemy dynasty in the post-Alexander era benefited because of a sustained effort to bring more land under cultivation, the introduction of cotton and wine-quality grapes, and more widespread irrigation. The dynasty also increased foreign trade, particularly in luxury goods. On the other hand, the hallmark of the following Roman conquest was a focus, not on increasing wealth creation, but on increased taxation needed to drain wealth. Substantial grain production was shipped out to the Roman garrison in Alexandria and onto Rome itself. Roman rule monetized the economy to make it easier to drain the wealth. The degree of manufacturing and foreign trade did indeed increase dramatically, but the benefit belonged to the Romans and not the Egyptians. If Achaemenids were the first to destroy an ancient, creative civilization, then Roman control of ancient Egypt is the world's first significant instance of systematic wealth drain from one civilization by another.

Transmission of creativity: Persians hardly had anything novel to transmit to ancient Egypt. The Greeks, however, had a major impact on Egypt, as they brought the evolving fruits of Greek-Hellenistic learning to Egypt, resulting in significant advances in astronomy as an example.

Impact on institutional structures and processes: While Persians, Greeks, and Romans impacted ancient Egypt's political system, economy, manufacturing, and scientific activity, none seriously impacted the Egyptian religion and social structure. Quite to the contrary, the Ptolemy kings adopted the trappings of Egyptian royalty and were mummified in classical Egyptian fashion. They also followed the Egyptian religion and gods. Magnificent temples were built. Similarly, the Romans adopted Egyptian goddesses as well. Such is the power of ancient culture. The political, military, economic, and legal systems may melt rather quickly after conquest but not the social structures and religious and cultural beliefs, which change much more slowly.

Net impact: The Persian Empire destroyed the old stable order in Egypt while the Greeks improved agriculture and brought science to Egypt. Romans, while improving manufacturing and monetizing the economy, drained Egypt of its wealth. The difference was that while the first two were empire builder settlers, the Romans were distant wealth drainers par excellence. It is indeed difficult to think of another civilization that prospered and remained independent for nearly three millennia and had foreign domination for nearly three more millennia to the present while being able to retain its identity in some measure! If the intersection of the mighty Nile and the brutal desert created conditions for a small, centralized, and insular civilization six millennia ago, the same geographical elements enabled its control by outsiders as other civilizations around its periphery grew stronger. Geography is no longer the destiny of civilizations to the same degree, but its dramatic role in early civilizations is hardly deniable. The Egyptian civilization proves that hypothesis.

Thus, only two of the four primary civilizations survived the current phase, with Greeks, Persians, and Romans arriving on the world stage.

History, Causes, and Outcomes of the Persian Empires

13.5 Brief Political History (539 BCE–224 CE)

We reviewed the origin of the Achaemenid Empire in the last chapter up to the ascension of Cyrus. Cyrus the Great, after overthrowing Asyages and consolidating his power, defeated Babylon in 539 BCE to incorporate Mesopotamia into his empire. The conquest of Egypt occurred in 525 BCE by Cambyses. Cyrus was followed by Darius I and Xerxes I, who died in 464 BCE. Lesser rulers followed Darius and Xerxes, and once again, the empire descended into corruption and decadence. It was overthrown by Alexander after a little more than two centuries after the beginning of the current phase. In conquering Mesopotamia, we witness, for the first time, the collision between an opportunistic empire builder and a civilization with a nearly favorable internal creative balance and world-class astronomy. The birth of the Persian Empire was literally a bloody event, with several centuries of conflict with Assyria and the amalgamation of different Indo-Aryan tribes.

The first war between the Persians and Greeks occurred at Marathon in 490 BCE. It was essentially a punitive Persian attack because Greeks had settled in Asia Minor had rebelled against the Persian rule. Later, the Greeks successfully checked the Persian force and were able to prevent a surprise attack on Athens twenty-five miles away. The next engagement occurred at Thermopylae in 480 BCE, which apparently the Persians won. In the following year, the Persians destroyed Athens. However, the Greek navy feigned retreat in the Bay of Salamis, luring the Persians into the narrow straits, where they rammed the Persian naval contingent, thus destroying it. In 478 BCE, the Greeks destroyed the remaining Persian army under Mardonius at Platea. The Persians, having sent the message, seem to have lost further interest in engaging the Greeks seriously, and eventually entered a treaty with the Greeks in 449 BCE that was mediated by the Athenian politician Callias. Nearly half a century later in 401 BCE, a rebel Persian prince named Cyrus the Younger, collected an army of ten thousand Greek mercenaries and marched into the heart of the Persian Empire and back, demonstrating the effectiveness of the Greek invention of the phalanx. This was perhaps a preview of the havoc Alexander was to heap on the Persian Empire decades later. The Persians did not learn from this warning and failed to modernize their military.

Western historians often portray the Persian–Greek wars as early examples of the superiority of a nascent European civilization. The reality, however, is more complex. That all Greek city-states combined were smaller in size compared to one of the twenty-three provinces of the Persian Empire would tend to substantiate their claim. However, when one understands the Persian objectives in these engagements, the claim does not hold water. It seems that Persian objective was to prevent Greek expansion on its western flank through playing one Greek city-state against another. Often, the Greeks, sympathetic to the Persians and known as Medized, fought under Persian command. The Persian Empire initially was a land empire supported by an army. The Greek city-states, because of their geography, had a more balanced military force, which together with home turf advantage explains their tactical success at Platea. The Greek-Persian wars until Alexander were fought primarily on Greek soil, more than two thousand miles away from the Persian home base.

It also helps to remember that our knowledge about these wars comes from the Greek historian Herodotus, who is regarded by some as not the "father of history" but the "father of lies." The Persian "defeat" of 2,500 years ago is comparable to the recent American "defeat" in Vietnam.

The Achaemenid Empire Cyrus and Darius built did not survive the onslaught of Alexander. Thereafter, Persia remained under Greek control for several decades. This defeat is clearly attributable to a lapse into luxury by Persian nobility and superior weapons, training of the Greek forces, and tactics by Alexander. Shortly after he began invading Asia, Alexander, perhaps sensing the strength of Persians and the relative weakness of Egyptians, turned southwest and conquered poor, hapless Egypt first. This allowed him to acquire additional resources before attacking Persia a year later. One must wonder what might have happened had he chosen to attack Persia right away, as was his first impulse. Clever empire builders have always used the resources of the one defeated people to defeat another.

In 248 BCE, the Parthians liberated Persia from Seleucid, one of the generals left in charge of Alexander's conquered territories. The Parthian Empire lasted from 248 BCE to 224 AD or nearly half a millennium. The Parthians supposedly came from the steppes east of the Caspian Sea, a convenient homeland for a whole slew of Indo-Europeans for Western historians. Thus, within a couple of generations, Persians successfully got rid of Greek influence with the Seleucid kingdom ceding the territory of the Achaemenid Empire to the Parthians. During a later period, the Parthian Empire was on friendly terms with the Hans in China, but it came under strong pressure from the Roman Empire in the west and the Kushan Empire in the east and did not eventually survive this pressure as an empire.

Like most imperial powers, the Persians represented their conquests of foreign peoples as liberation from previous oppression. For example, after conquering Babylon, Cyrus was quick to discredit Nabonidus, the last Babylonian ruler, as a tyrant. Because Achaemenid rulers did not subscribe to an uncompromising monotheism, they respected local religious traditions and successfully allied themselves with local priests in both Babylon and Egypt to gain political advantage.

13.6 Natural Causes

There were no significant natural disasters or changes in physical and ecological environment that impacted the Achaemenid and Parthian Empires during the current phase.

13.7 Intrinsic Causes

Institutional Systems, Structures, and Processes

Political system: The political structures and processes of the empire evolved considerably as it went through the process of absorbing the achievements of Egypt, Mesopotamia, and many other smaller civilizations in the process of conquest. The Achaemenid Empire was the first multicontinent, multicivilization, and multicultural empire of the world. It spanned Europe, Africa, and Asia. It did not, however, last long enough to evolve into a cohesive civilization, remaining a motley collection of diverse people to the end. Politically, it was headed by a monarch whose power was checked by key aristocratic families. At its height, the empire was divided into twenty-some provinces, each headed by a governor, an army commander, and a secretary, and all were appointed by the king in an attempt to keep power centralized. Like most empires, it had ill-defined succession rules, and military power was the basis of power. Like most monarchies, there was insufficient separation of legislative, executive, and judicial functions. The empire at its height consisted of about 30 million people (estimates range from 10 million to 80 million) though it covered an area of more than 10 million square kilometers or about 4 million square miles.

Military capability: Given the enormous eventual size of the Persian Empire, which consisted of diverse ethnic groups, a professional army was a requirement. Cyrus created a strong land force. Although Cyrus showed interest in developing a navy, this task fell to his son, Darius. The impetus for development of an imperial navy came from the maritime traditions in both Egypt and Greece. The reader may recall that Egypt was conquered by the Persian Empire in 525 BCE and remained in its control for nearly two centuries. Darias established the Persian navy in the fifth century BCE, and it would reach its zenith under Artaxerxes II in the fourth century BCE. The technology to build ships and even the personnel to operate the ships came from Phoenicians, Egyptians, Cypriots, and Greeks. A typical Persian warship was about 120 feet long and about 20 feet wide. It was fitted with metal blades in the front and hooks on the side for offensive purposes and was capable of carrying three hundred troops. Smaller ships carrying up to a hundred troops were used to patrol the rivers in the empire. The imperial navy invented the concept of a massive boat bridge over rivers and channels and used the concept successfully to cross Tigris River and the Bosporus. Alexander borrowed the idea of boat bridges to cross the Indus River in India during his invasion of a small kingdom in Northwest India. Both the army and navy had a strong offensive orientation.

Economic organization: The economy was divided into three sectors: royal, managed by temples, and private. The royal sector was significant in size and active in livestock and manufacturing. The temple sector existed mostly in conquered lands in Mesopotamia and Egypt, consistent with local traditions. Land was tenured out to soldiers and others since in theory the king was the owner of all land. The economy was primarily agricultural, and land was tilled by farmers or, if owned by the elite, by the slaves captured in wars. Irrigation was provided through the Qnant system or the underground irrigation system that transported water from aquifers in the mountains. The empire, unlike ancient Egypt, excelled in internal land transport, with the principal highway being over 1,500 miles long—a road Alexander was to use to invade two centuries later. The road system encouraged commerce, but more important, it was required to keep the huge empire together. It is difficult to ascribe more than modest growth to the sustainable surplus under the natural conditions that prevailed in most parts of the empire. Darius introduced the silver and gold coinage and introduced money-lending houses. The word "check" in English is derived from Old Persian. A standardized system of length, weight, and volume was introduced. International trade was controlled by Phoenician subjects of the empire, given their skills in sea navigation.

Systems of religious faith: The religious impulse was first systematized by Zarathustra probably in the eighth century BCE. He created a religion with good and evil as represented by gods Ahura-Mazda and Ahriman. Zarathustra conceived the world as a struggle between good and evil and independently formulated the important concept of free will. Early Persians did not create images of gods as they believed gods to be different from humans and offered sacrifices to the sun and moon, earth, fire, water, and the winds through a hereditary class of priest known as *magus*. This class evidently initiated changes to original Zoroastrianism. Thus, practical religion still had strong elements of polytheism.

Science-religion conflict in ancient Persia must be judged to be minimal because not only the doctrinal monotheism was absent there was little interest in science as well. The tendency toward monotheism embedded in Zoroastrianism was yet to impact this neutral attitude toward science.

Legal systems: The judiciary consisted of the king as the supreme court, a high court, and local courts spread throughout the provinces. The law derived its authority from the divine inspiration of Ahura Mazda and the king. In addition, arbitration was encouraged as a means to settle disputes. The Persian Empire may have been the first to have formal "lawyers" who educated the litigants in law before the case appeared in the courts where the parties in dispute personally presented their cases directly to the court. The legal code was partly based on the Egyptian legal system. The lawyers themselves did not argue the cases.

Social structure: Society was divided into four main classes: ruling elite and priests, warriors, traders, farmers, and slaves. Separate gods were associated with each class, with the *ahura*s, including Mitra and Varuna, representing the first class. Social structure did not change appreciably, and the social life of the elite in the Persian Empire continued to swing back and forth from austerity to decadence. Cyrus and Darius built the empire and seemed to have lived a Spartan life (eating one meal a day, for example), Xerxes sustained it, and his successors through decadence weakened it. For the masses, social life meant stressing family ties, communal unity guaranteed by religious freedom, and loyalty to the throne. The empire allowed slavery with war captives only. Inequality probably became worse as later Achaemenid rulers and the Parthian dynasty forgot the Spartan ways of early Achaemenid rulers.

Knowledge-Creating and educational institutions: There were no formal knowledge-creating institutions in ancient Persia during the present phase. Informal education was based on Zoroastrian ethics and consisted of good thoughts, words, and actions. Like the Egyptian Empire during its imperial phase, the Persian Empire lacked any pretense for a higher purpose and existed mainly to transfer wealth from the provinces into the central coffers, which were used to maintain the imperial army and the good life of the ruling elite. The source of wealth at the center was power, not industry.

Wealth allocation process: As noted above, the elite of the empire vacillated between a Spartan and decadent life, with the latter usually gaining the upper hand. The surplus was overwhelmingly directed into supporting the luxurious lifestyle of the elite and protecting the empire through a strong military and a centralized administration. The empire neglected the development of industry. However, with monotheistic tendencies, it was not necessary to invest the surplus to build elaborate temples and to support a priest class, a major improvement over the Mesopotamian and Egyptian civilizations. Thankfully, in contrast to the Egyptian civilization, building monuments for the afterlife did not exist either. However, magnificent palaces and courts more than made up for the difference. The focus of the Persian Empire was on a narrower version of practical creativity that made a good life for elites better. Thus, wealth allocation favored the elite lifestyles and military needs.

Social cohesion: Right from the start, the Achaemenid Empire was a collection of different peoples held together by a strong center that did not unduly interfere with the religion, tradition, and customs of the conquered peoples. It was interested in extracting a portion of the surplus through taxation and did not have a religious or economic ideology that it wished to impose. Thus, since the empire remained strong during the current phase, an extensive legal system coupled with a strong army and Zoroastrian ethics provided the social cohesion. However, social cohesion was top-down and political in character, not bottom-up or organic, social, religious, or cultural. Art sponsorship played a key role in projecting the powers of Achaemenids to diverse groups.

Internal wars: There were few major internal wars after the empire was established; however, decadence coupled with lack of succession rules resulted in periodic dynastic upheavals, as did rebellions in faraway conquered territories, such as Egypt. The highly efficient centralized structures ensured internal stability over extended periods.

The Parthian Empire, from our perspective, was not sufficiently different from the Achaemenid Empire in its institutional structures and processes. Both empires remained highly centralized; excelled in military strength, art, and architecture; and were disinterested in science and philosophy, preferring religion based on faith and not direct experience.

Formative Beliefs and Ideology at the End of the First Synthesis Phase

The relatively benign monotheism of ancient Persians, their relative lack of desire for knowledge as evidenced by their reaction to Mesopotamian astronomy, a social cohesion derived from political power, the oscillation between luxurious decadence and a Spartan lifestyle of the elite, their acceptance of slavery, their interest in trade, and their need to expand the empire as the singular means to grow state revenue all point to a belief system that may be summarized as follows:

- A belief in practical knowledge to increase wealth production and to expand the empire
- A belief in the relative equality among different ethnic groups within the empire despite significant wealth polarization and slavery
- An attitude of insularity toward the intellectual and religious creativity of others
- A belief in aggression toward other social orders

These beliefs, though derived in part from Mesopotamian and Egyptian civilizations, are important since as the first empire of any consequence, these beliefs strongly impacted the beliefs of other West Asian civilizations that followed the Persian Empire.

13.8 Extrinsic Peaceful Causes or Sum Total of Others' Constructive Outcomes

Impact of Indian Civilization

Channels of transmission: The principal channel was trade.

Transmission of creativity: Indian and Persian civilizations mostly reciprocally impacted each other as equals. However, Persia had a very practical and imperial orientation. It conquered Mesopotamian civilization but showed little interest in Babylonian science. Persia also did not learn from the Indian civilization because it concentrated her energies on civilizations it could conquer, and the Indian civilization did not afford that possibility during most of this phase. However, there is little-known interaction in practical technology, religion, art, science, or philosophy. Consequently, there was only modest fruitful contact between the two during this phase, except in trade.

Fair trade: After the Persian Empire was established in the late eighth century BCE, trade with the empire no doubt increased, replacing Mesopotamian–Indian trade. Old Persian cities also seemed to have played a role in the declining Indo-Mesopotamian trade.

Impact on productive outcomes: The annual value of tax levied on the northwestern Indian province of Sindh was gold dust equal in value to 4,680 talents of silver, with one talent being equivalent to about sixty-seven pounds. If one assumes the sixteen to one ratio for gold to silver price, this calculates to about twenty thousand pounds of gold. Alternatively, one talent of silver paid about ten years of wages for a skilled worker; thus the tax levied on the Indian province was equivalent to the wages of fifty thousand skilled workers!

13.9 Extrinsic Violent Causes or Sum Total of Others' Destructive Outcomes

Impact of Mesopotamian and Egyptian Civilizations-Persian Empire as Victor

The Persian Empire gained both prestige and treasury after absorbing the weakened Mesopotamian states and Egypt.

Transmission of creativity (practical creativity, astronomy, and art): Perhaps the biggest impact of Egyptian conquest was on architecture and art, practical technologies such as irrigation techniques, and weapons technology. During the current phase, Persians had the opportunity to access the Babylonian/Chaldean astronomy but did not show interest because of their practical orientation. Achaemenid art reflected the diversity of the empire it was borrowed from Assyrian, Egyptian, Greek, Phoenician, Lycian, and Cappacodian sources.

Impact on productive outcomes: The tax on an Egyptian province was 120,000 measures of grain and 700 talents of silver and enriched the treasury.

Impact on creative outcomes: Since the rule was based on force, the Achaemenid emperors used art as a glue to bind the empire together: the empire lacked commonality in language, religion, or ethnicity. Art played a huge role, buttressed further by luxurious lifestyle of several Achaemenid sovereigns: the Assyrian wall reliefs, depictions of the Assyrian god Ashur to represent the Zoroastrian god; human-headed, winged bulls; Egyptian paintings of conquered peoples in the form of the nine bows; and the Egyptian idea of using outer palace walls as billboards of victorious imperial power and Greek influence in the execution of details such as drapery, hair, eyes, and beards. The use of art as a propaganda tool and the shape of columns are some examples of the extensive foreign influence on Achaemenid art.

Impact on institutional structures and processes: The highly centralized structures of Egyptian civilization and the intelligent political, economic, and religious structure of the first intercivilization empire of the world had little in common. One is hard-pressed to think of an institution in the Achaemenid Empire that was modeled after the Egyptian civilization.

Impact of Ancient Greece–Persian Empire as Defeated

Transmission of creativity: Alexander tried to create a hybrid culture combining features of both Persian and Greek cultures by adopting Persian dress personally and insisting on thousands of marriages between Greek soldiers and Persian women, for example. This attempt, however, must be judged to be of little long-term consequence. Following Alexander's sudden death, most of this was undone rather quickly by his generals. One does not see any lasting synthesis in art, language, culture, philosophy, or science resulting from the encounter. Persian civilization was far too advanced and proud, and the Greek rule was far too short to have significant impact.

Fair trade: Geographically speaking, Persians were in the middle of it all during the current phase. As the trade between Asia and Europe opened up, Persians benefited greatly from the trade flow, yet they also squandered a lot of this wealth on imperial adventures or on protecting themselves from the enemies they had created. With the exception of Alexander's invasion, during the phase Persia was an instrument of control rather than being controlled by one. With the establishment of the Parthian Empire that was to last half a millennium, they demonstrated their resiliency.

Impact on productive outcomes: There was little known impact on productive outcomes.

Impact on creative outcomes: There was little in religious, philosophical, or scientific creativity that interested the practical-minded Persians. That even in the absence of a full-blown monotheistic faith, science did not interest the ruling elites of Persia over a thousand-year period through three of the greatest empires the world has ever seen, namely, the Achaemenid, Parthian, and Sassanian Empires is indeed surprising. Perhaps it points to the refractory nature of the inner nature of civilizations. We witness a similar situation in the Roman world through the Roman Republic and the Roman Empire, also over a millennium.

Impact on institutional structures and processes: Again, the geography-constrained model of city-states that necessitated the emergence of elitist democracy driven by commercial interest and colonization and the naïve polytheism of the ancient Greeks had little application in the rugged expanses of West Asia, ruled by a nearly monotheistic religious impulse.

13.10 Productive Outcomes

Given the population and the natural arid condition through most of the empire, it is difficult to envision easy internal wealth creation despite great communication, internal trade, and freedom. The land portion of the trade between Rome, India, and China was controlled by the Parthian Empire and added to its wealth. There were no significant migrations into or out of the empire during the current phase. However, the empire was eminently successful in eliciting the loyalties of the conquered peoples through religious tolerance and alliances with the religious and political elites.

It is probably fair to say that greater emphasis was placed on internal trade than on trade with other civilizations. We see evidence of that from the construction of Darius' palace in Persepolis, which required timber from Lebanon, Carmania, and Gandhara; gold from Bactria and Sardis, silver and ebony from Egypt; ivory from Ethiopia; and builders from Egypt, Babylon, Ionians, and Sardians. Persepolis, one of the four capitals of the Achaemenid Empire, was known as the "richest city under the sun." It was also the trading capital of the Near East. There was free movement of different peoples within the empire, as the building of palace in Persepolis suggests.

13.11 Creative Outcomes

Achievements in Practical Creativity

The well-to-do had a taste for fine clothes, food, and fragrances. The kings were said to not go to war without their personal fragrance carriers. The focus was on practical creativity to maintain the empire and to support the elite lifestyle. The key practical achievements of the phase must include development of the underground irrigation system to bring water from high mountains to the cities and farms and using high technology, such as the windmill and galvanic cell for electroplating, both having been acquired from the Mesopotamians.

Achievements in Religious Creativity

The religious creativity of the Persian civilization under Achaemenids may be summarized as developing religious tolerance and, perhaps based more on political necessity than religious orientation, further development of Zoroastrianism through incorporation of several concepts from the Indo-Aryan religion, such as naming the months and days after the divinities. A greater part of Avesta is believed to have originated during the Achaemenid Empire. There is little of Zoroastrian development that has come down from the Parthian period.

Achievements in Intellectual Creativity

During the current phase, art, architecture, and medicine received the greatest attention. Philosophy and other branches of science, such as mathematics and astronomy, did not receive much attention during the period.

Achievements in medicine: In *Vendidad*, which is part of the later versions of Avesta, three kinds of medicine are mentioned: knife, herbs, and sacred incantations, with the last being most important. Again, much later literature refers to an encyclopedia containing 4,333 diseases identified during the current phase. Darius rebuilt the school of medicine in Sais, Egypt, that had been destroyed earlier. The idea of organ transplant is also said to have originated in the Achaemenid period. Ancient Persia basically succeeded in organizing practical medicine away from superstition and magic.

Achievements in art: Ancient Persia produced great art and architecture, achieving a distinctly Persian style, although with significant absorption of foreign elements, such as tall, slender columns. The great hall of Xerxes covered a hundred thousand square feet, and its details were the finest ever created by an ancient civilization. Achaemenid kings were masters in using art as a force to glue the empire together lacking a linguistic, religious, ethnic, or cultural unity. It is interesting the art reflected different ethnic styles, artists came from different communities, and art was created at the center, often under royal supervision and sent to provinces. It functioned as billboards of imperial power and a powerful means of persuasion through the most effective contemporary visual media of the era.

Achievement in institutional structures and processes: It is important to emphasize the political innovation behind the Achaemenid Empire: the idea that a number of different dependent states can be ruled by a center with states retaining their individuality, including their peculiar political, economic, religious, and social forms; their languages; and their customs. It is the first instance in human history of unity among diversity that was provided by an impartial, enlightened center based on competent administration and a highly developed web of communications and transportation, making it possible for men to freely produce, trade, and travel. Early in the current phase, the Persians thus created the political, military, and social structures of an empire that have survived as a model for how diverse peoples with different cultures languages, religious faiths, legal systems, and economic organization can live in harmony under a central government. This, together with art and architecture, may be regarded as the greatest accomplishment of Persian civilization.

13.12 Achievements in Science

Unfortunately, this brilliant empire utterly failed to show significant intellectual creativity outside of art and architecture, since it never shifted its creative energies away from a near total focus on empire building, the good life for the elite, and a rising monotheistic religion, though it still remained tolerant of the different religious traditions of the conquered peoples.

Summarizing Achievements in Abstract Systems-Building Capability (ASBC)

By the end of the phase, the ASBC of the second great Persian Empire must be characterized as relatively underdeveloped: it had adopted alphabetical script and mastered the creative method, but it showed little interest in developing or adopting sound epistemology.

History, Causes, and Outcomes of the Roman Republic

13.13 Brief Political History (753 BCE–200 CE)

Roman Republic and Roman Empire

Legend has it that the Roman Republic was founded in 509 BCE by noblemen when they overthrew King Tarquinius after his son Sextus raped the daughter of one of the nobles. The "republic" was a small principality surrounding city of Rome and was founded in 753 BCE. It was the tribal tradition that if a king left office, his powers returned to the assembly of nobles, called the senate, until a new king was elected. Thus, the senate was not elected; it was a body consisting of the chiefs of the powerful families who inherited those positions. However, Tarquinius was so despised, he was not allowed to return. As a result, the senate evolved a system of choosing two consuls for a one-year term in place of a king, while retaining most powers. The two consuls had veto powers over each other.

A second assembly, called the plebs, consisting of the lesser wealthy landowners and merchants, also evolved over time. As the Roman Republic expanded on the Italian Peninsula, the power of the plebeians also grew and from 376 BCE onward, one of the consuls came to be elected by the plebeians. The plebs had the responsibility of passing laws, while the senate controlled the treasury, foreign policy, and military. This sharing of power between the top two layers of the Roman Republic set the stage for the Republic to expand in the coming centuries. Thus, the

Roman Republic was ruled by a club of hereditary nobles and wealthy landowners. By the middle of the fourth century BCE, the Roman Republic was still smaller than a small province of the Persian Empire and less than about four thousand square miles in area.

The Republic was really a city-state and was yet to enter the big league. South of Italy was dominated by Magna Graecia colonies. Lacking a standing army initially, the Roman nobles supplied legions, whose job was to conquer land. Over the next hundred years, the balance of power shifted to the plebeian assembly and the new nobility. The Roman Republic, in the wake of Alexander's death and his successors fighting over their Asian territories, entered an aggressive imperial era around the Mediterranean, employing the Roman legions and later a standing army. The Roman Republic could go on an imperial quest around the Mediterranean since Greeks attention remained focused in West Asia and Africa.

The Roman Republic's expansion actually started a bit before the death of Alexander in 323 BCE. The victory in the Latin and Samnite wars (340–268 BCE) allowed the republic to expand, and by end of the fourth century BCE, it butted against the city-states of Magna Graecia in south Italy. The inevitable conflict between Greeks and Romans resulted in the Pyrrhic War in 283 BCE. By 268 BCE, the Romans controlled the entire Italian Peninsula. The Roman Republic now set its sights on Carthage Empire, which controlled North Africa, France, and Spain. The empire had been established by the Phoenicians (the ones who had taught Greeks to write) and was a strong naval power in the Mediterranean. The saga of these so-called Punic wars was a long, drawn-out affair lasting nearly 150 years and was primarily a naval warfare. After many setbacks, the Romans finally prevailed, and as a result became the masters of the Mediterranean. However, in the process, the Roman Republic became thoroughly militarized. Even before the Punic Wars finished, the Roman Republic opened a second series of wars called the Macedonian Wars in 217 BCE.

By about 150 BCE, the Romans had finally conquered the Greek city-states as well. A decade or so later, King Attalus in Asia Minor willed his kingdom to Romans to forestall a civil war among potential heirs. With this gift, the Roman Republic was nearly 750,000 square miles, almost half of Emperor Ashoka's domains in India a bit earlier. This expansion, however, came at a huge price. In addition to the militarization of the Romans, it led to a shift in the power balance between the landed nobles and wealthy knights, resulting in declining public support for the republic that ended the Roman Empire.

The Roman Empire remained in a state of unending wars with Britain; with Germanic tribes; Jewish, Gothic, and Frankish tribes; Huns; and the Parthian Empire. The Roman Republic and Empire provided the first unified political structure to the continent of Europe; however, the internal surplus and the spoils of the conquest were both spent on military capability and on the high living of the elite. There was little left for intellectual creation, except as needed to support the lifestyle of the elite.

13.14 Natural Causes

The Italian Peninsula is mountainous but not impenetrable and is centrally located with respect to the Mediterranean. These factors made Rome a great staging area for the regions around the Mediterranean Sea. In addition, the soil in the Po valley was fertile, which remained the most productive area in Rome until the conquest of Egypt. Rome was easier to defend as it was surrounded by hills. Access to the sea through the Tiber River was also helpful. In addition, the Alps in the north protected the peninsula from the barbarians. It was indeed a great place to launch an empire in Europe and North Africa.

13.15 Intrinsic Causes

Institutional Systems, Structures, and Processes

Political system: Initially the Roman Republic was an elite democracy, as noted earlier. Later, it was expanded to include the plebeians into an assembly. These two bodies held all political power for a while until the political power came to rest with emperors after the fall of the Republic in 27 BCE. We will review the political structure of the Roman Empire in the next chapter in more detail.

Military capability: The military consisted of the infamous Roman legions. The idea behind the legions was simple. The landowners and noblemen would organize legions of small fighting forces of under five thousand men for offensive purposes. The early republic had no standing army; it only used legions as needed. This worked very well as long as the military campaigns lasted a few months. The senate did not have to fund a standing army. Later, when the republic grew and the campaigns lasted years not months, the republic had to resort to a standing army.

The Roman legions owed a great deal of their military technology and tactics to the Magna Graecia city-states in southern Italy. The Republic was indeed an efficient military machine, with established rules to divide the conquered lands among the privileged few. However, unlike the early Greek civilization, it did not always turn the conquered into slaves. This was probably necessary given the far-flung nature of the conquered lands compared to the compact city-states of Greece, consistent with geographical setting. Without question, the military capability was offensive in nature.

Economic organization: The economy of the Roman Republic was essentially agricultural and slave-based. It was focused on feeding the population. The legions scattered throughout the Mediterranean region maintained internal control. Agriculture and trade dominated the economy, supplemented by small-scale manufacturing. It has been estimated that 25 percent of the population were slaves, a significant improvement over ancient Greece. Extensive land and sea trade routes were established. While the transport of goods was a benefit of the large road network, their most significant purpose was the fast mobilization of the legions. The road networks are indeed one of the lasting legacies of the Roman Republic. The industry effort focused on mining stone and metals required for the construction and military hardware. The lifestyle of the rich required luxuries that in turn required imports of cotton, silk, spices, precious stones, and even slaves from all over the world. The imports were paid through gold when required. The global trade routes opened by the Hellenistic states and Kushans were helpful. Both barter and a cash economy supported by high-quality coins existed. Slave markets were common, where slaves could be bought and sold.

Systems of religious faith: The Roman Republic, ancient Greece, and the Roman Empire (initially) had a polytheistic religious orientation. During this period, we witness the rise of Christianity, mostly as a religion of the poor masses in the Hellenistic-Roman world. Christianity was founded by Jesus and was strongly monotheistic by contrast. Initially, because Christianity was primarily a religion of the masses, the Roman Empire persecuted the Christians with a vengeance. During the first century of its existence, it was managed by the apostolic church, which in practice meant a church run by the disciples and relatives of Jesus. The gospels and New Testament were compiled in this period. In the second century of its existence, a transition was made to the episcopal structure, through the positions of bishops and presbyters or elders.

The Roman Republic did not actively oppose science because of religious impulse. It was more like the ancient Persians in that both empires conquered or controlled peoples interested in science but did not understand its value. Thus, Romans could hardly be accused of harboring science-religion conflict or excessive spirituality, for they neither valued science nor were excessively religious.

Legal systems: Roman law was highly developed and was based on both customs and laws enacted. In later times, the will of the emperors also came to be seen as the law. The original contribution of Roman law was its focus on the exact formulation of law and on actions of the individual as the guiding principle and not intentions, since only actions could be verified.

Social structure and inequality: The social structure consisted of a senatorial class, who had a hereditary monopoly on political power; the equestrians controlling commerce; three classes graded by property-owning citizens forming the working middle class; nearly propertyless proletarians; and slaves. The status of women remained deplorable. Men were the absolute head of the family and lords of the wife, children, daughters-in-law, nephews, and slaves. Roman society was highly stratified, with extreme wealth at one end and slavery at the other end. It has been estimated that an average senator owned wealth several hundred times that of a proletariat.

The Roman Republic and the Roman Empire displayed excessive inequality. The expansionary phase of the Roman Republic reached its height by the end of the second century BCE, with significant wealth polarization based on the elite immersed in high living. This led to an extended period of the so-called servile or slave wars, which at one time involved over a hundred thousand slaves under the command of a gladiator named Spartacus.

Knowledge-Creating and education institutions: Few formal Knowledge-Creating or educational institutions existed—not even the Greek-style academies. The elite were educated by private tutors. Romans did not organize universities. They displayed little of the love of knowledge of the Greeks, remaining practical empire builders. The creative focus was architecture, art, law, and engineering directed toward the lifestyle of the elite, military needs, and ensuring food and water supplies.

Wealth allocation: Without a doubt, the majority of the wealth was allocated to supporting the high living standard of the elites and the maintenance of the military for expansion and defense. Romans did not build expensive monuments for emperors and did not significantly allocate religious activities. A priest class did not have to be supported. However, the support of elites and the military consumed everything. Romans had little interest in science. They were not actively antiscience, as evidenced by the continuation of intellectual activity in the Hellenistic world for a brief period under their control. They just did not see its value. After all, had they not defeated the intellectually minded Greeks?

Social cohesion: Roman society was a quintessential class society with a pretention of democracy. The patricians and the plebeians were at the top, the free citizens in the middle, and the slaves at the bottom. Religion played little role in managing social cohesion within Roman society. Roman law and Roman police and military did the job.

Internal wars: The Roman world was replete with internal intrigue and infighting, and an extended internal war ultimately resulted in the destruction of the Republic and its pretensions of democracy. The Roman Empire replaced it.

Formative Beliefs and Ideology at the End of First Synthesis Phase

The relatively primitive polytheism of the Romans, their relative lack of desire for knowledge as evidenced by their reaction to Greek achievements, a social cohesion derived from police brutality, their commitment to luxurious decadence, their acceptance of slavery and enjoyment of inhuman gladiator games, their interest in trade, and their need to expand the empire through militarism as the singular means to grow revenue point to a belief system may be summarized as follows:

- A belief in practical knowledge to increase wealth production and to expand the empire
- A belief in the fundamental inequality between Romans and non-Romans
- An attitude of openness toward the practical creativity of others and an equally insular attitude toward the intellectual and religious creativity of others
- A belief in violent aggression toward other social orders

These beliefs, though derived in part from the worst Greek impulses of aggression and inequality among its own citizens, are important since as the first European empire of any consequence, these beliefs strongly impacted the beliefs of other European empires.

13.16 Extrinsic Peaceful Causes or Sum Total of Constructive Outcomes

Reciprocal Impact of Rome-India Fair Trade

After the Roman Republic and Roman Empire defeated ancient Greece and Hellenistic states, the new round of interaction with Indian civilization at the beginning of the Common Era was trade-based, made possible in part through the Silk Route under the protection of Parthian and Kushan Empires and in part through coastal sea routes. This trade was in India's favor, and Romans had little interest in Indian epistemology, metaphysics, and religious creativity unless it related to the administration of the empire.

Science was still too immature to help in wealth creation during the current phase, and the worldly Romans wanted nothing to do with it. Knowledge for its own sake was hardly a Roman priority. Thus, interaction remained confined to trade.

Impact on productive outcomes: Romans, while depending on Indian manufactured luxury goods, bemoaned the outflow of gold as payment. It is doubtful that this trade with India had a material impact on Roman productive outcomes.

There was little impact on the creative outcomes or impact on the institutional structures and processes.

13.17 Extrinsic Violent Causes or Sum Total of Destructive Outcomes

The Impact of Ancient Greece and Hellenistic States—the Roman Empire as Victor

Transmission channels: The principal channels were the Greek colonies in southern Italy and around the Mediterranean that Romans conquered over centuries before the Common Era began.

Transmission of creativity (practical creativity, religion, art): The principal direction of flow was from Greece to the Roman world and consisted primarily of practical technology, architecture, military technology, and art. The impact of conquest of North Africa, Europe, Greece, and Hellenistic states on the Roman world was twofold: a substantial gain in controlling SGS of vast lands, acquisition of slave labor, and access to practical technologies of architecture, irrigation, and city planning from Greece, Hellenistic states, and Persians.

The transition to the Roman Empire and Christianity essentially occurred about the same time. Initially, since Roman religion was polytheistic and as Hellenistic states gradually became part of Roman Empire, under its oppressive rule, the common man turned to Christianity for solace. Christianity became popular with the masses in former Hellenistic states, and because Rome worked hard to conquer the Hellenistic world, it initially abhorred Christianity and persecuted Christians.

However, by the fourth century, the Roman state saw handwriting on the wall, and it had no choice but to adopt Christianity as a state religion and that led to a thousand year period of uncompromising antiscience attitude in the European civilization, a continuation of the attitude of the Roman Republic and Roman Empire but for religious and not imperial reasons.

It is easy to see why as the Parthian Empire reconquered Persia from Greek control and as Greece was defeated by Romans, the latter, as victors and the inheritors of the ancient Greek and later Hellenistic tradition, took only what was needed from the fruits of the Greek-Hellenistic synthesis so they could expand and maintain the empire. They took practical and weapons technology and the rhetorical skills for internal politics, since political elites in pre-Socrates Athens at its height were also interested in rationality as it related to politics, law, and acquisition of power. Romans destroyed ancient Greece; however, they could not destroy the Greek intellectual achievements of the post-Alexander Hellenistic world.

Fair trade: Significantly, Hellenistic states also helped in the creation of a single trading zone comprising of Europe and Asia.

Pact on productive outcomes: The source of Roman wealth was not industry; it was conquest and possibly trade. The impact on productive outcomes was indirect through practical and military technology transfer.

Impact on creative outcomes: There was material impact on the victors in the arena of art. The Roman Republic, however, did not value the scientific and philosophical tradition that Greece and Hellenistic states had nurtured over the previous two to three centuries, ever since it gained access to Mesopotamian astronomy. The victors, thus, ignored what was of real value in Greek heritage, and it had to take shelter on Asian soil to shield itself from the antiscience, empire-building Romans. Hellenistic states in turn had a major impact on Asia in such areas as art, astronomy, geometry, architecture, and town planning. And most importantly, Hellenistic states introduced Christianity into Europe.

On the one hand, Hellenistic states did succeeded temporarily in saving science from the Romans; yet, on the other hand, they facilitated the introduction of Christianity into Europe, thus preventing any interest in science in Europe for more than a millennium after the fall of Rome. It is noteworthy that Europe, with the exception of Greece, which was influenced by Indian science and philosophy, Mesopotamian astronomy, Phoenician script, and Egyptian art, has spent most of its existence as an antiscience civilization.

We need not belabor the extent of the interaction between ancient Greece and Hellenistic states and the Roman world. The continuity in art, architecture, language, political philosophy, slavery system, military technology, and imperial quest is obvious. What is equally obvious is the lack of continuity in philosophy, religious creativity, and science as we transition from ancient Greece and the Hellenistic world to the Roman Republic and Roman Empire.

To summarize, Romans did not value religious, philosophical, or scientific creativity. In this respect, the Roman world resembled the Persian world: both walked away from science, the former from Greek science and the latter from Babylonian science. Both eventually adopted intolerant monotheism, the former Christianity and the latter Islam. Romans took a lot from the world; their lasting contribution was just Roman law. Bottom line: the Roman Empire adopted Asian religion and Greek architecture, art, and practical technology but utterly neglected Greek science and philosophy.

Impact on institutional structures and processes: Greece and the Hellenistic states only had a marginal impact on Roman institutional structures and processes, except, as noted above, in practical and military technology and the institution of slavery. The Roman political system, so utterly different from the benign Persian model, was derived from its own tribal roots. Its economic organization was government-centered, with a weak merchant class, and its social structure even more stratified than that of ancient Greece. It is fair to say that until the emergence of European colonial power five hundred years ago, the world did not witness the shameless inequality between the conqueror and the conquered seen in the Roman world.

Impact of Egyptian and Mesopotamian Civilizations—Roman Empire as Victor

Channels of transmission: The conquest served as the principal channel of transmission.

Transmission of religious creativity: The cult of the Egyptian goddess Isis became popular in the Roman world. The powers of the Greek god Zeus and the Roman god Jupiter paralleled those of Enlil, the offspring of the god An and the goddess Ki in Mesopotamia. In both Enûma Eliš and Genesis, the primordial world is formless and empty; the only existing thing was the watery abyss that existed prior to creation. The sequence of creation was also similar to the one in the bible: light, firmament, dry land, luminaries, and man.

Impact: Apart from Egypt becoming the granary of the Roman Empire and the impact of the Roman religion in a minor way as noted above, there was little impact of Egypt. On the other hand, the impact on Rome on hapless Egypt was quite significant, due to wealth drain and destroying the Hellenistic science that had taken root in Egypt.

"Civilizing" Western Europe—the Roman Empire as Victor

Since we do not treat Western Europe as an independent entity yet and even though it was the violent aggression of Western Europe by Roman Empire and not the other way around, below we summarize the impact of Roman aggression on Western Europe.

Loss of sustained political independence (SPI): Taking advantage of Alexander's invasion and the subsequent Greek attention on its vast Asian territories, the Roman Republic expanded in Europe and North Africa. Over a period of four centuries, the Roman Republic (mostly) and the Roman Empire annexed North Africa, including Egypt, France, Spain, and England. These victories followed naturally in the aftermath of the defeat of Greece and were extended to western Hellenistic states. The Roman Empire wisely refrained from attacking Asia beyond the western Hellenistic states and stuck to empire building in the Wild West that northwestern Europe was. Thus, throughout the current phase, Rome played the role of an imperial aggressor in Europe and North Africa and its ambitions in Asia were held back by Parthians and for a while by Hellenistic states. Imperial Rome came to control the SGS of North Africa and Europe, and these states suffered the loss of sustained political independence.

Control of wealth or means of wealth creation: The Roman Republic and the Roman Empire were brutal in controlling conquered territories, even from long distance. The indigenous elite displaced, and the key objective was not settlement in the new territory but to drain its wealth and enslave its population. As mentioned above, this was the first time in history that drain of wealth by one civilization from another on this scale and enslavement of conquered population occurred. This pattern of control and wealth drain and enslavement remained a key aspect of subsequent European empires whenever opportunity arose.

Impact on productive outcomes: The ostensible impact on the productive outcomes on barbarous Europe was undoubtedly positive through an extensive road system; the introduction of new technologies and crops; mining operations in Spain, Gaul, Britain, Macedonia, and Thrace; and manufacturing techniques and increased trade. That these innovations did not benefit the Europeans of the day is equally true. Nonetheless, Romans did civilize Western Europe through conquest.

Transmission of creativity: Roman technology, architecture, and legal system became firmly established in the Roman provinces in Western Europe, depending on their ability to produce what Rome wanted. It is fair to say that Roman systems and Christianity civilized Western Europe.

Impact on institutional structures and processes: Rome imposed its political system, military methods, industry, religion, and legal system on Western Europe.

Net impact: Assessment of the net impact of Roman aggression on Europe is ostensibly positive as it helped to civilize Europe. However, it was at the expense of wealth drain, and the average western European hardly saw any improvement in his life. In this work, we take the view that the transmission of practical creativity, including production, building, transport, and communication technologies, happens spontaneously in the absence of aggression, since there is little ideological resistance to such transmission. It is true that aggression may accelerate the transmission, but it will delay its benefits to its population until after the political freedom is regained. Prehistory and history is full of such examples of the spontaneous flow of technology, right down to the nineteenth-century example of Japan. During the current phase, Rome forced technological and artistic creativity on Europe to allow it to extract its wealth. Thus, we would assess the net impact on Europe to be highly negative and highly positive on Rome.

13.18 Productive Outcomes

Production of wealth: The creative energies of Romans were, therefore, neither consumed by religion nor spent on intellectual creation. They did not have much left after managing the empire and good living for the elite. Like their Persian brethren, they seemed to have learned nothing except military technology, architecture, and art from the Greeks, Mesopotamians, and Egyptians, who were practically under their noses, and later, under their thumbs, for centuries. The Roman Republic, starting with humble origins, had a very aggressive external orientation and enjoyed a sustained political independence over several centuries. The productive outcomes in mining, metallurgy, and stone building were impressive.

Fair trade: As we mentioned before, the current phase witnessed the rise of the first global trade system. This system was developed in two stages. In the first stage, Seleucid rulers wrested the control of trade network from the Achaemenid Empire and worked with the Ptolemaic dynasty in Egypt to create a land trade route linking Europe and Asia. With the fall of the Seleucid Empire to the Maurya Empire, the Persian Empire to Parthians, and Ptolemaic Egypt to Romans, a direct sea route using Arabian Sea and Mediterranean Sea with a portion through Egypt was developed. In the second century, the global trade expanded to include Southeast Asia and China, with Rome sending an ambassador to China in 161 CE. Export from India included manufactured items, such as cotton and silk clothing, pepper, ivory, spikenard, agate, carnelian, lyceum, and more. In exchange, India imported tin, gold, silver, precious stones, glassware, and even girdles.

13.19 Creative Outcomes

Achievements in Practical Creativity

Practical technology, including transport and weapons technology, art and military technology, and architecture were adopted enthusiastically. The objective of the privileged few in the Roman Republic was a good life awash in luxuries, and they succeeded well in that for nearly three hundred years. The Roman Republic also contributed to the development of military technology, legal code, roads, architecture, and art. In other words, they created what was needed for conquest, the administration of conquered lands, and a good life. The Roman Republic was not too different from the Persian Empire in priorities. They too were focused on empire building, art, and architecture. However, for a while, like some city-states in ancient Greece, they had an elitist democracy.

Achievements in Religious Creativity

The Roman Republic and Empire remained mired in an intolerant polytheism that they never questioned. As a consequence, the Roman Empire actively persecuted believers in Christian monotheism during the latter part of the current phase. Roman civilization never even suspected the possibility of the doctrines of monism, agnosticism, or atheism. It simply was not interested in religious creativity. The Roman Republic was selective in adopting creative outcomes of other civilizations, such as ancient Greece,

Egypt, and Mesopotamia. At times, foreign religious elements crept in.

Achievements in Intellectual Creativity

However, science and critical philosophy rarely made the grade. Like the Persians, they remained focused on empire building and the good life for the elite. With the fall of ancient Greece by about 150 BCE, the center of scientific creativity in Greece began to shift to the Hellenistic world in Asia, as we discussed above, since the priorities of the Roman Republic were focused on physical expansion and administration of the empire and good life for the elite. They absorbed Greek military innovations, art, and architecture but stopped there. In other words, they took what they valued, choosing not to adopt nascent Greek science. Initially, the Roman Empire tolerated science in the Hellenistic world. However, as they consolidated their control, they naturally killed the spirit of science mainly through neglect.

13.20 Achievements in Science

Thus, we conclude that Europe under the Roman Republic and the Roman Empire was increasingly under the control of a highly centralized imperial form of government that persecuted the emerging Christians for most of the period under consideration in this chapter. These forms of social, religious, military, and political structures were successful in expanding the borders of the Roman Empire and in guaranteeing the nascent European civilization sustained political independence with respect to the external world. These same structures, however, tilted the internal creative balance either toward practical creativity to support the imperial needs, to challenge an emerging monotheistic religious dogma, or both. The stronger the Roman Empire became and the more it consolidated its power, the more it drove scientific activity into the background. By 200 CE, the job was nearly completed and the now-established European civilization failed to adopt science developed by the Greeks and Hellenistic states or to synthesize neo-Babylonian and Indian learning. This view, of course, is in stark contrast to the Western notion that science was a creation of ancient Greece and the Hellenistic states and that later the Roman civilization abandoned it. The Greek contributions to science inspired by Mesopotamia and Indian civilizations occurred prior to the birth of a continent-wide European civilization. Romans killed science twice, first in Greece and then in the Hellenistic states. And Roman civilization indeed suppressed its flowering for the third time through its adoption of antiscience Christian monotheism, as we shall discuss in the next chapter.

Summarizing Achievements in Abstract Systems-Building Capability (ASBC)

By the end of the phase, the ASBC of the Roman Empire must be characterized as moderate: it had adopted/modified alphabetical script and mastered the creative method but lacked sound epistemology.

History, Causes, and Outcomes of the Central Asian Nomads

13.21 Brief Political History (~150 BCE–200 CE)

Central Asian Nomads—First Wave of Invasions

Xiongnu spent a thousand years of uneasy and fluid relationship with the Chinese civilization, particularly the Han dynasty. Because the Xiongnu could not defeat China, they settled for raids to ensure a regular tribute from the Chinese. And they did this effectively for centuries with the Han dynasty as long as they remained united. Even the division was used effectively to reunite the confederation, with Chinese help. Ultimately, their division into northern and southern Xiongnu in the first century gave the Hans breathing room. The bottom line was the Xiongnu extracted tribute from China, and China maintained its independence.

Yeuzhi, another nomadic tribe, were defeated by Xiongnu in 174 BCE and were forced to move southwest. Their defeat of the Scythians shortly thereafter alarmed the Xiongnu, who chased them further west to the northern bank of Oxus River around 145 BCE. Yeuzhi next defeated the Greco-Bactrian kingdom and adopted Greek ways in the process. They moved further south, defeated the Indo-Greeks, and ultimately united to create the Kushan Empire that included a significant portion of northern India.

13.22 Natural Causes

The central Asian region is arid and cool but suited for agriculture and is natural for a nomadic lifestyle based on herding and attacking civilizations.

13.23 Intrinsic Causes

Institutional Systems, Structures, and Processes

We need not get into the intrinsic causes driving the central Asian nomads. Suffice it to say that at some point in history, central Asian nomads, having slowly acquired key weapons and transportation technologies from surrounding civilizations, would organize themselves under a capable leader and try their fortunes through invading faraway civilizations. Their time had arrived and would remain so for nearly two millennia. All that was needed was a great leader, an effective intelligence-gathering system, and a weakness in one or more of civilizations surrounding them.

It was empire building in its purest form, unencumbered by religion or any other ideology. From their perspective, perhaps attacking civilizations was the first step in settling down and becoming civilized. Why invent something when you can just take it? Internal conflict among different tribes and strong Chinese defense deflected one of the five tribes of the Yuezhi, the Guishuang, the origin of the name *Kushan*, toward distant South Asia, as we noted above.

Formative Beliefs and Ideology at the End of First Synthesis Phase

The relatively primitive religion, their focus on acquiring military technologies, a social cohesion derived from tribal equality, the Spartan lifestyle of the elite, and their singular focus in invading civilizations all point to a belief system that may be summarized as follows:

- An open-mindedness relative to religious and intellectual knowledge
- A belief in the relative equality among people
- A belief in aggression toward civilizations as their ultimate mission

These beliefs are natural for a nomadic people located in arid and cool geographical setting and surrounded by civilizations at a higher stage of evolution.

13.24 Extrinsic Peaceful Causes or Sum Total of Constructive Outcomes

Impact of Indian and Chinese Civilizations

Many central Asians attacked Chinese and Indian civilizations during the phase, including Xiongnu, Scythians, and Kushans. They experienced far more success with the Indian civilization, however. This success was proof that central Asian nomads had absorbed the transportation and weapons technologies from civilizations and under a capable leader had developed the ability to organize into a fighting force. Their long experience with the Chinese civilization had hardened them, and they sought to seek their fortunes elsewhere, mostly in India, during the current phase. This capability was highly significant since for nearly the next two millennia, central Asian nomads would overwhelm established civilizations of Europe and Asia in the east, west, and south repeatedly and upset the balance of power.

During the current phase, both Scythians and Kushans, lacking any religious or economic ideology, were absorbed into the Indian civilization after establishing short-lived empires in India.

13.25 Extrinsic Violent Causes or Sum Total of Destructive Outcomes

No violent causes materially and strategically impacted the central Asian nomads during the current phase. A tactical defeat meant their withdrawal into arid region awaiting the next opportunity.

13.26 Productive Outcomes

Given the lack of sustainable agriculture and a settled way of life, the productive outcomes were minimal.

13.27 Creative Outcomes

The creative outcomes all pertained to military technology and intelligence-gathering systems. Central Asian nomads were yet to acquire a written script, and there was little religious and intellectual creativity.

13.28 Achievements in Science

Similarly, there was little question of any scientific creativity from central Asians, given their stage of development.

Summarizing Achievements in Abstract Systems-Building Capability (ASBC)

By the end of the phase, the ASBC of central Asian nomads must be characterized as singularly underdeveloped: they lacked a written script, let alone an alphabetical script; had not quite mastered the creative method; and utterly lacked any understanding of epistemology.

History, Causes, and Outcomes of the Ancient Greek Civilization and Hellenistic States

13.29 Brief Political History (550 BCE–200 CE)

Ancient Greece

As we noted in the last chapter, the archaic period led to the emergence of city-states often at war and organized along radically different political structures. Starting with 550 BCE, the key events of Greek history up to the time of Alexander were the Greek–Persian wars (490–449 BCE) that temporarily united the Athenians and Spartans, followed by a bloody thirty-year war known as the Peloponnesian war (433–403 BCE) between the two. The immediate cause of this war was a desire to support respective allies who were at war with each other. However, the strategic cause of the war was imperial ambitions of both and the distrust of the other gaining power. Athens lost the war and went through another reign of tyrants and overthrow through establishment of elitist democracy again in 403 BCE.

In 399 BCE, this nascent "democratic" government executed Socrates on flimsy charges! Yet, this elitist democracy was the foundation of the golden age of Athens, the subsequent decline of Sparta, and the emergence of Athenian Empire. The long Peloponnesian war weakened both Sparta and Athens; fortunately, this occurred after the conflict with Persians was essentially over and the treaty had been signed in 449 BCE, as noted earlier.

Starting with Alexander, Greeks left home around 334 BCE for an imperial misadventure marked by speed and unparalleled success. Alexander established an empire on three continents; upon his death, his generals, Antigonus, Seleucus, and Ptolemy, divided the empire into three kingdoms. They lost half the territories to Indians and Persians by about 250 BCE in the first blow. In the second blow, initially the European and African territories were lost to the Roman Republic by about 150 BCE and then the Asian territories to the Roman Empire by 50 CE. The story of the ancient Greek civilization during this phase is the story of the rise of Alexander and the three Hellenistic states, their quick defeat at the hands of Indians and Persians, and their eventual destruction at the hands of the Roman Republic and the Roman Empire. Alexander single-handedly turned ancient Greece into an instrument of control that wreaked havoc in West Asia and North Africa until he was stopped dead in his tracks at the doorsteps of India. However, given the intellectual awakening in pre-Alexander Greece, this terrible invasion had the unintended consequences of creating a Greek-Hellenistic-Indian synthesis, something that was hardly Alexander's intent.

Hellenistic States (323 BCE–200 CE)

As noted above, Alexander's vast territories were divided into three kingdoms each ruled by one of his generals. His mother, Olympia, had desired to establish Alexander's infant son, with the Uzbek princess Roxanne, as king under her own protection. It took decades to establish the boundaries of the Hellenistic kingdoms because of continuing internal conflicts, even before any interference from the Roman Republic.

The successful standoff in the encounters with Persia in the fifth century BCE and little competition in the West, since the Roman Republic was still little more than a small principality; the fabled riches of the East; and a desire to teach the Persians a lesson were probably all important factors in the continued militarization of Greek society that pushed it toward imperialism. Although we will not get into the interesting story of the rise of Alexander's father, King Phillip, and his control over Greeks, this event provided the immediate spark needed for imperial adventure.

It is commonly believed that Alexander was a Greek. He was in fact a son of King Phillip, who was considered by famed Athenian orator Demosthenes (384-322 BC) "not only not a Greek nor related to the Greeks but not even a barbarian from a land worth mentioning." In 336 BCE, after King Phillip was murdered apparently at the instigation of his wife, Olympia, Alexander moved quickly by eliminating all rivals through murder and intrigue and proclaimed himself king at the tender age of twenty. Alexander was a young man with an exceptional military mind that was exceeded only by his ambition. He inherited a fighting machine honed by nearly hundred and fifty years of nonstop wars with Persians, the Peloponnesian War, and other internal wars between the Greek city-states over the period of 490–336 BCE. Alexander's dream was to conquer the known world, we are told. He did succeed in conquering a significant portion of it (larger than anyone else before him) in a very short time indeed.

In 334 BCE, Alexander led the Macedonian and Greek armies into Anatolia to fulfill his father's plan to avenge Greece by attacking Persia. After he crossed into Anatolia, he cast his spear into ground, claiming the Asian continent for himself before a single victory! This was clearly based on his rather understandably limited geographical knowledge. He defeated Darius in a battle but failed to capture him. For some reason, before heading straight to Persepolis, he detoured into Tyre in modern Lebanon and on to Egypt, where he founded the city of Alexandria in 331 BCE. Perhaps he needed additional resources before engaging the Persians again, and a weakened Egypt was an easier target. Later that year, he handed the Persians a crushing defeat at the battle of Gaugamela. Alexander now proceeded toward Afghanistan and Uzbekistan and ran into difficulty there against guerrilla tactics. He was forced to enter into an alliance sealed by his marriage to princess Roxanne of Bactria in 327 BCE.

At the doorsteps of India, his army faced unexpected resistance from a small regional king named Puru in Northwest India. The fight so terrified the tired and exhausted Greek soldiers that they refused to march further into India. Alexander won the battle, but Puru ended up doubling his domain since Alexander wanted to win his friendship. Alexander wisely decided to turn back, giving up his dream of world conquest, probably thinking of what the future would bring if he dared to continue his march into India. However, he did not want to go back the same way he came since he had so many enemies waiting for him, and it would be unsafe given the exhausted state of his army. He chose to return through Sindh, and there, in a minor engagement, he nearly died. Alexander died at age thirty-three in Babylon before he could return to Greece, but his misadventure and the resulting weakness of the Greeks had created an opportunity for the expansion of the small Roman Republic on the Italian Peninsula and beyond.

Alexander's military success in West Asia must be attributed to the superiority of the phalanx, tactics, and his unsurpassed generalship.

After Alexander's death, Antigonus's attempt to expand territory in the west was unsuccessful, and in the east, Seleucus had to cede most of Afghanistan to the powerful Mauryan king Chandragupta in India a few years after Alexander's death. Greek contingents there chose not to return to Greece and to remain under Chandragupta's rule. Decades later, the eastern kingdom lost Persian territories to the Parthians. Thus, within seventy-five years of Alexander's death, the three kingdoms together were reduced to less than one-fourth the original size: Ptolemaic Egypt in Africa, old Greece and Macedonia in Europe, and a much-curtailed West Asian kingdom centered in Syria. The imperial stretch of Alexander had taken the first blow and managed to survive for the time being, though in a much reduced form.

With the establishment of these three kingdoms, Greek civilization had entered the so-called Hellenistic era, continuing the tradition of internal wars among these states. Other blows came later from the Roman Republic and the Roman Empire. The loss of Egypt by 30 BCE and the final demise of Indo-Greeks a little later put the Hellenistic states on a path to oblivion and may be formally said to end in 330 CE when Constantine moved the capital of the Roman Empire to Constantinople in 330 CE. However, the last three centuries constituted painful decline.

The Hellenistic states caused plenty of destruction themselves for nearly two centuries following Alexander as they attempted to survive in foreign lands. They battled with Persian, Indian, and Roman civilizations. They lost to all three, and in the end, the Roman Empire put an end to the last surviving vestiges of the Hellenistic states. Perhaps the lesson is that an offsite empire, irrespective how much the victors adopt the culture of the conquered peoples, cannot leave a lasting imprint unless it is based on a powerful secular or religious ideology capable of converting the conquered population to new beliefs. The Greeks lacked such an ideology despite their art and military prowess.

Thus, the Hellenistic states lasted less than a millennium and never recovered from Roman conquest. Thereafter, the acclaimed birthplace of European civilization remained substantially under domestic or foreign domination for nearly two millennia. With the death of these Hellenistic kingdoms, ancient Greek civilization essentially ceased to exist.

13.30 Natural Causes

If one ignores that Alexander's invasion brought Greeks to lands of vastly differing natural conditions, there were no changes in natural causes of significance in either Greece or the Hellenistic states. Clearly, Greeks adapted themselves to these varied conditions well.

13.31 Intrinsic Causes—Hellenistic States

Institutional Systems, Structures, and Processes

The area the ancient Greeks occupied before Alexander invaded equaled the size of a state, not a civilization. Even this small area was split into city-states, which we covered in the last chapter. Below, we focus mostly on the Hellenistic states.

Political system: The Greeks were foreigners in the conquered territories far away from home. The political structures that evolved were partnerships among the Greek king, the Greek and Macedonian immigrants, and the local elites. Since democracy in Greece was a democracy of the wealthy and powerful, with nearly 75 percent of the population as slaves, naturally, this elitist democracy of the homeland was quickly forgotten in the conquered lands. Cities were the economic centers of the Hellenistic world and were governed by city councils strictly under the king. These councils and the wealthy were responsible for collecting the taxes in the countryside and the villages. The administrative structures of the cities often resembled the already existing local structures.

Military capability: To maintain a loyal army, the kings preferred Greeks and Macedonians troops, enticing them with land grants. However, earlier in Persia, Alexander married the daughter of Darius III and ordered ten thousand of his men to marry Persian women, wanting to create an army for his new empire. His military treated Persians and Greeks equally. The infantry was augmented in some Hellenistic states, with stone-hurling artillery technology capable of throwing 170 pounds a distance of two hundred yards, war elephants, and large naval ships.

Economic organization: The Greek conquerors introduced little innovation or change in the local economic organization. Their interests were in replacing the elites and controlling the surplus. World trade through the silk routes in India and China was an incredible source of revenues for the vanishing Hellenistic states as they shared the control of these routes. A greater portion of the India-Roman trade went through the sea, which the Hellenistic states did not control.

System of religious faith: The religion remained polytheistic and only toward the end did the common man began to be attracted to the emerging monotheistic Christianity in western Hellenistic states and to Buddhism in the east. It is worth noting that after defeating the Persians, Alexander demanded to receive the honors due a Greek god, and most Greek city-states back home complied and sent delegations to honor him on the battlefields. The kings of the Hellenistic world, however, displayed remarkable tolerance in the religious sphere; many Greeks converted to Buddhism in the Bactria region. Simultaneously, we see expansion of Hellenistic Judaism, which integrated Judaic monotheism with the Greek concepts of *logos* (reason) and *sophia* (wisdom). We also witness the decline of the Hellenic polytheism in the wake of the decline of Greek culture. Hellenic polytheism was based on twelve gods who were strongly identified with various cities. As Greek influence waned in these cities, so did the Hellenic religion, paving the way for the spread of Christianity, Buddhism, and Judaism in these cities, depending on their location.

There was little science-religion conflict in the Hellenistic states, since monotheism was yet to emerge. The death sentence prescribed to Socrates was a result of his social and moral critique of the Athenian elite and not for his views on religion. His unorthodox, inquiring mind was seen as a threat to the social order and a corrupting influence on the youth.

Legal system: Legal structures heavily drew on the local traditions, with the king's will reigning supreme. Unlike the Romans, the Greeks never developed a formal legal structure before or after they left Greece.

Social structure: The social hierarchy consisted of the king and his Greek elite, followed by the local elites, Greek soldiers, and the local hierarchy that existed before the conquest. The Greek society, as we saw in the last chapter, was highly stratified, with a high proportion of slaves and women definitely occupying a second-class status. However, the landholdings of aristocrats were modest compared to the Roman Latifundia. Although ancient Greece was essentially a slave-owning society with a low position assigned to woman, it was able to maintain its class conflicts within bounds in part because wealth polarization was not extreme. Several Greek states displayed a Spartan attitude. Unlike the Roman Empire, one does not witness slave revolts in ancient Greece, for example. In the Hellenistic states, the alliance with local elites, called the friends of the king, meant that the existing local ways of managing class stratification would continue. This task was essentially delegated to the local elites.

Since the elite, often with Spartan tendencies, and Greek soldiers ruled the Hellenistic states, and since, unlike back home, the conquered population could not be converted into slaves, wealth polarization was not excessive. Greek conquest, unlike Roman conquests, did not add to the existing inequality in conquered lands.

Knowledge-Creating and education institutions: In many conquered lands, after conquest, Greek teachers taught the local nobility. The true centers of Hellenistic science were Alexandria in Egypt and Antioch in Anatolia. The critical difference between intellectual speculations of Plato and Aristotle in ancient Greece and these new Hellenistic centers of knowledge were the support they received from the elite, who funded both the library and the museum in Alexandria. The support in turn was based on a much broader revenue base than what was possible in ancient Greece.

Wealth allocation: Military expenditures in the Hellenistic kingdoms were high because of the need to supplement the professional army with mercenaries who had to be paid regularly. A strong, loyal military was essential to survive in foreign lands. However, the Hellenistic kings lived a relatively modest life, not wasting the surplus on palaces and monuments. Similarly, the allocation to religion was minimal, as it was considered a personal affair. With large territories and a broad tax base, sufficient surplus could be allocated to intellectual creativity.

Social cohesion was achieved through a loyal army of Greek soldiers and an alliance with local conquered elites, guaranteeing religious freedom to the conquered populations and the continued use of local legal systems to dispense justice.

Internal wars: Internal wars among the Hellenistic states continued for decades but were not particularly damaging. However, unlike the city-states of ancient Greece, these conflicts and the geographical factors excluded the possibility of these states uniting against an external threat.

Formative Beliefs and Ideology at the End of First Synthesis Phase

The relatively benign polytheism of Greeks, their strong desire for knowledge, as their travels in search of knowledge and their enthusiastic adoption of Mesopotamian astronomy show; a social cohesion derived from slaves and the elite accepting slavery and as the lack of slave uprisings show; the relatively Spartan lifestyle of the elite; their need for trade; their aggressive orientation; and the fortuitous empire resulting from Alexander's military genius all point to a belief system that may be summarized as follows:

- A belief in knowledge that evolved from speculative idealism to one based on the union of sense data and reason in the post-Aristotle period
- A belief in the fundamental inequality among citizens based on the fact that as much as 75 percent of the population in some city-states during some periods were slaves
- An attitude of admirable openness toward the intellectual and religious creativity of others
- An abiding belief in aggression toward other social orders

These beliefs, though derived in part from Mesopotamian, Phoenician, and Egyptian civilizations, are important since as the first social order of any consequence to originate from European continent, these beliefs strongly impacted the beliefs of European empires that followed.

13.32 Extrinsic Peaceful Causes or Sum Total of Constructive Outcomes

Impact of Indian Civilization on Pre-Alexander Greece

Indian civilization was more advanced in practical, religious, and intellectual creativity during the pre-Alexander period. However, perhaps as little as a century after Alexander's invasion, ancient Greece had pulled ahead in several arenas, such as art, philosophy, geometry, and astronomy.

Transmission channels: Most contact occurred through direct, individual travel or was mediated through a third party. It seems that Indian civilization had a reputation for scholarship in Mesopotamia, and Greeks first became aware of Indian learning through Mesopotamia.

We discussed in the previous chapter how Greeks learned to write and how they learned the organization of city-states from Phoenicians who controlled Ionia during 1200–550 BCE, before the Persian excursion into Ionia. In the sixth century BCE, both the Phoenician city-states in Ionia and the Gadara region on the Indian northwest frontier fell under the control of Persians. In fact, Gandharans, Ionian Phoenicians, and Ionian Greeks took part in Xerxes's invasion of Greece in 480 BCE. In addition, the Persian Empire provided great travel facilities, including the great 1,500-mile royal road in the heart of the empire for traders and scholars seeking knowledge in faraway lands. There is also evidence of lively Indian-Phoenician trade through the Red Sea around the same time. Phoenicians may have lost political power to Persia, but Phoenician traders and sailors continued to prosper under Persian control. Thus, war, travel, and trade linked India and Ionia through the Persian Empire in the sixth through fifth centuries BCE. Before Alexander, Greek scholars such as Pythagoras and Democritus, likely traveled to Mesopotamia and India and were aware of Indian developments in philosophy, mathematics, and physics. Alexander's invasion only accelerated this process, and we know Buddha in the sixth century BCE knew of ancient Greece.

Transmission of intellectual creativity (philosophy and science): Current research has thrown a very interesting, though not unexpected, light on the relationship between pre-Socratic sophists in Greece and the Jain and Buddhist rationalism. We may study the impact of Jain and Buddhist rationalism on ancient Greek sophism through comparing Pythagoras (560–480 BCE), Empedocles (492–432 BCE), and Protagoras (490-420 BCE) on the Greek side and Mahavira (599–527 BCE) and Buddha (563–483 BCE) on the Indian side. Thus, one reaches the conclusion that Greek philosophers had the means and desire to learn of Jain and Buddhist rationalism, which they did. Athens had a need for wise men in the political arena, and Ionian wise men traveled to wealthy Athens in search of making a living, as scholars have always done. They likely needed need to hide the foreign sources of their "wisdom," since they and their wisdom needed to appear Greek to narrow-minded Athens.

Democritus (460–370 BCE) was a contemporary of Socrates (469–399 BCE) and is known for his contributions to atomic theory and geometry, although none of his works survive. He seems to have boasted that he was the most traveled man in Greece, having been to Mesopotamia, Egypt, and India, the latter according to Cicero's *De Finibus*, v. 19; Strabo, xvi, as well as recent research. His atomic theory resembles a theory of matter Indian thinker Kannada proposed a couple of centuries earlier. The contributions of Democritus and his teacher Leucippus were ignored in Athens and detested by Plato, as they represented nascent materialism or agnosticism.

Clearly, more research is needed in this area. However, it appears reasonable to us that Ionian rationalist philosophy was influenced by Jain and Buddhist rationalism, which, to the great credit of the ancient Greeks, took root in the post-Socratic Greek soil. After all, the Persians were hardly impressed by it. The similarity between Kannada and Democritus, between Jainism and Pythagoras, and between Indian medicine and Hippocrates cannot be brushed off as coincidental, as Western historians have carelessly done.

Impact of fair trade and peaceful migrations: There was little direct trade between ancient Greece and Indian civilization. Greeks, unlike Romans, were empire builder settlers and not wealth drainers. However, in the post-Alexander period, Greek soldiers and scholars migrated to Hellenistic states, including the ones founded by Indo-Greeks.

Impact on productive outcomes: There was little direct impact of Indian on Greek productive outcomes of wealth, as there was little direct trade, which was first controlled by Phoenicians under Persian rule followed by the Romans. More important, Indo-Greeks were cut off from their homeland shortly after Alexander died and were slowly absorbed into Indian culture.

Impact on creative outcomes: There are few instances in ancient history of a relatively obscure people who learned to write only a few centuries earlier being able to achieve what pre-Alexander ancient Greeks achieved. There was no European culture to draw upon. Thus, foundations of pre-Alexander Greece, exaggerated as they are by Western historians, have to be the achievements of great ancient civilizations, including the as-yet unrecognized intellectual debt to the Indian civilization.

Impact on institutional structures and processes: There was little direct impact.

Impact of Persian Civilization on Pre-Alexander Greece

Even a quick review of ancient Greek writings shows that Greeks thought highly of Persians; one might say they were obsessed with them. Roger Beck claimed that Greeks were "flagrantly dishonest" in much of their writings, since they often contradicted each other.

Transmission channels: Greek learned of Zoroastrian philosophy from priests known as the Magi between 600 and 300 BCE. In the first century CE, Pliny lamented that Zoroastrian philosophy gave Greek a "lust" for science, which he equated to magic. He also claimed that Pythagoras, Empedocles, Democritus, and Plato traveled abroad to study Zoroastrianism and returned to Greece to either disparage it or claim this knowledge as their own and teach it. The early Greek philosophers such as Thales (624–546 BCE), Anaximander (610–546 BCE), and Anaximenes (585–528 BCE) were all from Miletus in Anatolia, indicating a strong Persian influence. Pythagoras was Anaximander's student

Transmission of intellectual creativity (philosophy and science): It is said that Zoroaster believed there were three kinds of philosophy: physics, economics, and politics. Because Alexander burned the nasks (books of the Avesta) after translating them into Greek and killed all the Magi priests, no original Persian works survive except as references to Zoroastrianism in pre-Alexander Greek works. Two great Renaissance philosophers, Ficino and Pica della Mirandola, believed that Zoroastrianism is the only true philosophy passed on from the Persian Magi to Greeks and Indian sages. Professor Mary Boyce, in her *History of Zoroastrianism,* states the following:

- According to Pliny, mentioned above, Osthanes, who taught Democritus, had trained in the "monstrous craft" of Zoroastrianism.
- According to biographer Diogenes Laertius (third century CE), Alexander is among the authorities on the Magi or Zoroastrian priests.
- Colotes of Lampsacus (320–260 BCE) accused Plato of plagiarizing Zoroaster, since the framework of Zoroaster's *On Nature* narrative appears in Plato's *Myth of Er* in the Republic.
- Plato's disciples claimed that Plato was a reincarnation of Zoroaster.

Thus, what was specifically transmitted cannot be pinpointed. All that can be said is that Greeks respected and were jealous of Persian philosophy and science, acquired it, and used it, while some nationalist elements such as Pliny criticized those who acquired this knowledge. In the end, Alexander, in a fit of jealousy, destroyed Avesta and executed the Magi priests after Avesta was translated.

13.33 Extrinsic Violent Causes or Sum Total of Destructive Outcomes

Greece and the Hellenistic states were the first victors relatively briefly and then were slowly conquered by Indians, Persians, and Roman respectively.

In general, pre-Alexander Greek civilization must be considered a sea-based, aggressive colony builder and trader in the Mediterranean and for post-Alexander Greek-Hellenistic states, a violent empire builder-settler, in contrast to the Roman Republic and the Roman Empire, which remained empire-builder and wealth-drainer controls throughout their existence. This raises the question of why this change took place in Greek orientation. There were several reasons for this change:

- In the pre-Alexander period, the modest Greek colonizing efforts were around the Mediterranean, not unlike other peoples of the Mediterranean. It was in the underdeveloped regions that were close to homeland and not worth settling on, except in Anatolia and the Italian Peninsula.
- The presence of the Persian Empire in the east precluded an eastward land-based thrust until Alexander.
- Alexander's military skill defeated the Persians and made a land-based empire possible in relatively wealthy and developed Asia, and though far away from home, it was worth the effort.

By contrast, Rome remained limited to conquering Europe and North Africa around the Mediterranean by Greek strength during the pre-Alexander period and was limited to conquering the hapless western Hellenistic states in the post-Alexander period by the strength of the Parthian Empire. Thus, the Roman world remained Mediterranean-based and a wealth-draining instrument of control. It failed to produce the daring of an Alexander. In other words, Alexander belonged to an exceptionally rare breed of men, including Genghis, who succeed far beyond what could be imagined for them.

Impact of Mesopotamian Civilization—Ancient Greece and Hellenistic States as Victors

Transmission of creativity (astronomy): If Indian civilization influenced ancient Greece epistemology, metaphysics, physics, and religious creativity peacefully in the pre-Alexander period, the Mesopotamians handed achievements in astronomy and geometry to the Greeks and Ionians after Alexander's invasion.

Impact on creative outcomes: Alexander was quick to expropriate the Babylonian astronomy, had it translated, and sent it to Greece. This set the stage for further development in geometry and astronomy in the Hellenistic states, culminating in Euclid's geometry and Ptolemy's astronomy as the high watermarks.

Impact on societal structures and processes: Because the Greeks in Hellenistic states were empire–builder settlers who lost contact with the homeland rather quickly; there was little impact from Indian and Persian civilizations on the societal structures and processes on ancient Greece itself.

Ancient Greece and Hellenistic States after Defeat

Not surprisingly, the net impact on victorious Greece and the Hellenistic states was less than the loss inflicted on them as the conquered, if only because they no longer existed.

Loss of SPI of ancient Greece and Hellenistic states: Natural terrain had forced the Greek civilization to develop into city-states. With the Achaemenid Empire on its eastern flank and the Roman Republic on its western flank, Greeks were frustrated as Persians drove Greeks out of Anatolia, and the Romans drove Greeks out of the Italian Peninsula. Both earned Greek enmity.

The rising Persian Empire entered an era of an uneasy relationship with the rising Greek ambitions on its western flank, resulting in wars with Greeks during 490–449 BCE, where Persians had an upper hand. Eventually it was payback time for Persia, however. The Achaemenid Empire was destroyed by Alexander's invasion. Persians lost political independence and the control of its SGS for several decades through the invasion of Alexander that only ended with the establishment of the Parthian Empire in 248 BCE.

The Greek city-states had historically fought one another. However, they always managed to come together in the face of an external threat or when planning aggression against others. This was, of course, necessary, since each city-state was too small to deal with any significant external threat or opportunity. As long as Greece maintained a defensive posture, the civilization prospered. Alexander's imperial reach and brutal raids stretched the limits of Greek power, so that within less than a hundred and fifty years of his death, the Roman Republic succeeded in destroying the Greek power in part because of the exodus of significant Greek military and intellectual talent to greener pastures in the newly minted Hellenistic states. The Roman Republic won, with disastrous consequences for the Greek civilization as it entered a long period of irreversible decline and was eventually absorbed into the Eastern Roman Empire. That the Greeks managed to assert themselves despite the presence of two strong empires on its eastern and western flanks is a tribute to Alexander's military genius. He destroyed one of the empires in cruel and irrational manner and created Hellenistic states while sowing the seeds of the eventual destruction of ancient Greece at the hands of the other empire.

Since the strategy of internal unity could not be repeated in the case of Hellenistic states that were far bigger, spread out, and with large non-Greek populations as it turned imperial, its long-term survival could not be assured in the face of conflict with the Roman Empire. The broad parameters of this encounter were similar to the one between the Roman Republic and the Greeks. This is not surprising, given that each was a descendant of the previous two. Alexander's invasion, by establishing a Hellenistic world centered far away from the homeland and the later success of the Roman Republic against the Greeks, drained the resources in the form of both intellectuals and soldiers away from Greece. Had Alexander stayed home or returned after teaching the Persians a proportionate lesson without detouring to go to Egypt first and later onward to India, it might have been different.

Once the Roman Republic tasted imperial success, its successor, the Roman Empire, continued in the same vein and eventually succeeded in annexing the western territories of the Hellenistic world. The eastern territories had been ceded earlier to the Mauryan dynasty in India and to the Parthians in Persia. This encounter had very similar results.

The ultimate result of the Alexander's invasion was a slow destruction of ancient Greece and the Hellenistic states at the hands of Indians, Romans, and Persians.

Impact of Roman and Persian Empires and Indian Civilization Ancient Greece and Hellenistic States as Defeated

One needs to distinguish between ancient Greece and the Hellenistic states conquered by the Roman Empire and those destroyed or absorbed by Persian and Indian civilizations. The long-term impact of the Roman Republic and Roman Empire on ancient Greece and the Hellenistic states was a slow death of the Hellenistic tradition of science through resource starvation, while the long-term impact of Indian civilization was absorbing some of the scientific and artistic achievements of Hellenistic states into Indian culture.

Loss of control of wealth or means of wealth creation: Ancient Greece lost control of its wealth and wealth creation to Roman Empire. However, under the Byzantine Empire after the current phase, it recovered some measure of its independence, since it emerged as the center of the Byzantine Empire after the fall of the Western Roman Empire. Likewise, for Hellenistic states, control of the wealth and means of wealth reverted to Indians, Persians, and Romans over a period of about four centuries.

Transmission of creativity: In the east, the Hellenistic states fared better. The Indo-Greeks adopted Buddhism after transmitting their astronomy to the Indian civilization, and they were absorbed into the Indian civilization over time. The Indian civilization influenced interest in epistemology, metaphysic, open-ended religious inquiry, and science, and though the Hellenistic states added to it immensely, it was not a product with indigenous roots alone. Both the Roman Republic and the Roman Empire had a conflicting attitude toward ancient Greece and the Hellenistic states: on the one hand, Rome in general and several Roman emperors, such as Nero (who participated in an Olympics Games in 67 CE and won every contest he entered by bribing the judges), looked up to ancient Greece but also disliked Greece intellectual tradition and the early popularity of Christianity in Greece.

Impact on productive outcomes: Roman impact on the productive outcomes of ancient Greece after it became an eastern province of the Roman Republic in 146 BCE must be regarded as minimal for the practical technological knowhow was not all that different. We have already discussed the impact of Hellenistic Egypt above. The question of the impact of the Indian civilization on Indo-Greek productive outcomes is moot since the fundamental economic organization was hardly Greek in origin; it remained Indian throughout the short rule of Indo-Greeks in Northwest India. As Greece became part of the Byzantine Empire after the current phase ended, it did not experience Roman propensity to divide it. In fact, it became the center of the Byzantine Empire and became one of its most prosperous and highly urbanized provinces. Thus, its productive outcomes recovered under Byzantine rule, after stagnating under Roman rule.

Impact on institutional structures and processes: As Romans gained control of ancient Greece and the western Hellenistic states, they controlled the economy and trade to suit their objective of wealth drain. The impact on institutional structures and processes came through the Roman and the Byzantine Empires and Christianity after defeat. The political system and military were modeled after Romans. The economic organization did not change much. There was an attempt to reconcile Greek philosophy and religion with Christianity, which, given the more centralized nature of the Byzantine Empire, ultimately led to Orthodox Christianity with the power of the church highly circumscribed. The Roman legal system was quickly adopted. Similarly, Roman indifference to education and intellectual pursuits were slowly assimilated. It is fair to say that the emerging European civilization over time forgot what ancient Greeks had achieved until Francesco Petrarch (1304–1374) looked back with pride more than a thousand years after the destruction of Hellenistic states.

Assessing the net impact: The net impact of Persian, Roman, and Indian civilizations on ancient Greece and the Hellenistic states was their utter destruction as independent entities. They met the fate of Mesopotamian and Egyptian civilizations while transmitting architectural and artistic achievements to Rome and achievements in astronomy and, to much a lesser extent, in art, to the Indian civilization.

It is fair to conclude that interaction among ancient Greece, Mesopotamia, India, and the Hellenistic states was the most fruitful outcome of peaceful interaction in the absence or wake of war among civilizations in the arena of knowledge and formed the basis of a new synthesis in the current phase.

13.34 Productive Outcomes—Ancient Greece

Productive Outcomes

The nature of both peaceful migrations and trade in ancient Greece were determined by the relative infertility of Greek soil. The local production focused on cereals, olives, and grapes, and Greece depended on wheat from outside. And that explains the early Greek colonization in both fertile Italy and Asia Minor. There was little migration into the Greek mainland during this phase; it was always Greeks leaving to found colonies, usually peacefully before Alexander and by using forcing in the post-Alexander period. Thus, the Greeks were travelers and traders and learned a lot about other lands. The condition of the soil and terrain as well as rainfall thus explains the Greek propensity for migration and trade. Key commodities imported were wheat; papyrus; spices; shipbuilding materials, including wood and pitch; fabrics; linen; and metals. There is evidence that the trade volume increased significantly from 500 BCE forward, based on the number of shipwrecks found in the Mediterranean. We judge the Greek trade on the whole to be fair trade. Ancient Greeks did not use the control of territories and trade routes to drain them.

13.35 Creative Outcomes—Ancient Greece

It is difficult to say anything praiseworthy about the ancient Greek city-states that has already not been tiresomely repeatedly by Western commentators. In today's world, ancient Greek philosophers, mathematicians, artists, physicians, and scientists are household names even in the non-Western world. We even know how they appeared physically, mostly through images created a millennium after they had died! Speaking relatively, ancient Greek civilization was indeed a brilliant, if short-lived, flash. Its contributions in the early part of this phase were modest and influenced by Indian and Mesopotamian science. The greater independent achievements came after Alexander's death, initially in the independent Hellenistic states that drew freely from local cultures, and later under the control of the Roman Republic and Empire, both of which worked overtime to kill these achievements. Below we summarize pre-Alexander Greek achievements and how Indian and Mesopotamian science likely influenced them.

The emerging mainstream European civilization (though not the Hellenistic states that were hybrids of Greek and foreign cultures) did not value the achievements of ancient Greece until Arabs discovered Greek achievements centuries later and developed them further.

Achievements in Practical Creativity

Even during this phase, it is not always easy to trace the genealogy of inventions. Below, we summarize practical inventions often ascribed to ancient Greeks. Some, such as the screw and the so-called Archimedes screw, are known to have existed before. Some inventions were developed by Romans but have Greek, Persian, or Chinese origin. It is noteworthy that a greater proportion of these inventions took place in Hellenistic states in Asia, with presumable synthesis of Greek and local ideas and inventions.

Materials: New materials, such as marble for construction, parchment as an early form of paper, mercury and gold amalgam, and metal cable came into use.

Processes: The most significant new process invented was the use of a glass blowpipe, allowing unique glass shapes in modern-day Syria.

Tools: Tools such as locks, steam toys, sundials, screws, the convex lens, the lever, the compound pulley, the chain drive, roller bearings, and pipe organs have been associated with Greece and the Hellenistic states.

Energy: Candles were in use, and Greece also said to have spotted surface mineral oil in West Asia. One story here is rather grotesque: when Alexander was informed of the oil-like substance, he was incredulous and had a boy coated and torched with the substance to test the truth of it.

Construction: The key developments in the construction arena were aqueducts, tunnels through mountains, amphitheaters with designed acoustics, the Parthenon, planned cities like Alexandria, skylights, home heating, glass panes, the Coliseum, and Persian-style gardens.

Transportation: In transportation, the focus was on inventions of military significance, such as the floating pontoon to cross rivers, early maps, and ships with up to ten banks of rowers and designed by Phoenicians.

Infrastructure: Innovations in infrastructure include bridges such as the one across Danube, an atlas of the known world, and canals, such as one linking the Red Sea and the Nile.

Communication: Communication inventions were primarily of military significance and included optical and fire signals, newspapers, and shorthand writing.

Weapons: The new developments in weapons included thick armor, the catapult, and a double-armed catapult.

Achievements in Religious Creativity

Greek religious impulse never progressed beyond a naïve, unstructured polytheism practiced by Indo-Aryans several thousand years earlier and surpassed by Indian structured polytheism, monism, and agnosticism and Persian and Jewish monotheism. including Christianity, by the beginning of the Common Era.

The one exception is the religious thought of Pythagoras. The similarity between Pythagorean religious thought and Jain religious philosophy is striking: Pythagoras, like Jain, believed in the transmigration of soul, nonviolence toward all life, asceticism, and the nonexistence of God. None of these beliefs has roots in ancient Greek tradition. According to Xenophanes, perhaps because of his acquired belief in the transmigration of soul, Pythagoras is said to have heard the cry of his dead friend in the bark of a dog.

It is known that Pythagoras traveled to Babylon and possibly to India. He is also likely to have known about the Sulbha Sutras at Babylon, where he learned about the so-called Pythagorean theorem. It is noteworthy that none of his writings have survived. The geometry theorem began to be ascribed to him by Western commentators only in the fourth century CE or more a thousand years after he had died—a clear instance of assuming timelines. Pythagoras was also likely infatuated by Indian number theory but drew the wrong conclusion that the essence of the world consisted in the numbers. This is in stark contrast to Indian thought that numbers are nothing but useful abstractions or tools to understand the world.

Achievements in Philosophical Creativity

Greek philosophy began with the absurd notion shared by many ancient traditions that water is the basis of all existence.

Thales, Parmenides, and Zeno: The earliest Greek thinkers are called the Eleatics. They existed in the sixth century and included Thales, Parmenides, and Zeno. They rejected perception as a valid means of knowledge. Instead, they stressed logic as the standard of truth. They also stressed a monism completely at odds with long-standing Greek polytheism. The parallel with the philosophy of Upanishads, established centuries earlier, is again striking. Upanishad thinking, with its emphasis on Atman, Brahman, reincarnation, and karma, was a natural outcome of a millennia-long spiritual tradition and was used to justify the Indian caste system. However, such a philosophy in ancient Greece appears as a foreign phenomenon. Many Western commentators have noted this similarity but have refused to acknowledge its Indian origin. Some have instead ascribed this similarity to a shared human nature of philosophers!

Democritus: As a reaction to the Indian caste system and the Upanishads, India witnessed the rise of Buddhism in the sixth century BCE. Early Buddhism was rational.

Correspondingly, in Greece, in the fifth century, we witness a rise of rationalism associated with Democritus, Empedocles, and Protagoras. Recent research has raised the possibility that Democritus visited India. His theory of matter has a striking resemblance to Kannada's theory of matter.

Plato: The dogmatic idealist philosophy of Socrates and Plato in the fifth century was a temporary throwback to the earlier philosophical idealism in Greece. It developed not only the concept of preexisting ideal forms but also significant political and ethical theories. Plato is considered the greatest philosopher of ancient Greece. His philosophy of ideal preexisting forms, however, considers these ideal forms as existing independent of the object and the inquiring mind! Plato had little interest in astronomy, except to the extent it could substantiate his theory of ideal forms. It is fair to say that Plato's philosophy was a negative influence on science. As a consequence, Greek science in the post-Alexander period contributed to astronomy after it was able to set aside Plato's influence. This was primarily because Aristotle, under Indian and neo-Babylonian influence, rescued Greek philosophy from Plato's idealist, antiscience orientation. Aristotle brought the preexisting forms from heaven and made them reside in the object itself, an improvement in the ultimate quest of making them logical constructs residing in the rational mind.

Epistemology: In the fourth century BCE, Aristotle proposed in his theory of universals, where he stated that Plato's universals or ideal forms actually resided in the particular object, as noted above. He called these ideal forms the essence of an object. Thus, for Aristotle, knowledge moved from particular to universal and not the other way around, as Plato proposed. Aristotle's epistemology, while a quantum jump over Plato's idealism, stops short of the theory Kannada proposed Kannadanearly three hundred years earlier. In Kannada, universals were simply categories of mind to aid in understanding, with no intrinsic essence implied whatsoever. Although Aristotle brought Plato down to earth with his empirical outlook, his physics, however, are nothing more than speculations without an iota of experimental basis, as should be expected of all early physicists.

Achievements in Art

Greek visual art was representational in orientation and understandably lacked the concept of perspective. It excelled in sculpture, poetry, and drama. Greek sculpture heavily borrowed from Egyptian tradition. In fact, most Greek figurines, like the Egyptian figurines, were originally painted in color. Over time, the paint has disappeared. However, Western museums have steadfastly refused to restore the Greek statues to their original state, as that would reduce their artistic value in modern eyes because these statues would then look Oriental! Ancient Greek philosophers did not have an art theory. Greek civilization did not subscribe to monism and because, it was focused on nature and society, its art, like Egyptian art, was natural art and not religious in spirit. In music, Pythagoras is widely credited with recognizing the mathematical basis of musical harmony, but there is no evidence for that.

13.36 Achievements in Science—Ancient Greece

Unlike Mesopotamia, the main driver of interest in science in ancient Greece was not religious in nature. It was philosophical–political in nature. Unlike the neo-Babylonian gods, Greek gods were more humanlike. They interacted with humans, sometimes even producing children with them. And gods could be utterly helpful to humans; for example, Greeks had a god of metal craft, named Hephaestus. The planets represented gods, natural perfection, and beauty. Astrology was practiced on a significant scale. Thus, a contradictory attitude toward planets, which included both viewing them as gods who were generally helpful and as perfect natural objects, had a significant impact on how the ancient Greeks adopted the astronomy of the Babylonians and developed it further based on the new science of geometry, as we shall discuss a little later. The conflict between religion and science was modest, though the same could not be said of the conflict between pre-Aristotle idealist Greek philosophy and speculative natural science. The conflict was truly between idealism in philosophy or misguided epistemology and science.

Achievements in Formal Science

Mathematics: The geometric theorem that states that an angle inscribed within a semicircle is a right angle has been traditionally ascribed to Thales; However, there is no evidence of that. There is some evidence that he may have learned it from the Babylonians. Some ancient sources attribute the discovery of the Pythagorean theorem to Pythagoras, whereas others claim it was a proof for the theorem that he discovered. Modern historians believe that the principle itself was known to the Babylonians and was likely imported from them.

Zeno is credited with ten paradoxes, all derived from a lack of understanding of the infinitesimal and motion of a body, which is a differential of position of the object with respect to time. None of his writings is known to have survived.

Democritus was reportedly among the first to observe that a cone has one-third the volume of a cylinder with the same base and height; however, we only know this through much later citations of his works. The idea of mathematical proof is also ascribed to the Greeks, but there is little evidence except through much later citations.

Logic: Aristotle proposed a syllogism with two universal propositions containing a common term and an inference that follows from the two propositions. The system naturally does not work if the propositions are singular or particular instead of being universal. Developing such first-order logic was to come more than two thousand years later.

Achievements in Natural Sciences

Physics: Aristotle's speculative physics is yet another example of science without an experimental basis. The difference is that Aristotle's physics often contradict commonplace observations. Basically, Aristotle's physics consists of the five elements of earth, air, water, fire, and ether and four causes: material, formal, efficient, and final. The first represents matter without motion, the second the essence of things or their form, the third is initiating cause, and the fourth is that for the sake of which a thing exists. He further distinguished between proper causes and accidental causes. All elements are attracted to the center of Earth, which is the center of the universe.

What is fascinating about Aristotle was not his speculation about the nature of physical world but how he hung on to his assumptions about the physical world even when the conclusions he drew from them contradicted common experience. He claimed the following absurdities:

- The quickest runner can never overtake the slowest.
- Matter is not atomic; it is continuous.
- Without force, there can be no motion.
- Planets move in perfect circles.
- A vacuum is impossible since it means infinite velocity.
- Motion is impossible.
- A flying arrow is at rest.
- A force causes motion at a constant speed.
- Gravity can be attractive or repulsive.

Psychologically speaking, Aristotle's speculations get great respect today because he called his speculations physics, a name we use today for the modern, experimentally based understanding of the natural world. About the only thing the two have in common is the name. Democritus's atomic theory of matter has been alluded to above and was likely based on Kannada's theory of matter.

Astronomy: Plato discussed a geocentric model with a spherical Earth, a stationary Earth at the center, and a spherical heaven centered on Earth and containing the planets, moon, and sun. Hellenistic astronomy response.

Let us now move to the significant productive, creative and scientific outcomes of Hellenistic states.

13.37 Productive Outcomes—Hellenistic States

Hellenistic states did not make significant changes to the economies of the lands they took over, since their objective was not wealth drain. In general, Hellenistic states traded fairly to mutual advantage, colonized peacefully, or settled in the territories they won in war and became ultimately absorbed in the local civilizations, leaving little trace of themselves as a separate people. There was little choice, however, since it was impossible to maintain such long lines of supply and communication, and these lines were disrupted by the Parthian, Roman, and Maurya Empires.

13.38 Creative Outcomes—Hellenistic States

The term *Hellenistic* was invented in the nineteenth century to describe the eastern territories conquered by Alexander outside the Greek mainland. The three principal Hellenistic kingdoms that survived the Indian and Persian counterattack but eventually fell to the Romans were the Antigonid kingdom in the second century BCE; the Seleucid kingdom, by then centered in Syria by the middle of the first century BCE; and the Ptolemaic kingdom a couple of decades later with fall of Cleopatra in the first century CE. Both before their fall to the Roman Republic and Greece and for nearly two centuries after the rise of the Roman Empire, the Hellenistic world was an intellectually charged world. There are several interesting reasons for this unexpected development:

- With Aristotle, Greek learning had begun to move away from Plato's idealism and the excessive emphasis on ethics and philosophy. Greek intellectuals like Theophrastus, Aristotle's most creative pupil, who followed the Greek army, brought this orientation with them. Requirements of running vast kingdoms also made Greeks reject the philosophy of idealism in intellectual pursuits, thus turning their focus to technology and science in the absence of a monotheistic faith.

- The Hellenistic kings and their armies were a minority in far-flung lands, and they highly valued Greek immigrants to the conquered territories. In fact, the social hierarchy in these Greek kingdoms typically consisted of the king and his inner circle, the wealthy Greeks, wealthy locals, and the masses. Thus, kings of the Hellenistic world competed for talented Greeks in all fields.

- Greek became the language of the Hellenistic states, with locals learning the language. This resulted in a broadening of the base of people who could contribute to the scientific project. Perhaps the best example of this is the astronomer Ptolemy (90–168 CE) in Alexandria, Egypt. Though he took both Greek and Roman names, he was likely from southern Egypt.

- Vast territories meant a huge tax base, which allowed the kings to support learning as well as building projects.
- The flow of new ideas was a significant factor. The interaction with Babylonia, Syria, Egypt, and Anatolia was more enduring and uninterrupted. However, contact with India was also very strong during the Maurya Empire and still continued during the reign of Indo-Greek kings (200–0 BCE) on the northwest frontier of India and through Roman trade. We are literally talking about centuries of contact between Greeks and other peoples. When one reflects on the Indo-Greek culture through Gandhara art that survived until recently, one must conclude a similar level of fusion occurred in other fields as well.

The great age of Greek philosophy and art probably ended after ancient Greece lost its independence. The Hellenistic states were more focused on astronomy and geometry. In summary, Greece and the Hellenistic world, while eventually losing political independence to the Roman Republic and the Roman Empire respectively, developed the ability to do science in lands far away from Greece for centuries after Alexander. The pluralistic Hellenistic world managed to beat the relatively homogeneous Greek civilization at its own game by a wide margin, as we elaborate below. Calling these achievements exclusively Greek is the equivalent to calling all Indian achievements between the thirteenth and eighteenth centuries exclusively Muslim.

Achievements in Practical Technology

Some of the inventions attributed to the Hellenistic period include dry dock, air and water pumps, a Persian wheel gear, surveying tools, fire hose, vending machines, clock tower, automatic doors, and a form of an analog calculator used in astronomy.

13.39 Achievements in Science—Hellenistic States

Achievements in Formal Science

Geometry was the focus of formal sciences in the Hellenistic world. We see a minor emphasis on logic and epistemology and none on linguistic development. There was no development of algebra, trigonometry, or coordinate geometry by either Greek or Hellenistic mathematicians. Their contributions to the theory of numbers were limited by the absence of the place value numerical system. Greek illiteracy, with a more rational number system, forced them to focus on geometry, and this was fortunate retrospectively since the science of geometry was the need of the hour. The problem of the heavens was the first problem to be solved before natural sciences in general and physics in particular could be put on a firm basis, since that required mastering the experimental method. And the heavens afforded a readymade opportunity to study controlled uniform motion. Geometry was the key since it was essential to affirm the sizes of the earth, moon, and sun and the distances among them accurately. When the sizes and distances were established, their motion could be studied in a scientific manner. The key achievements of the Hellenistic world in formal sciences were:

- Euclid's geometry from the third century BCE, based in part on the works of earlier geometers, including Pythagoras, was an achievement comparable to Panini's grammar, which was developed in the sixth or seventh century BCE in terms of logic if not creativity.
- Archimedes in the third century BCE succeeded in calculating area bounded by a parabola and a straight line and stated it equal to 4/3 times the triangle of equal base and height. He also gave an accurate value for pi. The significance of Archimedes's method was his use of successive approximation, resembling a modern infinite series. Incidentally, this man also improved the screw pump and a heat ray using a concave mirror that was apparently used in the Punic wars.
- Hellenistic mathematicians also developed a theory of conic sections.

The geometric focus is plainly evident in the above short list. It is tempting to say that this focus was conscious since it was the need of the hour. However, this would not be entirely true. The focus on geometry was also driven by a lagging development in other areas of formal sciences and the absence of great religious creativity to suck in the intellectual resources. It was a happy and fortuitous coincidence that moved the cause of science forward.

Achievements in Astronomy

As we suggested above, the real achievement of the Hellenistic states was in the area of astronomy, where they went beyond observation and speculation to actual measurement and deduction using the newly minted science of geometry.

- Astronomer Aristarchus (310–230 BCE) tried to estimate the distance between the sun and the earth. His method required measuring the angle between the moon-earth axis and the sun-earth axis when the moon was at half phase in terms of the distance between the moon and earth. At the half-moon phase, the three form a right-angle triangle. However, the measurement of the angle could not be precise enough. His estimate of the distance was approximately twenty moon distances, with the actual distance being 390 distances. He also noted that the sun and moon have nearly equal angular sizes, so their diameters ought to be proportional to their distances. Thus, he concluded that sun is about twenty times the size of the moon, and therefore the sun must be about six to seven times the size of Earth since he knew the ratio of the diameters of Earth and the moon from observing the lunar eclipse. Because Aristarchus thought the diameter of the sun was at about six to seven times the diameter of Earth and was hundreds of times more voluminous and massive, he perceived the sun to be a solid. He believed the sun had to be stationary. He, therefore, proposed a sun-centered solar system and was the first person in history to do so based on reasoning and not intuition. As we saw in chapter 9, the idea of heliocentric solar system goes back to Vedic astronomy. However, Vedic astronomers gave no reason why. It is irrelevant that Aristarchus's reasoning was wrong (he assumed that the density of the sun and Earth is same because the sun was perceived as a hot stone), the fact that he gave an apparently sound reason is worth emphasizing.

- Eratosthenes (276–194 BCE) in the third century BCE used geometrical arguments and inspired observations to compute the diameter of Earth to within 1 to 2 percent, provided we assume that by stadia he meant the Egyptian stadia, which equals 157 meters, and not Olympic stadia, which equals 185 meters. Eratosthenes used data from difference in the angles made by the sun's shadow of a stick at two different points on Earth's surface with a known distance between them. It was indeed a brilliant geometrical achievement. This allowed the computation of a more accurate diameter for the moon and the distance between the moon and Earth. The accurate measurement of the sun's diameter and the distance between Earth and the sun had to wait until the seventeenth century, however. Eratosthenes also devised a system of latitude and longitude and invented the leap day.
- The Antithera mechanism, a device for calculating the movements of planets, dates from about 80 BCE. It was the first ancestor of the astronomical calculator.

These achievements in astronomy were a natural consequence of the marriage between geometry and both earlier and new astronomical observations and speculations. Inspired by rising Christian dogma, Aristarchus's heliocentric model was ignored, resulting in Ptolemy's Earth-centered model being accepted in the Hellenistic world in subsequent centuries. There were several "common sense" reasons: if the earth indeed moved, would we not feel the wind blowing? Further, if Earth moved, would we not see a shift in the position of the stars? Of course, air moves with Earth, and the stars were too far for the ancient astronomers to detect parallax as a result of Earth's motion. Ptolemy, therefore, worked out the earth-centered model but could not explain the backward or retrograde motion of the planet Mars as viewed from Earth. Such a motion would be impossible if Mars indeed circled around Earth. Thus, Ptolemy was forced to propose his theory of epicycles, which required a planet to not only go around Earth but also the point on the planets' orbit around Earth. The theory of epicycles "explained" the retrograde motion, but it also put astronomy on the wrong path until Aryabhatta in the fifth century rescued it, as we shall see in the next chapter.

We have been brief in describing Hellenistic creative achievements. However, it must be stated that the achievements of Hellenistic astronomers were without precedence. For once again in human history, an objective marriage between observation and logic was attempted in the realm of natural phenomenon. Yet, we can see how with Ptolemy this delicate marriage soon ended, destroyed by a tendency of over-explanation and under-observation and religious dogma.

Earth sciences: Pliny (77 CE) in his *History of Nature* makes a fuzzy distinction between the inorganic and organic worlds. He focused on both describing plants and animals and their usefulness to man. There was little attempt at systematic classification.

Medicine: Herophilus (third century BCE) was a notable anatomist and was followed by Erasistratus, who distinguished himself as a physiologist and correctly summarized the existence of blood circulation. Galen (129–199 CE) showed remarkable interest in anatomy. Because Roman law prohibited the dissection of dead bodies, Galen used dead animals. He seemed to have generally understood the function of the trachea, the larynx, differences between oxygenated and de-oxygenated blood, the respiratory system, and motor and sensory nerves in animals and by extension to humans. Galen successfully performed cataract surgery. However, Galen also used and defended bloodletting as a cure.

Summarizing Achievements in Abstract Systems-Building Capability (ASBC)

By the end of the phase, the successive ASBC of both ancient Greece and Hellenistic states must be characterized as highly developed: it had already adopted alphabetical script and mastered creative method in the previous phase and made great strides in epistemology.

History, Causes, and Outcomes of the Chinese Civilization

13.40 Brief Political History (481 BCE–220 CE)

The Spring and Autumn Period was followed by the Warring States period, where the power of the Zhou dynasty weakened even more, resulting in the slow emergence of the Qin dynasty. It took more than two centuries to unify China for a brief period of fifteen years under Emperor Shi and later his son, guided by the general able Li Si, until it was overthrown by the Western Han dynasty in 206 BCE, which lasted until 9 CE. Wang Mang's short reign was followed by the Eastern Han dynasty in 22 CE. It lasted until 220 CE and was followed by the Tang dynasty.

From our perspective, the most critical event of the period was the conflict between Xiongnu, a nomadic confederation of Mongolian, Turkish, or Iranian origin, and the Han dynasty. Xiongnu had earlier defeated yet another tribe known as Yuezhi, which forced the latter to move south and settle on the northern bank of the Oxus River in Uzbekistan. The Han dynasty tried to enlist the Yuezhi people in their conflicts with the Xiongnu confederation. This diplomatic mission failed, probably because the Yuezhi people had set their sights on moving further south. The great Kushans were a branch of the Yuezhi people. Thus, a failure of the Han dynasty to defeat the Xiongnu people forced Yuezhi to migrate toward South Asia, a move that was to have a profound impact on South Asia and the history of science, as we shall explore later in the chapter.

Like previous periods in their history, Chinese civilization remained busy dealing with internal splintering tendencies and the nomadic threats from the north; there were no significant conflicts between China and other civilizations during this period. A significant part of the Great Wall of China was built under the Qin dynasty to keep the nomads out.

13.41 Natural Causes

Under Wang rule, there were massive floods in the first decade of Common Era. Excessive silt buildup caused floods in the Yellow River, and it actually split into two branches. The flood converted thousands of farmers into homeless bandits who proved uncontrollable by Wang armies. Natural causes must be seen as a decisive factor in the overthrow of Wang rule and the emergence of the Eastern Han dynasty.

13.42 Intrinsic Causes

Institutional Systems, Structures, and Processes

Political system: The Han emperors reigned supreme as commander-in-chief, ultimate dispenser of justice, and head of bureaucracy. The emperor was assisted by three councilors responsible for state budget, public works, military matters, and disciplinary actions against officials. Below the councilors were nine ministers responsible for palace grounds, ceremonies, the palace guard, the imperial stable, justice, the imperial clan, protocol, treasury, and entertainment. One is struck by the number of ministers catering to the needs of the emperor and his family.

At the local level, the administration was divided into provinces, groups of counties, and counties and districts. The first three were headed by governors, administrators, and prefects respectively. The provincial governors had the authority to act without central government approval in important matters, suggesting a measure of decentralization.

Military capability: Han emperors had an army consisting of an infantry, a cavalry, and a navy. The military force was a small, standing army, also called the Northern Army; an army of conscripted soldiers of males over age twenty-three; or a volunteer army known as the Southern Army. During times of war, this force was supplemented with militia. The military was well-structured into divisions, regiments, companies, and platoons. Three significant developments that took place under the Han dynasty were the emergence of strengthened cavalry, the construction of the Great Wall, and moving tens of thousands of soldier-farmers to the western frontiers to successfully fight the nomadic invasions of the Xiongnu. The army had a clear defensive orientation.

Economic organization: The Han period was a period of population growth and substantial growth in manufacturing and commerce. Landlords increasingly controlled agriculture, manufacturing seems to have vacillated between private and government control, and commerce remained essentially in private hands. A census in 2 CE counted the population at 55 million in over 12 million households. A land reform in the second century BCE created a market for buying and selling land, which resulted in a concentration of land in the hands of aristocrats and reduced the majority of peasants to landless status by the first century CE. However, the tax base remained light on the small farmer, and the state tended to protect it through repeated tax reductions. The government moved to nationalize key manufacturing, such as salt and iron manufacture, when they became excessively profitable. The government also participated in the manufacture of cloth, silk, figurines, and gold, silver, and lacquer products. Commerce was in the hands of local and itinerant merchants, the latter conducted intercity and foreign trade and often became very wealthy and avoided paying taxes. The emperors often had to control grain markets and markets for other goods markets to curb the merchants' influences and prohibited merchants from buying land, a law that was difficult to enforce.

Han emperors also used conscripted labor to construct the Great Wall, temples, and irrigation projects. Foreign trade mostly consisted of silk, wine, horses, and weapons. Clearly, the economy was industrializing and urbanized, with a government very much concerned about the common man that remained its tax base. The government acted to curb the freedom of the big landowners and itinerant merchants, often unsuccessfully.

Systems of religious faith: During the Han dynasty, China did not have a homegrown, systematized religion. The common man strongly believed in the ritual offering of animals and food to please spirits and ancestors. It was commonly believed that a spirit-soul went to paradise after death, and a body-soul remained on earth upon death and could only be united with the spirit-soul through rituals and sacrificial offerings. Original Chinese metaphysics consisted of five elements (wood, fire, earth, metal, and water), whose transformation and balance in the heavens, earth, and society followed the principle of yin and yang and could be affected through ritual sacrifice. During the Han period, Buddhism arrived in China from India, and several Buddhist texts including the *Sutra* of forty-two chapters and *Perfection of Wisdom* were translated into Chinese. A Buddhist temple called the White Horse Temple was erected.

There was little science-religion conflict in China during the Han period because neither religion nor science was developed. The former remained at the level of animism and polytheism, and the absence of alphabetical script constrained the development of science and philosophy.

Legal system: The Han legal code was based on and derived from the Qin law and was compiled by Chancellor Xiao He. It is noteworthy that the code allowed a greater equality between genders than most legal codes of the era. The chief executive of a county also doubled as local judges, with more complex cases being referred to the Ministry of Justice. The legal code made a distinction between criminal and civil cases. Punishment ranged from fines to hard labor to death. The earlier practice of mutilations was replaced by more humane beatings. Thus, Hans had both a legal code and a well-developed legal system. Police maintained law and order in villages, cities, and marketplaces.

Social structure: At the top of the social hierarchy were of course the emperor and the kings that belonged to the royal family. At the lowest level were slaves, who constituted a small portion of the population. Those in between were divided into twenty classes, including nobles, officials, scholars, small landowners, tenants, wage laborers, physicians, pig breeders, butchers, artisans, merchants, contract workers, occultists, and messengers. The social hierarchy clearly shows that social status was biased toward the landowners and peasants, and the bureaucracy looked down on manufacturing and commerce.

As we noted above, class stratification was very granular; however, the landownership progressively got worse for the farmer after land reform. Similarly, the merchant class got rich through speculation in grain and goods trade and did not register and pay taxes. It was despised by both government and the common man. Chinese society was becoming a society with quintessential excessive inequality.

Knowledge-Creating and educational institutions: Like most civilizations of the period, there were no knowledge-creating institutions, though Han emperors supported scholar–philosophers. The Han dynasty was among the first to establish an imperial university that boasted thirty thousand students at its peak in the second century BE. A system of public and private schools provided a secondary-level education.

Wealth allocation: Improvements in practical creativity increased wealth. A significant portion of wealth allocation went to support the lifestyle of the elite (it was difficult for government to collect revenue from the wealthy); defensive military needs, such as building the Great Wall; and the military preparedness to fight the nomads, which remained a constant threat throughout Chinese history during this phase.

Social cohesion: Although the position of the common man deteriorated, a strong legal code, Confucian ethics, an organized police force, the government's responsiveness to the common man, and the never-ending threat of nomadic invasions provided sufficient social cohesion to hold together the Han state for centuries.

Internal wars: The Han dynasty went through two periods known as Western and Eastern Hans, punctuated by a civil war under Emperor Wang. The nationalization and distribution of the land and outlawing slavery directed against the landowning landlords elicited a strong reaction. The reforms, opposition from the landlords, and the rise of rebel groups, including the Red Eyebrows, led to Emperor Wang's downfall. He was killed by a mob that broke into the palace. Thus, there were periods of significant internal strife.

Formative Beliefs and Ideology at the End of First Synthesis Phase

Underdeveloped Chinese polytheism, the strong practical orientation of the Chinese, a social cohesion derived from the absence of slavery and a caste system, the relatively modest lifestyle of the elite, their single-minded focus in keeping nomads away, and their sense of being unique if not superior to others all point to a belief system that may be summarized as follows:

- A belief in practical knowledge based on observation and common sense
- A belief in the fundamental equality among citizens, based on absence of slavery and caste system and emperors who cared for the farmers
- An attitude of insularity toward the intellectual and religious creativity of others
- An abiding belief in peace and a defensive posture toward other social orders unless attacked

These beliefs, derived mostly from the absence of religious overgrowth, social cohesion, and unending wars with nomads, are important since, as the primary civilization to originate in fertile East Asia, these beliefs strongly impacted the beliefs of all later East Asian and Southeast Asian civilizations.

13.43 Extrinsic Peaceful Causes or Sum Total of Constructive Outcomes

Transmission of Religious Creativity

The transmission of Buddhism to China began toward the end of the current phase or more than half a millennium after its founding in India. There is debate about whether it was transmitted through the Silk Route or through a maritime route, with most evidence favoring the former. Since Chinese civilization was already established with a strong cultural and literary tradition, it was most influential in adapting Buddhism to its own needs as well as impacting the spread of Buddhism to lesser Southeast Asian cultures. The Kushan emperors were instrumental in transmission to China, where it interacted vigorously with Taoism and Chinese art and rituals. Opinion also varies concerning when the doctrine was first transmitted, with popular myths placing the date about a century earlier than documented evidence, which dates back to 148 CE. Ironically, a Parthian prince-turned monk translated the scriptures and built temples in Chinese, followed by a Kushan monk named Lokaksema, who brought Mahayana Sutras to China toward the end of the second century CE. Of the twenty-some schools of Buddhism that originated in India, the significant ones that reached and penetrated China were Dharamaguptaka (with its twelve-fold division of Buddhist teaching), Sarvastivada (literally, all that exists), Kasyapiyas (likely an offshoot of Sarvastivada), and Mahasamghika (likely earliest branch of Mahayana).

Fair trade: The second most significant component of extrinsic peaceful causes for the Chinese civilization during the phase was the land- and sea-based trade between Indian and Chinese civilizations. The invasion of Alexander and the establishment of Acheaminid, Parthian, and Kushan Empires played a great role in linking the Indian and Chinese civilizations to the empire in West Asia and Europe. Thus, for the first time, the world was linked through a broad-based global trade network. In parallel with violent interaction, this peaceful interaction increased the pace and content of the interaction among civilizations dramatically.

Pact on productive outcomes: The impact was indirect through trade efficiencies.

Impact on creative outcomes: The impact of Buddhism on Chinese art, iconography, and religious thought was still in the future. In the current phase, Buddhism merely succeeded in capturing Chinese imagination, probably because it shared some ideas with Taoism. In effect, Taoism expanded its belief about the universe and learned of Buddhist monastic structure. Buddhism gained vocabulary to teach Buddhism to the Chinese.

Impact on institutional structures and processes: As noted above, Buddhism began to impact the structure of Taoist monasteries during the current phase.

13.44 Extrinsic Violent Causes or Sum Total of Destructive Outcomes

Nomadic invasions impacted China during the phase, but none of the major civilizations invaded. However, the Han dynasty, though losing several engagements with the Xiongnu, was successful in containing the threat through a strong military and building the Great Wall. China, in turn, was able to expand its territory toward central Asia as well as the south, receiving tributes from several neighboring states, such as Burma, Japan, the Parthian kings, and the Kushans. Thus, we would characterize the impact on China as minimal, except for the drain of resources to build and maintain the Great Wall. China successfully contained the threat and retained control of most of its SGS.

Transmission of creativity (religion): With the exception of Buddhism, it is difficult to pinpoint what else of significance that China learned from other civilizations during the Han dynasty. It remains a mystery and lost opportunity that China did not show interest in alphabetical script, underscoring the complex relationship between the desire for cultural unity assured by a stable logograph and the positive impact of alphabetical script on creativity.

Impact on productive outcomes: There was little direct impact on the productive outcomes of China.

Impact on institutional structures and processes: There was little impact on the societal structures and processes as well.

Net impact: The net impact on the Chinese civilization was even less negative than on the Indian civilization, since the Chinese were successful in diverting the nomadic pressure toward India.

13.45 Productive Outcomes

Productive Outcomes

True to its inner nature, China was not open to peaceful migrations into China in this phase. However, during this period, China became part of the world trade system linking India, China, West Asia, and Europe. This came about because the invasions of Alexander and the Kushan Empire linked these areas and created safe trade routes overland. The external trade increased significantly as the Silk Route opened up and peaceful migrations mostly constituted Chinese colonizing the South of China.

13.46 Creative Outcomes

Achievements in Practical Creativity

Incredible progress in practical creativity was made in China during the Han dynasty.

Materials: Cai Lun invented paper and the papermaking process in the second century CE.

Processes: Chinese engineers extended technologies of blast and cupola furnaces to produce pig iron and cast iron, producing wrought iron by injecting oxygen (air) and steel through a refining process.

Tools: Key tools invented or further developed included the caliper, odometer cart, water wheel, reciprocator, bellows, pressure-compensated water clock, seismometer employing an inverted pendulum, bronze gears, rotating armillary sphere, and chain pumps.

Energy: Chinese engineers developed use of natural gas through bamboo pipe, ensuring its safe use through use of exhaust pipes and carburetors.

Agriculture technologies: Inventions of note include the mechanical seeds drill for planting, an iron plow with three plowshares, a seed box to feed the seed drill, and a tool that turned the soil. The device could plant eleven acres using one man and two oxen. Chinese engineers also invented a winnowing machine operated using a crank shaft. To protect crops from wind and drought, they used an alternating arrangement of furrows and ridges

Nonagricultural products: Salt production was mechanized using derricks to lift brine into iron pans, where the water was evaporated using natural gas. They developed low-temperature lead glazes and greatly improved silk weaving technologies.

Construction: Chinese construction engineers used domes, archways, and vaulted chambers. A drainage system using ceramic pipes, ditches, and brick arches were in common use around the capital city of Chang'an.

Transportation: Chinese cartographers during the era developed maps and raised relief maps using graduated scales and grids. Junk ships using a rudder for steering were first created during the Han era, thus making them seaworthy. The Chinese also invented the wheelbarrow. Finally, the heavy wooden yoke around a horse's chest was replaced by a softer beast strap, a precursor to the horse collar.

Infrastructure: Chinese engineers developed a greatly expanded bridge-building technology, including the arch, beam, suspension, and platoon bridges.

Achievements in Religious Creativity

In contrast to practical creativity, indigenous religious creativity was low. The Chinese focused on animal and food sacrifice to polytheistic deities and ancestors. There was little new in their metaphysics, which was based on the birth and destruction cycles of the five elements and based on the principle of yin yang.

Achievements in Intellectual Creativity

Music: Jing Fang created a musical scale consisting of sixty notes. He also suggested that fifty-three perfect fifths equal thirty-one octaves, a feat that was equaled in Europe in the seventeenth century only.

Art: The Han dynasty is notable for functional ceramics, which undoubtedly was a national industry. Han ceramicists invented low-temperature lead glazing in multiple colors using copper and iron. Ceramic figurines and scaled models of homes and animals including horses were produced for use in tombs. During the Han period, Chinese artists also began to produce paintings and sculptures of Buddha and bodhisattvas in the Indian art tradition.

13.47 Achievements in Science

During the present phase, Chinese science focused on three primary areas: early mathematics, astronomical observations, and practical tools for recording scientific observations. Below, we summarized these accomplishments.

Mathematics: In the third century BCE, Emperor Huang ordered all books outside of Qin state burned. As a result, not much about ancient Chinese mathematics is known with certainty. The most important mathematical work is *The Nine Chapters on the Mathematical Art* published in the second century AD. The book is actually a compendium on math, engineering, architecture, and other practical matters. It provided surprising proof of the Pythagorean theorem, accurate values of pi, an annunciation of the so-called Cavallieri principle on volume, as well as solutions to 246 word problems. In the second century, Heng provided the formula for computing the volume of a sphere. *Nine Chapters on the Mathematical Art* also used negative numbers. However, it is not known if Buddhists brought the concept was brought to China.

Astronomy: Chinese astronomers of the era subscribed to the geocentric model and believed that the sun, moon, and earth were all spherical in shape. They understood the cause of solar and lunar eclipses and believed that moon shined because of reflected sunlight.

- An atlas listing twenty-nine comets over a period of three hundred years, including the terrestrial events these comet visits corresponded to was called the *Book of Silk* and was written 300–400 BCE.

- The Chinese invented improved time-keeping devices, the water-powered rotating armillary for astronomical observations (~100 AD), and the seismograph (132 AD).
- Accurate calendars based on the sun and moon.

Earth sciences: Wang Chong accurately described the water cycle of water evaporation into clouds and back to water through rain.

Medicine: Chinese medicine during the current phase was based on the application of Chinese metaphysics and practical medical knowledge. Illness was viewed as disruption of the vital energy that was governed by the principle of yin and yang, the birth cycle (fire, earth, metal, water, and wood), and the destruction cycle (fire, metal, woods, earth, and water) of five elements. Each organ in the body, each season, and each taste was associated with an element. As an example, the liver is associated with wood and element metal with pungent taste. Alcohol has pungent taste, and therefore alcohol destroys the liver (wood), since we know metal destroys wood! In this scheme, the correct relationship between wood and metal is projected onto a known relationship between liver and alcohol to explain such a relationship. In parallel with this fancy diagnostic methodology, the practical side of Chinese medicine relied heavily on herbs, acupuncture, herbal smoke therapy, calisthenics, a strict diet, and surgery, including the use of anesthesia.

Summarizing Achievements in Abstract Systems-Building Capability (ASBC)

By the end of the phase, the ASBC of the Chinese civilization must be characterized as moderate. It had already mastered the creative method in the previous phase and continued to fail to adopt alphabetical script and move forward in epistemology, despite adopting Buddhism since the focus of Chinese civilization on Buddhism was purely religious and not intellectual.

History, Causes, and Outcomes of Indian Civilization

13.48 Brief Political History (550 BCE–250 CE)

As we saw in the last chapter, by the sixth century BCE, India had begun to make the transition from modestly sized republican monarchies to larger, centralized states and empires in northern India. At the beginning of the present period, north India was under the rule of the Nanda dynasty, which was centered in Patliputra in the northeastern region. After Alexander's hurried departure, North India was united by two men of exceptional ability: one a commoner (others question his humble origins) of great courage and ambition and the second a homely Brahmin of exceptional wisdom.

Chandragupta Maurya and Chanakya gave India its first great empire and an efficient administration beginning in 321 BCE. The administrative machinery they put together was copied by nearly all subsequent empires on the subcontinent. The Maurya Empire did not last long and ended less than fifty years after Chandragupta's grandson, Ashoka, who united nearly all of India for a brief shining moment, died in 232 BCE. After victory in the devastating war of Kalinga, Ashoka had converted to Buddhism, adopting pacifism, and significantly reduced the size and deterrent capability of the armed forces. Within fifty years of Ashoka's death, a Mauryan general named Pushyamitra Sunga put an end to the Maurya Empire and state sponsorship of Buddhism by deposing the last Mauryan king, Brhadrata, in 185 BCE, and proclaimed the founding of the Sunga dynasty.

The Sunga dynasty was followed by the Kanva dynasty for nearly one hundred years in the north, and these dynasties were under great pressure from the Satvahanas (230 BCE–300 AD) from South India and well as from nomads in the northwest. During the two hundred years (185 BCE–0 CE) after the Mauryan dynasty, the so-called Indo-Greeks (the leftover Greeks trapped between the Parthian Empire and India) and the Scythians invaded India from the northwest. Over the following two hundred years, the Parthians and Kushans invaded, again from the northwest. Of these two, the Kushans were most successful, creating an empire that stretched from Uzbekistan to central India. The great Kushan emperor, Kanishka, converted to Buddhism, while displaying great religious tolerance toward other faiths, and moved his capital to Mathura in central India. Under him, the Indo-Greeks converted to Buddhism as well, and the Gandhara School of Art flourished in the northwest. Kanishka is also remembered for calling the fourth Buddhist Council in Kashmir and built a monumental Buddhist Stupa measuring three hundred feet high at Peshawar. The ruins of this Stupa were discovered in early twentieth century. The Kushan Empire lasted well into the third century, when India was invaded again from the west, this time by Sassanians from Persia who correctly sensed the weakness of Kushans.

Thus, partly because of Ashoka's pacifism, North India remained in a weakened position to face the external threat from a never-ending stream of mostly nomads. Thus, in the post-Ashoka period, right up to the fall of the Kushans, we see:

- Multiple waves of invasions from the northwest in a period of weakened military strength. These waves, as noted above, included Indo-Greeks (239–130 BCE), Scythians (100 BCE–0), Parthians (0–100 AD), and Kushans (0–250 AD).
- The rise and fall in succession of states and empires, both indigenous and foreign.

- Alternating support for Hinduism and Buddhism, with the eventual reassertion of the supremacy of Hinduism and declining support for Buddhism, starting with the Gupta dynasty in the fourth century. The next chapter discusses the Gupta dynasty.

- The successful and complete absorption of the foreign invaders into Indian civilization over time. Typically, the foreign elements first converted to Buddhism and later into Hinduism. This was in part a reaction to Hindu caste system, which would assign a low rank to the foreigners. As Buddhism weakened in India, there was little choice for the invaders-turned-Buddhists but to convert to Hinduism, which would now assign them a higher social caste because they had been in the country for centuries and had been accepted.

Below, we review these four waves of invasions.

Indo-Greeks defy classification. They were the leftover contingents from Alexander's days on India's northwest frontier, Afghanistan, and Bactria and had chosen to make these areas their home. Their connection with Greece had been nonexistent for nearly a century, and they had adopted the religion, culture, and language of the local areas but were primarily under the sway of Buddhism and Indian civilization. As long as the Mauraya and Sunga emperors were strong, they were confined to Afghanistan and Bactria. The Fall of Sungas created a temporary opportunity for these Indo-Greeks. Perhaps, the most important Indo-Greek king was Menander, who converted to Buddhism and later became a Buddhist monk. He certainly conquered the territory east of Punjab and may have participated in raids as far south as Mathura. An important and lasting impact of the Indo-Greeks was the fusion of Indian and Greek art, known as the Gandhara School, with its sublime renditions of the Buddha. One may also speculate that this fusion was not limited to just art, although art is its most visible aspect. Hellenistic science and philosophy must have been brought to the region, although it is hard to find direct evidence of this. After their brief shining moment, Indo-Greeks turned Buddhists, later adopted Hinduism and were absorbed into the Indian society over the centuries.

Scythians or Sakas were a nomadic tribe from southern Siberia. In 177 BCE, the Yuezhi tribe was defeated by the neighboring tribe of the Xiongnu, as noted above. This historic event caused the Yuezhi to migrate west, displacing the Sakas further west and south. They attempted to enter India through northern Afghanistan. They were unsuccessful because of the entrenched Indo-Greeks there. The Sakas or Indo-Scythians ultimately entered India through Sindh and Saurastra near the mouth of the Indus around 110 BCE. Indo-Scythians then moved north and prevailed against the Indo-Greeks, displacing them to the northwest, and established a state with Taxilla as a capital and two satrapies centered in Mathura and Gujarat. Their efforts to expand to the east were repelled by Vikramaditya of Ujjain, who celebrated the event by establishing the Vikramaditya calendar in 57 BCE. Ultimately, a century later, they would be successful in an eastward expansion, raiding as far as Patliputra and included Ujjain in the long-lived western or Gujarat satrapy.

Indo-Scythians, like the Indo-Greeks, were followers of Buddhism and were ultimately absorbed into mainstream Indian society as Kshatriyas. In the first century BCE, the Indo-Scythian kings had names like Maues and Azes, and by the second century AD, the names had become thoroughly Indian. The power of the Indo-Scythians was checked by the Yuezhi or Kushans, who were advancing toward India right behind them, as well as by the Indo-Parthians. The last significant Indo-Scythian king was Western Strap Rudrasimha III, and Chandragupta of the Gupta dynasty defeated him in 395 AD. There is evidence that the original invasion of India by the Indo-Scythians not only included Indo-Scythians but also Pahlavas and Kambojas of Persia as allies.

The Parthian Empire flourished in Persia starting in 248 BCE. Around 20 AD, Gondophares, a Parthian governor, declared his independence and established the Indo-Parthian kingdom. The kingdom lasted less than a century, with Kushans conquering the northern territory in 75 AD. The Indo-Parthians did not convert to Buddhism and were probably directly absorbed into Indian society. There is also evidence that they may have migrated to the Andhra area in South India and were responsible for establishing the Pallava dynasty, which we touch on in the next chapter.

Of all the nomadic tribes that invaded India during this period, the Kushans were most successful. Probably around 30 AD, Kujala Kadphise of the Yuezhi tribe established himself as the king of Guishuang north of Oxus River. He conquered Afghanistan and died at the age of eighty after establishing a firm basis for the Kushan Empire. His great grandson, Kanishka, the greatest Kushan emperor, ruled from 127 to 147 AD over a vast territory that included the area from Uzbekistan and all of north India. These territories were administered from two capitals: Purushapura or modern Peshawar and Mathura, in addition to a summer capital at Bagram. The Kushan Empire was a multicultural and multireligious empire that slowly became Indianized. Kanishka converted to Buddhism, calling forth the fourth Buddhist Council in Kashmir as noted above.

In addition, early Kushan rulers accepted Greek deities, while later kings converted to Shaivism. Kushan kings also supported Gandhara art, and under them, it achieved great height. Perhaps the greatest long-lasting accomplishment of the Kushans was contacts with both Rome and China, which resulted in greatly expanded trade both through the

Silk Route as well as through India and the Arabian Sea. By the second century AD, Kushan emperors were thoroughly Indianized, as evidenced by the last great Kushan king named Vasudeva I. Vasudeva I ruled from 191 to 225 AD. Beginning with the third century, the Kushan Empire began to lose vitality, ceding territory to the Sassanians. Still later, they lost North India to the rising Gupta dynasty.

To summarize, North India's political history during this phase consisted of convincing Alexander to turn back after battles on the northwest frontier, the rise and fall of a strong Mauryan dynasty, followed by weaker dynasties unable to defeat the four successive waves of mostly nomadic invaders. They came to build an empire and gain India's wealth. They succeeded in both, but in the process they became completely absorbed in Indian civilization.

Brief History of South India during the Phase (230 BCE–200 CE)

The situation in South India was materially different. We mentioned the Satvahanas gained control of portions of North India, defeating the Kanvas just before the Common Era. Kushans and later Guptas pushed them back to the south. Further south of the Satvahanas in the Andhra territory, the so-called early Chola, Chera, and Pandaya dynasties (0–300 AD) were established during this period. When we compare the situation in north and south, we find several critical differences, including the absence of a Buddhist stronghold, the relatively stronger influence of the Brahmins, the absence of foreign invasions, an emerging curiosity relative to Southeast Asia, and a civilization with greater orientation toward a continued evolution of Hinduism. One sees greater propensity for large temple projects and relatively little propensity toward establishing great universities. One witnesses artistic, architectural, and literary works but within a strongly religious context. One does not witness an intellectual renaissance. Students typically traveled from south to north to study.

13.49 Natural Causes

There were no new significant natural causes affecting the Indian civilization during this period.

13.50 Intrinsic Causes

The political, religious, social, and economic conditions in the north and south of India during this period were materially different. Our focus will be on North India.

Institutional Systems, Structures, and Processes

Political system: Politically, we see alternating control by foreign and domestic dynasties while peace and local democracy continued to flourish at the village level. The empires remained responsive to the needs of common man, as evidenced by several large irrigation projects and a low tax burden. There was little question of the divine right of kings. Socially, the process of assimilating the foreign invaders was successful, without recourse to communal strife, since the foreigners, unlike later periods, had not brought a religious dogma with them.

Military capability: The Mauryan army, of which we know the most, consisted of infantry, cavalry, chariots, armored elephants, navy, and logistics. The army was structured into Patti, Gulma, Gana, Vahini, Pratana, Camu, Anikini, and Akshauhini. Patti consisted of one chariot, one elephant, three cavalry, and five infantry and was thus the smallest fighting unit of ten soldiers. Each successive division consisted of three lower units, except the Akshauhini, which consisted of ten Anikini. Thus, an Akshauhini was about 25,000 troops or a modern division. The entire military was about 750,000 troops or about thirty modern divisions, probably the largest army in the world at the time. The weaponry for the infantry consisted of the longbow made out of bamboo and steel, steel swords, javelins, and spears. Elephants were also mounted with archers and javelin throwers with a mahout guiding the elephant. Chariots were in decline, and the cavalry was perhaps the weakest element. The bodily armor varied from none to steel to silk clothing to block arrow.

The tactics relied heavily on highly complex formations known as *Vyuhas*. There were numerous formations that evolved, such as Lotus, Needle, Hawk, Eagle, Fish, Trident, and Wheel. Clearly, these formations were designed with an infantry-based enemy force in mind and would be less effective against a powerful cavalry. It is probably fair to say that the Indian army, even before the rise of the Maurya Empire, would have fared better against the Greeks than against the Persians. An encounter with the army of a small regional king was able to put fear in the heart of battle-hardened Greek soldiers. They had lost desire to march further.

Economic organization: While the central power in North India during this phase ebbed and flowed because of invasions and the rise and fall of empires, the tempo of economic life accelerated in part because invaders chose to identify with Indian civilization. The agricultural sector used an iron plowshare, and sickle and ladles were used presumably for irrigation. The state did not tell farmers what to grow or not to grow. The textile, silk, dyeing, mining and metallurgy, metal working, and ivory and glass industries had strong guilds associated with them. The economy was monetized, with interest rates typically at 15 percent. Minting machines were capable of turning out six coins at a time. There was vigorous trade within and with Rome through both the Silk Route and by sea with Indian ships as large as seventy-five tons carrying the goods. The local democracy in the villages functioned well, and the relationship between the villages and the central authority fluctuated, strengthening during periods of stability and centralized power. The periods of stability saw several great irrigation projects being undertaken, as mentioned above. Economically, the civilization progressed based on successful irrigation projects and well-organized industrial guilds in many industries. The subcontinent also benefited from trade wealth that poured in from the Roman Empire and Southeast and East Asia.

Systems of religious faith: As we have alluded to above, religious affiliation was primarily split between Hinduism and Buddhism. There was little interest in monotheism, even though Christianity is said to have arrived on the coast of Kerala in the first century. By the end of the period, Hinduism was again becoming ascendant, but slowly. There was ample religious freedom, as evidenced by the attitudes of later Sungas Emperors, the Indo-Greek king Menander, and Kanishka. Buddhism got a tremendous boost from several emperors in succession and successfully checked monism.

Because monotheism did not get a foothold on Indian soil, there was little science-religion conflict. In addition, since Buddhism successfully acted as a counterweight to monism, at least at the intellectual if not the social level, excessive spiritually was absent as well. Abrahamic religions of Judaism and Christianity required limits on freedom of thought and intellectual creativity. The Indian tradition of spiritual experimentation, polytheism, and agnosticism places no such limit on freedom of thought and intellectual creativity. However, as we shall note in the next chapter, by the end of the next phase, it was different: ascendant monism, while not antiscience, did not place a high value on the knowledge of natural world, which resulted in the relative decline of science.

Legal System: The prime minister of Chandragupta, Chanakya, compiled his *Arthashastra* in the fourth century BCE, and it includes a book of law that details a highly specific secular legal code containing contract law, including rescission of sale; marriage law, including marital relations and extramarital affairs; inheritance; property law, including sale and public property law; debt recovery; trusts, labor laws, slave laws, and laws concerning robbery, assault, gambling, and even defamation (!). This period also saw the codification of Hindu law by Manu somewhere between 200 BCE and 200 AD.

Manusmriti confirmed the origin of law on the concept of dharma and caste. It includes both acceptable social behavior for each caste and the punishment for violation. Manu Smriti did not have the authority of statutory law. It was more a formalization of the common law, and it was left to each state to enforce the code. Manusmriti may also have been a reaction to rise of Buddhism and an influx of nomads and other invaders into India. Many kings generally did not legislate, since Manusmriti was based on caste structure and dharma and did the job. The exceptions to this statement are Chanakya's legal code and Ashoka's law of piety. The latter was in fact a moral imperative requiring proper treatment of all. However, it never approached the status of a legal code. At the village level, the Panchayat system dispensed justice. In the cities, the highest court was the king's court, consisting of up to ten members, including up to five councilors, a bench clerk, an accountant, and a procedural clerk. A network of lower courts often existed. The trial process consisted of four parts: complaint, reply, trial, and decision.

Social structure: The social structure of Indian civilization continued to consist of the king at the top, followed by the Brahmins, Kshatriyas, Vaishyas, and Shudras. The caste classification, though hardening, was still flexible. For example, Chandragupta, the founder of the Mauryan dynasty, came from a lower caste of peacock-keepers. As foreign elements came to be absorbed into Indian society, the identification developed along two lines: caste or occupation based on birth and or tribal affinity It was possible for people with same tribal affiliation to belong to different castes.

Impressively, women enjoyed freedom and were engaged in many occupations. Kautiya even specified penalties for offenses against women in the workplace. Perhaps the best way to summarize the class stratification during the phase is that the caste system became more rigid while the class structure became more open. The codification of caste rules in Manusmriti strongly suggests the former while the political turmoil, successful absorption of foreign elements, and state sponsorship of Buddhism by several dynasties suggests the latter. It is believed that equality of opportunity did not get worse for several reasons: the political situation remained unsettled because of the successive influx of foreigners who challenged the cast system and because of the rise of anticaste ideologies of Buddhism, and to a lesser extent, Jainism, kept the caste system in relative check.

Knowledge-Creating and educational institutions: Taxilla, Ujjayini, and Varanasi were important universities, as were the Buddhist monasteries. Basic education was widespread and was the responsibility of the Brahmins. Education in the technical fields was organized by the guilds, which recruited students at an early age.

Wealth allocation: Although military expenditures went down during Ashoka's rein, they remained generally high due to both internal and external threats. The allocation to practical creativity also increased, as evidenced by large irrigation projects and a vibrant manufacturing sector. Thus, the allocation to religious activity was modest, with some exceptions, like the Stupa at Peshawar. We also do not witness an elite steeped in luxury. As a consequence, despite the unsettled political environment, many dynasties supported creative endeavors. Some of the oldest known universities of the world, such as at Taxilla, were established in this period.

Social cohesion: The rise of Buddhism, the Hindu concept of dharma, and a more formal codification of Hindu law by Manu all contributed to managing class and caste conflicts. The successful absorption of foreigners into the Hindu caste system also contributed to social cohesion.

Internal wars: During this phase, North India saw a succession of highly centralized states of both indigenous and nomadic or foreign origin interrupted by periods of political chaos. In addition, Satvahanas from the south took advantage of the political weakness in the north to penetrate up north. The frequency of internal wars during the phase must be judged high because of the response to external invasions. After more than six millennia of being left alone, the Indian civilization was being pulled into the world system.

Formative Beliefs and Ideology at the End of First Synthesis Phase

The highly developed tolerant monism and agnosticism; a strong spiritual orientation; a social cohesion derived from the absence of slavery and ironically the presence of caste system—the latter constituting fundamental inequality among men as sanctioned by religion; a strong element of renunciation in the lifestyle of the elite; and an attitude of openness and peacefulness toward other social orders founded on natural bounty and ideology of nonviolence all point to a belief system that may be summarized as follows:

- A continuing belief in knowledge based on the union of observation and reason
- A belief in the fundamental inequality among citizens based on the caste system and concepts of reincarnation and karma
- An attitude of openness toward the intellectual and religious creativity of others
- An abiding belief in peacefulness and a naiveté toward intentions of other social orders

These beliefs, derived from religious overgrowth, social cohesion, and an absence of conflict with other social orders for millennia because of the sea and Himalayan barriers are important because as the primary civilization to originate in fertile South Asia, these beliefs strongly impacted the beliefs of all South Asian social orders.

13.51 Extrinsic Peaceful Causes or Sum Total of Constructive Outcomes

No significant extrinsic peaceful causes impacted the Indian civilization during the current phase.

13.52 Extrinsic Violent Causes or Sum Total of Destructive Outcomes

Though Alexander's half-hearted attempt to conquer India failed, it opened the path for other nomads, including Yeuzhi or Kushans and Scythians as well as Indo-Greeks and Parthians to make trouble for the Indian civilization. Thus, for the first time, the Indian civilization faced an external threat.

We want to take a brief moment to address the issue of the Indian civilization's ability to defend against foreign invasions, since it is asserted by some that the Indian civilization has been unable to defend itself against these attacks. Beginning with the current phase, Indian civilization defended itself successfully against Alexander (the only civilization to do so) and Indo-Greeks and recovered from Scythians and Parthians after early losses. It also successfully absorbed these foreigners into its bosom.

Indian civilization defeated the Huns in the sixth century, defeated Arabs in the eighth century, held the Turkish Muslims at bay at its northwest frontier for two centuries, and resisted the conversion to Islam peacefully over five centuries. Finally, the British, with qualitatively superior weaponry, took over a hundred years (after begging trade concessions from Mughal emperors for 150 years) to conquer one-half of the civilization. They were allowed peace for a mere twenty-eight years, after which Indian civilization achieved independence in sixty-two years through largely peaceful means, but not before the cunning British got their way, as Churchill boasted, through dividing the civilization.

Assessing Sustained Political Independence (SPI)

Alexander's "invasion of India" was more like battles along the border that resulted in the presence of Greeks along the border for couple of centuries in the form of Indo-Greek states. It was not an extended military conflict between two civilizations, with neither side losing sustained political independence. Alexander was forced to turn back by the strength of a minor king at the gateway of Indian civilization. But the myth of Alexander weeping at the prospect of nothing left to conquer at the end of his Indian campaign is amusing and continues to be promoted. If the myth is true, it shows a delusional Alexander.

Persians interacted mostly peacefully with the strong and peaceful Indian civilization on its eastern flank, having admiringly watched the encounter of a minor Indian king with Alexander. There were three reasons for this: they were preoccupied on the western front, successive Mauryan and Kushan Empires in India, and the occasional buffer provided by the Indo-Greek states. Persians did not attack the Indian subcontinent until the early decades of the Common Era. Gonophores, a rebel Parthian governor, declared his independence and established the Indo-Parthian kingdom.

The kingdom lasted less than a century within the northern territory, and the Kushans conquered it in 75 AD. Thus, the impact of the brief Greece-India encounter was insignificant but interesting in that it made Greeks aware of the limits of their military power and Persians respectful of Indian military strength.

The phase also witnessed a strategic shift in the balance of power between the Indian civilization and the central and West Asian peoples and nomadic tribes, such as Scythians and Kushans. Indian civilization endured successive waves of nomadic attacks and eventually succeeded in absorbing these tribes into her bosom. Since China was able to hold its own relative to the nomads, thus diverting that pressure toward South Asia, Indian energies were diverted toward fighting these nomadic invasions. After the fall of the Kanva dynasty, the nomads generally succeed in establishing empires in North India during the current phase. This strategic shift reasserted itself in one form or another until the British control of India in the eighteenth century fortified the defense against attacks from Afghanistan and central Asia.

Control of Wealth or Means of Wealth Creation

Alexander did not exercise any control over Indian SGS. The main impact was control of SGS and continual displacement of Indian elites in North India by post-Alexander successive aggressors willing to be absorbed in the Indian civilization. The impact was military and political and ultimately not negative for the common man.

Fair trade: In addition, the Kushan rule, in concert with the Parthian Empire, was crucial in the emergence of the Silk Route and a first worldwide trading system. Since none of the empires—Roman, Parthian, or Kushan—were dominant on a global scale and despite large-scale aggression, the global trade remained surprisingly free; it did not evolve into coerced trade.

Migrations: Scythians and Yuehzi tribes from central Asia successfully invaded India and renewed the racial stock. It had a significant impact on the Indian caste system, in that it provided greater legitimacy to the mixed caste groups in north India. These invasions, which were a direct result of Ashoka's pacifism, had the impact of diverting surplus to fighting these invasions. Indian society absorbed these foreigners into the Indian civilization without a material impact on its core values. All the nomads were successfully absorbed into the Indian culture and were assigned a place in the caste structure.

Transmission of creativity: Impact on Indian civilization came through Alexander and nomadic invasions. Of these, only Kushans and Greeks may be judged to be open to the creativity of Indian civilization. The invasions by Scythians and Parthians had greater political significance. Nomads also introduced new military technology—particularly, faster horses—into the Indian subcontinent. Nomadic invasions strongly influenced the spread of Buddhism to central Asia and China. These invasions brought new ideas and vigor to the Indian subcontinent and in concert with Buddhist teachings, probably had a sobering impact on the Indian caste system.

Impact on productive outcomes: There was little change in land ownership or economic policies as a result of the invasions. However, new technologies were likely introduced, and the Indian civilization was linked to the central Asian region through trade. Thus, despite the terrible short-term impact of these invasions, the productive outcomes continued on their slow upward path.

In addition, renewed foreign trade was a very significant development, since after this phase, the rise of a global power would be accompanied by coerced trade as a means of extracting the SGS from civilizations without seeming to control it. Thus, successive nomadic invasions of India during the phase played a dramatic role in linking India, China, and Europe through a global trade network and spreading Buddhism outside India. Expansion of trade improved the economic conditions in China, India, and the Hellenistic states, probably at the expense of Romans, who lived beyond their means, and was a contributing factor in the decline of Roman power.

Impact on creative outcomes: If the earlier direction of transmission was likely from India to ancient Greece, the direction was reversed with respect to India and the Hellenistic states. Alexander invaded India expecting a hero's welcome, but in the end, it turned into a humiliating retreat. Indian civilization benefited in two areas: astronomy and art, though the exchange was unable to change the direction or values of Indian civilization. Alexander's invasion also led to a permanent Greek settlement on India's northwestern borders, where it did result in a synthesis of Indian and Greek cultures since both displayed openness. The Greek presence led to the Gandhara school of art and Indian influence led to its eventual adoption of Buddhism by the Greeks. After the fall of the Maurya Empire, the Indo-Greek king Menander, successfully carved out a kingdom that included all of Punjab. However, Indo-Greeks were gradually absorbed into the Indian culture and adopted Buddhist religion, losing their identity completely, in part because the Parthian Empire cut them off geographically from the other Hellenistic states to the west of the Parthian Empire. The short-term negative military and political impact of these invasions must be characterized as modest.

Though advances in astronomy and geometry likely came to India, the Indian civilization did not pay immediate attention to it as it was still preoccupied with metaphysical and epistemological issues raised by the Buddhist revolution in human thought. There is no direct evidence of diffusion of astronomical knowledge dating back to the current phase; However, the Varahamihira treatise, dating 575 CE, mentions five astronomical works, two of which were called Romaka Siddhanta and Paulisa Siddhanta. These works summarize Hellenistic and Egyptian astronomy. This transmission occurred in either the current phase or the next. The diffusion of Greek art to Afghanistan has been referred to above, and its influence is well documented. Excellent channels for such transmission in the form of Indo-Greek contingent left in the northwest frontier, later Indo-Greek kings in north India, and Indian-Roman trade existed throughout the period from about 300 BCE to 200 CE.

Impact on institutional structures and processes: One must judge the impact of Greeks and central Asians on the societal structures and processes to be modest. Politically, Indian civilization became aware of the theory of divine right of kings through Alexander, who unabashedly considered himself a god. However, this silly theory had little impact on political systems. Indian rulers did not adopt Greek military tactics. Similarly, there was little in economic organization that impacted Indian civilization. The legal system also remained tied to religion and caste orientation. Both the Greeks and central Asians, unlike the Romans, hardly had a developed legal system. Greek religious impulse had little impact in India. To the contrary, Indo-Greeks adopted Buddhism. The foreign invasions probably had the greatest impact on social structure and social norms. The influx of Greeks and central Asians probably loosened the caste system in the northeast and the Punjab region to make room for the newcomers. In the Punjab area, a new caste was created for the foreign rulers, that of Khatris, which are different from both Kshatriya and Kshatri (born of a Kshatriya and Vaishya). Khatris became a new caste for the warlike foreign invaders as they transitioned from their original religion to Buddhism to Hinduism. The returning vogue of wearing long hair was likely influenced by Greeks.

Assessing the net impact: Clearly the net impact of Greek and central Asian invasions on the Indian civilization was a lot less negative than the impact of Greek and Roman invasions on Mesopotamia, Egypt, ancient Greece, and Hellenistic states. On the negative side of the ledger, the invasions caused destruction and put control of the surplus in foreign hands. On the positive side, foreigners were small in number and willing to be absorbed into Indian civilization over time. They also brought new vigor, new technologies, new science, and, most significantly, did not bring new intolerant creeds with them. There was no wealth drain either.

We believe the two sides of the ledger are more evenly balanced compared to other civilization. We would assess the impact to be negative but not excessively so.

13.53 Productive Outcomes

Despite constant invasions, the current period in India remained prosperous mainly because the village remained immune to these invasions. These invasions were punctuated by long periods of peace because Indian society was able to successfully absorb the foreign elements without creating lasting ethnic tensions.

The current phase may be regarded as the first significant period of international trade. Because of the rise of the Parthian and Kushan Empires in the wake of Alexander's campaign and the resulting Hellenistic states, the landmass of Eurasia was becoming linked through land routes in addition to the existing sea routes. The principal trade occurred between the Roman Empire, India, and China with Parthians, Kushans, and the Hellenistic states keeping the trading lanes open. The balance of trade was in India's favor, partly because of the luxury that Roman elite were accustomed to.

The Roman sailor Hippalus learned that monsoons blew from northeast in the winter and from southwest in the summer from either Mesopotamian or Indian sailors, who had done this for thousands of years. This, coupled with larger ships, formed the basis of the India–Rome trade through Berenike, a port on the western coast of Egypt on the Red Sea. Romans preferred the sea route since overland routes had to go through lands not necessarily friendly to Rome. From Berenike, camel caravans carried the cargo of spices, incense, opium drugs, textiles, and herbs to the Nile, about 250 miles west, and from there, large boats took the cargo to the Mediterranean. The whole process was nearly a year-long affair. Thus, fair trade was beneficial to the Indian civilization.

13.54 Creative Outcomes

Achievements in Practical Creativity

Materials: Wootz steel (containing very hard carbide bands) originated in India more than two millennia ago and was exported to Europe, China, and the Arab world. It became particularly famous in West Asia, where it became known as Damascus steel. Early diamonds used as gemstones originated in India during this phase. Lamp black and metal zinc were developed during the period. Glass was also produced during the period.

Processes: Dyeing technology based on minerals (red lead, yellow ochre, gold powder, lapis lazuli, azurite, malachite, calcium sulfate, white lead, silver powder, and zinc) and vegetable (indigo and *mamjistha*) sources were developed and used in textiles.

Tools: Large construction projects required considerable advances in the technology of lifting, loading, and transporting construction materials; building construction ramps; and using scaffolding and led to development of related tools and implements.

Agriculture technologies: The *Arthashastra* describes dam construction. Rock-cut step wells were invented around 100 CE. Indian farmers developed nonchemical, ecofriendly pesticides and fertilizers still in use today.

Nonagricultural products: During the period, textile technology achieved new heights as evidenced by export of textiles to West Asia and Rome. Non-glazed ceramics were also manufactured during the period.

Construction: A three-hundred-foot Buddhist Stupa was erected at Peshawar and was probably the tallest building of its kind in the world at that time.

Infrastructure: The *Arthashastra* notes the construction of bridges. The use of suspension bridges using plaited bamboo and iron chains came toward the end of the current phase.

Achievements in Religious Creativity

The current phase was a period of unequaled religious creativity in the Indian civilization. It produced two great religions, Jainism and Buddhism, and continued developing monism.

Monism: We see continued development of Vedanta in India and the related creed of Gnosticism, which was based on the belief that human beings are divine souls trapped in a material world.

Agnosticism: During this period, we see continued development of Buddhism through the third and fourth councils and rise of the Mahayana branch. Perhaps the most significant religious event of this period was the rise of Buddhism as a peaceful world religion as it spread to central Asia, China, Sri Lanka, Burma, Thailand, Cambodia, and Vietnam.

Buddhism was not only an agnostic doctrine but also sprouted advances in logic, epistemology, and art. As a religion, it preached the doctrine of ethics or the eightfold path based on right view, right intension, right speech, right action, right livelihood, right effort, right mindfulness, and right concentration. It preached the abolition of caste system and instituted a nonhereditary priesthood in place of the hereditary priesthood of Hinduism.

Achievements in Philosophy

Epistemology: The current phase of Indian history was exceptionally creative from the standpoint of developing the broadest range of religious philosophies and metaphysics the ancient world ever experienced. It is a momentous tribute to the freedom of thought that existed in ancient India. Hindu metaphysics had reached a natural resting point with the Upanishads and Vedanta; however, that was not yet the case with Buddhism and Jainism. It is therefore natural that the current period in Indian history focused on working out the issues of ontology and epistemology consistent with Buddhist and Jain doctrines. We briefly describe the key developments below:

- **Jain relativism:** Jain relativism states that universe is made up of substances, each capable of infinite modes. These substances are interrelated and mutually influence each other. One can see that Jain relativism is conceptually consistent with later scientific theories, such as gravitation and relativity, which postulate that the weight and dimensions of an object depend on its location in space and how it is viewed respectively. Note that Jain relativism does not imply that world is unknowable, only that such knowledge is relative not absolute.

- **Jain Syadvada:** The word *syadvad* means theory of probability. The syadvada postulated seven possibilities with respect to an object: (1) may be, it is; (2) may be, it is not; (3) may be, it is and it is not; (4) may be, it is indescribable; (5) may be, it is and yet is indescribable; (6) may be, it is not and is also indescribable; (7) may be, it is and is not and is also indescribable. This led Jain mathematicians to develop the earliest known concepts in the theory of probability. Again, note that syadvad does not deny the possibility of knowledge; it only emphasizes the quality of existing knowledge about an object.

- **Buddhist dependent co-origination:** The concept of dependent co-origination states that everything in the universe is interconnected through the web of cause and effect so that the whole and the parts are mutually interdependent and interpenetrating. The character and condition of entities at any given time are intimately connected with the character and condition of all other entities that may appear to be unrelated. Because all things are thus reciprocally conditioned and transient (*annica*), they have no independent reality or inner being or essence or soul (*anatta*).

- **Nagarjuna and Sunyata:** Nagarjuna, who lived around 150 CE, is considered to be the greatest Buddhist philosopher and the greatest ever by some. His philosophy, because of the use of word *sunyata* or void is often misinterpreted as nihilism. Nagarjuna starts with Buddha's concept of dependent co-origination and logically extends it to the proposition that things do not have an essence or inner being; they come into being because of other things or prevailing causes and conditions. He felt that precisely because things do not have a fixed, permanent essence, that change is possible. Note how different this is from Plato's preexisting forms, Kant's thing-in-itself, or Hegel's absolute idea. Thus, for Nagarjuna, the empirical and physical objects exist and are capable of change but are devoid of any essence. Nagarjuna uses the word *self-nature* to denote the concept of essence. His *tetralema* was simply a dialectical method to show that essences do not exist. Sunyata, for Nagarjuna, thus, is not the absence of objects, only the absence of eternal essence or preexisting form in objects. He may rightly be regarded as the first great realist or materialist philosopher that the world has produced. The essence of his materialism is that things do not have a fixed, eternal essence or soul or form or a thing-in-itself and that they can be understood by understanding their causes and conditions—i.e., through observation and reason.

We note that Wittgenstein, probably the most influential Western philosopher of the twentieth century, came to conclusions unsurprisingly similar to those of Nagarjuna. Wittgenstein's analysis of language and reality concluded that language either represents facts of reality or it does not. When it represents reality, it is a form of science. When it does not, it is nonsense and often leads to problems in philosophy through concepts such as essence, which are outside the range of experience precisely because things do not have essence. Wittgenstein was an antimetaphysical positivist like Nagarjuna, only he arrived at it through analysis of the relationship between language and reality, whereas Nagarjuna arrived at it through an extension of Buddha's concept of dependent co-origination through logical means to sunyata. Wittgenstein was not concerned explicitly about causes of why things change, only how they are represented through language and how language itself can lead to bad philosophy.

Wittgenstein condemned his own statements as a mere ladder to see the real. Going against centuries-long Western philosophical tradition, he propounded no philosophical system. Similarly, Nagarjuna anticipated his own critique by those who would misinterpret him by saying, "Am I not yelling 'don't yell'?" He also proposed no philosophical system. Both denied philosophy the possibility of real knowledge, which only sciences can achieve. Wittgenstein only allowed philosophy the role of showing that when it goes beyond the senses—i.e., to fixed eternal essences—it is dealing in nonsense. In other words, it does not create knowledge and at best it can police itself. Nagarjuna could not have agreed more. It is indeed difficult to believe that Wittgenstein was not aware of Nagarjuna's work of nearly two thousand years ago; however, he is not acknowledged by him. This is particularly surprising since Wittgenstein admired Schopenhauer, who in turn was a great admirer of ancient Indian philosophy in general and had access to Nagarjuna's writings.

It is noteworthy that Buddhism came closest to developing a consistent scientific outlook but failed in an important aspect. Ontologically, it arrived at the concept of sunyata through the concept of dependent origination to affirm the existence of the real. Note how this line of reasoning supports the concepts of *anicca* or impermanence and *annata* or absence of essence. However, Buddhism primarily saw the problem of existence in psychological and ethical terms alone, not in intellectual terms, and in attempting to understand the natural and social worlds through observation and reason. Thus, it saw the end of suffering through meditation and mind control and not through a knowledge of the physical universe and progressive perfection of social order based on better material conditions. The *lokayata* or ancient Indian atheism, on the other hand, seemed more grounded in practical hedonistic atheism with shallow intellectual roots.

Jain dualism, in the absence of a theory of evolution, could not bridge the gap between matter and soul. Additionally, Jain doctrine believed that a Jain monk who has achieved perfection was capable of super-sensuous perception, thus negating the need for a controlled observation of the physical world. This line of reasoning was obviously not helpful in developing an experimental approach to knowledge. In other civilizations, the case against science was made through monotheism, but in the Indian civilization during the current phase, we witness instances of this case against science made unwittingly by not extending the insights to understand the universe or philosophy unable to fully free itself from a self-centered monism and other-centered agnosticism.

Ethics: Contributions to ethics came from Hinduism/Vedanta, Jain, and Buddhist quarters.

- **Hinduism/Vedanta:** The word *yoga* means to unite or to control: in this case, unite the self and the Brahman or to control mind as a necessary step to achieve this unity. Yoga thus is the practical means of achieving the ultimate meditative state postulated in the Vedanta school. Patanjali systematized yoga over two thousand years ago, and it contains the Hindu/Vedantic ethical precepts called *niyamas* and *yamas*. His entire system has the following ashtangas, literally eight elements, the first two comprising the ethics and the last six stages of evolution on the meditative path.

  Niyams or preparatory do's: cleanliness, contentment, austerity, study of scriptures, and an attitude of surrender.

  Yamas or preparatory don'ts: injury to life, lying, stealing, inappropriate sex, and acquisitiveness.

  Asanas or physical posture for meditation: comfortable, stable position.

  Pranayama or breath control: the first step to control the wandering mind.

  Pratyahana or sense control: the second step to control the wandering mind.

Dharna or concentration: a final step control the wandering mind.

Dhyana or meditation: as a first stage in meditation using an object to meditate on

Samadhi or state of absorption: union of mediator and the object of meditation

- **Jain Ethics:** Jain ethics were similar to Hindu ethics, with a focus on nonviolence, truthfulness, not stealing, nonpossessiveness, and chastity.
- **Buddhist Ethics:** Buddhist ethics were based on the eightfold path to nirvana by Buddha as noted above. It consisted of right knowledge, right motivation, right speech, right livelihood, right behavior, right effort, right mindfulness, and right meditation.

Achievements in Art

As we have seen in the previous two chapters, starting about 1000 BCE, the Indian civilization had turned the corner again; it was once again becoming more urban and had begun to evolve in two contradictory directions: the continued focus on monism and achievement of internal self-god union through meditation while enduring a strong protestant reaction from Buddhism and Jainism on the one hand and an interest in knowledge of external world on the other. The birth of science we witnessed in the last chapter was despite this contradiction. During the current phase, this conflict continued. In fact, we may rightly view Indian history as a continuous struggle between these two viewpoints, with one or the other gaining upper hand in a particular period. The development of art during this phase, particularly visual arts, must be seen in the context of this fundamental struggle. There is greater emphasis on art but through an objectification of inner world and not on representation of the external world. Thus, Indian art, particularly to unsophisticated foreign eyes, appears strange since it was not driven by a need to represent nature or society and does not conform to the rules of aesthetics. Indian art of the phase was interested in representing internal religious feelings as well as the protestant Buddhist and Jain reactions to this internal religiosity. Typical representational art, on the other hand, begins with external world and ends with its likeness.

It is interesting to compare Indian art to recent art movements such as expressionism, impressionism, and abstract art forms: all three are more interested in expressing the inner, though secular, world of the artist, and all three set aside the so-called rules of aesthetics and proportion. Indian art of the period is more like these forms of art except it was not secular; it was religious in nature and was a reaction against this religiosity.

Architectural construction often utilized wood. For example, Chandragupta's capital, Patliputra, in the fourth century BCE was made out of wood and had a forty-kilometer wall with sixty-four gates made entirely out of wood. Thus, the surviving Indian art from this phase are stone pieces, such as Ashoka's pillars proclaiming his Buddhist message, the rock-cut cave temples, and stupas. Wood was continued as the medium in the post-Ashoka period, and we do not have any surviving art in wood from the period.

Music: Pingala was also a musical theorist who wrote a book on prosody as noted before.

13.55 Achievements in Science

Achievements in Formal Sciences

The reaction to monist philosophy in the form of Jainism and Buddhism during the current period had modest impact on formal science development. Hindu scholars continued their focus on linguistics, mathematics, and logic. Jain scholars focused on speculative cosmology and that required development of new mathematical thought. Buddhist scholars during this period initially focused on elaboration of Buddhist doctrine and toward the end of the period focused on logic and epistemology as they attempted to further define and clarify Buddhist thought.

Mathematics: The fundamental direction of Indian mathematical thought in the post-Sulbhasutra period was set by the groundbreaking work of Panini on linguistics in the sixth century BCE or earlier, as we discussed in the last chapter. The underlying structure of Panini's grammar is very similar to how a mathematical function is defined today. There is also evidence that Panini may have originated the use of letters to represent numerals. Thus, the algebraic nature of Indian mathematics in the period under discussion may be said to originate from the mathematical structure of the Sanskrit grammar. In ancient Greece, mathematics grew out of philosophical speculations about the nature of reality; post-Sulbhasutra mathematics in India grew out of linguistics, leading over time to the development of algebra and trigonometry. Below, we first describe the work of Hindu mathematicians followed by Jain mathematics of this period.

Significant Hindu mathematicians of the period are Pingala and Katyana. It cannot be ascertained when Pingala lived. In Indian tradition, he is known as the younger brother of Panini, who lived in the sixth century BCE or before; others date him as late as 200 BCE. Pingala is credited with creating the binary number system in connection with a description of the patterns of prosody. His discussion of the combinatorics of meter corresponds to the binomial theorem. He was also the first to describe the so-called Fibonacci numbers. He is famous for his work, the Chanda Sastras, a treatise on prosody. Although he was primarily a linguist, Katyana composed a series of nine texts on geometry dealing with simple geometric figures in the second century BCE.

The famous Bakhshali manuscript was discovered in 1881 near Peshawar. It is devoted mainly to arithmetic and algebra. It is believed to date from 200 CE to 400 CE and is likely a copy of an earlier manuscript. Why is this manuscript significant? During 200 BCE to 300 CE, the Indian subcontinent was under continual political turmoil due to invasions from central Asian nomads. It is probably due to these political and military dislocations that not much has survived from this period. Thus, this manuscript stands out. In addition, the style of elaboration shows logical presentation: it presents a rule, elaborates it in words, and then gives examples through application.

The real significance of this manuscript is that it shows the earliest known attempt to represent the negative numbers, subtraction operations, and equations symbolically. Thus, it could rightly be considered the first known text on algebra. As a consequence, scholars from different cultures and of different persuasion argued differed dramatically about the date of the manuscript. Some scholars have even argued that it is not Indian in origin and is as recent as 1200 CE!

Earlier Jain surviving texts dating from the fourth century BCE are *Surya Prajnapti* and *Jambudvipa Prajnapti*. A later text, known as *Sthananga*, lists the theory of numbers, arithmetic operations, geometry, algebraic equations and permutations, and combinations as the key mathematical areas worthy of study. A text, *Bhagabati*, dating from the third century BCE, gives the rules for permutations. In the second century CE, Jain mathematics developed a theory of sets and logarithmic functions of base two. It is worth noting that these branches of mathematics were developed not because of interest in physics; rather, they were developed because of interest in cosmology. Because of cosmology, they also delved into the first known analysis of concept of infinity. In the history of science, it is not just mathematics leading to the development of physics and vice versa, but also metaphysical anxiety, leading to a development of mathematics through the interest in speculative cosmology.

- Jain mathematicians were the first to discard the idea that all infinites were the same or equal. Jain thinkers identified four different types of infinities: infinite in length, area, volume, and number of dimensions. The world would have to wait for more than two thousand years before Cantor would take up a definitive analysis of orders of infinity.

- In the Jain work on the theory of sets, two basic infinite numbers are distinguished. On both physical and ontological grounds, a distinction was made between asaṃkhyāta ("innumerable") and ananta ("unlimited") that is, between rigidly bounded and loosely bounded infinities.

- Jain mathematicians also developed the earliest known concepts in statistical theory through the theory of combinations and permutations.

- Jain mathematicians anticipated the concept of the logarithmic function of base two nearly two thousand years before Napier, through a clear understanding of the law of indices.

- Jain mathematicians also focused on solution of simple, cubic, and quadratic equations, thus laying the foundation of algebra.

Linguistics: In linguistics, we witness the emergence of two great contributors: Katyayana, mentioned above, and Pitanjali, who was also from the second century BCE. Katyayana believed that the relationship of the words to their meaning is eternal or Siddha, even though the object represented by the word is not. This has been misrepresented as akin to Plato's ideal preexisting forms. Katyayana simply seems to be saying that once the word and its meaning are fixed, by definition, the relationship is eternal from a logical point of view. Plato's concept of preexisting forms implies a prehuman ontological existence and not merely a logical existence within mind. This is clear from his insistence that a word represented a category or word universal. As an example, the basis of the word *cow* is *cowhood* and goes on to insist that to prevent an infinite regression, the basis of *cowhood* is nothing more than *cowhood*! Katyayana's analysis led later thinkers to formulate the notion that the word *universal* is a superimposition of the semantic and phonological components. Finally, Pitanjali's *Mahabhasya* or great commentary, written in 150 BCE, was an elaboration of Panini's work, with an emphasis on rules of grammar, philosophy of grammar, morphology, and etymology.

Logic: Probably the greatest name in the development of logic in ancient India was Aksapada Gautama, not to be confused with Medhatithi Gautama, whom we discussed in the last chapter. Aksapada Gautama is the founder of the Nyaya school in the second century BCE. The Nyaya school is more than a work of logic; it is in fact an epistemology based on a realistic ontology. Nyaya admitted four valid means of knowledge: observation, inference/deduction, comparison, and testimony. Note that comparison is to something already proved, and testimony is mediated knowledge presumably obtained based on correct means in the first place. Therefore, there are only two true means of knowledge: observation and inference/deduction. One can plainly see this by contrasting the five-part syllogism Gautama developed Gautama and Aristotle's three-part syllogism. As the analysis in appendix L makes this abundantly clear. In Gautama, we find a clear elaboration of the entire methodology of science, starting with inferring the major premise from observation and then applying the major premise through observation and deduction to obtain valid conclusions. It was a momentous achievement not equaled until two thousand years later in J. S. Mills's critique of Aristotle's syllogism. The epistemology inherent in Nyaya is thoroughly consistent with the Vaisheshika school discussed in the last chapter.

Achievements in Natural Sciences

As we discussed before, the lasting developments in natural sciences require an appreciation of the experimental method, which was historically first required a thorough understanding of solar astronomy itself as a grand, natural controlled experiment. Prior to understanding solar astronomy, natural sciences everywhere, of necessity, were speculative in nature and based either on under-observation and over-explanation or on evolving industrial practices.

Chemistry: The development of practical chemical and metallurgical industry did not have to wait for a theoretical understanding. The industrial practice typically became a form of evolving crude experimentation. Chemistry was known as *rasayan shastra*, *rasa-vidya*, *rasatantra*, and *rasakriya*, or the "science of liquids." The industrial houses were called *rasakriya-nagaram* or *rasakriya-shala*, which literally mean "place where liquids are activated." A chemist was referred to as a *rasadnya* and *rasatantravid*, which mean "person having knowledge about liquids." Thus, in ancient India, chemical science was known and practiced but without a theoretical understanding and controlled experiments.

There was a significant interest in alchemy to transmute base metals into gold primarily through using mercury and the manufacture of dyes.

Achievements in Biological Sciences

Parasara's *Vrksayurveda* appears to be the oldest stand-alone book on botany in ancient India. From indirect, literary evidence, it has been dated to as early as the first century BCE. Parasara classifies plants into *dvimatrka* (dicotyledons) and *ekamatrka* (monocotyledons). These are further classified into *Samiganiya* (Febaceae), *Puplikagalniya* (Rutaceae), *Svastikaganiya* (Crucifeae), *Tripuspaganiya* (Cucerbitacaea), *Mallikaganiya* (Aponcenaceae), and *Kurcapuspaganiya* (Asteraceae).

Although the focus on natural science in India suffered during the current phase, in particular, a follow-up on Vaisheshika's revolutionary ideas in physics and chemistry, it was not due to a conflict between science and religious doctrines. It was based on the diversion of intellectual resources toward the working out of the metaphysical, epistemological, and ontological implications of the doctrines of Buddhism and Jainism.

Achievements in Social Sciences

Political economy: More than two thousand years before Adam Smith, Chanakya wrote a treatise on political theory and economy called *Arthasashtra*, a title that may be translated as *Wealth (and Management) of Nations*. The book covered a much wider scope than the wealth of nations. It is unlike any book written in the ancient world. Chanakya, as we mentioned before, was responsible for the founding of the Maurya Empire through his advice and counsel to Chandragupta. He was, thus, a king-maker. We may call Chanakya's work the first text in political economy, but as we shall see below, it was much more than that.

Chanakya starts out by counseling an aspiring king about how to gain power. He bases this on political realism and harsh pragmatism. He sees a higher purpose in this pursuit of power, provided the king or future king is just and treats his subjects based on concept of dharma, clearly outlining in the process the qualities needed in a king. The political state he describes is an autocracy married to a meritocracy. Once power is attained, Chanakya focuses his attention on how to preserve it. He outlines in detail the qualities necessary for the prime minister and the council of ministers and defines how the princes ought to be trained to ensure continuity of the dynasty. Chanakya then proceeds to define the entire administrative apparatus needed for managing a state efficiently, including the duties of a king, such as how he should structure his day into sixteen parts, the superintendents of the various departments of centralized production, the duties of a city administrator, formation of new villages, and a spy network to gather information. The type of economic structure Chanakya recommends is what we would today call a mixed economy with a near complete freedom in the agricultural sector and a near complete monopoly in the nonagricultural sectors, such as mining, forestry, textiles, liquor, gold, slaughterhouse, and ship building. Presumably, these activities were capital intensive and city-based and required knowhow, and only the state was in position to organize these activities.

In addition, he described additional, nonproduction departments to manage passports, the state inventory of goods, weights and measures (outlining a unit of time, where the smallest unit was about one millionth of a day and a measure of time equal to $1/50^{th}$ of an hour by specifying the design of a water clock), tolls, taxation, prostitution, commerce, and agricultural policy. Chanakya also focuses his attention on foreign policy, describing six fundamental forms of relationship that can exist among states (war, peace, neutrality, alliance, war with one and peace with another, and threat of war) and the conditions under which they should be employed.

Chanakya discusses military strategy in detail, including a theory of geopolitical balance of power, fort construction, weapon production and maintenance, war tactics, and specialized departments for horses, elephants, and chariots, including training elephants.

Chanakya had a lot to say about tax policy, tolls, and their effects on production and prices. As mentioned before, Chanakya outlined a detailed legal structure, specifying the law of the land and punishment for each violation, monetary or otherwise. He discussed gender relations, contracts, sale of property, and rules of inheritance in explicit details. Finally, Chanakya balanced his tough-minded approach to affairs of the state with compassion toward the poor and women, arguing for liberal assistance during famines and a distribution of unused lands. He correctly saw land and agriculture as the basis of all wealth.

To summarize the creative and scientific achievements of the Indian civilization during the current phase, there was a strong challenge to the Upanishad philosophy of monism, reincarnation, and karma from Jain and Buddhist quarters as the former were being used to justify an increasingly rigid caste system. Initially, both the Jain and Buddhists had rational and supportive thinking toward new knowledge and science. However, over time, they impacted the Indian intellectual developments in three important ways: first, because of state sponsorship, both Buddhism than Jainism sucked in the intellectual resources away from science; second, the ethical, epistemological and ontological implications of Jain and Buddhist doctrines had to be worked out and that turned out to be a mammoth intellectual undertaking lasting centuries; third, as these implications were worked out, these doctrines, while starting out as agnostic, themselves became idealist in outlook. Thus while Jain thought made substantial contributions to math and logic and Buddhism to philosophy, logic and epistemology, neither focused on and further developed the speculative scientific theories of Kannada or Kapila except providing repeated, mostly sterile commentaries. As a result, physics and astronomy increasingly took a back seat to metaphysics and formal sciences in India during this period.

North India continued to lead in the arena of intellectual creativity in the subcontinent. North India not only was a leader of intellectual creativity in the subcontinent, by the end of current period, it was in fact the only place in the world that held the possibility of the pursuit of science. Europe was slowly passing into the grip of Christian dogma, Roman Republic had killed science in Greece and Roman Empire finished off the job in the Hellenistic world, China continued its focus practical creativity in its own peculiar, insular ways, Persia remained Persia, leaving north India alone to pursue science for more than five centuries until the Arab renaissance. This we shall focus on in the next chapter.

Summarizing Achievements in Abstract Systems-Building Capability (ASBC)

By the end of the phase, the ASBC of the Indian civilization must be characterized as world-class: it had already mastered creative method, adopted alphabetical script in the previous phase and made even greater strides in epistemology through the work of great Buddhist philosophers.

Summarizing the State of Civilization and Science

13.56 State of Civilization and Science at Phase End

Overview of the History of the Phase

The phase saw the destruction of the Achaemenid Empire and ancient Greece at the hands of Alexander and the Roman Republic respectively. It witnessed the emergence of the Hellenistic states from Alexander's Empire and their slow destruction successively by Indians, Persians, and the Roman Empire. It saw the Maurya Empire emerge in India and the Parthian Empire emerge in Persia in the wake of Alexander's invasion. It witnessed successive invasions of North India by Indo-Greeks, Scythians, and Parthians, and the first wave of central Asian nomads deflected by China toward the Indian subcontinent. The Chinese civilization maintained its independence by paying tribute to the nomads, and Indian civilization retained its soul by successfully absorbing the Greeks, Scythians, Parthians, and nomads into her bosom after successively losing to them on battlefields. With the Roman Empire, we witness the first extensive empire on the European continent. By end of the phase, the key powers consisted on the Indian and Chinese civilizations and the Roman and Parthian Empires. Both empires were past their peaks and would experience downfall or disintegration in the next phase.

As in previous chapters, we now summarize the state of civilization and specific sciences in the world at phase end.

Practical Creativity

Key materials invented or discovered in this period were malleable cast iron, steel, concrete, improved parchment, mercury, gold amalgam, and an early form of porcelain. Key process inventions included electroplating (!), lost wax process, and glass blowing. Humans invented the use of ox power, dual horse power, the undershot water wheel, and candles. They discovered the use of natural gas and petroleum and toyed with steam power. The water clock and sundial were improved. In addition, the following tools were invented: gears, screw, improved Archimedes screw pump, springs, chain and socket device, roller bearings, crank, water mills, belt drive, wheelbarrow, convex lens, adjustable calipers, water-powered bellows, chain pump, seismograph, and magic lantern. Key inventions included cylindrical grain storage, the first harvesting machine, grain winnower, insecticides, multitube seed drill, and whiffletree that allowed two oxen to pull a cart. The water organ and double boiler were invented. Key achievements in construction included several types of aqueducts, formal gardens, dome, a lighthouse, five-story buildings, central heating, the trestle bridge tunnel, designed harbors, window panes, skylights, deep wells, an iron suspension bridge, large naval vessels, and colossal statues. It also included the six-hundred-mile Chinese Grand canal, Magic canal, Great Wall, dry dock, fire signal, Silk Road, horseshoe, chest harness, collar harness, toe stirrups, parachute, ship rudder, star maps, maps with grids, and three-mast ships.

In short, we can discern significant breakthroughs in military and nonagricultural technologies during the phase.

Religious Creativity

The state of religious creativity during the phase may be summarized through the rise of Christian monotheism and the rise of Zoroastrianism in West Asia; Buddhism and Jainism in India as a reaction to monism and caste system; and Taoism in China, the latter was a statement of the lawfulness of the universe and moral conduct, and retained its focus on this-worldliness. Monotheism and monism led to serious implications for science to one degree or another, while others were generally positive for science.

As we have repeatedly emphasized, the conflict between Christian monotheism was fundamental in nature, whereas the conflict between monism and science was more a question of what is important in life: understanding the physical universe and the social order itself in an effort to make material life more comfortable or the union of the in-dwelling self and the true ultimate nonmaterial reality called Brahman. Buddhism clearly anticipated the ultimate solution to *Homo sapiens* existential anxiety through an agnostic metaphysics and an ethical system not dependent on divine grace. However, as we know, *Homo sapiens* as a whole would be hardly ready to accept that solution for a long time.

Philosophical Creativity

This phase was also a period of heightened philosophical activity. In epistemology, metaphysics, ethics, and logic, the essential insights were achieved through an interaction among Indian, Greek, and Hellenistic civilizations. The field of aesthetics as a discipline did not see significant new developments. A theory of beauty that explores the relationship of reason to imagination was still in future just as exploring the relationship of the beauty to emotions was in the past.

Artistic Creativity

The state of art, distinct from a theory of art, fared much better during the current phase. The greatest progress was made in architecture, sculpture, drama, and dance, with painting, music, and literature lagging behind. It is easy to see why painting lagged behind sculpture. Development in the art of painting requires perspective, which in turn requires the concept of zero and the derived concept of a vanishing point in a the two-dimensional work of art that a painting is. Sculpture and architecture are three-dimensional objects, and the very process of creating these art forms can provide the correct dimensional relationships through trial and error without a theoretical understanding. Thus, in our judgment, painting with correct perspective is a higher art form, and its full development was still in the future. The development of literature was held back, in part, not for intellectual but for physical reasons: paper. It is also easy to see why drama and dance could move forward. They required human motion and storytelling ability, the latter having been established millennia ago through myth creation. However, on the whole, art was making the progress one might expect.

Scientific Creativity

The greatest progress was made in the area of geometry and arithmetic, including the concept of zero and the decimal system. There was little new in arena of linguistics. Panini had already transformed the field of linguistics into science with sublime beauty. In logic, Gautama's five-part syllogism and Aristotle's three-part syllogism made considerable progress.

The present phase saw great progress in astronomy through the application of geometry. However, Hellenistic astronomy bogged down due to a tendency of under-observation and over-explanation. This probably occurred for political reasons. Hellenistic states lost their conquered territories to Persian, Indians, and Romans, losing revenues and control in the process. Persian and Romans had little interest in science, and Indian civilization was preoccupied with working out Buddhist and Jain doctrines and adjusting to and absorbing the great influx of nomadic invaders. Physics did not progress beyond Greek and Indian speculations. It was too early for chemistry to achieve the status of science, remaining tied to practical wealth creation activities, such as textile and metallurgical industries. We see modest beginnings in earth science—for example, simple observations on the water cycle.

Perhaps even more than astronomy, progress was made in the field of medicine. In classification of diseases, diagnosis, treatment, and surgery, medical science made impressive gains. In biology, we see several civilizations make rudimentary attempts to classify the vegetable kingdom.

Developments in social sciences focused on the maintenance of the social order, not attempting to consciously improve it through theoretical understanding. Thus, we see a focus on the legal system, judicial structures, effective acquisition and exercise of political power, the relationship between competing states, military tactics, and strategy. In addition, a great start was made in psychology and ethics in both religious and secular forms.

Mathematics: The principal developments took place in number theory and geometry. Existence of irrational numbers, the so-called Fibonacci sequence, and binomial theorem were established. The Chinese version of the decimal system and a method of exhaustion and summation of infinite series to determine areas of geometrical shapes using the latter two methods were developed. The latter was also the beginning of algebra and even calculus. The greatest development took place in plane, spherical, and conical geometry, with Hellenistic and Chinese contributions dominating.

Logic: The syllogisms of Gautama and Aristotle represent the highest development of logic during the phase.

Astronomy: The correct ideas that motion of planets and occurrence of the eclipses can be predicted, the phenomenon of the precession of the equinox, and the ideas of a heliocentric solar system, a rotating Earth, and that the sun is a star either originated or developed further during the phase using the new science of geometry. Unfortunately, Hellenistic astronomy's insistence on a geocentric solar system, no doubt influence by the worldview contained in Judaic-Christian religions, set back the course of astronomy by nearly half a millennium until the rise of Aryabhatta in India around 500 CE.

Physics: The state of physics hardly advanced beyond what Kannada had asserted centuries earlier, as we noted in the last chapter, in part because the progress in astronomy was stymied by Ptolemy's tendency of under-observation and over-rationalization. Thus, Aristotle's attempt at physics is noted for its imaginary leaps, with every claim contradicting common experience and even correct but subtle ideas of other physicists in the Greek tradition, such as Democritus.

Medicine: Medicine progressed dramatically in diagnosis and treatment strategies, including herbs, acupuncture, and surgical techniques. However, Indian, Chinese, and Greek medicine lacked the correct understanding of the specific causes of the diseases. The general belief of the physicians was that illness was caused by an imbalance in Indian doshas, Greek humors, or Chinese vital energy within the body. However, unlike Aristotle's physics, the inability of the physicians to understand the causes of disease may be overlooked since their explanations did not contradict common experience.

Political economy: The integration of the social sciences attained by Chanakya (he displays considerable understanding of economics, politics, psychology, ethics, sociology, military strategy, and law) must be considered one of the finest achievements of ancient world. It probably remained unequaled for nearly 1,500 years, until Ibn Khaldun founded the science of sociological and historical analysis in the twelfth century. However, the difference is that Chanakya, as a highly successful practitioner, focused on administration of a state, and Ibn Khaldun, as a scientist who had withdrawn from an unsuccessful public life, was more interested in the process of societal change.

To summarize, Indian civilization, on balance, while retaining interest in formal sciences, shifted its focus from natural science to philosophy during the current phase. Ancient Greece expanded greatly and declined irreversibly but not before making a mark on several civilizations. While Alexander was directly responsible for the expansion of Greek world, he was also indirectly responsible for its scientific achievements during the Hellenistic period and for its ultimate destruction. Alexander valued Mesopotamian learning, and the Hellenistic states founded by Alexander needed the Greek military and intellectual talent to emigrate from Greece. This talent, when leveraged by the local talent and tax base, produced breakthroughs in geometry and astronomy. The leadership in natural science, thus, passed from India to Greek and the Hellenistic world for several centuries until the Roman Republic and Empire succeeded in conquering Greece and the Hellenistic world, killing the spirit of science. This spirit returned once again to India, as we shall discuss in the next chapter.

State of Productive Outcomes

The current phase was characterized by a rise of manufacturing and the first global trade linking Asia and Europe. This trade was mostly fair trade, since while the trade was global in scope the empire building was regional in scope, and thus empires had to cooperate in order to link the regional trade networks. It should also be clear that global trade was made possible through growth in manufactured goods that did not spoil and that were less voluminous and less expensive to export. While civilizations were getting wealthy through improvements in agricultural productivity and concomitant growth in the manufacturing sector and trade, the surplus also became more susceptible to its destruction through extended wars accompanied by destruction and looting. The rate of technological change during the phase was obviously low by modern standards. As a consequence, a successful, vibrant public manufacturing sector developed to cater to the wealthy elites in nearly all major civilizations. Peaceful migrations primarily such as populating southern China continued eastward, and southern migration in India occurred primarily within civilizations.

State of Constructive Outcomes

In parallel with and often in the wake of violent conflict, the constructive peaceful interaction continued and played its part.

Transmission of practical creativity: Diffusion of practical creativity gained momentum through global trade in the wake of military conflicts and the resulting migrations. It is both not necessary and difficult to trace the specific diffusion of key technologies

We can see that several key inventions, such using the horse, as an effective instrument of long-distance warfare, war tactics, and high-grade steel weapons set the stage for extended military conflicts among civilizations and between a civilization and the nomads from the central Asian steppes attacking the Indian and Chinese civilizations during this period.

Transmission of religious creativity: Although this phase was responsible for the birth of Jainism, Buddhism, and Christianity and their influence on civilizations responsible for their birth was enormous, the impact of the diffusion of religious creativity must be judged to be modest at best. There are several reasons for this. Both Buddhism and Jainism were tolerant of other faiths and did not push for conversions. Christianity was not tolerant of other faiths as it regarded Jesus as the only savior; however, both Christianity and Judaism lacked state power to push them during the current phase. It remained a bottom-up religion of the masses, with limited geographical reach, and it was still busy working out the coherence of its message. Buddhism spread outside of India, particularly in the central Asian region, Sri Lanka, and other Southeast Asian countries through the efforts of the Mauryan and Kushan Emperors, while Jainism essentially (except its influence on Pythagorean philosophy in ancient Greece) remained confined within the Indian subcontinent. The intolerant monotheistic religions, such as Islam, were yet to emerge.

Buddhism undoubtedly played a played in opening up the Silk Route and contributed to international trade.

Transmission of intellectual creativity: Prior to and including Alexander, there was likely a flow of knowledge from India and Mesopotamia to Greece through the travels of Pythagoras, Democritus, and others. Trough Alexander's misadventure in Asia made the Greeks appropriated Babylonian astronomy. In addition, although Aristotle set Greek thought on a more rational path (though not more experimental) in the late fourth century BCE, significant development of science actually occurred in the post-Alexander and post-Aristotle Hellenistic states, far away from Greece, under Egyptian and Indian influence. Unfortunately, the Roman Republic, the Roman Empire, and Persia were utterly unable to see the value in Greek–Hellenistic–Indian intellectual achievements Mesopotamia, ancient Greece, the Indian civilization, and the Hellenistic states all made outstanding creative contributions. Unfortunately, of these only the Indian civilization survived the current phase. In philosophical creativity, we have already traced the impact of Indian rationalism on Greek sophist philosophy. In artistic creativity, the Egyptian civilization impacted Grecian art, and the latter in turn impacted Roman and Persian art and architecture. Similarly, Mesopotamia must be rightly considered to have set ancient Greece on a path of great contributions in astronomy and away from the nonsensical armchair speculations of a Plato based on preexisting forms.

Peaceful migrations and fair trade: The prosperity of Indian, Persian, and Roman civilizations became linked through global trade, and it was a major factor in supporting creative endeavors in general and science in particular in post-Alexander Greece, the Hellenistic states, and post-Buddha India imbued with agnostic stirrings. Yet this growing surplus failed to support science in Roman and Persian civilizations. As noted before, peaceful migrations mostly occurred within civilizations and not between them.

Fortunately, this global trade, unlike the global trade controlled by European nation-states since 1500 CE, was essentially fair trade because while the trade was global, the empire building remained regional in scope. Thus, the phase may be thought of as an early form of globalization in the history of the world characterized by free movements of goods but not significant labor or capital. The entire phase was driven by global trade on the one hand and regional empire building on the other. The former depended on the latter in large measure.

Strictly speaking, only the Chinese civilization and Roman Empire retained political independence throughout this phase, because China managed to push the nomadic threat toward West and South Asia. The Roman Republic, followed by the Roman Empire, remained successful aggressors. From London in England to Gandhara in Northwest India, violence and regional intercivilization empire building was the name of the game during this phase.

The bottom line is that as a result of violent interactions, China remained China; Indian civilization benefited marginally from Greek learning; Romans rejected the Greek and Hellenistic learning except in art, architecture, and warfare; and nomads were successfully absorbed into civilizations. Mesopotamia, Egypt, ancient Greece, the Hellenistic states and the Achaemenid Empire did not survive, and world trade linking continents and civilizations came into existence. The civilizations' fate had become irreversibly interlinked, for better or worse. Greece, the Hellenistic states, and Indian civilization pushed the cause of science forward, learning from one another.

State of Destructive Outcomes

There was a marked increase in the destructive violence from civilizations and nomads, with extended wars among civilizations and civilization and nomads becoming a norm. The internal wars also intensified relatively compared to the previous phase. Fortunately, these destructive tendencies, in contrast to the later phases, did not have an accompanying intolerant creed. As a result, after wars, there was a clear tendency on the part of nomads to absorb into the conquered civilization and lose the separate identity. Alternatively, some multiethnic empires showed tolerance toward ethnic, religious, and linguistic diversity. Similarly, the possibility of systematic global wealth drain did not exist, given the state of manufacturing and transport technologies. To summarize, the destructive tendencies of civilizations and nomads remained limited because of the state of monotheism and manufacturing, transport, and weapons technologies. The nature of the destructive tendencies of some future civilizations makes this first phase with intercivilization conflict rather innocuous.

Thus, the phase essentially witnessed the destruction of Mesopotamian and Egyptian civilizations, the Achaemenid Empire, ancient Greece, and the post-Alexander Hellenistic states. The survivors were the Indian and Chinese civilizations and the newly established Parthian and Roman Empires. It was indeed quite a shake-up. It is pattern that will repeat in the future: the aggressive violent nomads of arid central Asia and dry West Asia and the civilization of colder Europe ultimately destroy one another, while peaceful Indian and Chinese civilizations somehow manage to survive.

Assessing the Inner Nature of Participants

13.57 Inner Nature of the Persian Empires

Productive capacity: The sustainable growing surplus at the empire's command was considerable, but due to military victories and territorial expansion and not necessarily due to improvements in productivity resulting from new technology adoption. The vast lands the empire controlled had low population density. Similarly, the significant role of the state and the priest in the economy, frequent luxurious lifestyle of the elite, and significant allocations to military all tended to limit economic freedom. Wealth allocation tended to favor military spending and trade expansion. The elite of the civilization vacillated between austerity and decadence. Consequently, class conflicts and wealth polarization probably swung back and forth, reflecting the vacillating attitude of upper classes. The internal wars, after the period of the consolidation of the empire, were decidedly moderate, as evidenced by the relatively low frequency and an exceptionally well managed first empire in the history of world. Thus, shifting of the surplus due to internal wars was nonexistent given the centralized nature and strength of the state. The equality of opportunity was at least moderate, given the absence of caste and slavery systems. However, Persians were favored for high positions. Despite being a motley collection of groups, social cohesion was surprisingly moderate and not low because the state allowed people religious freedom and a moderate equality of opportunity because the empire was not driven by an ideology, except that of territorial expansion. We would judge the productive capacity to be at best moderate.

Creative capacity: Creative freedom existed, as evidenced by religious freedom and support of art and architecture by the elite but was constrained by a rigid social structure, centralized authority, practical orientation, and a monotheistic disposition toward religion. The Persian Empire was open to the practical creativity of other civilizations and tolerant of religious diversity as mentioned above. However, there was lack of awareness of the importance of philosophy and science, and both empires had a strong militaristic orientation. Zoroastrianism practiced by the elite was relatively tolerant, as it was a monotheism under construction and one that had not yet acquired a self-righteousness, intolerance, or violence. The extensive far-flung empire comprised of many different ethnic groups required this tolerant attitude. The science-religion conflict favored religion, but the issue was moot for all practical purposes. The empire inherited the abstract systems-building capacity from Mesopotamia but made only modest use of it. Thus, creative capacity was moderate and narrow.

Constructive orientation: There was little geographical or linguistic isolation and little question of early success or failure against nomads since Achaemenid roots themselves were nomadic. The Achaemenids, a practical warrior people showed little interest in the world-class science of astronomy developed by neo-Babylonian astronomers but did cultivate Mesopotamian (and later Egyptian) art and architecture and probably acquired weapons technologies from all, including the Greeks. The empires clearly had a defensive military capability for most of the phase. It expanded trade with Indian civilization; however, both empires remained relatively uninterested in Mesopotamian, Indian, and Greek developments in mathematics and astronomy. It is indeed puzzling that Persia, which took to science after the Arab conquest in the next phase, remained utterly uninterested in it during the current phase. Perhaps the explanation is that Arabs conquered and initially foisted science on Persia. Thus, the constructive orientation may be characterized as type 1 openness, as evidenced by lack of interest in Babylonian astronomy despite a long history of learning from Mesopotamians.

Destructive orientation: It is difficult to detect elements of institutional greed or the presence of intolerant creed in the Persian Empire. Clearly, early success against major and minor civilizations, its nomadic roots, and the low natural bounty of the region contributed to the violent and aggressive character of the empires. As we have noted above, the Achaemenid Empire conquered Mesopotamian, Egyptian, Assyrian, and Elmite civilizations. The external orientation was necessarily violent, required of an empire builder with nomadic roots.

Thus, these empires harbored an insular empire-builder nature or a type IV external orientation.

13.58 Inner Nature of the Roman Republic

Productive capacity: The Roman world's prosperity rested primarily on conquest and expansion. Its economy was agrarian and based on slaves. Manufacturing focused on luxury and military technology, with government playing a dominant role in trading within and with other civilizations. The economic freedom must be judged moderate at best, as would be the new technology adoption. The SGS remained low, but as the Roman Republic succeeded in conquering North Africa, Greece, and the Hellenistic states, the absolute magnitude kept increasing. Its wealth allocation definitely favored military spending and the elite lifestyle. The equality of opportunity must also be judged to be low. Slavery, slave revolts, and wars of succession continued to tear its social fabric apart. Surprisingly, its social cohesion was high during the current phase, because of its strong military and a formal legal code. As long as wars of succession were kept in check, the stability of SGS control remained high. It is often stated that the ensuing Roman Empire (discussed in the next phase in greater detail) declined because of decadence; however, the deciding factor was continuation of the decadent lifestyle in the absence of new conquests (result of rising strength of barbarians). We judge the fundamental productive capacity to be moderate at best both because of intrinsic and natural causes.

Creative capacity: What is curious about Roman world is that, despite modest creative freedom, little science-religion conflict and relative openness to the creativity of other civilizations, its contributions remained confined to art, architecture (derived mostly from ancient Greece), and law. It seems to us that this must be the fate of a social order whose existence depends not on industry and science but on power and conquest. The Roman Republic did not lack abstract systems-building capability. The entire structure of the Roman world was, however, fine-tuned to support new military campaigns and the lifestyle of those in power. It had no higher objective. Thus, its internal creative balance remained type A or practical, but unlike the Chinese in later phases, it was not particularly prolific except in law and military matters. Legal code and roads built for military campaigns may be the Roman world's only worthwhile legacy. Its creative capacity may be characterized as high but narrow.

Constructive orientation: The Roman Republic was not geographically or linguistically isolated, and it did not have to deal with nomads from a posture of weakness. Trade between Rome and India flourished. However, they showed little interest in Greek and Indian philosophy and science. The Roman Empire, as we shall see in the next phase, killed Hellenistic science through neglect, and it adopted Christianity to prolong the empire after its persecuted population embraced Christianity. It almost seems as if the Roman world was a reaction to ancient Greece and the Hellenistic states. The conquerors refused to value the science and philosophy of the defeated. If Greeks and the Hellenistic states loved knowledge, Romans were far more practical. If the Hellenistic states attempted to synthesize their polytheism with Christianity, the Roman Empire initially tried to persecute the Christians. If the Greeks did not develop overseas trade away from Mediterranean and chose to settle overseas instead, the Romans excelled in it. In short, the Roman psyche developed in reaction to Greek psyche, except in practical areas, such as military capability, architecture, and practical technology. Thus, the constructive capacity of Rome must be judged type 1 openness.

Destructive orientation: The city of Rome was founded around 753 BCE, about the time Greece established colonies in southern Italy. For several centuries, both the Roman monarchy and the Roman Republic watched the rise of Greek power in awe. After Alexander died and the center of Greek power moved east to Hellenistic states, Roman expansion began in earnest and absorbed the Greek colonies after the Pyrrhic wars. Here again, the Roman psyche reacted to the Greek psyche. If Greeks conquered and settled in foreign lands, Romans conquered and transferred the wealth to Rome by maintaining long-distance control. If Greeks went east in search of empire, Romans went west. If Greeks were often Spartan, no luxury was too much for Roman elites. If Greeks could not and did not convert the conquered population into slaves, Romans readily did. What they had in common, however, was the aggression, violence, and empire building to compensate for low natural bounty and population density. They differed in their attitudes toward intellectual and religious creativity, as noted above. Thus, the orientation was aggression and violence, though with a difference: Greeks were empire-builder settlers, and Romans were systematic wealth drainers through long-distance territorial control in part because their empire was in frigid Europe or in desert lands in Africa that they considered unworthy of settlement. The Roman world thus needed and developed institutional greed, though not an intolerant creed. The English copied this model two millennia later, but the English displayed type 3 openness.

The Roman world's external orientation was insular and violent or type VIII.

Bottom line: Between the Greeks and Romans, the pattern of aggression with or without openness to the creativity of other civilizations and with a propensity for wealth drain was set for the European civilization for next two millennia.

13.59 Inner Nature of the Central Asian Nomads

We need not work too hard to assess inner nature of early central Asian nomads. What makes a nomad a nomad is a very low productive capacity, low and narrow creative capacity (despite an admirable tribal equality) except in military technology, a relatively high constructive capacity, and an extremely high destructive capacity, often bordering on cruelty. As we shall see in the following chapters, successive waves of central Asians invaders became increasingly more sophisticated picking up writing, religion, technology, and city dwelling from civilizations. It would be indeed difficult to characterize Babur in the sixteenth century as a nomad.

13.60 Inner Nature of the Ancient Greek Civilization (Up to Alexander)

Productive capacity: The economic freedom in the Greek city-states was highly selective, given that as many as three-fourth of the population were slaves. (Even in the city of Athens at its height in the fifth century BCE, slaves constitute one-third of the population.) Women had a second-class status, despite limited government role in the economy and low taxation. The new technology adoption was probably modest as well since economic activity had low status in general. Similarly, nonagricultural production was subordinated to participation in the political, artistic, physical, and social activities, though ceramic, bronze casting, and wrought iron technologies were practiced. These follow from the high proportion of slaves and a very elitist social structure that lived off the countryside produce without participating in it, though controlling it. The balance in wealth allocation was good. Natural terrain was not very cooperative, resulting in terrible, long-lasting internal wars. The equality of opportunity was definitely very poor, given the number of slaves. Their belief in democracy was elitist at best.

We would judge the social cohesion to be moderate, given the absence of revolts among slaves. SGS control fluctuated because of ongoing internal wars. In their zeal to ascribe everything modern to ancient Greece, some Western historians have attempted to argue that ancient Greece had a market economy. Nothing could be farther from the truth. Internal trade was modest, but city-states controlled overseas trade states to ensure grain and timber to the cities and was paid for in silver. The economy was thoroughly monetized with wide circulation of coins. The economy was structured around the wealthy and foreign trade to create revenue to fight wars with other cities. The productive capacity must be judged as moderate.

Creative capacity: The economic structure did provide a small minority of males the needed time and money to engage or encourage creative endeavors such as sculpture, architecture, and philosophical debates when not fighting another state. Creative freedom for this group must be judged to be high but problematic in part because ancient Greek would not think twice about executing a Socrates. Science-religion conflict was low because Greek religion never went beyond naive polytheism despite attempts by Pythagoras to learn about Indian religious doctrines. The abstract systems-building capability was world-class. We would judge creative capacity to be high and broad.

Constructive orientation: Ancient Greece solved the problem of geographic isolation early on by developing seagoing capability and never had to deal with nomadic threat. As a result, Greeks were open to influence from Phoenicians in language; from Indians in religion, science, and philosophy; from Mesopotamians in astronomy; and from Egyptians in art throughout the existence of both ancient Greece and its progeny, the Hellenistic states. Ancient Greece clearly possessed defense military capability to engage in constructive interaction with other civilizations. However, it often chose the path of war and destruction. The openness must be characterized as type 4.

Destructive orientation: Right from the beginning, ancient Greece practiced local empire building on a massive scale. It had a pugnacious, destructive internal nature, and their need to establish colonies in Italy and Anatolia to meet population pressures and the military genius of young and charismatic Alexander formed the foundation of turning ancient Greece into a violent, destructive empire builder. Again, Western historians go into ecstasy describing Alexander's achievement, forgetting that central Asian nomads performed equal or greater feats. After all, during most of history, it only took few tens of thousands of soldiers and an able commander to bring down a peaceful civilization. Alexander does indeed rank up there with Timur and Genghis Khan in destruction and cruelty.

Thus, ancient Greece had an external orientation of an open empire builder or a type III external orientation.

13.61 Inner Nature of the Hellenistic States (Post-Alexander)

Productive capacity: In the Hellenistic states in West Asia and Egypt the synthesis of the Greeks and local cultures changed the scale and quality of economies with a greater emphasis on manufacturing, less on holding slaves, and a much enhanced role for the government. The Greeks did not interfere with Asian agriculture and manufacturing, and the economies of the Hellenistic states were becoming more monetized with greater overseas trade because of their location on the Silk Route. The economic freedom was high, with new technology adoption accelerating and wealth allocation becoming a little more balanced. Even equality of opportunity improved since the slavery system was not as pronounced and as elitist democracy withered. The social cohesion was not bad since Greeks showed willingness to both challenge and be ultimately absorbed into the local cultures. The SGS control was not particularly stable since there were unending wars because of Roman pressure and wars of succession in these states. Productive capacity in Hellenistic states far exceeded than what was possible in ancient Greece.

Creative capacity: Hellenistic states had a balanced role of religion and allowed creative freedom until they succumbed to Christian dogma. It had inherited the high abstract systems-building capability from the Greeks and clearly allowed local talent to emerge. Astronomer Ptolemy was of Egyptian origin, as an example. We would characterize the creative capacity during the post-Alexander but pre-Christian period as very high. Western historians often exaggerate the scientific contributions of the ancient Greeks before Alexander so as to downplay the post-Alexander outcomes by comparison. Mingling resulted in great strides in astronomy based on the new science of geometry and its application to astronomy in the Hellenistic states, away from the influence of Greek philosophical idealism. With the rise of the Christian faith and the resulting attempts at a religious synthesis, the creative capacity of the Hellenistic world began to slide even before they were conquered and absorbed into the Roman Empire. For the phase as a whole, creative capacity remained high and broad.

Constructive orientation: Hellenistic states had type 4 openness and were often strong enough to engage in peaceful interaction. They benefited from the opening of the Silk Route. The surviving Hellenistic states in Anatolia and Egypt fared a lot better than Hellenistic state under pressure from the Roman Empire. Greeks on the northwestern border of India converted to Buddhism and likely influenced Indian art and astronomy.

Destructive orientation: The Greek destructive impulse turned defensive during the Hellenistic period because its fighting capability was continually bested by Persians, Romans, and Indians in part because they were away from home base, though they had been established in new lands for centuries. However, they had set themselves as superiors and never fully integrated into local culture until it became necessary. The moderating influence of a compassionate religion like Buddhism was clearly limited to the Indo-Greeks, so clearly evident in the great Menander, the Indo-Greek monarch. Still, the destructive orientation remained violent. The Hellenistic states, not the Romans or even pre-Alexander Greece, set the template of aggression and openness for the European civilization when it was not under the sway of Christian dogma.

Thus, the external orientation was that of an open empire builder or type III.

13.62 Inner Nature of the Chinese Civilization

Productive capacity: Although there was great concentration in landholding toward the end of the phase, the Chinese farmer enjoyed a lighter tax burden, and government intervened to control prices from plummeting. The role of government in manufacturing was a heavy though often wise one. Government controlled trade most of the time. Thus, economic freedom for the famers and artisans was high, since traders and landlords were kept on a short leash. There was considerable use of new technologies in agriculture and manufacturing. We would judge new technology adoption to be high. Wealth allocation favored military strength and must be judged to have only a moderate balance. Equality of opportunity did not deteriorate and internal wars moderated except toward the end of the phase. Social cohesion also improved as power returned to the central authority through the Han dynasty. All this meant a more stable SGS. We would judge the productive capacity to continue to be high.

Creative capacity: The combination of protecting the small farmer from landlords and traders and the government role in manufacturing pushed for new practical technology to burst forth. We would characterize the creative freedom high in principle but held back in the religious, philosophical, and scientific arena because of the lack of alphabetical script, resulting in its expression mostly in the practical realm. Similarly, the science-religion conflict hardly existed since neither science nor formal religion existed, much like the Roman Empire. It continued to suffer from the lack of an abstract systems-building capability. It was so oblivious of the coming explosion of practical inventions in the next two phases, that we would assess the creative capacity of the Chinese civilization to be modest and narrow.

Constructive orientation: Despite geographic and linguistic isolation, Chinese civilization became open to religious creativity from the Indian civilization but not without internal struggle. China had sufficient defensive military capability to keep the nomads at bay and to engage constructively with other civilizations. The current phase was one of the few times the Chinese civilization was a bit open to the outside world. Chinese civilization displayed an uncharacteristic type 2 openness during the phase.

Destructive orientation: China remained peaceful and maintained only a defensive posture against the nomads who continued to challenge the civilization. Thus, China still continued to have an insular and peaceful or type II external orientation.

13.63 Inner Nature of the Indian Civilization

Productive capacity: With the exception of the Mauryan period, when government role in the economy was greater, the economy exhibited high economic freedom, as evidenced by the number of guilds, the extent of internal and external trade, the role of money, and the absence of landlords. The new technology adoption was also high, with widespread use of iron tools in agriculture. Equality of opportunity did not change significantly, since the impact of the influx of nomadic invaders challenged a hardening caste system. Earlier during this phase, the caste system showed signs of becoming more rigid and later becoming less rigid under the influence of Buddhism and foreign influx. The internal wars became more frequent because of internal empire building and external invasions through four separate waves in the post-Alexander period: resources had to be diverted to military preparedness, long periods of political instability had to be endured, and the foreign elements had to be absorbed into the Indian civilization. Social cohesion was high as well since foreigners and invaders successfully adopted Indian culture readily. Thus, the civilization exhibited a high sustainable growing surplus and a high productive capacity.

Creative capacity: Creative freedom remained high and broad, as evidenced by tolerant religious attitudes with Hinduism, Buddhism, and Jainism working out their philosophical positions through debate. There was no science-religion conflict, with scholars of entirely differing religious persuasion debating their differences in public. The idea of a Socrates being punished by death would have horrified Indians of the day. The abstract systems-building capability remained high. The creative capacity remained high and deep, though physical sciences tended to take a back seat to formal sciences and philosophy.

Constructive orientation: Clearly, the civilization exhibited type 4 openness as it integrated foreign elements and knowhow into the Indian civilization. Fortunately, foreigners had not brought an intolerant or violent religious ideology. The defensive military capability in the post-Mauryan period declined severely. As a result, constructive interaction typically took place in the wake of empire building by central Asian nomads, Persians, and Indo-Greeks. The Indian civilization exhibited a peaceful open external orientation during the phase, with a focus on trade with Europe, West Asia, China, and Southeast Asia. These were by no means entirely helpful factors as far as creativity is concerned. However, later diffusion of Greek art and Hellenistic astronomy were positive contributions, preparing Indian civilization for its next creative jump. In short, the openness existed despite a fluid political situation.

Destructive orientation: Indian civilization never indulged in empire building across civilizations despite multiple invasions that resulted in the rise and fall of several foreign empires in the wake of Ashoka's ill-advised pacifism. Despite coming in contact with inter-civilization empire builders, the Indian civilization did not adopt the ways of the invaders. It remained peaceful toward other civilizations. More pointedly, the invaders gave up dreams of conquest outside the confines of Indian civilization, perhaps because they could hardly conquer all of the Indian subcontinent, they got the control of the fertile land they wanted, or were influenced by Indian religiosity and openness.

The Indian civilization continued to display an open and peaceful or a type I external orientation.

The key parameters that measure the changing inner nature of key participants in the current phase are summarized in table 13.1.

13.64 The Inner Nature of Participants at the End of the First Synthesis

Persian Empires

The inner nature of the Persian empires during the phase consisted of moderate productive capacity as represented by its moderate internal SGS, a narrow type A creative capacity, a type 1 constructive orientation, and a violent, empire builder destructive orientation. It, therefore, had type IV external orientation.

Roman Republic

The inner nature of the Roman Republic during the phase consisted of moderate productive capacity, as evidenced by its moderate internal SGS, a continuing type A creative capacity, a type 1 constructive orientation, and a violent, empire builder destructive orientation. It also had a type IV external orientation.

Central Asian Nomads

The inner nature of central Asian nomads during the phase consisted of low productive capacity, type A creative capacity, type 4 constructive orientation, and a violent and cruel destructive orientation. It thus had type III external orientation.

Ancient Greece

The inner nature of ancient Greece during the phase consisted of moderate productive capacity, as evidenced from its moderate internal SGS; a type C creative capacity, a type 4 constructive orientation, and the cruel, destructive orientation of an empire builder with a type III external orientation.

Hellenistic States

The inner nature of the surviving Hellenistic states during the phase consisted of high productive capacity, a type 4

Table 13.1: Relative Values of Measurable Parameters of Social Orders
First Synthesis Phase, 550 BCE–200 CE

Measurable Parameters	Productive Capacity					Creative Capacity			Constructive Orientation				Destructive Orientation		
	NB	EF	NTA	WAB	SC	Creed	ASBC	WAB	GI	ESAN	LI	Creed	NB	IG	IC
Persian	Med	Med	Med	MS	Med	Bal.	Med	MS	Low	N/A	Low	Bal.	Med	Med	Yes
Roman Repub.	Med	Low	Med	MS/ED	Med	SRC	High	MS/ED	Low	N/A	Low	SRC	Med	High	Yes
Central Asian	Low	High	Low	MS	High	Bal.	Low	MS	High	N/A	Low	Bal.	Low	High	No
Ancient Greece	Med	Med	Med	CE	High	Bal.	High	CE	Low	N/A	Low	Bal.	Med	Med	Yes
Hellenistic St.	Med	High	Med	CE	Med	Bal.	High	CE	Low	N/A	Low	Bal.	Med	Med	Yes
Chinese	high	High	High	PE	High	Bal.	Low	PE	High	Yes	High	Bal.	High	None	No
Indian	High	High	High	CE	Med	ES	High	CE	Low	No	Low	ES	High	None	No

NB: Degree of Natural Bounty ASBC: Abstract Sys. Building Capability ED: Favors Elite Decadence ES: Excessively Spiritual
EF: Economic Freedom GI: Geographic Isolation MS: Favors Military Spending SRC: Sci. Religion Conflict
NTA: New Tech. Adoption ESAN: Early Success against Nomads PE: Favors Productive Endeavors Bal: Balanced
WAB: Wealth Allocation Bal. LI: Linguistic Isolation CE: Supports Creative Endeavors
SC: Social Cohesion IG: Institutional Greed
IC: Intolerant Creed

creative capacity, a type 4 constructive orientation, and a violent destructive orientation. Thus, it too had a type III external orientation.

Chinese Civilization

The inner nature of Chinese civilization during the phase consisted of high productive capacity because of high internal SGS, an intensified type A creative capacity, a type 2 constructive orientation, and a peaceful destructive orientation. It thus had a type II external orientation.

Indian Civilization

The inner nature of Indian civilization during the phase consisted of high productive capacity as represented by a high internal SGS, a type C creative capacity, a type 4 constructive orientation, and a peaceful destructive orientation. The external orientation is type I.

Table 13.2 summarizes the comparative inner nature of significant social orders at the end of the first synthesis phase.

Table 13.2: Comparative Inner Nature of Civilizations
First Synthesis Phase: 550 BCE–200 CE

Social Order	Productive Capacity	Creative Capacity	Constructive Orientation	Destructive Orientation	
	Internal SGS	ICB	O/I	P/V	SPI
Persian	Moderate	Type A	Type 1	Violent	Yes
Roman Republic	Moderate	Type A	Type 1	Violent	Yes
Central Asian	Low	Type A	Type 4	Violent	Yes
Ancient Greece	Moderate	Type C	Type 4	Violent	Yes
Hellenistic St.	High	Type C	Type 4	Violent	Mixed
Chinese	High	Type A	Type 1	Peaceful	Yes
Indian	High	Type C	Type 4	Peaceful	Mixed

Legend
SGS: Sustainable Growing Surplus
ICB: Internal Creative Balance
O/I: Openness/Insularity
P/V: Peaceful/Violent
SPI: Sustained Political Independence

The Evolution and Rationalization of the First Synthesis of Science

13.65 First Synthesis in Science

In this first of the four chapters that focus on the development stage of science, we want to draw attention to the Babylonian-Greek-Hellenistic-Indian synthesis of science, which covers a substantial period beginning around 550 BCE or less than two centuries before the founding of the Maurya Empire in India. It endured through the Roman Republic's success in extinguishing the flame of science in Greece around 150 BCE and ended when its successor state, the Roman Empire, delivered a similar, final blow to Hellenistic science by about 200 CE.

It was not just regional empire building and global trade that defined this phase; it may also be characterized by a third critical element, that of steady exchange of ideas and inventions among civilizations that occurred in the wake of empire building and trade. This exchange of ideas and inventions, the intensity of which the world had never witnessed before, though slow by today's standards, was often mediated and forgotten later. The key conduits for this exchange of ideas were pre-Alexander travel by Greeks to Mesopotamia and India, Alexander's invasion itself, Seleucid-Mauryan connection (320–185 BCE), Indo-Greek kingdoms (239–130 BCE), and Indian-Roman trade (200 BCE). No doubt, the quality and extent of these contacts and communications varied significantly over these seven centuries; however, there can be little doubt that, in sum, these contacts were highly significant, if forgotten. It is also difficult to ascertain how symmetrical these communications were, either since unlike Indians, Chinese, and Arabs, the Greeks and later European thinkers only infrequently acknowledged mediated or even direct foreign sources of knowledge. This was probably in part due to excessive individualism and in part due to the indirect nature of most such evolving, distant communications. We believe these contacted were rather one-sided, with information mostly flowing from Indian, Egyptian, and Mesopotamian sources to the Greek and Hellenistic world in the pre-Alexander period. The diffusion of knowledge definitely became more symmetrical about a century after Alexander's invasion.

This first synthesis was not a conscious and deliberate synthesis of Greek, Hellenistic, Indian, and historic Mesopotamian achievements in astronomy. It was perhaps too early in the history for conscious synthesis in part because the self-consciousness of civilizations was not yet that strong and in part because the origin and genealogy of ideas and inventions was not established in the eyes of the participating civilizations. Any discussion of this synthesis must include the achievements of the Indo-Greek branch of Hellenistic states that became trapped between the Parthian Empire in Persia and the Mauryan and its successor empires in India. Judging from Gandhara art alone, these achievements were substantial. It is also true that Indo-Greeks were cut off from the Hellenistic states early on and came to be substantially identified with Indian religion and culture. Thus, during the current phase, scientific creativity primarily refers to pre- and post-Alexander and parallel and overlapping achievements in Greece, Hellenistic, and Indian civilizations with each now consciously and unconsciously building on the success of others. In this respect, it was indeed a unique phase:

- The development of science took place in parallel with Indian and Greek civilizations and Hellenistic states, with each focusing on a somewhat different aspect of science.
- The linkages among these civilizations were substantial if unconscious. However, these linkages are often minimized by some Western historians.
- The linkages resulted from both peaceful and violent interactions.

Thus, this first synthesis differed from the syntheses that followed in important respects. The later syntheses, such as the Indian, Arab, Italian, and western Europeans that we shall discuss in chapters 14, 15, and 16 are different from this first synthesis in that these later syntheses were more conscious that they were synthesizing the scientific achievements of their own and other civilizations. The syntheses were continuous in time and were achieved by an undisputed emergent new leader in scientific creativity during that phase. By contrast, this synthesis had three distinct living, sequential, or parallel centers: those of ancient Greece, the Indian civilization, and the Hellenistic state as well as the foundational achievements of Mesopotamian civilization in astronomy and those of Egypt in art. There was no emergent undisputed leader, and the communication between these centers was far from perfect. Yet, there is no denying that sporadic communication existed and was responsible for cross-fertilization. If ancient Greece appears to dominate this phase retrospectively, it is not because other civilizations of the time recognized this or because Greece achieved all that they had achieved independently. It is only because of the unabashed attempt of modern Western civilization to write a revisionist history.

Linking Babylonian, Hellenistic, and Indian Science

As we have stated before, ideas do not respect civilization boundaries. It is not just marching armies that can carry the ideas. Travelers, both common people and scholars, as well as trade can achieve the same objective. In the latter case, it is usually difficult to trace the path of ideas since even the receiver may not be aware of the source, or if he is aware, he may not be willing to acknowledge the source. The true history of the birth of science, as we saw in the last chapter, suffers from a deliberate distortion of Indian history created by the hypothesis of the Aryan invasion in 1500 BCE by Max Mueller and British imperialists, with such distortion made possible by the existence of strong oral tradition in Indian civilization. These two, in an unholy alliance, had the effect distorting the chronology of Indian history by pushing it forward. Similarly, the true history of the Hellenistic-Indian phase suffers from an insufficient understanding of the linkages and communication that occurred among the Indian, Babylonian, Greek, and Hellenistic traditions. The Western story of this has been based on minimizing the importance of this linkage as well as on treating the ancient Greece and Hellenistic world as identical. Ancient Greece was a homogeneous single cultural entity that held the promise, while the Hellenistic states were a seething mixture of multicultural identities that actually produced science. Below, we summarize observations on the links among the scientific activities in India, Babylonia, Greece, and the Hellenistic states over the period 550 BCE to 200 CE in an attempt to draw a comprehensive picture.

- **Historic India/Babylonia communication:** Trade between India and Mesopotamia, as we saw earlier in chapter 10, can be traced back to 3000 BCE. The full extent of the relationship between Indian and Babylonian protoscience remains unclear, although Seidenberg (1961) concluded that geometry (including the Pythagoras theorem) with an essential proof by construction and mathematics in Sulbha Sutras contain codification of knowledge going as far back as 1700 BCE, and Babylonian mathematics has Indian roots. Given the similarities between Indian and Mesopotamian astronomy and given the existence of trade between Mesopotamia and India over the preceding millennia, Seidenberg may not be too far off the mark. However, the rise of the Achaemenid Empire substantially reduced direct India/Babylon trade and communication. It did not kill it, however.

- **India/ Greece communication:** As we have touched on before, the similarities between the Upanishads and the philosophy of Heraclitus, the religious leaning of Pythagoras and Jainism, the Hippocratic concept of three humors and Ayurveda's three doshas, and the science of Kannada and Democritus are too close to be lightly dismissed. Democritus is known to have visited Babylonia, Egypt, and Ethiopia, and recent research has claimed that he also visited India, though given the Babylonian/Indian connection, he did not have to go to India to learn the epistemology and atomism of Kannada. In addition, how does one explain the discontinuity between Plato's preexisting ideal forms and down-to-earth Aristotle's philosophy? Could that have occurred through the mediation of Kannada's epistemology? Incidentally, it is known that Plato hated Democritus and ordered all his books burned.

- **Greece/Babylonia communication:** Babylonian astronomical knowledge was transmitted to the Greeks through Alexander, who likely ordered Callisthenes to translate the astronomical records and have them sent to Aristotle. However, this is acknowledged only rarely; the translation was titled *Teresis*, meaning *guard* in Greek, which is a rough translation of the Babylonian title, *Massartu*! Why the reluctance to acknowledge the source? One wonders about the psychological motivation at work. Perhaps because there was little astronomy in Greece before that.

- **India/Hellenistic communication:** By the time of Alexander, the flow of ideas and knowledge between India and the Hellenistic states must have been like a perennial monsoon shower, yet we see little reference to foreign sources by the Greeks. Sure enough, the historians like Herodotus and ambassadors like Magsthenes to the court of Chandragupta knew a lot about Indian civilization and were admirers of its greatness; however, few Greek scientists acknowledged Indian or other sources. Could it be that a historian must, of necessity, show his superior knowledge of other cultures to be accepted as a historian, and a scientist must hide his? In addition to this, the Indian-Roman trade must have been a great source for transferring ideas and knowledge. The presence of the so-called Indo-Greeks, trapped between the Persian and Maurya Empires, were yet another source. Gandhara art points to a flow of Greek artists to Northwest India. Is it reasonable to assume that that this flow was limited to artists and was one way?

Clearly, a lot more research is needed to nail these communications down specifically. However, there can be little doubt that these communications and exchange of ideas were a potent factor underlying the first synthesis. Indian and Babylonian civilizations freely shared their knowledge with the Greeks, without the latter acknowledging that. Babylonia was absorbed into the antiscience Persian Empire, and Indian intellectual creativity took a temporary detour to focus on the working out the ethical, epistemological, and ontological implications of Buddhism and Jainism. Thus, during the current phase, the further development of natural science drifted toward the multicultural Hellenistic states, in effect living on borrowed time.

However, we must never forget that pre-Alexander Greek philosophical and scientific creativity (Pythagoras, Plato, and Democritus), to the extent it was not based on Indian rationalism represented by Jain and Buddhist doctrines and Indian science represented by Kannada and Zoroastrianism was pretty mundane, inaccurate, and speculative. Only in the post-Alexander Hellenistic states did breakthroughs in geometry occur after Greeks absorbed the Babylonian-India astronomy and beginnings in geometry. The rules inherent in Indian-Babylonian astronomy used to predict the motion of the planets and occurrences of the solar and lunar eclipses formed the basis for the new science of geometry. The science of geometry was in fact a brilliant generalization of the properties of linear space these rules assumed, governing the motion of planets and occurrence of eclipses. That is why we have called the current phase the Babylonian-Hellenistic-Indian synthesis.

13.66 Rationalizing the First Synthesis in Science

As noted in chapter 9, the rationalization of science in the violent interaction era will be carried out using the inner nature of relevant social orders, provided care is taken to distinguish between invaded, defeated, and aggressor civilizations or states thereof.

Why Persian Empires Did Not Give Birth to Science

Two distinct periods concern ancient Persian protoscience and aborted science. The first period spanned from Zoroaster (likely born around the tenth century BCE) to Cyrus, who unified the Median and Persian empires in 550 BCE or a period of about five centuries. The second period ended by Arab conquest in the seventh century CE or a period of more than a millennium. The destruction of Avesta and the mass killing of the Magi priests in a fit of jealousy by Alexander in the fourth century BCE, as noted earlier, not only makes it difficult to assess Persian protoscience but also explains why Persians did not move along the path that could have resulted in birth of science or at a minimum show interest in Indian and later Greek science. However, we did not consider ancient Persia during the protoscience phase for two reasons: little information of the period survives and the Zoroastrian system likely did not go beyond critical religion and philosophy to venture into formal and natural sciences.

Being sandwiched between the Indian and the Mesopotamian civilizations, it is indeed difficult to conceive that ancient Persia before the imperial period beginning 550 BCE was not influenced by both. The linguistic similarity between the Sanskrit of Rig Veda and Gatha of Avesta implies more than common origin and considerable reciprocal influence. Zoroastrianism's underlying belief is not different from Indian monism, with a self-creating universe that ultimately results in the emergence of consciousness. However, it is clear based on the writings of Greek authors themselves that Zoroaster was the original inspiration for philosophers of ancient Greece (just as Phoenicia was the inspiration for alphabetical script, ancient Egypt the inspiration for art, ancient Mesopotamia for astronomy, and ancient India for science).

Returning to the current phase, the Persian Empire was more of an empire and less of a civilization early in the phase but was becoming more of the latter by the end of the phase. The multiethnic civilization symbolized by the Persian Empire was the first warring civilization in history. In fact, the conquest of neo-Babylonian state and the expansion of the empire mark the beginning of the era of extended military conflicts in our framework. This turn to imperialism and Alexander's later destruction had a decisive impact on Persia. Let us look at the key elements driving the inner nature of the Persian empires/civilization:

Internal SGS: The internal SGS in the beginning was very low indeed, as the Amadai people from Anatolia were nomads. As they unified and conquered new territories, the SGS increased but remained moderate because of limited population and the productivity of the land, even after Achaemenids conquered Mesopotamia and Egypt.

Allocation of SGS: The SGS was not only moderate but also allocation since 550 BCE strongly favored military spending and a fluctuating, decadent lifestyle of the elite. In addition, allocation to imperial roads and waterworks was significant to keep the empire together and to provide water for the population and farms respectively. With the unification of the Persian and Median empires in 550 BCE by Cyrus, the influence of the Magi priests declined as the Persian culture turned imperialistic and devoted its energies to conquering Mesopotamian and Egyptian civilizations and the administration of the empire. The second and decisive blow came from Alexander, when he destroyed the Avesta and the Magi.

Nature of creed: Zoroastrianism had encouraged the development of philosophy and would likely have led to the birth of science. As noted earlier there are strong reasons to believe the original Greeks philosophers were reluctant and closet Zoroastrians. However, imperial focus won the day after 550 BCE.

State of its ASBC: The state of ASBC did not go beyond understanding the creative method and the existence of alphabetical script since the critical philosophy of Zoroaster remained in a state of suspended animation starting with Cyrus as it succeeded in educating the now famous philosophers of ancient Greece. With the emergence of the Parthian Empire (an empire that did not draw inspiration from Zoroastrianism, unlike the later Sassanians) less than a hundred years after Alexander's destruction, Persian culture continued to move away from critical thinking and focused on imperialism, right up to the Muslim conquest.

Openness/insularity: The turn toward imperialism strongly impacted the openness to the intellectual creativity of other civilizations. Achaemenid did not value Mesopotamian astronomy, for example.

Nature of violent greed: The empire-building enterprise added new territories and population, thus increasing the SGS considerably. However, this wealth was transferred to the center only to a modest degree to pay for administration, military capability, and an elite lifestyle. It thus did not increase poverty among the conquered, and their land was not usurped or their population displaced. The conquerors simply replaced indigenous elites.

Thus, throughout its thousand year-plus history from Cyrus up to Arab conquest, the imperial spirit of Persia continued to reassert itself time and again. That spirit is the spirit to build empires, create efficient centralized structures, a predisposition toward monotheism, interest in artistic and architectural creation, in short, a spirit of practical creativity and religious dogma. Although Persia was in living contact with Mesopotamia and came in contact with Indians and Greeks time and again, it was, despite the glorious Zoroastrian period, unable to light the flame of philosophical and scientific creativity during its long history until arrival of Islam, not counting a short exception in the sixth century CE that proved the rule. The answer lies in the combination of rigid, centralized social and political structures on the one hand and an increasingly dogmatic religion on the other, thus producing a culture that was devoid of both economic and creative freedom despite wealth and sustained political independence. Why Islam ignited the change in Persia is a question we must defer to later chapters.

To summarize, Achaemenid and the Parthian Empire were unable to give birth to science despite a glorious Zoroastrian past mainly because Persia turned imperialistic at the beginning of the current phase, thus impacting its SGS allocation and openness to others' creativity and because Alexander destroyed both the records of accumulated knowledge and the Magi priest-scholars. These empires represent an imperial and regressive period of Persian culture until it was shaken by the Arabs.

Why the Roman Republic and Roman Empire Could Not Give Birth to Science

Unlike the Persians, the Roman Empire cannot boast of a Zoroastrian interested in critical philosophy or reflective metaphysics. Quite the contrary, the Romans not only ignored the Greek science but also actively killed Hellenistic science, choosing to adopt Christian dogma instead, thus setting back the course of European civilization by more than a millennium.

Internal SGS: The government and landlords controlled large sectors of the economy, including mining and agriculture. The internal SGS remained moderate but was substantially augmented by conquest, slaves, and trade with other civilizations, including the Indian civilization. The source of Roman wealth was land acquisition through aggression and subsequent wealth drain and use of slaves, both Romans and those acquired through wars and not freedom-based industriousness.

Allocation of SGS: The elite decadence and military capability consumed most of the SGS. The whole purpose of the Roman Empire was territorial expansion and a good life for the elites. Its extensive roads, metallurgy, highly developed legal code, art, and architecture all served the needs of the elite, which did not care about intellectual creation.

Nature of creed: Throughout most of history, Roman experienced little science-religion conflict for they had neither to boast of. After initially persecuting Christians, they rejected their crude polytheism and adopted Christianity when it became expedient to do so.

State of ASBC: Roman abstract systems-building capability remained weak. It had mastered the creative method and possessed an alphabetical script. Its arithmetic capability was rather modest and did not develop epistemology. Its logic found expression in legal code and practical creativity but not in religious or scientific creativity.

Openness/insularity: Romans had highly selective openness to the creativity of others, mostly in practical technologies of interest to an empire-builder and luxury-seeker.

Nature of violent greed: The violent greed of Romans displayed a different character compared to that of Persians in that after Romans conquered a territory, they did not just replace the defeated royalty. Their control went deeper, with Roman families controlling the wealth of the territory through not just taxation in the name of empire but also the production of the wealth. Thus Romans engaged in systematic wealth drain, which they squandered on military capability and luxurious lifestyle of the elite senatorial families.

Thus, despite sustained political independence, substantial wealth, alphabetical script, and the absence of science-religion conflict, the Roman period was a colossal waste from the standpoint of science. The Roman world resembled the Persian empires in this respect, only worse. The absence of creed and the presence of wealth obtained through empire building did not help the Roman world give birth to or nurture science, since it lacked openness to the creativity of others unless that creativity directly helped in the expansion and maintenance of the empire.

Why Chinese Civilization Did Not Give Birth to Science

Again and again, we will return to this theme in Chinese history: relatively little scientific and religious innovation, great practical innovation and preindustrial wealth-creation ability, long stretches of sustained political independence, unending insularity, peaceful external orientation, and a stubborn refusal to adopt alphabetical script. China lacked destructive orientation, though internal conflicts were unending during periods when nomads weakened central authority. However, was not the case during the current phase. One sees the beginning of arithmetic, geometry, and algebra in *Nine Chapters* and an openness to Buddhism from India during the current phase but little else in other fields such as logic, astronomy, medicine (beyond the five-phase theory), and linguistics. Thus, a lack of openness to the creativity of other civilizations (including adoption of alphabetical language) despite lack of creed is why China could not give birth to science.

Why Ancient Greece Did Not Give Birth to Science

It is interesting but understandable that Greek historians and diplomats visited India and acknowledged Indian achievements. but Greek philosophers who likely visited India and freely learned from her rarely acknowledged their sources, or perhaps their acknowledgement was lost through multiple translations and commentaries. The intellectual evolution of early ancient Greece seems to have followed the Indian developments of about two centuries earlier.

Internal SGS: Internal SGS was probably low to modest, augmented as it was through peaceful colonization in Italy and Anatolia and a generally fair trade.

Allocation of SGS: The geographical terrain prevented the rise of a strong center in ancient Greece, thus continuing the city-state form of political organization at a time when rest of the world had moved beyond it. This political fragmentation led to unending wars among city-states that consumed a lot of surplus. However, SGS was indeed allocated to the academies, and its original motivation was to train privileged youth in a desire to retain political control in a system that was not based on merit.

Nature of creed: There was, however, little science-religion conflict in Greek society. The censoring of the thinkers resulted from a perceived threat to power structure and not from the force of a religious doctrine.

State of its ASBC: The state of ASBC in pre-Alexander Greece must be judged to be strong: it had mastered the creative method, had alphabetical script, and developed strength in science of logic and epistemology. However, this strength was reduced because of a tradition of speculation in the absence of common sense. It thus excelled in philosophical idealism despite a more grounded minority view.

Openness/insularity: Building on Indian and Persian achievements, the scholars of pre-Alexander Greek civilization did move toward type C internal creative balance during the phase despite the Greek political elite of the period—who meted out a death punishment to a Socrates and harassed other scholars.

Nature of violent greed: Thus, pre-Alexander Greece played the historic role of passing on science it received from other civilizations as well as its own contributions to the Hellenistic states, just as post-Alexander Greece came gradually to be dominated by the antiscience Roman Republic.

To summarize, achievements in science and greater achievements in fields such as philosophy, logic, and epistemology in pre-Alexander Greece are consistent with the absence of science-religion conflict, resource allocation to intellectual creativity, openness to the creativity of other civilizations, and political independence of the pre-Alexander Greek civilization. That it did not give birth to science is simply because the Roman Republic, taking advantage of Alexander's overreach in Asia and resulting weakness at home and diversion of attention, destroyed it.

Why the Indian Civilization Did Not Move Natural Science Forward

Internal SGS: Indian civilization continued to produce high internal SGS consistent with its natural bounty and large population. There was modest augmentation through fair trade with West Asia and the Roman Empire.

Allocation of SGS: The focus on formal and natural sciences declined compared to religion and philosophy, and this allowed the Hellenistic states to jump ahead based, in part, on transmitted Chaldean astronomy, Zoroastrian philosophy, and Indian science and mathematics.

Nature of creed: During the phase, North India was a seething cauldron of philosophical and religious creativity: monism, structured polytheism, agnosticism, and atheism competed in the free market of ideas. Fortunately, Indian civilization failed to develop monotheism. As a result, there was little danger of science-religion conflict. The danger of excessive spirituality was balanced by the emergence of agnosticism and atheism. The focus on linguistics, logic, and speculative natural science slowly gave way to working out the implications of the agnostic Buddhist and atheistic Jain doctrines and naturally failed attempts in synthesizing these doctrines with polytheistic Hinduism as well as monism. The attempt only succeeded in poisoning the revolutionary doctrines of Buddhism. It is true that this attempt itself produced great works in logic, philosophy, and epistemology, but it caused an unfortunate delay in a return to natural science and astronomy.

State of ASBC: Indian civilization continued to lead in ASBC during the phase, excelling in logic and epistemology, having mastered the creative method and alphabetical script in the earlier phases.

Openness/insularity: Indian civilization continued to remain open to the constructive outcomes of other civilizations as evidenced by the influence of Hellenistic astronomy and art and fair trade with the Roman Empire.

Nature of violent greed: Toward the end of the phase, it recovered its sustained political independence it had lost to the nomadic and other invaders after successfully absorbing the foreign invaders into Indian civilization. There was little wealth drain to other lands, since the invaders came to settle and adopted the Indian belief systems and norms over time.

During this period, North India continued to retain the internal creative balance more or less that originally gave birth to science in the previous phase. Buddhist and Jain ideas carried the day in the present phase. However, this was no free lunch, since it took the Indian intellectual class centuries to work out the profound doctrine of Buddhism in epistemology, ethics, and logic simultaneously fighting the invaders. The internal creative balance of Indian civilization remained favorable toward intellectual creation, though it tilted more toward critical philosophy and formal and social sciences and away from natural science. It was the age of philosophical creativity and nomadic conflict undergirded by a rising caste system. The Indian response was to address the issues around equality through religious innovation and internal stability through political consolidation, as it absorbed the foreign invaders, and in the process, the cause of science, relatively speaking, took a back seat.

Why the Hellenistic States Led the First Synthesis of Science

The stars were aligned for the Hellenistic states after the death of Alexander. Who would have predicted that science would find a home in North Africa and West Asia in the Hellenistic states?

Internal SGS: The internal SGS of the Hellenistic states was moderate to high and was augmented by trade and injection of new ideas and Greek immigrants, in part because of the pressure exerted by the Roman Republic on the Greek homeland.

Allocation of SGS: The Greek elite lived relatively simply in conquered lands. There were unending internal wars, which consumed substantial SGS. The force of Greek culture and the relative lack of opportunity in the homeland meant that the Greek elite were willing to support intellectual creativity, in particular astronomy, geometry, and philosophy.

Nature of creed: The Greek religion was rather unsophisticated polytheism, and they were willing to adopt new religious doctrines. Greeks on the northwest frontier of India adopted Buddhism. Later in the phase, there were unsuccessful attempts to synthesize Plato's metaphysics with Christian dogma, for example. Though unsuccessful, its impact was to delay and dilute Christian dogma in the Hellenistic land in West Asia and North Africa.

State of ASBC: The state of ASBC in the Hellenistic states was what was the Greek homeland had bequeathed. In logic and epistemology, Hellenistic states were world-class. They lagged only in arithmetic, but that was compensated by advances in geometry, which was what was required for breakthroughs in astronomy.

Openness/insularity: The Hellenistic states continued the Greek tradition of learning from all while acknowledging nobody! The egotistic creative personality was likely a creation of Greek culture, and such egoism encouraged openness to new ideas and adopting them.

Nature of violent greed: The Hellenistic states were as admirable an empire-building phenomenon as ever seen in the history. They conquered and displaced local elites, lived relatively simply, brought world-class capabilities and attitudes to the conquered territories, did not drain wealth, adopted local customs, and were absorbed into the civilizations they conquered. It is indeed difficult to find a better example of empire building in history! This is surprising since they were descendants of one of the most destructive conquerors in world history. Perhaps it resulted from the pressure exerted by the Roman Republic on the Greek homeland and drove the point that they cannot go back, that the conquered territory was their home, so they did not bring a destructive and intolerant creed with them. Both creed and greed (in the sense of wealth drain) were absent.

The Hellenistic states were at the leading edge of astronomy, geometry, and medicine throughout their half-a-millennium existence. They encouraged continual immigration from Greece to the kingdoms to ensure a loyal army, intellectual capability, and a Greek upper class overlaying the local elite. This trend of migration accelerated because of the pressures the Roman Republic was putting on the Greeks in Greece itself. The opportunities for Greeks were increasingly greater abroad. Thus, there was a confluence of ideas and scholars supported by an expanded tax base in the Hellenistic states. As a result, intellectual creativity took off, far beyond what the Greeks achieved in their homeland or could have achieved. The unintended consequences of Alexander's misadventures were a heightened interest in science, funded by the new phenomenon of global trade and an expanded tax base. The center of gravity for Greek intellectual creativity moved east to Asia and North Africa. Thus, openness to the creativity of other civilizations, absence of intolerant creed, and resources gained through greed without systematic wealth drain through empire building made it possible for the Hellenistic states to lead in science during the phase until Romans conquered them.

To summarize, of the six major civilizations, the Persians, Romans, and Chinese had little to do with science in the current phase, and the Greeks, Indians, and the

Hellenistic states entered development stage of science with Hellenistic states leading during the first synthesis in science. Unlike later syntheses, this synthesis was geographically dispersed, and civilizations were not fully conscious of this synthesis. Nevertheless, looking back, its existence is a pretty clear.

Shifting Center of Gravity of Science

The development of science during the phase was dispersed, but its center of gravity moved to the Hellenistic states. Indian civilization focused on formal and social sciences. The center of astronomy passed from Mesopotamia and India to the Hellenistic states. The focus of natural sciences also shifted from India to ancient Greece and the Hellenistic states.

13.67 Life Stage of Science Achieved by Civilization

Based on the inner nature of civilizations and the underlying parameters summarized in table 13.1, the five key civilizations achieved the following life stages in science.

- Indian Civilization: Development stage of science
- Persian Empire: Mature protoscience of science
- Roman Republic and Roman Empire: Mature protoscience of science
- Central Asian Nomads: Birth stage of protoscience
- Chinese Civilization and Persian Empire: mature protoscience of science
- Greek Civilization: Development stage of science
- Hellenistic States: Development stage of science

13.68 Role of Peaceful and Violent Interaction in Development of Science

Phase III is the first phase with significant peaceful and violent interaction among civilizations. Before leaving this chapter, it might be useful to review their comparative roles in the development of science during the phase.

Impact of Peaceful Interaction

As we have discussed earlier in the chapter, there was material contact between India and Greece before Alexander. This was essentially peaceful interaction based on curiosity and travels of individuals or mediated through West Asia: direct evidence is sketchy; the similarity between the creative outputs of the two civilizations leaves little doubt of this interaction. Thus the broad outlines of the peaceful transmission of knowledge in the ancient world up to the present phase likely occurred as follows:

- Transmission from Indian civilization began with Sulbha Sutras to Mesopotamia, probably around 1900 to 1700 BCE and presumably on an ongoing basis through Indian-Mesopotamian trade. Over a millennium and a half, this exchange evolved into Chaldean and Indian breakthroughs in astronomy. The Chaldean achievements were a critical foundation of Greek astronomy. It must be remembered that Plato openly discouraged the science of astronomy, except to the extent it would support his theory of ideal preexisting forms.

- Indian science and Zoroastrian philosophy diffused to ancient Greece directly or indirectly through travels by scholars, such as Pythagoras and Democritus, during 600 to 350 BCE.

- Alexander's transmission of the achievements of Chaldean astronomy directly to Greece is, of course, well documented. These streams of knowledge survived in the Hellenistic states after the Roman Republic conquered ancient Greece. Although the transfer of Chaldean astronomical works and the implied geometry was a result of Alexander's invasion, we characterize it as part of peaceful transfer, since there was no direct conflict between Mesopotamians and Greeks. The former had ceased to exist by the time of Alexander's invasion.

- These streams then underwent considerable development in the Hellenistic states before returning to India through the Romaka and Paulisa Siddhantas to form one of the pillars of Aryabhatta's astronomical breakthroughs during the next phase, when Indian civilization had picked up the scientific project after nearly a millennium of focus on Buddhist and Jain doctrines. As we have mentioned elsewhere, these doctrines constituted a form of protestant reaction to Indian monism, which had allied itself with caste divisions. However, unfortunately, the Buddhist and Jain doctrines had themselves become idealist over the centuries, showed only modest interest in natural science, and were primarily interested in logic, epistemology, mathematics, and metaphysics.

It is indeed a wonderful case of what goes around, comes around.

Impact of Violent Interaction

Civilizations went through quite an experience during this phase, and it was a foretaste of worse things to come. The march of science was not immune to the devastating impact of differing strains of instruments of control during this phase: empire builders with favorable internal creative balance or a practical one and who were either open or insular to the creativity of other civilizations.

- The Roman Republic did not adopt Greek science and succeeded in destroying it by ignoring it. The Roman Empire did not adopt the Hellenistic science and also succeeded in destroying it by ignoring it.

The Roman Republic and the Roman Empire learned and absorbed Greece military technology, architecture, and art but showed little interest in Greek science. It is amazing, though not surprising, that nascent European civilization was not impressed by Greek and Hellenistic achievements. Perhaps only in hindsight would the Greek accomplishments appear significant to later Europeans. Greeks also forgot their own achievements. In our framework, the Roman Republic and the Roman Empire would be characterized as antiscience wealth drainers who destroyed Greek and Hellenistic science through a lack of appreciation. This is a pattern that will be repeated frequently in the following chapters. In this encounter, science transplanted itself in the Hellenistic states on Asian soil, far from antiscience Rome.

- Persia became indifferent to science after turning imperialistic, despite having given birth to critical philosophy during the last phase in West Asia and despite being exposed to Mesopotamian and Indian civilizations and the Greece and Hellenistic worlds over these centuries. The Persian and Roman lack of interest in science underscore the fact that early in the history of science, science had little practical value, and interest in science had to come from the inner, deep values of a civilization. This was particularly true when a civilization or empire did not feel secure in its inner nature. That is why Persian and Roman Empires walked away from the science right under their noses and why Hellenistic empires did not, because the latter was an extension of ancient Greece, a civilization that, having absorbed all it could, loved knowledge. This attitude obviously changed in modern times since science has demonstrated its practical value through its link to wealth creation and its value in creating technology.

- The situation in India was different. It was already focused on science at the beginning of the phase. The question is what impact nearly four hundred years (200 BCE–200 AD) of intermittent nomadic invasions had on science in India. One the one hand, the dislocation caused by invasions and wars was obviously negative. However, on the other hand, there was no drain of wealth, and the invaders were successfully absorbed into Indian civilization and adopted the Indian religion, language, culture, and values. Thus, apart from temporary dislocations, these invasions probably had a modest impact in the longer term. The internal creative balance, though temporarily upset by these waves of invasions, quickly recovered each time. It also did not fall prey to an evangelizing monotheistic, antiscience creed, as Turkish Islam would later in history. True, there was a loss of sustained political independence during periods of invasions, but it did not last either since the invaders eventually adopted Indian core values. The entire period was shortly going to be capped by the reassertion of indigenous authority under Guptas in the next phase. Finally, we must count the inpouring of new ideas, cultures, and peoples as something very positive for the cause of science in an open civilization. It was truly a period of integration and assimilation of the new influences under the gentle agnostic, polytheistic, and pluralistic values of Indian civilization. Notwithstanding this, as we have noted above, Indian civilization during this period was too busy working out the ontological and epistemological implications of Jain and Buddhist thought to make a significant contribution to the development of astronomy and speculative natural sciences. Indian civilization made outstanding contributions in mathematics, logic, and philosophy during this period. However, in natural science, the legacy of Kannada and Kapila had to take a back seat because the monist philosophy of the Upanishad was a brilliant intellectual achievement; its social purpose in part, however, was the intellectual justification it provided to the institution of the caste system, which condemned a majority of the population to a second-class existence. The reaction to this inhuman inequality occurred through the birth of the protestant philosophies of Jainism and Buddhism. However, these doctrines, while initially rational, turned idealistic over centuries, and the net result, as we have discussed before, was to move the direction of Indian intellectual creativity away from physics and more toward metaphysics and philosophy. This was, without question, one of the significant missed opportunities in the history of science and in the history of Indian civilization. Science took a detour in India to focus on philosophy as a result of the invasions but was confined to mostly internal developments.

Through Alexander and Indo-Greeks, India likely benefited from contact with Greek and Hellenistic science, especially in astronomy and geometry. This learning was to flower in the next phase under the Guptas.

Although Alexander succeeded in destroying the Persian Empire, he also paved the way for the destruction of Greek science through an imperial overstretch unsupported by the inner economic strength and the size of the ancient Greek civilization. He was, thus, a flash in pan that ultimately set fire to the house! On the other hand, Alexander was also responsible for the rise of Hellenistic world, which gave a second chance to Greek science after the Roman Republic's conquest of Greece and before the Roman Empire's conquest of the Hellenistic world. Further, even though Greek civilization did not survive the combined weight of Alexander's misadventure and the invasions of Roman Republic, it brought the Greeks into greater contact with Mesopotamian and Indian civilizations, which certainly accelerated the process of significant cross-fertilization between the leading civilizations with an interest in science. On balance, however, we believe that the Roman conquest of Greece was detrimental to the cause of science.

As a result of the changes discussed above, relatively speaking, the leadership in science passed from the Indian and Mesopotamian civilizations to the Greek and Hellenistic world, since Persians destroyed the former and since Indian focus shifted temporarily to philosophy and metaphysics.

Looking Ahead

13.69 Emerging New Participants and Fate of Existing Participants

Central Asian Nomads—Second Wave

The central Asian nomads, after being frustrated by Chinese resistance, discovered South and West Asia and Europe, thus setting up a pattern of invasions over the coming millennium when the conditions were right. During the next phase, we shall witness the second wave of central Asian nomads, including Gokturks, European Huns, and Indo-Hephthalites.

Arab Nomads

No other new civilization emerged during the phase that deserves mention. However, two points need to be noted. First, a substantial portion of the Roman-Indian trade went through the sea, assisted by several ports on the Arabian Peninsula. Probably for the first time, the ports experienced influx of wealth that gave rise to the Mohammedan revolution and subsequent emergence of Arab nomads on the world scene toward the end of the next phase.

Fate of Existing Participants

Ancient Greece was in shambles at the end of the period under the rule of Roman Empire, which was long oblivious of its past greatness. The ephemeral Hellenistic states were absorbed into Indian, Persian, and Roman worlds by the end of the phase, though with materially different impact. Only Indian and Chinese civilizations and Persian and Roman Empires survived the phase.

13.70 A Peek into Coming Chapters

We have called this chapter the Greek-Hellenistic-Indian synthesis and the next three chapters the Indian, Arab-Persian, and Italian syntheses respectively. In the Greek-Hellenistic-Indian synthesis phase, there was awareness of other's achievements and a slow diffusion of ideas between India, Greece, and the Hellenistic states, but each side pursued science substantially independently. In the Indian synthesis phase, India alone pursued science, though it was modestly helped by the Greek achievements in astronomy and geometry from the previous phase. Similarly, in the two syntheses that followed, independent streams of knowledge from one or more areas fused and developed further, continuing to create something greater.

The next three chapters, therefore, will discuss the three syntheses that followed. The development stage that led to maturation science, thus, was a long and tedious process requiring more than two millennia of interrupted and often fortuitous effort through the following four phases after birth, with a shifting center of gravity of science:

- The Babylonian-Greek-Indian-Hellenistic Synthesis (550 BCE–200 CE): current chapter
- The Indian Synthesis (200–750 CE): chapter 14
- The Arab Synthesis (750–1200 CE): chapter 15
- The Italian/Western European Synthesis (1200–1600 CE) chapter 16

13.71 Summary

By about 150 BCE, the Roman Republic had succeeded in destroying the pre-Alexander nascent Greek science that integrated and further developed Mesopotamian and Indian science. Fortunately for science, Greek science in the post-Alexander world survived and flourished for several centuries in the Hellenistic world, away from destructive Roman control. Because during the current phase the intellectual energy of Indian civilization was focused primarily on formal and social sciences and philosophy, the leadership for the development of the natural sciences passed on to the Hellenistic states, the heirs to Babylonian and Indian intellectual creativity. There was significant but variable level of ongoing communications between these two leaders in science during this period through trade, travel, and invasions. Thus, the current phase saw significant developments in formal sciences and philosophy and the first meaningful steps (followed by the Ptolemy's diversion of epicycles) in astronomy by exploiting the newly developed science of geometry. Formal science had taken giant steps and natural science a first baby step. There was no turning back now—only the possibility of temporary interruption by greed and creed of destructive civilizations.

By the end of second century CE, the Roman Empire succeeded in repeating in the Hellenistic world the Greek fate at the hands of Roman Republic, thus killing science (which as we shall see essentially remained at the periphery of European world from the post-Alexander period until the twelfth century). With this, the scientific leadership returned again to the Indian civilization since by then Indian civilization had absorbed the nomadic invaders and had worked out the ethical, ontological, and epistemological implications of Buddhism and Jainism. The next phase in the history of science, which we have called the Indian synthesis, is what we cover in the next chapter. Persian civilization continued to show little interest in science, and China was starting to get exposed to Indian religious creativity through the spread of Buddhist doctrine by the end of current period and remained focused on practical creativity.

The inescapable conclusion is that Indian and Mesopotamian civilizations lighted and maintained the flame of science in both ancient Greece and the Hellenistic states while the Roman Republic and Roman Empire worked overtime and ultimately succeeded in extinguishing it, thus plunging Europe into its customary darkness for a thousand years, aided by an Asian import, Christian dogma, until the Arabs rescue it again, as we show in chapter 16.

Chapter 14

Violent Interaction Era—Fourth Phase: Development Stage

Second Synthesis of Science (200–750 CE)

14.1 Introduction

In this chapter, we continue exploring the development stage of science through the second synthesis of science, covering a substantial period. It began around 200 CE, after the demise of the Hellenistic states in West Asia and the declining Kushan Empire in India. It ended with a series of highly successful invasions by the Arab nomads armed with Islamic faith on multiple fronts, the beginning of the decline of Buddhism in India, the supremacy of Christianity in Europe, and the rise of monism and polytheistic Hinduism yet again on the Indian subcontinent.

Since it is more appropriate to consider the Arabs as conquering nomads and not yet a civilization in this phase, we could say the significant wars among civilizations during this phase were primarily between the Persian and Byzantine Empires and the Persian and Kushan Empire. On the nomadic side, Huns attacked the Roman Empire and India, and nomadic Arabs attacked just about everybody: Persians, Indians, nomads, and Europeans. Therefore, the phase is characterized by aggressive and mostly successful nomadic invasions and the absence of science just about everywhere except in India.

Ancient Greek and Hellenistic achievements were becoming a distant memory (though they were hardly important to Europeans even during their heyday). China remained prosperous and insular while demonstrating an outstanding level of practical creativity. And though it was not fully clear yet, the world was going to be overrun successfully for centuries by the most aggressive and uncompromising form of monotheism the world has ever seen, with disastrous consequences for several civilizations. Yet this aggressive monotheism also was to create third synthesis of science before becoming fully conscious of the fundamentalist and antiscience implications of its own faith, something we take up in the next chapter.

As in previous chapters, we will first identify all the essential players and affirm the broad nature of the phase. We then discuss brief political history; the significant natural, intrinsic, and peaceful extrinsic and violent extrinsic causes driving the evolution of each essential player during this phase; and summarize their productive outcomes (wealth creation, peaceful migrations, and fair trade), their creative outcomes (practical, religious, and intellectual creativity, including philosophy and art), and their achievements in (formal, natural, biological, and social) sciences. We then summarize of the state of civilization and science at phase end. Following this, we assess the changes in the inner nature of all key participants. Finally, we summarize the evolution of science and rationalize its evolution across different participants through the phase and its life stage at phase end. We end the chapter by providing a glimpse of emerging new participants, the coming chapters, and a chapter summary.

Affirmation of Era, Phase, and Essential Participants

14.2 Affirming Era of Civilization

During this phase, major civilizations continued to remain in the era of extended military conflicts, with transport and weapons systems undergoing significant developments, including better roads, better ships, faster horses, and improved weapons resulting from developments in iron technology. The phase was marked by the destruction of Sassanian, Roman, and Gupta Empires at the hands of nomads. This phase laid the foundation for a millennium-long domination of the world by nomads of central Asia, who slowly adopted Islam and Arabia through empires they created from civilizations they conquered.

14.3 Major Participants of the Phase

The major participants of the phase were Indian and Chinese civilizations and Persian, Roman, and Byzantine Empires. The significant nomads of the phase were Gokturks, Euro-Huns. and Indo-Huns from central Asia and the West Asian Arabs.

History, Causes, and Outcomes of Emerging European Civilization

14.4 Brief Political History (200–750 CE)

Roman Empire (200–476 CE)

As the reader will recall, after about a hundred years of instability and civil war, in 27 BCE, the Roman Republic died with Octavian emerging as a de facto emperor of what became the Roman Empire. The Roman Empire continued similar policies and values, though without the elitist republican form of government, underscoring the point that elitist democracy in the Greek and Roman worlds was either a result of the city-state political structure or tribal roots and was utterly different from modern democracy. It thus stretches imagination to link the two as western European historians are fond of doing. During the first century, with Roman Emperors Augustus and Trajan, the empire eventually included all of western Europe, most of England, most of southern Europe, Anatolia, Egypt, and territories in North Africa. It was the world's most extensive empire at its peak, covering over two million square miles, about a third bigger than the Indian subcontinent. Thus, the Roman Empire extended its control throughout the Hellenistic world, except of course the Persian Parthian Empire, Afghanistan, the northwest Indian territories, and through a string of drawn-out military conquests.

Throughout most of the third century, the Roman Empire again experienced a period of instability, primarily due to unclear succession rules, barbarian invasions, and mismanagement of the economy. In 285 CE, the empire was partitioned into two halves, creating two equal emperors under the title of Augustus. Valentinian II, the last head of the Western Empire, was murdered in 392 CE, and following this, Theodosius, the head of the eastern provinces, briefly united east and west under him.

Until the fourth century CE, the Western Roman Empire did not have to deal with a violent instrument of control; rather, civilizations such as Greek, Carthigian, and the Hellenistic states had to deal with the Roman Empire as a powerful and determined instrument of control. The Roman Empire had an uneasy relationship with the Parthian Empire on its eastern flank, but that did not erupt into extended wars. In 395 CE, after Theodosius died, after more than a decade of high drama around succession issues again, the Roman Empire was permanently split into two halves, one part going to each of Theodosius's two sons.

However, beyond the few hundred miles around the European side of Mediterranean, which effectively defined the Roman writ, lay the barbarians in Europe and northwest Asia. Valens had let the Visigoths, fleeing a migration of the Huns, settle within the borders of the empire, but they were mistreated by the local Roman administrators and rebelled. A large Roman army was defeated by the Visigoths (376 CE), and Emperor Valens was killed. The Vandals, Alans, and Suebi ravaged Gaul and Hispania in 405 CE. In 410 CE, the Visigoths sacked Rome and established themselves in Gaul and Hispania. This allowed Britain to become free of Roman domination. An invasion by Attila the Hun (434-453 CE) followed these attacks from Germanic tribes. Vandals sacked Rome in 455 CE and controlled North Africa. The plan to reassert control over North Africa failed miserably and resulted in the destruction of the Roman fleet in 461 CE, followed by another naval defeat in 468 CE. Finally in 476 CE, the mercenaries deposed the emperor, and the empire divided into seven kingdoms. Thus, as the empire expanded beyond the capability of its institutions, the Huns from northwest Asia and the European barbarians from the north finished the empire off—an expected result for a wealth-draining imperial power of humble origin that lasted for nearly a millennium.

The Eastern Roman Empire came under Greek influence in 610 CE and is called the Byzantine Empire by modern historians, starting with this date. It is discussed in later section. It is noteworthy that the Sassanian Empire was indirectly responsible for the fall of the Western Roman Empire as they deflected the Hun pressure toward western Europe. Later, they pressured and ultimately defeated the Byzantine Empire in 532 CE.

Western Europe (476–750 CE)

For more than three centuries after the fall of the Western Roman Empire, the political structures in western Europe remained highly decentralized, where the common man worked the land owned by the lord, who collected the tax and passed it on to the small princes to pay for state administration and wars. It also led to powerful landed nobility allied with the ascendant hierarchical Catholic Church. This was not the case in the Byzantine Empire. The difference may be attributed to the absence of papal authority and the presence of a stronger, continuing central imperial authority that escaped the nomadic destruction. This, however, was a difference of degree, not kind. Both parts of Europe were under the sway of an evangelizing monotheistic creed.

Finally, Charlemagne succeeded in organizing the Holy Roman Empire in the late eighth century in the eastern portion of the old Western Roman Empire. This Germanic Empire, with Christianity as a state religion, continued in some form until 1806, when Napoleon both put an end to it and crowned himself the holy Roman emperor! We will cover some of these developments in more detail in later chapters.

14.5 Natural Causes

We do not believe natural causes were of fundamental importance in the fall and decline of the Roman Empire. However, just about every imaginable natural causes has been invoked by one historian or another to explain the overanalyzed fall of the Roman Empire, including deforestation, Justinian plague, lead poisoning, and a volcanic eruption of Mount Krakatoa in 535–536 CE causing climate change, malaria, and droughts. The bubonic plague is estimated to have killed about 20 percent of the population in the third and fourth centuries.

14.6 Intrinsic Causes

Institutional Structures and Processes

Political system: The political power resided with the emperor, who typically needed to secure the support of the military through monetary awards at the time of ascension. Below the emperor remained the two hereditary classes: a senatorial order and an equestrian order. The political and military officers were chosen from these classes. The senatorial and equestrian elites were restricted to Italians only. Only rarely was a non-Italian person of ability outside these classes able to rise in the ranks. The newly acquired provinces along the borders were under the emperor's direct control, while the older, more stable provinces were managed by the old senatorial families. Most of the military legions were stationed in the imperial provinces. This division of the control of provinces, however, was liable to change if the emperor so desired. Thus, the political structure was autocratic, nonmeritocratic in general, and without any freedom for all except at the very top.

Military capability: The backbone of military capability in the Roman Empire continued to be the armies, consisting of legions composed of citizens and auxilla consisting of noncitizens who were rewarded with citizenship at the end of a shorter service. In addition, Augustus also created a police force stationed on the Italian Peninsula. The total strength of army may be as high as 300,000. The navy was not as prestigious and had the function of protecting the trade routes and ensuring supplies to the army. It was primarily stationed in the Mediterranean and Black Seas.

Economic organization and wealth creation: The economy of the empires was mainly agrarian. The manufacturing base was concentrated in mining and metallurgy and building industries. Large-scale mining operations used such innovations as hydraulic mining and produced iron (100,000 tons/year), copper (15,000 tons per year), lead (80,000 tons per year), silver (200 tons per year), and gold. These in turn served the needs of expanding trade, the armed forces, and the lifestyle of the elite: weapons and the infrastructure needed to maintain control and build palatial homes. Mining of gold and silver was necessary to pay for the fine luxuries imported from the East for the privileged classes and to mint the extensive coinage in circulation. The entire economic structure was designed to serve the needs of the very few at the top. It has been estimated that average Roman had an annual income of about one thousand dollars in 2010 dollars, and the empire had a population of about 50 million with the wealth creation equivalent to about $50 billion.

Systems of religious faith: The spread of Christianity was preceded by the Roman persecution of Christians. Christianity had spread rapidly from the bottom up and was beginning to be accepted by the emperors, but Roman emperors also had desired and often required the subjects to revere themselves and their families as gods. There was some continuing persecution of Jews and Druids as well. In 313 CE, the Roman emperor Constantine issued the so-called Edict of Milan, and later in 325 CE, he called the council of Nicaea legalizing Christianity. Once the religion was adopted by the Roman emperors, it spread rapidly in Europe using the excellent network of Roman roads. It spread from the urban centers to the countryside.

The fall of the Hellenistic states also contributed to the rapid rise of Christianity. This expansion was by and large peaceful, consistent with the message of love from Christ, who preached that God loved all and wanted you to accept Him voluntarily. As the religion shed its apostolic roots and became more hierarchical, it entered the monastic stage, which allowed an expansion in papal authority in Western Europe. It became rigid as well as continuing the Roman tradition of being staunchly antiscience.

Starting about the seventh century, a great schism developed in Christianity, leading over a period of several centuries, to distinct Orthodox and Catholic branches. The single most significant difference between the two branches, from our perspective, was the acceptance of a pope as the religious head of the Catholic but not the Orthodox branch. Later, this was to make it possible for pope in western Europe to not only interfere in the matters of state but also gain sufficient power to be both the virtual head of a state and the Catholic Church during several periods of western European history. Thus, a pope would be in a position to influence or even block scientific thought if it conflicted with Christian dogma.

On the other hand, the Catholic Church did not allow concentration of power in the state, the celibacy requirement prevented the rise of a hereditary priest class, and the church promoted equality in that all Christians were sinners before God. Thus the Western Roman Empire, the Eastern Empire, and later Holy Roman Empire all adopted Christianity. We shall develop these themes in subsequent chapters. Returning to the current phase, Europe was firmly in the grip of Christian monotheism by the fourth century.

There was little science-religion conflict in the Roman Empire until its adoption of Christianity in the fourth century. However, the demise of Hellenistic science after Roman conquest of the western Hellenistic states had little to do with Roman religion. It had more to do with the intense practical nature of the Roman civilization.

Legal systems: The enactment of the laws during the current phase passed from the hands of the senate to the emperors through edicts, causing great confusion in the legal arena. By 535 CE, legal scholarship under Trobanian systematized the Roman law into Corpus Juris Civilis. Under Roman law, all citizens were not equal. The law treated Roman citizens, foreigners, free citizens, slaves, and certain family members unabashedly as unequal. Roman law did not have a formal court system either. A private citizen could act like a judge if both parties agreed to such arrangement, much like arbitration. The code was both written and unwritten. The code also made an important distinction between public law and private law as well as between natural law, common law, and statutory law. Thus, laws were well developed but the courts and legal system were not.

Social structure: The social structure in the Roman Empire continued to be based on ancestry, six grades of property, and citizenship. Noncitizens were further divided into *peregrini* (foreigners) and slaves. The family was unabashedly patriarchal, with women born of Roman citizens classified as citizens but not allowed to hold office.

The Roman Empire intensified the Roman Republic tradition of a quintessential class society based on heredity and wealth with little justification provided by religion. Thus, Roman society had excessive inequality and was steeped in the tradition of slavery. There was no real middle class in the Roman Empire. The wealth stratification was extremely high. Religion did not play a significant role in managing class conflicts. Roman law and traditions, backed by a very strong military force, kept the social order and internal control, which was interrupted by frequent slave rebellions. Ultimately, the stubborn distinction between citizens and noncitizens was to prove the undoing of the empire.

Knowledge-Creating and educational institutions: The Roman Empire did not have formal knowledge-creating and educational institutions. Education was modeled after the Greek tradition but without the academies run by scholars and was primarily left to individual family. The focus of education for boys was reading writing and arithmetic, followed by law, customs, and public speaking. The mother was responsible for educating the girls, and education was limited to domestic needs, including sewing, spinning, and weaving.

Wealth allocation process: The surplus was basically squandered on the expansion and maintenance of the empire or the luxuries for the elite. An increasing amount of surplus was also beginning to be directed toward building elaborate churches and supporting the clergy toward the latter part of this phase. Unlike the pharaohs of Egypt, the Roman emperors were not interested in the afterlife. Consequently, the surplus, thankfully, was not typically wasted on royal monuments. Significant development of roads and water systems using aqueducts also took place to support military activity and urban needs respectively.

Social cohesion processes: Roman law and Roman police provided the social glue. Religion played little role in the process.

Internal wars: The Roman Republic had to contend with terrible slave wars, which were successfully dealt with. The Roman Empire, on the other hand, did not have significant internal wars, provided the foreign mercenaries are considered non-Roman. The Roman Empire did not have wars among states; it was far too centralized for that. The internal instability in the Roman Empire stemmed from the lack of clear rules of succession, and this resulted in internal wars that were in fact wars of succession limited to the elite families. By the end of the third century, as we mentioned above, it was clear that the empire was too large to be governed by one emperor. It was split into two halves to be governed by an Augustus and, in order to minimize the problem of succession, by a Caesar each. This system of four executives came to be known as a tetrarchy.

However, it is clear that military success expanded the empire beyond the capability of its social and political institutions by the fourth century. In other words, the rigid class stratification, as we noted above, caused the empire to spiral downward starting in the fourth century CE. The belated adoption of Christian doctrine proved insufficient to arrest the decline.

Formative Beliefs and Ideology at the End of Second Synthesis Phase

The relatively unstructured polytheism of pre-Christian Romans, their focus on practical knowledge as evidenced by their reaction to and suppression of Hellenistic science, a social inequality resulting from extensive slavery and decadent elite, their interest in trade and their need to expand the empire as the singular means to grow state revenue all point to a belief system that may be summarized as follows:

- A belief in practical and military technology as means to increase wealth production and to expand the empire and to sustain elite life style.
- A belief in the fundamental inequality among Romans and non-Romans, Italians and non-Italians, men and women, between slaves and freemen and divine right of kings.
- An attitude of insularity toward the intellectual and religious creativity of others through most of the phase.
- A belief in aggression toward other social orders.

These beliefs, derived in part from their Greek heritage, are important, since as the most consequential European empire until modern times, these beliefs strongly impacted the beliefs of other European empires.

14.7 Extrinsic Peaceful Causes or Sum Total of Constructive Outcomes

Impact of Indian Civilization

Transmission of creativity: There were marginal Indian influences in the Roman world, particularly in silver coinage, silk textiles, and ivory products. Buddhism and other Indian religions are mentioned in the writings of Clement of Alexandria (150–215 CE) and others.

Fair trade: As we discussed in the last chapter, Indo-Roman trade began and probably peaked in the first two centuries of the Common Era. However, it continued even after the fall of the Western Roman Empire. Gold coins of Justinian I (527–565 CE) have been discovered in South

India. This trade in all likelihood continued until the Arabs captured Alexandria in the middle of the seventh century, thus forcing South India to turn to Southeast Asian trade to make up the loss. Roman trade with other civilizations not part of the Roman Empire was essentially fair trade, since the Romans controlled neither the territories nor the trade routes linking civilizations.

Impact of migrations: Migrations into the center of the Roman Empire occurred primarily through slaves captured in the wars. Unlike the Greeks, Romans did not permanently settle in the conquered territories. These territories were administered through Roman military and other personnel assigned on a temporary basis, much like the British rule in India. The system to extract minerals and the produce of conquered territories through the well-developed road system, military control of the territories, and use of the slave system reminds one of the British strategies of more than a millennium later. It is doubtful scholars migrated from other civilizations into the Roman Empire either since Romans hardly valued them. However, one may safely assume Greek technologists and skilled craftsmen frequently migrated into the Roman Empire.

Impact on productive outcomes: The Indian impact on productive outcomes was probably negative as there was a continuing negative balance of payment, typically paid through gold.

Impact on creative outcomes: There was little impact on the creative outcomes.

Impact on institutional structures and processes: Likewise, there was little impact on the institutional structures and process. Given the distance, lack of sufficient firsthand knowledge, and totally different belief system, this is hardly surprising.

Impact of West Asia

Transmission of creativity: During the current phase, the greatest impact came from West Asia in the form of Christianity and various cults, including the cult of Mithra, which may be of Persian origin. It is also noteworthy that Rome ultimately chose to adopt Christianity, something that the Hellenistic states never accepted in totem. They remained bound to their polytheistic tradition and synthesis of their polytheistic tradition with Christianity and were attracted to rational Buddhism (if opportunity presented itself) as well as to dogmatic Christianity during the phase.

Impact on productive outcomes: The direct impact on productive outcomes was minimal.

Impact on institutional structures and processes: The impact of the arrival of Christianity both during and after the Roman period was profound. The movement was from the bottom up and was energized by the Roman persecution of Christian converts, who were clearly attracted to the Christian message of equality before God as they were unequal to Roman citizens. Romans were forced to acknowledge Christianity as a state religion. After the fall of Rome, in the absence of a strong political center, the church rushed in to fill the political vacuum, resulting in a highly decentralized feudalism in western Europe, with the church and kings vying for power. The political system, religious organization, social structure, position of science, and legal systems were profoundly impacted by Christianity. It is fair to say that the conquest of polytheistic Europe by a monotheistic foreign faith was complete and was a preview of the impact of Islam in Europe and Asia.

14.8 Extrinsic Violent Causes or Sum Total of Destructive Outcomes

In the previous phase, the Roman Empire essentially played the role of aggressor for over half a millennium, rather successfully. During this phase, it was mostly payback time in the fourth and fifth centuries, and it eventually led to the destruction of the Western Roman Empire. However, before that, we will briefly consider the impact of violent conflict with the Hellenistic states, where Rome was a conqueror and with the Persian Sassanianan Empire, where neither side lost.

Continuing Impact of Hellenistic States

Transmission of creativity: The interaction between the Roman Empire and the Hellenistic states was intense, prolonged, and selective. It was also a relationship between an aggressor and a victim. However, it was hardly fruitful from the perspective of transmission of creativity.

Impact on productive outcomes: It is unlikely for a multiethnic and multicivilization empire to rise without utilizing the achievements of surrounding civilizations and build upon their achievements. The Roman Empire was no exception. Its practical technology was built in part on the achievements of Greeks in Hellenistic states, Carthaginians, and Etruscans, among others. The Roman Empire continued to borrow all it could in architecture, sculpture, practical technology, and medicine from Hellenistic achievements. In all fairness, however, it must be stated that Hellenistic contributions in these areas, which go beyond what the ancient Greeks had accomplished, did not exactly eclipse what Rome was capable of on its own in these fields.

Impact on creative outcomes: What is significant is not where Rome surpassed Hellenistic world, but what Rome did not absorb and in fact what it actively discouraged and killed: Greek speculative science and Hellenistic astronomy and geometry. This is significant, since the lasting achievements of ancient Greece were mostly confined to art and philosophy, and it was only in the Hellenistic states that Greek tradition in union with Babylonian and Indian traditions led to breakthroughs in geometry and astronomy. The Roman Empire had little interest in these two sciences. The Romans chose to ignore the intellectual creativity of Greeks and the Hellenistic states, except in the arena of sculpture and architecture.

Impact of the Persian Civilization

The conflict between Sassanians and the Roman and Byzantine Empires was long and fierce. The first period was the conflict between the Roman Empire during the third and fourth centuries CE, and the second period was the conflict with the Byzantine Empire in the fifth, sixth, and early seventh centuries CE. In fact, these two periods were preceded by two earlier periods of conflict: ancient Greece and the Achaemenid Empire, the Hellenistic states, and Parthians as we saw in the previous chapter. These four periods constitute a millennium-long conflict between successive states, the last two of which had the unintended effect of safeguarding the rest of Asia from the Roman Empire.

If we ask the question that apart from terrible wars, what sort of interaction between Rome and Persia took place during the current phase, the answer is not much. They, of necessity, learned from each other in military matters. There was no doubt a diffusion of architecture and art forms, since both focused on these.

Impact on institutional structures and processes: Other civilizations little impacted the Roman Empire's political system, economic organization, legal systems, social structures, and knowledge-creating and educational institutions. The impact was confined to military and religious matters: imperial Rome, as it transitioned from republic to empire, borrowed heavily from the Persian court ceremonies, which later influenced the court ceremonies in modern Europe. Rome adopted the Persian heavy cavalry, and the Persians learned the Roman siege tactics and infantry tactics. The European armored knight of the Middle Ages can also be traced to Sassanian armored cavalry. This assessment is fully transparent when one recognizes that adoption of Christianity by imperial Rome was based on coopting a bottom-up popular movement, which in itself gained strength because of the early Roman persecution of Christians.

Impact of European Barbarians and Huns

Loss of SPI: Western Huns destroyed the Western Roman Empire while receiving substantial booty but failed to create an organized state, thus splintering Europe into small units and making it possible for the emergence of the Catholic Orthodoxy and a strong papal institution.

Nomadic Arabs conquered a vast territory from Spain to Sindh, controlling the SGS in all of West Asia, Iberia, and North Africa. They were far more successful in Europe and Sassanian Empire than in India. They were beaten back in India and only managed to hold on to minor pockets. China remained unscathed from Arab and Hun attacks; in fact their defeat of eastern Huns, once again, created nomadic pressure on India, West Asia and, Europe.

Europe was descending into political darkness while India and China were defending nomadic attacks much more successfully.

Loss of control of wealth and means of wealth: Huns were once looters interested in wealth drain. The Arabs were empire builder settlers, but fortunately their control was confined to Iberia and Sicily. Thus, loss of wealth and control of wealth must be assessed to be modest.

Assessment of Net Impact

The Roman Empire was both a conqueror and conquered, though we treat Rome primarily as conquered during the current phase. The Roman Empire met the fate of Mesopotamia, Egypt, Greek, and the Hellenistic states, though it lasted longer than any of those if we consider all its various incarnations. Thus, the net impact was clearly disastrous in its death at the hands of European barbarians and Asian nomads it looked down on, but one hardly wants to shed a tear when a former cruel victor is given a taste of the same medicine it mercilessly administered to others.

14.9 Productive Outcomes

Roman technological achievements and use of slavery meant a substantial increase in wealth creation. Though largely responsible for the birth of European civilization, the Roman Empire remained a motley collection of conquered states not deserving being called a civilization until the injection of foreign glue provided by adopting Christianity. It did not encourage migration, except for slaves as needed, and the Romans did not permanently settle in conquered territories. As we have discussed above, the Roman Empire excelled in trade, both internal, which was coercive in nature, and external, which was fair in nature, since the military reach of the empire even at its height was regional not global.

Thus, leaving aside religious, philosophical, and scientific innovation, we may give the Roman Empire high marks in such areas as practical creativity, military capability, architecture, art, and administration. Like the Persian civilization, it was an aggressive entity that excelled in practical creativity. It was indeed an incomplete civilization.

14.10 Creative Outcomes

We covered the substantial but declining creative achievements of Hellenistic states under coercive Roman rule in the last chapter. We also covered the outcomes of the

Roman Republic in the last chapter. Below. we focus on the significant outcomes of the Western Roman Empire.

Achievements in Practical Creativity

The focus of Roman creativity was practical technology. One would be hard-pressed to find serious interest in intellectual creativity in the heart of the Roman world. The outcomes in practical creativity were, however, impressive. Romans were engineers and builders at heart, building tens of thousands of miles of roads and hundreds of miles of aqueducts. They invented, improved, or adapted watermills, cranes, the screw press, bridges, dams, mining, sanitation, the arch, dome, a type of harvesting machine, lighthouses, the paddle wheel, the plow, glass blowing techniques, the spiral staircase, tunnels, concrete, and wood veneer, to mention the significant ones. Romans developed sanitation technology, including indoor plumbing and flushing toilets. In addition to engineering and building skills, Romans excelled in military technology and empire administration through political and legal innovation. Romans copied the cavalry saddle design from the Celtics and essentially inherited weapons technology from Greeks and others. However, the Romans did develop a light body armor that was more comfortable to wear and easier to manufacture than the Persian heavy armor.

Achievements in Religious Creativity

The emperor was divinely approved and encouraged a royal cult. Roman outcomes in religious creativity were limited to persecution, absorption, and control of foreign cults and religious systems to suit the needs of the empire. Traders, soldiers, and travelers brought foreign cults such as Mithras and Isis and were absorbed as long these did not threaten the empire. Initial Roman reaction was to treat Christianity as a superstition; however, by the time of Constantine, Christianity had been upgraded to the status of the only religion, and all other cults came to be defined as superstitions by the practical Romans. Thereafter, Constantine ordered a serious persecution of non-Christians, which included looting and temple destruction and was continued by his son. It never occurred to the Romans to treat religious questions intellectually.

The apostolic age of Christianity had ended by 100 CE and witnessed the emergence of the Episcopal Church, with bishops in charge as we saw in the last chapter. The next big step in the evolution of Christianity was its legalization in 325 CE. Following the legalization, four critical developments took place:

- Identification of text from the literature of Christianity that would later become the New Testament.
- Seven councils took place between 325 and 451 CE. These developments crystallized the Christian dogma and caused splits, such as the Assyrian Church of the East and Oriental Orthodoxy.
- The third significant development was the emergence of Christian monasticism under the leadership of Basil and Benedict, a development that was to have a great impact on the emergence of scholasticism in Western Europe centuries later.
- Finally, the emergence of papal authority in the sixth century. This became possible when the Byzantine Empire failed to protect the Italian Peninsula from the invasion of Lombards, and the papal state came to the rescue by paying protection money to Lombards, hiring mercenaries to fight them and enlisting the Franks in the west in the fight. Thus, Western Christianity became thoroughly politicized and was to remain so for nearly a millennium thereafter.

Achievements in Philosophy

There was a serious backlash against learning in the Roman Empire after the demise of the Hellenistic states. It is said that Theophilus destroyed all non-Christian books at the library in Alexandria in 391 CE. The job was completed later by Muslim general 'Amr ibn-al-'As in 646 CE. He is reportedly to have said if the books agree with the Koran, they are superfluous, but if they disagree, they are blasphemous and should be destroyed. The Roman Empire never considered philosophical inquiry a worthy pursuit.

Achievements in Art

The focus on Roman art was visual arts and to a lesser extent literature as opposed to performing arts. Roman architecture is exemplified by structures such as the Coliseum and Pantheon and use of mosaics. Roman sculpture is an outstanding example of realistic representational art. In literature, Vergil's epic *Aeneid* was composed before the Common Era and represents the high point of Roman literary achievement, but, unfortunately, it was written to justify Roman imperial expansion. Driven by the need of skill in political debates, Romans took the art of satire to new heights. Roman writers also excelled in epigrams that were used at funerals as eulogy.

14.11 Achievements in Science

The focus of "science" in the Roman Empire was consolidation of the first synthesis of science (described in the last chapter) and preservation of knowledge that was passed on to Indian and Muslim civilizations. However, some peripheral activity did continue.

Achievements in Linguistics

The Romans developed the Latin alphabet widely used in all the European languages.

Achievements in Mathematics

Although the Hellenistic civilization had passed its prime, there continued to be some activity in mathematics. Diophantus compiled the works of earlier mathematicians in algebra. He is incorrectly identified as father of algebra by later Western historians. Similarly, the earlier works of Euclid and Archimedes were compiled in the fifth century CE. Our knowledge of these ancient mathematicians dates from these sources, which were compiled a millennium after their deaths. Perhaps the singular Roman mathematical achievement was Roman numerals, whose conceptual limitation is clear to anyone who has tried to use the system for simple arithmetic operations. Its current use is reduced to highlighting segments of a written document. Roman numerals probably go back to the third century BCE, but the full development occurred around the beginning of the current phase.

Achievements in Physics

In the early sixth century, Philoponus of Alexandria performed experiments on falling objects. He showed that difference in falling times did not correspond to the ratio of weights, thus questioning Aristotle's speculations on the subject. In addition, he distinguished between matter, space, and motion.

Achievements in Medicine

Roman medicine was passive and included prayers, offerings, and sacrifice; however, their surgical knowledge was relatively sophisticated, primarily because of the achievements of Hellenistic physicians such as Galen.

Achievements in Social Sciences

Romans never viewed social sciences as an intellectual arena. One would be hard-pressed to find something comparable to the *Arthashastra* from the Roman Empire. However, their achievements in legal systems, political rhetoric, and administration of the empire were substantial. The innovations in these arenas in fact date back to the Roman Republic, are borrowed heavily from ancient Greece, and were initially designed for city-states. As the territory expanded during the empire phase, these institutions proved insufficient to administer a much larger territory.

Summarizing Achievements in Abstract Systems-Building Capability (ASBC)

By the end of the phase, the ASBC of the Roman Empire must be characterized as moderate: it had adopted/modified alphabetical script and mastered creative method in the previous phase but continued to fail to adopt or develop and thus lacked sound epistemology.

History, Causes, and Outcomes of the Byzantine Empire

14.12 Brief Political History (293–711 CE)

As noted above, the roots of the Byzantine Empire go back to 292 CE, when a tetrarchy consisting of two emperors and two Caesars was established, and the Roman Empire divided into and eastern and western halves, indicating an absence of clarity of succession rules and the limits of its institutions. This division did not last, and in the early fourth century, Constantine I established a single dynastic rule, moved the capital to Byzantium, and adopted Christianity as a state religion. In 395 CE, when Theodosius died, the empire was again divided between his two sons. Thus, 395 CE may be considered the founding of the Byzantine Empire, which consisted primarily of Anatolia, Greece, and Egypt. In a way, it was a reincarnation of the western Hellenistic states in Christian garb.

The Byzantine Empire escaped the destruction the Huns brought upon the Roman Empire in the west through tribute, bribery, and better defenses. After Attila's unexpected death in 453 CE, the Byzantine Empire enjoyed a century of peace. Thereafter, starting in 518 CE, Justinian I embarked on a reconquest of the western Roman provinces, with a good measure of success, adding the Italian Peninsula, parts of North Africa, and the Iberian Peninsula. By 600 CE, the Byzantine Empire resembled a reconstituted but shrunken Roman Empire at its height.

In a very real sense, Constantinople was chosen as the eastern capital and a gateway to trade and a way to get away from European barbarians; however, the move also succeeded in getting it closer to Asian barbarians. Fortunately, the Byzantine Empire successfully deflected the Huns toward the Western Roman Empire through bribes and diplomacy as noted above. Luckily for the empire, the Hun menace did not survive for long after it plundered the Western Roman Empire. The two empires never joined hands to fight the barbarians. Perhaps the Hun's tactics prevented the two empires from jointly fighting the Huns. Thus, the barbarian threat pressed on the empire from west and the north. From the east was the unrelenting threat from the Sassanians, which was followed by the Arab threat from the south. The Byzantine Empire was surrounded despite its success against western provinces.

Prolonged fighting with the Persian Empire under the Sassanians to the south in the sixth century exhausted both the Byzantine and Sassanian Empires considerably. Taking advantage of the situation, the Arabs handed a crushing defeat to the Byzantine Empire in 634 CE and laid siege to Constantinople during 674 to 678 CE. The empire never fell to Arabs, but several provinces, including Egypt, portions of the Iberian and Italian Peninsulas, and southeastern

Europe were lost to Arabs, European barbarians, and Bulgarian kingdoms during the seventh century CE. Leo saved the empire from Arab attack through the use of the so-called Greek fire, a form of a flamethrower. As we shall see in the following chapters, the Byzantine Empire went through several periods of expanding and shrinking borders in the following centuries until its demise in 1453 CE.

To summarize: Europe and North Africa saw the Roman Empire in its full fury for the first two centuries of the Common Era. During the early part of this phase, the process of conquest came to an end because distant new territories were harder to conquer and maintain, and the benefits were fewer. In the southwest, the Roman Empire was butting against the Parthians, who were rich and powerful, and in the northeast, nature was harsh. The barbarians, such as the Germanic tribes and Huns, were more poor and warlike. It was indeed payback for the Roman Empire during the current phase.

The decline, as we mentioned above, started with attacks by European barbarians from the north. In 434 CE, Attila the Hun attacked the Roman Empire and returned with a booty including nearly 250 pounds of gold. After a few years of absence, during which time Attila was defeated by the Sassanian Persians, Attila returned to Europe where he knew he would be more successful. Over the years 440 to 453 CE, he repeatedly attacked the Roman Empire, reaching as far west as France. He presumably died happy in Italy celebrating his marriage to a young Gothic princess named Lidico.

Like all empires, the Byzantine Empire was also responsible for destructive outcomes that impacted other civilizations. The Byzantine Empire was chiefly responsible for weakening the Sassanian Empire, which the Arabs defeated in 651 CE. Shortly thereafter, Arab armies attacked the Byzantine Empire and nearly succeeded. However, it survived in part because of the use of flamethrower technology. As noted above, it lasted with fluctuating fortunes for nearly seven centuries before succumbing to the Ottomans in 1453 CE.

14.13 Natural Causes

The epidemic of plague impacted the Byzantine Empire in 541 to 542 CE, and thereafter it continued to occur until the end of the current phase. Loss of population to plague must be viewed as a moderate impact on the empire, as it affected both the economic activity and recruits for military.

14.14 Intrinsic Causes

Institutional Structures and Processes

Political system: The Byzantine Empire naturally inherited the Roman political system of the fourth century CE. Emperors ruled as absolute monarchs and based their power on divine origin while assuming the role of religious head as well. In the beginning, the provinces had separate civil and military heads that were appointed by the emperor; however, a dramatic shift of political and legislative power from the senate to the bureaucracy under a powerful head of bureaucracy called a *sakellarios* was formalized. The bureaucracy was responsible to the emperor alone, which meant a centralization of the power since bureaucracy and not senators based on heredity became the preferred path to aristocracy. However, as the Byzantine Empire successively came under attack from the Sassanian Empire in the southeast, barbarians to the north, and Arabs to the south, the system of separate civil and military authority in provinces became ineffective and was replaced by unified governance under one leader called a *strategos*. The strategos had both civil and military authority. This led to further centralization, though it also led to faster decision making in provinces under attack. Thus, the Byzantine Empire, through creation of a central bureaucracy under sakellarios and provincial governance under strategos, became significantly more centralized than the Roman Empire to more effectively meet significant existential threats. An elaborate system of spies helped ensure loyalty and kept the bureaucracy on alert.

Military capability: Though inherited from the Roman military, the Byzantine army developed a couple of key differences over time. First, as noted above, was the appointment of powerful strategos in the provinces (or themes), and the second was the decline of the Roman legions on foot and the rise of armored cavalry fashioned after Persian cavalry. In addition, the use of mercenaries likely increased in both infantry and cavalry. The themes allowed the emperor to raise a large army without incurring expense from his treasury. Byzantine emperors also had a navy that was, however, confined to the Mediterranean Sea since international trade during most of the current phase was under Persian control.

Economic organization: Byzantine economy and wealth creation was centered on agriculture and trade with manufacturing except silk textiles playing relatively a diminished role. Agriculture concentrated on growing cereal crops, olives, and livestock and was not particularly productive as it remained mired in traditional techniques. A functioning grain market existed in Constantinople, with the state often playing the role of market maker to keep grain prices stable. The industry focused on silk weaving, including embroidery and tapestry, and marble, silver, and gold mining. The manufacture of silk was essentially an imperial monopoly, and its internal trade was severely restricted. International trade was the backbone of the economy. The empire exported silk, marble, silver, and gold and imported luxury items, such as perfumes, textiles, and spices. Constantine I had wisely moved the capital of the empire from Rome to Constantinople to not only get away from barbarian invasions but also position the empire as gateway between east and west, with Constantinople becoming the western terminus of the famed Silk Road. Taxes included sales tax, property taxes, income taxes, and import taxes set at ten percent. The state controlled international trade, interest rates, and silk production and managed an excellent circulation of coinage, which contributed to the economic integration of the empire. The financial sector, through public and private credit, was sufficiently developed to support international trade. Since economy was heavily dependent on trade, Arab conquest in the seventh century saw a dramatic reversal of fortunes toward the end of the current phase. In short, like its political system, the economy lacked freedom and was controlled by the state, which resembled state capitalism married to Christianity.

Systems of religious faith: Development of the Christian Church in the Byzantine Empire proceeded in the opposite direction compared to Western Europe where, after the fall of Rome in 476 CE, the church took advantage of the political and military fragmentation and established itself as a unifying authority in the form of Catholicism under the pope. In the Byzantine Empire, which had escaped destruction by the Huns and held its own against the Persians, the state remained strong and centralized. The emperor as head of the church prevented the rise of an independent, politically minded church. The royal practices from the pre-Christian era in Greece, Egypt, and Anatolia nicely supported this. However, this came at a price: Christianity in the east never found a unifying voice, and the Orthodox church did not represent all the Christians in the empire, with branches such as Assyrian and Miaphysite churches splitting off during the current phase. The emperor, who was considered a messenger of Christ responsible for conversions to Christianity, appointed the bishops, passed religious laws, and provided financial support to the church. The patriarch of Constantinople was the operating head of the Orthodox Church and had authority to appoint the metropolitan sees and archbishops through the empire. Minorities, such as Jews, were generally not persecuted, unlike in Rome. Thus, Christianity in the east was more mystical, liturgical, and more disunited and may have contributed to Arab success in the seventh century. A controversy, known as the Iconoclastic Controversy, over the use of religious images resulted in further fragmentation of the Orthodox Church. Greater unification was only achieved centuries later through the conversion of Russian, Bulgarian, and Slavic populations. The bottom line was, though not as united, the Christian faith was generally successful in converting the majority of the population in the empire.

If science-religion conflict was absent in the Byzantine Empire, it was so only because science was absent and not because the potential for such conflict did not exist. The location of the empire, while great from the standpoint of trade with Asia, also brought the empire in conflict with Asian powers. Thus, both the Christian worldview and unending military engagement extinguished interest in science, despite being closer to ancient Greek and the Hellenistic heritage, and that, not surprisingly, meant no overt conflict between science and religion.

Legal system: Emperor Justinian ordered a revision of Roman law completed from 529 to 534. The codex was first to be completed and consisted of past imperial edicts as well as legislation pertaining to religion, which included laws against heresy (requiring each citizen to uphold the Christian faith) and paganism, where the practitioner of pagan sacrifice may be indicted for murder. Next to be completed was a compendium of past legal opinions, and it was given the full force of law. The third piece was a book for training future jurists and dealt with principles of law. The fourth and final part was a collection of new laws enacted after 534 CE. This great effort ensured the survival of Roman law; it was introduced in Italy in 554 CE, and from there, it spread on to Western Europe. It also passed to Slavic Europe and Russia in later centuries. In the seventh century, as the empire weakened, the Justinian code fell into relative disuse and was replaced with new compilations in Greek.

Less than two centuries later, the code was modified again in 726 CE to reflect social and religious evolution in the empire. Leo III introduced the new code, called Ecloga, while establishing the concept of equality before law by expanding the rights of the poor, women, and children and took a tougher stand on criminals by introducing such punishments as amputation and blindness. Ecloga and the direct compensation of judges by the imperial treasury were meant to make the legal process more just.

During the current phase, other legal documents, such as farmer's laws, naval law, and revised canonical law also emerged. An interesting feature of the farmer's law was the collective responsibility of a village community to pay taxes. This implies a communal concept of property in the villages while an individual rights concept prevailed in the cities. Naval law specified the rules of profit sharing and responsibility of loss of property or ship among the crew. Canonical law consolidated the doctrinal teachings coming out of the first six religious councils and responsibilities of the clergy, monks, and non-Christians. However, in general, the bishops of the Orthodox Church interpreted its canonical law rather liberally, depending on local conditions.

Social structure: Not surprisingly, the social structure was very hierarchical and consisted of landed aristocrats, church officials, merchants and industrialists, and peasants and wage earners. Social schisms also existed between the rural and urban, Greek and non-Greek populations, aristocratic bureaucracy and nobility, and bureaucracy and church officials. The officials closest to the emperor were often eunuchs. The farmer was free, with a separate legal code as we noted above. Slavery still existed but on a much reduced scale. The four pillars of the Byzantine society—the military, bureaucracy, economy, and church—were firmly under the control of the emperor and ultimately defined the resulting social structure.

Formative Beliefs and Ideology at the End of Second Synthesis Phase

The dogma of Christianity, their relative lack of desire for knowledge as evidenced by their reaction to surviving Hellenistic science, a social division derived from the concentration of political power, and their continued acceptance of slavery, interest in trade, and need to expand the empire as a key to grow state revenue all point to a belief system that may be summarized as follows:

- A religious faith that hampered creative endeavors, except as related to faith itself, such as church architecture
- A belief in the inequality among different ethnic groups within the empire because of significant wealth polarization and slavery, despite the Christian message of equality before God
- An attitude of insularity toward the intellectual and religious creativity of others
- A belief in aggression toward other social orders

These beliefs, though derived in part from Roman heritage and Christianity, while denying Greek heritage, are important since as the first Christian empire of any consequence, these beliefs strongly impacted the beliefs of Christian empires that followed.

14.15 Extrinsic Peaceful Causes

It is difficult to point out significant extrinsic peaceful causes, except, of course, its inheritance of Roman traditions and Christianity impacting the Byzantine Empire. There were perhaps three contributing reasons: its own violent aggressive nature, its strong belief in Christian dogma, and its insular nature from being surrounded by hostile powers on its eastern, northern, and southern flanks and an entrenched and relatively less hostile Christian feudalism on its western flank.

14.16 Extrinsic Violent Causes or Sum Total of Destructive Outcomes

Assessing Loss of SPI

The Byzantine Empire survived much better than the Roman Empire, as it showed more flexibility in dealing with the western Huns and was aware of the strength of the Sassanian Empire. Still, the Sassanians put continuing pressure on the Byzantine Empire and weakened it considerably prior to the end of the current phase, making it easier for Arabs to circumscribe it. However, it never lost political independence. Quite the contrary—it attempted and even succeeded for a while to control of the former Roman territories, as noted before. It is probably fair to assess the impact as a loss of prestige and relative power. Though the empire survived these mortal threats, their net impact was a permanently unsettled, inward-looking state unable to harness the creative energies of its people.

Assessing Loss of Control of Wealth and Means of Wealth

The Byzantine Empire may have lost prestige and power, but it remained in control of its wealth (except doling out booty to the Huns and Persians as needed). Often it benefited from temporary territory expansion and a favorable trade relationship. And internally, it hardly showed progressive economic and technological thinking. Thus, its fortunes fluctuated, depending on the power of others surrounding it.

Fair trade: International trade with Asia was a major factor defining the wealth of the Byzantine Empire during the current phase. However, the Byzantine kings did not control international trade; they merely participated in it. Their naval reach was limited to the Mediterranean; the Persians controlled the trade during most of the phase and handed over the control to the Arabs toward the end.

Migrations: After the fall of the Western Roman Empire, the Byzantine Empire was the only game in town in Europe, and as a result, artists, architects, and scholars flocked to Constantinople and helped build the Hagia Sophia Church in Constantinople, the high point of Byzantine architecture. Byzantine scholars ventured abroad to the Sassanian Empire at Khusrau I's invitation but returned home soon after Khusrau died.

Impact on productive outcomes: The Byzantine Empire benefited from the trade being located at the western end of the Silk Route, which was, perhaps, the greatest source of its wealth, given the static nature of its agriculture and limited reach of its manufacturing.

Transmission of creativity from Rome, Greece and Hellenistic states: The Byzantine Empire naturally inherited all the Western Roman Empire's achievements in military technology, law, art, and architecture. Since it was surrounded by enemies, it was a highly centralized, bureaucratized state, and as such it lacked creative freedom, except in areas such as architecture. The net result was an openness to military technology, art, and architecture in the service of religion and being closed from all other Hellenistic achievements.

Impact on creative outcomes: As the center of European power returned near its ancestral home with the decline of Hellenistic states and the Western Roman Empire, it did not come alone; it brought a total commitment to Christianity. Thus, Roman militarism and practicality, Hellenistic and classical Greek achievements, and Christian faith struggled for control of the Byzantine soul, and Christianity won, hands-down. This outcome was singularly important in the attitude that the Byzantine Empire displayed toward the ideas and inventions of other civilizations. The Byzantine Empire had total access to classical Greek achievements and Hellenistic synthesis in science and had less reason to resist the Hellenistic achievement, as its people could historically identify better with these achievements. But it frittered away its relative trade wealth and urban soul to offensive and defensive campaigns while nurturing Christianity and rejecting science.

Impact on institutional structures and processes: The Byzantine Empire, of course, inherited all Roman institutions, but there were subtle differences: the absence of papal authority, a relative break with the slavery system, and a greater impact of Geek civilization and Hellenistic states. Before Christian dogma conquered the Byzantine state significantly, it was open to Greek intellectual tradition; the last Plato-style academy was closed only in the sixth century. It is a truism to say that Byzantine institutional structures and processes were inherited from the Roman Empire, influenced by ancient Greece and Hellenistic states, and ultimately defined by Christian dogma in a role subservient to the state.

Assessment of net impact: It is not accurate to classify the Byzantine Empire as conquered during the current phase. Perhaps "hapless" better describes its condition, not only in this phase but also during the next two phases. One is reminded of the fate of the Ottoman Empire in the eighteenth and nineteenth centuries. Conscious of its roots in the Roman Empire, unable to influence events and yet somehow surviving and refusing to die describes its state, certainly after the current phase, if not during this phase.

14.17 Productive Outcomes

Productive Outcomes

Wealth creation: Wealth creation got its edge from international trade, since agricultural innovation was relatively low and industry was mostly confined to silk weaving and was controlled by the state.

Fair trade: Despite continual wars with the Sassanians, the Byzantine Empire kept trade with Asia and Europe alive. The goods traded included pottery, tableware, marble, spices, silk, and metalware.

Peaceful migrations: Few peaceful migrations to other civilizations out of the empire were recorded; the only exception was scholars migrating to Gundeshapur, as discussed earlier. However, internal travel was significant for trade, medical treatment, empire administration, and pilgrimage and church affairs.

14.18 Creative Outcomes

Not surprisingly, the significant achievements of the Byzantine Empire were also in art, architecture, centralized administration, and weapons technology.

Achievements in Practical Creativity

When Barbarians disrupted the water supply to Rome in the sixth century, the Byzantine emperor, Belisarius, ordered the conversion of small ships with milling gear that used the river hydropower. Practical innovation in the arena of building construction included the invention of the so-called cross-in-square church architecture and pendentive, which allows a circular dome to be placed on a rectangular building. In the infrastructure area, the concept of the point arch was developed to support a bridge over a tributary of the Euphrates River in the sixth century. In the weapons technology area, two ideas deserve mention: the use of ancient Greek flamethrower technology as a land weapon that saved the empire from Arab onslaught and its grenade version, which was housed in a ceramic or stone jar and launched by hand.

Achievements in Religious Creativity

The process of the split among eastern, Orthodox, and western Catholic branches began during this phase and was completed formally in 1054 CE. The two branches slowly diverged in several key respects. The ultimate authority in Orthodox Christianity rested with scriptures and the councils and not the pope. Significantly, sin was seen as a barrier between God and man and not as a means of punishment. As a result, salvation came from a personal process and not a pardon sanctioned by church officials, who could also be bribed. The divine and not human nature of Christ was of greater importance in the Orthodox version of Christianity, and the process of uniting with God came to be mediated by the Holy Spirit. Orthodox worship began with the invocation of the Holy Spirit to aid in this process and became increasingly liturgical. In short, the Orthodox Christian Church continued to emphasize personal experience and not a legalistic or contractual approach, as its Catholic cousin had developed. This was mainly because the Orthodox church remained dependent on a centralized state and was never powerful enough to, in effect, become a parallel state under the popes.

Achievements in Art

The central feature of Byzantine visual art forms, such as churches, monasteries, mosaics, illuminated scripts, and icons, was its overwhelming Christian religiosity. The

Greek and Roman devotion to natural form was forgotten and displaced by religious imagination in creating art. The highpoint of Byzantine architecture occurred in 537 CE, with the construction of the highly ornate Hagia Sophia Church in Constantinople, complete with icons and mosaics constructed out of metal, wood, precious stones, silver, and gold. In literature, the Greek, Christian, Roman, and Asian elements combined to produce historical accounts; encyclopedias; secular poetry, including the epic *Digenis Akritas*; religious literature; and popular poetry. During the current period, religious literature dominated literary achievements. There was little further development in philosophy.

14.19 Achievements in Science

Achievements in Natural Sciences

Although Byzantine scholars maintained an interest in classical Greek learning throughout the phase, the combined burden of wars and dogmatic Christian faith meant little progress in science, in part because the Hellenistic achievements of second synthesis were ignored, and there was little awareness of the achievements of the second (Indian) synthesis of this phase. Thus, during the current phase, there was little original thinking in science in the Byzantine world. As we shall see in the next chapter, there was a renaissance of sorts in the Byzantine world after 10,000 CE, which was in fact a muted reaction to the third (Arab) synthesis we take up in the next chapter. However, this Byzantine renaissance is of great significance, as it was instrumental in passing on the results of the third synthesis to the Italians, Venetians (in contradistinction to direct transfer from the Arabs to western Europeans), and western Europeans, who spearheaded the fourth synthesis that we cover in chapter 16.

Achievements in Social Sciences

There was little new in the field of social sciences, except the Justinian I legal code and Ecloga that reflected the influence of Christianity on the Roman legal code. We have already covered these.

Summarizing Achievements in Abstract Systems-Building Capability (ASBC)

By the end of the phase, the ASBC of the Byzantine Empire must also be characterized as moderate, as it failed to go beyond the Roman achievement in epistemology.

History, Causes, and Outcomes of the Persian Civilization

14.20 Brief Political History (224–651 CE)

Sassanian Empire

The Parthian Empire, which lasted from 248 BCE to 224 CE or nearly half a millennium, was followed by the third Persian Empire called the Sassanian Empire from 224 to 651 CE. It was founded by a family from Parsa, the cradle of the Achaemenid Empire. Sassanians saw themselves as successors of the Achaemenid Empire after a Greek and Parthian interlude and wished to restore Persia to its greatness and, unlike the Achaemenid and Parthian Empires, must also be classified as a civilization and not just an empire. The Sassanians checked the expansion of the Roman and Byzantine Empires in the west and made a successful, though not lasting intrusion into India in the east with Emperor Shahpur I (240–270), who extended his authority eastwards into northwestern India. The previously autonomous Kushans were obliged to accept his suzerainty. Although the Kushan Empire formally ended by 270 CE to be replaced by the northern Indian Gupta Empire in the fourth century, it is clear that Sassanian influence remained relevant in India's northwest throughout this period. It became the largest empire in the world with the fall of the Western Roman Empire. The Sassanian Empire, though tolerant of Manichaeism, made Zoroastrianism a state religion, thus setting the stage to later adopt Islam. Like its predecessors, it sponsored great art and architecture.

In 427 CE, the Sassanians won a major victory over the Huns and drove them out of Persia. At its height under Khosrau I in 610 CE, the empire included Persia, Afghanistan, modern Iraq, and parts of Anatolia, Egypt, northwest India, and central Asia. Thus, the Sassanians had to deal with the Roman and Byzantine Empires (Byzantine Emperor Justinian paid 440,000 pieces of gold in 532 CE as a bribe to keep the peace) on its western flank. In fact, the Sassanian Empire was surrounded by empires equally keen on expansion on all sides: Roman Empire in the west, the Byzantine Empire in the north, China and central Asians nomads in the east, the Gupta Empire in the southeast, and Arab nomads in the south. The Sassanians handled all these empires with great diplomatic and military skill.

The cross-fertilization of Indian and Persian cultures led to the Indo-Persian culture in the North-West Frontier Province and Baluchistan. However, the Persian court under Khosrau II became decadent, and the treasury was exhausted in renewed fighting with the Byzantine Empire, with Byzantine Emperor Heraclius inflicting serious damage.

The fall came at the hands of Arabs abruptly over a period of a mere five years, primarily because of devastation resulting from the conflict with the Byzantine Empire as well as a succession-related civil war. While it maintained political independence until the end came, its conflict with the Byzantine Empire made its destruction by Arabs relatively easy and swift.

Internal conflicts were well controlled through centralized structures. Much like the Roman Empire, the Sassanian Empire consisted of a central homogeneous civilization surrounded by conquered territories with disparate ethnic groups. The empire was the union of a civilization and a motley collection of peoples. It was a powerful instrument of control, conquering territories from neighboring empires or checking their expansion. They were no different from other empires in this respect. The loyalty of some conquered territories and the Persian civil war of succession proved fatal, and toward the end, the empire fell to Arab armies. Persians slowly converted to Islam, there was little place left for the original religion of Zoroastrianism, and Zoroastrians became a persecuted minority and had to flee to India to save their religion.

14.21 Natural Causes

No significant natural events impacted the Persian civilization during this phase.

14.22 Intrinsic Causes

Institutional Structures and Processes

Political system: The political system of the Sassanians was even more centralized than the Parthian Empire was. Under the king, the structure consisted of provincial governors and a powerful central bureaucracy of military, agriculture, industry, and religion departments. There was a rigid caste system based on birth, with individuals of great talent from lower ranks only rarely able to escape it. The head priest, the military commander, and the chief of bureaucracy were great wielders of power below the monarch.

Military capability: The Sassanian military force further developed based on the strong Achaemenid and Parthian traditions. The military consisted of light infantry and heavily armored cavalry. Both the horse and the soldier were fully armored. The Sassanian military developed two key doctrines: using archers and elephants to create openings that heavy armored cavalry using both the lance and bow could exploit and the effective use of the so-called siege machines used to lob heavy stones into enemy positions. Clearly, the cost of maintaining the heavy armored cavalry was high.

Economic organization and wealth creation: The manufacturing and trading sectors of the economy developed significantly under the Sassanians. Manufacturing centered on metallurgy, woven silk, rugs, jewelry, and fragrance was organized into guilds. That they used labels signifying different brands shows that they were conscious of quality. The mining and metallurgical operations were centered in Armenia and Transoxania, and raw silk was imported from China. Foreign trade was facilitated by a network of roads, bridges, new ports, and Armenian, Syrian, and Jewish merchants that connected the Roman Empire with West Asia. Probably in the early fourth century, Sassanian merchants replaced Romans from the profitable trade routes to India. Thus, under Sassanian rule, Persia came to dominate international trade and kept the Byzantine Empire in check. Under Khosrau I, the petty landholding nobility were the backbone of the Sassanian provincial administration and the tax collection system.

Systems of religious faith: Zoroastrianism was essentially the state religion and was purged of its Greek polytheism, which had found its way into the religion after Alexander. Under Sassanian Emperors, orthodox Zoroastrianism was enshrined through a structured hierarchy of priests and a compilation of the Avesta, which was lost when Alexander burned the city of Persepolis in a fit of revenge half a millennium earlier.

A word about Manichaeism is in order. For a while, it seemed to be on its way to become a world religion that competed with Christianity and Buddhism. Mani was a Persian ascetic who founded Manichaeism in 241 AD. Mani followed the Indo-Sassanians to Afghanistan and the Indus valley to encounter a strong Buddhist culture in these places. Several Buddhist concepts, like the transmigration of the soul, became part of Manichaeism, as did the Buddhist Sangha structure. However, essentially, Manichaeism was a dualistic gnostic religion, with much in common with Christianity and Judaism. Mani returned to Persia, where the Sassanian emperors were tolerant of a new faith that was not dramatically different from Zoroastrianism. It spread rapidly, extending its influence from Europe to China but eventually died out slowly over the following thousand years under pressure from Christianity in the west and Islam in the east. Indo-Sassanians apparently did not convert to Manichaeism and were subsequently absorbed into the Indian mainstream society over time. Similarly, under Sassanians, Christianity also flourished on the western edge of the empire and in Baharain. The first Christian state was established in Armenia in 301. The Sassanian emperors, though less tolerant than the Achaemenids and Parthians, were not religiously intolerant.

There was little direct science-religion conflict during Sassanian rule because the focus on science was limited, and Zoroastrianism was not strictly monotheistic. It was based on dualism in that both good and evil had always existed and was not a uniquely eschatological monotheism yet. Unlike Vedanta, Christianity, and Hinduism, Zoroastrianism did not believe in monasticism. Thus, it did not exert a pull to renounce the world.

Legal system: There was no formal legal code, and the legal system centered on the emperor. This, in turn, required glorification, though not deification, of the monarch. The monarch primarily saw dispensing justice in terms of maintaining a stable social order and not individual rights.

Social structure: The Sassanian social structure consisted of five classes: the nobles, called Bazorgan, headed by a strong monarch; priests; warriors; intellectuals; and commoners. The commoners in turn were split into the Aryan freemen and non-Aryan peasantry. The Aryan commoners constituted the heavy armored cavalry of the Sassanians. Separate rules for different ethnic and religious groups existed, reflecting the tolerant nature of the rulers. These social classes were essentially hereditary, though exceptional individuals did move across classes. Membership in a class was based on birth, although it was possible for an exceptional individual to move to another class on the basis of merit. Zoroastrianism reinforced the social stratification.

Knowledge-Creating and educational institutions: Sassanians also promoted education. The great school in the capital attracted thirty thousand students at its peak, easily the largest university in the world at that time.

Wealth allocation processes: Like the Roman Empire, wealth allocation focused on manufacturing, trade, and military but probably allocated more resources to religion and education than the Romans did. Much like in the Achaemenid Empire, the Sassanian royalty vacillated between an unpretentious and decadent lifestyle. The latter contributed to its undoing, as we noted above.

Social cohesion processes: The social cohesion in the multiethnic empire was successfully maintained through a justice system that was tolerant of diversity, a powerful Zoroastrian religious hierarchy, and a strong military force. However, Sassanian rulers promoted Zoroastrianism right from the start and at times persecuted Christians. As a result, social harmony suffered. After the arrival of Islam, adherents of Zoroastrianism were persecuted and treated as dhimmis, with many migrating to India.

Internal wars: Strong centralized structures, strong military, and excellent infrastructure successfully prevented significant internal wars within the empire. Toward the end, the invasion by Byzantine Emperor Heraclius unglued the empire, with Khusrau being murdered by his son who agreed to end the war. Khusrau's death started a civil war and a war of succession lasting nearly two decades. This civil war created an opening for Arab armies.

Formative Beliefs and Ideology at the End of Second Synthesis Phase

The relatively benign monotheism of ancient Persians; their relative lack of desire for knowledge through scientific means except for a brief period under Khusrau I; a reduced social cohesion due to Zoroastrianism, followed by Islam as the state religions; the oscillation between luxurious decadence and Spartan lifestyle of the elite; their acceptance of slavery; their interest in trade; and their need to expand the empire as the singular means to grow state revenue all point to a belief system that may be summarized as follows:

- A belief in practical knowledge but not scientific knowledge
- A creeping belief in inequality among different religious groups within the empire, with continuing wealth polarization and slavery
- An attitude mostly of insularity toward the intellectual creativity of others
- A continuing belief in aggression toward other social orders

These beliefs were derived from earlier Persian empires and were reinforced through the active promotion of Zoroastrianism and adoption. The arrival of Islam to Persia was a crucial significance for both sides, but we address that in the next chapter.

14.23 Extrinsic Peaceful Causes or Sum Total of Constructive Outcomes

Impact of Byzantine Empire

Persia, of course, was not a peaceful civilization and was in constant struggle with the Byzantine and Roman Empires as well as local empire building in modern-day Israel, Iraq, Jordan, Armenia, Afghanistan, Turkey, Caucasia, central Asia, Arabia, and western Pakistan. In fact, the exhaustion after the war with the Byzantine Empire made it possible for Arabs to defeat Persia.

Transmission of creativity: There is little doubt that there was continuing diffusion of practical technology from the Byzantine and Roman Empires. However, Persians absorbed what they thought was important, limiting themselves to mostly practical innovations, art, and architecture. Throughout the half millennium of interaction between Sassanians and the Byzantine Empire, there is only one instance of known interaction in scientific arena: migration of scholars from Byzantine to Persia when the Byzantine Emperor Zeno expelled these scholars. However, even these scholars returned home as part of a treaty with Emperor Justinian, as they felt homesick. This short-lived unique experiment in science initiated by an enlightened Persian Emperor Khusrau I unfortunately died with him, since the experiment did not sprout from the Persian soil. During this brief period under Khusrau I, science was promoted, employing disgruntled intellectuals fleeing from the Byzantine Empire. A later treaty between the two allowed the intellectuals to return home and cut short the experiment in science. Persians were intensely practical empire builders without a wealth drain propensity. They borrowed practical technology, art, and architecture from all and rejected religion, critical philosophy, and science until the time of Khusrau II.

Impact on productive and creative outcomes: The impact of the transmission of practical and military innovations must be considered peripheral, and Persians probably influenced the Byzantine Empire as much as the Byzantine Empire influenced it.

Impact of Indian Civilization

The interaction between the Indian civilization and Sassanians was limited and somewhat forced. The Sassanians had established themselves in northwest India, taking advantage of Kushan's weakness before the rise of the Gupta dynasty and before the Hun pressure. They rose again after the collapse of the Gupta dynasty. During the second Indo-Sassanian period, interaction took place. However, it was limited to the exchange of practical technologies. Just as the Persians had walked away from Mesopotamian astronomy and geometry a millennium ago, Indian achievements in astronomy and mathematics hardly impressed them.

Transmission of creativity: The interest in achievements of the Indian civilization did awaken briefly during the reign of Khusrau I (532–579 CE). Khusrau I was a generous patron of literature and philosophy. Greek and Indian works were translated, and scholars from the Byzantine Empire and India arrived at his court. During the reign of Khusrau I, Indian scholars were invited to Gundeshapur, and several Sanskrit texts were translated. Clearly, the Sassanians had access to the works of Aryabhatta, Brahamagupta, and others. However, with the death of Khusrau I, the potential synthesis of Hellenistic science that was gathering dust in Constantinople and Indian science under the auspices of an enlightened king died as well. Unfortunately, his rule was followed by his son, who had little interest in the creative outcomes of other civilizations. Thus, the openness to others' intellectual creativity lasted for a short time during the reign of Khusrau I.

The impact of Indian civilization was also the cultural arena through such artifacts as Chess, with Persia changing its name from Chaturanga to Chatrang and one of Khusarau I's ministers translating Panchatantra into Pahlvi. The minister went to India in search of a plant that revived the dead but instead came back with Panchatantra!

Impact on Productive and Creative Outcomes: The impact must be considered secondary since it was voluntary and depended on the inner nature of Persian civilization.

14.24 Extrinsic Violent Causes or Sum Total of Others' Destructive Outcomes

Impact of Arab Conquest

Loss of SPI: For the most part, the Sassanian Empire was an aggressor and often a conqueror. Toward the end of phase, over a period of two decades, the Sassanian Empire successively lost Mesopotamia, central Persia, southern Persia, southeastern Persia, Azerbaijan, Armenia, and Khorasan to Umayyad Caliphate by 651 CE. About a century after the Umayyad conquest, the Abbasids Arabs, who were in competition with the Umayyad Caliphate, joined forces with non-Arab Muslims, particularly the Persians. They succeeded in establishing the Abbasid Caliphate and moved the capital from Damascus to Baghdad. Given their long history and imperial tradition, the Persians reasserted themselves in the Abbasid court in Bagdad very quickly after the Abbasid victory, and what emerged was a synthesis of Arab-Persian culture with religion and language supplied by Arabs and much else by Persians. Abbasids, though successful in destroying the Umayyad Caliphate with Persian help, ultimately paid the political price, and power slowly flowed from Arabs to the Muslim Persians. One surviving branch of the Umayyad family fled across North Africa to the Iberian Peninsula to establish a parallel Caliphate in Spain and Cordoba and remained a rival of Baghdad as one of the two centers of Muslim power for several centuries. Thus, we would argue that, though Persians were conquered by Arabs, their eventual acceptance of Islam and their own imperial tradition allowed them to emerge as near co-equals to their conquerors.

The contrast with the Indian experience with Islam during the next phase is instructive. Hindus largely refused to accept Islam (they considered their tolerant religious tradition far superior), and they lacked an imperial tradition, thus the Muslim Empires in India largely remained foreign and only ceased being so when an enlightened ruler such as Akbar came to power in the sixteenth century.

Loss of control of wealth and means of wealth: Arabs were empire builder settlers. Thus, there was little question of wealth drain. Additionally, except in religious matters, Arabs were keen, open students, and given their small numbers, they needed allies. They were much like Greeks in the Hellenistic states, only the Arabs were armed with an intolerant religious ideology. Thus, apart from replacing the Persian elite, there was little impact on the loss of control of wealth and means of wealth. Arabs were utterly different from Romans in this respect.

Fair trade: Perhaps the most significant impact came through trade with other civilizations. Sassanian merchants had dominated the trade, with Europe and India as not only middle men but also manufacturers of high-quality, value-added merchandise. Arabs continued and expanded this enterprise. However, it is to be noted that this trade mostly remained fair trade, since Arabs lacked the control of seas and territories in Europe (except Spain and Sicily), India (except Sindh), and China.

Transmission of creativity: Persians were beginning to be recipients of the fruits of second synthesis of science through the Arab presence in the Iberian Peninsula and Sindh.

Impact on productive outcomes: Like most empire builder settlers, the impact of Arab conquest on the productive outcomes of Persia was minimal, except for the short-term impact of property destruction and political instability.

Impact on creative outcomes: The full impact of this transmission was felt in the next phase, after Arabs consolidated their control and as Persia adopted Islam.

Impact on institutional structures and processes: Historically, since the Achaemenid days, Persia saw itself as the center of power and culture and all surrounding areas (including Greece for a while until Athens developed into a power center) came under Persian cultural influence to one degree or another. Persia was hardly influenced by other social orders until the arrival of Islam. In political organization, military capability, economic organization, systems of religious faith (Zoroastrianism, Manichaeism and Baha'I, and Mazdakism), legal systems, social structure, and knowledge-creating and educational institutions, one discerns little influence of other social orders. The only exceptions are Manichaeism and Mazdakism (the earliest known form of communism), where one detects the influence of Buddhist thought. The most significant impact came through adopting a foreign dogmatic religion, which necessitated the adoption of Arabic script. However, the Zoroastrian religion was not as distinct from Islam as, for example, Hinduism was. With Islam, there was little separation of religion and state, and the Isla-derive Sharia legal system had to be adopted once Islam took root. Thus, two Persian civilizations exist: the older, true Persian-inspired civilization through the Achaemenid, Parthian, and Sassanian Empires, and a Muslim Persian civilization through the Arab caliphate. Arab monotheism and conquest, however, was unable to extinguish the Persian culture, though they were able to put it on a different path. In the end, Persia made Islam thoroughly Persian and taught its Arab masters a lot while learning the value of science and critical philosophy from them.

Assessment of net impact: The negative impact was loss of SPI for a short while and the imposition of a new religion and the destruction of an old one. However, there was little wealth drain, and the victors were staunchly proscience. In fact, Arabs introduced Persians to science, and the latter took to science like ducks to water. Yet, as we shall see in the next chapter, Islam also killed science in twelfth-century Persia. On balance, we would regard the impact to be negative, and Persia was pulled from an Indian-Iranian-European sphere into the Arab sphere—an arena it dominated before as conquerors.

Arab conquest signaled the rise of a worldwide Arab Empire, by far the largest the world had seen to date. This instrument of control was responsible for shifting control of trade and setting the stage for the third synthesis in science for the first time under the auspices of a nomadic people, as we will discover in the next chapter. It was truly the age of barbarian and nomadic ascendancy just about everywhere because civilized social orders were weak as a result of the conflicts of the previous phase.

14.25 Productive Outcomes

Wealth creation: Sources of wealth were territorial expansion, industry, and trade, as noted above. Although the basic societal structures and processes continued to be Persian in inspiration and became more centralized, the Sassanians benefited from the expanding world trade, diffusion of religious ideas, and immigration of scholars from the Byzantine Empire and Indian civilization. Nonetheless, it must be acknowledged that the Persian civilization gave as much to the world during this period as it took in, if not more.

Fair trade: The Sassanian Empire built on the international trade the Kushans initiated. However, it is hardly surprising that this trade was not just taxed by the state for revenue but also under state control and was focused on luxury items, much like the Roman Empire. There was indeed a great network of roads, bridges, ports, and caravan rest houses to support the trade activity. Remains of Sassanian colonies on the Arabian Peninsula attest to the role the Sassanian Empire played in international trade. The empire mainly exported rugs, leather goods, textiles, and woolen products.

Peaceful migrations: Peaceful migration consisted mostly of the scholars from India and the Byzantine Empire.

14.26 Creative Outcomes

In many ways, the Sassanian period constitutes the highest achievement of Persian civilization before its defeat at the hands of Arabs and conversion to Islam. The sustained creative focus of the Sassanian Empire was on practical creativity, medicine and art, and architecture.

Achievements in Practical Creativity

The primary focus of the empire was on practical creativity, with a special focus on iron technology in part because infantry required the protective iron gear. Iran earned a well-deserved reputation as the armory of Asia. There was also considerable emphasis on technological innovations, such as the waterwheel and windmill, which are said to be of Persian origin.

Achievements in Religious Creativity

Religious creativity during the Sassanian period expressed itself in a revival of Zoroastrianism and Manichaeism and a tolerance toward other faiths. Neither Zoroastrianism nor Manichaeism was strictly monotheistic. Persian civilization had already left polytheism behind more than a millennium ago and was yet to show any interest in monism, agnosticism, or atheism. It is said that Sufism, later adopted by Islam, was born in Gundeshapur from its neo-Platonic roots.

Achievements in Intellectual Creativity

As Christian dogma took hold of the Byzantine Empire, intellectual creativity took a back seat. In 489 CE, Zeno closed the theological and scientific center at Edessa. As a consequence, many scholars left the Byzantine Empire in 529 CE, when Justinian persecuted the scholars. Khosrau I gave refuge to these scholars at Gundeshapur, which became a great center of learning, drawing scholars from Byzantine, Hellenistic, and Indian civilizations.

Achievements in philosophical creativity: Khosrau I commissioned scholars to translate Greek texts into the Pahlavi language and invited Indian and Chinese scholars to Gundeshapur. Achievements in philosophical creativity were, however, limited to becoming familiar with the Greek, Hellenistic, and Indian civilizations because the political support for intellectual creativity was short-lived. As we noted earlier, after Khusrau I, the financial support died down because of a decadent lifestyle, conflict with the Byzantine Empire, and civil war. Thus, the lamp of knowledge was indeed lighted but never burned bright. One is reminded of Moghul Emperor Akbar's attitude toward religion a millennium later. His religious tolerance in the face of resistance from the Islamic establishment only lasted as long as he was alive. Thus, we may ascribe the short-lived Gundeshapur experiment to Khusrau I and Zelo's expulsion of scholars and not resulting from the inner processes of the Persian civilization. It just never took root. With the treaty with Emperor Justinian, these homesick scholars returned home, thus hastening the decline of Gundeshapur.

Achievements in Art: The Sassanian Empire truly achieved greatness in art and architecture. It essentially rejected the Hellenistic influence, returned to its Persian roots of Achaemenid period, and laid the basis for the coming Islamic art and calligraphy. Its influence has also been traced to central Asia, China, and the Byzantine Empire.

Persian architecture of the period is known for its distinctive use of space that conceived a monument or palace in terms of masses and surfaces, creating a very expansive and calming feeling. The walls were decorated in stucco color. Monuments at Ctesiphon and Firozabad are massive, with the largest single span vault at the time. The dome chamber in the palace of Firozabad used the squinch, which allows building a circular dome on a square building. This was most likely a Persian invention adopted in the building of the Hagia Sophia. Clearly, painting and art are well developed, if one is to judge from later references. Artistic creation also expressed itself well through metalwork, gem engraving, pottery, sculpture, textile art, rugs studded with jewels, exceptional royal crowns of great symbolism, and decorative garments.

The Sassanians used Pahlavi as the state language. During this period, written tradition began to replace oral tradition. The written tradition primarily focused on the religious and historical matter, with little interest in the literary field. Thus, Avesta was written down and the compilation of history annals, such as *Book of the Deeds* of the Ardashir, Son of Babag which is not a work of historiography. Rather, it was a record of how the ruling elite wished to perceive the founder. As in science, many literary works were translated into Pahlavi. Even the Indian classic *Panchatantra* was translated from Sanskrit.

14.27 Achievements in Science

Formal sciences: There were few creative outcomes in mathematics, logic, or linguistics that deserve mention in this period.

Natural sciences: Similarly, in natural sciences, astronomical and astrological works were translated but little new knowledge was added during the short period of support.

Medicine: The medical treatises on medical diagnosis, herbal medicine, and surgery from Hellenistic, Greek, and Indian sources were translated and synthesized to create a flourishing school of medical treatment. The distinctive achievement of Gundeshapur is the achievements of its school of medicine and its hospital system. Recent research, however, has cast some doubt on the importance of this ancient learning center.

The Sassanian Empire was the high point of the classical Persian civilization, which was focused on empire building and vacillating between simple and decadent living.

Summarizing Achievements in Abstract Systems-Building Capability (ASBC)

By the end of the phase, the ASBC of the Persian Empire must be characterized as moderate: it had adopted/modified alphabetical script and mastered creative method but continued to lack sound epistemology.

History, Causes, and Outcomes of the Chinese Civilization

14.28 Brief Political History (220–618 CE)

Chinese Civilization

China went through centuries of fragmentation after the fall of the Han dynasty. The important dynasties during this phase of Chinese civilization were the three kingdoms of Wei, Shu, and Wu, which lasted until 280 CE. Under the three kingdoms, China went through a period of decentralization. This was followed by the Jin dynasty (265–420 CE), which unified the country. Civil war in the Jin dynasty encouraged rebellion by nomadic tribes settled in the north, which led to a non-Han Wu Hu Period (304–439 CE). The Wu dynasty was founded by nomads settled in the north. The Jin dynasty had invited these people to work as laborers to repair the badly damaged Chinese economy during the period of Three Kingdoms. Thus, the political fragmentation of the period may be attributed to both civil war toward the end of the Han and Jin dynasties and nomadic instruments of control. However, the invaders did not bring a monotheistic faith with them nor were they looking to drain the wealth; they were conquerors who wanted to replace the Chinese elite, settle down in the conquered territory, and adopt Chinese culture. They did this successfully and were absorbed into the Chinese civilization over time, very similar to the absorption of Kushans and Indo-Greeks into the Indian civilization. Wu rule again led to fragmentation into as many as sixteen states and a large-scale migration of the Han Chinese to South China. The Jin, who had been pushed south by Wu forces, collapsed in 420 CE, which led to southern and northern dynasties (420–589 CE). During the four centuries after the fall of the Han dynasty, China was fragmented into anywhere from three to sixteen states or kingdoms, a state of affairs that was only ended by the short-lived Sui dynasty from 589 to 618 CE, which revived many of institutions and central authority. A brilliant period under the Tang dynasty followed for nearly three centuries, and we cover that in the next chapter.

There is a theme that we constantly witness in the Chinese history: the founding of a dynasty, the rise of a highly centralized state resulting in a relatively long period of peace and prosperity, followed by collapse based on internal or external causes leading to at times a prolonged period of political fragmentation. China has been rightly described as a practical, insular civilization constantly in search of a state, finding it, and losing it numerous times, including in the current phase. In contrast, Indian civilization may be described as a profoundly religious, open civilization and only occasionally able to organize a subcontinent-wide state for short periods.

The Chinese civilization during most of this period remained mired in internal conflicts and sustained invasions from the eastern Huns, Xiongnu nomads, Tibetans, and the Toba tribe, who were probably related to the Gokturks. However, it did maintain its distinct identity for the most part through successfully absorbing these nomads, much like what had occurred in India during the previous phase. The instability, unfortunately, led to a general philosophy of hedonism and anarchy during the period, despite the adoption of Buddhism.

The outstanding features of this entire period in China's history were political fragmentation, outstanding practical creativity, and the spread of and resistance to Buddhism.

14.29 Natural Causes

There were no significant natural events that impacted the Chinese civilization materially during the current phase.

14.30 Intrinsic Causes

Except the political fragmentation and arrival of Buddhism, there was little significant change in societal structures and processes.

Systems of religious faith: The Chinese first became aware of Buddhist doctrine in 2 BCE through central Asian Yuezhi people. After the rise of the Kushan Empire and the conversion of Emperor Knishka to Buddhism in the second century AD, a Parthian monk by the name of An Shih Kao came to China in 148 AD and established the first Buddhist temple in Layang. In the fourth century, we witness the arrival of a great teacher named Kumarajiva to China. Kumarajiva was the son of an Indian father and a Kuchean princess. Kumarajiva was actually captured and brought to China and may have spent several years in prison. He eventually rose to become the teacher of Qin dynasty Emperor Yao Xing, the first Chinese emperor to convert to Buddhism. Prior to Kumarajiva's arrival in China, the Buddhist monks had translated the Buddhist sutras based on concept-matching translations. This meant that they tried to find the nearest equivalent concepts in Taoism and Confucianism and used those to translate Buddhist texts. Kumarajiva put an end to that practice, resulting in tremendous clarity in new translations. Buddhism spread in China because of not only the political instability but also certain similarity between Taoism and Buddhism. For example, the Tao concept of the three treasures of compassion, moderation, and humility are very similar to Buddhist concepts of Karuna, middle path, and Buddha's personal example of humility. Probably, the most significant impact of the spread of Buddhism in China was an advance in religious thought, from a mixture of crude polytheism and sophisticated Taoism to a softer version of Buddhist agnosticism. This advance was undoubtedly responsible, in part, for China's ability to withstand the challenge of Islam centuries later. The spread of Buddhism in China occurred during the long period of instability, from the beginning of the third century to nearly the end of sixth century. It is an irony that the birthplace of Buddhism rejected Buddhism and fell to Islam, and the adoption of Buddhism contributed to China successfully fending off Islam in the coming centuries. It is also noteworthy that the spread of Buddhism to China and other parts of Asia was completely nonviolent. It was based not on military might or even the will of the masses, as was the case in Christian Europe; rather, it was based on the intellectual appeal of the Buddhist doctrine itself to the elites in China. It was a top-down conversion as opposed to the bottom-up conversion in the case of Christianity or conversion based on military conquest in the case for Islam.

There was little science-religion conflict during the phase, since the religious impulse in both indigenous religion and Buddhism was not antiscience, and there was modest focus or interest in science. The focus remained on practical creativity and adoption of agnostic Buddhism.

Legal systems: A word is also in order concerning the development of legal systems in China. While the Chinese civilization produced a strong state on a civilization scale very early in its history, China failed to develop a rule of law that stood above the sovereign. The reason for this is two-fold: Chinese law was never grounded in religion and China did not experiment with any form of democracy at village, state, or federal levels. In most civilizations, emergence of legal systems was either rooted in religion or some form of democratic expression. China was strong when its center was strong. It was equally true that China lacked a caste system or any propensity toward slavery. It was perhaps the first civilization to open the doors of bureaucracy to the common man based on sheer talent and no connections. In many ways, China is a unique civilization. Like the Indian civilization, it never showed any interest in territorial expansion; its orientation was not geopolitical expansion but internal order and external defense. The emperor, bureaucracy, and common law served as de facto legal structure and legal code.

Social structure: There is little doubt that political fragmentation led to greater inequality, since much like the Roman Empire, the fragmentation gave rise to wealthy families without the presence of a central authority.

Internal wars: Internal wars resulting from the collapse of the Han, Jin, and Sui dynasties were a continuing theme of the phase as noted above.

Formative Beliefs and Ideology at the End of Second Synthesis Phase

The enthusiastic adoption of Buddhism, their continuing strong practical orientation toward knowledge, a high degree of social cohesion based on the absence of slavery and caste systems, their continuing focus on nomadic threat, their greater interest in trade, and their fundamental peaceful orientation toward other social orders all point to significant changes in a belief system that may be summarized as follows:

- A belief in practical knowledge based on observation and common sense
- A belief in a form of Buddhism strongly influenced by Hinduism
- A continuing belief in equality among citizens, now supported by Buddhism as well
- An attitude of continuing insularity toward the intellectual creativity of others
- An abiding belief in peace and defensive posture toward other social orders unless attacked

These beliefs were fundamentally derived from Chinese culture, and the adoption of Buddhism reinforced some, such as social equality and peacefulness.

14.31 Extrinsic Peaceful Causes or Sum Total of Constructive Outcomes

Impact of Indian Civilization

Trade and migrations: The Kushan dynasty developed and made safe the Silk Route in the first centuries of the Common Era. During the current phase, the Muslims or central Asians did not control the Silk Route, and the trade to Europe was conducted through the sea. Thus, the Silk Route was likely used primarily for China-India trade. The manufacturing sector under the Gupta kings was highly organized and contributed to trade with China.

Transmission of creativity: Chinese interest in Buddhism drove the interaction between Chinese and Indian civilizations during the current phase. Indian Buddhist monks visited China, and the Chinese Buddhist monk Xuanzang visited India between 629 and 645 CE. Over six hundred Buddhist texts, Buddhist relics, and statues were brought back to China on twenty-two horses. Upon his return to China:

- He organized a gigantic effort to translate the texts into Chinese with the help of scholars from all over East Asia.

- He founded a new school of Buddhism, known as the Faxiang school, which did not survive for too long but produced great scholars, such as Kuiji, a Chinese, and Woncheuk, a Korean.
- Through his personal interest in the Yogyakarta school, he succeeded in transmitting Hindu and Buddhist theories concerning perception, karma, rebirth, and consciousness to different schools of Buddhism in China. The reader may recall that by the seventh century, the original agnosticism of Buddha's message was a distant memory in Indian Buddhism, and Buddhist schools had adopted many of the concepts of Vedic religion into Buddhism.

It is curious that the Indian decimal place value system with the concept of zero was not transmitted to China, perhaps because of Xuanzang's religious focus. However, during his long stay, he must have noted the advantages of the Indian number system. China continued to use its own positional decimal system without zero (a system still superior to anything in West Asia or Europe). Muslims finally introduced the Indian numeral system to China the Yuan dynasty. The same applies to Xuanzang's reaction to Indian breakthroughs in astronomy under Aryabhatta and the alphabetical script he encountered in India. Thus, for inexplicable reasons, this transmission never broadened beyond religion. Perhaps the two cultures were very different with different priorities. On the surface of it, however, it truly remains a perplexing phenomenon.

Impact on productive outcomes: There was modest impact on productive outcomes except through trade efficiencies, which were likely secondary in importance. The greater impact came through the resources that the state spent in building monasteries and temples and the upkeep of the monks, who neither worked nor paid any taxes. Often, these construction projects caused materials shortages, particularly of precious metals. One gets the impression that Buddhism conquered the minds of the common man more than it conquered the elite, and the royalty undertook these projects largely to win the loyalty of masses. The spread of Buddhism also created the demand for Buddhist artifacts for the common man.

Impact on creative outcomes: The interaction between China and India remained peaceful. It is clear that despite Xuanzang visiting India for prolonged studies, his interest seemed to have been confined to Buddhism. Indian achievements in astronomy and linguistics did not seem to have made an impression on him. There are also no records of Chinese practical creativity reaching India. These must be regarded a great missed opportunity in the history of creative exchange.

Impact on institutional structures and processes: The interaction between a practical, worldly culture and the agnostic Buddhist doctrine which had been heavily influenced by Hinduism that arrived in in China was fascinating. Chinese monks, while they never achieved strong political influence, demanded and received a comfortable existence. The influence of Buddhism was confined to art, religion, and to some extent, the legal system. Chinese culture did not have a strong tradition of meditation before Buddhism; thus, it invented the concepts of Amitabha or selfless souls in and "Pure Land" to help the bring the Chinese to nirvana.

14.32 Extrinsic Violent Causes or Sum Total of Destructive Outcomes

Loss of SPI

Wu Hu barbarians controlled China and its SGS for over a century and were ultimately absorbed into Chinese civilization. China remained unscathed from Arab and Hun attacks; in fact, their defeat of eastern Huns, once again, created nomadic pressure on India, West Asia, and Europe. China maintained its tradition of taking the blows from nomads and successfully civilizing them.

Impact on China

Other civilizations impacted China primarily through the spread of Buddhism and trade during this phase, as China continued a strong preference for insularity. The impact of Buddhism was covered in an earlier section. Global trade actually suffered during the period because of the unstable relationship among empires and civilizations and because China itself experienced significant internal turmoil.

14.33 Productive Outcomes

Wealth: Despite being a kaleidoscope of rising and falling states as a result of internal divisions, civil war, and nomadic invasions, the current period of fragmentation must be characterized as prosperous. The emergence of a mechanical genius like Ma Jun attests to the use of new technology in wealth creation.

Fair trade: Foreign trade to Europe suffered as a result of fragmentation. However, there was a continuation of the trade with the Indian civilization in part because of the spread of Buddhism.

Peaceful migrations: The most significant peaceful migrations were the migration of the nomads to China at the invitation of the Chinese emperor to help repair the economy and the migration of the Han Chinese to the south later under pressure from these same nomads after they attained power in northern China.

14.34 Creative Outcomes

This period of Chinese history underscores the notion that a civilization need not be a politically united entity to be creative; reasonably stable states capable of ensuring internal creative freedom and sustained political independence are the only requirements.

Achievements in Practical Creativity

The Chinese civilization continued its amazing contributions in practical creativity. The highlights are:

Materials: Manufacture of steel by forging cast and wrought iron.

Processes: Wood block printing used to print *Dharani Sutra,* which was translated from Sanskrit and is the earliest block print discovered to date.

Tools: During the current phase, China witnessed the birth of a mechanical genius named Ma Jun in the third century CE. Many mechanical inventions, such as an ingenious puppet theater operated by hydraulic power, the crankshaft handle, chain pumps used in irrigation, a south-pointing compass, differential gear that allowed applying equal power to wheels rotating at different speeds, and automatic door openers that used a foot pedal resulted from his genius. The earliest possible development of the abacus in China and the earliest water clock using the escapement mechanism also date from this phase.

Energy: Use of methane gas to light the cities through bamboo gas cylinders, water-powered flour-sifting mills (reverse steam engine).

Agriculture technologies: Improved whiffletree, use of biological pest control, use of manure as fertilizer, row planting, hoe, weeding, and tea.

Nonagricultural products: Improved silk loom, improved ceramic techniques, matches to light fire, use of toilet paper, and use of banknotes or paper money.

Construction: One hundred thousand rock-carved statues of Buddha in Longmen, a nearly three-hundred-foot-high pagoda made out of cast iron, and a 1,325-ton cast iron pillar.

Transportation: Improvements in stirrup and horse collar design, a windmill-powered carriage, a wheelbarrow, and even a manned flight using kite.

Infrastructure: Stone arch bridge over the Jiao River and the Grand Canal linking Yangtze and Yellow Rivers completed.

Communication: First court newspaper published; first public newspaper published in 748 CE.

The substantial achievements of the Chinese civilization in practical creativity are summarized in table 14.1.

Achievements in Religious Creativity

Kumarajiva set the wheels of religious creativity in motion during the phase when he translated the Buddhist sutras. The absorption of Buddhism in the China school produced

Table 14.1: Significant Achievements in Practical Creativity
Chinese Civilization, 750–1200 CE

Category	Significant Achievements
Materials	Improved porcelain
Processes	
Energy	Gunpowder composition, use of petroleum
Tools	Improved escapement mechanism, fishing reel
Agricultural Products	
Non-Agri. Products	7-day week, paper money
Construction	40-ton cast iron pagoda
Transportation Technolog	Improved compass, 700-ft-long bridge, dry docks
Weapons Technologies	Gunpowder rockets
Infrastructure	
Communications	Movable type, first book printed, multicolor printing

several new schools, of which Pure Land Buddhism, Tiantai, and Chan deserve mention. Pure Land Buddhism originated in India and probably came to China in the second century. It stressed the attainment of mindfulness through recitation of the Amitabha Buddha to attain rebirth in the Pure Land. The Tiantai school drew inspiration from the work of philosopher Nagarjuna and placed great emphasis on mindful breathing as a method. The Chan school, which subscribed to several Buddhist sutras and was focused directly on the mental function to achieve Nirvana, was clearly derived from Raj yoga.

Achievements in Intellectual Creativity

Achievements in art: Chinese art focused on sculpture, painting, and calligraphy during this period. The initial impulse of depicting Buddhist motives of enlightenment and inspiration in a realistic manner gave way to a more abstract expression during the period of northern and southern dynasties. However, near the end of the phase, there was a reaction to this lifeless representation, which paved the way for the vibrant Tang Buddhist art we cover in the next chapter. Perhaps Gu Kaizhi was the most famous painter of the period. Gu Kaizhi was from the ancient city of Wuxi and wrote three books on the theory of painting emphasizing the importance of expression in the eyes. Painting was done on silk or brick walls in tombs and depicted religious themes or daily and court life. The Chinese have viewed calligraphy as a form of painting that embodies abstract line, rhythm, and structure more perfectly than painting. This may be an idea whose aesthetic value may be difficult to appreciate. Calligraphy initially used silk as medium, and paper later replaced it. Famous calligraphers of the period include Wang Xizhi, Lanting Xu, and Wei Shuo, the last being a woman.

Finally, we may mention Guo Pu, who wrote a history of the Jin dynasty and *The Book of Burial,* which defined the concept of Feng Shui (literally meaning water-wind) for the first time. Feng Shui has been applied in home decoration, gardening design, landscaping, and business transactions and has been used in the rituals of daily life since then.

14.35 Achievements in Science

Mathematics: Chinese mathematicians of the phase were describing large numbers using powers of ten and represented the negative and positive numbers using different colors. By 400 CE, Chinese mathematicians—possibly as early as five hundred years earlier—successfully developed a true position value decimal number system using bamboo rods and a board. Liu Hui (263 CE) used a 192-sided polygon to compute a highly accurate value of pi and proved the so-called Pythagorean Theorem. Chinese mathematician Sun Tzu (250 CE) discovered the remainder theorem, which can be useful in finding solutions to the polynomials through trial and error. Zhang Qiujian (450 CE) developed formula summing an arithmetical series and the solution of two linear algebraic equations. Zu Chongzhi (~475 CE) developed the correct formula for the volume of a sphere using the so-called Cavalieri method. Liu Zhuo (544-610) introduced the quadratic interpolation method.

Astronomy: The Chinese continued its fine tradition of astronomical observations. They produced star maps, identified the first nova, and correctly observed that the tail of a comet must always be away from the sun.

Medicine: Physician Chen Chuan identified symptoms of diabetes mellitus.

Summarizing Achievements in Abstract Systems-Building Capability (ASBC)

By the end of the phase, the ASBC of the Chinese civilization must be characterized as low: it had mastered creative method but continued to fail to adopt alphabetical script and lacked sound epistemology.

History, Causes, and Outcomes of the Central Asian Nomads—Second Wave

14.36 Brief Political History

The Central Asian Nomads—Second Wave (200 CE–774 CE)

In the last chapter, we witnessed the saga of the central Asian Xiongnu tribe, which came into conflict with the Han dynasty after successfully deflecting the Yuezhi branch toward India. The Yuezhi defeated the Parthians, ruled North India for two centuries, and became absorbed into Indian culture. Another central Asian tribe known as Huns moved west near the Caspian Sea in the early fourth century, after the Chinese successfully dispersed the Xiongnu toward northwest. "Western" Huns ravaged Western Europe, and another branch known as Indo-Hephthalites were defeated in India and were largely a spent force by the end of the sixth century. Following the Huns, we witness the rise of Gokturks, who were kept in check by the powerful Sassanian Empire in the West and China in the south and were ultimately defeated by Arab nomads. With that, the second wave of the invasion of central Asian nomads came to an end. In the last chapter, we covered the Xiongnu and Yuezhi or Kushan Empire, and in this chapter, we cover the Hun and Gokturk Empires. After a hiatus of five centuries, we shall witness yet another central Asian empire under the Mongol Genghis Khan and its subsequent offshoots in China and India over the following centuries. The central Asian nomads, like all nomads, rose to prominence when the following three conditions were met: sufficient diffusion of transport and weapons technologies from civilization to nomads, the rise of a charismatic leader able to unite different tribes into a fighting force exploiting the principal of tribal equality, and military/political weakness in nearby civilizations.

Nomads settled in the north, founding the Wu dynasty. These people had been invited by the Jin dynasty as laborers to repair the badly damaged Chinese economy during the period of the Three Kingdoms. Thus, the political fragmentation of the period may be attributed to both civil war toward the end of Han and Jin dynasties and nomadic instruments of control. However, the invaders did not bring a monotheistic faith with them and were not looking to drain the wealth; they were conquerors who wanted to replace the Chinese elite, settle down in the conquered territory, and adopt the Chinese culture. They were successful and were absorbed into the Chinese civilization over time, very similar to the absorption of Kushans and Indo-Greeks into the Indian civilization. The instruments of control, thus, did negligible permanent damage to the Chinese civilization.

Rouran Khannate (330–555 CE): Rouran Khannate was a central Asian tribal confederacy that created an empire north of China. It was defeated by an alliance of Chinese and Gokturks in 552CE. It seemed that Rouran Khannate was unsuccessful in threatening civilizations except indirectly by pushing western Huns toward Europe and Indo-Huns toward India. The relationship of the Rouran to the Xiongnu has not been established.

Western Huns (369–470 CE): While theories concerning the origin of Huns vary, most scholars consider them to be of central Asian origin. They settled near the Caspian Sea, possibly driven westward by Rouran Khannate, and by the late fourth century had conquered the European barbarians, such as the tribes of Alani, Ostrogoths, and Visigoths. In 395 CE, a Hun raid into the Caucasus resulted in their destruction of Armenia and even Syria. They were less successful in attacking the northern provinces of the Byzantine Empire. In the early fifth century, a charismatic leader known as Oktar created a unified federation. He was succeeded by Rugila, who became the first Hun to attack the Roman Empire in alliance with a Roman general. Rugila was followed by his nephews, Bleda and Attila, as corulers who plundered the Byzantine Empire. In 445 CE, Bleda died, leaving Attila fully in charge. In 447 CE, he began plundering the Byzantine Empire again, and this continued for three years until 449CE, when he received the promise of annual tribute. Only earthquake, famine, and plague saved the eastern empire from the Huns. Attila was on good terms with the Western Empire. However, in 450CE, a Roman princess asked Attila to save her from a forced marriage with a prominent Roman senator. Using this as a pretext, Attila claimed half of the Western Empire. When he did not receive the dowry, he invaded the Western Empire and had to retreat in 451CE after a tactical defeat. In the meantime, the Eastern Empire stopped paying tribute, and Attila planned to attack Constantinople but died in 453 CE on his wedding night after marrying a German princess. Attila's heirs sustained defeat at Nedao in 469 CE, and that effectively ended the Hun adventure in Europe.

Indo-Hephthalite Huns (400–550 CE): It is likely that Indian Huns, also known as Indo-Hephthalites, that invaded India in 480s CE, were not related to Huns that plundered Europe and may have chosen to call themselves Huns to frighten the enemies. Nonetheless, this branch harassed the Gupta dynasty for nearly fifty years until Narsimanhgupta led an alliance to defeat them in the 530s CE. However, the Gupta Empire was fatally weakened in the process.

Gokturks Empire (552–774 CE): About four hundred years after the fall of Xiongnu power at the hands of China, a branch known as the Gokturks (meaning "celestial Turks") under Bumin Qaghan of the Ashina tribe rose to power by rebelling against the Rouran Khanate. The Rouran Khanate was a confederation led by the Xianbei tribe, who had remained in the Mongolian steppes after most Xianbei had migrated south to northern China. At its zenith, the empire stretched from the Black Sea to within a thousand miles of the Pacific Ocean. It was confined to the north of China since rise of the Tangs (618–908 CE, to be discussed in the next chapter) made it difficult to expand in the south. Gokturks had similar traditions and tribal/political structures as the Xiongnu except that the council of tribal chiefs had sovereign authority to replace the Khans. Gokturks lasted from 552 to 745 CE, and a civil war in 584 CE resulted in a split into eastern and western pieces. The Tan dynasty dominated the eastern part; however, the western part continued to expand and came into conflict with the Arab Umayyad Califate and was ultimately defeated. By about 750 CE, the reconstituted Eastern Empire was ended by the Tang dynasty. These people were later conscripted as fighters by the Abbasids and were to play a dominant role in world history for centuries.

As noted before, the Huns were instrumental in weakening or destroying the Roman, Byzantine, and Gupta Empires. There was internal fighting and a major civil war. The Gokturk Khans were responsible to the Ashina tribal council, which retained the ultimate authority, and this tended to temper the infighting. Gokturks could have brought havoc to many civilizations. However, the Chinese and Persians successfully kept them in check, though they were later defeated by the Arab nomads. The Sassanians probably prevented them from invading India as the Yuezhi and Huns had earlier. In the end, their empires were nothing but millions of square miles of barren land and a few million inhabitants subsisting on plunder of and tribute from civilizations.

The bottom line is that the Hun groups, related or unrelated, plundered the Roman, Byzantine, and Gupta Empires, in part because the Sassanians defeated them in 427 CE, thus deflecting the Hun pressure toward Europe and India for over a century. After that, they essentially disappeared. But the damage was done. Hun plunder and the fighting between Persians and Byzantine Empire had opened the way for a more dangerous nomadic invader, the monotheistic Arab nomads.

14.37 Natural Causes

Nomads by definition exist on dry, hot, or arid lands incapable of supporting agriculture. What drives all nomads, including the Huns and Gokturks, is possession of land capable of supporting agriculture.

14.38 Intrinsic Causes

Institutional Structures and Processes

Like the rise of all nomadic people, the rise of Huns and Gokturks followed a familiar pattern: rise of a charismatic leader capable of uniting the different tribes based on personality and political skill, create a fighting machine, and sense weakness in neighboring tribes by initiating the campaign to win. There was little pretense of an ideology in the case of either Huns or Gokturks.

Formative Beliefs and Ideology at the End of the Second Synthesis Phase

The relatively crude animism of the central Asian nomads, their relative inability to develop intellectual knowledge, high social cohesion derived from tribal roots, charismatic leadership and egalitarian lifestyle of the elite, the absence of slavery and caste systems, their interest in trade, and their singular focus to attack civilizations all point to a belief system that may be summarized as follows:

- A belief in practical knowledge and a focus on military strength
- A belief in the relative equality among citizens without significant wealth polarization
- An attitude of openness toward the intellectual and religious creativity of others
- A belief in aggression toward civilizations

These beliefs derived from their tribal traditions are important, since as the second wave of central Asian invasion of civilizations, they passed these beliefs to the next wave of invasions when some tribes converted to Islam, significantly impacting these beliefs as we discuss in the next chapter.

14.39 Extrinsic Peaceful Causes or Sum Total of Constructive Outcomes

There were no significant extrinsic peaceful causes driving the central Asian nomads. There were few goods that could be traded or interchange of inventions or ideas with mutual benefit. Peace was simply a tactical retreat until a future perception of relative military strength.

Transmission of Creativity

During their reign, the Turkic language adopted a script commonly known as runic script. In fact, it seems the primitive Norse Elder Futhark or rune alphabet used by pre-Christian Scandinavian Germanic tribes descended from Gokturk script (likely through conquests of European barbarians by western Huns, as noted earlier). The Gokturks were religiously tolerant, like all central Asian nomads, except when they began to adopt Islam after the ninth century. When the latter happened, they turned into the most ferocious defenders of the faith. During the current phase, the Gokturks tolerated Buddhism, Christianity, and Manichaeism but continued to practice shamanism, animism, totemism, and animal worship. They likely absorbed practical technology from the civilized people they came in contact with, such as the Chinese, but there is no direct evidence of that. Europeans Huns also used Gothic as a language, did not have interest in religion, and never really settled down from plunder and tribute-seeking for us to assess their religious tolerance.

14.40 Extrinsic Violent Causes or Sum Total of Destructive Outcomes

Central Asian Nomads as Invaders but Not Conquerors

During the current phase, civilizations were relatively strong compared to central Asian nomads. Unlike the previous phase, when central Asian nomads established empires in West and South Asia, their success was confined to harassing civilizations and civilization-based empires. It is true they helped end the Roman Empire; however, they did that with the help of European barbarians and could not establish a lasting presence in Europe. The campaign of the Huns in India was a failure in that they were unable to establish lasting political presence there either. In China, the eastern Gokturks were under Tang control. Towards the end of the phase, the emerging Arab nomads defeated western Gokturks. The reasons for this state of affairs were both the relative military strength of the civilizations and lack of unity among the nomads. Multiple nomad groups were vying for control throughout the phase. Thus, the impact of central Asian nomads was limited to creating sizable internal empires in arid central Asia, collecting booty from civilizations, or retreating after attacking them.

Thus result of this Mexican standoff between central Asian nomads and civilizations was that central Asians did not build empires encompassing civilizations and provide them with political stability, bring in new technology, or reinvigorate the racial stock of civilization. They remained a nuisance, and as western Gokturks witnessed the swift rise of Arab nomads armed with a new creed toward the end of the phase, they understood they could no longer compete with Arabs and wisely chose to join the Arabs as mercenaries in the next phase. As luck would have it, the eastern central Asian nomads would rise one more time under Genghis Khan to overwhelm the Muslim civilization by then controlled by the erstwhile mercenaries now converted to Islam. However, for this interesting turn of events, we must wait until the next chapter.

Bottom line: the impact of violent aggression by central Asian nomads was marginal on the invaders but considerably more on civilizations and empires they attacked.

14.41 Productive Outcomes

For a while, Gokturks played a dominant role in ensuring the global trade through the Silk Road, and it was a very profitable enterprise for them. Many Gokturks settled in the conquered territories in the western empire and later were conscripted into the Arab armies after their defeat, and their descendants played a dominant role in the control of Muslim civilization in the eleventh century.

14.42 Creative Outcomes

It is difficult to assign any significant creative outcomes to the Huns, Gokturk, and other Turkish nomads during this period. Their energies were focused on absorbing practical technology from civilizations they came in contact with and using their military strength to expand the territories.

14.43 Achievements in Science

Summarizing Achievements in Abstract Systems-Building Capability (ASBC)

By the end of the phase, the ASBC of the Chinese civilization must be characterized as low: it had mastered the creative method but continued to fail to adopt alphabetical script and lacked sound epistemology.

History, Causes, and Outcomes of the Indian Civilization

14.44 Brief Political History (200–750 CE)

At the beginning of this period, Kushan power had begun to decline in North India. By the end of the second century AD, the Kushans were exhausted, and their demise was hastened by Indo-Sassanians who had declared their independence from the Sassanian Empire in Persia and managed to carve out an empire in North India that lasted over a century. The Indo-Sassanians were in turn weakened by attacks from the Indo-Hephthalites in 410 AD, and this paved the way for the expansion of the Gupta Empire. This ushered in a second golden age of Indian civilization and science. The Gupta dynasty lasted nearly three centuries and spanned almost all North India at its height.

The Indo-Hephthalite broke through again by the end of the fifth century, causing trouble for the Guptas. They did unsettle the Guptas but were unable to establish an empire of significance. The Huns invaded India and succeeded in advancing to the Ganges valley, leaving behind a trail of looting, rape, murder, and destruction. They temporarily overthrew the Gupta Empire but an Indian coalition eventually defeated them in 528. A coalition of Hindu dynasties finally drove them out in 557 AD.

Guptas began to lose steam after this period and were replaced by Indo-Sassanians in the northwest for a second time and by the so-called Turki Shahi dynasty in the Punjab area. The Turki Shahi dynasty (550–870 AD) was actually an Indian Buddhist dynasty despite the name. In the seventh century, we also witness the rise of Harsha Vardhan (590–657 CE) in north central India. The Hindu Shahi dynasty (870–1050 CE) replaced the Turki Shahi dynasty. Meanwhile the Western part of India, after the Guptas, came under the control of the Pratihara Rajputs, who were dominant from the sixth to the eleventh centuries (in the east and northeast, the Pala dynasty held sway from 750 to 1174 CE).

The evolution of North Indian dynasties was a result of three forces: the attacks by Indo-Sassanians, Indo-Hephthalites, and indigenous reaction to it. This resulted, as noted above, in several regional kingdoms and two great empires, one long-lasting and the other rather short-lived, (Guptas and Harsha, respectively) during the period. The short-term success of Arabs in the Sindh was politically marginalized over a time. Therefore, the North Indian civilization, though taking several blows, was able to resist Persian, Hephthalites, and Arab expansion successfully. The invaders were, once again, successfully absorbed into the Indian civilization under the big tent of Hinduism or were successfully checked.

It is noteworthy that the Arab army had been victorious throughout Eurasia; however, it had to struggle for seventy years to relatively succeed in India. In the next century, they pushed forward in several provinces of northern and western India. But at the end of it all, India was far from being conquered militarily or assimilated culturally. Nagabhata I of Malwa handed a defeat to Arab armies in 725 CE and the Chalukya ruler, King Vikramaditya II, defeated Arab armies in 738 CE. The Arab advances into the Punjab and toward Kashmir were driven back by

Lalitaditya Muktapida (724–760 CE) of Kashmir. He was in alliance with Yasovarman of central India. The Arab invasion of India, thus, ended in a more or less a failure, as contrasted with its success in Iberian Peninsula. Arabs, therefore, suffered a much worse fate in India than in Europe and in a shorter time. Despite some early success, their adventure must be judged to be a failure. They seemed to have lost interest since they were eminently more successful in Europe, Anatolia, West Asia, and even western portions of central Asia. Consequently, they decided to leave India and China alone and to focus on building a civilization in the conquered territories. Their consolation prize was a few trading posts and Multan on the Indian subcontinent. It is important to remember that the Arabs took all of seventeen years to conquer the Persian Empire and all of seventy years to conquer Iberia, but they never tasted lasting success in India. It is also interesting to read later Arab historians' derisive accounts of the Arab failure to conquer India, which they attributed to the presumed Hindu practice of voodoo and black magic! Centuries later, when Muslims would make a successful second attempt to invade India through the Turks who had converted to Islam, these outposts would come handy as sources of information of military significance. But for now, these outposts seemed of little strategic significance. It was the third time in a millennium that India had successfully repulsed or civilized the nomads. But it would be the last time.

The history of internal conflicts among Indian states during this phase is too diverse to be captured in a few paragraphs. And it is not particularly relevant to our purpose. Between the periods of centralized empires, there was continual warfare. However, it is important to recognize that such warfare did not destroy intellectual creativity. The land grants to the universities, for example, were recognized by successive states. The warfare did not destroy the economy. The change in political leadership through warfare had little long-term impact on intellectual creativity. Aryabhatta, the astronomer, did his most creative work during the turmoil caused by Hun invasions! True to its core values, the Indian civilization did not attack another civilization; its external orientation remained peaceful and open. It shared its science freely with others.

There were no naval powers yet capable of threatening the Indian civilization either.

14.45 Natural Causes

There were no significant natural disasters or gradual changes that impacted the Indian civilization during this phase.

14.46 Intrinsic Causes

Institutional Structures and Processes—North India

Political systems: At the height of their rule, the Gupta kings ruled through an extensive administration headed by ministers in charge of military, judicial, and financial affairs. Governors controlled twenty-six provinces, each subdivided into districts called *vishayas* and headed by a *vishayapati*. Each district was further divided into several *vithis*. Each vishayapati was assisted by a four-person council representing the city mayor, merchants, noble families, and bureaucracy. However, the administrative structure was a far cry from the centralized model in Roman, Chinese, and Persian civilizations. It depended on the collaboration between the central regional and local officials.

Military capability: The Gupta's military capability consisted of armored infantry employing javelins and long swords, infantry archers, armored cavalry, a division of elephants, and a navy to patrol coastal waters. The steel bow the archers used had both high penetration and long range due to the high tensile strength of the steel. Unlike the invading Huns, cavalry archers were rarely employed; however, the long bows were highly effective against the horse-mounted archers. Guptas also used catapults and fire arrows. The war tactics combining the infantry, cavalry, and elephant division were highly developed. The military force was disciplined and understood the importance of logistics. This fighting force defeated the invading Huns, and the decline of the empire must be attributed to internal division and not inferior weapons, command, or tactics.

Economic organization and wealth creation: Village life remained unaffected by the military campaigns, by and large. Village democracy and self-sufficiency continued. During the emergence of a strong state such as the Gupta Empire, the economic exchange between villages and cities increased. The Gupta Empire employed a detailed system for land measurement and taxation. There also existed urban-based merchant and artisan guilds that had separate administrative organizations, attesting to the vigor of the commercial and manufacturing sectors. The prosperity under the Guptas reached new heights, with the wealthy and middle class gaining ground. There were rest houses for travelers and merchants along India's highways. External trade expanded to both Europe and Southeast Asia, bringing wealth to north India.

Systems of religious faith: In general, Buddhism began dying slowly after 600 CE in India, and Brahmanism and Hinduism were asserting themselves again. However, it was a peaceful transition based on debate and reason and not violence; nonetheless, it was a transition of monumental consequence for the future of science as we see later.

In addition to Hinduism, Gupta kings and Emperor Harsha extended patronage to Buddhism and Jainism.

There was no science-religion conflict in North India during the phase. Islam and Christianity, though both present on the subcontinent, were on the sidelines. Monism remained subdued until toward the end of the phase. Hindu polytheism and agnostic Buddhism were ascendant, and both were fully reconciled to science.

Legal systems: The law of Manu, straddling the religious law and common law, formed the basis of social behavior. The royal edicts formed the basis of statutory law that distinguished between civil and criminal law, and the judicial apparatus implemented the statutory laws. The people were generally law-abiding, and punishments for crime were relatively lenient and mostly monetary. Rarely, punishments such as a death sentence or having one's hand cut off were applied against obstinate, professional criminals.

Social structure: The caste system was alive and well, tempered by absorption of foreign elements and the impact of Buddhism and formed the basis of social structure. The class structure, based on wealth differentiation, was superimposed on the caste system. Law did not recognize the equality of sexes. If slavery existed, it was not on a large scale; the existence of a caste system mitigated its need. Numerous charities created by the wealthy existed, offering free care to all, and the capital possessed an excellent, free hospital. Thus, the caste and class inequalities were compensated a little by the charitable inclination of the wealthy.

It is difficult to assess the degree of class stratification during the phase in North India. Increasing prosperity tended to hide it, and the caste system tended to make it acceptable. On the whole, it is difficult to see how class and caste stratification got any worse than in the previous phase.

Knowledge-creating and education institutions: Knowledge was highly valued, as evidenced by the number of great universities and observatories. Nālandā was a Buddhist center of learning in eastern India and was founded in 427 CE. It has been called the first of the great universities in ancient recorded history, and Bakhtiyar Khilji sacked it. This event is seen by scholars as a late milestone in the decline of Buddhism in India. He is said to have asked if there was a copy of the Koran at Nalanda before he sacked it. Nalanda had 10,000 students and 1,500 professors and a significant contingent of foreign students. Takshashila was an early center of learning dating back to at least the fifth century BCE in the northwest. Ujjain had a famous observatory during the reign of Harsha in the seventh century. These were by far the biggest and the best universities that world had seen to date. It is worth noting that both Buddhist and Hindu scholars worked in the same universities side by side.

Wealth allocation: Speaking relatively, Indian monarchs of the age lived modestly. One hears of Gupta kings bowing their heads in public gatherings, acknowledging that they served the public. One hears of Harsha emptying his treasury every five years in an attempt to help the poor and return the people's wealth back to the people. Gupta kings recognized talent by appointing nine individuals of exceptional achievement in diverse areas as jewels to the court. This was a practice adopted by the later Mogul king Akbar. Undoubtedly, surplus was diverted to defending against the nomadic invasions and internal conflicts; however, it was not excessive, and the increase was typically of short duration.

Social cohesion processes: The Gupta period was a period of political freedom: people were free to travel without passports. Government did not need espionage for internal stability and cohesion. Caste rules and the concept of dharma and Buddhist ethics based on the eightfold path contributed to a social cohesion with little crime.

Internal wars: Internal wars were intense during both the early and last part of the phase. The decline of the Kushans and the Indo-Sassanian invasion created instability, which the rise of Guptas put an end to. After the decline of the Guptas, under Hun pressure and internal squabbling, the provincial governors revolted against the Gupta Empire. However, it must be stated that during this phase, nomads were far less successful in India than in Europe and China under Hans. A century or so later, the western part of north India came under the Pratihara Rajputs and the eastern part under the Pala dynasty, both of which we cover in the next chapter.

Institutional Structures and Processes—South India

At the beginning of this phase, South India entered a dark age under the Kalabhras, who ruled most of the south for over three centuries. Following the decline of this central authority, we see a kaleidoscope of dynasties, including Pandaya (560–820 CE), Chaluka (543–753 AD), Pallavas (335–800 CE), and Rashtrakutas (753–982 AD) emerging on the South Indian scene.

The best of the South Indian dynasties were centrally administered where there was autonomy for the villages and a direct contact between the farmers and the empire officials—in other words, the absence of a landowning class. The main crops included wheat, rice, and barley. There was considerable attention given to irrigation projects. The Kallanai dam, which dates back to the fourth century and spans the Cauvery River, must be considered an engineering wonder of its time.

The stronghold of religion and the caste system was tight, and most education was connected with religion. Temples were the main centers of education. There were no centers of higher learning anywhere near comparable to Nalanda in the north. Students often went to North India to pursue higher learning. The Shaiva or Vaishnava forms of Hinduism prospered.

There was continual warfare among dynasties but with little impact on village life.

Formative Beliefs and Ideology at the End of Second Synthesis Phase

The tolerant structured polytheism and monism of Indian civilization and the relative decline of Buddhism toward the phase end, belief in knowledge through union of reason and observation, deteriorating social cohesion because of the caste system, their continuing openness, and peacefulness all point to a belief system that may be summarized as follows:

- A belief in possibility of knowledge through the union of observation and reason on the one hand and a challenge to that from monism, which shunned observation
- A belief in the fundamental inequality among different castes
- An attitude of openness toward the intellectual and religious creativity of others
- A belief in peacefulness toward other social orders

These beliefs were mostly continuation of internal traditions impacted by the changing balance of power between a retreating Buddhism and an ascendant monism and structured polytheism.

14.47 Extrinsic Peaceful Causes

Impact of Hellenistic States

Although we have called the current phase the Indian synthesis, there were two likely significant Hellenistic influences on the Indian civilization.

Transmission of creativity (science, art): The diffusion from the Hellenistic states probably continued during the early part of this phase, but it soon dried out as the Hellenistic states were absorbed into the Roman Empire and as Christianity became the state religion of both western and eastern Roman Empires. It is known that several Hellenistic texts on astronomy were translated into Sanskrit. Yavanajataka or sayings of the Greeks was probably translated in the second century and was particularly used in astrological calculations. Paulisa Siddhanta was another translation of Hellenistic astronomy and was based on the work of Paul of Alexandria in the late fourth century. Finally, Romaka Siddhanta was another work that was translated in the sixth century. How specifically these works influenced Indian science is not known with certainty; however, they were clearly thought valuable by Indian astrologers and astronomers. Aryabhatta probably knew of Ptolemy's contorted epicycles. However, it is curious that Euclid's geometry does not appear to have diffused to India, probably because it first existed in published form in the fourth century, authored by Theon of Alexandria. Thus, Aryabhatta had to invent both plane and spherical trigonometry (which are a marriage of geometry and algebra) in order to do astronomy. Yet, Aryabhatta rejected Ptolemy's epicycles and went on to propose a heliocentric solar system. It is known that Romaka Siddhanta did influence the work of Varahamihira in the seventh century in the development of his tropical system of astronomy. We may not be certain about their specific genealogy; however, it would be foolish to bet against such an occurrence.

Hellenistic art also found its way into northwest Indian Kushan kings, decades after the fall of Indo-Greeks, who had converted to Buddhism and created the Gandhara School of art, which flourished until the seventh century CE. There is archeological evidence of such transmission.

Impact on productive outcomes: There was little impact on the productive outcomes.

Impact on creative outcomes: Indian astronomers certainly knew of Hellenistic achievements in astronomy. However, it is also clear that they did not pay too much attention to its results and followed an independent path. How Greek realism in art affected the Mathura-centered Kushan art and the paintings in Ajanta is a matter of debate, however.

Impact on institutional structures and processes: There was little impact on Indian institutional structures and processes, which followed the Mauryan tradition.

Impact of Southeast Asian Civilizations

There were extensive religious, trade, and cultural exchanges between India and several countries of Southeast Asia, both during and following the Gupta dynasty. Cultures of present-day Indonesia, Burma, Cambodia, Sri Lanka, and Vietnam were profoundly affected by the Indian civilization, creating what has been called Greater India. What is truly remarkable about greater India is that it was not based on military power and political control; rather, it was based on soft power. For over a millennium, starting with the current phase, this soft power resulted in states, dynasties, and magnificent Hindu and Buddhist temples whose ruins are scattered all over Southeast Asia. During the current phase, as North India fragmented politically following the fall of Gupta dynasty, dynasties in southern India continued the expansion of Indian culture to Southeast Asia, including Java and Sumatra, as we shall note in the next chapter.

Impact on productive outcomes: Impact was confined to South Indian dynasties and resulted from trade efficiencies.

Impact on creative outcomes and institutional structures and processes: The impact was primarily from the Indian civilization to the Southeast Asian states, principally in religion, art, architecture, and language. We cover more of this in the following chapters.

14.48 Extrinsic Violent Causes

Assessing the Loss of SPI

The Sassanian Empire weakened the Kushan Empire in the third century CE, thus allowing the rise of the Gupta dynasty, much as Alexander's invasion provided some impetus for the rise of Mauryan dynasty more than half a millennium ago. However, in the sixth century, the Huns failed to conquer India and gain control of its SGS and were absorbed into Indian civilization. The strategic impact of the instruments of control on Indian civilization was significant since it resulted in the decline of the Gupta Empire and ushered in another period of the fragmentation. Nomadic Arabs conquered vast territory from Spain to Sindh, controlling the SGS in West Asia, Iberia, and North Africa. They were far more successful in Europe and against the Sassanian Empire than they were in India. They were beaten back in India and only managed to hold on to minor pockets.

It is fair to say that although Sassanian pressure and nomadic invasions caused a lot of destruction, unlike the previous phase, these invasions were hardly able to seriously impact the sustained political independence of the Indian civilization.

Loss of Control of Wealth and Means of Wealth

Because the invaders during the phase were empire builder settler types (Kushans, Huns, and Arabs), there was little drain of wealth to the outside and because these invaders were followed by indigenous rulers (Guptas, Harsha) and because the invaders (except the Arabs, who did not succeed) hardly brought with them a religious or economic ideology, the impact of these invasions, apart from temporary destruction of life and property and the displacement of elites, was not substantial.

Impact of Huns and Arabs

Fair trade: The trade continued to prosper during most of the current period, though it suffered with the demise of the Roman Empire. It picked up again because of Southeast Asian trade, Sassanian control of the international trade, and the rise of Arabs toward the end of the current phase. Arabs had begun to participate in trade during the current phase but did not control it yet.

The interaction during the current phase was mostly limited to Arab invasion, and trade control passed into Arab hands through small trading colonies the Arab merchants established. The invasion of India was a strategic failure, and Arabs were too preoccupied with carving out an empire from the decaying body politic of the Sassanian, Byzantine, and Roman Empires to remain engaged in India after a few decades. Their interest in Indian science would actually awaken later in the next phase through continued commercial contacts and control of trade based on their now extensive global empire.

Impact of migrations: The most significant peaceful migration into India originated in Persia after the Arab invasion and the conversion of its population to Islam. Although the conversion was a slow process lasting hundreds of years, several Zoroastrian groups saw the handwriting on the wall and chose to migrate to western India in 715–936 CE, the exact date not being certain. This was not particularly significant at the time. However, the Parsees, as the emigrated Zoroastrians came to be known, were one of the first communities to show interest in European culture during British rule and were instrumental in developing modern Indian industry. Huns impacted Indian society by loosening the caste system and the political hierarchy of the ruling dynasties. The Huns who chose to stay were absorbed into Indian culture over time.

Transmission of creativity: Invaders who came into India were mostly nomads, such as the Huns and Arabs. These invaders brought a strong tradition of armored cavalry and new war tactics. Perhaps water mills and windmill came to India from Persia during this time. Both Christianity and Islam were introduced in India, the former peacefully in South India and the latter through aggression in North India. However, neither made a significant impression of Indian religiosity during the phase.

Apart from ideas and inventions in the military arena and religion, the obvious flow of creativity was from the Indian civilization to nomads. Arabs had shown exceptional aggression and success in West Asia and Europe but were not a civilization yet and did not have much to contribute to Indian learning. As a result, there was little diffusion of intellectual creativity into India; rather, it was out of India.

Impact on productive outcomes: The impact was marginal except through trade and an uncertain flow of practical technology. However, Indian civilization was also strong in manufacturing and production of wealth as the widespread existence and power of manufacturing guilds shows.

Impact on creative outcomes: There was little impact on creative outcomes either, for India was undoubtedly the leader in formal sciences, astronomy, philosophy, and religious creativity.

Impact on institutional structures and processes: Except in the military arena and through the marginal introduction of Christianity and Islam, there was little impact of the institutional structures and processes as evidenced by the structures and processes of the Gupta and Harshvardhan dynasties. Both Islam and Christianity remained confined to local pockets in modern-day Kerala and the Sindh/Multan area respectively.

Assessment of net impact: The net impact of invasions on the Indian civilization, when considering both positive and negative aspects, must be assessed as marginal except for the immediate loss of life and property. Indian civilization took a second blow and bore the brunt of nomadic invasion but held its own while leading the world in science.

14.49 Productive Outcomes

Wealth production: Indian civilization continued to generate wealth as evidenced by repeated invasions and desire to trade with India by Huns and Arabs. The current phase was a period of great prosperity in India. Wealth polarization was likely modest, considering how well various industrial guilds were organized and considering the humble, public-oriented attitude of the Gupta monarchs. It was also a period when the monarchs and polity valued meritocracy. The Gupta period was a period of peace, where people lived in an environment free of crime and poverty. The existing political and religious structures and customs managed the class conflicts well without killing the incentive for individual achievement. There was a remarkable entrepreneurial culture and a broad middle class under enlightened monarchs.

Fair Trade: Decline in travel resulting from the dominance of Brahmanism resulted in a steady decline in the shipbuilding industry, as we indicated earlier, and opened the door for Arab traders. India continued to be a manufacturing powerhouse of the world, even after the fall of Guptas, leading the world in textiles and mining and metallurgy; however, the job of moving the merchandise out of the country had now fallen into Arab hands. In the following centuries, the Arab merchants would be the source of much information the Turkish invaders needed to attack India starting in the eleventh century. The attack came from the northwest, when the civilization was weaker militarily after having gone through centuries of political divisiveness.

Migrations: There were no major migrations into or out of India during this phase. True to its inner nature, India welcomed Christian missionaries and Zoroastrian refugees. Many Arab Muslim traders also made India their home and were treated well.

14.50 Creative Outcomes

Achievements in Practical Creativity

Based on archeological research to date, it seems the focus of practical creativity during the current phase was not in agriculture and transportation technologies but primarily in manufacturing technologies. Perhaps agriculture and infrastructures were already relatively developed, and the focus had shifted to manufacturing sector.

Materials: Vegetable dyes from indigo and cinnabar, sugar refining and crystallized sugar, rust-free iron, and cashmere wool

Processes: Dyeing process, distillation process, and development of diamond mining

Tools: Bow instruments for carding of cotton, a magnetic compass called *machha-yantra* or fish machine, spinning wheel, and single roller cotton gin

Energy: Water mills

Nonagricultural Products: Perfumes

Construction: *Vastu shastra* manual, showing and understanding of materials, architectural techniques, and hydrology

Achievements in Religious Creativity

The impact of the life-and-death struggle between Buddhist agnosticism and the monism of Vedanta during the current phase was monumental for the future of Indian science. Buddhist thought was turning idealistic, and the Buddhist focus had shifted from the original social concerns to doctrines of Buddhism itself. The Brahmins took advantage of that in two ways: first, polytheism found resurgence under the Guptas, as evidenced by the composition of Puranas during the current phase and second, systematized monism drove Buddhism out of India and turned the country in a conservative direction, including injunctions against foreign travel. Philosopher Sankara played an outsize role in this monumental change.

Achievements in Philosophy

Metaphysics: There are two outstanding names in metaphysics during this phase: Dignaga (also called Dinnaga) and Sankara. Unfortunately, both eventually lapsed into idealism. Dignaga arrived at his idealism through reductionism as follows: what we see as an object is analyzable into smaller parts. We may regard smaller parts as real. However, they can be broken into still smaller parts. This means that smaller parts do not exist except in our minds. The object, therefore, exists only in consciousness. Here, Dignaga, through reductionism, projects the analytical nature of mind on to the object and reaches a conclusion that sensation does not exist, thus contradicting the very method he outlined in epistemology, where he give priority to sensation over inference.

Sankara, perhaps the greatest Hindu philosopher, was more subtle. Sankara agreed that starting point of knowledge of external reality is indeed sensation. But he believed what we sense is not true reality but reality transformed by our organs of sensation and thought. This sensation-based knowledge is a delusion and is a form of ignorance. True reality is not the multiplicity we see in the external world but an external unchanging dynamic unity he called Brahman. But how do we access Brahman? Apparently not through sensation and mind. His answer was that something higher than senses and mind was trapped in lower being or ego—the Atman—is directly capable of communion with the Brahman, bypassing the senses and the mind. Of course, Sankara did not outline or propose any mechanism through which this communion takes place or provide any objective proof that this external unity he called Brahman exists. Judging from his remarks, it appears that the existence of all was matter, energy, and a presumed cosmic spirit. His philosophy is similar to Emanuel Kant's philosophy, who thought the structure of the mind itself changes our perception of external objects, and therefore we can never know the thing-in-itself. Of course, Kant did not formulate a unitary external reality that is beyond mind or a higher self within. Thus, Kant may be regarded as a philosopher-scientist and Sankara as a religious philosopher, both sharing common prejudice.

Sankara's system had no place for a personal God, thus moving away from both polytheism and monotheism. The existence of God was also no problem for Sankara, since for him existence is God; God is not transcendent, he is imminent in the world and knowable here and now. Sankara is regarded as the philosopher responsible for re-establishing philosophical monism in India. The first significant period of Indian science or the birth phase of science from 750 to 500 BCE started with a successful challenge to monism, and the current phase of the second synthesis of science, unfortunately, ended with ascendant monism under Sankara's relentless leadership. However, Indian monism was never overtly antiscience; it just did not value science as much. It was more interested in spiritual enlightenment.

Epistemology: Dignaga, a Buddhist philosopher, made the outstanding contribution to epistemology. He is said to have written at least fourteen philosophical works, and nine of them survive. But none of them are in the original Sanskrit; they survived only in Tibetan and Chinese translations. These books were destroyed by ignorant Muslim-Turkish invaders in the twelfth and thirteenth centuries because they assumed the presence of the statues of Buddha in Stupas and universities and the absence of the Koran meant idol worship. However, had they bothered to study the content of these books, they would have likely found them to be even more offensive and blasphemous.

In a work called *Nyayamukha* or *Introduction to the Method* and later in *Pramanasamuccaya* (meaning *A Compendium of Theory of Knowledge*), Dignaga, following the Visheska school, emphasized that there are only two means of knowledge: sensation and inference, the latter including both induction and deduction. However, most importantly, he emphasized:

- Sensation is knowledge uncontaminated by imagination.
- Inference is knowledge gained through the middle term of a syllogism, with the constraints discussed below in the section under logic. He goes to great lengths to emphasize that in inference, the sensation belongs to a class that shares the middle term. The sensation may belong to many other classes. Only sensation is real, and all classes are just mental categories.
- Sensation must take precedence over inference, if one must choose.

Thus, his early epistemology is consistent and thoroughly realist and free from imaginary concepts like preexisting forms, eternal idea, or thing-in-itself, which appeared real to many Western epistemologists before and after Dignaga.

Let us move on to creative outcomes in science.

As we have noted before, North India bore the burden of Hun invasions from the northwest and the Arab nomads from mostly southwest but also from northwest. It was successful in repelling or containing both invasions. The crucial difference was that it was able to absorb the former into Indian civilization but not the latter. The pockets of control the Arabs maintained after they retreated continued to adhere to an uncompromising monotheistic faith that would not hesitate to use any means to achieve its political and religious objectives. It was to rear its head, as mentioned above, in later centuries in the form of Turkish invasions from the northwest, as we shall discuss in the next chapter. For the moment, India, unlike Europe, was mostly able to protect its political independence from the invaders. It would, however, be for the last time. As a result, the centers of learning and science continued to prosper in the north despite political fragmentation after the decline of Guptas. Great universities, both of Hindu and Buddhist persuasion, dotted the north. Students from overseas and the south flocked to these universities to learn and to teach.

One such great student and teacher was Sankara, who systematized the Vedanta philosophy. Another was the Chinese traveler Fa-Hein, who came to learn about Buddhism and has left a very favorable account of Indian society of the period. There was a real flowering of arts, literature, and architecture during the period, as the Ajanta and Elora caves demonstrate.

Thus, we see that Indian civilization successfully co-opted the foreigner invaders for the third time (Alexander in fourth century BCE, Yuehzi/Kushans/Indo-Greeks/Indo-Scythians over next half a millennium, and Indo-Sassanians/Huns/Arabs over the following half a millennium) through a combination of military resistance and cultural/religious absorption during the current phase. The relatively gentle agnostic values of Indian civilization triumphed once more. Again, as before, these invasions were a disruption to the cause of science, but only relatively speaking. The absence of a monotheistic creed in Huns, containment of the Arabs, the presence of internal creative freedom, and highly productive land all made certain that progress in science resumed once peace and stability was reestablished after invasions or internal wars. During this entire phase, India was the only civilization contributing to the march of science despite the periods of instability noted above. In this respect, the period was no different from the modern era in that despite terrible, continuous wars over two hundred years notwithstanding, science continued to move forward.

Achievements in Art

The Gupta period was perhaps the golden period of Indian art, with excellent sculpture, painting, architecture and literature, dance, and drama. Unfortunately, most of the temples of the period are no more, the only exception being the Ajanta and Elora caves that were carved out in the fifth century CE and later. Ajanta has forty-eight rock-cut caves with Buddhist themes. The thirty-four caves at Elora represent the high point of rock architecture that has Hindu (seventeen), Buddhist (twelve), and Jain (five) themes. These caves are not only architectural and sculptural wonders but also depict the high point in Indian wall painting.

Kalidasa reached the high point in Indian drama and poetry was reached during this phase under the Guptas, as during the current phase. We do not know with certainty about the life of this great figure of Sanskrit literature. Kalidasa, who was a master of simile, wrote three plays ("Malavikagnimitram," "Abhijnanasakuntalam" and "Vikramorvastyam"), two epic poems (*Raghuvansa* and *Kumarasambhava*), and two lyric poems ("Meghduta" and "Ritusamhara"). Several other lesser-known poets composed poetry in both religious and secular themes.

From this brief summary of creative achievements of Indian civilization in the current phase, the following is abundantly clear: despite having to continue to divert a significant portion of intellectual resources to working out the doctrines of Buddhism and Jainism, science made substantial progress in all facets. Logic, epistemology, and linguistics were well developed. There was a fundamental breakthrough in solar astronomy by Aryabhatta, and one could find real progress in terrestrial physics after more than a millennium since Visheska, However, Aryabhatta's work did not gain traction perhaps because it was too far ahead of its time. The Hun invasions from the north and the Arab invasion from the west, though both were successfully defeated and contained. The resulting weakening and ultimate disintegration of central authority did not help the cause of science either. The flame of science burned bright in India without exploiting other civilizations when there was indeed darkness and ignorance in the rest of the world.

14.51 Achievements in Science

Creative Outcomes in Formal Sciences

Mathematics: The present phase was a period of unequaled progress in number theory, in algebra, the birth of trigonometry, development of geometry, and the concept of coordinate geometry.

- **Number system**: The positional representation was known to Indian scientists at least as early as the Bakhshali Manuscript, which dates back to the third century CE. It used meaningful pictorial symbols to signify the numbers—for example the moon for number 1 and wings for the number 2. They were written from right to left. However, Aryabhatta was the first person to devise a positional system that had a basis of a hundred, used shorter syllables, and had an implicit zero, taking initial crucial steps in the development of a true decimal system. Brahmagupta made the second advance, probably before 629 CE when he actually used a symbol for the number zero. Bhaskara I took the third step when he devised a number system that had a basis of ten, used the nine Brahmi numerals and Brahmagupta's zero, and wrote the numbers from left to right. The fourth and final step was taken again by Brahmagupta when he devised accurate rules for positive and negative numbers and for division and multiplication by zero. He got these nearly right. Until Bhaskara I, scientists did not use the known Brahmi numerals to represent numbers, probably because they were used in commerce and were thus too commercial to be used in science. The use of notation of right to left was more rational because they had to have a means of distinguishing the pictorial numbers from the words in a verse. Undoubtedly, these three gentlemen created perhaps the single most amazing and sublime invention to come out of human mind.

- **Algebra:** Aryabhatta provided solutions of the so-called Diophantine equations. Brahmagupta was the most prolific mathematician of his time. In *Brahmasphutasiddhanta*, he developed general solutions for linear and quadratic equations, developed computational rules for fractions, and gives sum of squares of the first n integers as $n(n+1)(2n+1)/6$ and the sum of the cubes of the first n natural numbers as

$(n(n+1)/2)$ squared. Brahmagupta also gives a solution of the so-called Pell equation through a multiple-step process he called a pulverizer.

- **Trigonometry:** Aryabhatta gave the formula for the area of a triangle and developed the concept of sine and cosine functions. He called the sine as *ardhajiya* or half chord. This was abbreviated to *jiya*; the Arabs called it *jiab* and wrote it *jb* since Arabic lacks vowels. Later writers, realizing that *jb* was an abbreviation of *jjaba*, called it *jiab*, which means a bay or cove. This was literally translated into Latin as *sinus*, meaning bay. From there, in English it became *sine*. Aryabhatta developed sine tables at an interval of 3.75 degrees. Varahamihira extended the science of trigonometry further by developing the fundamental relationships between sine and cosine functions. In *Mahabhaskariya*, Bhaskara I give a remarkable formula to compute the cosine function from pi alone.

- **Spherical trigonometry:** Aryabhatta's book also contained rules for spherical trigonometry.

- **Geometry:** Aryabhatta gave an accurate value of pi. But more important, he saw pi as an irrational number and realized that any number that represented pi would simply "approach" the true value. This may be the first realization of the concept of limit in the history of mathematics. While Aryabhatta's interest was primarily in astronomy, Brahmagupta's interest was in arithmetic, algebra, and geometry. We have mentioned his contributions in the first two above. In geometry, Brahmagupta developed formulas for area of cyclic quadrilaterals, which is a more general result than Heron's formula for triangles. Finally, Brahmagupta developed a theorem to the compute area of rational triangles.

- **Calculus:** During his research on the lunar eclipse, Aryabhatta introduced the concept of infinitesimals—i.e., *tat-kalika gati* or instantaneous motion of the moon. His description of moon's motion may be thought of as the first basic differential equation ever written. His equation was commented on by Manjula (tenth century) and Bhaskaracharya I (twelfth century), who incidentally derived the differential of the sine function as cosine function. Later mathematicians used these ideas in deriving the areas of curved surfaces, thus anticipating integral calculus.

- **Coordinate geometry:** Ninety years after the current phase ended, in 840 CE, Vacaspati Misra stated that the position of a point in space could be fixed by three coordinates, thus taking the first step toward coordinate geometry, which was simply a marriage between algebra and geometry.

The above brief description of the groundbreaking work in several areas of mathematics demonstrates the revolution in mathematical thought brought about by these men. It laid the foundation for coordinate geometry and calculus for future mathematicians. It is no exaggeration to claim that science would not have gone anywhere without these men.

Logic: The well-known Buddhist logicians of this phase were Asanga (290–360 CE), Vasubandhu (400 CE), Dignaga (480–540 CE), and Dharmakirti (600–660 CE) and Hindu logicians from the Nyaya school were Vatsayana, who wrote *Nyaya Bhashya* (400 CE), and Uddoy Takara (sixth century), who wrote *Nyaya Varttika*. There was healthy competition between these two schools. The Hindu logicians were inspired to study logic in part because they wanted to use logic as an axe to grind in metaphysical debates. The usual approach in the books Buddhist logicians wrote during this period was to focus on the Buddhist sutras with rules of debating and epistemology included as appendices. Dignaga's work was an exception; its primary focus was logic and epistemology.

In his first independent work on logic titled *Hetucakradamaru*, which literally means "the sound of an unstoppable wheel." The title conveyed Dignaga's conviction that he had discovered something stupendous in the field of logic. What he had discovered were the necessary conditions required in using middle terms in a syllogism to prove differing propositions. In other words it was how to prevent falsehood from creeping into proof by analogy. Table 14.2 summarizes his momentous discovery: only in two of the nine cases can one be certain that middle term has been correctly used. Dignaga defined three conditions for valid use of the middle term in new situations:

- The middle term must be a valid characteristic of the minor term.

- The middle term must be present in agreeing examples where it is relevant and must be absent in those agreeing example where it is irrelevant.

- The middle term must be absent from all differing examples.

It is worth noting that John Stuart Mill, who spent more than three decades in the employment of the East India Company as the chief examiner in charge of all correspondence with princely states not under company control, proposed very similar criteria called the joint method of agreement and difference. The question of his awareness of Dignaga work while in India is an open question requiring further research.

Thus, during this period, Indian logicians went beyond the development of the simple syllogism used during the previous phase; they defined the conditions under which the deductive part of the syllogism is susceptible to deliberate or unintentional errors.

Table 14.2: Dinnaga's Truth Table
Concomitance between Major and Middle Terms for a Given Minor Term

Middle Term	Present in Differing example	Absent from Differing Example	Present in Some but not Other Differing Examples
Present in Agreeing Example	UNCERTAIN	VALID	UNCERTAIN
Absent from Agreeing Example	INVALID	UNCERTAIN	INVALID
Present in Some but not Other Agreeing Examples	UNCERTAIN	VALID	UNCERTAIN

Achievements in Natural Sciences

Solar astronomy: The most significant Indian astronomers of the period were Aryabhatta, Brahmagupta, and Varahamihira. Aryabhatta was likely born in the central Indian region in 476 CE, did his research at Kusumpura or Patliputra, and died in 550 CE. Varahamihira was born in the Bengal region in 505 CE and died after 587 CE. He was one of the nine jewels in the court of Chandragupta II.

To understand Aryabhatta's monumental accomplishments, we first need to understand the following two key points:

- There was no tradition of geocentrism in the history of Indian civilization. This is clear as daylight both from the reading of ancient astronomy and as well as spiritual and philosophical deliberations lasting over nearly two millennia before Aryabhatta. Satatpatha Brahmana clearly stated "the sun strings these worlds, the earth, the planets, and the atmosphere to itself on a thread." In philosophical deliberations, we find, "there are countless universes diverse in composition and space-time structures," which clearly spells out the nongeocentric idea. The question then is why did the Indian philosophical tradition not fall prey to the seemingly natural geocentric idea? The answer is the Indian religious tradition always had a fundamental distaste for the idea of monotheism. Geocentrism is a natural child of monotheism because monotheism starts with the presumption that there is an almighty God who created the earth and by implication, the stars, sun, and moon for man and his enjoyment. And as we have seen in previous chapters, the idea of monotheism in West Asia goes back to Ikhnaton in Egypt, was picked up by Jews in Palestine and then by Zarathustra in Persia and again by Jesus in Palestine. When the good news of Christianity came to India nearly two thousand years ago, it did not find fertile ground. It took Islam eight centuries and great physical violence to convert just a third of the Indian population. By contrast, it took Islam hardly fifty years to convert a sizable fraction of population in Persia and nearly all population in Iberia. That the ancient Indian astronomical text was called Surya-Siddhanta and not Earth-Siddhanta was not without reason!

- Aryabhatta was aware of Ptolemy's astronomy and erroneous epicycles. After the fall of the Hellenistic states, the Indo-Greeks were absorbed into India by 200 CE, Persian empires existed from 248 BCE to 651 CE as a buffer, and Roman-Indian trade diminished, so the opportunity to exchange of ideas was severely limited except as noted above. At the same time, even if Aryabhatta was aware of Ptolemy's work, he probably did not think much of it. Thus, Indian astronomy was not poisoned by the concept a geocentric astronomy and therefore had no need to claim a revolution in astronomy when it naturally developed the idea of heliocentric universe in the scientific context. Discovery of a heliocentric doctrine constitutes a world-shattering revolution only in a monotheistic and geocentric cultural context of Europe and West Asia.

What did, then, Aryabhatta discover? From Aryabhatta's perspective, it was quite simple. He was able to account for the daily apparent movement of the fixed stars by the hypothesis of the rotation of the earth and not the rotation of the sun, provided the period of the rotation of earth is taken to be equal to one day. Now skeptics would say that the earth can also rotate in a geocentric model if the sun takes one year and not twenty-four hours to rotate around the earth. However, that notion is unable to explain the position of planets as observed from the earth. Aryabhatta probably considered that idea and rejected it based on actual observations. The revolutionary thought of Aryabhatta was that earth rotated on its axis with a period of sidereal day and that idea is fundamentally incompatible with geocentrism. And because Aryabhatta belonged to a tradition that never subscribed to geocentrism, he was able to conceive of the idea a thousand years before anyone else. From a history of science perspective, this situation is not dissimilar from Einstein's explanation of why only he was able to conceive of the theory of special relativity in 1905. He attributed it to his belated intellectual development during childhood and as a result was not prejudiced by the cultural and common sense bias against the nature of space and time. He also happened to be at the right place at the time. Aryabhatta, who did not have to deal with the cultural baggage of the geocentric concept, also did not to make a big deal of his idea of heliocentric world. After all, who would he be trying to prove wrong—the pope?

Aryabhatta was the first astronomer to assign the start of each day to midnight and stated that moon shines because of reflected light from the sun. Aryabhatta also explained the eclipses result from shadows falling on earth cast by the sun or moon. He devised computational methods for eclipses that were superior to any known methods, and no other methods were known until the middle of the eighteenth century. Aryabhatta also calculated the diameter of the earth to be 39,968 kilometers, which is within 0.2% of actual value. Finally, Aryabhatta calculated the rotation of earth with respect to stars, or sidereal day, to be 23 hours 56 minutes, and 4.1 seconds, and he calculated the value of sidereal year to be 365 days, 6 hours, 12 minutes, and 30 seconds. The former is accurate to within .08 (!) seconds, and the latter to within 3 minutes and 20 seconds or 0.062%. There is, however, no mention of elliptical orbits in Aryabhatta. We could confidently state that, in 500 CE, Aryabhatta has taken astronomy to where it would be after Copernicus in the fifteenth and *before* Brahe in the seventeenth century. Aryabhatta's work had profound impact on Muslim astronomy and through it, on European astronomy.

Naturally, there is considerable irrelevant debate whether Aryabhatta proposed a heliocentric model of the solar system nearly a millennium before Copernicus, all of which appears to us as nitpicking and a refusal to give up five hundred years of delayed credit. This refusal to give Aryabhatta his due, of course, is quite understandable since if Western historians relent on this point, the entire edifice of who invented modern astronomy falls apart. Hence, this refusal will continue, just as the Aryan Invasion Theory is adamantly being adhered to more than one hundred years after even its originator agreed that it was an outright fabrication!

Varahamihira lacked Aryabhatta's originality. He is remembered for his Pancha-siddhanta, which attempts to bring together all known knowledge: Indian, Egyptian, Roman, and Greek. It may be thought of as an encyclopedia. He made no attempt to reconcile the different systems. His encyclopedia is an indirect confirmation that Aryabhatta's groundbreaking work was not being taken as seriously as it should have been.

Brahmagupta was the head of the astronomical observatory at Ujjain, and he wrote four books on mathematics and astronomy while at Ujjain: the *Cadamekela* in 624 CE, the *Brahmasphutasiddhan* in 628 CE, the *Khandakhadyaka* in 665 CE, and the *Durkeamynarda* in 672 CE. The *Brahmasphutasiddhanta* is most well-known and discusses methods of calculating the position of heavenly bodies over time, their rising and setting and their conjunction, and the computation of eclipses. At the end of the book, he devotes chapters to instruments and units of measurement. The book was translated into Arabic in 770 CE. Al-Biruni also transmitted Brahmgupta's ideas in *Ta'rikh al-Hind,* which was translated later into Latin as *Indica*. Brahmgupta believed the earth moved but did not rotate. He is also known as the father of zero. While an exceptionally gifted mathematician with great originality, his refusal to accept Aryabhatta's heliocentric model was a real setback in the history of astronomy.

Indian astronomers of this phase used a variety of instruments to make the measurements, including the *sanku* or sundial, *ghati yantra* or water clock, *gola yantra* or armillary sphere, and early versions of the astrolabe.

However, history is full of irony. The subsequent weakening and fall of the Guptas and the decline after Harsha dried out the support for science. Harshavardhan converted to Buddhism, Hinduism turned to monism again, and the Muslim invasions began, starting with the Arabs and followed centuries later by Turkish tribes. A great tradition in mathematical astronomy remained on a permanent declining path. Temporary interest in mathematics rose again with Bhaskara II in the twelfth century in the north and in Kerala School of astronomy and mathematics with the Madhava school in the fourteenth century that we shall pick up in chapter 16.

The groundbreaking work in mathematics and astronomy also deepened the speculation concerning terrestrial physics. However, the problem of solar astronomy was far from being solved without the concept of elliptical orbits and quantitative theory of gravitation. Aryabhatta's heliocentric system had not gained traction among other scientists. The experimental method was yet to be developed and awaited the fuller understanding of solar astronomy. All this notwithstanding, budding Indian physicists put forward an impressive number of speculative physical theories and concepts. Below, we cover the most significant contribution made by Prasastapada in ~600 CE.

Laws of motion: In the late sixth or early seventh century, Prasastapada took up the first real analysis of motion. His work is summarized in table 12.3. Prasastapada's work may be reviewed in three categories: classification of types of motion, force/mass interactions, and energy/mass interactions:

- Types of motion: Prasastapada identified rectilinear (implied in inertial motion), curvilinear, rotary, and vibratory motions.

- Force/mass interaction: Prasastapada also identified seven different force/mass interactions listed in the middle portion of table 12.3. We also take the liberty to render his concepts into modern equivalent in an attempt to show the earliest conceptualization of the ideas of inertia, impulse, and relative motion. Prasastapada, not having conceptualized momentum and force, uses the word *motion* for motion as well as for momentum and force, perhaps because motion is the common element in all three. Prasastapada was also aware of motion caused by elasticity. While stating that a solid object is capable of only one motion, an object like a leaf was capable of complex motion pattern, and thus he anticipated the field of solid mechanics.

- Energy/mass interaction: Prasastapada went further, having realized that sometimes motion causes chemical and physical changes, one type of motion in one body may cause a different kind of motion in another body, or a motion might "disappear." Thus, here he uses the word motion for motion as well as energy. An intuitive understanding of kinetic energy can be seen in his work.

- Relative motion: Aryabhatta stated: *"Bhakthe vilomavivare gathiyogenaanulomavivare dvow gathyantharena labdow dviyogakaalaavatheethaishyow."* Translated, it means that whenever two bodies are traveling in the opposite directions, the distance between them is to be divided by the sum of their speeds. If they move in the same direction, the distance is to be divided by the difference of their speeds. This gives the time required for the bodies to meet or the time elapsed after motion began.

With hindsight, these were baby steps, unlike the giant leap of Aryabhatta in astronomy. We may rightly regard Prasastapada as the first physicist to take up the issue of motion in general and through observation and analysis get some of its aspects right. However, significant progress on planetary motion and motion under gravity were a prerequisite to understanding general laws of motion and the concept of force. Motion under gravity is motion under a single constant force that produces constant acceleration, a naturally occurring, controlled experiment that Galileo used to understand the laws of motion in the sixteenth century. However, after Prasastapada, Arab scientists in the tenth and eleventh centuries took the next decisive steps in the laws of motion, and we shall take that up in the next chapter.

Optics: Aryabhatta had already supported Sushruta's notion that light enters the eye and does not emanate from it. Chakrapani viewed light as a wave form that spreads in circles in all directions. On the contrary, the Mimamsaka schools had viewed light in the form of particle. The modern theory of light combines both views. Reflection and refraction of light were understood. Vaharahamihira called reflection *kiranavighatna*, a term whose literal translation is more akin to scattering of light. Another scientist, Vatsyayana, called reflection *rasmiparavartna*, a term whose literal meaning is more appropriate. Uddyatakara studied refraction in the seventh century and attempted to explain it by analogy of water seeping through porous matter. Both slow down as they travel through matter. He called the phenomenon *Tatra parispanda triyaagamanam parisravah pata iti*. However, there was no attempt to quantify these phenomena. Similarly, there was no theory of color.

Sound: In the seventh century, Pasastapada theorized that since the *akasa* or sky is incapable of motion, air must carry sound. The intensity of sound was seen as resulting from the magnitude of vibrations of the air molecules, a phenomenon termed *kampasantana-samaskara*.

Gravitation: In the seventh century, Brahmagupta clearly stated the impact of gravity: Bodies fall toward earth, as it is the nature of earth to attract bodies. Although Brahmagupta made the fatal error of not believing the rotation of the earth, he believed the earth was a sphere, was moving, and attracted objects toward it.

The above all-too-brief summary of advances in natural and exact sciences makes it abundantly clear that Indian scientists were deeply interested in both observation and mathematics and combined the two to understand physical phenomenon. They were centuries ahead of any other civilization at the height of the current phase.

Chemistry: Chemistry remained a practical technological field with strong roots in textile dyeing, mining metallurgy, and casting technologies. One of wonders of premodern metallurgy is the iron pillar erected during Gupta times. It is nearly twenty-two feet high and weighs six tons. It withstood 1,500 years of exposure to heavy rain with little corrosion

Earth sciences: As we also note below, the astronomer Varahamihira produced an encyclopedia that included diverse subjects as weather (clouds, wind, forecasting, and measurement of rainfall),

Achievements in Biological Sciences

Medicine: Vagbhata was the greatest physician of the era. Vagbhata was born around 500 CE in the Sindh on the western coast and was taught medicine by his father and a Buddhist monk. He wrote two books, the first called *Astanga Samagraha* or the *Encyclopedia of Eight Branches of Medicine* and the second called *Astanga Hridaya* or the *Summary of the Encyclopedia of Eight Branches of Medicine*. Vagbhata may be regarded as one of trio of the great Indian physicians, the other two being Sushruta and Charaka. The encyclopedia was written in 7,120 verses and included diagnosis and therapies, often going beyond what Charaka had summarized neatly a millennium ago. It included sections on personal hygiene, the influence of seasons, disease classification and diagnosis, individual differences, and therapies, including the *panchkarma* or digestive system therapy consisting of induced vomiting, laxatives, two kinds of enemas, and nasal cleansing.

Madhav was the second physician of great importance in the early 700s. He discovered the cure for smallpox by inoculating a small amount of pus from a person who already had small pox into a healthy person. Madhav wrote a seventy-nine-chapter book called *Nidana*, which lists diseases, symptoms, and complication. His preventive treatment of smallpox is described in a special chapter in *Nidana*.

However, there was little progress made in anatomy and physiology since the dissection of dead bodies was not allowed.

Achievements in Social Sciences

Science of pleasure: In Indian civilization, pursuit of pleasure is one of the legitimate goals of life with no implication of sin associated with it. It is therefore hardly surprising that Indian civilization would produce a systematic work on the science of pleasure. Mallanaga Vatsyayana authored *Kamasutra* probably in the fourth century AD. The work consists of thirty-six chapters and about 1,250 verses. The book focuses on a broad range of sensitive subjects in a morally neutral tone much like a social scientist, a sexologist, or a psychologist would today. The chapters range from introductory material (five chapters); how to make yourself attractive to the other partner (two chapters); how to get a sexual partner, wife, another woman, or a courtesan (seventeen chapters); arousal of sexual desire and different methods of sexual union (ten chapters); and rules of conduct for female partners (two chapters). There is a distinct male bias in the book as it refers to simultaneous multiple partners for men and not for woman. However, for its time, it was a remarkable book and shows the Indian civilization during its golden age as a society fully engaged in pleasure in a socially sophisticated manner but without sliding into hedonism.

One would have to work hard to find a book concerning sexual pleasure after Vatsyayana in the fourth century until Masters and Johnson's books in the twentieth century. It is interesting to note that nearly four millennia after the invention of writing, Indian scientists continued to express their findings in verse form, a tradition that dates back before the fourth millennium BCE, prior to the invention of writing. Such is the power and force of tradition in human civilizations.

Encyclopedias: Indian civilization has had a long tradition of producing encyclopedias but mostly pertaining to religious and medical matters. In the sixth century, astronomer Varahamihira produced an encyclopedia that not only contained basic astronomy but also such diverse subjects as weather (clouds, wind, forecasting, and rainfall measurement), architecture (town planning, water-divination), family life (marriage and domestic relations, cleansing of teeth), plants (growth of crops, flowers, trees), commerce (commodities, prices, and traders), manufacture of perfume and precious stones (gems, pearls, and gemstone evaluation). The *Samhita* had 106 chapters and went through multiple editions.

Summarizing Achievements in Abstract Systems-Building Capability (ASBC)

By the end of the phase, the ASBC of the Indian civilization was world-class: It continued to have the world's most scientific alphabetical script. In addition, it advanced the frontiers of epistemology and logic, the experimental method in the heavens through invention of trigonometry and spherical geometry, and developed the decimal system, including the concept of zero. It was indeed the greatest advance in abstract systems-building capability the world had yet witnessed. It clearly laid the foundations of the third and fourth synthesis we discuss in the next two chapters.

Summarizing the State of Civilization and Science

14.52 State of Civilization and Science at Phase End

Overview of History of the Phase

Briefly put, Sassanians deflected the Huns, who then overran the Western Roman Empire in the north and exerted considerable reciprocal pressure on Byzantine Empire in the west and Kushan Empire in the east. This resulted in the fall of Roman and Kushan Empires, the rise of the Tang dynasty in China, and the rise and fall of the Gupta dynasty in India. Mutual weakening of Byzantine and Sassanian Empires created a short-term opportunity for Huns and opened the door for a long-term opportunity for

Arab nomads, who overwhelmed the Sassanian Empire and Western Europe, which had been weakened by Huns and Byzantine Empires respectively. Civilizations were ready to hand over the control to a new aggressor driven by an intolerant creed for nearly a millennium.

Let us now summarize the state of creative, productive, and destructive outcomes of all essential players taken together at the end of the phase.

State of Practical Creativity

The achievements in practical creativity were broad and led by the Chinese civilization. Key materials invented or discovered in this period were ceramics, parchment, and improved steel. Key processes invented were the water-powered saw mill, cotton gin, and spinning wheel. Key forms of energy invented were the windmill, the water wheel, the use of coal, and methane gas. Key new tools invented were the compass, differential gear and water clock, and abacus. Significant agricultural products invented or discovered were pest control using ants, crops in rows, and a flour-sifting machine. New nonagricultural products invented were knitted fabric, matches, and toilet paper. Significant construction-related breakthroughs included improved aqueducts, canals linking rivers, arches supported by columns, and construction of large monoliths like the 120-foot Buddha statue. Many inventions of significance include two-oxen-driven carts or Whipple tree, the horse harness, the stirrup, iron chains in suspension bridges, wind-driven land vehicles, the segmented arch bridge, canals linking rivers, newspaper, and book blocks for printing.

We can see that several key inventions that made horse a more effective element in warfare and long-distance attack set the stage for the nomads from central Asian steppes and Arabia attacking Indian, European, and Persian civilizations during this period. By far, the Chinese civilization and, to a lesser extent, the Roman and Sassanian Empires and the Indian civilization, made the greatest contributions in practical technology during this phase.

State of Religious Creativity

The current phase witnessed the development of Christian dogma and its politicization under the popes, evolution of Buddhism toward philosophical idealism, the reestablishment of Zoroastrianism, and the birth and decline of Manichaeism. The phase also witnessed the expansion of both Christianity and, to a much greater extent, Buddhism. Despite the expansion, the current phase could hardly be characterized as creative as the previous two phases, which resulted in the triumph of monism and agnosticism respectively. This was a phase with ascendant monotheism in West Asia and Europe, thus setting stage for the coming terrible science-religion conflict.

State of Philosophical Creativity

Buddhist and Hindu philosophers did the most significant work in philosophy, with both ultimately lapsing into idealism as we noted above. Buddhist philosopher Dignaga arrived at his philosophical idealism through reductionism, and Hindu philosopher Sankara arrived at his realism through epistemological reasoning, stating correctly that absolute knowledge is not possible through science. However, he went a step further and claimed that the route of trained intuition and meditation to absolute knowledge was far superior to the path of experimentation and science to relative knowledge. Hindu monism killed Buddhism in India, and thus Indian religiosity returned to a contradictory mixture of polytheism and monism. On the Christian front, Augustine essentially destroyed the value of Greek and Hellenistic science by asserting that there was no point in probing into nature, and it was sufficient for Christians to believe that the only cause of all creation is one true, loving, transcendental God. Though philosophy failed on the metaphysical front, it made significant progress on the epistemological front under Dignaga who, despite his creeping idealism, laid out the essential epistemology, which consisted of the union of sense data and reason. There was little creative achievement in the theory of aesthetic and secular ethics during the phase.

State of artistic creativity: The greatest artistic achievements during the phase pertain to painting (Ajanta), sculpture (Roman), rock-carved art (Ajanta,) literature and poetry (Kalidasa), and calligraphy (Chinese). Music and dance did not make comparable progress in any civilization.

State of Scientific Creativity

Several sciences made excellent progress. However, full solution to the problem of astronomy and the development of experimental method remained in the future.

Formal sciences: There was considerable progress in arithmetic and number theory, algebra, and both plane and spherical trigonometry. Aryabhatta conceived the idea of the first derivative in his concept of instantaneous motion. Clear formulation of the concept of coordinate geometry was still in the future. Dignaga made significant contribution to logic by defining the necessary conditions required in using middle terms in a syllogism to prove differing propositions or what is needed to prevent falsehood from creeping into proof by analogy. There was little groundbreaking work in linguistics; however, using Greek and other languages as model, Latin script was finally developed, thus laying the foundation for the emergence of modern European languages.

Astronomy: Aryabhatta went beyond Ptolemy's epicycle to propose the correct architecture of the solar system, but his work was ignored by later Indian astronomers. Brahmangupta put forth the concept of gravity.

Physics: Progress toward understanding the laws of motion through an understanding of types of motion, different force/mass interactions, and different energy/mass interactions. These are the earliest glimpse of the ideas of inertia, force, momentum, energy, and the relativity of motion conceived by the human mind. Sound was understood as propagation through air, laws of reflection of light were understood, and the existence of terrestrial gravity was understood, though it did not extend to its universal nature. In optics, Aryabhatta understood the role of eye as a receiver and not a source of light.

Medicine: Biological sciences including medicine declined after the fall of Hellenistic achievements in anatomy and physiology and after Indian achievements in diagnosis and treatment, including surgery. The only bright spot and groundbreaking discovery during the current period was that of inoculation for smallpox.

Social sciences: There was little progress in the arena of social sciences during the current phase, with one glaring exception: the science of pleasure developed in the Indian civilization. It is indeed difficult to imagine Christian Europe during the current phase with its "sex is sin" mentality to create something comparable. Both Roman and Gupta rulers made considerable progress in the art of administration. Roman and Manu laws must be considered outstanding examples of practical law of the current period for a class and caste society respectively.

State of Productive Outcomes

Driven by steady improvement and the diffusion of practical creativity, improvements in wealth creation in Indian, Chinese, and Roman civilizations continued, interrupted as they were by both internal fighting (particularly in India and China) and nomadic invasion in all three cases. World trade was driven by Romans, Guptas, Sassanians, and Arabs in succession. Notable migrations were those of Byzantine scholars to the Persian Empire and the Zoroastrian Persians to India.

State of Constructive Outcomes

Although central Asian and Arab nomads succeeded in destroying Roman, Persian, and Gupta empires, wars among major civilizations were not decisive. Persian control of the international trade during Sassanian rule seemed to be limited to their role as middlemen rather than a genuine control of commodity prices backed up by control of the entire trade route. In short, the wars were indecisive and trade was fair, and these limited the intensity of interaction among civilizations to somewhere between peaceful and violent.

Impact of the diffusion of practical creativity: It is difficult to assess the diffusion of practical technology during this phase with certainty. During most of the period this chapter considers, most civilizations were not in active communication, and thus the diffusion was likely slower. What we can say with confidence is that significant breakthroughs in practical technology had been achieved in China, Europe, and India, and faster diffusion of these technologies occurred during the next phase through the Arab nomads conquering West Asia, Iberia, and the beachhead on the Indian subcontinent or the area lying between these three major civilizations in western, eastern, and southern Eurasia. Yet, we can glimpse the diffusion of silk manufacture, horse stirrup, and compass out of China; textile and steel technology out of India; and architectural breakthroughs and sculpture out of Roman and Byzantine Empires.

Impact of the diffusion of religious creativity: By the end of this phase, for the first time, all major religions were in existence. Christianity saw significant expansion, and its center of gravity moved from West Asia to Europe. Buddhism began a slow decline in India and a steady rise in East Asia. Hinduism reasserted itself in India and drove Buddhism out. And we witnessed the birth of Islam, and with it, an aggressive, expansionist push by zealot nomadic Arabs.

Christianity: The western Europe adoption of Christian dogma strengthened the antiscience attitude that existed during the Roman Empire. Between the tradition of the practical orientation of the Roman Empire and Augustine's formulation of clear, uncompromising monotheism, science had little support left on the European continent. Europe was being set up for a millennium-long period characterized by its modern historians as dark ages, except these were dark ages for Europe and not humanity.

Buddhism: Buddhism had shown remarkable success in civilizing the first wave of nomads from central Asia, who invaded India, as we saw in the last chapter. However, in the process, Buddhism was transforming itself from its original pristine agnostic outlook to philosophical idealism. Its social message of equality among castes was becoming diluted as it focused itself more on philosophy, metaphysics, Buddhist doctrine, and logic and not on the actual social conditions in India. It was thus becoming less relevant socially. However, it also began a second lease on life through expansion in East Asia and Tibet. The Brahman priests took full advantage of this transformation in Buddhism and drove it out of India. Buddhism would also suffer a retreat in northwest India and central Asia at the hands of Islam, as we shall discuss in the next chapter. This had monumental consequences for Indian science as Indian civilization turned once again toward monism and spirituality.

Islam: Arabian history before Islam is one of intertribal fighting and destruction, and their dependence on trade as middlemen for survival in the harsh climate of Arabia. Political union of these tribes had proved difficult because of the tradition of tribal honor, which prevented one tribe from accepting the authority of another. However, if political union could possibly be based on celestial or divine authority, it could act as a face-saving unifying device. The political genius of Mohamed, disguised as a religious doctrine, was to recognize this central fact. Islam was thus born in Arabia through Mohamed and was uncompromisingly monotheistic from the start. As the Koran says, Allah does not love those with no faith. However, the focus of Islam during this phase was not religious expansion; rather it was political integration and territorial expansion. Arab armies fought eighty-seven significant wars during the first 150 years of Islam's existence.

Fortunately for the Arabs, Islam was born into a power vacuum. The Indian and Chinese cultures had always been and were peaceful with respect to other civilizations. The Huns dealt a severe blow to the western Roman Empire. The Byzantine Empire survived unscathed but was not particularly strong as a result of its prolonged wars with Persia. And the Persian Empire had been weakened as well by these wars. One group of central Asian nomads had migrated to India and were absorbed into Indian culture. It would take centuries for them to regroup. Another group, the Gokturks, was weakened by internal division. Thus, Arabs, imbued with an aggressive and uncompromising faith, found themselves at the center of a relative political and military vacuum, which they exploited to the fullest. By 750 AD, the Arab domains stretched from Spain to Sindh. The doctrine of Islam played a critical role in this. It is indeed hard to imagine a people with an Arab pedigree to become masters of the largest empire the world had seen to date in such a short time without a faith like Islam. Thus, the focus of early Islam was not conversions; that was to come later. The focus of early Islam was successful territorial expansion ostensibly in the name of Allah, the only God. The faith of Islam was not an important faith except for the Arabs during this phase. Early Islam was a motivational force for expansion and not yet a self-conscious monotheistic doctrine that fully understood its own antiscience nature.

Monism: The subtle idealist philosophy of the Upanishads had been eclipsed by Buddhism earlier, as the former intellectually supported the caste system through concepts of soul, reincarnation, and karma and as the latter led a social protest against the caste system. Buddhism was openly critical of the caste system as well as the Upanishad philosophy, as we mentioned above. However, the practical focus of Buddhism during the current phase had begun to shift from social equality to doctrinal metaphysics, and as we noted above, this not only resulted in significant development in epistemology and logic but also drained resources from natural sciences and created an opening for Hinduism to reassert itself. The Gupta emperors ardently supported Hinduism but were tolerant of other faiths. Harsha, during most of his reign, supported Hinduism and may have converted to Buddhism toward the end. However, since his empire did not survive him, his conversion to Buddhism was rather inconsequential. Toward the end of this phase, Sankara solidified this gain through his clear annunciation of the philosophy of monism and a Hindu cultural unity emphasized through establishing places of pilgrimage in the four corners of India. At the same time, in southern India, the devotional Hinduism or Bhakti movement was taking shape. Thus rise of monism also played a role in challenging monotheism brought by the Arabs. In the face of this monism, monotheism did not seem convincing to the Indian masses, even at the bottom of the social order. Contrasted with the earlier expansion of Christianity in Europe, the absence of monism is indeed instructive.

Thus, religiously speaking, this phase saw expansion of Buddhism in East Asia, Islam in West Asia, Christianity in Europe, and reassertion of Hinduism/monism in India. This set up the coming conflict between hard monotheism, soft monotheism (or Sufism), and monism/Hinduism on the Indian subcontinent and conflict between two major forms of monotheism—that is Judaism and Christianity—in Europe.

Impact of the diffusion of intellectual creativity: It is probably fair to say that diffusion of artistic creativity was only significant between Byzantine and Persian civilizations; however, scientific knowledge from Greek-Hellenistic states and the Indian civilization to Arabs had begun to trickle. The diffusion of philosophical systems fared a little better, primarily because Buddhism spread. The beginning of the acquisition of scientific knowledge from Sindh in India and Iberia in Europe by Arabs constitutes the most dramatic outcome in diffusion of intellectual creativity during the current phase and laid the foundation of the third synthesis of science during the development stage of science, as we shall discuss in the next chapter.

Peaceful migrations: One significant migration took place from Persia to India and consisted of those Persians who had refused to convert to Islam in the seventh century.

Fair trade: Trade during the current phase went through several stages. In the first two centuries, it was the India-Rome trade through sea that was dominant. This was followed by the land-based Persian-dominated trade linking Europe and Asia under the Sassanian rulers. Trade among civilizations suffered in the next century because of disruptive invasions of West Asia, Europe, and India, first by the Huns and then by Arabs. Finally, with Arabs established as masters of an empire that stretched from Iberia to Sindh, trade began to recover again with bigger impact in the coming centuries. Thus, waxing and waning trade between Europe and Asia continued during this phase and got a boost from Arab conquest toward the end. The trade, which supported Roman elite lifestyles, favored both India and China.

Arabs had learned shipbuilding technology from the Romans and would learn the technology of papermaking and heavy armament from the Chinese. This allowed the Arabs to control the sea lanes starting with the late seventh century, which resulted in flourishing sea trade between South Asia and Europe. This shifting trade pattern caused a decline in the shipbuilding industry in India, and many Indian states gave a welcome mat to the Arab traders. These states granted land outside many large Indian cities on the west coast of India to the Arab traders. Indian shipbuilding eventually turned conservative; a book on shipbuilding dating back to the sixth century explicitly forbids using iron nails and mixing different timbers. The Arabs also controlled major portions of the northern leg of the Silk Route between China and Europe by the middle of the seventh century. What the Arabs could not achieve militarily in India, they achieved partially through their control of the sea routes.

The trade volume and trade routes during the phase, therefore, were defined by the changing fortunes of Byzantine and Sassanian Empires and the invasions of Hun and Arab nomads.

In summary, the key impact came through diffusion of religious creativity and access of Greek, Hellenistic, and Indian science to Arabs.

State of Destructive Outcomes

The phase continued to see dramatic increase in destructive outcomes, both infighting and external invasions. China, India, and Persia were attacked by Gokturks, Huns, and Arabs. India and China survived, but Persia did not. Similarly, the Roman and Byzantine Empires often initiated war against the others. Hun invasions contributed to the fall of the Roman Empire, and the Byzantine Empire saw its borders and fortune fluctuate during the phase. With the rise of Arabs and Islam, we witness the emergence of a new phenomenon in history: the combination of greed and creed as the driving motive to build an empire.

Assessing Changes in the Inner Nature of Participants

14.53 The Inner Nature of the Roman Empire until 476 CE

Without doubt, the driving causes of Roman Empire through most of the phase remained intrinsic: a military strength that had exploited the diversion of Greek attention toward Asia and a very effective control of conquered territories through a highly stratified social structure based on heredity and property but with unclear rules of succession. Romans learned from their neighbors and conquered territories they valued. The psychology of the Roman upper classes was living the good life through conquest, internal inequality, and enormous practical creativity. The ultimate end for the Western Empire came through nomadic instruments of control. The Eastern Empire survived the onslaught of the Huns since the Huns used the Eastern Empire as a buffer between them and the powerful Sassanians at whose hands they had experienced defeat. They differed in that the Western Roman Empire, while it lasted, had a stronger external orientation and higher productive capacity. The Byzantine Empire was more laid back in these matters.

Productive capacity: Internal economic freedom was rather limited since the state or elite families controlled both manufacturing and trade. New technology adoption was slow, except in areas essential for the survival of the empire, namely military matters, including weapons and roads, and water supply, using aqueducts. Construction and manufacturing skills were high, judging from architecture and quality of coinage. The wealth allocation balance was tilted in favor of military and elite lifestyles. Little surplus was allocated to intellectual or even religious pursuits. We would judge the inequality to have moved in the positive direction in the eastern wing compared to the Roman Empire because of the rise of an educated bureaucracy based in part on talent and not heredity, the relative freedom of the farmer, the relative disappearance of slavery, and state intervention the economy through control of grain prices. Several of these changes were driven by Christian view of universality of sin in front of God. Social cohesion was low, despite strong military and legal components since Roman society was highly stratified with little organic unity holding it together, except success on the battlefield. Internal wars were confined to wars of succession and slave revolts and either did not play a determining role until the threat of nomads and European barbarians. Thus, SGS control did not shift. We would judge the productive capacity of the Western Roman Empire to be high and of the Eastern Empire to be modest.

Creative capacity: Creative freedom until the adoption of Christianity in the fourth century was hampered by deep social inequality and a reaction to the Greek and Hellenistic tradition of intellectual and, to a lesser extent, religious creativity. Perhaps, the Roman world saw Greek interest in knowledge as a weakness. Thus, Roman talent migrated into military, political, and legal arenas. After the adoption of Christianity, particularly in the Eastern Empire, Christian dogma and the resulting science-religion conflict further limited creative freedom. The Roman world inherited the abstract systems-building capability from Greeks and used it well in limited areas such as the legal system. We would judge the creative capacity of the Roman world as high but narrow.

Constructive orientation: The Roman world, though bound by the Mediterranean to the south and by a frigid north inhabited by barbarians, could not be classified as geographically isolated. Roman success against the barbarians, the northern Africa and Greek adventure into Asia, and the need for trade with Asia meant that Roman world was open to trade and practical creativity, particularly in military and architecture. toward the beginning of the fourth century CE, Rome world also became open to the foreign religious doctrine of Christianity that had been making inroads into the heart of the common man. Thus, only in philosophy and science did the Roman world remain not only insular but also actively working to destroy it. The Eastern Empire did that to Greek spirit of science, and the Western Empire did the same to Hellenistic science. The constructive orientation of the Roman Empire is judged to be type 1.

Destructive orientation: The Western Empire developed trade as it needed finished products for its elite that it could not produce locally. The trade system essentially developed into institutional greed as the leading families controlled. Likewise, the leading families also controlled the provinces. Although the Western Empire persecuted Christians for centuries, it never developed the intolerant creed it was interesting in imposing on others. The Eastern Empire was different: the power quickly centralized from senatorial families into an emperor and was prevented from oozing out into Christian Church. Thus, it did not seem to have developed institutional greed since, relatively speaking, leading families did not control manufacturing and trade. Although the Eastern Empire embraced Christianity wholeheartedly, it displayed little capacity to export it, since it faced a powerful Persian Empire to the east, and the west was already in the orbit of Christendom. Both the Western and Eastern Empires had great early success against smaller, weaker civilizations and nomads. Thus was no fundamental change in the destructive orientation within the Roman world during the phase as it went through defeats on the battlefield and through internal convulsions. Such is the power of beliefs acquired early during the growth cycle by a civilization or empire and reinforced through success.

14.54 The Inner Nature of the Byzantine Empire after 476 CE

Productive capacity: The land was owned by farmers, manufacturing was rather modest, and trade was primarily in silk and grain. Government controlled the trade and manufacturing of silk. Thus, we would characterize both economic freedom and new technology adoption as low. Wealth allocation balance favored military capability and supported religion. The social cohesion was moderate, as slavery was not as prevalent since landlords used indentured labor, and nearly all the population shared the unifying fear of the Christian faith. However, the most significant blows came from emperor Khosrau I, who demanded significant tribute, and later from Arabs who reduced the territory to a third. Thus, sustainable growing surplus often went through periods of precipitous decline. We would judge the productive capacity to be moderate and fluctuating.

Creative Capacity: The situation was not any better with respect to creative freedom. Creative freedom demands that doubts concerning existence knowledge be respected and encouraged and thereby make it possible for creative individuals to bring forth solutions concerning these doubts. With the exception of weapons technologies and architecture, creative freedom was hardly encouraged. Christian faith made the science-religion conflict worse despite easier access to ancient Greek learning within the Byzantine Empire. Significantly, the Platonic academy was closed in 529 CE, though interest in ancient Greece continued at some level. However, abstract systems-building capability remained high because of Greek and Roman heritage. The creative capacity must be judged to be high but narrow.

Constructive orientation: The Byzantine Empire stood at the interface of Asia and Europe: there was hardly any geographical isolation. It did not have to deal with nomad threat in any significant manner. However, it inherited its insularity to religious and its intellectual creativity from the Roman Empire and did not rise above it. It probably had a softer corner for Greek and Hellenistic learning compared to the Roman Empire and supported it until the Platonic Academy was closed in 529 CE. The openness in the closed Byzantine world was at most type 1.

Destructive orientation: Unlike the Western Roman Empire, the internal destructive aspect was rather mild because of greater internal equality and a less luxurious elite lifestyle. The succession wars were also milder by comparison and with the exception of the Nika riots in 532 CE, internal stability prevailed during the phase. Externally, the Byzantine Empire behaved like the Roman Empire and went through a territorial expansion after the fall of the Western Empire. This was followed by both Persian and Arab invasions.

Evolution of the Dynamic Inner Nature from the Roman Republic to the Two Roman Empires

The Roman Republic was a curious mixture of relative equality among the leading aristocratic families, coupled with extreme wealth polarization and inequality among the rest. This worked well to ensure expansion and conquest. However, after the "Republic" rooted in tribal traditions gave way to essential monarchy, the internal structures of the empire became more centralized and, toward the end, in the grip of monotheism.

This change resulted in declining rate of practical innovation and that, coupled with end of expansion and the cost of maintaining the distant vast holdings, put severe pressure on the resources, causing increasing inequality and infighting. The German and Asian nomads exploited this weakness and put an end to the western empire. Thus, we see mostly practical innovation during the early part of this phase. By the fifth century, even practical innovation had slowed down dramatically.

These centralized structures also ensured that the internal creative balance remain tilted toward practical creativity to support the imperial needs or toward the religious creativity to meet the requirements of a monotheistic religious dogma or both. Romans excelled in law, administration, architecture, and engineering skills, and had a practical internal creative balance. With Christianity firmly established, the conflict between religion and science, now hidden and now open, continued in Europe with the balance quickly shifting in favor of religion. The two activities of science and religion continued to increasingly become polar opposites, preventing the spirit of free inquiry in Europe from taking root after the Romans killed it in ancient Greece and the Hellenistic states, both of which never fell prey to Christianity. The Roman Empire remained open to the practical creativity and reluctantly to the religious creativity of other civilizations.

The external orientation of Europe in the centuries after the fall of Western Roman Empire became defensive under the triple burdens of Christianity, papal meddling that exploited internal divisions, and Persian and Arab pressure and aggression.

14.55 The Inner Nature of Persian Civilization

Dominant causes that drove the Persian civilization must also be assessed to be intrinsic causes and its actions as an instrument of control. Natural and extrinsic causes played a modest role during most of the phase. The end came at the hands of Arab nomads when the empire had been weakened due to wars with Byzantine Empire and internal divisions. For the first time in its history, the Persian Empire showed, despite a never-ending military conflict with the Byzantine Empire, a broad creative orientation and an open external constructive orientation. There was little change in its external destructive orientation

Productive capacity: Given the expansion of manufacturing, emergence of guilds, relatively little government interference in the economy, and product branding, internal economic freedom must be judged to be high. It is believed new technology adoption was high, at least in some periods, as evidenced by infrastructure construction that included bridges, dams, and underground aqueducts. This also indicates that government played a key role in large projects. The king also supported farmers and artisans if only to counterbalance the nobility. Persian artisans achieved high skill levels during the period, judging from art and architecture. Wealth allocation balance got progressively better, judging from the rise of the Gundeshapur complex. Though the social structure was stratified, Sassanian rulers, until the time of Khusrau II, managed the social and ethnic tensions and inequality very well as they consciously worked to balance the interests of different classes and ethnic and religious groups. Social cohesion fluctuated, depending on government investment in irrigation schemes, control of international trade, and balance of power among the nobility, the king and central bureaucracy, and the farmer/artisans. It seems that, for a while, the kings even used a popular "socialist revolution" that advocated equal ownership of wealth to destroy the power of the nobility. The inner wars were limited to wars of succession, and therefore the SGS control was stable. We would thus describe the productive capacity, though fluctuating, to be high under favorable political conditions.

Creative capacity: Creative freedom in practical manner was abundant and supported by royalty. The role of religion was more nearly balanced, and the abstract systems-building capability existed, as evidenced by the emergence of literature in alphabetical script. The question arises why the spark that initiated the interest in science and intellectual creativity required an exodus of scholars from the Byzantine Empire. This is indeed a difficult question to answer. The fact that the academy did not survive means it was the vision of one man, Khusrau I, the chance emigration of Nestorian Christians bearing Greek medicine, neo-Platonist philosophy and translation of Indian books. Even Gundeshpur achievements were confined to medicine and philosophy. Little was achieved in astronomy and mathematics. On balance, we would judge the creative capacity to be deep but narrow, in part because Gondishapur was short-lived and inspired by foreign learning and did not go beyond it.

Constructive orientation: Sassanians did not face geographical isolation, West Asia was indeed a melting pot, the regime was in a prolonged struggle with the Byzantine Empire, and occasionally struggled with the Indian civilization. They did not deal with nomads on an ongoing basis, having defeated and deflected the Huns toward Europe. Thus, fundamentally, the Sassanians were open to trade and practical creativity, including art and architecture and military technology. Their interest in intellectual creativity came in the last stages of its existence through foreign influence, as noted above. We would characterize their constructive capacity as type 3 or even type 4 because of their support of Menichaenism despite their commitment to Zoroastrianism. The short-lived Gondishapur experiment must be regarded as a missed opportunity in the tortuous history of science.

Destructive orientation: Persian civilization during the phase lacked both institutional greed and an intolerant creed but clearly enjoyed military success against minor civilizations. Its protracted struggle against the Byzantine Empire exhausted both, making them ready to be toppled by rising Arabs. The Persian civilization under the Sassanians was a true heir to the millennia-old Persian tradition of violent aggression, beginning with Achaemenids and continued by Parthians and Sassanians.

14.56 The Inner Nature of the Chinese Civilization

The dominant causes of Chinese civilization were the intrinsic causes, peaceful extrinsic (spread of Buddhism), and the nomadic instruments of control settled in northern China. The successful rise of a centralized, united Chinese state under the Tangs in the seventh century is consistent with a recurring theme of Chinese civilization. The fundamental change in the inner nature of the Chinese civilization during the phase was its focus on practical creativity, resulting in remarkable explosion of practical inventions.

Productive capacity: The productive capacity in China during the period was high because of high economic freedom and breakthroughs in agricultural technologies with high new technology adoption. The internal equality must be judged to be moderate as in previous phase. Despite political fragmentation, social cohesion remained high with a continuing ability to absorb the nomads into Chinese culture. Chinese civilization during this phase experienced plenty of internal wars and instability of SGS control.

Creative capacity: Apart from outstanding contributions in the arena of practical creativity and the adoption and internalization of Buddhism, there was no significant change in Chinese creativity, except modest contributions in math. China continued to resist adoption of alphabetical script and continued its insular ways with modest creative freedom in intellectual creativity in part because of a lack of abstract systems-building capability and in particular the alphabetical script. One does not detect interest in astronomy and physics by Chinese intellectuals despite contact with India. Chinese monks came to India to primarily learn about Buddhism and do not seem to have shown much interest in Indian mathematics, astronomy, and linguistics. Thus, the internal creative balance continued to be practical with a keen interest in Buddhism as it mirrored many features of Taoism despite creative freedom and an absence of science-religion conflict. The creative capacity may be judged to be narrow but deep.

Constructive orientation: China remained insular to the creativity of other civilizations, with adoption of Buddhism a glaring exception, thus earning it a type 2 openness for the first time.

Destructive orientation: Chinese civilization did not develop institutional greed for raw materials, land, or foreign markets and did not develop an intolerant creed. On the contrary, it showed openness to a tolerant creed such as Buddhism. Staying true to its peaceful nature, it did not engage in aggression against any civilizations with the intent of SGS control, colonization, or systematic wealth drain. It dealt with nomads and smaller civilizations around its periphery to ensure its own defense and to obtain nominal tributes.

14.57 The Inner Nature of Central Asian Nomads—Second Wave

The important central Asian nomads of the phase consisted of two separate groups: the western Huns that helped to destroy Western Roman Empire and Indo-Huns who weakened the Gupta Empire in India. Both the Rouran Khannate and the Gokturk Empire, however, remained satisfied in creating a nomadic empire in central Asia and did not and could not attack civilizations. The rise of Gokturks resulted from a successful internal revolt against the Rouran Empire and their abilities as a military power. The end came at the hands of Chinese and the Arab nomads. Gokturks had inner nature befitting central Asian nomads. Below, we assess the inner nature of the historically more important Huns.

Productive capacity: Because of limited population and dry climate, both Indo-Huns and Western Huns naturally had a low productive capacity and a low sustainable growing surplus and questions of economic and new technology adoption, except in military matters, were not exactly relevant. Both Indo-Huns and Western Huns had a high level of internal equality based on tribal tradition, which was essential for military discipline, and they displayed limited internal aggression, in part because the Khans never acted like an absolute sovereign.

Creative capacity: Like all nomads, Indo-Huns and Western Huns had creative freedom with no science-religion conflict (they neither had science or an organized religion). Clearly, the abstract systems-building capability was low, and they were open to the creativity of other civilizations.

Constructive orientation: The constructive orientation of both Western Huns and Gokturks was likely open as they did not have or adopt an intolerant religious creed and by tradition were open to adopting civilized ways.

Destructive orientation: Like all nomads of the period, Huns had a natural "institutional greed" for fertile lands.

And like all nomads until that point in history, Huns lacked an intolerant creed. However, like all nomads from central Asia, they remembered success in devastating civilizations and in fact succeeded in destroying the Roman Empire and weakening the Gupta Empire in India, They possessed exceptional aggression and violence driven not by creed but by greed.

14.58 The Inner Nature of the Indian Civilization

Productive capacity: The sustainable growing surplus remained high in part because of the emergence of a strong manufacturing sector in private hands, economic freedom and new technology adoption, and strong and favorable though fluctuating international trade. Indian society though largely free from the institution of slavery, experienced increasing wealth polarization, once again becoming more caste-prone, which was supported by an ascendant monism by the end of current phase. During this phase, Indian civilization experienced considerable internal fighting among the various states before the emergence and during the decline of the Gupta and Harsha Empires.

Creative capacity: North Indian civilization definitely continued the tradition of creative freedom, experienced no science-religion conflict, was open to creativity of other civilizations, and continued to have a high abstract systems-building capability.

Constructive orientation: Indian civilization remained open to the creativity of and trade with other civilizations.

Destructive orientation: Indian civilization remained true to its core value of external peacefulness during this phase as well.

The key parameters that measure the changing inner nature of key participants in the current phase are summarized in table 14.3.

14.59 The Inner Nature of the Participants at the End of the Second Synthesis Phase

Roman Empire

The inner nature of Roman Republic during the phase continued to consist of moderate productive capacity, as demonstrated by its moderate internal SGS, a type A/B creative capacity as Christian dogma overlaid its practical orientation, a type 1 constructive orientation, and a violent, empire builder destructive orientation, giving them a continuing type IV external orientation.

Byzantine Empire

The inner nature of the Byzantine Empire during the phase continued to consist of moderate productive capacity represented by its at best moderate internal SGS, a type B creative capacity, a type 1 constructive orientation, and a violent, empire builder destructive orientation. It thus had a type IV external orientation as well.

Persian Civilization

The inner nature of the Persian empires during the phase consisted of moderate productive capacity evidenced by its moderate internal SGS, a type A creative capacity, a type 1 constructive orientation, and a violent, empire builder destructive orientation. It, therefore too had a type IV external orientation.

Table 14.3: Relative Values of Measurable Parameters of Social Orders
Second Synthesis Phase 200–750 CE

Measurable Characteristics	NB	EF	NTA	WAB	SC	Creative Capacity			Constructive Orientation			Destructive Orientation		
						Creed	ASBC	WAB	GI	ESAN	LI	NB	IG	IC
Roman Empire	High	Med	Low	MS	Low	SRC	High	MS	Low	High	High	High	High	High
Byzantine Empire	High	Med	Low	MS	Mod	SRC	High	MS	Low	High	High	High	High	High
Persian Civilization	High	High	High	MS	Med	Bal	High	MS	Low	Med	High	High	Low	Low
Chinese Civilization	High	High	High	PE	High	Bal	Low	PE	Med	High	Low	High	low	Low
Cent. Asian Nomads	Low	High	Low	MS	High	Bal	Low	MS	Low	Low	N/A	Low	High	low
Indian Civilization	High	High	High	CE	High	Bal	High	CE	Low	High	High	High	Low	Low

NB: Degree of Natural Bounty
EF: Economic Freedom
NTA: New Tech. Adoption
WAB: Wealth Allocation Bal.
SC: Social Cohesion

ASBC: Abstract Sys. Building Capability
GI: Geographic Isolation
ESAN: Early Success against Nomads
LI: Linguistic Isolation
IG: Institutional Greed
IC: Intolerant Creed

ED: Favors Elite Decadence
MS: Favors Military Spending
PE: Favors Productive Endeavors
CE: Supports Creative Endeavors

ES: Excessively Spiritual
SRC: Sci. Religion Conflict
Bal: Balanced

Chinese Civilization

The inner nature of the Chinese civilization during the phase consisted of high internal SGS that corresponded to its high productive capacity, a world-class type A creative capacity, a type 2 constructive orientation, and a peaceful destructive orientation. It therefore had a type II external orientation.

Central Asian Nomads

The inner nature of the central Asian nomads during the phase consisted of low productive, type A creative capacity; a type 4 constructive orientation; and a violent and cruel destructive orientation resulting in a type III external orientation.

Indian Civilization

The inner nature of Indian civilization during the phase continued with high productive capacity, a type C creative capacity, a type 4 constructive orientation, and a peaceful destructive orientation. It continued its type I external orientation.

The inner nature of all participants during the phase is summarized in table 14.4.

The Evolution and Rationalization of the Second Synthesis of Science

14.60 The Second Synthesis in Science

During the current phase, the development of science had the following characteristics:

- Took place primarily in the Indian civilization.
- The linkages between Indian science and outside world were modest, in part because of the absence of science elsewhere despite thriving world trade. Chinese civilization was focused on practical creativity while Roman, Byzantine, and Persian Empires remained focused on empire building, practical technology, architecture, and art.
- These modest linkages relative to science were essentially peaceful in nature.

The phase was unusual in that the only civilization where advances in science took place was peaceful and was not seriously impacted by aggressive invasions. It funded its advances in science through its internal resources and not based on conquest.

14.61 Rationalizing the Second Synthesis through Causes

As in previous chapters, we will rationalize the state of science in each civilization based on their intrinsic and extrinsic causes and how well they satisfied the necessary and sufficient conditions of the corresponding stage of science.

Table 14.4: Comparative Inner Nature of Participants
Second Synthesis, 200–750 CE

Social Order	Productive Capacity	Creative Capacity	Constructive Orientation	Destructive Orientation	
	Internal SGS	ICB	O/I	P/V	SPI
Roman Empire	High	Type A/B	Type 2	Violent	No
Byzantine Empire	Moderate	Type B	Type 2	Violent	Yes
Persian Civilization	High	Type A	Type 3	Violent	No
Chinese Civilization	High	Type A	Type 2	Peaceful	Yes
Cent. Asian Nomads	Low	Type A	Type 4	Violent	Yes
Indian Civilization	High	Type C	Type 4	Peaceful	Yes

Legend
SGS: Sustainable Growing Surplus
ICB: Internal Creative Balance
O/I: Openness/Insularity
P/V: Peaceful/Violent
SPI: Sustained Political Independence

Why the Roman Empire Remained in the Mature Protoscience Stage

Internal SGS: Given the extensive expanding territories, systematic wealth drain capability, the lifestyle of the elite, and estimates made by different authorities, the internal SGS must be judged to be high.

Allocation of SGS: A substantial portion of the SGS continued to be invested in military capability, a decadent elite lifestyle, art and architecture, and infrastructure and police force needed to hold the empire and maintain internal cohesion. Thus, what was left for intellectual creativity was rather modest.

Nature of creed: Roman polytheism was tradition-bound, ritualistic, practical, and contractual in relation to its innumerable deities, but it was also open-ended, as evidenced by the incorporation and equation of the gods (for example Zeus with Jupiter) of ancient Greece into Roman pantheon after 146 BCE. Toward the end, the Roman Empire adopted Christianity as state religion after persecuting Christians for centuries and leading to science-religion conflict.

State of ASBC: The state of the ASBC of the Roman Empire remained weak despite conquest of Greece, since Romans only incorporated the art, architecture, and religion of ancient Greece and not its speculative philosophy and astronomy, even though the Greek mainland was the center of gravity of science. The center of gravity of science later shifted to Hellenistic states in West Asia and Egypt precisely because the Roman Empire did not value science. Later when Romans conquered Hellenistic states, the die had already been cast and they likely did not consider the breakthroughs in astronomy and geometry on par with art and architecture and ignored them. Besides, these developments had taken place away from mainland Greece in lesser nations! They must have seemed foreign, non-Greek and non-European to Romans. Thus, epistemology and arithmetic remained weak in the Roman world.

Openness/insularity: The Roman world was remarkably open in practical military and nonmilitary technology, art and architecture, trade, and religion—essentially those aspects that helped in the empire-building project and luxurious lifestyle for the elite. It was not open to philosophical and scientific creativity mainly because these arenas had little impact on empire building and wealth-producing capability.

Nature of violent greed: While sharing some features with ancient Egypt, the Roman Empire resembled the British Empire more fully in how it viewed the conquered territories, only the Roman Empire's reach was more extensive and broader. Egypt used its colonies and power to extract the raw materials it did not possess. However, the Roman (and British) Empire took over territories and exerted political and economic control to extract the SGS. Toward the end, territorial aggression no longer yielded new greener pastures because of the intense pressure exerted by European barbarians and the Asian nomads. Thus, SGS was stagnant precisely when military and decadent living demanded more.

In short, the Roman world remained in the state of mature protoscience, and it ensured the emerging European civilization would remain bound to Christian dogma for nearly a millennium. In short, its abstract systems-building capability remained subpar; it adopted a monotheistic, dogmatic creed; it remained closed to the intellectual creativity of other social orders; and when successfully extracted wealth from others through violent greed, it squandered it on decadence. It ultimately lost its SPI before the phase end.

Why the Byzantine Empire Remained in the Mature Protoscience Stage

Internal SGS: The internal SGS of the Byzantine Empire was moderate at best because of relatively low productivity of the agricultural sector; underdeveloped manufacturing, except silk, with heavy dependence on trade, which in turn was dependent on military struggle with the Sassanian Empire; and because of state control of economy.

Allocation of SGS: The Byzantine Empire allocated its SGS in military capability and religious endeavors. Constant wars with the Sassanian Empire took its toll.

Nature of creed: Creative freedom was confined to elaboration of Christian faith. There were precious little resources left for science after paying for wars and religious activity. Its science-religion conflict was high, as evidenced by the statement of its high priest, Saint Augustine, who claimed that "we should not be alarmed lest the Christian be ignorant of the force and number of elements; the motion, and order, and eclipses of the heavenly bodies; the form of heavens; the species...." Christian dogma unquestionably held back science despite the empire's Hellenistic heritage. There was an essential lack of scientific and philosophical creativity exhibited by the Byzantine Empire during the current phase.

State of ASBC: The abstract systems-building capability was not different from that of Roman Empire, for similar reasons.

Openness/insularity: The Byzantine Empire was open to the creativity of other civilizations mostly in military and manufacturing technologies. Again, a lack of scientific activity in the Byzantine Empire is consistent with these driving causes. The Eastern Empire was perhaps a bit more open to intellectual creativity toward the end of the phase than Western Europe perhaps because the Eastern Empire escaped the nomadic invasions and was geographically closer to the Hellenistic centers of learning.

Nature of violent greed: The Byzantine Empire dreamed of expanding its domains to that of the Roman Empire after the latter's fall. For a while, it succeeded. However, constant pressure from the Sassanian Empire made it difficult to hold on to the territories in the west. Thus, the contribution of the external SGS through systematic wealth drain was not very high and was costly.

Thus, similar to the Roman Empire, the abstract systems-building capability of the Byzantine Empire remained subpar; it adopted a monotheistic, dogmatic creed; it remained closed to the intellectual creativity of other social order, and when it successfully extracted wealth from others through violent greed, it squandered it on military capability and churches. Consequently, the Byzantine Empire remained in the mature protoscience stage.

Central Asian Nomads Failed to give Birth to Protoscience

Central Asian nomads attacked both the Roman Empire and the Indian civilization during the phase. Like all nomads, they had low internal SGS, which they allocated predominantly to building military capability. They had a rather primitive religious creed that did not oppose science in principle and therefore, they were open to the intellectual and religious creativity of civilizations. Their ASBC was very weak. What is unique about the central Asian nomads during the phase is that while they helped destroy or weaken both the Roman and Gupta Empires, they were unable to establish a stable empire in either place. Thus, while they looted, they never established a stable stream of SGS for themselves in places they helped destroy.

The absence of science in central Asians of the phase is absolutely consistent with their low internal SGS and inability to control the SGS of civilizations, their subpar abstract systems-building capability despite their openness to the creativity of civilizations; and their sustained political independence. One hardly expects science from a nomadic social order bent on aggression and that has the objective of looting and raiding.

Why the Persian Civilization Remained in the Mature Protoscience Stage

Internal SGS: Internal SGS was likely high because of several breakthrough technologies, including water transport, the windmill, and the water mill.

Allocation of SGS: A significant portion of SGS was squandered on wars with the Byzantine Empire and the nomads.

Nature of creed: It did not succumb to Christian faith, revived Zoroastrianism, and was more accommodating to intellectual freedom. There was little science-religion conflict during the current phase until the arrival of Islam. Only under Khusrau I did science receive state support resulting in diffusion of Hellenistic and Indian science. But this was too little too late.

State of ASBC: It was no different from that in the previous phase.

Openness/insularity: Persian civilization under the Sassanians was open to practical and artistic creativity of other civilizations.

Nature of violent greed: The Sassanians were a bit more successful than the Byzantines in controlling the SGS of other surrounding civilizations

The lack of achievements in science by the Sassanian Empire during the phase is consistent with its modest abstract systems-building capability, its essentially monotheistic creed, and its closed attitude toward others' intellectual creativity despite access to the SGS of conquered peoples Ultimately, the Sassanian Empire belongs in the same class of empire builders that failed to develop science despite being next door to a center of gravity of science either because of limited ASBC or insularity to philosophical and scientific creativity.

Why the Chinese Civilization Continued in the Mature Protoscience Stage

Internal SGS: The industrious Chinese civilization continued to create high SGS through several significant practical innovations.

Allocation of SGS: China was internally fragmented and under attack from Huns and other nomads during most of the current phase. Thus, a significant portion went into military capability, followed by Buddhist temple-building, followed by practical creativity.

Nature of creed: Buddhism was well established in China during the current phase after initial resistance from both Confucianism and Taoism. However, the Buddhism that arrived in China was ritualistic and had been fragmented into many schools that had been impacted by Hinduism to one degree or another. Its metaphysics resembled philosophical idealism. Though it did not actively oppose science, it did not encourage it either. Its focus remained on ethics and mental peace and not an understanding of the natural and social worlds. There was little science-religion conflict in China.

State of ASBC: There was little change in the abstract systems-building capability of the Chinese civilization, and it continued to fail to adopt alphabetical script, choosing instead to translate the Buddhist literature into Chinese.

Openness/insularity: For the first time in its history, Chinese civilization though Buddhism in general and gentry Buddhism in particular, opened up to both the religious and philosophical creativity of the Indian civilization but remained insular to its scientific creativity. The only reasonable explanation is the absence of alphabetical script and an apparent lack of relationship between science of the day and wealth production in the practical Chinese mind, which oddly enough was becoming more philosophical through the introduction of Buddhism.

Nature of violent greed: Violent greed did not conquer the Chinese civilization in this phase either. It fought the nomads vigorously while being internally fragmented. It maintained its sustained political independence during the phase and neither benefited nor suffered from wealth drain. The only impact of others' violent greed was diversion of SGS to military capability.

In short, subpar abstract systems-building capability, its insularity, and adoption of a corrupted Buddhism were responsible for its continued failure to develop science. As a result, its energies remained focused on practical creativity, internalizing Buddhism, and defending against nomads. Chinese civilization was eminently successful in these ventures. The limited outcomes in mathematics and observational astronomy and outstanding achievements in practical creativity are consistent with the inner nature of Chinese civilization during the phase. China remained in the stage of mature protoscience.

Why Indian Civilization Led the Development of Science

Internal SGS: The internal SGS was evidently high, particularly under the Gupta rule.

Allocation of SGS: Given relative peace until the sixth century, there was significant allocation of the surplus to creative endeavors as is evident from existence of universities and observatories as well as emphasis on the arts and literature.

Nature of creed: There was little science-religion conflict, and the economy was highly organized and productive, resulting in wealth creation. The political establishment was highly supportive of science, as evidenced by number of universities and observatories. With Buddhism neutralized by Hinduism and Vedanta, the focus of creative impulse once again returned from metaphysics and philosophy to science. Indian civilization led the second synthesis in science. Indian civilization had a world-class abstract systems-building capability; a tolerant, personal experience-based religious creed; and an openness to the creativity of others. All of these boosted the cause of science when the rest of the world slept.

State of ASBC: The state of abstract systems-building capability was indeed world-class because of significant development in logic and epistemology through the efforts of Buddhist scholars and because of the emergence of the decimal system, including the concept of zero.

Openness/insularity: In addition, Indian civilization remained open to the creativity of other civilizations, particularly the achievements of Hellenistic states, and enjoyed sustained political freedom through defeating both the Huns and the Arab aggressors.

Nature of violent greed: Indian civilization too remained peaceful and true to its nature. It was able to preserve its sustained political independence, defeating both central Asian and Arab nomads. Thus, it did not suffer from or benefit from systematic wealth drain.

There are indeed numerous examples of civilizations developing science by expropriating wealth and science of other civilizations, but there is hardly an example in history of a civilization, while under continuous attack from nomads, developing world-class science using primarily its own scientific traditions and its own wealth. The achievement of Indian civilization during the phase presents an alternate model of success to history's empire builders, violent colonizers, and wealth drainers.

The Shifting Center of Gravity of Science

The center of gravity of science returned to the land of its birth during the current phase. Intrinsic, extrinsic peaceful, and extrinsic violent causes all favored this development. Let us see how:

- Indian rulers under the twin influence of Buddhism and Hinduism not only created an atmosphere of creative freedom but also supported creative endeavors financially.
- Indian civilization remained open to the creative outcomes of other civilizations. It also benefited from peaceful and fair trade with other civilizations. Naturally, Christianity, because it arrived in India peacefully in the second century CE, had little chance to convert the agnostic, monist, and philosophical Indian mind.
- The Sassanian Empire's preoccupation with the Byzantine Empire and the failure of both Huns and Arabs to conquer India resulted in prolonged periods of sustained political independence during the phase.

14.62 Confirming the Stage of Science for Each Civilization

Based on the inner nature of civilizations and the underlying parameters summarized in table 14.1, the five key civilizations achieved the following life stages in science:

- Indian Civilization: Development stage of science
- Persian Empire: Mature protoscience of science
- Roman and Byzantine Empires: Mature protoscience of science
- Central Asian Nomads: Birth stage of protoscience
- Chinese Civilization: Mature protoscience of science

Looking Ahead

14.63 Emerging New Participants and Fate of Existing Participants

At phase end, we see the emergence of two new players: Europe-wide Christian civilization and Arab nomads.

European Civilization

The Roman Empire until its end and the Byzantine Empire in Europe continued to be under the control of a highly centralized imperial form of government and increasingly under a rigid Christian dogma during this phase. These forms of social, religious, and political structures were largely successful in creating European civilization out of the dissolution and breakup of the Western Empire, the emergence of papal authority, and a determined stand against the Persians by Byzantine Empire. The term "Europe" was first used by Saint Columbanus in 600 CE in a letter. However, the boundaries of the states in the west and in the Byzantine Empire continued to be rearranged after the demise of the Western Empire and nomadic invasions brought havoc to Europe; however, by and large, Europe succeeded in creating cultural cohesion through Christianity, a unifying stand against the Islamic conquest of Iberia in the west, and successful standoff against the Sassanians in the east. The political independence was, however, shattered by the Arab conquest of Iberia, which we shall take up in the next chapter.

Monotheistic Arab Nomads (632–750 CE)

By far, the most significant new player to emerge during the phase were the Arabs. Persians and the Byzantine Empire had weakened or destroyed Persian, Roman, Byzantine, and Gupta Empires, thereby opening the way for an even more dangerous invader, the Arab nomads. Moved by an uncompromising faith, a power vacuum left by the demise of Romans, reciprocally assured weakness of the Byzantine and Sassanian Empires, and a strategic location with respect to international trade, Arabs rose like a mythical creature out of the Arabian Desert to become masters of the greatest empire the world had seen in a span of less than hundred years. It would be another half a millennium before Genghis Khan would exceed this accomplishment, if only for a fleeting moment.

The death of Mohammad in 632 AD was a period of crisis for the fledging Muslim community in Arabia since the rules of succession were not clear. The first four Caliphs, Bakr, Umar, Usman, and Ali are collectively known as the "rightly guided" ones. Taking advantage of the weakened Persian Empire in the east and a weakened Byzantine Empire in the west due to prolonged conflicts between the two as well as a Western Europe in disarray due to the fall of Western Roman Empire, the "rightly guided" ones greatly expanded the Arab territories, while putting down internal revolts and facing dangers of infighting (last three of the "rightly guided" were murdered). The message of absolute confidence that they were doing God's work transmitted by Mohammad to these four personally before he died, must be considered a decisive factor in these swift victories in difficult and opportunistic times. Another key factor in early victories was the effective use of "sea desert" as a place to withdraw to regroup in a tactical retreat, comparable to the use of sea in a conflict between a land power and a sea power. By 660, in less than thirty years, Arabs had snatched Syria, Egypt, Tunisia, and Palestine from the Byzantines; Iraq, Afghanistan, and Iran from the Sassanians in Persia; and Turkestan from the Chinese. It was indeed a feat more durable than feats pulled off by Alexander a millennium earlier and by Genghis Khan more than half a millennium later.

Civil war led to the rise of the house of Ummayads of the Quraishi tribe in 660 after the battle of Nahawan. This started the second phase of expansion, leading to Arab intrusion into the Iberian Peninsula and India. The former was fully successful and the latter essentially failed except as a beachhead. Further expansion in both east and west proved difficult due to resistance from Turkish tribes in Samarkand and Tokhaistan, defeat at the battle of Tours by Franks in Europe, and severe resistance and defeats in India. The Ummayads are also remembered for converting Islam from a religious community bent on territorial expansion to a royal dynasty bent on territorial expansion.

Arab designs on India actually date back from 634 CE. However, the first four expiations sent by the "rightly guided" Caliphs resulted in total failure. The succeeding Caliph over next twenty years sent as many as six expeditions by land. All were repulsed with great loss, except the last one, which succeeded in occupying Makran in AD 680. For the next twenty-eight years, the Arabs did not dare send another army against Sindh. The next expedition in 708 CE was sent to conquer the port of Debal, near modern Karachi. Its commanders were killed, and the Arab army was routed again. Again, the Arabs under Mohamed Bin Qasim, in their desire to secure the Silk Route, attacked the Turki Shahi dynasty in Punjab but failed to break through. They then tried to approach again from the south near Sindh. This attempt was successful, resulting in a stronghold going as far north as Multan in southern Punjab.

However, with Bin Qasim's murder at the behest of Caliph because of the intrigue by a captured Indian queen in Damascus, the conquered territory was under constant pressure, with successor states shrinking in size and influence. When the Abbasids came to power in Bagdad, the two successor states, Mansurah in the south and Multan in the north, declared independence from Baghdad. In 738 CE, the Chaluka king, Vikramaditya II handed an Arab army a convincing defeat. For the next three centuries, they remained under pressure from the surrounding Hindu states and remained politically and militarily irrelevant in the Indian subcontinent.

By contrast, in Europe, by 750 CE, the Arabs controlled nearly eighty percent of the Iberian Peninsula. However, by 1300, it was reduced to less than twenty percent. The expansion beyond the Iberian Peninsula was stopped when the Frank king Charles Martel handed Arabs a defeat at the battle of Poitiers in 732 CE. We cover the Muslim golden age, which began on the Iberian Peninsula with the help of Jewish scholars and then moved east to Baghdad, where it was nurtured mostly by Persians and Indians, in the next chapter. During the current phase, the Arab nomads were successful in conquering deserts lands of West Asia, including defeating the Sassanian Empire, and Iberia and Sicily in Europe. But in the Indian subcontinent, their campaign must be judged as an overall failure.

By 750 CE, another civil war broke out in Arab inner circles, leading the Abbasids to remove the Umayyads using a non-Arab, Persian alliance. The Abbasid Caliphate was created by Abbas Muttalib, who shifted his capital from Damascus to Baghdad, thus ushering in the Baghdad phase of the golden age of Muslim civilization. This age was to last over three hundred years. In the meantime, the Umayyad dynasty continued to flourish on the Iberian Peninsula. The current phase may be regarded as the phase that established the foundations of a coming Muslim civilization in Asia, North Africa, and Europe. We take up the Islamic civilization in the next few chapters.

Finally, it is important to note the distinction between the nature of central Asian and Arab nomads. Previously, we had mentioned three necessary conditions for the rise of a nomadic power. These conditions also apply to Arab nomads. However, what distinguished the Arab nomads were two additional characteristics: belief in an uncompromising monotheism and long though uneven experience as middlemen in land and sea-based trading with civilizations. The significance of the latter is that once Arabs attained control, they automatically controlled both the sea and land-based international trade. Thus, their power was more durable than that of land-bound pastoral nomads like the central Asians.

Fate of Some Current Participants

The current phase saw the destruction of the Roman, Rouran Khannate, and Gokturk Empires. The Persian civilization began the process of adopting Islam. Only the Indian and Chinese civilizations and the Byzantine Empire survived the phase intact.

14.64 A Peek into Coming Chapters

Toward the end of the phase, Arabs begin to show interest in science based on what they learned from the Indians and from the debris of the Hellenistic achievements gleaned through their conquest of Iberian Peninsula and their struggle with the Byzantine Empire. This absorption of Greek, Hellenistic, and Indian science by Arabs formed the basis of the third synthesis that we take up in the next chapter.

Specifically, Arabs came in contact with Indian mathematics, astronomy, chemistry, and physics. Similarly, Arabs in Spain encouraged the development of the nearly forgotten Greek and Hellenistic philosophy, geometry and astronomy. By the end of the phase Arabs became the only people in the world to have full access to the entire scientific tradition of the world, despite having none of their own. The vast empire and extensive control of trade and surplus ensured the resources to pursue whatever creative endeavors they fancied. Pressure from the Huns and Arabs had a very dramatic impact on European psyche. It withdrew inward in terms of external orientation and immersed itself into Catholic and Orthodox Christianity. Thus, newly emerging European civilization closed itself intellectually and allowed the scientific leadership to pass to the Arabs. The impact of Arabs and Islamic monotheism on India was more indirect: it probably gave a boost to monism, and thus, relatively speaking but not completely, turned Indian civilization away from science.

14.65 Summary

The fourth phase was a phase when only the Indian civilization produced significant science, making outstanding contributions in mathematics and astronomy though relatively modest contributions in physical and social sciences. Other civilizations either did not show any interest in science or were in the process of adaptation and learning. We witnessed the end of Western Roman Empire at the hands of the Huns and European Barbarians and the rise of the nomadic Arabs, who created an empire from Sindh in India to Spain in Europe in a short period, though we discuss that in the next phase when we shall witness both the land and the sea trade coming under Arab control. The economies of India and China were based on agriculture and a vibrant manufacturing sector, and Arabs had a mercantile orientation backed up by newly acquired strong naval and land forces and an uncompromising faith. China continued her strong tradition of practical inventions of immense value. In the Indian civilization, we see a precipitous decline of Buddhism and a return to monism and Hinduism. Perhaps, the most critical aspect of the phase was the rise of uncompromising monotheism, which had already overwhelmed significant parts of the world, with the worst yet to come.

Chapter 15

Violent Interaction Era—Fifth Phase: Development Stage

Third Synthesis of Science (750–1200 CE)

15.1 Introduction

In the last chapter, we witnessed the demise of the Western Roman Empire and the swift rise of the Arab Empire through a skillful exploitation of military and political weaknesses of the Sassanian and Byzantine Empires and a politically fragmented Western Europe. We also saw how the Indian civilization, though it was more successful than Europe in containing Arabic nomads, had remained politically fragmented because the weakened Gupta Empire did not survive the defeated Hun invasions, and the post-invasion Harsha Empire was far too short-lived. This political vacuum once again created an opening for religious monism (a recurrent theme of Indian civilization), resulting in precipitous decline of Buddhism, in part because Buddhism itself had moved away from social concerns and agnosticism and toward philosophical idealism. Monism and the Bhakti movement were only too eager to exploit the opening through doctrines of karma and reincarnation and the institution of the caste system.

This chapter is mainly a story of continuing violence based on both creed and greed that Arab nomads unleashed on Europe, North Africa, and West Asia and the rise of an Islamic civilization that, building on the foundations of Greek and Hellenistic science in Europe and the second Indian synthesis of science, created a new synthesis before Islamic monotheism under Turkish leadership essentially killed any chance of the further progress in science by the late twelfth century. Nevertheless, we count this highly successful endeavor as the third of the four syntheses during the development stage of science; the final being the two-part Italian and the West European synthesis that we shall cover in chapter 16. Equally important, this chapter is also the story of the fortunate escape of Chinese civilization from the Muslim conquest and the beginning of the process of conquest of Indian civilization by Turkish Islamic invaders. It is also the story of the beginning of the end of Arab rule in Western Europe and the beginning of Turkish conquest southeastern Europe. Finally, it is the story of an introverted Europe remaining under the sway of Catholic dogma and feudalism in the west, the birth of an aggressive Venice as a mercantile state in the center, and of a declining Byzantine power (though it successfully ignited a short-lived Byzantine renaissance in art) under Turkish pressure from the east. The Venetian experiment was to turn out to be a dress rehearsal in the Mediterranean of the coming dominance of the high seas by a few states perched on the Atlantic coast of Western Europe as well as the foundation for the Italian Renaissance funded through wealth based on control of trade between Asia and Europe.

As in previous chapters, we will first identify the major civilizations, empires, and nomadic formations of the phase and examine the causes driving their evolution, then review their significant productive, creative, and scientific outcomes, and summarize the state of civilization at phase end. We then assess changes in their inner nature. Following this, we briefly describe the third synthesis and the state of specific sciences at the phase end and rationalize the scientific achievements of each participant. We end the chapter by identifying the new emerging characters, peek into the coming chapters, and summarize this chapter.

Affirmation of Era and Essential Participants

15.2 Affirming the Era of Civilization

During this phase, civilizations as a whole naturally remained in the era of expanding military conflicts since transportation and weapons technologies continued to expand the scope of land-based empires and land- and sea-based trade. In addition to greed, we also witness, for the first time in history, the rise of a violent, intolerant and self-assured creed in the form of Islam. Thus, for the first time, the devastating combined force of greed and creed by a nomadic people fast on their way to becoming a civilization in its own right was employed in the empire-building enterprise.

15.3 Essential Participants of the Phase

Major civilizations of the phase continued to be Indian, Chinese, and European civilizations, and starting with this phase, Muslims, which had evolved through distinct Arab, Persian, and Turkish periods. The phase thus witnessed Arab and Turkish nomadic tribes adopt civilized ways. The pressure of central Asian nomads toward West Asia and Europe was kept in check by the expanding Muslim Empire during the phase. As a result, the central Asian nomads from the southern tier of central Asia, who had converted to Islam, turned toward South Asia. As we shall see in the next chapter, central Asian aggression did not end during current phase. The invasions of non-Muslim Genghis Khan and his Islamic descendants were still in the future, though it would be the last time. Several secondary civilizations in South and Southeast Asia also came into prominence under the influence of Chinese and Indian civilizations during the phase.

History, Causes, and Outcomes of the European Civilization

15.4 Brief Political History (750–1200 CE)

Starting with this phase, because of the glue provided by Christian monotheism, we may speak of a European civilization rather than ancient Greek city-states, a Roman Republic, transplanted Hellenistic states, or a Roman and Byzantine Empire. The current period of European civilization may be analyzed in three distinct geographical areas, each undergoing different political, religious, and intellectual and trade experience: the west, the center, and the east.

In the west, the Iberian Peninsula remained under Arab control throughout most of this period, while the part to the east of the Iberian Peninsula was united by Charlemagne and the pope in 800 CE. However, this political union was short-lived. By the mid-ninth century, the Vikings in the north and the Magyars from the east were in control. In 1054, the Christian church formally split in two parts, which further weakened political unity. The defenseless British Isles, often referred under historical amnesia as Fortress Britain, were conquered a fourth time in 1066 by Normans (the other three times being Romans from 54 BCE to the fifth century, Anglo-Saxons from the fifth to eleventh centuries, and Vikings from the ninth to the eleventh centuries, bringing England ever closer to continental Europe. Often, disparate territories came under the control by a single monarch. However, this was often a result of a carefully arranged marriages among the royalty of Europe and not military strength. For example, in the twelfth century, Sicily was ruled by a German prince because he had married a Sicilian princess. The pope held the real power behind the throne through the ever-present threat of excommunication.

In the eighth century, the Byzantine Empire suffered the loss of Italy due to a religious dispute concerning iconoclasm mentioned in the previous chapter. As a consequence, in the center on the eastern seaboard of the Italian Peninsula and on the western seaboard of Greece, we witness the rise of the maritime Venetian state, founded by Italians fleeing the Italian Peninsula from the invading barbarians. They remained in control of the Mediterranean trade for some period after the current phase. The relationship between Venetia, the Byzantine Empire, the Crusaders, and the Muslim states during the current phase was one of naked opportunism. The Venetian navy protected the Byzantine waters in exchange for trade privilege and both often jointly fought against the Muslims. Yet the Byzantine Empire strongly resented the growing power and wealth of Venice. Venice, while supporting the Crusades against the Muslims, generally was not above using them against the Christian Byzantine Empire if it was required!

In the east, under the Macedonian dynasty, the Byzantine Empire initially grew stronger and handed a number of defeats to the Abbasid Arabs. In the early eleventh century, the Balkans were added, and the empire was at its second peak and was stretched from Armenia to the Italian Peninsula (the reader may recall the first peak occurred in the sixth century under Justinian). However, Arab control of Sicily remained a thorn in the side of the Byzantine Empire. The eleventh century was a period of trouble because of the great schism in 1054 CE and the Normans' invasion of Italy, resulting in Seljuk Turks handing the empire a crushing defeat in 1071 CE. By the end of the eleventh century, the Seljuks controlled Anatolia and founded the capital city of Nicaea merely fifty miles east of Constantinople. The Byzantine Empire once again saw a revival of sorts in the twelfth century, while the Seljuks were preoccupied with internal infighting under emperors John and Manuel, who added territories in both Asia and Europe. In 1204 CE, ironically, the capital Constantinople was captured by the army of the Fourth Crusade, which intended to recapture Jerusalem from the Muslims. However, Constantinople continued nominally in Byzantine hands until 1453, when Ottoman Turks put an end to its misery by capturing it.

A word about Crusades is in order. In all, there were nine Crusades between 1095 and 1272 CE. The religious goal of the Crusades was the capture of Jerusalem and Holy Christian lands from Muslim control. However, the strategic political and military purpose was to create a political consensus to drive out and put the Muslim civilization on the defensive. The Roman Catholic Church organized the Crusades and helped the pope who, at times, ruled much of Western Europe. The aggressive spirit of the Crusades was inherited by the Reconquista that we discuss in the next chapter. However, during the current phase, the Crusades did not change much politically. It fact, it pointedly strengthened the Anatolian Turkish perception that Europe was weak and disorganized and encouraged the later Ottoman aggression against southeastern Europe.

The emergence of nation-states in Western Europe and the control of the high seas was still centuries away. During much of this phase, Europe was disunited politically and weak militarily and like Indian civilization was, therefore, on the defensive with respect to Islam despite occasional successes. However, toward the end of the phase, just as Europe was gaining an upper hand with respect to the Muslim threat after nearly five centuries of subjugation, Indian civilization was on the verge of losing its political independence to Islam for an equal number of centuries. It was indeed a dark age for the newly emerged European civilization, with Venetian trade and the mini Byzantine renaissance in arts in the twelfth century as rays of hope.

To summarize: internally, the panorama of the states was constantly shifting, resulting in local wars as mentioned earlier. The state of internal aggression must be characterized as high as it was constantly stroked by the jockeying for power between the pope and the royal houses, the Norman conquests, the rise of Venice, and intermittent Byzantine westward territorial expansion.

By and large, Europe was at the receiving end of external aggression from the Muslim civilization during the current phase. As the Arab power in the west started to wane after about halfway through the phase, the Seljuk Turk power began to wax in the east. The aggressive impulse in the Crusades was essentially a defensive religious reaction against Arabs and Venetian expansion was essentially mercantile in essence and was directed against limiting the naval expansion of the Byzantine Empire and the Seljuk Turks. Venice, surprisingly, was very successful at that during this and next phase. Similarly, the Charlemagne Empire centered in France and Germany and northern Italy confined its aggression to internal European territorial expansion. It was hardly a sea power. Thus, with the exception of the Crusades starting end of the eleventh century, Europe was essentially on the defensive in land warfare. However, the sea warfare was a bit different. Both Arab and Seljuk Empires were primarily coastal sea powers, thus allowing the emerging Venetian state to control Mediterranean trade by the end of the current phase. Though the Ottomans corrected this in the fifteenth century, this strategic blunder allowed the trade wealth to begin to flow into Venice and other European cities, setting the financial foundation of the Italian Renaissance in the coming centuries.

15.5 Natural Causes

No significant natural causes affected European civilization during the current phase. The second round of bubonic plague was still in the future.

15.6 Intrinsic Causes

Intrinsic Causes—Institutional Structures and Processes

Political system: Political structures in the west consisted of royalty or high nobility at the top, followed by the feudal lords who had large amounts of land. Serving under the lord were the knights, the farmers, and the serfs. However, overtly or covertly, often the real power resided with the pope.

In the center, the case of Venetia was interesting. During the twelfth century, the Venetian principality severely restricted the power of the Dodge through two councils, a major one consisting of 480 members chosen from prominent families and minor council consisting of six members to "assist" the Dodge. It was perhaps the first instance, before the Magna Carta, where political power passed from the king to his nobles and where political power passing from an absolute ruler to a business class. It set the stage for the rise of a mercantile Venetian power in the following centuries. With hindsight, the coming Venetian adventure was a dress rehearsal in the eastern Mediterranean for Western Europe's dominance of the high seas and world trade centuries later. In the east, the Byzantine Empire continued to follow its theme system, but the Orthodox Christian religious authority never equaled or rivaled the political authority of Byzantine rulers. Though the political structure in the west and the center was relatively decentralized, the church was becoming highly organized and centralized. Thus, in the west, the pope as religious authority reigned supreme; in the center, the Venetian business class reigned supreme, and in the east, political authority reigned supreme.

Military capability: Gone was the military supremacy of the Roman and Byzantine Empires. In the west, heavily armed cavalry following Persian designs formed the backbone and employed lances. The knights in fact were highly respected and formed a distinct class. The light cavalry employed the crossbow. However, militarily, West Europeans even lagged the Hungarians and often prayed "Lord save us from the arrows of the Hungarians." The infantry, which used spears and archers, was the largest section and often employed mercenaries. There was a steady decrease in the importance of the knight. The navy remained very traditional and used galleys employing flamethrowers. The principal tactics were fortification based on castle, city walls, and siege warfare. The former became necessary in the face of fragmentation and barbarian invasions, and the latter often employed catapults, scaling ladders, siege towers, and tunnels to undermine the city walls. Adoption of the stirrup from China boosted the cavalry; however, in the absence of explosives technology, military capability remained pretty static. Unlike the Muslim civilization, there was no offensive religious motivation for European military, the Crusades essentially being a defensive reaction born of anger and frustration.

Economic organization: The economy was agrarian, naturally. The slavery of Roman times had more or less disappeared, partly due to the impact of Christianity, but it was replaced by the landless serf who was bonded to the landlord in untold ways. The feudal lord felt some sense of responsibility for the serf. The feudal system in Western Europe was in fact a system where the land was parceled out into district-size chunks handed out to nobles in exchange for tax collection and military service. The king had little direct say in the local economic matters. The situation in the cities was better, particularly toward the end of the phase: the manufacturing and commercial sectors were getting organized into guilds, which regulated and monopolized the internal trade. The guild apprenticeship started at the tender age of seven. These craft guilds were the precursors of the future capitalism that we shall encounter in chapter 16.

It was not yet a class system in that there was minimum mobility across various strata. It was more akin to a caste system, with serfs having the least mobility, followed by the guilds. Nonetheless, it was a stable system and resulted in a significant increase in European population; the surplus was not wasted on territorial expansion in faraway lands. The wars were limited to the continent, unlike in Roman times. On the eve of the second millennium, Paris had a population of twenty thousand and Rome a mere thirty-five thousand in a world that had cities ten times as large. There was no large navy to support either. In the center, in 1198, CE Pope Innocent III granted a license to Venice to trade with the Saracens or Arabs. In the east, the Byzantine economy was not feudal and was more centrally controlled. It saw an economic revival in the eleventh century with increased urbanization. Trade flourished through efforts of both Venice and the Byzantine Empire.

It should be noted that starting in the current phase, two types of money were in circulation: traditional coin money used for retail buying and selling and so-called money of account, which had a large value and was used only for large-scale commercial transactions. A money changer could convert the money of account into coinage if needed. What we see here is the early development of a credit system based on mutual trust. The unit of the money of account was *Libra* in Latin, pound (with Latin symbol £) in English, *livre* in France, and *Pfund* and *mark* in Germany.

Systems of religious faith: By about 800 CE, nearly all of Europe was Christian. The church presented as a strong voice in political affairs, with the pope as the head of a vast network of churches and monasteries manned by the clergy and monks. The roles of both the clergy and the monk were not hereditary. Only clergy could administer the sacraments, while the monks focused on theological study in the monasteries. This role differentiation was important since the monks' focus on theology in the current and next phase eventually turned Scholastic. The church had a tax-exempt status and significant property rights, participated in crafts, and often administered its own criminal law for its members. Through Christian doctrine, the church held sway over the masses to a point where it could absolve the sins in exchange for money. The inclusion and elevation of Mary, the mother of Jesus, into a nurturing mother status was evolved to soften the austere masculine image of Christianity. This was a late development, as we find no such status given to Mary in the old bible.

During the current phase, through all regions of Europe in the west, center, and east, science-religion conflict remained high. There was some movement away from Augustine's uncritical adoption of Christianity. The early Scholasticism, (eleventh through twelfth century), though, was focused on giving a rational form to Christian doctrine but not challenging it.

Legal system: The legal code of Roman and Byzantine origin reinforced and supported the position of the elites: clergy and nobility. While it gave some protections to others, it rarely gave them privileges. The law also served to help define who were outside society. Women had very limited rights, for example, they could not hold public office.

Social structure: In the west and center, the social structure derived from feudalism. At the top of the pyramid was the pope, followed by the king. The king made land grants to nobles and powerful military chiefs called vassals. The former swore to protect the king, and the latter agreed to fight for him in return. At the bottom were the serfs, who were given land to work on and paid the noble or vassal the tax and promised loyalty. In the beginning, the feudal system was somewhat meritocratic, and it was possible for men of ability to move up. However, over time it became hereditary, static, and complex. There was little change in the social structure in the Byzantine Empire during the current phase.

European civilization during the current phase continued to have excessive wealth polarization in the west under an entrenched feudalism in bed with the church, in a rising Venetia controlled by prominent business families, and to a somewhat lesser degree in Byzantine Empire under the centralized theme system where farmers appear to have a little more breathing room.

Knowledge-Creating and educational institutions: There was not much by way of knowledge creation in medieval Europe, and early education was conducted in either monasteries or cathedral schools by monks and bishops respectively. Priests from Chantry schools also helped educate children when not dispensing religion or acting as paid prayers for the dead. Some Cathedral schools, such as in Paris, later evolved into great universities. Students typically sat on the floor. Knights were required to attend school and girls from wealthy families were allowed to attend schools. Latin grammar, rhetoric, astronomy, music, arithmetic, geometry, and logic constituted the seven liberal arts. Further studies in medicine, law, philosophy, or theology were possible in monasteries, cathedral schools, or in several early universities such as Bologna, Reggio Emilia, and Salerno in Italy in the twelfth century. Most medieval Europeans were illiterate.

Wealth allocation process: The surplus was not squandered on military campaigns and on the elite to the same extent as during the Roman period. The name of the game was not expansion; it was reclamation and defense. On the other hand, considerable surplus was spent on elaborate churches and castles that dotted the countryside and to support the pope, the grandeur of whose lifestyle rivaled or exceeded that of royalty. Monasteries were another outlet for the surplus. All in all, we could surmise that what was saved from excessive military expenditures was channeled into religion. Little of the surplus was directed into intellectual activity, with the exception of monasteries. Future great universities of Europe only began to come into existence toward the end of this phase, just when great universities in North India were going out of business.

Social cohesion processes: In Western Europe's feudal system, the basis of social cohesion was the mutual obligations between the king and his nobles and vassals (tax collection and military service), the nobles and the serf (wealth production), and the glue provided by the Christian faith. Often, the conflict between the kings and pope regarding authority to appoint bishops and abbots and the papal ability for excommunication (hence barring entry into heaven after death) destabilized the system. In the center, in Venetia, the merchant class provided social cohesion with both religion and politics playing a subordinate role. In the east, the centralized provinces and the theme system provided social cohesion, and the head of Orthodox Church depended on the emperor for financial support and hence lacked political power. The customs and the legal and religious structures thus created a very stable system, with each strata or caste knowing its place in the system and accepting that position. The bond between lord and serf went beyond the economic arena, further increasing the social stability.

Internal wars: The current phase was marked by intense internal wars resulting from the conflict between the kings and pope in the west, and the struggle for dominance between Venice and the Byzantine Empire in the Adriatic Sea in the center and the Byzantine goal of westward territorial expansion in the east. Often, these three competing power centers combined forces to fight the Arabs in the Iberian Peninsula and the Ottomans in the east. Thus, the goals of land grab and sea control, fueled by intolerant monotheistic creeds of Christianity (Crusades) and Islam and insatiable Venetian greed, made internal stability and peace an elusive goal. It was a preview of the terrible drama of the coming centuries.

Formative Beliefs and Ideology at the End of Third Synthesis Phase

The entrenched and intolerant Christian dogma, the continuing antiscience attitude made worse by political power enjoyed by the pope in the west and Christianity throughout, a social inequality resulting from the master-lord relationship embedded in a strange and uniquely European feudalism despite the Christian message of equality before God, and the tradition of violent aggression kept in check by Arabs in the west followed by Turks in the east all point to a belief system that may be summarized as follows:

- A belief in Christian salvation and turning away from an interest in practical let alone intellectual knowledge
- A belief in the fundamental social and economic inequality
- An attitude of insularity toward the intellectual and religious creativity of others
- A continuing belief in aggression toward other social orders, betrayed by the Crusades despite inability of overt empire building

These beliefs, derived in part from their Roman heritage, in part from Christian dogma, and in part due to Muslim power, are important since they defined both the emerging attitude toward science and other social orders.

15.7 Extrinsic Peaceful Causes

Impact of Indian, Chinese, and Islamic Civilizations

Europe directly interacted with the Islamic and indirectly with the Chinese and Indian civilizations through Arab mediation. Like the Chinese civilization, European civilization during the current phase was insular, though in different arenas. While the Chinese civilization was insular across all creative endeavors except perhaps religious creativity, by contrast, European insularity extended primarily in religious matters alone. Because of the relative openness and Muslim presence in Iberia, European civilization reacted to the impact of extrinsic causes faster.

There were monumental peaceful causes at work behind the scenes that set the stage for profound changes to European civilization in the coming centuries. The first was the Latin translation of Arabic works of ancient Greece and the Hellenistic states, or the first synthesis of science, by men like Peter the Venerable and Peter Abelard. The second was the translation of the achievement of the third (Arab-Persian) synthesis in mathematics, optics, astronomy, chemistry, medicine, and architecture, which itself was based, in part, on the second (Indian) synthesis in science. Third was the byproduct of the Crusades, which resulted in greater trade and in turn brought many products unknown or extremely rare and costly, including a variety of spices, ivory, jade, diamonds, improved glass manufacturing techniques, early forms of gunpowder, oranges, apples, other Asian crops, and many other products.

Transmission of Creativity to European Civilization

Practical creativity: The diffusion of several key Chinese practical inventions such as paper, gunpowder, the compass, the stirrup, and movable type printing likely mediated through the Arabs. Although the history of wood block printing goes back nearly two millennia in Chinese, Egyptian, and Indian civilization, ceramic movable type was invented in China in 1040 and metal movable type in Korea around 1240 CE. We know that movable type was not available in Europe as late as Marco Polo's return in 1295 CE. The oldest book that used movable type to print it was called *Jikji* and was printed in Korea in 1377. It seems the idea of movable type reached Europe through Marco Polo and through a long evolutionary process that eventually led to the Gutenberg press in 1457.

Because the Arabs controlled Iberia early in their expansion, the diffusion of Chinese technology into Europe through the Muslims occurred earlier than in India and was much more extensive, judging by the diffusion of additional key technologies, such as rigid horse collar and saddle, whiffletree, crank handle, the arch, block printing, windmills, the canal lock, the artisan well, mechanical clocks, the stern-mounted center rudder, and paper manufacture.

Religious creativity: Arabs brought Islam to Spain, and over time succeeded in converting nearly 85 percent of its population through the usual Muslim approach of both positive and negative economic incentives.

Intellectual creativity: The diffusion of the results of third synthesis from Muslim civilization in philosophy and science from Iberia to Western Europe and Italy and the diffusion of art of the Byzantine renaissance into Italy in the eleventh century set the stage for the fourth synthesis of science in Venice and Italian city-states. Perhaps the conquest of Toledo from Arabs in 1085 CE was the turning point from an intellectual standpoint. The astronomical tables and algebra of Khwarizmi (1122 CE), medical encyclopedias of Ali ibn al-Abbas (1127 CE) and Avicenna (1130 CE), and Euclid's elements (1142 CE) were translated from Arabic into Latin. In addition to translations, the travels by scholars such as al-Biruni and traders also helped diffuse the achievement of Muslim civilization.

Impact on Productive Outcomes

Wealth creation: With the exception of Venice, wealth did not see a change in Europe during the current phase because of oppressive feudalism in the west and a highly centralized state in the east under Byzantines. Both sapped the creative initiative and entrepreneurship in the face of new practical technology pouring into Europe through the Arabs.

Fair trade: The Arab control of Spain and Sicily, coupled with the control of land routes through Persia, had a profound impact on European trade, which came to be dominated by Muslim traders. Only toward the end of the phase do we witness the rise of Venetian power in the eastern Mediterranean Sea that began to cut into the profits of Arab traders. During the eleventh and twelfth centuries, Venice became extremely wealthy by exploiting the conflict between the Byzantine Empire in eastern Europe and the Arab Empire in Western Europe. Venice controlled the western end of the Europe-Asian trade through its control of the Adriatic Sea. However, this trade wealth may still be characterized as resulting mostly from fair trade because Venice only controlled the western terminus of this trade with respect to the Byzantine Empire and the Ottomans. Its control hardly extended to Asian terminus in the east, which, though was coming increasingly under the dominance of the Arabs.

Migrations and travel: Apart from the significant internal migration of Germans into central and eastern Europe and Vikings and Anglo-Saxons into England, the most significant peaceful migrations from outside Europe took place from Indian subcontinent and North Africa. The former were Rajasthani or Jat stock, later called gypsies, fleeing the Ghazni invasion of India in the eleventh century and migrated through North Africa into the Iberian Peninsula. The latter were Arabs from North Africa, who came into Spain in the wake of the Moors conquest, much like the Greeks immigrating to the Hellenistic states. Jews who had been persecuted by the Roman Empire also migrated to Muslim Iberia and fought the Crusaders alongside the Muslims. However, by the eleventh century, Muslims no longer welcomed Jews in Granada because of the reaction against the powerful and ostentatious Jewish Vizier. This was followed by the fundamentalist Almohads, who had wrestled control of the southern part of the Peninsula, resulting in the migration of Jews eastward into the heartland of Europe. In summary, the current phase saw peaceful migration of Arabs, Indians, and Jews into Europe. Even today, one may glimpse a perfectly Arab face in southern France.

The Muslim defeat of the Byzantine Empire had the profound consequence of peaceful emigration of scholars from Byzantine to Italy. These people were to prove critical in igniting the fourth synthesis of science, also known as the Italian Renaissance, that we take up in chapter 16.

Impact on Creative Outcomes

There was little overt impact on creative outcomes during the phase. The focus of creativity remained religious architecture and refining the Christian dogma. However, beneath the surface, Europe was absorbing the world's practical and intellectual heritage, sinking deep into Christian dogma and was on the verge of discovering and linking to the heritage of ancient Greece and Hellenistic states through Arab mediation. Thus, perhaps the most significant impact of peaceful extrinsic causes on Europe was the diffusion of the fruits of the Arab-Persian synthesis of science into Europe and infusion of Chinese practical technology.

Impact on Societal Structures and Processes

To all outward appearances, European civilization remained backward and feudal in nature. However, the diffusion of world's practical technology and the Arab-Persian synthesis of science introduced through Islam was beginning to stir both the religious and business-minded Europeans. During the following centuries, the changes in economy, trade, and legal structures, of course, came a lot sooner than in religious and political structures because the most advanced proximate civilization was the Muslim civilization, which, like the European civilization, supported the marriage between state and religion and had become antiscience by the end of the current phase.

European civilization, with the exception of Venice, lacked institutions that allowed individual initiative because of feudalism, papal authority, and the theme system in the eastern Byzantine Empire. Knowledge gathered through Crusades and Arab rule in Iberia initiated the development of decentralized bureaucracies that ultimately led to the creation of nation-states under powerful sovereigns. The societal structures and processes remained fundamentally unaffected by the extrinsic causes during the current phase, however.

With the exception of the Crusades, which were a defensive reaction in some ways, European civilization remained hidebound during the current phase. However, the Crusades and Venetian commercial empire were a dress rehearsal of the horrors of Reconquista and the control of high seas by a few western European nation-states in the coming centuries.

The Muslim presence in Iberia and Sicily did eventually manage to unite the Europeans around the existing political and religious structures. This resulted in limiting the extent of Muslim conquest as well as their eventual retreat. The humiliation of conversions to Islam in Iberia and the resulting Crusades and violent Reconquista had a major role in the reigniting the aggressive tendencies lying latent in Europe since the fall of the Roman Empire.

15.8 Extrinsic Violent Causes

Assessing the Loss of SPI

During most of this phase, Western Europe in general and the Iberian Peninsula and Sicily (for a much shorter period) in particular remained under Arab hegemony. It is significant that Arab power was confined to the part of Europe nearest to African continent, as it implied both a relatively weak Arab naval power and the internal struggles between the Umayyad and Abbasid factions. The Arabs were to maintain the control of at least a part of the Iberian Peninsula throughout the entire current phase. Eastern Europe under the Byzantines had a somewhat easier time against the Arabs but was not so fortunate when Arab power passed on to the Turkish in the eleventh century. Turks were successful in eventually destroying the Byzantine Empire, as we shall take up in the next chapter.

Loss of Control of Wealth and Means of Wealth

Thus, Arabs were successful in only controlling Iberia and Sicily in Europe, and Iberia greatly benefited from the allocation of surplus to creative endeavors. Elsewhere in Europe, the loss of territory in Iberia, diverting a shrinking surplus into necessary defense, and building elaborate churches and massive castles for feudalism to survive further reduced the surplus available for creative endeavors, which were not encouraged by the Catholic Church regardless.

Impact on Productive Outcomes

Arabs were empire builder-settlers in Europe. There was little question of wealth drain or an impoverished population. They were also open to practical creativity and created a diversified economy through encouraging textiles, glassware, ceramics, and metalwork industries and through introducing new crops such as hard wheat, rice, watermelon, eggplant, and banana. They also introduced better irrigation techniques, such as the water wheel.

Impact of fair trade: Arab victories impacted free trade, and Europe benefited from linking the Iberian Peninsula with rest of Europe through the Mediterranean and later the shifting of Turkish focus toward east. Arabs controlled the Mediterranean Sea, which resulted in both the Byzantine and Holy Roman Empires to cede the trade control to the Arabs. Exactly the opposite began to happen toward the end of the phase.

Impact of migrations: Earlier in the phase, there was significant movement of talent from both outside Europe and within Europe to Iberia. As Arab power in Iberia waned, the scholars began to diffuse out of Iberia into Europe, and as Venice gained control of the eastern Mediterranean, the trade and scholars began to return to central Europe, though focused in the hands of the tiny state of Venetia.

Transmission of Creativity

Although the Arab conquests were swift, as we saw in the last chapter, the expulsion of Arabs from Europe only occurred slowly over the centuries, with the final victory coming after the end of the current phase. Thus, the Arabs left a significant legacy of creativity in Europe.

The strategic orientation of the victorious Muslim civilization in Iberia was one of adopting the practical technology and intellectual ideas they encountered. The orientation of the defeated European civilization elsewhere in Europe was that of sheer disinterest toward strides occurring in practical and intellectual creativity in Iberia under Muslim domination through most of the current phase.

On religion: Arabs, after initial tolerance during the founding decades, imposed Islam on Iberia with little impact elsewhere. In the center, Sicily met the same fate at Arab hands in 826 CE until the Normans reconquered it in 1091 CE, an event many historians, with some license, consider as the first Crusade.

Practical Creativity

In addition to the agricultural innovations alluded to above, architecture and language stand out as key examples of practical creativity that influenced Iberia. Moorish architecture, with its horseshoe arches; fine, slender columns; and spacious buildings dot the Peninsula even today after a thousand years. They had a major influence in Iberia. Muslim craftsmen monopolized the building trade in Spain for centuries.

Arabs, of course, did not introduce the alphabet in Spain; however, Arabic became the court language slowly. It impacted the Spanish language and poetry dramatically and enriched it with several thousand words.

Intellectual Creativity

There was little interest in science in Europe when the Arabs arrived; rather, the Holy Roman Empire, the Byzantine Empire, and the Christian church had actively worked to extinguish the Greek and Hellenistic science that had managed to find shelter in Asia and Africa. However, as mentioned above, once Muslim military focus under the Turks shifted from west to the east, Europeans were successful in driving the Muslims out of Western Europe, mastering the Mediterranean Sea again. Having watched the Arabs do science in Iberia for centuries and having failed at integrating Christian dogma and Greece philosophy that had been spilling out of Muslim Iberia (The tenth-century library of al-Hakam was one of the largest libraries in the world, housing more than four hundred thousand volumes.), they were ready to look at science in a more open-minded manner. Thus, the instruments of control, though destructive of the European civilization and Christianity in the earlier centuries of the phase, was responsible for creating an opening for science in the dogma-soaked European mind still living in the dark ages.

Ready or not, Muslim civilization offered a gift of immeasurable value to the European civilization. Arabs-Persians had created the third synthesis of science based on and by extending Greek-Hellenistic-Indian achievements. By the end of this phase, it resulted in several independent developments coming together that favored European civilization. The Arab-Persian control of Muslim civilization passed into the hands of antiscience Turks in the eleventh century. This resulted in weakening the Arabs and their control of Iberia and Sicily since the Turks had greater interest in weakening the neighboring Byzantine Empire and expanding their control toward central Asia (and South Asia), where their ancestors had come from centuries earlier. This shift in the focus of Muslim power from west to east and Islam turning fundamentalist not only resulted in bringing the golden age of Islam to an end but also made it possible for the Europeans to drive the Arabs out of Europe but also made possible the emergence of Venetia as a sea power in the eastern Mediterranean for several centuries beginning the end of the current phase. Thus, as Arabs retreated from Europe they left the fruits of the third synthesis of science for an unsuspecting and unprepared Europe and left a vacuum in Mediterranean that was quickly filled by a rising Venice. Once again, trade wealth started trickling into Europe, the wealth that would combine with the fruits of third synthesis and the Byzantine scholars fleeing to Italy to lay the foundation for the fourth synthesis, better known as the Italian Renaissance, in the coming centuries.

The strategic response of the European civilization toward the end of the current phase was the Scholasticism (absorbing Islamic synthesis), Crusades, and Reconquista, all of which we take up in the next chapter.

Impact on Institutional Structures and Processes

The impact of Muslim empire building in Europe had significant long-term consequences on the societal structures and wealth production and allocation processes. Most notable were the impact of Muslim legal system, adoption of new technology, and the rise of learning centers in Paris, England, and Italy to support Scholasticism.

There was perhaps a modest impact of Arab conquest on the nature of class conflict and wealth polarization. Loss of trade wealth and successful defense against the Arabs needed resources. This burden likely fell on the poor in Europe. However, Arab conquest also brought together the Holy Roman Empire and the Christian church in western and central Europe, thus moderating the internal fighting. Finally, this internal unity against the aggressor also resulted in awakening the historical tendencies of aggression within the European civilization, which manifested itself in the Crusades and the rise of the maritime Venetian state.

Assessment of Net Impact

Lack of creative freedom under Christian dogma and the continuing impact of the Roman Empire (which had little interest in the philosophical and scientific outcomes of ancient Greek and Hellenistic civilizations centuries earlier) drastically impacted the creative impulse, lest the reader think that only Arab invasion caused all the damage to European civilization. Thus, the impact of Islam on Europe during the current phase was an acceleration of the tendencies inherent from the debris of the Roman Empire, a deepening hold of Christian dogma within a defensive

Europe, and the beginning of a creative awakening during the current phase.

Summary

Arab encounters initially shell-shocked Europe into accepting a loss of territory and influence. However, it later fought back through the Crusades and Reconquista and ultimately succeeded in driving Islam out of Europe but only after centuries of Muslim adoption and further development of Indian, Greek, and Hellenistic science. The central impact of Islam on both the Holy Roman Empire in the west and the Byzantine Empire in the east was to put both of these empires and the European civilization on the defensive and make them mostly inwardly oriented during the current phase, Crusades notwithstanding, European civilization suffered at the hands of the Arabs in the beginning of this phase but was fortuitously positioned very well indeed by the end of this phase to enjoy the gifts of Muslim achievements. Arabs were the conscious destroyers of Europe's political independence and inadvertent givers of their creativity. In short, after an initial loss, the ultimate impact of instruments of control on European civilization was to expel the Muslims while gaining technology, science, and an aggressive external posture after more than half a millennium of introverted existence—quite the opposite of what the Indian civilization was to experience *after* the current phase.

15.9 Productive Outcomes

Wealth creation: The driver of wealth creation in Europe during the current phase was not the improvement in agricultural productivity, which remained low. Rather, it was population increase, greater urban activity, and international trade. Comparatively speaking, wealth creation remained modest.

Fair trade: Arabs dominated Mediterranean trade, and Venetians dominated toward the end. Up in the north, near the end of the phase, Baltic trade by the Hanseatic League, which bound together Russia, Germany, England, and Nordic countries, expanded considerably. The two trading regions were overlapping and helped, much like Christianity in the previous phase, to knit the European continent together. Ironically, the Crusades also helped boost trade through new contacts. Cities such as Genoa, Pisa, Toulouse, and Venice were thriving port cities.

Peaceful migrations: The peaceful migrations of Indians, Arabs, and Jews into Europe during the current phase have been mentioned earlier. In southern France, it is not difficult to identify the Arab facial type in a crowd even today. The migrations also occurred through wars and Viking invasions of England and Norman invasion of regions as far apart as England and Sicily.

15.10 Creative Outcomes

The creative history of Europe during this phase consisted in developing Christian dogma, absorbing practical technology from other civilizations, displaying modest interest in philosophy, and significant development in art. So absorbed was Europe in its Christian dogma that at the start of the phase western Europe had retained little active, continuous memory of Greek and Hellenistic traditions. The center of European art had shifted to the Byzantine Empire in the east, which, though under attack from Islam, managed to hold on.

Achievements in Practical Creativity

Europe was a net receiver of Chinese, Indian, and Muslim practical technology. Such innovations as the stirrup, arched saddle, windmill, blast furnace, horizontal loom, cotton gin, grindstone, watermill, and improved shipbuilding technology were absorbed into the European civilization. The significant achievements of European civilization in practical creativity are summarized in table 15.1.

Achievements in Religious Creativity

Early in this phase, the mythology of Christianity, consisting of the concept of the holy trinity, death, resurrection, and ascension of Jesus, communion and holiness of saints, the second coming, judgment, and salvation of the faithful, had all been pretty much worked out. Likewise, the hierarchy of the church in the west—with the Roman bishop as the pope and local bishops and lay priests established—was also in place. The Byzantine Bishops did not accept the pope as the head, and that led to a split between the Catholic and Orthodox branches. The key relevant aspects of Christianity during the current phase from our perspective were the conflict between the pope and the state and the development of monasteries, since both had significant impact on the development of science in Europe after the current phase.

State and Christianity: The fundamental difference in the western Holy Roman Empire and the eastern Byzantine Empire was that the Byzantine Empire had survived the Huns, as we saw in the last chapter. As a result, the state was stronger in the east than in the west. The pope in the west took advantage of the weakened political situation and during several periods and became a force equal or greater than the kings. The pope had the power to levy taxes, maintained an army, took part in wars, and initiated the Crusades. By winning the investiture controversy in the eleventh century, the pope generally controlled the appointment of head of churches or bishops and the head of monasteries or abbots. This religious interference in the matters of state is not too different from the state in which modern-day Islam in some countries finds itself in. Papal power reigned supreme between the eleventh and thirteenth centuries. It was during this period that Popes

Table 15.1: Significant Achievements in Practical Creativity
European Civilization, 750–1200 CE

Category	Significant Achievements
Materials	
Processes	Early blast furnace, Catalan Forge
Energy	Use of coal
Tools	Several clock designs
Agricultural Products	Improved wine making
Non-Agri. Products	Use of forks for eating
Construction	Notre Dame, use of engineering drawings, cross-ribbed vault dry dock, keel and framework design for ships
Transportation Technologies	Ultra-fast Viking ships, lighthouses, concept of glider
Weapons Technologies	Gravity-based catapults
Infrastructure	Paved roads
Communications	

initiated the Crusades. Toward the end of the current phase, the Catholic church helped establish the institutions of Inquisition to suppress heresy, achieve doctrinal unity, and convert Muslim decedents of ex-Christians in Iberia under the threat of persecution, including being burned alive at the stake.

Since Augustine in the fourth century, the focus of Christianity had been love of God and denial of the pleasures of flesh thought of as sin. St. Benedict's rule in the sixth century had emphasized obedience to God. None of the thinkers of medieval Europe during the current phase had dared question Christian monotheism.

Rise of monasteries: At the beginning of the current phase, Charlemagne founded schools to address the problem of illiteracy among the clergy, thus making it possible for monasteries and monks devoted to understanding Christianity to emerge. The Clinic reform of the monasteries starting 910 CE resulted in the pope directly controlling the abbots in place of the feudal lords. Over time, this expanded the scope of monasteries, and they came to operate all schools and libraries. Later, in the twelfth century, as these schools separated into grammar schools and centers of higher learning, monasteries naturally evolved into universities at Bologna, Paris, and Oxford. The Cistercian movement of the late eleventh century affirmed a return to the austere life for the monks outlined earlier by St. Benedict including hard manual labor. The monks in due course also became the main force in spreading technological innovations in agriculture, metallurgy, and water management in Europe. In the late twelfth century, yet another monastic reform was initiated by the Mendicant order, which focused on a life of poverty, chastity, begging, education, and missionary activity for the monks in seclusion. It appears that this change was driven by increasing wealth polarization and allowed the monks to get closer to the common man. Throughout medieval times, monasticism displayed an ability to adapt in response or in reaction to conditions occurring in the society, the church, or even within its own body. These changes often brought about needed reform and helped to serve the church as a whole.

Thus, the three faces of medieval Christianity—those of bishops, monks, and priests—were in stark contrast. All three positions were nonhereditary, required celibacy, and were mediators between God and common man. However, that is where the similarity ends. The bishops were wealthy and lived like princes and kings. The monks lived the life of austerity and were budding teachers and intellectuals, though within the limits prescribed by the Christian dogma. The priests did not live like the princes, take a vow of poverty, possess power, or engage in intellectual pursuits. They represented the frontline of mediation between God and ordinary man.

Evolution of Christianity and Islam: It is interesting to contrast the early evolution of Christianity and Islam, for they were fundamentally different. Islam, though communicated through a humble angel of God, emerges in the seventh century as a complete militaristic religion with no separation of state and religion. Christianity, though brought to Earth by God's only son, had a more tentative beginning, but it managed to slowly crawl itself into a position of similar power over the first half millennia of its existence. Part of the reason for this difference is of course that Islam was born into a political vacuum, and Christianity faced one of the world's more powerful empires.

To summarize, religious creativity in Europe during the current phase was highly circumscribed. Christian monotheism was naturally beyond polytheism; however, the ideas of monism, atheism, and agnosticism would strike the European mind as blasphemous during the phase.

Achievements in Philosophy

Perhaps the most significant philosophical activity in Europe during the current phase was the attempt to reconcile Christian dogma with Greek philosophy—a task that was, of course, doomed to failure but also a task that set the stage to absorb and further develop the results of Arab synthesis in sciences. This was a task the monks undertook in the dark, cold monasteries of medieval Europe. It is perhaps inaccurate to call this effort a philosophy, since the focus here was not open-ended inquiry; rather, it was the justification of an existing faith through reason or to dress up monotheistic faith in the garb of reason.

Johannes Scotus Eriugena—who was of Irish origin—in the mid-ninth century was one of the earliest of such attempts to synthesize Christian dogma and neo-Platonism. On the one hand, he claimed a substantial identity between philosophy and religion, and on the other, he claimed philosophy as primary and religion as secondary or derived. His basic claims, thus, were self-contradictory. To Scotus, all life reflected God's attributes and was evolving toward a harmonious union with God. Thus, his worldview of evolution of the universe is one of religious evolution on an automatic pilot.

In the late eleventh century, Anselm (1033–1109 CE) of Canterbury, England, attempted to reconcile faith and reason through ontological proofs of God's existence as follows: first, God is conceived as a being higher than any other being. No greater being can be conceived. Second, if no such being existed, then a greater being or a being greater than that which no greater being than be conceived, can be conceived. Third, but that is absurd and hence God exists! Such reasoning today would hardly pass the logic test.

Perhaps, the most significant development occurred under the philosophy of nominalism, and French theologian Roscellinus (1050–1125 CE) was an early proponent of this in the early twelfth century. He conceived of philosophy as separate from both religion and science. He saw philosophy as consisting of ethics and logic and termed sciences as mechanical philosophy. Roscellinus also turned Plato on his head by claiming that universal categories of mind are only concepts and not real, thus echoing Kannada's epistemology nearly two millennia ago.

Petrus Abaelardus (1079–1142 CE), also a French theologian, is known for conceiving faith in rational terms and continued the position Roscellinus took in establishing the authority of Aristotle over Plato. Abaelardus was perhaps the only medieval theologian to consider the ethics from a philosophical perspective in Europe. He emphasized the role of intention over any rules in defining the moral value of an action.

Peter the Venerable (1092–1156 CE) is known for his study of Islam based directly on the Islamic sources in Arabic he obtained in Toledo. He successfully portrayed Islam as a heresy and in negative terms. His translations were the basis of the beginning of a serious scholarship of Islam in Europe, but only after Islam had been in Europe for nearly four centuries! The other significance of Peter the Venerable's work is that he appears to have opened the floodgates to translate Arabic works in philosophy, medicine, and science into Latin. Gerard of Cremona (1114–1187 CE) went to Toledo in search of Arabic works. Avicenna's encyclopedia, *Kitab al-Shifa*, was translated in 1180 CE. Its influence was phenomenal. Quickly, translations of other works followed. In western Europe at this time, the terms "Muslim" and "philosopher" could be used interchangeably.

Thus, what we witness is an interesting contradiction: a heightened interest in Muslim philosophy and religion while simultaneously rejecting the Islamic monotheism and a forced reaffirmation of Christian faith. The last century of the phase, Europe simultaneously conducted the Crusades and absorbed the third synthesis of science from the Muslim civilization, much like absorption of European science and anticolonial struggles of twentieth-century Asia against Europe.

Achievements in Art

There was a small surge in literature, art, and architecture in the ninth century that is known rather expansively as the Carolingian renaissance of northern Europe. It was nothing more than northwestern Europe attempting to adopt the Roman language and art forms. European art was still captive of the dark ages with the one exception of Gothic architecture, with its delicate columns supporting a massive arched roof made possible by shifting the weight to outside buttresses and its sublime stained glass windows. It is claimed that Carolingian renaissance in art formed the basis of Gothic art and even the Italian Renaissance. It is difficult, however, to see the connection.

The next great period of European art occurred in the Byzantine Empire in the twelfth century. The successful expansion of the eleventh century, despite setbacks against the Seljuk Turks, had led to increased trade and wealth, and this wealth flowed into art since the center of philosophy and science in Europe was too far away in Spain and the church in the Byzantine Empire was under state control and lacked widespread monasteries. Thus, while Muslim influence was reawakening the spirit of philosophy and inquiry in Western Europe, art flourished in the Byzantine Empire during the eleventh and twelfth centuries. This art took the form of distinctive church architecture, mosaics, and silk embroidery. Western Europe, Venice, and Italy all looked east for artistic inspiration. Iberian-Moorish art also derived inspiration from Byzantine art. Clearly, the focus was on architecture and decorative art as opposed to sculpture and painting. Similarly, the focus was on visual art forms and not performing arts or literature.

To summarize, in the west, the creative impulse focused on absorbing Muslim philosophy and science in the monasteries and the affirmation of Christianity. In the east, creative focus was primarily on art and literature, and it also helped preserve Greek texts. In the center, the Italian Peninsula and Venice were getting ready to receive the creative achievements of the east and west during the next phase to bring about the fourth synthesis of science.

15.11 Achievements in Science

By 750 CE, at the start of the current phase, Christianity, had already gone through the apostolic, Episcopal, and state adoption stages and was in the monastic stage, with the power of the Bishop of Rome or pope increasing dramatically. There were three critical developments in Christianity during the current phase. All but one of these was negative for the cause of science.

First, the split between the western and eastern branches became more or less final. The contributing factors were disputes over iconoclasm, papal authority in general, and papal primacy in jurisprudence in particular. Byzantine emperors being against all three. This resulted in the church becoming a determining political factor in western Europe.

Second was the Christian reaction against Muslim expansion and the perceived excesses in Iberia and Sicily. This took two forms: Crusades to reconquer the holy land, starting in 1095 CE, and the start of the Reconquista movement in Iberia in the twelfth century.

The third and most significant from our perspective was the evolution of cathedral schools in western Europe into theological universities at Paris, Oxford, and Bologna starting about the eleventh century. These universities would later emerge as centers of science after absorbing the lessons of the third synthesis. It is ironic that in western Europe, the retrogressive rise of the pope as a political force coupled with a strong monastic tradition ultimately evolved into theological universities and still later into centers of science. In part this was because the pope did not have to depend on the state for funding the monasteries. Often, it was the state. In the Byzantine Empire, this did not happen since the church depended on the state for funding, and the Byzantine Empire had to constantly invest in defending against the rising Turkish tide throughout this phase and beyond. The fleeing of scholars from the Byzantine Empire to the Italian mainland due to Turkish pressure contributed to these developments also.

Europe had little interest in science despite the Arab achievements in Iberia. Translation of Arabian books into Latin had begun toward the end of the phase; however, the weight of Christian doctrine was too stifling to yet take the achievements of the Arab synthesis too seriously.

Summarizing Achievements in Abstract Systems-Building Capability (ASBC)

By the end of the phase, the ASBC of the European civilization was improving. It continued to have alphabetical script. In addition, it began to dabble in epistemology, watching Arabs in Iberia, and it adopted the decimal system, including the concept of zero, after a good Christian fight. However, one would hardly classify it as world-class.

History, Causes, and Outcomes of the Chinese Civilization

15.12 Brief Political History (618–1279 CE)

The two key dynasties of the Chinese civilization during the phase were the Tang and Song dynasties. The Tangs had been successful against the northern nomads through a combined strategy of military buildup, trade, and opportunistic marriage relationships. At the height of their power, the Tangs received tribute from diverse adjoining kingdoms, such as those of Kashmir, Nepal, Champa in Vietnam, Japan, and Korea.

Early in this phase, however, the Tang dynasty faced the An Shi Rebellion (755–763 CE), which was successfully put down with help from the Turkish nomads and Abbasids from Persia. This, however, weakened the central authority and gave rise to strong provincial governors. A persistent famine followed in 873 CE, undermining Tangs who, severely weakened by these two events, ultimately lost power in 918 CE followed by a short period of chaos called the five dynasties and ten kingdoms period (907–960 CE).

The Han rule is comparable to the Roman Empire in some respects. Both excelled in technological achievements, law and administrative skills. Both were threatened by barbarians externally and internally through the rise of a degenerate nobility that owned large estates.

Tangs were followed by the Song dynasty in 960 CE. It was to last for over three hundred years. The Song period is divided into Northern Songs (960–1127 CE) and Southern Songs (1127–1279 CE). In the later part of the eleventh century, the Song court became politically divided between the so-called reformers and the conservatives. The reformers under Wang attacked state corruption through land tax reform, higher standards for civil service exams, and the creation of several government monopolies. The nomadic Jin confederation in the north took advantage of this political division within the Song court and invaded China, driving and confining the Song dynasty to the southern half of China, thus initiating the Southern Song period. While the Tang period was generally a period of stability and prosperity, the Song period is considered by many to be the golden age of Chinese technology despite its defeat at the hands of the Jin.

Uncharacteristically, the Chinese civilization during the phase pursued an expansionist military policy in its immediate neighborhood while pursuing an expansionist trade policy on a global basis. China during this phase was forced into both defensive and offensive postures with respect to northern nomads, Tibet, Korea, and Japan. The Tangs were forced to contain the Jins through trade and marriage relationships and forced to collaborate with the northern nomads such as the Uyghur khan Moyanchur in helping to put down the An Shi Rebellion. There was, however, little violent colonization or policy of systematic wealth drain from other civilizations.

15.13 Natural Causes

The famine of 873 CE was so severe that harvest was no more than half the normal size. This shook the foundations of the Tang Empire. Other than this event, there were no significant natural causes that impacted the evolution of Chinese civilization during the current phase. Fortunately, the substantial Chinese iron industry switched from charcoal to coal, thus significantly slowing down the process of deforestation with its potentially significant adverse impact.

15.14 Intrinsic Causes

Intrinsic Causes—Institutional Structures and Processes

Political system: There was one significant change in fundamental political structures, which continued to consist of a central ruling dynasty and a centralized structure to rule the provinces. This change was the rise of imperial examinations under the Tangs, which substantially reduced the reliance on the aristocratic families to supply the talent needed to run the affairs of the state. Graduates could be appointed state officials in the central, provincial, and local administrative posts. These competitive examinations succeeded in drawing the best talent into government. The Tang government had two departments to respectively draft and review the state policy and six ministries, including personnel administration, justice, finance, rites, military, and public works to implement the policy. This administrative model would last until the fall of the Qing dynasty nearly a thousand years later. The Song dynasty in turn significantly accelerated the transition from an aristocratic to a bureaucratic administration. The Song dynasty was perhaps the first instance in history where a broad middle class participated in running a civilization on a meritocratic basis and helped usher in an enormous expansion in practical technology and economy.

Military capability: Military consisted of infantry, cavalry, and crossbowmen and was organized into platoons, companies, and battalions and had as many as one million soldiers. Infantry also included an elephant division, which fell into disuse after the tenth century as the range of fire lances improved. The Songs also established China's first permanent navy. During the Song dynasty, military strategy was treated as science, and soldiers were tested for endurance and fighting skills. However, the absence of a unified command remained a startling weakness since the military was commanded by three independent marshals. Crossbowmen were employed against the cavalry and employed long-range bows and fire lances. In the eleventh century, use of bombs was initiated. The navy used pontoon bridges, large ships, and faster paddlewheel ships. In the early eighth century, Emperor Xuanzong had created a professional army instead of relying on conscripted soldiers, thus ensuring success against nomadic invasions. Tang emperors continued the tradition of an imperial guard garrisoned in the capital and palaces from the time of the founder of the dynasty. Land was assigned to the farmers in exchange for military service; however, the status of the military professional remained below the scholar-official bureaucrats.

Economic organization: The early Tang government lowered both the grain tax and the cloth tax thus encouraging tax compliance. The Chinese population shifted dramatically from north to south, creating a more balanced geographical distribution, but 90 percent of the population continued to remain agrarian. During the Song period, the Chinese population doubled to 100 million, primarily because of greater yields and increase in land under rice cultivation in central and southern China. China under the Songs was one of the most prosperous economies of the world, excelling in agriculture, manufacturing, and both domestic and foreign trade. Industrial and commercial guilds came into existence during the Song era and worked with the state on tax, wage, and price policies. Internal trade was facilitated by the Grand Canal in particular and the wider canal system in general and the resulting reduction in transportation costs. An excellent postal system covering twenty thousand miles of roads or rivers routes facilitated trade and communication. The Tang dynasty government undertook perhaps the first census of the population anywhere in the world. Under Song, agriculture was marked by better seeds, tools, and fertilizers with enormous increase in yield and acreage under cultivation. The key industries were iron, gunpowder, porcelain, and textiles. Expanded internal and international trade brought great fortune to merchants.

Systems of religious faith: Before the persecution of Buddhism in the ninth century, both Buddhism and Taoism were accepted by the emperors. Under emperor Xuanzong (reign 712–754 CE) imperial examinations were based on Taoist texts while relying on Buddhist rituals to, for example, avert droughts and ensure victories in wars. Chinese monks also visited the court of Japanese Emperor Tenji (reigned 661–772 CE) in the seventh century to spread Buddhism. Tang emperors were religiously tolerant, as evidenced by their recognition the Nestorian Christian Church. However, Christianity died in China after the Tangs lost power in the tenth century. Buddhist scholar Xuanzang had traveled to India in the seventh century and returned after seventeen years with valuable Sanskrit texts translated into Chinese. In the early ninth century, under the Tangs, short-lived suppression of Buddhism began. Both Confucianism and Taoism objected to Buddhism. Confucian scholar Han Yu put it bluntly: "Buddha was a man of the barbarians who did not speak the language of China and wore the clothes of a different fashion. He understood neither the duties that bind sovereign and subject nor the affections of father and son." By one record, 4,600 monasteries and 40,000 temples were destroyed and a quarter million nuns and monks laicized by the mid-ninth century. Buddhism saw a revival during the Song period, with more Buddhist monks visiting to and from China than in the Tang period. However, no religious beliefs system gained an upper hand: Confucianism, Taoism, Buddhism, and Chinese folk religions existed side by side and had a profound impact on the daily life of the common man.

Song emperors continued to be tolerant of other religions such as Islam (Ethiopian Muhammad Sa'd ibn Abi-Waqqas established China's first mosque during Emperor Gaozong's reign, and it still stands today) and Christianity both of which, however, remained as fringe religions. In a real sense, China was a laboratory for peaceful and violent competition among world's major religions.

There was little conflict between science and religion because of the absence of monotheism and an essential lack of focus on scientific activity.

Legal systems: In 624 CE, Emperor Taizong issued a new legal code composed of twelve sections and five hundred articles that subsequent Chinese dynasties would model their legal codes after. The code had its roots in the Zhou, Wei, and Jin dynasties. It includes laws concerning internal travel, peasants, state enterprises, forgery and counterfeiting, apprehension of the guilty, corruption of the officials, and the legal process itself. The code had clear and commensurate punishment ranging from flagellation to decapitation for each crime. It was considered liberal and did not rely on heavy punishment. However, the punishment may be different for the same crime, depending on the social relationship between the offender and the victim. Thus, the code did not see all men equal before law. It has been viewed as an admirable composition of faultless logic by French Sinologist Jacques Gernet. Often the magistrate acted as an investigator as well. Song emperors continued to use the legal code and judicial system of the Tang dynasty.

Social structure: The social structure under both Tangs and Songs consisted of nobility at the top followed by a powerful meritocratic bureaucracy, merchants, artisans, and peasants. The peasants either owned the land outright, paid rent, or were hired hands at large estates. There was little slavery in China, and women enjoyed considerable power both within the home, in business, in entertainment, and even in government. The most striking was the position of women during the Tang period. Women in the countryside managed the weaving and silk production. Urban and elite women at times acquired wealth and were allowed to become Taoist priests. The courtesans were sophisticated, highly respected and were often accomplished in arts. Men respected assertive women. Women even played polo, often wearing male clothes. The bureaucratic gentry, though it looked down upon the merchant class and commercial activities, secretly engaged in the same activities they publicly looked down upon. The government, the Song government in particular, funded hospitals, retirement homes, and graveyards for the poor. China seems to have had a very vibrant social life during this period. The status of women improved considerably. They had many legal privileges, including status at home and owning small businesses. Many forms of entertainment, including theater, acrobats, puppeteers, musicians, legalized prostitutes, and restaurants were commonplace. The bureaucrats helped make life bearable for China's middle class.

Because the role of landed aristocracy was diminished due to the rise of a meritocratic bureaucracy, class stratification was moderate by the standards of the era. If the upper classes enjoyed sports like polo, football, and of course, archery and hunting, the bureaucracy had their well-defined holidays and vacation for significant family matters, such as marriages.

Thus, the status of bureaucracy, the modest control of land by feudal lords, and the position of women all point to a moderate wealth polarization in China and the emergence of a relatively prosperous middle class.

Knowledge-Creating and educational institutions: Although China had a strong established imperial examination tradition and thus many schools teaching the classics, one does not witness the rise of great universities as the knowledge-creating centers in China during this phase.

Wealth Allocation process: The sustainable surplus increased dramatically in China during this phase because of an increase in population, the area under cultivation and increased yield, the rise of the manufacturing sector, and expanding domestic and foreign trade. The surplus also seems to have been allocated in a balanced manner among opulence, military, and creative endeavors. However, the allocation within the creative endeavors was heavily tilted toward practical creativity. The religious and intellectual creativity were short changed. This, coupled with the absence of alphabetical script, continued to prevent progress in science.

Social cohesion processes: During the Tang rule, social cohesion was ensured through a strong centralized administration, a well-defined and reasonably fair legal code, and a bureaucracy selected through meritocratic imperial examinations. Religion and physical force played a relatively minor role in ensuring social cohesion.

Internal wars: After the defeat of warlord Liang Shidu in 626, the Tang period remained a period of internal stability. The entire phase consisting mostly of two powerful dynasties must be characterized as enjoying internal peace in large measure.

Formative Beliefs and Ideology at the End of Third Synthesis Phase

The violent persecution of Buddhism, their continuing strong practical orientation toward knowledge, the high degree of social cohesion based on continuing absence of slavery and caste systems, their continuing focus on nomadic threat, opening trade with India and the Muslim world, and a more aggressive defensive posture with respect to nomads that never quite turned imperialistic all point to significant changes in a belief system that may be summarized as follows:

- A belief in practical knowledge based on observation and common sense
- A relative openness toward Christianity and Islam while persecuting Buddhism because unlike Islam and Christianity, Buddhism had become too strong and was in a position to eclipse Taoism
- A continuing belief in equality among citizens, supported by pro farmer policies
- A continuing, mostly insular attitude toward the intellectual creativity of others
- An aggressive but fundamentally defensive posture toward northern nomads

These beliefs were fundamentally derived from Chinese culture, the insecurity of Taoists, and greater aggressiveness on the part of central Asian nomads.

15.15 Extrinsic Peaceful Causes

China had the most interaction with central Asian nomads, Arabs, and Persian and Indian civilizations.

Impact of Central Asians

In its dealings with central Asians, Chinese civilization only shared its technology, albeit reluctantly. They did not receive anything of significance in return probably because of distance.

Impact of Muslim and Indian Civilizations

Fair trade: Trade links over the sea and the Silk Road were instrumental in bringing new practical technologies and products to China, such as new types of ceramics, fashions, furniture, and metal working techniques from India, Persia, and West Asia. Several musical instruments, such as oboes, flutes, drums, and cymbals were imported. Use of chairs and table learned from other lands replaced the old habit of sitting on floor mats. In its interaction with India, it was primarily interested in Buddhist texts.

Migrations and travel: During the Tang era, Buddhist monks continued to travel from India and Sri Lanka. The monks brought the Buddhist sutras and artifacts of South Asian culture to China. Significant migrations only occurred through nomadic invasions of the Jin nomads from the north. However, thousands of Indians, Sinhalese, Jews, and Nestorian Christians came to live in China to manage the trade.

Practical creativity: In the arena of practical creativity, China was not impacted significantly since China was the inventor of many of the key practical technologies during this period.

Religious creativity: China's indigenous religious systems of Confucianism and Taoism during the current period were potentially exposed to two new religions of Islam and Christianity while continuing to experience the impact of Buddhism. However, Christian missionary activity was practically nonexistent, since Europe was not exactly in a position to undertake such an activity during the current phase five thousand miles away. Buddhism was only mildly interested in missionary activity but had the advantage of an established base in China, and China had a thirst for Buddhism. This continuing diffusion of Buddhist thought from the Indian civilization took place through individual travel by the Chinese. Finally, because of established Buddhism and northern China being under the influence of the Jin for considerable period; the preoccupation with and success of Islam in Europe, West Asia, and Northwest India during the current phase; and the physical barrier of the Tibetan plateau, Islam was mostly unsuccessful in China except on its western-most fringes.

Intellectual creativity: In the arena of intellectual creativity (art, philosophy, and science), the Chinese civilization did not benefit directly from other civilizations because of its practical and insular nature and lack of alphabetical script. However, the indirect impact came through the impact of Buddhism on neo-Confucianism. Classical Confucianism was principally a system of ethics that lacked any serious metaphysics, and Taoism, like the Indian Vedanta, believed in an external reality that was independent of the sensual world of matter and energy. The Buddhism that came to China, though agnostic, had Hindu ideas of reincarnation and karma. Neo-Confucianism bravely rejected the Taoism and Buddhist ideas of reincarnation and karma and created a more practical metaphysics based on the concepts of li and qi, which may be roughly translated as universal law and external, sensate matter-energy complex. Thus, the net effect of this cross-fertilization of Taoism, Buddhism, and Confucianism was to combine a practical and materialist metaphysics and Confucian ethics into the emerging philosophy of neo-Confucianism, a philosophy that was to rule the Chinese mind for the next thousand years. However, it must be added that this very scientific outlook once again failed to give birth to science because of the absence of alphabetical script, the insular nature of Chinese civilization, and an internal creative balance that remained intensely practical. Chinese civilization refused to consider the achievements of Indian and Muslim achievements in astronomy, mathematics, and experimental method that were clearly available to it through the trade and travel channels. It is unlikely that the Chinese did not learn of Aryabhatta's astronomy through the travels of Chinese scholars to and from India; however, it does not seem to have impressed them.

Impact on Productive Outcomes

Wealth creation: Wealth creation in China increased during the current phase but that was exclusively because of an intrinsic reasons, such as opening the south, greater use of techniques to enhance agricultural productivity, and increased trade.

Impact of trade: The impact of fair trade with Indian, Muslim, and European civilizations, on the other hand, was more vigorous; based on both land and sea routes; and touched many more lives. The old Silk Road reached its golden age under the Tangs, and China during the Tang rule gained new technologies and products such as ceramics, silversmithing, and fashion from Persian and Indian sources while selling porcelain and lacquerware. Trade resulted in the creation of strong export-oriented manufacturing sectors, government-owned factories (much like China today), and the emergence of joint stock companies to finance the mercantile ships that carried goods and were considered high-risk ventures. It was not just the Silk Road that contributed to international trade. Maritime trade using large junkets capable of carrying up to seven hundred passengers to South Asia, Southeast Asia, West Asia, and eastern Africa boomed through the port of Guangzhou, which was often attacked by foreign and Chinese pirates because of its wealth. Trade with Korea and Japan also increased through the Yellow Sea. The principal exports were ceramics, jade, gold, silverware, iron swords, velvet, and textiles. China developed a cosmopolitan culture in the coastal cities that supported a large population of traders from all over the world. This interchange exposed China to new forms of furniture, fashions, ceramics, and musical instruments. However, fluctuating control of western lands between Tibet and China and bandits undermined the effectiveness of the Silk Road during the Tang period. China traded with Persia, India, Arabia, Iraq, and eastern Africa. Increased trade activity undoubtedly had a significant impact on the wealth and surplus. Increased wealth from trade may have contributed to China's uncharacteristic aggressive external posture under the Tangs. On the other hand, it is likely that the Jin nomads attacked and successfully conquered northern China during the current phase because of its increased prosperity.

Impact on Societal Structures and Processes

It is indeed difficult to imagine the extrinsic causes directly impacting the Chinese societal structures, knowledge and wealth creation, and wealth distribution processes during the current phase.

Summary

Chinese civilization created the doctrine of neo-Confucianism and gained wealth through fair trade as a result of peaceful extrinsic causes during the current phase. However, apart from this, there were no fundamental changes brought about by these extrinsic causes to the outcomes, intrinsic causes driving the Chinese civilization, or Chinese attitude toward science. China indeed remained China during the current phase and was fully confident of its cultural superiority. Thus, while China shared hard practical technology (gunpowder and printing) with the rest of the world, China in turn received and created artifacts of soft cultural value. There is little evidence of the greater wealth being channeled to scientific creativity. We also believe that the insular nature of Chinese civilization ensured that the impact of extrinsic causes was slower than the norm and in the long sweep of history, not lasting.

15.16 Extrinsic Violent Causes

Assessing the Loss of SPI

As we noted in the last chapter, the Tang period was an unusual military period in Chinese civilization since it displayed both a defensive and aggressive posture with its neighbors, including the Gokturks and other central Asian Turks, Koreans, Japanese, and Tibetans. The Tangs were generally successful in these battles. In the twelfth century, nomadic Jins conquered the northern half of China and maintained that control until conquered in turn by the Mongols in the early thirteenth century. The one great unintended consequence of the Jin conquest was to protect China from Muslim invasions. Islam made little impact on China, thanks to central Asian and non-Muslim control of northern and western China in the eleventh century and the consequent diversion of Turkish Muslim pressure toward India. Subsequent to the current phase, after the Mongols drove the Jins out, China dealt with non-Muslim Mongols as it had periodically done in its history: by absorbing them into the Chinese mainstream.

Fortunately, China's loss of sustained political independence remained confined to the north and only for the latter half of the phase. The Song state was partially able to compensate for the loss of northern territory through increased agricultural output in southern China, thus continuing its commitment to practical creativity. Even in the northern territory, conquering Jins did not possess an intolerant and antiscience monotheistic faith like Islam, such as the Turkish tribes that had adopted Islam held. Thus, they were more prone to being absorbed into the mainstream Chinese culture, as other nomadic conquerors were.

Loss of Control of Wealth and Means of Wealth

Jins, much like other invaders of the period, were empire builder-settlers with little interest in wealth drain. Jins in particular brought no new creed, technology, or science with them. Thus, apart from displacing the Songs and destroying life and property, there was little fundamental impact on means of wealth creation.

Impact on Productive Outcomes

The successful attempt to put down the An Shi Rebellion with the help of Turkish nomads and Abbasids as well as the northern conquest of the Jins linked China to Asia and Europe for land-based trade. This nicely complemented the increasing sea-based trade. Thus, the impact of foreign intervention appears to have been positive for the Chinese trade while not impacting the migration pattern except for the arrival of a limited number of invaders.

Impact on Creative Outcomes

Transmission of creativity: Only the Jin military conquest was swift but because the Jins did not possess any superior creative technology, religion, or science, their impact on Chinese civilization was insignificant, and the speed of impact was irrelevant.

It is clear that foreign occupation had an impact on the Chinese creative endeavors and its golden period of prosperity because the Songs were pushed to the south and because of the willingness on the part of the Jin to adopt Chinese ways, as the Kushan had done in India a millennium ago. Some historians believe that Song development of explosives technology resulted from their desire to defeat the Jins after they had lost the northern territory.

Impact on science: There was no impact of Jin conquest on Chinese science in part because there was little focus on science in China during this period except astronomical observations and some mathematics, but mostly because the conquerors possessed no antiscience bias. China had a weak tradition in science because of its practical orientation and because it lacked alphabetical script. Since China did not fall under Arab control or Turkish control, it remained more interested in practical creativity by far when compared to its interest in intellectual creativity.

Impact on Institutional Structures and Processes

Foreign conquest did not materially impact internal class conflicts or internal political division. Chinese civilization did not change its essential defensive and peaceful orientation during the phase. The aforementioned external aggression under the Tangs was purely internally generated. Jins did not have an impact on the societal structures and wealth creation and allocation processes either, so there was no indirect impact on creative endeavors. Perhaps the most significant impact was in the military capability through cavalry, which depended on faster horses, heavy armor, and innovative tactics such as using a team of horses attached to one another through chains.

Assessment of Net Impact

The conquering nomads possessed little superiority in any arena except in the military when compared to the Chinese and were open to the practical, religious, and intellectual creativity of the Chinese civilization. Thus, the strategic response of the Chinese civilization was to civilize the invaders, and the Jins, over time, too had little choice. Since China was lucky to have lost its sustained political independence in a portion of its territory and only for a part of the phase to a non-Muslim invader, the impact of instruments of control on Chinese civilization was small and not lasting. Indian and European civilizations were not so lucky.

15.17 Productive Outcomes

Wealth creation: Both the Tang and Song periods were largely periods of internal stability and sustained political independence. During the Tang period, population increased from 50 million to 75 million, with a more balanced distribution between north and south. During the Song period, the population increased again, by some estimates it was as large as 200 million by the end of Song period. Increased population, an explosion in new technologies, enormous expansion in internal and international trade, expansion in money stock, increase in the area under rice cultivation, decentralization and deregulation of the economy through lower taxation, the rise of a responsible bureaucracy, and limiting excessive role of metaphysics all combined to dramatically increase wealth creation. China was perhaps the wealthiest country in the world by the end of the Song dynasty.

15.18 Creative Outcomes

Achievements in Practical Creativity

China continued to produce unmatched world-class technology during this phase. Key Chinese innovations of the phase included printing, gun powder, the compass, and paper money.

Gongliang and Weide compiled known gunpowder technology in 1044 and described its use in bombs that were lobbed from a catapult. Prisoners of war passed this technology on to the Mongols, who used it the thirteenth century. It was one of the reasons for their military success. In addition, the use of the grenade, firearm, cannon, and landmine were also developed.

Bi Sheng invented ceramic movable type printing in 990 to 1051. Extensive encyclopedias were compiled on history and practical technology. Woodblock printing dated from the seventh century.

The first banknotes were produced in 1023. Under Emperor Shenzong, Chinese mints in 1080 alone produced 5 billion coins or about fifty per Chinese citizen. These coins were so durable that they were still be in used in the eighteenth century.

Architecture during the Song period reached new heights of sophistication through the use of building codes and architectural innovations, such as slanting struts, improved mortar, corbel brackets, the cantilever, and tie beams.

Shen Kuo wrote *Dream Pool Essays* 1088 AD and described a dry dock to repair boats, the navigational magnetic compass, and the discovery of the concept of true north.

China not only continued to develop amazing practical technology during the current phase but also, like a modern corporation, worked very hard to keep it from following into the hands of the foreigners successfully for long periods. The technology, however, continued to leak out of China through travelers and invading nomads.

The amazing Chinese achievements in practical creativity during the phase are summarized in table 15.2.

Table 15.2: Significant Achievements in Practical Creativity
Chinese Civilation, 750–1200 CE

Category	Significant Achievements
Materials	Improved porcelain
Processes	
Energy	Gunpowder composition, use of petroleum
Tools	Improved escapement mechanism, fishing reel
Agricultural Products	
Non-Agri. Products	7-day week, paper money
Construction	40-ton cast iron pagoda
Transportation Technologies	Improved compass, 700-ft-long bridge, dry docks
Weapons Technologies	Gunpowder rockets
Infrastructure	
Communications	Movable type, first book printed, multicolor printing

Achievements in Religious Creativity

Religious creativity did not extend beyond translating Buddhist literature and a tolerance toward Christianity and Islam. Religiosity remained a crude mixture of Taoism, Confucianism, Buddhism, and superstition.

Achievements in Philosophical Creativity

The upsurge in Buddhism during the Tang period was followed by another reaction in the form of neo-Confucianism against Buddhism during the Song period. Though its roots were in the Tang period, neo-Confucianism prospered during the Song period by expunging the mysticism and superstition inherent in Confucianism. The focus of neo-Confucianism was not religious enlightenment, but rather the focus was on rational ethics. Thus, the movement was a return to the traditional Chinese emphasis on ethics and not metaphysics. The practical Chinese spirit was reasserting itself in both philosophy and technology. Buddhism's influence might have waned in philosophy due to the increasing importance of imperial exams during the Song period. Its sway, however, over artistic creation and monasteries continued. Ouyang Xiu (1007–1072), a historian and statesman, referred to Buddhism as a "curse" and strongly advocated replacing it with Confucianism.

Achievements in Art

The Tang dynasty witnessed the Golden period of Chinese literature with a focus on poetry, the eight-line Jintishi poetry, short stories, travelogues, classical prose, and persuasive writing associated with neo-Confucianism. By contrast the Song period witnessed the birth of landscape, panoramic, and portrait painting and further development of calligraphy. Chinese courts of the phase were filled with painters, poets, historians, storytellers, and calligraphers. The Chinese opera can also trace its roots to the Song dynasty.

To summarize the creative outcome, China was outstanding in practical creativity and artistic expression during the current phase. It was weak in religious, philosophical, and scientific creativity.

15.19 Achievements in Science

Astronomy: Statesman Su Song developed the astronomical clock tower of Kaifeng in 1088 AD. The clock tower was driven by a rotating waterwheel and included world's first escapement mechanism. The clock tower included a large bronze, mechanically driven, rotating armillary sphere. However, Chinese astronomy primarily remained interested in describing the heavenly motions and not explaining them through mathematical reasoning and model building. In addition, star maps using cylindrical projection were produced.

Earth sciences: Shen Kuo also devised a geological theory for land formation, or geomorphology, and theorized that there was climate change in geological regions over an enormous span of time. China also excelled in cartography and produced excellent maps often using a grid and a scale of about an inch for 100 li. There are excellent description of sea routes to West Asia, references to Iranian lighthouses and travels to India. Similarly local land maps known as "fangzhi" became popular during the Song dynasty.

Biology: In 1070, Su Song also compiled the *Ben Cao Tu Jing* or *Illustrated Pharmacopoeia*, in 1058 to 1061 AD, working with a team of scholars. This pharmaceutical treatise also discussed a wide range of other related and unrelated subjects, including mineralogy, botany, zoology, and metallurgy.

Medicine: The main focus of Chinese medicine during the Tang period was a compilation of the medicinal substances prepared from plants, herbs, animals, and vegetables. The practice of medicine was controlled by the state, which supported a medical college. In the seventh century, Zhen Qian diagnosed diabetes and suggested avoiding starch foods and alcohol. Shen Kuo (1031–1095 CE), who must have been an anatomist, suggested the existence of two throat valves instead of three. The physician and judge Song Ci (1186–1249) wrote the world's first book on forensic medicine aimed at identifying the causes of death.

Historiography: Several historiographies, including the *Old Book of Tang*, were completed in the tenth century. The history of the Song dynasty was completed in the eleventh century, and universal history of China consisting of three million Chinese characters and covering 404 BCE to the beginning of the Song dynasty was also completed. During the Tang and Song dynasties, several encyclopedias covering astrology and many other subjects were published.

Summarizing Achievements in Abstract Systems-Building Capability (ASBC)

By the end of the phase, the ASBC of the Chinese civilization made significant progress: it, however, continued to fail to adopt alphabetical script. In addition, its state of epistemology remained underdeveloped, and it did not feel the need to adopt the Indian decimal system since it had its own cumbersome but ingenious physical position value system consisting of bamboo rods and a board. There was little appreciation of planets, moon, and sun as a controlled experiment in the heavens, and consequently, Chinese astronomy remained limited to making brilliant observations about the stars, sun, comets, and supernovas.

History, Causes, and Outcomes of the Indian Civilization

15.20 Brief Political History (750–1200 CE)

Arabs attacked North India in the seventh and early eighth centuries from the Sindh, as we noted in the last chapter. Their objective seems to have been to control the sea trade between India and Europe. For a number of reasons that we discussed in the last chapter, they seemed to have succeeded in that objective. Control of North India was contested by a kaleidoscope of several Indian dynasties with fluctuating fortunes during the current phase: Palas of Bengal (765–1175 CE), Gurjara Pratiharas (805–1036 CE), Paramara (949–1088 CE), Chauhans (seventh through fourteenth centuries), Chandella (950–1203 CE), Haihayas (895–1150 CE), and Sena (1070–1230 CE). In Kashmir, the Karkota (600–850 CE) and Utpala dynasties (855–939 CE) stand out during the phase.

The Pala dynasty at its height controlled the entire northern subcontinent, from Afghanistan to Bengal. It was followed by the Sena dynasty, though in the east only. In the northwest, two dynasties followed the Pala: the Buddhist Shahi and the Hindu Shahi during the eighth to eleventh centuries. After 975 CE, the Hindu Shahi came to an end, and Jayapala became the first ruler of the Hindu Shahi dynasty, whose domains extended to Kabul. Jayapala had the foresight to see the strategic menace from the northwest since the Ghaznivids, who were being pushed southward by the Seljuks, in turn had their eyes set on the fertile plains of Punjab. Jayapala was defeated in 1001 CE and had to cede a significant portion of his empire to Mahmud Ghazni. Subsequently, Ghazni raided northern and western India; however, only a portion of Punjab came under his control, and the Ghazni dynasty ruled for 175 years. Parallel with the Shahi Dynasties, Gurjar Pratihars dynasties ruled much of lower northern India east of Punjab from the ninth to the eleventh centuries. Chauhans, a branch of the Pratiharas Rajputs, ruled portions of the upper part of north India from the eighth to the twelfth century. At its peak (836–910 CE), Pratiharas rivaled the Gupta Empire in the extent of its empire. In 1160, the Ghuris, a Turkish-Afghan group, conquered Ghazni from Ghaznavids, and Mahammad Ghuri became governor of Ghuri. Under the leadership of Rajput Prithviraj Chauhan, the Chauhans repeatedly defeated him, and he was let free in a foolish display of misconceived magnanimity. Ghuri ultimately succeeded in capturing Delhi and the old Shia'ite Arab pocket of Multan. He made Delhi his capital and before dying appointed his most able general and former slave Qutub I-Din Aibak as sultan, thereby initiating the Delhi Sultanate or Slave dynasty in 1206 CE. Thus, the conquest of North India took more than two hundred years. Indian armies had defeated and checked the invaders on several occasions, much like they had defeated the Arab armies earlier. But they had not quite done so this time. The year 1206 CE may be considered the beginning of the Muslim rule in Indian history.

Though politically the civilization appeared strong, having defeated the Arabs and holding the tide against the Turks in the north during most of the current phase, the situation beneath the surface was not healthy. No long-lasting central imperial power appeared. Creeping conservatism was clear in military technology, manufacturing, religion, and social attitudes. These changes were beginning to have a profound impact on the North Indian civilization. Muslim invaders, after the Arab failure, had to wait patiently on the sidelines for nearly three centuries (an often overlooked fact) for North India to fragment beginning about 1000 CE and took another two hundred years to establish Muslim rule in North India. It was, by no means, a duplication of their quick success in Persia or Europe or North Africa. India put up a far stronger resistance to the Muslim invasion than any other civilization. And perhaps that is why when it fell, it did not recover for over five centuries.

Simultaneously, South India was also an ever-changing kaleidoscope of Hindu dynasties with fluctuating borders and changing fortunes during this phase: Yadavas (850–1334 CE) on the upper western coast, Rashtrakutas on the lower western coast (753–1189 CE), Cholas in the deep south (849–1279 CE), Hoysalas (1026–1343 CE) and Kakatiyas (1083–1323 CE) in the middle south, the Nolamba dynasty (800–1050 CE) in the deep south, eastern Ganga (1078–1434 CE) on the upper east coast, Western Ganga on the upper western coast (450–1000CE), and the Chaluka dynasty ruled parts of southern and central India between 941 and 1197 CE.

South India was not only unaffected by the Muslim invasions during this phase but also getting into an expansionary mode, establishing peaceful colonies and trading posts throughout Southeast Asia. For the first time in history, Indian civilization was showing an interest in the world beyond its southern shores. However, this was in part necessitated by the loss of control of European trade to the Arabs. South Indians expanded the influence of Indian culture to Cambodia, which produced a great Hindu empire known as Khmer or Angkor. It lasted from 820 to 1432 CE.

In Java, two successive Hindu empires known as Sailendra (700–800 CE) and Mataram (800–1000 CE) came into existence. Finally in Sumatra, the Buddhist Empire of Srivijaya lasted from about 700 to 1250 CE. The Chola Empire at its height in the eleventh century controlled the entire Malaysian Peninsula. With Arabs controlling the trade to Europe, South Indian dynasties had to find a new outlet, and this led to their generally peaceful maritime expansion in Southeast Asia. It was one of several overlapping regional trade systems that bound the world economy. They exported Indian culture and religion but in a fundamentally peaceful way. There was no violent colonization, forced relocation, or extermination or forced religious conversions of the indigenous peoples. This expansion was based on mutual benefit and trade under the leadership of the Cholas. The Chola court exerted considerable diplomatic influence over the Cambodian, Java, and Sumatra courts. It is ironic that while North India was losing the land-based war to violent monotheistic invaders, South Indian dynasties were creating the world's first maritime open sea consortium to expand trade and commerce throughout Southeast Asia and peacefully exporting Indian polytheism and Buddhism. The ironies of history never cease to surprise its student.

It is perhaps inaccurate to say that wealth polarization and class conflicts worsened during the current phase; however, it is accurate to say that the caste system became more rigid and affected creative freedom indirectly. Fortunately, slavery was not practiced, but that did not matter much; the damage done by the increasingly rigid caste system was bad enough.

The real change was in the state of internal aggression. Both the north and south was a changing kaleidoscope of dynasties of varying duration that were insecure because of a rather fluid military and political situation internally and on the west coast and northwest borders.

However, the Indian civilization was not destructive or violent with respect to other civilizations. The Arab and Turkish presence in the southwest and northwest respectively did not afford the opportunity to be aggressive anyway. However, South India exported Indian culture and religion to all of Southeast Asia in a peaceful manner maintaining strong trade and diplomatic relationships. This was the first time in over two millennia that Indian civilization was venturing abroad. True to its inner nature, this venture remained largely peaceful. There were no exterminations of indigenous peoples, no racism, no economic incentives to induce religious conversions, and no economic exploitation. This expansion was based on transplanting of Indian culture and its voluntary acceptance by the indigenous people for mutual benefit, much like the universal acceptance of Western science today.

15.21 Natural Causes

There were no significant natural causes affecting the evolution of Indian civilization during this phase.

15.22 Intrinsic Causes

Intrinsic Causes—Institutional Structures and Processes

Political system: There was no fundamental change in the political structures of dynasties that arose in both the north and the south. However, one does detect that greater concerns of the common man seems to have declined in considering the public policy.

Military capability: The backbone of North Indian armies remained infantry and elephant divisions. The emerging new technologies based on gunpowder were either not in sight or ignored. There was no significant advance in tactics or command structure either. The Cholas influence in Southeast Asia was backed up by perhaps the world's first blue-water, open-sea navy consisting of three fleets of about a thousand ships each. The navy had two objectives: to safeguard the sea lanes from sea pirates and to maintain a strategic balance of forces in the eastern Indian and western Pacific Oceans. The hull of these ships was reinforced with iron plates, the ships were equipped with flame-throwing technology, used a compass, and were powered by both wind power and oarsmen. The naval force consisted of one hundred thousand men and was highly organized. In table 13.4, we show a brief list of naval officers to give the reader an idea of its sophistication. In short, the upgrade of land forces in the north needed to defend against the Muslims invaders was nowhere in sight, while the south was developing a world-class navy to peacefully pursue its commercial interests oversees!

Economic organization: There was a relative decline of the manufacturing sector compared to the Gupta times. One does not hear about the industrial and commercial guild any longer. The Arabs took over overseas trade, and there was a considerable decline in the commercial ship-building industry in the north. There was little change in the economy at the village level. It continued its relative self-sufficient mode. Caste increasingly determined the position and profession of the individual. Meritocracy applied only within the caste context, if that.

Systems of religious faith: Religious attitudes continued to go through the changes that began in the previous phase. Buddhism was in decline despite its adoption by the early Pala emperors. Although Islam had been temporarily checked, religion evolved along two different directions: monism was gaining ground against outwardly polytheistic Hinduism, and within Hinduism, spurred by South Indian religiosity, the devotional attitudes were gaining ground. There was greater sanctification of the caste system by religion. Thus, science-religion conflict must be judged to have increased despite a precipitous decline in scientific pursuits.

Legal systems: There was little development in formal legal code. Manu's religious code defined the relationship among the castes and the behavior of the individual within a caste.

Social structure: Social conservatism, sanctioned by religion and caste system, was ascendant during the phase.

Thus, the social structure consisted of the royalty and nobles followed by the four castes.

North Indian civilization during the phase was static. Political fragmentation, Muslim threat or invasions from the northwest, decline of Buddhism, rise of monism and creeping devotional religiosity from the south, and the absence of a secular legal code all resulted in a growing conservative outlook and a hardening of the caste system. Though slavery was absent, the position of women and lower castes continued to deteriorate during the phase. During the next phase, the arrival of Sufism and increasing caste inequality would provide an opening to start the process of conversion of the population into Islam.

The inequality worsened significantly, not because of wealth polarization or class conflicts but because of the caste system, declining Buddhism, and political fragmentation. For seven centuries since the fall of Gupta dynasty, Indian civilization remained fragmented politically. The role of science declined throughout the phase commensurate with declining state support and rising monism which though not antiscience, did not value the understanding of the natural and social phenomenon since it did not regard them as real knowledge. Real knowledge was only possible through trained intuition and meditation and not through senses and reason as Kannada more than a millennium ago and Dignaga more than half a millennium had labored to advocate.

Knowledge-Creating and educational institutions: With the demise of the Pala dynasty in the tenth century, the age of great universities was coming to an end because of lack of support precisely around the time the great universities of Europe were struggling to be born. Turkish invaders finished the job and controlled most of North India in the century following the end of current phase. Thus, sciences, in particular astronomy, starved of state support, suffered.

Wealth allocation process: The sustainable surplus likely stopped growing since the number of large public works seems to have declined. There were increased internal wars since no long-lasting imperial authority comparable to the Kushans and Guptas emerged during this phase. Emergence of devotional Hinduism meant building great temples. Thus, internal wars and religious activity consumed a substantial portion of the surplus, resulting in a declining share for both public works and creative endeavors.

Social cohesion processes: Since there was little development in the legal code, social cohesion was based on religious ethics, caste rules, and antiquated judicial structures in the villages and cities.

Internal wars: In the north and south, a unifying political force failed to emerge during the current phase, and as a result, the intensity and sheer number of internal wars increased. Unlike China, the centrifugal tendencies in the Indian and European civilizations have always been far stronger than centripetal forces. This has been more so in the case of Indian civilization because of both linguistic and hence ethnic fragmentation as well as insufficient glue provided by a caste-ridden religion. Europe seems to have fared better because of the (caste-free) glue provided by Christian dogma. The hard truth is that political and social fragmentation has been a natural state in the case of world's oldest civilization and a great unifying force (Maurya, Kushans, and Guptas) only arose or failed to arise in response to external events. The default political outcome in the Indian civilization has been political fragmentation punctuated by occasional unification under a powerful dynasty. In contrast, the default political outcome in the Chinese civilization has been a strong central authority punctuated occasionally by political fragmentation. This phase was no exception. However, the price was going to be greater this time around, as we shall see in the next chapter.

Formative Beliefs and Ideology at the End of First Synthesis Phase

The tolerant structured polytheism and monism of Indian civilization and the essential decline of Buddhism early in the phase, a belief in knowledge through the union of reason and observation, relentless pressure resulting in steady loss of territory on the northwest frontier, deteriorating social cohesion because of the caste system, and their continuing openness and peacefulness all point to a belief system that may be summarized as follows:

- Belief in the possibility of knowledge through a union of observation and reason lost ground because monism shunned the importance of observation in knowledge creation.
- A belief in the fundamental inequality among different castes.
- An attitude of openness toward the intellectual and religious creativity of others.
- A belief in peacefulness toward other social orders.

Rising monism argued uncompromisingly by Sankara and the precipitous decline of Buddhism were the principal drivers of change for the belief system of Indian civilization during the phase.

15.23 Extrinsic Peaceful Causes

During this phase, Indian civilization was in interaction with Arabs in southwest Asia, Turks in the northwest, China, and with many peoples in Southeast Asia. The direct contact with Europe had declined precipitously. Interaction with China too had declined and appeared one way and confined to religion. Indian civilization failed to acquire practical technology from the Chinese, just as the Chinese failed to acquire Indian mathematics and astronomy.

Impact of Arabs and Turks

Although Indian civilization shared its mathematics, astronomy, and medicine with the Arabs, Indian civilization failed to learn anything from Arabs in return partly because of distance and the Arab failure to establish an empire in India. However, more important, the cause of this state of affairs may be attributed to conservatism of the civilization brought about by the changes in religious attitudes, dictates of the caste system, and perhaps a sense of false superiority. In religion, Indian monism was unimpressed with Islam. The lack of political leadership in the north allowed such conservatism to flourish. Though the Indian civilization managed to hang on to political independence for most of the phase, it ceded the control of its trade to the Arabs.

Transmission of practical creativity: The diffusion of Chinese and Muslim practical technologies mediated through Turkish invaders in India was less profound than in Europe and came later. The diffusion of Chinese practical technology, such as papermaking, gunpowder, printing, and the compass into India occurred through the Ghaznavids, and India failed to learn anything of significance in military technology from the Turks until after the Ghaznivid control of North India, mostly in the next phase. Ghaznavids sultans had adopted Persian court culture, and they brought it to India There was an important reason these technologies found a warmer reception in Europe than in India. The Arabs, both during their presence and as they retreated from Europe, created and left a strong legacy of science and practical technology about the time Europe was beginning to question, ever so gently, Christian dogma and open itself to science and when the Christian monks in the monasteries were receptive to the new technology, allowing science and technology to play off each other.

By contrast, Turkish dynasties that controlled north India toward the end of this phase were antiscience and not as advanced technologically. The bottom line: while the Muslim golden age left a strong legacy of practical technology and science in Europe, it was the bearer of relatively substandard technology and religious fundamentalism to India.

Transmission of religious creativity: Despite the continuing Arab presence in the provinces of Sindh, Multan and Cochin and Turkish conquests in the northwest, and deep raids into North India, Indians were not impressed with Islam and its message of intolerance during the current phase. Conversions to Islam by the end of the current phase were miniscule and probably similar in levels to conversions into Christianity, which had arrived on the western cost of India as early as the second century. In the absence of sustained force and economic incentives, there was little interest in Islam during the current phase. Sufism was still in the future.

Transmission of intellectual creativity: The diffusion and impact of intellectual creativity followed the pattern we saw in practical technology. In the arena of science and philosophy, translation of Indian works into Arabic occurred early in the phase. However, following centuries of development by Arabs, the translations back into Sanskrit were sporadic and occurred after considerable delay.

Fair trade: Land trade was in decline and sea trade was increasing during the current phase. Overland trade to West Asia declined because of the Muslim control in the northwest. However, there was sea trade to the west, and Arabs controlled trade through the Arabian Sea. Indian civilization also began to surrender the control of its trade to the Muslim civilization as it no longer controlled the pricing of its products and the shipping lanes and did not maintain the strength of its shipbuilding capability. Simultaneously, sea trade through the Indian Ocean to Southeast Asia and China was controlled by South India dynasties, in particular, as mentioned above, the Chola dynasty, whose influence extended to the entire Indian Ocean. Chola kings sent an embassy to the Song court in the eleventh century and conducted a highly profitable trade with the Chinese. Highly organized merchant and manufacturing guilds existed in the south to support such activity. One organization of such guilds was named "Five hundred from the four states and thousand directions," indicating the size and scope of its ambition. It was probably the world's first international chamber of commerce. The South Indian trade focused on spices, textiles, and glass articles in exchange for copper and gold. The wealth resulting from this trade activity resulted in a flourishing literature and architecture in South India but not science.

Impact on migrations and travel: Perhaps the most significant migrations and travels consisted of the gypsies migrating out of India mentioned above; Indian mathematicians, astronomers, and physicians going to Baghdad; Arab traders establishing trading colonies on the western coast of India; and Indians establishing trading colonies in Malaysian Peninsula, Java, Sumatra, and China.

Impact on productive outcomes: Wealth creation remained static since relatively few new technologies were adopted and trade control was ceded to Arabs, which meant that Indian merchants lost the pricing power for their exports.

Impact on creative outcomes: There was little impact on creative outcomes. Both precipitous decline in intellectual creativity and a revival in religious and artistic creativity were in the future under Muslim domination.

Impact on societal structures and processes: Similarly, there was little impact of the extrinsic peaceful causes on the political scene and societal structures and processes within the states during the phase. While several large and powerful empires, such as Palas, Shahis, and Pratiharas came into existence, Indian civilization remained utterly divided toward the end of the phase as the Turkish pressure mounted and the societal structures and processes remained unchanged.

Impact of Southeast Asia

The Interaction with Southeast Asia occurred through South Indian dynasties and was thus confined to a one-way transfer of religion, architecture, and culture. Indian civilization did not succeed in transplanting its tradition of science to Southeast Asia since it had not succeeded in transplanting this to South India either during the current phase. The diffusion of Hinduism and Buddhism from India into Southeast Asia occurred, and the diffusion of Buddhism was essentially complete by the time it lost influence in India.

Summary

The impact of extrinsic causes on Indian civilization, therefore, followed a pattern similar to that of the Chinese civilization: it came through religious creativity and shifting trade patterns. However, there were important differences too. It was too early for a Hinduism-Islam synthesis to emerge in India, and Arabs exerted greater control on trade routes with India than with China. In short, during the current phase, India influenced the world through its past scientific accomplishments but was unwilling or unable to be influenced by the world through its creative achievements.

15.24 Extrinsic Violent Causes

Assessing the Loss of SPI

Although the ultimate Arab position in India after the battle of Rajasthan hardly mattered, they did manage to retain a pocket in Sindh and Multan for several centuries and thereafter seemed satisfied with the trade benefits. Thus, at the end of the current phase, the political situation in North India with respect to Muslim control was comparable to that in Europe after 700 CE.

The rise of Turks in the bosom of Muslim civilization and its shifting focus from west to Southeast Asia and the success of central Asian nomads in snatching northern and western China from the Songs, the Seljuks pushing the Ghaznivids south, and the unattractiveness of the Tibetan plateau all combined to concentrate Turkish Muslim pressure on India, resulting in the breach in Punjab toward the end of the current phase. Thus, after nearly a millennium of sustained political independence, North India was in the process of losing it to Ghaznis and Ghauris, thus initiating the Muslim era in South Asia. The Turkish Muslim tide, aided by internal treachery, overwhelmed the brave Rajput defenses after a struggle that lasted for nearly two centuries. Mohammed Ghauri captured Multan in 1175 and Lahore in 1186 and defeated Prithviraj Chuahan in 1193, thus laying the foundation for Muslim conquest of India. As the Khwarezmid Empire took over the Ghauri Empire in 1225, the attention of Ghauris focused exclusively in India as it was the biggest prize of them all. The full impact of Turkish victory on Indian civilization was yet to unfold at the end of the current phase.

The fragmented north could claim sustained political independence during most of this phase; however, the stage was also set for its long-term decline.

Loss of Control of Wealth and Means of Wealth

There was little loss of control of wealth during the current phase except on the northwest frontier.

Impact on Productive Outcomes

Similarly, apart from destruction of life and property resulting from Muslim invasions, there was little impact on the productive outcomes during the current phase.

Impact of fair trade: There was likely modest impact on the trade through the Silk Route because of constant invasions and wars in the northwest and later in Punjab.

Impact of migrations: This impact too was in the future.

Transmission of creativity: Indian civilization remained mostly cut off from both Chinese and European civilizations during the phase. During the current phase, the backward Muslim states in Northwest India controlled the access to both the world-class Chinese technological knowhow and great progress being made in science in the more progressive successive Muslim centers in Cordoba, Bagdad, and Samarkand. The modest impact, which came toward the end of the phase, was confined to practical technology, military technology, and religious creativity.

Impact on institutional structures and processes: There was little discernible impact on the institutional structures and processes during the current phase. Control of trade routes by Arabs probably resulted in drain of the wealth and surplus. It probably did not impact the wealth polarization but did have considerable impact on resources available for creative endeavors because of diversion to military needs in north India. Unfortunately unlike in the eighth century, to fight the Arab aggression, Turkish Muslim invasions of the north did not result in internal unity to fight the aggression. Quite the contrary, aggressors were able to create divisions and benefit from it.

Assessment of Net Impact: There was little visible impact of aggression on the Indian civilization until the very end of the phase. Its return toward monism, expulsion of Buddhism, political fragmentation, and adoption of Bhakti movement were all of its own making. The long-term impact was to come in the next phase after the Muslim Empire became established and became a centuries-long struggle and accommodation with the Indian civilization, a struggle that the British were only too willing to exploit in the nineteenth and twentieth centuries.

However, appearances can indeed be deceiving. The future, with hindsight, was bleaker indeed, for it was not the Arabs in the morning of Islam that conquered India; rather, the relatively backward Turkish tribes conquered India after Islam had turned them fundamentalist and anti-science. The ultimate impact of this conquest, though far short of destruction, was as profound as that of any civilization on another in history, and we cover this in more detail in the next chapter.

15.25 Productive Outcomes

Wealth creation: According to Angus Maddison, in 1000 CE, India was the world's largest economy with a share of just under 30 percent. India also had 30 percent of the world's population. By contrast, India's share of GNP in the first century was 33 percent, and its share of population only 21 percent. One explanation of the change is that the trade no longer favored Indian civilization. Another contributing factor may be political fragmentation and the rise of Bhakti movement with its focus on devotion to God. Thus, as Indian civilization faced the threat of Islam in 1000 CE, it was the largest economy in the world, though it no longer led the world in per capita GNP, if Maddison's research is to be believed. By comparison, when the British left India after partitioning it, its share of world GNP was 3 percent, and it population share had fallen to 18 percent because of systematic British policy of wealth drain, which led to famines, poverty, and arrested development.

Fair trade: There was considerable trade activity during the phase as manufacturing, though in relative decline, was still in the forefront by world standards. Indian products in textiles, ivory, metalwork, woodwork, soap making, and glass blowing were in great demand. However, the trade was now mediated through the Arabs and the Venetians, who controlled access to West Asia and Europe respectively and thus pricing powers increasingly was out of Indian hands. This was a fundamental change compared to trade under the Guptas, when Indian and Roman ships carried the goods to Europe. Southern trade with Southeast Asia fared much better, as mentioned before.

Migrations and travel: There were significant peace migrations into India during the current phase. Migration occurred in the wake of Arab invasions and trade activity and through successful Turkish incursions. The Chinese visits in search of Buddhist texts was replaced by Muslim scholars such as al-Biruni who were interested in Indian scholarship and civilization.

15.26 Creative Outcomes

Achievements in Practical Creativity

The focus on practical achievement was relatively broad-based, as shown in table 15.3. Jute began to be cultivated and sugar refining process was improved. In textiles, muslin was created in what is Bangladesh today. It was named so because Europeans first encountered in Masul in what is now Iraq. Bhoja's *Samarangana-sutradhara* (~1100 CE) describes chiming chronometers (*putrika-nadiprabodhana*). Other achievements in practical technology were water supply plants, astronomical models, vehicles, wooden robots, and designs for flying machines centuries before Leonardo da Vinci. In his *Yuktikalpataru*, Bhoja warned shipbuilders about using iron along the bottom of the vessels, for this would render them vulnerable to magnetic rocks at sea.

Achievements in Religious Creativity

Monism: Hinduism's ascendancy on the Indian subcontinent in this phase witnessed two conflicting and concurrent and mutually reinforcing developments: expansion of monism based on Sankara's teachings and challenges to this uncompromising, though tolerant, monism from the migration of the Bhakti movement that originated in the south. Sankara's epoch-making synthesis of Upanishad worldview was based on the impossibility of real knowledge through senses and intellect. This sense-based knowledge, according to him, was in fact ignorance; true knowledge was only possible through intuition and mediation and resulted in a communion of the higher nonmaterial self within and the equally nonmaterial Brahman without. In the eleventh century, Ramanuja, in opposition to Sankara's view, stated that both the inner self and the sense knowledge are real, permanent, and independent modes of knowing God. However, theistic philosophy of Ramanuja, though it asserted the reality of world under the control of an omniscient God, continued to focus on moksha and knowledge of the world as the principal aim of life. Moksha, according to him, does not come from theoretical knowledge of God through either mode but from devotion to him. Therefore, his epistemologically better view of the reality did not prevent him from lapsing into spirituality. The difference between Sankara and Ramanuja ultimately was not one of objective but only of how to get there. Ramanuja's philosophy strengthened the hand of the Bhakti movement, which had sprouted in the south in the fifth and sixth centuries. Its migration north was undoubtedly welcomed by the Brahmins in their fight against Buddhism and in their knowledge that masses were more likely to welcome Ramanuja's devotional approach

Table 15.3: Significant Achievements in Practical Creativity
Indian Civilization, 750–1200 CE

Category	Significant Achievements
Materials	
Processes	
Energy	Perpetual motion machine concept
Tools	Bhoja's jet plane design, Bhoja's mechanical devices, chiming chronometers, wooden robots
Agricultural Products	
Non-Agri. Products	12-month calendar
Construction	Angkor Temple complex, astronomical models
Transportation Technologies	Vehicle designs
Weapons Technologies	
Infrastructure	Water supply plants
Communications	

to Sankara's abstract approach in achieving moksha. Thus, the process of continued decline of the Buddhist philosophy of agnosticism and social protest against the caste system and Hinduism's return to the central focus on moksha as the aim of life on this earth continued. Throughout its history, to the extent Indian civilization emphasized the effort toward attainment of moksha, it implicitly deemphasized the interest in pursuit of science, art, and philosophy. However, a belief in moksha, unlike strict monotheism, does not forbid science; it just makes it proportionally less relevant. Indian civilization has had to fight this tendency throughout its history. In the current phase, it was once again losing this battle. Finally, Hinduism and Islam on India's northwestern border made little impact on each other during this phase. However, Hinduism and Buddhism both made a profound impact in Southeast Asia during the current phase.

Buddhism: Theravada Buddhism with its emphasis on the cessation of samsara and the attainment of nirvana through original Buddhist teachings continued to be practiced in Sri Lanka and Southeast Asia. The Mahayana school, developed in India in the early centuries of the first millennium, placed greater emphasis on motivation to liberate all other beings from samsara as well as oneself. It therefore placed greater emphasis on compassion than the Theravada school did. Mahayana Buddhism continued to prosper in China during the early part of this phase in two forms: Chan or Meditative and Pure Land. The latter is distinguished by the Amitabha, who resides in the Pure Land and helps ordinary folks achieve nirvana as it was indeed a difficult task. The Buddhists (as well as Zoroastrians and Manicheans), however, were persecuted under Emperor Wuzong starting in 845 CE when he needed the wealth of monasteries to fight the Uyghur nomads.

A third school of Buddhism developed in India by combining the Mahayana branch and yoga. This school came to be known as the Vajrayana Buddhism and spread to Tibet during the eighth century. This was fortunate since Tibetan Buddhism was able to safeguard Buddhist literature from Turkish invaders of India in the eleventh and twelfth centuries. In Japan, the first Buddhism to arrive was the Chan Buddhism, which evolved into Tendai to accommodate local Shinto tradition, and Zen, which emphasized experiential wisdom. The Vajrayana branch also arrived in Japan and was known as Shingon.

Buddhism also spread to the Srivijaya Empire in Sumatra under the Sailendra dynasty during the seventh to thirteenth centuries. In addition, Mahayana Buddhism was an important religion under the Khmers in the Southeast Asian peninsula. Jayavarman VII (1181–1219), built large Mahayana Buddhist structures at Angkor. The Buddhist religion also shielded Southeast Asia from adopting an extreme version of Islam later when Muslim traders from India took Islam to Indonesia.

Buddhism had little success against the Christian or Muslim variety of monotheism primarily because Buddhism is agnostic and did not fit into cultural settings that had a long history of intolerant monotheistic thinking. It was ahead of its time for such a setting. The only interesting impact that Buddhism had on monotheism was through lending the life story of Buddha to the legend of St. Josaphat. The name *Bodhisattva* changed to *Bodisiva* in Persian in the seventh century, to *Budhasaf* in an eighth-century Arabic document, to *Lodasaph* in Georgia in the tenth century, to *Loasaph* in Greece in the eleventh century, and finally to *Josaphat* in Latin!

Achievements in Philosophical Creativity

The key focus of philosophical creativity was in religious context covered above. Epistemology, ethics, and aesthetics essentially remained in the background during the current phase.

Achievements in Art

Perhaps the most outstanding feature of Indian art during the phase is the construction of elaborate temples in both North and South India, a tradition that continued in the south in the next phase even as great temples were being razed to ground in the north by Muslim rulers to rob material for mosques and palaces. This expression of religiosity away from the focus on the rock-cut caves in the previous phase may be understood from the cultural synthesis taking place driven by the Bhakti movement. These temples comingled the Jain, Shaiva and, Vaishnava, and Shakti strains of the Bhakti movement. Religious life was moving toward elaborate rituals, differing modes of worship, and daily processions of the deities. The great temples of the era that survive are in fact complexes, called the Parivara system. A large temple is surrounded by shrines and is built over multiple generations and at times by multiple dynasties. While in the rock-cut temples of the previous phase, the focus was on separate identity of different religious beliefs (Buddhist, Jain, and Shaiva and Vashnava), the focus in medieval period shifted to an architectural synthesis through use of ground-level temples with highly decorated exteriors. The reason for this shift is obvious: the cave temples were designed for the monks and priests, away from the intrusions of life. The temples during the current period were designed to be immersed in the life of the common man and depicted life images (including erotic images) on external walls. The theme of the life images on the outer walls and deities inside was meant to convey the idea that the devotee must leave his worldly life outside the temple to realize God.

The two issues concerning temple art of the current phase were it did not develop new architectural forms on the one hand and the artistic expression remained hostage to too many traditional stylistic constraints on the artist on the other hand. Despite these serious limitations, the artists managed to convey the force of the underlying Bhakti movement, which was derived from the demise of Buddhism, the rise of monism in the north, and the rise of Bhakti movement in the south. Southern religiosity was conquering the north, just as the northern science was failing to make any impact on the south.

We want to mention the two outstanding examples of Indian art during the current phase: the Khajuraho temples in central India built by the Chandella dynasty and the images of Nataraja. The Khajuraho complex originally consisted of eighty-five temples, of which only twenty-four survive the natural and Muslim destruction. However, they remain among the finest expression of man's creative urge. Architecturally, these temples were constructed out of sandstone assembled together without mortar using the mortise and tenon technique, which required grinding precision surfaces. Stylistically, the sculptures represent representational art and are inspirational to artists even today. The statues of the famous Nataraja date back to the tenth century in the south, and artists used stone, wood, and bronze as the medium. Nataraja represented the cosmic energy in the universe as well as within the heart and their union, and in that sense, it may be considered as expression of monist philosophy. In 2004, a six-foot-high statue of Nataraja was unveiled at CERN, unifying the cosmic dance of the Nataraja and the cosmic dance implied in the equations of modern atomic physics.

Clearly, literature and performing arts probably regressed compared to its golden age in the previous phase.

15.27 Achievements in Science

Achievements in Formal Sciences

Mathematics: Almost eight centuries before Descartes (1644 CE), Vacaspati Misra (840 CE) conceived the foundations of spherical coordinate geometry. In *Nyayasuchinibandh*, he states that the position of a particle in space could be established by measuring along three imaginary axes. In 850 CE Mahavira wrote a book of algebra called *Ganita Sarasa Magraha* in which he described solutions of indeterminate linear equations and rules for the use of permutations and combinations. He also described a process for calculating the volume of a sphere and one for calculating the cube root of a number. He developed formulas for some geometrical figures, including right-angled triangles with rational sides. Around 900 CE, Sridhara wrote two books, *Trisatika*, describing the solution to quadratic equations, and *Pataganita*, which seems to have been written for the layman and gives rules for arithmetic operations and deals with ratios and fractions. Prthudakasvami (830–890) named the emerging science of algebra Bijaganita, which means a science of calculating the unknowns. He was the first to use symbols to denote unknown quantities. Brahmdev (1160–1130 CE) made contributions to trigonometry.

Bhaskara II: Bhaskara II may be considered the greatest mathematician of the Middle Ages. He wrote three major works: *Lilavati*, named after a daughter he loved very much; *Bijaganita*, and *Siddhanta Shiromani*. The first work is primarily on arithmetic but includes sections on plane and solid geometry as well as solutions of indeterminate equations. The second work focused on algebra, which gave methods of solving the so-called Pell's equation as well as other quadratic and cubic equations using a cyclic or Chakravala method. In *Siddhanta Shiromani*, he developed important relationships between trigonometric functions and founded the branch of spherical trigonometry. In this work, we can find his ideas concerning calculus. He provided an early version of the fundamental theorem of differential calculus, namely Rolle's theorem. He went as far as to calculate the derivative of the sine function as the cosine function.

Achievements in Physical Sciences

Astronomy: Lalla (720–790 CE) wrote a two-volume book on astronomy. The first volume covered mean and true longitudes of the planets, issues with diurnal rotation, lunar and solar eclipses, syzygies, risings and settings, and the motion of the moon. In the second volume, Lalla examined topics such as graphical representation, the celestial sphere, the principle of mean motion, the terrestrial sphere, motions and stations of the planets, geography, and instruments.

Vijayanandi wrote *Karantilaka*, about astronomy, toward the end of the eleventh century and discussed similar topics as Lalla above: mean and true longitudes of the sun, moon, and five planets; the length of day; issues concerning diurnal rotation; lunar and solar eclipses; time of first visibility and conjunction of the planets; phases of moon; and units of time measurement.

Bhaskara II was not only a great mathematician but also a competent astronomer. He seems to have followed the heliocentric model of Aryabhatta. He calculated time required for Earth to orbit the sun to be 365.2588, which was achieved without sophisticated instruments and using the naked eye. Siddhanta Shiromani also covered all the standard topics of Indian astronomy.

Physics: Sankara Misra observed electrostatic forces between straw and amber. In Upaskara, Sankara Misra also discussed the properties of heat; however, the absence of instruments prevented any quantification. In the tenth to eleventh centuries AD, Udayana recognized solar heat as the heat-source of all chemical changes. Bhaskara II, the mathematician, was also the first person to conceive of a perpetual motion machine. The notion of conservation of energy obviously did not exist.

Earth sciences: Polymath Ksemendra in the eleventh century was also a cartographer and two maps produced by him were incorporated in Francesco Pulle's *La Cartografia Antica dell India*, produced in the early thirteenth century.

Achievements in Biological Sciences

Medicine: Physician Madhav wrote a seventy-nine chapter book, *Nidana*, describing diseases and symptoms, including smallpox and inoculation against it.

To summarize, during this phase, North Indian civilization was increasingly preoccupied with a religious revival and fighting the Turkish invasions, particularly after 1000 CE. Science took a back seat, undoubtedly. However, like a body in motion, science also has its own momentum, once it is set in motion. The loss of sustained political independence only occurred toward the end of the phase and was recent and limited to the Punjab. Any resulting changes in internal creative balance were obviously not instantaneous. To a large extent, changes in internal creative balance depend on the nature of the religious and political change and on the passage of time. Punjab had begun to come under the rule of Turkish Muslims after 1150 CE; the rest of North India was free, although it felt the Turkish pressure and no doubt the states diverted resources to military buildup. Despite this uncertain and changing military environment, there continued to be a steady stream of world-class contributions in mathematics in North India. However, not surprisingly, the quality of creativity in astronomy had begun to deteriorate significantly as it required greater support from the state. One also cannot help wonder why there was little research done in physics and terrestrial laws of motion during this phase; there was no follow-up to Prasaspada's work in the seventh century. We suspect this was in part because the work in astronomy, with the few exceptions like that of Bhaskara II, had become routine and was driven partly by astrological and religious needs. The interplay between research in astronomy and terrestrial motion under gravity tend to feed on each to the benefit of both. As astronomy became routine, research in terrestrial physics never sprouted. The Indian mathematical tradition, on other hand, had the strength to continue on its own, and it did not require excessive resources in the form of observatories and instruments from the state. Undoubtedly, the religious changes and creeping importance of Bhakti, spirituality, and otherworldliness discouraged a focus on physical universe to the detriment of physics. However, it is clear from the above summary that there were still flashes of creative fire here and there. but the earlier golden age of creativity had lost steam.

Summarizing Achievements In Abstract Systems-Building Capability (ASBC)

By the end of the current phase, the ASBC of the Indian civilization was no longer world-class: it continued to have the world's most scientific alphabetical script. In addition, it advanced the frontiers of mathematics. However, the need of the hour, the next great advance in ASBC, was developing controlled experiments here on earth. The Indian civilization did not keep up advancing frontiers, and the Muslim civilization led the way.

History, Causes, and Outcomes of the Central Asian Nomads—The Third Wave

15.28 Brief Political History (800–1206 CE)

As we have discussed in previous chapters, people of Turkish and Mongol extraction originated in central Asia. Central Asia may be said to consist of five countries that belonged to the former USSR (Kazakhstan, Kyrgyzstan, Tajikstan, Turkmenistan, and Uzbekistan) and Mongolia. The Sanskrit word "stan" (which means "place") in the names of the four former USSR republics attests to either the westward influence of millennia old Indo-Aryan culture or a central Asian origin of the Aryans, which assumes, incorrectly in our judgment, that Aryans did not originate in India and the neighboring northwest region. The name of nearby Afghanistan comes from "Upa-Gana-stan," which means in Sanskrit "The place inhabited by allied tribes."

This conflict between central Asian nomads and surrounding civilizations in the east, west, and south occurred whenever population pressure increased and a charismatic leader united the different tribes to create a fighting force. The nomadic lifestyle is also suited to long-distance warfare once the art of horse riding was mastered. The central Asians were on the north central edge of the Silk Road used to transport goods from India and China to Europe and back. The lure of controlling the Silk Road within a stone's throw to the south was a great incentive for central Asian tribes to unite. Thus, the saga of central Asia is the saga of conflict between nomads and settled peoples, lasting nearly two thousand years, and ending in nomads themselves becoming civilized over time. Over time, they were influenced by the people they conquered, and they, in turn, strongly influenced civilizations in West, South, and East Asia as well as Europe. What can be said about these people? It is clear that they were always fearless fighters, and they had no tradition of agriculture, science, or any organized religion of their own. They were intensely practical people focused on military technology.

Recalling the first and second waves: It is useful to briefly recall the pattern of central Asian attacks against civilizations. We may recall from chapter 11 that in phase III, Kushans or the Yeuzhi tribe from central Asia, who were pushed south and west by the Chinese, had overwhelmed northwest and northern India. These nomads did not engage in looting, were interested in empire building, and were religiously tolerant. They eventually converted to Buddhism and Hinduism and developed uncharacteristic wisdom under the gentle doctrine of Buddhism.

The second wave, which consisted of Huns, Huna, and Gokturks, was initiated by European Hun tribes organized by Attila and his predecessors of both central Asian and East European extraction. In 435 AD, Attila besieged the Byzantine capital, extracted tribute, and retreated. He attacked the Sassanian Empire in Persia, but they defeated him in 440 AD. In 445 AD, he again attacked the Byzantines, extracted tribute, and retreated. In 451, he attacked the Western Roman Empire after his request to cede half of the empire to him as dowry (Roman princess Honoria had sent him a marriage proposal!) was denied. Ho marched as far west as modern France successfully but was apparently defeated in the battle at Chalon, though not decisively. Two years later, he attacked Italy, making anew his dowry demand. At the request of the Roman emperor, Pope Leo met Attila and convinced him to turn around in peace in exchange for a promise of a holy crown for one of his successors. He died in 453 AD, apparently murdered by his wife, according to one version.

The second wave of attacks was continued by group of central Asians known as Huna or Hepthalites. They attacked India in the latter part of the fifth century. A Hepthlite king, Toramana, overran the great Gupta Empire in India in 500 AD. However, a Hindu coalition drove the invaders out by 530 AD. Hepthalites are believed to be a mixed horde consisting of Turkish and possibly some Iranian elements. Huns also attacked China at about the same time. The second wave was more interested in looting, and the nomads were unsuccessful in stable empire building this time around. It was probably the reorganized descendant of Huns and Hephthalites that constituted the vast Gokturk Empire, which, however, was unable to threaten Persian, Indian, or Chinese civilizations on its eastern, western, and southern borders respectively because these civilizations remained strong. The north, Siberia, was too cold to be useful. The Gokturk Empire was the largest central Asian confederation that utterly failed conquer civilizations since, for a change, the central Asian nomads were surrounded by strong civilizations!

One of the chief villains of history in our judgment resulted from the unholy synthesis of Islam and Turkish nomads who were hired as mercenaries by the Arabs. Earlier waves of central Asians in history had been civilized by Buddhism, Hinduism, and the Chinese culture. Similarly, Christianity had tamed the barbarians from northern Europe. Nomadic Arabs were civilized by Indian and

Hellenistic science and Persian culture since they needed to adopt it for commercial and political reason as they ventured into Iberia and Sindh. In the eleventh century, Muslim Turks, as descendants of central Asian nomads, were once again standing at the crossroads of history as the leading military force they inherited from the Arab-Persian Muslim civilization. The descendants of Turkish nomads appeared set to the control great civilizations in Asian, Europe, and Africa by the end of the current phase. The world history of the next several centuries will be the story of their adventures and eventual decline.

Brief History of the Third Wave— Ghaznavids and Selkuks

The Ghaznavids: With the fall of the Gokturk Empire, Gokturks in the western region converted to Judaism, a fact that puzzles some historians even today, though it should not since central Asian nomads have not been particular about picking a religion to adopt. They, at different times, have adopted Buddhism, Hinduism, Christianity, and Manichaeism. Yet, for a third time in a little more than a millennium, a migration from western fringes of the old Gokturk Empire began in the ninth century, this time to serve in the Arab armies of the Abbasid Caliphate in Persia. Central Asian nomads now had decided not to attack but join the civilizations Arab nomads controlled. This was an entirely new phenomenon from a West Asian perspective, for it was conscription and not invasion. It was, however, this conversion of the eastern tribes to Islam that was to prove much more significant historically, though they had converted to Islam for the practical reason of allowing them to be conscripted into the Arab-Persian armies of the Abbasid Caliphate. These Turks put an end the Persian Sammanid dynasty by 1000 CE and established the Ghaznivid Empire as we saw in section 13.8 above.

The Seljuks: While the Ghaznavids became part of the Persian culture and conquered it from within, yet another Turkish tribe under the leadership of a chieftain called Seljuk migrated from the Steppes to northern borders of the Samminid Empire when it was in decline. Like the Ghaznivid, the Seljuks adopted Islam. Their stepping stone to power was not through invading a civilization, at least in the short run; rather, it is through attacking the Ghaznavids since they were in the way. When Mahmud Ghazni died in 1030 CE and his son was focused on Indian campaign in the Punjab, a grandson of Selkuk named Togrul Beg defeated the Ghaznivid army in 1040. By 1055 CE, the Seljuks were in control of Baghdad without firing a shot, and the nominal Sunni Caliph of Bagdad gave Togrul the title of Sultan, which marked the beginning of the Seljuq Empire. Suddenly, the Seljuks were transformed from nomadic raiders to masters of a vast and sophisticated Islamic empire.

The Seljuk drove the Ghaznavids further south toward India, which ultimately led to the founding of the slave dynasty, as we noted earlier. Seljuk rulers now had the dual mission of unifying Islam and expanding its frontiers, and thus they invaded Fatimid in Egypt and Palestine and the Byzantine Empire. In 1064–68, Sultan Alp Arslan invaded Armenia and Georgia, the frontier regions of the Byzantine Empire. These acts of aggression elicited response from Byzantine emperor Romanus, and he was defeated by Seljuk in a key battle in 1071 CE. Over the next thirty years, the Seljuk pushed into Anatolia in the heart of the Byzantine Empire and began to call their empire the Sultanate of Rum—the name Seljuk had for the Byzantine Empire. They eventually settled in Asia Minor or Anatolia on the eastern edge of the Byzantine Empire. Several sultans spent time in Constantinople, married Byzantine princesses, and widened their worldview. During the twelfth century, Anatolia, while becoming thoroughly Turkish, became mired in turmoil because of infighting among different Turkish tribes. This infighting and the Mongol invasion in the mid-thirteenth century gave rise to the Ottoman Empire that we take up in the next chapter. Seljuk rulers fought the Crusades in the eleventh century and after Malik Shah's death in 1094 CE but struggled to contain the Crusaders. The last of the Iranian Seljuk ruler died on the battlefield in 1194, and by 1200, Seljuk power was at an end everywhere except in Anatolia. They lost control of Persia to yet another Turkish tribe known as Khwarezmia, setting the stage for a successful Mongol invasion.

15.29 Natural Causes

Central Asian land is too dry for farming. In premodern times, the grasslands of central Asia were capable of supporting humans through herding livestock. Thus, the people living there developed a nomadic lifestyle that often came in conflict with settled people around the periphery of the Asian steppes. The natural cause remained the driving force for central Asians to seek conscription in Arab-Persian armies. The difference was the absence of political vacuum in China, West Asia, and South Asia in the ninth century. The same natural causes were also behind the westward Seljuk migration and the struggle against the Ghaznavids.

Below, we focus on the Seljuk branch, the most successful of the nomads in the current phase. It is perhaps more accurate to consider the Seljuqs as nomads at the beginning of the phase when the Arabs and Persians hired them as mercenaries. However, at the end of the phase, they controlled the Muslim civilization, having learned culture and court tradition from Persians. Given their roots, we have chosen to classify them as the third wave of nomads from central Asia to invade and control civilizations.

15.30 Intrinsic Causes

Intrinsic Causes—Institutional Structures and Processes

Political system: The empire was divided into provinces ruled by a family federation. In such an appanage state reflecting the tribal sensibilities, the ruler assigned provinces to family members. The family in effect was the executive and legislative branches. The administrative system and court rituals were copied from the Persians. The sultan was the ruler and was assisted by his tribal elders. One constant problem was the absence of well-defined succession rules, and it often led to infighting among leading families when a ruler died.

Military capability: The military force was drawn from Turkish tribal sources consisting of infantry and lightly armed cavalry archers as well as a standing army consisting of slave soldiers drawn from Kurds, Armenians, Georgians, and Arabs. The standing army was typically heavily armored infantry, and the cavalry was fashioned after the Persian model and carried swords, bow arch, and spears. The fearlessness and ability to absorb new military technology and riding skill played an essential role in the military's success. A system of land grant supported the warriors and their horses.

Economic organization: The Seljuk did not change the economic system except for the land ownership pattern and sometimes encouraged a trend toward pastoralization in northern Persia and eastern Anatolia. During their peak, the Seljuk rulers repaired old Roman roads in Anatolia, built roadside inns, and instituted state insurance for trade losses in an effort to build commerce. External trade was expanded based on links with the republic of Genoese, a onetime rival of the Republic of Venice. The surplus expanded as a result of trade and territorial expansion and not improvements in productivity through improved technology. The increased wealth allowed Seljuk rulers to absorb other Anatolian principalities.

Systems of religious faith: Although Seljuk Turks converted to Islam, they were initially more tolerant of religious diversity. Most of the population was Greek-speaking Christians with a significant Jewish minority. Unlike the Arabs in Iberia, the Jews did not rise to positions of power under Seljuk rulers. That role was carved out for the Persians, whose culture and court rituals and language the Seljuk rulers had adopted. Churches, synagogues, and seminaries were built. Seljuk rulers supported the Sunni Hanafite instead of the Persian Shi'ite sect and tended to be conservative fundamentalists in matters of religion.

There was little science-religion conflict initially. Omar Khayyam developed his astronomy and al-Ghazali formulated his antiscience philosophy during the Seljuk rule. They were contemporaries and were active in the early period of Seljuk rule. Seljuks did not prevent the slide of Islam into an antiscience stance in the post-al-Ghazali period.

Legal system: Under Seljuk rule, further development of sharia law in worship, contract law, family law, and criminal law continued to take place. Theologian philosopher al-Ghazzali stated that the purpose of sharia law was to preserve faith, life, family, and wealth and knowledge creation. Notwithstanding the potential conflict between new knowledge creation and faith, al-Ghazzali's attempt to systematize the legal code based on a few basic principles must be regarded as a landmark achievement in the evolution of legal code.

Social structure: The social structure consisted of Turkish noble families at the top, followed by Persian elite, religious leaders, wealthy merchants, peasants, and slaves. The position of women was definitely low since women did not hold any official positions except occasionally in the ruling family hierarchy.

Although Seljuks had converted to Islam, they had retained memory of their tribal roots and traditions. Thus, the Seljuk reign did not produce excessive inequality.

Knowledge-Creating and educational institutions: In the eleventh century, Nizam al-Mulk, a prime minster in the Seljuk dynasty, established Madrasas for educating the young and founded several universities staffed with scholars and supported by government grants only decades before the Seljuk dynasty turned conservative.

Wealth allocation process: The Seljuk rulers squandered the surplus on internal wars, territorial expansion, and building mosques and palaces. During its peak years, creative endeavors were indeed supported. However much like Persian under Khusrau I centuries earlier, it was insufficient to continue the Arab-Persian synthesis.

Social cohesion processes: The social cohesion must be judged to be weak despite the strong presence of sharia law since the empire was a hodgepodge of various competing Turkish tribes, and the conquered ethnic groups were of differing religious persuasion. The external borders of the empire were hardly secure either, thus providing constant fodder to internal instability. The empire, surrounded by enemies, was inherently unstable and was kept together by military force.

Internal wars: After the death of Malik Shah in 1092, the Seljuk Empire remained mired in internal wars of succession, which encouraged revolts through the empire. The empire was put to an end by the governor of the vassal state of Khwarezm.

Formative Beliefs and Ideology at the End of First Synthesis Phase

The adoption of Islam by Seljuk rulers, their relative lack of engagement in the Arab-Persian science project, declining social cohesion derived from tribal roots but impacted by internal political divisions, the emergence of a slavery system, and their singular focus on aggression as means of growth all point to a belief system that may be summarized as follows:

- A continuing belief in practical knowledge, a focus on military strength, and a lack of interest in supporting science
- A declining belief in the relative equality among citizens as they became civilized and settled down
- An attitude of insularity toward the intellectual and religious creativity of others, consistent with their Islamic beliefs
- A continuing belief in aggression toward Islamic states and civilizations

These beliefs derived from surviving tribal traditions but were strongly impacted by the evolution of Islam. They are important since these beliefs influenced the Ghaznavids, who succeeded in conquering India.

15.31 Productive, Creative, and Scientific Outcomes

Productive outcomes: The focus of the Seljuk Empire was adding territory through wars and not production of wealth through adoption or development of new technology. However, they did encourage internal trade through construction of caravanserais or resting places for trade caravans.

Seljuks were fearsome and brutal. They were outstanding fighters but were not good at governance. Their empire was based solely on military might and was thus short-lived when other nomadic tribes gained the upper hand. So much energy was expended in offensive and defensive wars and on the good life that little emphasis was placed on the production of wealth. The basis of wealth increase was conquest and nothing else.

Creative outcomes: In the creative arena, there was little focus on practical technology and philosophy. There was indeed a focus on architecture in the form of mosques and tombs. Under Seljuk rule, the mosque evolved to a new form with four minarets and dome, and it served as the prayer hall. The tombs of the empire consisted either of elaborate circular or star-shaped towers with elaborate inscriptions or domes with brilliantly colored glazed tiles. Clearly, both innovations had a major impact on Muslim architecture, particularly in Iran and Turkey.

Scientific achievements: As late as the ninth century, most Turks as conscripts in the Muslim armies had not converted to Islam. Had they come to power at that time and when Islam itself had not closed the door on science, like many nomads, they may have contributed to science. However, a change in Islam's relationship to science and the adoption of Islam by Seljuk Turks meant the Seljuk rulers had little interest in science.

History, Causes, and Outcomes of the Muslim Civilization

15.32 Brief Political History (750–1200 CE)

A Focus on Persia

As we noted in the last chapter, with the fall of Sassanian Empire in 651 CE at the hands of the Arabs, the long tradition of independent Persian empires effectively came to an end for nearly a millennium until the rise of the Islamic Safavid Empire in the sixteenth century. During this interim period, the proud Persians had to accommodate the Arabs and Turkish nomads. They slowly accepted Islam and played an indispensable role in civilizing both Arabs and Turks. The Sassanian Empire was followed by the Umayyad Arab rule during 651 to 750 AD. The rule of the Umayyads Arabs was overthrown by the Arab Abbasid dynasty, which, through an alliance with the Persians, ruled the Muslim Empire until 945 CE. However, from at least the mid-ninth century, Abbasid rule in many parts of the empire was nominal. Palestine and Syria were in revolt, hoping to bring back Arab rule, North Africa came under Berbers, and eastern Persia came under two Persian dynasties, the Safavids in 870 CE and the Sammanids starting about 900 CE. Under the Sammanids, the Persian culture triumphs again.

However, the Persians made the same mistakes as the Arabs and conscripted Turkish tribes in the east in the army and slowly entrusted provincial power to Turkish governors who expanded their power as the Sammanid dynasty crumbled by 1000 CE. In 962, one Turkish slave, Alpitigin, established the Ghaznivid dynasty that was to last for over two centuries, and Seljuks overthrew this empire by the mid-eleventh century. Seljuk pressure ultimately pushed the Ghaznavids toward India in the eleventh century and finally led to the establishment of Delhi Sultanate in 1206 CE. Thus, Persia bounced around from Umayyads to Abbasid to Persian to Ghaznivid to Seljuk rule during this phase. And the worst was still to come through the Mongol invasion in the thirteenth century.

Sometime early in the current phase, the old Zoroastrian Persian civilization came to an end, and only two of the six ancient civilizations survived. Mesopotamian and Egyptian civilizations were gone by 500 BCE, ancient

Greek was gone by the beginning of the Common Era, and Persia was gone before the beginning of the second millennium.

Arabs temporarily but not fundamentally changed the Persian civilization through the introduction of Islam. They succeeded in converting Persia to Islam because Persian religious sensibilities were not too far from monotheism to begin with. Perhaps the most profound impact of Arabs on Persia was to pull Persia into the scientific project. Persians took to science like ducks to water, and by the eleventh century, they came to dominate the scientific activity in the Muslim world and indeed the entire world. We shall cover the substantial creative, productive, and destructive outcomes of the Persian civilization under Muslim civilization in section 13.16.

Muslim Civilization

From the rise of Abbasids and the shifting of the capital of the empire to Baghdad, we may date the beginning of the process of birth of a Muslim civilization proper. It was no longer just an Arab Empire created in a fit of monotheistic drunkenness. The Abbasid Caliphate, which was a Sunni Arab-Shia-Persian alliance, lasted until 945 CE. Another Arab Shia'ite dynasty called Fatimids arose in Tunisia in 909, and it expanded to include all North Africa, including Egypt. In 1059 CE, it came remarkably close to controlling the entire Muslim world. Thereafter, it declined and was terminated in 1171 CE. In parallel, in 945 CE, Shi'ite Buwayid princes from Southwest Iran seized political control of the caliphate from the Abbasid Caliph, reducing his authority as a mere religious head. Significantly, the Buwayid rulers called themselves kings as opposed to Caliphs. This dynasty was to last for 110 years. The Abbasid Caliph, reduced to the position of religious head, allied with Seljuk Turks. Seljuk Turks had been conscripted in the late ninth century, as we mentioned above, to the personal guard of the Abbasid Caliphs. They succeeded in overthrowing the Buwayids. However, the Sunni Seljuk Turks retained the political power as sultans while the Abbasids remained as Caliphs, with their role reduced to religious matters. From the middle of the eleventh century to the beginning of the fourteenth century, Seljuk Turks, interrupted rather inconveniently by the Mongol invasions in the thirteenth century, controlled the Muslim Empire in West Asia. This was followed by Ottomans, Mamluks, and Safavids in the west; Ghaznavids and Timur Lane in east; and the Delhi Sultanate and Moguls in the south, right down to the twentieth century in some cases.

Thus, Arab expansion took one hundred and fifty years to reach its peak; it experienced an Arab-Persian golden age of about two hundred years that declined in the following hundred years, followed by nearly seven centuries of fiercely and ferociously Muslim-Turkish dynasties mostly barren of science.

Islam also unleashed wars and terror on the non-Muslim world with a hitherto unknown ferocity and consistency. The war on other civilizations and belief systems was driven by the concept of the world divided into the house of Islam, and the house of war underscored the idea that those who were not Muslim deserved an ongoing war unleashed upon them. During the current phase, the harm caused by these wars was at least partially balanced by the diffusion and development of science, technology, and trade among major civilizations. However, as Islam turned conservative at the end of the current phase, there was little compensation for its continued terror on the non-Muslim world.

15.33 Natural Causes

In a fundamental sense, natural causes were the key to the rise of Muslim civilization. Arabs, like all nomads existing in arid environs, looked at established civilizations and dreamed of conquering them. It was simply a matter of the right opportunity through a combination of a charismatic leader, ideology of conquest, and military weakness in the surrounding civilizations. Central Asia and West Asia are at the crossroads of Indian, Chinese, and European civilizations. In the seventh to twelfth centuries, Europe was weak and fragmented, and India was weak after the tenth century. Consequently, both fell to Islam, one after another. China under the Tangs and Songs remained strong and survived the Islamic fury. Thus, while natural causes lie at the root of the rise of Muslim civilization, much like all nomadic empires, there were no significant specific natural causes that impacted the Muslim states during the current phase.

15.34 Intrinsic Causes

Intrinsic Causes—Institutional Structures and Processes

Political system: The political system in all Islamic states and empires derived from the word of God as revealed in the Koran through the Prophet Mohammed and as elaborated later in sunnah, hadith, and sharia. The purpose of political structures was to abide by Allah's will and do Allah's work under Allah's sovereignty, following his instructions and within the limits and injunctions prescribed by him. Clearly, such a structure could only be as good as the underlying political concepts in the Koran and sharia. The key political concepts in the Koran are:

- All Muslim free men are created equal
- Muslims must always expand the sphere of Islam because that is what God wants
- God will judge a Muslim by this after death

Thus, it is easy to see that non-Muslims, slaves, and women are not equal to free Muslim men, and Islam is activist, expansionist, politically dynamic, and religiously conservative by its very nature. The purpose of the state is to use all means at its disposal to achieve the ideal life required of a Muslim and to expand the house of Islam. It was from the start an unabashed case of self-righteous theology preaching political activism and was not bashful about using military power. In practical terms, the king and his prime minister, aided by a consultative council (elected in theory by the people but never in practice), held all executive and legislative powers and made judicial appointments in Muslim states. However, religious establishments retained the right to pass judgments on legislative and judicial outcomes. In other words, political structures were never allowed to contradict or innovate beyond the Koran and sharia as interpreted by the religious establishment. Thus, Islamic political structures may be thought of as God's dictatorship based on revelations to a particular man living in a particular cultural context at a particular time in a particular place. It was, therefore, one man's wisdom masquerading as God's word.

However, because it was God's word, it was applicable to all times, places, and cultures, a conviction it shares with all self-righteous ideologies. These were the strength and weakness of Islamic political structures. Political tolerance when it existed in Islam was not a belief. It was a tactic.

Military capability: Islam was a religion born in violence, and war is an integral feature of Islam. Without the military capability of its founder and early leaders and the existing power vacuum in Eurasia at the time, it could not have succeeded. Early wars were required by revelations, by the desire to loot the caravans of other tribes, and the refusal of a nearby tribe to pay taxes.

A careful study of the early wars during Mohammad's life and the following decades clearly points to two sets of reasons for their success. On the military strategy side, the key innovations were a unified command and careful strategic and logistical planning; the latter was of great significance because of the prevailing geographical conditions. On the psychological side, there was great motivation and unity resulting from uncompromising religious zeal and lure of heavenly reward after death. Later, Arabian nomads learned and absorbed the weapons and transportation technologies of the civilizations they came in contact with or conquered. The most developed arm of Islamic military was undoubtedly the cavalry, whether horse or camel mounted, followed by infantry. The navy was not well developed until quite late by the Ottomans. Muslim empires were all land-based. Strong commercial fleets for trade never translated into a blue-water navy until the Ottoman Empire faced the Venetian power. Today's Islamic states are a legacy of the early success of this militaristic religion and subsequent decay because of creeping fundamentalism.

Economic organization: Islamic civilization was the world's first long-lasting worldwide, multiracial, multiethnic civilization spanning three continents. The economic structures varied dramatically from place to place and over time. Yet certain principles behind these economic structures are clear: although Islamic revolution had an urban base, the needs of agriculture were critical to the revenues. Many societies in Asia in particular were characterized by an absence of landed property either in law or in fact. Islam created a social transformation through a much broader ownership, sale, mortgaging, and inheritance of the land for farming or commercial purposes, thus increasing incentives for increased production. Because Islamic empires linked many civilizations, hundreds of "new" crops and domesticated animals were introduced throughout the Muslim-conquered territories where they were hitherto unknown. The underexploited lands were developed, and the output of those already under cultivation were increased through improved methods and seeds.

Islamic states were also responsible for faster diffusion and development of practical technology. Steel and metallurgy from India and China; glazed ceramic technology, paper, and later gunpowder from China; and chemical and textile technology from India were imported and developed further. In several Muslim states, artisan guilds developed early, which later gave way to the factory system in some industries. Arabs by nature were traders and developed a strong shipping industry. Often, only Arab and other Muslim merchants knew the prices of various commodities in different parts of the world and became wealthy by exploiting these price arbitrations. Muslim commercial fleets and armies increasingly controlled the land and sea routes between Asia and Europe and worked in conjunction with Venetians to create a global trading system for the second time in history.

However, Islamic religious law did not allow debt and considered interest as evil. This undoubtedly played a role in checking the concentration of capital and prevented the rise of capitalism and credit markets in Islamic states. Islamic economics did not treat Muslims and non-Muslim as equal. In many Muslim states and empires, the non-Muslims had to pay a tax called *jezia*, ostensibly to protect non-Muslim minorities or even majorities from, of course, the Muslims, much like the British taxed Indians centuries later to protect Indians from the British!

Systems of religious faith: Islam is structured around the concepts of belief in Allah as the only God, five daily prayers, charity to fellow Muslims, fasting, and pilgrimage to Mecca called Hajj. The first two define relationship to God, and the last three confirm and consolidate the relationship to fellow Muslims. The mosque is the pace of worship, study, and for the community to gather in Islam. Unlike Hinduism, Islam does not have a hereditary priest class, and unlike Christianity, Islam does not require celibacy of its religious leaders. In the Sunni sect, an Imam often led the prayers in the mosque while a Sheikh gave the sermon. The legal and religious questions and disputes were settled by scholars known as *ullema* in accordance with the Koran, sunnah, and sharia. In the Shia branch, the Imam of the mosque takes on the roles of leading the prayers, sermon, religious/legal scholarship, and even political leadership. The twelve historical Imams of Shi branch are believed by the Shi'ites to have been chosen by God to lead all humanity in all aspects and are considered sinless.

Islam makes a clear distinction between Muslims and non-Muslims. This distinction invariably led to a division of the world into *Dar al-Islam* (the House of Islam under Muslim control) and *Dar al-Harb* (the house of war) under non-Muslim control. One must admire the innocent frankness with which the religious objective of Islam and the means to achieve it are spelled out in embarrassing details. There was little of the hypocrisy usually associated with other ideologies.

During most of the current phase, surprisingly there was little conflict between science and religion in Islamic states. There were several reasons for this temporary state of affairs: Islam was in the phase of absorbing knowledge from the Indian, Chinese, Persian, and European civilizations; the implications of the Koran had not been fully worked out; the need for astronomical data to assist in planning trade routes; the need to establish credentials with the conquered peoples; and the infantile state of biological and cosmological sciences during the phase. The latter was important because theories such as biological evolution would clearly contradict the Muslim precepts of the origin of life, which had been copied wholesale from Jewish and Christian traditions.

Legal system: The criminal and personal laws were derived from sharia under the watchful eye of the religious establishment through issuing fatwas. However, developing business and contract law was dramatic and groundbreaking. The concepts of written contracts, joint stock companies, agency, and trusts were fully developed for the first time in human history. Modern business law is rooted in Muslim business law, which was passed on to the Europeans. Legal scholars, who also functioned as religious scholars, derived the laws based on the following priority: Koran, Sunnah, consensus of Ullema, and Qiyas or analogical reasoning. Thus, society did not determine the law in Islam; God did. Ullemas only have the right and obligation to interpret it. In non-religious matters, Islamic states often used so-called grievance courts to settle conflicts. Thus, legal innovation could not go beyond the Koran either.

Social structures: Socially, Islam was not as progressive as was believed by its adherents. It is true that Islam never believed in racism. It is also true that all free Muslim males are equal. However, there are deep inequities in Islam between slaves and free men, men and women, and Muslims and non-Muslims. Islam encouraged the creation of empires by any means since it would lead to expanding the house of God or house of Islam. Since, in the beginning, non-Muslim and slaves constituted a majority in nearly all early Muslim states that have existed, all early Muslim states were highly discriminative, though Muslims tended to believe that their ideology provides equality to all human beings. In marriage, in property and in government, the position of women was decidedly inferior to Muslim males, though it was a significant step forward compared to Arab nomadic traditions.

All Muslim states exhibited a high degree of social inequality among free male Muslims on one hand and non-Muslims, women, and slaves on the other. Women were generally required to be secluded and only rarely held a position of power or worked outside home. Polygamy was allowed, as was the system of slavery for both men and women. The economic exploitation of non-Muslims was practiced where politically possible and conversion to Islam was rewarded everywhere. Ironically, in the face of this outrageous inequality, Muslim scholars and rulers believed their administration to be just because it was consistent with God's word in the Koran. The equality among the free Muslim men was helped by the Koran's injunction against interest, which prevented the concentration of wealth.

Knowledge-creating and educational institutions: Early Islam from the eighth to twelfth century was definitely forward-looking with respect to knowledge. Through adopting Indian and Greek science, technology, and production methods from all over the world; the introduction of paper, gunpowder, and later printing from China; and the creation of world-class universities in Iberia and West Asia, Islam led the world in knowledge creation for centuries. Many Islamic states were highly literate as Islamic states left basic education to the private sector.

Wealth allocation process: It is clear that absorbing practical agricultural and other technology from several civilizations and initiating land reform allowed several Muslim states to create a growing surplus. Early in the history of Islam, before the Sharia had been fully worked out, the Arab rulers in Iberia and West Asia, in part because of Persian influence, supported creative endeavors. It is true that a significant portion of the growing surplus was diverted to the military campaigns by several states. However, even that worked in the favor of Islamic civilization since Muslims kept winning and expanding to the new lands. Muslim dynasties were not shy of living well either. To re-emphasize, on the whole in the early centuries, in the morning of Islam, Muslim rulers supported creative endeavors, and Muslim states showed considerable creativity in adopting and developing Greek and Indian science and Chinese practical technology.

Social cohesion processes: Without question, the detailed Sharia, highly developed judicial system, and shrewd and often discriminatory policy toward non-Muslims for unfair taxes and exploiting social divisions ensured social stability in Muslim states.

Internal wars: Internal wars among Muslim states were intense and unending. If the war against other civilizations was driven based on a self-righteous creed and greed, the internal wars were driven by pure, old-fashioned succession wars and power grabs. The control of Muslim civilizations passed from Arab to Persian to Turkish (see below) control during the phase, and the dynastic succession was ill-defined and was often determined through war. The tribal divisions and traditions of the Arabs and Turks and the long history of Persian empire building only added to intensity of wars. Yet its adherents always regarded the religion as peaceful. Perhaps they meant the world would be peaceful after it was transformed into a caliphate; however, the never-ending conflicts among the Shia and Sunni and among the Muslim dynasties and states hardly inspired that confidence.

Formative Beliefs and Ideology at the Beginning of Third Synthesis Phase

The beliefs and ideology of Muslim civilization started out as remarkably different from those it had at phase end. It was quite a rapid transition, and perhaps it is in the nature of ascendant monotheism to eventually lead to conservatism. Early in the phase, Islam was open to science and knowledge based on observation and reason, it espoused social equality, Arabs were by nature city dwellers and traders, the Muslim civilization was not excessively fragmented, and success on the battlefields had filled the treasuries of the Muslim states, before Muslim jurists and philosophers had worked out the relationship between science and Islam. Thus, in the morning of Islam, the beliefs and attitudes of evolving Muslim civilization may be summarized as follows:

- A belief in knowledge as union of observation and reason derived from past achievements of the Indian and Greek civilizations
- A belief in the fundamental equality among Muslim males, coupled with inequality among men and women and among Muslims and non-Muslims
- A attitude of openness toward the practical and intellectual creativity of others, coupled with insularity toward others' religious creativity
- A belief in aggression and conquest toward other social orders

These beliefs fundamentally resulted in a need to gain allies in conquered territories and the results of the second synthesis or the Greek-Indian heritage were highly instrumental in pushing the cause of science.

Formative Beliefs and Ideology at the End of Third Synthesis Phase

The intolerant, aggressive, and self-assured monotheism with an excessive focus and obsession on conversions to Muslim faith; a focus shifting from knowledge creation to mysticism of sorts; imposition of taxes on non-Muslims; and the existence of separate legal codes for different communities all point to a belief system at the end of the phase that may be summarized as follows:

- A belief in practical and military technology as means to increase wealth production and to expand the empire and to sustain elite lifestyle
- A belief in the fundamental inequality between Muslim males and everyone else, in effect similar to European racism of the last five hundred years
- A attitude of insularity toward the intellectual and religious creativity of others
- A continuing belief in aggression toward other social orders

These changing beliefs, founded on hadith and the interpretation of Koran by Muslim jurists are important, since after killing science within Muslim civilization, they successfully killed it in the Indian civilization, thus handing over its leadership to Western Europe for the first time in its history.

15.35 Extrinsic Peaceful Causes

If the reader intuitively senses how there could have been extrinsic peaceful causes affecting the emerging Muslim civilization, the reader would not be far off the mark. This is because no civilizations could interact peacefully with the rising Arab nomads, who attacked just about everybody around them: the Indian civilization (634 CE), the Sassanian Empire (632 CE), Syria (637 CE), Armenia (639 CE), Egypt (639 CE), North Africa (652 CE), Transoxiana (662 CE), the Byzantine Empire (703 CE), Iberia (711CE), the Gokturks (712 CE), China (751 CE), southern Italy (831 CE), and Anatolia (1060 CE). These conflicts were largely successful and brought Arab nomads in contact with great civilizations and the world's heritage. What followed was incredible inflow of creative achievements of all significant civilizations to the Arab Empire. This transfer of creativity and glue of Moslem religion succeeded in creating the Muslim civilization. However, this transfer of creativity was immediately in the wake of violent aggression and therefore cannot be considered peaceful interaction.

15.36 Extrinsic Violent Causes (651–1200 CE)

Muslim Aggression

Muslim civilization faced no significant instruments of control during the current phase, except the temporary inconvenience of the Crusades. In fact, Islam did not face any significant threat until the discovery of the new sea routes in the sixteenth century, with the exception of Mongols in the thirteenth century and to a lesser degree, the rise of Venetia. Muslim civilization was the instrument of control par excellence unleashed on Europe, Asia, and Africa during the current phase. Muslim aggressors experienced military defeats in Europe as well as in India; however, no offensive attacks on Islamic states occurred during the current phase. Islam and Muslim civilization were ascendant. In Europe, Arabs continued their hold on the Iberian Peninsula and converted the vast majority of its population to Islam, but its influence remained confined geographically and declined during the latter part of the phase. In India, however, the victory was not within reach, and the conversion of population to Islam was in the future. By the end of the current phase, Islam was under pressure from a resurgent Europe.

By contrast, India was coming under increasing Muslim pressure and was getting ready to surrender its political independence to Muslim invaders. North Africa and West Asia also fell to Muslim aggression, with relatively speedy and full conversion to Islam.

Evolution of Power in Muslim Civilization

Arabs were perhaps too weak to conquer and hold Persia since the Persians themselves were empire builders and fighters par excellence. Arabs consequently allied with Persians to conquer Persia and used the conversion of Persia into Islam to hold on to Persia. The latter was not too difficult since Persia had monotheistic tendencies to begin with. Because of Persia's full, though slow, conversion to Islam and because of power passing from Arab to Persian hands, the negative impact of the Arab conquest of Persia was short-lived and quickly mitigated. The losers had joined the victors and outdid them in the end. The aggression of Arab nomads against Persians, the Arab decision to hire Turkish mercenaries, and the conversion of Persians and Turks into Islam resulted in the leadership of the Muslim civilization passing successively from Arab to Persian to Turkish hands through centuries of internal conflicts, as discussed earlier.

Changing Priorities of Muslim Power

Muslims states, naturally, controlled the surplus wherever they conquered. During the Arab-Persian period, there was balance in allocation to opulence, military, and creative endeavors and increasing productivity through adoption and integration of world's practical technology increased surplus. With Turkish control, the situation began to change in part because of changing focus in Europe. Turkish dynasties did not react to the slow loss of Muslim control in Western Europe and focused on the Byzantine Empire and Asia requiring significant change in allocation to military. This, coupled with the reinterpretation of the relationship between Islam and science, resulted in a significant decline in allocation to creative endeavors.

Thus, Arab conquests signaled the rise of a worldwide Muslim Empire, by far the largest the world had seen to date. This instrument of control was responsible for shifting control of the trade and setting the stage for the third synthesis in science for the first time under the auspices of a nomadic people by cross-fertilizing mostly the Greek/Hellenistic, Indian, and Chinese achievements since there were little European achievements to speak of.

Transmission of worldwide practical creativity: As Arab conquests brought the Indian and Chinese civilizations, central Asian nomads, and the debris of the Hellenistic world together, the world entered a new creative phase in practical technology. China had hoarded paper, printing, gunpowder, compass, porcelain, glazing, horse riding, and superior iron technology. Europe had inventoried a whole range of mechanical tools, such as gears, pulleys, levers, and the astrolabe from the Hellenistic period that had either been forgotten or fallen into disuse. Similarly, Indian civilization had a superior cotton gin, the spinning wheel, dyeing, textiles, and iron and glass manufacturing technology. The essential impact of Arab invasions was to learn, cross-fertilize, and further develop these technologies and diffuse them throughout West Asia, central Asia, and Europe through trade in goods that required these very technologies. Central Asian nomads played a pivotal role in diffusing the technology of gunpowder and the stirrup to rest of the world and were instrumental in diffusing other technologies such as papermaking, printing, textile, and mining technologies without adopting them. Their interest was primarily in technologies of military significance.

Seljuk mercenaries had been conscripted in the Abbasid armies starting in the ninth to tenth centuries, and they continued to have strong connections with their fellow tribesmen in the east. The Chinese first used Gunpowder in 1132 CE, and we know that the Arabs knew of gunpowder by 1240 CE. Thus, between 1132 and 1240, the Seljuk mercenaries likely transmitted the knowledge of gunpowder to the Arabs. This knowledge was further reinforced during the invasion of West Asia by Genghis Khan in 1258 CE during the next phase.

One of the most significant military technological inventions in the medieval times was the invention of the stirrup in China in the fifth century, as we noted in the last chapter, since it allowed the rider to deliver a deliver a much greater thrust to the spear or to stand in the saddle for more effective close combat. The invention likely was passed to central Asian Turkish tribes to Persia to the Byzantine Empire to Germany in the eighth century and changed the relative importance of cavalry and infantry.

Although paper had been invented in the second century CE, after the Arab Abbasids defeated the Tang Empire in the battle of Talas in 751 CE, the Chinese prisoners of war taught the Arabs the art of papermaking. From Abbasids, it reached Iberia quickly and ultimately reached France by about 1400 CE.

It seems that the magnetic compass invented in China in the third century BCE and somewhat later in India was used for navigation by the tenth century. It reached Europe by 1190 CE, and we find its first mention in Islamic literature about half a century later. However, we believe the Arabs may still have been the intermediaries in bringing this invention to Europe in the twelfth century.

Within the Islamic sphere, Persia greatly influenced Arab court culture, arts, and architecture, and Arabs drew Persia into their scientific project that had taken root in Iberia under Ummayads and spread out from there.

The lasting contribution of the Byzantine Empire to the Muslim civilization was advancing the art of the dome, which the Arabs adopted, as did eastern Europe, including Russia.

Transmission of Indian intellectual creativity: During this phase, Indian astronomical works, such as *Surya-Siddhanta* and the works of Brahmaguta, were translated into Arabic by al-Fazari about 777 CE. It appears that the pioneering work of Aryabhatta outlining the heliocentric model of planetary motion was not translated perhaps in part because it was ignored in India, particularly by Brahmaguta, who was very influential at the end of seventh century. Brahmagupta's work in trigonometry, astronomy, arithmetic, and medical treatises was transmitted to the Arabs. The Arabs, in turn, introduced Indian decimal system in Spain in the eighth century, with Pope Sylvester II imposing the new arithmetic system on Europe in 1000 CE. Indian algebraic trigonometry was introduced into astronomical calculations.

Transmission of Greek/Hellenistic intellectual creativity: The case of Europe–Arab interaction was exactly the opposite of Arab-Indian interaction during the phase. The invasion of Europe was a strategic success in that Iberia was conquered and remained under Arab control for several centuries.

As Abbasids came under the influence of Persian culture, they first became aware of the Greek/Hellenistic tradition in philosophy and science in Persia followed by a similar discovery by Moors in Iberia. The reader might remember Sassanian emperor Khusrau I, who had given shelter to fleeing Byzantine scholars in the sixth century. Thus, Persians were perfectly positioned to create a synthesis of Greek and Indian heritage. It is useful to remember that the substantial conversion of Persians into Islam took place only in the eleventh century. Persians were looking for a way to "upstage" the Arabs, and in the process sponsored the translation of the Greek and Hellenistic works into Arabic since Arabic had to become the language of scholarship even though Persian emerged as the court language.

Surrounded by enemies, Arabs in Iberia needed local cooperation, and the local Jewish population was the first to cooperate with invaders. Arab rulers employed the Jewish scholars to translate Greek and Hellenistic texts in philosophy, geometry, and astronomy. Not surprisingly, Arabs also encountered the Greek and Hellenistic philosophy and science in Egypt and Syria, where the scholars carrying this tradition could still be found. Euclid's elements, Ptolemy's *Almagest* and the works of Aristotle and Plato were translated into Arabic as well.

Attitude of Arabs concerning religious creativity: Arabs during the phase showed great openness to the practical and intellectual creativity of all civilizations they conquered. However, since Arabs were absolutely convinced that Islam was the final word of God, later Muslim Turks showed little interest in the religious creativity of other civilizations. They were, therefore, at their destructive best in the matter of religious creativity. Destruction and looting of the places of worship and taxes were used unabashedly to induce conversions. By the end of the period, the conversion of Persia and the Turkish tribes in West Asia into Islamic faith was nearly complete. The conversion of Iberians to Islam and Arab control of trade had profound impact on European psyche and had two major historical consequences: Crusades against Islam and rise of the small but highly successful state of Venice. The first was essentially a failure except as a signal of rising European consciousness against Muslim domination. The second was a great success and was a key first step in the rise of the Europe in the following centuries. However, both had to wait for the Muslim power in Iberia to wane, which happened when the control of Muslim power passed onto Turks, and Turkish attention turned eastward toward the Byzantine Empire.

Fair trade: The previous spurt in global trade during the centuries of the unified Roman Empire had been controlled in part by the Romans. Now, Europe-Asia trade came under the control of the Arabs, and the greater Muslim Empire was in a position to bypass the Byzantine Empire and eastern Mediterranean Sea to create land trade routes completely dominated by Muslim states. Muslim states collectively controlled both the land trade and sea trade between India and West Asia and Europe. Abbasids conducted the sea trade through the ports of Alexandria, Aden, and Siraf in the Arabian Peninsula and cities such as Mogadishu on the east African coast. In addition,

Indian commerce with Southeast Asia also proved vital to Arab and Persian merchants. Thus for the first time, China, Southeast Asia, West Asia, and Europe came linked into a worldwide trade network. Muslim navigation science was well developed, introduced the three-mast merchant ship and a smaller boat called *qarib*, and used an earlier version of the sextant. Trade not only brought economic benefits but also accelerated the diffusion of ideas and inventions. The land-based trade was probably more important in the early centuries of the phase, and sea trade became increasingly more important during the phase. Muslim states controlled the Silk Road as well as sea travel through the Arabian Sea and the Persian Gulf. There was great demand for silk textiles, spices, marble, sandalwood, porcelain, incense, precious stones, musk, and camphor in West Asia and Europe. This trade was temporarily interrupted because of the Crusades in the eleventh century, however. Muslim states not only traded products, but also were the first to do long-distance slave trade, with slaves captured from Caucasus, Berbers from North Africa, Slavic eastern Europeans, and the English and Nordic from northern Europe. The letters of credit acceptable from China to Iberia were easier to obtain for Muslim traders, and Muslim states successfully created maritime fleets after absorbing shipbuilding technology from other civilizations. Thus, the worldwide trade-based wealth accumulation process shifted from European and Indian hands to Muslim hands, though Venice continued to play a strong regional role.

Migrations and travel: Migrations occurred in the wake of invasions and through invasions. Large peaceful migrations were indeed rare. Muslim traders traveled to India, Southeast Asia, and China and established merchant colonies as far as China. Scholarly travel occurred as well. Jews traveled from Africa and West Asia to the Iberian Peninsula to offer their services to Arab rulers, and scholars from India were invited to Baghdad to translate Indian works in mathematics and astronomy. One famous scholar named al-Biruni, a man of encyclopedic erudition, came to India in the eleventh century with Mahmud Ghazni and stayed for several years in Punjab. He translated many Sanskrit books and wrote extensively about Indian civilization. Thus, scholars from many civilizations worked in Baghdad and Cordoba for many centuries and helped create the third synthesis in science. During the Arab-Persia period, Muslim states attracted Indian scholars from India and Jewish scholars from throughout Europe. Later, during the Turkish period, the scholars fled the Byzantine Empire and took shelter on the Italian Peninsula. This transfer of talent was a great contributor to the Italian synthesis.

Impact on productive outcomes: Muslims were not colonizers in the sense of large-scale movements of people to new or conquered territories because there was little population pressure. Their conquest model was to put together an army, overwhelm and conquer a frontier state, and displace the local elite in the name of Islam. Most significantly, Muslim conquerors introduced the new practical technologies they acquired from other civilizations to the conquered civilizations.

The impact of diffusion and integration of practical technologies, legal code protecting private property systems, innovative taxes, and land acquisition policies had great impact on agricultural and manufacturing productivity in conquered territories. One can only imagine the impact of gunpowder and the stirrup on military success, the compass on navigation, paper on recordkeeping, and the indirect impact of all of these on wealth production. Never in the history of mankind had a technology transfer occurred to a victor on this scale and at this speed. That, coupled with the control of trade and territorial expansion, allowed the Muslim state to leapfrog other civilizations in wealth creation. The Achilles heel of the Muslim civilization with respect to wealth creation was its injunction against interest, which prevented the development of credit markets and the accumulation of capital needed for a capital-intensive factory system.

Relatively free trade also grew during the Arab–Persian period and was both land- and sea-based since Arabs controlled the Mediterranean and had a strong presence in the Arabian Sea. This was a great contributor to the wealth of Muslim states. However, during the Turkish period, Muslim civilization lost control of the sea routes and focused on land routes alone. This first created an opening for Venice during the current phase and later for western European states after the current phase.

Impact on creative outcomes: During the Arab-Persian phase, as trade wealth poured in and as Muslim states integrated the world's technology and science, wealth grew and was directed toward both conquests and creative endeavors. The results were spectacular in practical and intellectual creativity. Practical creativity resulted in great improvement in agricultural productivity as well as in manufacturing. Intellectual creativity produced the third synthesis while philosophical and religious deliberation led to the realization that Islam and science were fundamentally incompatible.

During the current phase, Persia evolved from being enthusiastic students to influential teachers and eventually became the leader of the golden age of Islam as the center of learning moved from Iberia to Baghdad. For the first time in its history, Persia showed interest in science and produced world-class science. Indian and Greek achievements in science had not impressed the Persians in the past. However, the Arabian imposition of Islam on Persia and later of science was difficult to ignore as it came with military conquest. The impact of this instrument of control on science in Persia was positive and dramatic in the end. Nonetheless, it was short-lived. As Islam's innocent experiment with science ended, so did Persia's infatuation with science, and Persia quickly fell back into its historical habit and disposition toward science. The conflict between science and Islam was apparent and indeed pinpointed by Persian scientists and philosophers by the twelfth century. It took root since the linkage between science and the production of wealth did not yet exist. Control of Muslim civilization passed from Arab-Persian to Turkish hands. The Turks, unlike the Persians, had never bought into the Arab-Persian scientific project, and were only too happy to move back to its historic orientation of empire building and the good life for the elite, with a focus on art and architecture. The inner nature of Persian civilization reasserted itself as soon as the forcing function of Arab conquest had weakened and the true nature of the relationship between Islam and science had become clear.

Like the Europeans, the Turks were latecomers to science or a systematic religion for that matter. In the early centuries of the phase, Turks probably had no opinion on rising Arab-Persian science. They were naturally more interested in military, political, and state matters. However, as the Turks converted to Islam and as Islam shed its innocence with respect to science, Turks, who by now had come to control the Muslim civilization, became ferociously antiscience. Thus, the impact of Turks on science during the current phase was only slightly negative, but it was ready to kill already weakened science in India and thus hand the leadership in science to the Europeans, building on the fruits of the Arab-Persian synthesis.

The Turks had rejected science and accepted Islam in part because Islam itself was rejecting science. And this combination of antiscience and pro-Islam Turkish attitude proved disastrous for world history and science. Turkish dynasties brought religious intolerance and an antiscience attitude to the Indian subcontinent beginning with the thirteenth century. The latter, however, is something we explore in future chapters. As far as the current phase is concerned, it must be said that Islam was a Godsend for the Turks. After spending a couple of centuries in the wilderness as conscripts in the Arab-Persian armies, the Turks migrated into Anatolia and made Asia Minor their stronghold. By the eleventh century, Turkish conscripts had asserted themselves and became the dominating force. Not being fully comfortable on the sea and having concentrated in Anatolia, they shifted the focus of awesome Muslim power from west to east to put pressure on the neighboring Byzantine Empire. This shift had major consequences for Indian, Chinese, and European civilizations as we noted above. The fighting spirit of Turks, invigorated by the infusion of Islam, had reasserted itself as the leading power of the Muslim civilization as if to forcefully and dramatically confirm the inherent conflict between monotheism and science.

In the ensuing centuries, this knowledge was to comingle with Indian achievements in arithmetic, algebra, trigonometry, and astronomy to produce the third synthesis in science at two Muslim centers of learning in Bagdad and Cortoba before Muslim philosophers realized the fundamental incompatibility of science and Islam. However, it is important to note that Arab conquests and contacts in Europe and India during the current phase set the stage for the highly significant third synthesis of science. We also hasten to add that the third synthesis started out as an Arab venture and ended as a Persian and to a lesser extent a Turkish project as political power evolved in the Muslim civilization.

Impact on societal structures and processes: As we have emphasized above, Muslim states not only possessed the world's heritage in science, art, and technology but also took the best from different administrative systems, developed legal codes, instituted land and tax policies, and created structures and processes that were innovative as long as they did not conflict with the tenets of the Koran. Thus, the Imams had a great say in the legislative and judicial systems through the fatwas, just as the pope had through the threat of excommunication in Europe. Political and religious innovation was impossible, but economic and legal innovation was possible.

Islam is perhaps the world's first written, expansive, and extremist ideology and theology. The societal structures and processes of the Islamic states during the period were impacted by both the conquered peoples and the working out of ideas in the Koran by Muslim scholars and integration of the world's technology and science. Muslim states adopted military structures and economic organization and tolerated the social structures of the non-Muslim populations they controlled as needed. Arabs, Persians, and Turks forcefully imposed Islam on conquered civilizations and states and insisted on the identity of political and religious authority as required by the Koran, imposed the writ of sharia law on Muslims, and retained Arabic as the language of religious thought.

Summary: The Muslim civilization is deeply indebted to Indian, Greek, Persian, and Chinese civilizations. It is indeed hard to imagine the Muslim civilization without the wholesale adoption of the science, technology, and administrative systems from these civilizations. The independent Arab contribution was an inflexible and intolerant religion that sanctioned violence in the name of God and the idea of a unified military command. Most civilizations, consciously or unconsciously, slowly or rapidly, are naturally impacted by extrinsic causes or the diffusion of practical and intellectual creativity. However, in the case of Islam, it was just about the entire starting point beginning after a string of early military victories. Yet, Arabs deserve the credit for their openness to the practical and intellectual creativity of other civilizations in the early centuries, even if they were sometimes forced into such openness in foreign lands surrounded with enemies. Significant diffusion of practical technology, philosophy, art, and science from China, India, and Europe occurred, thus enabling Arabs to become the most significant military force on the globe as well as bring about the third synthesis of science and unique Muslim art and architectural forms.

During the Arab-Persian period, the impact of empire building on the Muslim civilization itself was highly positive in terms of gains in technology and science, wealth creation, and control of trade wealth and territories. The same cannot be claimed for the Turkish period. While the Muslim civilization continued to gain territories and converts, its creative impulse had fallen victim to its internal science-religion conflict. The orientation of Turkish dynasties as the ultimate power center of Muslim civilization was a result of this evolution, and it accelerated this evolution. Thus, during the current phase, Muslim civilization was the most significant and successful instrument of control, and its leadership during the phase changed from Arab to Persian to Turkish hands while it evolved from a civilization that was unaware of the contradiction between its religious theology and science to a stark and conscious realization that Islam and science are fundamentally incompatible.

The impact of empire-building activity on the Muslim civilization during the Arab-Persian period was rapid and tended to slow down during the Turkish period as the civilization settled down, despite continuing successes on the battlefields.

This situation began to deteriorate dramatically by the last decades of the twelfth century once the implications of the message in the Koran had been worked out and once the control of Muslim civilization passed from Arab/Persian hands to the Turkish hands decades before Baghdad was sacked by Genghis Khan's descendants. The marriage of creeping Islamic religious fundamentalism and the Turkish nomadic psyche produced a conservative outlook with disastrous consequences for the future of Muslim civilization and science. As we shall see in following chapters, the Islamic civilization still produced brilliant discoveries after the twelfth century; however, they were not a result of state sponsorship. They were sporadic and based on individual genius and a lingering momentum, reminding one of mathematical achievements of Bhaskara in twelfth century. Turkish dynasties had very different priorities with respect to the allocation of the surplus. It was not science; it was exclusively territorial expansion and control of land trade between Asia and Europe.

15.37 Productive Outcomes

Productive Outcomes

Wealth creation: The secret of wealth creation in Muslim civilization was through trade monopoly, and the secret to expansion in wealth was the control of surplus through empire building, an activity whose longevity was assured by encouraging conversion to Islam and punishing non-Muslim populations through the infamous jezya tax and other discriminatory practices in state employment and business opportunities. Only when Muslim rulers were a very small minority and lacked internal talent or rarely when an enlightened ruler came to power did non-Muslims have an opportunity to compete on merit. The preference was always given to Muslims, but regardless of race, since Islam, unlike Western Europe centuries later, is completely devoid of racial bias.

Fair trade: Islam was responsible for a renewed expansion of world trade between Europe and Asia, which had declined with the fall of Roman Empire. This trade took place both through the old Silk Road and sea-based spice routes. The sea routes mostly hugged the coasts for safety since Arab shipbuilding technologies had not mastered the open seas. In addition, Islamic expansion opened northern, eastern, and West African areas to world trade, in not only goods but also the slave trade. Since horses and camels could not carry heavy loads, most land trade was in high-value, lightweight goods, such as silk, jewels, spices, and perfumes. Ships, however, could carry large cargoes of low-value heavy merchandise, such as timber. As the Muslim civilization developed, it found a better balance between sea and land routes.

Arabs had a strong tradition of trading. The original Arab culture had been city-based and periods of prosperity in Arabia before Mohammad had coincided with periods of flourishing trade. As Arabs absorbed shipbuilding technology, navigation, and astronomy, they evolved from merely providing safe passage for goods through and around Arabia to controlling the entire process. Often, Arab and later Muslim merchants pooled investment to reduce trade risk.

Spice trade played a powerful role in the spread of early Islam and was made possible through trading posts in India and control of the sea routes linking India and West Asia. It is doubtful that without the spice trade Islam would have become a major religion outside of the Arab world since the spice trade was a source of wealth that would be diverted toward building stronger military capability to control the far-flung territories. Control of trade led ultimately to the control of territories. The new spice trade pattern was very different: in Roman times, the spice trade was indirect and resulted from an overlapping network of local traders. However, because of Muslim conquests, the entire spice route had become a Muslim trade route, resulting in the elimination of middlemen profits. This not only increased the trade volume but also increased the profits for the Muslim merchants, who often had a monopoly on such trade.

Muslim merchants traded in goods and had a flourishing slave trade as well. However, Muslim slave trade was different in nature and purpose compared to later European slave trade. Muslim slave trade focused on mostly women for domestic servants or as sex slaves in the harem, and it was not racial in its focus. This difference makes a lot of sense, since Muslims were not looking for field labor as no new unpopulated or sparsely populated lands capable of agriculture had been discovered. They were looking for domestic help, and Islam did not need a racial bias since religion itself could be used as a unifying force.

Trade was extremely important to the growth of Muslim civilization. Muslim merchants enjoyed a monopoly on global trade throughout the current phase. The secret of the expansion of Muslim civilization was a monopoly in world trade, religious zeal, and an open-minded attitude toward the practical creativity of other civilizations for several centuries. Growth in trade and the expansion of Muslim civilization went hand in hand. This was not too different conceptually from the western European experience centuries later, where growth in trade went hand in hand with the expansion of colonialism. Only mercantilism and capitalism had replaced religion as the guiding light. God followed by greed would replace greed followed by God.

Peaceful migrations: The story of migrations in and out of Muslim states during the current phase is also instructive. With the exception of Turkish mercenaries, there were no mass migrations into West Asia, since it lacked the capacity to support large populations. Likewise, migrations out were also relatively small and consisted of soldiers in Muslim armies. Since Islam required effort to convert others to Islam, allowed multiple wives, and lacked a racial bias, the invading armies often married the local women and settled in the conquered lands. Thus, there was substantial migration into Iberia, Northwest India, and northern Africa during the current phase. Islamic expansion also encouraged travel for business and intellectual reasons. Muslim trades had a strong presence in ports from China to the Mediterranean. Muslim dynasties during the current period encouraged intellectual creativity in science, art, and sciences. Often, Indian and Jewish scholars were invited, and often Muslim scholars traveled to Muslim and non-Muslim lands for scholarly reasons.

15.38 Creative Outcomes

Let us review the Islamic (Arab, Persian, and Turkish) achievements during this phase, including its golden age and the third synthesis.

Table 15.4: Significant Achievements in Practical Creativity
Muslim Civilization, 750–1200 CE

Category	Significant Achievements
Materials	
Processes	Improved distillation
Energy	Windmill with horizontal axis
Tools	Astrolabe, planisphere, Mercetor projection for maps, mechanical devices in Kitab al Hiyal, camera obscura, chain drive use common
Agricultural Products	
Non-Agri. Products	Medical licenses granted
Construction	
Transportation Technologies	
Weapons Technologies	
Infrastructure	
Communications	

This golden age had two centers: those on the Iberian Peninsula and those in Baghdad. It also had two foundations: Greek and Indian science, one dead and long forgotten and the other alive but not so well. Greek heritage was accessed indirectly with the help of Jewish and Christian scholar-translators in Spain, and Indian science was accessed more directly through Arab outposts in Sindh, the translation of Indian works, and actual travels by Indian astronomers, mathematicians, and physicians to Baghdad.

Achievements in Practical Creativity

The significant and substantial achievements of Muslim civilization in practical creativity during the current phase are summarized in table 15.4.

Achievements in Religious Creativity

Islam went through a significant evolution during the current phase, which may be understood through the evolution of sharia or Islamic law since every Muslim must follow sharia to the letter, with no exceptions allowed. The original sources of sharia were the Koran and sunnah or Mohamed's living example. These together may be regarded as the canonical law of the Muslims. Arab experience and constraints in Iberia as well as interaction with the Persian civilization had a profound moderating impact on sharia evolution. Legal scholars recognized the validity of *ijma* or the consensus of Mohamed's companions and *qiyas* or various forms of reasoning to derive legal judgments. This recognition was an implicit admission that the Koran and sunnah were not specific enough to meet the demands of an expanding empire that included an expanding circle of communities and peoples. This resulted in the emergence of *fiqh* or Islamic jurisprudence or common law, based on independent interpretation of the Koran and sunnah. In addition, the edicts of Muslim sovereigns formed a third leg of the legal system. By the eleventh century, this process was leading the legal system so far away from the Koran and sunnah that philosopher al-Ghazali formally closed the doors of an independent interpretation of the Koran and sunnah or the process of *ijtihad*, thus drastically slowing further evolution of Islamic law. The Shia branch had rejected these innovations altogether.

Interaction with Persia helped to civilize early Islam and made the administration of Islamic states driving the golden age of Islam more efficient. Islam later reversed this process and became more conservative. Control of the Islamic empire by the Turkish tribes and a declining Jewish and Persian influence in the eleventh century reinforced this trend. The Turks were comfortable with this change since their nomadic origins were closer to those of the Arabs of Mohamed's time. Turks, by their own admission, had made Islam more ferocious, conservative, and intolerant. This Turkish face of Islam, pushed south by the Seljuk Empire, reached South Asia in the eleventh century.

Sharia may have turned conservative but not before making monumental contributions to legal theory. Concepts like *aqd, lafil, hawala,* and *waqf* directly correspond to contracts protected by collateral, jury, agency, and trusts. Many legal scholars believe that the structure of English common law was directly copied from Muslim law after the eleventh century.

Thus, Islam managed to convert the sparsely populated civilizations of central and West Asia and Iberia to its fold early in the phase and put the Indian civilization on the defensive and European civilization in an offensive mood toward the end of this phase. Islam had little impact on China or Southeast Asia, with both remaining under the influence of Hinduism and Buddhism during this phase.

Manichaeism: Manichaeism, as we saw in the last chapter, was a dualistic gnostic religion that had carved a nice niche for itself in central and West Asia. However, tolerant monotheism preached by Manichaeism had no chance against the aggressive, uncompromising monotheism of the Islamic variety, and by the end of this phase, Manichaeism had just about disappeared from the face of the earth.

Achievements in Philosophical Creativity

Metaphysics: It is impossible to do justice to great Muslim philosophers without a clear understanding of the Muslim theology within the confines of which their thought progressed. The four key premises of Islamic theology are the existence of God as a personal being, his creation of a fixed but lawful nature for man's enjoyment, his creation of man with free will, and his judgment (heaven and hell) of man's actions. Thus, Islamic theology is a theodicy and is theocentric and anthropocentric. It is essentially similar to Christian theology, except it lacks the concepts of holy trinity and original sin, the omission of both must be considered as improvements. The question of this theology being influenced by any other system did not arise, as the Koran itself was the last word of God. Thus, when Muslim scholars came in contact with the intertwined Indian religious and philosophical systems ranging from polytheism to monism to agnosticism to atheism, they were brushed aside. It was, of course a different matter with Indian science. Thus, Muslim philosophy turned to Greek sources, where philosophy was separated from theology and where theology was less developed. We may, therefore, think of Muslim philosophy as fundamentally deriving from Greek philosophy. It was indeed a safe foundation to begin from, given the Koran's revealed nature. Below, we review the thought of the four great Muslim philosophers: al-Farabi (873–950 CE), Avicenna (980–1037 CE), al-Ghazali (1058–1011 CE), and Averroes (1126–1198 CE). These men were not only philosophers but also great polymaths and greatly contributed to many other fields, as we shall see below.

Al-Farabi, a Persian, was a polymath excelling in many fields. Of his surviving 117 books, 43 are on logic, 11 on metaphysics, 7 on ethics, 7 on political science, 11 commentaries, and 17 on music, medicine, and sociology. As a philosopher, he believed in neo-Platonism, which is a form of idealistic monism. Not surprisingly, he differed from Plato in that his ideal state would be ruled, not by a philosopher-king but by an Imam-prophet. His main focus was to synthesize Muslim theology with the thought of Plato and Aristotle—an impossible task in that the three systems conflict with one another. However, his efforts did help pave the way for the emergence of Sufism later. To his credit, al-Farabi recognized the importance of logic, physics, mathematics, and metaphysics in philosophy.

Avicenna, also a Persian, clarified the relationship between Aristotle's concepts of existence and essence, arguing that existence is contingent and is brought about by the action of a cause on the essence. His belief in reconciliation between neo-Platonism and Aristotle's thought is based on this notion. This is difficult to understand, since Aristotle believed that essence or universals resided in the object (he had brought Plato's preexisting forms from heaven to earth, so to speak) with only the particulars apparent to us. Neo-Platonism postulates the existence of preexisting essences outside the object and to which visible object owes its existence. Avicenna never suspected that that universals and essence may only belong to the mind and may only be a means to understand the object, as Kannada had postulated fifteen hundred years earlier.

Al-Ghazali, again a Persian, is most remembered for writing the book *Incoherence of Philosophers,* in which he totally rejected both Plato and Aristotle. He was perhaps the first Muslim philosopher to suspect the incompatibility of critical philosophy and a closed revealed religion. He denounced both the Greek tradition and the Muslim philosophers who ascribed to that tradition and thought that the work of Plato and Aristotle was incompatible with Islam. It is curious that on the one hand, he believed that material substances cannot be the cause of natural events, and on the other hand, he supported scientific methodology. In other words, the cause of events is God, and nature appears lawful because God is rational and consistent. Thus, he was not antiscience, only antiphilosophy since the philosophical question for him was already settled by the Koran. The claim that he discovered philosophical skepticism appears exaggerated to us, since al-Ghazali attributed the cause to God and was not unsure about it. It is also interesting to note that once we question the notion that God is the cause of natural events, we are led, rather quickly, to the doctrine of dependent co-origination, which simply says that substances are one another's reciprocal causes. There is no transcendental cause of events. Thus, while Islam forced al-Ghazali to rightly reject the philosophical idealism inherent in Greek philosophy, it also made al-Ghazali reject critical philosophy since it would lead him away from Islam and toward agnosticism and possibly materialism.

A century later, Averroes, an Arab, wrote a rebuttal to al-Ghazali in *The Incoherence of Incoherence.* He spelled out his belief that religion and philosophy were two different ways of approaching the truth; the former cannot be tested, and the latter is only open to the intellectually gifted. That, of course, presupposes that there can be no conflict between the two, which is not true. Averroes is closer to the mark when he brilliantly states that existence precedes essence or essence resides in existence. However, perhaps it was too late by then, as political control had passed into the hands of Turks, and a sharia-dictated way of life had thoroughly penetrated the Muslim mind.

From this rather brief description of Muslim philosophy, we can discern three separate streams of thinking: an unsuccessful attempt to synthesize Muslim theology to the Greek idealist philosophical tradition, an insistence that theology and philosophy must be kept separate, and theology must dictate philosophy. The first resulted from a desire to provide a status to the Muslim theology, the second from a desire to further science, and the last from a realization that this was an impossible task given a refusal to give up the revealed truth in the Koran. The Koran, therefore, defined the limits of philosophical speculation by Islamic philosophers. It is hardly an unusual fate for religious philosophers refusing to give up an a priori belief system.

There was yet a fourth line of thinking, where an attempt was made to severely restrict and reduce philosophy to jurisprudence, notably by al-Raziq. Again, this line of thinking assumed the philosophical truth to be already revealed in the Koran, and it was simply a matter of working it out through jurisprudence—i.e., how should a Muslim live in society on this earth? In the end, ultimately, critical philosophy lost and Islam won. Any time in monotheistic civilization, if critical philosophy loses, it spells the end of science, for science and monotheism are incompatible, and critical philosophy has been a time-tested weapon of choice to attack monotheism.

Epistemology: Muslim epistemology is quite impressive, but it ultimately suffered from the same limitations as Muslim philosophy: it wanted to be consistent with the Koran, and it was unable to move beyond clarifying Plato and Aristotle. As al-Kindi, al-Farabi, Ibn Bajja, Averroes, Avicenna, Ibn Tufayl, and Ibn Yaqzam developed it over centuries, Muslim epistemology may be briefly summarized as follows: True knowledge is essential for human happiness, and this knowledge may be obtained through two different means: prophetic revelation or philosophical reflection. The former is effortless and complete, and the latter is progressive and slow. Knowledge may also be viewed as self-evident or mediated by senses and logic. Both prophetic knowledge and mediated philosophical knowledge requires the acquisition of the essence, not superficiality, of things. These essences or universals exist independent of the ordinary objects existing in the world (Plato's preexisting forms). If one follows the path of philosophical reflection to knowledge, these essences come to the human mind in an impure form mixed with the sense data (that is, Aristotle's universals residing in the object). The internal senses of imagination and reason then extract these pure essences or universals from the sense data. This process of extraction goes through two phases, called the explanatory phase and the proof phase. The explanatory phase consists of identifying a structure relevant to the universal (genus, species, and difference) and accidentals (specific and generic) properties of the universal. The proof phase that helps in understanding of the essence of things is one that moves from known to the unknown universals.

One can see that Kant is absent, but Hegel is present in full force. However, Kannada is also conspicuous by absence. True knowledge is the essence of things. It is preexisting and possible through God's grace and reflection. The idea that universals are a product of the human mind to aid and understand is absent. This is a somewhat limiting epistemology. It must be stated and did not prevent Muslim scientists from achieving dramatic results in many fields as long as they did not conflict with the Koran's revealed truth.

Ethics: There are two trends in the history of Islamic ethics: an early one that amounts to commentaries on Plato, Aristotle, and other Greek writers and second an Islamic ethics derived from the Koran. The commentaries reinforce the Aristotelian distinction between moral and mental virtues. They, however, insist that evil is only a result of human action and has no independent existence. Islamic ethics starts with the presumption that human beings are naturally inclined to submit to Allah and become Muslims; however, this is subverted by the desire for material possessions and greed. Thus, personal ethics in Islam are focused toward character building through the five principles of Islam: submission to Allah, daily prayers, charity, fasting, and pilgrimage. It is not just belief and acceptance of Allah; it is the actions that matter. Through its early centuries, Islamic ethics shows developments in environmental ethics, medical ethics, military ethics (rules of engagement, treatment of prisoners of war), and political ethics (peace and justice, rule of law, and social welfare) were all driven by an underlying limited humanism (equality of free Muslim men) of global scope and ambition.

The philosophical and religious strands were brought together by al-Ghazali in the following manner: the goal of ethics is happiness. Happiness is either otherworldly or this-worldly. However, this-worldly ethics are necessary for otherworldly happiness, and happiness in this world depends on mental virtues (courage, wisdom, temperance, and justice), physical virtues (health, strength, longevity, and strength), social virtues (family, wealth, status, and noble birth), and divine virtues (guidance, counsel, direction, and support).

Closer examination of Muslim ethics leads to three fundamental problems: the gap between theory and practice by nearly all Muslim states, particularly with regard to the treatment of non-Muslims (and in particular non-Muslims who were not People of the Book), slaves, and women. It is indeed difficult to reconcile the theory of Islamic ethics with the practice of a frequent tax on non-Muslims, polygamy, violent aggressions, and jihad.

Thus, similar to metaphysics and epistemology, Muslim ethics were bound by its Greek heritage and the Koran, with the latter always having the last word.

Achievements in Art

Two aspects of Muslim art stand out during its formative period: it borrowed heavily from the people it conquered, most notably from Christian Spain and Persia, and since Persian art was influenced by Byzantine art under the Sassanians, Muslim art also owes a great deal to the Byzantine Empire and hence Roman art. Secondly, the impact of Islam forbidding certain art forms, such as representing images of God, music, and dance.

Visual arts: The focus of Islamic architecture was the mosque, tomb, forts, and palaces. Early mosques were constructed in hypo style and included one minaret and a prayer hall, such as the great Tunisian mosque of Kairouan, which is done in Arab style. Later mosques evolved into more elaborate forms under Christian and Persian influence and included four *Iwans* or entrances, multiple domes, a courtyard or *sehan*, fountains, and gardens. The mosques used geometric decorative design, sublime calligraphy, often bright colors, and paid special attention to both interior and exterior space in the Persian manner by creating an impression of openness, light, and breeze welcomed in. Notable examples are the Great Mosque at Cortoba, which was converted from a church over a period of two centuries; the Mosque of Ahmad ibn Tulun; and the Mosque of al-Hakim, which was built in the eleventh century in Egypt.

The early palace design was copied from Roman villas, incorporating a bathhouse, residential area, a mosque, and garden, including an irrigation system. These palaces were to evolve into the grandeur of Alhambra in Spain and Akbar's Fatehpur Sikiri Palace in India under Persian inspiration that we cover in the next chapter. Sometimes, the palace, fort, mosque, and tomb existed within a fort setting.

Performing arts: Islam did not encourage performing arts. There was little by way of developing dance, music, and theater in the early Muslim world. As Islam adopted different cultures, the attitude toward the performing arts was strongly influenced by the conquered culture. Thus, we witness the emergence of Sufism's adoption of dance and music as Islam came in contact with mystical traditions that used music and dance as a way to reach God. In these circumstances, Islam had to balance what was a cultural norm and what religion forbid. However, puppet shows and passion plays were popular in the early Islamic world.

Literature: Literature was not ignored in Islamic civilization during the current phase. The book of *1001 Arabian Nights* was compiled from Persian folk tales and must be classified as fantasy. The first ever murder mystery story is included in *1001 Arabian Nights*. On the other hand, Sindbad the sailor and Aladdin were inspired by Arab imagination. The tragic-romantic poem "Laila Majnun" was probably written in the eighth century in the Ummayad caliphate in Spain. Umar Khayyam wrote *Les Rubbayats*, or one thousand four-line verses, in the twelfth century. The Persian epic *Shahnameh* was composed in the tenth century. The satirical poem known as *hija* was also introduced during the current period by al-Jahiz, who developed the notion that a serious subject could be made easy to learn if it was made humorous. On the nonfiction side, early Muslim writers produced manuals of facts, history, and geography. Biographical writing included the *Book of the Genealogy of the Noble* by Persian scholar al-Baldhuri, and Ibn Khurdadhbih, a postal clerk, wrote the world's first travel book. Ibn Battuta wrote another about his travels in non-Muslim countries. Ibn Tafil may be considered the father of philosophical novels. *Hayy ibn Yaqdhan* is based on a boy who lives alone in the desert with animals and discovers civilization.

15.39 Achievements in Science

Achievements in Formal Sciences

During the early centuries of the phase, both mathematical and physical sciences were relatively free from the Koran's limitations, and building on Greek and Indian foundations, they made outstanding progress.

Mathematics: Muslim mathematicians made outstanding contributions to all known fields in mathematics and pioneered new fields.

Arithmetic: Al-Khwarizmi (?–846) wrote the book *al-Jamwal-tarriq ibn-hisab al-hind*, introducing the Arabic world to the Indian numeral system, replacing the cumbersome Roman numeral system. Within a century and a half, the system was transmitted to the West as well.

Algebra: Al-Khwarizmi, again based on the Indian algebraist Brahmagupta's work, defined rules to solve algebraic equations algebra through two concepts of *jabar* (transposition) and *muquabla* (reduction). The science of algebra continued its remarkable process over the next three centuries, with solutions of equations with five unknowns by Abu kamal Shuja, cubic equations by al-Khazin and Khayyam (1050–1123) in the twelfth century, and al-Tusi developing the concepts of a mathematical function and founded the branch of algebraic geometry. The Arab word *sei* (thing) written in Europe as *xei* became the symbol x for the unknown variable in algebra.

Al-Khujandi (1000), Nasir al-Din, and al-Biruni all made significant contributions in number theory.

Geometry: The Banu Musa brothers translated Greek works on geometry into Arabic and wrote on conical sections. *Thabit ibn Quarra* generalized the Pythagorean theorem and provided a proof. Abu'l-Wafa and Abu Nasr Mansur pioneered the spherical geometry needed in astronomy. Several Muslim geometers critiqued the Euclidean parallel postulate.

Calculus: Al-Haytham found the integrals for polynomials of fourth degree and was a key contributor to the development of calculus. In the twelfth century, the Persian mathematician Sharaf al-Dīn al-Tūsī discovered the derivative of cubic polynomials, thus contributing to the development of differential calculus.

Trigonometry: Arab and Persian mathematicians translated early Indian works on trigonometry. Several Muslim mathematicians developed it significantly and produced correct trigonometric relationships for plane and spherical trigonometry.

Logic: Much like philosophy and epistemology, the science of Muslim logic had its origins in Greek tradition, with many authors writing commentaries on Aristotle, starting with al-Farabi. He also introduced the theory of conditional syllogism and analogical inference needed in qiyas and made the study of logic easier by dividing it into two categories: *takhayyul* (idea) and *thubut* (proof). Avicenna had a decisive influence on the development of Islamic logic. He developed the theory of hypothetical syllogism, propositional calculus, temporal modal syllogism, and made contributions to inductive logic. Al-Raji also developed a system of inductive logic. Finally, al-Din Suhrawardi developed the concept of decisive necessity, where all modalities must collapse into one. The age of innovation in logic came with Ashari school of philosophy, which held that comprehending God was impossible, faith is more important than reason, and God is the reason behind the change that humans interpret as reason. This was the beginning of the closing of the Muslim mind. This view also found support with Ottoman later, who took the Muslim strategic advantage in practical technologies for granted and turned away from science. The science of logic suffered right along.

Linguistics: The earliest Arabic grammarian is Abi Ishaq, who died in 735. Sibawayh is the greatest grammarian of the Arabic language, and his study of Arabic phonetics is precise, leading some to compare his achievement with Panini's work of nearly a millennium and half earlier. His contributions greatly helped spread Arabic language throughout West Asia.

Achievements in Physical Sciences

Astronomy: Muslim astronomy has had a brilliant past and raised serious questions about the accuracy of the geocentric Ptolemy model of planetary motion with epicycles during this phase and came very close to overthrowing it all together, as we shall see in the next chapter.

We may summarize the progression of Muslim astronomy during the current phase in two stages. The earliest stage was when Muslim astronomers absorbed the Indian and Greek astronomy and through the latter the results of Babylonian astronomy. This period lasted for nearly a century and was essentially over by the early decades of the ninth century. The second stage lasted well into the eleventh century and was marked by two fundamental developments: a collection of astronomical data and seriously questioning the Ptolemy planetary model.

- Jafar ibn Musa (803–873) proposed the concept of gravitation force and suggested that laws that govern the celestial bodies also govern the motion of objects on earth.
- Al-Balkhi (787–886) did not claim a heliocentric theory, but defined the orbital motions around the sun and not earth. For some unknown reason, his work was not followed up. Unlike Aryabhatta, he did not talk about the earth's rotation on its axis, however.
- Al-Khwarizimi (780–850) mapped motions of the sun and motion of five planets.
- Al-Battani (853–929) proposed elliptical orbits and calculated the precession of the earth's axis.
- Al-Khujandi (940–1003) calculated the tilt of the earth's axis.
- Al-Haytham (965–1039) was the first to criticize the Ptolemy model on an empirical basis.
- Al-Sijzi(945–1020) stated that the earth rotates on its axis, and according to al-Biruni proposed a heliocentric model.
- Ibn Bajjah (1085–1139) proposed a planetary model without epicycles with eccentric orbits.
- Al-Biruni (973-1048) discussed heliocentric model but was neutral with respect to its advantage over the Ptolemy model.
- Al-Zarqali (1029–1087) revolted against the Ptolemy model and proposed elliptical orbits.
- Averroes (1126–1198) also proposed elliptical orbits and a concentric model.
- Al-Khazini incorrectly proposed in early twelfth century that the force of gravity is inversely proportioned to distance.
- Al-Rahman (903–986) sited a galaxy and mapped the stars, and Ibn Ridwan (982–1061) observed a supernova.
- The idea of elliptical orbits was also put forth by Abu Ishaq al-Zarqali in 1080 CE.
- It has been suggested that Omar Khayyam advanced the concept of heliocentrism and the earth spinning on its axis.

Thus, it is clear that there was a general consensus that the Ptolemy model of planetary motion was wrong, and initial steps (elliptical orbit, the earth's rotation, and the idea of heliocentric model) were taken in an attempt to correct it.

Laws of terrestrial motion: It is in the laws of motion that Muslim physicists came closest to the correct view, going way beyond the Greek and Indian speculations. Muslim physicists felt free to go beyond the Greek speculations because, unlike in philosophy, ethics, and epistemology, there was little constraint from Islam. All the scientists mentioned were devout Muslims and believers.

- Al-Haytham maintained that a body continues in uniform motion unless acted by a force (Newton's first law).
- Avicenna discovered the concept of momentum as equal to mass times velocity.
- Al-Baghdadi discovered that force varies proportional to acceleration (Newton's second law).
- Ibn Bajjah stated that each force has a reaction to it (Newton's third law).
- Averroes was first to introduce the concept of inertia and that of force as the rate at which work is done to change the motion of a body.(Newton's first and second laws).

We do not know if Prasaspada's work from the seventh century was translated or transmitted to the Muslims. Muslims contributions in the laws of terrestrial motion stand more than halfway between Prasaspada's work and the pioneering achievement of Galileo and Newton's final formulation.

Optics: Al-Haytham (965–1040) was indeed the father of optics. He developed a correct theory of vision and studied the eye as an optical system, though providing a wrong explanation of the eye lens as the receptor of light. He formulated laws of reflection, studied refraction, and experimented with lenses and mirrors. He provided correct explanation of the camera obscura and moon effect—i.e., why the moon appears larger when near horizon. Al-Haytham also studied the rainbow but provided a wrong explanation of why rainbows occur. Finally, he correctly surmised that velocity of light must be finite. Avicenna (960–1037) proposed a particle theory of light and also believed that light had a finite speed.

Hydrodynamics: Al-Khazini wrote *The Book of the Balance of Wisdom*, in 1121, which discussed theories of statics and hydrodynamics. The book discusses the construction and uses of hydrostatic balance including the instruments, such as the aerometer and pycnometer flask. He was an outstanding maker of scientific instruments.

Chemistry: Experimental chemistry as a science was single-handedly created by the Muslims, who introduced controlled experiments and precise measurements to chemistry. They distinguished alkalis and acids and investigated their reactions. Alchemy, though itself misdirected, made possible numerous incidental discoveries and new experimental methods. The ninth century chemist, Geber (Jabir ibn Hayyan), was a pioneer of chemistry and introduced the experimental method in chemistry through processes such as distillation, filtration, evaporation, liquefaction, crystallization, purification, and oxidization.

Botany/zoology: Aristotle's works were well known to Muslim zoologists. Muslim biologists developed theories on evolution, which were widely taught in medieval Islamic schools. Muslim biologist al-Jahiz (781–869) developed a theory of evolution and environmental determinism in explaining different skin colors and studied the effects of the environment on the survival of animals and the struggle for existence. Al-Jahiz also studied food chains. Ibn al-Haytham proposed a theory of evolution, though without the concept of natural selection.

Geography and earth sciences: Many books on environmental sciences and pollution were written by Muslim scientists, such as al-Tamimi, al-Masihi, Avicenna, al-Kindi, al-Razi, Ibn al-Jazzar, Ali ibn Ridwan, Abd-el-lati, and Ibn al-Nafi. For the first time, a world atlas was produced in 1154 CE by Arab geographer Mohammed al-Idrisi, interestingly, by Norman king Roger II of Sicily.

Achievements in Biological Sciences

Medicine: Building on the works of Indian and Greek medical achievements, both of which were translated into Arabic, Muslim physicians made significant contributions in anatomy, ophthalmology, pathology, pharmacy, pharmacology, physiology, and surgery. Muslim states set up some of the earliest dedicated hospitals. Hundreds of new drugs were extracted from plants.

Avicenna established experimental medicine and wrote *The Canon of Medicine* (1025) and *The Book of Healing* (1027), both standard textbooks in many parts of the world until the eighteenth century. He studied the nature of infectious diseases and their spread through water and other mediums. He was responsible for developing the concept of clinical trials. He wrote on the importance of diet and climate on health. We owe him a clear description of sexually transmitted diseases, dermatological disorders, tuberculosis, and nervous ailments. He also pioneered the use of ice to bring fever down.

Averroes wrote a seven-volume medical encyclopedia entitled *Kitābu'l Kulliyāt fī al-Tibb* (*General Rules of Medicine*) in 1162 and twenty other books on medicine. He had thorough knowledge of anatomy, physiology, pathology, diagnosis, and general therapeutics. He seemed to understand the human immune system intuitively and observed that no one can suffer from smallpox twice. He was also first to understand the correct function of the retina.

Ibn Zuhr introduced the experimental method into surgery through refining surgical procedures on animals. He studied anatomy through dissection and post mortems.

There were many other talented Muslim physicians, too numerous to be mentioned, who made great contributions to medical science.

Achievements in Social Sciences

Political science: A book by Niza al-Mulk in the twelfth century called *Siyasatnama* discusses political theory and administration of the state.

Summarizing Achievements in Abstract Systems-Building Capability (ASBC)

By the end of the phase, the ASBC of the Muslim civilization must be characterized as world-class: it had alphabetical script, had mastered creative method and sound epistemology, adopted the decimal system, absorbed the importance of controlled experiments in the heavens, and broke new ground in creating the experimental method here on earth, particularly in optics and chemistry. What they lacked was a science of calculus and hence the ability to quantify the results of their experimental observations in astronomy and motion here on earth.

Summarizing the State of Civilization and Science

15.40 The State of Civilization and Science at Phase End

Overview of History of the Phase

The current phase began with ascendant Arab nomads unable to succeed in India but who continued their significant success in Europe. The Chinese civilization was overwhelmed by Jin nomads from northern China. However, by the end of the phase, the leadership of the emerging Muslim civilization had passed from Arabs to Persian to Turkish groups, whom the Arabs had originally hired as mercenaries. The Chinese civilization successfully absorbed the Jins. By the end of the phase, while the Arabs were losing control in Europe, Muslim Turks were gaining a strong foothold in the Indian subcontinent. For the first time in history, two groups of central Asian nomads had converted to a self-assured, intolerant monotheistic religion.

State of Civilization

As in previous chapters, before leaving the significant outcomes section, it is useful to pause and summarize the state of civilization at the end of phase V. We will do so by summarizing the state of knowledge, success in applying knowledge to practice, and state of *Homo sapiens* conflict. Knowledge is what separates *Homo sapiens* from other life forms—knowledge not applied is essentially useless and conflict prevents some *Homo sapiens* from achieving these two objectives.

If the current phase belonged to Muslim civilization, the Muslim civilization was shaped by the two-millennia-old Persian culture. Persian Islam and not Arab Islam, which by the ninth century had exhausted itself, influenced both central Asia and the Turkish people already in West Asia and through them, India. It is not an exaggeration to see the area from Anatolia to India as area under the influence of Persian culture propagating itself through Islam through architecture, poetry, medicine, philosophy, and literature. Arabic script remained confined to religion. Great names, such as Omar Khayyam, al-Ghazali, and Avicenna were all Persian.

State of Practical Creativity

Practical technology made outstanding progress in several key areas, including textiles, mining, architecture, energy sources, and tools, thanks primarily to the Chinese civilization. Since the rising Muslim civilization was the geographical and political center surrounded by Indian, Chinese, and European civilizations and since the Muslim civilization had the upper hand in trade by far during the current phase, the Muslim civilization was the key mediator in spreading practical technology.

State of Religious Creativity

The state of religion had also taken a step backward. No new systems of faith were created, and no syntheses of existing faiths were attempted. Monotheism in the form of Christian and Islamic dogma was ascendant, as was monism in India. Even though new Buddhist states came into existence in Southeast Asia, Buddhism was on a long-term trajectory of decline since these states were too small to make a global impact. Clearly, peaceful agnosticism was in retreat in the face of aggressive and violent monotheism. Despite great openness, the one creative endeavor that was not open to unbiased analysis in the Muslim civilization was religion. Islam is God's final world to humanity for the Muslims, and it was not subject to interpretation and evolution. Thus, as Muslim civilization took the lead in developing scientific outlook and began to extend its thinking to areas such as astronomy and biology, it came in fundamental conflict with the Koran's teaching. If the universe and life are based on immutable laws and do not apparently require an imminent or transcendental deity, the Koran's teaching may be called into question. In fact, this is what happened to Muslim science and the fate of the third synthesis when the great al-Ghazali closed the door on science in the second half of twelfth century.

State of Philosophical Creativity

The state of philosophy was not good. Decline of Buddhism, the rise of monism and monotheism, and an unholy alliance between monotheism and Platonic philosophy was not good for critical philosophy. Philosophy in effect had become subservient to religion in European, Muslim, and Indian civilizations and remained focused on ethics in China under neo-Confucianism.

State of Artistic Creativity

The state of art improved primarily in the Byzantine, Persian, and Muslim civilizations. Indian art remained hostage to religious impulse. More specifically, visual arts and, to a lesser extent, literature, made progress; however, performing arts remained mostly static.

State of Scientific Creativity

The state of science also made great progress in mathematics, astronomy, and physics under the leadership of Muslim civilization but further progress was coming under pressure because of the conflict between Islam and science. Thus, during the current phase, natural science, with formal sciences making the greatest progress, did not succeed in freeing themselves from the clutches of religion. Laws of heavenly motion were not fully understood, with other natural sciences remaining underdeveloped. Since science was not yet in a position to directly impact the wealth-creation process because technological innovation was essentially independent of science, the impact of diffusion and development of science was indirect though still profound in our judgment.

State of Productive Outcomes

Civilizations and nomadic confederations were highly effective in spreading new developments in practical technology through travel, migration, and trade channels, resulting in significantly increased wealth creation, population increase from about 350 million to about 450 million, and a global trade system. However, the scope of sea travel remained confined to the Mediterranean Sea and Indian Ocean. There was migration of scholars from India to West Asia from the Byzantine Empire to Persia and the Italian Peninsula and from West Asia to India. As scientific creativity took root primarily in the Muslim and to a lesser extent continued in the Indian world, its impact on state administration, manufacturing, trade, legal systems, and war was considerable as all these activities were now open in principle to analytical fact-based analysis.

However, the relatively underdeveloped state of science and critical philosophy allowed religion to play a larger-than-life role in the affairs of the word. Monotheism used faith to control people of differing faith, and monism encouraged believers to shift focus away from science, critical philosophy, and art.

State of Constructive Outcomes

There were few constructive outcomes that did not occur in the wake of aggression of Muslim and central Asia converted to Islam.

State of Destructive Outcomes

The purpose of knowledge of the natural and social worlds and faith is human happiness. However, if the process of creating knowledge and applying it is based on excessive conflict, it becomes self-defeating. The present phase witnessed a significant increase in social inequality within a state, and wars among states within a civilization and extended conflicts among civilizations intensified. Social inequality within states was driven by Islamic faith, where only Muslim males were equal; a caste system where inequality was hereditary; and by feudalism, where only the wealthy and powerful were equal. Similarly, wars among states intensified because of greed and competition for control among states within the ascendant Muslim civilization, because of political fragmentation within Indian civilization and because of religious interference in politics. Finally, the conflict among civilizations also began in earnest. In the past, a powerful state, empire, or nomadic group attacked civilization and even conquered a good chunk of it. It was never a civilization against other civilizations. However, the unprecedented rise of a civilization that saw itself as different from other civilizations based on a faith that sanctioned violence to great power status was something new in the history of the world. The acquisition of transportation and weapons technology from other civilizations made such a rise possible and lasting.

All in all, good or even excellent progress in knowledge creation and its application in practice were made, but they were also accompanied by intensified conflicts at class, state, and civilization levels.

State of Scientific Creativity

Formal sciences: Arab and Persian mathematicians took algebra, number theory, and trigonometry to new heights while the Indian civilization made significant contributions to the development of infinitesimal calculus. Arabic grammar was put on a sound basis. Logic in the Muslim world was put on firmer ground through developments in the theory of hypothetical syllogism, propositional calculus, and temporal modal logic.

Astronomy: Astronomers exposed Ptolemy's planetary model as wrong and took early corrective steps, such as establishing the notions of elliptical orbit, the earth's rotation, and a heliocentric solar system.

Physics: All three laws of motion were stated, though not systematized or experimentally verified. This was a monumental achievement, given that the problem of solar astronomy had not yet been solved decisively. By contrast, the field of optics was put on a firm scientific basis.

Chemistry: The science of chemistry was put on a firm experimental basis, though it was still haunted by the ideas of alchemy.

Earth science: A world map was produced for the first time while Muslim scientists paid attention to environmental concerns and pollution.

Medicine: The experimental basis of medicine was firmly established, and a systematic approach to disease identification and treatment established.

Social sciences: For the first time since Chanakya in the fourth century BCE, a book, *Siyasanama*, was written about political science and the theory of a state.

Assessing Changes in the Inner Nature of Participants

15.41 Changes in the Inner Nature of European Civilization

Productive capacity: The societal structures and processes remain static with the exception of the evolving function of monasteries. Most of the population remained literate and had low skill. Thus, European civilization continued to lack economic freedom as it struggled under feudalism in the west and highly centralized structures in the east. Allocation to wealth creation was not valued, and foreign technology with the exception of military technology was more of a curiosity. Thus, the rate of new technology adoption was near zero. European civilization scored better in the area of internal inequality because of the abolition of Roman slavery system and Christian dogma that preached a questionable concept of equality in that all, not just Christians, were equal sinners in front of God. The social cohesion, despite excessive inequality, science-religion conflict, and internal wars, was good, thanks to the glue provided by the uncritical acceptance of Christian dogma in the west, and Christian faith and centralized bureaucracy in the east. Because of the internal wars, stability in control of SGS worsened for a number of reasons: the religious schism between east and west, the competition between Venice and the Byzantine Empire, the constant pressure of the Muslim civilization, and the active and effective role played by the pope to keep European polity fragmented. Thus, destructive internal wars were frequent, and sustained political independence was a mixed bag because of Muslim pressure. The western flank had lost political freedom to the Arabs at the beginning of this phase, and the eastern flank had been checked by Seljuk Turks toward the end of this phase. Only the center was able to hold its independence (except for Arab control of Sicily), and this center centuries later would rise to produce science during the Italian synthesis and pass the results on to the western European synthesis. We cover these in chapter 16. We would judge the productive capacity of the European civilization to be at a low point during this phase.

Creative capacity: Allocation to creative endeavors was primarily in religious creativity through building churches, palatial residences for religious leaders, and monasteries. Christian dogma stymied creative freedom and openness, though one sees definite attempts to rise above it during the last decades of the phase in Christian monasteries egged on by Muslim achievements next door in Iberia. In this lack of openness, it was much like South India: thoroughly religious and uninterested in the intellectual achievements of North India. Christian creed ensured a mind-numbing science-religion conflict and even modest scientific discovery at variance with religion could only be published at great personal peril. Of course, there was little danger of such a breakthrough coming out of the European mind during the current phase.

It is fair to say that up to this point in its history, central, western and northern Europe had shown little interest in science; rather, it had actively and repeatedly walked away from Greek and Hellenistic achievements centered in Greece, Egypt, and Asia. On the other hand, the abstract systems-building capability was improving because of the Arab presence and their import of decimal numerals. Thus, creative capacity must be judged to be low and narrow.

Constructive orientation: European civilization has roots in Mesopotamian, Egyptian, and Phoenician civilizations; ancient Greek city-states; the Roman Republic and the Roman Empire, and the Hellenistic states. All these actors have had aggression and imperial tendencies to one degree or another. However, they differed considerably in their openness to the intellectual creativity of other civilizations (Mesopotamian and Greek civilizations and the Hellenistic states were quite open while the Roman Republic, Roman Empire, and Egypt were markedly less so). To be specific, there was little linguistic or geographical isolation. The question of early success against nomads leading to insularity as a factor is also irrelevant. The unreflective adoption of Christian creed determined the constructive orientation of the European civilization during the phase. Ironically, openness to religious creativity of others made Europeans insular to all three forms of creativity: focus on religion and salvation meant little interest in practical creativity; the notion of Christianity as the only valid metaphysics meant little openness to other religions anymore; and since even a modest challenge from science to Christian dogma was met forcefully, intellectual creativity with the exception of art was not valued. Thus, the European civilization may be generously characterized as having type1 openness during the phase.

Destructive orientation: The external orientation of European civilization during the current phase was decidedly more defensive and inward. The aggressive manifestation came late in the phase through the Crusades, rebellion against Arab control of Iberia, and the strength of the Venetian state. The former did not amount to much, except it intimated an aggressive stance in the making that would manifest itself more thoroughly centuries later. The rise of the Venetian state was highly significant, as we indicated above, but it was confined to the eastern Mediterranean. It too, however, intimated a coming control on the high seas centuries later by leading European states. The combination of a long history of institutional greed perfected through Roman imperialism, Christian dogma, and low natural bounty though kept in check by Muslim power did not bode well for other civilizations if European civilization ever attained power.

During the current phase, its aggression and imperial ambitions remained checked by the power of the Muslim civilization while its openness to the creativity of other civilizations remained hampered by its relatively newly adopted Christian faith. It was the worst of times for the young civilization.

15.42 Changes in the Inner Nature of the Chinese Civilization

Productive capacity: The sustainable growing surplus for the Chinese civilization must be judged to be high, given the improvements in practical technologies and resulting high new technology adoption as well as the continuing economic freedom championed by the first Song emperor and high social cohesion under the Tang and Song dynasties. Internal inequality was relatively low, and there were long periods of internal stability during this phase. The productive capacity must be judged high.

Creative capacity: Creative freedom was high in principle but remained confined to practical creativity since the Chinese civilization continued to underestimate the importance of alphabetical script. The first Song emperor created political institutions that fostered creative freedom, resulting in the growth of technology and achievements in arts and literature. Trade flourished both within China and overseas. Chinese technologists created a number of practical inventions of exceptional significance. However, as in previous periods, Chinese sensibilities remained practical, constrained as it was by the lack of alphabetical script in particular and abstract systems-building capability in general. There was little science-religion conflict despite limited religious persecution. The creative capacity too remained narrow but deep.

Constructive orientation: China could hardly be characterized as geographically isolated. The record against the nomads during the phase was mixed. China only displayed type 2 openness, remaining insular with respect to intellectual creativity of other civilizations.

Destructive orientation: China enjoyed political independence through most of this period, spared of the havoc Islamic aggression was causing in Europe and West and South Asia. China went through periods of aggression against neighboring states and civilizations with an uncharacteristic aggressive posture (though driven by defensive motives) during the phase.

Given its constructive and destructive orientation, the external orientation of Chinese civilization remained type 2.

15.43 Changes in the Inner Nature of the Indian Civilization

Changes in the Inner Nature of the North Indian Civilization

Productive capacity: The aftermath of the Hun invasion and resulting prolonged political fragmentation and the absence of large irrigation projects meant less state support and continued economic freedom, if only by default. However, technology wealth synergy and social cohesion suffered, which probably resulted in a slower growth in the sustainable growing surplus. North Indian civilization was also becoming less open, with less internal equality and increased internal aggression. The productive capacity remained high.

Creative capacity: The creative freedom existed despite precipitous drop in state support of the creative endeavors and creeping religious conservatism. The science-religion conflict, nonexistent in the previous phase, was raising its head and may be characterized as moderate. Thus, creative capacity may be judged to be less deep and less broad compared to the last phase fundamentally due to internal causes.

Constructive orientation: Likewise, openness suffered with religious injunctions against foreign travel rearing its head and may be characterized as type 1. This was a dramatic change for the Indian civilization.

Destructive orientation: Still with a mostly peaceful external orientation, North Indian civilization may be characterized as type I-B or externally a peaceful orientation and internally a religious orientation.

Given its constructive and destructive orientation, the external orientation of the Indian civilization was an unusual mixture of peacefulness and type 1 constructive orientation.

Changes in the Inner Nature of the South Indian Civilization

Productive capacity: South India was in a different mode during the current phase. Economic freedom made it possible for the agriculture, manufacturing guilds, and international trade to expand, resulting in wealth creation and a high sustainable growing surplus. Increasing overseas trade and manufacturing guilds also point to high-technology wealth synergy. Hinduism and the absence of foreign aggression ensured high social cohesion. Inequality in the south was more moderate than in the north in part because of increasing wealth. However, internal stability was at best moderate; the south continued to be a kaleidoscope of states through the phase. No single state became powerful enough to control all of the south. The South Indian civilization exhibited openness with respect to trade and religion.

Creative capacity: However, the creative freedom left a lot to be desired. Despite wealth, South India did not see an emergence of great universities during the current phase. The wealth from overseas trade was not invested to establish centers of learning or to give shelter to intellectuals from the north facing lack of financial support since North Indian kingdoms were under pressure from the Turkish invaders in the northwest; rather, it was spent to build magnificent temples and to support literary achievements. The surplus was, thus, directed into religious and artistic creativity. Consequently, one would be hard-pressed to see a dramatic change in its internal creative balance, which continued to focus on a religious-aesthetic orientation. There was little science-religion conflict since science was not pursued, and monism was not as strong even though the great Sankara, who systematized monism, hailed from the south.

Constructive orientation: If a change occurred in its inner nature, it was perhaps in the direction of openness to maritime trade and wealth creation. In this respect, it was similar to the rising Venetian state in the landlocked Mediterranean, except, the South Indian civilization was not violent. Venetia went on to build more palaces and palatial homes than churches, and Venetia was smaller and did not operate on the open seas. They both, however, wasted the surplus they created to support the elites here on earth. Where the two differed was in their religiosity. Venetia and Italy eventually inherited the fruits of the third synthesis taking place in Iberia, and South Indian states did not seek to take the mantle of North Indian science.

Destructive orientation: The external orientation remained essentially peaceful but with a strong motivation to keep the trade routes open based on diplomacy and force if needed. It was not, however, an orientation of outright empire building and continued to maintain its sustained political independence. North India was under pressure from Islamic tribes from the southern tier of central Asia, who were in turn under pressure from the Seljuk. It was falling under the sway of monism and the Bhakti movement, ironically imported from the south. As a result, while retaining its external peaceful nature, it was becoming a more conservative, religious, and spiritual, though without science-religion conflict. The South Indian civilization, on the other hand, was not under threat from Muslim invaders and was engaged in mostly peaceful expansion in Southeast Asia, exporting its culture and religion while expanding fair trade. Thus, while looking dramatically different in the north and south, Indian civilization remained with its peaceful external orientation and remained open under difficult circumstances.

15.44 Changes in the Inner Nature of Muslim Civilization

Three sequential contributors to the inner nature of Muslim civilization were Arab nomads, Persian civilization, and Turkish nomads.

Dynamic Inner Nature during the Phase

The early conquests in West Asia, Iberia and North Africa, and Sindh had a profound impact on the nomadic psyche of the Arabs. Most of these conquests occurred after the completion of the Koran but much before the completion of sharia. These conquests took Arabs to new lands, where they were a minority surrounded by enemies. They needed both friends and converts from the intellectuals and political classes as well as from the common man. As control of Muslim lands shifted from Arab to Persian to Turkish hands, there was little change in the productive and destructive aspects of the dynamic inner nature. However, the creative aspect underwent dramatic change.

Productive capacity: Under Muslim rule, economic freedom flourished as it encouraged broader land ownership and brought new lands under cultivation. Arabs by tradition were city dwellers and traders and thus encouraged commerce and foreign trade. Adoption of new practical technologies was helpful in wealth creation. Earliest Islam was admirably egalitarian with respect to free Muslim males with focus on God's work through fair and foul means. However, within a century, as the empire expanded, all that egalitarianism was quickly forgotten. The ruling dynasties and upper classes began to live in luxury and assembled royal courts and harems, much like Persians and Romans. The requirement of charity and the inflow of trade wealth and loot as well as an injunction against interest meant that wealth polarization was not excessive. There were few mass rebellions in Muslim states, primarily because the state was seen as an instrument of God's will and as God's instrument. How could a common man, who had swallowed the Islamic message, engage in rebellion against the state? Thus, we would characterize the state of internal equality in most Islamic states during the present phase as moderate for its Muslim population. Internal equality among Muslim men must be judged relatively high despite the existence of slavery because all Muslim men were equal before God, there was an injunction against interest in Islam, and there was a need to befriend the political and intellectual classes in the conquered lands, giving rise to a sensible meritocracy. The overall internal equality under Muslim civilization started out as high, and by the end of this phase, because of the increasing importance of slavery and the deteriorating position of women and non-Muslims must be characterized as low. The wars among Muslim states were a different matter, however. Islam was born in violence and remained mired in internal violence throughout the current phase. The leadership of Muslim civilization passed from Arabs to Persians to Turks in a highly violent manner. In addition, the wars of succession were often brutal because there were no rules of succession in place. Similarly, there was little tolerance among the different sects within Islam, in particular the Shia and Sunni. We would characterize internal aggression among Muslim states as high throughout the current phase. This however, is not different from any other externally aggressive civilization in history, since the opportunity for conquest leads to internal competition, much like the British-French rivalry in the eighteenth and nineteenth centuries. The productive capacity, despite a strong position in trade, must be characterized as moderate.

Creative capacity under the Arabs: In this process of gaining friends and converts, Arab conquerors saw fit to support the Persian, Greek, and Indian achievements and ensured creative freedom. Political support of Greek learning was helpful in winning over the intellectual classes. Since the Koran's interpretation of the period favored new knowledge except in matters of religion, the Arabs adopted a type 3 openness to the creativity of other civilizations. The science-religion conflict was yet to emerge since the existing science and foreseeable limits of future science was yet to contradict the Koran.

Creative capacity under the Persians: With Arab conquest in the seventh century and the subsequent Persianization of the Arab rule under Abbasids and Buwayids, Persia was pulled into the third synthesis of science, thus benefitting from the Arab renaissance. The Persianization of Arab courts occurred relatively fast; however, conversion to Islam in Persia was a somewhat slower process. In the ninth century, only 40 percent of Persia was converted to Islam, with the number rising to essentially 100 percent by the end of the eleventh century. Thus, the internal creative balance of Persia turned intellectual during most of this phase, but it was so for the first and last time. Persia's experience with science-religion conflict and its openness to the creativity of other civilizations mirrored that of the Arab experience during this phase. It is a historic fact that even after the Persians freed themselves from Turkish influence in the sixteenth century, they never returned to science; instead, they returned to their pre-Islamic inner nature, in part because of a conversion to Islam and a changed interpretation of the Koran. Muslim civilization experienced severe science-religion conflict toward the end of this phase. The internal aggression among Muslim states remained high

Creative capacity under the Turks: Thus, after the eleventh century, as they assumed firm control of Muslim civilization, we would characterize the Turks as a people with a practical internal creative balance and severe science-religion conflict.

Constructive orientation: Not surprisingly, given the nomadic roots of the Arabs and Turks, Muslim civilization had a very constructive external orientation and remained open to the creativity of other civilizations and trade. This may be explained through several reasons: the nomadic background of Arabs and Turks implies openness, Islam was a young religion, all the implications of the Koran had not been worked out, and openness was a means to create allies in conquered lands. The constructive orientation of Seljuk must be described as open. They adopted Persian culture and supported literature, art, architecture, and science. They adopted Persian as court language and retained Arabic as the language of scholars. The Seljuk period may be seen as a hybrid of Iranian, central Asian, and Anatolian Turkish cultures and was the last major Muslim Empire in West Asia to show openness to science. However, by the end of the phase, the tide had turned against openness, and religious fundamentalism and an antiscience attitude had crept in.

As we shall note in the next phase, after this phase, central Asian nomads such as Genghis Khan and, to a lesser degree, other central Asians farther removed from the center of Muslim civilization, were the only ones who actively supported science. The open-minded Arabs of Iberia, the Moors, had vanished from the scene by the end of the phase. Muslim civilization exhibited type 1 openness toward the creativity of other civilizations.

Destructive orientation: We would characterize the Muslim civilization under Arab, Persian, and Turkish phases as extremely aggressive with respect to other civilizations. Muslim civilization as a whole retained its political independence during the current phase. All three incarnations of the Muslim civilization during the phase—Arab, Persian, and Turkish—had aggression against other civilizations in common, if nothing else. This is hardly surprising, given their nomadic and empire-building roots. The destructive orientation of Turkish Islam remained aggressive to the end, given their nomadic roots and their adoption of Islam. In their own words, they brought a fighting spirit and fanatical aggression.

Given its constructive and destructive orientation, the external orientation of the Muslim civilization was clearly transitioned from type III to type IV during the phase.

15.45 Changes in the Inner Nature of Central Asians

The most important central Asian group of the current phase were the Seljuk, who were hired as conscripts in the Abbasid armies in the ninth century and succeeded in taking over the Muslim caliphate in West Asia.

Productive capacity: Because of a temperate climate, the natural bounty was moderate but better than in arid central Asia. The Seljuk would hardly be classified as nomads any longer. They had lived a settled existence for couple of centuries when they came to power and had adopted the agriculture, manufacturing, and commerce of the conquered populations. Social cohesion based on tribal loyalties had suffered, despite the glue Islam provided. The focus of wealth allocation was military spending and monuments. Thus, given a low population density, the productive capacity was moderate, and increases in surplus remained highly dependent on conquests.

Creative capacity: Unlike all previous nomads groups, the Seljuk were the first to adopt Islam as Islam turned its back on science and thus faced a science-religion conflict. Clearly, the abstract systems-building capability was high, and they were open to the creativity of other civilizations.

The creative capacity was bequeathed by the third synthesis and was deep and broad except for the religious pressures.

Constructive orientation: The constructive orientation of the Seljuk rulers was open in matters relating to military and practical technologies and trade only. Adoption of Islam had ensured an insular nature relative to the religious and intellectual creativity of other civilizations.

Destructive orientation: The Seljuk, after settling down and adopting Islam during the second half of the phase, were no different from other empire builders had a natural "institutional greed" for fertile lands. However, like all nomads from central Asia, they had a memory of success in devastating civilizations and in fact succeeded in destroying the Roman Empire and weakening the Gupta Empire in India. They possessed exceptional aggression and violence, driven not by creed but by greed for more fertile land.

The key parameters that measure the changing inner nature of key participants in the current phase are summarized in table 15.5.

15.46 The Inner Nature of Participants at the End of Third Synthesis Phase

The current phase witnessed dramatic changes in the productive and creative capacity and constructive and destructive orientation of all major participants, except the central Asian nomads.

European Civilization

At the end of the current phase, European civilization had a low productive capacity as indicated by its low internal SGS, a type B2 creative capacity, a type 1 constructive, and a rekindled violent destructive external orientation as revealed through the Crusades.

Chinese Civilization

During the current phase, China continued to demonstrate high productive capacity with high internal SGS, a continuing type A creative capacity, and a type 2 openness. Uncharacteristically, Chinese civilization exhibited a modestly violent external orientation. Yet, we would hesitate to characterize the Chinese civilization as a warring civilization since its principal posture was defensive and was in response to the aggression of others.

Indian Civilization

During the current phase, North Indian civilization witnessed a decreasing productive capacity though still with a high internal SGS, a transition to type B1 creative capacity, and a greater insularity with type 3 openness and continuing peaceful external orientation. Indian civilization experienced a precipitous decline in its creativity capacity because of the Islamic ideology of the victors, political fragmentation, the decline of Buddhism, and a resurgence of excessive spirituality.

The South Indian civilization took a different direction, showing a high SGS, a type B1 ICB, a less destructive internal orientation, and a very assertive, though largely peaceful external orientation.

Muslim Civilization Including Seljuk

Muslim civilization, of course, achieved high moderate productivity with a moderate internal SGS, supplemented with trade profits and conquests, a creative capacity that transitioned from type C to type B2, a constructive orientation with a type 3 openness (until implications of the Koran

Table 15.5: Relative Values of Measurable Parameters of Social Orders
Third Synthesis, 750–1200 CE

Measurable Characteristics	Productive Capacity					Creative Capacity			Constructive Orientation			Destructive Orientation			
	EF	NTA	WAB	NB	SC	Creed	WAB	ASBC	GI	ESAN	LI	Creed	NB	IG	IC
European	Low	Low	ED	Mod	Mod	SRC	ED	Strong	Low	N/A	None	SRC	Mod	Low	High
Chinese	High	High	PE	High	High	Bal	PE	Weak	Low	Y/N	High	Bal	High	Low	Low
Indian	Med	Med	MS	High	Mod	ES	MS	Strong	Low	No	None	ES	High	low	None
Seljuks	High	High	MS	Low	Low	SRC	MS	Strong	Low	N/A	None	SRC	Low	Low	Low
Muslim	High	High	CE	Low	Low	SRC	CE	Mod	Low	N/A	None	SRC	Low	Low	Low

NB: Degree of Natural Bounty
EF: Economic Freedom
NTA: New Tech. Adoption
WAB: Wealth Allocation Bal.
SC: Social Cohesion
ASBC: Abstract Sys. Building Capability
GI: Geographic Isolation
ESAN: Early Success against Nomads
LI: Linguistic Isolation
IG: Institutional Greed
IC: Intolerant Creed
ED: Favors Elite Decadence
MS: Favors Military Spending
PE: Favors Productive Endeavors
CE: Supports Creative Endeavors
ES: Excessively Spiritual
SRC: Sci. Religion Conflict
Bal: Balanced

Table 15.6: Comparative Inner Nature of Participants
Third Synthesis, 750–1200 CE

Civilization	Productive Capacity Internal SGS	Creative Capacity ICB	Constructive Orientation O/I	Destructive Orientation P/V	SPI
Indian	Moderate	Type B1	Type 3	Peaceful	Yes
Chinese	High	Type A	Type 2	Peaceful	Yes
European	Low	Type B2	Type 1	Violent	No
Seljuks	Moderate	Type B2	Type 2	Violent	Yes
Muslim	Moderate	Type C ⇒ Type B2	Type 3	Violent	Yes

SGS: Sustainable Growing Surplus
ICB: Internal Creative Balance
O/I: Openness/Insularity
P/V: Peaceful/Violent
SPI: Sustained Political Independence

were understood), and a destructive orientation combining an intolerant creed and violent aggression. In this phase, Indian and Muslim civilizations essentially switched roles relative to creative capacity, just as Muslim and European civilizations will be switching roles in the next phase.

The comparative inner nature of participants is summarized in table 15.6.

The Evolution and Rationalization of the Third Synthesis of Science

15.47 Third Synthesis in Science

Like the previous phase, this phase also saw development mostly within one civilization. Muslim civilization led the charge with modest continuing contributions from the Indian civilization. The Byzantine Empire had been significantly weakened by Muslims, Indian civilization remained politically fragmented and had rediscovered monism and devotional Hinduism, Europe remained on the defensive with respect to Muslim civilization and under the stifling influence of Christianity, and the Persian civilization whole-heartedly joined the Muslim world in the science project and even led it for a while.

Thus, the rising Muslim civilization alone was in a position to carry forward science for several centuries until toward the end of the current phase, when they discovered their own version of doctrinaire monotheism. Science therefore:

- Moved forward mostly in Muslim civilization with an occasional significant contribution from the Indian civilization.
- There were strong linkages between the Muslim civilization and all other past contributors to science: Indian civilization and Greek and Hellenistic learning preserved in Europe.
- These linkages resulted mostly in the aftermath of violent aggression by Muslim civilization against both Europe and India. These linkages among civilizations, in the wake of violence, are summarized in figure 15.1.

Thus, science remained in the development life stage and completed the third of the four syntheses primarily under the leadership of Muslim civilization. Indian and Muslim civilizations remained open to the creativity of other civilizations and retained political independence, but it was Muslim civilization, by far, that led in contributions toward the development of science and the scientific method. European and Chinese civilizations remained relatively insular. While the former continued to experience a loss of political independence at the hands of Muslim civilization, the latter remained free. However, neither made notable contribution toward science and the development of scientific method.

Linking Indian, Greek, Hellenistic, and Muslim Science

Readers will recall the religion of Islam was born at a time of a worldwide power vacuum: the Byzantine and Sassanian Empires had weakened each other, the Huns and European barbarians had destroyed the Roman Empire, the Gupta and Harsha Empires in India had perished, and China suffered from famine and An Shi Rebellion. Both Europe and India had remained politically fragmented.

Chapter 15 · Third Synthesis of Science (750–1200 CE)

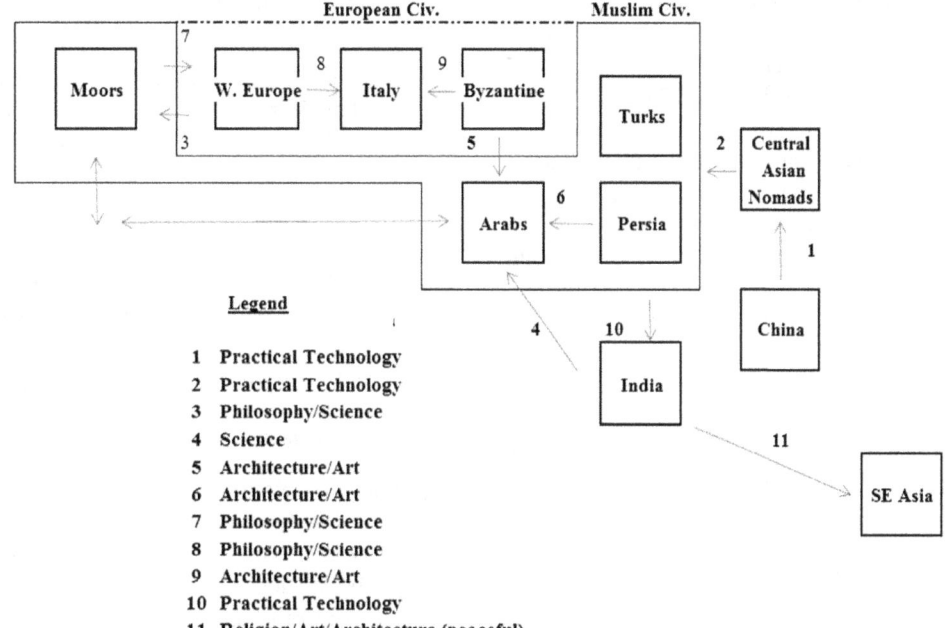

Figure 15.1: Interaction in the Wake of Violence
Third Synthesis, 750–1200 CE

Legend
1 Practical Technology
2 Practical Technology
3 Philosophy/Science
4 Science
5 Architecture/Art
6 Architecture/Art
7 Philosophy/Science
8 Philosophy/Science
9 Architecture/Art
10 Practical Technology
11 Religion/Art/Architecture (peaceful)

Between 760 and 750 CE, Arabs invaded, conquered, or controlled, to one degree or another, the entire region from Iberia to Sindh in India as well as Egypt. Thus, Arabs had access to Indian, Greek, and Hellenistic science at a time when there was little dynastic support for science in the world and at a time when fledging Arab states needed local support to legitimize their existence in the eyes of the conquered populations. Thus, the Arabs quickly assimilated the culture and knowledge of the people they conquered while holding fast to their religion and language. In the process, we witnessed the transformation of a people with little history in science into the leading proponents of science.

The Koran enthusiastically supported new knowledge with little premonition that only a few short centuries later, it would turn against it with equal enthusiasm:

- They built schools, libraries, hospitals, and observatories throughout the Islamic states, ensuring adequate staffing and funding.
- They invited scholars to Damascus and Baghdad from all over the world.
- They translated books from all over the world into Arabic and produced commentaries on them.
- They internalized the newly acquired knowledge they had acquired, and by the end of the eighth century, they were in a position to claim the leadership and push forward with the third synthesis of science based on Indian, Greek, and Hellenistic achievements. The Indian civilization had begun this process in the previous phase but cut short because of the fall of the Gupta and Harsha Empires.

If the reader needs further proof that science is innate in *Homo sapiens* and will come into existence time and again when the conditions are right, it is right here before our eyes. Who would have guessed in the sixth century that science would move forward under Arab leadership?

Let us look at the specific linkages that made this transformation possible:

- Closest to home was the Nestorian Christian community that was oppressed by the intolerant Byzantine Empire and had taken shelter in Persia. This community had helped to establish the Gundeshapur academy, which was modeled after the Hellenistic academy in Alexandria under Khusrau in the sixth century. This academy, which apparently used the Syrian language and not Persian, had a hospital and an observatory. Caliph al-Mansoor invited two astronomers (Nawbakht and Masha'allah) when he founded Baghdad in 762 CE. When he fell ill in 765 CE, he invited the head physician at Gundeshapur, Bukhtyishu, to cure him. Thus, Hellenistic astronomy and medicine traveled to Baghdad through Nestorian Syrians and Persians.

- Arabs invaded Sindh in the latter part of the seventh century and were defeated by an Indian coalition in 738 CE but remained in the era as traders, thus ensuring ongoing contact. The assimilation of Indian mathematics and astronomy took place in three steps.

The first step was the translation of books, such as *Sindhind* and *Kand Khanak,* based on Brahmagupta's *Brahmasphutasiddhanta* around 750 CE. This book introduced Indian astronomical computation methods and Indian numerals. The visits by Indian scholars to Baghdad, probably in 772–773 CE was the second step. The third step was several books written by Arab scholars elucidating both the computation method and the numeral system, including Tarqueeb al-Alfaaq on *Arrangements of Orbits* by Yakub ibn Tariq in 778 CE. In the ninth century, the famous al-Khawarizmi (780–850 CE) wrote two books. The first was *Zij al-Sindhind,* and it was based on Indian astronomical methods. The book consisted of thirty-seven chapters and 116 tables, including a table containing sine values. It described the orbits of all seven heavenly bodies at the time. This work defined the direction of Muslim astronomy. The second book was *Hisab al-Hind,* and it was written in 825 CE, which was translated into Latin in 1126 CE as *Liber Algotizmi de Numero Indurum.* This book popularized the Indian decimal system in the Muslim world. Thus, over a hundred years, Muslim civilization internalized Indian astronomy and mathematics.

- In parallel, in Iberia under the Moors, Arab rulers established a close alliance with Spanish Jews who had a long history of being discriminated against by Visigoths. The Sephardim or Spanish Jewish scholars translated Greek and Hellenistic texts into Arabic. One famous work on neo-Platonic philosophy was produced by ibn Gabirol, a Spanish Jew.

Thus, what we see is a conscious synthesis of Indian, Greek, and Hellenistic learning. It is to the credit of Caliphs like al-Mansoor that intellectual freedom flourished, and in a short period, Baghdad became the foremost center of learning in the world. The Muslim world would remain in the vanguard of science for over three hundred years, until it was effectively killed by a more self-conscious Islam.

15.48 Rationalizing the Third Synthesis in Science

Why Science Continued to Elude the Chinese Civilization

The continuity in the inner nature of the Chinese civilization is indeed sufficient to explain the great outpouring in practical technology and the continuing absence of science.

Internal SGS: Despite substantial conflict with nomads and in part because of a somewhat decreased wealth polarization resulting from the rise of a meritocratic bureaucracy and control of the merchant class, the internal SGS remained high during the phase.

Allocation of SGS: It seems the allocation was focused on military capability and practical creativity. The phase of building Buddhist temples had come to an end.

Nature of its creed: Despite significant persecution of Buddhism undertaken by Confucianism and Taoist nationalists and modest openness to both Islam and Christianity, there was little conflict between science and religion because persecution of Buddhism was short-lived and monotheism hardly appealed to the Chinese and remained a fringe religion.

State of ASBC: China continued to fail to develop world-class abstract systems-building capability despite brilliant flashes in mathematics. It did not adopt an alphabetical system or make progress in critical philosophy, decimal systems, and the experimental method. It showed little interest in the science being the Muslim civilization developed.

Openness/insularity: It was not dictates of a creed or loss of SPI that prevented China from giving birth to science; it was its insular nature and a belief in its superiority, a belief derived from its interaction with nomads and not with other civilizations. Even as late as modern times, China continued to hold the view of its superiority. One is reminded of the letter that Chinese monarch Qianlong wrote to King George of England in 1793. The letter betrays an unwarranted belief in the inferiority of England and China's superiority.

Violent greed: Chinese civilization was not only largely successful against the nomads but also displayed elements of aggression against its neighbors, including Tibet and Japan. However, it seems that this aggression was motivated by a desire to secure the borders and a feeling of superiority and not territorial expansion or wealth drain. Chinese emperors were satisfied if conquered territories acknowledged Chinese oversight.

Thus, continuing weak ASBC and insularity fully explain the absence of significant science, just as high SGS and its allocation explain the outpouring of world-class practical technology.

Why Science Declined in Indian Civilization

Internal SGS: Internal SGS remained high despite unending Muslim invasions in the northwest front and the slow loss of territory.

Allocation of SGS: There was a significant change in SGS allocation. A greater proportion was being diverted toward religion and military capability, because of external attacks and internal fragmentation.

Nature of its creed: Shifting the religious focus from Hinduism/Buddhism to monism and the Bhakti movement resulted in weakening scientific activity in North India. The question is why Buddhism lost out to Hinduism and why Hinduism lapsed into monism and the Bhakti movement, which represented excessive spirituality for the intellectual and the common man respectively. The answer is that, relatively speaking, the Gupta Empire weakened Buddhism, and after the demise of the Gupta dynasty and the resulting political fragmentation, the Brahmins found an opening to reassert their position. And they found in Sankara a man of exceptional genius to make the case. Simultaneously, the arrival of the Bhakti movement from the south completed the transition from a polytheistic/agnostic creed to a monist creed whose stated purpose in life is to achieve union with the Brahmin through training of intuition and meditation and not understanding the real world through union of observation and reason. Thus, once more Indian civilization fell into the trap of excessive spirituality. The conservative Brahmins, whose ancestors had created the science of astronomy more than two millennia ago, succeeded in carrying the day. It was indeed a sad day for the Indian civilization.

State of ASBC: Indian civilization retained a world-class abstract systems-building capability, despite a high internal SGS. The twelfth-century Indian mathematician Bhaskara understood the concept of infinitesimal, calling it *truti,* meaning exceedingly small; enunciated the Rolle theorem; and calculated the derivative of sine function before anyone else. The state of epistemology and logic remained strong, but the civilization was falling behind in astronomy due to reduced support and as a result was falling behind in developing the experimental method, both in the heavens as well as on earth.

Openness/insularity: Political divisiveness, military weakness and an inability to hold back determined invaders, creeping religious conservatism, an increasingly inflexible caste system, and declining support of learning centers by the state all slowly but surely contributed to declining creative freedom. And creative freedom was increasingly directed toward religious revival. Though we witness openness to practical technology and overseas trade with Southeast Asia resulting in increased prosperity and religious revival, artistic, scientific, and philosophical creativity was on a decline in the north. Scientific creativity was largely confined to formal sciences, and even that was sporadic and required the emergence of a world-class genius such as Bhaskara. No breakthrough occurred in astronomy as no astronomer dared pick up where Aryabhatta had left off centuries earlier.

Coming loss of sustained political independence: The political landscape in North India after repelling the Arab invasion had remained divided, with internal instability increasing markedly. In addition, beginning with the eleventh century, Turkish pressure in the northwest mounted. Parallel with these political developments, Buddhism lost ground, and monism asserted itself again. Turkish invasions from the northwest and political disunity as evidenced by the inability to come together to face the invaders, unlike what they had done during the Arab invasions four centuries earlier, and the treachery of some brought North India close to loss of SPI. In fairness to the courage of Indian defenders, it must be stated that Muslim/Turkish invaders succeeded not just in India but also about everywhere else during the phase, for they were armed with fast horses, better weapons, and a belief that they were doing Allah's work. The net result was that North Indian civilization was on the verge of losing its political independence to anti-science invaders, who fervently believed in an intolerant monotheistic creed. One can imagine the persistent drain of resources needed to fight Turkish invaders.

Thus, the decline of science in India is easily rationalized through changes in the nature of its creed, openness, and the destructive orientation of others (loss of SPI) despite a high SGS and despite a world-class abstract systems-building capability. Scientific developments in North India from here on will be sporadic and mostly in formal sciences and would occur mostly through men of exceptional genius. State support of science would die. The destruction of temples and associated looting of the wealth, closing of universities, and burning of libraries undertaken by the Turkish dynasties were other contributing factors. Indian science was entering a dark age. The states would still be prosperous for centuries to come, but Indian civilization was entering an age of a long, slow decline in creative endeavors. Under Muslim rulers, it would produce great art and architecture but no science.

Thus, Turkish Muslim dynasties not only killed science in West Asia but also managed to do the same in the very birthplace of science. The changes during this phase were to set the course of Indian civilization for the coming six centuries. Despite occasional bright spots, these six centuries must be regarded as the intellectual and spiritual dark age of the Indian civilization, despite a flowering of architecture, dance, and music. It was initiated by an internally generated lapse into religiosity and sealed by an antiscience, violent aggressor who was absolutely sure of its nomadic monotheism and had the zeal of a recent convert to both civilized ways and a new religion.

Why Interest in Science Was Born in the Western European Civilization for the First Time

Though not obvious, the impact of extrinsic causes on the European civilization was profound toward the end of the phase. Western Europe in effect benefited from the world's technology and science at the end of the most creative period of Muslim civilization. Just when Indian civilization was on the threshold of losing its political freedom, Islam was walking away from its golden age of science, and the Chinese civilization remained self-absorbed, Europe became the unwitting beneficiary of what the world had achieved in technology and science. Half a millennium later, Western historians would develop amnesia and claim science as their exclusive creation.

Different parts of Europe witnessed different scenarios during and toward the end of the phase. In the west, substantial liberation of the Iberian Peninsula occurred toward the end of phase from Arabs who had been full of confidence and blissfully ignorant of the conflict between their monotheistic faith and science. In the center, we see the quarreling Holy Roman Empire and papal states with entrenched feudalism; in the east, the rise of a Venetian sea power toward the end of this phase; and in the Far East, a centralized Byzantine Empire successfully keeping Muslims from West Asia at bay during the early part of the phase but in retreat in the latter part of the phase. As Arab power waned, Western Europe witnessed a renaissance of learning-based Arab synthesis. In the east, a highly aggressive Venice controlled Asian trade and would lead to an Italian Renaissance based on both Muslim synthesis and the discovery of ancient Greece in the next phase. In the Far East, centralized structures entrenched in Christian dogma continued to exist, awaiting their demise, also in the next phase.

It is as if fate had wanted to force-feed science to Europeans: science unfolding in the Iberian Peninsula under the Arabs (who were themselves unaware of the coming conflict between science and Islam) probably baffled Europeans as they watched the unfolding drama from a safe distance under the shackles of Christian feudalism in the west or under a highly centralized Byzantine Empire fully conscious of the conflict between science and Christianity in the east or in the middle by Italians fleeing the Italian Peninsula under barbarian pressure to found the mercantile state of Venice desiring to profit from Europe-Asia trade and giving shelter and resources to the scholars fleeing from the Byzantine Empire under Muslim pressure.

Irony in history does not get any better than this: a mild scientific renaissance in the Western wing of Europe under foreign auspices and a continuation of traditional European attitude toward creativity in the rest of Europe. As we shall see in the next chapter when Europeans did manage to gather political and military courage, they would not only be indeed ready to absorb the lessons of this grand foreign experiment in science in their backyard but also would have absorbed the importance of controlling the sea routes from Venetian experience in the Mediterranean.

For the moment, let us focus on western Europe.

Internal SGS: The internal SGS in western Europe was definitely low given its natural bounty and low expertise in technology.

Allocation of SGS: The focus of SGS allocation was naturally religious creativity and military capability to liberate Iberia from Arabs. However, as we noted earlier, there was substantial interest in translating Arabic books into Latin in the eleventh and twelfth centuries.

Nature of its creed: The pull of Catholicism was great indeed. It is fair to say that during this early period of Scholasticism, scholars interested in science and critical philosophy period were thoroughly Christian in their beliefs. The question arises why the Christian dogma did not hold them back. The answer is that they intended the new knowledge in the form of dialectical reasoning to enable them to defend the dogma more vigorously. Early leaders came from England, which was a bit removed from the papal stronghold.

State of its ASBC: The state of ASBC for western Europe had begun to improve because of Scholasticism. The nascent philosophy and import of decimal system was beginning to strengthen the epistemology and science of logic reasoning, though they were hardly in the service of critical philosophy and science.

Openness/insularity: Western Europe, for the first time in its history, was opening up to intellectual and practical creativity of other social orders. It was clearly not open to the religious creativity of others as it was busy developing Christian doctrine. It was open to indeed open to fair trade, but there was little opportunity since the Atlantic side was unexplored and Mediterranean was controlled by the Republic of Venice. Fortunately, after initial resistance, it showed openness to the decimal system.

Nature of violent greed: By the end of the phase, western Europe had essentially succeeded in defeating the Arabs, thus liberating Iberia and Sicily from Arab control. There had been no wealth drain; however, the population had mostly converted to Islam, and the purpose of the Reconquista was to reconvert the population back to Christianity. Thus by the end of the phase, Western Europe could be said to have sustained political independence.

Different parts of Europe were differentially gaining abstract systems-building capability, becoming a bit open about the Muslim, Greek/Hellenistic, and Indian intellectual achievements and Chinese practical technology while remaining immersed in Christian dogma and attempting to recover its loss of sustained political independence through the Crusades, Iberian victories, and Venetian maritime trade. The foundations of both the Italian Renaissance and the following western European Renaissance that were to flower in the next phase were in fact laid in the current dark age through access to Muslim science and Venetian naval exploits on a local scale.

Why the Muslim Civilization Led in the Development of Science

At the start of this phase, the Muslim civilization may be said to have come into existence under Arab-Persian leadership. Arab conscription of Turkish fighters in the ninth century and the earlier conquest of Persia laid the groundwork for the emerging and evolving character of the Muslim civilization. As the control of the center of Muslim civilization passed from Arab to Arab/Persian to Persian/Turkish to Turkish hands, the nature of Muslim civilization changed dramatically. The key factor impacting this evolution was the concomitant completion of sharia by the tenth and eleventh centuries. Since sharia was the detailed working out of the Koran, sunnah, and hadith, it was bound to have a great impact on all aspects of Muslim civilization. Muslim civilization has always been based on the understanding and interpretation of the word of God as laid out in the Koran and as exemplified by the life of the prophet and statesman Mohammad. Accordingly, we have dwelt on the inner nature of Muslim civilization during the Arab, Persian, and Turkish periods as well as the impact of completion of sharia to understand the evolving inner nature of the Muslim civilization. By the end of the phase, Muslim civilization was still an aggressive, violent civilization and had not lost any of its religious zeal. What had changed by the end of the phase was its relationship to science. Serious doubts about the continuation of the science project had arisen and tended to be resolved in favor of religion, but it was, by no means, a done deal.

Internal SGS: The internal SGS was naturally low but supplemented through expansion.

Allocation of SGS: During the early centuries of the phase, when Arab territories were expanding at a fast clip and there was no perceived conflict between the Koran and science, Muslim rulers were quite generous in supporting creative endeavors including science despite military capability consuming significant part of SGS.

Nature of its creed: With hindsight, it is clear that the Judaic-Christian metaphysics in the Koran was in fundamental conflict with science, but it was hardly obvious to early Muslims because science itself was too weak to question the metaphysics of a seven-day creation and the Koran as the word of God. Early breakthroughs in mathematics, physics, chemistry, and medicine could hardly dethrone the Koran or cast a doubt on its accuracy. Significantly, early Muslim scientists did question the geocentric solar system; however, like Aryabhatta, their work was not taken seriously. Only in the eleventh century did philosophers reflect on the potential discoveries of science and metaphysics in the Koran. Thus, science prospered in the morning of Muslim civilization because it was not accompanied by critical philosophy. As critical philosophy developed, it sided with Islam and against science.

State of its ASBC: Muslim civilization during the phase had world-class ASBC, having absorbed successfully Indian and Greek achievements while adding considerably to them, particularly through developing the experimental method.

Openness/insularity: Since Islam was oblivious to science-religion conflict through most of the current phase, Muslim civilization showed remarkable openness to the practical and intellectual creativity of other civilizations.

Nature of violent greed: Muslim civilization retained its aggressive, violent orientation toward other social orders throughout the phase. It was a new type empire builder that did not want to be absorbed into the conquered populations. Rather, it was focused on spreading Islam though without wealth drain. Thus, with few exceptions, Islam created religious friction but not poverty and economic misery in the conquered territories.

Below, we briefly trace the fascinating evolution of the Muslim attitude toward science during the phase.

Why Arabs were able to initiate the third synthesis in science: Arab expansion took West Asia by storm. It is instructive to reflect on how religious, militaristic, and tribal nationalism of Arabs coped with their own military successes. Arabs were small in numbers in relation to the lands they conquered, and they had little history of learning. The first issue was how to deal with non-Arabs who had converted to Islam and their other non-Muslim subjects. Arab rulers, after Abbasids came to power, accepted non-Arab Muslims. There was little choice, given their numbers. They grudgingly accepted non-Muslims but made a distinction between People of the Book: Christians and Jews and all others. Thus, the rank order was Arabs, non-Arab Muslims, People of the Book, and all others. They imposed tax on non-Muslims as a price for protecting them from invaders or themselves. This tax naturally created an ambivalent attitude toward conversions as it tended to reduce state revenue. Muslim dynasties everywhere would utterly fail to understand the separation of state and religion. This, of course, is not too surprising, for wasn't the initial impulse of expansion to spread the word of God?

The grudging acceptance of the conquered people was to have a profound impact on the Arab attitude toward learning and science. Unlike the European and Persian empires centuries earlier, the Arabs did not have a home base (because the home base was hot and dry) and elites to maintain back home. They were conquerors/settlers in foreign lands. Under Abbasids in Baghdad and Umayyads in Spain, Arabic language flourished as a court language. It was centuries before the rigid Islamic sharia fully emerged. Their subjects included large numbers of Christians and Jews, particularly in Spain, who learned the court language of Arabic and translated many of the ancient Greek books into Arabic. Islam was young and knowledge in a broad range of subjects was welcomed based on Greek, Hellenistic, and Indian learning. Universities gained academic freedom. As a result, science in West Asia and Iberia stirred again after half a millennium.

The foreigner introduced the Arabs to a fossilized science in Iberia and a living science (though it was living on borrowed time) in Sindh. The Arab rulers allowed it to prosper by providing political support and resources during the critical period before the sharia would bring the conflict between Islam and science out in the open. Doing so helped legitimize their rule in the eyes of the intellectual classes.

Why Persians continued to carry forward the torch of science: The question is why Persians under Arab influence were able to continue the third synthesis of science and not the ancient Persians, who had historically greater access to these Indian, Greek, and Hellenistic learning. The answer seems to lie in the fact that the Arab Empire was centered in faraway lands with hostile foreign populations. By contrast, historic Persian empires were always centered in Persia and on Persians. Because Persians, unlike Indians, had a predisposition toward monotheism, they eventually underwent a 100 percent conversion to Islam after the Arab conquest of Persia. Consequently, the Arabs were successful in transplanting science in the Persian soul. Eventually, the student outdid the teacher. The Renaissance lasted for nearly three hundred years until it was extinguished by Seljuk Turks in West Asia and by Reconquista in Spain. The Arab rule in Iberia finally came to an end in the fifteenth century with the conquest of Granada on the Mediterranean. The Arabs get the credit for reviving Greek and adding to both Greek and Indian learning. After the recapture of Grenada, the books were once again translated, this time, however, into Latin.

This golden age of Islam is sandwiched between the pre-sharia morning of Arab-Persian Islam and the control of Muslim civilization by the antiscience Seljuk Turks. Once this period of about three centuries died out, Arab-Persians never regained their interest in science. It was a great golden age for science nonetheless. Yet, in the long span of history, this golden age must be regarded as fortuitous since it was undertaken for practical necessity and before Islam recognized science as its nemesis. Centuries later, in its full consciousness and maturity, Islam rejected science, having correctly realized that science would undo Islam. When presented as a conscious choice, Muslim civilization chose Islam and rejected science. It was the first conscious and full recognition in history that monotheism and science are incompatible. Europe was to prove this again in the coming centuries before ultimately rejecting Christianity and embracing science after a lengthy struggle.

Why Persia could not ultimately sustain flame of science: Throughout the long history of Persia, including the conversion to Islam, the spirit of Persia continued to assert itself time and again. That spirit is the spirit to build empires, create efficient centralized structures, is predisposed toward monotheism, and has a taste for artistic, literary, and architectural creation, in short, a spirit of practical creativity and religious dogma. This spirit triumphed under Persian dynasties, ebbing under the Turks and triumphing again in the sixteenth century under the Persian Safari dynasty. Thus, considering the entire span of Persia's long history, one is forced to regard the enormous contribution to science by Persians under Arab rule to be more of an exception and not a rule. However, as we noted earlier, it was, no doubt, a powerful exception. This was so because Turkish rule to one extent or another spanned the last century of the current phase and nearly all the next phase and simply reinforced the Persian historical disposition toward rigid centralized structures, the good life, artistic and architectural creation, and monotheistic creed but without the force of Arab interest in intellectual creation. Persia's historically aggressive external orientation had not manifested itself since the fall of Sassanian Empire. It has been kept in check successively by Arab, Turkish, and Mongol pressures and still later by Russian and western European expansions.

Why Turkish dynasties killed science: The association of Turkish nomads with Islam seemed to have been most detrimental from the perspective of other civilizations. They adopted Islam enthusiastically as it seemed to fit with their warlike and conquering ways, only now they would do it for both God and greed. While adopting Islam from Arabs, who initially conscripted them in their armies, as we mentioned above, they quickly destroyed the Arab-Persian interest in science once they acquired leadership of Muslim civilization. After converting to Islam, they extended their control into Persia and Afghanistan and moved toward India in three separate waves: the Ghaznivad branch attacked India during the current phase in the eleventh century, the Timur branch in the fourteenth century, and the Babur branch in the sixteenth century, with the latter two being the descendants of Genghis Khan who had converted to Islam by then. In both India and West Asia Turks did the greatest damage to the cause of science. In a relatively short period, they managed to kill science in North India, and science moved to the south to escape their tyranny. As if in hot pursuit, they killed the surviving kernel of science in India a second time in the south by the seventeenth century.

Summary: The bottom line is that because of a dogmatic belief in the Koran, Arabs, Persians, and Turks appear fundamentally as antiscience in history, but they made great contribution to science before the contradiction between Islam and science became transparent. Where Islam failed and has continued to fail even to date is in the religious reformation required to create metaphysics compatible with science.

During the highly dynamic current phase, Muslim civilization produced science when it did not allow conservative interpretation of the Koran to stand in the way of science and when it displayed openness to the creativity of other civilizations thus acquiring practical technology, abstract systems-building capability, and knowledge in specific sciences through scholars from different civilizations. It enjoyed SPI throughout the phase with a minor setback, not critically important. Of these, the critical factor in the beginning was openness and toward the end the changing creed. Below we emphasize the critical importance of openness early in the phase.

Arabic conquests were quite successful in increasing the diffusion of practical agricultural and nonagricultural technology, including the spread of domesticated plants. This undoubtedly increased wealth production and surplus creation, resulting in the potential for a greater allocation to creative endeavors, including science in Muslim states in Iberia and West Asia during the Arab-Persian period

The diffusion of intellectual creativity in art, science, and philosophy was breathtaking by historical standards. Arabs succeeded in adopting Indian and Hellenistic science, Hellenistic philosophy, and Persian art, resulting in the third synthesis. Of course, historically, the most fruitful impact of this diffusion was exposing the central and western Europeans to the fundamentals of science for the first time in their history. Greek-Hellenistic science of a millennium or more ago was confined to Greece, Egypt, and other Hellenistic states in West Asia. Europeans under the Romans had rejected this learning as it was too early for the West European mind to be interested in it. Europe had taken what it needed from the fruits of this first synthesis (art and architecture and military technology) and roundly rejected the rest. However, after centuries of development of science during the third synthesis under the tender loving care of the Arabs and Persians, European civilization began slowly to question Christian dogma and consider scientific enterprise toward the end of current phase.

Migrations, though not mostly peaceful, were plenty and were supplemented by travel from traders and scholars, resulting in providing channels for the diffusion of creative outcomes including science.

Trade among civilizations increased dramatically and because Arabs controlled the trade routes and important territories, they were the principal beneficiaries. This increased wealth concentration in Arab hands undoubtedly helped the cause of science for several centuries.

Future impact of Islam on science in other civilizations: The impact of the Arab-Persian-Turkish empire building on science was profound as well. The Arabs discovered and developed Greek science, integrated it with Indian science, and took it to greater heights. It made Persians interested in science for centuries, with Persia producing world-class scientists.

It also helped create a western European consciousness in science through diffusion of the fruits of third synthesis.

And it laid the foundation for fourth and fifth syntheses of science in Italy and western Europe, through destruction of the Byzantine Empire, the rise and fall of Venetia, and the launch of the process to discover sea routes to India and the resulting accidental discovery of the Americas. Turks, on the other hand, began the destruction of the tradition of Indian science.

There was little lasting impact of Islamic science or aggression on China.

The impact on India appeared minimal but with a severe and long-lasting impact awaiting the Indian civilization in the next phase: after conversion to Islam and arrival in India, Hinduism, with the exception of the period of Akbar, had little impact on Turkish religiosity. We must, however, remember that in early years, like Umayyads in Iberia centuries ago, Akbar was trying to establish an empire. He knew that he was weak and had to accommodate the Indian sensibilities to succeed against both the Hindu kings and the Sultanate. Turkish aggressiveness and violence did eventually manage to convert a third of the Hindu population into Islam over a period of six centuries. They seemed to us to be the only people, who, though playing a dominant role on the world stage for literally eight hundred years and coming in contact with Indian, Arab, and Western science, managed to essentially remain aggressively antiscience until modern times. Such is the enduring nature of inner nature of civilizations and entities. The occasional scientific contributions made under Ottomans as well as the Mongol/Mogul dynasties during the twelfth to nineteenth centuries must be considered as occasional flare-ups of Arab-Persian or Indian flames of science that they themselves had more or less extinguished.

The Arab-Persian-Turkish Empire during the current phase not only lasted throughout the current phase but also could continue expansion for another five hundred years in Europe, India, and Indonesia when the Muslim civilization continued as a multicivilization entity through Ottoman, Safavid, Delhi Sultanate, Mamluks, several Indonesian sultanates, and Mughal Empire. However, this was expansion of an antiscience Muslim civilization.

The spread of Islam under Turkish leadership, the continued stronghold of Christian dogma in Europe, and the resurgence of monism in India were ultimately detrimental to the cause of science. Christian dogma was openly antiscience; Islam discovered its inherent antiscience bias, and Indian monism, though not antiscience, simply did not value the real knowledge of the real world as it once again focused on the ultimate liberation of the soul through meditative or devotional practices.

Bottom line: under the political necessity of creating alliances with conquered foreigners in foreign lands and before the completion of sharia, Arabs displayed an openness to the learning of other civilizations and transmitted this openness to the Persians. Once they were entrenched in part through converting the foreigners to Islam and as sharia was completed, openness began disappearing into thin air. The changing attitude to creativity in general and to science in particular was captured in the evolving dynamic inner nature of Muslim civilization.

Shifting Center of Gravity of Science

The center of gravity moved from Indian to Muslim civilization, and by the end of the period, it was ready to pass into European hands as Arabs began to retreat from Europe. The European mind became a little more open to science, the Indian mind was a lot less so, and the Muslim mind was beginning to reject science when forced to choose between science and Islam. And China remained China as far as science was concerned.

15.49 Confirming the Stage of Science for Each Civilization

Based on the inner nature of civilizations and the underlying parameters summarized in table 15.5, the five key civilizations achieved the following life stages in science.

- Indian civilization: Regressing but still in development stage of science
- Muslim civilization: Leader in development stage of science
- European civilization: Regressing but still in mature protoscience of science
- Seljuk central Asians: Regressing but still in development stage of science
- Chinese civilization: Mature protoscience of science

15.50 Emerging New Participants and Fate of Some Participants

Since the central purpose of the book is to understand the relationship between civilizations and science, we need only focus on civilizations that have impacted science through mutual interaction since science was not born or develop within an isolated civilization. Thus, we have felt justified in focusing on Eurasia and North Africa in the chapters so far. The Americas, Australia, and Africa were either isolated or were at an earlier phase of human development. Africa, excluding Egypt, clearly played a dominant role in the early development of *Homo sapiens*; however, over the last ten millennia, its impact on major interacting civilizations of Eurasia civilizations has been rather limited.

Yet, Eurasian and North African theaters have not only been the home of major civilizations in China, India, West Asia, central Asia, and Europe but also to smaller peripheral civilizations such as those of Japan, Korea, Russia, and Southeast Asia. Fortunately for us, these civilizations, while displaying significant creativity, have been relatively unimportant to the birth and development of science, and these civilizations did not materially impact major civilizations. In fact, an additional characteristic that these peripheral civilizations share in common is that they have been enormously impacted by Indian, Chinese, Muslim, central Asian, and European civilizations.

Below, we make a few remarks about these civilizations and probably will not deal with these civilizations explicitly in the following chapters.

Southeast Asia and Greater India: Southeast Asia witnessed several kingdoms and empires: in south and central Vietnam, the Champa kingdom (700–1832), Angkor kingdom (1200–1431) in Cambodia, Ayutthaya kingdom (1350–1767) in Thailand, Sailendra (700–800 CE) in Sumatra, and the Majapahit kingdom (1300–1500) in Java. In general, Southeast Asia was impacted militarily by the Mongols and Chinese and culturally by the Indian and Chinese civilizations. It is probably a fair assessment that Mongol/Chinese military campaigns did not succeed and the Indian religious, cultural, technological artistic, and linguistic influence carried greater influence than the Chinese, despite considerable disparity in geographical distances. Since the principal impact came from South India, Indian Muslim states, and China, these civilizations were not exposed to significant scientific ideas of Indian, Muslim, and European civilizations. Their creative impulse was expressed in practical technology, art, architecture, and in adaptation of religion. In the modern period, these states all fell to European aggression. Southeast Asian civilizations may be characterized as practical, with no science-religion conflict, and were very open to outside influences, with moderate internal equality, high internal aggression, and a low external aggression.

The spread of Buddhism had a significant impact on East Asia: for centuries, it shielded them from the attraction of Islamic monotheism and shifted the focus toward a goal of nirvana and otherworldliness. We do not believe that it helped the cause of science either. Buddhism possessed powerful epistemology, but the objective of nirvana, like that of moksha, did not allow science to be considered seriously. In history, one witnesses Buddhist philosophers, logicians, and ethicists but not Buddhist scientists despite the fact that Buddhism is not antiscience. Besides, most of East Asia lacked an alphabetical script, and it rejected the alphabetical script that came with Buddhism. Science is unlikely to develop in the absence of an alphabetical script. Since Muslims and Islam could not penetrate the Far East, in part because of entrenched Buddhism, the Indian subcontinent had to bear a greater brunt of Muslim invasions. The impact of Genghis Khan was opposite: his penetration into China and West Asia meant he spared South Asia, in part because of a strong presence of the Delhi Sultanate, as we discuss in the next chapter.

Korea: Not surprisingly, geography allows Korea to exist as a separate entity. Koreans claim their history goes back ten millennia to have founded the Chinese civilization. In more recent times, Korea went through a three kingdoms (Silla, Goguryeo, and Baekje) period from 57 BCE to 668 CE, followed by a unified period under the Silla, Balhae, Goryeo, and Joseon dynasties right to the end of the nineteenth century, bearing repeated invasions from China and Japan. Korean culture was strongly influenced by Buddhism and Confucianism from India and China respectively. Creative impulse in Korea, which must be characterized as stronger than in Southeast Asia, expressed itself in arts, painting, calligraphy, dance, pottery, and music. It is noteworthy that Korea was the only civilization in the Far East to develop an alphabetical language called *hangul*, consisting of fourteen consonants and ten vowels during the reign of king Sejong in the fifteenth century. Korean civilization may also be credited with the invention of movable metal type, an iron hull ship, a system of musical notation, and the first novel. Korea also developed sun dials, water clocks, rain gauges, astronomical maps, mechanical representation of the solar system, and celestial globes during the reign of Sejong.

Japan: The Japanese are a mixed racial stock from Asia. The Chinese civilization strongly influenced the Japanese civilization; the Indian civilization influenced its religious belief system. Being an island, Japan has retained its political independence throughout its history, leading to a unique culture. Japan became unified in the eighth century during the Nara period. Creativity in Japan until modern times was expressed through art and poetry. Japan developed its own syllabic language, called *Kana*, after relying on the Chinese language for centuries. In the seventeenth century, a Japanese mathematician came close to conceptualizing integral calculus through development in the method of exhaustion used in determining the area of geometrical figures.

The inner nature of Japanese civilization may be characterized as practical, with no science-religion conflict, an oscillating openness to the outside influences, relatively high internal equality, low internal aggression, and a strong, though controlled, streak of external aggression that leads it too often attempt to achieve beyond its capability. The Japanese record of creativity until the twentieth century pales in comparison to Korean achievements.

Russia: Russian racial stock is a mixture of eastern slaves and northern Scandinavians. Its culture is a composite of Slavic and Byzantine cultures that also provided the orthodox Christian faith. Mongols brutalized Russia, and Russia succeeded in defeating the Mongols a hundred and fifty years later. Over the next several centuries, the little Grand Duchy of Moscow had become a huge empire stretching from Moscow to the Pacific Ocean. This enormous expansion came at a cost as Russia moved farther from western Europe and was slow to participate in scientific, cultural, religious and political developments that occurred in western Europe over the last five centuries. Achievements of Russian civilization until the modern period were confined to art, architecture, and religion. We may characterize the inner nature of Russian civilization as religious, with moderate science-religion conflict, open to external influence, low internal equality, low internal aggression, and a strong external aggression.

Most of these "secondary" civilizations have not been central to the story of science throughout history; however, it is noteworthy that in the twentieth century, these "minor" civilizations have been more successful than the major Indian, Chinese, and Muslim civilizations that were under greater control of European civilization.

Fate of Some Existing Participants

All four major civilizations—Indian, European, Chinese, and Muslim—survived the phase with parts of Europe still under Muslim control. The Indian civilization was about to be overrun by the Muslim civilization and Muslim and Chinese civilizations by the Mongols.

15.51 A Peek into Coming Chapters

The internal Persian-Turkish encounter during the phase was to have most profound influence on world civilizations during the current and succeeding phases. We digress briefly to note the strategic impact of the rise of Muslim-Turkish dynasties on world civilizations. First, as we have noted above, the Turks, after adopting Islam, usurped power from Arabs and Persians. Turkish dynasties used this power to attack both Europe in the west, Egypt in the South, and India in the east, where they founded the Delhi Sultanate. Turks ultimately conquered most of southern Europe, the Black Sea, and the lower Caspian Sea and thus controlled the lucrative land trade to the east. Their strategic mistake was to allow Venetia to rise as a Mediterranean sea power that later proved to be the financial foundation of the Italian Renaissance. They attempted to correct that mistake in the fifteenth century, but it was, thankfully, too late. Their near destruction of Venetian power and total control of land and sea trade to the east forced the West Europeans to seek sea routes to India that were safe from the Turks. This led to the discovery of America and European colonialism. Turks held sway over Egypt and most of West Asia. No matter how one looks at it, the impact of Turkish control of the Muslim civilization on world history during this phase and the following centuries was profound. It led to changes that turned out to be extraordinarily positive for Europe, equally extraordinarily negative for the Indian civilization, and marginally negative for the Chinese civilization in the long run. These changes must be attributed to the unholy marriage between an uncompromising monotheism of Islam, fearless courage and riding skills, and nomadic destructiveness of the Turks that were honed on the vast, empty plains of central Asia. Turks began the process of the death of science in both Muslim and Indian civilizations.

In this phase, for the second time in history an attempt was made to establish an empire across Asia, Europe, and Africa. The first attempt was of course Alexander's, and though it was greater in fury and speed, it was not particularly successful, partly because Alexander died too soon and did not have an ideology, just personal ambition. This second attempt, however, succeeded because the centrifugal forces in empires to splinter and exhaust their resources were bested by the glue provided by Islam in an era when monotheism seemed unassailable by immature science. Thus, it was perhaps the first time in human history that a sustained empire across the world's major civilizations was created. However, success did not mean that, on balance, this empire did any less harm than the empires before or since. It is in the nature of empires to conquer, exploit, and retard growth of the civilizations they conquer while pretending to do the opposite. As we discussed in part III of the book, empire building was a specific form of the instruments of control to achieve this objective through controlling densely populated and wealth-producing territories. The objective of an empire is not to drain the wealth of a civilization, for early empires generally did not possess the technology to drain this wealth to produce greater wealth in the home territory. Rather, their objective was always to replace the indigenous elite, control the wealth already being produced, and to channel this surplus based on the victor's inner nature.

In the case of the Muslim Empire, Islam as God's word and its superficial message of equality provided the needed cover. By contrast, Alexander had no universal message, for did the Greeks not think of him as a Macedonian barbarian? He was driven by personal ambition and was, historically speaking, a flash in the pan. The Greek migrations more than a century after Alexander's death created Hellenistic states in less than a third of the territory originally conquered by Alexander, as we discussed in the previous chapters. The harm Alexander did to civilizations was marginal and not lasting. We could not claim that for the Muslim civilization.

15.52 Summary

This phase witnessed monumental changes in all four major civilizations. The Muslim civilization, founded by Arabs, successfully pulled Persians and Turks into its sphere and saw dramatic territorial expansion and the birth and decline of its golden age of science. Indian civilization began a long downward cycle because of political disunity, religious revival internally, invasions of central Asian/Turkish tribes, and conquest externally. Europe, though outwardly quiet and introverted, seemed to be signaling a return to its aggressive orientation through the Crusades and the aggressive Venetian state. It had also begun to discuss its Christian dogma in its monasteries and its budding universities just about the time al-Ghazali was announcing the closing of the Muslim mind. Chinese civilization produced amazing practical technology that would indirectly alter the course of conflict among civilizations as well as the progress of science and learning.

In short, by the end of the current phase, the Muslim mind was closing fast, the European mind was opening slowly, the Indian mind was calcifying, and the Chinese mind, well, it remained highly productive in a very uniquely Chinese manner, that of practical creativity and wealth creation.

The focus of the Indian and Chinese civilizations remained internal, the European civilization remained defensive, and the Muslim civilization remained offensive throughout the phase. We believe that seeds of the relative position of the four major civilizations of the world today—namely, Chinese, Indian, European (Western), and Muslim—were sown during the current phase. It was truly a game-changing phase for the next millennium.

Chapter 16

Violent Interaction Era—Sixth Phase: Development Stage

Fourth Synthesis of Science (1200–1600 CE)

16.1 Introduction

The current phase may be said to begin with yet another bang from central Asia. The Mongols arrived on the world stage out of nowhere and overwhelmed the established Turkish-Persian Muslim dynasties and the Chinese civilization, which, unlike the Indian civilization, had managed to largely remain insulated from Muslim aggression. The Mongols faded away equally fast in a little more than hundred years, only to have their descendants, Timur Lane and the Moguls, create havoc again less than a hundred and two hundred years later respectively.

The first invasion of this fourth wave of central Asians was by non-Muslim nomads; however, the next two were by those who had converted to Islam. The reader can by now appreciate that overwhelming civilizations every few centuries on average through cruelty and destruction had become part of the genetic code for countless generations of ambitious young central Asian men, who no doubt dreamed of assembling armies and raiding civilizations in the east, west, and south to loot wealth or to establish empires on their soil. But fortunately it would be the last time. The current phase, which assured the coming ascendancy of European civilization and mature science, may be said to end with a symbolic whimper when the little-noticed East India Company was established in 1600 CE, five years before the great Akbar passed away.

The current chapter, therefore, has two parallel developments in the post-Mongol period: Turkish Muslim domination in southern Europe on the one hand and West and South Asia and North Africa on the other. Both developments cover about the same time period, and in both, several contemporaneous or sequential Turkish and allied dynasties, working in substantial independence, played a critical global role. The principal reason to highlight the two parallel developments, then, is to focus on the differing impact of Turkish Muslim domination in Europe on the one hand and West and South Asia and North Africa on the other. In Europe, the actions of Ottomans had very positive, though thoroughly unintended, outcomes that helped bring about the fourth synthesis of science in western Europe. In West Asia and North Africa, Khwarezmian, Safavid, Ottoman, and Timurid dynasties continued the Ghazanvid and Seljuk policy of undermining Arab-Persian science.

In India, the Delhi Sultanate, followed by the Mongol (Mogul) branches of Turkish Muslims, greatly contributed to the final death of Indian science. In short, the *unintended* consequences of Turkish world domination in West Asia, India, and Southeast Europe for over half a millennium turned out to be positive for central and Northwest Europe, while the *intended* consequences were overwhelmingly negative for Asia and North Africa. Without exaggeration, the foundation of the modern world, including the final maturation of science and the coming domination of the world by the European nation-states through mercantilism, colonialism, and systematic wealth drain, may be traced to the antiscience attitudes of Turkish dynasties. It was also nurtured by the science-religion conflict inherent in their adopted religion of Islam and their nomadic preference for land-based empires. Thus, in many ways, the current phase is pivotal in the history of science, since it marked the beginning of the belated birth of science in western Europe and its precipitous decline in Asia. This period may appear as a golden age to Turkish historians for Turkish Muslim dynasties truly dominated the world stage during this phase. We hope to convince the reader that it was hardly so from a broader historical perspective and, more particularly, from the perspective of science.

As in previous chapters, we will first affirm the era and phase through applying the relevant necessary and sufficient conditions to leading-edge participants and then identify the essential participants or major civilizations and nomadic confederations of the period. We then briefly summarize the political history, natural intrinsic, peaceful extrinsic and violent extrinsic causes driving the evolution of each participant. Next, we summarize the state of civilization at the phase end. We then assess the changes in the inner nature of the participants. Following this, we outline the evolution of science and rationalize the scientific outcomes of each participant during the phase based on their inner nature. We end the chapter by providing a summary.

Era and Essential Participants

16.2 Affirming the Era of Civilization

Civilizations continued to remain in the era of extended military conflicts during the four hundred years that comprise the current chapter. If anything, weapons and transportation technologies were becoming more devastating through the invention of explosives and navigation technologies. Muslim civilization, with an intolerant creed that had turned fundamentalist, though chastised by Mongols, remained powerful enough to gain control of Indian civilization. European civilization, an upstart with an equally potent ideology of greed and an intolerant creed, found an opening to successfully challenge the Muslim civilization, while the Indian and Chinese civilizations essentially remained oblivious to this global conflict. The Mongols and the Muslim civilization defined the era at the beginning of the phase, and toward the end of the phase, the European civilization took the lead in the military conflicts among civilizations.

16.3 Major Participants of the Phase

Major civilizations and nomadic confederations of significance in this phase are the Chinese civilization, with Mongol and Ming Empires; the Indian civilization, with the Delhi Sultanate and Mogul Empires; the Muslim civilization, with Sejuk, Mamluk, Ottoman, and Safavid Empires; the European civilization, with rising nation-states in the west, the Venetian city-state and the Holy Roman Empire in the center; and the final demise of the Byzantine Empire in the east after a millennium of fluctuating fortunes. The invasions of the non-Muslim Mongol nomadic confederation played a key role in Muslim and Chinese civilizations. In addition, we see the rise of Majapahit and Khmer civilizations in Southeast Asia, which we will touch on briefly, if only to convince ourselves that the story of these peaceful extensions of Indian civilizations is not central to our story.

History, Causes, and Outcomes of the Central Asian Nomads—Fourth and Final Wave

16.4 Brief Political History (1200–present CE)

Much like earlier waves of nomads from central Asia, there were no instruments of control that exerted pressure on the Mongols for civilizations never needed anything from the nomads in dry, cold terrain; they were free to build their military strength and plan their attacks in isolation. Mongols themselves became the most successful instrument of control the civilizations had ever faced. Probably the mythic memory of earlier waves of central Asian successes played a role in their collective consciousness. No doubt, central Asian young men dreamed about plundering civilizations for nearly two millennia. However, the success of all nomadic misadventures always depended on the relative weakness of civilizations, peaceful or not. Once again, the combination of the rise of a charismatic leader and the weakness of the surrounding civilization proved disastrous. It had not been that difficult for nomads to produce a great general every few hundred years for nearly two millennia since cruelty and destruction remained essentially unchecked in the central Asian nomadic mind. And they did it again at the dawn of the current phase.

For the fourth time in history (Yuehzi, Huns, and Seljuks/Ghaznivids as the first three), we see the rise of central Asian nomads, this time like the first three waves, without the Muslim creed Seljuks/Ghaznivids adopted Islam afterward), though only initially. The rise of Genghis Khan (1155–1227) followed the previous pattern. Through unification of various Mongolian tribes, he became the undisputed leader of Mongolia, and in 1206 started, at the age of 51, his military campaigns. He quickly established his dominion in central Asia, attacked the Qin Empire in 1211, and in 1218 dealt a severe blow to the Khwarezmian Empire (1194–1220), which was also of Seljuk origins and a brief successor to the Rum Seljuks. Genghis Khan's older son, Ogedei Khan (1186–1241), invaded and conquered Russia, Poland, and Hungary and completed the destruction of the Qin Empire in China. His son, Guyuk Khan (1206–1248) planned to continue conquering Europe and very quickly advanced into the heart of the Holy Roman Empire. However, before invading Vienna in December 1241, the news of Ogedei's death reached commander Batu, who was ordered to withdraw. The death of Ogedei saved Europe from impending disaster in the nick of time. Alcoholism played a role in the death of several Mongol heirs.

After Guyuk's death, the control of the empire passed on to Genghis's grandsons and sons of Tolui (1190–1232), who was the fourth son of Genghis Khan, named Mongke (1208–1258), Kublai Khan (1215–1294), and Helagu Khan (1217–1265). Helagu Khan established the Ilkhanate in West Asia after sacking the great city of Baghdad in 1258. Kublai Khan expanded the empire to include most of East Asia, including China, Vietnam, Khmer, Burma, Champa, and Korea as either conquered or vassal states and established the Yuan dynasty. Two invasions of Japan in 1274 and 1281 failed due to bad weather. After the death of Kublai Khan, whose adoption of Chinese culture created family disputes, the empire disintegrated into four chunks: Golden Horde (eastern Europe), Chagatai Khanate (central Asia), Ilk Khanate (West Asia), and the Yuan dynasty (China and Southeast Asia). Over the next century, these pieces were absorbed into emerging local empires. The descendant of the Chagatai Khanate, Timur Lane and the Babur, were eventually successful in India in the sixteenth century. The word *Timur* means *iron* in the Chagatai language and is probably derived from the Sanskrit word *Cimara*, probably a lingering influence of Buddhism in central Asia from the days of the Kushan Empire.

Mongols slowly adopted the local culture, religion, and language and were culturally absorbed into them within less than two centuries. Thus, it took less than a century to build the Mongol Empire and less than a century for it to disintegrate.

Repeated Mongol invasions of India were unfortunately (!) repulsed by rulers of the Delhi Sultanate, for had the Mongols succeeded, Islam in India would have been nipped in the bud, and Mongols would have been absorbed into Indian culture, much like in China, thus remaining relatively strong in the face of European imperialism focused on draining wealth. In the extreme west, the Mamluks of Egypt also were successful in checking the Mongols.

At its height, the Mongol Empire ruled a fifth of the entire landmass of Earth (one-half of known landmass) and 100 million people. It stands as the largest contiguous empire in the world and is likely responsible for over 40 million deaths or 10 percent of the world population at that time and unimaginable property loss. Western Europe escaped conquest by sheer luck. South Asia and Egypt, under the Mamluk and Slave dynasties respectively, both offshoots of the Seljuks, successfully defended against the Mongols. Clearly, the Mongols' military success depended on open spaces and grasslands for the horses.

Mongols had an admirable internal equality one would expect from nomads based on meritocracy for all except the ruling family. This seemed to have been a great factor in their military success as it was a great morale booster and resulted in exceptional courage in the face of danger. Similarly, internal conflicts were kept to a minimum, and rules of succession, unlike the Muslim civilization, were relatively clearly laid out. Both of these elements meant the Mongols could focus their attention on conquering civilizations. Mongols were undoubtedly the most aggressive and successful nomads in history.

Genghis Khan and his empire represent the non-Muslim half of the fourth wave of nomadic invasions. The world had barely recovered from Genghis Khan when his descendants, who had converted to Islam by then, unleashed more destruction upon West and South Asia, first through Timur Lane (1336–1405 CE), who descended from Changtai Khannate, and a century later through Babur (1483–1530 CE) in India. This time, China escaped since it was strong under the Ming dynasty, and once again Europe was lucky. However, we shall cover these below in the Muslim and Indian civilizations. It was by far an unequaled destruction of human lives and property the world had witnessed until European aggression started in the next phase. During the postempire period, the destructive inner nature of the most destructive nomadic confederation in history melted and transformed under the influence of Tibetan Buddhism in one of the most remarkable turnarounds.

Mongols who had established the Yuan dynasty in China were expelled in 1368 CE and remained under Ming control. They spent more than a century in disarray until united in the late fifteenth century by Queen Mandukhai (1449–1510 CE). Uneasy relations with the Ming continued; however, the Mongols continued to gain strength as their population recovered. In the sixteenth century, Mongols felts strong enough to invade Tibet and gave an ultimatum to destroy or surrender. If it was the latter, the Mongols would adopt Buddhism and help spread it.

The Tibetan clergy acquiesced and thus began a cultural renaissance for next two centuries. Thereafter, Mongolia came under Manchu control until 1911 CE and became a republic in 1924 CE.

Below we focus on Genghis Khan and his descendants.

16.5 Natural Causes

It is indeed difficult to imagine the rise of Genghis Khan, and indeed all successful central Asian invasions, without the open spaces needed to develop exceptionally skilled cavalry and the grasslands of central Asia for breeding horses. The sea, the extreme desert terrain, and cultivated plains were problematic.

16.6 Intrinsic Causes

As before, with central Asian tribes, we are not as interested in the causes that made their rise and conquest possible, since they neither created science nor were antiscience. Our chief interest lies in their direct or indirect impact on the Chinese, Indian, Muslim, and European civilizations, for once again, the central Asians had upset the balance of power among civilizations in Eurasia.

Intrinsic Causes—Institutional Structures and Processes

Clearly, Mongols' success was made possible by supreme political and military leadership required to unify the various tribes to create a fighting force, with each family required to contribute at least one able-bodied young warrior. Once this force was created, its continued success depended on an effective system of military intelligence and the use of the resources of the defeated entities. Their strengths were tribal equality, horsemanship, archery, sheer courage, cruelty, loyalty, and discipline. and their weakness was the sea and the extreme desert or mountainous terrain. The tribal equality may be assessed by the Mongol code of law, which, among other things, included death punishment for lying intentionally, sodomy, and sorcery, adultery, spying on tribe members, and becoming bankrupt three times. Their curse was an addiction to alcohol. Unlike civilizations, nomadic confederations were not hampered by excessive inequality or science-religion conflict. Tribal traditions and the absence of both organized religion and science assured that. And the rise of the nomadic confederation meant that internal wars had been settled and different factions were united behind a charismatic leader who was ready to pounce on civilizations. Mongols were no exception.

Formative Beliefs and Ideology at the End of Fourth Synthesis Phase

It is instructive to compare the beliefs and ideology of Mongols and the transformation of one branch under the influence of Buddhism and another branch that adopted Islam in the ensuing centuries. If the reader is interested in understanding the impact of religion on the human psyche, there is hardly a better controlled the experiment than this in human history.

We have already referred to the formative beliefs and ideology of the nomadic mind in chapters 12 and 13 in the context of the first two waves of central Asian nomads that overwhelmed civilizations, and we have referred to the formative beliefs and ideology of some nomads who adopted Islam.

Below, we focus on the formative beliefs and changing ideology of those Mongols who returned home after much destruction and who, centuries later, adopted Tibetan and Chinese Buddhism in contrast to the Mongols, who were situated closer to West Asia and adopted Islam.

The religious openness of the returning Mongols, the natural tribal equality of the nomads without a slavery or caste system, the impact of Buddhism on historic aggression, and the cruelty of nomads despite a continuing harsh nature eventually led to the emergence of a new nomadic man in the nomadic setting—something the world had not witnessed before.

- A new belief in knowledge based on abstract systems-building capability brought about by Buddhism
- A strengthened belief in the equality of citizens through Buddhist egalitarianism
- A continuing attitude of openness, reinforced again by Buddhism philosophy
- A renunciation of violence and aggression toward civilizations based on Buddhist ideas

These beliefs, derived from surviving tribal traditions but strongly impacted by adoption of Buddhism, are important since they allow us to study the comparative impact of two diametrically opposite religions, those of Islam and Buddhism, on the relatively unencumbered nomadic mind.

16.7 Extrinsic Peaceful Causes

The most significant extrinsic peaceful impact on Mongols was adoption of Buddhism by one branch and the adoption of Islam by another branch, as noted above.

16.8 Extrinsic Violent Causes—Mongols as Victors

Mongols were the most successful empire builders of history. Mongols and their descendants controlled Muslim civilization for about nearly three centuries (Ilkhanate and Chagatai), Chinese civilization for about a century (the Yuan dynasty), the Indian civilization for nearly three centuries (Mogul dynasty), and parts of European civilization for nearly three centuries (Golden Hordes).

The fate of all nomadic conquerors without an ideology is to be absorbed by the very civilizations they attacked. The Mongols were no exception. The Ilkhanate and Chagatai branches were a minority in the Muslim civilization. Consequently, they converted to Islam which only added to their ferociousness. The Yuan dynasty in China did not have to contend with Islam, for China had escaped Islam, precisely because of the Mongols themselves. The Yuan dynasty had to contend with the weight and tradition of Chinese culture. The Yuan dynasty was completely absorbed into Chinese culture in a few decades and was overthrown in less than a century, as we noted earlier.

Finally, the Golden Horde continued to control parts of southeastern Europe and Russia until the end of the fifteenth century. Thereafter, the Golden Hordes led a precarious existence sandwiched between the Ottomans and the Russian State and were ultimately put out of business by Catherine of Russia in 1783. Both Christians and Muslims wooed the Golden Hordes, and they chose to adopt Islam in the early fourteenth century under the rule of Uzbeg Khan (1312–1341).

Mongols and other central Asians were impacted mostly by the Chinese civilization and the Ottoman Empire in practical and intellectual creativity, Muslim civilization impacted them directly through Islam, and Indian civilization indirectly through Tibetan Buddhism.

Transmission of practical creativity: The phase started with the Mongols showing great interest and flexibility in acquiring the latest military technology from surrounding civilizations, particularly Chinese explosives technology, construction, and siege machines capable of being dissembled and reassembled on the battlefield.

Transmission of religious creativity: Central Asians including Mongols and Timur Lane, who conquered West Asia, had adopted Islam but others did not. Thus, eastern Mongols, those in China and Mongolia, though aware of Islam, were not sufficiently impressed by it to consider adopting it.

Transmission of intellectual creativity: The Mongols did not show much interest in the religious and intellectual creativity of civilizations with the exception of borrowing the Uyghur and Arabic alphabet to create a written script for the Mongol language. Genghis Khan's effective integration of different central Asian tribes into a fighting force played a key role. As the territory expanded through a succession of military campaigns, trade wealth played an increasingly important role in consolidating the empire and future victories. These changes took place at lightning speed during the last decade of the twelfth century and early decades of thirteenth century. The true and unintended significance of the Mongol invasion was to bring the civilizations into greater contact and to reinvigorate the old Silk Route and trading between Asia and Europe, which in the fourteenth century, came to be dominated by Ottomans and Italians, though at great destruction and violence.

Impact on creative outcomes: Timur, the Turkic-speaking Mongol of the Barla tribe, as we noted earlier, conquered central, West, and South Asia in the latter part of the fourteenth century after Mongol power had waned. Though a Muslim, he styled himself as the heir of Genghis Khan, and in cruelty and destruction, he indeed was. His grandson, Ulugh Beg (1394–1449), was probably the greatest astronomer central Asia ever produced. He built the great observatory at Samarkand, which was comparable to Tycho Brahe's at Uraniborg and Taqi Din's at Istanbul. Unlike the former, it lacked the telescope. As a child, he had traveled through Persia and India as part of his grandfather's and father's military campaigns. Lacking a telescope, Beg compiled an extensive catalogue of stars using a huge, 118-foot-long sextant and wrote trigonometric tables of sine and tangent accurate to eight decimal places. Thomas Hyde translated his work was translated into Latin in 1665.

From Genghis to Hulagu (1217–1265) to Timur (1336–1405) to Beg is an amazing story of destructive and cruel nomads becoming sponsors of great science under the influence of Muslim achievements, returning to cruelty and destruction, and producing a great scientist all within a couple of centuries. Significantly, Beg was not a particularly effective ruler.

Impact on institutional structures and processes: Like all nomads, over time, the Mongols adopted the institutional structures and processes of the Muslim or Chinese civilizations. Only those who remained in Mongolia naturally retained their distinct identity, even after voluntarily adopting Tibetan Buddhism in their homeland.

Assessment of net impact: As we have noted, the Mongols not only directly or indirectly impacted all major civilizations but also were immensely impacted by them as well. Ultimately, the impact on the Mongols was no different from most victorious nomads. They enjoyed the fruits of their victories, but those who settled in conquered lands lost their identity as the civilizations they conquered completely absorbed them.

16.9 Productive, Creative, and Scientific Outcomes

Productive Outcomes

We are on solid ground in highlighting the productive outcomes of the Mongols in relocated lands. The mass migration of Mongols and their descendants in the wake of invasions into the surrounding civilizations in China and West Asia and to a lesser extent Europe rejuvenated the racial stock of these civilizations. Mongol conquest also *directly* linked Chinese, Muslim, and European civilizations and indirectly linked the Indian civilization through trade, much like the central Asians had done on multiple occasions earlier. Thus, Mongols encouraged land trade. During their reign, Marco Polo traveled to China and learned of Chinese practical technology. Under Mongols, religious freedom was the norm. They tended to support several religions at the same time. They provided the world with the most efficient mail system over very long distances, probably because of its military significance. Their impact on military technology was substantial. They excelled in mobile forces (horseback archers), siege, trebuchet, and lance forces, and effectively used engineers to build equipment using local material during extended campaigns far away from home. The Mongols had little impact on the sea trade. The key unintended impact of the Mongols was to bring the different parts of the Eurasia in greater communication with one other and increase trade. Thus, it helped lay the groundwork for the fourth synthesis of science. The fall of the Mongol Empire disrupted the land-sea routes, and its subsequent control by Ottomans created a need to discover sea routes.

Creative Outcomes

Below, in the interest of continuity, we describe the creative achievements of the Mongolians up to the eighteenth century.

At the time of Genghis Khan, aside from war strategy and tactics, it appears there is little that Mongols acheived in practical creativity. They were a practical people who had little interest in science, philosophy, or religion. Genghis consulted the blue sky when in doubt. However, there was one fortunate or fortuitous exception. His son, Helagu Khan, was convinced by the great Persian astronomer al-Tusi to fund an observatory at Maragheh in Persia. In Maragheh, the astronomical concepts of the Tusi couple and Urdi's Lemma were conceived. Without these concepts, Copernicus could not have developed the heliocentric model of the solar system. We hope the irony of this is not lost on the reader. Apart from funding the observatory in Persia and their openness toward all religions, it is indeed difficult to point out any significant achievements in philosophical, scientific, artistic, or religious creativity during the empire phase.

The Mongols who returned to Mongolia, having firsthand witnessed the world at large, helped create a renaissance of Mongolian culture under the influence of Tibetan and Chinese Buddhism, and it flourished. Mongolia produced great architecture, silk painting, and sculpture in the fifteenth and sixteenth centuries. In the seventeenth century, a new script called *Todo bichig* was developed by Pandita Namhaijamto (1599–1662). In the seventeenth century, Zanabazar, who was head of Buddhism, created incredibly beautiful sculptures of Sita Tara and Siyama Tara, inspired by the Sanskrit gods of Tibetan Buddhism. Finally, in the eighteenth century, a great polymath named Ming Antu (1692–1765 CE) developed nine trigonometric equations and wrote forty-two volumes of *The Roots of Regularities*, five volumes in linguistics, and fifty-three volumes in mathematics. He discovered the infinite series to calculate pi and the arctan, which Madhva of the Kerala school in the fourteenth century discovered. In the seventeenth century, Lubsandanzan wrote a book, *Altan Tobchi*, on statecraft. Huang Taiji, also known as Abahai, wrote a Mongol history book known as *Erdeniin Tobchi*, and Ligdan Khan translated literally hundreds of books about Buddhism into the Mongolian language.

Here, we have an instance where, a half a millennium later, a descendant of Genghis Khan under the gentle influence of Tibetan Buddhism and Chinese culture discovered the idea of limit and infinitesimal behind differential calculus. The genius indeed can sprout even in a nomadic mind under right conditions.

If the reader needs proof that the societal structures and processes in combination with natural and extrinsic causes act to dramatically change the inner nature of a people, the proof is right here in the Mongol experience during the twelfth to eighteenth centuries. First, the formative impact of the harshness of nature, followed by the impact of an intolerant creed and the impact of agnostic creed that valued all life over all laid bare for the reader to examine. However, such change occurs over centuries and is not visible to a particular generation except through historical analysis. And such change may result from intrinsic or extrinsic causes or a combination thereof. It cannot be predicted; it can only be explained.

History, Causes, and Outcomes of the Chinese Civilization

16.10 Brief Political History

Mongol period: The Mongol conquest of China occurred in stages, culminating in the defeat of the Song dynasty in southern China in 1279. That led to the founding of the Yuan dynasty, which lasted until 1368.

The longer-term fate of all Mongol kingdoms after the conquest in Asia and Europe heavily depended on their successful integration into and adoption of local culture, and this clearly failed in China despite heroic attempt by Kublai Khan, mostly due to the divergence of nomadic and settled cultures but also due to the insular nature of Chinese civilization. Mongols who adopted Islam in other parts of Asia were guaranteed instant integration. They had no such luck in China. Thus, the Yuan dynasty was one of the shortest-lived significant dynasties in the history of China. Under Kublai Khan's rule, the winter capital was moved from Mongolian territory to the Chinese City of Dadu, which is modern-day Beijing. He established the summer capitol in Shangdu, which is also referred to as Xanadu.

Clearly, Mongol conquest shook up China through the destruction of the agricultural base and human life. However, Mongols also improved the infrastructure and secured the Silk Road. Their contradictory behavior of attempting to adopt Chinese culture while putting down the Chinese contributed to the rise of Ming dynasty. After the fall of the Yuan dynasty, the Mongol intrusions into China were a periodic feature of Ming period. This required considerable surplus allocation to the military and the fortification of the Great Wall. These actions reinforced the insular nature of Chinese civilization. Mongols protected China from potential Muslim aggression. Thus, China lost sustained political independence and control of its surplus to the Mongols for about a century, and its strategic response was twofold: to defeat the Mongols and absorb them into Chinese culture, much like civilizations had always done. Following the overthrow of the Mongols, China clearly went through a period of military assertiveness and sea exploration in the fifteenth century, followed by a return to its historic insularity in part because the constant threat from the Mongols and other nomads required constant vigilance.

Ming period: Neglect of agriculture by the Yuan dynasty resulted in many peasant revolts that ultimately led to its downfall. The Ming dynasty, founded by Zhu Yuanzhang, a former Buddhist monk, came to power in 1368. Ming emperors, at the behest of the merchant class, financed the naval expeditions of Admiral Zheng He in early fifteenth century. Superficially, China, like the Muslim-Turkish empires in India and Persia and the Ottoman Empire, appeared prosperous during this phase; however, beneath the surface, a different future was slowly unfolding. Ming emperors were not greatly interested in territorial expansion. They had a relationship of loose suzerainty with Tibet, a conquest of Vietnam was short-lived, and a war with Japan was fought in 1592, which, however, was initiated by a Japanese warlord Hideyoshi, who had dreams of conquering China. Though the Mongol Yuan dynasty was toppled in 1368, the Mongol threat never quite vanished during Ming reign, particularly during the fifteenth century. Fortification of the Great Wall was not of much help; it only tended to reinforce Chinese insularity.

Violent traders from western Europe: With the exception of the Americas, where western European brutality and double-dealing knew no bounds, the approach to Asia in the sixteenth century was different, and China was no exception. The Portuguese and Spanish were hardly in a position to dictate terms to Ming rulers, although the Portuguese tried the military approach for a while unsuccessfully. They resorted to culling favors, such as becoming intermediaries in Chinese-Japanese trade, defeating troublesome pirates in an effort to win trade concessions. Eventually, substantial trade in silk, porcelain, and embroidery developed in exchange for silver, mostly from the New World but also from Japan. Trade based on the Spanish and Portuguese slowly developed control of the trade routes. Although China was open to relatively fair trade with Europe, it was hardly open to European science as we noted below. Thus, European aggressors did not impact the sustained political independence control the surplus. They were happy biding their time and enjoying trade profits. The Chinese response was to indulge them.

Manchu conquest: The Manchus from the northeast, however, were an altogether different matter. Once again, a "remarkable" tribal leader called Nurhaci united the Jerchen or Jin tribes in 1586 in northeastern China. The tribe had ruled China before the Mongols overthrew them. His son, Huang Taiji, renamed the new confederation the Manchu. Jerchen spoke a language called Tungus, which is a derivative of the Altaic language family that includes Turkic and Mongolian languages families. The group is named after the Altai Mountains in central Asia, underscoring that the Jerchen are an offshoot of central Asians who had settled in northeastern China, just as the Huns were a branch of the central Asians settled in West Asia near the Ural Mountains and Caspian Sea. A Japanese warlord named Hideyoshi initiated the Sino-Japanese War in 1592. The Chinese and Korean armies jointly defeated the Japanese, by the Chinese on land and the Korean navy on the sea. However, this greatly weakened the Ming dynasty, thus creating an opening for the Manchus in the early decades of the seventeenth century. The Manchus eventually succeeded in 1644 in conquering China and laid the foundation of yet another nomad empire in China, known as Qing dynasty, which lasted until 1911. Thus, once again, the recipe of a civilizations' weakness combined with a charismatic nomad leader proved fatal. The Qing controlled the surplus and integrated into Chinese culture but forced the Chinese to maintain the Queue hairstyle as a symbol of submission. The strategic response for the Chinese was to accept the foreign rule since the Manchu kept the imperial civil service mainly staffed by the Han Chinese and continued the Chinese court ritual.

China was *mostly* a recipient of aggression during the phase. There was unending harassment from the Mongols in the north; however, Ming emperors dealt with it relatively effectively until the end. The Japanese tried to attack China unsuccessfully, which allowed China-Japan trade to fall into European hands. Increasing wealth during the middle period of the current phase saw rare but short-lived Chinese land- and sea-based assertiveness. China attacked Vietnam, created a massive migration of Hans into Southwest China to change the demographic balance, and extracted tributes from Tibet and many other nations in the Southeast Asia. It is fair to say that China's civilization always focused on defending the Chinese landmass throughout history but became a somewhat reluctant aggressor for a brief, inglorious period during the current phase.

16.11 Natural Causes

Loss of population under Kublai Khan was followed by the black plague in the early fourteenth century, which killed another 30 percent. Toward the end of Ming period, the damage to the economy through inflation was compounded by the so-called little ice age, resulting in crop failure and famines, particularly in the north. In addition, the deadliest recorded earthquake occurred in 1556, and it killed nearly a million people. These two upheavals, combined with a ruinous agriculture, resulted in a breakdown of authority and opened the door to the Manchu invasion in the 1644 CE.

16.12 Intrinsic Causes

Intrinsic Causes—Internal Destructive Outcomes as Causes

Political system: Under the Yuan dynasty, the empire was divided into a central region and eleven branch secretariats. The latter were subdivided into circuits, prefectures, sub-prefectures, and counties. The Ming emperors continued this political structure. A traveling inspector monitored each provincial administration, and the inspector reported back to the emperor. Three departments of policy draft, review, and implementation were consolidated into a grand secretariat, and six ministries—personnel, revenue, rites, justice, war, and public works—continued. The ministries, headed by a minister and run by a director, were under the direct control of the emperor. The ministries and provincial governments were staffed with a meritocratic nine-grade civil service consisting of two thousand to four thousand high-ranking scholar-officials selected through merit exams and about a hundred thousand lesser officials. Eunuchs ran the imperial household. The eunuchs rose to positions of great power under the Ming emperors and were equal in rank to scholar-officials of civil service, though they had only four grades. The royal family and princes were given large estates but had nominal military commands and served no administrative functions. During the Han and Song dynasties, princes functioned as local kings.

Thus, the Ming political structure was highly centralized, consisting of a powerful monarch, a highly efficient meritocratic civil service, and a royal house dependent on powerful eunuchs.

Military capability: Ming emperors maintained a standing army estimated at one million troops and assembled a vast navy; however, the size of their naval force went down significantly after the mid-fifteenth century, after the naval expeditions of Admiral Zheng He. This was a strategic blunder since the Portuguese and other West European states, especially the Portuguese, were getting ready to visit China soon. Interestingly, the position of military generals was hereditary and was generally considered to be below the merit-based scholar-officials.

Economic organization: Emperor Hongwu instituted land reforms and reduced taxes on farmers to as low as 1.5 percent, in part because the first Ming emperor, Wong-Hu, was himself a peasant. This resulted in self-sufficient rural communities throughout China. In addition, many new crops such as corn, potatoes, and tomatoes were introduced to China from the New World discoveries through the Europeans in the sixteenth century. As a result, the population boomed once again, rising by some estimates to two hundred million by the early seventeenth century.

Once agriculture was brought under control, later, Ming emperors focused on industry. The industry was privatized and with the abolition of forced labor, a wage-earning labor class emerged. It is said that during the Ming period, iron production increased significantly and exceeded that of Europe. Manufacture of iron, porcelain, alcohol, and handicrafts, especially silk stockings, made great progress.

The roads and canals built during the Yuan dynasty facilitated trade. After the death of Emperor Hongwu, the restrictions on trade were loosened, resulting in an expansion of commerce, which led to a vibrant merchant class in Chinese cities. Exports boomed and although the Chinese occasionally demanded payments in the form of weapons imports, they mostly got paid in silver. It has been estimated that the Chinese share of world GNP under later Ming emperors was about 30 percent. The increased alliance between the merchants and landed gentry resulted in a weakening of the state. It is claimed, with some justification, that industry privatization, rise of wage labor, rising production, and exports led to the decline of feudalism and the beginning of a market economy.

The great failure of the Ming dynasty was the failure to manage the money supply in paper, copper, and silver. In what may be the first experiment in deregulation, early Ming emperors significantly increased the amount of paper currency in circulation and deregulated the production of salt in the early fifteenth century *while* accepting silver as a payment for licenses to manufacture salt. A natural preference for silver as a medium of exchange as well as an increase in its supply destroyed the value of paper currency, reducing it by as much as a factor of hundred in less than thirty years in the early fifteenth century.

The increase in foreign trade in the sixteenth century, which was settled in silver, and the acceptance of silver by the government further increased the amount of silver in circulation dramatically through exports and increased domestic illegal mining activity. Economic activity came to be conducted in silver and copper coins. However, in the sixteenth century, as foreign trade declined and because King Phillips of Spain blocked the flow of silver from the Americas to China, the amount of silver from overseas dropped, resulting in a three- to fourfold increase in the value of silver relative to copper coins. Since farmers had to pay taxes in silver but could only sell their crops in copper coins, this in effect meant a ruinous tax increase on farmers. This, coupled with a mini ice age in northern China and its resulting famine and lost harvest, meant a dramatic decline in economic activity and led to the downfall of the Ming dynasty. However, as the wealth increased in the later Ming period before the arrival of the Europeans, the internal wealth polarization again tended to increase. The net effect of European trade was to ruin the Chinese economy, precipitate fall of the Ming dynasty, and allow nomadic conquest of China once again in its tortured history.

Systems of religious faith: Kublai Khan provided religious freedom, and the Ming emperors continued the practice of religious tolerance. There was minimal intrusion of religion in the matters of state. Religion was an individual affair, and the practice of religion included ancestor worship, folk religions based on polytheism, Buddhism, and Taoism. Though Christianity and Judaism had long existed in China, the Ming period saw the arrival of missionaries from Europe, such as Matteo Ricci and Nicolas Trigault. There was no science-religion conflict in China during the current phase because both Taoism and Buddhism believed in a lawful self-sustaining universe.

Legal system: There was little change in the legal code inherited from the Song dynasties and derived from neo-Confucianism. Although there were no separate civil and criminal codes in theory, in practice, large sections and subsections of the legal code would be characterized as civil code and was used to establish torts. Confession rather than objective evidence was required to convict a person and that led to excessive torture at times.

Social structure: The social hierarchy of the Mongols with the order ranked as Mongols, non-Mongol foreigners or Semuren, Han Chinese, and the Song Chinese. Kublai Khan worked hard to adopt the Chinese culture, which resulted in the non-Chinese Mongol groups no longer considering him a Mongol, and the Chinese continued to consider him a non-Chinese. The tenfold social hierarchy instituted by Yuan emperors, where the Confucian scholars were rated at number nine, just below the prostitutes at number eight and just above the beggars at number ten, did not endear Kublai Khan to the Chinese.

Under the Ming emperors, the traditional social classification of gentry, farmers, artisans, and merchants became very fluid because of increased social mobility resulting from changes in agriculture, industry, and commerce. The most dramatic change was the increased status of the merchant class, which had begun to fuse with landed gentry. Thus, during the current phase, the internal inequities witnessed several periods of dramatic change. With Mongol victory, for over a century, the Chinese were discriminated against and remained second-class citizens. Following the establishment of the Ming dynasty, the internal inequities took a turn for the positive because of wise agricultural and manufacturing policies.

Knowledge-Creating and educational institutions: No formal universities focused on new knowledge existed in the Ming period. The focus continued on Confucianism and neo-Confucianism and the training of the scholar-officials to meet the needs of civil service.

Wealth allocation processes: The improvement in infrastructure, agriculture, manufacturing, and commerce increased the population and wealth creation severalfold. The rise of a strong merchant class even pulled in the landed gentry, resulting in increasing wealth polarization though increasing surplus. Most of the surplus went into supporting the elites, military needs, and the maintenance of the civil service and empire administration. Not much was directed toward religious or intellectual creativity.

Social cohesion processes: Chinese civilization remained cohesive, capable of fully absorbing foreign invaders. The internal cohesion of Chinese civilization continued to be founded on the absence of a caste system, slavery, and serfdom in the extreme such as in medieval Europe. The concept of an equal field system continued to restrict concentration in landholdings. Thus, the social cohesion in Chinese civilization did not depend on physical control but on a central tendency to return the concentration of wealth to a healthy mean.

Internal wars: Fortunately, internal wars were modest during the current period, except, of course, during the rise and fall of the Yuan dynasty. By and large, China was internally peaceful during the current phase.

Formative Beliefs and Ideology at the End of Fourth Synthesis Phase

There are several aspects that point to significant changes in a belief system. These are continuing strong practical orientation toward knowledge, being impressed with European practical technology but not Christianity and European science, the high degree of social cohesion based on the continuing absence of slavery and caste systems, losing SPI to nomads at the beginning and getting ready to lose it again at the end of the phase, substantial trade with Europe and its colonies toward phase end, a more determined posture with respect to nomads, and the naval expeditions of General He. The changes may be summarized as follows:

- A belief in practical knowledge based on observation and common sense.
- A relative openness toward religion. The major religions were Taoism, Buddhism, limited Christianity, and even Islam in the northwest; the Mongol and the Ming emperors tolerated them all.
- A continuing belief in equality among citizens and supported by the pro-farmer policies of the Ming dynasty.
- A temporary relaxation of the attitude of insularity toward others' practical creativity as well as naval exploration.
- A continuing aggressive but fundamentally defensive posture toward northern nomads.

These beliefs were fundamentally derived from Chinese culture and lessons learned from the Mongol rule.

16.13 Extrinsic Peaceful Causes

With the exception of Jin and Mongols, who controlled China for about a century each during the twelfth through fourteenth centuries, China remained independent and insular during the balance of the current phase. Its interaction with both Indian and Muslim civilizations had declined significantly. Because the impact of European mercantile states was based on the control of the high seas and coerced trade, it cannot be classified as peaceful, even though there is actual territorial control except the island of Macau by Portuguese. This would turn out to be a good assumption as the intentions of European states became clear during the next phase. About the only peaceful impact came from Southeast Asia through Chinese initiative.

Impact of Southeast Asian Civilizations

In the early fifteenth century, we see a brief period of China venturing outside the middle kingdom through the naval voyages of Zheng He, a Muslim eunuch whose father had been to Mecca. The seven different voyages were designed to extract tributes from kingdoms throughout Southeast Asia and involved building over two thousand large naval vessels. However, defeat in Vietnam in 1428, a strong continuing threat from the Mongols in the north, and the dictates of Chinese insular nature forced China to turn inward once again. China's profound sense of superiority was reinforced through interaction with minor civilizations that ended the Zheng He plans to explore several other parts of the known world. The strength of reaction against these voyages can be judged from the fact that all court records of the voyages were burned in 1479. China had, once again, proved its insularity and its sense of superiority. This was a good omen for the European civilization.

16.14 Extrinsic Violent Causes—As Defeated

In the previous phases, China was impacted by Buddhism from India and the opening of the free trade through the Silk Road as it occurred in the early centuries of the Common Era. Chinese, much like India, had managed to keep the nomads at bay more or less through strong defense, bribery, marriage alliances, cultural absorption, and building the Great Wall.

Impact of Mongols

Loss of SPI: China experienced a complete loss of sustained political independence resulting in the Mongol rulers completely controlling SGS.

Loss of control of wealth and means of wealth: Thus, land-based empire-building Mongols conquered China and controlled its sustainable growing surplus but without systematic wealth drain though squandering it on elite decadence. Within a century, the non-Muslim Mongols were absorbed into the Chinese civilization or expelled to Mongolia.

Fair trade: The Yuan dynasty brought the land-based Silk Road to life again, resulting in greatly increased trade. It helped increase the wealth of China during the Ming period after agricultural reform took hold.

Impact on productive outcomes: Mongols made the strategic error of concentrating on trade and manufacturing as noted earlier. Kublai Khan's transformation from conqueror to ruler led to many changes in agriculture. The population of China suffered dramatic loss during the decades of Mongol conquest, reportedly decreasing from 120 million to 60 million. He, however, created aid agencies, increased the use of postal stations, established paper currency, reorganized and improved roads, and expanded waterways. Yuan dynasty emperors, who ruled all of China for the first time from Beijing, seemed to have neglected the agriculture and focused on urban life through encouraging industries such as ceramics and arms manufacture through renovating the capital and linking Beijing and Hangzhou by extending the Grand Canal. However, the Yuan emperors failed to maintain the canal during their decline.

Impact on institutional structures and processes: The response of the Chinese civilization to Mongols was classic, as noted above: over time, convince the uncivilized invader to adopt Chinese culture and be assimilated. This was theoretically possible since the invader did not have a religious or economic ideology of its own. In practice, however, it probably did not happen because Mongols were established world-conquerors when they invaded China. The Yuan emperors built the Forbidden City, combining Arab, Iranian, Mongolian, and Chinese architectural elements. The sprawling complex had a large area for nomadic tents and in fact became a sanctuary of Mongolian culture that insulated the emperors from Chinese culture. Early Yuan emperors did not learn the Chinese language and used translators. Yet they eventually adopted a Chinese name for the dynasty and reinstituted the civil service exam. They were wise enough to not impose the Mongolian lifestyle, religion, and culture on China. The Yuan dynasty also showed intolerance toward certain Muslim practices of Halal slaughter and circumcision.

Assessing net impact: The net impact of the Mongol rule on the Chinese civilization was horrible: destruction of agriculture through neglect, squandering of SGS on an elite decadent lifestyle and overt or covert discriminatory policies toward the Chinese. These policies contributed to its quick decline and the emergence of Ming era.

Impact of European Civilization

It seems that Marco Polo's visit to China had managed to impress Marco Polo and not China. Undoubtedly, the strategically most significant extrinsic violent causes to impact the Chinese civilization during the phase were the arrival of Portuguese and the Dutch in the sixteenth century.

Assessing loss of SPI: Portuguese explorer Jorge Alvares arrived in China in 1513 about fifteen years after they landed in Calicut, India. In 1557, the Portuguese set up a trade monopoly and established themselves in Macau. Because the Chinese were not allowed to trade with Japan, the Portuguese acted as middlemen and traded Japanese silver for Malacca paper and Chinese silk.

Loss of control of wealth and means of wealth: The Portuguese lacked the power to control China politically or militarily since the Ming dynasty, like the Mughals in India, was too strong. However, the Portuguese had the power to control its foreign trade as the trade pattern shifted from land to sea because sea transport was faster, cheaper, and relatively safer. Thus, the Portuguese began to slowly drain Chinese surplus, starting toward the end of the current phase. There was not a lot that the Chinese could do, since the European powers, though fighting among themselves, collectively controlled the high seas. Their control of trade, the discovery of silver in the New World, and the Chinese fascination with silver, much like the Indian fascination with gold, caused waves of high inflation in China. This was a significant cause in the weakening of the Ming dynasty and led to its overthrow by Manchu in 1644. That China did not develop naval power in response to western European invasion is perhaps understandable because of the weakness of the Ming dynasty in the sixteenth century and the Manchu invasion in the late sixteenth century.

The practical, religious, and intellectual creativity was transmitted primarily from Europe to China through Jesuit priests who billed themselves as soldiers of God since its founder, Ignatius of Loyola, had a military background.

Practical creativity: The Ming emperors were awed by European clocks that were spring-driven and unlike Chinese clocks, which were weight-driven. In fact, the first audience with emperor was granted to Ricci because the bell of European clock the emperor owned had stopped working! The incident highlights the leap in the clockmaking capability of sixteenth-century Europeans—after all Chinese invented clocks and the escapement mechanism hundreds of years earlier. Europeans also introduced the celestial globe, telescope, and the altazimuth, a mounting device that can swing vertically and horizontally. The Chinese were more concerned about the military use and abuse of the telescope and not its use as an astronomical instrument. Ironically, some original Chinese inventions, such as clocks, were imported into China during the Ming dynasty after considerable foreign improvements.

Transmission of religious creativity: The Portuguese also brought Christian missionaries; however, Chinese were not impressed with Christian faith since it conflicted with the Chinese belief systems of ancestor worship, folk polytheism, Taoism, and Buddhism. As a consequence, the Christian missionaries mostly presented themselves as monk-scholars in order to extract trade concessions. St. Xavier, who was a cofounder of the Jesuit Order, brought Christianity to China and established a Jesuit beachhead in China but was far more successful in Japan. St. Xavier died in Macau and was buried in Goa, India, though his arm was cut off and sent to the pope as a gift. Ming emperors were hardly impressed with Christianity and kept Jesuits on a short leash as far as Christianity was concerned.

Intellectual creativity: If St. Xavier failed in the religious mission in China (probably because the self-proclaimed soldier of God lacked gun power), later Jesuits, in particular Matteo Ricci (1552–1610), dazzled the Ming emperors with European scientific knowledge, particularly in geography and astronomy. In geography, Ricci challenged the Chinese notions of a square, flat Earth and round heavens, with China as the largest nation and China as "everything under sun." It was indeed a shock to the Chinese that China was but a part of the east. He thus challenged the Chinese notion of other nations as "barbarous and unreasoning animals." Ming emperors sought the advice of the Jesuits in astronomy to set the date for key rituals and the seasons. Soon Jesuits replaced Muslim astrologers in the Ming court after the Jesuits correctly predicted the timing of the solar eclipse of 1629. The Muslim astronomers had predicted it to occur an hour earlier. Matteo Ricci also translated Confucian writings into Portuguese and developed a method to write Chinese characters in Latin. Jesuits also brought European mathematics, including the decimal system.

Fair trade: In 1557, the Portuguese, after several unsuccessful attempts, managed to establish a trade colony on the island of Macau. When the Ming dynasty banned trade with Japan because Japanese warlord Hideyoshi had declared his intention to conquer China in 1592, the Portuguese became the trade intermediaries between China and Japan.

Impact on productive outcomes: The impact of Portuguese on productive outcomes was indirect but profound. The Portuguese created a demand for Chinese products such as silk and tea. Their monopoly of the trade meant it was coerced and not free, thus extracting unreasonable profit despite heavy export duties. The Portuguese also confirmed how the Chinese foreign trade completely dried out under Ming. Finally, foreign trade flooded China with silver, causing high inflation and thus distorting economic activity. Thus, during the late Ming period, China benefited from an infusion of practical technology, scientific knowhow, and a flourishing trade with the Portuguese. However, the practical Chinese mind remained more interested in practical technology and trade and not in science under highly unstable political conditions. Europe learned much from China early in the phase; however, China did not absorb what Europe offered late in the phase through German missionaries.

Impact on institutional structures and processes: There was little impact on the Chinese institutional structures and processes during the phase, despite strong exposure to Europeans.

Assessment of net impact: Ming emperors were selectively interested in European creativity, as it impacted them immediately. One gets the impression that they failed to understand its strategic importance since there was no immediate big price for such a failure. The impact remained confined to trade. As the Manchus replaced the Ming dynasty in the next phase, they made China militarily strong but more insular. As nomads, they understood even less the profound changes taking place in Europe and Europeans were hardly in a position to control a strong centralized China until the mid-nineteenth century, unlike a divided India beginning in the mid-eighteenth century. Thus, trade impact was negative. Chinese insularity drove the real negative impact.

16.15 Productive Outcomes

Productive Outcomes

Wealth creation: The current period was a prosperous period in China as it utilized the technology developed in the previous phase to create wealth under the peace and stability provided by the Ming emperors. However, the Ming policy to control the economy through trade restrictions and price control was not helpful.

Peaceful migrations and travels: There was little by way of large-scale peaceful migrations into China during the current phase. In 1275, Marco Polo, along with his father and uncle, the Venetian explorers, visited the Yuan capital, modern-day Beijing, and a relationship of trust was formed between Marco Polo and Kublai Khan. Of course, Marco was not the first European to visit China; however, his travelogue left a strong impression on the European mind and sparked further interest in Eastern world exploration. The famous 1453 map, the greatest achievement of medieval European cartography, was derived from a similar map Marco brought from China.

In the early fifteenth century, we see a brief period of China venturing outside the middle kingdom through the naval voyages of Zheng He, a Muslim eunuch. The seven different voyages were designed to extract tributes from kingdoms throughout Southeast Asia and involved building over two thousand large naval vessels. However, defeat in Vietnam in 1428, strong continuing threat from the Mongols in the north, and the dictates of Chinese insular nature forced China to turn inward once again. A profound sense of superiority also contributed ending the Zheng He effort to explore several other parts of the known world. The strength of reaction against these voyages can be judged from the fact that all court records of the voyages were burned in 1479.

Peaceful migrations: There was little by way of peaceful migrations into China during the current phase. Only Mongol and European missionaries and traders came to China; the former were hardly peaceful, and the latter were travelers and visitors.

Fair trade: During the Mongol period in the thirteenth and fourteenth centuries, external trade and exchange of technology expanded because of the links of the Yuan dynasty to the vast Mongol khanates throughout Asia. In the fifteenth century, Zheng He's voyages opened sea trade for a while; however, as China turned inward, sea-based trade declined due to a declining shipbuilding industry and sea piracy conducted by Japanese and Chinese themselves. The reaction of Ming emperors was to bring trade under state control and to restrict the sea trade to the ports of Ningbo, Fuzhou, and Guangzhou. In 1557, after initial defeats, the Portuguese established a permanent trading colony at Macau. Sea trade, with the Chinese exporting silk and porcelain, began to thrive again; however, it increasingly came under Portuguese and Dutch control. This trade initially brought an enormous amount of silver into the country, replacing paper currency. Later, when the supply of silver diminished because of a ban on silver export by King Phillip of Spain, it ultimately led to inflation and the downfall of the Ming dynasty. The Chinese benefited also from exposure to New World crops and animals (maize, sweet potato, and peanuts) the Europeans brought to China.

Portuguese and Dutch control of Chinese trade was part of a worldwide trend of trade leadership shifting from the Ottomans to western Europe. Western Europe had succeeded in making an end run against the Ottomans, who had controlled the overland trade throughout Asia and eventually even Mediterranean trade by defeating the Venetians in the early sixteenth century. The fourth synthesis of science or the Italian Renaissance (which we discuss in a later section) was funded through the Venetian trade. When that died out under Ottoman pressure, western Europe's control of world trade funded the fifth synthesis or western European synthesis (that we discuss in the next chapter) and was ready to support science in western Europe for the first time in its history.

16.16 Creative Outcomes

Not much changed concerning nature of outcomes from the Chinese civilization. The focus remained on practical creativity, practical religion, and art. China did not adopt alphabetical script, and its philosophical and scientific creativity remained limited despite exposure to budding European science through Portuguese traders toward the end of the phase. The Mongol and the Ming eras hardly matched the Song era.

Achievements in Practical Creativity

The initial reaction of the Ming emperor Hongwu to practical technology such as clocks and mechanical automation devices embedded in the Khanbaliq palace was one of disgust, and he had them destroyed. Fortunately, the director of the ministry of public works carefully preserved the details of these ingenious devices. Ming emperors, in contrast to the Yuan dynasty, though, were highly successful in reforming agriculture, manufacturing, and commerce but must be regarded as not supportive of new practical technology including military technology. For example, *Huolongjing*, a late fourteenth-century manual, describes canons, simple hand guns, and multistage rockets. However, there was limited innovation in gunpowder technology in China from the fifteenth century onward. The innovations came from Turks, Mongols, and Europeans after they learned about the original Chinese inventions. The birthplace of gunpowder had fallen behind in what it had given the world. The same may be said of clock-making technology. The Portuguese judged water clocks, incense clocks, and sand clocks inferior to European designs in the sixteenth century.

What was true of the mechanical devices and military technology was definitely not true for the application of existing technologies to agriculture and manufacturing. In a detailed encyclopedia compiled by Song Yingxing in seventeenth century, we find descriptions of mechanical and hydraulic devices for agriculture and metallurgical technologies.

Table 16.1: Significant Achievements in Practical Creativity
Chinese Civilization, 1200–1600 CE

Category	Significant Achievements
Materials	
Processes	Textile machines
Energy	
Tools	Kite as a war communication tool
Agricultural Products	
Non-Agri. Products	Toothbrush
Construction	1,100-mile grand canal
Transportation Technologies	Large junk ships
Weapons Technologies	Bombs with shrapnel and sound, first known gun
Infrastructure	
Communications	

Thus, during the Ming period there was a subtle shift in the direction of practical innovation: it did not break new ground anymore; it basically supported the creation of wealth through application. Below we list the key inventions or improvements.

Processes: During the Yuan dynasty, hydraulic-powered bellows were significantly improved, resulting in more efficient iron manufacture as they helped create a higher temperature furnace. In addition, crucible melting and quenching processes were developed, and the textile looms were improved.

Tools: Pearl diving equipment was developed.

Agriculture technologies: The Chinese invented a crank-operated winnowing fan for separating chaff from grain and developed the process for hydraulic irrigation.

Nonagricultural products: The Chinese invented or improved many board games and playing cards. The restaurants during this period also began to use menus for their customers. The Chinese also invented a toothbrush using pig hair that functioned much like the modern bristle toothbrush.

Construction: The 1100-mile Grand Canal was constructed.

Transportation: Chinese engineers built large Junk ships.

Communication: Wang Chen invented ceramic movable type and used it to print a treatise of agriculture in 1313, though the first metal type was used in Korea in 1390.

Weapons: Following the invention of gunpowder during the previous phase, Chinese engineers during the Yuan dynasty invented cast iron bombs, exploding cannonballs, hand cannons, signaling flares, landmines, and multistage rockets with aerodynamic wings. They also used kites for military signaling. Thus, practical creativity remained world-class during the Yuan dynasty.

The significant achievements of the Chinese civilization during the current phase in practical creativity are summarized in table 16.1.

Achievements in Religious Creativity

There was little by way of religious creativity in China during the current phase. Generally, the Chinese had a negative reaction to the Christianity brought in the Portuguese missionaries and Dutch/German Jesuits and continued to be unimpressed by monotheistic Islam. The Buddhist doctrine had been completely absorbed and adapted to Chinese sensibilities. A Chinese brand of Buddhism, Taoism, ancestor worship, and crude polytheism all competed for their share of Chinese religious mind. There was no interest in developing metaphysical doctrines, much like what had occurred throughout Chinese history. The practical Chinese mind did not see value in such speculation in the current phase either.

Achievements in Philosophical Creativity

Metaphysics: The Ming dynasty adopted the philosophy of neo-Confucianism based on the concepts of universal law and external sensate energy-matter complex developed during the Song period. However, one important philosopher, Wang Yangming (1472–1529), proposed an idealist philosophical doctrine reminiscent of Kant stating that objects do not exist independent of the mind and the mind shapes the objects. He, however, correctly claimed that absolute knowledge was not possible and the teachings of great masters like Confucius were not the source of truth but a guide to the truth. Conservative officials in the Ming court strongly objected to this mode of thinking, believing that this line of thinking reflected the impact of Chan Buddhism.

Epistemology: Wang modified the neo-Confucian epistemology of extending knowledge through careful investigation of objects and events. He believed that knowledge was impossible without action. The question of using knowledge for action did not arise because knowledge and action are unified in the knowledge creation process. His great contribution to epistemology was to realize that the process of gaining knowledge was open to all regardless of socioeconomic backgrounds, thus underscoring the universality of mind and reason. Thus, he comes close to the modern view that in order to gain knowledge of the world, one must interact with it and not just think about it. However, he failed distinguish between an action needed to gain knowledge and actions that might be undertaken to change the world based on new knowledge.

Ethics: Wang drew another startling conclusion from neo-Confucianism: he postulated the existence of an innate knowledge of good and evil and that every human being knows this difference from birth. He claimed such knowledge to be intuitive and not rational. Thus, the process of forming a value system was not entirely rational for him.

Aesthetics: Chinese philosophers did not develop any specific theories of aesthetics during the current phase.

Achievements in Art

There was a great resurgence in literature, music, theater, painting, porcelain wares, lacquer wares, jade carvings, and calligraphy during the Ming period. Because of increasing wealth and wealth polarization, a significant market for these works of art developed during the Ming period. Xu Xiake published his voluminous travel diaries.

Chu Tsai-Yu invented equal temperaments in music by dividing the octave into twelve equal parts, stating that this was necessary to reconcile differences in harmony between the fifth and an octave in 1584, independent of the same invention by Galileo's father in 1581.

In summarizing the creative outcomes of Chinese civilization during the current phase, we may assert that extraordinary Chinese practical creativity became more practical and less ingenious. There was little religious creativity, philosophy made progress under Wangming but was squelched, and the Chinese civilization blew a great opportunity to benefit from the outcomes of the fourth (Italian) synthesis that the missionaries brought to China. Perhaps if the Ming dynasty had not fallen, things might have been different, although we doubt that. The lack of alphabetical script remained a great hindrance to clear conceptualization and building mathematical models of scientific phenomenon. Of course, in today's world, all civilizations, including Chinese and Muslim, are pro science since the linkage between science and wealth creation is firmly established. However, in the premodern period, the inner nature of a civilization or an invader was critical to the acceptance of science.

16.17 Achievements in Science

Achievements in Formal Sciences

Yuan Emperors continued the Chinese tradition of practical creativity but did not encourage science by attempting to link China to the Islamic science, as an example. Of course, it would be illogical to expect them to do so. Even during the Ming period, the pace of science was slower than in the Song period (which was mostly observational in nature without development of mathematical modeling in any case) despite very strong diffusion of science into China through monks and Jesuits.

Math: In 1235, Chiu-Shao in Nine Sections treats equation of fourth and higher degree. Chinese algebraist Chu Shih-chieh mentions the so-called Pascal's triangle based on an earlier Arab work in 1303. The most notable achievement was the publication of a book on trigonometry with a Portuguese monk as the co-author in 1607.

Logic: There was little original work done in the areas of logic and linguistics in China during the current phase.

Achievements in Physical Sciences

It was indeed difficult for the insular and superiority-minded Chinese to believe that Europeans had superior science in their possession when they arrived in the sixteenth century. One short-lived reaction was that this science must have been derived from the Confucian philosophy. However, this belief was soon abandoned, as it was too ridiculous to retain.

Astronomy: Astronomer Guo Shoujing built a simplified instrument weighing several tons that was mounted to revolve parallel to the earth's axis in 1270, and he built a twelve-meter-high gnomon to measure the sun's shadow.

Achievements in Biological Sciences

Biology: Li Shih-Chen's great pharmacopoeia containing over a thousand plants and animals with eight thousand uses in 1593, far surpassed any other such encyclopedia of its time. He also described the distillation process in detail.

Medicine: Chinese medicine, continuing its tradition, did not place an emphasis on anatomical structures and continued to define body using semiempirical concepts such as *qi* (life energy), *xue* (blood), *jinye* (bodily fluids), *zang fu* (physiological functions), and *jing luo* (channels), with an emphasis on disease identification and treatment through herbs, acupuncture, massage, exercises, skin abrasion, and suction therapies.

Li Shizhen (1518–1593 CE) wrote *Benaco Gangmu,* which described 1,800 medical drugs. During the Ming period, inoculation against smallpox was very common.

Chinese physicians discovered the cause and treatment for goiter, practiced smallpox inoculation, and knew the cause of diabetes. Chinese physicians also recommended using a toothbrush with bristles as part of oral hygiene.

Achievements in Social Sciences

The singular Chinese contribution to social sciences was taking a population census and was continued in the Ming period.

Thus, China not only walked away from the results of the fourth and early results of the fifth syntheses of science but also mismanaged its sea trade. Its inward policy created a great opening for western Europe in East and Southeast Asia during the current period. Had naval exploits of Commander He been followed through, European control of world trade might not have happened or its domination might not have been so complete.

Summarizing Achievements in Abstract Systems-building Capability (ASBC)

During the current phase, the ASBC of the Chinese civilization stood still: it continued to fail to adopt the alphabetical script. In addition, its state of epistemology remained underdeveloped and did not feel the need to adopt the Indian decimal system. It continued to use its own cumbersome but ingenious physical position value system, consisting of bamboo rods and a board. There was little appreciation of planets, moon, and sun as a controlled experiment in the heavens, and consequently Chinese astronomy continued to remain limited to making brilliant observations about stars, sun, comets, and supernovas. Likewise, the notion of differential calculus remained foreign to the Chinese.

History, Causes, and Outcomes of the Indian Civilization

16.18 Brief Political History

North India

The Sultanate Period: With the death of Mohamed Ghauri in 1206, since he had no sons, one of his slaves named Aibak ascended the throne, thus initiating the so-called Slave dynasty. The concept of equality naturally did not extend to slaves within Islam, though the concept of meritocracy obviously did in this case. The Slave dynasty lasted from 1206 to 1290 and was followed by the Khilji dynasty until 1320. This was followed by the Tuglaq dynasty (1320–1413), unimaginable plunder by another Turkish Muslim invader, Timur Lane (1398), the Sayyid dynasty (1414–1451), the Lodhi dynasty (1451–1526), and the eventually the Mogul dynasty (1526–1857) founded by Babur and Hamayun and secured by the great Akbar (1542–1605). The Mogul dynasty was briefly interrupted by the rule of an exceptionally wise ruler in north India named Afghan Sher Shah.

Following the Slave dynasty, the Khilji dynasty came to power. The Khiljis, also of Turkish origin, settled in Afghanistan before coming to India, much like the Slave dynasty, had ruled Bengal and snatched power in a coup that put an end to the Slave dynasty. During the Khilji dynasty, that Sultanate first established the short-lived Madurai Sultanate in the south. All three of the Khilji sultans are remembered for their ferocity, deceitful character, and religious fundamentalism. Historians generally agree that the second ruler, Alauddin Khilji, was successful in holding back the forces of Mongols and saved South Asia from the destruction Genghis Khan's descendants caused in China.

The Khilji dynasty was followed by the Tughlaq dynasty, with two interesting rulers: Mohammad bin Tughlaq and Firuz Shah. The former, though full of ideas including a failed invasion of Persia, an unsuccessful attempt to shift his capital to southern city of Devgiri, and the introduction of a failed brass and copper currency (supported by gold and silver in the treasury) was ultimately unsuccessful with a much reduced territory by the time he died in 1351. By contrast, Firuz Shah, born of a Hindu princess, was relatively liberal and lacking in ambition and was a successful reformer.

Timur Lane invasion: Timur Lane attacked India in 1398, ostensibly incensed by the relative tolerance the Tughlaq Sultanate displayed toward Hindus, but he was motivated by its great wealth. During his brief stay of seven months, he slaughtered over a hundred thousand Hindus and returned with immense wealth that included ninety fully loaded elephants to carry precious stones for his mosque at Samarkand. The Madurai Sultanate also declared its independence during the reign of the Tughlaqs.

Sultanate continues: The Sayyid dynasty ruled North India as vassals of Timur for about thirty-seven years, and the last ruler voluntarily abdicated in favor of Bahlul Lodhi, who was governor of the Sindh province. The last Lodhi king was Ibrahim Lodhi, who attempted to centralize authority. His reign was marked by constant infighting between Turkish and Afghan rulers in and out of the Lodhi Sultanate. The governor of Punjab and Ibrahim Lodhi's own uncle invited the Timurid/Mongol prince Babur from Afghanistan to invade India. Babur's invasion succeeded in decisively defeating Ibrahim Lodhi in the first battle of Panipat in 1526, thus establishing the Mogul dynasty.

The Founding of the Mogul dynasty: What the Mongols could not achieve in the thirteenth century, they tasted only briefly, toward the end of the fourteenth through Timur Lane's brutal raid. Babur, who claimed to be a descendant of Genghis Khan, succeeded in defeating the Sultanate at Panipat in 1526 after his plans to conquer Persia under Safavids did not succeed. He was lucky to defeat a Rajput coalition one year later in 1527 because of internal treachery.

The shining interlude between the Sultanate and Mughal periods: Babur died soon and his son, Humayun, suffered defeat in 1540 at the hands of the great Pashtun ruler Sher Shah from the Bihar region. Fortunately for Humayun, Sher Shah died five years later in an explosives accident, allowing Humayun to return to India in 1555. He succeeded in capturing Punjab, Delhi, and Agra, and a few months later, he too died in an accident. In the meantime, during the ten years since Sher Shah's death, a remarkable self-made Hindu entrepreneur turned great general named Hemu brought under control or defeated the rebellious-minded Afghan nobles of the Sher Shah court, captured Delhi from the Moguls, and was crowned king on October 6, 1556. A month later, the Mogul army under Bairam Khan and Humayun's fourteen-year-old son Akbar and Hemu's army met at Panipat. Hemu seemed near victory when a stray arrow injured him, and he lost the battle. Thereafter, Akbar consolidated the Mughal Empire and ruled wisely for half a century until his death in 1605.

Violent traders from western Europe: The Muslim dynasties that ruled India had earlier been successful in holding back the Mongol invasions in the thirteenth century (though not in the late fourteenth century) for they understood the land wars and Indian geographical setting favored the settled dynasties against the nomadic Mongols. However, these same dynasties did not understand the menace from the sea and ignored it, never developing a powerful navy.

Thus, after Vasco de Gama reached India in 1498, the Portuguese established trading posts along the west coast at Kollam, Goa, Dieu, Daman, Salsette, Chaul, Bacaim, and Mumbai, mostly through successful skirmishes with Muslim rulers. These were insignificant in terms of territorial mass; however, their commercial importance was significant since, comparatively speaking, the land trade through the old Silk Road was slow, risky, and costly compared to sea trade around the Cape of Good Hope. Thus, a foreign power had come to control the foreign trade of an entire civilization. The Portuguese strategy was to dominate the Asia-Europe trade by setting up colonies in key locations in India, China, and the Persian Gulf. The Portuguese, therefore, did not control the surplus directly; they only controlled the trade wealth through dictating unfavorable prices. None of the Sultanate rulers had foreseen a need to develop naval power and were caught unprepared when the Portuguese arrived.

In addition to trade wealth, the Portuguese, being children of the Inquisition and not having gone through the Protestant Reformation, unlike the Dutch, the English, and the French, displayed a strong will to push Christianity and were quite successful within the small territories under their control. The Portuguese were religiously intolerant: they passed anti-Hindu laws, forced conversions to Christianity, and were equally discriminatory to Indian Jews, Muslims, and even Syrian Christians. Like Muslims, they destroyed temples and synagogues, and in the absence of naval strength, there was little the Indian dynasties could do. The Portuguese dominated the Indian trade throughout the sixteenth century, and with the arrival of the Dutch and the English, their influence declined thereafter. Indian Portuguese colonies progressively lost support from Portugal as Portugal lost interest in the Indian territories and diverted its attention toward Brazil. In essence, the Portuguese opened the door for British control of India; their impact was quite limited. By successful and unsuccessful behavior, the Portuguese taught the British the rules of being a successful systematic wealth drainer in India: a strong naval force, playing local states against one another, not pushing conversions to Christianity, and not intermarrying.

South India

Bahmani Sultanate: Within a century of establishing themselves in the north, the Sultanate moved to conquer the south. The first attempt by the Delhi Sultanate to penetrate the south after the decline of the Cholas was short-lived: the South Indian kingdom of Kakatiya fell in 1323, followed by the defeat of the Hoysal dynasty in 1333 CE. Malik Kafur established the Madurai Sultanate in 1333, but it was ended by the Vijayanagara army in 1378. In 1347, Bahman Shah revolted against Tughlaq rule to establish the Shi'ite Bahmani Sultanate, with a capital at Gulbarga, which lasted until the end of the fifteenth century. The Bahman kings believed they descended from the legendary Persian king Bahman and were patrons of Persian culture. Following this, five separate kingdoms emerged in the early sixteenth century, namely, Bijapur, Golconda, Ahmadnagar, Bidar, and Berar, making it possible for Vijyanagara to survive for three centuries.

Vijayanagara: The Kingdom of Vijayanagara was founded when Harihara I defeated the Madurai Sultanate and consolidated the smaller Pandaya and Kaktiya kingdoms in 1336. The empire reached its zenith under Krishnadevaraya (1509–1529 CE). Vijayanagara armies annexed territories from the Sultanates and extended the domain to Kalinga. The five Sultanate kingdoms generally competed with one another; however, in 1565, they combined their forces to defeat the Vijayanagara kingdom and reduce its capital to ruins. The empire survived until 1686 in a much weakened form. The Vijayanagara kingdom was the last Hindu stand against Muslim invaders before the rise of the Maratha power in the eighteenth century.

Thus, by the mid-fourteenth century, about two-thirds of India was under Muslim control. The only pockets of resistance were the Rajputs in the western desert and Vijayanagara in the south. The loss of sustained political independence was essentially complete by the end of the fifteenth century, except in the two areas mentioned, and its completeness may be appreciated by the fact that power struggles in the conquered areas occurred not between Indian states and the invaders but between different groups of invaders. We may count only the reigns of Sher Shah, Hemu, and Akbar (collectively about half a century) in the north and the state of Vijayanagara (about three centuries) in the south as the only islands of peace and stability during these tumultuous centuries in India.

As if the internal instability was not enough, three major waves of external invasion occurred during the period: the Mongol invasions of the thirteenth century, which the Sultanate repelled; Timur's invasion and looting at the end of the fourteenth century; and the Moghul invasions of the sixteenth century. Indian civilization, true to its peaceful nature, did not attack other civilizations. Even the conquering invaders did not attack other civilizations because they did not succeed in stabilizing the internal situation, and given the wealth-creation capacity of the land, there was little need for it. Who from the fertile plains of Punjab, which were capable of producing multiple crops a year, would want to conquer central Asian grasslands?

Thus, during the current phase, Indian civilization experienced internal conflicts and external aggression. Only toward the end of the phase did the political situation stabilize because Akbar chose to work with the majority Hindu population and discriminate against them.

Yet, on the surface, all seemed well, and Indian civilization probably enjoyed one of the highest standards of living in the world. The surplus, however, was beginning to be drained through trade or used to support the foreign elites. There was little left in attitudes or resources to support creativity. With hindsight, the future did not look good.

16.19 Natural Causes

During the current phase, it is fair to say that all crises were manmade. Unlike in China, Mother Nature did not cause any significant famine, floods, or earthquake in South Asia.

16.20 Intrinsic Causes

Intrinsic Causes—Institutional Structures and Processes

Political system: The political structure the Muslim dynasties employed during the phase was no different from other Muslim states. The sultan had the legislative and executive powers and acted as the highest court of appeal. Some of the early rulers sought investors from the Caliph to improve their standing and adopted titles indicating their nominal subservience to the distant Caliph. The sultan was assisted by a crown prince, commander of the army, and four ministries constituting the treasury, economic policy, judicial affairs, and religious affairs, and at times by a regent, collectively known as council of advisors. The legislative authority of the sultan was circumscribed by the religious scholars or *ulema*, who ensured the consistency of the legal edicts with the sharia, and nobles, who blunted the absolute political power of the sultan. The latter occurred when the sultan was weak or underage.

The empire was divided into provinces and the provinces into districts. The provincial governors had a responsibility for law and order and had military obligations. Below the foreign elite, things did not change much and remained traditional. At the district level, there existed officials performing the functions of revenue collection, treasury, civil law, criminal law, police chief, military attaché, and maintenance of land records. At the village level, the administration consisted of a *panchayat*, with responsibilities for tax collection, local justice, land records, and revenue collection.

Military capability: The military force of the Sultanate comprised of infantry and cavalry, with increasing use of explosive weapons. The invading force was typically small (ten thousand to thirty thousand) and consisted of a fast cavalry. There was little emphasis on building a naval force even under Akbar. The unsettled political situation, attacks on the south, and the demise of the Cholas had destroyed the world's first blue-water navy under the Cholas. Brilliant on-field military tactics by invaders like Babur and others resulted in a string of victories for the invaders. Sher Shah organized one of the most disciplined armies of the period. It consisted mostly of Pashtun soldiers that had a modern artillery division.

Economic organization: It is difficult to imagine increasing economic prosperity during times of an unsettled political situation. The village communities draw inward, manufacturing stagnates, and commerce shrivels. This is what happened during the Sultanate dynasties.

However, there were flashes of effective policies here and there. It was too long a period to not witness at least some positive developments. Muhammad bin Tughlaq improved roads and built roadside inns. Firuz Shah built five canals to bring more area under cultivation. Sikandar Lodhi reduced taxes. By the time the last Lodhi king came to power, however, internal trade had collapsed, and the economic situation asked for yet one more invader, the Moghuls.

However, between the Sultanate and the Moghul period, Sher Shah improved and expanded the Grand Trunk Road; introduced the tri-metallic currency system, which consisted of a silver *rupiya*, a gold *mohr*, and a copper *dam*; instituted an effective tax collection system; and provided needed social services, such as a postal system, hospitals, free kitchens, and police. Alas, he ruled for a mere five years. It was as if history consigned the role of reversing the bad management of the Sultanate centuries and creating a set of policies that the Moghuls would use for effective governance for the following couple of centuries to an able ruler like Sher Shah. It is doubtful if the productivity and surplus decreased during these centuries because of internal political instability and the constant threat and reality of invasions by Turkish and Mongol groups. It is likely the rate of increase probably slowed down significantly.

A study of Mughal society by the end of Akbar's reign reveals the existence of a class distinct from the landholding class and the peasantry, comprised of physicians, architects, scholars, teachers, poets, painters, musicians, and a large number of craftsmen, apart from merchants, who made their living by selling their professional skills. Conspicuous by their absence were scientists focused on understanding nature.

The great prosperity of Vijayanagara Empire was based on technology of harvesting and storing surface water for use in agriculture as well as commodity-based foreign trade with China and other countries.

Systems of religious faith: In general, the Sultanate dynasties had religious bigotry in common, though there were exceptions, such as Muhammad bin Tughlaq. Sikandar Lodhi frequently destroyed Hindu temples to erect mosques in their place and had discriminating policies against Hindus. Thus, Islam gained a number of converts from lower castes who saw this as a way to improve their situations. This was also the period when Suffi saints and Hindus worked together to attempt a synthesis of Islam and Hinduism. The Sikh religion was born from this effort but was completely devoid of Islamic intolerance and fundamentalism. Native faiths continued their tradition of tolerance and an absence of missionary zeal, though increasingly they were turning away from science. The new faith of Islam showed intolerance and missionary zeal and continued the antiscience posture they brought with them.

Legal system: There was little by way of developments in the legal code, given the general stagnation during the phase. The Sultanate implemented the Muslim sharia as the basis of legal code for the Muslims and essentially allowed Hindus to live by their caste rules. In the commercial sphere, typically a Muslim judiciary handled disputes for both Hindus and Muslims. Sher Shah is remembered for making several operational improvements in the judicial system.

Social structure: The Sultanate imposed a distinct social rank order: Turkish tribes, Afghan tribes, converted Muslims, and Hindus, and the stratification of the caste system. Most of the political and military positions went to Muslims. Even an enlightened monarch such as Akbar could only show about 10 percent of the high level positions occupied by Hindus while they comprised about 85 to 90 percent of the population. Yet, the Sultanate saw a gradual cultural synthesis in the north. Many Hindus learned Persian, which became the language of court and commerce. It is probably fair to say that wealth polarization, inequality, and slave trade increased because of the Delhi Sultanate due to tax policies, discrimination against majority populations, and need to support both the defeated indigenous elite and the victorious foreign elite.

In the south, the Vijayanagara rulers encouraged enlightened policy with respect to women, the caste system, and religious rights of the minorities, despite that the empire came into existence to defend Hinduism against ascendant Islam.

Knowledge-Creating and educational institutions: From the day the Slave dynasty general Bakhtyar Khilji sacked Nalanda University in Bihar because it did not contain a copy of the Koran, we may date the beginning of the end of rational enquiry in North India. To escape the invaders, Indian science had to take shelter in the only Hindu state of significance during the current phase, that of Vijayanagara. It is interesting and heartwarming to note that during the pre-thirteenth- century period, South Indian intellectuals were content to travel to the north to learn and teach; however, after the thirteenth century, after witnessing the destruction of places of learning in the north, they rose to the occasion and established new centers of learning in South India.

Wealth allocation process: Until toward the end of current phase, it is probably safe to assume that the surplus did not grow materially despite some large public works irrigation projects, primarily because of political-military instability and mismanagement. Most of the surplus in the north was directed toward military needs both internal and external and to support the lifestyle of the foreign elites. There was little allocated to creative endeavors. Thus, despite glittering monuments based on the Indo-Muslim synthesis in architecture and despite the liberal rule of Akbar, North Indian civilization had indeed entered a dark age with respect to intellectual creativity.

Social cohesion processes: Indian civilization was hardly cohesive: its deep divisions of caste and ethnicity were further accentuated by the arrival of Islam, which imposed the infamous *jizya* tax on non-Muslims and discriminated against the majority Hindu population. The principal methods used for social cohesion among Hindus continued to be the Manu code that governed relations within and between castes, sharia law for the increasing Muslim population, the creative attempts to develop a synthesis between Hinduism and Islam, the Muslim judicial system in criminal matters, and physical force against the Hindu population.

Internal wars: Again, as implied above, because of the unclear rules of succession for the Sultanate, its strong desire to complete the conquest of India, and strong resistance from the Indian states, **internal wars** and aggression increased dramatically, with dynasties typically lasting less than a century.

Formative Beliefs and Ideology at the End of the Fourth Synthesis Phase

The domination of the internally inconsistent metaphysics of structured polytheism (Hinduism) and monism, further deterioration in social cohesion because of the caste system, creeping insularity as evidenced by injunctions against foreign travel, and relentless pressure resulting in steady and substantial loss of territory to Muslim invaders all point to a changing belief system that may be summarized as follows:

- A weakening belief in the knowledge through the union of reason and observation brought about by monism's rejection of science and insistence on the possibility of true knowledge through trained intuition and meditation

- A continuing belief in the fundamental inequality among different castes

- An attitude of insularity toward the intellectual and religious creativity of others

- A continuing belief in peacefulness toward other social orders

These beliefs set the stage for the domination and success of the antiscience philosophy of Turkish Muslims on the northwest frontier.

16.21 Extrinsic Peaceful Causes

There were no significant peaceful extrinsic causes impacting Indian civilization during the phase, except the positive impact of trade with Southeast Asia in the early centuries of the phase, before European colonizers took control of it.

Impact of Southeast Asian civilizations: Here, we may discern three periods. The first period was a continuation of the previous period, with continued diffusion of Buddhism, Hinduism, art, and architecture. In the second period, probably starting in the fifteenth century, Muslim traders brought Islam to Southeast Asia, resulting in the arrival of Indo-Muslim art and architecture and continued fair trade with the Indian civilization. The third period began in the sixteenth century, with the violent arrival of Portuguese and Dutch hungry for trade wealth and armed with Christian dogma and gunboats. The European aggressors did not succeed in replacing one form of monotheism with another but succeeded in cutting off the direct trade with India and became controlling middlemen.

16.22 Extrinsic Violent Causes—As Defeated

The Indian civilization's singular misfortune was to witness the presence of all four forms of the instruments of control during the current phase: empire builders in the form of Turkish Muslim invaders, looters in the form of Timur, violent colonization and plunder by Portuguese colonizers on the west coast, and the founding of the East India Company in 1600, which was to evolve into a systematic wealth drainer par excellence over the next two centuries. In the current phase, however, the first three forms were primarily relevant and only the first that was significant. It is indeed difficult to cite another major civilization that has ever faced such a formidable combination of instruments of control as the Indian civilization faced in the current phase. Yet, superficially, all was well and the Indian civilization, like the Chinese civilization across the Himalayas, was one of the most prosperous in the world.

Impact of Muslim Conquest

Loss of SPI: The invasion of Timur Lane did not have an immediate impact, except the horrible destruction it caused and the looting. However, in the longer term, it probably inspired Babur to attack India a century later. The Indian civilization lost SPI during the first century of the current phase, more completely in the north and largely in the south later. The strategic response of the Indian civilization to Muslim control was to continue to politically and militarily resist the invaders-turned settlers through Rajputs enclaves and the Vijayanagara Empire. The former was neutralized by Akbar's policy of reconciliation, and the latter was defeated in 1646 by an alliance of southern Muslim states. Essentially, despite the resistance, which never died, Indian civilization had lost its sustained political independence.

Loss of control of wealth and means of wealth: The conquerors fortunately were empire builder-settlers and not wealth drainers but, unfortunately, they were closed-minded religiously. Sultanates in the north and south controlled the sustainable growing surplus, and the allocation of surplus was now in the hands of foreign elite infused with an intolerant monotheistic antiscience ideology. At the end of the phase, the Muslim dynasties controlled SGS in all regions except the western desert and extreme south while the European traders had begun to drain wealth from the sea enclaves they controlled.

Transmission of practical creativity: Indian civilization had itself turned conservative and less open during the previous phase, and as result, there was little internal pull. New inventions and technology primarily came through the Turkish-Mongol invaders from the northwest, who inherited some of the fruits of the Arab-Persian synthesis. We may count the introduction of paper manufacture (Turks), hydraulic technology (Persia), and weapons technologies such as explosives, firearms, and cannons (Turks and Mughals) as the Sultanate introduced new technologies into India. These technologies, not world-class and introduced long after their inventions, were absorbed and probably increased the sustainable growing surplus. India was not in direct contact with Chinese or European civilizations or the leading states of the Muslim civilization in the early part of the phase. Access into India was controlled by the technologically second-rate, antiscience Turkish-Mongol dynasties. Thus, little Muslim science trickled into India. The key channels were post-invasion peaceful interaction and travel by individuals.

Transmission of religious creativity: In western and central Asia, Islam met civilizations or tribes that were equal to Arab aggressiveness but open to Islam since they either had a monotheistic tradition or were religiously underdeveloped. In Europe, Islam met a politically and militarily weak but equally dogmatic monotheism. In China, non-Islamic Mongols met a cohesive civilization that preferred a Buddhist agnostic belief system adopted from the Indian subcontinent. And much like India a thousand years earlier, China successfully absorbed the non-Muslim invaders in her bosom. In India, Arabian invaders in the seventh century faced a strong Indian civilization that found monotheism distasteful and held its own against the invader. However, Turkish Islamic invaders in the thirteenth century found the Indian civilization in a much weaker position politically but religiously tolerant. In India, Islam found both an open-minded population and a weakened resistance, the combination of which led to a significant attempt at both conversion and synthesizing Islam and another religious tradition. For centuries, this attempt absorbed the Hindu mind with its penchant for inclusivity. However, in the conquered majority of the subcontinent, the focus of the Sultanate remained the conversion of the Hindu population to Islam using the cover of Sufism. The heroic effort at the synthesis of the two religions resulted in an Indo-Muslim culture in art, architecture, and music. Clearly, by the end of the fifteenth century, the Sultanate was thoroughly Indian but fiercely Islamic within the context of the developing Hindu-Muslim cultural synthesis.

The Muslim empire builders brought monotheism with new vigor into India during current phase. Earlier attempts of forcing Islam had not been successful. Now they were more successful because of military and political control and loss of sustained political independence in large sections of the civilization.

Transmission of intellectual creativity: Intellectually, Muslim dynasties in the sixteenth century never showed any interest in European learning. Thus, the strategic response of the politically subjugated Hindus was to fight Muslim domination, and the strategic response of the Muslim dynasties was to push for Islamic conversions and ignore the European naval threat and opportunities inherent in their science. It was indeed a deadly combination.

Impact on institutional structures and processes: The impact of Muslim invaders was profound on institutional structures and processes. Gone was the political system that separated political power and religion. In the military arena, Muslims brought explosives technology and new fighting tactics. The fundamental economic organization remained unchanged; however, the emphasis changed from agriculture to manufacturing, external versus internal trade, greater use of money, and internal trade passing from the Vaishyas to Khatris in the north. Similarly, Muslims introduced a more structured religious organization to the Indian civilization, going all the way to the Sultanate while destroying Hindu temples to make place for mosques. The business legal system came to be derived from Muslim law while the social law for Hindus remained caste-based. Islam also challenged the Hindu social structure by challenging caste-based inequality. While the caste system survived by becoming even more conservative, the social structure added one more layer: Muslim nobility, followed by the Muslim-dominated military and bureaucracy and the caste-based Hindu social structure. Perhaps the biggest damage was done to the institutions of higher learning and the great universities. There were two reasons for this: first, the invaders had little interest in science, and second, these universities were also centers of Hindu philosophy and religion, which the invaders saw as a threat to Islam.

Assessment of net impact: With hindsight, the Indian civilization was entering a long, dark night, losing its SPI and becoming exposed to an intolerant ideology from an antiscience invader. Yet the superficial Indian civilization appeared healthy. Perhaps the best way to describe the impact of Muslim invasion was that the Indian civilization lost its soul but saved its body, as there was little wealth drain.

Impact of European Civilization

Assessment of the loss of SPI: The Portuguese built their first fort at Pulicat in 1502 with the help of the lone Hindu kingdom of Vijayanagara, which was surrounded by Muslim states. Thus, right at the outset, the cunning Europeans began to build their strength on the subcontinent, exploiting internal divisions. The Portuguese again allied with Vijayanagara to defeat the Bijapur Sultanate in 1510, thus securing permanent settlement at Goa and later acquiring new territories of Daman (1539), Diu (1535), and Bombay (1534). These and other territories constituted a strip of land about fifty miles long and twenty miles wide, less than 0.1 percent of the landmass of the subcontinent, being the first successful bloodsucking leech a European colonizer implanted on the body of the Indian civilization. It is important to understand that the Portuguese were defeated multiple times in India, which is hardly surprising. However, because the Indian rulers lacked naval power and were internally divided, the Portuguese retreated to the sea and successfully staged a return. Naval artillery made the Portuguese successful. The whole affair was highly organized by the House of India and funded by the Portuguese crown, which sent annual armadas to India, sparing no expense to get the best European naval guns. The following years, the armadas were organized based on the information brought by last year's armada.

Strategically, throughout the sixteenth century, politically and economically, the dominant Indian states saw the Europeans as marginally important and suffered their coastal attacks as nothing more than nuisance and often ignored their requests for trade concessions. Indian civilization once again failed to protect its interests on the western coast in 1500 CE, just as it had failed to protect its interests on northwestern frontier three centuries ago.

Loss of control of wealth and means of wealth: Even the first expedition Vasco de Gama organized was successful beyond the wildest dream of the Portuguese. It brought cargo equal to sixty times the cost of the expedition! The Portuguese had tasted Indian blood and liked it. The Portuguese had rules for dividing the loot befitting a sophisticated plunderer: about half for financing the future expeditions, 20 percent for the crown, and 30 percent to the crew and captain. Each crew, in addition to a salary, was allowed to bring a "liberty chest," four feet by three feet by two and a half feet, for personal profit to Lisbon free of duty to be sold at preset prices. It is worth mentioning that the Portuguese sold spices to northern Europe since Venetian merchants, who were supplied spices by Arab and Indian merchants through the Arabian Sea, Red Sea, and Alexandria, controlled the southern European market. The difference is that the former was loot and coerced trade and the latter was free trade. The sale to northern Europe must have excited the imagination of other would-be plunderers in Europe. Why pay full price when you can plunder?

Interesting as these details are, during the current phase, they had little impact on the wealth of India as a whole, though they had a devastating impact on those looted and a major impact on the Portuguese. The population of Portugal in 1500 CE was one million, with a per capita GDP of about five hundred dollars in 2000 dollars. India had a comparable or higher GDP per capita. If the Portuguese were able to coerce half the produce of, say, 2 million Indian peasants on the western coast of India, it would have doubled the GDP of Portugal and would have increased its surplus by an order of magnitude. Such was the power of a wealthy civilization enriching a tiny plunderer.

Transmission of practical creativity: The Portuguese arrived in India in 1498 in Calicut and brought the printing technology with them.

Transmission of religious creativity: Portuguese traders brought monotheism with new a vigor into India and used printing technology as an aide to spread Christianity. Earlier attempts of Christianity had not been successful. Now they were more successful because of military and political control and the loss of sustained political independence in small coastal sections of the civilization.

Transmission of intellectual creativity: Unlike China, German missionaries did not arrive in Calicut. They were Portuguese and were hardly at the forefront of the fruits of Italian Renaissance. Thus, it does not seem that either Euclid's geometry or Copernicus's heliocentric model of the solar system arrived in India during the current phase. One wonders what might have resulted from the fusion of European geometry and astronomy and the Kerala school of mathematical astronomy during the strong Vijayanagara state The reader may recall the empire suffered defeat in 1545 but lingered until 1646.

Impact on productive outcomes: Trade control began to shift from being free trade to coerced trade, thus starting the process of wealth drain. In addition, the trade with Southeast Asia had also dried out because of the decline of a naval presence toward the end of previous phase and the emergence of naval states of Europe, such as Portugal and Netherlands in the Indian Ocean and Arabian Sea. Indian civilization's march toward insularity was accelerated by internal Muslim control and the beginning of European trade control.

Assessment of net impact: With the arrival of Europeans, the civilization was getting ready to lose its body, with Muslim dynasties remaining in blissful ignorance. Only in the second half of the twentieth century, would the civilization begin to revive its body and soul, ironically using achievements of mature science and institutions of political economy.

16.23 Productive Outcomes

Productive Outcomes

Wealth creation: We know Indian civilization had world-class iron, textiles, and dyeing technologies and had significant glass and pottery technologies. This technological base, together with new incoming technologies, was sufficient to maintain world-class prosperity during the current and following phases, leading to an unhealthy complacency.

Migrations and travels: At the beginning of the current phase, the great period of Arab and Chinese travelers to India had essentially come to a close, with the significant exception of Ibn Battuta, and the period of European sailors was yet to begin in full earnest. Battuta came to India during the reign of Muhammad bin Tughlaq, probably in 1333, and spent the next nine years in India. Muhammad bin Tughlaq appointed this thirty-year-old with little legal background judge of Delhi. His annual salary was 12,000 dinars. The significance of this appointment was that it was a symbol of ethnic engineering and empire consolidation on the part of the Delhi Sultanate. Battuta mentions in his memoirs that at Calicut port, he saw a ship about to sail for the gulf to enlist as many Arabs as possible. We may thus assume that there was ongoing migration into the Indian portion of the house of Islam during the current phase. It also suggests that the dynasty was still not secure after being in control of North India for over a hundred years. It was not too different from what the post-Alexander Greeks did in the conquered Hellenistic states. We do not know if Battuta liked it, but based on his memoirs, the Indian custom of chewing beetle leaves with lime and crushed areca nuts at least goes back to Battuta's time. Battuta left India to take up the post of ambassador in the court of Yuan emperors in China.

Fair trade: It is probably accurate to characterize the trade as mostly fair during the phase. Land and sea trade were controlled respectively by the Turkish regime on the northwest borders and Arabs. The Arab presence in and around the Arabian Sea and the Muslim states in Asia, Africa, and Southeast Asia, including Malacca and the Straits of Malacca, formed a worldwide Muslim network of trade relations after the fall of the Hindu and Buddhist empires of Southeast Asia at the beginning of the current phase. It is important to note that Malacca was a very influential trading state and was not just in the business of collecting duties. It was the lynchpin of the trading network that stitched together the islands to the trading centers in Malayan Peninsula, India, and Burma. At the start of the sixteenth century, the real struggle was between this established Muslim-controlled trade network and the Portuguese challengers.

Vasco de Gama arrived at Calicut in May 1498, helped by an Indian sailor named Ahmed ibn Majid, who was hired in Africa by Gama, returned with goods valued at sixty times the cost of expedition in part since he refused to pay the custom duty and full price of goods in gold. This clearly must have made the Portuguese salivate. The failed mission of Pedro Cabral in 1500 CE followed, and he accidentally discovered Brazil after being blown off course on the way to India. In India, he misjudged his strength, entered into a fight, and lost nine of his thirteen ships before returning. Gama returned again in 1502, bombarding the city, looting the rice ships, and, like the barbarian he was, cutting off the hands, noses, and ears of the crew. Over the next thirty years, through sea battles and diplomacy, the Portuguese succeeded in establishing several colonies on the west coast with the capital at Goa. By this time, the Portuguese controlled trade routes around Africa and India as well as South America and were in a dominant position for the next hundred years, before competition from the Spanish, Dutch, and English. Thus, trade that was relatively fair trade until about 1500 had become a coerced trade by the end of the sixteenth century and was dominated by the Portuguese. Just as Hindu Kingdoms nearly eight hundred years ago had failed to protect their trade routes from Arab invaders and traders, coastal Hindu and inland Muslim kingdoms in India failed to protect their trade routes from Portuguese onslaught. Their long supply lines and small numbers were more than compensated for by their superior naval power. The sea for the Portuguese was an area of tactical retreat, just as the desert had been for the Arabs nearly a millennium ago.

Although shipbuilding had declined, it was not dead yet. Arab traders purchased their boats in India, as did the Portuguese later. In fact, the Indian shipbuilding industry continued even under the British until the British banned it with the rise of steam ships.

16.24 Creative Outcomes

At the end of the last phase, the Indian civilization was still capable of producing a giant like Bhaskara in the great learning centers of North India. In the current phase, the loss of political independence to the five bungling anti-science dynasties of Delhi Sultanate and the Moghuls, the political instability of the Sultanate, discrimination against the majority population, and allocation of resources away from creativity and toward luxury for the foreign elites drained the scientific and philosophical creative impulse of the North Indian civilization. The creativity during this phase had to remain confined to architecture and religious synthesis or by taking shelter in the Vijyanagara Empire in the south, which had escaped Muslim control. Thus, during the current phase, creativity was defined by the inner nature of foreign invaders and in effect hiding from them.

Achievements in Practical Creativity

It is difficult to point out significant achievements in

practical creativity during the current phase because creativity was not valued on absorption of the foreign technologies that had come to India with the invaders was emphasized and because the research in this area to date is limited.

The technologies of military significance, such as pyrotechnics (thirteenth century), firearms (fourteenth century), and extensive use of gunpowder (fifteenth century) were mastered.

Achievements in Religious Creativity

To understand the religious dynamic in the North Indian civilization during the current phase, we need to review the background of Islam and the religious situation at the beginning of the thirteenth century.

Arrival of Sufism: When the Turkish Slave dynasty brought Islam to India with full force in 1206, Islam itself had changed into a closed system. The early evolution of Islam took the form of explaining the canonical law believed to be contained in the Koran and sunnah. In parallel, the disciplines of theology and philosophy heavily influenced by Greek rational philosophy also attempted to rationalize Islamic faith through philosophy. However, by the twelfth century, it was clear that this was not only logically impossible but also threatening to the revelation in the Koran. Consequently, the great Persian philosopher and theologian al-Ghazali formally closed the door on independent interpretation of the Koran by jurists, theologians, and philosophers. The growth of Sufism may be thought of as the inner, mystical reaction to this closing of the Muslim mind while attempting to stay within the parameters of the Koran. Thus, the Islam that arrived in India was both closed-minded on mainline religious questions and yet contained a seed of open-mindedness in the form of rebellious Sufism. Sufism, therefore, has even a stronger component of social service for the poor, the sick, and the seeker himself. Sufism may also be thought of as Islam without aggressiveness or intolerance and its imbedded inseparability of state and religion.

Bhakti movement: In North India, meanwhile, the populist movement of Hinduism was the Bhakti movement, which had originated in the south and became a grassroots phenomenon in the north that aimed at directing the Hindus along a devotional path toward a universal God. The biggest proponent of the Bhakti movement in the south was Madhva (whose philosophy we discuss below), for whom only God was completely independent. All other entities, though separate, are dependent on God for their existence. Madhva advocated a devotion to God through the Bhakti path. Madhva's religious views deviated significantly from Hinduism, particularly his concept of eternal damnation. He conceives souls in three categories: souls that qualify for moksha, souls subject to eternal reincarnation, and souls condemned to eternal damnation. It is not clear if this reflects the impact of Islam or Christianity. For the first time, a Hindu thinker had postulated eternal damnation in opposition to universal moksha.

Hinduism-Islam synthesis: Thus, in the early thirteenth century, Islam, Sufism, and the Bhakti movement met head-to-head on the plains of the Ganges. This colliding of the uncompromising and victorious Islam, its emerging softer face in the form of Sufism, and the rising Bhakti movement in the defeated North Indian civilization, which was steeped in the caste divisions, produced a very potent and powerful mixture, resulting in great religious creativity in North India that lasted several centuries. Thus, in the north, we witness the emergence of great saints and poets, such as Kabir, Nanak, Surdas, Chaitanya, Mira Bai, and Tulsidas, who were great proponents of the Bhakti movement.

Kabir (1440–1518), though born of or at least raised by Muslim parents, expressed a reformed version of Hinduism through poetry. He believed in the Hindu concepts of *jivatma*, *parmatma*, karma, reincarnation, and Brahman as an imageless God. Like Buddha, he strongly objected to the caste system. Nanak (1469–1539) believed in an incomprehensible and indestructible Godhead who was capable of personal and impersonal forms. Like Christianity, salvation is possible only through the grace of God. Nanak emphasized awareness of God through chanting, honest living, and serving others, very much in the mold of Sufism. The philosophy of Surdas (1478–1583) is a reflection of the times. He was very much immersed in the Bhakti movement that was sweeping North India. This movement represented a grassroots spiritual empowerment of the masses.

The corresponding spiritual movement of the masses happened in South India in the first millennium. Chaitanya (1486–1534) was another saint from the Bengal region who emphasized awareness of God through public chanting and singing in groups. Mira Bai (1498–1547) represented the Bhakti movement with a feminine perspective. She composed great poetry based on her complete surrender to God as her lover. Tulsidas (1532–1623) remained more within traditional Hinduism and was not interested in religious distinctions. Thus, be believed in both Ramanuja and Sankara. His focus, like that of Nanak, was on the practice of religion through constant awareness of God. He is remembered for compiling the immortal Ramayana, which extols the story of the ancient Aryan king, Rama.

It is instructive that early proponents of Bhakti movements, Kabir and Nanak, were more revolutionary social reformers who wanted to do away with the caste system and tried to synthesize Hinduism and Islam. However, the latter proponents—Surdas, Chaitanya, Mira Bai, and Tulsidas—represent a return to Hinduism and appear more comfortable with a caste system. Thus, Islam's impact during the period continued to be the slow and steady conversion of lower-caste Hindus into Islam under economic incentives and limited persecution. The reformist movement in Hinduism had just about fizzled out by the end of the sixteenth century. This was the third great missed opportunity, since Buddhism nearly succeeded in doing so two millennia ago and since central Asian conquerors were successfully converted first to Buddhism and then to Hinduism a millennium ago. The caste system continued to show its resilience by successfully withstanding both internal and external attacks on it. One is forced to ask why the caste system appears as such a constant in the Indian civilization for at least four thousand years. The answer seems to be that the caste system has exceptionally strong ties to both mainline religious convictions of the Indian civilization through the concepts of reincarnation and karma as well as to the socioeconomic system. It is India's version of both a class system and a system of slavery that was present in most other civilizations until the rise of modern times. As we shall see in the following chapters, what agnosticism, monotheism, reason, and military might could not accomplish, technology and industrialization would achieve, since these forces have the potential to change the very foundation of the Indian economy through functioning markets that allow equal opportunity and hence destroy the economic basis of the caste system.

Parallel to this, there was effort made to translate Hindu religious works from Sanskrit to Persian. Sultan Firuz Shah had a large personal library of manuscripts in Persian, Arabic Sanskrit, and other languages.

Sufism, on its part, developed several aspects in common with the Bhakti yoga in Hinduism, such as the indispensability of a teacher, meditation, and pilgrimage to the tombs of dead saints. Some Sufi groups even granted the possibility of bypassing sharia and attempted to reach God directly. Sufism is so close to Bhakti yoga that we consider it a decisive factor in the spread of Islam, particularly in India and Southeast Asia.

For its part, Islam was happy to let Sufism and economic discrimination to lead the process of convincing lower-caste Hindus to consider conversion to Islam.

Buddhism: There was little significant doctrinal development or expansion of Buddhism during this period. It had already had its run in India and reigned supreme in East and Southeast Asia. Buddhism attracted the Mongols in the thirteenth century. However, they were religiously tolerant and supported several religions until their ultimate conversion into Islam.

Hinduism: The story of Hinduism during the current period is a story both of the continuation of the Bhakti movement started during the previous phase as well as, through it, a response to Islamic monotheism. The Bhakti movement that originated in the south became a grassroots movement in the north aimed at directing the Hindus along a devotional path toward God in an era of foreign rulers with an uncompromising alien faith. The biggest proponent of the Bhakti movement in the south was Madhva, who founded the philosophy of dualism, different from both Sankara's monism and Ramanuja's qualified monism. Madhva advocated the devotion to God through Bhakti.

Achievements in Philosophical Creativity

The fate of practical creativity was also shared by intellectual creativity, particularly in North India under the control of the Sultanate. Intellectual creativity had begun a decline during the last phase under the influence of monism and the Bhakti movement from the south. At the end of the current phase, intellectual creativity in Indian civilization had slowly died, though not before making world-class contributions, precisely at a time when it was growing by leaps and bounds in Europe.

Metaphysics: Madhava (1238–1317) founded the philosophy of dualism, which is different from both Sankara's monism and Ramanuja's qualified monism. Madhava had identified five fundamental differences concerning the entities in the universe: those between self and God, matter and God, one self and another self, between matter and self, and between matter and matter. Thus, Madhva's philosophy was realist, unlike that of Sankara's monism, Mahayana Buddhism, and Pitanjali's Yogachara (all idealist schools of philosophy) and was more akin to the ancient Visheshka, Nyaya, and Samkhya schools. For Madhva, only God is completely independent; all other entities, though separate, depend on God for their existence. It is important to note that Madhva's dualism is different from European dualism more than three centuries later, since only God is independent in Madhava. In Descartes, for example, both mind and matter are independent entities, with the former being nonmaterial in that he equated to consciousness and differentiated from the physical brain.

Epistemology: One might expect that no new ground was broken in epistemology during the current phase, that it must have been a period of endless commentaries on older works, much like the last phase and much like centuries of European epistemology with an uncritical adherence to Aristotle and Plato. There was little thought given to the experimental method, since, after all, a civilization generally develops its epistemology consistent with its physical and intellectual resources, both of which, in North India, had dried out under the Turkish Islamic rule that had destroyed great libraries at Nalanda, Varanasi, Vikramsila, Srinagri, Kanyakubja, Valabhi, and Jagaddala. One would be hard-pressed to find the equivalent of a Fredrick II to support a Tycho Brahe in India during this phase. This was true for North India during the current phase, with one exception: the Jagaddala school, which flourished in Mithila, the capital of the Kingdom of Tirabhukti in eastern India. It alone had succeeded in maintaining its independence through the current phase.

The Navya-Nyaya school insisted that fields of ontology (what can exist and therefore knowable), means of knowledge (perception, reason, comparison, and verbal testimony), rules of logic (inferential knowledge), and how can we be sure that knowledge is true and an unambiguous means of representing acquired knowledge are necessary for developing a complete epistemology.

The Navya-Nyaya School (founded earlier by Udayana and extended by Ganesha Upadhaya in the thirteenth century) produced creative work of highest order in the fields of logic, epistemology, and precise language representation. Ganesha wrote *Tattvacintamani* (*A Thought Jewel of Truth*) to defend the challenge to Nyaya realism by Advaita Vedanta of Sriharsa. Raghunath (1450–1525) wrote forty books, including his important commentary, Tattva-chintamani-didhiti. His other books include Pratyaksamani-didhiti, Anumana-didhiti, Padartha-khandana, Dravyakiranavali, Prakashadidhiti, Gunakiranavali-didhiti, Atmatattva-viveka-didhiti, Nyaya-lilavati-prakasha-didhiti, Krtisadhyanumanadidhiti, and Vajapeyavada.

Ganesha theorized on the means of acquiring true knowledge, and his unique contribution in logic was developing restrictive conditions for the universals (such as vicious infinite regress) necessary in the syllogism. This was a turning point in Indian logic. Gangesha's contribution may be compared to the development of modern logic breakthroughs of Boole, Frege, and Russell. He steadfastly held to realism in strong opposition to the idealism of Vedanta. The principle of economy or *laghava* (equivalent to Ockham's razor in the thirteenth century) was very important to Ganesha in his analyses. Concerning the certainty of knowledge, Ganesha made a distinction between knowledge and knowledge of knowledge and was emphatic that not all knowledge claims can be sustained or that knowledge is fallible. However, he did not fall into the trap of skepticism, since the doctrine of fallibility is restricted to specific instances, and skepticism degenerates into generality. Finally, as we shall note below, he developed an unambiguous means of representing knowledge.

Raghunātha's commentaries focused on the true nature of abstract numbers and its inseparability from natural phenomenon. His studies of metaphysics dealt with proving the nonexistence of a complex reality. The Navya-Nyaya school remained active in India until the eighteenth century.

Ethics: During the current phase, ethics was elaboration of what was already known. No new thinking emerged. Indian mainstream ethics remained driven by the basic metaphysics of Hinduism, namely, reincarnation, the law of karma, free choice, and the four great aims of life.

Aesthetics: The field of aesthetics was no different from that of ethics in that no new theories were put forward.

Achievements in Art

There was considerable progress made in architecture because the Muslim Sultanate and other dynasties supported it, and literature was stimulated by the religious synthesis and creativity. The significant monuments of the period include Qutab Minar (1193–1368), several tombs, and the city of Fatehpur Sikri (1570). The architecture increasingly displayed a synthesis of Muslim and Hindu architecture.

The developments in literature were significant and significantly different compared to the Gupta period. Gone was the emphasis on drama. The focus now was on religious literature. Kabir is remembered for his engaging folk poetry, and Tulsi Das composed the epic *Ramayana* in the prominent language of Indian heartland, Avadhi.

Deccan Sultanates had a number of cultural contributions to their credit in the fields of art, music, literature, and architecture. Famous examples of the latter include Char Minar (1591) and Gol Gumbaz. The Sultanates were also responsible for developing *deccani urdu,* which became the spoken and literary language.

There was also considerable development in music, both religious and secular, and because of the greater control of the north by Muslim dynasties, the musical traditions of the north and south diverged though retained basic elements of *sruti* (relative pitch), *swaras* (individual notes), *raga* (melody), and *tala* (rhythm), though the ragas and talas in the north and south differed considerably. The southern tradition, known as Carnatic music, was mostly vocal and systematized by Purandara Dasa (1484–1564). The northern branch, called Hindustani music, had a greater role for instruments. In the north, the ragas were influenced by Arabic, Sufi, and Persian forms, leading to a sort of fusion, much like in architecture, though in music, Indian elements had a much greater participation. Great composers like Tansen flourished. Religious music flourished under Vaishnavites and individuals like Meera Bai and Chaitanya. Toward the end of the current phase, the Gharanas dominated music in the north and focused on a particular style of singing. New instruments like the sitar and table came into existence. Architecture and music displayed creativity in the current phase, in stark contrast to practical and intellectual creativity.

Thus, we may summarize the state of Indian creativity during the current phase as follows:

- The practical technologies, including military technologies, came through the Turkish invaders and were fully absorbed.

- The invaders placed a high emphasis on architecture and music, and these two areas of creativity flourished. They discouraged all other creativity by burning libraries and by drying up state support to creative individuals.
- In religion and medicine, indigenous and foreign knowledge were synthesized to the extent possible, resulting in the birth of Sikhism and the Tibb system.
- Domestic elites were able to keep only two regions outside the reach of invaders: the kingdoms of Tirabhukti and Vijyanagar. These two regions, significantly, produced world-class creativity in logic, epistemology, mathematics, and astronomy, despite the sea of Islamic fundamentalism, political instability through most of the phase, and a focus on luxuries for the elite.
- Physics, chemistry, biology, and earth sciences remained ignored because of the influence of Vedanta (which takes the focus away from nature and toward moksha) and the lack of interest shown in science by the Muslim dynasties.

Creative impulse within the Indian civilization was on its death bed with the demise of Vijyanagar and Tirabhukti. By the time the Europeans arrived in India with superior technology and the fruits of the Italian Renaissance, the Indian subcontinent was thoroughly under the control of a fundamentalist, antiscience ideology with little interest in new learning. Science in India went into a coma.

Little of the fruits of the third synthesis came to India since the invaders were themselves antiscience and did not value scientific creativity. The Turkish rulers, the Portuguese, or the Dutch were not at the forefront of scientific revolution. The Arab-Persian or European intellectual breakthroughs also did not take root: Islam had walked away from science before it came to India. The Turks had shown nominal interest in astronomy, and Moghuls were nomads with little interest in creativity except in military technology. European science also did not take root because of substantial Muslim control, the destruction of places of learning, political instability, and the religious nature of Muslim dynasties.

16.25 Achievements in Science

Achievements in Formal Sciences

Mogul emperor Akbar, the grandson of Babur, reversed some of the ills of the Sultanate, for he was a tolerant man raised in a Hindu environment in the Rajput town of Umerkot, while his father, Humayun, was in an extended political wilderness from 1540 to 1555. However, Akbar, an illiterate, was hardly in a position to understand the significance of the long-declined Arab science in the Muslim tradition, the nascent European science, or the surviving Indian science (that had been driven to a southern outpost in Kerala and an eastern outpost in Bengal, where the Navya-Nyaya school of logic had originated), for was he not a descendant of the Mongols. He pulled the country together, created prosperity, and even attempted a personal synthesis of all religions in the best Hindu tradition but did not encourage and support a return to the tradition of Indian science.

Under the Vijayanagara Empire, the Kerala school of mathematics and astronomy prospered since Indian science in the fourteenth century was forced to take refuge in South India as Turkish rule consolidated its hold in North India. Madhavan founded the Kerala school of mathematics, and it flourished for about 250 years, producing a string of mathematicians and astronomers such as Narayan Pandit (1340–1400), Parameshvaran (1370–1460 CE), his son Nilakantha (1444–1544 CE), Chitrabhanu (1530–1600 CE), and Jyesthadeva (1500-1600 CE).

Geometry and algebra: The Kerala school had several significant recoveries in the field of geometry and algebra to their credit during their short existence, including the so-called Newton-Gauss method of interpolation and other iterative solutions of algebraic equations, the formula for the ecliptic and the so-called Lhuillier formula for the circumradius of a cyclical quadrilateral figure. Nilakanta discovered the so-called Newton infinite geometric progression convergent series.

Calculus: Jyesthadeva was the author of *Yuktibhasa*, based on the groundbreaking work of Madhava (1340–1425 CE). It has been hailed as the first textbook on calculus. Madhava's discoveries include the infinite series for trigonometric functions, the transcendental function of pi, and computing the value of pi to ten decimal places. The work, rediscovered in 1835 by Englishman C. M. Whish, remained neglected until reinvestigated by C. Rajgopal in 1944. In Whish's words, "Kerala mathematicians had... laid the foundation for a complete system of fluxions...and their works...abound with fluxional forms and series to be found in no work of foreign countries." Madhava is now recognized as one of the world's foremost mathematicians and the inventor of differential calculus. Yet, an achievement as great as this has not been without criticism, since it is viewed as empirical and algebraic and without rigorous proof, unlike Greek mathematics, which is geometric and antiempirical. However, such a viewpoint itself suffers from ethno-centrism as it assumes that mathematical traditions in earlier stages of development can employ very different methods, concepts, and structures.

Logic and linguistics: Tattnacintamani of Ganesha (1474–1550) also developed a methodology for a precise semantic analysis of language based on six basic relations that clarified many traditional philosophical issues. These formulations are the equivalent to modern mathematical logic. Navya-Nyāya methodology to represent knowledge proved to be so effective that they were used by philosophers, linguists, and legal theorists during the centuries that followed.

Achievements in Physical Sciences

Astronomy: Madhavan developed a method to determine the position of the moon every thirty-six minutes.

Indian astronomy had never fallen into the trap of what may be aesthetically appealing (uniform circular motion), theologically required (Earth created by God as center of the universe). or forced constructions as a reaction to the latter (Ptolemy's epicycles). Rather, in the spirit of true science, it remained wedded to what is verifiable based on observation. Traditionally, ever since at least Aryabhatta, Indian astronomy had applied two corrections to compute the longitude and altitude of the interior and exterior planets: the correction for eccentricity (*manda*) and a conversion from a heliocentric to geocentric reference (*sighrocca*). Before Nilakanthan, the correction to compute the longitude was the same, and the correction for latitude were different for the interior and exterior planets. Nilakanthan realized that the latitude of a planet results from the divergence of the planet from the ecliptic. Therefore, he reasoned that the sighrocca of the interior planets is identical to the mean path of the planet, and the manda correction ought to be applied to this mean path of the planet and not the mean sun. This change meant that the method to compute latitude was now the same for interior and exterior planets. Based on this brilliant insight, Nilakanthan developed a consistent theory for the motion of interior and exterior planets for the first time in the history of astronomy. His physical or geometric model was based on all planets except orbiting around the sun and the sun orbiting around a spinning Earth. All that remained was to have the earth also rotate around the sun. Both the earth rotating around the sun and the sun rotating around the earth are computationally equivalent as long as all other planets orbit around the sun.

Nilakanthan, thus, proposed a model of solar astronomy, where all planets except the earth rotated around the sun in elliptical orbits, the sun rotated around the earth in an elliptic orbit, and the earth rotated on its axis. He beat Copernicus by having computationally superior equations of motion for the planets and beat Kepler by over a century.

There also was significant flow of Muslim astronomical works into India. In 1370, Indian astronomer Mahendra Suri translated the existing Muslim works on astrolabe into Sanskrit. In the sixteenth century, a team of scholars at Akbar's court translated the writings of Ulugh Beg at Samarkand. Half a century later, Nityananda translated Muslim treatises into Sanskrit. What direct or indirect impact these translations had on the Kerala school astronomers is not known with certainty.

Parameśvara was a prolific writer and authored some thirty works. These include original treatises and commentaries on other works of astronomy and astrology. Among his original works on astronomy might be mentioned the following *Dṛgganita* (1430); a work on spherics, *Golādīpikā* (1443); and three works on the computation and rationale of eclipses, *Grahaṇāṣṭaka*, *Grahaṇamaṇḍana*, and *Grahaṇanyāyadīpikā*. He also commented on a large number of astronomical works, including the *Āryabhaṭīya*, *Sūryasiddhānta*, *Laghumānasa*, and *Līlāvatī*. Many of his works are yet to be published.

The seamless celestial globe was invented in Kashmir by Ali Kashmiri ibn Luqman in 1589 CE and twenty more were produced later.

Physics: Prasastapadda's analysis on motion centuries earlier was not followed up again and there was not a diffusion of Arab-Persian breakthroughs in the physics of motion. There was little attempt to conceptualize the "unseen" causes of motion through a mathematical approach. Vallabhacharya (thirteenth century) noticed the resistance of water to a sinking object in his *Nyaya-lilavati* in the thirteenth century, just as Sankara Misra (fifteenth or sixteenth century) noted the electrostatic, evaporation, kinetic energy, and capillary phenomena in his *Upaskara*. He conceptualized about surface tension and viscosity (*sanrata*). However, by and large, the great breakthroughs in logic remained confined within their own narrow fields.

Thus, Indian civilization probably had the most sophisticated epistemology during this phase but failed to extend it to an analysis of nature. It was used primarily to settle disputes among various schools of philosophy.

Chemistry: The focus of chemistry was on metallurgy, dyeing, medicinal chemistry (use of mercury in particular), and the alchemy of gold making and elixir synthesis. Metallurgists developed extraction techniques, and processes of distillation and calcinations were employed to develop alkalis, acids, and salts for medicinal purposes. Interestingly, the twin goals of gold making and elixir synthesis converged in mercury, which was used in the transmutation of base models into gold. Its preparations were used to purify, rejuvenate, and transform the body into an immortal state. Toward the end of the phase, there was a definite shift from alchemy to medicinal chemistry since it was clear that alchemy did not deliver.

A rather large number of books on alchemy date from the current phase in several Indian languages.

Earth sciences: Following the likely lead of Muslim cartographers, maps of world "suitable for human habitation" and the city of Amber with house-by-house detail were produced in the seventeenth century.

Achievements in Biological Sciences

Biology: There was little interest in developing the science of biology during the current phase.

Medicine: Early in the phase, religious prejudice against touching corpses and loss of knowledge of anatomy led to a decline in surgery. With the establishment of the Sultanate, Galenic–Arab medicine arrived in India. This has two significant outcomes. First, gradually, a fusion of Indian and Galenic-Arab systems of medicines known as Tibb resulted. *Madin al-Shifa-i-Sikandarshahi,* authored by Mian Bhuwah in 1512, was based on this synthesis. Typically, old Sanskrit texts were translated into Arabic but not the other way around. Second, a class system developed, where the physicians who practiced the Tibb treated the well-to-do, and the vaidyas practicing the Ayurveda treated the poor. With the Mughal dynasty, the practice of medicine entered a period of relative growth: *hakims, tabibs* (the word for physician in central Asia), and *jarrahs* (surgeons) were specialized into ophthalmologists, pharmacologists, veterinarians, anatomists, and sex therapists. Shaikh Bhina, Mulla Qutbuddin Kuhhal, Hakim Biarjiu, Hakim Bhairon, and Chandrasen were well-known surgeons of the Akbar period. Herbal medicine was entrenched with physician owning herbal farms and being responsible for preparation of medicines whose compositions were kept secret.

There was little by the way of systematic medical education. It seems that dynasties did not bother to set up medical colleges and relied on Persian universities for the purpose. *Shifakhanas* (hospitals) were run by the state, employing physicians for the purpose.

Medical research was hampered by the lack of anatomical research. In 1550, Bhave Misra discovered blood circulation. It is not known if the earlier discoveries of Muslims al-Nafis and al-Lubudi, discussed below, influenced him.

With the Portuguese and the French coming, kings and princes recognized the superior medical knowledge they brought with them, and a close personal relationship between a European physician and royalty often developed.

Achievements in Social Sciences

There was little interest in developing social sciences during the current phase.

Summarizing Achievements in Abstract Systems-building Capability (ASBC)

By the end of the current phase, the ASBC of the Indian civilization continued to fall behind except in one arena: it continued to have the world's most scientific alphabetical script. However, the need of the hour, the next great advance in ASBC, was developing controlled experiments here on earth. Indian civilization did not keep up the advancing frontiers, and European civilization led the way. The one area Indian civilization led in was developing the foundations of differential calculus in the fourteenth through the sixteenth century.

History, Causes, and Outcomes of the Muslim Civilization

16.26 Brief Political History

Mongol Destruction of the Seljuk Empire

As we saw in the last chapter, the Seljuks, who were descendants of the Turkish mercenaries recruited by the Arabs in the ninth century, were in control of their masters by the mid-eleventh century. As they consolidated their power, they split into at least three branches. The first branch was called the Rum Seljuks, and they controlled Anatolia with a capital at Konya. The second branch, called the Khwarezmids, ruled over Iran, Iraq, and Syria with a capital at Isfahan. A third branch held sway over Afghanistan and Northwest India and established the Delhi Sultanate in India in 1206. The eleventh and twelfth centuries truly belonged to the Seljuks; they ruled from Anatolia to all of northern India. Like all central Asian nomads, they adopted the local language, religion, and culture to varying degrees. All Seljuks adopted Sunni Islam. Persian culture and language was the culture of the courts, and Arabic culture retained its supremacy in matters of theology and law. They also learned from the Byzantine Empire; several sultans spent time at the Byzantine court and married Byzantine princesses. At the same time, they put enormous pressure on the Byzantine Empire. Thus, the Seljuks as a group were inheritors of Arab, Persian, Byzantine, and Indian traditions. In 1218, Genghis Khan's brutal invasion severely weakened Seljuk power in Anatolia and West Asia, though not in India as we discussed above.

A second blow came in 1258 with Helagu Khan's sacking of Baghdad, and with that, Seljuk power effectively came to an end. Like earlier waves of nomads from central Asia, Mongol motivation was control of trade through Silk Road and, in parallel with the control of the global trade system, the physical control of Chinese, Indian, European, or Muslim civilizations if the latter's weakness allowed that. Mongols under Genghis Khan were in a position to execute both strategies with respect to Chinese (as we noted above) and Muslim civilizations in the thirteenth and fourteenth centuries, encouraged as they were with the difficulties among the Seljuk in the west and the Songs in the east. Mongol invasions destroyed Seljuk power, paving the way for Ottomans in Anatolia. The Mongol invasion had two significant outcomes: establishment of the Ilkhanate in Persian for over a hundred years and the rise of Ottoman Empire in Anatolia in the early fourteenth century, which was to last until the twentieth century.

Safavids and Timurid Dynasties

The Mongol control of Persia ended in the early fourteenth century, with the region undergoing a long period of civil strife. This was ended by invasion of an exceptionally cruel, even by Mongol standards, descendant of Genghis Khan named Timur Lane in 1381 as noted before. The reign of Timur and his son lasted until 1447 when Persia came under the control of the so-called Turcoman federation. In 1500, the Safavids, a group of Turkish and Persian ancestry, came to power and ruled Persia until the mid-eighteenth century. Meanwhile, the Timurid dynasty continued to flourish outside of Persia in Mesopotamia and Caucasus. Timur was followed by his son, Shah Rukh, who was followed by his grandson, Ulugh Beg, who was a far greater scientist than a ruler.

Ottomans

Ottomans rose to power in the early fourteenth century under the leadership of Osman, a gifted leader and brilliant general. He achieved this through consolidation of the splintered Seljuk Empire into the so-called Ghazi states in Anatolia. The Seljuk Empire had been severely weakened by the Mongol attacks. The focus of the Ottoman Empire was westward, on the weakened Byzantine Empire. This struggle lasted for nearly 150 years and ended with the fall of Constantinople in 1453, a seminal event in European history. At the height of its power in the sixteenth and seventeenth centuries, Ottoman territories spanned southeastern Europe, western Asia, and North Africa.

The six-hundred-year Ottoman history may be divided into two nearly equal periods. During the first three hundred years, Ottomans were the most successful instrument of control in the world, conquering territories comparable in size to the Roman Empire. However, as European states made a run against the Ottoman trade starting in the sixteenth and seventeenth centuries, and they pulled ahead in science, technology, religious reform, and manufacturing prowess. Although Ottomans were successful in defending their empire for some period, it was not necessarily a tribute to their staying power; rather, it was because the rising new European powers had bigger fish to fry in Siberia, Americas, Australia, South Asia, and Africa respectively. By the end, the Ottoman Empire had become a joke because it had lived on borrowed time for too long.

16.27 Natural Causes

There were no catastrophic natural causes that impacted significantly the evolution of the Ottoman Empire. It mostly escaped the Black Death that raged in Europe in the fourteenth century. As we mentioned above, the a majority of the lands conquered by the Ottomans were not blessed with natural bounty, being of arid climate.

16.28 Intrinsic Causes—Ottoman Empire

In analyzing the causes of Muslim civilization, we focus primarily on the Ottomans as the leading Muslim empire of the phase, drawing in the Persian civilization as appropriate.

Intrinsic Causes—Institutional Structures and Processes

Political system: The Ottoman sultan or *padishah* (lord of kings) was also the caliphate, the highest political-religious-military position in Islam, though he ruled through delegation of authority. The Ottoman dynasty is unusual in Muslim history for its continuity and longevity in part because it showed a willingness to absorb non-Turkish ethnic groups through intermarriages over the centuries. Its territories expanded, and it solved the traditional Muslim problem of rules of succession. Executive control was exercised through a council of ministers called Divan or Porte, which included tribal leaders, religious leaders, military officers, and, after 1320, a prime minister or a grand vizier. During the sixteenth century, the sultan receded into the background, and the grand vizier became the de facto head of the state. The treasury department under the Ottomans was the most developed in the world during this phase. A bureaucracy of professional accountants trained by the ulema greatly helped to manage the affairs of the state. This great body succeeded in providing perhaps as much stability to the affairs of state as the dynastic continuity.

The Ottoman Empire consisted of twenty-nine provinces and numerous tributary states, some later absorbed into the empire, while others retained a degree of autonomy over centuries. The administrative apparatus was divided into civil and military units. The civil administration was a mixture of administrative practices from Islamic Iran and the influence of the Byzantine Empire, with considerable local autonomy reflecting the diverse nature of the conquered territories that included Muslims, Christians, and Jews. Ottomans aimed to achieve peace, prosperity, and security within their borders, within the overarching context of Sunni Islam and dynastic continuity while always attempting geographical expansion.

Military capability: The Ottoman army included *janissary* (the Sultan's bodyguards), *sipahi* (infantry), *akıncı* (light cavalry), and *mehterân* (the oldest military marching band in the world). The Ottoman army for centuries was the most advanced fighting force in the world and was one of the first to employ small firearms and cannons. During the current phase, the Ottomans also had one of the strongest navies used to conquer Egypt and Algeria.

Economic organization: At its height in the sixteenth century, the Ottoman Empire was an agrarian economy with vast land holdings and a limited population of fewer than 20 million people. The majority of the land may be characterized as unsuitable for agriculture with the technology of the day. Yet it was surrounded by civilizations with thriving agriculture and manufacture. Thus, the Ottomans evolved an economic structure based on small, private farms; limited manufacturing; and extensive commerce through the control of land-based trade routes. Nearly half of state revenues came from agriculture and the rest from import/export taxes. The manufacturing sector steadily increased its presence in the economy, and by the end of the sixteenth century, manufacturing guilds had become established. Many cultivators dabbled in both agriculture and small-scale domestic manufacturing. The state followed a deliberate policy of establishing great commercial centers at Bursa, Edirne, and Istanbul by attracting merchants and artisans into these successive capitals.

As long as the Ottomans had a monopoly over the trade routes before the discovery voyages of the Europeans, this geopolitical-based economic structure served the Ottomans well. We may measure the decline of Ottoman power in direct proportion to the opening of parallel sea routes that bypassed West Asia and the Mediterranean after the current phase.

The economic objective of the Ottomans was to consciously seek to increase state revenue without damaging social cohesion and through maintenance of traditional structures.

Systems of religious faith: The Ottomans had a highly differentiated religious policy toward people of different religions. Having adopted Islam centuries earlier and having conquered vast non-Muslim lands, they developed a three-layered approach to different religious communities under their control. At the top was the Muslim community, headed by the sultan himself, who was both head of state and indeed the self-appointed head of the worldwide Muslim religious community. This was the group that had access to the best opportunities. Its behavior was regulated by sharia and the Koran. In the middle were the Christian and Jewish *dhimmis* (the Ahl al-Kitab), who were allowed to practice their religions subject to certain conditions through the millet system. At times, the Ottomans required the people of the different millets to wear specific colors of, for instance, turbans and shoes. At the bottom were the agnostics and polytheists, who were subject to the jizya tax and were never granted a millet. This three-tier structure remained permeated by a persistent contempt for dhimmis, who had willfully chosen to refuse to accept the truth of Islam despite the opportunity to do so. It is no secret that Ottomans perceived Islam as a superior belief. Ottomans did not forcibly convert non-Muslims; however, non-Muslims had very limited opportunities in the administration of the state. Thus, the Ottoman religious policy was neither secular nor enlightened but was guided by practical considerations. On balance, the Ottoman religious attitude looks good only in comparison to Christian Europe and only with respect to the People of the Book. It hardly approached the religious tolerance displayed by Hinduism, Buddhism, or Jainism, and we would not expect it to. Finally, we must note that the Ottomans practiced an inhuman system of forcefully snatching young Christian boys from their families in southeastern Europe and providing them with an Islamic education for an eventual career in military or administrative system. This was done under the concept of *devsirme*, which roughly means the right to collect blood tax, a conceptual cousin of the notorious *jizya tax* on those not considered the People of the Book. This horrible practice exposed their underlying lack of respect for other religions and their practical attitude.

Both the gradual decline of science and rising conservatism fed on each other to increase the science-religion conflict, culminating in the destruction of the great astronomical observatory founded by Taqi al-Din Muhammad in 1580 under the pretense of prognostications from the heavens claimed by the Muslim clerics. Again, the Ottomans were successful in maintaining internal stability primarily through a policy of territorial expansion spoils that were distributed. This worked well until the end of the current phase.

Legal system: The legal structure in the Ottoman Empire corresponded to the three-layered religious structure plus the needs of commerce. Ottomans had three distinct court systems: a court system for regulating the social and religious conduct of Muslims based on sharia, a court system for non-Muslim People of the Book based on the concept of dhimma, and a trade court system to facilitate the conduct of commerce, including property and contract law. The sultan appointed the judges for each court system and for the first two, from the specific communities. The administrative Kanun, derived from Turkish traditions from the pre-Islamic era, was superimposed on these layers. It dealt with issues unresolved by sharia. However, the dhimmis were under restrictions in dress, building codes, and openness of worship (much like modern-day Saudi Arabia) and could not inherit property from Muslims. The non-Jewish and non-Christian dhimmis were subject to, as we mentioned above, the jizya poll tax. It is true that, unlike Christian Spain during the Inquisition (in part a reaction to Moor conquest), dhimmis did not have to choose between exile, death, or apostasy; however, without question, discrimination against non-Muslims under Ottomans was institutionalized in a clear, well-thought out, and graduated manner to serve the needs of the empire.

Ottoman law allowed slavery. Ottoman sultans routinely converted the war prisoners into slaves and forced them to convert to Islam. In a process called the "harvesting of the steppes," Slavic peasants were converted into slaves. Thus, under Ottomans, "whites" had white and non-white slaves. Like Islam in general, Ottomans did not discriminate on a racial basis, only on ethnic and religious basis.

From the standpoint of the legal code, the Ottoman system was a patchwork. Given the fundamental distinction between Muslims and non-Muslims required by the Koran and sharia, development of an integrated legal code for a multiethnic empire was out of question.

Social structure: Social life in the Ottoman Empire was a result of many competing influences: sharia, Persian culture, Turkish folk culture, and Byzantine culture. Istanbul was very cosmopolitan because it had been the capital of both Roman and Byzantine Empires. In a sense, a cultural fragmentation resulted, with the sophisticated elite Ottoman culture tending to assimilate the Byzantine and Persian cultures through intermarriages and through inheriting the court culture from Persians on the one hand and a folk culture derived from sharia and dhimma system on the other. The same fragmentation appeared in gender roles. Elite women in harems played a commanding role, at one time even running the empire; however, participation of ordinary women outside the home was limited.

The Ottoman harem was a highly developed institution consisting of several grades each of women (*valide sultan* or queen mother, four kadims, an unlimited number of concubines, and odalisques or servants) and eunuchs (penis and testes removed, only penis removed, and only testes removed). Often, the most beautiful women were presented to the sultan by his governors.

Ordinary women, provided their work did not involve association with men, were allowed to earn a living. The most widespread forms of employment for women, both in the cities and in rural areas, were weaving and embroidery. Door-to-door selling, which was widespread, was an acceptable trade for middle-aged women. Women labored in the fields as needed. Thus, it appears that Ottomans had a more relaxed attitude about women than earlier Muslim societies, allowing low-level participation in the economic and social life but still based on the concept of gender separation. Surprisingly, female surgeons existed as the illustration in the fifteenth-century book titled *Cerrahiyyetu'l-Haniyye* (*Imperial Surgery*) depicted. The social pecking order under Ottomans was Muslim-Turkish elite, ordinary Turkish Muslims, non-Turkish Muslims, People of the Book, other non-Muslims, women, and the slaves.

One would have to give relatively high marks to Ottomans compared to earlier Muslim empires since they had evolved a system of self-management of different ethnic communities. There was discrimination against non-Muslims and women, but there were relatively few revolts against the state, unlike the Roman Empire. Thus, we conclude that excessive inequality must be judged to be an improvement over earlier Muslim states.

Knowledge-Creating and educational institutions: One has to look hard to find world-class universities in the Ottoman domains. It is a fair assessment to say that they did not support the great Arab-Persian learning centers either. Instead, the Ottomans focused on the religious and military/administrative education needed to run the empire. Although Madrasah came into existence during the Seljuk period, it reached its most widespread development during the Ottomans. Similarly, the palace schools achieved distinction as the training schools for the young Christian boys snatched from parents as a tribute. These schools located in the Edirne, Galata, and Pasha palaces provided a seven-year training, after which the young men were inducted into serving as personal guard of the sultan, other high officials, and cavalry units or sent to Topkapi palace for further training to become high military or administrative officials of the empire.

Wealth allocation process: The most salient features of the Ottoman Empire were large landholdings and sparse population. In addition, a significant portion of the land was not productive but had to be defended against Persians in the south, Venetia in the west, the Ming Empire in the east, and other Turkish rivals, such as Timur Lane, in the south. This required significant military expenditures, both of an offensive nature early in the phase and of an increasingly defensive nature later in the phase. In addition, the Ottoman elite lived in high style, hardly resembling early Islam, a religion of which the sultan saw himself as the head. Thus, while the wealth production increased in proportion to the population, military and luxurious living easily outpaced it. Ottomans were always chasing additional revenues to support military and their styles. Fortunately, the Islam they had inherited from Arab-Persian days had walked away from creative endeavors in most areas, except those required for high living and military needs, such as architecture, some forms of art, and military technology development. As a result, by the end of the phase, the Ottoman power had already peaked, even if it was not obvious to the Ottomans.

Social cohesion processes: Cohesion was insured by Islam and the second-class status of the non-Muslims under the concept of dhimmis and worse still, the people belonging outside the Abrahamic religions. Separate legal codes and strong states played a key role in insuring social stability.

Internal wars: As trade wealth began to dry out, territorial expansion stopped, and European powers increased pressure on Ottomans, the internal stability declined because of a disruption in the established trade patterns.

Formative Beliefs and Ideology at the Beginning of Fourth Synthesis Phase

The beliefs and ideology of the Ottomans were inherited from the Arabic/Persian empires toward the end of the last phase plus the remnant tribal traditions of the Turks. It thus inherited a monotheism turned fundamentalist, turned mystic under the Sufi saints, and had an antiscience attitude. Mongol invasions shook the Muslim civilization to its foundation, but the Ottomans saved it. Given the rise of Safavids in the east, there was little room for imperial designs in the east, and thus Ottomans focused on hapless southern Europe and the Byzantine Empire and finished it off in several bites. To their credit, the Ottomans evolved the following social pecking order: male Muslims, female Muslims, Christian and Jewish communities, and all heathens. Thus, social cohesion was contrived and managed, not organic. Ottomans acquired Muslim insularity to others; creativity, except that of military and practical significance died. The attitude of aggression continued unabated. The combination of Islam and the nomadic past was unbeatable when it came to aggression, fierceness, and sheer bravery. All these factors led to the following uniquely Ottoman belief system:

- A belief in practical knowledge at the expense of scientific knowledge
- A continuing belief in the fundamental equality among Muslim males coupled with inequality among men and women and among Muslims and non-Muslims, softened a little through the dhimmi system
- A attitude of insularity toward religious and intellectual creativity of others
- A belief in aggression and conquest toward other social orders

These beliefs reinforced the direction and evolution of Muslim civilization for three centuries after the current phase, since the Ottomans were the biggest Muslim empire of the phase.

16.29 Extrinsic Peaceful Causes

The drama of the fourth synthesis began in Iberia at the start of the phase and finished in Italy toward the end of the phase. Copernican revolution, made possible in part by the achievements of Arab/Persian science, was a stone's throw away. However, these achievements seemed irrelevant to the practically minded Turks and were ignored, and they shut down the Istanbul observatory. Thus, there was little impact of the extrinsic peaceful causes on Ottomans except the participation in the Asia-Europe land-based trade, the trade that was being replaced by sea-based trade by the end of the phase.

This was an unforgivable strategic error, driven no doubt by their understanding of the precepts of the Koran. One sees a desperate and ineffective attempt by Turks in the nineteenth century to catch up with Europe, except perhaps Germany, as they understood the connection between science and industry. But it was too late, since Europe except was bent on humiliating the Ottomans to avenge the loss of Constantinople.

16.30 Extrinsic Violent Causes— As Victors and Defeated

During this phase, Muslim civilization was both under attack and attacked other civilizations, as we have covered above. At the dawn of the eighth phase, Muslim civilization as an instrument of control par excellence in the previous phase was at a turning point: its creative phase was behind it; it faced a resurgent Christian Europe, which, though not fully recovered from its bruising battle with Muslim civilization, had dared attack its center through Crusades; Seljuk power was divided; and Ottomans, that were a creation of the Mongol invasion, were still in the future. However, Ottoman rulers saved the Muslim civilization: they destroyed Byzantine Empire and checked Venetian power in the Mediterranean and disintegrating Mongol power in West Asia, even as the Arabs lost the Iberian Peninsula.

Impact of Mongols as Victors

Loss of SPI: It was indeed payback time for the Muslim civilization. The greatest instrument of control was at the mercy of an even greater instrument of control, at least in its home base in the early part of the phase, as it faced Mongol and Timur Lane invasions in the fourteenth century. The Muslim states in West Asia, though of nomadic origin, were no longer nomadic. They were settled and were a civilization in every respect. Consequently, their response to the Mongol invasion was also a classic: resist the invasion with full might and after defeat, absorb the nomadic invader into the civilization. Thus, over time, both the Ilkhanate and Chagatai Khanate converted to Islam and became absorbed into Muslim civilization. The net long-term impact of the Mongol invasion was creating three great Muslim empires: the Ottoman Empire in Anatolia and Southeastern Europe, the Safavid Empire in Persia in West Asia, and the Mogul Empire in India. Muslim civilization seemed to have taken the Mongol blow and not only survived but also expanded its domain by converting central Asian invaders to Islam.

Loss of control of wealth and means of wealth: Clearly, Muslims lost Iberia. However, the Mongols and Timur Lane were classic empire builder-settlers, and there was little wealth drain. Gradually, the Mongols were absorbed into Muslim civilization.

Transmission of practical creativity: It seems that Muslims acquired explosives technology between 1240 and 1280 CE. The diffusion of explosives technology was fast and very effective since cannons were apparently used in 1248 in Seville and 1260 by Mamluks in Egypt against the Mongols themselves. The driving reasons were clearly military and the effectiveness of the technology to change military balance.

Transmission of intellectual creativity: The great

Persian astronomer al-Tusi was able to convince Helagu Khan, son of Genghis Khan to fund the great observatory at Mehgrab. Here, al-Tusi developed the idea of the so-called Tusi couple, essentially doing away with the idea of equant in Ptolemy's convoluted epicycle theory. Clearly, Mongols were not particularly impressed with Islam as a religion as it would be more than hundred years before some of them would adopt Islam.

Impact on productive outcomes: As Mongols lost China, and as their descendants converted to Islam and expanded influence in South Asia, as Ottomans established themselves in southeastern Europe and came to control the Mediterranean, and as Chinese technological breakthroughs leaked out, once again the Eurasian world was linked more fully through trade after a millennium. The treasuries of Muslim states from South India to Greece began to overflow again, the loss of Iberia notwithstanding.

Assessment of net impact: The net long-term impact of invasions must be considered positive in the sense that it brought new technologies to the Muslim world and gave the Muslim civilization a second wind. But if the first wind was pro science, the second wind was antiscience. From a longer historical perspective, the impact was disastrous since it reinforced the antiscience fundamentalism of Islam through conversion of the nomads to Islam. The resulting territorial expansion of Islamic states proved that Islam was indeed a superior ideology given by God himself.

Impact of Europe as Victors

Loss of SPI: In 1212 CE, a Christian coalition under Alfonso VIII defeated Muslims and drove them from central Iberia, the north having been already liberated. Less than four decades later, Alfonso III of Portugal liberated all of modern Portugal. Granada in the south continued to exist until 1492, when the Muslim armies surrendered to army of a united Spain under Ferdinand II of Aragon and Isabella I of Castile. In 1501, a united Spain gave an ultimatum to Muslims and Jews of Granada to convert to Christianity or be expelled, thus extending the horrors of the Reconquista to all of Spain. This was followed by edicts to change Arabic names and attires in 1567 CE.

Transmission of intellectual creativity: Muslim civilization was not only defeated by Mongols and driven out by European civilization, it had turned conservative. Its leader had fallen firmly into Turkish hands, and, other than practical creativity military significance and architecture, there was limited interest in the creativity of other civilizations, particularly after the thirteenth century. The speed of peaceful interaction had slowed down dramatically compared to the last phase, the only exception being technology of military significance.

Impact on Productive Outcomes: The loss of Iberia had little impact on the rest of Muslim states, for the loss was slow and the Moors had long been cut off from Muslim centers in West Asia. It is doubtful any Muslim state shed a tear at the slow, painful death of the Moors; certainly no Muslim state came forward to help. The impact of Mongols and Timur Lane, while destructive in the short run, was actually beneficial, for it linked the pieces of the old Silk Route more completely at a time when new, more efficient sea routes were yet to be discovered.

Impact on institutional structures and processes: Apart from the slow and beneficial impact of military and other technologies on the institutional structures and processes, it is indeed difficult to see the significant impact of defeats in Iberia and at the hands of Mongols and Timur Lane. Quite the contrary—Muslim civilization converted the nomads to Islam and civilized them.

Impact of Ottomans as Victors

Transmission of practical creativity: Ottomans during the current phase were primarily open to the practical creativity of military significance and increasing state revenues through customs duties on expanding land trade they controlled after the Mongol power had declined. And they worked hard to acquire the former and encouraged the latter. The key interaction with the Byzantine Empire, punctuated by wars as it was, was a continuation of the previous phase, with the continued diffusion of art and architecture. After Constantinople was toppled, the magnificent Hagia Sophia was converted to a mosque. The mosaics were covered with plaster and the marble floors with prayer carpets.

Transmission of intellectual creativity: Ottomans showed only a modest interest in intellectual creativity and little interest in religious reform, both of which were accelerating in the Italian city-states of Venice and Florence toward the end of the phase. Being next door to Italy and Venetia, the Ottoman elite clearly had a ringside seat to the fourth synthesis of science taking place during the Italian Renaissance, much more so than the Chinese or Indian civilizations, where the fruits of this synthesis came in fragments, late, or coupled with wealth drain through coerced trade. By contrast, after destroying the Byzantine Empire and conquering southeastern Europe, the Ottomans had an early, clear view of the fourth synthesis at a time when they had wealth and ruled the eastern Mediterranean. However, religious convictions stood in the way, and the Ottomans never made a commitment of resources to seriously reignite creative impulses. This was dramatically highlighted by the destruction of the Istanbul observatory in 1577 CE. Interaction with Europe was limited to trade and wars.

Impact on institutional structures and processes: Ottoman institutional structures were essentially Muslim, Persian, or nomadic in origin and remained during the current phase. The political, military, economic, religious, legal, social, and educational structures remained Muslim, Persian, or nomadic in origin. The only exceptions were the janissary and the dhammi system. The former was an army corps created from abducted Christian boys, and the latter was necessitated by need for social cohesion in non-Muslim majority communities in several conquered European territories.

16.31 Productive Outcomes

Wealth creation: The Ottoman Empire must be judged poorly as far as internal wealth creation was concerned. The agriculture was based on tenet farming with high taxes. Slavery was legal. The empire did not develop manufacturing and industry, and the means of internal transportation were inadequate. Lack of manufacturing development, in part due to the absence of a credit market in part because Islam prohibited interest, meant that land reform (often frustrated by ulema) and limiting the power of landed nobility could not happen. The central idea behind the empire's early success was territorial expansion and control of the spice route Genghis Khan opened. Thus, a significant portion of revenue went into supporting the elite and maintaining a strong military and naval force. Consequently, the empire prospered as long as the spice route and eastern terminus in the Mediterranean remained a monopoly and as long as manufacturing and industry did not develop in western Europe. The source of wealth was the trade monopoly as the empire stood between east and west and territorial conquest and not industry and productivity gains.

Peaceful migrations and travel: The outward expansion of Islam was so great during the current phase that travels by Muslims completely eclipsed any migrations into Islamic territories. Trade, pilgrimage, and knowledge were the most powerful reasons to travel, Muslim traders and students traveled the length and breadth of Muslim territories, and ordinary Muslims often traveled to Mecca. We covered one such famous traveler, Ibn Battuta, earlier in the chapter. Several Ottoman emperors like Mehmed and Bayzeid welcomed Jews to migrate from Europe to Ottoman territories because Christians mistreated them and because of their skills.

Fair trade: Trade was a pillar of the Ottoman Empire. It was located on the trade routes between Asia and Europe, and several European states, such as Venice and Genoa, paid hefty sums to access these trade routes. The commodities trades were vast, including spices (sugar, salt, saffron, ginger, cinnamon, cloves, and pepper), drugs (opium, arsenic, mirobolani, and perfumes), textiles, dyes, luxury goods (gold, copper, coral, porcelain, precious stones, mirror, glassware. and wallpaper), and, of course, the slaves. It has been estimated that nearly half of the revenue of the Ottomans was derived from trade, which would equate to around 6,000,000 ducats in 1600. The present value of this amount is in excess of $2 billion. The difficulties began toward the end of the current phase once the sea routes to America and Asia were discovered. This severely disrupted the Ottoman economy, causing inflation because the trade became imbalanced resulting in considerable social consequence since the government raised taxes to make up for the lost revenue. However, as the mercantile era gave way to the manufacturing era in Europe, the Ottomans did not learn from revolutionary changes happening next door and began a long downward slide from the declining trade and cheaper manufactured goods. Thus, what was true in the arena of intellectual and religious creativity was also true for trade and manufacturing.

16.32 Creative Outcomes—Muslim Civilization

The Ottoman Empire was far more successful than Seljuks were in territorial expansion and thus had a greater interest in practical technology, particularly military technology. In many ways, the Ottoman Empire was an Islamic successor to the Byzantine Empire, which was clearly focused on practical creativity and art and had diminishing interest in scientific and philosophical creativity. However, the Ottomans inherited the mantle of the Arab-Persian synthesis, however much diminished by the closing of the Muslim mind. Muslim civilization produced great scientists and philosophers, including Persian astronomer al-Tusi in the thirteenth century, great inventors like Turkish Taqi al-Din, Mongol Ulugh Beg, the grandson of Timur (yes, Timur the plunderer) in astronomy and mathematics, and Persian philosopher Mulla Sadra (1571–1641) during this period. However, in the last analysis, these achievements were the final hurrah of the Muslim civilization (much like the Indian achievement in mathematics and astronomy through the Kerala school and in logic and epistemology through Navya-Nyaya) since these great achievements were spatially isolated and were not followed through due of lack of commitment and uneven belief in the value of science.

Achievements in Practical Creativity

The focus of practical creativity was weapon technologies and mechanical inventions. The emphasis of agricultural, manufacturing, and transport technologies was limited.

Tools: Ottoman engineers invented clepsydras or water clocks and linear astrolabe. Taqi al-Din invented astronomical clocks capable of an alarm at specified time and a clock capable of showing time in hours, minutes, and seconds that was highly useful for astronomical observations.

Non–agricultural technologies: Three other mechanical inventions by Taqi al-Din deserve special mention. Taqi al-Din invented the first steam turbine in 1551 and put it to a practical use in rotating a spit nearly seventy-five years before a similar invention by Giovanni Branca in 1629.

Table 16.2: Significant Achievements in Practical Creativity
Muslim Civilization, 1200–1600 CE

Category	Significant Achievements
Materials	
Processes	
Energy	
Tools	Clepsydras, suction piston pumps, reciprocating mechanism linear astrolabe, impulse steam turbine
Agricultural Products	
Non-Agri. Products	
Construction	Alcazar built
Transportation Technologies	
Weapons Technologies	Cannon with 600-lb balls, matchlock muskets, military bands
Infrastructure	
Communications	Pigeon relay

Interestingly, he called the book describing his inventions *Sublime Methods of Spiritual Machines*. In 1559, Taqi al-Din also invented a far more impressive six-cylinder monobloc suction pump using hydro power to raise water. The pump incorporated valves, pistons, pin joints, cams, and a reciprocating mechanism. Taken together, these two inventions constitute the possibility of a steam engine. These inventions show Taqi al-Din's mechanical genus; however, these inventions were not fully followed through.

Construction: Several beautiful alcazars were built-in Spain.

Communication: A sophisticated pigeon relay system was developed for long-distance communication.

Weapon technologies: A treatise on gun powder was completed in 1327 that indicated an early interest on the part of the Ottomans in cutting-edge military technology. By the fifteenth century, Ottoman armies were accomplished in the use of guns, cannons, and matchlock muskets and were using them with devastating effect in the siege of Constantinople in 1453. However, it must be noted that bombarding technology used during the siege was provided by a Hungarian named Orban and was invented in Europe earlier. Orban had earlier offered his services to Byzantine Emperor Constantine XI, but the poor emperor could not afford Orban's salary or provide the needed materials to manufacture the guns. Orban died in an explosion during the siege. Ottomans also invented the marching and military bands, underscoring their understanding of the role of music in instilling the will to fight and win. Ottoman engineers also invented cannons with six hundred balls and matchlock muskets.

Table 16.2 summarizes the significant achievements of the Muslim civilization during the current phase in practical creativity.

Achievements in Religious Creativity

As we discussed in the last chapter, the early evolution of Islam took the form of explaining the canonical law believed to be contained in the Koran and sunnah. In addition, the disciplines of theology and philosophy, heavily influenced by Greek roots, also attempted to rationalize the Islamic faith through philosophy, which led to the emergence of Sufism. Thus one may view the practice of sharia for the Muslims immersed in practical life and the pursuit of wealth and power and theology, and philosophy for those intellectually inclined and Sufism for those who focus on the spirit and are disengaged from pursuit of wealth and power. Sufism, therefore, has a very strong component of social service for the poor, the sick, and the seeker himself. Sufism may also be thought of as Islam without aggressiveness, intolerance, and the imbedded inseparability of state and religion. Sufism grew to be a movement that spread throughout Muslim domains.

The most significant event in Islamic thought during this period was a contradictory continuation of restrictions on free inquiry on the one hand and the growth of Sufism on the other.

Thus, most significant event in Islamic thought during this period was a contradictory continuation of restrictions on free inquiry on the one hand and growth of Sufism on the other.

The issue of religion was settled for the Ottomans, Persians, and central Asians. Any creativity ran the risk of heresy. However, under the Ottomans, we witness the expansion of Sufism and the associated whirling dervishes. Originally, Islam focused on good living and meeting a judging God in heaven. Sufism believes it is possible to realize God in this world. During the present phase, Sufism was interpreted as not contradicting Islam and was instrumental in the spread of Islam, particularly in South Asia, since realizing God in this life is a central goal of Hinduism. Sufi lodges were funded through trusts in perpetuity and were very active with social work and charity, including hospice, food for the poor, and Sufi education. Dervishes were Sufis who attempted to realize God through their whirling dances and music aimed at producing a trance.

There were great religious Islamic scholars throughout the current period, such as the father-son duo of Taqi al-Din (1295–1378 CE) and Taj al-Din Sabuki (1359–1393 CE) of the renowned Sabuki family in Egypt, to mention just two. However, their focus was preserving Islam and not religious innovation.

Achievements in Philosophical Creativity

Islamic philosophy developed along three lines during the current phase: mysticism, existentialism, and traditional view. The mystical view is best represented by Rumi and Sufism, and the existential was developed by Persian Suhrawardi and Mulla Sadra.

Mysticism and Sufism: Rumi (1207–1273 CE), a Persian, is better known as an outstanding poet. However, the ideas expressed in his poetry are remarkable indeed and hint at his simple, direct metaphysics: the spirit after devolution from the divine undergoes an evolutionary process by which it comes nearer to the same divine entity from which it devolved. His poem below comes very close to the philosophy of Indian thinker Madhva (1238–1317 CE), who simply emphasized that we do exist, have individuality, and can know things; God exists; and the ultimate goal is union with God. One can also interpret that in this poem Rumi is expressing his belief in reincarnation, provided one equates the ultimate nonexistence with Indian concept of moksha or liberation from cycle of reincarnation.

> *I died as a mineral and became a plant,*
> *I died as plant and rose to animal,*
> *I died as animal and I was man.*
> *Why should I fear? When was I less by dying?*

> *Yet once more I shall die as man, to soar*
> *With angels blessed; but even from angelhood*
> *I must pass on: all except God doth perish.*
> *When I have sacrificed my angel-soul,*
> *I shall become what no mind ever conceived.*
> *Oh, let me not exist! for nonexistence*
> *Proclaims in organ tones,*
> *To Him we shall return.*

In parallel with philosophy of mysticism, the concepts of Sufism, such as psychological organs (*Lataif-e-sitta*), spirit (*ruh*), the astral (*nasma*) and physical body, consciousness (*haal*), stages of consciousness (*manzil* or *maqam*), and the state of union with God (*fanna, baqaa*) also continued to develop.

Existentialism: While the golden age of Islamic philosophy was over by the beginning of the current phase, the school of illumination founded by Persian Suhrawardi (1155–1191 CE) was based on principles of sufficient reason and the impossibility of actual infinity. It was further developed by Mulla Sadra (1571–1641 CE), who wrote forty-five books, including *al-Hikma al-muta'aliya fi-l-asfar al-'aqliyya al-arba'a* (*Transcendent Wisdom of the Four Journeys of the Intellect*). Mulla Sadra developed two key concepts. First, he believed that existence preceded essence (thus turning Plato on his head) and has three planes: material, spiritual, and an intelligible form. He believed that the spiritual form comes into existence at birth but survives death. Second, he developed the concept of substantial motion and self-flow in all existence without any help from God, the latter resembling the Buddhist concept of codependent origination. Taken together, Sadra used these concepts to defend the Koranic metaphysics of a transcendental God and resurrection at the time of death when only spiritual and intelligible forms survive and the material form does not.

In his epistemology, Sadra was a realist, believing in the possibility of knowledge in which reason and imagination played a decisive role. He emphasized that reality exists independent of the mind and is knowable through reason. He did not comment explicitly on the role of perception in his epistemology. He also believed that existence simply is or, is necessary; the accidental essences attach themselves to existence and are the object of knowledge. It is important to note that primacy of existence in Sadra should not be confused with the existentialism of Nagarjuna or modern Western existentialism, for they are not identical. Finally, the spiritual form in man strives for perfection through an understanding of the essences based on intellectual reflection—a concept that resembles the Jnana yoga in Hinduism.

It is clear that Sadra correctly assessed the possibility knowledge of the world through reason but felt compelled to create metaphysics to prove the claims of the Koran. Thus, unlike Buddha, he never arrived at the philosophy of agnosticism and skepticism concerning metaphysical questions. In the last analysis, he remained an apologist for Islam while going from essentialism to existentialism and remaining a true believer in the possibility of knowledge. It may be said that he represented the highest peak in philosophy possible by a believer in Islam.

On the Ottoman side, there were hardly any new breakthroughs except a form of the practice of Sufism through the whirling dervishes, who practiced whirling as a way to remember God. Philosophers like Shamsud al-Din Pashs (1528) popularized philosophy. Shamsud is said to have written two hundred books.

Islamic philosophy tried to break through Islamic dogma through Sufism and existentialism. However, these philosophies were always positioned within an Islamic context to avoid a backlash from the religious establishment.

Achievements in Art

Of all the Muslim states during the current period, not surprisingly, the Ottoman Empire achieved the greatest heights. In architecture, Ottomans achieved a synthesis of Arab, Persian, Turkish, and Byzantine motifs, resulting in mosques with hemispherical domes; slender, pencil-shaped minarets of great delicacy; and palaces of great architectural achievement. Architects from all over, including western Europe, flocked to Istanbul after 1453 CE. Busra was known for its fine silk, Iznik for ceramic art, Baghdad for book calligraphy, and Cairo for fine carpet weaving. Injunctions against painting the human form were cleverly bypassed through miniature painting so as to not offend the religious sentiment of the masses. Similarly, Ottoman music was based on Arab, Persian, Turkish, and Byzantine elements and was organized around *usul* (rhythm) and *makam* (melody). It was religious, military, and secular as well as vocal and instrumental, with thirty different instruments. Later, after the current phase, violin and piano were added. Turks enjoy classical Ottoman music even today. Finally, performing arts were not totally ignored, unlike most Muslim states. The shadow theater was conceived during the Ottoman period and was used effectively to criticize the government.

Undoubtedly, the Ottomans were patrons of arts, and unlike their attitudes in religious and intellectual creativity and in practical military technology, did not hesitate to incorporate foreign influences to achieve their own unique synthesis. Yet, they did not wander too far from Islamic restrictions. Full-scale painting and sculpture were hardly developed.

To summarize creative achievements, there were indeed world-class breakthroughs in philosophy and astronomy by thinkers like Mulla Sadra and al-Tusi. However, as the center of the Muslim civilization came to rest with the Ottomans, a change of focus took place: Ottomans, under pressure from Venetians, and due to an interest in territorial expansion, diverted resources from intellectual creativity to practical creativity. Similarly, we see the emergence of a mechanical genius like Taqi al-Din, a focus on observational astronomy, and the refinement of instruments with developing theoretical models. The destruction of both Samarkand and Istanbul observatories was the final visible blow to Muslim science. Without a solution to the problem of the heavens, the problem of terrestrial motion could hardly be solved. The idea of momentum first conceived by al-Baghdadi had lost momentum, so to speak.

16.33 Achievements in Science (Muslim Civilization)

Achievements in Formal Sciences

It is true that the golden age of Islamic science had drawn to a close. However, it would be natural to expect continued scientific creativity from the Muslim civilization for a some time after decline set in. The tradition of science and knowledge infrastructure cannot just disappear because the state or religious power centers have stopped supporting science with the old fervor. The case of Islamic science during the current phase is hardly different. Besides, Mongols provided a shot in the arm to the scientists.

Geometry: Molla Lutfee (d1512) compiled a book on geometry, *Tad'eef al-Madhbah* (*Duplication of Cube*), which was in part a Greek translation.

Trigonometry: Al-Tusi (1201–1274) in the thirteenth century was the first one to give a systematic treatment of spherical trigonometry. He is also well known for his law of sines for planes triangles. Ulugh Beg of the Timurid dynasty in central Asia compiled sine and tangent tables accurate to eight decimal places. Jamshid al-Kasi (1380–1429 CE), a Persian patronized by Ulugh Beg, developed the law of cosines.

Algebra: Sharaf al-Tusi wrote a treatise on cubic equations and developed the so-called Horner's rule for solving any algebraic equation in 1209 CE. Al-Qalasadi (1412–1486) lived in Spain and Tunisia and made significantly original contribution toward introducing the algebraic notation. Al-Kashi developed an iterative method to solve cubic equations. In *Key to Arithmetic*, al-Kashi defined the properties of binomial coefficients and the so-called Pascal's triangle.

Logic: Great figures of Islamic logic in the previous phase were al-Ghazili and Avicenna (Ibn Sina), with the latter refuting simplistic Aristotelian logic through classifying the premises in a syllogism possible, probable, contingent, and necessary qualifiers. These were followed by Fakhar al-Din al-Rizi, who developed a system of inductive logic (which, in distinction from deductive logic, allows the possibility of the conclusion to be wrong even if all the premises are correct). His work was challenged by Nasir al-Din al-Tusi (1201–1274 CE), who founded the school of Neo-Avicennian logic. Naim al-Din al-Qazwini al Katibi (d. 1276 CE) wrote a text on logic in which he extended the number of modalities or qualifiers considered by Avecenna. This text was used in Muslim religious institutes right down to the twentieth century. Finally, Ibn Taymiyyah (1263–1328) argued that inductive logic is far from certain and elevated the role of analogy in reasoning, particularly in jurisprudence.

Thus, developments during the current phase examined inductive logic, constraints on deductive logic, and analogy as means of drawing valid conclusions. The most important development remained the extension of Avicennian modalities.

Linguistics: Al-Suyuti (1445–1505 CE), an Egyptian linguist and philologist wrote *The Luminous Work Concerning Sciences of Language and its Subfields,* which discussed semantics, morphology, and phonetics. It was based on two earlier works by Ibn Jinni and Ibn Faris.

Achievements in Physical Sciences

Astronomy: The great names in Muslim astronomy during the current phase were Persian al-Tusi (1201–1274 CE); Persian Qutab al-Din Shirazi (1236–1311 CE); Arab al-Urdi (?–1266 CE); Arab Ibn al-Shatir (1304–1375 CE); the central Asian grandson of Timur Lane, Ulugh Beg (1393–1449 CE); Persian al-Kushi (1403–1474, also known as Ali Kuşçu; and Turk Taqi al-Din (1526–1585 CE).

If the focus of Muslim astronomy in the previous phase was refining the Ptolemy scheme, the focus in the current phase was to question it and provide competing models. In Ptolemy, the concepts of epicycle and equant solved the problem of anomalous retrograde planetary motion but at the expense of the uniform circular motion of the planets, which was allowed only around the imaginary equant and not around the deferent or the orbit.

By the early thirteenth century, as we saw, Seljuk and other Turks were firmly in control of the Muslim civilization from Anatolia to India. A decade or so later, Mongols overran most of the Eurasian landmass except South Asia. In 1256, Hulagu Khan, grandson of Genghis Khan, founded the Ilkhanate in Persia and became a patron of astronomer al-Tulsi (1201–1274 CE), who established a world-class observatory near Maragheh, including a library containing four hundred thousand books. There, al-Tusi developed the concept of the Tusi couple, a conceptual scheme to resolve linear motion into two circular motions or vice versa. The Tusi couple may be visualized by imagining two nesting spheres touching at one tangential point, with the inner sphere half the size of the outer sphere and rotating in the opposite direction at twice the velocity. Under these conditions, the tangent point will oscillate back and forth along the diameter of the larger sphere. The significance of the Tusi couple was that it allowed for both the retrograde motion of the planets while allowing uniform circular motion around the deferent and eliminating the imaginary equant.

About the same time, an Arab astronomer named Urdi (1250 CE) formulated Urdi's Lemma. It demonstrated that if two equal lines originate from a third line at equal internal or external angles and are joined with another straight line, the two lines will be parallel. A parallelogram results if the equal angles are external.

Qutab al-Din Shirazi (1236–1311 CE), a disciple of al-Tusi, developed new models for the motions of Mercury and the moon. His work is often considered the high point of Maragha observatory.

Finally, Ibn al-Shatir achieved a breakthrough about 1350. By using theorems of al-Tusi and Urdi, al-Shatir succeeded in eliminating the Ptolemy's equant and epicycles, thereby laying the foundation of nested and mechanically acceptable orbits for the planets.

The theorems of al-Tusi and Urdi were critical for Copernicus (1473–1543 CE) nearly two centuries later to transition from Ptolemy's geocentric model to a heliocentric model. The theorems were translated into Greek at the beginning of the fourteenth century and found its way to Copernicus. Copernicus, it is claimed, was not aware of Shatir's work

Ulugh Beg, who became a ruler of Samarkand as a teenager, built a great observatory called *Gurkhani Zij* in 1428. Using a fifty-meter-high gnomon, he determined the length of sidereal year within an error of twenty-five seconds in 1437, a more accurate measurement than that of Copernicus a hundred years later. He also measured the tilt of the earth's axis at 23.52 degrees, again with better accuracy than that of Tycho Brahe. His work at Gurkhani was followed by al-Kashi, who was a master of astronomical instruments and advocated a purely empirical view of astronomy independent of philosophy and theology. In his *Treatise of Astronomical Instruments*, he described simple, equinoctial, and solistical armillaries; sine and versine instruments; and various sextants. He invented two instruments: the plate of conjunctions to determine planetary conjunctions and the plate of Zones for predicting positions of the sun and planets. He also proposed a model for the motion of Mercury and found evidence for the rotation of the earth through his observations of comets. In 1430, the observatory published new tables depicting star positions using world's largest astrolabe, which measured forty meters. This observatory was destroyed by religious fanatics in 1449 CE, the year Beg died, and was rediscovered only in 1908.

Ottomans were late in getting into astronomy, beginning in

the fifteenth century and producing astronomers like Rumi (1440 CE) and Celebi (1525 CE). However, the greatest Ottoman astronomical observer was Taqi al-Din, who built the great observatory at Istanbul in 1577. Like the observatory at Samarkand, this one also focused on the measurements producing star catalogues that took into account the effect of precession and were used by European astronomers well into the eighteenth century. It is quite clear that he invented the telescope. In a book published in 1574 called *Book of the Light of the Pupil of Vision and the Light of the Truth of the Sights*, he described an instrument that brings faraway objects closer. He also explained how he had made the instrument prior to 1574. Unfortunately, the great observatory did not survive because his prediction of a comet as bearer of "well-being and splendor" was followed by devastating plague in many parts of the Ottoman Empire, and this observatory, which rivaled the ones at Samarkand and Uraniborg, was destroyed in 1580 because of the objections of the Muslim clerics. Taqi al-Din was devastated and died five years later at age fifty-nine.

It is noteworthy that the achievements of Mongol and Ottoman astronomy were essentially in measurement aspects while the Persian-Arab achievements were in conceptual breakthroughs and model building. This is not surprising, however, since Turks and Mongols were newcomers to the game.

It is clear from the above brief history of Muslim astronomy during the current phase that astronomy thrived in the Muslim civilization because of the central Asians, who were either non-Muslim Mongols or Mongols who had converted to Islam recently. These dynasties funded the observatories at Maragha and Samarkand. The Ottomans belatedly joined the game in full force in the late sixteenth century but quickly walked away because of religious conservatism. The conflict between Islam and science had been resolved in favor of Islam ever since Ghazili saw clearly that ultimately science would undo the monotheistic faith he loved so dearly. The Arab-Persian momentum of the golden age fortunately took advantage of Mongol generosity, but Muslim astronomy was clearly living on borrowed time.

Physics: The developments in Islamic physics were much more limited during the current phase. Al-Kashi emphatically rejected Aristotle's physics and emphasized the experimental method as the only path to knowledge. The most noteworthy development took place in optics by Taqi al-Din. In a three-volume work on optics, Taqi al-Din discussed nature and propagation of light, formation of sight, composition of light, laws of reflection, and laws of refraction. Interestingly, Taqi al-Din used astronomy to prove that light does not originate from the eye. Arguing that since the speed of light is constant, stars are millions of miles away, and we see the stars as soon as we open our eyes, light must originate outside the eyes.

Chemistry: Al-Tusi was the first to state the law of conservation of mass that "a body of matter cannot disappear completely. It only changes its form and other properties band turns into a completely different complex or elementary matter."

Biology: Al-Tusi studied biology extensively and believed in an evolutionary universe, starting with the physical evolution of a uniform universe leading to development of minerals, plants, animals, and humans. He anticipated Darwin by six centuries, stating that organisms that gain new features have greater survival value. Organisms change as a result of internal and external interactions. The ideas of natural selection and the survival of the fittest are plainly evident in his writings.

Earth sciences: In cartography, maps drawn by the Ottoman cartographer and admiral Piri Reis in 1513 included the Americas and Antarctica and was considered the most accurate in the sixteenth century. Ibn Battuta explored India, Sri Lanka, China, and Sahara, becoming the most traveled person of his time in 1326–1352. If Ottomans did not excel in natural science, they did nurture the disciplines of geography and cartography. A book by an unknown author in the sixteenth century refers to voyages of Columbus, Cortes, and Magellan. Ottomans adopted European cartography techniques. Piri Reis (1555 CE) drew the oldest surviving map based on Columbus's original map, including Antarctica. Seydi Ali Reis (1562) wrote a book on navigation in the Indian Ocean, apparently using a German compass. The profession of surveying was well recognized and organized in the Ottoman Empire from the seventeenth century forward.

Achievements in Biological Sciences

Medicine: Mamluk Sultan built a sophisticated hospital in Cairo in 1284. There were several Muslim physicians who made startlingly original contributions to medical science. Among them was Ibn al-Nafis (1213–1288 CE) who accurately described the blood circulation system, including coronary and pulmonary circulation. He also refuted the ancient Greek theory of three humors and many other inaccurate theories about the body's anatomy and physiology. Another great Muslim physiologist was Ibn al-Lubudi (1210–1267 CE), who established the pumping action of veins as independent from the heart. Based on his study of the fetus, he established that heart is the first organ to form and not the brain, as was supposed at that time.

Ibn Ilyas was a great anatomist in the late fourteenth century who accurately described many features of the circulatory and nervous systems. His encyclopedia, *Anatomy of the Body*, contained a description of most systems in human body. Muslim physicians also developed concepts of metabolism, infection, and immune system.

As in astronomy, medicine during the Ottoman period did

not break any new ground: Şerafeddin Sabuncuoğlu (1385–1468 CE) published the surgical atlas, *Cerrahiyyetu'l-Haniyye* (*Imperial Surgery*). Sharaf al-Din (1468) was an important figure in the development of Ottoman medical literature. Jalal al-Din Hajee Pasha (d.1417) wrote two books in Arabic, *Shifa al-Askam wa Dawa al-Ala'am* (*Treatment of Illnesses and the Remedy for Pains*) and *Kitab al-Taleem fil Tibb* (*Teaching of Medicine*). Musa b. Hamun (1554), a royal physician of Suleman the Magnificent, wrote the first book on dentistry in Turkish. Tadhrika al-Antaki compared Islamic and Western medicine in 1599 CE. Finally, Shamsuddin Itaki wrote *Risala Teshrehay Abdan* (1632), which introduced European anatomy in Turkish medical literature.

Achievements in Social Sciences

Ibn Khaldun (1332–1406 CE) may be rightly considered the father of several fields of study, among them: philosophy of history, sociology, cultural history, demographics, and economics. Many commentators have credited him with such original and modern concepts as social conflict, social cohesion, social capital, social networks, feedback loops, systems theory, corporate social responsibility, and historical method. Throughout most of his life, Ibn Khaldun was a man of action who considered himself, ultimately, a failure. During the years of withdrawal and reflection on his failures, he wrote an autobiography and several other books in which he developed these and many other concepts in detail. He was truly a genius.

Summarizing Achievements in Abstract Systems-Building Capability (ASBC)

By the end of the phase, the ASBC of the Muslim civilization was no longer world-class: in the previous phase, it had alphabetical script, mastered creative method and sound epistemology, adopted the decimal system, absorbed the importance of controlled experiments in the heavens, and broke new ground in creating experimental method here on earth, particularly in optics and chemistry. What it continued to lack was the science of calculus.

History, Causes, and Outcomes of the European Civilization

16.34 Brief Political History

The history of Europe during this phase consists of four interrelated developments: first, evolution of the Holy Roman Empire in the west and center into nation-states through Reconquista, the Inquisition, the demise of feudalism, Scholasticism, and the Reformation; second, the growth and decline of the city-states of Venice and Florence and the Italian Renaissance in the south; third, the final painful death of the Byzantine Empire and loss of the southeastern Europe to the Ottomans, Russian expansion in the east, and finally the Portuguese and Spanish discovery of sea routes to the Americas, Africa, Australia, and Asia, setting the stage for the western European domination of the world's civilizations to the present time. Below we consider each of these developments.

Evolution of the Holy Roman Empire in the West

As we saw in the previous chapters, the Huns destroyed the Western Roman Empire in the sixth century, and the Eastern Roman Empire came into conflict with the Persians in the seventh century but managed to hold its own. The Holy Roman Empire, the successor of the Western Roman Empire, was initially strong in what are France, Germany, and Italy and Benelux countries today but was under constant threat from Vikings and Hungarians. In the east, the Slavic states of Moravia and Belarusian reigned supreme. We saw how "France" became more or less independent of the authority of the Holy Roman Empire since the tenth century and how "Spain" and southern "Italy," being closest to North Africa, were annexed by Arabs. This fragmentation was further accentuated by the split of Christianity into Catholicism and Orthodox Christianity in 1054 CE. Finally, Normans invaded England in 1066, linking the royal houses of the island and mainland. This combination of external threats and internal dissension (reinforced by papal interference in the political affairs) was responsible for the feudalism in medieval Europe.

Probably the most significant event in the history of western Europe during the current phase was the emergence of several nation-states destined to play a disproportionate role in the history of the world following the current phase. Below, we briefly trace this development.

At the start of the current period, the Holy Roman Empire, though splintered into counties, duchies, and small states, had gained strength because it had begun to benefit from the rise of Venetian trade and had fortuitously escaped the wrath of the Mongols. Thus, it initiated the Crusades against the Christian holy lands in Palestine, supported Reconquista in Iberia, and initiated the Inquisition in many parts of western Europe. Portugal became the first European nation-state in 1249 CE as one of the consequences of the success of Reconquista.

Peasant wars in France and England and the French-English Hundred Years' War (1337–1453 CE), together with royal marriages, helped crystallize the nation-states of France and England. The Holy Roman Empire, which by now had been reduced to the territories of Germany, bits of eastern France, Benelux countries, northern Italy, and Austria today, had a weak political structure and was forced by the princes to organize into "imperial circles" for the purpose of common defense and tax collection. The Hanseatic League of the northern region helped increased the trade between eastern and western Europe, helping the Holy Roman Empire economically once again. The unification of the crowns of Aragon and Castile through marriage in 1469 laid the basis for modern Spain. Thus, by the end of the fifteenth century, Portugal, Spain, France, and England had essentially emerged as nation-states. By the end of the sixteenth century at the conclusion of eighty years' of war between Spain and the so-called seventeen provinces of Nederland, the Netherlands also emerged as a nation-state independent of the Holy Roman Empire. By the end of the current phase, the Holy Roman Empire, directly or indirectly, had spawned nation-states of Spain, Portugal, France, the Netherlands, and England, states that would be the future sea powers in the coming age of discovery of sea routes. Unfortunately, Germany, Italy and other states of central Europe would have to wait until the nineteenth century to fully achieve what nation-states of western Europe achieved three hundred years earlier. This, in effect, in our judgment, had unwittingly set the stage for the world wars of first half of the twentieth century.

Escaping Mongols

We noted earlier how Europe escaped Mongol invasion. Later, an attempt was made to form an alliance between the Crusaders and Mongols against the Muslim empires. It was based on a common belief that a king from the east would help Christians against the scourge of Islam. However, because the Ottomans' focus on southeastern Europe made it possible to liberate Iberia without external help, the alliance fizzled out despite years of gifts and embassy exchanges.

Growth and Decline of Venetian State in the South

Before the beginning of the current phase, Venice controlled several colonies on the eastern Adriatic Sea. In 1204, Venice sponsored the Fourth Crusade, which established the short-lived Latin Empire, replacing the Byzantine Empire. Venice looted Constantinople and became its chief financier. It replaced the Byzantine Empire as the chief trade mediator between Europe and Asia and built a huge navy consisting of over three thousand vessels. When Constantinople fell to Ottoman Emperor Mehmet in 1453, it not only further strengthened Venice but also brought it in direct conflict with Ottomans. By the end of the fifteenth century, defeats at the hands of the Ottomans, discovery of new sea routes, and the plagues of 1575 and 1630, which killed more than a third of Venice population, Venice lost its position in world trade, the source of great wealth to very few families. Venice never had a population of more than three hundred thousand people, and its glory days were sandwiched between the decline of Arab power, the rise of Ottoman power, and a disintegrating Byzantine Empire. Under normal circumstance, a city-state like Venice could only dream of the wealth it had managed to acquire. However, this wealth acquisition played a critical role in developing science since it funded the Italian Renaissance, as we shall see below.

Demise of the Byzantine Empire and the Rise of Russia in the East

We have already alluded to the difficulties the Byzantine Empire found itself in. Having escaped the Huns in the sixth century and having rejected the papal institution, it was in a stronger position than the Holy Roman Empire, despite its defeat at the hands of Seljuks in 1071 CE during the previous phase. The Latin Empire, in the aftermath of the Fourth Crusade initiated by Venice, was replaced by the Palaeologan dynasty, with Emperor Michael VIII as ruler. Michael retreated from Asia Minor and increased taxes on the peasantry to fund the repairs of the capital from the destruction the Fourth Crusade caused as well as to finance his European expansion campaigns. The strategy did not work, resulting ultimately in a devastating civil war that opened the door for Ottoman mercenaries in the mid-fourteenth century. By the end of fourteenth century, the Ottomans had established themselves in Serbia, and the Byzantine Empire was now surrounded. The emperor sought help from the pope, but he demanded a reunion of Catholic and Orthodox branches under his leadership in return. Sensing the opportunity, Ottomans captured the city and put an end to the painfully suffering empire in 1453 CE. The last days of the empire eerily reminds one of the final days of Mughals in Delhi before it fell to the British in 1857.

Discovery of the Sea Routes by Portuguese and the Spanish

As the five nation-states of western Europe began taking shape, as feudal decentralization replaced centralized nation-states, and as the power of Venice and the Byzantine Empire was dealt a severe blow by the Ottomans, western Europeans were at the mercy of the Ottomans for trade. The trade not only provided the needed spices for meat preservation during the winter months and to overcome the monotony of the diet but also was a potential source of wealth for defense, creative endeavors, and supporting the lifestyle of the elite. These were major factors in European monarchs funding discovery voyages to India, which ultimately led to the discovery of the Americas and Australia. Portugal initiated the age of discovery because of its geographical position on the west coast of Iberia; its stable and supporting monarchy, which provided tax incentives and insurance for sea voyages; and because its population of a little over a million solely depended on maritime economy and trade. On the personal side, it was the desire to establish their knightly honor in the absence of opportunities for war (King Jaoa had just concluded a 101-year nonaggression pact with Spain in the early fifteenth century) and desire to spread Christianity that prompted King Jaoa's son Henry to capture the Moroccan city of Ceuta in 1411. The city became a natural launching pad for the sea voyages. It took acquisition of Arab navigation skills, Arab maps, and hordes of astronomers, geographers, cartographers, and sailors who had migrated into Portugal from Europe to make the project successful.

The first break came in rounding Cape Bojador in 1434, killing the prevailing myths about the "sea of darkness" to the south. However, Ceuta's fortunes declined because land trade began to bypass Ceuta to use Tangier, and the entire project became a drain on Portuguese treasury. Prince Henry was forced to invade Tangeri and lost very badly in 1437. Prince Henry died in 1460, and exploration slowed until King Joao II came to power in 1480. He personally sponsored four expeditions that resulted in Bartolomeu rounding the Cape of Good Hope in 1488, thus laying the foundation for Vasco de Gama's discovery of the sea route to India. Thus, it took Portuguese essentially three generations to reach the Cape of Good Hope.

In the meantime, the Spanish Queen Isabelle funded Christopher Columbus's expedition to reach India, and he accidentally discovered America in 1492. Columbus had understood the counterclockwise wind pattern in the Northern Hemisphere better than anyone else and took advantage of that to reach the New World and return home. Pedro Alvarez Cabral discovered Brazil while on a voyage to India. He had been blown off track in 1500 by the clockwise winds in the Southern Hemisphere. Spanish explorer Ferdinand Magellan completed first circumnavigation in 1519–1522, going around South America.

As the knowledge of these discoveries spread and sailing wind patterns and maps began to leak out, England, the Netherlands, and France got into the act. A half a century later, the English and sometime-pirate Francis Drake successfully repeated the Spanish feat of circumnavigation in 1580. Finally, Dutch explorer Willem Janszoon explored Australia and New Zealand in 1606. Though the French did not take an early lead in discovery of sea routes, they became very active in the colonization of North America and Africa in the early seventeenth century.

Thus, by the end of the sixteenth century, these newly minted five nation-states of Europe had put an end to the Ottoman-Europe-Asia trade monopoly, just as Ottomans had dealt a blow to Venetian trade earlier and as the two together had destroyed the Byzantine Empire before that. In the meantime, Russia had become the master of northern Eurasia through land exploration. The nation-states of Europe were now in a position to make an end run around the great Indian, Muslim and Chinese civilizations about the time science had essentially died in these civilizations, as we saw above.

On the other hand, science had begun to thrive in western and central Europe for the first time in their histories, first through Arab-inspired Scholasticism in the west and then through the trade-funded Italian Renaissance in the center. The center of gravity of science was ready to move back to western Europe toward the end of the phase because Venetian trade was destroyed and sea routes to Africa, Asia, and the Americas were discovered. Trade wealth was drying out in Venice and beginning to pour into the treasuries of these five nation-states. These nation-states probably could not believe their eyes at the reversal of their fortunes from the dark days of Black Death; dark, cold monasteries; dispersed political and military power through feudalism; and being hemmed in by a "sea of darkness" hardly two centuries ago. All this was because in part Prince Henry of Portugal had no war he could fight to prove his valor!

These developments, particularly the sea power, led to wars of supremacy of the high seas in the race to control trade and increase colonization among the five nation-states. The Portuguese were first to be knocked off, when they suffered a defeat at the hands of combined Spanish, French, and English navies. The next key naval war occurred in 1588, when the English navy defeated the Spanish armada, which established English supremacy. The four Dutch-English wars came after the current period, with the English winning the first and last and the Dutch second and third.

16.35 Natural Causes

During the first half of the fourteenth century, Europe experienced a mini ice age, resulting in an agricultural crisis. And as if that was not enough, black plague began in 1345 through fleas on rats in Italian ships killing at least 25 million or a third of European population.

16.36 Intrinsic Causes

Intrinsic Causes—Institutional Structures and Processes

Political system: The current phase was a period of four great political developments:

1. Evolution of the political structure of the Venetian state from autocracy to aristocracy to elitist democracy around the Adriatic Sea
2. Consolidation of power under monarchies, the breakdown of feudalism, and weakened papal authority in the evolving nation-states in the west
3. Continued shrinkage and weakening of the Holy Roman emperor relative to princes as nation-states grew independent
4. The end of Byzantine Empire at the hand of Turks in the east

As we saw in the last chapter, Venice was the first state

to restrict the absolute power of the ruler. Its small size probably had something to do with it. Key political developments in the early thirteenth century were consolidating the six members of the Minor Council, three leaders of the Quarantia tribunal, and the Dodge into Signoria. Shortly after that, a senate was created, whose sixty members were elected by the Great Council, consisting of 480 members selected from the leading families of Venice. These developments had the net effect of stripping the power of the Dodge and placing power in the hands of the major council that represented the interests of leading families of Venice. In Venice and northern Italy, protected by the Alps from German princes, several large city-states such as Venice, Florence, and Naples emerged and retained a republican form at a time when the rest of Europe was developing nation-states in an old-fashioned imperial form and struggling to shed feudalism.

Thus, an opposite development took place in the political structures of the five emerging nation-states of western Europe. In these states, the power migrated from the feudal lords and the pope to royalty, with the pope creating mischief at every possible opportunity. The increased power of royalty in the west and smashing of feudalism occurred through three changes: transfer of power from nobility to royalty through the creation of a national standing army and a parliament of the nobles; challenging papal authority through the Reformation in England (Henry the VIII), France (John Calvin), Germany (Martin Luther), and the Netherlands (Arminius), all in the first half of the sixteenth century; and creation of an organized bureaucracy to manage the state affairs.

The emerging alliance was between the royalty and the merchants. Thus, the merchants supported a strong central government in these states. It is important to understand that Venice, with its miniscule population and its Mediterranean theater, needed the political power to reside in the leading families because their aim was to simply collect the duties on goods and protect that through a strong navy as long as possible. The nation-states of western Europe, which had begun to compete with one another on the open sea and in their attempts to establish trading colonies or permanent settlements overseas, needed a strong central government at home to fund these endeavors through taxes on a significantly greater domestic population. Thus, while the power in Venice was snatched from the Dodge and transferred to a few leading families, in the five newly minted nation-states, it was centralized and continued to reside in a strong king supported by these merchant traders and bureaucracy.

The religious reformation did not take place in Iberia and Italy: in the former because of the lingering excesses of the Inquisition and in Italy because of the stronghold of the pope. Fortunately, in Iberia, despite the absence of Reformation and the presence of the Inquisition, a strong monarchy emerged in the fifteenth century because of Isabella and Ferdinand, who created a strong Spanish state, funded Columbus, and made Spain Christian again. Thus, a strong centralized state emerged in England, Spain, Portugal, France, and the Netherlands but not in Italy and Germany, which remained feudal and split into principalities with a weak, nominal emperor. Reformation by itself could not help Germany organize into a nation-state since the political changes did not take place. Thus, the center under the shrinking Holy Roman Empire stagnated politically in part because it did not have the pull of lucrative trade that Venice and western Europe enjoyed in succession despite a religious reform movement. In short, the political development in Europe was highly uneven and driven by geographical factors.

Military capability: There were several key developments of military significance within Venice and the five new nation-states during the current phase. First, Europe absorbed the new technology of explosives that was transmitted from China to Muslims to Europeans. This technology was further developed through firearms and guns. Several books, such as Konrad Kyeser's *Bellifortis* in 1405 and Roberto Valturio's *Weapons Technology* in 1455, were written during the period and attest to this development. Second was the absorption and further development of shipbuilding technology and cartography. The ships became large, one hundred to three hundred tons, and had capacity to carry guns with speeds of six to eight knots for larger square-rig sailing ships and up to seventeen knots for the smaller clippers. Third, there were outstanding achievements in cartography, covered under the Outcomes section. These developments combined to produce the awesome naval power of Venice and later of five nation-states. Fourth, for infantry, the idea of organizing soldiers into small units under a low-ranking commander and the units into still larger units provided a superior structure and control both off and on the battlefield. And lastly, the Spanish introduced the use of biological warfare through prostitutes when the French army attacked Naples in 1495. The Spanish probably got the idea from the Tartars, who had used plague-infested bodies during a siege of Kafka in 1345. The disease was brought to Italy by Genoa merchants stationed in Kafka. Unlike the Mongols, the cavalry was not nearly as important and had reached its limits as a fighting force.

Economic organization: The peasants continued to revolt in the late fourteenth century in England (Wat Tyler) and France (Jacquerie) as life became hard due to the plague. As feudalism began to break down in the west and as the impact of Scholastic learning undertaken by monks and abbots began to spread scientific and technological know-how, these states saw the rise of guilds and city burgers, who applied this knowledge to manufacturing in the fifteenth century, and the merchants who, with the discovery of sea routes, focused on trade wealth beginning in the sixteenth century. However, successful trade required government interference through protectionism, monopolies, high taxes, higher prices, and war. The guilds and city burgers were growing but were still too weak to challenge the merchant/ royalty alliance. Their day would of course come when the Industrial Revolution came of age in the eighteenth century.

The fifteenth, sixteenth, and seventeenth centuries were the age of mercantilism, which was founded on the discovery of the sea routes that had knitted the world, and it required strong, centralized political structures in these five nation-states to exploit the opportunities. In short, the agricultural technologies had benefited from Arab rule and had become widespread, manufacturing methods improved because of growing guilds in the west, and trade boomed in the earlier centuries in the Italian city-states and in the sixteenth century through the discovery of sea routes. The Reconquista in the thirteenth century, strong monarchies developing in the fourteenth to sixteenth centuries, the republican city-states of Italy that provided much financial innovation including banking and the double-entry system, the Spanish Inquisition in the fifteenth century, and Reformation and the discovery of sea routes in the sixteenth century all contributed toward a strong Christian mercantile Europe by the end of the phase, snatching the control of the trade from Muslims while hanging on to the science and technology they left behind.

Religious systems of faith: As implied above, the key religious developments were short lived: the strange phenomenon of multiple popes in the late fourteenth and early fifteenth centuries at the instigation of French King Philip IV; the Spanish Inquisition, which made Europe Christian again; and the Reformation, which sealed the weakening papal authority substantially and gave rise to the Protestant branch that was in fact a protest against the excesses of the Catholic Church and the pope.

In his *Ninety-Five Theses* in 1517 CE, Luther questioned the papal right to sell indulgences to raise money to build the Basilica and argued that atonement can only come from the grace of God without intermediation. The next year, the pamphlet was translated from Latin into German and was widely circulated with profound impact. In France, John Calvin, a contemporary of Luther, also denied the papal right to indulgences, argued for separation of state and church, and criticized using passages in the bible against charging interest because conditions had changed. In England, even before these ideas spread, the church had divorced itself from papal authority because the pope refused to grant a divorce to Henry the VIII. Christianity was shedding feudalism in western Europe and getting ready for capitalism. Significantly, both Luther and Calvin had turned anti-Semitic before they died but were more tolerant of faraway Islam. Calvin's message spread to England and led to the Presbyterian movement.

By the end of the phase, science had, as we shall see in the Outcomes section, had made great progress, and the laws of heavenly and terrestrial motion were close to being laid down (all that remained was the science of calculus) based on works of Copernicus, Brahe, Kepler, Descartes, and Galileo. Yet, science-religion conflict was alive and well. The Catholic Church and forced Copernicus to delay the publication of his book and forced Galileo to recant his support of the heliocentric theories. But the church was on the losing side. Perhaps the best way to characterize the science-religion conflict was that it was on the decrease and toward the end of the phase, it was putting up a last, desperate losing battle as far as physics was concerned. The conflict with biological sciences, as we shall note in future chapters, was three centuries into the future since there was little in biological sciences of the day that contradicted the bible.

Legal system: As we noted in chapter 12, the Theodosian Code was the high point of Roman law, and during the current phase, it continued in the centralized Byzantine Empire, supplemented with the Germanic customary law as Germanic tribes became part of the empire. With the Holy Roman Empire, the legal system in Europe had become centralized, giving rise to case law. As the Holy Roman Empire weakened and feudalism became the norm, the legal system also became decentralized, local, and customary again. In the twelfth century, the Crusades had an unintended impact: they brought back the Roman legal code to the west. During the current phase, the newly discovered and forgotten Roman law as well as Muslim legal concepts in Iberia competed with customary law in continental Europe, common law in British Isles, and canon law everywhere. However, in parts of Europe as nation-states became stronger, the judicial structures also became more uniform and centralized, with such innovations as jury systems and circuit judges, even borrowing procedures from existing ecclesiastical courts. Similarly, customary and common laws became supplemented with regulatory law and legislative law as parliaments became more functional.

The merchant law of the northern Hanseatic League played an important role in the development of contract and property law. Thus, Europe was the battleground of the ancient and foreign, customary and statutory, and secular and religious legal systems, structures, and procedures during the current phase. The potent mixture was struggling to give birth to a rational, secular legal code, judicial structure, and procedures. The rate of innovation and their immediate practical value resulted in first formal patent law in 1474 in Venice, which allowed protection against infringement for ten years. Interestingly, Galileo was granted a patent for raising water in 1594 CE.

Social structure: If reader is getting the idea that Europe during the current phase was hardly homogeneous, the reader is not far off the mark. The social structure of European society was no exception. In the west, strong centralized states had smashed feudalism, and the rough social rank was royalty, landowning nobles, rising merchants, bureaucracy, manufacturing guilds, and the peasants. In the center of the Holy Roman Empire, it was the petty princes, nominal emperor, struggling knights (who had been made obsolete by the explosive technology), the wealthy clergy (resented by the increasingly impoverished knights), town patricians (resented by the rising guilds-based burgers), city workers who worked for the guild owners, and the peasants. In the small republican city-states, the social pecking order was nearly entirely determined by wealth since political power coincided with wealth and religious influence was kept at bay. The wealthy families controlled the political structure and the elitist democracy. Thus, the social order was the elected members of the wealthy families: bankers and wholesale merchants and high administrators at the top, followed by retail merchants and guilds that controlled production monopolies, skilled craftsmen, unskilled workers, and the peasants. Italian republics were most urbanized (about 20 percent) in Europe, boasting cities as large as in Asia.

There was little change in the social structure in the Byzantine Empire, which ended in 1453 CE. Thus in the west, social position was increasingly determined politically; in the center through land ownership, in the Italian republics by wealth, and in Byzantine through the closeness to imperial dynasty. In all cases, there was steady, though uneven, decline of religious authority throughout the phase.

This was a period of spreading sophistication in manners, as evidenced by the fast adoption of forks and knives Catherine de Medici of Venice brought to France. By the end of the phase, the status of women actually suffered compared to previous centuries: women were expected to stay home, a sexual double standard persisted to an extent that rape was not considered a serious crime, women were expected to be subservient to men, and the Renaissance was nearly exclusively man's affair.

Thus, inequality was excessive, though for different reasons in the different regions of Europe. The first Atlantic slavery system began within a decade after Columbus discovered the New World and during the current era remained limited, amounting to barely 3 percent of the entire slave trade because the newly discovered colonies had not become big slave-dependent plantations. Unlike Islam, Christianity discouraged domestic slaves. The caste system was obviously absent; however, the wealth polarization was excessive. The only difference was whether the source of wealth was land ownership or control of emerging manufacturing capability through guilds or foreign trade. Merchants were probably the wealthiest class in the west and in the Italian republics, and landed gentry were wealthiest in the center and east. The status of women was second-class and was hardly impacted by the Italian Renaissance. The minority Muslim and Jewish communities were treated in an inhuman manner through the Inquisition process. Even religious reformers, such as Martin Luther and John Calvin, had turned anti-Semitic toward the end of their lives. The humanism of the Renaissance essentially remained a theoretical concept.

Knowledge Creation and educational institutions and processes: The knowledge creation institutions went through two separate periods. In the first period, France and England followed the lead of the Italian Republics and encouraged the monasteries and Abbeys to evolve into center of Scholasticism. Universities of Paris, though in existence before 1200 CE, received its charter from the Catholic Church in 1200 and banned teachings of Aristotle in 1210. This was followed by Universities at Padua (1222), Naples (1222), Toulouse (1224), Cambridge (1244), Rome (1244), Sorbonne (1253), Heidelberg (1386), Leipzig (1409), St. Andrews (1409), Louvain (1426), Leiden U. (1575) as first secular universities in Europe, Edinburgh (1583), and Academia de Ciencias Matematica in Madrid (1575). Just when the Turkish dynasties were destroying great Indian universities, new were being founded for the first time in western Europe. Monks and friars staffed these universities.

Wealth allocation process: Both sustained surplus growth and its allocation differed widely by region. Toward the end, the growth in the west had resumed after being affected by plague, famine, and civil wars; as agricultural productivity improved; and as the sea trade routes to Asia were discovered. However, its allocation was still focused on religion, commerce, and building the institutions of the emerging states, such as the military and the bureaucracy. In the center of the lands of the Holy Roman Empire, it was probably stagnant and was usurped by the landed gentry and religious establishment. In the Italian republican states, the surplus grew dramatically in the current phase. For example, average incomes in Venice were said to have tripled during the fourteenth to the sixteenth century, and its allocation was more balanced since the wealthy merchants became great patrons of art and science, in part because of great wealth polarization. They had accumulated too much wealth. There was little need for a land-based military; the source of wealth was the control of trade based on coastal colonies supported by a strong navy in the eastern Mediterranean. In the east in the Byzantine Empire, the surplus also stagnated in part because defense required greater allocation because of Ottoman pressure and the allocation to creative endeavors declined.

Social cohesion processes: In the west, strong states, nationalism based on the idea that those who speak a common language are brothers, and increasing trade wealth in the sixteenth century provided the cohesion. In the center was feudalism (the serf had to obtain the lord's permission to marry) and the Christian church provided cohesion. In the freewheeling Italian republics, it was laissez-faire capitalism, the control exerted by the guilds, and the compactness that provided the glue. In the east, the church and feudalism provided the glue until the end.

Internal wars: The internal wars were fought with ferocious intensity and frequency. The final battles of Reconquista; the English and French civil wars; the conflicts with the pope; the Hundred Years' War between the French and English, whose roots can be traced to the Norman Conquest of England; wars as a continuation of commerce by Spain, Portugal, and Venice; and the horrors of the Inquisition make the current phase as one of the most violent periods in European history. After the current phase, internal wars would metamorphose into relative cooperation, and European aggression would be directed toward Asia, the Americas, Africa, and Australia for several centuries.

In the next section, we look at the relatively peaceful interaction among civilizations during the phase. However, such interaction generally occurred in the wake of war and under conditions of control.

In the following section we will then look at the external violent causes that resulted in different forms of one civilization controlling another: empire building, violent colonization, and systematic wealth drain—the latter typically with control of trade routes and in its most effective form with territorial control.

Formative Beliefs and Ideology at the End of the Fourth Synthesis Phase

Though it was not obvious, Christian dogma and its antiscience attitude were under examination through Scholasticism and the results of third synthesis in the universities that in fact grew out of monasteries. Scholasticism demanded reason before accepting dogma, thus creating the possibility of real knowledge based on observation and reason. However, Scholasticism did not prevent a relapse in the barbarity of Reconquista in Spain. In addition, the master-lord relationship inherent in the European brand of feudalism was under attack with the emergence of guilds and city burgers. These changes created an openness to others' creativity. At the same time, Venetian success in the Mediterranean was awakening the old impulse of violent aggression. These beliefs can be summed up as follows:

- A belief in Christian salvation and a parallel emerging belief in real knowledge through observation and reason derived from the fruits of third synthesis and "discovery" of Greek heritage
- A belief in increasing social and economic equality among citizens, at least in urban centers
- An attitude of openness toward the intellectual and religious creativity of others
- A strengthened belief in aggression toward other social orders based on Venetian experience in the early centuries and the control of high seas in the last century of the phase

These beliefs, derived from achievements of the third synthesis, which were wrapped in Greek/Roman heritage, were at odds with Christian dogma. This struggle was resolved slowly through steady scientific progress during the next phase.

Readers may ask why the European civilization managed to take early steps during the current phase that led to the successful resolution of the science-religion conflict inherent in Christian dogma, while half a millennium earlier, the Muslim civilization utterly failed to do so. Although we deal with question at length in the next chapter, here we provide a brief version: we think the critical difference was nature of aggression unleashed by Muslim and Christian civilizations on the world and not the Protestant Reformation of the sixteenth century as is commonly believed. The Protestant Reformation simply reduced the intermediary role of the clergy, which was absent in Islam to start with. Muslim aggression was that of an empire builder-settler type, while European aggression, beginning with the current phase, was a systematic wealth-drainer type. This meant that capital began pouring into Europe (as we noted in the case of Portugal earlier), leading to the emergence of capitalism followed by the Industrial Revolution in some *mercantile states,* which in turn made the connection between science and wealth creation both stronger and increasingly clear. Thus, there was no turning back on science. Islam, on the other hand, placed an injunction against charging interest, thus making the process of even internal capital accumulation and concentration difficult. The question of why capitalism and the Industrial Revolution first occurred in the Netherlands, England, and France but not Spain and Portugal on the one hand and Germany and Italy on the other is a question we must defer until the next chapter.

16.37 Extrinsic Peaceful Causes

It is difficult to characterize any extrinsic causes that impacted the European civilization during the current phase as peaceful. Despite the destruction of the rotting Byzantine Empire on the eastern flank, most of central and northwestern Europe was regaining its historical aggressive impulse, initially through the Crusades, followed by the rise of mercantile Venice, expulsion of Moors in Iberia, and the horrible Reconquista. Thus, we may see the current phase as the period in which European civilization managed to rise from ashes and push back the Muslim tide successfully through controlling the high seas and with a bit of help from Genghis Khan. No doubt, creativity flowed to Europe in the overt absence of war, and Europe gained control of world trade for the first time in its history. Both occurred in the wake of wars and at gunpoint. Thus, all extrinsic causes impacting Europe in the current phase must be regarded as violent.

16.38 Extrinsic Violent Causes

Extrinsic Violent Causes—Europe as Victor

Liberation of Iberia: The response to the European Reconquista and the Inquisition was meek. Given the Mongol attack and the rising strength of the nation-states of western Europe, there was little that Moors could do as they were literally pushed into the sea. The glory of the Moors was simply reduced to a memory in the Muslim mind.

A lucky break: Thankfully, Europe was saved from Genghis Khan in the nick of time and was successful evicting the Muslims from Iberia. However, as we noted before, one of the consequences of the Mongol invasion was the emergence of the Ottoman Empire centered in Anatolia. Both the eastern and central regions, the Byzantine Empire, and the Republic of Venice had to contend with the Ottomans. In essence, while western Europe was evicting Moors out of Iberia, emerging successfully from feudalism, and getting ready to dominate the oceans of the world, Ottomans were strong enough to not only destroy the Byzantine Empire but also severely limit the Venetian state and its financial foundation of Mediterranean trade, but not before Italian city-states succeeded in creating the fourth synthesis in science based on trade wealth.

Conquest of the Americas: This was rather straightforward and disastrous. The native populations of the Americas were hardly in a position to resist European onslaught. Throughout the sixteenth century, native populations in central and South America lost land to the Spanish and Portuguese and often faced extermination. The net result was the great exodus of gold and silver from the Americas, which helped sustain the new global trading system being built by the West Europeans based on control of the seas. The response of the natives was to fight when they could. The Spanish and Portuguese were not opposed to interracial marriages, and the natives were open to Christianity, more or less. As result, the extermination and relocation were kept at a minimum, and Europeans dominated the synthesis of European and native cultures.

The bottom line is that at the end of the current phase, the once-dominant Muslim civilization, despite formidable Ottoman successes during the phase, had been put on notice and was beginning to be circumscribed. The Indian and Chinese civilization and Southeast Asian states were being set up for systematic wealth drain, Africa for slave trade, and the Americas for absolute land-snatching.

By the end of the phase, the western European civilization was in a position to control all other major civilizations because it had, under conditions threatening its very survival (bubonic plague, Ottoman control of the land trade, and Ottoman control of eastern Mediterranean), accidentally discovered the sea routes linking all civilizations at a time when no other civilization had the naval power to resist it. Thus, it exclusively controlled the seas that connected all these civilizations and was in a position to force trade concessions from these civilizations, using the trade wealth to create stronger naval force to extract more concessions. The process inexorably led to territorial control, which led to an even greater drain of wealth or the acquisition slaves and indentured labor from civilizations and peoples. The European civilization had hit on a sadistic cycle, and unlike Muslims, it rationalized its actions not through a creed but through the ideology of racism. In other words, it was not chosen by God but nature and was simply engaged in a civilizing mission.

European civilization lost in the east to the Ottomans as we note above, finally got its act together in the west, conquered the Americas through the superiority of sea power, and prepared to make an end run against the Ottomans in the coming centuries through sea power.

For the first time in history, unrelated events conspire to bring the world heritage to one civilization. Western Europe received practical technology from the Mongols, Chinese, and Muslim civilization; new crops and vegetables from the Americas; philosophy and science from ancient Greece as discovered, preserved, and developed by the Muslim civilization; and from scholars from the defeated Byzantine Empire, key mathematical concepts of the decimal system including the all-important zero and differential calculus, from the fruits of the fourth synthesis from Italian city-states (otherwise known as the European Renaissance.)

Europe had learned all it could from the Chinese and Muslim civilizations at the beginning of the current phase, and by the end of the current phase, it had pulled ahead of all major civilizations in most creative endeavors if not in wealth production.

Transmission of practical creativity: The phase started with Mongols showing great interest and flexibility in acquiring the latest military technology from surrounding civilizations, particularly Chinese explosives technology, and dispersing it to the Muslim and European civilization. It seems Muslims acquired explosives technology between 1240 and 1280 CE, and European civilization acquired explosives technology through William of Robruck, who was an ambassador to the Mongols in 1254–1255 CE or earlier, since gunpowder was mentioned by Bacon in 1247 in *Opus Majus*. Simple firearms first made the appearance in Europe in 1247 CE. Clearly, European acquisition was peaceful, and Muslim acquisition came as a result of Genghis Khan's invasion or through the Silk Route trade. In either case, the diffusion was fast and very effective, since cannons were apparently used in 1248 in Seville and 1260 by Mamluks in Egypt against the Mongols themselves. The driving reasons were clearly military, and the effectiveness of the technology was to change military balance.

Perhaps Marco Polo (1254–1324) was the true motivator of Columbus, who discovered the sea route to Americas while attempting to go to India. Marco Polo reached China over land in 1274 at the age of seventeen, accompanied by his father and uncle (who also had traveled to China earlier, 1266–1270), and spent the next seventeen years in Asia, mostly in China. The stay in China was facilitated by the fact that China was ruled by Mongol Kublai Khan at the time. The Polos were traders looking for profit and used the Mongol Hulagu Khan and land routes pioneered by the Mongols to reach China. When Columbus reached America, he had a copy of Marco Polo's account of his travels. Marco Polo's account dazzled the medieval European mind. Among the information or artifacts Marco Polo brought with him included: a beautiful nautical map of the known world that introduced Europeans to the art of cartography, silk, spices, noodles, porcelain, coal, gunpowder, paper money, printing technology, and chopsticks. Here is an example of a vivid account by Marco Polo that made a strong impression on European minds: "All over the country of Cathay, there is a kind of black stone existing in beds in the mountains, which they dig out and burn like firewood. If you supply the fire with them at night and see that they are well kindled, you will find them still alight in the morning, and they make such fine fuel that no other is used throughout the country. It is true that they have plenty of wood also, but they do not burn it, because those stones burn better and cost less."

During the latter part of the phase, ancient Chinese practical inventions and ideas continued to trickle into Europe, including the matchbox invented by Chinese court ladies in 577 CE (which reincarnates as an English invention in the early nineteenth century), Pascal triangle (1527), kites (1589), and seed drill (1565) and ceramic enamel (1575).

The primary advantage of discovery of North and South America, apart from gold and silver and of course the land itself, was the knowledge of a variety of fruit, vegetables, and animals, such as the rubber tree (1492), maize and turkey (1518), potatoes (1553), sunflower seeds (1569), vanilla (1520), cocoa (1520), tobacco (1560), chili paprika (1493), and tomatoes (1544). In addition, Martinus de la Cruz compiled Aztec knowledge in the field of medicine.

Thus, there was slow and steady diffusion of practical technology from West Asia and Iberia into Europe, and it was often mediated by the monks in the monasteries. Examples include gardens inspired by Islamic and Moorish traditions (through Crusades ~1200), silk thread technology (1220), wheelbarrow (1220), the first paper mill in Italy and Germany (1277) and Troyes, France (1355), spinning wheel (referenced in the statutes of a German guild in 1280), the first mechanical clocks driven by weight and not water (1286), eyeglasses (1286), rocket (1380), suction pump (1400), windmill (1414), genuine flintlock small arms (1425), belt drive (1430), movable type printing based on Chinese and Korean ideas (1440), and the blast furnace (1456).

Transmission of religious creativity: Having been bitten by Islam and still consumed by Christian dogma, the European civilization would have to wait until the twentieth century to appreciate the tolerance and universality of Hindu and Buddhist religious thought.

Transmission of intellectual creativity: While the Arabic translations of Greek works in philosophy had been translated from Arabic into Latin in Iberia, an independent effort in the late fifteenth and early sixteenth centuries was undertaken by Manutius beginning in 1498 in Venice to publish the Greek classics in literature and philosophy in the Greek language, including five volumes of Aristotle, nine comedies of Aristophanes, and works of Thucydides, Sophocles, Xenophon, Herodotus, Demosthenes, and Euripides all within a period of two decades.

Europe could still learn from the Indian civilization in religious creativity and mathematics. It was hardly possible that it would do so in the former; however, it was fortunate for Europe that it did in the latter. Below, we briefly discuss three key mathematical ideas.

As we noted in an earlier chapter, the so-called Fibonacci numbers (1202 CE) have been known in India since at least 200 BCE, and Virahanka clearly summarized them in 700 CE. These were transmitted from Arabs to Persians to Byzantines to Venice through Leonardo of Lisa, who was also known as Fibonacci.

The decimal system reached Europe at least by 1220 and likely earlier through *Arithmetica of Jordanus Memorarius*. The rules of using the decimal system were popularized much later in 1478 in *Treviso Arithmetic*. Fibonacci popularized the use of zero in Europe in *Liber Abaci*. Incidentally, the concept of zero was initially rejected by the Christian church, and only when its commercial and not scientific value became clear did the Catholic Church reluctantly accept it. Fibonacci was the man who pushed for its use. Fibonacci learned his mathematics from Muslim mathematicians.

When Europeans arrived on the west coast of India in the

sixteenth century, the Jesuits needed to understand how Indian calendars were constructed using the arithmetic calculations using the decimal system and astronomical data using trigonometric values calculated through the use of infinite series. In addition, accurate values of the trigonometric functions were essential in developing improved navigational techniques, which were required as part of the get-rich-schemes based on trading with India. The Jesuits had learned Malayalam and were in fact teaching Malayalam to Indian children. The Jesuits came across copies of Yuktibhasa written by Jyesthadeva in 1530, consolidating the work of Madhava (1350–1425) and Nilakantha Somayaji (1444–1544). Madhava laid the foundations of calculus, including differentiation, term by term integration, and the theory of area under the curve. What is remarkable about these infinite series is that Madhava understood that the correction term he developed for these infinite series had a limited nature. Madhava's work shows up in Taylor and Gregory series about a century later but remained forgotten until the early nineteenth century and remained unacknowledged until mid-twentieth century. Thus, Europe resisted two key Indian ideas in mathematics. The first was the concept of zero that was considered heresy and probably lasted several hundred years. The second was the idea of infinitesimals, which were considered improbable, and war that raged from the seventeenth to the nineteenth century, despite the formal use of calculus for more than two hundred years.

Muslim civilization transmitted the ideas and invention not only from its own but also from the technologies learned from the Chinese as well as mathematics, astronomy, and medicine they learned from the Indian civilization in the previous phase. The one to have a profound impact on European intellect was, of course, the decimal system, without which progress in science and some arts would hardly be possible.

There was little direct interaction between Persia and western Europe. Persian astronomy achieved its greatest height in the thirteenth century, with the outstanding work of al-Tusi in the aftermath of the Mongol invasion and control of West Asia. The likely route of the transmission of Persian astronomy to Europe was mediated through the Byzantine Empire, where some of al-Tusi's works, including the critical idea of the Tusi couple, which allowed Copernicus to discard the idea of equant in planetary models, were translated into Greek and are still preserved in Italy. Michael Scot translated al-Ishbilt's astronomy, the works of ibn Rashid in 1217 while at Toledo, and Aristotle's *De animalibus,* completed at Toledo before 1220. Avicenna's *Canon of Medicine* was translated into Latin in 1473.

With the fall of the Byzantine Empire at the hands of Turks in 1453, scholars and skilled workers fled from Constantinople and took shelter in Italian city-states, boosting the creative potential of these states. These scholars undoubtedly brought some of the fruits of the Arab-Persian synthesis with them.

After the discovery of sea routes and the resulting shift in trade patterns, the wealth of Italian city-states had begun to decline precipitously while the exact opposite was occurring in western Europe and to a lesser extent in northern Europe through the Hanseatic League. The merchants of the Hanseatic League partly mediated the gradual transmission of the results of the fourth synthesis in art and science from Italian city-states to the universities in western Europe in the sixteenth century. This transmission was to fuse with key developments in philosophy in western Europe based on the Moor legacy and would form the basis of the fifth and last synthesis of science, as we will discuss in the next chapter.

It is incredible to realize that during the current phase, first the tiny Italian city-states followed by newly emerged nation-states in western Europe acquired the entire knowledge base that civilizations had painstakingly accumulated up to this point in history, and neither of these had shown any interest in science and philosophy. Western Europe had no heritage in science, philosophy, or art, and the precursor of the city-states, the Roman Empire, only adapted art and architecture from Greece, did not adapt science or philosophy, and developed practical technology, weapons, and a legal system. In succession, these two entities acquired the Arab-Persian synthesis in science, Indian mathematics, and Chinese practical innovations primarily because of the Mongol invasion, which had weakened the Muslim civilization and created a Europe-Asia dialogue. The singular western European contribution was discovering sea routes and was brought about in desperation by the plague and destruction through internal wars, the emergence of nation-states that arose to check the obscene power of the pope, and Ottoman control of the land trade. Western Europe was straight-jacketed internally by the pope and externally by the Ottomans. Ideas follow wealth, so they first reached Italian city-states, followed by western Europe.

Impact on institutional structures and processes: It is fair to say that while Europe was the recipient of the creativity of all major civilizations during the phase, the political, economic, religious, and educational structures were its own invention. The exceptions are a legal system that derived many key concepts in contract and trust law from Muslim civilization and military capability from the Ottomans.

It is critical to recognize that after the dismal failure of Crusades to recover the "Holy lands" from the people who invented Christianity in the first place (!), European military capability was hardly world-class. The terrorizing Turks, with their reach as far north as Iceland (1627), moved a complacent Europe to build its military capability through better fortifications and new military tactics to repel the Turkish cavalry. Most important, after losing the Mediterranean Sea to Turks, Europe had to focus on discovering sea routes with African, Muslim, and Indian sailors.

Assessment of net impact: The net impact was negative in the east and ultimately highly positive in the west. In the east, the Ottomans killed the aristocracy and liberated the peasants from landlords without a wholesale destruction of religion and culture. In the west, the Ottomans initially exploited the political disunity (German princes exploited the Ottoman threat to gain concessions from Charles I and Frances I, inviting Turks to attack the Hapsburgs). The resource drain required by the Spanish resistance to Ottomans under Phillip II in the late sixteenth century allowed the Dutch revolution to gather momentum. In short, the failure of Crusades followed by Turkish expansion had a dramatic impact on western Europe that had only recently recovered the Iberian Peninsula from the Moors after five centuries of domination. They were not about to repeat history without a fight to the death. Similarly, competition to control the sea routes from the Turks, who had control of the Red Sea, Arabian Sea, and the Mediterranean on the one hand and from friendly enemies like the Spanish, English, and the Dutch on the other, forced the Portuguese to be more innovative in naval technology. Finally, Turkish pressure on Venetian city-states resulted in English and French traders receiving Turkish privileges to compete with Venetian traders (much like the farmans or royal decrees the English had received from Mughals in India). The net result was French control of trade in the Mediterranean, Dutch control in East Africa, and English control in India. In short, the Turkish-Venetian wars and mutual weakening opened the door for small states perched on the Atlantic coast, precisely when world heritage in technology and science was washing ashore. This combination of wealth and knowledge had no precedence in world history. One is tempted to say that something along these lines had to happen sooner or later to one civilization.

It is incredulous to think that, in the fourteenth century, when Petrarch (1304-1374) looked back at the last thousand years of European dark ages, he consoled himself by lumping the Greek and Roman experiences together! Rome had walked away from the Greek accomplishments in science and philosophy for a thousand years. Greek accomplishments had to take refuge in Asia and North Africa, and even there, the Romans killed the Greek spirit in hot pursuit. Petrarch may be forgiven for not understanding the Babylonian, Egyptian, and Indian precedents for key Greek accomplishments; however, he can hardly be forgiven for lumping together Greek and Roman heritage, for these are as different from each other as day and night. He was indeed desperate to see continuity between ancient Greece and Italian city-states when there was hardly any as far as science and philosophy were concerned.

A new vigor based on trade wealth and developments in science and technology and a questioning of the Christian dogma had energized the European aggression that had been dormant since the fall of the Western Roman Empire at the hands of the Huns more than a millennium ago. However, this aggression was not the typical empire building of an Alexander or the Arabs, Persian, or Turks, where the invader conquered lands, relocated to conquered lands, and displaced the indigenous elites to control the surplus. It was of an entirely different nature: for sea routes had created two diametrically different opportunities for Europeans. In the Americas (and after this phase, Australia), the indigenous population, which was at an earlier stage of development (somewhere between the hunting-gathering and Neolithic stages), could be displaced or exterminated and supplanted with a European population and African slaves, who were also at an earlier stage of development, to create new states focused on commodity production without deploying large armies. This was the path of violent colonization—an entirely new form of inhumanity for the civilized man.

The second opportunity was afforded by Asia and parts of Africa where sophisticated, phoneme civilizations existed with a high rate of wealth creation but with weak naval forces. The strategy European powers developed for this second set was to create trading posts along the coast and extract increasing levels of surplus through coerced trade based on the control of sea routes. Both strategies were in their infancy at the end of the current phase.

Extrinsic Violent Causes—European Civilization as Defeated

Destruction of the Byzantine Empire: By the fifteenth century, with the rise of Ottomans, Muslim civilization again challenged Europe, this time in Southeastern Europe and in the Mediterranean in the fifteenth and sixteenth centuries. The Byzantine Empire was defeated in 1453, and a period of great growth followed in the sixteenth and seventeenth centuries, during which most of southeastern Europe, including the Balkans and Hungry, the Caucuses, Iraq, and North Africa, were added to the Ottoman domains. The loss of sustained political independence for the Byzantine Empire was complete and permanent as it ceased to exist. The Ottomans controlled the sustainable growing surplus in all regions.

No states came to assist the Byzantine Empire in its hour of need. The European response was acceptance of foreign rule in part because the Ottomans were less forceful in conversions to Islam, unlike the Moors.

Decline of the Republic of Venice: The struggle for supremacy in the Mediterranean between the Ottomans and the Republic of Venice lasted nearly three centuries, from 1423, when Ottomans initiated the seven-year wars to control the Aegean Sea to 1714 CE. They destroyed the great Venetian merchant fleet and naval forces. Neither western Europe nor central Europe came to assist Venice in any significant manner. Western Europe, busy expanding into the Americas and Asia/Africa, and central Europe, also under pressure from the Ottomans, hardly their acts together. Rising Russia was busy expanding into Siberia, pushing into Muslim states to the south, and positioning with respect to Ottomans. All the Venetian colonies were slowly lost to Ottomans.

To summarize, western and central Europe preserved their SPIs, but eastern Europe, including the birthplace of European civilization, Greece, could not.

Loss of control of wealth and means of wealth: The destruction of the Byzantine Empire and Venetian naval presence in the Mediterranean, through devastating, was more than compensated by gains in Asia, Africa, and the Americas. The strategy of western Europe was to keep focus on Asia, Africa, and the Americas and deal with Ottomans later, after the destruction of the source of their trade wealth. Thus, western Europe abandoned eastern Europe.

Impact on productive outcomes: There was indeed little impact on Byzantine and Venetian empires. The Byzantine Empire was confined to small area around Constantinople by the fifteenth century, and Ottoman victory actually brought more stability and vigor to southeastern Europe. Venice already controlled trade with Asia. The fall of Venice by the early eighteenth century, after the current phase ended, could have been a severe blow to the European civilization. However, as we mentioned above, trade with the Americas and Asia and slaves from Africa more than compensated for the land/Mediterranean trade.

Impact on institutional structures and processes: As western Europe was successfully shedding its feudal past and exploring Muslim achievements, the Byzantine Empire remained mired in religious orthodoxy, divine right and the absolute authority of rulers, and decadence as the Muslim civilization shaped its power, fortune, and evolution. Likewise, the Byzantine Empire in effect isolated western Europe from West Asian powers, such as Persians, Seljuks, and Ottomans. Consequently, there was little impact on western Europe from the rising Ottomans. The prestige of the Byzantine Empire was such that Sultan Mehmet, after victory in 1453 CE, declared himself "Kaysa-i-Rum." Since the Byzantine Empire was destroyed, there was little question of impact on its institutions.

Assessment of net impact: European civilization, in effect, sacrificed its left arm to preserve its right arm. The net impact of the loss of the decaying and fractured Byzantine Empire cannot be considered a great loss since it gave an opportunity to even the score with the Ottoman Empire in the next phase.

16.39 Productive Outcomes

Wealth creation: In the first half of the phase, European civilization had its share of difficulties in the form of a mini ice age, the bubonic plague, extended internal wars between emerging nations, civil wars, the declining position of the Republic of Venice and the defeat of the Byzantine Empire. However, by the mid-fifteenth century, things were looking good: no natural calamities occurred and Muslim, Indian, and Chinese technologies had been absorbed and mastered. Agricultural productivity was rising, and manufacturing guilds were prospering. The commodity and credit markets were developing, and precious metal from the Americas had begun to pour in to lubricate internal and external trade, the latter becoming a monopoly of a handful of nation-states based on control of sea routes. The decimal system had been absorbed, which further facilitated commerce. Emerging nation-states had a strong bureaucracy dedicated to improving the national economy. Internal wars had settled down and rivalry between established sea powers, such as Portugal and Spain, and the challengers, such as England, France, and the Netherlands had moved to the race to control the open seas. Since the German states had not united to form a nation-state, German cities along the northern coast formed the Hanseatic League, which focused on facilitating trade concessions for city merchants from foreign rulers. It remained effective throughout the phase and excelled in trading timber, amber, wheat, rye, resins and wax. Most importantly, no civilization was in a position to challenge western European nation-states. It is hard to envision another period in history when such a powerful confluence of factors affecting wealth creation occurred. Thus, wealth creation increased dramatically, particularly in the emerging nation-states of western Europe.

Peaceful migrations: There were relatively few peaceful migrations during the period. One can think of Russian Afanassi Nikitin, who reached India via Persia in 1466, and the migration of Byzantine scholars, who brought the knowledge of Muslim creative achievements.

Fair trade: Because the European states controlled the sea routes and because sea routes were far superior in terms of cost, time, and safety, the control of international trade became a monopoly in the hands of these states. Though they competed with one another, they cooperated to maintain the monopoly. Thus, free trade died for nearly the four following centuries by the end of the phase. In fact, things would get a lot worse before they could get better for the rest of the world since control of trade routes was going to be followed by territorial control after the end of the phase.

16.40 Creative Outcomes

The focus of European creativity during the phase was on absorbing and extending new technologies introduced by the Arabs, adopting the fruits of third synthesis in science in philosophy and science, rescuing art from Christian dogma, and containing the power of Catholic Church.

Practical Creativity

The focus of practical creativity during the current phase was broad in Europe.

Materials: Whiskey; paper mills in Italy, France, and Germany; graphite for writing; platinum was discovered; mirrors were made with metal backs.

Processes: Prefabricated assembly (1320), blast furnaces, saline curing, spinning wheel flyer, standardized production of ammunition, rolling mill, ribbon loom, silver from copper/lead, and early refrigeration.

Tools: The hydraulic saw machine, PMM, silk-throwing machine, ball bearings, the triangulation survey method, a clock in Westminster, the compound crank handle, drift nets, a spring-loaded watch, the combination lock, theodolite, the lathe (1569), water turbines (1582), pencils, and an early knitting machine.

Energy: Windmill and water mills.

Agriculture products/technologies: Tobacco was identified, refined sugar, potatoes, and doughnuts.

Nonagricultural products: Buttonholes, stoneware, spectacles, reading lamps, and the flush toilet.

Construction: The sixteen-mile Ticinello canal (1209), forty-five-meter high vault in France(1225), West Minister Abbey, canal lock, Cathedral of Pisa, perpendicular Gothic church, forty-mile canal, forty-four-meter-wide dome, galley assembly line, Onion domes, raising of the obelisk.

Transportation: A lighthouse 1,610 feet high, suspension shock absorbers, four-wheel cart with turning front wheels, parachute, Lateen rig, 1000 ton ships, crane boat, Wipmolen, Caravel ship, tunnel, folding canal locks, helicopter design, glass globes for diving, topmast for ships, ship speed measurement, fluitschip cargo ship (1595), and ironclad ship.

Infrastructure: Segmented arch Ponte Bridge, elliptical arch bridge, and new aqueduct built.

Communication: Movable type printing, postal system, and encryption code.

Weapon technologies: Primitive firearm assembled, flax-strung longbows, cannon, single piece bronze cannons, steel crossbow, breech-loaded cannons, and exploding cannon projectiles,

Since the printing process was perfected in the middle of fifteenth century, the book publishing business took off. It has been estimated that in a mere five decades or by 1500 CE, over thirty-five thousand books had been published, with three-fourths of them Latin and one-half on religion. The first book in German was published 1440, in French in 1476, in Italian 1465, in English in 1474, and in Portuguese in 1556. Below, we list a random sampling of the books printed: *Clocks (1364), fireworks (1420, 1489), the bible (1454), architecture (1470, 1485), Euclid (14xx), Glass (1499), Distillation (1500, 1512), Ship building (1536), and Navigation guide (1545).*

The significant achievements of the European civilization during the current phase in practical creativity are summarized in table 16.3.

Religious Creativity

At the start of the phase, religion had a stranglehold on the European mind, royalty, and masses. The story of European religious creativity during the current phase is a story of varying degrees of success in freeing European masses and royalty from religious stranglehold.

The Holy Roman Empire founded by Charlemagne had come increasingly under papal authority, as we saw in the previous chapter, throughout Europe including the British Isles. The first split occurred in 1054 between Catholicism and Orthodox Christianity, because while western Europe had degenerated into a highly decentralized feudal system, the east under Byzantine Empires had a strong central authority capable of resisting the pope. For the next five centuries or from the split in Christianity to Reformation, papal authority reigned supreme in the west. The feudal structure worked to the great advantage of the church and clergy: clergy either owned land or shared profits with the nobles because they held the peasant masses under their religious spell. Sins could be absolved through money, and most clergy, though required to be celibate, had housekeepers who performed more than domestic chores. With new technologies and new learning from the third synthesis knocking at the doors and a weakened Muslim civilization devastated by Mongols, the need and opportunity to redefine the social order was obvious. Thus, the three great movements in the sphere of religion were Reconquista, the Inquisition, and the Reformation. Their collective objective, in concert with rise of nation-states in western Europe, was to make Europe Christian and to expel church and papal authority from state and science. They succeeded in the first objective but failed in the second during the current phase.

Reconquista: Reconquista from 1085 to 1249 CE years had reduced the Moor Empire to little Granada, ushering in nearly 250 years of peace between the Castile crown and Granada. The dynastic union through the marriage of Ferdinand II of Aragon and Isabella of Castile in 1469 CE strengthened the Spanish royalty and spelled trouble

Table 16.3: Significant Achievements in Practical Creativity
European Civilization, 1200–1600 CE

Category	Significant Achievements
Materials	Whiskey; paper mills in Italy, France; graphite for writing; platinum discovered; mirrors with metal back; pencil
Processes	Prefabricated assembly (1320), blast furnace, saline curing, spinning wheel flyer, standardized production of ammunition, rolling mill, ribbon loom
Energy	windmill
Tools	Hydraulic saw machine, PMM, silk-throwing machine clock in Westminster, compound crank handle, drift nets, spring loaded watch, Polymetrum (survey) combination lock, theodolite, lathe (1569), water turbine (1582)
Agricultural Products	Tobacco identified, refined sugar, potato, doughnut
Non-Agri. Products	Buttonholes, stoneware
Construction	16-mile Ticinello canal (1209), 45-m vault in France(1225) Westminster Abbey, canal lock, Cathedral of Pisa, perpendicular Gothic, 40-mile canal church, 44-m wide dome, galley assembly line, onion domes, obelisk raised
Transportation Technologies	161-ft-high lighthouse, suspension shock absorbers, 4-wheel cart with turning front wheels Lateen rig, 1000 to ships, crane boat, Wipmolen, caravel ship, tunnel, folding canal locks, helicopter design glass globes for diving, topmast for ships, ship speed measurement, fluyt ship (1595), ironclad ship
Weapons Technologies	primitive firearm assembled, flax-strung longbows, cannon single-piece bronze cannons, steel crossbow, Breech-loaded cannons, exploding cannon projectiles, cast iron cannon balls, wheel-lock musket, rifling in guns
Infrastructure	Segmental arch Ponte Vecchio bridge, elliptical arch bridge, new aqueduct built
Communications	

for Granada, the shrunken Moor Empire in Iberia. The war, initiated in 1482 and completed in 1492 by complete annexation, was clearly a religiously inspired war with full support from the pope. At least a hundred thousand died.

Inquisition: The European Inquisition has a long history and went through medieval, Spanish, Portuguese, and Roman periods. The medieval period occurred during the thirteenth through the fifteenth century and was directed against Christian groups such as Cathars (who wanted a return to early Christianity and did not recognize the church establishment) and Waldensians (who also did not recognize the church establishment and the saints) in France and the Knights Templar (a powerful military group tied to the Crusaders and resented by the French king) and the Beguines (who were mystics) in Germany and North Italy. These groups were charged with heresy, idolatry, apostasy, corruption, and homosexuality and were often burned on the stake, including the Joan of Arc, who led several victories in the Hundred Years' War and fell victim to politically motivated charges of heresy. The Medieval Inquisition was often a local affair.

The Medieval Inquisition was followed by the Spanish Inquisition in 1478 CE before annexation of Granada. Reconquista is easily justified—after all for this is what the Muslims did in the eighth century during their conquest. However, the horrors of the Spanish Inquisition that followed the annexation of Granada were inhumane and was ordered by Ferdinand and Isabella. The Jews were expelled from Spain with the pope's approval or converted to Christianity (called *conversos*). All remaining Muslims were converted to Christianity (called *moriscos*), ordered to leave. or prosecuted. The objective of the Spanish Inquisition was to ensure that conversos and moricos did not revert to their earlier faith. If suspected, they were falsely accused of witchcraft, blasphemy, bigamy, and sodomy. They were tortured and sentenced in Kangaroo courts, often in absentia, to public admission, whippings, jail, galleys, confiscation of property, and burning at the stake.

The Portuguese Inquisition followed similar lines.

The purpose of the Roman Inquisition was different: it was directed against the intellectuals in an attempt to control thought that might question Christian dogma. The Inquisition drew an index of forbidden books in 1559, burned Giordano Bruno at the stake in 1600, and forced Galileo to recant his belief in the heliocentric theory in 1633. It also confined Tommaso Campanella to twenty-seven years in prison beginning in 1599. He wrote his important books in prison. The first scientific society established by architect Giacomo della Porta was also suppressed by the Inquisition in 1560.

Reformation: If the Inquisition was directed against the nonbelievers by the royalty and the church, the Reformation was directed against the church for corruption, moral lapses on the part of clergy, and the monopolization of the role of clergy in salvation. The two outstanding figures of the Reformation are Martin Luther (1483–1546) and John Calvin (1509–1564). Luther challenged the establishment by stating that salvation comes, not from good deeds but from Jesus alone through grace and all baptized Christians are holy priests. The bible was translated into the language of the masses, and the clergy were allowed to marry. For his actions, the pope excommunicated him. In his later years, Luther turned anti-Semitic.

Calvin questioned the biblical injunction against charging interest in combination with political change. The European civilization succeeded in making Europe Christian and separating state and church; however, separating church and science was not successful, as, the death of Bruno, imprisonment for Campanella, and the trial of Galileo shows. Yet, one can see a softening of attitude toward science.

Achievements in Philosophical Creativity

Metaphysics: Developments in metaphysics during the phase may be looked at as the final culmination of Scholasticism under Thomas Aquinas (1225–1274 CE) and the attack on Christian dogma through pantheism, astrology, and Hermeticism in support of science's struggle against the church during the Renaissance period.

Thomas Aquinas's metaphysics was realistic, much like that Aristotle, who had maintained that sensible things had reality of their own. The question then became the relationship of sensible things in particular and nature in general to God. Here, Aquinas goes back to Plato's idea of preexisting forms with a twist: things have reality because they participate in existence or God. Each finite thing had its own essence, which depended on its participation in the existence. Aquinas cannot rise above his faith in the Christian God, and his metaphysics, therefore, are limited by that faith. There was no question of even considering agnosticism and the doctrine of dependent co-origination, which clearly state things have no essence and their existence depends upon mutual interaction in the here and now. Under Aquinas, Scholasticism reached its height and laid bare the contradictions inherent in Christian monotheism dressed up in Greek idealism. The freer inquiry during the Renaissance would be an attempt to assert the independent powers of man, which would lead to the enlightenment period and critical philosophy. However, only in the twentieth century would Western metaphysics discover agnosticism after growing beyond the philosophy of skepticism. We must note in passing that Aquinas also conceived the transcendental unity of truth, beauty, and goodness, combining metaphysics, ethics, and aesthetics, something also embedded in the Indian concepts of satyam, shivam, and sundram, with truth being an imprint on the mind, goodness on the will, and beauty on emotion.

Therefore, one would indeed be disappointed if one looked for critical philosophy during the Renaissance. The focus was not to rationalize Christian doctrine using a method of philosophy, as was the case with Scholasticism in western Europe along the lines of the Muslim philosopher who had attempted and failed to reconcile Islam and rational philosophy. The practical and cultural focus was, instead, the discovering the literary heritage of Greeks and Romans and spreading it through the newly invented printing press to the middle classes. The philosophical emphasis was on recovering original works of Greek philosophy. However, the recovery of classics also laid bare a time in history when the leading European minds (Greek) were not in the clutches of Christian dogma. Thus, one of the outcomes of the entire process was to reassert the independence of man and his powers. It was not a time of great leaps in philosophy but a time of recovery:

- Giovanni Pico della Mirandola (1463–1494 CE) wrote about the dignity of man and the possibility of magic.
- Marsillio Ficino (1433–1499 CE) was another humanist who pushed for painting, sculpture, architecture, music, and literature. He was an ardent believer in astrology.
- Nicholas of Cusa, a German philosopher, preached pantheistic beliefs or the unit of God and nature, implying an imminent but not transcendental God. For some reason, he was not declared a heretic by the church, possibly because he did not live in Italy, a papal stronghold. He also preached that suprarational understanding was a condition to understanding God. He was closer to the philosophy of Vedanta as Sankara outlined half a millennium earlier.
- Giordnno Bruno (1548–1600) was found guilty of heresy and pantheism. Like Nicholas, he believed in an infinite, immobile universe that could not be completely understood by rational means. He influenced philosophy indirectly through his intuitive cosmology.
- Michel Montaigne (1533–1592) who popularized the essay form of writing subscribed to the philosophy of skepticism and thus marks the earliest beginning of transition from Scholasticism and Renaissance to the period of Enlightenment.

Thus, the focus of metaphysical speculation of the phase became challenging the Christian dogma through pantheism and Hermeticism, and toward the end of phase supporting philosopher/scientists who both anticipated and agreed with the heliocentric theory of Copernicus. Their effort laid the foundations of critical philosophy in the next phase.

Epistemology: In contrast to modest innovations in metaphysics, which never arrived at fully developed skepticism, let alone agnosticism, the developments in epistemology were quite impressive and led to the formulation of the scientific method based on sensation, inference, and controlled experiments. The key figures of this development were Roger Bacon (1214–1294), William of Ockham (1285–1349 CE), Bernardino Telesio (1509–1588 CE), Tommasso Campanella (1568–1639 CE), Francis Bacon (1561–1626 CE), and, of course, Galileo (1564–1636 CE).

Roger Bacon emphasized and used the experimental method to study the phenomenon of the rainbow-extending the work of Muslim experimentalists such as al Hazen. He took issue with Aquinas and Magnus concerning using the experimental approach in understanding nature but lost the battle. Current scholarship around the originality of his *Opus Majus* is divided. However, there is little doubt that within the context of European civilization, he was a great proponent of the experimental method. However, from a global perspective, there was nothing original about Bacon's proclamation that "without experience, it is impossible to know anything completely." The statement is only revolutionary within the narrow context of European Scholasticism. Bacon never explicitly stated the importance of induction in the scientific method. He remained at the level of stating the importance of reasoning and experience.

Ockham emphasized the importance of simpler explanations of natural phenomenon as better than more complex ones. His formulation, which was not original, has indeed stood the test of time and is indeed guiding science seven centuries later. **Bernardino Telesio** was an intermediate figure who emphasized that the importance of sense data actually contradicted his own epistemology in developing his theory change based on matter, heat, and cold as he injected the idea of a higher impulse impacting natural change, much like Kapila nearly two millennia earlier. Nevertheless, he must be regarded as someone who sided with reason over scripture and with sense data over reason.

Tommaso Campanella was more coherent in arguing that sensation alone is the source of knowledge in his *Philosophia sensibus demonstrate*, published in 1592. He was a vocal opponent of Aristotelian philosophy. Campanella was also a believer in astrology and was sentenced by the Roman Inquisition to twenty-six years in prison, as we noted earlier.

The man who finally rescued the science in Europe from Aristotle's exclusive reliance on deductive reason was of course **Francis Bacon**. Unlike Aristotle, where knowledge resulted from an axiom through deduction, Bacon in effect asked where the axiom came from and where it should come from. The answer he provides is that facts or sense data must lead to axioms through inductive reasoning and that in turn leads to physical law. He was the first person in European history to correctly integrate sense and data to create an epistemology—a feat that Kanada in India and Mozi in China accomplished two millennia ago, Dinnaga accomplished in India one millennium ago, and Ibn al-Haytham accomplished half a millennium earlier. We cover the epistemological implications of Galileo's work under Scientific Creativity below.

Ethics: The development of ethics in Europe during the current phase may also be understood through the injection of ancient Greek ethics into a thoroughly Christian dogma and the opportunities opened by discovery of new sea routes. The latter's reference point was the bible, while the former depended on resolving the tension between virtue and happiness through action. The net impact was a slow secularization of ethics and its divorce from Christian theology, at least for the intellectual class, in itself a no mean task. This was accomplished through a renaissance in intellectual life supported by the enhanced availability of books because of the printing press. Yet while the Greek ethics argued for the autonomy of an individual and a virtuous life, Machiavelli in his *prince* argued that politics has nothing to do with ethics.

The question then became how to the resolve the contradiction between individual ethics of virtue and practical political ethics. This conflict was partially resolved through the related ideas of racism against nonwhites and the idea of the blue blood of the aristocracy and an opportunistic use of the continuing influence of Christian dogma. Since the Renaissance postulated the essential equality and autonomy of the human being, the issue arose how to treat the natives in Americas and peoples in Asia. Juan Gines de Sepulveda (1489–1573 CE) a Dominican philosopher, argued that native Indians were natural slaves who did not possess a soul (presumably Christian) and therefore reducing them to slavery was consistent with Christian theology. He stated that natives are "as children to parents, as women are to men, as cruel people are from mild people." That deoxygenated blood is blue as seen in the veins against pale white skin was sufficient proof for Spanish noblemen fighting the Moors during the Reconquista, showing that their pedigree had not been contaminated by darker-skinned persons, not realizing, of course, that if blue blood existed throughout their bodies, they would be dead! Thus, the ideas that whites are superior to nonwhites and that blue-blood aristocrats are superior to ordinary masses were born toward the end of the Renaissance period and were to serve as a justification for plundering the world and instituting a system of slavery focused not on domestic chores but on plantations and wealth creation. Later, in the eighteenth and nineteenth centuries, the ideology of racism would be strengthened through the emerging science of biology.

Thus, individual morality began a transformation from Christian morality to an autonomous individual morality while the political morality, rather unceremoniously, adopted the ideology of racism and blue blood and drew part of the justification from Christian theologians such as Sepulveda. This ideology was to serve the imperial needs of the coming domination of the globe by the nation-states of western Europe.

Aesthetics: If, from a historic aspect, Aquinas was nothing more than an apologist for Christian dogma dressed in philosophical garb, he did put forward a rather interesting theory of religious aesthetics or transcendental beauty. Aquinas identified three conditions of transcendental beauty: proportion, integrity, and clarity. If art consists of form, content, and emotion, then Aquinas was close to the mark in his theory of religious aesthetics, for form is proportion, clarity is content, and integrity is related to the emotion of morality. Of course, good art has no necessary relationship with integrity or clarity and only unfettered imagination that has appeal. But Aquinas may be forgiven for not anticipating the modern view of aesthetics.

Achievements in Art

Three important developments took place in performing arts in Europe: ballet, plays, and opera. The first fully developed ballet, "Ballet Comique de la Reine" was staged in France in 1581 for Catherine Medici. England took the lead in theater, with Shakespeare (1564–1616) plays becoming popular by the end of the sixteenth century. Jacopo Peri composed the first opera in 1597. He also wrote "Eurydice," performed at Henry IV's wedding to Marie Medici in 1600. The pipe organ was invented in 1360 and the dulcimer in 1400; the piano was still in the future. Michel de Toulouze published the first book using musical notation in 1496.

In visual arts, the key developments were recovering Greek and Roman heritage in sculpture and architecture, achieving great mastery in both technical and aesthetic terms in both, and the beginning of oil painting in 1400. These developments began in Italy in the fourteenth century since Italy was in a position to support artists. In painting, Leon Battista perfected the concept of perspective using the idea of zero or a vanishing point to create a three-dimensional effect in 1436. Art also became more secular as the hold of Christianity weakened a little. Master artists like Michelangelo, da Vinci, Raffaello, and Titian thrived. Art as a profession had come into existence. The new styles moved north through efforts of artists like Albrecht Durer at the end of the fifteenth century. Gothic art of the north was giving way to Renaissance art.

Developments in literature were driven by the printing press and interest in Greek and Roman heritage. Short story as a literary form in Europe began with publication of *Canterbury Tales* and Giovanni Boccaccio's *Decameron*. Petrarch popularized the sonnet form of poetry, and Montaigne invented the essay form.

16.41 Achievements in Science

Achievements in Formal Sciences

Arithmetic: European achievement in arithmetic during the current phase was resistance and acceptance of the Indian decimal system that reached Europe through the Arabs. While the idea of the decimal system had been known in Europe, at least by the late tenth century, it was also, not surprisingly, resisted by the Catholic Church and favored by wealth merchants who saw its value in accounting and compound interest calculation. It was formally introduced into Europe by Fibonacci (1170-1250 CE) through his book, *Liber Abaci*. It replaced Roman numerals by the fifteenth century. Leon Batista wrote a treatise on zero in 1471. In 1484, Nicholas Chuquet had difficulty accepting negative numbers and zero as a root of an equation. Filippo Calandri introduced an algorithm for long division in 1491. Negative numbers finally found acceptance in Cardan in 1545, nearly a thousand years after they were conceived by Brahamagupta. Simon Stevin's" the art of the tenths" was published in Dutch in 1585 and contained a systematic notation of the Indian system in Europe.

Nicole Oresme (1360) proved that the harmonic series is divergent based on comparison to another obviously divergent series.

The practical contribution of Europe in arithmetic was developing symbols for various mathematical operations: Pello used a dot to represent division in 1492, Hoecke used symbols for +/- in 1514, Robert Recorde introduced the equal sign in 1557, stating beautifully that "what could be more equal than two parallel lines?" Rudolph Christoff introduced symbols for square root in 1525. The modern form of the numerals was also finalized when they entered typesetting after the invention of the printing press.

There were significant contributions to number theory, such as when Hudalrichus Regius discovered (33550336) as the fifth perfect number (a positive integer equal to sum of its divisors) in 1536 and Francesco Maurolico's proof that sum of first odd numbers is $n2$ in 1575. As an aside, since six is the first perfect number, Augustine had claimed in the fourth century that the number six is perfect since God created the world in six days!

The last great achievement in arithmetic during the current phase was the discovery of logarithms by Napier in 1594 to simplify calculation, since a logarithm can convert the problem of multiplication and division to the much simpler problem of addition and subtraction. The idea of logarithms was first proposed by Indian mathematician Virasen in 816 CE, as the reader will recall.

Algebra: In algebra, the focus was on summarizing and mastering the existing knowledge:

- German mathematician Michael Stifel (b1567) summarized algebra and arithmetic knowledge in 1544.
- Rafaek Bombeli used complex numbers to solve equations in 1572.
- Franciscus Vieta used vowels for variables and consonants for constants in 1591.
- In Italy, during the first half of the sixteenth century, Ascipione Del Ferro and Niccolo Fontana Tartaglia found solutions for cubic equations. Tartaglia's student, Lodovico Ferrari, found solutions to quadratic equations.
- In 1572, Rafel Bombelli showed how to deal with imaginary numbers arising in the solution of cubic equations in his *L'Algebra*.

Geometry: Pi was computed to an accuracy of six decimal places in Europe for the first time in 1600, a thousand years after Aryabhatta had calculated it to eight decimal places. For the first time since Vichaspati, Nicole Oresme (1360) gave glimpses of the idea of plane coordinates.

Trigonometry: Trigonometry was in great demand because of the needs of navigation and commerce and grew to be of major importance. Johann Muller, also known as Regiomontanus, wrote a summary of trigonometry in 1461 that was published in 1533 CE. He was the first to include the tables for sine and tangent function in European history. However, much of the spherical trigonometry formulation was taken from the twelfth-century work of Jabir ibn Aflah. Another book, called *Trigonometria* was published in1595 by Bartholomew Pitiscus (1561–1613 CE). Pitiscus was first to use the term *trigonometry*.

Probability: Levi ben Gershon (1288–1344 CE) was a Jewish mathematician who wrote in Hebrew and established the formula for permutations and combinations in 1321 in France. This is the first great advance in probability since al-Kindi used frequency analysis to decipher an encrypted message. He proved the sine law for triangles and produced sine tables. In 1526, Cardano, who was an accomplished gambler and was always broke, wrote *Book on Game of Chance*, which included the first systematic treatment of probability. The book also included advice for how to cheat in gambling.

Thus, it was in probability theory that European mathematics broke new ground.

Logic: The field of logic, surprisingly, made significant progress in three areas and actually went beyond simply recovering and reciting Aristotle. Pope John XXI, William of Ockham, John Burdian, and Albert of Saxony were some of important figures:

- In placing restrictions on the range of a predicate in a proposition taken as truth. For example, in all men are mortal, does men refer men alive today or yet to be born? One can see seeds of first-order logic in this formulation.
- Clear identification of terms necessary for logic such as *and*, *if*, or *etc*.
- A theory of consequences developed by William of Ockham that distinguishes between material and logical implication, which highlighted the pitfalls in using if-*P*-then-*Q* logic, as it can give erroneous results.

Linguistics: There was little interest in fundamental linguistics in Europe during the current phase.

Achievements in Physical Sciences

Astronomy: We may summarize the progress in astronomy under observational astronomy, the confluence of correct and incorrect ideas, and the final emergence of correct solar astronomy through Copernicus, Tycho Brahe, and Kepler.

In observational astronomy, the following deserves mention: Alfonse constructed astronomical tables in 1250. The Milky Way was recognized as stars by Albertusi in the mid-thirteenth century. Chaucer wrote a book astrolabe in 1391. Toscanelli sighted and reported a comet in 1433 and reported Halley's Comet in 1456. Regiomontanus builds an observatory in Nuremberg in 1471 and studied comets. Picolomini produced a star atlas with stars labeled with letters in 1540. Europe discovers the comet tail is always away from the sun nine hundred years after the Chinese in 1540. Frisus (1508–1555 CE) describes a method to determine latitude from comparing clock time and sun time. Girolamo Cardano establishes that comets are real through parallel measurements. Reinhold publishes astronomical tables using the Copernican model in 1551. Tycho Brahe observes what turned out to be a nova in 1572, but it was first noted by the Chinese in 1006. David Fabricius noted the first variable star in 1596.

This was also a period of a great confluence of ideas, both from within Europe and outside: Jean Burdian claimed in 1350 that initial impulse was sufficient to explain the planetary motion, and it was unnecessary to invoke God. The idea of infinite universe with uniform bodies was conceived in 1436. Peurbach thought the sun controlled Ptolemy's epicycles in 1471. Nicholas of Cusa turned Plato on his head and thought there were no perfect circles in heaven and questioned a geocentric universe, thus supporting Giordano Bruno, who believed that stars have planetary systems and that the universe is infinite. Fracastoro took a wrong turn and extended the Eudoxus's model of solar astronomy to seventy-nine spheres in 1537. The idea of a Tusi couple reached Europe after the fall of the Byzantine Empire, and was developed as an alternative in place of the equant, an imaginary point placed halfway between the center of the deferent and the center of the epicycle.

The story of heliocentric astronomy starts with Copernicus in the early part of the sixteenth century. It placed the sun at the center, with planets in circular orbits around the sun and the moon around the earth. The apparent motion of distant stars was due to the rotation of the earth. Thus, he had it right except for the shape of the orbits. He was hesitant to publish his theory for nearly thirty years. He finally published *De revolutionibus orbium caleestium* in 1543 as he lay on his deathbed. The idea of a Tusi couple was critical in discarding the idea of equant, which forced Copernicus into the heliocentric model.

As luck would have it, the Protestant revolution placed land and resources in the hands of the Danish king, who bankrolled Tycho Brahe. Brahe was given an island with forty families as his subjects, and he built an observatory on the island. Though a great observational astronomer, Tycho was hardly convinced of the Copernicus theory based on his own observations starting in 1576 CE, thirty-three years after Copernicus published his theory. He believed that the sun and moon orbited the earth while other planets orbited the sun. He also believed in astrology.

Tycho Brahe was also very secretive and refused to share his data with Kepler who came to work for Tycho in 1600 CE. Kepler was a much better theoretician and believed Copernicus's theory. Recently, C. K. Raju advanced a theory that Tycho possessed the data from Indian astronomer Nilakanthan (which had been transmitted to Europe by Portuguese missionaries, along with the concept of differential calculus through the infinite series for trigonometric functions). Since Tycho, who was a competent observational astronomer and not a competent theoretician and did not believe in Copernicus, he was unable to deduce the laws of planetary motion from his and Nilakanthan's data. He did not want to give Kepler access to the data for two possible reasons: he did not want Kepler to know part of the data was not his own or he believed Kepler would deduce the planetary laws and outshine him. As luck would have it, Brahe died in 1601, and the data came to Kepler's possession. According to Raju, Kepler took Nilakanthan's data and transformed his orbits to a heliocentric concept. Once he did that, the variable epicycles in Nilakanthan's data came out as ellipses, and the rest, as they say, is history. Kepler, who may not have known that part of the data was not Tycho's, was also a professional astrologer and thus made the story that he arrived at his laws of planetary motion using Tycho's data. All this, even if true, does not detract from Kepler's accomplishments and his three laws. The first two were published in 1609 and the third in 1619:

- The orbit of all planets is an ellipse, with the sun located at one of the two foci
- Planets sweep equal areas in equal time
- The period of a planet's revolution around sun is proportional to the cube of the semi-major axis of the planet

The laws were indeed a momentous discovery since, unbeknown to Kepler, the third law contained in it the law of gravitation, because all that was needed was determining the acceleration experienced by a body in uniform circular motion, and that in turn required knowledge of calculus, which Kepler did not have. Galileo put his seal of approval on Copernican views in 1597 in a letter written to Kepler and almost died for his crime.

The bottom line was Copernicus conceived of a consistent heliocentric system with help from al-Tusi, and Kepler affirmed Copernicus with possible help from Nilanathan's data. A grand theoretical theory that explains the solar system was still in future, however.

Using astronomical observations, Pope Gregory reformed the calendar in 1582, with the Julian day count established in 1583. January 1, 4713 BCE, was the first day.

Physics: The most significant development in physics during the current phase was better understanding of terrestrial motion. The first step was to dethrone Aristotelian physics, which was conceived without an experimental basis. Throughout the sixteenth century, physicists questioned Aristotle's physics. Peter Ramus (1515–1572 CE) attacked Aristotle's, physics as did Giovanni Benedetti, who supported the impulse theory. In 1545, Domingo de Soto recognized that falling objects accelerate, and Galileo observed and analyzed the pendulum phenomenon in 1581 CE.

Thus, by the time Galileo began his experiments on an inclined plane, and both principle of inertia and acceleration during free fall were established. Even the time square law or the distance traveled under gravitation being proportional to square of the elapsed time was known. What had not been stated explicitly was that gravitational acceleration was constant. This is precisely what Galileo's experiments established, not in algebraic form but through geometrical constructions. He also stated more explicitly that a body stays in constant motion unless acted on by a force. Thus, Galileo formulated the first law of motion and made progress toward the second law. Galileo's experiments finalized the critical importance of the experimental method about the time Francis Bacon gave theoretical foundations final form.

With Galileo and Francis Bacon, European civilization had achieved what no other civilization had achieved before: a theoretical understanding of the scientific method and its successful use to deduce a law of nature here on earth about the time Kepler was annunciating the laws of solar system. Newton would achieve the grand synthesis of the heavenly and earthly realms in less than a century.

Optics did not progress much beyond where Muslim scientists had left off. The phenomenon of reflection and refraction and rainbows were studied in the thirteenth and fourteenth centuries, as was the camera obscura in 1550 CE. Similarly, magnetism was studied experimentally, with Gilbert publishing the first book on magnetism in 1600 CE. Surface tension was observed by Leonardo da Vinci. Both Galileo and Andrea Palaadio studied the strength of materials. Simon Stevin studied the phenomenon of hydrostatics in 1586 CE. Galileo invented the first telescope in 1600 CE.

Chemistry: Chemistry remained chained to alchemy despite the latter being banned by Pope John in 1317, not for the Catholic Church's enthusiasm for science but for alchemy's association with non-Christian mysticism. It is interesting to note how the Catholic Church burned Bruno at the stake for pursuing astronomy and yet encouraged chemistry by banning alchemy since the former contradicted the bible and the latter did not. The experimental basis of chemistry was laid by great Muslim chemists and was hardly followed up. Yet there were discoveries. Albertus Magnus discovered arsenic in 1250 CE, alchemist Arnold prepared pure alcohol in 1270 and came close to discovering carbon monoxide, the photochemical reaction for silver salts was noted in 1565 CE, and Libvius prepared hydrochloric acid, tin tetrachloride, and ammonium sulfate in 1597 CE. The real progress remained practical, tied to textiles and metallurgy. Rosetti wrote a treatise on dyeing in 1548 and another on perfume and soap making processes. Georgius Agricola published his highly influential *De re Metallica* in 1556, summarizing the state of knowledge in mining (fire-setting and thermal-shocking methods) and extractive metallurgy.

Thus, the focus in chemistry during the current phase was rising above alchemy and bringing out the practical chemical processes kept hidden by guilds and practitioners out in the open. Only in the seventeenth century will chemistry begin to develop a theoretical basis.

Earth sciences: The clear focus of earth sciences in Europe during the phase was world geography, which was driven by an almost obsessive need to discover a sea route to India. That in turn gave birth to rigorous cartography.

Ptolemy's *Geography* was translated from Greek into Latin by di Scarperia in 1405. Nicolo Conti reached India by land in 1418 and probably underscored the importance of discovering sea routes. The fifteenth century is a catalogue of geographical discoveries with increasing tempo: Ceuta Island (1415), Madeira (1418), Azores Islands (1432–1444 CE), Caribbean Islands (1492), the sea route to Calicut (1498), Brazil (1500), Spice Islands (1512), circumnavigation through Pacific Ocean (1513–1529), and Japan (1543). Sebastian published a major compendium on world geography in 1551.

The earliest sea *navigation* was based on using landmarks, local knowledge, and maps. In high seas when no landmarks were visible, they navigated using the course or direction and the distance traveled. The former came from celestial bodies or a compass and the latter by a ship log and a sand glass. These techniques would be sufficient for coastal navigation. However, open sea navigation required astronavigation based on an almanac of the geographical position of the celestial object, an accurate sextant to measure the altitude of the celestial object, accurate maps and chronometer, and a highly accurate table of trigonometric functions. The European explorers did not have the latter, and this created Jesuit interest in the infinite series invented by the Kerala school of mathematical astronomy in the early sixteenth century since these series made accurate tables of the trigonometric functions possible. Thus, Portuguese and Spanish navigators succeeded in putting navigation on a firm scientific basis toward the end of the current phase.

Cartography was of critical importance and saw fantastic development: Toscanelli prepared a map of the Atlantic in 1474, suggesting Asia was only 2,500 miles away, prompting Columbus's voyage. The first global map was produced by a European in 1492, and another cartographer Martin Waldseemuller named America after Americus Vespucius, who explored it between 1497 and 1504. It showed Americas to be not part of Asia in 1507 as Columbus had believed. The first globe was constructed in 1515, showing Americas forty years before Copernicus's theory; a book on cartography was published in 1524 by German astronomer Apian; Alonzo de Santa Cruz produced a map of how magnetic field departs from true north, thus aiding in more accurate latitude determination in 1530; and Geradus Mercator introduces maps based on the Mercator projection, which diminishes the size of countries near equator in 1568.

William Merlee of England attempted *weather forecasting* in 1337. Nicholas Cusa invited the hygrometer in the mid-fifteenth century, and Galileo invented an early thermometer toward the end of the sixteenth century.

Agricola discussed the existence of ore veins in the ground, thus making an early contribution toward developing *geology*. He also coined the word *fossil* in 1545. Leonardo deduced from sea fossils on land that the earth underwent transformations. The hexagonal nature of snowflakes was noted in Europe for the first time in 1591 by mathematician Thomas Harriet.

Achievements in Biological Sciences

Biology: With the advent of the printing press, the first book on *botany* was not about plants but typically on herbs. Botany went through a period of sample collection and compilation with illustrations. Otto Brunfels (1488–1534) published an illustrated book on 230 plants. Leonard Fuch described five hundred plants, including some from the New World in 1542. Valerius Cordus (1515–1544) took matters one step further with more botanical descriptions of plant reproductive anatomy. This was followed by a period of classification of the plants: Jerome Bock attempted plant classification in Germany in 1539, followed by one based on roots and fruits by Andrea Cesalpino in 1583. This naturally led to botanical gardens (first in Italy in 1543), where the plants could be observed under controlled conditions. In 1580, Prospero discovered plants have two sexes. Several workers in the field could boast of vast collections of plants, sometimes numbering the thousands (Ulisse Aldrovandi, 1522–1605).

Aristotle's *Zoology, History of Animals*, where he classified animals according to their known physiology and behavior, was two millennia old by the end of the current phase. The fundamental change toward the end of phase was a collection of creatures as opposed to anecdotes about them. This allowed careful observation under controlled conditions and led to publication of the so-called *Bestiaries* or compendiums summarizing the knowledge concerning animals. Artists such as Albrecht and Leonardo da Vinci worked with naturalists to draw or etch animals.

Konrad Gesner went a step further and produced a magnum opus in the form of five emblem books, starting in the mid-sixteenth century. They focused on four-footed mammals; egg-laying, four-footed animals; birds; fish and aquatic animals; and snakes and scorpions. The book was added to the list of prohibited books by the Catholic Church! Ulisse Aldrovandi published the first volume of his zoology encyclopedia in 1599. Several workers noted the similarity in the organs of higher animals and humans, including Pierre Belon, who noted the similarity in the bones of all vertebrates.

Medicine: Medical science remained in its infancy during the current phase. The phase started with translations of Arabic and Greek texts into Latin. William of Moerbeke (1215–1286) translated Galen's works from Greek into Latin. New diseases were diagnosed: minor's disease by Paracelsus in 1530, influenza in Paris in 1414, syphilis by Fracastoro in 1530, and appendicitis by Jean Francois Fernel in 1542. From Bacon in 1260 to Peracelsus in 1522, several thinkers postulated that disease was caused by natural agents and could be cured chemically. This was necessary to reiterate since the prevalent notion was that disease was caused by evil spirits.

The highlight of European medicine in the current phase was anatomy, after the pope allowed dissection in 1235. Mondino De'Luzzi's *Anatomia* was published in 1316 based on dissections and was used for two centuries in teaching anatomy, signifying the slow pace in anatomical research. In 1543, Andreas Vesalius truly replaced Scholastic thinking in medicine with an empirical approach in anatomy and physiology through his publication of *Human Anatomy*. This was followed by detailed description of several organs: Francois Fernel described contraction in the digestive processing in 1542, Gabriel Fallopio described the female reproductive system and inner ear details in 1561, Bartolomeo Eustachi described adrenal glands in 1563, Costanzo Varolio described cranial nerves, Varolli described the pons, part of brainstem, in 1573, Arcangelo Piccolomini distinguished between the cortex and cerebral hemispheres in 1586, and Hieronymus Aquapendente studied fetal development in 1600. Blood circulation was described by Michael Servetus in 1553, and Realdo Colombo claimed blood circulated from the right chamber to the lungs and to the left chamber from the lungs. Harvey finally settled the question in 1628.

There was progress in disease treatment as well: Henri de Mondeville advocated cleansing and suturing wounds in 1320, Guy de Chauliac described the treatment of fractures and hernias, Benedetto Rinio's book on medicinal herbs discusses 440 plants, gold was used to fill teeth in 1450, the first surgical treatment of a gunshot wound was in 1497, Swiss Jacob Nufer performs the first recorded Caesarean in 1500, the first prosthetic hand was developed by Von Berlichingen in 1508, tincture of iodine was used as a disinfectant by Swiss physician Paracelsus in 1520, Ambroise advocated soothing cream in place of boiling oil for wound treatment in 1545, and the glass eye was invented in 1579.

The field of medicine was getting organized into a profession, as evidenced by books and associations and the founding of midwives association in 1452 in Germany and the Royal College of Physicians in 1518 by Thomas Linacre. Heinrich von Pfolspeundt published the first German book on surgery in 1460, the first book on dentistry was published in 1530 in Germany, and *Dispensarium* sums up European knowledge of drugs, chemicals, and their preparation in 1535.

Last, but not the least, the microscope was invented in 1590 by Zacharias Janssen.

Thus, the greatest creative achievements of European civilization during the phase were in astronomy closely followed by physics. The era of Scholasticism, which focused on preserving Christian dogma, had also exhausted itself. In most other areas, such as practical inventions, mathematics, art, and medicine, the achievements of Chinese, Indian, and Muslim civilization were discovered, modestly developed, and adopted. As China fell under nomads, India under antiscience Muslims, and the center of Muslim under the Turks, Europe was all that was left to pursue creativity in general and science in particular. The destruction of observatories in Istanbul and Samarkand and the destruction of Vijayanagara Empire by a coalition of South Indian Sultanates and the end of mathematical astronomy in India stand as testimony to this monumental change.

Achievements in Social Sciences

Only in political science and economics did European civilization develop in new directions

Political science: The essential thesis of Machiavelli (1469–1527) was that aside from the unpredictable influence of fortune, the success of a state depended on the skill and energy of its leader and that individual ethics had little to do with political ethics. His position on the former may be explained in part by the size of the states in northern Italy at that time, the level of wealth polarization that existed, and his desire to win favor with the Medici family. Machiavelli was a materialist who had read Democritus and Epicurus and did not believe in the power of gods but held politics in high esteem, much like Socrates. However, unlike Socrates, he had little use for virtue in a ruler. The ruler was allowed freedom without moral constraints as long as his objectives were acceptable. The book *Prince* explaining his philosophy earned the term *Machiavellian* as equivalent to deceit, cruelty, and fear. He was not too far off in describing the way world operated, only he also stated that is the way it should or can operate. He was a realist without a streak of idealism. Perhaps the true political philosophy of Machiavelli is more apparent in a commentary he wrote on the Roman historian Titus Livus (59 BCE–17 CE). In the *Discourses on Livy*, Machiavelli focused on the structure of republican form of government, warfare, and political leadership. However. even in this more serious work, he could not help being a Machiavellian.

Economics: If Machiavelli favored the expulsion of morality from politics, Lessius (1554–1623) wanted to bring morality into business and finance but without the uncritical injunctions of the Catholic Church. Thus, he favored charging modest interest in lending money as a compensation for loss of liquidity and promoted a free rein in price for commodities and insurance risk. Martin de Azpilcueta (1493–1586) noticed the relationship between prices and scarcity of precious metal. thus anticipating the quantitative theory of money put forward formally by Jean Bodin (1530–1596). On commodity pricing, Luis de Molina and others argued for a use-value theory of price, which was a precursor to the free market theory of price based on supply and demand.

Thus, the basic ideas behind micro- and macroeconomics were being laid out toward the end of the current phase, clearly indicating the development of capitalism and markets in labor, money, and products.

Summarizing Achievements in Abstract Systems-building Capability (ASBC)

By the end of the phase, the ASBC of the European civilization was indeed world-class: it continued to have alphabetical script and had already adopted the decimal system. It led in understanding the controlled experiments in the heavens and was indeed on the verge of duplicating them here on earth. There were significant strides in epistemology based on the works of several philosophers and scientists.

Summarizing the State of Civilization and Science

16.42 State of Civilization and Science at Phase End

Overview of the Political History of the Phase

Thus, Anatolia, West Asia, North Africa, North India, and portion of South India during this phase remained under the control of various Turkish tribes, who, as the reader will recall, were direct or indirect descendants of the mercenaries from central Asia conscripted by Arabs. The only exceptions to the above statement are Genghis Khan's conquest of West Asia in 1218 CE, who was followed by his descendant Timur in 1383 CE, and Babur's conquest of North India. Babur founded the Mogul dynasty in 1526 CE and was a descendant of Timur. However, the Mongols outside of China had converted to Sunni Islam by Timur's time. Thus, the entire region from Anatolia to India was under Turkish or Mongol hegemony by the end of the phase; both were or had become absolute believers in Sunni Islam.

China was spared Islamic aggression, though not nomadic aggression. India was not spared either. Fortunately, this time, Europe escaped both nomadic and Islamic aggression because, unlike the Huns nearly a millennium earlier, Mongols weakened the Muslim civilization and put it on the defensive, the vast Muslim domain acted as a buffer, and Mongols conquered China instead of western Europe. Europe was lucky and could now focus its energies on extricating itself from feudalism, Arab control, and its own history of disinterest in science. Meanwhile, the Southeast Asian civilizations continued to develop their great Hindu and Buddhist kingdoms under the gentle influence of Indian and Chinese civilizations in complete isolation from Muslim and European civilizations until about the fourteenth century. Muslim and European control gradually followed.

State of Practical Creativity

In the technology arena, what stands out are movable type printing and explosives technologies, the benefits of Columbian exchange and refinement of manufacturing technologies such as papermaking, wine fermentation, metallurgy, woolen textiles, and shipbuilding. Transportation technology also took a leap forward and included canals, locks, aqueduct improvements, and tunnels. Builders experimented with architecture, and the Cathedral of Pisa was built during this time.

State of Philosophical Creativity

In philosophy, classical Greek philosophy failed to put both Islamic and Christian dogma on a rational basis. The Scholastic project failed, which laid the foundation for the emergence of critical philosophy. Critical philosophy was largely absent during the phase, but the focus of metaphysical speculation became challenging Christian dogma and supporting philosopher/scientists who held other theories about how the universe worked.

State of Scientific Creativity

In science, we see the most development: the intellectual basis of science of the infinitesimal was laid out, the architecture of the solar system was defined, and significant progress was made toward understanding laws that govern terrestrial motion. Chemistry still awaited the application of the experimental approach. Geography, cartography, and science of navigation expanded greatly, and a good start was made toward understanding the principles behind microeconomics and macroeconomics. Clearly, understanding the scientific method reached new heights.

State of Religious Creativity

The state of faith, however, remained dismal. Islam, upon collision with science, gave up on the latter. Christianity tried to co-opt science through classical philosophy but failed miserably. In Indian civilization, monism, mysticism, and the devotional approach made a comeback, and a synthesis between Hinduism and Islam was modestly successful but failed to make an impact on the caste system. Buddhism and agnosticism were on the defensive in India and Southeast Asia. Furthermore, Buddhism continued to evolve away from agnosticism by absorbing elements of monism and polytheism as it spread across cultures.

State of Artistic Creativity

In performing arts, new musical instruments and musical notation came into existence, and oil painting with perspective developed by leaps and bounds. Ballet and opera came into existence. Arts in Europe at least began to take on secular themes. In literature, buoyed by the printing press, new forms in poetry, short stories, and prose came into existence.

Productive Outcomes

Absorption of technologies from all major civilizations brought in part by Mongol invasions, increased productivity in Indian, Chinese, and European civilizations. By the end of the phase, fair trade essentially was replaced by coerced trade based on control of sea routes. This was beginning to impact productivity and wealth creation in Indian, Muslim, and Chinese civilizations by the phase end. Peaceful migrations had dwindled and were replaced by violent colonization. A significant migration of scholars from Byzantine and Italy played a key role in the birth of the Renaissance.

Constructive Outcomes

The most important constructive outcomes were transmission of creativity and emergence of a new world trade system based on linking the world's oceans. We have described the transmission of creativity in detail already. Though the oceans were controlled by a few western European states, the state of trade between Asia and Europe may be characterized as partly coerced since these powers did not control significant Asian territories. The same cannot be said of goods or the slave trade among European civilization, the Americas, and Africa. Such trade must be characterized as coerced beginning in the sixteenth century. To underscore the impact of interaction among civilization on the fourth synthesis of science in western Europe, we summarize all significant interaction in figure 16.1.

Destructive Outcomes

The current phase was full of conflict: Indian civilization remained unable to solve caste division and fell victim to Muslim aggression after holding it back for two centuries. The aggression in turn generated conflict between the invader and the Indian dynasties. The Muslim and Chinese civilizations were devastated by Mongol invasion. The invasion resulted in the rise of the Ottomans, who destroyed the Byzantine Empire. The Ming dynasty put an end to the Mongol Empire in China but fell victim to Qing pressure toward the end of the phase. The European civilization, though it successfully pushed the Moors out, its eastern flank, the Byzantine Empire, and Venice suffered at the hands of the Ottomans. Europe also experienced internal struggles related to civil wars and wars among nation-states, in particular the Hundred Years'

War. In addition, the nation-states, once they controlled the sea routes, initiated the violent colonization of America, slave trade with Africa, and coerced trade with Asia and made an end run against the Ottomans through encirclement. In short the state of creativity and productivity for civilizations was excellent; however, the state of conflict took a turn for the worse.

State of Specific Sciences at Phase End

Formal sciences: The most significant achievements in mathematics were systematization and further development of arithmetic, algebra, and logarithms and laying the foundation of the probability theory. Similarly, the field of logic was systematized through better understanding of conditions on syllogism through the use of operators such as and, or, if etc.

Astronomy: Kepler conceived a consistent heliocentric model of the solar system, including his three laws of planetary motion with possible help from Indian astronomer Nilakanthan. It was based on Copernican theory, which in turn required the critical concept of the Tusi couple that had been put forth by Persian astronomer al-Tusi.

Physics: The critical achievement in terrestrial physics was the experimental proof that acceleration due to gravity on earth is constant for all bodies, independent of size. It was indeed a monumental achievement.

Chemistry: Chemistry was slowly freed from the clutches of alchemy, ironically with help from the pope, leading to better understanding and the manufacture of several key chemicals. However, it would be an exaggeration to say that chemistry, like astronomy and physics, was put on a firm experimental basis. The state of chemistry did not advance significantly beyond what the Muslim civilization had achieved.

Earth sciences: The clear focus of earth sciences in Europe during the phase was world geography, cartography, and navigation on the high seas driven by an almost obsessive need to discover the sea route to India. That in turn gave birth to rigorous cartography. Very preliminary steps were taken to develop the science of geology and weather. The progress in earth sciences went significantly beyond what was achieved by Muslim civilization in the third synthesis.

Medicine: Great progress was made in anatomy after the pope allowed dissection in the thirteenth century. Several sound treatment methods were discovered, such as for gunshot wounds, fractures, and hernia. Much like chemistry, medicine also remained in its infancy, probably not too far ahead of what Muslim physicians had already accomplished

Social sciences: A ruler-centered political theory devoid of any ethical foundation was put forth by Machiavelli, which only deserves to be included as science since it

Figure 16.1: Peaceful Reciprocal Interactions
Sixth Phase: 1200–1600 CE

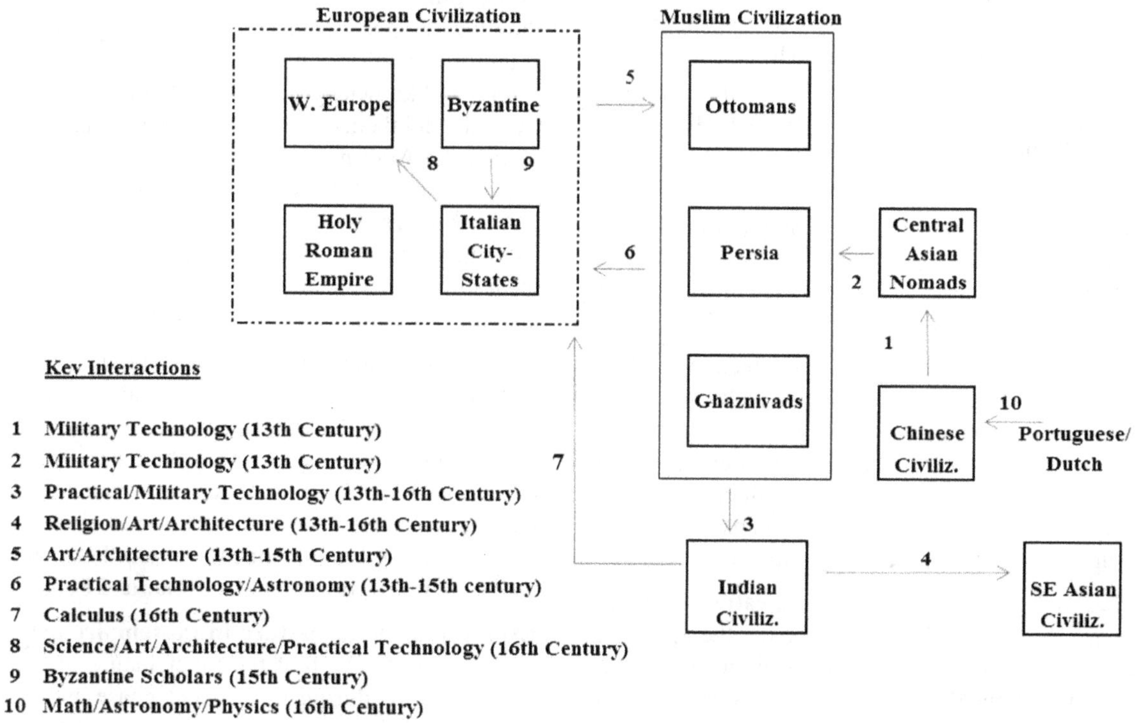

Key Interactions

1. Military Technology (13th Century)
2. Military Technology (13th Century)
3. Practical/Military Technology (13th-16th Century)
4. Religion/Art/Architecture (13th-16th Century)
5. Art/Architecture (13th-15th Century)
6. Practical Technology/Astronomy (13th-15th century)
7. Calculus (16th Century)
8. Science/Art/Architecture/Practical Technology (16th Century)
9. Byzantine Scholars (15th Century)
10. Math/Astronomy/Physics (16th Century)

reflected the political condition of Italian city-states at the time. In economics, however, we see scholars arguing for charging interest and market-based pricing. Most interestingly, the relationship between the general price level and money supply (or precious metals) was observed. However, given the enormous increase in supply of precious metals because of the discovery of the Americas, it is hardly surprising.

Assessing the Inner Nature of Participants

We have consistently argued the creative and productive capacity of a social order depends on its evolving institutions and processes, natural bounty, and the impact of the sum total of all external peaceful and violent engagements. In this section, as before, we deduce the inner nature of key participants.

16.43 Inner Nature of Central Asian Nomads

Central Asian Nomads—the Fourth Wave (1200–1800)

Productive capacity: The productive inner nature of Mongolian nomads did not differ much from earlier waves from central Asia. Agriculture was secondary to herding. There was indeed economic freedom, but Mongols lacked agricultural technology, rudimentary markets, and natural conditions to create a sustainable growing surplus despite a high degree of internal equality based on tribal traditions and the social cohesion created through Genghis Khan's considerable leadership skills. Consequently, the question of new technology adoption was moot. Thus, like all nomads, internal productive capacity was low and in fact formed the basis of their aggression. The changing SGS came from controlling the surplus of conquered civilizations during the empire period and reverted back to the nomadic level after the empire period was over. Productive capacity was necessarily low.

Mongols that returned home after disintegration of the empire had acquired many of the norms of civilization, including agriculture and settled life. They displayed a higher productive capacity.

Creative capacity: The primary focus of creative freedom within the Mongol culture was military technology; the interest in religious and intellectual creativity was modest at best, after all, when in doubt, Genghis Khan consulted sky. The question of science-religion conflict was moot. Thus, they had a low and narrow creative capacity. Wealth allocation primarily favored military capability.

After the empire period was over, creative capacity underwent a dramatic transformation under the influence of Tibetan Buddhism and creative freedom flourished. There was no science-religion conflict under Buddhist agnosticism, and great strides were made in abstract systems-building capability. The creative capacity, surprisingly, underwent a dramatic change. However, since the population base was small and the surplus was limited and inconsistent, the creative output was at the mercy of the chance emergence of a great genius and not the systematic allocation of resources to creative endeavors that produced a base of talented artists, scientists, and philosophers to sustain ongoing development.

The Mongol branch adopting Islam underwent no such renaissance and produced tyrants such as Timur Lane and Babur. It was clearly antiscience and had a practical internal creative balance.

Constructive orientation: The Mongols were hardly isolated but were without any significant ideology. It was in their soft genetic code to conquer civilizations, learn from them, and be absorbed into them over time. Thus, not surprisingly, the Mongols exhibited openness to trade and the practical and religious creativity of civilizations they plundered. However, as their descendants converted to Islam, the openness turned into insularity to both religious and intellectual creativity, reflecting the nature of Muslim civilization after the twelfth century.

Destructive orientation: The destructive orientation, like that of other central Asian nomads, was aggressive, cruel, and violent in the extreme during the empire period, based on low natural bounty and a long history of institutional greed for productive land and people. The purpose of internal equality was not creative or productive endeavors but to create a highly motivated, aggressive force to invade and capture the sustainable growing surplus of civilizations, followed by a relatively equitable distribution of the plunder. Once again, Mongols simply confirmed the fragility of civilizations, the lack of focus on producing wealth and knowledge, and civilizations' historic inability to defend themselves against well-organized nomads. Unlike the Arab nomads, the destructive orientation of Mongols was not derived from religious faith; rather, it was more of a reflection of generic *Homo sapiens*' destructive nature amplified by harsh natural conditions and often made invincible by the emergence of a charismatic military leader, military technology, and military doctrine.

Destructive inner nature also underwent a dramatic shift under the Buddhism-inspired cultural renaissance. Mongols transcended their aggressive impulse to a considerable degree since they adopted Buddhism and became a peace-loving people. By contrast, the branch that adopted Islam also excelled for a short while in artistic and scientific creation because of momentum but continued to produce ruthless invaders like Timur and Babur.

Evolution of inner nature in postempire period: It is worth emphasizing that the inner nature of the central Asian nomads during the current phase and extending into the next is an interesting example of the dramatic impact of a religious belief system. Genghis Khan and his descendants brought havoc to the world, killing 10 percent of the world's population. After the Mongol Empire disintegrated, not all Mongols returned to Mongolia. One of the branches that did not return was the Barlas tribe. It remained in Turkestan, adopted Islam and Persian culture, and produced Timur Lane in the fourteenth century. The Mongols who returned to Mongolia, on the other hand, came under the influence of Tibetan Buddhism and perhaps Chinese culture, experienced a cultural renaissance, developed a peaceful orientation, and produced remarkable creative outcomes, including coming close to independently inventing calculus in the eighteenth century as we noted earlier. This reminds one of what had occurred to Kushans in India more than a millennium ago. Thus, during the postempire period, the inner nature of the Mongols evolved along two different lines: one group adopted Buddhism, transformed its destructive nature, and produced a cultural and even scientific renaissance, and the other group adopted Islam, continued its destructive ways, and became wedded an antiscience attitude. The differing evolution of the two Mongol branches affirms that ideology or belief system, particularly religious beliefs, is all-important and that even before the modern era, a nomadic people could travel far from barbarianism and reach heights of creativity within a span of ten generations under the right circumstances.

16.44 Inner Nature of the Chinese Civilization

Productive capacity: Destruction under Kublai Khan was followed by the black plague in the early fourteenth century, which killed another 30 percent of the Chinese population. During the Ming period, Chinese civilization was extremely successful creating wealth through application of existing practical technology and good agricultural, manufacturing, and trade policies coupled with high demand for its products in Europe through the Silk Route, which was made secure and safe by Mongols. The experiment in deregulation initiated by Ming emperors succeeded beyond their wildest imagination. It increased economic freedom by putting an end to state involvement in iron and salt industries and focused instead on completing irrigation projects to help agriculture. This, coupled with the fruits of the Columbian exchange and the use of agricultural tools during the latter part of the phase on large plantations, resulted in a great increase in surplus and the creation of rural, rural-urban, and even a national market for some commodities. After an initial period, the trade restrictions and taxes were eased, and both internal and external trade expanded. New technology adoption was high, and despite increasing internal inequality, social cohesion remained in part because of relatively stable control of surplus. Wealth allocation remained focused on defending against nomads and practical creativity. For a while, Mongols diverted the surplus to expensive palaces and residences. The productive capacity was high and increasing. China accounted for nearly a third of the world economy at the end of current phase.

Toward the end of Ming period, the damage to the economy through inflation was compounded by the so-called little ice age resulting in crop failure and famines, particularly in the north. In addition, the deadliest recorded earthquake occurred in 1556 and killed nearly a million people. These two upheavals, combined with a ruinous agriculture, resulted in a breakdown of authority. As a result of these driving factors, the Chinese civilization handed the trade leadership to the Europeans, whose actions, coupled with the wrath of Mother Nature eventually destroyed the Chinese economy through inflation. Thus, in the sixteenth century, economic freedom, knowledge-wealth synergy, social cohesion, internal inequality, control of surplus, and openness all suffered. The productive capacity was in a free fall when Manchus conquered China in 1644 CE.

Creative capacity: The Chinese civilization, after a deadly experience with the Mongols and a short-lived attempt to reach beyond its shores under Ming rulers, returned to its eternal comfort zone: a practical orientation and insularity. The creative freedom suffered under Ming emperors compared to the Song dynasty since Ming emperors did not value the practical technology to the same degree. The resources were there but not applied, in part because the lack of alphabet inhibited developing complex philosophical and scientific systems. China continued to exhibit minimal science-religion conflict, often displaying a profound sense of cultural superiority. As a consequence, China became disinterested in the scientific and religious creativity of other civilizations. How can we explain these outcomes based on specific causes? First, the founder of the Ming dynasty came from a peasant background and showed opposition to even practical technology; he had the mechanical automations in the palace destroyed. This slowed down the development of new practical technology. Second, the superiority complex built into the Chinese civilization prevailed, and China turned away from both European science (the results of the fourth synthesis) and an assertive or even aggressive impulse with respect to the outside world. Third, China's abstract systems-building capability remained stymied under Ming emperors as they focused on traditional Chinese endeavors. Its creative capacity continued to be narrow and deep but not as deep as before, since even a focus on practical creativity took a hit. Greater focus existed on arts, sophisticated living, and mannerisms.

Constructive orientation: The constructive orientation did not change materially, essentially exhibiting Type 2 openness but that did not seem to hurt the productive capacity much.

Destructive orientation: China also continued to retain, despite several half-hearted attempts at territorial expansion and naval expeditions, an essentially defensive posture though fought hard when attacked. Thus, China's destructive orientation remained quintessentially Chinese one more time, and it maintained its sustained political independence fairly well during this phase, by first absorbing the Yuan dynasty into Chinese culture, followed by a revolt against it while defending against intermittent Mongol attacks that continued after the fall of the Yuan dynasty. The economic ruin from famine caused by the mini ice age, earthquakes, rampant inflation, and excessive concentration of wealth in the hands of merchants toward the end of the phase created an opening for the Manchu from the north to conquer China in the seventeenth century.

Thus, China's destructive orientation remained defensive and mostly peaceful. It did not excessively engage in empire building, violent colonization, or systematic wealth drain. However, its internal policies once again ended up inviting external aggression.

16.45 Inner Nature of the Indian Civilization

Islam had an enormous impact on the Indian civilization during the current phase. Though British colonial rule in the coming centuries after the collapse of Mughal rule was going to have a greater physical and intellectual impact on the Indian civilization through wealth drain and the reintroduction of science, Islam had a far greater psychological impact through Islam on the Indian civilization during the four centuries of this phase.

Productive capacity: The agriculture, industry, architecture, and commerce materially benefited through the introduction of new practical technologies and a strengthened monetary economy managed by the Sultanate. Textile, metalwork, stonework, and other industries prospered. The middle class in the cities was grateful for keeping the Mongols at bay and for new economic opportunities. However, the Sultanate was unable to create a fair land revenue system and had to engage in parasitic tax collection that brutalized the peasantry often. External trade picked up because of the worldwide Muslim network and because Islamic rule tended toward a tax policy that favored the manufacturers and traders at the expense of the farmer. Therefore, under Islamic rule, trade with other countries expanded again, in part because of the acceptance of letters of credit in many parts of the Islamic civilization, since all had a common legal code. Because of tax and trade policies, manufacturing gained. On balance, the Sultanate increased the focus on the economy and economic freedom increased.

Turkish invaders introduced new technologies, such as printing, paper making, gun powder, guns, bookbinding, ceramic tiles, the Persian waterwheel, and Islamic architectural style, to name the important ones. However, these technologies were not up to world standards and came in late. Still, the new technology adoption clearly accelerated and had a strong impact on economic activity.

The internal equality, however, suffered a great deal. Islamic rulers, particularly in the north, practiced religious discrimination through the jezia tax on Hindus, the destruction of Hindu temples, the destruction of Buddhism through cutting the support for monasteries, using economic and religious incentives through Sufis saints to accelerate conversion, and imposing an administration based on sharia law. This phase naturally produced a great number of saints in North India, who attempted a synthesis of Hinduism and Islam and promoted the message of tolerance and diversity. Yet, this message failed to root out caste inequality since the caste system was too firmly integrated into the economy and its support from the Hindu religion was absolute. This failure at reform turned the Hindu majority even more religious and unwittingly stiffened the caste system as a last defense against Islamic attack on its religiosity.

With hindsight, the attempt at synthesis was not successful and over centuries, nearly a third of the Hindu population in the subcontinent converted to Islam. Considering the long span of nearly eight centuries, the Indian experience with Islam is perhaps the best record of resisting Islam while trying to accommodate it than anywhere else in the world, where Islam either had a near total victory or near total defeat. Islam also introduced slavery into India. Sultan Tuglaq is said to have had 180,000 slaves.

Islamic rulers were big spenders on palaces, tombs, and gardens. Undoubtedly, this created a burden on peasantry. Islamic rule also clearly increased the wealth polarization between cities and villages. From a social point of view, Islamic rulers treated the Hindus as second- or third-class citizens. Thus, the inequality between Hindus and Muslims was institutionalized and increased among Hindu castes, both derived from religion. We would characterize internal inequality as relatively high and social cohesion as moderate.

Throughout this phase, the political situation in India remained extremely fluid. There were several reasons for this instability. First, compared to the Arabs, the invading Turks were much more ruthless and destructive and brought their tribal rivalries from the Afghan base into India. This resulted in constant infighting, wars of succession, and treachery, which never allowed any particular dynasty to last more than a century or feel secure enough to undertake sustained development. Second, continual invasions during the Slave dynasty by Mongols, during the Tughlaq dynasty by Timur Lane, and during the Lodhi dynasty by Babur kept the political situation unsettled as each of these intrusions was more successful than the one before it. Third, the Hindu resistance to these dynasties, though not successful, in part because of internal treachery and in part because of superior weapons technology and fast horses, added to instability. The three-way struggle consisting of infighting within the Sultanate, periodic invasions from the northwest, and Hindu resistance explains the political fluidity and relative lack of sustained economic development. External invasions continually weakened the Sultanate but still did not allow Hindu resistance to succeed, since the Sultanate and the invaders shared the same objective. This dynastic instability was balanced by the self-sufficient democratic and caste-bound village communities that also tended to withdraw inwardly during periods of political instability and reduced trade with the cities. Thus, we would characterize internal wars as substantial, resulting in a shifting control of surplus and changing policies that interfered with the objective of increased wealth creation.

The contrast with China during this period, incidentally, is instructive. The Mongols, who were not Muslim and not yet splintered, conquered China. Lacking a coherent ideology, they tried to assimilate into Chinese culture. They were overthrown within a century by the Ming dynasty, which provided three centuries of peace and stability. The Islamic ideology of the Sultanate provided the decisive difference with respect to China during the same period.

The impact of Islam and the Sultanate on south was different than in the north. The Deccan Sultanates had to rely on the Hindus to a greater extent for administrative work. The Deccan Sultanates, having been in the country for a while, were relatively more relaxed about conversion, fewer people converted to Islam in the south, the hold of Sultanates was not as strong, and the impact of the devastating foreign invasions were not as closely felt. Thus, the mix of Sultanate strength, invaders, and Hindu resistance had a different dynamic that led to the rise of the Vijayanagara Empire. In the Vijayanagara Empire, all key dimensions of the productive capacity were superior: more economic freedom, better new technology adoption, less inequality, more internal stability, and better social cohesion. Thus the Vijayanagara Empire was the most prosperous empire within the Indian subcontinent, with high sustainable growing surplus. Its wealth provoked such jealousy that a coalition of Muslim kingdoms invaded and destroyed it in 1646 CE, about the time Manchu conquered China.

Indian civilization continued to have a high productive capacity despite political instability and had one of the highest standards of living in the world. But under Muslim control, it was woefully unprepared to meet the challenges ahead.

Creative capacity: Indian society underwent a dramatic change during this phase. It lost its political independence to a foreign power with a dramatically different belief system and values. The values of Indian society encouraged intellectual and religious knowledge and had an open and peaceful attitude toward other civilizations. The invaders, in contrast, were religiously intolerant, disinterested in intellectual pursuits, and had answers to all religious inquiries through a revealed faith. In addition, their cousins had witnessed the fundamental incompatibility between a revealed faith and the pursuit of open-ended science toward the end of Arab-Persian golden age of science. They were not about to risk it again. Besides, they could not see how science could add to their wealth and power. Hindustan had too many workers available at low wages to build their palaces, forts, and gardens. Thus, the long history of creative freedom came to be suppressed with the arrival of Islam in both religious and scientific endeavors. Muslim invaders began the destruction of science right at the start, as evidenced by Nalanda University being razed to the ground and Bakhtiar Khilzi burning its library. (He is said to have asked before burning the library if it had a copy of the Koran.)

Science-religion conflict increased dramatically compared to the last phase and civilization became less open to its own creative past and those of the fruits of fourth synthesis brought by Europeans. This occurred despite breakthroughs in abstract systems-building capability because these breakthroughs remained confined to Hindu states in the South. Thus, throughout the phase, Indian civilization was falling behind in science and technology (despite infusion of new technologies) because of the strong pro-religious and equally strong antiscience views of the invaders. Creative freedom was under attack because of discriminatory policies toward the majority and the focus on conversions. This turned the creative capacity of the North Indian civilization from broad and deep to low and narrow. The intolerant religious orientation of Muslim rulers pushed for conversions into Islam (while great Hindu saints attempted a religious synthesis) and a strong artistic focus, which resulted in a renaissance in architecture and music as science and critical thinking died. In other words, the creative impulse was reduced to syntheses in art, religion, and architecture, which reflected the priorities of the victor.

It was different in the Vijayanagara Empire in South India, which gave shelter to the North Indian science fleeing from Muslim rulers. The creative impulse of the south under the Vijayanagara Empire evolved from religion and artistic focus to including a focus on science. Thus, we would characterize its creative capacity as favorable to science. The Bahmani Sultanate and its five descendant states were no different than the Sultanate in the north and remained focused on religion and architecture, with limited artistic creation, resulting in a narrow but deep creative capacity. South India had struck a more balanced deal with its Islamic rulers than the north was able to. The South Indian civilization retained its cultural heritage better than the north under Islamic aggression in part because Islamic rulers could not do a wholesale destruction of temples or impose the hated jezia tax mainly because the population balance was different.

Constructive orientation: There was no geographical isolation or any insularity due to the success against nomads. The changes in the constructive orientation of Indian civilization during the phase was a mixed bag and a result of Islamic conquest: there was greater openness to international trade and in adoption of practical technologies, architecture, and music. However, openness in religious and intellectual creativity clearly declined.

North India was overwhelmingly Hindu, which was a majority but lacked political power. The miniscule minority had all the political power. The Muslim minority displayed a type 1 constructive orientation and a very severe destructive orientation. It was naturally expended, even after the victors had become a part of Indian civilization, adopting its ways in all arenas except religion and court culture, toward completing the conquest of the subcontinent (and not against other civilizations) but never quite achieving that goal.

The Hindu majority population, on the other hand, suffered a setback in its constructive orientation because of the attitude of the victors toward science and religion. However, the victors brought a number of practical technologies, such as paper making and explosives, and these were readily integrated. The Hindu majority under foreign rule probably behaved as if they too had type 1 openness.

Destructive orientation: The North Indian civilization remained peaceful with respect to other civilizations during the phase. It did not indulge in empire building, violent colonization, or systematic wealth drain. The South Indian civilization remained peaceful while losing some of commercial aggressiveness of the Cholas. It essentially lost its political independence toward the end of the current phase. The Sultanate successfully defended South Asia against Mongol attacks for nearly a hundred years from the early thirteenth to the early fourteenth century. The destructive orientation of the majority Hindu population underwent no change as they remained peaceful with respect to other civilization, at most exporting religion and culture peacefully.

Bottom line: at the end of the current phase, Islam and the Indian civilization were at a classic standoff, with each side convinced of its viewpoint. Muslims were convinced about their political and military control and absolute faith in Islam and Hindus of their tolerant faith and were mindful of their numerical strength and of their ultimate victory. Indian civilization was, thus, different from Persia, the Iberian Peninsula, or Southeast Asia in this respect. It too had lost to Muslim invaders but refused to abandon its faith and join the victors.

16.46 Inner Nature of Muslim Civilization

The leading empire within the bosom of Muslim civilization during the current phase was the Ottoman Empire, straddled as it was across Asia and Europe. As the one that destroyed the Byzantine Empire, it came close to conquering central Europe and successfully whittled away Venetian control of Mediterranean. Below, we focus on the inner nature of Ottoman Empire during the current phase that was the period of unequaled ascendancy.

Productive capacity: The focus of Ottomans remained territorial and on expansion and extracting surplus through taxation during the current phase. The surplus was used in military expansion under the theory of territorial expansion revenue equals more territorial expansion. Still, at the end of the sixteenth century, the population base of the empire was a mere 15 million people scattered over two million square miles, and the Ottomans favored agriculture and commerce over manufacturing. Thus, the economy was land-rich, with deficient capital and labor resources. Farmers often had a mix of agriculture, animal husbandry, and handicraft manufacture to survive. Economic freedom existed; however, it was meaningless given state policy. Similarly, new technology adoption was low since capital formation was preempted by the state policy of applying surplus to military. Yet effort was made to do irrigation projects and increase agricultural productivity. Social cohesion was good despite the complex ethnic mix since most conquered groups were given the freedom to manage their own affairs. The same was not true for internal inequality: non-Muslims were treated as second-class citizens, slavery existed, and young Christian boys were forcibly removed from homes and trained as imperial guards. SGS stability was outstanding, however. There was little question of the control of surplus moving around in a haphazard manner. Thus, what we see is the sustainable growing surplus totally dependent on territorial expansion and not an increase in internal productivity through development in agriculture, manufacture, and commerce. Once the process of expansion came to an end as the Ottomans butted against the Safavids in the east, central European resistance in the west, and Russian resistance in the north, the empire's productive capacity stagnated. The focus of wealth allocation remained practical and on military creativity.

Creative capacity: The story of creative freedom in the Ottoman Empire during the thirteenth through sixteenth centuries mirrors the story of creative freedom during the Arab-Persian period of Muslim civilization. What we witness is a relative flowering of creative freedom in practical and intellectual creativity throughout the phase, only to be curtailed at the end. Several factors contributed to this underappreciated (compared to the Italian Renaissance) modest renaissance in Muslim civilization. Ottomans were far removed from Hulagu Khan's support of Persian astronomy (thirteenth century), the boost in learning from the Byzantine Empire (fifteenth century) and the Italian Renaissance (fifteenth and sixteenth centuries), and the surge in wealth from trade and territorial expansion. However, much like the previous phase, Islamic fundamentalism once again took creative freedom hostage. In 1580, the great observatory at Istanbul was destroyed because fundamentalists claimed heavenly prognostications of impending disaster if the astronomical work was continued. Thus, at phase end, the creative freedom must be judged to be low because of continuing, severe science-religion conflict and religion once again gained an upper hand. Yet the Ottomans were strong supporters of practical creativity, including military technology during this phase, and remained so after the current phase. Thus, creative capacity at phase end must be characterized as moderate and narrow with a strong religious policing function. No longer could the crown jewel of Muslim civilization be considered as having world-class abstract systems-building capability. The focus of creativity was practical creativity, particularly with military significance.

Constructive orientation: Openness to European creative outcomes declined by phase end, despite the absence of geographical isolation. That must be attributed to the rise of Islamic fundamentalism. It is doubtful if the Copernicus' *De revolutionibus orbium coelestium,* published in 1543 CE, ever reached the chief astronomer of the destroyed observatory, Taqi al-din. The constructive orientation started out as relatively open but by phase end turned insular.

Thus, the construction orientation of the Ottomans must be characterized as type 1 or open to practical creativity and trade despite the absence of linguistic or geographic isolation. Ottomans, being empire builders, were more interested in coerced trade; however, since they did not control the land trade routes in their entirety, they could only participate in it as the most significant but not dominant or controlling entity. Right from the start in the early fourteenth century, Ottomans, like the Seljuq dynasty they replaced, remained either disinterested or neutral to science, though they had a ringside seat to what was slowly emerging in Europe. In destructive orientation, they carried on the aggressive and violent tradition of both Muslim civilization and central Asian nomads.

Destructive orientation: Ottomans emerged in the aftermath of the Mongol invasion and were central Asian nomads who had adopted Islam and a settled way of life centuries earlier. Through Islam, they acquired religious zeal. Ottomans throughout this phase indulged in classical empire building in the Persian and Roman style: they did not relocate to conquered territories and conquered areas around their home base and managed the territories long distance. They extracted the surplus of the conquered territories and substantial trade revenue and used it to conquer other territories. Thus, the impact of their empire building was not only destruction through unending wars but also wasted surplus that might have gone into economic development under a wiser policy. The Ottomans did not indulge in violent colonization either since land was plentiful in relation to population size. Consequently, systematic wealth drain was not their cup of tea since they failed to match western Europe in developing naval force, though they bettered the Venetian state in the Mediterranean in that respect. Systematic wealth drain requires, as we have seen, a sea-based trade monopoly over a large productive population with or without territorial control but using the trade wealth to manufacture goods to increase the trade in a virtuous cycle of growth. Ottomans not only lacked naval strength but also never developed strong manufacturing prowess. The destructive orientation throughout the phase remained violent.

16.47 Inner Nature of the European Civilization

Like some other civilizations, different regions of Europe showed significant differentiation with respect to creative and productive capacity and constructive and destructive orientation. This is to be expected during periods of rapid change. Below, we focus on the nation-states of western Europe and the Italian city-states, fully recognizing that even within western Europe, there were significant differences between Portugal and Spain on the one hand and France, England, and the Netherlands on the other. Similarly, the German-centered Holy Roman Empire was different as well. However, our focus below will be western Europe and the Italian city-states. It is also useful to distinguish between the early part of the phase, when Italian city-states were awash in trade wealth, and the latter part of the phase, when western European states began to taste the sweet fruits of trade wealth as the source of trade wealth shifted from the Mediterranean to the Atlantic and Indian Oceans. Yet, despite the mere lip service given to it, the Arab-Persian heritage (which in turn was further development of Indian-Mesopotamian, Greek, and Hellenistic heritage) in western Europe that was the true basis of renaissance in Italian city-states.

Productive capacity (western Europe): Western Europe went through an economic catastrophe during two-thirds of the phase because of the black plague, Hundred Years' War, and a mini ice age. Yet it was a period of absorbing technologies and knowledge from all other civilizations, as we noted in an earlier section. By the end of the fifteenth century, the manufacturing activity had grown and vigorous internal and external trade developed, the former facilitated by the Hanseatic League in the north and the latter controlled by northern Italian states. Increased tax revenue and an alliance with the rising city burgers allowed the kings to create the strong armies needed to bring the feudal lords under control and challenge the powerful role of the pope. The royal house succeeded in both objectives. This led to nation-states, and with the opening of the sea routes to Asia and the discovery of the New World, the trade wealth started to pour into western Europe and not northern Italian city-states. Thus, by the end of the phase, the proud nation-states of western Europe, bound by a common language and administered by a competent bureaucracy, had developed a culture of economic freedom, high rate of new technology adoption, high social cohesion, relatively less social inequality, and skill to engage in coerced trade. In addition, something else happened. The internal fighting among the states, fueled by papal interference, also lessened because of ample opportunities in the New World, Asia, and Africa. In other words, their conflict/cooperation occurred on the high seas, resulting in stable control of internal surplus and from coerced trade. The sustainable growing surplus increased dramatically, more so in France, England, and the Netherlands than in Spain and Portugal, who relied more on coerced trade and were more successful in the Americas than in the population centers of Asia.

Productive Capacity (Italian City-States of Venice, Florence, and Genoa): The same process of defeating feudalism in fact began earlier in the city-states of North Italy, as reported by a visiting German monk in the twelfth century. The difference was one of scale and timing: these were city-states, not nation-states; their trade reach was regional, not global; and the process began much earlier in the city-states of northern Italy. The other difference was the inability to challenge the church establishment. The state of agriculture improved significantly through an increased area under cultivation and the flow of capital to agriculture because of rising grain prices. Manufacturing, particularly wool and textile industries, took off, and commerce was helped by expanding banking and credit, both internal and external expanded dramatically. However, the entire process was driven by expanding external trade, whereas in western Europe, the process was driven by internal changes in response to the inflow of ideas left behind by the Muslim presence in Iberia. Thus, economic freedom existed, new technology adoption was high, social cohesion remained high, internal inequality was high because of the status of women and high wealth polarization (domestic slaves were also plentiful. Records show that ten thousand Balkan young women were sold as slave during a decade beginning 1423 CE.), and internal stability in the control of surplus existed. The sustainable growing surplus was high and growing because of external trade.

Creative capacity (western Europe): Creative freedom in western Europe during the current phase was a mixed bag, though it was moving in the right direction. The monks and professors in monasteries and universities were absorbing the fruits of the third synthesis as well as new technology through translations, travels, and the Crusades. The influence of the pope was declining and institutions of state bureaucracy were developing under powerful monarchs. There was little interference from the Catholic Church in this nascent learning process during the thirteenth and fourteenth centuries, for it was too innocuous to pose a threat to Christian doctrine. However, due to the bubonic plague (fourteenth through seventeenth century, with peak in the fourteenth century) and the Hundred Years' War 1339–1353) between France and England, this process slowed down considerably. The Inquisition in Spain, following the Reconquista in 1249 CE, peaked in the late fifteenth and early sixteenth centuries. However, it was a reaction to the Moor conversion of Christians to Islam centuries earlier and Jewish complicity in it. It was mostly confined to Spain while the creative process was concentrated in France, Germany, and England. Again, in the sixteenth century, the Protestant Reformation in France, England, and Germany gave another boost to religious freedom in that it questioned the authority of the religious establishment, if not Christian doctrine. Thus, we would characterize creative freedom in western Europe as positive and growing. Science-religion conflict existed in principle, but it did not stop practical and intellectual creativity in part because critical philosophy did not challenge Christian doctrine but helped rationalize it. Similarly, openness to the creativity of other civilizations, trade, travel, and migrations was excellent, religion being the only exception. The abstract systems-building capability improved steadily, based on the translations of third synthesis left by Arabs.

Creative capacity (Italian city-states): As we noted in the last chapter, Venice already had its Magna Carta moment before the Magna Carta was signed. Italy was divided between the kingdom of Naples, the papal states in the middle, and small city-states in the north; Venice in the east; Florence in the center; and Genoa on the west coast of the Italian Peninsula. If the focus in western Europe was philosophy, science, and religion, these three city-states were hardly driven by lofty motives. They were driven by commerce and wealth creation through trade and were based on an enormous expansion in banking and credit markets. Both Genoa and Venice had trading colonies in North Africa, Greece, and the Black Sea area. Venice focused on commerce with Asia in spices, silk, and dyes, constantly competing with the Ottomans in the eastern Mediterranean and with Genoa in the western Mediterranean. Florence developed a booming woolen industry (with wool from northern Europe) while Genoa concentrated on the silk industry based on dyes from the east and textile designs from the Byzantine Empire and Persia. This combination of a focus on manufacturing coupled with control of the Mediterranean Sea increased the wealth of these states immensely. It has been estimated that income in Venice tripled between the thirteenth and sixteenth centuries. This combination of manufacturing development and trade wealth killed feudalism in these city-states. The needs of commerce required developments in cartography, and an enormous concentration of wealth made it possible for wealthy families to become patrons of art, architecture, and literature, all of which created a genuine interest, not in Greek philosophy and science, but in Greek and Roman artistic, architectural, and literary heritage. Thus, the so-called Italian Renaissance was almost exclusively focused on art and not philosophy, religion, or science. And in these matters, creative freedom was unparalleled.

The arrival of Byzantine scholars in the late fifteenth century supplemented this. They were bearing fruits of Arabic-Persian science in West Asia. Thus, we see western Europe focusing on philosophy and religious and scientific creativity while the northern Italian city-states focused on art, architecture, and literature followed by a focus on science. The so-called Italian Renaissance has been employed as a cover by Western historians to underestimate the role of Arab science and overestimate Greek heritage, which the European civilization proper had never valued. Science-religion conflict was strong, but it did not matter since the initial focus was on art, architecture, and literature, and the church establishment supported these activities. In fact, the popes were great patrons of art themselves. Both the size of the city-states (often under a few hundred thousand) as well as the nature of intellectual activity also prevented any reformation movement in these city-states. There was great openness to the practical creativity of other civilization as well as a willingness to trade with them.

Thus, European civilization as a whole had creative freedom and openness to the creativity of other civilizations in part because of the Crusades. It was beginning to challenge the hold of the church establishment over religion and saw a steady improvement in its abstract systems-building capability based on slowly extending the fruits of third synthesis.

Constructive orientation: The constructive orientation under church control experienced an opening as the source of wealth shifted from land and peasants to trade wealth and manufacturing and as Byzantine scholars poured in after 1453 CE. This change occurred in Italian city-states without a religious reformation while in western Europe it occurred in conjunction with the Protestant Reformation, because of the Catholic Church's overreach, greater trade wealth in the sixteenth century, and the distance from the Vatican.

Destructive orientation (western Europe): By the end of the fifteenth century, western Europe had discovered sea routes to the New World and Asia and was ready to surpass the aggression and violence the Italian city-states in the Mediterranean exhibited. The early focus was to get gold and silver from the Americas and use it to trade with Asia through controlling sea routes, thus making an end run against the trade the Italian city-states and Ottomans conducted. During the sixteenth century, the strategy was naked violence in America against the native population and more limited violence in Asia and Africa to create fortified trading posts in an attempt to extract trading profits. Thus, western Europe was working overtime to cut the basis of prosperity in both Italian city-states and the Ottoman Empire.

Destructive orientation (Italian city-states): The coastal Italian city of Genoa and the Venice states were highly aggressive and established colonies violently, not for land but in an attempt to control trade routes through and around Mediterranean while Florence focused on building manufacturing prowess and banking. There was little desire or ability to build land empires, unlike the Romans did. They faced the Ottomans and Safavids to the east, and the memory of Ottoman destruction of the Byzantine Empire was fresh in memory. These states were so small, they were mere dots on the maps. Consequently, the experience of Italian city-states was a dress rehearsal in the Mediterranean of the coming drama on the high seas orchestrated by the nation-states of western Europe.

The changes in the parameters that define the inner nature of participants are summarized in table 16.4.

16.48 Inner Nature of Participants at the End of Third Synthesis Phase

Central Asian Nomads (Non-Muslims)

During the current phase, central Asian nomads demonstrated low to medium productive capacity, type A creative capacity, a type 4 openness, and a violent destructive nature.

Chinese Civilization

During the current phase, China continued to demonstrate high productive capacity with high internal SGS, a continuing type A creative capacity, and a type 2 openness. Uncharacteristically, Chinese civilization exhibited a modestly violent external orientation. Yet, we would hesitate to characterize the Chinese civilization as a warring civilization since its principal posture was defensive and was mostly in response to the aggression by others. Thus, it continued to display a type II external orientation consisting of peacefulness and insularity.

Indian Civilization

During the current phase, the North Indian civilization witnessed an increasing productive capacity because of new technology diffusion. Thus it had high internal SGS,

Table 16.4: Relative Values of Measurable Parameters of Social Orders
Fourth Synthesis, 1200–1600 CE

Measurable Characteristics →	Productive Capacity					Creative Capacity			Constructive Orientation				Destructive Orientation		
	EF	NTA	WAB	NB	SC	Creed	ASBC	WAB	GI	ESAN	LI	Creed	NB	IG	IC
Mongols*	High	Low	Low	Low	High	Bal	Low	Low	Low	N/A	No	Bal	Low	High	None
Chinese	High	High	Low	High	High	Bal	Low	Low	Low	Yes	Yes	Bal	High	Low	None
Indian	High	High	Mod	High	Low	ES	High	Mod	Low	No	No	ES	High	Low	High
Ottomans	High	Mod	Low	Med	Mod	SRC	High	Low	Low	N/A	No	SRC	Med	High	High
European	Mod	High	High	Med	High	SRC	High	High	Low	N/A	No	SRC	Med	High	High

NB: Degree of Natural Bounty
EF: Economic Freedom
NTA: New Tech. Adoption
WAB: Wealth Allocation Bal.
SC: Social Cohesion

ASBC: Abstract Sys. Building Capability
GI: Geographic Isolation
ESAN: Early Success against Nomads
LI: Linguistic Isolation
IG: Institutional Greed
IC: Intolerant Creed

ED: Favors Elite Decadence
MS: Favors Military Spending
PE: Favors Productive Endeavor
CE: Supports Creative Endeavors

ES: Excessively Spiritual
SRC: Sci. Religion Conflict
Bal: Balanced

* Buddhists

a transition to type B1 creative capacity on the part of the majority Hindu population; a type B2 creative capacity on the part of rulers, with the latter being the determining factor; a type 1 constructive orientation; and continuing peaceful external orientation despite terrible internal violence. The Indian civilization experienced a precipitous decline in its creativity capacity because of the Islamic ideology of the victors, political fragmentation, the decline of Buddhism, and a resurgence of excessive spirituality. Indian civilization continued to have a mild form of type II external orientation, combining peacefulness and a significantly reduced form of openness to others' creativity.

The South Indian civilization took a different direction, showing a high SGS, a type B1 ICB, a less destructive internal orientation, and a very assertive though largely peaceful external orientation.

Muslim Civilization under Ottomans

Ottomans, of course, achieved high moderate productivity with moderate internal SGS, supplemented with trade profits and conquests; a type B2 creative capacity; a type 2 constructive orientation; and a destructive orientation that combined an intolerant creed and violent aggression. Ottomans thus displayed a type V external orientation, combining religious insularity with violent empire building.

European Civilization

At the end of the last phase, European civilization had moderate productive capacity as indicated by its moderate internal SGS, a type B2 creative capacity, a type 3 constructive capacity, and an extremely high violent destructive orientation to support its wealth drain strategy as revealed through its conduct in the Americas and Asia. It thus had a type VII or type VIII external orientation consisting of a violent systematic wealth drainer and religious insularity.

The comparative inner nature of participants is summarized in table 16.5.

The Evolution and Rationalization of the Fourth Synthesis of Science

16.49 Fourth Synthesis in Science

The key questions, as we have noted before, are the following:

- Did the progress of science take place in one or several or all civilizations?
- Did this development take place in a linked matter or an independent manner? Was the linkage explicit and conscious or unconscious and mediated?
- Were the linkages peaceful or violent?

There were strong linkages between Muslim and European civilizations. These linkages strengthened in the aftermath of defensive aggression by European civilization against Muslim control. The Chinese civilization remained hostage to its own long tradition of focusing on practical creativity, and Indian civilization came under the control of Turkish Muslims who had turned antiscience toward the end of last phase. Thus, like the previous phase, this phase saw development mostly within one civilization.

Table 16.5: Comparative Inner Nature of Civilizations
Fourth Synthesis, 1200–1600 CE

Civilization	Productive Capacity	Creative Capacity	Constructive Orientation	Destructive Orientation	
	Internal SGS	ICB	O/I	P/V	SPI
C. A. Nomads (Muslim)	Low	Type A	Type 4	Violent	Yes
Chinese Civilization	High	Type A	Type 2	Peaceful	Mixed
Indian Civilization	High	Type B	Type 1	Peaceful	No
Ottomans	Moderate	Type B	Type 1	Violent	Yes
European Civilization	Moderate	Type B ⇒ C	Type 3	Violent	No

Legend
SGS: Sustainable Growing Surplus
ICB: Internal Creative Balance
O/I: Openness/Insularity
P/V: Peaceful/Violent
SPI: Sustained Political Independence

Linking Muslim Science to the Rise of Science in Western Europe

The process of liberating Europe from the control of Muslim civilization, as the reader will recall, began in the previous phase when Roger of Hartville liberated the Sicilian outpost of Muslim domination of Europe in 1060 CE, Alfonso VI conquered Toledo in 1085 CE, and Geoffrey of Bouillon led the first Crusade to Jerusalem in 1099 CE. These were purely politically developments that initially gave rise to a sustained effort in Europe to distort the life of Prophet Mohammed and the religion of Islam. However, Europeans also discovered the achievements of Muslim science and through it, Indian, Greek, and Hellenistic achievements. The first step was translating Arabic books into Latin, starting perhaps with Pedro de Alfonso, a Spanish Jew who converted to Christianity and translated books on astronomy as his ancestors had translated books from Greek into Arabic centuries earlier. This was followed by Peter the Venerable (1094–1156 CE), who financed a company of translators and translated a series of astronomical and mathematical texts and their own compilations. The scientific text also created a need for scientific methodology, logic theory, and non-religious metaphysics or, in short, philosophy. Here, western Europe discovered both the Muslim analysis of Aristotle as well as the original Aristotle in translations from Arabic to Latin (by Gerard of Cremona, 1114–1187). Finally, toward the end of the twelfth century, Ibn Sine's encyclopedia of medicine, *Ki tab al-Shia*, and later, his works on philosophy, were translated.

Thus, at the beginning of the current phase, western Europe had gained access to the most up-to-date knowledge in mathematics, astronomy, physics, chemistry, earth science, medicine, and philosophy. It is wrong to think that western Europe only rediscovered its heritage. This acquisition of knowledge is more akin to the Arabs acquiring knowledge from Indian, Greek, and Hellenistic sources, for, much like Arabs, western Europeans had no prior tradition in science. Worse, they had completely ignored Greek and Hellenistic learning in their backyard through the Roman Republic and Roman Empire for over a millennium. Europeans today like to think of ancient Greece and the Hellenistic states as their own. However, the truth is that Greek and Hellenistic learning found greater acceptance in India and with nomadic Arabs than within the Roman Republic, Roman Empire, and Byzantine Empire both before and after adoption of Christianity. Success has many fathers, as they say.

16.50 Rationalization of the Fourth Synthesis in Science

As in previous chapters, we now ask the question why a particular civilization pursued or did not pursue science in the phase. It is easier to answer why Indian and Muslim civilizations did not continue developing science and why the Chinese civilization continued to not take the scientific project seriously. A bit harder to answer is why the European civilization finally got engaged in science, given their long history of ignoring and suppressing science. Below, we answer these important questions.

Why China Failed to Give Birth to Science

Internal SGS: Internal SGS remained high despite the early disruption, destruction, and mismanagement of the

Mongols. The economy recovered nicely under the Ming dynasty.

Allocation of SGS: However, even the emphasis on practical technology, which had been China's claim to fame for more than a millennium, took a hit under the Ming dynasty, with focus shifting to art and literature.

Nature of Creed: Chinese creed remained pluralistic and essentially non-monotheistic. Thus, it continued to offer little resistance to science on religious or metaphysical grounds.

State of ASBC: Fortunately, there was discernible improvement in the abstract systems-building capability despite the continuing absence of alphabetical script, focus on the controlled experiment in the heavens beyond mere observations, and no breakthrough in the concept of the infinitesimal and calculus. The Indian numeral system was introduced during the Yuan dynasty by Hui Muslim people in the thirteenth century and later by European missionaries in the sixteenth century. However, there is little evidence of its use in scientific work despite the attempted injection of European science in mathematics and astronomy in the sixteenth century by missionaries in the hope of gaining trade concessions.

Openness/insularity: China remained insular to the intellectual creativity of other civilizations and retained a strong belief in its superiority, a belief that was derived from its long interaction with nomads, and it was a belief that early exciting breakthroughs in science European colonists and missionaries brought to China could not break. The letter of Chinese monarch Qianlong to King George of England in 1793 that we mentioned in the last chapter highlights China's belief in its unwarranted superiority.

Nature of violent greed: Despite Mongol invasion early in the phase, Manchu aggression toward the very end of the phase, and the success of European violent traders in the sixteenth century, China managed to retain its sustained political independence during the phase since it successfully absorbed the non-Muslim Mongols and kept violent European traders confined to the margins of the Chinese coast. It neither added to its internal SGS nor lost control to any significant degree.

Thus, the essential outline of the story for why China failed to develop science during the current phase did not change much. It was not a creed mired in science-religion conflict or the loss of SPI (despite a relatively short Mongol rule, China recovered nicely) that prevented China from giving birth to science. It was the lack of an alphabetical script and insularity to others' intellectual creativity (critical philosophy and breakthroughs in mathematics and astronomy) that were responsible for China never going beyond the mature protoscience phase until modern times.

Why Muslim Science Died

During the phase, the domain of Islamic science shrank to mostly astronomy and medicine, where it did make some world-class contributions. But it was living on momentum and borrowed time. Islam no longer had a heart for science. More than Persians and Ottomans, the central Asians (particularly in the second half of the phase) moved science forward in the Muslim world, as non-Muslims or as recent converts who perhaps did not fully appreciate the conflict between Islam and science, much like the Moors in the Iberian Peninsula in the eighth century. Probably, funding science for them was a matter of prestige than a broad-based conviction. If doubts about science reigned supreme in the Muslim mind at the beginning of the phase, the rejection of science was complete by the end of the phase. Thus, as a last hurrah, Muslim civilization during the current phase pushed the frontiers of science in astronomy and medicine while completely failing to resolve science-religion conflict. There was no Scholasticism or Protestant Reformation for the Muslim mind in the current phase. The substantial achievements in astronomy can be explained through momentum from the previous phase and the short-lived Ottoman and central Asian commitment to science. Born in a culture with centuries-long tradition in science, the scientists did not have to listen to religious philosophers, at least for a while.

Let us review the evolving picture of Muslim science through its Persian, Ottoman, and central Asian science, keeping in mind its steady secular decline throughout the phase.

Persian science: Persian astronomy got a big boost from the generosity of Mongol Helga Khan, who funded the Maragheh observatory. This observatory produced, among other things, the concept of the Tusi couple, which proved essential in deposing of the epicycle theory by Copernicus. Central Asian nomads throughout history, starting with Kushans, Gokturks, Huns, and Mongols, though they displayed unspeakable cruelty, were open to the religion, language, culture, and science of the civilized peoples they conquered. Did not Knishka convert to Buddhism and supported the cause of science in North India? Helagu Khan financed the Maragheh observatory, and Kublai Khan continued to support the Chinese tradition of world-class practical inventions at some level. It was not the state of abstract systems-building capability or the loss of SPI (despite Mongol invasion) that killed Persian science; rather it was the intellectual insularity Islamic creed demanded, as al-Ghazali stated so eloquently toward the end of the last phase. Persian withdrawal set the stage for later Ottoman and central Asian withdrawals.

Ottoman science: Seljuk Turks had been exposed to Islam, including during its golden age under Arab-Persian rule, for the longest period. They witnessed firsthand the closing of the Muslim mind in the twelfth century, after brilliant golden age lasting for four centuries when Islamic thinkers realized that Islam and science in particular and a revealed faith and science in general are ultimately incompatible. Seljuqs learned the lesson well and transmitted the notion to Ottomans, who pushed practical creativity, including aviation and military technology and explosives, producing mechanical geniuses like Taqi din at the expense of science. In this, they were hardly different from Romans and pre-Islamic Persian dynasties. Even after the current phase ended, the Ottomans, Safavids, and Moguls had the world's best explosives technology. Ottoman interest in science was only skin-deep because of Islam and ended with the destruction of the Istanbul observatory in 1577 at the instigation of Mullahs, even though they had a ringside seat to what was going on in Europe. Ottoman astronomy still achieved well during the current phase because of its connection with the calendar, astrology, geography, and cartography. It got the necessary support, but not the study of terrestrial motion and biological sciences. That must have seemed totally useless to the religious-minded yet practical Ottomans. The Muslim thinkers in the twelfth century, as we saw in the last chapter, came close to discovering the laws of motion and the theory of evolution. Muslim Turks effectively put an end to science in their domains from Anatolia to India for nearly seven centuries. It is telling that after Constantinople fell and even before that, its scholars did not hurry to relocate to Turkish territories; instead they headed to Italy, where they would help ignite the Italian Renaissance. This happened despite relocation to Italy meant moving away from the church of their choice, whereas they might be allowed more space as a religious minority in Ottoman domains. Contrasting this with the Indian men of science who would travel thousands of miles to Baghdad half a millennium earlier is telling. Again, it was not the state of abstract systems-building capability or the loss of SPI (despite the Mongol invasion) that killed Persian science; rather it was the intellectual insularity demanded by Islamic creed.

Central Asian science: If the Ottomans inherited the Seljuk legacy, the central Asians inherited the Persian legacy in science. Contrary to popular notion, they did not always actively destroy science. On occasion, an exceptional Muslim Turk like Sultan Ulugh Beg in the fifteenth century even supported astronomy, perhaps because he himself was an accomplished astronomer. However, after Beg died, his observatory at Samarkand met a fate similar to the one at Istanbul.

Islam remained closed to the religious creativity of other civilizations because the question of religion and metaphysics was settled in the Koran since it was God's word. Destruction of science throughout Muslim domain is easily explained through the Islamic creed and its fear of science as it held the potential for an agnostic or even a Godless universe, and that was just not possible.

Why Indian Science Died

Indian science took shelter in Vijayanagara and thrived there for three centuries, producing calculus and perhaps even the astronomical data Kepler used to prove and modify Copernicus' heliocentric orbits. None of the five Sultanates in the coalition that destroyed the Vijayanagara Empire in a fit of jealousy came forward to support the Kerala school of mathematics and astronomy. As a result, the Kerala school withered with the decline of Vijayanagara, and with that, the last flame of science in India was extinguished after gloriously burning for 2,500 years. Thus, Indian science entered a coma or suspended animation after a 2,500-year tradition of science and was to remain dead for nearly three centuries.

Internal SGS

Allocation of SGS: Thus, development of science in North India came to screeching halt, not because of a lack of surplus but because of the changing pattern of wealth allocation under the Sultanate and Moghul dynasties. The primary focus of the Sultanate was to bring the entire subcontinent under Muslim control, conversion of the Hindu population, and luxurious living. The Sultanate expressed little interest in the fruits of the Arab-Persian renaissance, what was happening in Vijayanagara, or the emerging European synthesis. The creative impulse was largely absorbed in the Hindu-Muslim synthesis in religion and arts and the absorption of practical technology. The ruling Muslim dynasties could hardly be expected to mourn the death of science they did not value.

Nature of creed: Indian science was in decline before the Muslim conquerors because of the rising tide of monism and the Bhakti movement. It was not a case of conflict between science and religion; rather, it was more akin to neglect of science prompted by spiritual overgrowth. This period of Indian civilization was sandwiched between the establishment of the Sultanate and western European control of India.

Unlike the Arabs and Persians, Turkish Muslim rulers of India had showed little interest in science. As noted before, by the thirteenth century, Islam as a whole had concluded that its revealed faith was ultimately incompatible with agnostic science. The Seljuk Turks and Ottomans inherited that point of view from Arabs and Persians (after conversion to Islam), and they passed it on to all branches of Turks, such as Ghaznivids, and those Mongols who later converted to Islam, such as Timur Lane and Babur. Creativity impulse during the phase was confined to what the victor valued: syntheses in arts, medicine, and religion, and as a result, science migrated to pockets where Muslims did not exercise control. Turkish invaders did not just destroy temples; they destroyed universities in India as well.

State of its ASBC: Indian civilization continued to fall behind in abstract systems-building capability, having failed to adopt the experimental method because of an excessive spirituality and domination by an antiscience conqueror. One sees flashes of brilliant hypotheses, such as Misra's blood circulation hypothesis; however, these were not tested using experiments.

Openness/insularity: Openness to the intellectual creativity of other civilizations also took hit in most of India during most of the phase, again because of excessive spirituality and conquest by an antiscience invader. The reader will recall that the origin of excessive spirituality is traceable to previous phase when political fragmentation, Arab invasion in the Sindh, and the fundamentalist reaction against Buddhism turned Indian civilization once again inward and toward monism. This trend was continued through an alliance between Indian spirituality and Sufism, resulting in an attempted synthesis between Islam and Hinduism.

Sustained political independence: Indian civilization experienced a loss of sustained political independence throughout the period but without wealth drain. The continual invasions and control of India by the Turkish Muslims tribes in the twelfth and sixteenth centuries was of global significance in the sense that it accelerated the death of Indian science. Had Mongols conquered India, Indian civilization would have eventually (no doubt after paying a huge price, as China did) absorbed the secular Mongols, much like China did, and would have escaped the antiscience Turkish Muslim rule and the debilitating western European economic control, just as China did.

Thus, it was not abstract systems-building capability that killed science. It was excessive spirituality, followed by the loss of SPI to invaders with an antiscience creed and religious and intellectual insularity that killed science after it valiantly tried to remain lit in Vijayanagara.

Why the Fourth Synthesis Occurred in Europe

We first review the fourth synthesis in Europe as a whole, followed by its detailed development in different parts of Europe, much like the Arab, Persian, and Turkish periods of Muslim science in the last phase. The latter experienced a secular decline while Europe experienced secular growth.

Internal SGS: The internal SGS, despite the injection of new technologies from Asia, was not much better. Bubonic plagues and bitter religious wars hardly helped.

Allocation of SGS: Much SGS was diverted toward religious creativity and wars, including religious wars.

Nature of its creed: Christian dogma was indeed a problem. However, astronomy and mathematics were highly valued by the aggressive, emerging nation-states in western Europe because of its linkage to navigation. Whoever controlled the seas controlled the trade and whoever excelled in navigation and cartography controlled the high seas. Thus, a contradiction existed between using Christian dogma to justify existing wealth disparity and the need to support science to extract new wealth from the world through coerced trade. Fortunately for Europe, the potential for new wealth was so much greater that it had a fighting chance even in the current phase.

State of ASBC: The abstract systems-building capability was truly world-class by the middle of the phase. With the understanding of the experimental method in the heavens complete, the focus shifted to its development here on earth, first in navigation and cartography and then the laws of terrestrial motion, which Muslim scientists had achieved centuries earlier.

Openness/insularity: Control by Muslim civilization and reaction in the form of Crusades in the previous phase, the Venetian experience in the Mediterranean, discovery of the Greek/Roman heritage, and the possibility of immense wealth through coerced trade in the current phase all conspired to open the European minded to the creativity and the wealth of other civilizations.

Nature of violent greed: Coerced trade based on violence saved Europe during the phase. They used ships designed after African fishing boats (with an enhanced ability to tack or align the sails to the wind, and it used lateen sails that allowed luffing) loaded with guns powered by Chinese explosives technology in the Mediterranean. Venice used this first, followed by the Portuguese and the Spaniards in the New and Old Worlds. This wealth turned European fortunes around. The first fed the Italian Renaissance and the second, though it did not support the cause of science directly, did so indirectly as it opened the door for the Dutch, English, and French in the next phase. Thus, the internal SGS of leading western European traders, the Portuguese, and the Spanish probably jumped by an order of magnitude during the sixteenth century. However, because these states did not go through religious reformation, this wealth was plied into the control of the New World. It did, however open the door for others, Dutch, English, and French to control the Old World in the next phase.

Strengthening abstract systems-building capability, newfound SPI, the declining hold of Christian dogma (with tactical reversals along the way), and a resulting openness to the creativity of other civilizations underlie the fourth and last western European synthesis in science as it moved from failed Scholasticism in western Europe to the Italian Renaissance to its temporary home in central Europe and then returned to western Europe under the protective cover of religious reformation.

A common perception is that Italian Renaissance was responsible for the birth of science in Europe. The reality is far more complex. The story of the fourth and final synthesis of science that occurred in Europe during the current phase has five sequential parts:

1. Scholasticism stalled in western Europe because of the bubonic plague and religious wars.

2. The rediscovery and development of ancient Greek philosophy and arts by the city-states of northern Italy lead cultural pride. It was made possible by the trade wealth resulting from Venetian control of the eastern Mediterranean.

3. Astronomy and physics in developed central Europe because of the discovery of the ancient Hellenistic heritage and the influx of scholars from the Byzantine Empire who brought Muslim science into Italian city-states and Central Europe.

4. The reformation of Catholicism in northern and western Europe created a favorable environment for science to prosper in northern and western Europe.

5. The center of gravity of science returned to its Scholastic home, softened by the Reformation and enriched by the new trade wealth based on control of sea routes to the Americas and Asia.

Thus, the true story of the fourth synthesis has its origin in western Europe, its inspiration in Venice, its breakthrough in central Europe, and its flowering in back in western Europe. Below we consider each of these.

Why Scholasticism failed in western Europe: Western Europe was the natural place for the birth of Scholasticism in Europe, for it was closest to one of the centers of the Arab-Persian synthesis. Based on the Arabic to Latin translations of Greek philosophy and considerable results obtained by Muslim scientists in mathematics, physics, and medicine, thinkers in western Europe proceeded along two directions: to attempt to put the Christian faith on a rational basis through Greek philosophy and to pursue science. The first effort was represented by theologians such as Thomas Aquinas and Albert Magnus, and the pursuit of science was represented by early secular-minded thinkers like Roger Bacon. It was a classical struggle between science and monotheism—a struggle that had already failed within the Muslim civilization. This struggle did not focus on whether the world was lawful or not. Aristotle helped win that battle in the European world a long time ago. The struggle was whether the world worked without any interference from a transcendent power. Roger Bacon's analysis of a rainbow resulting from refraction—a natural phenomenon versus being a work of God—is a case in point.

There was much translating of the Arab-Persian synthesis in science and philosophy from Arabic to Latin in the eleventh and twelfth centuries, as we noted in the last chapter, with greatest interest from scholars at newly established universities in Paris and Oxford, which were themselves an evolution of monasteries steeped in rationalizing Christian dogma. In the thirteenth century, we see the rise of scholars like Roger Bacon, who wished self-promotion based on a new knowledge pouring in.

Unfortunately, Roger Bacon and other like-minded thinkers failed, and Thomas Aquinas succeeded. There were many reasons for it: the Catholic Church was too strong and controlled by the French at critical times, and Thomas Aquinas was French. In addition, the nation-states of western Europe were yet to emerge with local political power residing with bishops and feudal lords, who were in an unholy alliance, and western Europe was poor and illiterate with no trade wealth pouring in. The failure of Scholasticism was cemented in the fourteenth century through natural calamities such as the bubonic plague and the mini ice age as well as destructive internal wars, such as wars of succession and the infamous Hundred Years' War. It seemed as though the science was going to have a stillbirth in western Europe.

Bacon may have lost to Aquinas, but that did not entirely kill the project. One book translated from Arabic to Latin was *Kitab-al-Mu'tabar,* by Abul-Barkat. It explained projectile motion as violent inclination (*mayl qasri*) imparted by the mover to the object that diminished as the object distanced itself from the mover. Kean Burdian (1300–1558) and Albert Saxon (1316–1490) employed this early concept of momentum to explain the acceleration of falling objects and still later was adapted to explain the motion of heavenly bodies through circular impetus.

Italian Renaissance: The creative impulse of the Muslim civilization declined because of inherent science-religion conflict and as Muslim invaders accelerated the demise of Indian science, and asChinese practical creativity was beginning to lose steam because it continued to lack a much-needed theoretical foundation. The northern city-states of Italy, including Venice and Florence, successfully came to assert control of the eastern Mediterranean and began to develop a manufacturing base that freed them from the feudal lords, who had been in alliance with the Catholic Church. The Alps provided shelter from German princes to the north. These changes were also taking place in western Europe to one degree or another.

However, the critical difference was the degree of trade wealth pouring into Venice and the Italian city-states. Thus, while resource-starved, war-ravaged, and plague-infested western Europe buried science and proclaimed the Christian faith in dark, cold monasteries, the Italian city-states took the lead in artistic creativity based on the discovery of original Greek philosophy and art scholars brought into these city-states byscholars fleeing the Byzantine Empire, which was defeated by the Turks after 1453. Both western Europe and the Italian city-states had left the Byzantine Empire to the mercy of the Turks, who, of course, had a long score to settle with the Byzantine Empire.

During the thirteenth, fourteenth, and fifteenth centuries, western Europe was preoccupied with civil wars, internal conflicts among the states, bringing the Catholic Church and aristocracy under royal control, developing a centralized bureaucracy, creating a state-funded army, and all the changes required for to emerged as centralized nation-states on the geographical scale of an old imperial province, with common ethnic links, such as language, culture, and history. Spurred by trade and manufacturing, Florence and Italy became extremely wealthy. By some accounts, the incomes tripled over the fourteenth and fifteenth centuries. As a consequence, the center of innovation moved to Italian city-states that had already accomplished the creation of effective states on a much smaller scale and controlled Mediterranean trade. The trade allowed the Italians to develop credit markets to an unprecedented degree. Because both Arabs and Turkish did not excel in sea power at that time, the city-state scale was sufficient until the rise of larger states in the west and the opening of the high seas.

Renaissance spreads to central Europe with a focus on science: The Italian Renaissance focused initially on art, literature, and architecture as it discovered the ancient heritage and took newfound pride in it. It did not display much interest in science as yet. However, it did establish great universities staffed with Byzantine scholars who had brought not only the Greek heritage but also the results of the Muslim heritage from the West Asian center. One key concept was that of the Tusi couple, which scholars brought to Italy when fleeing Constantinople after 1453. This concept, coupled with the concept of the circular impetus, helped Copernicus to develop his heliocentric theory.

These universities and the Byzantine scholars trained early scientists and philosophers in Italy during the late fifteenth and early sixteenth centuries. Copernicus, who was Polish, and Nicholas of Cusa, who was German, were trained in Italian universities. Thus, Italians excelled in art, literature, and oratorical skills, in contrast to the Scholastic period when the focus was on mathematics, philosophy, and astronomy since that is where the money was. The northern Europeans mostly took on the science project cut short earlier by failed Scholasticism. However, these scientists ran the great risk of being burned at the stake because the Protestant Reformation was yet to happen. Their efforts led to the breakthrough in astronomy and culminated in Copernicus's heliocentric theory, which challenged the Catholic Church's geocentric theory. It should be noted that the Catholic Church only cared about the geocentric theory because the bible said the universe was geocentric.

The Protestant Reformation: About the time Copernicus labored on his heliocentric theory, Luther was challenging the Catholic Church from a religious perspective, protesting the sale of indulgences. The net effect of the Reformation was to give the independent thinkers in central and western Europe a cover. At the same time, the trade wealth pouring into Italian city-states slowed down as Venice began to lose its preeminent position to the Ottoman navy. Simultaneously, the new sea routes to Asia and Americas meant the wealth instead began to pour into western Europe. Finally, by the fifteenth century, several western European states had become strong with bureaucracy, a strong military, and the city burgers who sided with the royalty, thus weakening the landed nobility and that peculiar arrangement called feudalism. The center of gravity of science moved back to its Scholastic home, encouraged by more secular states and a more circumscribed church.

Western European Synthesis: The Copernican revolution of 1543 was ignored for a full generation. The banner was taken by Tycho Brahe, who, incidentally, did not believe in the heliocentric theory. It is likely that this belief colored his data gathering. He was unable to make sense of his data and did not want to share the data with others, and with Kepler in particular, as he was afraid of being upstaged since he rightly sensed his conceptual weakness. Recent research, as we mentioned before, has claimed that Tycho may have been in possession of the data from Indian astronomer Nilakanthan, which cried out for elliptical orbits and not circular orbits as Copernicus had proposed. Tycho died without resolving anything, and his data fell into Kepler's. Kepler was a much better conceptualizer and was not held back by the geocentric view. Thus, Kepler enunciated his three planetary laws, closing a three-millennia-long quest to solve the problem of the heavens. Directly or indirectly, acknowledged or not, it was the culmination of efforts in four civilizations over three millennia: Indian, Mesopotamian, Muslim, and European.

How Does Galileo Fit into This Story?: The story outlined above makes sense except for one detail, if the center of gravity of science had moved back to western Europe, how does one explain Galileo, who was Italian and Florentine and a giant of terrestrial physics?

There are several possible explanations. First, the discoveries he made were not exactly original. The law of uniform acceleration and the kinematic law stating that distance traveled by a body is proportional to the square of time were already known to Nicole Oresme in the fourteenth century. The laws of inertia had been enunciated by Arab physicists centuries earlier. Whether Galileo had knowledge of this is unknown. Galileo did not use the language of mathematics to express these laws. He used geometric constructions. It is more appropriate to think of Galileo as an outstanding experimentalist (and an instrument-maker, such as the telescope and thermometer), confirming earlier observations. Significantly, Galileo did not take the decisive step of force as a product of mass and acceleration since he did not possess and could not develop the science of calculus. This does not, in our judgment, diminish the stature of Galileo but puts it in correct historical perspective. In other words, the home of science in Europe was northern and western Europe and remained so through the various phases of Scholasticism.

Its birth was pushed by the Arab-Persian achievements, its fundamentalist turn under Aquinas, its defiant turn in northern and central Europe away from the center of papal authority, and its final death at the hands of Reformation and nation-states of western Europe. Italy and the Italian Renaissance simply facilitated the birth of science in Europe through its wealth, universities, shelter of Byzantine scholars, and Greek and Hellenistic heritage. Galileo is better explained as an individual phenomenon rather than as an Italian phenomenon. That is why it is difficult to name another Italian scientist in the same league as Galileo. That Italy was the center of Catholic dominance and that Catholic Church was fully supportive of the renaissance in arts but not science would seem to substantiate this view.

The truth is that just as all European empires (the Roman Republic, Roman Empire, and Byzantine Empire), prevented the birth of science in Europe for a millennia and half, Muslim civilization, after it turned its back on science by the end of last phase, killed science within the Indian civilization as well. The collision of the dogmatic Christian faith and nearly mature science handed to Europe the Muslim civilization and made Europe proper take interest in science *for the first time in its history*. This fact makes Europe's journey from one who was given the gift of science by an invader to a claim of science as its unique invention all the more astounding. The same contradiction that turned Muslims away from science now made Europeans turn toward science. Who could have predicted that at the start of the second millennium?

To summarize, through failed Scholasticism in western Europe, followed by the confidence-inspiring discovery of its Greek-Hellenistic heritage, Venetian trade wealth in Italian city-states, the reformation of Christianity, and a return to its Scholastic home with wealth from coerced trade based on discovering new sea routes, science made its home in western Europe for the first time in its history.

The Shifting Center of Gravity of Science

We have already alluded to all the reasons the center of gravity of science has moved around from the last phase to the current phase. Very briefly:

- Muslim civilization walked away from science because it could not face the conflict between science and Islam.
- Turkish Muslim dynasties killed science in most of India except in Vijayanagara, where it prospered until the end of this phase.
- Chinese civilization failed to adopt an alphabetical script, becoming more insular in the latter Ming period, followed by Nomadic conquest by the Qing dynasty, which lasted into the twentieth century.
- European civilization threw off the yoke of Muslim civilization while becoming heir to its scientific achievements. It moderated its religious impulse, defeated feudalism, developed its manufacturing capabilities, and succeeded in capturing wealth through coerced trade by controlling the Mediterranean Sea and the Atlantic and Indian Oceans.

Thus, science made western Europe its home for the first time in its long history. Recognition of this fact puts in perspective the almost obsessive need of western European historians to rewrite the history of Europe as exclusively a European phenomenon since if science was a purely European phenomenon, western Europeans would not have to explain their late entry into the science project.

16.51 Life Stage of Science Achieved by Civilization

Based on the inner nature of civilizations and the underlying parameters summarized in table 16.5, the five key civilizations achieved the following life stages in science:

- Indian Civilization: Regressing but still in development stage of science
- Persian Empire: Regressing but still in development stage of science
- European Civilization: Leader of the development stage of science
- Seljuk central Asians: Regressing but still in development stage of science
- Chinese Civilization: Mature protoscience stage of science

Looking Ahead

16.52 Emerging New Participants

No new participants emerged during the phase, except the greater role for those mentioned in the last chapter: Southeast Asia, Northeast Asia or Korea and Japan, and North Asia or Russia.

Fate of Participants

All key participants survived the phase except the Mongol Empire. As we have noted before, the Mongol Empire may not have survived; however, the Mongols continued to a significant factor in world history through the branch that converted to Islam.

Southeast Asian Civilizations

Southeast Asia saw several old kingdoms and empires continue and witnessed new ones rise: the Champa kingdom (700–1832) in south and central Vietnam, the Angkor kingdom (1200–1431) in Cambodia, the Ayutthaya kingdom (1350–1767) in Thailand, and the Majapahit kingdom (1300–1500) in Java. All these kingdoms were Indian in culture, religion, and language to one degree or another. It is inaccurate to think of these as colonies since there was little displacement and destruction of the indigenous people. Indian merchants and Brahmins, unlike later Europeans in the Americas, simply provided superior culture to the local population. Apart from the local kaleidoscope of the changing fortunes of these kingdoms, three seminal events from outside affected the region during this period.

The first of these was the Mongol invasion we covered above and the naval expeditions of Chinese Admiral Zheng He in the fifteenth century and European naval invasions in the sixteenth century. The Ming dynasty sponsored a number of naval expeditions between 1405 and 1433 to reinforce the Chinese presence and control trade. The real impact of Zheng He, who was in fact a Chinese Muslim, was to help strengthen the Malaccan Sultanate (1403–1511) established by an Hindu prince from Srivijaya named Paramesvara. He is said to have converted to Islam after marrying a Muslim princess. The Malaccan Sultanate prospered because of trade with India through Muslim merchants from West India. Thus, the second event was the conversion of Malaysia and Indonesia to Islam, and it was brought about by Chinese and Indian Muslims and not Arabs, Persians, or Turks.

The third event was the arrival of the Portuguese and the Dutch in the early sixteenth century. The Portuguese put an end to Malaccan dynasty in Java, and the Dutch became active traders of spices in Indonesia. We will pick up their stories in the next chapter.

European civilization was standing at the cusp of history by the end of fifteenth century. After the Turks and Mongols cut off the overland trade routes, the price of spices had jumped dramatically for a number of reasons, including supply and cost of transportation. Once the new sea routes were discovered and the nation-states of Europe smelled a historic opportunity, the question was how to use this power. A three-prong strategy was developed that remained effective in not only the sixteenth century but also the seventeenth and eighteenth centuries. In the Americas and Australia, the strategy was territorial control achieved through displacement, intermarriage, and the extermination of the population if necessary and control of gold and silver to ensure adequate money supply for the expanding commerce. In Africa, the strategy was to acquire slaves to work in the new territories. In Asia, the strategy was to control the coastal areas to ensure they could engage in coerced trade. The African slave trade actually began in 1440, violent colonization in the early sixteenth century, and coerced trade with India, China, and Southeast Asia about the same time. Because the territories controlled by Muslim states was sparsely populated and lacked natural wealth (in relation to the technological knowhow of the time), the western European states left West Asia alone for the time being.

Thus, the nation-states of western Europe were not interested in one-time raiding, looting, or indulging in classical empire building. Rather, the strategy was violent colonization of lands inhabited by peoples at an early stage of development, a shameless and inhuman slavery system, and mercantilism or the state control of foreign trade for continuing prosperity and security through tariffs, export subsidies, use of staple ports to control the market, banning the export of precious metals, wage control, consumption control, and trade monopoly. They monopolized trade through exclusive colonies, encouraging piracy, and banning foreign shipping.

Thus, during the phase, Southeast Asian civilizations became beneficiaries of mostly peaceful interaction with Indian, Chinese, and Muslim civilizations and the violent interaction with European civilization. However, they did not develop to a point where they would engage in serious science because the impact of Indian civilization was mostly from South India and not North India, the impact Muslim civilization came from the antiscience Indian Muslim dynasties, and the wealth drain came from European civilization.

16.53 Summary

Muslim civilization had conquered most of the surrounding civilizations during its heyday in the last phase and the current phase through its Arab, Persian, Turkish, and Mongol (Muslim) incarnations. Now the European civilization had begun the process of making an end run against Muslim civilization during the last century of the current phase through the emerging nation-states of Portugal, Spain, the Netherlands, Britain, and France. The greatest instrument of control at the beginning of the phase, the Muslim civilization, was getting ready to lose its ill-gotten gains, not on land but on the high seas by the end of the phase. Of course, it remained oblivious to the mortal threat.

These two developments would now mingle and cross-fertilize to determine the fate of science and civilizations in the coming centuries: science would become an exclusively European phenomenon; the wealth of the world would wash on the shores of Europe. Africa, Asia, and the Americas would be brutalized and impoverished. It would be claimed that science has been in its golden age since then and that the world was civilized. However, we would be asking the question that given one civilization controlled the entire worlds' resources and given that science, at the end of the current phase, was toward the end of its development stage after a two millennia-long development period, why has the progress in science had been so slow? More than a century lapsed between Copernicus and Newton in creating the first grand synthesis of heavenly and terrestrial motion through gravitation; nearly a century between Newton and Maxwell in the second grand synthesis of electricity and magnetism; half a century between Maxwell and Einstein in the third synthesis of gravity, electricity, and magnetism; and a century of waiting for the fourth grand synthesis of gravity, electricity, magnetism, and quantum mechanics. Is it precisely because science came under the exclusive control of one civilization—a civilization that has been and continues to be violent, greedy, self-indulgent, and with strong residual belief in monotheism, including its political exploitation, with the resulting inadequate support of science? Is it because it always supported technology over science in its unending chase of wealth? We will ask these questions in the final chapters.

Chapter 17

Violent Interaction Era—Seventh Phase: Mature Stage

Mature Science (1600–1950)

17.1 Introduction

If the last phase laid the foundations for the European civilization to dominate the world through militarily and commercially circumscribing the Muslim civilization based on the discovery of sea routes to the Americas and Asia and the death of science in Indian and Muslim civilizations, the current phase transformed that foundation into a reality unimaginable at the beginning of the phase. It was the phase that put an end to Ottoman ambitions, witnessed five relatively small or even tiny nation-states of western Europe controlling most of the world directly or indirectly, saw the beginning of successful revolt against this control in the Americas, saw Russia sneakily exerting control over most of North and central Asia, and saw the Qing dynasty in China grabbing Tibet and Western China.

In the second half of the phase, as England, France, and the Netherlands ushered in mechanized manufacturing through the Industrial Revolution, the nature of the relationship between the civilizations of Asia and these nation-states began to change from one of coerced mercantilism to the export of manufactured goods from Europe to Asia. Thus, Asian civilizations began losing their manufacturing base and increasingly became mere suppliers of commodities to the industrializing countries of western Europe. The world's resources came to be controlled by these small nation-states of Europe and the most advanced of these (and others, such as the German states) continued the tradition of science that began in the previous phase, culminating in the five grand unifications in physics and several others in other branches of science, starting with unification of laws governing heavenly and terrestrial motion. What is truly unique about the current phase is reducing the civilizations in Asia to the status of commodity providers, five grand unifications in physics based on results of the fourth synthesis leading to maturation of science at the end of the first unification, the conscious application of the science and its methods to the wealth-creation process, and the near absence of scientific activity in Asia until the twentieth century for the first time in history.

If the phase began symbolically with the establishment of the East India Company in India, it may be said to finish with the liberation of most of Asia and Africa from European imperialism, beginning in the second half of the twentieth century. American and French revolutions and the rise of Napoleon signified the coming irrelevance of the European monarchies and provide a convenient midpoint of the phase. Even though most of Asia and Africa saw political independence toward the end of the phase, the world has continued to be controlled by the economic, military, technological, and institutional power of a handful of the leading states of newly christened "Western" civilization (named to set it apart from all other Eastern civilizations) through economic, military, political, and financial institutions such as G-8, NATO, the UN, the IMF, and the World Bank since the end of World War II. The new name itself reflects the geographical metamorphosis of a subcontinental European civilization to a world entity.

During the standalone era (6500–3000 BCE), a civilization could excel without controlling other civilizations and without even being aware of its superiority. During the peaceful interaction era (3000–500 BCE) a civilization could excel, though it was likely aware of its superiority. However, during the era of extended military conflicts among civilizations (500 BCE–present), an era that implies the existence of instruments of control across civilizations, a militarily superior civilization may be controlling one or more civilizations and be aware of its superiority. An example of the latter case is the Muslim civilization that dominated the Indian civilization and to a somewhat lesser extent European civilization but did not control the Chinese civilization. Following the Muslim civilization, the present and last phase of science represents an extreme example in that one civilization dominated *all* other civilizations. It was made possible by the European civilization's control of the sea routes, thus allowing it to extend its military, economic, and political control to all major and even minor civilizations. The world had never witnessed the likes of this ever before. It is tempting to say that this was bound to happen sooner or later with the discovery of planetwide sea routes linking all civilizations (a fact made possible by the geographical layout of earth's surface), but that would be wrong since several contingencies could have prevented it, for nothing is inevitable in history. What actually happened can be rationalized, but it was not necessarily inevitable—a fact that becomes even more transparent when we analyze the critical contingencies in the current phase.

Thus, the uniqueness of the final phase is that one civilization managed to exert control over all other civilizations at a point in history when Muslim civilization had walked away from science and had managed to kill science in Indian civilization. It is also when the Chinese civilization had come under the control of nomads who, while protecting it from European aggression during the eighteenth century, neglected to even sponsor the traditional Chinese technological tradition and rejected European science the Christian missionaries brought to China. However, even the Qin nomads could not keep the European wolves at bay during the nineteenth century. Thus, because of the absolute dominance of one civilization over all others, the approach in this final chapter is different, and the organization reflects this.

- It is obviously important to understand the driving causes of all civilizations, as in previous phases, particularly the causes driving the key western European states and their controlling impact on other civilizations. More specifically, it is important to understand how the European civilization, or more precisely, how a few small states in western Europe, came to control all major civilizations through control of sea routes and how the military and political struggle that allowed these small western European states to dominate mammoth civilizations unfolded through coerced trade and wealth drain.

- Unlike previous chapters, it is not necessary to be as detailed in describing the creative and productive outcomes of civilizations. The overwhelming creative and productive outcomes originated in European civilization principally, not because it suddenly developed a monopoly on creativity but because it controlled the wealth of all other civilizations (with a few exceptions, such as Japan, which escaped colonial control). This control allowed it to increase the pace of its knowledge creation and effectively ensure that such processes in other civilizations remained stillborn. The reader may thus assume, as a first approximation, that these accomplishments of European civilization and its colonies in newly discovered continents essentially equal the difference between the creative, productive, and destructive achievements at the end of the present phase, minus what existed at the beginning of the present phase. This does not mean that contributions from other civilization were nil. It only means that these contributions pale in comparison because of the *linked* nature of relatively fast change in a few small western European states and their colonies in the New World and static or declining nature of all other civilizations during this phase. It is as if a few western European states and all other civilizations constituted the two inseparable poles of a magnet: power, creativity, and change at one pole and stagnation, increasing poverty, and loss of self-determination at the other pole. We will be *relatively* brief in describing the creative and productive outcomes of European civilization because these are well known. However, we will comment on its religious achievements in sufficient detail because of its independent nature and its connection to attitudes toward science.

- It is however important, as in previous chapters, to continue to define both the inner nature of each major civilization as it unfolded during the phase through changing relative importance of causes.

- Finally, it is obviously critical to describe and rationalize the scientific achievements of civilizations. We will have an opportunity to ask how one civilization that controlled the resources of the entire planet did in pushing the cause of science further. Or more precisely, how its commercial, aggressive, and religious tendencies impacted not only its own creative tendencies, including the forward march of science, but also the creative impulse of other great civilizations. Would science be farther along today without such control? Would Higg's boson have been discovered a couple of centuries earlier and be known today as the "Lee boson" or the "Gupta boson"?

Era and Essential Participants

17.2 Affirming the Era of Civilization

Civilizations have continued to reside in the violent interaction era that began around 550 BCE and went through empire-building period until 1500 CE. This was followed by the mercantile (violent colonization) and systematic wealth-drain periods. The onset of an era is defined by the characteristics of the leading civilization, which was European civilization during the current phase. European civilization easily satisfied the requirements of the range of transportation technologies, weapons technologies, and an aggressive orientation based not on creed, though creed played a secondary role, but on greed. Its aggression based on creed actually moderated considerably during the phase and was displayed by its Catholic branch in the New World mostly during the violent colonization phase.

17.3 Essential Participants of the Phase

Major civilizations of the phase are:

- Chinese: Manchu Empire (1644–1911)
- Indian: Mughal Empire (1526–1857), Maratha Empire (1674-1818), and British Empire (1857-1947)
- Muslim: the continuing Ottoman (1399–1921) and Safavid (1501–1736) Empires
- European, with the European nation-states, the short-lived Napoleon Empire (1804–1814), the Russian Empire (1721–1917), the USSR (1917–1989), and the New World states, such as Canada, the United States, Mexico, Brazil, Argentina, and Australia (1600–2000)

The current phase is distinguished by the fact that the Arab and central Asian nomads had been civilized, absorbed into civilizations, or rendered powerless with the rise of sea power. Both technological change and the discovery of sea routes linking civilizations meant that nomads could arise as nomads again. Thus, a two-millennia-long period of violent era punctuated and often dominated by nomads, such as Kushans, Huns, Arabs and Genghis, Moguls, and the Manchu finally passed into ages shortly after the present phase started.

The significant secondary civilizations of the phase were either in the Northeast Asia, such as Japan and Korea, or in Southeast Asia, such as Vietnam, Indonesia, and Thailand etc. The distinguishing feature of the secondary civilizations in Northeast Asia is that they escaped the European colonialism and thus bounced back rapidly after European imperialism collapsed. However, Southeast Asian civilizations had no such luck because of size, climate, and population.

History, Causes, and Outcomes of the European Civilization

17.4 Brief Political History (Europe, the Americas, and Australia)

In the interest of brevity, we shall *mostly* refrain from getting into the detailed country-specific history of European civilization since it is hardly necessary from our perspective. Instead, we shall summarize broad developments and key events within these broad trends, only lightly touching country-specific details. As we shall see, it is impossible to understand European history during the phase without a thorough understanding world history and vice versa.

Colonial Expansion in the New World (1600–1775)

As we have noted in the previous chapter, European colonial expansion began around 1500 with the discovery of sea routes to Asia and Americas, and it reached its peak during the early part of the current phase. Modern violent colonial expansion is a European invention and may be said to exist when a foreign invader with an attitude of racial, religious, or cultural superiority succeeds in military and political control of an indigenous population at an earlier stage of development and pursues its interests without any cultural compromise. In the New World, this colonial expansion occurred in conjunction with population migration from Europe, slaves from Africa, and indentured labor from Europe and Asia. It resulted in displacement or obliteration of the local population to one degree or another.

During the first two centuries of this phase, the focus of colonial expansion was the new continents of North America, South America, and Australia. By 1775, Spain and Portugal had transferred substantial populations to the colonies mostly through immigration, indentured servants, and displaced, enslaved, or exterminated indigenous populations. It established control over South America and Central America and the southern half of North America. England had established control over the northern half of eastern North America and over Australia.

Coerced Trade with the Old World (1600–1800)

Contrary to popular belief, western European nation-states, though in a militarily strong position, did not control significant territories in Asia and Africa at the midpoint of current phase. This was in part because their attention had been focused on easier successes in Americas and Australia, partly because there was little need for it during the mercantile period, and partly because some of the states and civilizations, particularly in Asia, were too strong to mess with except near shorelines.

In addition, the nation-states of western Europe needed to be stronger and the timing had to be right on a case-by-case basis. The Portuguese, French, Spanish, Dutch, and English only controlled the coastal areas in Africa, South Asia, and Southeast Asia. The only significant exceptions were Bengal (to the surprise of the British) and the Philippines, which fell under British and Spanish control respectively. However, within the following century, western European nations controlled nearly all of Africa, South Asia, and Southeast Asia. Only East Asia escaped significant territorial control. However, even China, which remained strong in the seventeenth century, did not escape unequal treaties comprising of the forced opening of thirteen ports and the loss of Hong Kong after the defeat in the First Opium War of 1842 with the British.

It is worth noting that the western European states not only fought with the states and civilizations in Asia and Africa but also with one another, often agreeing to carve out territories. Thus, the British controlled South Asia, the entire eastern half of Africa, parts of West Africa, and coastal Arabia were controlled. France controlled most of the northern half of West Africa and Vietnam, the Portuguese and the Dutch controlled the southern half of West Africa, and the Dutch controlled most of Southeast Asia.

Mercantilism with the Old and New World (1600–1800)

The question arises why the western European nation-states pursued two different types of colonialism in the New and Old World states during the current phase and what was the relationship between the two. The answer lies in the differing commodities each area produced or was capable of producing and the differing capacity to turn these commodities into products in New World colonies, Europe, Africa, and Asia. In general, we may identify two differing sets of relationships with western European nation-states at the nexus:

- A triangular relationship between the New World, Africa, and Europe, where Europe and Africa supplied immigrants, indentured labor, and slaves to the New World; the New World supplied commodities such as sugar, tobacco, cotton, gold, and silver to Europe; and Europe supplied rum, textiles, and other manufactured goods to Africa.
- A second reciprocal relationship between Europe and Asia, where Asia supplied manufactured goods to Europe in exchange for silver and gold obtained from the Americas, with the Chinese preferring silver and the Indians preferring gold.

This allowed a few nation-states in western Europe to create revenue through taxes and duties, with the balance going to the merchants. The economic, political, and military implications were staggering. Economically, the wealth of merchants began to exceed those of the landowning aristocracy, which resulted in the emergence of early capitalists. These economic changes resulted in political changes in Britain, France, and Holland and to a far lesser degree, in Spain and Portugal), where the merchants gained political power at the expense of the aristocracy. Militarily, the mercantile system gave enough revenue to these governments in western Europe to create powerful navies to not only fight it out with other western European nation-states but also more important to assert increasing control in Asia through coastal colonies and become increasingly significant players in the domestic political scene first in South and Southeast Asia, followed by Africa, China, and Arabia.

Thus, the mercantile period witnessed an economic policy of trade monopolization through high tariffs, import restrictions, export subsidies, manufacturing subsidies, wage controls, government-controlled monopolies, forbidding the use of foreign ships, and exclusive trade pacts on the one hand and wars among the leading mercantile states on the other. This has been the history of today's promoters of nations advocating free trade.

The English-Dutch wars and the French-Dutch wars deserve mention, the wars with the Spanish and Portuguese having been settled in the previous phase. The purpose of these wars was to damage the other's economy. The restriction on imports had one positive impact, converting the wastelands into agricultural lands in some areas of Europe. Free markets, about which the nation-states of western Europe led by Britain were to rhapsodize toward the end of the phase, were nowhere to be seen.

The land-based empires in Europe, such as the Habsburg, Holy Roman, Russian, and Austro-Hungarian also tried their hands at mercantilism, but their scope was local, not global. Thus, they remained second-tier players. Only the nation-states of western Europe located on the open seas had the opportunity to participate in the global mercantile system. It was clearly a cause of resentment and envy.

There was a fundamental difference between the colonial expansion of the western European states in the New and Old World. The former was driven by the needs to access commodities and the latter was driven by the need to access products. The coming industrialization in western Europe was going to change this pattern dramatically in the second half of the phase.

Political Revolutions in the New World (1775–1850)

Not all colonies continue to remain profitable as the colonies founded by indentured labor and slavery under the guidance of the mother country for several reasons: the local consumption of local commodities increased, commodities production decreased due to soil exhaustion, and mercantile policies were circumvented through encouraging piracy and smuggling. In addition, some colonies began to assert themselves politically as they matured, as their manufacturing capacities were built, and as their overall dependence on the mother country decreased. The English colonies in America thus came to manage their own internal affairs by the middle of the eighteenth century, a fact that Great Britain resented. Thus, the period of 1775 to 1825 was a period of revolt by these colonies against their European masters. In 1776, British colonies in North America revolted and gained independence, followed by Mexico (1810–1821), Argentina (1810), Chile (1818), and Brazil (1822), which took advantage of rise of Napoleon and his defeat of Spain. However, unlike the British colonies in North America named the United States of America, which established a democratic and free enterprise form of government, the Spanish and Portuguese colonies in South and Central America chose a form of government with strong military rulers, feudal land ownership, and strong ties to the Catholic Church. In other words, both more or less followed the organizational forms of their erstwhile colonial masters. Independent New World states reflected European political structures to one degree or another.

Key Political Developments in Europe during Mercantile Period (1600–1800)

The political developments in the leading states of western Europe, Britain, France, and the Netherlands resulted from a unique mix of religious, political, military, and economic causes in each case. The latter were dependent upon their levels of success as mercantile powers since greater success meant greater power to the merchant class at the expense of the aristocracy and greater revenue for the government.

England and United Kingdom: In the case of Britain, the religious causes were more important than in the other two. Since Tudor queen Elizabeth I died in 1603 without an heir, England and Scotland came to be ruled by James VI of Scotland and James I of England under a dynastic union of crowns. His son, Charles, married Catholic French princess Henrietta-Marie Bourbon in 1625, raising alarm bells in Protestant England. At the same time, Charles I needed money to send a force to force to participate in the Thirty Years' War fought in the Holy Roman Empire between Catholic and Protestants. He could not get the money without the parliament of aristocrats (which could be dissolved by the king anytime) and the aristocrats who collected revenue. He called the parliament in 1628. The new parliament extracted the Petition of Right from Charles I, prohibiting the king from infringing upon certain rights. The king needed to call a second parliament in 1640, this time to put down a rebellion in Scotland against his plan to unify the church. The conflict led to three civil wars during the ensuing decade and later to the so-called Glorious Revolution, when parliament invited William of the Netherlands to invade England in 1688. The result was finally in parliament with a decisive win. The struggle between the Protestant aristocrats and the Catholic king was won with the help of the Dutch military and the rising merchants, who supported the aristocrats. During the second half of seventeenth century, Great Britain went through a period of dictatorship with a strong parliamentary leader such as Cromwell and was without a monarch. The English monarchy was restored in 1701 by the parliament to James I's daughter and son-in-law and extended to Scotland through the Act of Union in 1707. Clearly, monarchy was restored and remained powerful in part because of English conservatism but since the merchants were too weak to govern on their own and did not want the aristocrats to have an upper hand. The fifty-year civil war had set England and Scotland on the path of parliamentary monarchy with aristocrats in control for the time being. The merchants and the budding capitalists, of course, would replace the aristocrats as the force to reckon with in the next phase, as the mercantile system gave way to the Industrial Revolution and mechanized production, thus transitioning from mercantile period to the period of systematic wealth drain.

During the eighteenth century, the United Kingdom was ruled by the three Georges of German ancestry, with George II strengthening the constitutional monarchy and George III losing the American colonies. England and the United Kingdom engaged in nonstop warfare between 1600 and 1815, with number of wars probably numbering 150. This reminds one of the wars the Arabs fought in the first two centuries after Islam was born.

France: During the sixteenth century, France under the Valois and Bourbon dynasties, though a latecomer to the colonial game, managed to create colonies in North America, India, and West Africa (Senegal), often in opposition to the British interests. Simultaneously, it created a highly centralized state under a strong monarchy. Following religious wars of the previous century (1562-1598), France participated in the thirty-year Religious War (1618–1648), War of Three Henrys (1627–1628), War of Devolution (1667) against Spain, Franco-Dutch wars (1672-1678), War of Reunions against Spain and the Holy Roman Empire (1683–1684). The net effect of these conflicts was the defeat of Protestants in France, circumscribing the power of Spain and the Holy Roman Empire, and the emergence of the Dutch as a Republic. France remained under a strong monarchy, bypassing the political developments in England and the Netherlands. France, unlike England, could not always choose the conflicts with other European states. Throughout the most of the eighteenth century, France continued to remain a centralized monarch under Louis XV's long reign.

If the religious causes were one of the drivers of the political changes in seventeenth-century England, religious wars on mainland Europe actually strengthened the centralized state in France, partly because France was surrounded by land-based neighbors. The power of merchants in France never equaled that of seventeenth-century English merchants, and the French monarchy never went through a period of weakness. The wars in Europe and the smaller colonial/mercantile empire meant that France was unable to create a navy to match the British navy and paid a price when the Seven Years' War (1757–1763), which ought to be called World War I, broke out between France and Britain in North America, Central America, India, West Africa, and the Philippines over the overlapping colonial/mercantile empires. Britain won decisively, and France lost its first colonial empire.

A little more than a decade later, when the English colonies of North America rebelled against Britain, France was still smarting from the loss of its colonial empire and enthusiastically supported the colonies, exhausting its treasury in the process. Louis XVI was forced to convene the Estates-General, consisting of nobility, clergy and common people in 1789 after a gap of 175 years. The Estates-General over three years evolved into the National Assembly, executed Louis the XVI, and declared France a Republic in 1792.

Comparison with England is interesting: the political change was delayed by a century, and when it finally came, it grandly went beyond constitutional monarchy. However, the revolutionaries could never get their acts together, which gave Napoleon an opportunity. Napoleon was a highly successful military general to come forward in a military coup in 1799 and crowned himself emperor in 1805. Napoleon succeeded brilliantly on land wars in Europe, even though the British defeated him on the sea at the Battle of Trafalgar in 1805. In 1812, he invaded Russia with an army of seven hundred thousand. The campaign was a disaster, and Napoleon was forced to abdicate in 1814. He staged a minor comeback but a coalition of European states defeated him at Waterloo in 1815.

The Netherlands: The Duke of Burgundy united the seventeen provinces of the Low Counties in 1433, thus forging a separate non-German identity. These seventeen counties were either under French or Holy Roman Empire rule. In 1548, Holy Roman Emperor Charles V gave some level of autonomy to these provinces. Further differences developed as the provinces enthusiastically adopted the Protestant religion while the Holy Roman Empire under Philip II, the son of Charles, remained devoutly Catholic. Philip II initiated religious persecution and the centralization of tax collection and judiciary. The ensuing Eighty Years' War between the provinces and Spain had the first fifty years as a war of independence from Spain and the last thirty as part of the broader thirty years' religious war. The Netherlands declared independence in 1581 and achieved independence in 1648.

Three characteristics defined the new nation of the Netherlands: it was a republic ruled by an aristocracy of merchants, which brings to mind the city-states of northern Italy that led the Renaissance; its Protestant faith; and its policy of open doors to wealthy entrepreneurs as varied as Portuguese and German Jews, English rebels against the Church of England, and French and Flemish Protestants.

The entrepreneurial energy of this melting pot soon created a vast trading empire and the world's most powerful navy by 1650, replacing the Spanish and Portuguese as the dominant trading nations. The Netherlands conflicted with the other rising power, Great Britain. Early in the seventeenth century, the Dutch trading company VOC replaced the Portuguese as the dominant trader in Indonesia, following the Portuguese brutality but with better weapons, ships, and organization. The trading company came to control Indonesia as one of the most lucrative colonial possessions during the second half of the seventeenth century. The Netherlands fought two wars with the British and a war with the French and the British combined that ended in 1674. The wars brought realism to the tiny Netherland's ambitions as a great power. The Netherlands had to pay a substantial indemnity and cede New York to Britain. Over the next century, the Netherlands remained a minor player in the colonial game, political power came to be centralized under a stadtholder, and it fought a fourth war with the British during 1780–1784. The war in effect ended the Netherlands as a great colonial power.

Spain and Portugal: We will not get into Spanish and Portuguese history; suffice to say that their colonial empires remained established in South and Central America, and they lost North America to the United States of America.

The Spanish and Portuguese intermingled with the local population to one degree or another and forged their separate noncolonial entities, much like the United States of America. Spain, and Portugal, as we noted above, lost much of their influence over the colonies through wars of independence in the early nineteenth century. In Europe, Spain drifted into constitutional monarchy, never quite developing a republican form of government until the twentieth century.

The Prussian Empire: In 1525, the monastic states of Teutonic knights were consolidated by Albert into the duchy of Prussia, initially as a Polish fiefdom with Lutheranism as the state religion. Through marriage, Brandenburg and the duchy of Prussia merged in 1618 to create the Brandenburg-Prussia state. The entity slowly evolved into Prussia, and in 1701, Fredrick I was recognized as king of Prussia by the Holy Roman emperor and became increasingly independent of the Holy Roman Empire in the eighteenth century.

The Fate of the Holy Roman Empire: The reader will recall the Holy Roman Empire traces its history to Charlemagne in 800, who unified Europe east of Arab control of the Iberian Peninsula. The western lands evolved into independent France, and the eastern lands became the Holy Roman Empire when Otto I took over in 962 and remained powerful until thirteenth century. Thereafter, the duchies and counties became more powerful, and a process of electing kings through archbishops and princes was instituted through the Golden Bull in the fourteenth century. This essentially reduced it to the Holy Roman Empire of the German nation, while the Italian Peninsula assumed a separate identity under papal influence. Since the fifteenth century, despite the existence of the elective body, the Holy Roman Empire came to be ruled by the house of Habsburg. The process of fragmentation, fueled by the Catholic-Protestant division, geographical factors, and geopolitics continued until 1806, when the empire was dissolved. For a brief period, because of inheritance rules, the empire included Spain as well in the sixteenth century. The Swiss federation was first to separate (it was already quasi-independent in 1499), followed by the Netherlands in the seventeenth century and the Prussian state in the eighteenth, reducing the empire to Austria and eastern Europe lands ruled by the Habsburg dynasty and the still-independent small German states. In the eighteenth century, Voltaire correctly remarked that the Holy Roman Empire was not holy, Roman, or an empire.

Polish–Lithuania commonwealth: We only need mention that King John Sobieski II of the Polish-Lithuanian Commonwealth allied with Holy Roman Emperor, Leopold I, to defeat the Ottomans in 1683 and save Europe from Islam.

The Russian Empire: After Ivan the great established the duchy of Moscow and defeated the Golden Hordes., Ivan IV, the Terrible, centralized power in the monarchy and exhausted the treasury through wars. He crowned himself a tsar in the mold of a Byzantine emperor. This was followed by the Polish invasion of Moscow, which led to a popular revolt against invasion and the ascension of the Romanov dynasty, which ruled until 1917. Fortunately, both the Polish-Lithuanian Commonwealth and the Swedish empire were engaged in bitter conflict, allowing the Romanovs to consolidate power. A series of peasant revolts followed and were crushed.

Peter the Great (1686–1725) was a commanding autocrat who was nearly seven feet tall. He defeated the Swedes, founded a new capital on the Baltic, defeated the Ottomans, and expanded into Siberia. He brought a western European model of bureaucracy to Russia and essentially transformed Russia into an empire before he died at age fifty-three. The next great ruler was Catherine II. She was of German origin and ruled from 1762–1796.

The history of Europe during this period is a history of a scramble for land and commodities trade in the New World and the Old World, coerced product trade with the Old World, and relatively unsuccessful attempts at a transition from a monarchy to a democratic form of government, with the sole exception of the formation of the United States of America. However, just when the exploitation of the New World colonies was ending, the systematic wealth drain of the Old World colonies in Asia and Africa began in earnest.

Political Developments in Europe during the Systematic Wealth Drain Period (1800–2000)

United Kingdom: By the end of the Napoleonic wars, the people of Fortress Britain had emerged victorious against all rivals in the colonial game: Spanish, Portuguese, Dutch, and French. But they sustained the loss of their largest colony, which resulted in the creation of the United States of America. This ended the first British Empire, but the British were already expanding a second one with their victory over Marathas in 1813 in India. This new empire was going to be more sinister since it was not focused on trade and conquering territories with sparse populations at an earlier stage of development, as in the New World, but on controlling the ancient, populous civilizations in the Old World through systematic wealth drain in the interest of industrializing the United Kingdom.

The history of the United Kingdom is too well known to describe in detail. The high points to be noted are the following:

- The ill-fated union with Ireland (1800)
- The flow of power from the monarchy to the prime ministers, starting with George IV
- The Reform Acts of 1832, 1867, and 1884 to extend democracy, whereby the number of electorates increased from 366,000 (~2% of the voting population) to 8 million or about two-thirds of the population
- The Antislavery Act of 1833
- Vastly expanded territorial control in India and Africa
- Substantial independence for Canada (1867), New Zealand (1907), Australia (1926), Irish home rule (1886–1893), and Irish independence and partition (1920s)
- World War I, the Great Depression, and World War II
- Independence to Asian and African colonies (1947–1970), including the partition of India and creation of Pakistan
- The formation of the Commonwealth
- The Suez crisis

The second British empire ended much like the first empire: in disaster, only this time it was destroyed violently by competing German, Italian, and Japanese Empires through two world wars and mostly peacefully by the peoples of the territories and dominions they controlled.

France: Following Waterloo, the monarchy was restored in France briefly between 1815 and 1830. This was followed by the eighteen-year July monarchy controlled by the French bankers, traders, and the rising bourgeoisie. The process of creating the second French colonial empire began with invasion of Algeria in 1830. The second republic followed and lasted from 1848 to 1851, when Napoleon III seized power and declared himself emperor and continued empire building into Indochina from 1867 to 1874. But the monarchy collapsed following the Franco-Prussian war of 1871, and the third republic was born. It lasted until 1939. France acquired additional colonies or strengthened influence in Indochina, North Africa, and West Africa during this period. Thus, while British colonies had begun rebelling against unjust colonial rule, the French were acquiring new colonies.

The fourth republic came into existence after World War II in 1946 and lasted until 1958, when the fifth republic was born. The fifth republic continues to the present day. It seems that the French have been always a century behind the British in several respects, the key drivers being a weaker mercantile system, a weaker naval force, a highly centralized state, a strong monarchy, a stronger aristocracy, and an incomplete Protestant revolution or its equivalent.

The Netherlands: In the nineteenth century, the Netherlands eventually adopted a constitution monarchy, but the minority Catholic population broke away as the separate nation of Belgium. The VOC went bankrupt in 1800, and the Netherlands' main colony, Indonesia, was taken over by the Dutch government. The government introduced a system of forced cultivation and indentured labor, bringing enormous wealth to the Netherlands. Unlike France, the Netherlands was not a late joiner in the colonial game when compared to the British; however, its smaller size undoubtedly played a role in ending its ambitions.

Spain: During the Napoleonic wars, Spain mostly fought against France, and eventually the people of Spain defeated France in 1813 through guerilla tactics. However, the monarchy was restored and continued until 1873. A two-year first republic followed, and after that, the restoration of monarchy and a second republic in 1931. The second republic lasted until 1939. The civil war in Spain led to military dictatorship, which lasted until 1975. The transition to democracy was complete by 1982, and Spain finally joined several other western European nations as a constitutional monarchy.

Austrian, Prussian, and German Empires: Francis II dissolved the Holy Roman Empire in 1806 after his disastrous defeat by Napoleon and founded the Austrian Empire. Austria played a huge role in the defeat of Napoleon, and Francis II continued to rule the Austrian Empire, which included Italy, Poland, and the Balkans. It was a multi-ethnic empire. The 1815 Congress of Vienna also created the German Confederation, consisting of the kingdom of Prussia, the Austrian Empire, and smaller independent German states. The Prussian-Austrian war of 1866 resulted in Austria's defeat, and Austria left the Confederation, which was now renamed the Northern Confederation. A year later in 1867, Austria united with Hungary to create the Austro-Hungarian Empire. The Northern Confederation evolved into the German Empire in 1871under a Kaiser and consisted of Prussia, small German states, and four territories from Austria. It lasted until 1918, when Germany became a Republic. The German Empire industrialized rapidly after 1850; however, it was too late for Germany to get into the colonial game. The end of World War I marked the end of the Austro-Hungarian Empire. The Czechs declared independence, followed by Hungary, and Romania. Both Hungary and Austria became republics, and the southern Slavs became a kingdom of Serbs, Croats, and Slovenes.

Thus, the Holy Roman Empire that lasted for just about a millennium successively shed France, Switzerland, the Netherlands/Belgium, Prussia, Czechoslovakia, Hungary, and Romania. It spawned a host of monarchies, constitutional monarchies, and, eventually, republics.

Russia: Russia successfully stopped Napoleon as he invaded Russia in 1812. She brought western European art, science and culture to Russia. However, Russian Empire became strong and large, in fact several times larger than entire continent of Europe, it sent alarm bells in England and France who entered into the war between Russia and Ottoman in 1856 on the pretext of maintaining the balance of power and probably saved Ottoman Empire from destruction. The absolute rule of Tsars continued through the rest of the nineteenth century, refusing to allow any form of political change. The rise of German Empire in the second half of the nineteenth century led to World War I between Britain, France and Russia against Germany, Austria-Hungary, Italy and Ottomans primarily because Germany was denied colonies in Asia and Africa and resulted in the destruction of Russian, German, Ottoman and Austro-Hungarian Empires.

World War I brought communists to power in Russia. The communists reorganized the Russian Empire into a Union of Soviet Socialist Republics. The rise of Fascists in Germany, Japan, and Italy led to World War II, leading to the defeat of Germany, Japan, and Italy with the help of the United States. After World War II, the USSR emerged as a superpower, engaged in decades-long cold war with the United States, and imploded in 1989. It reverted back to a Russian democracy of sorts.

Italy: From the mid-sixteenth century to the end of the Napoleonic wars, Italy was controlled by Spain, Austria, and France. Between 1841 and 1861, Italy was unified by driving the Austrian and French out with the help of Prussia under the generalship of Giuseppe Garibaldi.

After half a century of experimentation with liberalism and opportunism during World War I, Italy turned fascist and imperialist, conquering Libya and Ethiopia. It, allied with Germany and Japan in World War II, and the Allies defeated them in 1943. The first republic was formed after the war and lasted until 1992. It included the last two decades of political and social upheaval fought by the extreme right and left and often turned violent. The second republic came into existence in 1992 following the fall of the Soviet Union, when the Communist Party of Italy abandoned socialist ideology. This continues to the present.

The United States: During the nineteenth century, the United States occupied itself with extending its domain from the Atlantic to Pacific Oceans through displacement of indigenous people, the "Louisiana purchase" from France, purchase of Alaska from Russia, and initiating wars with Mexico and Spain. At the same time, it managed to preserve its unity through a devastating civil war and managed to rapidly industrialize the state. By the end of the nineteenth century, the United States was the largest economy and had a larger population compared to any European or South American nation.

During World War I, the United States sided with the British and took the lead in creating the League of Nations.

The League of Nations failed in its mission but succeeded in institutionalizing the relationship among nations of the world. Until then, the only way to settle disputes was through international law, bilateral negotiations, or war, without the assistance of a world body.

During World War II, the United States again sided with Britain and France after initial hesitation. At the end of the war, the United States and the victors established the United Nations, complete with veto power for the five permanent members of the Security Council, World Bank, and International Monetary Fund. In 1946, the United States had half the productive capacity in the world, had developed nuclear weapons, and saw itself as a bulwark against the Soviet Union, with Europe and Japan as junior partners. It fought Korean, Vietnam, and Afghan wars, ultimately defeating the Soviet Union. Simultaneously, it established a relationship with China, exploiting differences between China and the Soviet Union, with India to balance Chinese power in Asia.

Thus, what we witness is a painful transition from absolute monarchy to some form of democracy for most nations of Europe and their colonies in the New World, with the exception of Britain and the United States. We also see a shift in relationship with ancient civilizations in Asia, where the leading nation-states of Europe succeeded in territorial control and as they industrialized, reduced these civilizations to suppliers of commodities and buyers of manufactured goods under conditions of coerced trade. In the mercantile period, they had mostly bought manufactured goods from Asia and commodities from the New World colonies. Thus, they drained Asian civilizations of enormous wealth.

17.5 Natural Causes

There were no significant natural causes that impacted European civilization. The impact of environmental pollution and potential climate changes resulting from the industrialization of European civilization and its offshoots came in the second half of the twentieth century. This impact was both local (quality of water, air, and soil) and global (climate change). The local impact was effectively addressed through regulation and pollution control technologies, while the global impact of climate change was mostly resisted for scientific and political reasons.

17.6 Intrinsic Causes

Institutional Structures and Processes

Political system: At the beginning of the phase, we either witnessed strong, centralized seafaring monarchies, mostly in western Europe, highly fragmented princely city-states, mostly in Italy and Germany, a resurgent Russia land-locked on the western front, or Ottoman imperialism in southeastern Europe. The political system in each of these areas evolved quite differently during the current phase. In western Europe, the evolution from monarchy to democracy was largely determined by the extent of the continued hold of Catholic ideology and in the Catholic center as well as Orthodox Christian Russia in the east, where there was little opportunity of colonial exploitation, the focus was to create strong, centralized land-based empires with little predisposition toward democracy. In southeastern Europe, after the Ottomans were weakened by western European states by the end of the eighteenth century, the focus was national liberation with little regard to the political system. The colonies of the western European states in the Americas simply reflected the political system of the mother country. Thus, we see democracy in Britain, France (after Napoleon's misconceived attempt to outdo Germans and Russians in land-based European empires), and the Netherlands; continued monarchy in German and Russian states until the twentieth century; and liberation of southeastern Europe from the Ottoman yoke, followed by military dictatorships of one hue or another.

The North American states colonized most successfully by France and Britain adopted a democratic political system while central and South America colonized most successfully by Spain and Portugal adopted military dictatorships. Only in the twentieth century did Russia, Germany, and Central and South American states move toward the democratic political system. Thus, we may conclude that the political systems in European civilization moved decisively from monarchy to democracy; however, the paths taken were dramatically different and involved different speeds.

Military capability: During the last phase, gunpowder had begun to end the superiority of the horse, sword, and bow on land while the discovery of sea routes began the age of sail. Thus began a three-century period in which explosives, steam power, and the standardized production of weapons assisted by scientific and industrial revolutions changed the face of the military power of key European states on both land and sea. We cannot begin to provide the reader with a detailed history of these developments. However, the key developments in the land armies were: superior firearms, mounted riffles, and field artillery cannons of increasing range and precision. These developments were supported by breakthroughs in metallurgy, standardized parts manufacturing, chemistry, and mechanics. Considerable development in war doctrine and strategy also took place through Napoleon (disrupting enemy supply lines), Clausewitz (war of attrition), and Jomini (operations and intelligence). A key issue for European states was the relative emphasis on the army versus the navy and that depended on the need to protect colonies in Americas and Asia. Here, Britain had an unfair advantage in that it could develop a stronger navy without exposing itself to the land forces of other European states, and this simple fact goes a long way in explaining the ultimate success of Britain against its rivals in the age of sail. The key developments in naval force may be summed up in "from wood and wind to steam and steel" and included using steam power, big guns on ironclad ships, submarines, and torpedoes.

In the twentieth century, the short-lived concept of trench warfare was developed, followed by automatic rifles. The internal combustion engine made both the tank and the airplane possible. Use of nuclear energy produced large submarines and large aircraft carriers, while developments in electronics and rocket science led to intercontinental missiles capable of carrying nuclear weapons. Breakthroughs in biological sciences opened up an entirely new form of warfare, that of chemical and biological warfare. By the closing decades of the twentieth century, European civilization and its satellites in Americas had assembled enough power to destroy civilizations many times over.

The story of the military capability of the leading states of European civilization paralleled the development of science and technology and may be summed up as the steam, internal combustion engine, and nuclear power replacing the horse; precision guns replacing cannons; and missiles, chemical, and biological agents, and nuclear devices replacing the gun, bow, and catapult. Advanced use of computers games in military strategycoordination among the military units, and intelligence operations significantly enhanced military capability.

Economic system: The transformation of the European economy from its agrarian base to modern information economies occurred in stages and at different rates for different nation-states. In what follows, we focus on Britain and the United States as the leading nation-states in this process. As we have noted in the history of European civilization above, the economic history of these two nation-states may be understood through the mercantile (1600–1800) and systematic wealth drain (1800–2000) periods. During the latter period, the impact of the Industrial Revolution on agriculture and manufacturing occurred.

During the mercantile period, the key drivers in agriculture were the emphasis on colonization of Americas and use of African slave and European indentured labor in New World plantations to produce and import agricultural products. This accelerated the process of urbanization without a proportional increase in agricultural productivity in home countries. Nevertheless, there was impact of improved transportation, Columbian exchange, and loans to farmers from Bank of England after 1700. There was also better irrigation through canals and improved livestock through breeding. However, these improvements must be considered secondary to the bonanza from new colonies and slave or indentured labor. Colonies in turn received manufactured products. During the systematic wealth drain period, the introduction of new technologies in both Britain and the United States dramatically improved agricultural productivity, thus accelerating the process of urbanization. These technologies included better tools, such as plows, cultivators, mowers, threshers, balers, harvesters, chemical fertilizers, and combines. Other innovations contributing to agricultural productivity included the following:

- The use of the steam engine or internal combustion engine
- Improved transportation of produce by using ships and railroads
- Improved storage techniques, such as root cellars, granaries, packaging, and refrigeration
- Better methods, such as crop rotation and professional management of farms
- New knowledge from botany and other sciences
- Communication technologies, such as the telegraph that made up-to-date information of worldwide market conditions

This process occurred in both Britain and the United States more or less simultaneously and was so successful that by the mid-twentieth century, only a small percentage of the population needed to work on the farm to support the entire population.

Manufacturing was a direct beneficiary of the increase in agricultural productivity since it freed a greater proportion of the population in Britain to engage in manufacturing and technological innovation earlier than would have been possible in the absence of the colonization of America. The Industrial Revolution in England and Scotland occurred between 1750 and 1825 and was characterized initially by the application of steam power and metallurgical breakthroughs in high-quality iron production. British iron production probably exceeded one million tons per year by 1840, the equivalent to over a hundred pounds per person. Textiles could be produced in factories staffed by industrial workers who could be hired or fired based on demand, unlike the older guild system where the number of workers was independent of the demand in the short run. Thus, the early inhuman factory system ran on profit and return on capital. As the factory system took hold, it initiated a dramatic change in worldwide trade.

During the mercantile period, Asia was the manufacturing powerhouse, albeit it was based on the guild system and handicrafts traded with commodities, including gold being supplied from the Americas. The key states of western Europe, including Britain, that controlled the high seas used gold from the Americas to buy Asian manufactured products from India and China. However, with the advent of the factory system, it became possible to reverse the relationship with Asia, particularly with India, which had fallen under colonial control by the end of the eighteenth century. The manufacturing base in Asia was destroyed through tariffs, and its status reduced to that of a commodity supply with dictated prices. The result of this process based on mastery of the high seas and coerced trade was increasing poverty in Asia and increasing prosperity in Britain.

The post-Civil War United States became the beneficiary of British investment and technology, and by the end of the nineteenth century was ready to teach the old master a thing or two in manufacturing.

With manufacturing beginning to dominate the national economy, the role of commerce and markets also began to expand. International commerce began to focus on importing commodities and exporting finished goods. Internal commerce focused on developing a distribution and retail system to keep up with expanding product markets. The stock exchange (set up in 1857 and modeled after the Dutch exchange) and credit markets as well as the banking system expanded to channel the savings and trade surplus into investment in both Britain and the United States.

The role of government in Britain and the United States during the second period was quite different. In Britain, the role of government was to maintain control of the seas and colonies in Asia (having lost the thirteen colonies in America) in support of coerced trade consisting of commodities and manufactured goods. In contradistinction to the global orientation of Britain, the United States was more inwardly focused through selective immigration from Europe, expanding the colonies from Atlantic to the Pacific through wars with Indian tribes and Mexicans, and developing agriculture through the plantation system and a world-class manufacturing base to meet the needs of internal markets while using its power for controlling small, defenseless countries in Central America.

While we have above summarized economic developments in Britain and the United States, other European states, including Nordic countries, Germany, France, Poland, Italy, Canada, and Australia had caught up by the time of World War I. Russia experienced an industrial revolution in the twentieth century after communist takeover. However, southeastern Europe remained agrarian until the mid-twentieth century.

Religious systems of faith: The primary religious faith of the European civilization continued to be Christianity with a Protestant sect dominating the north, the Catholic sect the middle, and the Orthodox sect the east and southeast. This phenomenon reflects the influence of the Lutheran Reformation as well as the differing speed of industrialization.

During the current phase, the new Protestant sect was most dynamic and sought to establish a direct relationship between man and God, bypassing the church. It was driven by scriptures and not tradition, allowing all Christians to become priests with salvation only possible through divine grace; one need not be a Christian to receive divine grace. There was little fundamental change in Catholic and Orthodox sects during the current phase. Orthodox Christians continued to believe in the equality of all bishops and reject papal authority and the concept of purgatory, the primacy of the scriptures, and the irreconcilability of faith and reason. Generally, only the Protestant sect allowed the freedom to pursue knowledge of the natural world even if it apparently contradicted the biblical doctrine. Thus, Newton could formulated the law of gravity and use his differential calculus to "prove" that earth was created by God in 4004 BCE.

The Protestant sect lacked central authority and splintered into many subsects based on minor doctrinal differences during the current phase, with each subsect having a national or international association. The Catholic sect remained united, and the Orthodox Church continued to have many branches often based on an ethnic nationality (Greek, Russian, etc.), each headed by a bishop and all bishops having one vote at an ecumenical council.

European civilization finally achieved a compromise between science and its Christian faith toward the end of the nineteenth century. Luther's Reformation of the Christian faith, breakthrough in geology and biology through Darwin, and astrophysics combined forces to chip away at the Christian metaphysics elaborated in the bible. Science, for the first time, finally a decisively gained an upper hand in a civilization steeped in a monotheistic faith. It was indeed a momentous achievement. This does not mean, however, that the primacy of science is accepted at the individual level by all or equally in all states of the European civilization. On the contrary, most individuals in most states of European civilization continue to believe in the Christian faith and go to church. However, the church has lost power to sanction science because it is valued by the elite as essential to prosperity and because the intellectual class is no longer able to justify Christian dogma. Thus, Christian faith has been circumcised and confined to the lower strata of populations in at least Protestant states, which in fact are the most advanced states of the European civilization.

Legal system: Again, as the reader might imagine, the legal systems saw considerable development, with different parts of Europe taking somewhat different approaches. Britain continued to strengthen its tradition of common law, with equity law representing royal conscience derived from its long judicial and executive traditions respectively. These included both civil and criminal laws. The common law and equity law tradition was supplemented with statutory law as the legislative bodies came into existence in England, Scotland, and Ireland. Thus, the English legal system is based mostly on judicial experience over centuries. On continental Europe, the tradition of a formal common law was weaker and a greater emphasis was placed on codified law derived from previous royal edicts and their periodic codification going all the way back to Roman codes. Similarly, the development of elected bodies was also slower, and as a result, a significant body of legislative law did not exist until the end of the nineteenth century. Thus, the Code Napoleon (1804), German civil code (1900), and Swiss code (1907) were developed. Russia, also lacking a strong common law tradition and legislative bodies, produced a number of codes during the current phase.

The judicial structure has also varied considerably in different parts of Europe and has included common law courts, equity courts, courts of appeals, and supreme courts.

All European legal systems ultimately denied the applicability of religious law and produced strong legal systems comprising of property law, contract law, property transfer law, tort law, and criminal law irrespective of the judicial, executive, or legislative origin of these different legal systems. English common law and the Code Napoleon form the basis of legal systems in significant parts of the world today, reflecting their colonial history.

Social structure and inequality: Social structure in states comprising the European civilization both evolved and varied by state. At the beginning of the phase, the rough social rank would be as follows: the monarch, followed by landowning aristocrats, the religious elite (religious elite stumped monarchy and aristocracy during certain periods in some Catholic states), merchants, manufacturing guilds, soldiers, peasants, slaves, and nonwhites. Women had a low status unless they belonged to the aristocratic class. Over four centuries, the impact of the Industrial Revolution and the democratic form of government on social structure has been dramatic: the loss of aristocratic status, slave emancipation, equal rights for women and nonwhites, and the emergence of manufacturing elite and the middle class.

We noted in the last chapter how the ideology of racism was a logical necessity in reconciling the ideology of humanism that came out of the Renaissance and imperial designs of the colonizing states of western Europe. Thus, at the very beginning of the current phase, a global concept of inequality was born for the first time, exposing the global ambitions of western European states situated on the Atlantic coast. By the end of the mercantile period, the concepts of racism and slavery were firmly rooted in the heart of European civilization. The position of women remained secondary while class prejudices of the feudal era transferred the prejudices against workers in the age of industrialization. However, an important countertrend was the democratization of political power, which, over a century-long process, markedly improved the position of women, nonwhites, and the working class in several states of European civilization. Thus, excessive inequality at the beginning of the phase had turned into relative equality among genders, races, and religious groups. However, paradoxically, the process of globalization with the transfer of capital and technology to Asia and Africa to seek higher profits is now threatening the very middle class in several states of the Western civilization, resulting in increased wealth polarization.

Knowledge Creation and educational institutions and processes: As we noted in the last chapter, Europe had evolved several great universities in France, England, Spain, and Italy beginning with the thirteenth century. Toward the end of the last phase, these universities, much like the monasteries, focused on Christian scriptures and Scholasticism or analysis of older works of philosophy in the hope of discovering the truth. However, both the Renaissance and Reformation had great impact on these universities, and they began to shift focus to knowledge creation, not through God as guarantor of knowledge but through man as he conquered internal doubt to reach certainty using observation and reason, particularly in astronomy and laws of terrestrial motion.

The University of Pisa and Padua provided employment to Galileo. Wandering Descartes did not need employment as he came from a wealthy family, and Cambridge University supported Newton. The success of these seventeenth-century pioneers pushed newer European universities from a focus on knowledge transmission to knowledge advancement throughout the eighteenth century. The nineteenth century saw this phenomenon take a step further when science became the focus of well-equipped and organized German universities, whereas the French and British universities were less focused and relied on private and individual scholars. This German model ultimately won and was a forerunner of the industrial research now sponsored by private and governments in most industrial countries. Thus, by the end of the nineteenth century, for the first time, a civilization had developed a sustainable, organized, and funded structure to ensure creation of new scientific knowledge on an ongoing basis. Science was no longer dependent upon the chance emergence of genius and improbable support of that genius by either a state or a wealthy patron. It had taken humanity three millennia to get to this stage.

On the other hand, technology development remained at the mercy of individual inspiration and interest a little longer, often needing a partnership with an entrepreneur with financial resources, such as James Watt's successive partnerships with John Roebuck and Matthew Bolton to manufacture and commercialize the steam engine. Only in the twentieth century do we begin to see an organized effort to develop technology, beginning with industrial labs followed by universities and government labs and government initiatives, such as nuclear energy and space programs.

The education system also evolved dramatically: from mostly religious to mostly secular, from merely primary to secondary to professional, from merely for elites to universal to compulsory, from mostly male to male and female, and from mostly private funding to mostly public funding. However, until the nineteenth century, most teachers remained incompetent, employing cruel discipline as an aid in teaching. The most influential early educators during the phase were John Comenius (1592–1670 CE), who advocated naturalist education, organized schools, and created entirely different type of textbooks. Rousseau (1712-1778) insisted education must be child-friendly, and Maria Montessori (1870–1952) developed the concept of child-friendly education further through ideas such as mixed-age classes and encouraging students to discover knowledge in an atmosphere of relative freedom. During the nineteenth century, several states also developed national school systems.

Wealth allocation process: During the mercantile period, with its extensive colonization of the New World and coerced trade with established civilizations in Asia and during the period of systematic wealth drain from the same established civilizations of Asia and Africa, the sustainable growing surplus in the leading European states grew dramatically. However, when one looks at how growth in surplus was allocated to wars among states of European civilization, wars with other civilizations, and the coddling the European elites on the one hand and creative endeavors, elimination of poverty and illiteracy on the other hand, the answer is very disappointing, particularly during the mercantile period. Apart from throwing a few crumbs to established universities, it is fair to conclude that states in Europe wasted this growth in usurped surplus on internal and intercivilization wars and providing luxuries to its elites. The situation, however, improved significantly during the period of systematic wealth drain because of the devolution of power to the middle class through gradual the democratization of politics and the spread of education. Thus, in the twentieth century, in many states, particularly the United States of America, we witness the rise of a middle class because of rising productivity and the unbroken allocation of a relatively high proportion of the surplus into creative and productive endeavors, at least until the Great Depression.

Social cohesion processes: During the mercantile period, the cohesion within the states was founded typically on strong centralized monarchies, support of the state by the church, extermination, displacement or alliance with indigenous populations of the New World and proslavery laws where needed, profit extraction from coerced trade with established civilizations of Asia, and strong legal and judicial systems. These realities stand in stark contrast to the proclaimed age of enlightenment in the eighteenth century, whose reach remained confined to academic circles.

The internal cohesion of European states during the period of sustained wealth drain was achieved additionally through the democratization of politics as well as by investment of wealth drain from Asia and the growth of internal surplus into a productive endeavor until the advent of two world wars in the twentieth century, when the colonial and noncolonial states of Europe (and Japan) fought for supremacy.

Internal wars: There was little desire for peace and cooperation among states within the European civilization because of the superior military power compared to established civilizations in Asia and a few states controlling the high seas throughout most of the phase until the rise of communism in Russia and China. Thus, Britain, France, Spain, Portugal, and the Netherlands probably fought more wars with one another to gain territories in the New World and to get trade concessions from Asian dynasties during the mercantile period than the nascent Muslim civilization did in its early centuries.

The period of sustained wealth drain from the established civilizations of Asia became possible when Britain, Spain, Portugal, and the Netherlands tacitly accepted existing colonial divisions. France under Napoleon was the sole exception, resulting in loss of French colonies in the New World. Half a century later, France was able to create a second colonial empire in Africa and East Asia. Wars among the colonizing states of Europe had now come to an end since they had succeeded in dividing up the world among them. However, a new dynamic began soon: a two stage process began to unfold to create contradictions between the colonizing and the non-colonizing states of Europe (Germany, Italy, Austria, Ottoman Empire, and Russia). During the first stage of the nineteenth century, a century-long struggle among the non-colonizing state in Europe for land supremacy led to the defeat of Ottomans and Austria, the victory of Germany and Russia, and the unification of Italy. In the second step, in the twentieth century, the conflict between the colonizing states in western Europe and victorious non-colonizing states in central Europe culminated in two world wars, with Russia and United States allying themselves with the colonizing states. The colonizing states, United States, and Russia won both wars, and in the process, the colonizing states were pushed to the sidelines, initiating an era of cold war (necessitated by nuclear weapons and logic of mutual assured destruction) between Russia and United States. The cold war came to an end at the beginning of the last decade of the twentieth century, resulting in essential internal solidarity among most states of European civilization except perhaps Russia, still smarting from defeat in cold war.

Thus, the four-century phase went through internal conflict among the colonizing states along the Atlantic coast followed by relative peace among them. But conflict among the states in central and eastern Europe was followed by conflict (two world wars) among the western colonizing states and eastern non-colonizing states, cold war between the United States and Russia, and generally an era of solidarity among all European states except Russia and occasionally France, as evident in Korean, Vietnamese, Yugoslavian, Afghan, and Iraqi wars in the twenty-first century.

Formative Beliefs and Ideology at the End of Fourth Synthesis Phase

Advances in geology and forming the theory of evolution dealt a fatal blow to Christian dogma. Increasingly open political systems coupled with opportunistic violence and backed by improving weapons technologies and the application of science to wealth production and leading to mechanized manufacturing and wealth drain from both Old and New Worlds all point to a belief system that may be summarized as follows:

- A profound belief in real knowledge through observation and reason, controlled experimentation, and solid epistemology
- A belief in increasing social and economic equality among citizens
- An attitude of openness toward the intellectual and religious creativity of others
- An abiding belief in aggression toward other social orders while claiming to be a civilizing force

These beliefs, derived from Greek, Roman, and Venetian traditions of violence against other civilizations, western European leadership in science, and its application to production of wealth and control of worldwide trade, formed the basis of the most complete system of exploitation the planet has known to date.

17.7 Extrinsic Peaceful Causes

Once western European states discovered sea routes and the Old and New Worlds and tasted the potential of these routes in controlling world trade, the issue of peaceful causes receded into the background. These states directed violence against each other and sophisticated civilizations in Asia an order of magnitude larger in size as well as the hapless peoples in the Americas, Africa, and Australia, which were at earlier stages of development. Extrinsic peaceful causes were both secondary and only occurred in the wake of violence.

17.8 Extrinsic Violent Causes—European States as Victors

In this chapter, we come across a totally different species of conquerors: they were either violent colonizers who destroyed or displaced populations they conquered or were systematic wealth drainers. They also represented a civilization that had leapfrogged ahead of the civilizations they wished to control. Thus, by and large, the issue was not transmission of creativity from the conquered to the conquerors but transfer of wealth from the conquered to the conqueror and the impact it had on the productive and creative outcomes of the conquerors. This was a change of gigantic proportions: the victor was not a brute but a self-centered creative entity. He was not moved by creed or compassion but clearly understood the connection between increasing wealth drain and knowledge. This new species engaged in systematic wealth drain and was indeed very dangerous since wealth drain from the conquered could be used to create science and technology by the conqueror and superior science and technology could be used to increase wealth drain resulting in wealth polarization of hitherto unknown proportions.

The entire gambit of the European conquest ran from a focus on land grab and coerced trade (Spanish and Portuguese) to systematic wealth drain (French, British and the Dutch) to export of capital and technology in search of cheap labor (the United States) while taking on rhetorical forms focused on spreading Christianity, a racially superior European civilization, and free markets (for capital and goods but not labor) respectively.

Thus, when one compares the violence a few European states unleashed and the violence the Muslim civilization and central Asian nomads unleashed during this phase, one is struck by:

- The worldwide character of the former and regional character of the latter
- The greater magnitude and sustained nature of the former and relatively limited magnitude and duration of the latter
- The objective of wealth drain of the former by allying with indigenous elite and displacement of indigenous elite and control of surplus of the latter
- The control of both underdeveloped continents and established civilization by the former and control of established civilization by the latter
- The much greater role of greed by the former and significant role of creed in the latter

These monumental differences can be easily explained by two factors: control of worldwide sea routes throughout and the rise of mechanized manufacturing in the second half of the phase by European states.

Thus, below we focus on wealth drain and control of the means of wealth creation and its impact on the productive and creative outcomes. We may then ask the question if the conqueror managed the immense resources at his disposal wisely or what was spent on weapons and wars and supporting the lifestyle of the elite versus investment in productive tasks and creative endeavors.

Extent of Wealth Drain and Control of Means of Wealth

The story of wealth drain and the control of the means of wealth during the current phase is a worldwide story that began with a few western European nation-states pitched against rest of the world or about 25 million people in less than two hundred thousand square miles versus 500 million people over tens of million square miles. It would take a whole volume to describe the story in detail, and we do not intend to do it, and it is not necessary. Instead, we shall focus briefly on the approach the most successful of these states took, namely Britain.

The story begins by asking how Britain, which had been ruled and invaded successively by Romans, German Anglo-Saxons, Vikings, Danes, and the French, acquired world-class naval power. The answer lies in adopting two naval innovations: replacing the oar-driven galleys by full-rigged ships with three or more masts and equipping them with large guns during the reign of Henry VIII in the first half of the sixteenth century. Neither of these was a British invention. These innovations, when applied judiciously, converted the British navy from a floating army to an effective naval fleet able to operate from a safe distance and not depend on sailors boarding enemy ships.

The second key question to ask is why the British did not focus on religious conversions as they began colonizing the New World. The answer lies in the second mover advantage. The Portuguese and Spanish began the colonization project before the Reformation and the English after the Reformation. Thus, the English had gotten rid of their Catholic impulses or at least it was well under control.

Thus, after defeating the Spanish Armada in 1588, the British arrived on the world stage to compete with the Portuguese, Spanish, Dutch, and French. The British succeeded because they took a highly differentiated approach to extract the surplus from different parts of the world. The more numerous and larger colonies a particular nation-state succeeded in, the more surplus it extracted and the more money it could spend on further enhancing naval power to keep competing states at bay, resulting in a "virtuous" feedback.

The differentiated British strategy was based on three externalities:

- The population density of the prospective colony, reflecting the productive use of the land
- The stage of development prior to colonization
- The climatic considerations

Using these factors, the British developed the following distinct approaches in different parts of the globe.

- **For a sparsely populated region with a warm climate at an earlier stage of development:** Disperse and obliterate native population, import slaves, and produce commodities while discouraging development of local manufacturing and using trading monopoly through shipping restraining acts. This is pure colonialism coupled with slavery with the rebellious future United States of America as an end point.

- **For a sparsely populated region with temperate climates at an earlier stage of development:** Disperse and obliterate native population, substantial British immigration to produce commodities, and use trade monopoly and market manipulation to extract surplus while discouraging development of local manufacturing. This is pure mercantilism, with a white colony typified by New Zealand, Australia, and Canada.

- **For a densely populated region with a warm climate at a comparable stage of development:** Military and political control coupled with coerced trade to extract wealth through the purchase of manufactured goods followed by converting the colony to a commodity producer and buying off goods through taxes, tariffs, and duties. This is mercantilism followed by systematic wealth drain and is typified by the relationship with the Indian civilization or simply mercantilism involving the Chinese civilization.

- **For a sparsely populated region with a dry climate at a comparable stage of development:** No economic interest; leave it alone unless it interferes with above objectives. This is geopolitical strategy is typified by the relationship with Muslim civilization until the discovery of oil.

These approaches were coupled with the following strategies to deal with the colonies and the competing states of Portugal and Spain in the sixteenth and seventeenth centuries; the Netherlands and France in the seventeenth, eighteenth, and early nineteenth centuries; Russia in the mid-nineteenth century, and Italy, Germany, and Japan in the twentieth century:

- Privateering or government-sponsored looting of Spanish ships carrying gold
- Constantly shifting alliances among the eight principal enemies to gain advantage in controlling the colonies

Table 17.1: Impact of British Colonial Wealth Drain

	1750	1914	1940
(1) Population of Britain, millions	7.5	44	47
(2) Population of all British colonies	50	400	450
(3) Tax imposed on the colonies, % of wealth created	60	50	50
(4) Administrative cost, % of tax Revenue	10	10	10
(5) Defense costs, % of tax Revenue	15	20	30
(6) Net Tax Revenue, % of wealth created in colonies	45	35	30
(7) Wealth drain in millions of colony workers equivalent	22.5	140	135
(8) Productivity ratio in Britain to colonies	1	4	5
(9) Wealth drain in British workers equivalent, millions	22.5	35.5	27
(10) SGS as a % of wealth creation in Britain	20	15	20
(11) British saving in British workers, millions	1.5	6.6	9.4

- Dealing with the principal enemy first
- Allowing the defeated to continue to prosper in a circumscribed manner
- Divide-and-rule policy in the colonies
- Balance economic and geopolitical interests
- Grudgingly introduce limited political reform to extend control through pacifying the emerging nationalist sentiment

How successful were the British in drain wealth from the colonies? The following approach to guestimate wealth drain is believed to be accurate within +/-100 percent.

Let us look at the numbers in table 17.1 in some detail for 1750 CE. The population of Britain was about 7.5 million, and Britain directly or indirectly controlled colonies with about 50 million people. The British imposed a revenue tax ranging from 40 percent to 83 percent. For our purposes, we assume an average of 60 percent. We further assume that the cost of collecting revenue, both administrative and native middlemen, is 10 percent of the revenue collected. Let us further assume that cost of "defending" the colonies, which the British were careful to have the colonies pay for, was 15 percent. Thus, the net revenue is 75 percent of the revenue tax of 60 percent or 45 percent. Thus, the wealth drain in the number of colony workers is 45 percent of the number of workers in the colonies or 22.5 million. If we assume the productivity of the British worker to be equal that of the colony worker in the pre-Industrial Revolution era, that translates to 22.5 million British workers. Further, if one assumes that British sustainable growing surplus was 20 percent of the wealth created, it was equivalent to 1.5 million British workers. Thus, the multiplier effect on the SGS is simply the ratio of 22.5 and 1.5 or 15. This means that British saving rate was fifteen times what it would have been without the colonies, after paying for administrative and defensive costs and after accounting for the difference in productivity of British and colonial workers. Note that we did not account for the difference between the total population and the working age population. However, since we did that for both Britain and the colonies, it cancels out. If anything, it underestimates the multiplier effect on SGS considerably since a greater proportion of the population in the colonies started work at an earlier age.

This simple calculation—which has numerous limitations, such as not considering capital outflows from the colonizing state, the pressure from colonies and other competing colonizers, or the internal turmoil on maintaining a façade of being a civilizing mission, to name a few—nevertheless can be used to understand the evolution of the history of British colonialism, mercantilism, and imperialism over two centuries.

Based on a century and half of effort at colonization, by 1750, Britain was in a strong position relative to its key competitors of the French, Spanish, Dutch, and Portuguese. The British position was so strong that it would easily compensate for the coming loss of first empire based in North America over the next decades by one based in Asia and Africa. In the middle column, table 17.1 focuses on the second empire at its peak in 1914 to its demise after World War II. Because the mercantile inflow of surplus resulted in the Industrial Revolution and the resulting increase in British productivity, the impact, though still substantial, went down with passing decades as the table shows. By the end of World War II, because of much higher defense spending to fight Germans, Italians, and Japanese; the national liberation movements in the colonies, including potential revolts by military forces that the British had been careful to nurture; the internal psychological difficulty in maintaining the façade of a civilizing mission; and American pressure and American debt, it was clear that the second colonial empire was becoming a burden. The British saw the handwriting on the wall and decided to dismantle it while still playing a dirty divide-and-rule endgame to maintain influence in the post-colonial world before they would be forcibly thrown out, as the French and Portuguese were.

It is obvious that waves of European colonizers—Portuguese and Spanish followed by the French, British, Dutch, Russians, Germans, and Italians—punctuated by terrible wars such as the Spanish-English War (1588), the four Dutch-English wars (seventeenth and eighteenth centuries), the Seven Years French-British wars (1756–1763), Napoleonic wars (1800–1815), Crimean war (1953–1956), World War I (1914–1918), and World War II (1939–1945), all engaged in the above approach and strategy to one degree or another. They shared the same intentions, but they succeeded in differing degrees. In a larger sense, these European states had to balance their intense competition for colonies by the desire to not destroy one another. They succeeded in this until World War II. With hindsight, it is easy to predict this outcome.

Impact on Productive Outcomes

Around 1750, the inflow of surplus was twice the wealth (wealth, not SGS!) Britain was capable of producing internally and was fifteen times the internal SGS. One can imagine the impact on the American economy if it received $15 trillion of wealth inflow for supporting the lifestyle of the wealthy, fighting wars, investing in industry, and supporting science. Never in the history of civilization had this occurred before. This inflow of wealth was a result of private effort with state military support and was driven by commerce and not a desire to create an empire. A significant portion of this inflow was directed toward investment in manufacturing and technology.

Internally, Britain provided the legal framework (patent protection) and sanctity of contracts to unleash entrepreneurial energy. The government provided the protection of domestic industries through duties on imports. The natural setting provided mineral wealth (coal and iron) and navigable rivers for internal trade. Similarly, internal peace through the union of crowns provided political stability. The English Channel and British navy played roles in providing natural protection from European armies.

The result was a burst of technological breakthroughs in agriculture, textile, mining, metallurgy, chemical, glass, and paper making industries. This was accomplished through key inventions in energy and tools. The former involved moving from wood to coal and from water power to steam power, and the latter involved hundreds of innovations across all industries, including such key inventions as the spinning jenny, flying shuttle, and cotton gin for textiles; coal reverberatory furnaces that made higher quality metal production; deeper mines in mining and metallurgy; railroads in transportation; and more efficient processes to make key industrial materials, such as sulfuric acid, hydrochloric acid, alkalis, and cement. In the energy arena, the steam engine and a host of machine tools, such as the lathe, milling machines, and boring machines capable of making interchangeable parts needed to construct more complex machines, was the stuff of the first Industrial Revolution (or more accurately industrial evolution) headed by Great Britain.

Germany spearheaded the second industrial evolution in specialty chemicals, electrical, and optical technologies. The third industrial revolution was headed by United States through innovations in communications (telegraph), air travel (planes), nuclear energy, solid-state electronics, computers, biotechnology, and the internet.

The collective impact of three industrial revolutions was an order of magnitude greater productivity in the leading states of the European civilization. The process of continuous innovation had become self-sustaining both economically and culturally by the beginning of twentieth century. The European civilization and the worldwide states it spewed to far corners of the planet, of course, never acknowledged the indispensable role of wealth drain from Asia, Africa, and Americas in igniting this process of the Industrial Revolution. Today, even decades after end of colonial control, the productive outcomes per head in former colonies is an order of magnitude smaller than the ex-colonial powers. Such was the degree of wealth drain from coerced trade and the psychological damage inflicted through destruction of indigenous education systems by the colonial powers.

Transmission of Creativity

The burst of creativity from European civilization was truly astounding from a technological standpoint, noted above and in a later section about religion, science, philosophy, and art. Yet the phase was not without continuing transmission from other civilizations in the form of critical ideas that remain unacknowledged even today, particularly in popular consciousness.

Practical creativity: Chinese practical technology had already been incorporated into Europe in the previous phase through Muslim intermediaries.

Intellectual creativity: The European mind, as it liberated itself from Christian dogma but was still unwilling to let go of religion, was naturally attracted toward monism, such as Vedanta and philosophy in Gita.

Works of Confucius were also translated into European languages by Jesuit scholars, such as Matteo Ricci and Prospero Intorcetta. These translations had considerable impact on the philosophy of enlightenment including moral philosophy. In the field of economics, the concept of laissez-faire was in all likelihood inspired by the Chinese concept of Wu Wei. Wise men of eighteenth-century Europe, such as Frenchman Francois Quesnay and German Goethe, were widely believed to represent Confucius of Europe and Confucius of Weimar respectively.

The European civilization had absorbed the dynamism of Islam in science and technology in the previous phase. It is perhaps no exaggeration to state that Islamic science, technology, and cartography, which all represented a synthesis and development of the Indian, Greek, and Chinese achievements as we have noted in preceding chapters, helped transform Europe from an ignorant backwater into a powerful and dynamic continent. It has been observed that the 1671 translation of Ibn Tufail's work, *Philosophus Autodidactus* inspired the first English novel, *Robinson Crusoe*, Robert Boyle's *The Aspiring Naturalist*, Kipling's *Jungle Book,* and the story of Tarzan.

As we saw in the previous chapter, in contradistinction to the indirect route mediated by Islamic civilization through which Europe had acquired Indian trigonometry and decimal system, the newly discovered spice trade route led to a direct channel through which European civilization likely gained knowledge of fundamental concepts of calculus and science of the infinitesimal that lay sheltered in the only significant Hindu state, that of Vijayanagara. We must note that most European scholars do not naturally accept this view. Many of them continue to manipulate dates to prove a Eurocentric viewpoint of mathematic, using terms like Hindu mathematics, which imply that the mainstream mathematics is of European origin. That this statement is ridiculous is evident from such seminal Indian contributions as the decimal system, zero, trigonometry, algebra, and foundational concepts of science of the infinitesimal. It should be hardly surprising that a civilization that invented and developed comfort with the idea of zero on philosophical, epistemological, and mathematical grounds over nearly two millennia would be a natural to develop the science of infinitesimal. However, European scholars, having succeeded in the "fabrication of ancient Greece" (in Martin Bernal's words) by minimizing the impact of African, Semitic, and West Asian roots of Greek civilization, could hardly be expected to not use the methodology to knock off the achievements of other civilizations to the extent possible.

During the early seventeenth century, the infinite series of the *Yuktibhasa* (which was transmitted to Europe in the sixteenth century) began to appear in the works of European mathematicians, such as Cavalieri (1598–1647), Pascal (1623–1662), Fermat (1601–1665), Gregory (1638–1675), and Taylor (1685–1731), all of whom had access to Jesuit archives. Though this work played a central role in the developing calculus, even in the second half of the twentieth century, Eurocentric scholars such as Whiteside intentionally attempt to date the *Yuktibhasa* to the seventeenth century.

Impact on Institutional Structures and Processes

There was little that European civilization needed to learn from other civilizations with respect to institutional structures and processes. The rate of change fueled by the extraordinary transfer of wealth from the world over was so great that ancient static structures and processes of other civilizations seemed quaint compared to what was needed to manage the changing face of society. European civilization had to conceive new structures in the political system (democracy, separation of powers, and free press), military capability (military doctrine, strategy, unified command structures, and better tactics), economic organization (free markets for not just credit and products but also labor and equity), legal structures (independent judiciary), dynamic social structure, and educational (universal education to high school) and knowledge-creating (universities, industrial labs, and government sponsorship of research) structures.

Differing Strategies Employed in the New World Colonies

Earlier, we noted the fourfold strategy the British employed to extract surplus from different parts of the world. Below, we briefly describe how European states differed in their strategy to control the New World or sparsely populated regions at an earlier stage of development.

As we noted before, the Spanish, Portuguese, French, Dutch, and British competed for control of the Americas and Australia. Broadly, this three-century-long struggle resulted in British supremacy in North America (except present-day Mexico) and Australia and Spanish and Portuguese supremacy in South America. In the mid-eighteenth century, the French controlled perhaps a third of North America, only to lose it through defeats and sale. A second French Empire followed in Africa and Southeast Asia. We also described how these European colonies struggled to gain freedom from their European masters.

In the present-day United States and Canada, where the British ultimately succeeded against the French and the Spanish, the British policy consisted of wars, broken treaties, slavery, displacement to reservations, and deliberately spreading disease to decimate the population (British supplying small pox-infested blankets to the natives as an example) while avoiding intermarriage and religious conversions. The response of the natives began with naïve welcome to armed struggle to resignation against an overwhelmingly superior force. The native populations mostly retreated to reservations in the West, and the United States belatedly agreed to provide special rights and limited autonomy to Native Americans. The British approach to colonization was family centered and resulted in smaller colonies, large plantations, and corporate structures that ultimately grew first into small states and a federal form of government, either formally under the British Crown or as independent states. The aim was to take control of the land and extract the surplus through production and trading commodities while keeping the colonies dependent on the mother country for as long as possible.

The Spanish and Portuguese in Mexico and central and South America followed a somewhat different approach, reflecting their differing beliefs and institutions. It resembled an imperial attack employing large institutions, bureaucracy including a legal system to regulate native labor, military power, an emphasis on religious conversions, and intermarriage. It was an approach based on state and church rather than a family-based approach. The response of the natives was armed struggle followed generally by the emergence of a sizable Christian Mestizo population in several regions (either natives and European or African slaves and European) with an identity entirely distinct from the colonizing countries. However, even today, this mixed population is often at an economic and political disadvantage. The ultimate objective of the aggressor was not different; only the approach was different in part because of an abundant supply of gold and precious metals of significance in trade.

The case of Australia provides a still different perspective. The native population numbered only in hundreds of thousands and was at an even earlier stage of development compared to the native populations in North and South America. The climate and terrain were more hostile. There was indeed violence against the aboriginals, who were unable to put up any kind of armed struggle; however. later their helplessness also created both sympathy for them, mostly through Catholic Church organizations, and a policy of assimilation motivated by a racist policy to "eliminate the full-blood and permit the white admixture to half-castes and eventually the race will become white" executed through the policy of removing children from parents well into the second half of twentieth century. Thus, Australia's location and low indigenous population made it ideal as a penal colony of the British Empire since English prisons were overcrowded and a new continental-size, unabashedly Anglo-Saxon-only state was built by the convict labor with little knowledge of family history.

Never in the history of civilization had a civilization brought so much misery to so many through instruments of violent colonization, coerced trade, and systematic wealth drain. The potential loss of direct and indirect lives, if tabulated, must amount to hundreds of millions of lives through extended military conflicts and global wars, famines, slavery, and inflicted poverty in North America, South America, Africa, Australia, India, China, and Southeast Asia. The most remarkable thing, however, is that, the European civilization continues to believe that it has had a civilizing impact on the world. Perhaps it should bother to ask those affected.

We hope that above brief description gives reader an appreciation of the uniqueness of violence unleashed by five small European states during the last half a millennium.

17.9 Productive Outcomes

Wealth creation: Never before in the history of civilization did all that is required to create wealth come together in one civilization. The European civilization controlled more than half the land mass directly and most of the rest indirectly. It had technology developed using principles of science. Its capital formation process got an unbelievable boost through controlling trade and systematic wealth drain from all other civilizations. Its population multiplied dramatically, and its labor pool was further enhanced by the cruel slavery system and indentured labor from other civilizations. Because of breakthroughs in technology and science, most states within the European civilization created excellent infrastructure and developed labor, product, and capital markets. As a result of the confluence of events, productivity in at least the leading-edge state increased at a steady rate, and by the end of the nineteenth century, it had surpassed all other civilizations by a wide margin. European civilization by 1950 had become more productive compared to Indian, Chinese, and Muslim civilizations by anywhere between one and two orders of magnitude. Japan was the only exception, as if to prove the rule because it had escaped colonial control.

A word is also in order about European states that did not play the colonizing game. These states in eastern and central Europe achieved comparable but not the same or higher wealth creation capability without an empire. We have argued that wealth drain from other lands made the colonizing states wealthy. How do we explain the comparable wealth creation capability in these states without an empire? The answer is their sustained political independence, the inevitable diffusion of existing science and technology, relatively insignificant outlays on a blue-water navy, and the absence of wealth drain from these countries. Much as Japan achieved comparable wealth creation capability between 1867 and 1905, or in a mere generation, starting from a lower base, the countries of central and eastern Europe, once they settled their political differences, achieved similar results in the eighteenth and nineteenth centuries. Given already developed technology and SPI and the absence of a history of colonial exploitation, it is normal for a lagging state to approach the wealth creation capability of states that are leaders in both science and exploiting others within a mere generation. In the second half of the twentieth century, this phenomenon has been again repeated numerous times in East Asia.

Fair trade: The words "fair trade" became a joke at the hands of the leading states of European civilization. Never had the world witnessed such shameful and exploitative control of world trade by a few colluding states of one civilization. And this control was achieved through military might, the resulting control of the high seas, and starving the traditional land-based trade routes by circumscribing the Ottoman Empire.

Migrations and Travel Out: Again, never had world witnessed the migrations to new lands and travels to the known world to the degree that European civilization engaged it. However, given the state of transportation technology and control of the high seas, this was completely understandable. Europeans settled North and South America and Australia, and they traveled to Asia and Africa in large numbers. At the peak, nearly two hundred thousand British had made India their temporary homes and were engaged mostly in administrative functions.

17.10 Creative Outcomes

As indicated earlier, we shall not detail the achievements of European civilization since the reader can safely assume they equal the state of civilization today, less what existed at the start of the phase and the rather modest contributions from Indian and Chinese civilizations resulting in part from the interaction with European learning. Nevertheless, a summary follows.

Achievements in Practical Creativity

It is indeed difficult to summarize the state of European technology that existed at the end of the twentieth century in a few paragraphs. During the current phase, scientific knowledge was used for the first time to develop and optimize technology itself. This not only made it more efficient to develop technology but also made the process of developing technology quicker and more scientific than merely experimental approach of trial and error. Thus during the current phase, the following significant technologies were developed in the rough chronological order: steam power technology, Transport technologies (railroads, steam navigation, the internal combustion engine, and the automobile), chemical technologies, electrical technologies (light bulb, electrical motor), agricultural technologies (tractor, planter, transplanter, chemical fertilizers, pesticides, harvester, and genetically modified seeds), communication technologies (telegraph, telephone), electronics technologies (television), advanced transport technologies (automobile, aviation, and superhighways), nuclear technology (nuclear power), computer technology (hardware and software), biotechnology, internet technology (optical fiber, cable, and radar). These technologies required inventing a host of materials and processes. Several technologies were combined to not only create weapons systems of awful destructive power (tanks, automatic weapons, missiles, submarines, fighter planes, aircraft carriers, and fission and fusion bombs) but also to develop an array of household machines that increased creature comforts (washing machines, air-conditioning, refrigeration, elevators, sound systems, and security systems) and reduced drudgery.

Achievements in Religious Creativity

Christianity remained in the crosshairs of science throughout the phase. Until perhaps the seventeenth century, some scientists (such as Newton, using differential calculus to prove the biblical assertion that the earth was created in 4004 BCE!) used science to promote Christianity and several philosophers linked Christianity to philosophical idealism (see philosophical creativity below). The breakthroughs in geology (age of the earth), materialism promoted by Marx and Engels, Darwin's theory of evolution suggesting a natural evolution of life rather than a creation by God, and theories of the evolution of the universe undercut Christian metaphysics in particular and the monotheism project in general. By the twentieth century, the intelligentsia no longer believed in Christian dogma, though a significant fraction of masses continued to, making them useful allies in conservative political parties.

The spectacular failure of monotheism in the face of science resulted in the spiritual impulse to be directed toward atheism, agnosticism, and Indian monism.

However, atheism did not take root since science has only addressed the issue of evolution of the universe, Earth, and life but not the question of why they exist, and atheism, which was originally based on the now-defunct assumption of a steady-state universe, hardly answered the question of why. The attraction toward Indian monism, with its concepts of unity of Atman-Brahman, reincarnation, and the law of karma seemed to fit better with the ideas of evolution. Thus, the birth of the Theosophical Society in India by British spiritualists may be understood as a reaction to the demise of Christian doctrine and an insistence that man must presume the primacy of consciousness over matter, even though science has insisted that consciousness arose out of the structure of matter at a given stage in its evolution. The more modern European man has realized that all religious beliefs are psychological assertions first and foremost, the more he has realized that monotheism and monism are the two sides of the same coin: the former believes that God is everything and man is nothing, there is one life, and a judgment day, and the latter believes man is everything. The latter believes there are potentially infinite lives and man must become God through his own effort. Agnosticism and its clearest expression, the thought of Buddha (not historical Buddhism), has also found adherents in the bosom of European civilization, though the numbers are hardly impressive. However, it seems to us that as monotheism and monism destroy credibility in monotheism and monism, European civilization in the coming decades will rediscover agnosticism.

Achievements in Philosophical Creativity

Metaphysics: The critical figures of European civilization relative to metaphysics, from our perspective, are Emanuel Kant (1724–1804) G. W. Hegel (1770–1831), several existentialists (Kierkegaard, Sartre, and Nietzsche), and Ludwig Wittgenstein (1889–1951). Kant's philosophy suggested that belief in a universal God is a practical necessity to be happy and live a moral life whereas Hegel postulated the existence of an absolute idea that first alienates into nature and then finds itself in the human mind (!). Only Wittgenstein clearly stated that all metaphysical statements are nonsensical, thus rediscovering Buddhist thought after 2,500 years. Thus, Kant was reluctant and modest, Hegel was pompous and nonsensical, and Wittgenstein was clear and bold.

Disenchantment with idealism and the rejection of materialism and Christian dogma led to the rise of Existentialist philosophy, with a focus on thinking, feeling, and living individual, thus reversing Plato's and Hegel's precedence of the essence over existence and a realization that life has no meaning other than what we choose to give it. For European civilization, it was momentous break from the unverifiable assumptions of monotheism and Christian dogma. However, it fell short of agnosticism since it failed to realize the importance of compassion toward other beings, thus leading the individual in the abyss of despair and angst while rescuing him from philosophical idealism. It is easy to see how existential metaphysics led to the nihilism of Nietzsche since it only points to human suffering without suggesting a solution. Interestingly while campaigning against morality, he thought of Buddhism as a successful religion since it fostered critical thought!

Thus, the main evolution of European metaphysics during the phase is from Christian dogma to a universal God to philosophical idealism to materialism to analytical philosophy (middle ground between idealism) to existentialism to nihilism to its utter rejection in positivism that rejects metaphysics—quite a smorgasbord and good enough for every palate except agnosticism.

Epistemology: If, in metaphysics, the key question is the primacy of matter versus spirit, the key questions in epistemology, on the other hand, are is knowledge possible and how does it come about? Much like the majority of philosophers over the ages, during the current phase European philosophers affirmed the possibility of knowledge of the world but differed on the process that results in knowledge. Below, we trace its tortuous development during the phase.

Modern European epistemology starts with Descartes and French Rationalism by paying woefully insufficient attention to or perhaps as a reaction to earlier thirteenth-century British empiricists such as John Scotus Dunn and Roger Bacon. Scotus Dunn had already dared to wonder if matter could think, and Bacon had inherited the spirit of the Arab-Persian experimental method. But French Rationalism of the seventeenth century brushed aside the nascent British materialism of the thirteenth century.

Rene Descartes (1596–659) based his epistemology on a firm belief in the power of logical deduction, which in turn was grounded in the only certainty he felt: "I think, therefore I am." Equally firmly, he doubted the ability of sense perceptions to provide true knowledge. Induction played little explicit role in his theory of knowledge despite that his founding principle of "I think, therefore I am" emerged from inductive reasoning. It is also interesting to note that Descartes, a physicist, successfully furthered the concepts of quantity of motion, also called momentum, and rate of momentum transfer, also called force. Muslim scientists originally formulated these concepts centuries earlier and could only have been further developed based on unconscious induction and conscious perception. The great French Rationalist severely underestimated the role of both perception and induction in epistemology, focusing mostly on deduction.

The next great figure, British empiricist David Hume (1711–1776), was very familiar with Descartes's work. Yet he came to the opposite conclusion. He believed that sense perception is all we can really trust as a means of knowledge. Furthermore, while he tolerated induction as a method since induction could be experience-based, he detested deduction, which he felt could not lead to any real knowledge. He believed that the mind that erroneously provides the connection between two events we observe and has no justification for linking the cause and effect. Thus, his epistemology focused on perception and blamed the tendency of mind to provide a causal connection when none is justified. In effect, he believed in no epistemology.

Immanuel Kant (1724–1804), a German and a pivotal figure, was deeply bothered by the destruction caused by Hume's stinging analysis of epistemology. Kant started out by making a distinction between analytic (all bachelors are unmarried) and synthetic (all bachelors are fools) propositions. He further distinguished between a priori (prior to experience) and posteriori (after experience) propositions. In his scheme, an analytic a priori proposition is same as deduction, and a synthetic posteriori proposition is identical to sense perception (this tree is green). Analytic posteriori statements by definition do not exist. This leaves the a priori synthetic propositions that Kant made pivotal in his epistemology. He believed that knowledge is possible because of the knowledge inherent or "a priori" in the very structure of the human mind! Thus, Kant, in addition to perception and deduction, introduces a third element to epistemology, the structure of the mind itself. He ignored the power of induction based on perception, deduction, and imagination.

An example of a priori synthetic proposition is the sum of the three angles of a triangle is 180 degrees. In this example, Kant seems to not have realized that the axioms of geometry from which the statement is derived, in turn, had to be based on sense perceptions, imagination, and deductive resulting in abstractions concerning the nature of space. This process of abstraction is nothing other than induction or inductive reasoning. Since Kant believed that knowledge is inherent in the mind, particularly of space and time, defined the process of knowing, he underestimated the value of induction and had to come to a sorry conclusion that the thing-in-itself or the essence of the object under study was unknowable. Note that knowledge of the object at a given time is necessarily imperfect, but it is possible to progressively improve it. However, according to Kant, the thing-in-itself was not knowable, now or ever. He was forced into this position because he could only convince himself that the mind only had a priori knowledge of space and time but not of the specific objects in the universe!

Of course, today we know that the axioms of geometry were based on the implicit assumption of a linear space. In reality, because of the presence of matter, space curves, thus disproving Kant's belief concerning inherent knowledge of space in the human mind. Kant also believed space and time to be independent, a proposition that has also not stood the test of time in the twentieth century. These examples clearly show the absence of inherent accurate knowledge concerning space and time in the human mind. What they show is that the human mind has inherent powers of perception, imagination, and reason (inductive and deductive) that may be employed to produce progressively better knowledge of natural or social phenomena.

As an aside, Kant's reluctance concerning the possibility of knowledge through the union of reason and observation or his formulation of the concept of the thing-in-itself is not too far from the conclusion reached by the great eighth-century Indian philosopher Sankara, who claimed that senses and reason cannot reveal external reality, but a reality transformed by our senses, a reality distorted by space and time. Of course, Sankara, being a monist, also proposed an alternate solution: intuition and meditation, and thankfully Kant stayed away from that.

The next great figure was **Fredrick Hegel (1770–1831)**. He totally disagreed with Kant, stating that it is better to say that the object has a soul than being the unknowable thing-in-itself that Kant had postulated. However, Hegel was an idealist, a Christian philosopher. He believed that God's desire for self-actualization resulted in an Absolute Idea that self-alienates and appears as nature, and the unfolding of this self-alienated Absolute Idea as nature creates consciousness through an unending cycle of thesis, antithesis, and synthesis. The further unfolding through a similar cycle of thesis, antithesis, and synthesis is how the mind or rational self-consciousness evolves and comes to possess complete knowledge of the object of interest. Hegel described this developmental process in great detail through the concepts of contradiction, the unity of opposites, the law of qualitative change, and negation of negation. Hegel's process simultaneously described the unfolding of nature, society, consciousness, and knowledge the latter possesses through the unfolding of the Absolute Idea in idealistic and religious terms since he believed in the primacy of spirit versus matter. Of course, Hegel had absolutely nothing concrete to say about this Absolute Idea. Hegel expressed his idealism in his famous statement: all that is real is rational, and all that is rational is real. Perception had little role in Hegel epistemology.

Karl Marx (1818–1883) inverted the idealist epistemological portion of the Hegelian system to create an epistemology that focused on the fusion of sense perception, induction, deduction, and imagination to create verifiable knowledge in both natural and social realms.

Significant contributions also came from Austrian philosopher **Carl Popper (1902–1994)**, who correctly insisted on the falsifiability of a scientific theory to be an essential and therefore a key element of epistemology. Popper introduced the idea of humility in epistemology that Descartes and Hegel sorely lacked.

To summarize, Descartes ignored the role of perception and induction, thus ignoring earlier British empiricists; David Hume disagreed with Descartes for ignoring the role of deduction and underestimating the role of induction; Kant disagreed with Hume and imagined knowledge to actually reside in the human mind rather than the mind being an instrument of knowledge; Hegel undermined the role of perception, and for him knowledge was a purely mental phenomenon fully capable of producing knowledge through unfolding of the Absolute Idea. Finally, Marx had to turn Hegel on his head and bring him back to real world so to speak; and Popper injected a much-needed dose of humility into Western epistemology.

With hindsight, of course, the whole three-hundred-year project handled by towering intellects looks rather ridiculous and reflects the softening conflict between science and monotheistic Christianity. Because the European civilization held other civilizations in contempt during this period, there was little possibility of corrective action from other civilizations. For example, Visheka or Buddhist epistemologies developed respectively over two one and a half millennia ago, and if available and studied could have shortened the entire process.

Less than a generation after Hegel died, Darwin proposed his theory of evolution, creating an alternative to the divine origin of man. Through biological evolution, we are given inherent powers of perception, imagination, and reason. The first two nearly fully developed and the third requiring substantial development through social evolution. With sense perception, imagination, induction, deduction, experimental, or what is in effect controlled perception, and Popper's humility at our command, the remarkable end product of European epistemology may be stated as follows:

1. The senses perceive data from the external world directly or through instruments with an inherent possibility of error. Properly designed experiments can reduced this error considerably.
2. The desire to go from sense data to develop generalized knowledge, that is going from particular to universal, from concrete to abstract or from specific to general, requires the mind to develop a hypothesis to explain the sense data. This sometimes semiconscious process using sense data, imagination, and deductive reasoning is termed *induction*.
3. The hypothesis thus developed must have the property of falsifiability, i.e., it must contain the possibility of being disproved. Thus, there is no a priori guaranty that induction will lead to a correct hypothesis.
4. Deductive reasoning is now applied to the hypothesis to predict new phenomenon or new conclusions from the hypothesis.
5. More sense data are now collected in an attempt to prove or falsify the hypothesis by verifying the predicted new phenomenon or new conclusions.
6. The acceptable hypothesis is the one that continues to survive attempts at falsification and is successful in predicting new phenomenon and new conclusions.
7. The whole process is repeated as many times as needed to reduce the error to the desired level, with each step producing an improved hypothesis.

In this scheme, all knowledge is relative and gets progressively better. Humans cannot be the heirs to perfect knowledge because we are not gods. This is even true of a formal science like mathematics, as Kurt Gödel (see below) proved through his incompleteness theorem in 1931. The bottom line is European civilization arrived at the correct epistemology through a tortuous path because of its Christian roots.

Ethics: Theories of ethics can be centered on the individual or society. In the former, they may be driven by character, intention, or result, and in the latter, they are always driven by result. The classical theory of virtue in European civilization was based on desired virtues such as wisdom, courage, or honesty in the character of an individual. Such theories were entirely consistent with the Buddhist approach to ethics. This approach, in effect, said to decide what is right and follow it.

During the current phase, several new theories of ethics were proposed, the most important being deontological, Utilitarian, and pragmatic. The most important proponent of the deontological theory of ethics was Immanuel Kant, who argued that morality means actions based on duty that has the capacity to become a universal law without contradiction, thus arguing that it is not the consequences but intention that is critical. Following such duty, whose essential component is goodwill, will lead to freedom. The most important proponent of the Utilitarian theory of ethics was John Stuart Mill, who measured the appropriateness of an action based on the happiness it gave to the parties concerned. It is easy to see how this theory can condone unethical behavior: if murder gives greater happiness to the murderer than pain to the murder, then murder is ethical! The most important proponent of the pragmatic theory of ethics is that John Dewey focused on the impact on society, not individuals, for he believed all action is social and moral criteria is not unchanging though it is more or less objective in a given situation or period.

Clearly there is a greater deal of overlap among the character-based (assuming character is not anti-social), deontological (if the intention is translatable to a universal law), and utilitarian (if correct assessment is made of the net impact of an action) theories of ethics. One is reminded of the parable of the elephant and six blind men.

Aesthetics: There is an interesting parallel between theories of ethics and aesthetics developed by European civilization with little agreement among the key thinkers. For Alexander Baumgarten, aesthetics may be defined as the science of sense experience. For Kant, aesthetic is entirely subjective and relates to an internal feeling of pleasure. Friedrich Schiller saw aesthetic appreciation as the most perfect reconciliation of the powers of observation and reason. Hegel, in a typical Hegelian manner, saw aesthetic experience as the result of the union of absolute spirit and senses and is therefore objective, not subjective. Still further, Arthur Schopenhauer saw aesthetic experience as intellectual without the bounds of will. Anthony Ashley-Cooper saw beauty as a sensory equivalent of morality. Ludwig Wittgenstein was perhaps the most honest in that he could not describe what is beautiful. Most interestingly, William Hogarth saw beauty as unity of design, variety, symmetry, simplicity, intricacy, and magnitude. However, such a description of aesthetics is too analytical and too modest for most European philosophers.

It is, however, perfectly understandable that despite centuries of concentrated effort, theories of ethics and aesthetics leave a lot to be desired. European philosophy has been has been most successful in epistemology and least in metaphysics, with ethics and aesthetic lying in between.

Achievements in Art

The current phase was perhaps the most significant period in the art history of European civilization since the Greek period, because of the changing socioeconomic conditions (control of global trade, devolution of political power from monarchy, and industrial revolution), changing intellectual climate (science, religion, and critical philosophy), the internal dynamics of the art itself, and because Renaissance art was mostly a discovery and celebration of classical Greek art.

Visual arts: The visual arts of painting, sculpture, and architecture went through several periods: Mannerism, Baroque, Rococo, Neoclassical, Romantic, Realism, Impressionism, Modern, and Contemporary, with painting exhibiting these periods in greater clarity.

Mannerism (early seventeenth century) was a reaction to the perfection in art from the Renaissance period and may be said to be driven by the internal dynamics of the art itself. The baroque period (early seventeenth century to mid eighteenth century), on the other hand, was a reaction of the monarchy and the Catholic Church against the Protestant Reformation, and the art was gaudy, sentimental, and emphasized grandeur. Rococo (mid-eighteenth century) in turn was a reaction to the excesses of the baroque period and was lighter and not overbearing and often employed asymmetrical representation. It continued to be elaborate, like the baroque period, and excelled in aesthetics without conveying a deeper meaning. The neoclassicism period was a reaction to the continued elaborate and empty nature of rococo art. It drew inspiration from the Renaissance and Greek art and represented the reaction to emerging science and critical philosophy. The importance of simplicity and symmetry came roaring back and had a strong political element to its themes of war and bravery. If the period of neoclassicism was a response to objectivity inherent in eighteenth-century science and critical philosophy. The romanticism period (late eighteenth century to the mid-nineteenth century) rebelled against such objectivity and instead emphasized the subjective, the emotional and the individual. The next period of realism (nineteenth century) in art was supportive of the romantic themes but was also influenced by the poverty and suffering resulting from industrial revolution. The periods of impressionism (creative use of light not possible for a camera), post-impressionism (use of dots in painting), and fauvism (use of exaggerated strokes in painting) all represent a reaction to the invention of photography in the early nineteenth century. Thus, until the nineteenth century, European art was primary representational or expressive. In the twentieth century, with the rise of relativity and nuclear physics, art experimented with cubism or emphasizing the relativity of perception through multiple views of an object superimposed on one other. Freeform modern art that was not representational, and expressive forms of art free from political, religious and philosophical constraints followed. The high point of modern art is abstract art that uses form and color to create engaging art based purely on imagination. Abstract art includes geometric abstract art, abstract expressionism, and lyrical abstract art, among others. Finally, contemporary art is irreverent, mixes high and low art, is full of humor and irony, and abhors any absolutism.

European art at the end of the twentieth century may justly claim that it has freed itself of history.

Music: Achievements in European music paralleled those of visual arts. The music of the baroque period was nothing if not grandeur, thus voice gave in to boisterous instruments, and major forms of European music, such as the sonata and concerto were defined. Though mostly instrumental and written with layered polyphony, baroque music continued to encourage improvisation and produced great composers, such as Johann Bach (1685–1750) and George Handel (1685–1759). The classical period (1750–1820) was a reaction to breakthroughs in science and critical philosophy, and music responded through a greater emphasis on structure and clarity and produced melodic music with subordinated harmony. Thus, classical music was, unlike baroque music, harmonious and highly structured and allowed little improvisation.

The classical period produced Joseph Haydn (1732–1809), Wolfgang Mozart (1756–1791), and Ludwig Beethoven (1770–1827). The classical period was followed by the romantic period (1810–1900), which was a modest reaction to the order and structure of the classical European music and was highly expressive and emotional. The support of the growing middle class assured not only the independence of the composers from wealthy patrons but also created an industry in music education. Piano saw great advances in part because of metallurgy and became very popular. The famous composers of the period were Fredric Chopin (1810–1849), Johannes Brahms (1833–1897), Poytr Tchaikovsky (1840–1893), Giuseppe Verdi (1813–1901), and Richard Wagner (1813–1883). Composers like Handel, Mozart, Verdi, and Wagner also wrote music for operas.

Contemporary European music, much like contemporary European art, is relatively free of history and experiment and is responsive to popular culture. It is primarily a result of the fusion of European and African music traditions. Just as photography impacted painting in the nineteenth century, radio and other recording technologies impacted music in the twentieth century, making music portable. Twentieth-century music includes blues (African-American tradition), jazz (fusion of African and European music), rock 'n roll (based on blues, jazz, and classical music), disco music (a reaction to rock 'n roll), and hip-hop music, which originated as an improvisation to existing popular music by disk jockeys.

Drama: The rebirth of European theater coincided with the restoration of monarchy in England, Scotland, and Ireland in 1660, where it narrowly escaped the sanction of the puritans who wanted no theater. The fear of the plague also played a role in the English renaissance in theater since the city of London shut down theaters in city for fear of spreading plague, and as a result, permanent theater buildings were constructed outside the city of London. If creativity in music was essentially a German enterprise, the rebirth of theater was largely English phenomenon. And it began as raucous, explicit sexual comedy as if to taunt the puritans and actually became more gaudy, elaborate, and spectacular. It often had elements of opera with the role of music often being secondary and borrowed from the more elegant French opera next door. The gaudy, raucous nature of theater of this period parallels the grandeur of the baroque period. The neoclassical period followed in visual arts and music and reflected the order and structure demanded by the enlightenment period while still continuing to reflect the grandeur. The themes had, however, toned down: comedy was no longer sexual but political. The period also saw censorship of theater in England. The objective, organized nature of theater changed again in the romantic period, when the emphasis shifted to the inner emotional life and individual in part a reaction to the Industrial Revolution and rising middle class. However, unlike visual arts and music, the romantic period in theater was tempered by the naturalism movement that drew inspiration from Darwin's theory of evolution. The theater became melodramatic, and its center moved to Germany. Theater in the late nineteenth century and early twentieth century reflected the taste of the middle class through the popularity of musical comedy.

European theater in the twentieth century has not only retained naturalism and realism but has also began to reflect the essential degeneration or loss of moral values in European civilization because of the slow but sustained of loss of religious faith without a compensatory development, loss of meaning, and a long history of cruelty through colonialism and racism. The trend in realism gave rise to epic theater, where the goal was to make the audience was fully aware that it was watching a play, unlike the romantic period where the audience was encouraged to fantasize.

The loss of the meaning of life and the emergence of the philosophy of existentialism gave rise to the theater of the absurd and the philosophy of nihilism, whose chief proponent was Nietzsche. That gave rise to the theater of cruelty, and its chief proponent was Artuad, who believed it to be the essence of life and used the theater of cruelty to create the experience of cruelty and brutality and the "thrill" associated with it. Finally, the twentieth century also witnessed experimental theater, which attempted to soften the distinction between the audience and the actors.

Dance: If Germany dominated the art of music and England dominated (to a lesser degree) the art of theater, France and, to a lesser degree, Italy dominated the early development of the art of dance during the current phase. Early dance forms, such as volte, became more elaborate and developed into baroque dances including the courante, tambourine, and forlana in the seventeenth century. Simultaneously, ballet moved from Italy to France and became the court dance under Louis the XIV, who was himself a dancer. In England, more informal folk dancing, including cushion dance and the hunting fox, were popular. By the eighteenth century, ballet had moved out of French court and had become established as an art form in Paris. It was appreciated by the rising middle class, and folk dancing became more popular, indicating increasing urbanization and a softer distinction between the big cities and villages. In the nineteenth century, dance became much more complex, with further development of volte into waltz, polka, and quadrille. These dance forms continued to penetrate the lower classes. Puritan England frowned upon the waltz as it required physical closeness.

In the twentieth century, concert ballet continued to develop in neoclassical, post-structural, and contemporary, and the couples dancing came under strong African and Latin influence, creating many fusion dances, such as jazz, cha-cha, tango, swing, tap dancing, and the fox-trot, to name a few. Dance education, including ballet, under the middle and lower classes continued to expand.

Thus, European nobility expropriated the dance of the lower classes, refined it, and gradually returned it to the middle and lower classes during the current phase. Like visual arts and music, European dance in the twentieth century became relatively free of history and tradition and became more experimental, willing to absorb foreign elements.

Literature—fiction: The world of literature in Europe around 1500 CE consisted primarily of epic and religious poems, as we noted in the previous chapter. Although other cultures had invented the novel and sophisticated plays, it was mostly absent from European literary tradition. The first to separate from epic poetry was play writing, with Shakespeare (1564–1616) as the outstanding example. Poetry was also impacted by the new understanding of nature through science and attempted to examine the origin of the phenomenon of love or religion through poems. It had a decidedly intellectual and not religious air about it. Simultaneously, John Milton (1608–1674) wrote the last great epic poem *Paradise Lost,* recounting the biblical dogma. The considerably older but underdeveloped short story writing tradition, such as the *Canterbury Tales,* a "novelty" in epic poem writing style, gave rise to the novel. The first novel appeared in the early seventeenth century. Thus, the literature of the baroque period was decidedly anything but baroque as it moved away from the pompousness of epic poems, religion, and tradition, with *Paradise Lost* being an exception and last hurrah. The experimental and investigative trend in literature was fueled further by critical philosophy during the age of enlightenment in the eighteenth century. Writers explored individual and social themes of changing fortunes, political satire, and declining superstition in European culture as it absorbed the teachings of science and critical philosophy.

With the nineteenth century, literature also entered the period of romanticism when the emphasis shifted from social analysis to the inner life of the individual. This was clearly visible in the Russian novel (Tolstoy and Dostoevsky), Russian and German (Goethe) poetry, as well as the incorporation of existentialism into literary works by Soren Kierkegaard.

Much like the rest of the art of European civilization, literature also began moving away from the emphasis on the emotional and subject to realism or a happy medium between the objectivity of enlightenment and the subjectivity of the romantic periods. In addition, much like other art forms, European literature of the twentieth century began reflecting the loss of certainty and meaning through cubism, surrealism, expression, and symbolism during the modern period up to World War II. The postmodern literature embodied science fiction, storyline fragmentation, examination of the states of the inner world, exploring the devices of fiction to expose its illusion, and a self-conscious satire of previous literary works, purposely combining the pieces of previous works in a disorganized manner. The post-modern literature of European civilization, like all of its art, is experimental, free of history and tradition, and open to fusion with the world's other literary traditions. The technology of printing and advent of electronic publishing has expanded the reach of literature dramatically.

In in short, European art went through the following periods:

- A baroque period characterized by pompousness and grandeur
- A neoclassical period that was characterized by simplicity
- An enlightenment period characterized by a focus on the objective
- A romantic period characterized by a focus on the subjective
- A modern period characterized by the loss of the meaning of life
- A post-modern period characterized by freedom and experimentation that sometimes border on the irrational during the current phase

It is indeed easy to see how European art during the phase has, on the one hand, responded to a breakthrough in philosophy and science and the breakdown of Christian dogma and on the other hand, moved from being the domain of the nobility to something created by the common man for the common man, in line with both the devolution and delusion of political power from monarchy to the common man.

17.11 Achievements in Science

Achievements in Formal Sciences

The history of mathematics across civilizations may be understood as three related developments: an ongoing development of numerals and number theory; the invention of seemingly independent branches, such as logic, geometry, algebra, trigonometry, and calculus; and the creeping realization that these separate branches are in fact different aspects of the number theory. During the current phase, European civilization not only developed new branches of mathematics based on earlier breakthroughs but also began the process of integrating these branches and its limits.

Coordinate geometry: Coordinate geometry is the marriage between algebra and geometry and was the earliest indication that geometry could indeed be related to number theory. Building on many earlier foundations stretching many hundreds of years, Rene Descartes (1596–1650) succeeded in giving the ideal a consistent basis. This was the first great breakthrough of European mathematic in the current phase. Using coordinate geometry, Euler developed the graph theory in the eighteenth century.

Probability theory: Blaise Pascal (1623–1662) and Pierre Fermat (1601–1665) laid the foundations of probability theory through combinatorics in gambling context. The theory matured from a focus on a discrete event to continuous variables. In 1933, Andrey Kolmogorov used ideas of sample space and measure theory to reformulate the probability theory on an axiomatic basis.

Calculus: The idea of the infinitesimal dates back to Aryabhata, Bhaskara, and Madhva in the Indian civilization and has a long pedigree in the European civilization, including Isaac Newton's teacher, John Barrow. Both Newton and Leibniz are thought to have independently invented calculus, and we have addressed the issue of transmission of Madhva's work on infinite series being transmitted to Europe by the Portuguese in the sixteenth century. It is uncertain what role it played in the formulation of calculus in the seventeenth century. Leibniz is especially remembered for its notation in calculus, considering how unattractive Newton's notation was. Surprisingly, calculus was not put on a rigorous basis until toward the nineteenth century through efforts of Augustine-Louis Cauchy (1789–1857), Bernhard Riemann (1826–1866), and Karl Weierstrass (1815–1897). In the twentieth century, calculus was extended to processes with stochastic or random behavior.

Functional analysis: The eighteenth century saw an explosion of functional analysis after the invention of coordinate geometry. Geometry and calculus had become established fields. The concept of a complex variable integrated the fields of algebra and trigonometry, yielding the beautiful Euler's identity. Lagrange developed the calculus of variations to find the maxima and minima of functions. Taylor popularized the Madhava series to represent a function through infinite series. Pierre Laplace (1749–1827) developed the Laplace transform, which essentially converted a differential equation into an algebraic equation to solve differential equations. The theory of complex discrete and continuous dynamical systems was developed, including the Chaos Theory, when the system behavior is highly dependent on initial conditions. Rene Thom (1923–2002) extended the analysis of complex dynamic systems where the stability may disappear, making it impossible to use traditional calculus. However, when such an occurrence is looked at in a larger context, such instability is related to the underlying geometrical structure, making analysis of complex unstable dynamic systems possible. Finally, the functional analysis was extended to the stochastic systems. Interestingly, Robinson brought back the notion of the infinitesimal championed by Newton and Leibniz and abandoned by mathematician for three centuries under philosophical criticism based on their nonexistence. Thus, the notion of continuous change went through an infinite series of Madhava to the infinitesimal of Newton and Leibniz to the limit theorem of Cauchy and back to infinitesimal based on hyper real numbers

Arithmetic and number theory: Simon Stevin (1585) developed the decimal notation capable of describing rational and irrational numbers. Combining with Indian numeral system, this created a method to describe any number in shorthand for the first time in history. Euler (1707–1783) established notation for complex numbers and the ratio of circumference for the diameter for a circle. Euler also clarified the distinction between algebraic numbers and transcendental numbers (all transcendental numbers are irrational, but all irrational numbers are not transcendental) and proved that numbers such as e and π are transcendental. Joseph Lagrange (1736–1813) made several contributions to number theory, including the four-square theorem, which states that any natural number or integer can be expressed as sum of four integer squares. Gauss proved the fundamental theorem of arithmetic (any integer greater than one is either a prime number or is product of prime numbers) using modular arithmetic, first developed by Euler. Gauss (1777–1855) proved the asymptotic distribution of prime numbers. Finally, toward the end of the nineteenth century, Georg Cantor proved that all infinite sets of numbers (integers, rational, and irrational) are not equal, thereby creating the theory of infinite sets.

Algebra: While calculus and number theory dominated eighteenth-century mathematics, the nineteenth century was truly a century of algebra, which focuses on not numbers or numerical calculation but on complex though well-defined structures of numbers with defined operations and processes. It may be thought of as generalizing arithmetic. Gauss proved the fundamental theorem of calculus, namely an nth degree polynomial with complex coefficients has n complex roots. The next great step was taken by Evariste Galois in 1819, when he showed that there is no algebraic method to solve polynomials of the fifth or higher degree. This astonishing result laid the foundation of group theory and the associated field of abstract algebra, which led to field of vector spaces, noncommutative algebra, and Boolean algebra. The latter, in turn, became the starting point of mathematic logic, which we take up later in this section. Finally, the twentieth century witnessed the rise of universal algebra, which focuses not on a particular group to study but the theory of groups.

Geometry: Throughout the ages, geometry had rested on the hypothesis of parallels and on linear space, where the three angles of a triangle added up to 180 degrees. In the nineteenth century, three great geometers, namely, Nikolai Lobachevsky, Janos Bolyai, and Bernhard Riemann, developed hyperbolic and elliptic geometries. Later, Riemann generalized the three geometries (Euclidian, hyperbolic, and elliptical) and laid the foundations of differential geometry Einstein used in his theory of relativity. In the twentieth century, the field of topology studies those characteristics of geometric figures that are independent of such actions as twisting, stretching, knotting, and bending. In 1975, Mandelbrot created the field of fractal geometry, which is characterized by detailed, discontinuous (non-differentiability) repeating patterns whose dimensions are greater than topological dimensions. The four-color theorem was proved in 1976.

Mathematics at a Crossroads: Throughout the seventeenth through nineteenth centuries and the early twentieth century, mathematicians were busy focusing on numbers, algebraic structures, new geometries, and continuous and stochastic change believing in the absolute truth of their results. In fact, David Hilbert dreamed on making all mathematics complete and consistent if only the remaining twenty-three problems could be solved. Kurt Godel's first incompleteness theorem dealt a mortal blow to this dream, for it proved that any consistent system of axioms is incapable of proving the truth of all its theorems, and worse yet, the system could not prove its own consistency. It thus challenges the notion Gauss had of mathematics: Mathematics is the queen of sciences, and number theory is the queen of mathematics. In other words, European mathematicians are coming to realize there is no absolute truth, not even in mathematics. The integration effort, however, continues: for example, the model theory studies mathematical structures such as groups, fields, and sets using mathematical logic. It is indeed a contradiction that mathematical conclusions, though they seem compelling, can hardly claim the mantle of truth. In that sense, mathematics is no different than other sciences. However, it has begun to realize this uncomfortable truth only now.

Linguistics: During the current phase, the science of linguistics in Europe developed along three entirely different lines: to put the regional language on a firmer grammatical foundation, to study the evolution of language or historical linguistics, and the field of comparative linguistics as Europeans came in contact with languages of other peoples.

In the eighteenth century, as regional languages replaced Latin, the grammars of these languages was put on a firm foundation, though nothing was comparable to the Sanskrit grammar. Dictionaries had been composed and published. Throughout the nineteenth and twentieth centuries, the rules of vernacular grammars of Europe remained stable and were strictly followed. However, social attitudes, globalization and the internet threaten the stability of these grammars, as indeed they do any grammar.

The second area of focus is historical linguistics, which has studied the classification of languages, historical change in languages, and the meaning of words. A notable area within comparative linguistics is that of Indo-European language studies, which aims to understand the hypothetical proto-Indo-European language.

Logic: Historically, the development of logic has been the responsibility of logicians and philosophers. As we noted in the previous chapter, the Navya-Nyaya school in India in the sixteenth century must be regarded as a precursor to modern symbolic logic and set theory in that it placed restrictive conditions for the universals. George Boole's wife, Mary Boole, who was herself a self-taught mathematician, wrote in 1901 of "the effect of Hinduizing (or more appropriately Indianizing) such men as Babbage, De Morgan, and George Boole in the mathematical atmosphere of 1830-1865." Toward the middle of the nineteenth century, logical syllogisms came to written in algebraic notation, though still obviously in non-quantitative manner. The impact of symbolic logic on both logic and mathematic was enormous. Aristotelian logic, to put it politely, was reformed and put on a more firm Navya-Nyaya-like foundation. For the next seventy-five years, symbolic logic dominated mathematics since it was believed that mathematics could be put on a firm foundation through symbolic logic. Two key works toward this effort are Gottlob Frege's *Begriffsschrift* and Russell and Whitehead's pompously named *Principia Mathematicia*, which attempted to derive mathematical truths from axioms and inference rules using symbolic logic. However, this considerable effort came into question with Kurt Godel's incompleteness theorems in 1931. Since the mathematical logic has evolved into zero-order logic that limits the truth values, the first-order logic uses quantified variables and second order logic extends over the set of elements to new areas including model theory, proof theory, recursion theory, and set theory.

Achievements in Physical Sciences

Astronomy: Astronomy has moved away from the solar system. The existence of different types of galaxies was confirmed as well as the evolution and eventual fate of stars into red giant, white dwarfs, neutron star, and black hole. The evolution of the universe has been traced back to the Big Bang event, followed by an expanding universe. The existence of multiple universes connected through wormholes has been postulated to account for the existence of extremely low likelihood events such as the emergence of life.

Physics: Physics went through three dramatic unifications: the first one involved unification of terrestrial and heavenly motion and required invention of calculus and was achieved in the seventeenth century by Galileo and Newton. The second unification occurred in the second half of the nineteenth century, and it unified electricity and magnetism. The third unification occurred in the early twentieth century, and it unified the theories of electricity-magnetism and gravity. We are near the fourth unification, comprised of electricity-magnetism and strong and weak nuclear forces. The "end of physics" or fifth unification that would integrate the theories of gravity, electricity, magnetism, and strong and weak nuclear forces may not be too far in the future.

Chemistry: Theoretical foundations of chemistry got a great start from Robert Boyle in the seventeenth century. He suggested that observable properties of matter result from properties of the atoms or corpuscles. Chemistry had to wait for another century to arrive at the laws of conservation of mass and the law of definite proportions as enunciated by Lavoisier (1743–1794) and Proust (1754–1826). The synthesis and analysis of numerous inorganic chemicals and the inability to do the same for organic chemicals led to the debate concerning Vitalism, which was debunked by Wohler's synthesis of urea. The atomic basis of chemistry was firmly established with Mendeleev (1834–1907) in 1870 by his periodic table. Understanding of the structure of atoms gave rise to quantum chemistry, where the properties of a material can be understood in terms of its atomic structure. Quantum chemistry was the grand unification of chemistry and physics. Meanwhile in the nineteenth century, organic chemistry made progress. and in the twentieth century, use of quantum chemistry accelerated understanding of biological molecules.

Earth sciences: Geology was born during the current phase for all practical purposes and answered the two related questions of rock formation and the age of the universe. The key milestones were the law of superposition, the principle of original horizontality, and the principle of lateral continuity by Nicolas Steno (1638–1686). James Hutton's (1726–1797) theory of earth in 1785 asserted a much greater antiquity for the age of earth, and the theory of uniformitarianism by Charles Lyell (1797–1875) in 1830 argued that geological processes have been occurring throughout the history of earth. In the twentieth century, the question of the age of the earth was settled through radioactive dating to be 4.5 billion years, and the theory of plate tectonics based on observations of continental drift was confirmed in the 1960s through the efforts of great many geologists. Plate tectonics explained both the phenomenon of volcanic rock formation as well as earthquakes. Geography made great advances during phase as well: the shape and size of landmasses and the geographical features of the continents were defined and oceans were mapped. The geophysics branch theorized the internal structure of the earth while oceanography and hydrology studied the ocean and water cycle. Atmospheric science developed models to predict climate and weather throughout the globe. For the first time in history, *Homo sapiens* had a scientific understanding of the earth's history and structure and the impact of the geological processes on the earth's morphology, climate, and weather.

Achievements in Biological Sciences

Biology: Much like astronomy in the preceding centuries, biology had to overcome the theological prejudice inherent in a monotheistic religion. After the earth was shown to not be the center of universe and had little use for God's intervention to maintain the universe, European theology drew a second red line in sand: the lawful universe and life were created by God. The development of biology greatly suffered as a result. Nevertheless, the scientific method had shown its power in astronomy and was making strides in physics, chemistry, and earth sciences during the early chemistry of the current phase, as we noted above. Thus, progress in biological science could only be slowed and not prevented.

The first interesting discovery was that of the cellular structure of plants in 1665, and Robert Hooke made it using a primitive microscope. As the power of telescope improved, microorganisms such as bacteria and spermatozoa could be seen. While fossils were identified in the seventeenth century, their acceptance had to await the question of the age of the earth.

The next significant, though theologically uncontroversial, step was taken by Carolus Linnaeus in 1735 when he classified all known plants and animals based on similarities and differences—a feat comparable to the periodic table in chemistry. The classification project continued as European travelers and scholars collected species and samples from all over the globe. The field of biogeography focused on the distribution of species across the globe and through geological time. In the eighteenth century, biologists continued to believe in an unchanging species, the malleable nature of species (Lamarck, who believed that environment causes changes in species) or even common descent (Comte de Buffon) in the animal kingdom.

The painstaking work done in biogeography was bound to bear fruit sooner or later. Charles Darwin in 1859 hesitatingly published *Origin of Species* based his research that spanned decades. Darwin showed how species change through the process of natural selection and explained the diversity of species through a branching pattern of evolution, thus arguing for common descent.

Natural selection and common descent seemed reasonable, but no one understood the process through which species changed. Fortunately, strides were being made in both cellular biology, which identified nucleus, chromosomes, mitochondria, and chloroplasts by examining the cell structure, and the macroscopic laws of genetics by Gregor Mendel (1822–1888) in 1865, though they became known in 1901. Huge de Vries proposed the mutation theory in 1900–1903 as the mechanism underlying the process of natural process, thus arguing that natural selection by itself could not explain evolution.

In the meantime, advances in genetics and a broader acceptance of Mendel's chromosome theory created the so-called modern synthesis combining natural selection and genetics by the mid-twentieth century while rejecting both mutation theory and inheritance of acquired characteristics or Lamarckian theory. The modern synthesis has restored the importance of natural selection, though it was tempered by barriers to gene flow (geographical, ecological, or social), resulting in genetic drifts that were clearly and explicitly recognized.

However, by no means, is the theory of mutation dead. Some biologists continue to regard mutation as the fundamental process in the production of more efficient genes through the elimination of duplicate genes and by combining genes. Thus, the three pillars of evolution are natural selection, genetic pooling, and gene mutation. Their relative importance is still debatable. At the same time, the creationists who reject theory of evolution based on theological belief can hardly be said to have evolved their views.

In the second half of the twentieth century, advances in biochemistry have led to molecular biology, which aimed at understanding all the cellular processes, such as protein synthesis, energy production, and the process of cell division. Thus, the broad structure of chromosomes (DNA) and the microstructure of chromosomes or the identification of genes, protein synthesis, energy production, and cell division are today largely understood.

The breakthroughs in biology have led to biotechnology, which is aimed at developing new drugs for diseases. Stronger hybrid plants to increase food production are based on changes recombinant DNA technology. The science of biology is now confidently moving into biophysics, astrobiology, cloning, bioinformatics, and synthetic biology or creating new life forms.

Medicine: Though, unlike astronomy, earth sciences. and biology, progress in medical science was not slowed by theological prejudice (most confirmed believers like medical science) it needed breakthroughs in cell biology and physiology. Thus, until the beginning of the nineteenth century, medical science remained static except in the field of anatomy.

During the nineteenth century, simple methods such as clean hands advocated by Ignaz Semmelweis (1818–1865) dramatically reduced disease. The next great step was linking microorganisms and diseases that occurred through the work of Louis Pasteur (1822–1895). The last great step was the professionalization of the field of nursing. Thus, it was improved nutrition and hygiene and not new drugs or procedures that dominated medical science in the nineteenth century.

Physiology took a great step in Europe with William Harvey's experimental demonstration of blood circulation, though the idea was not new. In the eighteenth century, Herman Boerhaave (1668–1738), his pupil Gerard van Swieten (1700–1772), who fought against superstition of Vampers and Pierre Cabanis (1757–1808), who incidentally was a not only physiologist but was both a materialist and a believer in vital theory, were both practicing physicians and important physiologists.

During the nineteenth century, the emergence of cell theory in 1838 accelerated research in physiology. Walter Cannon (1871–1945) developed the concept of homeostasis or physiological equilibrium. During the twentieth century, using insights from microbiology, biochemistry, and molecular biology, the key components of human physiology, such as circulation, respiratory, gastro-intestinal, unitary, reproductive, immune, endocrine, nervous, and integumentary systems were identified, analyzed, and understood. It became clear that the endocrine and nervous systems play key roles in physiological homeostasis.

The twentieth century not only saw great strides in physiology but also saw great progress in development of drugs and surgical techniques. The key breakthroughs on the drugs side were germicides, sulfa-antibiotics, penicillin, DDT, and vaccines for measles, mumps, polio, cholera, certain kinds of influenza, and HIV.

There has been a great explosion in the development of medical testing, including blood testing, x-ray imaging, ultrasonic imaging, CT scans, magnetic resonance imaging, and genetic mapping in the twentieth century. New therapies such as chemotherapy, radiation therapy, hormonal therapy, gene therapy, and stem cell therapy have come into existence as infectious diseases have been replaced by cancer, diabetes, and cardiovascular diseases.

On the surgical side, key innovations have been the development of cardiac surgeries; transplantation (liver, eye, kidney); reconstructive, laparoscopic, arthroscopic, and natural orifice surgery;, microsurgery; and robotic surgical techniques. Other innovations include prosthetic devices including artificial limbs, pacemakers, and a neural prosthesis.

The field of mental illness lagged behind until the twentieth century. During the nineteenth century, mentally ill people were confined to asylums with little possibility of treatment as psychiatrists could not make up their minds whether mental illness was biological or social. The focus was on classifying psychiatric diseases. The first breakthrough came through psychological theories of the early twentieth century, and these theories became popular with psychiatrists since they carried the potential for a cure. In the last forty years, biological psychiatry has reemerged because of advances in drugs, such as acetylcholine (neurotransmitter), chlorpromazine schizophrenia), and lithium (bipolar disorder) as well as testing techniques like neuroimaging.

The achievements of the European civilization in the twentieth century have been staggering indeed.

Achievements in Social Sciences

It is perhaps fair to say that until the current phase, with the few exceptions we have noted in previous chapters, civilizations had been mostly busy adapting to or understanding Mother Nature while using greed or creed to control other civilizations and hardly took time to understand *Homo sapiens* and its social organizations. It almost seems that evolution of social structure of civilizations was unconscious, dependent on the rise of charismatic and innovative leaders and a slow accumulation of knowledge. Certainly, by the end of the first century of this phase, the first grand unification in physics had taken place, and the scientific method had crystalized after nearly three millennia of often interrupted effort by major civilizations. And at the start of the eighteenth century, European civilization, which brought about the first grand unification of physics, was ready to apply the scientific method to *Homo sapiens* and their social organizations, resulting in the emergence of such social sciences as sociology, economics, political science, anthropology, psychology, and history. And if the early pioneers in these fields did not fully appreciate the fundamental difference between natural and social sciences and that of existence of free will, it is understandable since these pioneers were swept by the success of scientific method in the natural science arena. Perhaps less forgiving is the conscious and unconscious development of hypotheses paraded as theories and laws, designed specifically to justify the European civilization controlling other civilizations. We shall encounter these themes in most of the social sciences discussed below.

Sociology: During the current phase, the field of sociology emerged slowly as one dedicated to the study of society encompassing individual behavior (drawing heavily on psychology) to social structure to macro-level systems analysis.

The pioneers, such as Auguste Comte (1798–1857), applied the scientific methodology (also called positivism) to social evolution and defined three stages: theological (based on presumptions), philosophical (based on challenging the presumptions), and scientific (based on empirical data)—something very true for the evolution of European civilization. His focus was entirely on social evolution and not the behavior of an individual or the social structures. In essence, he saw an evolution or a history to a society.

If Comte focused on the evolution of society, David Durkheim (1858–1917) focused on its stability while retaining the positivistic methodology Comte pioneered. He also developed the structural functional approach that clarified sociological analysis from psychological and philosophical analysis.

Comte had died before the *Origin of Species* was published. Herbert Spencer (1820–1903) used the Lamarckian theory of evolution (use leads to inherited characteristics) to propose a theory of social evolution from a militant stage based on a fixed hierarchy to an industrial stage based on free markets. He rejected Comte's three-stage evolution. Not surprisingly, he believed that knowledge could be transmitted to the individual through knowledge gained by his race—a racist idea in Lamarckian garb that questions his status as a serious contributor to the theory of structural functionalism. He is also erroneously believed to be a social Darwinist, in part because he coined the term "survival of the fittest."

The positivist approach tended to accept the status quo. Karl Marx (1818–1883), however, saw little point in analyzing social evolution per se and believed in critical analysis would lead to change and produced the concept of class struggle as the engine of social evolution. In Marx, sociological analysis became self-conscious, capable of analysis and social action simultaneously. If Marx emphasized a specific course of social action based on his sociological analysis, Max Weber (1864–1920) did not go that far but agreed with Marx that the present social action of individuals is the proper field of sociology and not past evolution.

Today, the science of sociology is caught between the structural functionalism that has learned to emphasize quantitative methods and sees society as system of institutions and processes to create social cohesion and critical analysis initiated by Marx and others. This critical analysis sees conflict an essential aspect of society.

Political science: If the evolution of European sociology during the current phase aspired for both understanding social structures and their evolution as well as action aimed at changing these structures, political science was definitely more academic by comparison and simply reflected the changing political structures within European civilization.

We saw in the last chapter how European political thought was centered on the divine right of kings, a political ideology worse than the heavenly mandate entrenched in the Chinese civilization. We also saw how Machiavelli brought this political doctrine down to earth by frankly advocating that the ends justify means or that political power may be obtained through any means, thus disassociating political science from ethics. The next key figure in the evolution of political science was Thomas Hobbes (1588–1679), who felt the necessity of a strong central authority to whom the population cedes rights in order to create social order. In the absence of such authority, the inherently selfish nature of man will result in chaos. This was certainly true of Hobbes's England at the time.

For John Locke (1632–1704, however, human nature was reasonable, and the introduction of currency and social structure itself turned men into selfish means as it allowed accumulated of economic power. He believed that in a natural state, all men were equal and independent. Locke's lasting contribution to political theory was the idea of natural rights (to defend life, health, liberty, and property) and the separation of powers among the legislative, executive, and judicial bodies.

For Jacque Rousseau (1712–1778), the population ceding rights to a political authority is transformed into social contract that creates the general will to enforce the laws, laws that are created through direct and not representative democracy. Like Hobbes, Rousseau recognized the selfish nature of man. The main criticism of Rousseau's form of Republicanism has been that it becomes impractical as one goes beyond a city-state. Rousseau was born and lived in his beloved city-state of Geneva.

The analysis of political thought thus far had been focused on the relationship between social cohesion and political authority and had reflected the changing fortunes of monarchy, landed aristocracy, and the rising entrepreneurial class. Karl Marx upset the applecart and focused on the instability and injustice through his concept of class struggle. His notion of the essential goodness of man led him to advocate a dictatorship of the proletariat as an interim form of political organization before transition to a classless society.

A century-long experiment with Marxian idealism showed that it led both to relative economic stagnation as well as to a concentration of political power in the hands of a minority. In parallel with the socialist experiment, European civilization also advanced the political doctrine of liberal democracy consisting of representative democracy based universal franchise, separation of powers, a political constitution and free press, and multiple political parties representing different interests, thus legitimizing the class struggle. Liberal democracy, however has often led to tyranny of the majority and special interests and the influence of money hijack the political.

Academic political science today recognizes that it is an observational and not experimental science and, unlike natural sciences, cannot be quantified. The foundational question of whether *Homo sapiens* are good or selfish remains unanswered. However, there is evidence from evolutionary psychology that *Homo sapiens* have mechanisms to deal with small-group politics but behavior within larger structures is learned. Yet it has been claimed that "all politics is local."

Economics: If there is one social science that aspires to emulate natural sciences and comes close to doing so, it is economics. This has earned it the unfair title of dismal science.

The earliest consistent economic doctrine European civilization developed during the current phase was that of mercantilism. It reflected the rising success of colonialism based on control of the high seas and a brutal competition among the key European states perched on the Atlantic coast.

Not surprisingly, the theory of mercantilism advocated using military power to protect the domestic markets and control international trade. Thus, its chief tools were duties on imported goods and tariffs on exported goods to gain economic advantage while providing a military cover to achieve this.

The theory of mercantilism was followed by its opposite, laissez-faire and free trade. David Hume (1711–1776) saw the folly of mercantilism most clearly, as did others such as Locke and Dudley, who argued that the goal of the trade surplus mercantilism desired was impossible since it would have to be paid in gold or silver, which would increase money supply, resulting in a price increase, which would balance the trade. Of course, the British talked about free trade and practiced coerced trade for the following two centuries.

Although the Industrial Revolution was in the early stages, the factory system based on extensive division of labor, particularly in Britain, had replaced guild-based manufacturing. Adam Smith (1723–1790) published *Wealth of Nations* in 1776, and it argued that the selfish motivation of *Homo sapiens* was actually good since it required entrepreneurs to produce better products and the market kept prices low through competition. Thus, producers benefited because of improved efficiencies, and buyers benefited from lower prices through competition. It is as though an invisible hand made everything work out. The system, Smith argued, would work as long as the property rights were safe and as long as entrepreneurs invested capital in the enterprises. It was the first time someone had clearly explained how markets worked under the best conditions.

As national economies of key European states, such as Britain, France, and the Netherlands, expanded driven by industrial revolution, the debate shifted from trade policy to domestic economic policy. There was a great need to understand how a free market economy functioned in detail and how to make it better. The late eighteenth and nineteenth centuries still had a rather modest rate of innovation compared to modern standards, despite the accelerating Industrial Revolution. As a result, the economies were predominantly a commodities economy, where participating firms survived or failed based on price competition through substantial numbers of buyers and sellers. The conditions were therefore ripe for the rise of classical economic theory and thinkers like Jeremy Bentham (1748–1832), Jean-Baptiste Say (1767–1832), David Ricardo (1772–1823), and John Stuart Mill (1806–1873). Bentham developed the concept of utilitarianism; Say claimed there could never be a demand deficit in a free market; Ricardo clarified the factors of production (land, labor, and capital) and mathematically showed free trade to be better than protectionism, and Mill attempted to find middle ground between the doomsayers like John Malthus (1766–1834), realists like Ricardo, and optimists like Adam Smith. Malthus believed that population would rise faster than output, leading to falling wages and higher profits while Smith believed the rate of capital accumulation would outstrip population increase, leading to wage increases. Ricardo thought, based on his labor theory, that capital accumulation and population would remain in balance, and wages would remain stable. One can sense these all the classical economists sensed that capitalism was evolving, only no one knew where it would go.

Karl Marx (1818–1883) wrote his doctoral thesis on Greek philosophy at age twenty-three and seemed destined for an academic life. His admiration for Greek materialists like Democritus and Epicurus and idealist philosopher Hegel somehow conspired to turn Marx away from philosophy to develop concepts of historical materialism and class struggle as the motivating force in all history and from historical materialism to analysis of capitalist economy. If all his predecessors analyzed the stability of a commodity-based economy, Marx focused on its increasing instability. Using the labor theory of value and equal rates of return on capital in all segments of the economy, Marx showed that a closed commodities-based economy is inherently unstable and will lead to a revolutionary takeover by the workers, which in turn leads eventually to a classless state. It was indeed a powerful analysis based on inner workings. He forecast declining wages, a concentration of wealth, and booms and busts with each bust more terrifying. And for a while, it seemed that his predictions were coming true.

Leon Walras (1834–1910), perhaps the most underappreciated economics thinker, represented the most significant contribution toward the quantification of economics in the latter part of the nineteenth century. Between1874 and 1877, he published his theory of general equilibrium outlining the equations that determined the economy's equilibrium. In a way, Walras's general theory is the culmination of classical economics, and he ignored the instability of the capitalist economy that Marx addressed. Joseph Schumpeter (1883–1950) took this up and analyzed the instability of a commodity-based economy. He agreed with Marx that a commodity-based economy is indeed unstable, identified four cycles that created instability, and ultimately traced it to innovation. He also agreed with Marx that capitalism will self-destruct, not because of a working-class revolution but because the intellectual and social climate (and through it, government policy) will handcuff entrepreneurs and innovators and that will kill capitalism. The innovators are the creators and destroyers, and without them, advanced capitalism will slowly die.

Simultaneously, in the Soviet Union, which was under communist control since 1917, considerable work was done in how to manage a centrally planned economy.

The Great Depression swept aside the different economic theories and created an urgent need for fixes. This is what John Keynes did in 1936. Keynes was the engineer who suggested a way to manage the inherently unstable business cycle through government controlling the money supply and demand. Thus, if government action reduced interest rates, it would stimulate investment. If government engaged in deficit spending, it would create increased demand in the face of high employment. In other words, he created tools to manage and moderate the business cycle.

As the memory of the Great Depression faded away, the forces of the self-regulating nature of markets raised its head again and had two proponents. Milton Friedman (1912–2006) argued against the manipulation of interest rates and money supply and suggested it should expand at the rate equal to the expansion of the economy. Fredrick Von Hayek argued that a centrally planned economy must necessarily lead to political tyranny and that price signals in a free market are the only assured way to communicate what is generally known and what is individually known concerning supply, demand, and investment decisions.

During the first decade of the twenty-first century, the phenomenon of globalization and the emergence of highly sophisticated financial instruments made possible by information technology and computers have once again upset the apple cart. Both of these forces, the former through a global imbalance between savings and consumption through large trade deficits and latter through creation of financial instruments of uncertain evaluation, have once again created the dreaded instability, resulting in the Great Recession. No theoretical fix has emerged to handle this issue yet.

Thus, one can see that economic science the European civilization developed during the current phase not only put forth theories describing the equilibrium of a laissez-faire economy but also analyzed its inherent instability and developed ways to moderate the economic cycle. Globalization and power of information technology has created challenges in both the functioning the market (millisecond trades) and government policy (moral hazard of bailing out banks).

Anthropology: The field of anthropology is child of European colonialism and was formally born in the late eighteenth century. Beginning with linguistic anthropology, it has expanded to include cultural anthropology, physical anthropology, and archeological anthropology. Anthropology has gone through two stages: the first stage served the interests of colonization and slavery system and was overtly racist. The examples include the Aryan invasion of the Indian hypothesis promoted by Max Muller, who was in the service of the British, and the American School of Anthropology that championed the doctrine of multiple origins of *Homo sapiens* races, both in the nineteenth century. In the second half of the twentieth century, there has finally been a modest self-examination of the short history of anthropology in the light of the theory of evolution, new findings on the origin of *Homo sapiens,* and the decline of racist ideologies in general and criticism of Nazism in particular.

Thus, in the second half of the twentieth century, anthropology is emerging from under its own former self and is developing the capacity to understand different cultures more objectively. It is based on the realization that culture separates *Homo sapiens* from other species and culture defines what individuals learn, what they think, and how they act. Thus, it is no longer the European anthropologists' perspective that alone matters; it is also the perspective of the culture being studied. Apart from the concept of cultural relativism, European cultural anthropology has adopted the approach of structural functionalism and has moved away from the positivist approach it long ago abandoned in studying its European culture. The positivist approach continues to make sense in other areas of anthropology, such as archeological and physical anthropology.

Psychology: Psychology, which may be defined as the study of the human mind and human behavior, has a rather short but impressive history in European civilization beginning in the last third of the current phase. The older European achievements in psychology are modest when compared to Indian and Muslim contributions, as we noted in earlier chapters. Mental powers, such as perception, reason, imagination, emotion, memory, and will had long been known and analyzed to one degree or another. The question was how could these powers explain mental illnesses and mental health?

During the current phase, European psychology may be said to begin with Wilhelm Wundt (1832–1920), who tried to relate abnormal human behavior to damaged parts of the brain. Given the understanding of the anatomy and the physiology of the brain, this was an impossible undertaking; however, Wundt did succeed in establishing the science of psychology as a distinct discipline and firmly set the focus of psychology on understanding mental illness.

The opposite to the nascent structuralism of Wundt was represented by the functionalism of William James (1842–1910). It was probably the forerunner of the school of behaviorism (see below). James focused on empirical research on consciousness and the mental processes and how humans adapt to their environments. James's functionalism was thus descriptive, qualitative, passive, and without a theoretical underpinning. It was an alternative to emerging structuralism and perhaps nothing more.

Given the absence of detailed anatomical and the physiological understanding of the brain, the focus in the emerging science of psychology naturally shifted to creating models of the mind (as a process) to explain psychological illnesses. The first important figure to attempt this was Sigmund Freud (1856–1939), who began with topological models that divided the mind into conscious, preconscious, and unconscious components. He soon gave up on this division and charted the concepts of conscious, preconscious, and unconscious into:

- Id, which is a disorganized collection of desires and passions arising from instincts and is completely in the unconscious
- Ego, which is the organized part of mind with executive function through most mental powers such as perception, reason, imagination, emotion, memory, and will and has conscious, preconscious, and unconscious parts
- Superego, which is organized part of personality representing socially acquired conscience and is mostly unconscious

The relationship Freud postulated between the three structural parts of the mind was straightforward: id is autonomous and does not care about the constraints of reality and social norms; superego acts in opposition to id's desires, fantasies, and passions; and ego mediates between the two, often succumbing to the dictates of the id through preconscious rationalizations (denial, projection, rationalization, compensation, repression, sublimation, and reaction formation and admonishment of the superego (shame, guilt). Thus, a relationship between instincts, mental powers, and social norms was conceived. It is hard to disagree with this schema as long as one remembers that superego is a strong function of cultural norms, and therefore the specific dialectic between the id, ego, and superego is a strong function of culture as well and is not universal. However, Freud did not clarify this and proposed his theory as universal. In addition, the manifestation of id up to adulthood was conceived in oral, anal, and genital stages and implied that maladjustment of the id was part of universal human condition. Several psychologists challenged this aspect of Freud's system. Nevertheless, on the whole, it was a great start for the science of psychology.

Carl Jung (1875–1961) was a favorite disciple of Freud, but they disagreed when Jung tried to link part of the superego to an inherited collective unconscious in which archetypes imprinted like instincts in the brain resided. Thus, archetypes as well as the socially acquired superego defined the constraints on the id and drove ego. Apart from dream analysis, Jung provided little proof of his hypothesis. The second achievement of Jung was his classification of personality based on the ego's orientation (introverted or extraverted) and the principal mental powers (through thinking, feeling, sensing, and intuition), that ego used, thus leading to eight personality types (4x2).

Similarly, Karen Horney (1885–1952) theorized three different ego types, namely, moving toward others, moving against others, and moving away from others or compliant, aggressive, and withdrawing personality types. Horney suggested that people have different ego types because they are trying to satisfy different psychological emotions, such as affection (compliant), power (aggressive), and perfection (withdrawing). Thus, Jung's classification of personality types is based on perceptual, sensual, reason, and intuition (which is in effect reason plus imagination) and emotion while Horney mostly bases her classification on the preferred mode of driving emotions.

For some psychologists, however, the approach of structuralism was too much analysis of instinctual baggage and botched-up upbringing without commensurate benefits. Gestalt psychology, founded by Friedrich (1893–1970) and Laura Perls (1905–1990), instead claimed that mind functions holistically (meaning structuralism is unnecessary and useless) and the present moment is more important than past upbringing. In other words, humans are able to recover the inherent pristine mental powers regardless of the instincts and upbringing, bringing Gestalt close to Raj yoga. One corollary of Gestalt psychology is that by forcefully reliving past experiences in the present, they can be transcended.

In addition to structural, functional, and holistic theories, European psychology also developed the theory of behaviorism, made most famous by B. F. Skinner (1904–1990). Skinner was a strong believer that behavior was solely a function of environmental reinforcement and claimed that when behavior is attributed to what is going on the inside the mind, it is essentially the end of explanation. Thus, philosophically, behaviorism, like Gestalt, believes in the power of the present. Unlike structuralism, it believes in the reinforcing power of the environment. In Skinner, there is no mental illness per se, only behavior.

European psychology in twentieth century also put forth theories of the development of mental powers in addition to structuralism, functionalism, holistic, and behaviorist theories of mental illness and behavior. We have already referred to the development of id in early years Freud proposed. Jean Piaget (1896–1980) developed a theory of cognitive development in children. Piaget identified the ability of the mind to organize and store learned information in a schema that can be readily recalled in the appropriate situation and four stages of development as well as the processes associated with transition from one stage to the next (assimilation and accommodation). The four stages he identified were:

- Sensorimotor stage (0–2 years), when the infant senses the world without reflection and reacts to it through reflexes
- Preoperational stage (2–7 years), when the child believes in magical and anthropomorphic thinking and egocentrism
- Concrete operational stage (7–11 years), when the child begins to think in terms of cause and effect
- Formal operational stage (11+ years), when the child acquires an ability to think in abstract terms

If Freud theorized the development of id, and Piaget studied the cognitive development, Erick Erickson (1902–1994) studied the emotional development in an individual. Unlike id and cognitive development, ego (emotional) development, Erickson found, was a lifelong process, and he delineated eight self-explanatory stages whose outcomes depended on environmental factors:

- Trust versus mistrust (0–2 years), when a healthy child develops trust
- Autonomy versus shame and doubt (2–3 years), when a healthy child develops autonomy and self-direction
- Initiative versus guilt (3–6 years), when a healthy child learns to initiate projects on his own
- Industry versus inferiority (6–12 years), when a healthy child will learn the value of hard work
- Identity versus role confusion (12–18 years), when a healthy young adult develops a direction in life and believes his goals are attainable
- Intimacy versus isolation (begins at 18 years), when a healthy adult acquires capacity for intimacy in a I-thou relationship
- Generativity versus self-absorption (adulthood), when a healthy adult learns to be productive
- Integrity versus despair (old age), when a healthy person is able to face impending death with acceptance and feels his life has been well-spent.

Finally, Kohlberg (1927–1987), through his studies using structured moral dilemmas, proposed a six-stage theory of moral development, which, like emotional development, can be a lifelong process. The six stages organized into three levels are:

- Level 1: Preconventional morality
  Obedience and punishment stage
  Self-interest orientation
- Level 2: Conventional morality
  Interpersonal accord and conformity orientation
  Social order maintenance orientation
- Level 3: Postconventional morality
  Social contract orientation
  Universal ethical orientation

Thus, for Kohlberg, the development of superego is a lifelong process developing the cultural norms.

Development of European psychology mostly focused on explaining the development of id, cognition, ego, superego, and behavior mostly in the context of illness. Abraham Maslow (1908–1970) asked a different question and redirected psychology away from illness and toward achieving the potential in each human being. He called this self-actualization, thus founding the branch of humanist psychology. Not surprisingly, Maslow focused his research on healthy individuals and not on those with mental illness. He found such people to be in harmony with themselves and others and often enjoyed "peak experiences." They had transcended the physiological, safety, affection, and esteem needs and arrived at the self-actualization stage. Later, Viktor Frankl (1905–1997) added the self-transcendence stage or mystical stage to the list.

In summary, it is fair to conclude that to the extent the European science of psychology has not focused on the upbringing and mental illness of the individual and focused on the untapped potential inherent in the present and future, it approaches the science of present moment enshrined in Raj yoga.

History, Causes, and Outcomes of the Indian Civilization

17.12 Brief Political History

Mughals dominated Indian civilization in the sixteenth to eighteenth centuries. When the Moghuls declined, Indian civilization began to fragment into regional empires while the subcontinent came under attack through both Khyber Pass by the Persians and Afghans and from the sea by the Portuguese, British, and French. The difference with respect to China should be obvious to the reader immediately. China was weak in the seventeenth century *before* the relatively small nation-states of western Europe became strong enough to take on large civilizations. India became politically weak *after* the western European nation-states had become strong. The strategic significance of this difference is that while India had to suffer under European imperial control for two centuries, China suffered for less than one. Further, since China did not fragment in the nineteenth century, unlike what happened to India in the eighteenth century, the European powers controlled Indian civilization much more completely than they did the Chinese civilization.

Expansion and decline of Mughal Empire: The relatively wise rule of Akbar did not come to an end in 1605 with his death, for his son and grandson both generally continued his policies. The Mughals did not have accepted succession rules, and even when there was only one male heir, blood was spilled between father and son, resulting in destruction and uncertainty. Akbar was followed by his son Jahangir (1605–1627) and his grandson Shah Jahan (1627–1658). Both continued Akbar's policies, extending the empire by adding or securing Bundelkhand, Mewar, Kangra, and Kashmir while gaining and losing Kandahar. Shah Jahan's son Prince Aurangzeb (1658–1707) added the southern Sultanate of Ahmadnagar and nearly succeeded in adding the Sultanates of Bijapur and Golconda but was stopped in 1657 by the war of succession when Shah Jahan fell ill.

Aurangzeb's long reign of forty-nine years may be divided into two nearly equal halves, probably demarcated by the untimely death of Maratha Emperor Shivaji in 1680. He spent the first half attempting to consolidate the hold of Islam in North India and fighting rebellions in the north and south. Aurangzeb, unlike his father, grandfather, and great grandfather, was a religious fanatic who viewed himself as a soldier of Allah. He alienated the majority Hindu population by attempting to impose Muslim sharia law; instituting a jizya tax; destroying places of Hindu worship; banning music, dance, alcohol, prostitution, and castration; ordering Muslims to dress like Muslims; and banning Muslims from attending Hindu religious discourses.

Under Aurangzeb, India may be divided into three types of states: where the Mughal control was absolute (the heartland), where the control was moderate (Bahmani Sultanates, such as Bijapur and Golconda), and where the control was absent (Mysore Kingdom and Ahom Empire in Assam). Fanatic that he was, Aurangzeb's strategy was to conquer areas where his control was moderate and put in place punitive measures for the Hindu majority where his control was absolute. Clearly, very early in his reign, he began to overplay his hand.

The independent-minded Jats in in areas not too far from Delhi were the first to rebel. Aurangzeb had centralized administration, dramatically increased taxes, restricted Hindu religious practices, and aggressively promoted Islam, including forced conversions and destroying Hindu temples. The result was a decade-long armed rebellion 1669–1678) by Jats under the leadership of Gukula, and following his death, under Raja Ram. Although the rebellion failed, it was a harbinger of things to come.

Next to rise were the Maratha clans in Ahmednagar (present-day Maharashtra). The Deccan Sultanates had been weakened by Aurangzeb's military campaign when he was governor of the Deccan before becoming emperor, and this gave Marathas an opportunity to gain power. Shahji, a general in the Ahmednagar Sultanate (present-day Maharashtra), led numerous battles against Aurangzeb's military campaign from 1633–1636. His son Shiva Ji succeeded in carving out an empire from Muslim sultans of Bijapur (present-day Karnatka) and Golconda (present-day Andhara). Shivaji, who was double-crossed by Aurangzeb in the former's attempt to negotiate peace, managed to reestablish a significant kingdom before he died. However, it remained vulnerable to Moghul armies.

Aurangzeb's policies also created militant Sikhism in Punjab. The ninth Guru of Sikhs, Teg Bahadur, was a man of peace who resisted the designs of Aurangzeb to convert India to Islam supported by the philosophy of Naqshabandi Ahmed Sirhindi. These designs were implemented in Kashmir. However, Kashmiri Brahmins resisted converting to Islam and approached Teg Bahadur for help. The ninth guru told them to tell Aurangzeb that they would convert to Islam if the guru did. Aurangzeb had him arrested, brought to Delhi, and beheaded him in 1675. His son, guru Gobind Singh, fought the Mughals, converted the Sikhs into a fighting force, and died in 1708 at the age of forty-three from the wounds inflicted by a hired Mughal assailant. Before he died, the last guru wrote a letter to Aurangzeb, chiding Aurangzeb for his broken promises and weakness as a human being and thundered that "all modes of redressing wrongs having failed, raising swords is pious and just."

It is noteworthy that Aurangzeb's fanaticism pushed all three communities into militancy. He managed to put down the Jat and Sikh uprisings, struggled with Marathas, and did not succeed in invading the Ahom Empire in northeast India or in putting down the Pashtun rebellion in the northwest.

Thinking perhaps naively, he had achieved his objective of imposing Islam in North India and was enraged by his son Akbar defecting to the Deccan Sultanates or perhaps sensing an opportunity after Shiva Ji died in 1680 at age fifty-three, Aurangzeb returned to south during the second half of his reign to complete the conquest of Bijapur and Golconda, thus extending his control to nearly the entire subcontinent for a brief moment, though never quite succeeding against the Marathas. It was only the third time in history, after Ashoka (third century BCE) and Khilji (thirteenth century) that this happened.

On a personal level, Aurangzeb accused his rival brothers for not being true Muslims, accused his elder brother of poisoning the grand vizier, poisoned his sister Roshanara and her lover, and accused his father of incest with his older sister Jahanara, declared his father incompetent to rule and placed him under house arrest, and denied his father a state funeral. He had to murder all three of his brothers to assure his ascension. Yet, on occasion, he allowed existing temples to be repaired if it was politically expedient and made up with Jahanara after their father's death. He lived simply, supporting himself by sowing caps and copying the Koran. He was indeed a complex man combining military skill, tactical flexibility, lack of human compassion and family feeling, and an overabundance of religious fanaticism.

Aurangzeb's religious fanaticism in the north and military expansion in the south effectively sealed the fate of the Mughal Empire. Provincial Muslim governors and the majority Hindu population began rebelling after he died in 1707 at age eighty-nine, in part because he did not dare have a succession plan, for he never forgot what he had to do to achieve the throne. After his death, the country came under attack from the northwest and from the European powers, which had been insignificant players for two hundred years, perched along the coast of the subcontinent, patiently begging trade concessions from the Mughals.

British control of India: Eighteenth-century India, in contradistinction to eighteenth-century China, presents a compelling picture of domestic and foreign forces vying for control:

- In 1717, ten years after Aurangzeb died, the Nawab of Bengal declared his independence.

- This was followed by the Nizam of Hyderabad, who declared his independence in 1724.

- Sensing a weakened Mughal Empire, Nadir Shah of Persia raided India in 1739 and took back enormous loot, further weakening the Mughals.

- Earlier, Shivaji's grandson Shahuji, who was released by the Mughals in an attempt to divide the Marathas, succeeded in taking control of the Marathas. In 1713, taking advantage of Moghul discord, the Marathas marched to Delhi under Balaji Vishwanath, a general of Shahuji, and negotiated a treaty to gain substantial independence and revenue-sharing for the Marathas. By 1761, the Marathas under Peshwas or their hereditary prime ministers controlled nearly half of the subcontinent.

- Afghan king Abdali conducted a series of eight invasions from 1748 to 1766, surprisingly defeating the Marathas at the third battle of Panipat in 1761.

- The impact of the Abdali invasion was putting ending the Peshwa era and creating six autonomous Maratha states of Pune, Baroda, Indore/Malwa, Gwalior/Ujjain, Nagpur, and Dhar, thus creating an opening for the British to play one Maratha state against another.

- Sikhs ultimately put an end to Afghan ambitions in 1766 in a battle near Amritsar that killed five thousand Afghan soldiers.

- Mysore, a vassal state of Vijayanagara, expanded dramatically during the seventeenth century under the Wodeyar dynasty and became effectively controlled by Haider Ali 1761–1782), a general in the army, who was followed by his son Tipu (1782–1799).

Thus, by 1750, the stage was set for a hundred-year-long epic struggle among the breakaway provinces of Bengal in the east, Nizam of Hyderabad in the south, the Maratha states in the center, Mysore in the deep south, the shrunken Mughal Empire in the north, the Rajputs in the west, the Sikhs in the Punjab, and the French and the British along the coastal areas. While we will not get into the details of how the British ultimately succeeded in controlling most of India through shifting alliances, creating and using discord among Indian states, deceit as necessary, and superior weapons, we will mention briefly that Bengal fell in 1757, Mysore fell by 1799, Marathas were neutralized by 1818 through three wars, Sikhs fell by 1851, and the Mughals fell by 1857. Throughout this struggle, Nizam of Hyderabad and several Rajput states betrayed their own civilization and became allied with the British.

Independence struggle: The failed first revolutionary war in 1857 allowed the British a generation of peace that began to weaken with founding of meek, pro-British Indian National Congress in 1885. The Congress was transformed into a national liberation force by leaders like Gokhle, Tilak, and Gandhi. India was forced to join

World War I on the British side; however, Gandhi refused to support World War II. The peaceful struggle eventually succeeded in 1947 with British departure but not before partitioning the subcontinent into a predominantly Muslim Pakistan and a predominantly Hindu India. According to the unapologetic and imperialist Winston Churchill, Britain had the last word in India because they succeeded in partitioning it. After the partition, India adopted democracy coupled with socialistic economic policy, which failed miserably, and did not align in the struggle between the capitalist United States and western Europe and the USSR. Economic reforms took place in 1991, and since then the Indian economy has performed well. Indian foreign policy aligned itself with US policy after the fall of the USSR.

Looking back, the history of Islam in India from 1200–1857 was a struggle to convert India into a Muslim state that ultimately failed, and there has been no dearth of Muslim poets and historians who have shed tears over this failure. Islam succeeded in nearly full and speedy conversion of populations in every significant territory it conquered, except India. It is indeed a tribute to Hindu tenacity and fighting spirit that Islam ultimately failed and managed to convert less than a fourth of its population to Islam after five centuries of political and military power. Islam met its Waterloo twice: in the battle of Rajasthan and in the Iberian Peninsula in Europe. It is equally untrue to state that the Mughal Empire was replaced by the British Raj. The political power had already flowed into anti-Mughal Hindu and Muslim states when the British started their imperialist game. The political power then slowly flowed **from** Marathas, Sikhs, Haider Ali, Tipu Sultan, and others **to** the British, in alliance with Nizam through effectively using the divide-and-rule policy and superior weapons. The ninety years since 1857 were a struggle against British imperial control, at the end of which the power flowed from the British to the Indian people through establishing democracy.

17.13 Natural Causes

A devastating famine broke out in Bengal in 1770 that wiped out 5 percent of the Indian population. The famine was brought about by the East India Company raising the land tax from 10 percent to 50 percent on traditional crops to encourage a switch to opium and indigo and forbade food grain reserves. However, the company was spending enormous sums on imperial conquest and suffered financially. This forced the British Parliament to raise import duties on tea imported into America which, incidentally, precipitated the American Revolution.

17.14 Intrinsic Causes

Institutional Structures and Processes

Political system: The most significant political innovation of the phase was the emergence of more a meritocratic rather than hereditary leaders as the Mughal Empire went into decline. The emergence of a Haider Ali in Mysore and Shivaji and the early Peshwas in the Maratha Empire testify to this phenomenon. Apart from this, there was little significant change in the political structures that emerged during the current phase.

Military capability: Several innovations of military significance formed the foundation of rebellion against the Mughal Empire. The first, several new states, Marathas and Sikhs in particular, encouraged all castes to participate in the military profession. The Marathas constituted a blue-water naval force that included cannon-mounted ships called Pal, thereby correcting a strategic mistake of the Mughals. The navy kept the Portuguese and British off balance for several decades in the early eighteenth century. On the tactics side, the Shivaji introduced and developed the concept of guerilla warfare, which overcame the Mughal advantage of size and resources by exploiting knowledge of local geography, high mobility, and hit-and-run tactics. The great General Baji Rao, who won all forty-one battles he fought, perfected conventional battlefield tactics. He is said to be one of the few generals in history to never lose a war. Hyder Ali introduced rockets with iron shells, a technology used by the British against Napoleon as Congreve rockets.

In addition, pioneer Shiva Ji introduced other changes, including a standing army, state ownership of military horses, the concept of a part-time soldier, an intelligence department, and a clear chain of command.

Economic system: With the exception of Bengal toward the last decades of the eighteenth century under East India Company mismanagement, the Indian economy did rather well in the current period despite political and military chaos. However, there was little innovation and introduction of new techniques in agriculture, manufacturing, or commerce. Much like the Chinese economy, it achieved and maintained previously achieved highs throughout most of the first half of the present phase. During the early eighteenth century, Indian civilization accounted for one-fourth of world GNP and about one-fourth of world trade. During the second half, because of agricultural, industrial, and education policies the British imposed, the Indian economy declined to a point so that by the mid-twentieth century, it accounted for barely 1 percent of world trade.

Systems of religious faith: European missionaries reintroduced Christianity into the subcontinent. In the pockets the Portuguese controlled, there were forcible conversions. The relationship between the majority Hindu and Muslim populations took a turn for the worse because of Aurangzeb's fanaticism, which led to the fragmentation of Mughal, creating an opportunity for the British to play a divide-and-rule game. It is noteworthy that the Maratha

Empire was religiously tolerant.

The question of science-religion conflict during the current phase in the seventeenth and eighteenth centuries in particular is irrelevant since there was little support for science after the Vijayanagara Empire was destroyed. The Mughals were hardly interested in science, and the rising Hindu states, such as the Marathas and Sikhs, were too preoccupied to fight the Moghuls and Afghan, Persian, and European invaders. During the nineteenth century, as the British organized the universities, the Hindu population took to European science enthusiastically. The Muslim population, however, lagged in adopting the new learning. During the latter part of the nineteenth century, the Indian civilization produced a string of homegrown world-class scientists, including Prafulla Chandra Ray (chemistry), Jagdish Chandra Bose and S. N. Bose (physics and biology), and C. V. Raman (optics).

Legal system: Toward the end of the eighteenth century, three legal systems were competing: the Hindu legal system based on caste, sharia law, and the British legal code. The latter was established in steps: Madras (1652), Bombay (1672), and Bengal (1772). From 1772 to 1864, mostly British judges used the Anglo-Hindu legal code and expert advice of the Indian Brahmins, who knew traditional Indian law, to dispense justice. By the mid-nineteenth century, because of accumulated cases, the pundits and their advice had become redundant. Anglo-Hindu law was well received and highly appreciated by the Hindu majority population. The same, however, could not be said of sharia law and the Muslim population.

Social structure: The social structure of the different states became even more complex: in most states. The caste system remained intact, as did the preferential treatment given to the Muslim population in states under Muslim dynasties. The one great exception was the Maratha Empire, where the caste rules were not adhered: Brahmins became prime ministers, a shepherd became the ruler of Indore, and rulers of Baroda and Gwalior were of peasant origin. Still another layer was the Europeans: Portuguese in Goa and British in Madras, Bombay, and Bengal replaced the Moghuls or other dynasties as the ruling class. With the fall of Indian dynasties in 1857 and the arrival of the British wives, the social hierarchy became even more complex: the British ruling elite followed by local dynasties allied to the British, an anglophile class of Hindus, educated upper-caste Hindus, the Muslim population, and lower-caste Hindus.

Internal equality undoubtedly suffered under Aurangzeb's fanaticism, took a turn for the better under the Marathas, and took a turn for the worse as the British began to transform themselves from traders to rulers in Bengal, Madras, and Bombay. This pattern continued until the departure of the British. The British inculcated preferred communities such as Gorkhas from Nepal, the Anglo-Indian community, the Parsi community, and the converted Christian community.

Knowledge-Creating and educational institutions: The present phase continued to lie between the age of great Hindu and Buddhist universities Muslim invaders destroyed and the rise of westernized universities under the British control. There was an extensive system of traditional education, however, in India as late as the nineteenth century. In the late eighteenth century, before British rule began to systematically devalue (James Mill) and defund the indigenous system, in Bengal itself, there were a hundred thousand schools or a school in each village. Thus, basic education was more widespread in India than in England in 1800. Significantly, this education was not confined to the Brahmins but was spread across all castes and both Hindu and Muslim populations. The education took place in *pathshalas*, *gurukulas*, and *Madrassas*, which were more than mere schools; they were "cultural watering holes." Education of the Muslim population in Madrassas or religious schools took a balanced approached of religious and secular curriculum but though a step down from the time of Akbar, indicating the continuing poisonous impact of Aurangzeb's policies. The wealthy continued to rely on private tutoring. In addition, there were schools for higher learning such as medicine. Sketchy records indicate there were there were 1,101 schools of higher learning in the Madras presidency, 16 schools of higher learning in Ahmednagar, and 164 in Poona at the end of the eighteenth century. From a historical perspective, the Muslim invaders destroyed great Indian universities but left basic educational structure intact, and the British destroyed systems of basic education but created institutes of higher learning that looked down on Indian culture with the objective of creating half-baked anglophile Indians to serve the needs of the British administration. In that effort, the likes of Macaulay succeeded beyond their wildest imagination by the mid-nineteenth century.

Wealth allocation process: Despite the famine of 1770 brought about by British policy, the sustainable growing surplus achieved a previously demonstrated high point with essentially stagnant technology. As the British gained a foothold in Bengal, the limitless British hunger for revenue extraction became obvious. The first beneficiary of this revenue was the military personnel (paid on the first of each month in a brilliant tactical break from past practices) needed to maintain and expand the territory under British control. This starved the education system and the wealth creation process of any investment. The investment also began to pour into infrastructure needed to move the commodities. Thus, the sustainable surplus increasingly came to be under the control of a foreign invader with a clear policy aimed at destroying Indian agricultural patterns, Indian industry, and Indian education and draining of surplus out of the civilization to feed the Industrial Revolution in their island home.

Societal cohesion process: Social cohesion of Indian society, already under attack by a religious fanatic in the person of Aurangzeb, further deteriorated through the British policy of divide and rule. Despite the breakdown of the caste system initiated by the Maratha Empire, the British policy enflamed both religious and caste divisions. Education began to be limited to higher classes of Hindus in areas under British control. The destruction of education system began to alienate the educated from their roots, further weakening the social cohesion.

Internal wars: Most of the phase was full of terrible internal conflicts: the terrible Mughal wars of succession, Aurangzeb's twenty-six-year effort to conquer the south, the struggle between the Mughal emperors and rebellious provinces, and the struggle between the Mughals and Marathas. By the end of the eighteenth century, the Portuguese and the British had been in India for two centuries and clearly regarded themselves as "Indian" powers. They were the instigating factor in the intensity and frequency of internal wars until 1857. One is tempted to call the period between 1680, when Shivaji died, and 1857, when the British won the first war of independence, as a continuous, 177-year war-torn period. The British were subsequently allowed a generation of peace until the creation of the Indian national Congress, and in 1911, when King George held a pompous durbar in the Mughal court in Delhi, the British were scarcely a generation away from being thrown out but only after they extracted their price through horrible division of the subcontinent.

Formative Beliefs and Ideology at the End of Fourth Synthesis Phase

The beliefs and ideology hardly changed during the first half of the phase. Nearly all of India came under Muslim control. This was followed by a transitional period during which Marathas came close to unifying India under indigenous royalty. However, Afghani and European invaders upset the political balance. In the final third of the phase, belief systems and ideology evolved under the influence of European science and institutional structures and processes.

- A continuing belief in knowledge, through trained intuition and meditation on the part of the majority Hindu population and the antiscience attitude of Muslim rulers in the first half of the phase followed by the Hindu reformist movement sparked by European learning and the continuing insistence by Muslim population on the Koran as the word of God in the latter part of the phase
- A strengthened belief in the fundamental inequality among different castes
- An attitude of insularity toward the intellectual and religious creativity of others
- A continuing belief in the peacefulness toward other social orders by Hindu population in principle and by Muslim rulers in practice

These beliefs set the stage for antiscience philosophy of Turkish Muslims in the subcontinent, followed by a reaction against them.

17.15 Extrinsic Peaceful Causes

There were no peaceful causes impacting the Indian civilization during the phase.

17.16 Extrinsic Violent Causes

Loss of SPI

Indian civilization faced utmost challenges during the current phase: Aurangzeb's fanatic and frantic effort to expand the territory and force conversion to Islam was followed by invasions from the northwest and de facto British control of India. The Indian response to these challenges varied. Briefly, it failed in the first and third and nearly succeeded in the second, despite what some historians would want you to believe.

Aurangzeb's fanaticism: Reaction to Aurangzeb's fanaticism was the emergence of militancy and political fracture leading to the substantial weakening of Mughal power in India and the rise of revolutionary Sikhs, Marathas, and Mysore Empires. The majority Hindu population experienced some level of freedom after five centuries of Muslim oppression to one degree or another, mirroring the experience of the Iberian Peninsula in Europe. However, the resulting Moghul weakness created an opening for both the opportunistic Persian/Afghan raids and British control of India.

Persian/ Afghan invasion: Persian Nader Shah simply looted and departed. Abdali was from Afghanistan, which is contiguous to India, so he was interested in building an empire. He was, however, not successful in that effort and was ultimately defeated by Sikhs in 1766. However, Abdali handed a decisive defeat to Marathas in 1761, ending the Peshwa period and fragmenting the Maratha Empire. It made British conquest during the second half of the eighteenth century a lot easier.

British control of India: Indian civilization became politically fragmented shortly after Aurangzeb's death and paid a price for it. Until 1750, European powers, despite a very strong naval presence, had been forced to confine themselves in coastal enclaves, focusing on extracting wealth through trade.

As the Mughal and Maratha Empires splintered under invasions from the northwest, direct territorial control and accelerated drain of the wealth became possible. Given the military strength, particularly sea power, of the British and the alliances they created and deception they employed, the Indian states of Bengal (1757), Mysore (1799), the Marathas (1813), Sikhs (1851), and Mughals (1857) challenged the British and lost while the Nizam and Rajput states allied with the British. This hundred-year struggle gave the British exactly twenty-eight years of peaceful reign until the Indian National Congress was born in 1885 to challenge the British, this time through largely peaceful means eventually under Gandhi's leadership.

In short, Aurangzeb's fanaticism opened the gates for both invasions from northwest and loss to the British with Marathas coming close to uniting India under a Hindu dynasty before losing to the British.

Loss of Control of Wealth and Means of Wealth

During the post-Aurangzeb period in the eighteenth century, the surplus stayed mostly within the civilization, except what was looted by Persian Nadir Shah and by the British in Bengal. However, it was necessarily channeled into military activities or toward the lifestyle of the elite, and its control shifted constantly.

Impact on Productive Outcomes

Mughal emperors, beginning with Jahangir, were probably justified in granting trade rights to the Europeans before the advent of the Industrial Revolution, since Indian manufacturing had a differential advantage over European manufacturing in several key industries and since the Dutch, French, and British were engaged in a worldwide conflict for superiority. However, the process of weakening of the Mughal Empire after 1757, a period when European states hardly needed the permission of Mughals or other Indian rulers to control trade, also coincided with the Industrial Revolution coming of age: the rise of steam power, iron technology, and the rise of factory system based on a hired industrial worker and task specialization within and across the system of factories. The later Mughal rulers, much like the Ottoman and Safavid Empires, acted as if they were unaware of the strategic impact of loss of trade. Thus, the process of reversal of the Indian advantage in manufacturing and increasingly coerced trade based on tariffs and duties (following Colbert's theory of mercantilism), and agricultural policy and military defeats of Marathas, Mysore, and Sikhs, as well as the treachery of Nizam and some Rajput states, went hand in hand. By the early nineteenth century, the British had gained complete control over the trade of a civilization that was twenty times larger.

Thus, the British took exactly a century (from the 1757 battle of Plessey in Bengal to the first war of independence in 1857) to extend their control over India, and in the process they systematically destroyed Indian agriculture, industry, and education and built the infrastructure to extract its wealth, thereby bringing poverty and destitution to a civilization that had hardly known this phenomenon before. In 1757, the Indian civilization had a self-sustaining agricultural sector and a highly developed though unmechanized industrial base. Europeans never sold anything to India in seventeenth century; they only bought and paid in gold. India had nearly a quarter of the world export market, the needed mineral wealth for the eighteenth century (oil was not needed then), and a significant surplus. Added to this was the British technology, concepts of market economy, and business management. This would seem to be a marriage made in heaven for an economic growth. The question arises: what went wrong? The answer is indeed simple if unflattering to the conquerors, for it exposes their hypocrisy. While the conquerors talked of a civilizing mission, their actions spoke louder than their words. Below, we list specific British actions in agriculture, industry, and trade:

- Having failed in direct collection of revenue, they abolished the hereditary and customary right of peasants to the land to a landlord system of ownership in 1793 in Bengal, Bihar, and Orissa, followed by the Ryotwari system of direct revenue collection in Bombay and Madras Presidencies and the Mahalwari system in the Ganges Plain and parts of Punjab. As the British entrenched, they collected revenue directly and at nearly two to three times what was prevalent before them.

- In Bengal, land revenue was doubled between 1762 and 1765. Under the Mahalwari system, the revenue collection reached as high as 83 percent of the produce.

- On the industrial side, as mechanized production driven by steam power took off in England in the early nineteenth century, Britain began to dump cheap manufactured goods into India through a serious of tariffs and duties and made a concerted effort to destroy the textile industry that produced superior quality cloth. Historian William Digby has estimated that population of Dhaka declined by 60 percent between 1787 and 1817. During the same period, the population of London doubled and the export of muslin declined from rupees eight million to zero.

- To meet the burgeoning needs of textile mills in England, agricultural production was shifted from grain to cotton, thus creating a food shortage and thirty-two documented famines during British rule in India.

- In the trade sector, since India became a market for British goods, it transformed India from a manufacturing powerhouse into a commodity supplier.

Apologists rationalize British actions by saying that the British did not understand the difference between an Indian landlord and a British landlord. This view hardly is tenable when one considers what the British did in China with opium, with the African slave trade, or to Indian textile industry. The ugly reality is that until the Industrial Revolution, the British bought Indian goods using gold and silver from the Americas, and with the Industrial Revolution, control of India, and the American Revolution, it was more profitable to drain wealth directly from India.

As we noted in the last chapter, Indian Muslim merchants brought Islam to Southeast Asia, and by the beginning of the current phase, most of Indonesia and Malaysia were converted to Islam and ruled by Sultanates. However, the Portuguese and the Dutch took over trade during the sixteenth and seventeenth centuries, each outdoing the other in brutality. Though neither gained full control of Indonesian and Malaysian territory, the Dutch nearly controlled all aspects of the trade, exploiting the internal divisions. Thus, there was little direct contact between the Indian civilization, which had inspired Southeast Asia for a millennium, and Southeast Asia.

The productive outcomes in India suffered e3normously both because of the wealth drain and lack of investment except needed to get raw materials and commodities out.

Transmission of Creativity

At the start of the current phase Islamic rule had existed for four centuries in North India with pockets in the south and Muslim converts probably constituted 10 percent of the population and a new Indo-Muslim culture in art, architecture, music and even religion had sprung forth. Muslim civilization in India had become thoroughly Indian. However, there was little ongoing impact of Muslim civilization outside of India. Moghul had maintained diplomatic relations with Safavid Empire but the Ottomans were too far. Only in the eighteenth century did Muslim states outside India attempted raids after the Moghul Empire began disintegrating to be replaced by the British. Thus, there was little impact of Muslim civilization from outside; it was more a question of Muslim ideology impacting the civilization internally through Indian Muslims and of the latter, there was plenty.

Similarly, there was little interaction with the Chinese civilization during the current phase. During the seventeenth and eighteenth centuries, China was too busy pursuing imperialism on its western and northern borders and in the nineteenth and twentieth centuries, both India and China were preoccupied with fighting European imperialism. Thus, there was little exchange in practical, intellectual, and religious creativity or trade and migrations.

The interaction between India and Europe during the current phase was extensive. The interaction may be described in two parts: during the mercantile period, when interaction centered on trade and the diffusion of weapons technology, and during the period of systematic wealth drain. Systematic wealth drain occurred through the "peaceful" destruction of Indian industry, agriculture, and education, followed by the diffusion of modern science and manufacturing and transport technologies and British political and legal systems.

Practical creativity: Because of the territorial ambitions of competing European states and Indian states being drawn into the global French-British conflict (often called World War Zero), there was significant diffusion of weapons technology from Europe to India, often through French traders, technicians, and soldiers well into the nineteenth century. Most Indian dynasties resisted the invader, including accessing superior weapons technologies. This has been well documented for the reigns of Haider, Tipu, and Ranjit Singh.

Religious creativity: Christianity got a modest boost through the emergence of the Anglo-Indians.

Intellectual creativity: The real intent of the British educational initiative in India after 1857 was twofold: create the class of half-baked intellectuals needed to run bureaucracy and impress the Indians with the superiority of European intellectual achievements. The destruction of the Indian education system was followed by the inevitable diffusion of European science, manufacturing, and transport technologies. The British legal system and later political institutions were foisted on India, coinciding with the rise of an anglophile, Western-educated upper class and a clerical middle class. Thus, the British encouraged the spread of universities that taught not only science but also the superiority of European civilization and the honesty and altruism of the British (as exemplified by the creation of railroad network), thus creating subservient class of clerks and limiting the rise of industry.

Impact on Institutional Structures and Processes

The impact of the British on stagnated Indian civilization under antiscience Muslim dynasties was as profound and quick as the world has ever witnessed.

Political system: The constitutional monarchy of Britain with its hollow democracy was hardly at the cutting edge of political thinking, though it never prevented British political scientists from regarding it as the apex of human political development at a time in the world when France had rejected monarchy, Americans had defeated monarchy and adopted constitutional government, and Germany had glorified its patchwork of princely states. Also, the British had treaties with several Indian states that had committed treason during 1757–1857. Thus, even as developing political ideas of representative democracy reached India, the British could hardly allow these ideas to take root on their own, both because of the aforementioned treaties and the need to maintain control. While Indians clamored for political reform beginning in the late twentieth century, the British controlled its introduction to avoid a mass revolt. Only after independence was India able to implement the concepts of representative e democracy in one fell scoop.

Military capability: The British had the utmost impact on Indian military capability in weapons, command structure, tactics, and strategy. It was needed to maintain control of India and to keep the French and Portuguese at bay.

Economic organization: While the British destroyed Indian agriculture, industry, and trade, they also allowed the development of the modern business methods and instruments of market economy, such as the beginnings of capital markets, stock exchanges, and the central banking necessary to govern.

Systems of religious faith: The British shrewdly stayed away from either preaching Christianity or reforming Hinduism, with the exception of the custom of Sati as an obvious symbol of their progressive agenda. However, in other religious matters, on either Hindu or Muslim side, they remained uninvolved. The task of religious reformation was carried by the Indians themselves.

Legal systems: The British had the highest impact in transforming the legal system. The religious and caste basis of the legal system was cast aside and was replaced by British common law and executive orders designed to modernize the system and maintain control as discussed elsewhere in the chapter. A court system along British lines was established using English law. The government also required registration of birth, death, marriage, and the recording of deeds, wills, and trusts.

Social structure: It should come as no surprise to the reader that the highly class-conscious British with an ideology of racial superiority added layers to the already caste-ridden and religiously divided Indian civilization. The specter of Indian princes petitioning the British government to increase the number of gun salutes they deserved is as comical as the British holding a Moghul-style *darbar* in Delhi.

Educational structure: The British established a university system in India in 1857 through universities in Calcutta, Bombay, and Madras, focusing on liberal arts and law and not science and technology since the focus was to create recruits for bureaucracy and to develop an inferiority complex. Listen to McCauley's speech to the Parliament in 1835 concerning the purpose of education reforms: *"I have traveled across the length and breadth of India, and I have not seen one person who is a beggar, who is a thief. Such wealth I have seen in this country, such high moral values, people of such caliber, that I do not think we would ever conquer this country, **unless we break the very backbone of this nation**, which is her spiritual and cultural heritage, and, therefore, I propose that we replace her old and ancient education system, her culture, for if the Indians think that all that is foreign and English is good and greater than their own, they will lose their self-esteem, their native self-culture, and they will become what we want them, a truly dominated nation."*

Assessment of Net Impact

It is indeed superfluous to state that after the litany of aforementioned charges of hypocrisy and self-serving actions in the name of a civilizing mission, that the net impact of the British Raj in India was highly negative. In fact, it would indeed be hard to find a comparable example of such sickening proportions in world history when a small state was able to inflict such damage to the body, heart, and soul of a major civilization. Fortunately, Britain was unable to give Indian civilization a fatal blow; that was, of course, hardly in British interest. The patient must not die but must remain alive not for transfusion but to calculate the rate of drawing blood. In that, the British succeeded. The fatal blow was reserved for people on the other side of the world; people who were erroneously called Indians because a sailor named Columbus thought he had landed on Indian shores in 1492 CE.

17.17 Productive Outcomes

Wealth creation: The Indian civilization was one of the richest civilizations in the world until around 1750, despite being faced with coerced trade. It probably produced 25% of the wealth in the world, and its share of foreign trade was in a similar range. The wealth-creation capacity of Indian civilization, however, declined precipitously during the systematic wealth drain period because of British policy of keeping Indian agriculture hostage to British needs and the conscious destruction of Indian industry. By the time the British had left India, India had been transformed from one of the richest countries in the world to one of the poorest. Such was the impact of the self-proclaimed British civilizing mission. After the departure of the British, the Indian economy remained mired in socialist policies for nearly a generation and was derided by the Western press as stuck in a "Hindu-rate of growth." However, since 1991, the economy was liberalized, and Indian economy has demonstrated the capacity to grow at 10 percent a year. It seems that the economy will take its rightful place in the world by 2050 or after a lapse of three hundred years.

Migrations and travels: During the twentieth century, probably 2 percent of the Indian population migrated to Europe, England, United States, West Indies, Fiji Islands, Africa, and United States in conditions ranging from indentured labor to highly educated engineers, scientists, and physicians. These emigrants have adopted so well to their new homelands that it has become an adage with obvious exaggeration to claim that Indians succeed anywhere except in India.

Fair trade: British Departure has meant a two-century legacy of coerced trade finally came to an end. Though India's share of world trade is quite small at present, it is increasing at a good pace.

17.18 Creative Outcomes

Achievements in Practical Creativity

Modest achievements in the practical creativity of the Indian civilization essentially occurred during the mercantile period, before the planned and well executed destruction of Indian industry, irreparable damage to Indian agriculture, and ruin of indigenous education system took their tolls during the systematic wealth-drain period. However, creative endeavors, even during the mercantile period, were severely handicapped by stagnation that resulted from Aurangzeb's fanaticism and the resulting fragmentation of the political system as well as general stagnation from centuries of rule by dynasties steeped in intolerant monotheism and luxurious living.

The Mughal dynasty's focus was military strength and management of economy. Toward the former, a volley gun was developed by a Persian immigrant to Akbar's court in 1582. In addition, there was a two-century effort to develop metal cylinder rockets, which allowed greater propulsion, during the times of Akbar, Shahjahan, and later in Mysore under Haider Ali and Tipu Sultan. Tipu reportedly had a Rocket corps numbering five thousand and had considerable success against the British. Toward economy, the principal contribution of Akbar reign was land survey in the empire and the systematization of the land tax.

On the technology front, Indian agriculture used the seed drill and mammooty plow. These seed drill designs were sent to England. It remains unclear how long these instruments had been in use or when these inventions took place. The strength of the Indian textile industry was legendary. Dacca muslin was so fine, seven yards of the muslin rolled could be passed through an ordinary finger ring. There were highly efficient processes to make mortar, paper, iron, and steel. Isaac Pike described the mortar-making process in 1775 and compared the quality of Madras mortar to plaster of Paris and found the former to be superior. Similarly, the iron-making processes in central India were described by Major James Franklin of the Bengal Army in 1829, who found Indian wrought iron to be superior to Swedish wrought iron, which was thought to be of best quality in Europe. He goes on to describe the existence of mobile furnaces requiring little capital investment and capable of producing twenty-five tons of iron per year at a cost equivalent of two pounds and six shillings per ton and the cost of malleable iron at five pounds and ten shillings per ton. Similarly, in 1774, Lieutenant Colonel Edmund Ironside described the paper making process and instruments using the Indian plant known as San. Finally, Helenus Scott described the processes for making soap, gunpowder, indigo ink, cinnabar, vitriol, alum, and fossil alkali.

One item of interest was the introduction of "champo" or therapeutic massage to head to Europe by Indian traveler Sheikh din Mohammed. The modern word *shampoo* is derived from Hindi word Champo. His business became so successful in England that he was appointed shampooing surgeon to Kings George IV and William IV.

The general impression one gets from these descriptions is a country with technological diversity and sophistication—a sophistication that often impressed foreign observers. This indigenous technology was destroyed through products of the Industrial Revolution coupled with a policy of tariffs and duties. After the British gained control of Bengal in 1765, the company oppressed highly skilled weavers and dictated prices, and those who refused were subject to repression including, it is said, such sinister methods such as cutting hands of these textile guild workers.

Achievements in Religious Creativity

During the period of systematic wealth drain beginning with British control of Bengal, the Hindu elite in Bengal came to believe that Hindu religiosity had been corrupted by Buddhist agnosticism and manipulation by the Brahmins. Thus, Brahmo Samaj was founded by Ram Mohan Roy and Dvinder Nath Tagore with the intention of purging Hinduism of these influences. It preached one God as the source of all creation, love, and the importance of righteous conduct based the teachings of Upanishads. At the social level, it advocated the abolition of caste system, dowry system, and child marriage and the emancipation of women. The movement was split by Keshab Chander Sen, who not only viewed Christianity favorably but also thought of the British rule as a divine gift to India! The movement was strongly associated with the Tagore family in Bengal and influenced Ramakrishna; Vivekananda, who represented India at World Region Council in Chicago in 1893; and Mahatma Gandhi. It also gave birth to the Arya Samaj movement in Punjab and North India.

Thus, Hindu religiosity during the phase focused on protecting religion from Aurangzeb's fanaticism and responding to the challenges posed by both Christianity and European enlightenment. Thus, Hinduism survived Aurangzeb, tackled the challenge posed by Christianity, and sought refuge in its Upanishad roots while continuing its millennium-long tradition of distancing itself from Buddhism.

Orthodox Sunni and Shia sects of Indian Islam remained essentially closed as befitting a revealed religious doctrine.

However, attempts were made to create a synthesis of Islam and Hinduism, as we noted in the last chapter. Akbar tried and failed. Sikhism is thought by many to have been influenced by Islam, as we noted in last chapter. After 1650, the Hindu majority population was in a mode to preserve its religion as it struggled against the fanatical religious policies of Aurangzeb.

If Islamic thought affected Indian religiosity, the reverse was also true, though to a limited extent. In 1889, Mirza Gulam Ahmed founded the Ahmadiyya movement, which questioned the mainstream Muslim view of Mohammed as the last prophet, the justification of Jihad as a violent struggle, and claiming himself to be the last avatar of Hindu god Vishnu. Ahmadis are treated in India as Muslims but not in most other Muslim countries, including Pakistan. Consequently, Ahmadis are persecuted and discriminated in many Muslim countries and have been forced to immigrate to other countries.

Sikhism, as we noted in the last chapter, is monotheistic and believes in a God that is shapeless, unseen, timeless, omnipresent, and omnipotent. The omnipresence of God and Nanak as the prophet distinguishes Sikhism from Islam. The cosmos came into existence when God willed it to be. There was little evolution in the basic tenets of Sikhism during the phase. The key achievements were compilation of the teachings into Adi Granth by the fifth guru, Arjun, and creating a politicized and militarized Khalsa community by the last and tenth Guru Gobind Singh in 1699 in response to the fanaticism of Aurangzeb.

Achievements in Philosophical Creativity

If the reform movement of the Hindu religion focused on eradicating the accumulated social ills of the caste system and the position of women, developments in Hindu philosophy were essentially a reaffirmation of traditional metaphysics. There was no new ground in epistemology, ethics, and aesthetics.

Metaphysics: It is difficult to claim that the Indian civilization broke new ground in metaphysics during the current phase. Much like religious creativity, philosophic creativity was a response to the challenge of Western philosophy by reasserting the validity of Upanishad teaching and Vedanta worldview through the works of Vivekananda (1863–1902), Aurobindo (1872–1950), Raman Maharishi (1879–1950), and Radhakrishan (1888–1975). Raman Maharishi was most accommodating: while preferring Jnana yoga to achieve liberation, he believed it was possible to achieve that objective through other paths and other religions. Even Coomaraswamy advocated Perennial philosophy (1877–1947), since the fundamental concepts of Perennial philosophy are not different from Vedanta, the precedence of spirit over matter, or unity of individual spirit and the Brahman or universal spirit. Perhaps the closest it came to such a claim on new a contribution was through the work of Aurobindo, who introduced the concept of evolution into the Vedanta system, arguing that the initial contradictory material universe came out of a spiritual reality and existence as we know it resulted from this contradictory material universe through evolution. However, it is difficult to see how this concept is different from Hegel's system, which claimed the existence of the Eternal Idea that "alienates" into nature (or acquires a contradictory existence) and recovers itself in human consciousness at a certain stage in its development.

Epistemology: In epistemology, Radhakrishnan promoted the power of intuitive thinking over reasoning in his book, *The Idealist View of Life*. Despite his claim of being an agnostic, this is consistent with fundamental Vedanta idealism, which sees the birth of ultimate knowledge as based on intuitive awakening. However, if intuitive thinking is seen as a combination of powers of reasoning and imagination, with imagination providing the possibilities and reason (and fact) sorting out the possibilities, it is difficult to accept the uniqueness Radhakrishnan assigns to intuitive thinking.

There were no significant achievements in ethics or aesthetics.

Achievements in Art

Visual arts: Unlike science and philosophy, the Delhi Sultanate actually contributed significantly to developing architecture based on Indian and Persian traditions, as we noted in the last chapter. During the Mughal period, Persian tradition influenced both Indian painting and Indian architecture but still not Indian sculpture, which retained the classical Indian tradition since Islam did not permit the sculpture form of art. The miniature painting tradition during the Mughal period developed considerably as it became realistic in style and developed a greater use of perspective and as its subject matter expanded to include, animals, and plants while continuing the Islamic tradition of illustrating books and calligraphy. After the decline of Mughals, the miniature painting tradition migrated to the Rajput courts and from there to other parts of the country, such as the Kangra district in Himachal Pradesh. It finally evolved into "company painting" under European influence. Kangra paintings are based on Hindu religious themes, nature, and graceful feminine form. The Indo-Persian synthesis in architecture achieved great heights as evidenced by the Taj Mahal. In the east, during the British period, the Bengal school of art was created, which emphasized indigenous styles. Later twentieth-century artists such as Amrita Sher-Gill introduced European avant-garde style into Indian art. Post-independence saw a resurgence of indigenous themes in painting (M. F. Hussain and S. H. Raza) followed by a greater influence of artistic style from all parts of the world.

Performing arts: In the north, under the Moghuls, the classical *kathakali* dance form underwent significant development through Persian (straight legs) and Turkish (spinning, possibly from whirling dervishes) influence. Later, Mughals supported several *garanas* or schools, particularly at Jaipur, Lucknow, Benaras, and Raiharh. The British disparaged the *kathak* form, and it only survived in houses of ill repute until independence, when it has regained its old glory in part through Indian cinema. In the south, *Bharatanatyam*, which had remained confined to the temples, gained respectability in the twentieth century and became accepted in broader mass culture through efforts of individuals like Rukmani Devi Arundale. In the twentieth century, the medium of cinema popularized not only Indian classical dances but also folk dances such as *bhangra* and Garba dances as well as many Western dance forms.

Both in the north and south, Indian, classical forms of Carnatic and Hindustani music respectively dominated the music scene during most of the current phase. Indian music has remained monophonic and mainly vocal, raga-based, and dependent on a highly developed rhythm, while encouraging improvisation and is aimed at evoking universal emotions. Much like dance, it evolved through Gharanas supported by the nobility. While ragas may trace their origin to antiquity, Hindustani music underwent considerable development under Mughal period, which produced great vocalists like Tansen. Carnatic music may trace its distinct form to Purandara Das (1494), followed by Syam Sastri (1762–1827) and Tayagraja (1767–1847). In the twentieth century, mostly through cinema, Western melodies have crept into Indian music, and Indian music has become better known outside India, mainly in European civilization, through efforts of numerous talented musicians. There have been efforts to create fusion music with limited success.

Literature: During the Mughal period, Persian was the sole court and administrative language followed by an Urdu and Persian period, followed by English, while the Indian languages retained their regional influence and continued to develop their own literature.

Thus, during the Persian period, old literary works in Sanskrit were translated into Persian, and the Indian civilization produced several notable literary figures who wrote in Persian, such as poet Mohammed Iqbal (1877–1938), who wrote in Persian and Urdu.

The major regional languages in North India after the decline of Persian have been Urdu, Hindi, Bengali, and Gujrati, while the main languages in the south have been Telgu, Tamil, Kanada, and Marathi. Each region developed its own distinct literature during the current phase.

Urdu literature included significant developments in highly popular poetry known as *ghazal* (which was introduced into India from Persia and Sufi mystics) that covered romance, religion, and philosophy, and the emergence of the first significant Urdu novel, *Umrao Jaaan Ada*, in 1899, was written by Mirza Hadi Ruswa (1857–1931). Urdu short stories also blossomed in the twentieth centuries through the efforts of Premchand and Krishan Chander.

The Bengali literary movement in the nineteenth and twentieth centuries may be considered as part of the Bengal renaissance and included such prominent poets and novelists as Rabindranath Tagore, Sarat Chandra Chattopadhyay, and Bankim Chandra Chattopadhyay.

Similarly, Hindi literature saw considerable development in the twentieth century through efforts of Premchand, Mahadevi Verma, Harivansh Rai Bachchan, and Maithali Sharan Gupt.

In the south, the twentieth century also witnessed the rise of Telau, Tamil, Marati, and Orriya literature.

After a brief period in post-independence India, there was an effort to make Hindi the national language, an act the non-Hindi speaking population resisted. This was eventually abandoned with English, a language understood by the educated segment from all linguistic groups in India, becoming a de facto national language. This furthered the development of Indo-English literature through the efforts of writers such as R. K. Narayan, Vikram Seth, Chetan Bhagat, Khuswant Singh, Gita Mehta, and Nayantara Sehgal, to name a few. Several of these writers have achieved international acclaim. In addition, Indian immigrants settled in different parts of the English-speaking world and produced great writers such as Salman Rushdie, V. S. Naipaul, and Jhuma Lahiri.

To summarize, the creative achievements of Indian civilization in practical creativity, religious creativity, science, and philosophy did not amount to much during the Mughal period. However, the arts, particularly architecture and music, achieved new heights. During the British and systematic wealth drain period, there was a concerted effort to reinterpret the Hindu heritage in the light of European achievements and a modest renaissance in science, dance, and literature. In the latter part of the twentieth century, overseas, the Indians achieved world-class results in science and technology in particular, giving a psychological lift to the Indian civilization.

Destructive Outcomes Impacting Other Civilizations

True to its eight-millennia history of peaceful existence, Indian civilization did not attack any other civilization—not that it had an opportunity to do so. India, however, was attacked by newly created Pakistan three times and by China once after British departure. Today, India remains the only major civilization in the world that has never attacked other civilizations.

17.19 Achievements in Science

Achievements in Formal Sciences

Mathematics: The Indian mathematical tradition essentially had died with the Kerala school. During the current phase, mathematical contributions came from two foreign-inspired sources: the first took place through the work of two remarkable, self-taught mathematicians Ram Chundra (1821–1880) and Ramanujam (1887–1920) under the impact of the spread of British education in India. Ram Chundra developed a highly original algebraic method of finding maxima and minima of function through algebra without using calculus. Ramanujam had little training in mathematics and literally rediscovered a century of European mathematics, including work in number theory, infinite series, and functional analysis. He developed nearly four thousand mathematical identities. His work was not terse and involved such intellectual gymnastics that it was difficult to follow for even talented mathematicians. An international journal known as *Ramanujan Journal* has been launched to bring attention and understanding to his legacy. He is probably the only mathematician to have a journal devoted to his work, and he died at age thirty-three! He is considered by many to be in the same league as Gauss and Euler and may even be in a league by himself. It is perhaps no exaggeration to state that mathematical genius like Ramanujan is born once a millennium.

The second source resulted through Indian immigrants to Us universities and included names such as Harish Chandra (1923–1983), Srinivasan Vardhan (1940–), and Manjul Bhargava (1974–). Vardhan worked on stochastic differential equations and large deviations theory in statistics and was director of the Courant Institute of Mathematical Science from 1980 to 1984. It has been said that a remarkably large fraction of postwar mathematics came out of this institute. Bhargava is a highly decorated young mathematician who has made significant contributions in number theory and composition laws for quadratic and higher level forms. Harish Chandra developed the theory of arithmetic groups.

Logic

The Indian civilization achieved little in the field of logic during the current phase. However, during the nineteenth century, European logicians discovered Indian logic and analysis of inference and realized that Aristotle's syllogism could not account for the more sophisticated Indian syllogism. Further research is needed to understand the extent to which discovery of Indian logic and analysis of inference influenced nineteenth-century European pioneers such as Boolean, Cabbage, and de Morgan. There has been an increasing appreciation of the impact of Indian mathematics on European mathematics through number theory, algebra, trigonometry, and infinitesimal analysis, and these branches broke new ground from a geometry-centered Greek mathematics in the twentieth century. The same cannot be definitively said about Indian logic at this point.

Linguistics

What is true for logic is also true for linguistics. The discovery of the perfection of Sanskrit grammar by European scholars and its relationship to European languages has opened a new research field of comparative linguistics. In the 1950s, the process of designing computer language made it abundantly clear that Panini grammar was world's first formal system or a well-defined system of abstract thought applied to language. Panini has been called an Indian Euclid or more appropriately, Euclid is a European Panini.

The moving camps of the Mughal army also produced a new language during the current phase combining Persian, Arabic words, Hindi grammar, and Arabic script, called Urdu.

Achievements in Physical Sciences

Astronomy: During the Mughal period, the focus in astronomy remained on observational astronomy with little theoretical advance, which essentially took place in the Vijayanagara Empire under the Kerala School of Mathematics and Astronomy. After the five surrounding Muslim sultanates destroyed the Vijayanagara Empire and before British control, the science of astronomy had essentially died in India until it was taken up by Hindu king Jai Singh of Amber, who used Muslim instruments and older Hindu computational methodologies and built several large observatories at Delhi, Mathura, Ujjain, Jaipur, and Benarus. One of his observatories was visited by a Jesuit who brought astronomical tables compiled by Philippe de La Hire. La Hire was chair of mathematics at College Royal in Paris in 1702, giving Jai Singh an opportunity to compare his data with that of Hire. Jai Singh concluded that his instruments and computational methodology were superior to those of Hire. It is worth noting that Hire's astronomical observations were taken decades after Tycho Brahe. Jai Singh also stated in the Zij-i-Mohammad Shahi that he used locally produced telescopes for astronomical data. Thus, it is fair to conclude that before the British, the state of Indian observational astronomy was world-class. It appears that Jai Singh was not aware of the work of the Kerala school (whose results possibly reached Europe through the Portuguese in the sixteenth century) and its essentially heliocentric view of the solar system as he was in the north and relied on Muslim and older Hindu astronomy. Equally, he was not aware of Newton's achievements. This must be considered a great missed opportunity in the history of Indian astronomy. The north did not know what the south had accomplished.

With the establishment of the British (who established the Madras Observatory in 1792) in the second half of the eighteenth century, by which time Newton's theories had become thoroughly established, Indian astronomical traditions were replaced by European astronomy through efforts of Indian astronomer Mir Muhammad Hussain, who traveled to England to study astronomy. He predicted the existence of galaxies in 1777, probably a decade before their existence was confirmed through Herschel's monstrous forty-foot-long telescope. The last Zij was written by Gulam Hussain Jaunpuri (1760–1862) in 1838 and printed in 1855, two years before the first war of independence against the British in 1857. However, both Indian freedom and the independent tradition of Indian astronomy died thereafter. Additional observatories were established at Kodaikanal in (1900) and at Hyderabad, which was called the Nizamiah Observatory after the sixth Nizam. Several centers of astronomical research were established, notably at Calcutta, Allahabad, and Benaras. After independence, Indian astronomical research in key areas has continued.

During the twentieth century, Indian contributions to astronomy came from Indian immigrants to Britain and the United States. Two names deserve special mention: Jayant Narlikar (1938–), who championed the steady-state universe model in the 1960s as an alternative to the Big Bang theory, and Chandrasekhar (1910–1995), a leader in the structure and evolution of stars. He is known for the Chandrasekhar limit, which defined the size of a star destined to become a neutron star and black hole.

Physics: Achievements of Indian civilization in physics during the current phase were almost entirely due to the impact of European civilization. In the late nineteenth century and early twentieth century, Indians produced two world-class homegrown physicists: J. C. Bose (1858–1938), who invented wireless signaling before Marconi, who is generally given the credit for the invention of radio and was first to use a semiconductor junction to detect the signal. The second was C. V. Raman (1888–1970), who discovered the phenomenon of the scattering of light. It has been acknowledged by Nevill Mott that Bose was sixty years ahead of his time in the use of semiconductors and in anticipating the existence of P-type and N-type semiconductors. Raman discovered the phenomenon of scattering of photons after a collision with an atom or molecule.

Of the Indians who conducted research in Britain or the United States, two names are worth mentioning. The first is George Sudarshan, who made pioneering contributions in quantum physics, including laying the foundation of the third fundamental force of nature, the electro-weak force, for which Wienburg, Glashow, and Salam were awarded the Nobel prize in 1979, and a quantum theory of coherent light, for which Glauber was awarded the Nobel prize in 2005. He has also postulated the existence of tachyons, which are particles that travel faster than light.

Chemistry: There was little new achieved in the field of theoretical chemistry during the early centuries of the current phase. It is worth mentioning that North India practiced an ice-making technique that used boiled water since dissolved gases and solids lowered the freezing point, making it difficult to freeze water under local conditions even in winter. Thus, they had a practical understanding of the depression of freezing point. Indian chemical technology in dyeing and metallurgy remains ignorant of the new experimental and quantitative basis being created in chemistry until the arrival of British education in the second half of the nineteenth century. In the nineteenth century, the most important chemist was P. C. Ray (1861–1944), who synthesized several interesting chemical compounds and wrote a definite book on the history of Indian chemistry to the middle of the seventeenth century. Other famous names included colloidal chemist Jnanendra Nath Mukherjee (1893–1983) and Nagendra Chandra Nag.

Earth Sciences

Cartography: Achievements in cartography pale in comparison to world-class achievements. We mention only two to underscore the point that it was not forgotten despite the fact that need was minimal as European states controlled the civilization's coast during most of the phase. Sadiq Isfahani compiled a world atlas of sorts in 1647. A remarkable map measuring twenty-two feet by twenty-one feet showing a house-by-house detail for the Rajput capital Amber.

Achievements in Biological Sciences

Biology: There was little focus on biological sciences before the advent of British education. The invention of the microscope (late sixteenth and early seventeenth centuries) and breakthroughs in plant classification and Darwin's theory did not generate immediate interest. J. C. Bose, after his groundbreaking work in signaling mentioned above, invented a crescograph that demonstrated the similarities between the plant and animal tissue to external stimuli.

Two names deserve mention among the Indians who migrated to United States. The first is H. G. Khurana, who helped show how the nucleotides in nucleic acids control the synthesis of proteins. The second is Venkatraman Ramakrishnan, who helped understand the structure and function of ribosome, the molecule responsible for catalyzing the reactions to produce proteins. Both of these scientists were awarded the Nobel Prize.

Medicine: During the current phase, the science of medicine also remained tradition-bound before the advent of British education in the nineteenth century. Indian physicians knew how to cure small pox and regularly performed cataract surgery. There was little new knowledge in anatomy and physiology. As modern medicine came to India in the nineteenth century, it was enthusiastically adopted, along with the continuation of the old Ayurveda system.

Achievements in Social Sciences

Psychology: In psychology, we need to mention J. Krishnamurti (1895–1986), who was discovered and groomed by the leaders of the Theosophical Society and Order in the Star of the East to preach Vedanta worldwide. He broke off with them in 1929 after an experience of "awakening." If he preached Vedanta or the union of Atman and Brahman before his awakening, he taught the importance of mind and thought. He claimed that truth must be found through the mirror of relationships and by understanding the contents of the mind. He pointed out the potential dangers of thought that can prevent understanding through clinging to past and an insecurity about future. It is not an exaggeration to state that Krishnamurti was close to a Buddhist sage, though he denied being a Buddhist because he believed being a Buddhist meant not understanding Buddha, as is evident from his sayings:

- Nobody listened to Buddha; that is why there is Buddhism.
- In my heart, there is a continual thought of Buddha.
- Buddha might have said there is intelligence that has nothing to do with thought (imagination and memory).
- Buddha's teaching comes closest to realizing the ultimate truth.

Krishnamurtis's life journey from rejecting Jnana yoga and Vedanta and accepting Raj yoga and Buddha, though not Buddhism, is instructive. He attempted to recover the science of psychology from the clutches of Vedanta. However, it must be said that he was not particularly successful since the idea that all religious beliefs are psychological in essence had not taken root.

Economics: There was little creative thought in economic theory in India during most of the phase. Significant contribution came through Indians who migrated to United States. Again, two names deserve mention: Jagdish Bhagvati, who is a well-known theorist in international trade, and Amartya Sen, who has developed theories for causes of famine, human development theory from a socio-economic perspective, social choice, and welfare economics in which an economic policy is evaluated in terms of community welfare. He has stated that right with a corresponding capability to properly exercise it meaningless. He won a Nobel Prize for his work in 1998 and has been called by some as the Mother Theresa of economic profession, a comparison he finds unfair to Mother Theresa.

Political science: The Indian civilization may be justly proud of developing the political philosophy of nonviolent struggle against a rational but exploitative aggressor. This philosophy was nourished by Indian religiosity as well as by writers such as Tolstoy and Thoreau, who were influenced by Indian philosophy. The philosophy of nonviolent struggle was used successfully both in the United States and South Africa by Martin Luther King Jr. and Nelson Mandela respectively to fight racism.

History, Causes, and Outcomes of the Muslim Civilization

17.20 Brief Political History

The Muslim world since the 1600s essentially witnessed two great empires, the Safavid and Ottoman, and has been increasingly under attack from the Europeans including the Russian, Austro-Hungarian, and British Empires and in the twentieth century by the Americans. After expelling the Muslims from Europe, Europeans took the war to Muslim homelands during the present phase, much like they did to the Indian and Chinese civilizations. However, similar to the Manchu Empire, Muslim empires were relatively strong in the eighteenth century and weakness crept in only during the nineteenth century. Consequently, the Muslim civilization, unlike the Indian civilization, had to endure European control for one and not two centuries. Unfortunately, the discovery of oil in several key Muslim states in the early twentieth century meant that Muslim states in West Asia remained under European/American control after World War II through puppet governments supported by European and American interests.

Safavid Empire: As we saw in the last chapter, after the demise of the Il Khananate in 1335, Persia remained divided until arrival of another despot, Timur Lane. The Timurid dynasty survived for less than seventy-five years and was followed by lesser Mongol dynasties until 1502, when Shah Ismail I from northwestern Iran conquered Persia and most of modern-day Iraq and Afghanistan. Under Shah Abbas I (1587–1629), the Persian Empire expanded to include Uzbekistan and fought to hold Iraq against the Ottoman pushback. He also successfully defeated the Portuguese and the British from the Persian Gulf but expanded trade with the Dutch and English. Shah Abbas left no able heirs as he had his ablest sons murdered for fear of rebellion. Thus, the Safavids declined in the following century, and Ottomans and Russians took advantage of the decline to reconquer part of the territory. Safavids were deposed by Nader Shah, a commander of Mongol origin in the army. Nader Shah invaded and terrorized Delhi in 1739 and was assassinated in1747 for his cruelty and destructiveness. He was followed by the Zand (1750–1794) dynasty in the west and Ahmed Shah Abdali (1747–1772) in the east in present-day Afghanistan. Following the Zand dynasty, Persia witnessed the rise of the Qajar dynasty (1796–1925), which was founded by another Turkic tribe. During Qajar rule, Persia lost wars to Russia and Britain, losing Uzbekistan and Turkmenistan to Russia and control of the Persian Gulf to Britain. Unsuccessful attempts at democratic reforms failed, and Russians and the British occupied Persia after World War I. Another military commander, Reza Khan, took advantage of the fluid situation and established the Pahlvi dynasty in 1921. Meanwhile, oil had been discovered in Persia, and the British occupied Iran during World War II to ensure oil supply lines. There was hope that Iran would evolve into a constitutional monarchy. However, when Prime Minister Mohammed Mosaddeq tried to nationalize the oil industry in 1951, the CIA engineered a coup against him, thereby derailing evolution toward a constitutional monarchy. The Shah survived until 1979 with American and British support, when the monarchy was overthrown and replaced by an Islamic Shia Republic that continues to date to struggle against American–British economic sanctions.

Ottomans: As we saw in the previous chapter, as Europe pulled ahead in science, the Ottomans focused primarily on military technology. However, just as the Ottomans had dealt a severe blow to Venice and conquered significant portions of Hungarian kingdom in the fifteenth and sixteenth centuries, the Ottomans succeeded in conquering portions of eastern Europe in the sixteenth and seventeenth centuries from Habsburgs and the Polish-Lithuanian Commonwealth. The Ottomans were first defeated in 1683 in the battle of Vienna by the Holy League, which consisted of the Polish Commonwealth and Austrian and Russian Empires. It lost Hungary in 1699. During the eighteenth century, Ottomans fought several wars with Russian and Austrian Empires and were often supported by Prussians, British, and French in a classic geopolitical fashion since Prussia did not want Austria to succeed, and the British and the French wanted to deny Russia access to Mediterranean. The Ottoman Empire survived in part because the British, French, and Prussians wanted it to survive. The nineteenth century was a period of rebellion: Greece and Serbia declared independence in the 1820s, and Romania rebelled in 1867. Unending wars were fought with the Russian Empire, including the Crimean War in 1853–1856. Romania declared independence in 1877. Balkan wars continued prior to World War I. Turkey lost in World War I and lost all its possessions in Europe save Istanbul as well as Egypt and Sudan, which Britain annexed.

Thirty-nine new countries were created from the dissolution of the Ottoman Empire. The Republic of Turkey came into existence in 1923 after 623 years of Ottoman rule under Kamal Ataturk, who championed secularism and gender equality. Following Ataturk's death in 1938, Turkey observed neutrality in World War II, except near the end when Turkey gestured solidarity with the winning side. As the cold war started, the United States guaranteed Turkey's security, and Turkey joined NATO and was mostly ruled by military dictatorships during the balance of the twentieth century. Turkey became a functioning democracy in 2002 under the Justice and Development Party. Turkey's considerable effort to join the European Union failed, and despite that it has made remarkable economic progress and is touted as a model Muslim democracy in the Middle East.

17.21 Natural Causes

Black Death had weakened both the Mongols and Europeans in the fourteenth century, allowing the Ottomans to conquer southeastern Europe. The scrooge of the plague continued in the nineteenth century, forcing European powers to impose a quarantine against the Ottoman Empire. The quarantine was welcome since it also prevented British commercial penetration into Ottoman territories. In addition, Ottoman territories often experienced insufficient rain in its mostly unfertile lands, resulting in uneven grain production.

17.22 Intrinsic Causes

Institutional Structures and Processes

Political system: Throughout most of the phase up to 1876, the Ottoman political system did not go through fundamental changes that might decentralize when the first short-lived Ottoman Parliament was elected but was suspended by Sultan Abdulhamid two years later. The second Constitutional Era in 1908 followed and was ushered in by the Young Turks Revolution, reviving the 1876 constitution and effectively abolishing Ottoman rule. Following World War I, when the Ottoman empire finally lost its territories and a three-year-long war of national liberation headed by Kemal Mustafa, the Republic of Turkey was established. It was ruled by a single party until 1945, and a multiparty democracy followed, punctuated by military coups and a fairly standard multiparty parliamentary democracy by the late 1990s. A national anthem and a national flag had been adopted in the mid-nineteenth century under Ottoman rule. However, President Kemal Mustafa had changed the color of the flag from green to red to signify the political and religious break from Muslim Ottomans.

Military capability: The Ottoman military has a glorious early history befitting one of the longest-lived empires in human history. The military consisted of infantry, the standing Janissary corps (a special musket-carrying infantry), a light cavalry called *Akinci*, and the world's first organized military band called *Mehteren*. Until the end of the seventeenth century, the Ottoman navy reigned supreme in Black and Mediterranean Seas and had operations in Persian Gulf, Arabian Sea, and the Atlantic and Indian Oceans. After stagnation in the eighteenth century, the military was reorganized in 1826 when the Janissary corps was dissolved and a standing army was created through regular recruiting and training of salaried soldiers, who were required to serve for a fixed duration. The Turkish Air force was quickly established after the Young Turk's revolution, when European pilots demonstrated flights in the Ottoman Empire.

Economic system: Though controlling vast territories at least until the beginning of the nineteenth century, the population (probably 25 million at its peak in 1800, with most in the Balkans, and the first male-only census conducted in 1844) and the fertility of soil in most territories of Ottoman Empire (except the Nile Delta and western Anatolia) left a lot to be desired. Agriculture output was uneven, even though 80 percent or more of the population engaged in agriculture. Ottoman agriculture did not experience mechanization. Most of the land was owned by small farmers though after the middle of the eighteenth century, large estates became more common. Cereals, grapes, olives, and timber constituted most agriculture output. The state often neglected agriculture (with insufficient irrigation and lack of mechanization after the eighteenth century), most farmers supplementing income through dairy production and handicrafts.

One of the great achievements of the Ottoman economy was the organization of manufacturing guilds before the rise of industrial revolutions. Though the guilds discouraged competition, they were highly organized with strong government supervision, were internally democratic, had a strong apprentice system, and developed product standards. The guilds had strong links to both a religious sect and the Janissary corps. Much like agriculture, manufacturing suffered from a failure to mechanize; however, unlike agriculture, the guilds suffered from too much government interference and were dealt a severe blow with the abolition of the Janissary corps in 1826. The guilds also focused disproportionally on war materials.

Trade was the true backbone of the Ottoman economy before the discovery of sea routes by western Europeans and continued to be so for a couple of centuries during the current phase, albeit with a declining importance. The empire secured land trade routes and caravan stops or *sarai* and developed commercial centers within the empire, with Istanbul being at the crossroads of the trade. However, trade remained the monopoly of the state with little possibility of either opportunistic mercantilism or industrial production. This simple fact explains the Ottoman decline over the last two centuries as Europe surged ahead. The trade continued to be based on silk, porcelain, fur, grain, amber, leather, wool, and coffee.

The establishment of modern industry was neglected but not absent. The first telegraph was established in the mid-nineteenth century as were the railroads. Guilds began to be replaced with factories, the first bank notes were issued in 1840, a central bank was established in 1856, and the stock exchange was established in 1866. Similarly, the commerce code was revised in 1850 and land code in 1857. Private printing and publishing was also established in 1857.

As we have noted above, the government played a strong role through strong treasury, bureaucracy staffed by so-called men of the pen, strong regulation (trade licenses, profit control, restricted staffing, and tax on non-Muslims), talented immigrants, Sultan ownership of all land except mosques, and internal and international trade development. The system worked very well until the discovery of sea routes and the Industrial Revolution in Europe. The Ottomans were slow to react to these changes in part because they had rejected science, as we noted in the previous chapter. The entire focus of the Ottoman Empire was territorial expansion, trade wealth, and a stable social order with relatively benign attitude toward religious minorities for a Muslim state. One gets the sense that Ottomans woke up belatedly and hesitatingly to the technological and financial revolution brought about in Europe by the discovery of sea routes. The economic and political changes initiated by Ottoman sultans in the second half of the nineteenth century were insufficient to fend off the Russian and British determination to break up the empire.

In summary, the economic basis of the empire was control of land trade and a system of production based on a guild system with highly restrictive labor practices. As Europe forged ahead in industrialization and control of sea routes, Ottoman exports were reduced to commodities, and its tariff revenue declined precipitously, thus destroying its guild system.

Systems of religious faith: Islam remained the state religion throughout the Ottoman period. However, a majority of the population was Christian and Jewish with a highly developed monotheistic tradition of their own. Thus, unlike India, where Turkish dynasties pursued a policy of conversion, the Ottomans crafted a policy of limited tolerance of non-Muslims through the Dhimmi and millet systems, the former for all non–Muslims and the latter for specific ethnic groups. The Dhimmi system was based on unabashed inequality between a Muslim and a non-Muslim, as we have noted in earlier chapters. Non-Muslims paid Jizya tax, could not carry weapons, could not join the military or ride horses, and their houses could not overlook a Muslim house.

However, because non-Muslims were crucial to the economic life of the state, under the Millet system, non-Muslim communities were not subject to Muslim law and could have their own religious and social laws to govern themselves. The Christian communities, however, paid a blood tax in the form of stolen young boys who formed Janissaries.

It is worth recalling that the Ottomans were equally intolerant of Shi'ites; Sultan Selim I had massacred forty thousand Shi'ites in 1534.Thus, one must draw the conclusion that Ottomans retained the Muslim prejudice that Islam is superior and actively implemented the concept of Dhimmi system but were constrained by economic realities of the empire and were forced to develop the Millet system for dominant non-Muslim majorities.

Having destroyed the Istanbul observatory in the previous phase under pressure from religious fundamentalists, the Ottomans never looked back on science. The conflict between science and Islam remained alive and well and determined the Ottoman attitude toward developments in science next door in Europe. However, the Ottoman Empire, like all empires with territorial ambitions or who were later under attack from European powers, was more enlightened toward military technology, and they were quick to acquire shipbuilding and explosives technologies and later showed keen interest in telegraph and airplane technology. Critical questioning on Islamic metaphysics was never done.

Legal system: Until the nineteenth century, there was little fundamental change in the Ottoman legal system, which accepted the priority of sharia law for Muslims and Millet-based legal systems for Christian and Jewish communities. In addition, a trade courts system was secular in nature and was derived from a pre-Islamic Turkish tradition. However, religious courts could also settle trade disputes. Much like the economic and political change, the changes in legal system came to Turkey in the second half of the nineteenth century and were insufficient and late. The civil and criminal codes were modeled after the French legal code over 1840–1853 that led to European-style courts and a supreme court council. The laws regulating press and journalism were established in 1864.

Social structure: Prior to the mid-nineteenth century, the social structure consisted of a sultan followed by bureaucracy, the Muslim population, and the non-Muslim millets. Within the Muslims and millets, different classes were based on economic, political, and military power. The limited self-governance of non-Muslims helped the longevity of the empire but eventually led to Balkanization in the nineteenth century as it prevented the assimilation of different religious groups into a national identity. After the mid-nineteenth century, efforts were made to soften the Muslim/non-Muslim divide through the abolition of the jizya tax, a uniform tax code, and permitting non-Muslims to serve in the military. In addition, slavery and slave trade were theoretically abolished in 1847.

Clearly, the Ottomans and the Millet system never addressed the issue of equality between genders, Muslims and non-Muslims, and slaves and nonslaves, and religious law served to hide this inequality. Islam only recognized equality among male Muslims, just as Europeans recognized the equality among white males until modern times.

Knowledge-Creating and educational institutions: There was little change in the education system until the mid-nineteenth-century reforms: A council of public education and a ministry of education were established in 1845 and 1847 respectively. The first modern university was established in 1848, teacher schools in 1848, an academy of sciences in 1851, and the School of Economic and Political Sciences in 1859.

Wealth allocation process: During the current phase, the sustainable surplus was on a severe declining path because of increasing European control of trade, constant wars with Russia and western European states, loss of European territory throughout the nineteenth century, and little sustained and serious effort to restructure the economic, political, and religious institutions. Most of the surplus was allocated to elite luxuries and funding the wars and little was left for creative and productive endeavors. Ottomans were fascinated by new technology and acquired it. However, these acquisitions remained as ornaments of the empire, without a deep connection to the economic life of the empire. These only served to make the sultans feel adequate, though they were unwilling to allow meaningful change through devolution of power through strong political and economic institutions.

Social cohesion process: The development of the Millet system to buy the loyalty of the non-Muslim population worked for several centuries and kept internal peace within the empire. However, as western European states and Russia became strong, the Millet system came under severe pressure and led to the Balkanization of the empire in the nineteenth century.

Internal wars: One of the key accomplishments of the Ottoman Empire was internal peace for the first two centuries of this phase, and it was achieved through the Millet system. However, once key European states began exerting pressure on the empire, the Christian and Jewish majority took the bait and began a century-long process of national liberation movements in the European part of the empire. It took World War I for the British and French to seize and reconfigure the Asian part of the empire as their sphere of influence. This, as we noted before, was followed by a brief British occupation of Istanbul, the subsequent victory of Mustafa Kemal's forces, and the founding of the Republic of Turkish in Anatolia.

Formative Beliefs and Ideology at the Beginning of the Fourth Synthesis Phase

There was little significant change in Ottoman beliefs and ideology during the phase, despite strong pressure from European powers including Britain, Russia, and France during the eighteenth and nineteenth centuries, and steady loss of its European territory. There were attempts to acquire militarily relevant technology from Europe (telegraph, planes etc.) but without a change in political, religious and economic structures, these imports were only window dressing with little real significance.

As Ottomans who sided with Germany lost World War I and the empire dissolved, a man of exceptional foresight, Mustafa Kemal, set Turkey on a path of modernization, albeit through military dictatorship, believing that a period of secular-minded military dictatorship was essential to ensure the development of institutions capable of withstanding a rearguard attack from reactionary Islamic forces. Thus, Mustafa Kemal embarked on a different ideology born out of the ashes of the last Muslim Empire of significance. Today, Turkey has risen above its dictatorial past and is attempting to reconcile modernity and Islam. The beliefs of the Turkey as the leading-edge of Muslim civilization may be characterized as follows:

- A belief in science and knowledge through union of observation and reason along with a contradictory and abiding belief in metaphysics implied in the Koran
- A significant progress in equality between genders
- A continuing belief in the Koran as the word of God in the majority of the population, along with the emergence of a secular minority
- An attempt to transcend belief in aggression and conquest toward other social orders required by new global realities

These beliefs, though leaving a lot to be desired, represent the most progressive beliefs of any Muslim state in West Asia today and are an example of sorts for other Muslim states in the region. Clearly, the Islamic world is still awaiting its Luther and none appears to be in sight. The adaptation of the Muslim world to the challenges of modernity has been slow and difficult because of the religion of Islam and because the center of Muslim world in the Middle East is oil-rich, thus inviting determined western interference. Thus, Muslim states such as Turkey and Indonesia on the western and eastern flanks of the Muslim world with low to moderate oil revenues espouse a moderate approach based on a secular political constitutional democratic setup, an Islamic dictatorship model in Saudi Arabia and to an lesser extent in Iran in the oil-rich center, and an Islamic brotherhood model in oil-poor states such as Egypt, Syria, and Jordan. These differing strategies are supported or challenged by deep Western interests. As of now, there are no large effectively secular and democratic Muslim majority states, though Turkey has both a secular constitution since 1937 and a current Islamic-leaning government. There are over twenty small Muslim majority states in Africa, central Asia, and Southeast Europe that have a secular constitution, and the most populous Muslim state of Indonesia professes religious neutrality, which is indeed a great step forward. Clearly, the long Hindu and Buddhist past of Indonesia has something to do with this distinction as they developed a softer version of Islam and religious tolerance. Given this state of affairs, Islamic beliefs and ideology in the fifty or so Islamic states are in flux today.

17.23 Extrinsic Peaceful Causes

There were no peaceful causes impacting the Muslim civilization during most of the phase. It bears remembering that during the first half of the phase, European powers ended up controlling the periphery of the Muslim world from West Africa to the Philippines. This was followed by Napoleon's invasion of the Muslim heartland of Egypt in 1798, its self-proclaimed civilizing mission, and its utter rejection by Egypt of everything European and French. A century later, it was followed by Anglo-American control of oil in West Asia, the creation of Israel, and support of fundamentalist governments and dictatorships by the West, led by United States. Thus, the Muslim world has been at war with European/Western civilization throughout the phase. This is hardly surprising when one imperial power replaces another. The peaceful extrinsic causes, however, have played a role in the twentieth century through diffusion of science and technology and European political economic institutions. It was no longer possible for the Muslim world to ignore the connection between science and the production of wealth and political/military power in the twentieth century. Thus, different states of the Muslim world have attempted to blend the fruits of the mature science and technology and modern political and economic institutions with Islam in differing ways, ranging from a desire to establish a traditional, sharia-based Islamic caliphate to a secular democracy. While some of these approaches allow for a smoother transition from an intolerant monotheistic caliphate that the Islamic world was end the end of the nineteenth century to a modern, secular democracy, ultimately Islam must yield in the process. At the moment, understandably, Islam, with a proud imperial and creative history, is unwilling and that in addition to Western interference sets the pace for the impact of peaceful extrinsic causes.

17.24 Extrinsic Violent Causes—As Defeated

Muslim civilization did not change its destructive orientation during the current phase since the Koran still rules the hearts and minds of the majority of the world's Muslims. Nothing comparable to religious reformation of Christianity is on the horizon. Thus, if Muslim civilization has not engaged in empire building or colonization or systematic wealth drain, it is not because of lack of desire but a lack of opportunity. The concept of world conquest and a Muslim planet, however unlikely, still moves the Muslim believer as God's command. During the current phase, it was mostly a payback time for the Muslim world at the hands of its old nemesis, the European/Western civilization.

Outside of India, two empires constituted the stronghold of Muslim civilization: the Safavid Empire in Persia and the Ottoman Empire during the current phase.

Assessment of Loss of SPI

Ottoman–Venetian conflict: Beginning with the middle of the seventeenth century, for nearly a hundred years, the conflict between two waning powers in the Mediterranean, the Venetian Republic and Ottomans, raged. It effectively ended Venetian control of island of Crete, Morea, Tinos, Aegina, Corinth, Nauplia, Modon, Corone, and Malvasia, and Venice ceased to be a Mediterranean power after several centuries.

Russian–Ottoman wars: Much like Waterloo, the Crimean War (1853–1856) was of historic significance. The erstwhile enemies, France and Britain, saw the Russian desire to control straits linking Black Sea to the Mediterranean and success against the Ottoman navy using exploding shells (Russian-Ottoman War in 1829, which allowed Russians to close the straits to all foreign ships) by exploiting the national and religious sentiment against Ottomans as a threat and declared war on Russia. Russia was defeated, and its expansion to the west was halted. France emerged as the preeminent power in Europe. It led to reforms in the British army and the modernization of the Russian army, including abolition of serfdom. It contributed mightily to the unification of Italy and Germany and to the purchase of Alaska by the US when the US bought Russian debt. The net effect of the war was to halt Russian advancement into Ottoman territories, thus holding off the disintegration of the Ottoman Empire until after World War I. The weakness of the Ottomans led to a clamor for reforms and democratization by the Young Turks, which also failed, much like in China and Persia. After defeat in World War I and a brief war of national liberation, Turkey lost the balance of its empire and opted for a government of national unity under a single party and military control. Only in 1995 did a true and secular democracy emerge in Turkey.

Russian conquest of central Asia: The Crimean War postponed Russia's territorial advances in central Asia until the beginning of the 1870s. With a modernized army in the post-Crimean war period, Russian conquest of central Asia was a cakewalk, with little-known campaigns against Tashkent, Turkmen, Bukhara, and the Persian, Chinese, and Afghani territories. It only stopped when the British intervened to create Afghanistan as a buffer between Russia and the British Empire in India.

European wars in West Asia: The imperial phase of the Safavid Empire, as we noted above, came with the Qajar dynasty at the end of the eighteenth century when Persia came under British and Russian pressure and lost its eastern wing to Russia and control of the Persian Gulf to Britain. The response of Persia to these losses was similar to the Chinese response to the Opium Wars: that of failed reform and democratization during the nineteenth century. However, unlike China, where failed reforms was followed by a lengthy civil war leading to communist victory, in Muslim Persia, because there was little possibility of communist ideology taking root, there was a return to an absolute monarchy under the Pahlavi dynasty through British and American intervention. This dynasty continued until 1979, when it was replaced by a Muslim fundamentalist revolution against a foreign-supported regime.

Thus, the status of the SPI of the Muslim civilization may be said to go through three periods during the phase: in the first period, Ottomans successfully overpowered Venice in the Mediterranean and thus drying out the trade profits for Venice and Italy. In the second period, France and Britain allied together to successfully check Russian expansion, assisting Ottomans. This accelerated Ottoman decline, and the Ottomans transitioned from being the terror of Europe to the sick man of Europe in popular European psychology. Russia's westward expansion was halted, thus forcing Russia to expand eastward. In the third period, the discovery of oil in the latter part of the nineteenth century, shifted the focus of Britain, France, and the United States from Ottoman holdings in Europe to Saudi Arabia, Iraq, Egypt (which had no oil but was center of Muslim civilization), and Iran. During this period, the objective was to control oil through supporting the reactionary regimes in these countries, killing any democratic movements, and the creation of Israel.

Today, while European civilization has lost political and military control of the Chinese and Indian civilizations, it continues to maintain substantial control of Muslim states in West Asia. Only in the last twenty years has the Muslim civilization begun to successfully challenge this foreign control through the independence of Muslim states in central Asia after the collapse of the USSR, fundamentalist revolution in Iran, terrorism directed against the European civilization, and the emerging democratic revolutions in North African Muslim states.

Loss of Control of Wealth and Means of Wealth

Muslim civilization, which has been an empire-building civilization from its birth, got a taste of its own medicine with the rise of European civilization during the phase. In Anatolia, after initial success, the Ottoman state lost its holdings in Europe except for a toehold as if to remind Europeans of their humiliation at its hands. In central Asia, it lost to Russians. It South Asia, it lost to the British. In Indonesia, it lost to the Dutch. In Africa, it lost to the French. And in West Asia, it lost to the British and the United States. From Indonesia to the Iberian Peninsula, a thousand years of empire building fell in a mere hundred painful years preceding 1918, and it lost control of its own newly discovered means of wealth in oil as well. All this occurred at the hands of European civilization—a superior empire builder and a systematic wealth drainer par excellence. Though one feels sorry at plight of its population, it is hard to shed a tear at the demise of this civilization based on its intolerant, antiscience creed.

Transmission of Creativity

Much like the Indian and Chinese civilizations, Muslim civilization mostly interacted with the European civilization. However, the interaction was limited for several reasons: speaking relatively, the Muslim lands in Asia had little to offer compared to India, China, and Southeast Asia. Discovery of oil and its sustained need would have to wait until the twentieth century. The Muslim lands were unattractive, and the whole point of European sea power was to confine the Muslim states and empires (Safavid, Mughal, and Ottoman) and squeeze the life out of them by dominating the trade with India, China, and Southeast Asia. Finally, the Islamic ideology with its presumed superiority meant an absence of openness to the European breakthroughs in science and technology and a devolution of political power away from monarchy and religious organizations. Even Muslims on Indian subcontinent, who formed the largest Muslim concentration, displayed the same attitude. Loss of trade routes to European and the inherent conflict between science and Islam meant a low likelihood of the emergence of manufacturing elite to rise against religious establishment, monarchy, and landed aristocracy. Thus, the strategy of leading European states was to circumscribe the Muslim civilization and let it fester. The only exception to this were the Muslim states in India and Southeast Asia that were neither the center of Muslim civilization nor very strong but were essential to domination of world trade. This straightjacketing meant that peaceful interaction of Muslim civilization with all civilizations suffered, particularly with Indian and Chinese civilizations.

The discovery of sea routes around the Cape of Good Hope (good hope for whom?) had destroyed the trade basis of the Ottoman Empire through the irrelevance of the Silk Route and made it entirely dependent on the wealth extracted from its territories on the European continent. Similarly, the Persian Gulf, Gulf of Aden, and Malacca Straits fell under the British control eventually. The British role remained confined that of merchant-adventurer and not that of colonizer, a role that blossomed in the twentieth century with the discovery of oil and the disintegration of Ottoman Empire.

Aside from trade, perhaps the Muslim Empire that peacefully interacted most with European civilization was Ottoman Empire because of proximity. Until the nineteenth century, Ottomans were most interested in weapons technologies and did acquire them from Europe. Ottomans were slow in recognizing the importance of European breakthroughs in science and manufacturing technology and more importantly, Ottoman sultans were unwilling to liberalize political control and deregulate the economy. As a result, although Ottomans acquired key technologies such as railways, telegraph, and even aviation generally within a generation of inventions, they were unable to modernize their economy because of the bureaucratic control of the economy, Europe-sponsored national liberation movements in its European territory, and relentless pressure from Russia, Britain, and France. Thus, despite having a ringside seat to the breakthroughs in Europe, the Ottomans failed to take advantage of them.

We would summarize by noting that although Muslim land had escaped colonial control, for reasons noted above, the fruits of European breakthrough remained elusive because of being cut off from trade and because of Islam. The Indian Muslim population and the Southeast Asian Muslim lands gained the most from peaceful interaction because of trade, territorial control, and openness to new knowledge. Next, the Ottomans benefited some (though too little, too late) from the diffusion of practical and intellectual creativity, though within the confines of a rigid political structure and unbending religion. The Muslim lands that gained the least from peaceful interaction were West Asia because of its religious fundamentalism and political rigidity.

Of course, all this would begin to change after 1900 because of the slow evolution of political structures and a clear awareness of the connection among science, technology, and wealth creation. However, in the twentieth century, it was now in European and American interests to keep the Muslim states and empires mired in political backwardness and confined to the role of supplying oil to the economies of the European civilization.

Impact on Productive Outcomes

The impact on productive outcome was disastrous indeed. The pressure from the high seas by European civilization on the Muslim empires in Europe, North Africa, central Asia, South Asia, and Southeast Asia was relentless, and it squeezed its control of land-based trade until it died a parched death. The surplus in the Muslim states, much like in the Roman Empire, depended on territorial expansion and trade since both science and technology remained stagnant after the twelfth century. With both killed by European expansion, the civilization was bound to decline precipitously. By the end of the nineteenth century and even today, all Muslim states except those blessed with high oil production, low population, and a strategy to cooperate with worldwide European civilization (otherwise called Western civilization) match South Asia and Africa in poverty and squalor. Never has a worldwide empire fallen this this fast.

Impact on Institutional Structures and Processes

The impact of Islam was so strong that the impact of the European civilization on the structures and processes of the Muslim civilization remained the slowest. The self-image of Muslim states as erstwhile empire builders also came into play. Discovery of oil and interference of the European civilization also played a critical role. Thus, while the Indian civilization began the process of addressing the challenges posed by European achievements in the nineteenth century because of British presence and the Chinese civilization in the twentieth century, Muslim civilization continued to believe in the Koran and its teaching. Fortunately, the exception is its acceptance of technological and scientific achievements of the European civilization. This is because of its visible and demonstrated connection to the wealth creation process. That is in fact the silver lining as a Muslim civilization. The resolution of the conflict between Islam and science will move the Muslims forward, much like what moved Christians forward.

Assessment of Net Impact

The impact on the Muslim civilization was highly negative. It not only lost its privileged position as empire builder but also lost control of its territories to European civilization.

17.25 Productive Outcomes

Productive Outcomes

Wealth creation: There was little change in the wealth creation activity in Muslim lands until perhaps 1750. After that, a decline set in because of European control of trade.

Peaceful migrations and travel: There was little travel and migration until the second half of the twentieth century. Subsequent to that, Muslims from West Asia, South Asia, and North Africa migrated to Europe in large numbers. Probably more than 10 percent of the Muslim population of West Asia and North Africa now live in Europe.

Fair trade: The periphery of the Muslim civilization remained hostage to coerced trade controlled by European states beginning in the seventeenth century. In the twentieth century, the oil-rich heartland of the Muslim world has been controlled by Britain and the United States through supporting dictatorships in several Muslim countries. This was altered through the oil embargo of 1973, which allowed an oil cartel to emerge and balance scales a bit. Under the implicit deal, oil prices have been set by the cartel, with the understanding that a significant portion of the oil revenue will be invested in the Western world.

17.26 Creative Outcomes

Creative Outcomes

By 1600, Muslim dynasties controlled vast lands in Asia consisting of the Ottoman, Safavid, and Mughal Empires. It is fair to say that in the arena of practical creativity, the focus of these empires remained on land-based military technology, which we have covered under Ottoman and Mughal Empire descriptions. These empires indeed paid a huge price at the hands of European civilization. There was little by way of religious creativity, since Islam was a closed system with minimal interpretation of the Koran. The only area where Islamic civilization continued to nurture creative impulse was in the arts, particularly in architecture and music, by further developing the local tradition in these fields. The Muslim Empire in India probably achieved greater heights in these fields in part because of the influence of Persian art and has been covered elsewhere.

17.27 Achievements in Science

The age of scientific and philosophical inquiry had died centuries earlier due to perceived conflict between Islam and religion during a time when the linkage between science and wealth creation was obvious only to the visionaries. It is a telling comment that more Muslims have received a Nobel Prize in trying to make peace in war-ravaged Middle East than in science, where one South Asian Muslim and American-Egyptian scientist won the prize in physics and chemistry each.

History, Causes, and Outcomes of the Chinese Civilization

17.28 Brief Political History

The last decades of Ming rule were a period of turmoil caused by three interlocking factors: the persistent nomadic aggression from the north, the great famine of 1626, and the resulting peasant revolt. In the early seventeenth century, a charismatic leader named Nurhachi consolidated the Jurchen tribes in the north, posed a threat to Ming rule, and achieved some military success against the Ming Empire. Using the European designs of cannons acquired from Ming sources, Nurhachi's son Hong Taiji built his artillery capability and successfully defeated Ming forces in a series of battles during 1640 to 1642, thus weakening the Ming military considerably. In 1644, taking advantage of the weakened Ming state, a peasant soldier named Li Zicheng led a coalition of peasants and soldiers and sacked the Ming capital of Beijing. However, an opportunistic alliance between Jurchen and the Ming defeated the peasant rebellion, following which the Jurchen easily established the Manchu dynasty in Beijing, also named the Qing (which literally means clarity) dynasty by Hong Taaji. It took another seventeen years to bring the so-called southern Ming holdouts in various parts of China under control.

The first Chinese-born Manchu emperor, Kangxi, ruled from 1661 to 1722, longer than any other Chinese emperor. He successfully put down the rebellion by three of his governors with Ming roots in South China, added Tibet and Outer Mongolia to his domains, and annexed Taiwan from the Dutch. Emperor Kangxi was followed by his hardworking son Yongzheng (1723–1735) and grandson Qianlong (1735–1796).

The eighteenth century was a period of relative peace and prosperity. Manchu Empire controlled 13 million square kilometers, and Chinese population had doubled to 300 million when compared to the disastrous late Ming period.

The nineteenth century was a disaster for the proud Chinese civilization: the Manchu administration decayed internally and was threatened externally by European powers waiting for such a scenario to develop. The Opium War was thrust upon China by Britain in 1840, because Britain wanted to profit from doping the Chinese people. The internal rebellions, such as Taiping and Boxer against the Manchus, cost twenty million lives. Unequal treaties imposed by European powers that controlled the coast further weakened the Manchu. All this led to the 1911 revolution, which overthrew the Manchus after a series of failed reforms and defeat by the Japanese in 1895. This was followed by a brief attempt to restore the monarchy by Yuan Shikai. His death created a power vacuum filled by the democratic forces under Sun Yat-sen and Chaing Kai-shek and the left-leaning protest movement aroused by harsh conditions imposed by European imperial powers on China. The ensuing civil war between the forces of Chaing Kai-shek and the Communist Party founded in 1920 lasted a generation, with Communist victory in 1949 and the founding of the People's Republic of China. After unsuccessfully chasing the communist utopia for a generation, China adopted free market system in 1978 and is on its way to becoming a modern superpower.

17.29 Natural Causes

Like much of the northern world, China experienced the Little Ice Age at the beginning of the seventeenth century, resulting in severely curtailed agricultural production. This was further exacerbated by famine and drought beginning in 1626. It is interesting to note that both the Yuan and Qing Empires ended similarly: natural calamities led to decreased food production, which led to peasant revolts resulting in the fall of the ruling dynasty. The revolts were fueled by the idea of the mandate of heaven, which asserted that heavens showed their displeasure with a dynasty through large-scale natural disasters.

17.30 Intrinsic Causes

Institutional Structures and Processes

Political system: The fundamental Chinese political structure did not change much under the Qing dynasty, which was the second dynastic family of non-Chinese Origin. At the top was the non-Chinese emperor with absolute legislative, executive, and judicial powers and under best of circumstances, a mandate of the heaven. He was assisted by six boards or ministries: finance, civil appointments, rituals, war, crime, and public works. The Ministry of the Rituals often served as foreign office, clearly indicating a superior, insular attitude with respect to outsiders. There were eighteen provinces and four territories of Mongolia, Manchuria, Taiwan, and Tibet, each headed by a governor. The early Qing emperors were highly successful in ruling China: they ensured each position was held by a Manchu and a Chinese with the Manchu having more power and used a highly integrated and centralized bureaucracy to run the administration. The bureaucracy was selected based on a double standard using a quota system: a fully meritocratic civil service exam for an aspiring Chinese and far less so for a Manchu aspiring to be a civil servant. The bureaucracy remained paralyzed by top-down control, a flood of paperwork, a system of payback by the officials to his local sponsors, insufficient personnel, and postings in an unfamiliar area. The political system was essentially Chinese but was tweaked to maintain control of a foreign conqueror.

Military capability: Military organization reflected the foreign domination even more clearly. The eight Banner troops consisted of the Manchu and Mongolian groups and were differentiated by color. Banner troops were segregated from the Green standard army consisting of the Han Chinese. The latter outnumbered the former by three to one. Banner troops formed the cavalry and the Greens the infantry. Three Banner troops were garrisoned in the capital and were under the command of the emperor. The remaining five were distributed to the big cities, mostly to intimidate the Han population. However, the long peaceful period in the eighteenth century meant that soldiering became just another means of income for the conscripted soldiers and consequently their training and preparedness suffered enormously. The military appointments, unlike the civil appointments, were mostly hereditary. There was little change in command structure or tactics. During the current phase, there was a modest effort to upgrade the artillery based on European designs. Military capability, therefore, weakened throughout the eighteenth century, despite success in territorial expansion, which in fact served to mask it.

Economic system: If the Qing emperors worked overtime to create a centralized bureaucracy and an ethnically divided army, they also worked equally hard to improve the economy. And they succeeded in this through land distribution to landless peasants, lower taxes, repairing public works such as the Grand Canal, encouraging new crops (the fruits of Columbian exchange such as maize, peanuts, and potatoes), monitoring prices, and controlling merchant greed through licenses. All this led to increased domestic trade, strong functioning of markets, and consistently improving foreign trade throughout the eighteenth century. The trade balance remained in favor of China and was paid through silver bullion, which increased money supply that in turn caused further economic growth as well as a doubling of population. At the end of the eighteenth century, vastly expanded China appeared prosperous, peaceful, and stable. Despite efforts to the contrary, merchants gained prominence and built great fortunes. This success in economic management and economy had simply recreated the past. The mechanization of agriculture through innovations, weakening of the guilds, and manufacturing breakthroughs were largely absent from the scene.

Systems of religious faith: Taoism, Buddhism, and Confucianism remained the principal religions during the current phase. The differences between Confucianism, with its emphasis on family and social cohesion, and Buddhism, with its emphasis on individual salvation, had moderated at the beginning of the phase. However, there was a great effort to purge Confucianism of any Buddhist or Taoist influence and Confucianism played the greater dominant role in bureaucratic administration. However, the Qing emperors, who originally had brought shamanism with them, adopted Tibetan Buddhism and essentially ignored Taoism as a religious doctrine. Christianity was reintroduced through the Jesuits. However, during the late seventeenth century, Christianity was downgraded in the Qing court as it took its orders from Rome and not from Emperor Kangxi. Russian Orthodox Christianity was introduced in 1715, and Islam remained a peripheral religion of the conquered territories in the northwest.

There was no change as far as the science-religion conflict was concerned. Monotheism, thankfully, remained a fringe phenomenon, and the Qing emperors never viewed science as more than an inferior foreign curiosity. The reaction of Qing emperor Quinlang to the gifts and embassy sent by King George of England is instructive of the Qing attitude toward foreign products, technology, and science.

Legal system: The Tang code remained the legal code. Although the code appeared as exclusively a criminal code with clearly stated punishments, it was also used to establish tort in civil cases. The judicial process continued to remain sensitive to local customs in rendering judgments and continued to see its mission in not only enforcing the law but also reforming the criminals. Thus, torture was used to obtain confession in an effort to set the criminal on a moral path. Death sentences required the emperor's personal approval. Complaints were often settled out of court under the threat of probable court decision.

Social structure: Qing emperors banned intermarriage with the Han Chinese, separated the duties of Manchu and Chinese soldiers, and continued to speak their own language. Qing emperors also used a policy of both intimidation and benevolence: a policy of forcing Manchu dress on the Chinese, shaving the head and wearing queues was enforced for males, and Chinese women were forbidden to bind their feet; however, the emperors also recognized that they could only rule the sophisticated Chinese culture by being perceived as protectors of the Chinese culture. In the military, a clear second-class status was given to the Han Chinese. Similarly, as noted above, a double standard was practiced in selecting the civil service officials. Slavery was practiced on a limited basis: Han Chinese and Muslim criminals were sold as slaves or exiled to Xinjiang. Thus, the social hierarchy was the Manchu elite, followed by the Han Chinese civil service officials, merchants, by the good commoner, and "mean" people, comprising prostitutes, entertainers, and lowly governmental officials. "Mean" people could not take imperial exams and could not marry good commoners. Thus, there was economic and religious freedom, particularly to the peasants, but the political freedom did not exist since the Manchu elite wanted to retain control and their identity.

Clearly, the internal equality under the Qing suffered dramatically. The Han Chinese majority were made to feel inferior. The Manchu-Mongolian-Han distinction permeated through the military and bureaucracy. The military positions became hereditary. All this was required for the Manchu to maintain control and a separate identity.

Knowledge-Creating and educational institutions: The focus of the education system remained on Confucianism, learning which was necessary for the functioning of the bureaucracy. The primary purpose of the education system was not the creation of new knowledge or development of the individual; it was the identification of talented bureaucrats to ensure a well-functioning social system. This was so important that the Qing emperors personally supervised the final imperial exams in the capital, and a golden list of the successful candidates was posted outside the palace gates. Private academies also existed to prepare students for these exams. Jesuits brought European breakthroughs in geometry and astronomy but these never took root. A medical school, however, was established.

Wealth allocation process: There is little doubt that the Qing dynasty succeeded in reversing the economic decline during the late Ming period and ushered in a century of prosperity in China, much like Akbar's India. However, there was a price to be paid: a significant portion of the surplus was consumed by bureaucratic overhead since often a Han Chinese and a Manchu were appointed to the same position. Qing emperors also expanded military as they pushed for territorial expansion, and Manchu, who were outnumbered thirty to one by the Han Chinese, enjoyed a much higher standard of living. The Qing did not value creativity except perhaps in the military arena. Consequently, surplus grew in part because of population growth and not productivity improvements and was allocated to military, luxurious living, public works, and military and not to creative endeavors with some exceptions in artistic endeavors.

Societal cohesion process: The Chinese society returned to its classical stable form during the eighteenth century but with a twist: the majority Hans became second-class citizens were allowed to succeed economically but not politically. The coercion was forced on the majority through dress code, military might, and discrimination in imperial exams and military service. Qing emperors, in an effort to preempt rebellion, banned private ownership of firearms. Thus, social cohesion was assured through a mixture of coercion and ingrained Confucian ethics.

Internal wars: The Qing state after the initial wars during the early seventeenth century must be characterized as relatively free of internal wars and rebellions during the mid-nineteenth century. As the trade position of China worsened because Europeans controlled sea routes and as a result of treating the Han Chinese as second-class citizens, the Qing states became weak. China went through a century of internal upheaval from the mid-nineteenth to the mid-twentieth century.

Formative Beliefs and Ideology at the End of Fourth Synthesis Phase

If the reformist movement in Indian civilization started in the late eighteenth century, the Chinese civilization really got started in the late nineteenth century simply because strong central government managed to keep the European wolves away until the mid-nineteenth century. This was followed by internal rebellions that severely weakened the Qing government, and European and Japanese colonists controlled China to one degree or another. Thus, China had a choice of democratic capitalism or authoritarian socialism. In fact, China chose both and fought a bloody civil war that resulted in communist victory. Thus, in China the beliefs and ideology of an agrarian Qing society, which had not changed materially since the seventeenth century, leapfrogged to that of communist ideology, the first time ever in world history.

As an aside, it is interesting to compare the Indian, Chinese, and Muslim response to European colonial domination and to European science and social organization during the current phase. Broadly speaking, there are two key variables: the timing and extent of European domination of each civilization and the nature of the religious creed of each civilization. The first civilization to fall to under near complete European domination was the Indian civilization, with its tolerant, non-monotheistic creed. Its response was religious reformation, nonviolent struggle to achieve independence, and adoption of a secular, capitalist democracy with a dose of socialist planning. The next civilization to come under European control, though to a lesser degree, was the Muslim civilization with a deep faith in an intolerant monotheistic faith. Since it was sparsely populated and oil was not an issue, it was slow to respond, and when it did, it sought to combine European science and economic institutions with Islam. Chinese civilization had a rather practical attitude toward religion and was the major last civilization to fall under European domination, to an even lesser degree, and its response was to initially pick both democratic capitalism and authoritarian socialism but ultimately chose authoritarian communism. India fell in the eighteenth century, China in the nineteenth century, and the oil-rich Muslim civilization in the twentieth century. Religious attitude determined Indian civilization adopting secular democracy and capitalism, China adopted communism followed by free market reforms, and the Muslim world essentially rejected communism.

Returning to the beliefs and ideology of Chinese civilization in the current phase, formative beliefs and ideology underwent a dramatic shift only in the twentieth century. Adoption of the "scientific socialism" ideology, the concept of class struggle, and the rejection of insularity implied in adoption of a powerful foreign ideology and China's civil war all meant:

- A belief in knowledge through experimental method based on observation and reason
- A rejection of religion, a complete openness toward science and technology, and a rejection of institutions of free market capitalism until 1980
- A continuing belief in the equality among citizens required by communist ideology
- A n uncharacteristically assertive attitude toward neighboring states concerning territorial lines drawn by European imperialists

Since 1980, China has slowly embarked on a process of adopting the institutions of free markets while maintaining a dictatorial political system. The combination has worked well, just as it did in the case of Japan, South Korea, Taiwan, and Singapore.

17.31 Extrinsic Peaceful Causes

No lasting extrinsic peaceful causes impacted China during the current phase. It was few decades of relative openness followed by nearly three centuries of insularity and a century of European and Japanese invasions.

Transmission of Creativity in the Early Decades of the Seventeenth Century

Although the Portuguese were the first Europeans to reach China in 1513, the Jesuit missionaries first brought Christianity, European inventions, and science to China during the last decades of the Ming dynasty, bringing discoveries in astronomy and mathematics. The Ming court was interested in the new knowledge. Johann Schreck published *Diagrams and Explanations of the Wonderful Machines of the Far West* in 1627. Xu Guangqi translated Euclid's Elements in 1607. Johann Schall brought European astronomical techniques for calendar making and eclipse prediction. The Chinese calendar was updated using European methods in 1629. The old calendar was inaccurate since it lost one day every 128 years. Although the ideas of Copernicus were rejected by both the early Catholic missionaries in China and the Chinese, the ideas of Johannes Kepler and Galileo were also brought to China through later Protestant and Jesuit missionaries. Johann Adam Schall Bell, a German Jesuit, was the director of the Imperial Observatory and published the first Chinese book on telescope, called the *Far Seeing Optic Glass* in Chinese in 1634. Of course, the Catholic missionaries themselves did not believe in the Copernican system and therefore did not preach it. However, the work of Kepler and Galileo was not unknown to the Chinese in early seventeenth century near the end of the Ming period. The Ming Court honored these missionaries, gave them significant posts, and allowed them to build churches and preach.

If the Ming emperors were not fully onboard with pursuing science, the incoming nomadic Manchu had no interest in astronomy. There was little interest shown in Galileo's physics in China once the Ming dynasty lost power to the invading Manchu. Similarly, there was little theoretical work in chemistry, earth sciences, or biology in China during the current phase when the Ming court was wrapped up in luxuries and facing external threat. It took a tougher position against the Jesuits, requiring them to accept Confucianism and ancestral rites. During this period, the notion of perspective and representational art found acceptance among Chinese artists as an effective device for "documentation" purposes. The curtailed Jesuit activity continued until 1773, despite the building of the Beitang Church in Beijing in 1703. During the last decade of the eighteenth century, two diplomatic efforts were made by the British and Dutch to expand trade to Emperor Qianlong and both were rejected rather unceremoniously. The European diplomats were offended by the requirement to kowtow before the emperor. The British and Dutch wisely withdrew to pursue their imperial designs in India and Indonesia respectively since China under Qianlong was a militarily strong and highly effective state that small European nation-states could not afford to tangle with at that time. Thus, the brief period of openness to European creative achievements under the Ming dynasty came to an end, and China under Qing dynasty reverted to the traditional Sino-centric notions, oblivious of the fact that European power was on a steeply rising curve and would forcefully return to China with imperial designs in the future and impose its will. China would be torn by internal dissension by then and be ripe for easy picking, much like India was in the second half of the eighteenth century.

Only in the twentieth century was China again open to European intellectual tradition in science and philosophy, failing to successfully establish democracy in First Republic of China under Sun Yat-sen in part because of Japanese Imperialism and civil war, adopting the communist ideology, followed by capitalism and hopefully by democracy.

17.32 Extrinsic Violent Causes

Assessing Loss of SPI

Qing conquest: Until the rise of Islam, China often deflected the central Asian Nomadic pressure toward South Asia, West Asia, or Europe rather successfully. After the rise of Islam, ironically, successful nomadic invasions of Mongols and Manchu saved China from Islam, thus allowing a continuation of unparalleled cultural cohesion in China.

The routing of the peasant leader Li in 1644 led to the installation of five-year-old Shunji under the protection of regent prince Dorgon, who followed a policy of massacre and submission of the Han Chinese. He was behind the Yangzhou massacre and the humiliating haircutting order, stating boldly that "You keep hair, you lose the head; to keep the head, you cut hair." Fortunately, he died soon in 1650 and the policy toward the Han Chinese became less confrontational: it combined adoption of Chinese institutions while institutionalizing the second-class status of the Han Chinese. The court rituals, Confucian philosophy, and civil service examinations system were adopted as we noted above. The strategy was to align Qing rulers with the peasants and the intelligentsia while controlling the landlord and merchant power. At the same time, Manchu worked hard to ensure their separate identities through retaining their languages, keeping the Han Chinese from entering the Manchu homeland, forbidding intermarriages, preventing Manchu from engaging in manual labor and trade, using the dual appointment system, and barring the Chinese from highest offices. Thus, the Manchu strategy was to employ the traditional Chinese system of administration while maintaining political and military control through a range of policies and actions.

British wars in China: China was a tougher nut to crack than politically fractured India in the eighteenth century. So why not use India to profit in China? The first step was to introduce opium mixed with tobacco for smoking. The second step was to monopolize the production of opium in India by cutting out the Indian merchants. The third step was to purchase tea on credit in Canton with auction of opium in Calcutta, and the fourth step was the delivery of opium to the Chinese merchants illegally for sale within China. The Chinese emperor correctly saw this as an attempt to turn the Chinese into drug addicts and banned the trade, causing Britain to initiate two Opium Wars (1839–1842 and 1856–1869) to protect its opium profits. By the early nineteenth century, the British were selling nearly a thousand tons of opium, roughly five grams of opium for every Chinese. When the Chinese people revolted against the sell-out Qin dynasty in 1851–1871, with a revolution called Taiping, the British and French worked with the Qin dynasty to suppress it, killing 20 million people.

Japanese imperialism in China: Imperialism for Japan began close to home a generation after the Meiji revolution. The first attempt was to rid China's influence in Korea through the first Sino-Japanese War in 1894 to 1895, in which the Japanese succeeded since its military had adopted European technology and tactics and had occupied Taiwan. However, Korea came instead under Russian influence, which led to War with Russia in 1905 and which Japan also won. Japan entered World War I on the British side, seizing German military bases in the Pacific and China. Postwar Japan experienced prosperity, benefitting from British technology, but abandoned its democratic experiment and turned fascist. It attacked Manchuria in 1931 and China in 1937, occupying coastal cities, and it set up puppet regimes in both. The occupation resulted in a three-way struggle between Imperial Japan, Chinese Nationalists under Chaing Kai-shek, and communists under Mao Tse-tung, which the communists won.

Loss of Control of Wealth and Means of Wealth

Thus, during the current phase, China experienced two entirely different forms of control: it was first conquered by Qing dynasty, which became absorbed into Chinese culture, and second, European and Japanese imperial control followed. The former was a traditional empire builder settler and the latter systematic wealth drainers. Consequently, China lost control of surplus to nomads but remained prosperous, followed by control by the industrial nations bent on wealth drain, resulting in an impoverished China for more than half a century.

Impact on Productive Outcomes

There was little impact on the productive outcomes and prosperity during the Qing dynasty after China recovered from the wars of the early seventeenth century. Just as the Delhi Sultanate had protected India from Mongol invasion, the Qing dynasty saved China from European wealth drain throughout the eighteenth and early nineteenth centuries. China actually benefited from Columbian exchange through the introduction of peanuts, sweet potatoes, and maize. Foreign trade and population actually grew during the eighteenth century, as did government control of the economy. However, through the Opium Wars, drugging the Chinese population, and controlling coastal areas, the British were successful in destroying the Chinese economy.

Impact on Institutional Structures and Processes

A focus on the impact on political system: Qing dynasty was the last imperial dynasty of China and was founded by invading Manchus. It is useful to look back and assess the history of the peaceful interactions of Chinese civilization. The most consistent political beliefs in China throughout the ages have been the concepts of Middle Kingdom with all surrounding civilizations being barbarians, vassals, or tributaries who must acknowledge Chinese superiority. It is indeed curious that the Chinese civilization believed this about itself despite making only modest contributions in religion, sciences, linguistics, philosophy, and logic since the main outlet of the enormous Chinese creative and productive impulses has been practical creativity, art, architecture, creating an ethical social order, wealth creation, and fair trade. These are, however, understandable beliefs in the light of China losing its political independence to the nomads thrice (Jin, Mongols, and Qing) during the twelfth, thirteenth, and seventeenth centuries. Prior to that, China had been successful in diverting nomadic pressure to south, West Asia, or Europe.

We argue that these political beliefs arose precisely because of not valuing intellectual and religious creativity and because of success in dealing with nomads before the Jin and Mongol invasions. Thus, the insularity and notions of Middle Kingdom and the Mandate of Heaven, however immature they might be as political doctrines, are perfectly understandable in the context of Chinese historical experience, protected from the desert in the west, the sea in the east, and success in holding back the barbarians from the north. The only modest exceptions to Chinese insularity have been Chinese travelers coming to India to collect Buddhist literature and a naval expedition of Muslim Chinese General He during the Ming dynasty to Southeast Asia, though the latter was not followed through. The insularity and concept of superiority explain China's peaceful interaction during current phase as well. The foreigners came to China, peacefully or forcefully, to obtain the products of the Middle Kingdom or to impose their own. The current phase is both a continuation as well as laying a foundation for the eventual repudiation of these political beliefs. However, these beliefs continued to mostly define peaceful interactions with the world during most of the current phase.

The Qing dynasty negotiated the Treaty of Nerchinsk in 1689, demarking the common border not through ministry of Tributary Affairs but through a foreign office acknowledging Russia as a nontributary nation, thus opening Chinese diplomacy to the concept of relationships with nontributary states for the first time.

Likewise, in military weapons and command structure, economic organization (through eventual adoption of market economy), legal systems, and education and knowledge-creating structures, Chinese institutions have been deeply affected by European civilization. Only in religion did the Chinese civilization remain not materially impacted.

Assessment of Net Impact

During the current phase, China's principal interaction took place with the European civilization. China had little peaceful interaction with Indian, Muslim, and Southeast Asian civilizations during the current phase, since access to these European powers controlled access to these and the sea. The Qing dynasty was isolated but was happy and prosperous in its isolation, successfully pursuing its own imperial designs in Tibet and the northwest.

The net impact until the nineteenth century was marginal. However, in the nineteenth century and the first half of the twentieth century, the net impact on the Chinese civilization was substantial and negative.

China as Imperialist Power

Earlier dynasties were content to have the smaller states outside the Great Wall and China proper to remain as tributaries and vassals. The Qing dynasty was the first Chinese dynasty that went beyond the diplomacy of kowtow. The Qing emperors conquered Inner and Outer Mongolia, Xinjiang, and Tibet and forced other smaller states in vassal or tributary status. They ruled over an enormous territory of 13 million square kilometers at the end of the eighteenth century. The Roman Empire at its zenith was half that size. Qing imperialism was highly successful for the time being since Mongol and Muslim powers in central Asia had been weakened in part by imperial Russia, Tibet was weak having been attacked by Dzungars, European sea power was still evolving, and Russia sought peace with China to allow it to focus on the Ottoman Empire to the west and south. In addition, as we noted above, the Qing emperors had managed to get the economy growing again. They had doubled the territory, the GDP, and the population of China within a century without an industrial revolution. This remarkable feat was made possible by a combination of Han insularity and Manchu aggression. Much like the majority Hindu population under Mughals, the majority Han population, minority Muslim population, and Buddhist Tibet accepted their second-class citizen status as long as peace and prosperity existed.

Qing attempted a similar approach with the European nation-states as they approached China in a contest of two diametrically opposing views of the world: China as an insular middle kingdom and the world as an open trading system under European control. The rise of European states and control of sea routes ended Chinese aggression. As the economy and internal cohesion faltered in the nineteenth century, European states would be back, mischief in their heads and gun in their hands.

17.33 Productive Outcomes

Wealth creation: If creative endeavors during the current phase attempted to only scale earlier heights, wealth creation easily matched earlier heights. Iron, cotton, and ceramic industries blossomed along with increased agricultural production of wheat, rice, millet, tea, and silk. The population recovered and doubled to 300 million as noted earlier. Ceramics, silk, and tea became Chinese exports that were highly valued in Europe. The favorable trade balance paid in silver further increased economic development through increased money supply. The Shanxi banks also helped develop credit markets, further contributing to economic development. It is estimated that up to 20 percent of the produce reached market, thereby helping develop commodities markets as well. Internal trade also boomed as Qing emperors improved infrastructure. Wealth creation in China was at its highest in its history, based solely on agricultural economy, about the time Europe was undergoing an early phase of the Industrial Revolution. The Qing emperors never suspected the coming storm. One negative feature of the economy by the end of the phase was systemic corruption within the civil bureaucracy.

Peaceful migrations and travels: There were hardly any significant travel and migrations out of or into China from the Indian and Muslim civilizations. The greatest travels occurred into China from Europe through the Jesuit missionaries and foreign embassies. In the latter part of the nineteenth century, indentured Chinese labor was brought into the United States and several countries in Southeast Asia. Today, these countries have prosperous Chinese communities.

Fair trade: China practiced fair trade with its trading partners in that it was not backed by gunboat diplomacy.

However, internal market and external trade were not free, and a few merchants controlled the latter. The British and Dutch embassies in the last decade of the eighteenth century, which the Chinese spurned, were an attempt to influence Chinese trade policy. These European efforts were directed at opening Chinese trade, which was channeled through these merchants, resulting in a high price for tea in particular. Since the embassy failed, the British began importing tea from Japan until the plantations newly acquired Bengal could start producing tea. The failed diplomatic missions were a real setback for China since Europeans would be back in half a century, this time with guns.

The present phase of the Qing Dynasty is the culmination of two thousand years of a Chinese tradition of centralized bureaucracy, literature, and art, and its creative and productive achievements as a whole may be said to show "quantitative growth but a qualitative standstill."

17.34 Creative Outcomes

Achievements in Practical Creativity

One of the great puzzles of Chinese history is the incredible practical achievement during the Han, Tang, and Song eras and its equally incredible absence during the Yuan, Ming, and Qing dynasties. Was this because something fundamental changed in Chinese institutions or beliefs? Or was it because the impact of nomadic invasions that established the Yuan and Qing dynasties and their inability to value creativity except in military technologies? Was it the Ming dynasty, sandwiched as it was between the two nomadic dynasties, was unable to shake foreign influence on Chinese institutions and its processes? Or was it because further technological innovation required a scientific culture to emerge to support the next stage of technological innovation? We are inclined to believe the latter as the driving cause since both nomadic dynasties were quite willing to the absorbed into Chinese culture as long as their control of China was not threatened. In other words, they recognized the superiority of Chinese culture and mostly adopted its institutions.

Achievements in Religious Creativity

Religious creativity (it was never world-class in China) also took a tumble during the current phase. The driving force behind this decline in religious creativity was undoubtedly the Qing dynasty. The Qing rulers, while accepting the Chinese political doctrines of Middle Kingdom and Mandate of the Heaven and accepting Confucian precepts to achieve the ideal of a well-managed state, did not initially adopt either Taoism or Buddhism because they had brought central Asian Shamanism with them. Qing Shamanism, like animism, believed the visible world was permeated by spirits affecting human existence and required the expertise of a Shaman to control these forces. Thus, the Qing brought a primitive set of religious beliefs with them.

In addition, the Chinese intellectuals blamed neo-Confucianism, which had incorporated Buddhist and Taoist ideas, for the fall of Ming dynasty. Thus, both Buddhism and Taoism got a bad name with Chinese intellectuals, who pushed for the classical Confucianism through the Hanxue or Han learning movement. The eighteenth-century Imperial library established by the Qing emperors excluded all Taoist books. As a result, both Buddhism and Taoism began to degenerate since they exclusively became the religion of the masses without any intellectual guidance. Taoism, which aims for the immortality of the body and the soul, became increasingly focused on both supernatural forces as well as elixirs derived from mercury, lead arsenic, and sulfur. Similarly, Buddhism degenerated into the White Lotus cult under Taoist influence and preached chanting Buddhist sutras to enter Pure Land. Later, the White Lotus cult renounced mediation as a means of achieving nirvana and began to believe in a messiah, which further increased imperial persecution of the group, culminating in 1796 rebellion by the group against the Qing rule.

In short, under the twin influences of Shamanism and a desire on the part of Chinese intellectuals to purge Taoist and Buddhist influences from Confucianism, both Buddhism and Taoism degenerated into folk religions with increasing superstition. It was indeed an ignoble degeneration of the superstition-free agnosticism that the great Buddha had preached more than two millennia ago.

Achievements in Philosophical Creativity

There was little by way of developing critical philosophy in metaphysics, epistemology, ethics, or aesthetics during the current phase. The focus, as noted above, was on recovering classical Confucianism and to purge its Taoist and Buddhist influences. This was successful and supported by the Qing rulers for obvious reasons: Confucianism emphasized altruism, the obligations to the family and the emperor. and reinforcing rituals with almost religious overtones. While the Qing ignored the Confucian preaching of superiority of nobility of action over blood, they adopted the Confucian notion of meritocracy embedded in imperial examinations to strengthen the bureaucracy.

Achievements in Art

The Qing emperors were anxious to support scholars and artists in their efforts to gain respectability and acceptance in foreign lands. The key achievements of Chinese art during the current period consisted of developments in opera, painting, porcelain, literature, and architecture.

Opera: Beijing opera was developed toward the end of

the current phase and used voice, dance, music, acrobatics, and mime movements to depict great stories from Chinese history. It is perhaps appropriate to think of the Beijing opera as comprising theater, opera, athletics, and ballet. The opera typically had leading male and female actors, a clown, and an authoritative figure such as a warrior or a god and was rich in symbolism with hundreds of stylized movements. Actors often wore heavy makeup. The opera, which was a consolidation of regional traditions, was developed to commemorate the eightieth birthday of Emperor Qianlong.

Painting: The Qing painters during the current phase developed two schools of painting: orthodox and individualist. The orthodox school consisted mainly of the "four Wangs," who followed the great Ming expressionist Dong Qichang (1555–1636) and emphasized the technical skill in brushstrokes and calligraphy. Although European representational painting style had penetrated China, it was never considered high art. Dong Qichang's renowned landscapes never aimed at capturing natural realism. If the four Wangs were predictable in their expressionism, the individualist school represented by Shi Tao was revolutionary and irreverent, often drawing attention to the act of painting in an impressionistic, abstract. and even surreal manner. Shi Tao was undoubtedly the most innovative artist to emerge from China during the current phase. Qing emperors employed artists to create immense landscapes of great beauty. Illustrated books on the art of painting also appeared, such as *Jieziyuan Huazhuan,* published in 1679.

Porcelain: Porcelain ceramics were already a highly developed art in the Ming dynasty, and the ceramic industry suffered greatly because of civil war and Manchu invasion. Fortunately, emperor Kangxi built the porcelain industry beginning in 1683. The newly constituted industry developed opaque enamel colors, allowing artists to create a great variety of shades.

Literature: Emperor Qianlong created a library containing thousands of books and thousands of volumes. It was the largest collection in Chinese history. Persecution of writers was not uncommon if their writings were considered a threat to the Manchu rule. The key literary achievement of the period was broad publication of the four novels: *Outlaws of the Marsh* (thirteenth century) by Shi Nai'an, *The Romance of the Three Kingdoms* by Luo Guanzhong (fourteenth century), *Journey to the West* (sixteenth century) by Wu Cheng'en, and *A Dream of Red Mansion* (1791) by Cao Xueqin. The last was the only one written during the current phase. These novels, among the oldest in the world, are long and considered the greatest achievement of Chinese literature, and the current phase contributed one of these novels. Note that *A Dream in the Red Mansion* replaced *A Plum in the Golden Vase* because of latter's explicit sexual descriptions.

Architecture: Architecture, much like porcelain, painting, and literature, was primarily a continuation of the Ming tradition. The Mukden palace built by Nurhaci was modeled after the Forbidden City built by Ming emperors. The Qing rulers added the summer palace and expanded the Forbidden City but continued to use the Mukden Palace as a regional palace.

Thus, clearly in porcelain, literature, architecture, and painting, the Qing period followed the traditions developed during the Ming dynasty. Only in opera and in the individualistic style of Shi Tao, were artistic innovations visible.

17.35 Achievements in Science

Achievement in Sciences

There was little progress in formal and physical sciences during the current phase. However, there was modest progress in the field of medicine, primarily by extending traditional Chinese medicine.

- Anatomy began to undertake an experimental approach largely through the work of Wang Qingren (1768–1831) toward the end of the current phase. He described the pancreas, abdominal aorta, and diaphragm and showed the brain as the seat of thought and memory. He also dispelled such traditional notions of urine originating in excrement and lungs having twenty-four holes.

- In diagnosis, Wu Youxing published Weiyiliun in 1642 and had considerable influence on diseases associated with fever. Several physicians such as Ye Gui and Xue Xue made further contributions. Li Yongcui published a book called Zhengzhi huibu on diagnosis in 1687. In addition, books were published in ophthalmology, pediatrics, skin diseases, and gynecology.

- In treatment, Chinese physicians learned to inoculate against smallpox by injecting dried powder extracted from scabs into the nose. The process was copied by European physicians.

- Zhao Xuemin wrote an encyclopedia on herbs listing 921 herbs, their preparations, and uses.

- Qi Kun wrote a book on external medicine in 1665 that described various surgical diagnoses and techniques.

- Several medical encyclopedias were also published. Two that deserve particular mention are Golden Mirror of Medicine by Wu Qian in 1742 and an encyclopedia titled Collection of Ancient and Modern works that included 520 chapters on medicine and was published in 1726.

Achievements in Social Sciences

Social sciences in general and political science and ethics in particular remained tradition-bound with a continued belief in the twin concepts of Middle Kingdom and Mandate of Heaven and Confucianism. Confucianism emphasized virtue, loyalty to a righteous ruler, filial piety, proper etiquette, and social relationships and was perceived to be consistent with the Mandate of Heaven. It had the following beliefs:

- Heavens grant the right to rule China
- The ruler must be virtuous
- The right may be passed from father to son but only if the second condition is met

The idea of China as a middle kingdom was reinforced by the existence of barbarians and lesser vassal or tributary states around the Chinese state. Together, the three ideas of Middle Kingdom, Mandate of Heaven, and Confucianism purged of its Buddhist and Taoist beliefs, all describe an ideal of an insular social stability and harmony based on virtuous individuals and a virtuous ruler, for social stability required "prince to be prince, minister to be minister, father to be father, and son to be son." Such a system would not seek change and growth, and at the end of the eighteenth century, the Chinese civilization once again achieved a prosperous, stable state approximating these ideals: absolute monarchy with a mandate of heaven with vassal state surrounding it and Confucianism returning to its classical roots. There was little place for advancement of social sciences under these conditions.

Brief History of Other Key Players

17.36 Brief Political History of Northeast and Southeast Asia

Southeast Asian Civilizations

We will briefly focus on Indonesian history. The great age of Hindu and Buddhist Empires had come to an end by 1500 to be followed by gradual spread of Islam and emergence of Muslim states and Malacca, Demak, Aceh, Pagaruyung, Banten, and Mataram Sultanates (1257–181). The Portuguese were the first Europeans to arrive and established themselves through superior weapons, ships, and a divide-and-rule policy. They created a parallel sea-based spice trade channel, thus disrupting the trade network consisting of Muslim merchants and their Venetian Christian partners in the Mediterranean that had monopolized spice trade to Europe. The Dutch, who had established the Dutch East India Company in 1602, two years after the British East India Company was established, followed the Portuguese with better weapons, organization, and financial resources with a sole commercial focus, unlike the Portuguese who had both a commercial and religious focus. The Dutch were enormously successful, and by 1800, The Dutch East India Company was abolished and replaced by direct Dutch rule, more than half a century before a similar change in India. The Dutch ruled until 1949, except during 1942–1945. The national liberation movement against Dutch rule began in 1908 and led to independence in 1949 under the leadership of Sukarno (1901–1970) after a four-year armed struggle against the Dutch and their British allies. However, Sukarno increasingly turned to socialist policies and the communist party of Indonesia (founded in 1914 by an exiled Dutch Socialist). This alarmed the United States, which engineered a military coup in 1965 through General Suharto, a coup that destroyed both the Communist Party and democracy in Indonesia. Suharto, weakened by the 1998 financial crisis, remained in power until 1999, after which Indonesia returned to democratic form of government in 2004 essentially along the American model with a directly elected president, a People's Representative Council, and a Regional Representative Council.

The history of Vietnam parallels that of Indonesia; only we need replace the Dutch with the French, who controlled Vietnam from 1802 to 1945, followed by national liberation armed struggle against the French, who were defeated in 1954. They handed control to the United States, which effectively partitioned the country and fought a losing war for twenty years. In 1975, The Socialist Republic of Vietnam was founded, and it has followed the Chinese political model.

Northeast Asian Civilizations

Japan: Prior to the beginning of the current phase, Japan had been united by General Toyotomi Hideyoshi (1536–1598), who exposed the tendencies of imperialism inherent in Japanese civilization through his unsuccessful invasion of Korea. He was followed by Tokugawa Ieyasu (1543–1616). Japan went through the Tokugawa period (1603–1868) when political power remained in the hands of hereditary shoguns (much like Peshwa under Marathas in India) who renounced imperial ambitions, regulated the economy and taxation, and created a bureaucracy and a judiciary while suppressing religion and subordinating the aristocratic families. It was a remarkable period that brought peace and prosperity, in part because rest of Asia and Africa kept European states busy.

The imperial display of power by the United States and consequent signing of unequal treaties, including control of tariffs on imports, shook up Japan, spelled the end of Shogun rule and isolation, and restored monarchy. This was followed by a rapid economic progress based on adopting European technology. By the end of the nineteenth century, the imperial tendencies resurfaced again, and Japan fought China (1894–1895) conquered Korea and Taiwan, and by 1931, Manchuria. This led to tension with the United States, with Japan entering World War II on the German side when the United States blocked oil supplies to Japan. Defeat followed by dropping of atomic bombs on Hiroshima and Nagasaki and the loss of territories and occupation by US forces that helped transformed Japan into a demilitarized and democratic state.

Once again, with imperial tendencies having gone into hibernation, Japan turned to rebuilding and became a great economic power exceeding its benefactors in manufacturing excellence and has remained allied to the United States and European powers.

Korea: Korea was invaded by the Japanese in 1592–1598 and by the Manchus in 1627 and 1636. Korea followed the Japanese example of isolationism in the face of European aggression in the eighteenth and nineteenth centuries. Between 1866 and 1888, there were several skirmishes with the French, American, and British adventurers. This was also a period when, like Japan, Korea modernized rapidly. Korea was the unsuspecting beneficiary of the Sino-Japanese War of 1894–1895 as it became free of China's control. But not too for too long as Japan annexed Korea in 1910. Japan ruled Korea until 1945, a period that led to both democratic and communist political movements to liberate Korea. Following the end of World War II, the politics of the cold war dashed the hopes for a unified Korea, with the north under communist rule and the south under democratic rule. In 1950, the Korean War broke out and an armistice was signed in 1953, leading to permanent division. Since then, South Korea has made dramatic, Japan-like economic progress under US capital and technology transfer while north has languished under Chinese protection.

Summarizing the State of Civilization and Science

17.37 State of Civilization and Science at Phase End

Overview of the Political History of the Phase

As we noted in the last chapter, during the previous phase, European civilization successfully expelled the Muslims from Europe, became heirs to the fruits of the Arab-Persian synthesis in science, absorbed Chinese technological achievements of the previous millennium, discovered and celebrated the cultural and literary heritage of ancient Greece, created the European syntheses in science, established several centralized nation-states primarily on the Atlantic coast that turned over the political power from the feudal lords and Christian church to merchants and monarch, began a process to challenge Christian dogma, and discovered sea routes needed to control the world trade that had come to be controlled by the Ottomans.

From this foundation, in the first century of this phase Europe proceeded to successfully control world trade with the Old World and the newly founded colonies in the New World. This trade, coupled with slaves from Africa and indentured labor from Europe, created enormous wealth for the emerging nation-states. No doubt, a great portion of this wealth was wasted on wars among the competing nation-states and fighting the civilizations in both the New World and the Old World. Yet a small portion was also allocated to both wealth creation and knowledge creation.

The latter resulted in the first grand unification in science, that of gravitation and terrestrial motion through the work of Galileo and Newton.

In the eighteenth century, this led to several key developments: the control of Indian civilization, circumscribing the influence of Muslim civilization, successful rebellion by the colonies founded by the emerging nations of Europe in the New World, starting with English colonies in North America in the latter part of the eighteenth century (in part made possible by English success in India, French failure in India, and active French support of the American Revolution) and was followed within fifty years by Spanish and Portuguese colonies. The eighteenth century really came to an end with Napoleonic wars, which made the Spanish and Portuguese colonies able to gain independence. The process of transition from a strong centralized monarchy to a constitutional monarchy with a democracy of merchants also started in Great Britain and the Netherlands.

During the nineteenth century, this process of evolution toward constitutional monarchy and democracy continued haltingly in France and Spain while Germany, Austria, and Russia went through a phase of creating empires, gorging on their land neighbors, feasting on the crumbling Ottoman Empire, or in the case of Italy, internal unification. Both Muslim and Chinese civilizations experienced internal weakness, much like the Indian civilization did in the eighteenth century, and were attacked by nation-states and fell under their control. Simultaneously, the process of industrial revolution based on mechanical power and mechanized production spread throughout Europe. This served to alter the trade pattern between Europe and Asia from one where Europe bought manufactured goods to buying commodities, converting these into products, and selling them back to Indian, Chinese, and Muslim civilizations, thus destroying the indigenous industry. The result was increasing poverty and misery in these civilizations. Europe also managed to create the second grand unification in science, that of electricity and magnetism.

In the first half of the twentieth century, the process of evolution toward democracy continued, interrupted often by military strong men in the Spanish and Portuguese New World and in eastern Europe. It was now supplemented by national liberation struggles in Asia and Africa against French, Dutch, and British control. Simultaneously, the advanced colonizing nation-states of Europe met new competition in unified Germany and Italy; industrialized Japan, which had escaped European control; Russia; and, of course, the behemoth, the industrialized United States of America. This competition led to the two world wars that devastated Europe. It resulted in independence for Indian and Chinese civilizations, continued control of Muslim states from Libya to Iran by the oil-hungry Europeans and United States of America, transformation of the Russian Empire into the USSR under communist ideology, and emergence of the United States and USSR as two dominant powers.

Einstein brought about the third unification of science between electricity/magnetism early in the twentieth century, and a generation later quantum mechanics was born to explain the mysteries of the infinitesimally small.

In the second half of the twentieth century, USSR, China, South American states, Southeast Asia and India remained misguided by socialist ideology while Europe and United States forged ahead based on astonishing breakthroughs in technology. At the same time, Muslim civilization, refusing to give up outdated religious ideology, remained under American control through puppet governments. Led by China in 1978, Asia and Latin America slowly shed the socialist ideology and by the end of first decade of the twenty-first century were on their way to achieving parity with Europe, Japan, and United States in the coming decades. The fourth and presumably last grand unification in science between gravitation, electricity, magnetism, and strong nuclear forces at least seems within grasp.

Thus, a process that started with questioning the creed and accidental discovery of two continents by several small emerging states of Europe remained true to the ideology of greed: evolving from coerced trade based on control of coastal areas to systematic draining of the wealth of states and civilizations in the New World and destruction in the Old World based on military and political control of the territories with their internal rivalries, ultimately leading to the demise of empires they had built. One might say that it evolved from controlling the prices of traded commodities in the seventeenth and eighteenth centuries to controlling territories to draining the wealth of others in the nineteenth century and the first half of the twentieth century to controlling finance capital and the flow of technology in the second half of twentieth century. The end of the four-century domination of the European civilization is finally within sight. As periods of domination go, it will be one of average duration.

State of Creative Outcomes

As we noted before, we may safely assume the state of knowledge and art at the end of the phase was essentially equal that of European civilization. The state of faith is somewhat different. A significant minority in the European civilization has turned to atheism and agnosticism. However, both Islam and Catholicism had expanded particularly in Africa and continue to be dogmatic and hidebound. In India, Hinduism is going through both a slow reformation as well as a revival of Vedanta, initially promoted through the Theosophical Society founded by the British. It is estimated that vast majority of individuals in the world today continue to have blind faith in the religion they are born into or the religion they have chosen or adopted.

At the start of the phase, while the European civilization had more or less succeeded a millennium of stagnation, other civilizations were entering a period of stagnation. The Muslim civilization had been reduced to a shadow of its former self in terms of its creative endeavors, though ostensibly, all three major centers, Ottoman, Safavid, and Mughal Empires, were doing rather well. The impact of Muslim civilization and its close-minded religiosity and antiscience posture had managed to kill creative endeavors in the Indian civilization except in the arts. Similarly, the Chinese civilization was about to fall victim to nomad invasions. The nomads, though they hardly encouraged creative endeavors, managed to keep European wolves at bay for couple of centuries. Such was the situation among the major civilizations when the European civilization, smarting from bubonic plagues and Ottoman control of trade with Asia, discovered sea routes and began to tighten the noose around the other three civilizations through coerced trade. This was followed by more direct control and systematic wealth drain. All this reduced these proud civilizations to a status of poverty only imaginable during prolonged natural disasters in their histories. This killed any remaining vestiges of creativity in these civilizations.

The final impact came through the response of the three major civilizations to European learning. It is probably fair to say that Indian civilization was most responsive to European learning, in part because it was controlled more completely by a European state. Thus, the creative outcomes of Indian civilization during the current phase were a bit better than those of the Chinese and Muslim civilizations. Today, Indian and Chinese civilizations have regained autonomy and are beginning to contribute creatively. However, Muslim civilization continues to be under the control of United States and Europe because of discovery of oil in several Muslim states. Thus, Muslim civilization continues to lag in creative contributions. Consequently, in what follows, we focus on rather modest achievements of Indian and Chinese civilizations since the achievements of Muslim civilization are inconsequential and the achievements of European civilization are the overwhelming balance, so there is little need to elaborate on these from our perspective.

State of Productive Outcomes

The state of productivity is somewhat different from state of creativity in that a few economically advanced states like Japan and Korea surpassed the European productivity in some traditional or static industries.

State of Constructive Outcomes

Given the control of trade by a handful of European states and stagnation resulting from wealth drain, the creative endeavors in all civilizations except European civilizations dropped precipitously. Similarly, peaceful migrations from Indian, Chinese, and Muslim civilizations came to standstill except through indentured labor late in the phase. Thus, constructive outcomes only occurred from European civilizations to other civilization under conditions of economic and political control until the twentieth century.

State of Destructive Outcomes

As we have detailed above, most of the phase experienced unprovoked wars initiated by European civilization against all other civilizations.

At the end of the twentieth century, it is fair to say that Indian, most Southeast Asian, and Chinese civilizations have attained a considerable measure of political but not necessarily economic freedom from European/Western civilization. The same cannot, however, be said of the Muslim civilization in West Asia because of fossil energy politics. Thus, the Muslim civilization continues under indirect European control. The global Muslim "terrorism" is a direct result of this control.

The second source of conflict has actually been within the European civilization: cold war among its communist and capitalist states. Fortunately, that conflict never became hot and has been resolved.

At the same time, the European civilization has never hesitated to use its enormous military power in local conflicts of global significance, such as the Korean War, the Vietnam war, installing dictators in the West Asian Muslim states, the Serbian war, the Iraq war, the Afghan war, and the Libyan war. Nor has it not used its economic power to punish states that pursue an independent policy.

On the positive side, slavery officially no longer exists, and the Indian caste system is in the early stage of dying. The class war within the economically advanced states has moderated because of the emergence of a middle class that was necessary for the survival of capitalist free enterprise system. However, since 1975, the middle class in economically advanced civilizations has begun to experience a reversal in its fortunes since globalization has reduced the dependency of the capitalists in the advanced states since it can now buy and sell to the emerging middle classes in emerging counties.

Assessing the Inner Nature of Participants

17.38 Inner Nature of the Chinese Civilization

Productive capacity: The story of the productive nature of Chinese civilization during the current phase runs parallel to the one in previous phase. After initial chaos, natural calamities, and destruction caused by nomadic invasion, the economy began to recover under sound traditional management based on providing relief to peasants, creating a strong bureaucracy sensitive to local needs, keeping a watchful eye on the merchants, and upgrading irrigation and transport systems. This resulted in increasing production, expanding internal and external trade, and an expanding population. Thus we would characterize economic freedom in Qing China as modest since merchants and manufacturers faced restrictions, the new technology adoption was probably lower than in the previous phase but still positive, decreasing internal inequality for the Han Chinese majority, sustainable surplus as growing and under stable control, and high social cohesion achieved through a centralized, integrated, and meritocratic bureaucracy and Confucian ethics. The sustainable growing surplus was increasing because of population increase and productivity gains, and China once again accounted for nearly a third of the world's GNP and population by the end of the eighteenth century. The productive capacity of the civilization had once again arrived at its natural uniquely Chinese resting point, that of preindustrial prosperity and the absence of dynamism. Clearly, by the nineteenth century, the relative productive capacity had declined precipitously.

Creative capacity: The creative inner nature of the Chinese civilization under the Qing dynasty during the current phase fared much worse compared to the Ming dynasty. The Qing rulers did not value creative endeavors except when they helped in maintain control, such as in explosives technology, and their need to gain acceptance through art and preservation of the classics. The wealth allocation was directed toward economic management and territorial expansion, and for a while, the Qing rulers succeeded equal or better than all other Chinese dynasties, foreign or domestic. The Ming rulers seemed to value European learning the Jesuits brought to China; however, the Qing rulers with a nomadic background did not. The resources for scientific endeavors were indeed in short supply, though artistic creativity was valued. Yet, Qing rulers censored political writings and frowned on scholarly societies, and the persecution of artists that did not tow the Qing dynasty was not uncommon. There was little science-religion conflict. Creative capacity remained stagnant due to a stagnant abstract systems-building capability (a continued absence of alphabetical script, formal logic, and formal decimal system) and the economic straightjacket imposed by European civilization.

Constructive orientation: Thus, creative freedom was hardly valued despite the continued absence of the science-religion conflict. The Qing rulers had swallowed the Chinese political doctrines of Middle Kingdom and the Mandate of Heaven and used them successfully in reviving economy and greatly expanding the Chinese territory while suppressing its creative impulse even in practical technology. The civilization that produced the compass, paper, explosives, and printing press during the first millennia failed to produce an encore during the Qing dynasty as well. The linguistic and geographical isolation did moderate because of European Jesuits and traders, but China continued to have type 2 openness to the creativity of other civilizations.

Destructive orientation: If the productive and creative inner nature did not differ remarkably from the previous phase, it was a dramatically different matter with the destructive inner nature imprinted on the Chinese civilization by its foreign rulers, who worked hard at adopting a Chinese persona. The Yuan dynasty in the fourteenth century could not very well expand the borders of China since it would be fighting against its own Mongol brethren. This was hardly the case with the Qing, who had acquired the latest European cannons and explosives technology from the Ming rulers. Thus, for the first time in its history, China entered a period of naked aggression, not to defend its borders but to expand territorially. The three-millennia-long relatively peaceful and defensive posture lay in ruins under Qing aggression. One can argue that the foreign nomadic rulers displayed this aggression before they internalized the Chinese culture, and such an argument, in our judgment, would be largely true. For the first and last time, Chinese civilization under a foreign ruler displayed an aggressive, violent destructive nature and absorbed Inner and Outer Mongolia, Xinjiang, as well as Tibet into her bosom. It acted like the European and Muslim civilizations for a brief inglorious period.

Chinese civilization spent a majority of the current phase under a foreign invader, which was, once again, absorbed into the Chinese culture. Chinese civilization returned to high productive capacity. However, the foreign rule had two significant consequences: China ceased being the technology powerhouse that it had been during the previous millennium and thus its creative capacity was reduced to narrow and low, and China displayed an aggressive, violent external nature. It also continued to remain insular. Perhaps, both these changes, the latter for sure, can be attributed to the inner nature of the invader. Or perhaps, the decline in technological innovation may be explained through the fact that technological innovations now required using science that China did not possess.

17.39 Inner Nature of the Indian Civilization

Productive capacity: We may also analyze the productive inner nature of Indian civilization during the current phase into mercantile and systematic wealth drain periods. This division is more relevant for the present phase than the north/south division we have followed in previous chapters. During most of the mercantile period (1600–1800), the Indian economy performed well despite internal strife and religious fanaticism of some Mughal emperors and terms of trade increasingly negotiated or dictated by European merchants, who paid for Indian manufactured products with gold from the Americas. Indian civilization displayed economic freedom despite nonstop warfare. However, these wars and increasingly the coerced trade consumed most of the surplus, and reinvestment into industry and public works was probably modest and declined. Several technologies, such as firearms, explosives, irrigation methods, woolen textiles, and paper making had been introduced by Muslim invaders during the previous phase.

During the current phase, India benefited from European heavy cannon manufacturing and explosives expertise. The methods and tools employed by agriculture did not change appreciably, and by the end of the period, industry came under heavy tax burden in Bengal under the British control. However, in manufacturing, there was continuing improvements in textile, mining, metallurgical, firearms, and explosives industries. In 1750, India probably produced the best textiles and had highest iron production (though not highest per capita production) in the world. The *new technology adoption*, therefore, was a mixed bag, resulting in only spotty improvement productivity. Social cohesion had been badly damaged by Aurangzeb's fanaticism and the British divide-and-conquer policy; however, its deleterious effects on internal inequality were still in the future since the pattern of land ownership and manufacturing remained in private hands. Indian civilization remained open to trade and new manufacturing technologies and was one of the most productive civilizations in the world during the mercantile period.

All this was to change dramatically during the period of systematic wealth drain that began in the latter part of the eighteenth century in Bengal because the control of the Indian subcontinent by the British and the Industrial Revolution that occurred in parallel in England. This development changed the rules of engagement, and India slowly came to be seen as a commodities supplier and buyer of manufactured goods and not a supplier of manufactured goods, resulting in the destruction of Indian industry on an unprecedented scale and the realignment of agriculture away from grain production. It strengthened the transport and postal networks based on railways to efficiently move the commodities out and products in. One can imagine the loss of economic freedom, low technology knowledge synergy, an insular attitude, increasing internal inequality, and drain of wealth that resulted. If in 1750, Indian civilization accounted for 25 percent of the world trade, the number sank to 1 percent by 1947. Indian civilization had become one of the least productive civilizations in the world and least productive in its entire history. It was indeed the lowest point in Indian productive capacity, thanks to British policy.

Creative capacity: The creative impulse of Indian civilization that had remained protected in the Vijayanagara Empire for three centuries had died as Vijayanagara fell to surrounding Muslim states. It is fair to say that until the end of the nineteenth century, the creative inner nature of Indian civilization lay dormant, having fallen victim to Muslim rule that curtailed creative freedom in science, religion, and philosophy (though not in art, architecture, and music). As long as Muslim dynasties retained control, the science-religion conflict inherent in Islam affected both creative freedom and openness. The creative capacity remained low despite high abstract systems-building capability.

As the British consolidated their control of the subcontinent and felt secure enough to establish a universities system to create a clerical class to run the empire, and as the Muslim dynasties ceded control to the British, the Hindu population (initially in Bengal) enthusiastically welcomed European science and liberal education. Once again, after a lapse of several centuries, the Indian soul stirred with creative impulse and several produced world-class scientists. However, the spread of new learning remained confined largely to upper-class Brahmins. Thus, the creative inner nature both died and was reborn under British control during the current phase.

The magnitude and local availability of the surplus varied through the phase, going from a high to a low as Indian civilization became a commodity supplier as noted above. Ironically, the ICB moved in the opposite direction. It was type B2 under Muslim control while under Bengal renaissance; it clearly returned to type B1 with the possibility of returning to type C after a lapse of more than a millennium as it tasted European learning.

Constructive orientation: The British dealt a blow to the Muslim dynasties or rendered them powerless while keeping them as allies (Nizam, for example). The impact of European learning was to counter centuries of insularity imposed on the civilization by Muslim rule through both challenging Islam and challenging Hinduism, which had become conservative under Muslim pressure, to reform itself. The constructive orientation of leading segments of Hindu India slowly recovered its traditional type 4 openness by the twentieth century. However, the majority of the civilization in rural settings remained quite insulate and insular.

Destructive orientation: Indian civilization continued to demonstrate a peaceful external orientation during the mercantile period. However, once it fell under British control, its external orientation reflected the invaders' priorities with respect to stopping Russian response in the northwest frontier, enlisting India in two World Wars, or having to deal with several wars with Pakistan created by the British in 1947. This prompted the by-then ex-prime minister and Nobel Peace Prize-winning Winston Churchill, who was opposed to Indian independence, to honestly and carelessly observe: "We finally got our way in India."

During the current phase, as in the previous phases, the soul of the Indian civilization remained peaceful and did not engage in destructive behavior through invasions, control of trade, control of surplus, or wealth drain from civilizations, and it was not in a position to do so. It would be factually accurate to assert that the Indian civilization is the only major civilization in history to have remained peaceful during its eight-millennia history. China under Qing, as we noted above, did turn imperialistic in this phase. Perhaps the Chinese civilization may be excused since it merely failed to tame her nomadic invader. If so, then it is factually accurate to say that Indian and Chinese civilizations do not have a destructive inner nature directed at other civilizations. And such nature does exist in abundance for the Muslim and European civilizations, as we shall confirm once more below.

17.40 Inner Nature of Muslim Civilization

All states or empires within a civilization obviously do not and cannot have identical productive, creative, and destructive natures since their historical experiences, though shared, are not identical. They also have differing natural environments and institutions, though they would most certainly have common features, and different extrinsic circumstances. More than any other civilization during this phase, the Muslim civilization demonstrated this reality.

During this phase, Sunni or Shia Muslim ideology continued to drive the hearts and minds of Muslims in West Asia, central Asia, South Asia, and Southeast Asia. Below, we shall primarily focus on the productive, creative and destructive inner nature of the Ottoman Empire and make some brief remarks about other Muslim lands along the way.

Productive capacity: During the first two centuries of the phase, when Ottomans still had trade revenue, though it was declining, and despite fighting many wars with the

Venetian Republic, the economy of the Ottoman Empire performed well, comparatively speaking. The principal reason for this was expanding territory in southeastern Europe. Economic freedom during this period must be characterized as modest because of the powers the guilds exercised, and social cohesion was low because of the Millet system. Internal inequality was high because of the religiously circumscribed Dhimmi system. New technology adoption was low because new technology acquisition was relatively low. However, the empire was stable and control of sustainable growing surplus was in unchanging hands. The situation changed dramatically as the hold of European colonizers on world trade tightened toward the end of the eighteenth century, depriving the Ottoman Empire of trade revenue, as the Ottoman Empire came under combined British, French, Austrian, and Russian pressure, and internal social cohesion and the Millet system began falling apart. Ottomans reacted to this new set of circumstances by refusing to change and adopt new breakthroughs in science and technology from Europe even though they had the freedom to do so, unlike the Indian and Chinese civilizations. This "refusal" at one level is thoroughly understandable since change would have required the devolution of power away from the Sultanate, and the population was too mired in tradition to force this change.

During the nineteenth and twentieth centuries, economic freedom suffered further relative to what existed in Europe. The adoption of new technology was too little too late because of the tightly controlled nature of its industry through guilds and trade restrictions. Social cohesion took a nosedive. There was, however, marked improvement in internal inequality on paper as slavery was abolished, a uniform legal code was developed, and a halting movement toward centralization of political power began. However, it was again too little, too late create a modern economy to save the empire surrounded on all sides by enemies, and the result was pieces of empire achieving independence.

The declining relative productive capacity of the Ottoman Empire during the second half is reflected unmistakably in its half-hearted attempts to modernize based on developments in science and technology but without a willingness to undergo the necessary and painful political and economic changes. Lest the reader is too hard on the Ottoman elite, it is critical to keep in mind that the merchant class in Europe—which became wealthy through control of trade routes and thus spearheaded political changes—was necessarily absent in the Ottoman Empire because sea-based trade destroyed even the relatively smaller profits to Ottoman merchants. The economic and productive stagnation of the Safavid Empire was even more pronounced.

Creative capacity: If one is generous, one would be inclined to commend the Ottoman attempt to modernize its productive capacity. However, such generosity would be entirely misplaced when examining its creative endeavors. In science and critical philosophy, there was hardly any effort made to learn from European civilization. Creative freedom must be characterized as low except in matters of practical and military technology and long-standing science-religion conflict. Most significantly, the abstract systems-building capability was at a standstill because the emphasis was on acquiring technology and not its emerging scientific foundation. Consequently, the intellectual infrastructure behind science or the abstract systems-building capability was not valued. The creative capacity was narrow but deep during the first half of the phase and was narrow and shallow during the second half.

The Ottoman Empire continued to stand by the rejection of creativity by Muslim civilization since the twelfth century. The empire could not reject its Islamic roots and its creativity remained hostage to the prevailing interpretation of Islamic ideology. It was no different for the Safavid Empire.

Constructive orientation: Despite the absence of linguistic and geographical isolation and a memory of openness to the practical and intellectual creativity of other civilizations, openness to new ideas (except in military technology) was low as it was driven by religious beliefs. The constructive orientation remained type 1.

Destructive orientation: Both Ottomans and the Safavids faithfully followed their historically conditioned destructive inner natures. The Ottomans grabbed Southeast Europe after defeating the Venetian Republic and engaged in a long struggle to keep control of Arabian Peninsula and Egypt. The Safavids annexed Afghanistan and Uzbekistan and conducted raids on the Indian subcontinent. The difference this time around was that they could not hang on their possessions beyond the eighteenth century and in some cases beyond the nineteenth century because of the overwhelming strength of the European states. Nevertheless, if ultimate success was denied to these empires, the destructive inner nature to control others and to benefit from coerced trade or territorial control remained alive and well in the heart of Muslim civilization.

17.41 Inner Nature of European Civilization

If the Ottoman Empire in particular and Muslim civilization in general were plagued by declining trade tariffs and were hemmed in territorially by leading European states perched on the Atlantic coast and controlling key sea routes during most of the current phase, precisely the reverse was true for these European states: the profits from coerced trade with Asia, Africa, and the Americas (up to the eighteenth century), followed by continued systematic wealth drain based on territorial control, increased dramatically and progressively throughout the phase.

This centuries-long, highly successful extraction of the surplus by a few leading states in Europe from major civilizations (often more than an order of magnitude larger) and from sparse, hapless populations at an earlier stage of development (on lands often two orders of magnitude larger in size), a critical attitude toward religion through rejection the church's mediation role between man and God, separation of church and state, and a progressive devolution of power away from the monarchies set the stage for profound changes in the productive, creative and destructive inner nature of European civilization during the phase. Below, we focus primarily on the inner nature of the leaders among these leading states: Britain, France, and the United States. The inner nature of a few minor states hardly changed during the phase, while in most the states, it changed slowly through diffusion of technology and the existence of SPI.

Productive capacity: The productive capacity of European man probably did not change dramatically during the mercantile period except that the foundation for the coming profound political, economic, and religious changes were laid during the period. The leading states in European civilization such as France and England did not have a materially higher productivity than India or China toward the end of the eighteenth century as evidenced by the nature of trade patterns.

However, the changes in political (increased power of merchants, followed by manufacturing entrepreneurs, mass democracy, and effective separation of church and state) and economic and financial institutions (labor, credit, and product markets linked by emerging transport and communication technologies; banking systems; and stock exchanges), transition from the guild system to manufacturing based on task specialization, and mechanical power during the nineteenth century were dramatic and never before witnessed in the history of mankind. These changes led to national economies based not on a fixed relationship among the citizens but on an innovative, forward-looking, and competitive environments that allowed the potential of upward mobility for an increasing number of citizens with talent and ambition. The old social relationships based on religious beliefs, stagnant technology, and traditions were slowly replaced by those dictated by market forces. Thus, the economic foundation evolved from being static and stable to inherently dynamic and unstable by the end of the nineteenth century. During the first half of the twentieth century further changes in the political and economic institutions, such creating an industrial lab that focused on applying science to develop new products and processes to avoid brutal price competition; the federal reserve bank to manage money in circulation; and the safety net for the old, sick, and unemployed helped to restore dynamism and stability to the economy.

After World War II, creating supranational institutions such as the United Nations, the World Bank, and International Monetary Fund under American and British control continued this process of dynamism and progress, albeit with terrifying hiccups, such as the panics of the nineteenth century, the Great Depression of the 1920s, the stagflation of the 1970s, and the Great Recession of 2008.

The economic freedom increased dramatically and progressively during the phase. There was little technology diffusion from other civilizations during the phase. This was neither required nor needed. The new technology adoption through internal development achieved unheard-of heights, graduating successfully from chance dependence on an individual inventor to organized research labs. Social cohesion remained high, internally through the gradual emergence of a middle class and externally through the ideology of racism nurtured as it was through the use of extracted surplus from other civilizations. Finally, the requirements of a competitive marketplace ensured openness to new technologies and the mortal risk of ignoring innovation in the new competitive economic environment.

These institutional changes created a new productive capacity in the European man and in some of the states in the New World not seen in *Homo sapiens* before: productive, competitive, and relentlessly innovative with rational, unrelenting self-interest not tempered by fear of God. This man did not wear religious beliefs on his sleeve; he wore them in his heart while entertaining a profound internal doubt about their validity. He transitioned from being a soldier of God to a mercenary for profit. Never before in the history of civilization had humans attained such single-minded profit orientation. It had not happened in China, where loyalty to father and the sovereign was valued above all for millennia; in India, where personal salvation through God-realization was order of magnitude more important than all else; in the Muslim civilization, where the spread of Islam and living by the example of prophet were far more important than profit; or in the European civilization itself, where faith in God and His grace had mattered more than all else. In an ironic sense, it was a return to a focus on productive orientation not seen since the hunting-gathering era ten millennia earlier or before religious doctrines began to profoundly affect the natural *Homo sapiens's* productive orientation. At last, the actions of a civilization, if not its words, had managed to pierce through the clutter of religion.

Creative capacity: Given the high praise above, the reader might anticipate that we would be equally complementary about the creative nature of this new man created by European civilization. We are afraid we would be less so. Let us see why.

During the mercantile period, which included the first grand unification of science and the so-called age of enlightenment, support to science and critical philosophy was insufficient and often depended on an inconsistent support of wealthy individuals; though support for artistic creation by the wealthy individuals and religious establishment was plenty. This was because the elite was focused on global territorial conquest; the religious establishment still opposed science, though with decreasing effectiveness; and the linkage between science and wealth creation remained tenuous and was visible only to visionaries. Knowledge creation remained an activity not considered crucial but was highly appreciated when it happened.

Institutions for science, philosophy, and art took a turn for better in the nineteenth and twentieth centuries as the linkage between science and wealth creation became transparent, art became commercialized, and as religious faith faded further into background. Thus, universities became better funded and governments took it upon themselves to fund large research projects of little immediate commercial value. These projects in the twentieth century included harnessing nuclear energy (though the initial driving force was military power, not science), space programs (where the initial driving force was political), astronomy, quantum mechanics (where driving force has been genuine curiosity), and the genome project (where the driving force has been human health and commercial potential).

Clearly, creative freedom gets high marks still, in part because the science-religion conflict inherent in the Christian faith has been well managed and was not allowed to dictate the process of scientific inquiry—a dramatic change from Galileo's trial for heresy in 1600 at the onset of the current phase. The strides made in abstract systems-building capability through the experimental method, developing calculus, logic, epistemology, and the scientific method were indeed phenomenal.

The resulting creative capacity for the intelligentsia may thus be characterized as curious, aggressive, relatively free of religious constraints, and agnostic in effect. However, the commitment of the masses to creative endeavors continued to leave a lot to be desired. And because genuine scientific research is no longer the domain of an individual and because is very expensive, it must be supported by government, which requires the support of the masses. The prevailing view of public-funded research in the nineteenth century was exemplified by Gregory Airy, Astronomer Royal of Britain, who maintained that any research paid by the public should be demonstrably utilitarian. Even today, governments in advanced stages of the European civilization spend considerably less than one percent of GNP on pure research.

The conflict between the intelligentsia and the common man continues to remain the Achilles heel for the creative endeavors in European civilization fueled by the increasing consumerism of the common man.

Constructive orientation: There was little linguistic or geographical isolation. The combination of trade wealth and scientific breakthroughs had circumscribed the power of Christiana dogma. Thus, the European civilization achieved a constructive orientation approaching type 4 in the twentieth century, when its leading intellectuals opened their minds to such foreign creeds as Vedanta and Buddhism.

Destructive orientation Changes in the destructive orientation of the European civilization and its far-flung states in the New World were as uninspiring as the changes in its productive and creative capacity and its constructive orientation were. European civilization has a long and inglorious history of aggression, intolerance, and greed, though considerable progress was made in shedding religious intolerance during the current phase. The world, however, had never before witnessed the level of aggression and greed displayed by the leading states of European civilization: the reach of their aggression and greed extended to all continents and all civilizations: small and big, simple and advanced, rich and poor, and Christian and non-Christian. These states continued the tradition of Alexander and the Roman Empire and succeeded in outdoing both nomads (Huns and Genghis Khan) and the Muslim civilization in terms of impact. They hollowed great civilizations in India and China, destroyed or displaced the natives in Americas and Australia, enslaved the people of Africa, and prevented most of humanity from participating in the greatest expansion in human knowledge and creativity—an expansion that stood on the shoulders of the four great syntheses of science discussed in the last four chapters.

The leading states of the European civilization consistently sought control other civilizations' sustainable growing surplus, through coerced trade, territorial conquest, and systematic wealth drain during the phase.

Thus, the destructive inner nature of European civilization explicitly returned to its historical roots after a millennium of hibernation imposed by Muslim civilization. It evolved from coerced trade through the control of sea routes to a systematic wealth drain through territorial control, to control of technology and capital flows through the UN, IMF and World Bank, backed by military power. The instinct of aggression has not been moderated by an awakening of compassion, and greed has remained in high gear because of the built-in profit motive in its economic institutions. Only the religious intolerance has moderated. Further, these states, incredibly, sought to rationalize their greed and aggression through ideologies of racism, Nazism, cultural superiority, and a blatant fabrication of history and in so doing, the leading states and their historians have forgotten their own ordinary pasts.

In summary, we may celebrate the changes in the productive and creative nature of the European civilization and abhor its continuing destructive nature. It has shown the

Table 17.2: Relative Values of Measurable Parameters of Social Orders
Mature Phase, 1600–1950 CE

Measurable Characteristics →	Productive Capacity					Creative Capacity			Constructive Orientation				Destructive Orientation		
	NB	EF	NTA	WAB	SC	Creed	ASBC	WAB	GI	ESAN	LI	Creed	NB	IG	IC
Chinese	High	Low	Low	ED	Med	Bal	Low	ED	Low	Low	Yes	Bal	High	Low	None
Indian	High	Low	Low	ED	Low	ES	Med	ED	Low	N/A	No	ES	High	Low	High
Muslim	Low	Low	Low	MS	Low	SRC	Med	MS	Low	N/A	No	SRC	Med	High	High
European	Med	High	High	CE	Med	Bal	High	CE	Low	N/A	No	Bal	Med	High	High

NB: Degree of Natural Bounty
EF: Economic Freedom
NTA: New Tech. Adoption
WAB: Wealth Allocation Bal.
SC: Social Cohesion

ASBC: Abstract Sys. Building Capability
GI: Geographic Isolation
ESAN: Early Success against Nomads
LI: Linguistic Isolation
IG: Institutional Greed
IC: Intolerant Creed

ED: Favors Elite Decadence
MS: Favors Military Spending
PE: Favors Productive Endeavors
CE: Supports Creative Endeavors

ES: Excessively Spiritual
SRC: Sci. Religion Conflict
Bal: Balanced

way to conquering the lethargy and helplessness injected into the *Homo sapiens* social orders by religious doctrines but not the instincts of greed and aggression still haunting the species. European civilization, through the very institution that transformed its productive and creative nature, has fanned its destructive nature. Loss of religious faith, while freeing creativity from the shackles of metaphysical presumptions, has in fact bolstered the fires of greed since European man may no longer fear judgment day.

The relative values of the parameters assessing the dimensions of the inner nature of civilizations during the current phase are shown in Table 17.2.

17.42 Comparative Inner Natures of Participants

As we have alluded to above, the current phase is really a split phase: in the first half of the phase, the productive capacity of Indian and Chinese civilizations was higher than Muslim and European civilizations. However, the creative capacity of the European civilization was leapfrogging all other civilizations. By the end of the first half, a handful of European states managed to increase their stranglehold on all other civilizations, thus leapfrogging them in productive and creative capacity and constructive orientation while sharpening its destructive orientation. Beginning the second half of the twentieth century, the rest of the world has played a catch-up game expected to last several decades.

Having said that, below we summarize the "average" inner nature of civilizations during the phase.

Chinese Civilization

During the early part of the mercantile period, the natural calamities and external violent causes were in the driver's seat. As the Manchu rule settled down and adopted Chinese traditions and institutions, the intrinsic causes became more importance in wealth creation and trade. However, in creative and destructive aspects, the foreign ideology of the Manchus continued to a play a disproportionate role, as is evident in China's newfound imperialism on its northern and western borders and reduced emphasis even on its tradition of practical innovation. The external peaceful causes, which for a brief shining moment seemed to take root under the last Ming emperors, also played a secondary role since Manchus remained unable to shake the insular nature of the Chinese civilization; if anything, they strengthened it through their uncritical acceptance of the doctrines of Middle Kingdom and Mandate of the Heavens. Under Qing, China remained China except for the second-class status of the majority Han population and its rare display of imperialism, albeit of nomadic inspiration. Beginning in the mid-nineteenth century, the violent extrinsic causes became more significant as European states succeeded in asserting control over China. And again in the twentieth century, as the European powers became entangled in World War I and World War II, intrinsic causes through civil war became dominant and have remained so since.

On the average, during the current phase, China had a low productive capacity with a low internal SGS, a continuing type A creative capacity, and a type 1 openness. Uncharacteristically, Chinese civilization continued to exhibit violent aggression. Yet, we would hesitate to characterize the Chinese civilization as a warring civilization since it was its nomadic ruler. Thus, it continued to display an external orientation consisting of aggression and insularity.

Indian Civilization

During the mercantile period, the principal driving causes were the intrinsic causes. The Mughal Empire increasingly became obsessed with expanding control throughout the subcontinent, resulting in terrible conflict with both Muslim and Hindu states. The chief result of these internal land-based wars was that the defense of the vast coastline was utterly neglected, creating opportunity for European invaders. Nobody saw the connection between the loss of coastal areas and the coming territorial control inland. Muslim dynasties, which had controlled most of the subcontinent, hardly saw the need to learn from the Europeans during the seventeenth century. Even the fanatically religious Aurangzeb in his old age lamented and rebuked his childhood tutor, who asked for a reward for teaching Aurangzeb, telling him that he had given him factually inaccurate education in most practical subjects.

During the systematic wealth drain period, the situation reversed, and the extrinsic causes became dominant. Initially, the violent extrinsic cause throughout the late eighteenth and nineteenth centuries were dominant. Once British control was established, the reformation of Hinduism and introduction of European learning (type 3 openness) and wealth drain determined the evolution of Indian civilization. In the second half of the twentieth century, once again, the intrinsic causes, such as caste and ethnic divisions, politics of corruption, and the foreign ideology of socialism remained dominant. Only in the last decade of the twentieth century did the Indian civilization see the socialist straightjacket loosen because excessive mismanagement of the economy forced the issue.

On the average, during the current phase, North Indian civilization had comparatively low productive capacity with low internal SGS, a transition to type B1 creative capacity on the part of the majority Hindu population, a type B2 creative capacity on the part of substantial Muslim minority, a type 1 followed by type 3 constructive orientation, and continuing peaceful external orientation despite terrible internal violence. The Indian civilization experienced a precipitous decline in its creative capacity because of Islamic ideology, Hindu conservatism, and wealth drain by the British. The Indian civilization continued to have a mild form of type II external orientation, combining peacefulness and a significantly reduced form of openness to others' creativity.

Muslim Civilization under the Ottomans

At the beginning of the phase, to all appearances, Muslim civilization seemed riding high through the Ottoman, Safavid, and Mughal Empires and seemed driven by intrinsic causes. However, both Ottomans and Safavid Empires had a small population base and stagnant technology and depended on the trade between Asia and Europe and territorial expansion. The Mughal Empire, on the other hand, had a large population base and was not nearly as dependent on trade. In the seventeenth century, the Ottoman and Safavid Empires were the first to be impacted by extrinsic causes through control of sea routes by European states. The Safavid Empire was to suffer more since it was smaller and did not have a population base in Europe. However, Ottoman expansion was checked by Polish and German forces in 1683. In the eighteenth century, the Safavid Empire fell apart because of trade revenue loss, and the Ottomans were hemmed in by Russians. Thus, in the seventeenth and eighteenth centuries, violent extrinsic causes emanating from the European civilization were dominant. In the nineteenth century, again, net European pressure determined the evolution of the Ottoman Empire. Differing interests among European powers kept it alive. The Ottoman Empire finally collapsed in 1921 when it lost all territories and intrinsic causes largely determined the evolution of the Republic of Turkey. The dominant causes driving the Mughal Empire were intrinsic until its fragmentation around 1750, when violent extrinsic causes began controlling the events.

On the average, the Ottomans too had low productive capacity with internal SGS supplemented with trade profits and conquests, a type B2 creative capacity, a type 2 constructive orientation, and a continuing destructive orientation that combined an intolerant creed and violent aggression. Ottomans thus displayed a type V external orientation, combining religious insularity with violent empire building.

European Civilization

Genghis Khan and his descendants dealt a severe blow to Muslim civilization, and although it recovered through the Ottoman and Safavid Empires, it never reached its earlier relative military dominance even on land. The limited Chinese imperialism under the Manchus remained confined to around China. And Indian civilization remained controlled by Mughals who were confined to the subcontinent and never could complete their control over all of the subcontinent and were a land-based empire. This left the field wide open to European states to redefine the military and commercial trade dominance used on control of the seas that inked all civilizations. Once the process of controlling the sea routes began, it fed on itself: more trade wealth meant greater control of the sea route, which in turn brought more wealth. And this process went on for nearly 450 years. Thus, throughout the phase, the intrinsic causes and successful imperialistic nature dominated the evolution of European civilization.

By 1800, the Industrial Revolution was in full swing in Great Britain with unbelievable development in electrical, chemical, aviation, biological, nuclear, and information technologies during the nineteenth and twentieth centuries. The case for religion was weakened further through theory of evolution and developments in molecular chemistry. The second and third grand unifications in physics took place, and several new sciences such as sociology, thermodynamics, molecular biology, psychology, nuclear science,

Table 17.3: Comparative Inner Nature of Civilizations
1600–1950 CE

Civilization	Productive Capacity Internal SGS	Creative Capacity ICB	Constructive Orientation O/I	Destructive Orientation P/V	SPI
Chinese Civilization	Low	Type A	Type 1	Peaceful	No
Indian Civilization	Low	Type B1	Types 1/3	Peaceful	No
Muslim Civilization	Low	Type B2	Type 1	Violent	No
European Civilization	High	Type C	Type 3 ⟹ Type 4	Violent	Yes

Legend
SGS: Sustainable Growing Surplus
ICB: Internal Creative Balance
O/I: Openness/Insularity
P/V: Peaceful/Violent
SPI: Sustained Political Independence

and anthropology came into existence while in-depth developments took place in earth sciences and medicine.

The greatest destructive outcome of the period was systematic wealth drain from 75 percent of the world's population through military power, racism, Nazism, and two terrible global wars that killed close to 100 million people, 25 million to 30 million in World War I and 60 million to 70 million in World War II, which is equal to half of the entire population of the world at the end of the Roman Empire in 500 CE.

The significant outcomes of European civilization (which now renamed itself as Western civilization to reflect acquisition of continents to its domain and a desire to see itself as fundamentally different from other civilizations) were establishment of dynamic and unstable market economies, a slow and grudging evolution toward democracy, a breakdown of Christian faith for intellectual elites together with its continuing adherence in the lower classes, enormous creative outcomes yet a feeling it could have been greater, ownership of most of world's continents, and control of most of world's resources while draining wealth from established civilizations and keeping their productive and creative potential in shackles are consistent with its evolving dynamic inner nature. The reader only need look at a minor civilization such as resource-poor Japan, which escaped European control for obvious reasons during the phase, to be convinced of the truth of above statement.

The European civilization had high productive capacity as indicated by its high internal SGS, a type C creative capacity, a type 3 constructive orientation, and an extremely high violent destructive orientation to support its coerced trade and wealth drain strategy as revealed through its conduct in the Americas and Asia. In the twentieth century alone, wars initiated by the European civilization are responsible for 100 million deaths. It thus had a type VII or type VIII external orientation consisting of a violent systematic wealth drainer and religious insularity.

The comparative inner nature of participants is summarized in table 17.3.

The Evolution and Rationaliation of Mature Science

17.43 Grand Unifications Leading to Mature Science

The evolution of science in during the current phase is the story of science with grater backing in absolute terms than ever before in history and in a civilization protected from other civilization at a point in the history of science when it had achieved maturity after nearly 2,500 years of development across Indian, Greek-Indian, Arabic/Persian, and Italian civilizations, or the four syntheses discussed in chapters 12, 13, 14, and 15. It is an evolution that proceeded along logical stages of science whose pace was determined by the support it received from European civilization as a whole.

Given these remarks, the grand unifications of physics during the phase are thoroughly understandable.

The first unification in physics, consisting of heavenly and terrestrial motions, needed the differential calculus invented by Madhava and later, Newton and Leibniz. The laws of planetary motion Kepler deduced from actual data implied the law of gravity; all that was needed was a formula for the acceleration experienced by a body in circular motion and the second law of motion stating that force is equal to mass times acceleration. Calculus made this was made possible through the formula V2/R, which Newton deduced, where V is the velocity and R is the radius. Thus, if the square of the period is proportional to the cube of distance, it can be shown easily that the acceleration V2/R is inversely proportional to the square of distance, which through the second law leads to a law on gravitation, thus uniting terrestrial and heavenly motions. Newton used the motion of the moon around the earth to verify the law, arguing that if the moon is sixty Earth diameters away from the earth, its gravity must be 1/3600 that of earth or 32/2600=0.0088 feet/sec2. However, the velocity of the moon going around the earth at a distance of 12.6 million feet in a near circular motion is approximately 3,300 feet/sec. Therefore, its acceleration is 3300x3300/12,600,000 or 0.0864, which is very close to the calculated figure. The law of gravity was, of course, conceptually flawed since it implied action at a distance without providing the underlying mechanism. It is, in reality, no more than an empirical law that happened to be accurate enough. But at the moment, it was incredible that the same law quantitatively linked heavenly and earthly motions. But how could not they not? Is not earthly motion heavenly notion if one was on moon?

In the intervening century between Newton and Maxwell Clerk, the understanding of the laws of electricity and magnetism was built through experimental data and conceptualization. It was known that changing the magnetic field created an electric field. Maxwell Clerk postulated that changing electric field must also create magnetism based on symmetry, and when he plugged that term into the equations governing electricity and magnetism, its solution was a wave form with alternating electric and magnetic fields at right angles to each other and velocity too close to velocity of light to be a coincidence. Thus, Maxwell Clerk unified electricity and magnetism through a second grand unification.

Less than fifty years later, Einstein created the third unification, consisting of electromagnetism with gravity through his general relativity and altered the concepts of space and time as absolute quantities. His theory led to the idea of an evolving universe and the idea of the Big Bang that got the universe going.

Over the next half a century, the structure of an atom consisting of protons, neutrons, and electrons was discovered: protons with positive charge and neutrons with zero charge clustered in the nucleus, and the number of electrons with negative charge whirling around the nucleus at a sufficient distance to create a stable atom. There were two problems with this micro solar system model. One was how could all positive charges carry on a peaceful existence inside the nucleus, and second, why at times this peace was shattered in the form of radioactivity. Thus, strong and weak nuclear forces were postulated to respectively explain these phenomena. This led to resolving protons and neutrons into combinations of even smaller particles called quarks and abandoning the action-at-a-distance concept proposed by Newton postulating force-carrying bosons such as the graviton (that carries force of gravity though it was yet to be discovered), photons (that carries electromagnetic force), gluon (that carries strong nuclear force), and W and Z bosons (that carry the weak nuclear force). In this scheme, protons, neutrons, and electrons have mass, carry charge, and spin while the force-carrying bosons have energy and momentum.

In parallel with the structural and force transmission architecture, quantum mechanics, which deals with the motion of particles where action is on the plank scale, physical quantities such as momentum and energy can only change discrete amounts and not infinitely small amounts, and where matter and energy exhibit characteristics of both a particle and a wave.

Thus, by the mid-twentieth century, there were two theories: Einstein's theory of gravity for the universe as a whole and the quantum mechanics for the microscopic world. All they have in common is electromagnetism. It was an awkward period in science, and despite forty years of effort by Einstein and fifty years since his death, the gap has been narrowed but not bridged.

More than half a century had to lapse before the fourth unification, that of electromagnetism and weak nuclear force through the discovery of W and Z bosons.

Today, we seem to be on the verge of the fifth unification: that of electromagnetism and strong and weak nuclear forces through the discovery of the so-called Higgs particle. The Higgs particle mediates the process through which particles acquire mass or how energy/momentum condenses into mass, thus breaking the original symmetry in forces in the early universe. This has become known as the grand unification theory (GUT).

The sixth and final unification called the theory of everything (TOE) unites all four forces of gravity, electromagnetism, and weak nuclear and strong nuclear is on the drawing board, and the most promising idea is that of exceedingly small (10 to 33 cm) vibrating superstrings. The theory predicts graviton to be a superstring with wave amplitude of zero.

It is not just in physics that unifications took place during the phase. All chemical changes could be derived from quantum mechanics, thus uniting chemistry and physics. Similarly, in biology, classification schemes and biogeography led to the first unification in Darwin's theory of evolution and a second unification combining natural selection and genetics, which turn tied biology to molecular chemistry. In earth sciences, a unified theory of the evolution of the earth's surface features was developed, spanning nearly five billion years of history while plate tectonics supported this through the unified theories of rock formation and the phenomenon of earthquakes.

In each of these branches of science, we can discern a broad logical development coupled with blind alleys and missteps along the way. The blind alleys and missteps dissolved in the wake of new data and new conceptualization. Such is the stepwise social nature of science when the process is protected from destructive forces of history.

17.44 Rationalization of Mature Science

It would be anticlimactic to discuss why European civilization produced mature science while all other major civilizations regressed to earlier development stages. However, in the interest of completeness, we must do so.

Internal SGS: Clearly, the internal SGS of the now-heterogeneous Western civilization, from Chile to North America to Europe to Australia, has grown by leaps and bounds because of better land, a population increased by more than an order of magnitude, improved technology, and industrialization followed by post-industrial developments in information, nuclear, and biological sciences with agriculture slowly but steadily becoming a relatively small component of wealth production.

Allocation of SGS: Most SGS from internal and external sources was squandered on internal fighting and the lifestyle of the wealthy. Only a small portion was allocated to science, though this proportion has dramatically increased since World War II because of the nature of science and the Cold War that resulted in the space and arms race.

Nature of creed: As this capability was employed successfully to understand that the solar system and terrestrial motion was followed nearly two centuries later by the evolution of Earth, and life on earth can be easily explained through laws, Christian dogma began to lose its hold on European mind, thus furthering the cause of science.

State of its ASBC: The abstract systems-building capability of the European civilization through development of experimental method, calculus, sound epistemology, and the scientific method was unquestionably world-class. The fruits of the fourth synthesis and an enormous amount of trade profits during the mercantile era followed by persistent systematic wealth drain, despite resource drain on horrible internal conflicts, the decadence of the elite classes, and wars thrust upon other civilizations, proved sufficient to move forward in abstract systems-building capability.

Openness/insularity: As Christianity weakened, and even before that, European intellectuals developed openness to the creativity of other civilizations. However, this was a marginal factor since the fruits of the fourth synthesis were handed to Western Europeans on a platter at the beginning of the phase. Right from the start of the current phase, wealth drain, the hold of Islamic ideology in the Muslim and Indian civilizations, and nomadic control of China ensured that creative outcomes in all three civilizations were rather inconsequential. This naturally fed the theories of superiority and racism in European civilization that conveniently ignored that their control, and exploitation was the driving cause of that. To prove this assertion, we need not go beyond the example of Japan, which was never colonized because of its location and ecological attractiveness.

Nature of violent greed: The internal SGS grew throughout the phase and was supplemented by systematic wealth drain and the use of slaves and indentured labor. During the preindustrial period of the phase, the small Western European states saw more than an order of magnitude increase in their SGS because of systematic wealth drain. The military and political control of the world indeed paid handsome dividends to the European and now Western civilization. Finally, European civilization was the only civilization that enjoyed sustained political independence during the phase and was responsible for its absence for all other major civilization during the phase. While the political control of these civilizations was over by the mid-twentieth century, economic and financial control is continuing.

From our perspective, the progress in science the European civilization achieved during the current phase is not something unexpected or surprising. It is what could have been achieved in science had one civilization not controlled all other civilizations of the world at a time when science was ready to reach adulthood. And the process of control has not ended; only its form has changed. What was accomplished through violent colonization and dispossessing others of their land and means of wealth and through systematic wealth drain based on military and political control is now accomplished through control of technology and capital through undemocratic institutions. Thus, we conclude that while the maturation of science occurred in European civilization, it is also responsible for not allowing it to reemerge in most of the world.

Shifting Center of Gravity of Science

Needless to say, the center of gravity of science, which had moved to Western Europe during the last phase, remained anchored because it successfully executed the strategy of a focus on science combined with the political and economic control of most of the world's civilizations.

17.45 Life Stage of Science Achieved by Civilization

Based on the inner nature of civilizations and the underlying parameters summarized in table 17.2, the four key civilizations achieved the following life stages in science.

- Indian civilization: Development stage followed by mature stage in the twentieth century
- European civilization: Leader of the mature stage of science
- Muslim civilization: Development stage followed by mature stage
- Chinese civilization: Development stage followed by mature stage

Of course, achieving the mature stage does not necessarily mean making world-class contributions in science. It simply means that science is not resisted, its connection to wealth production is understood, and all civilizations have abstract systems-building capability that underlies science. Regressive religions still control segments of all civilizations. However, that is a rear guard action that will die its slow death despite efforts to reconcile science with monotheism and monism.

17.46 Summary

Any detailed summary of the chapter would seem superfluous at this point as well.

It is sufficient to say that taking advantage of the weakness in Muslim civilization (seventeenth century), Indian (eighteenth century), and Chinese (nineteenth century) and paralleling the approach of the Muslim civilization nearly a millennium earlier, European civilization not only controlled these civilizations through coerced trade and systematic wealth drain by exercising military power but also increased its landmass by an order of magnitude through the permanent displacement of indigenous peoples in Americas and Australia.

To its credit, using the world's heritage of science, it created mature science resting on firm foundations. It is also accurate to state that by the end of the phase, western European states had done more to push science forward than any civilization in history—a statement that would indeed constrain imagination at the beginning of the fifteenth century.

To its discredit, it most definitely slowed the march of science compared to what should have been possible through not only underfunding science but also preventing all other civilizations from participating in science by political control and wealth drain, reducing them to abject poverty by the mid-twentieth century.

Also to its discredit, it claimed, in the face of overwhelming evidence to the contrary, that it was solely responsible for birth and development of science because it was culturally and racially superior. In reality, it has only matched the Muslim civilization in aggression and desire for control and greed.

Chapter 18 | Evolution of Civilizations, Their Science, and Their Inner Natures

18.1 Introduction

In the preceding seven chapters, we have outlined the history, natural, intrinsic, peaceful and violent, and extrinsic causes and significant productive, creative, and scientific outcomes of major civilizations and nomad groups that have been significant to the intertwined story of civilizations and science over the last 8,500 years. There were two key assumptions in the analysis:

- Hypothesis of fixed yet flexible inner nature of *Homo sapiens*
- Hypothesis of the inner nature of social orders that founded the *Homo sapiens*

We also used a framework consisting of a tripartite division of *Homo sapiens* creativity, three eras of civilization and seven historically observable phases of science, ten key participants, and the concept of a social system consisting of interlocking social orders with reciprocal impact. No doubt, the facts we have presented have many significant gaps or even inaccuracies; however, more important, the main line of interpretation of the known facts by generations of Western historians is even more troubling.

This chapter takes at a look back at the last seven chapters to review the "forest" now that we have examined the "trees." There is no new data or interpretation presented in this chapter; it is simply an integrating chapter that hopes to provide a broader perspective that perceptive readers may already have appreciated. We achieve this simply through examining the evolution of each civilization, its science, and its inner nature

Evolving Dynamic Inner Nature of Social Orders

18.2 The Evolving Inner Nature of Social Orders

Let us look back and review how we assessed and applied the concept of inner nature consisting of productive and creative capacities and constructive and destructive orientations to historical analysis.

We first established the concept of a fixed yet flexible inner nature of the species through the unique species-specific physical and mental attributes within a social context. It consists of self-awareness; free will; the necessity of beliefs; conscious creative, productive, and constructive powers; and conscience and claimed that we need not take this fixed yet flexible inner nature of the species in the historical analysis since the intrinsic and extrinsic causes already reflect it. We then focused on the differences among social orders through their differing and evolving societal structures and processes and corresponding beliefs and attitudes to assess these capacities and orientations of each social order in each phase in chapters 11 through 17 and used them to rationalize the state of science achieved by each social order in each phase.

In table 18.1, we summarize the evolving capacities and orientations of key participants and through the seven phases.

Destructive Orientation of Social Orders is Quite Stable

Table 18.1 clearly shows that the destructive orientation of social orders, once formed or inherited, remains remarkably stable. Peaceful social orders remain peaceful and violent social orders remain violent.

Table 18.2 categorizes the world's civilizations and empires (nomads are only significant when they created empires) based on their aggression and internal creative balance. Table 18.2 highlights the remarkably stable destructive orientation of major civilizations over millennia despite a profound change in their internal creative balance. European civilization with or without the acquired Christian faith has exhibited a strong orientation of external aggression and greed through empire building, violent colonization, and systematic wealth drain while entertaining a varying orientation toward the creativity of other civilizations and religious affiliation.

The West Asian civilizations and central Asian nomadic federations too have displayed external aggression through empire building with an openness toward the creativity of other civilizations except after adopting Islamic faith, which resulted in religious insularity. The East Asian civilizations, with or without the acquired Buddhist faith, have depicted a peaceful external orientation coupled with abiding intellectual insularity until recent times.

Finally, the Indian and Southeast Asian civilizations with or without Hindu and Buddhist faiths have consistently shown a peaceful external orientation coupled with openness to both religious and intellectual creativity of other civilizations. These comments are a broad generalization and must be viewed as such with occasional exceptions

It is indeed remarkable that over the entire period during which these major civilizations have existed, professing differing faiths and with varying openness, a stable external aggression/peacefulness is evident in every civilization. Yet, it is hardly surprising that these tendencies remain very stable because their underlying forces, driven

Table 18.1: Evolution of the Inner Nature of Major Social Orders

Major Social Order	Capacity/ Orientation	6K BCE / I	1.0K / II	0.55K / III	0.2K CE / IV	0.75K / V	1.2K / VI	1.6K / VII	1.95.0K CE
Indian	Productive Cap.	High	High	High	High	Moderate	High	Low	
	Creative Cap.	Type C	Type C	Type C	Type C	Type B1	Type B2	Type B1	
	Construct. Orient.	Type 4	Type 4	Type 4	Type 4	Type 3	Type 1	Type 1	
	P/V	Peaceful	Peaceful	Peaceful	Peaceful	Peaceful	Peaceful	Peaceful	
	SPI	Yes	Yes	Mixed	Yes	Yes	No	No	
Chinese	Productive Cap.	High	High	High	High	High	High	Low	
	Creative Cap.	Type A	Type A	Type A	Type A	Type A	Type A	Type A	
	Construct. Orient.	Type 1	Type 1	Type 1	Type 1	Type 1	Type 1	Type 1	
	P/V	Peaceful	Peaceful	Peaceful	Peaceful	Peaceful	Peaceful	Peaceful	
	SPI	Yes	Yes	Yes	Yes	Yes	Mixed	No	
Mesopotamian	Productive Cap.	High	High						
	Creative Cap.	Type C	Type C						
	Construct. Orient.	Type 3	Type 3						
	P/V	Peaceful	Violent						
	SPI	Yes	Yes						
Egyptian	Productive Cap.	Moderate	Moderate						
	Creative Cap.	Type B	Type B						
	Construct. Orient.	Type 1	Type 1						
	P/V	Violent	Violent						
	SPI	Yes	Yes						
Greece/ Hellenistic	Productive Cap.		Moderate	M/H					
	Creative Cap.		Type A/C	Type C					
	Construct. Orient.		Type 4	Type 4					
	P/V		Violent	Violent					
	SPI		Yes	Yes					
Persian (Pre-Islam)	Productive Cap.		Moderate	Moderate	High				
	Creative Cap.		Type A	Type A	Type A				
	Construct. Orient.		Type 3	Type 1	Type 3				
	P/V		Violent	Violent	Violent				
	SPI		Yes	Yes	No				
Central Asian Nomads	Productive Cap.				Low	Low	Low	Low	
	Creative Cap.				Type A	Type A	Type A	Type A	
	Construct. Orient.				Type 4	Type 4	Type 4	Type 4	
	P/V				Violent	Violent	Violent	Violent	
	SPI				Yes	Yes	Yes	Yes	
European (Rome/Byzantine Europe)	Productive Cap.				Moderate	High/Mod	Low	Moderate	High
	Creative Cap.				Type A	Type A/B	Type B2	Type B/C	Type C
	Construct. Orient.				Type 1	Type 2	Type 1	Type 3	Type 3/4
	P/V				Violent	Violent	Violent	Violent	Violent
	SPI				Yes	Mixed	No	Yes	Yes
Muslim	Productive Cap.					Moderate	Moderate	Low	
	Creative Cap.					Type B2	Type B2	Type B2	
	Construct. Orient.					Type 2	Type 1	Type 1	
	P/V					Violent	Violent	Violent	
	SPI					Yes	Yes	No	

by differences in natural bounty and a response to these in the form of imperialist ideology (which in its basic form is lust for SGS control, land, slaves, raw materials, or markets), have persisted.

We need not remind the reader that aggression is not limited to other social orders alone. All civilizations have witnessed terrible internal wars. Such internal wars among the states of a civilization simply shift the control of sustainable surplus to a different state with more or less similar values and beliefs. Thus, the far less corrosive impact of internal wars still impacts a civilization's creative and productive powers, though to a different degree and in a different manner, and is dependent on the frequency and ferocity of these internal conflicts.

Constructive Orientation is Relatively Stable

The constructive orientation or openness/insularity of a social order can evolve but slowly and under unusual circumstances since it is determined by geographical isolation from other civilizations (a given in most of history), linguistic isolation (self-imposed but difficult to rise above because of the intimate relationship between language and culture), early wars against nomads (a given which when combined with geographical isolation from other civilizations can create a feeling of cultural superiority), and religious creed, which can indeed work to make a social system more open or insular. Monotheistic creed makes a social order more insular, all appearances to the contrary, while monism and agnosticism make a social system more open. However, since monism and agnosticism either have no need for conversions or their conversions are peaceful and hence less effective, monotheistic creeds in general have tended to make social orders more insular. Therefore, monotheistic social orders have shown a greater propensity to become insular more often than becoming more open until monotheism is challenged.

Table 18.2: Enduring Aggression of Social Orders through History

	Type A	Type B	Type C
Violent Systematic Wealth Drainer	Roman Republic/Empire (500 BCE–476 CE)	Ottoman Empire (1300-1922 CE) Byzantine Empire (330-1453 CE) Venetia/ Italy (1200–1600 CE)	English/French/Dutch Empires (1750–950 CE) American Dominance (1950–present)
Violent Colonizer		Spanish/Portuguese Empires (1500–1900 CE)	English/French Empires (1600–1750 CE)
Violent Empire Builder	Persian Empires (550 BCE–650 CE) Mongol Empire (1213–1368 CE) All Pre-Islam Nomads (500 BCE–750 CE)	Seljuk Turk Empire (1050–1300 CE) Delhi Sultanate/Mogul Empires (1200–1757 CE)	Hellenistic States (300 BCE–200 CE) Moors (Spain) (750–1492 CE) Arab-Persian Empire (West Asia) (650–1050 CE) Greek Civilization (750–334 BCE)
Peaceful	Chinese Civilization (all through history) Indian Civilization-Harappa (3750–2000 BCE)	Medieval European Civilization (476-1450 CE) Indian Civilization-Vedic (6500–3750 BCE)	Indian Civilization-Ganges (2000 BCE–1200 CE)

Internal Creative Balance

Creative Capacity Is Relatively Dynamic

Again, looking at table 18.1 clearly shows the extent to which internal creative balance is dynamic. All major civilizations except the Chinese civilization have experienced all three types of ICB during their history.

The creative capacity is determined by SGS allocation, abstract system-building capability, and the nature of its religious creed. Clearly, both SGS allocation and religious creed can change relatively dramatically through internal development or adoption. Significant breakthroughs in abstract system-building capacity (ASBC), on the other hand, are the work of extraordinary gifted geniuses and probably less than hundred individuals have made fundamental contributions to ASBC in the entire human history. There is a natural progression in the development of ASBC since an alphabetical script cannot be invented before rudimentary logograph, and the scientific method cannot be fully formulated before the invention of calculus. By its very nature, a social system cannot plan breakthroughs in abstract system-building-capability. To the extent an extraordinary genius is a chance statistical phenomena, he is likely to appear in civilizations with large populations, provided they have an alphabetical script and openness. This explains the disproportionately high contributions made by the Indian civilization in ASBC because of its openness and the disproportionately low contributions made by Chinese civilization despite a large population because of its insularity and refusal to adopt alphabetical script. Thus, fundamental breakthroughs in abstract systems-building capability are rare and largely outside the control of the social order. The social order is a recipient of breakthroughs in ASBC either through internal development or adoption from another civilization. No social system can stage the emergence of a Panini, a Madhva, or a Ramanujan. Through openness, wise allocation of SGS, and challenging monotheism social orders have been able to increase their creative capacity.

Productive Capacity is Highly Dynamic

Table 18.1 also shows that productive capacity to be highly dynamic. Changes in the productive capacity of a social order are first determined by changes in its economic freedom, adoption of new technology, the role of government in the wise allocation of SGS, its social cohesion, and its response to gradual or abrupt changes in nature. It is adversely impacted by excessive inequality and unnecessary or lengthy internal wars. Aggression and violence had a direct bearing on the surplus available to a social order during the era of violent interaction. If it goes up for one social order, it may go down for others, depending on the extent and duration of violent control. The controlling social order will have more than it produced internally or through peaceful interaction while the controlled social order will have less than what it produced internally or through ethical peaceful interaction.

The Concept of A Stable yet Dynamic Inner Nature

Like the fixed yet flexible inner nature of *Homo sapiens* at the individual level, the inner nature of social orders has both dynamic and stable aspects, though not as fixed and flexible as the *Homo sapiens* inner nature but sufficiently dynamic and fixed to be meaningful in historical analysis. Its enduring aspect is its destructive orientation. Its constructive orientation is relatively stable, its creative capacity is dynamic, and its productive capacity is highly dynamic. The above statement only pertains to the relative propensity to change; all social change is difficult and slow. Thus, the term *enduring* applies over the lifespan of social orders consisting of millennia, *stable* allows the possibility of change over a lifespan under unusual circumstances, *dynamic* is meant to convey significant change over centuries, and *highly dynamic* is meant to convey the possibility of change over decades. The stable yet dynamic inner nature of a social order is nothing other than its evolving productive and creative capacity and its relatively stable constructive and destructive orientation.

Social Orders as Magnifiers of the Inner Nature of *Homo sapiens*

We then demonstrated how this fixed yet flexible inner nature is magnified substantially by a social order based on the emergence of beliefs concerning creative and productive outcomes (truth or falsehood), conscience (concerning right or wrong), and division of labor. These developments led to creative, productive, constructive, and destructive behaviors.

It is indeed axiomatic to state that complex social orders including nomadic confederations act as supreme magnifiers of *Homo sapiens* inner nature since these social orders have proven to be far more creative and destructive than individual *Homo sapiens* as well as precivilization hunting-gathering tribal formations.

The question may be asked why complex social orders act as magnifiers of the *Homo sapiens* inner nature: they make creative and productive outcomes more creative and productive and make the constructive and destructive outcomes more constructive and destructive. The answer to this question is actually quite simple:

Civilizations in particular, compared to earlier social orders, require a much finer division of labor to both manage and further develop agricultural and nonagricultural technologies they are based on. The finer division of labor and the necessary coordination of the tasks, either through markets or government but typically both, mean a higher and increasing productivity in both creative and productive endeavors since a finer division of labor means each task is performed increasingly better because of continual learning and improved tools. Thus, civilizations heighten the cooperation among its members through a finer division of labor and the coordination among the finer tasks, which magnifies creative and productive outcomes.

However, a finer division of labor extends within not just productive and creative tasks but also political, religious, military, financial, educational, and legal structures and processes. Over time, this results in a vastly unequal power distribution among individuals within the civilization. Those who are enmeshed in the political, military, religious, intellectual, financial, and legal tasks attain more power and control. When this power combines with self-interest, opportunity, and an ethical conscience toward another civilization, constructive behavior gets magnified a well. However, when and if this power combines with self-interest, opportunity, and unethical conscience, the destructive behavior too gets highly magnified since the more powerful are in a position to gain more and lose far less through destructive behavior. This destructive behavior may exist within the states of a civilization in the form of excessive social, economic, and ethnic equality or intellectual, economic, or religious classes. It may exist *among* various states of the civilization in the form of internal wars or a at certain stage of development, *across* civilizations in the form of extended wars among civilizations. Thus, the finer the division of labor within a complex social order, the greater is the possible magnifying impact on the creative, productive, constructive, and destructive behaviors and outcomes the *Homo sapiens* are capable of. There is no free lunch indeed.

Dynamic Inner Nature and Evolution of Civilizations

18.3 Evolution of Social Orders through Inner Nature

There are three fundamental ways we can track the evolution of civilizations through history:

- Through their productive, creative, constructive, and destructive outcomes
- Through their evolving fixed yet dynamic inner nature

The first approach can be studied through data provided in chapters 11 through 17 and has the advantage of being plainly visible. In this section, we will track the evolution of major civilizations through the evolving inner nature, specifically through productive and creative capacities and through constructive and destructive orientations. Since productive capacity generally follows the creative capacity and can never go beyond it, though admittedly with a lag, below we will use the creative capacity and constructive and destructive orientation to graphically show how the civilizations have evolved through the standalone, peaceful interaction, and violent interaction eras. Further, we will use internal creative balance or ICB to represent the creative capacity, use openness/insularity as a measure of constructive orientation, and peaceful or violent (with its three aspects of empire building, violent colonization, and systematic wealth drain) behavior as a measure of its destructive orientation. This set of assumptions is the basis of the evolution of Indian, Chinese, pre-Islamic Persian, Muslim, and European/Western civilizations over their entire existence as shown in figures 18.1 through 18.5.

The Indian Civilization

The Indian civilization has remained peaceful and open when free from domination of outsiders throughout its long history of 8,500 years. Its wealth and creativity are not tainted by the blood of others, though it has benefited enormously from a creative exchange with others. It successfully maintained its political independence for over 7,500 years, thanks in part to the Himalayan barrier. It gave birth to science and retained a rational though at times excessively spiritual outlook until Turkish Islam broke through its defenses in the early thirteenth century. Earlier, it had successively repelled Arab aggressors. Over four centuries, as the antiscience Turkish tribes slowly felled a gentle, proud civilization divided by caste distinctions, science took its last breath in the place of its origin. As worldwide Islam lost out to European aggression beginning in the seventeenth century, Indian civilization felt the second punch through the opportunistic British waiting patiently in the wings for over a century. If the Muslim invaders killed science, the British impoverished the civilization while exposing it to European science, resulting in the short-lived Bengali renaissance. Today, Indian civilization is rebuilding after eight centuries of aggression by the Turkish tribes and the British systematic wealth drainers. It is a task that will take at least another half century. No other major civilization has taken such a one-two punch and survived yet still looks forward to renewal.

Thus, during its 8,500-year history, the external orientation of the Indian civilization remained true to its peacefulness and openness toward civilizations with respect to trade and practical, religious, and intellectual creativity. The internal creative balance, however, shifted dramatically from one phase to the next due to both intrinsic and extrinsic causes. Until 750 CE, the internal creative balance was type C or showed a steady move toward type C. After 750 CE, there was religious revival with internal creative balance moving toward type B1, a tendency reinforced by the success of central Asian Turkish invaders after 1200 CE. Whereupon the internal creative balance shifted to type B2 until the twentieth century, when it began its slow journey back toward type C after more than a millennium in the self-created excessive spirituality and Muslim/European domination.

Figure 18.1: Evolution of Indian Civilization

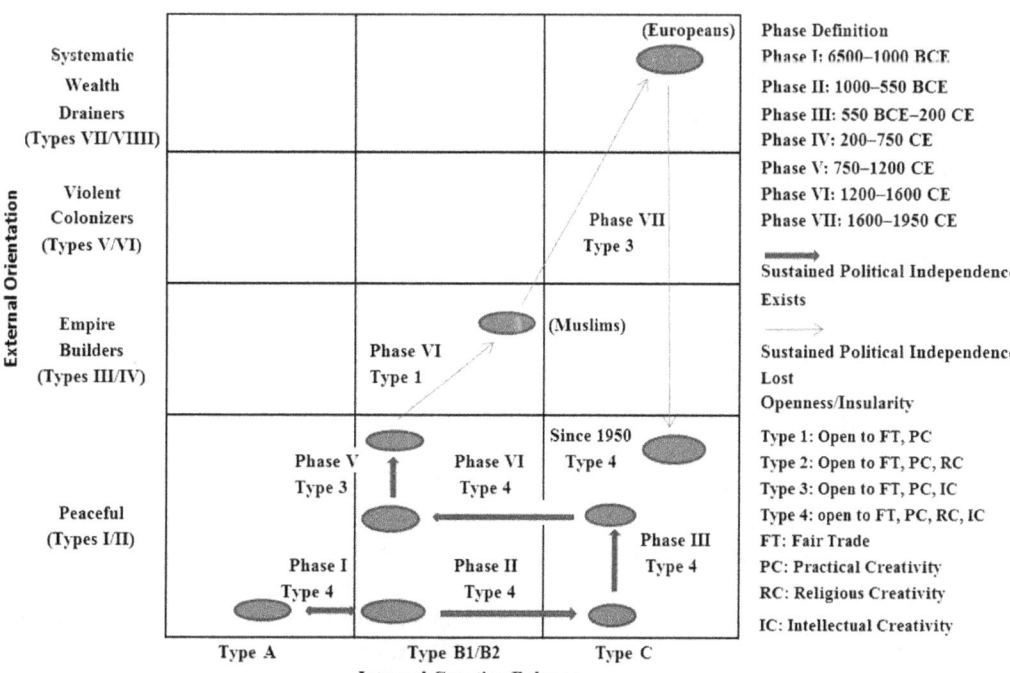

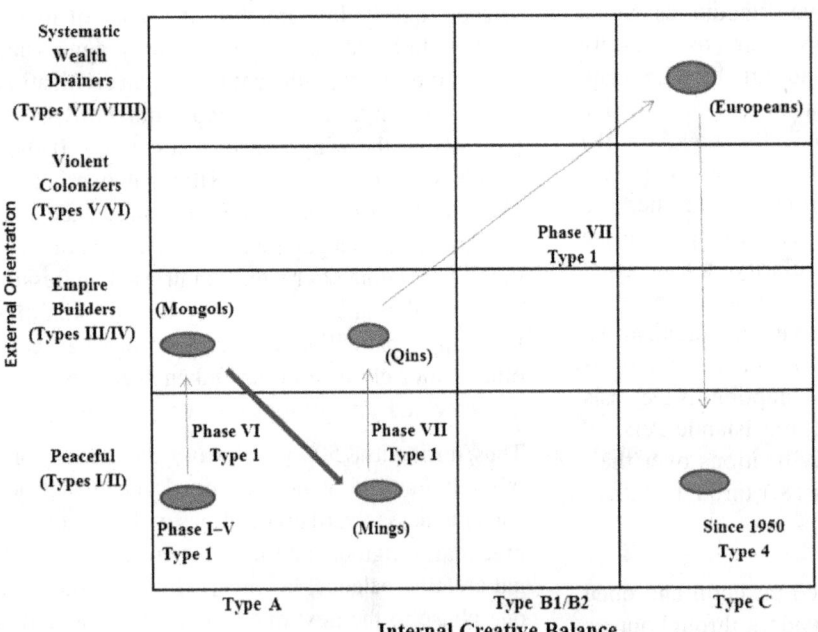

Figure 18.2: Evolution of Chinese Civilization

The Chinese Civilization

The evolution of the Chinese civilization over last five to six millennia is very different indeed. Lacking the Himalayan barrier, the Chinese civilization had to contend with the nomadic threat early and regularly. It made the Chinese civilization insular and imparted it with a sense of cultural superiority based on practical, ethical living. Unless controlled by nomads (such as Mongols and Qings) the Chinese civilization remained peaceful throughout its history. It was China's singular fortune that it never fell to Muslim aggression. Consequently, it never experienced a serious religious division. China's greatest weakness—the failure to adopt alphabetical script—was ironically its greatest strength. It never experienced linguistic and ethnic divisions. Its inability to develop a major religious doctrine meant China never experienced religion-sanctioned divisions. Thus, the Chinese civilization, insular and largely independent, remained a strong, central state through its long history. It showed little interest in science and comparatively less interest in metaphysics. Its enormous creative energies were channeled into practical creativity, which is an area in which China excelled more than any other civilization until the rise of modern Europe. China was not conquered by Muslims and was "only" humiliated by Europe, not conquered or hollowed. It has not followed the democratic free market path as it ventured on the path of development. Thus, its rise in the last half century has been dramatic. The constants of the evolution of the Chinese civilization are its peacefulness and its insularity masquerading as superiority. Thus, Chinese civilization has existed for at least five millennia and possibly longer.

The external orientation of the Chinese civilization during its entire existence has remained true to its essential peacefulness and insularity. Chinese civilization also displayed a remarkable consistency in its internal creative balance as well and remained type A. Only after the communist takeover did it begin to move toward type C under the influence of European science.

Pre-Islamic Persian Civilization

The pre-Islamic Persian civilization is a little over a millennia long. To Persian civilization belongs the dubious distinction of ushering in the era of violent interaction among civilizations. Its history is one of practical, tolerant empire builders slowly becoming increasingly religious but never showing any interest in science except through the import of Byzantine scholars. Pre-Islamic Persian civilization may be summed through its three empires, its final destruction of ancient Mesopotamian and Egyptian civilizations, and its transformation by Arabs. Persian civilization excelled in art and architecture. As Arabs invaded Persia successfully in the seventh century, Persia adopted Islam since it suited its warlike ways and the streak of monotheism it had harbored.

Muslim Civilization

Muslim civilization has been in existence for less than one and half millennia, a mere one-sixth as old as Indian civilization. Right from its birth, it has been highly aggressive, ostensibly in the name of God, like all empire-building civilizations driven by greed. It started with practical but open-minded Arabs, became sophisticated after

Figure 18.3: Evolution of Pre-Islam Persian Civilization

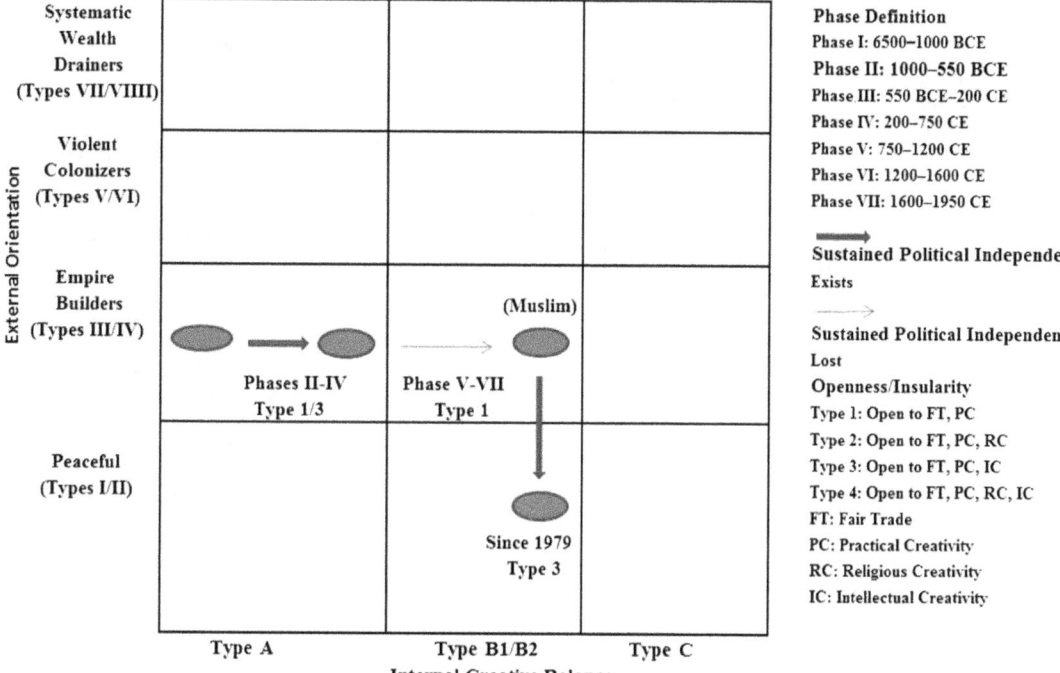

conquering Persia, and got into the science project after it came in contact with Indian science in Sindh and Greek/Hellenistic science in Iberia. For four centuries, Muslim civilization achieved type C internal creative balance, making incredible contributions to science. However, the rise of fundamentalist Islamic monotheism in the twelfth century followed by the European end run against land-based Ottomans pushed the civilization back into arid lands until the discovery of oil beneath the desert sands brought in European imperialism. Today, Muslim civilization is still struggling to free itself from European/Western control. It is the only major civilization that is yet to free itself from Western control. Throughout history, the Muslim civilization, as a child of West Asian heritage, remained aggressive with type B2 internal creative balance, except the brilliant period of four centuries. Muslim civilization has nomadic, Arabian, Persian, Egyptian, Mesopotamian, and Turkish roots. During its relatively short life, Muslim

Figure 18.4: Evolution of Muslim Civilization

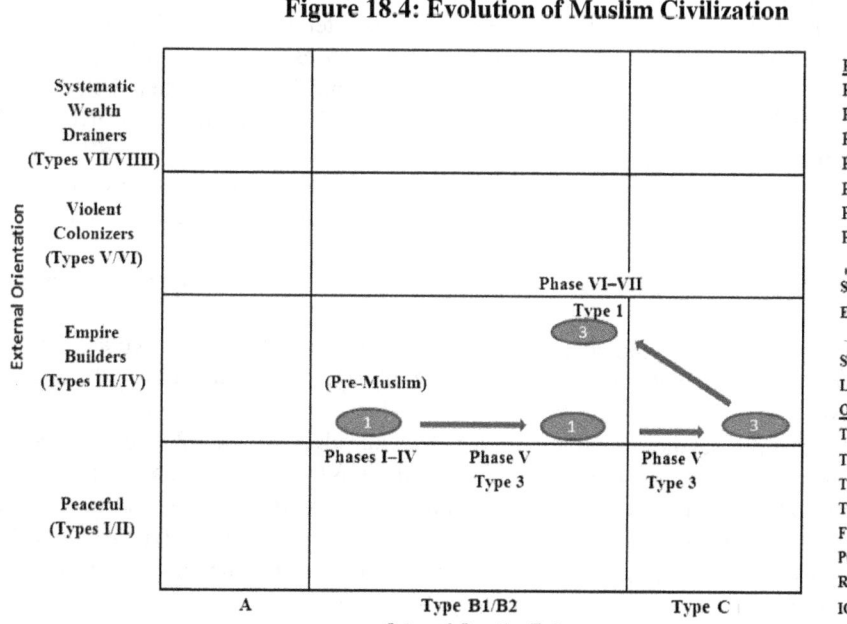

Figure 18.5: Evolution of European Civilization

	Type A	Type B1/B2	Type C	Phase Definition
Systematic Wealth Drainers (Types VII/VIIII)	● →	Phases IV-VI Type 1/3 → ● →	Phases VI-VII Type 3/4 ●	Phase I: 65000–1000 BCE Phase II: 1000–550 BCE Phase III: 550 BCE–200 CE Phase IV: 200–750 CE Phase V: 750–1200 CE Phase VI: 1200–1600 CE Phase VII: 1600–1950 CE
Violent Colonizers (Types V/VI)	Phase III Type 1	Phase II Type 4		──→ Sustained Political Independence Exists
Empire Builders (Types III/IV)		● →	Hellenistic States Phase III Type 4	──▷ Sustained Political Independence Lost
Peaceful (Types I/II)	Pre-Roman Phase I-II ●	Greece Phase I ●		Openness/Insularity Type 1: Open to FT, PC Type 2: Open to FT, PC, RC FT: Fair Trade PC: Practical Creativity RC: Religious Creativity IC: Intellectual Creativity

External Orientation (vertical axis) / *Internal Creative Balance* (horizontal axis)

civilization has also remained remarkable close to its core beliefs. Externally, it has displayed remarkably consistent aggression, nourished both by its faith and its nomadic roots, type 1 openness/insularity, and internally, an intolerant type B2 internal creative balance. This statement flies in the face of the remarkable golden age of science within Muslim civilization for nearly four centuries and the grudging Turkish acceptance of religious minorities in Europe for an equal number of centuries. However, it was unusual conditions under which Muslim civilization displayed either a pro-science or a religiously tolerant character. The inner nature of Muslim civilization has rested on aggression, type 1 openness/insularity, and a type B2 intolerant religious creative orientation.

The European/Western Civilization

European civilization started out in ancient Greece as a peaceful and open civilization, willing to learn alphabetical script from Phoenicians, art from Egyptians and Mesopotamians, and science from Indians. It all changed with Alexander reacting to earlier Persian "aggression." Alexander's success had a major impact on the European psyche: it learned that aggression pays both in wealth and in knowledge, which in turn creates more wealth. Thus, civilization has remained aggressive through all phases and remained open in several phases. The pro-science empire building and open Greek/Hellenistic world, which lasted for half a millennium, was destroyed by a practical, insular Roman world that in turn turned religious and more insular under pressure from Muslim aggression. Venetian control of the Mediterranean created an opening for European civilization, which led to the Italian Renaissance and the discovery of Greek/Hellenistic heritage, thus regaining its openness and type C internal creative balance after a millennium. As the Ottomans bettered the Venetians, European civilization, suffering from religious wars and Bubonic plagues, was in trouble once again but was rescued through discovery of sea routes. This led to renewed aggression, continued openness, and support of science, building on what the Arabs left in Iberia. The wealth pouring into the small western European states perched on the Atlantic (for the most part) and the resulting superior military strength and scientific knowhow allowed European civilization to control all other civilizations for last three centuries and extend itself on half of the land mass of the planet. In the process, it has maintained its aggression yet relinquished control partially when the option was defeat and bloodshed. The world today still lives in the shadow of European aggression and European science. European civilization, much like the Muslim civilization and the nomads, has shown remarkable consistency in aggression against other civilizations. However, its openness/insularity and its internal creative balance have both fluctuated significantly over the two and half millennia it has been in existence. Ancient Greece displayed an open and aggressive violent orientation and achieved a type C internal creative balance by about 500 BCE, followed by type A under Roman rule and type B2 when Europe adopted the foreign religious creed of Christianity. It went back to type C beginning about 1600 CE. Thus, the internal creative balance evolved from type C to type A to type B to a hard-won type C again. The openness evolved from type 4 to type 1 to type 3 to type 4.

Chapter 18 · Evolution of Civilizations, Their Science, and Their Inner Natures   551

Table 18.3: Evolution of Science Across Stages

Major Social Order	6K BCE	End of Phase I 1.0K BCE	End of Phase II 550 BCE	End of Phase III 200 CE	End of Phase IV 750 CE	End of Phase V 1200 CE	End of Phase VI 1600 CE	End of Phase VII 1900 CE
Laggers in Science								
Mesopotamian		PS-M	~S-B					
Egyptian		PS-D	PS-D					
Persian				PS-M	PS-M			
Central Asian Nomads				PS-B	PS-B	PS-B	S-D	
Ancient Greece			PS-M	S-D				
Roman/Byzantine				PS-M				
Chinese		PS-D	PS-D	PS-M	PS-M	PS-M	PS-M	PS-M
Leaders in Science								
Hellenistic States				S-D				
Indian		PS-M	S-B	S-D	S-D	S-D	S-D	PS-M
Muslim						S-D	PS-M	PS-M
European					PS-M	PS-M	PS-M	S-D	S-M

Life Stages of Science

PS-B: Birth of Protoscience   S-B: Birth of Science

PS-D: Developing Protoscience   S-D: Dev of Science

PS-M: Mature Protoscience   S-M: Mature Science

Leader of the phase

Dynamic Inner Nature and Evolution of Science

In this section, we highlight the consistency between the life stage of science and the inner nature of significant social orders in each phase.

18.4 Evolution of Life Stages of Science across Civilizations

In table 18.3, we summarize the stage of science for each significant social order over all seven phases. We may summarize the following general observations concerning evolution of science across civilizations:

- All four significant civilizations during the protoscience stage made contributions to protoscience.
- Indian civilization gave birth to science.
- Civilizations jumped from the mature protoscience stage to the development stage by acquiring and absorbing known science, thus bypassing the birth process of science.
- Mesopotamian and Egyptian civilizations, but not all of their learning, were absorbed into the Persian Empire; Greece gave way to Hellenistic states, which were absorbed into the Roman Empire and bequeathed their achievements to Indian, Muslim, and European civilizations. Persian civilization was absorbed into Muslim civilization. central Asian nomads primarily learned from Indian, Chinese and Muslim civilizations.
- Hellenistic states and Indian civilizations led in the early development of science, followed by Muslim civilization.
- Civilizations often reverted to an earlier stage under certain circumstances, particularly when controlled by other civilizations.
- Only the European civilization reached the maturity stage by the end of phase VI.
- Until the last phase, when European civilization controlled all other civilizations through high seas, all significant civilizations made contributions to

science. However, during the last phase, was the European civilization geographically expanded to become Western civilization made the overwhelmingly disproportionate contribution to science. Thus, phase VII stands out as a very unusual phase. This uniqueness, derived from control and wealth drain, explains the superior attitude of the European/Western civilization toward itself and a condescending attitude toward other civilizations.

The civilizations that led science in each phase are highlighted in table 18.3.

18.5 Summary

In this chapter, we first studied the changing inner nature across phases. Then, using the concept of inner nature, we tracked the evolution of each civilization and the stage of its science through phases. Our purpose was to highlight the stable and dynamic aspects of inner nature and to provide a bird's eye view of the evolution of civilizations and their science through the concept of inner nature. The chapter simply constitutes an integration of chapters 11 to 17.

KEY CONCEPTS

Dynamic yet stable inner nature of social orders
Evolution of civilizations
Evolution of science

Chapter 19 | Conclusions and Lessons of History

19.1 Introduction

We hope we have accomplished the twin tasks of validating the theory and rationalization of history of science. It has been a long journey: in first two chapters, we raised issues concerning civilizations and science, we then developed the needed theory, concepts, and tools in the next eight chapters; followed by seven chapters that laid out the intertwined story of civilizations and science over the 8,500-year history of civilization. In the last chapter, we looked back to gain perspective on this long history.

In this chapter, we simply want to summarize the key conclusions concerning the evolution of science and the key lessons of history, though it is somewhat repetitive of what has been said before. In the next and last chapter, we look at the future of science.

19.2 Science through Phases and Across Civilizations

Broad Evolution of Science

As we saw in chapter 11, all four primary civilizations participated in the development of protoscience with remarkable contributions though with differing emphasis with respect to practical, religious, and intellectual creativity, with Egypt and Mesopotamia producing strong states with centralized power and India producing decentralized institutions glued together through loosely bound spirituality. China remained isolated and produced a strong state as well, though it was under constant attack from nomads. The focus of Egyptian and Mesopotamian science was practical and commercial while focus in India remained spiritual and progressively became intellectual without a significant science-religion conflict. These differences resulted in a focus on different sciences. There was trade and exchange of ideas and migration between India, Mesopotamia, and Egypt. Recent research has suggested the possibility of the Indian origin of Mesopotamian mathematics.

Egyptian and Mesopotamian civilizations began declining, and their disintegration was complete by 500 BCE when great ideas in epistemology, mathematics, linguistics, and speculative natural science including astronomy and religion had sprouted out of the Indian civilization. The achievements of Mesopotamian and Egyptian civilizations were reduced to becoming the foundations of new civilizations in West Asia, Anatolia, and Greece. Thus, only the Indian civilization fully participated in the birth of science since it took a while for the new civilizations to absorb, accept, or reject the achievements of these two parent civilizations as well as the Indian civilization. The birth of science proper took place in Indian civilization between 1000 and 500 BCE and could also have easily taken place in the neo-Babylonian state of Mesopotamian civilization had it not been destroyed by world's first empire, the Persian Empire.

For the next two millennia, science went through four syntheses, becoming hostage to a never-ending conflict among civilizations and essentially becoming a foster child being shunted from one civilization home to another: now appearing as a Greek, Hellenistic, and Indian affair; an Indian affair; an Arab-Persian affair; and a European affair.

The cross-fertilization during the Greek-Indian-Hellenistic phase clearly began centuries prior to Alexander's invasion and continued after Alexander through Indo-Greeks on the northwest frontier of India and through India-Rome trade. In particular, recent research suggested the diffusion of Jain metaphysics, Buddhist rational philosophy, and Indian speculative physics to ancient Greece. This third phase, as we saw, led to considerable developments in geometry and earth-centered solar astronomy in Hellenistic states that was derived from Mesopotamian astronomical achievements harvested by Alexander and sent to Greece. The earth-centered astronomy set the course of astronomy on wrong path for over a millennium in in West Asia, North Africa, and Europe.

The Indian Synthesis or fourth phase led to several breakthroughs in mathematics, including the decimal system; number theory, including the concept of zero and negative numbers; trigonometry; the earliest notions of differential calculus, a heliocentric astronomy; and the concept of relative motion through Aryabhatta's groundbreaking work that unfortunately Brahamagupta rejected a century and a half later.

The fifth phase or Arab synthesis of Indian, Greek, and Hellenistic learning resulted in development of the critical concept of force as a rate of momentum transfer and other critical ideas including the Tusi couple Copernicus exploited in the next phase in creating heliocentric solar astronomy among many other achievements nurtured by the Venetian trade with Asia. Muslim civilization walked away from science toward the end of the twelfth century in a fit of fundamentalist backlash, and Muslim-Turkish invaders destroyed science in the Indian civilization, including in Vijayanagara, where science, under hot pursuit, had found a temporary safe haven.

The sixth phase or European synthesis occurred in stages and began on the foundation of the achievements the Muslims left behind in the Iberian Peninsula, and the

Scholastic work mined in Christian monasteries led to a second broader and complete formulation of the Copernican heliocentric model and Galileo's articulation of the laws of motion in Italy and central Europe followed by return of science to western Europe awash with new trade wealth. Northwestern Europe, as it first received the gift of science from the Arabs, was in dire economic straits because of the bubonic plague and religious wars, while Venice controlled trade profits before losing its control of the Mediterranean to the Ottomans. Fortunately, Northwestern Europe, assisted by Africans and Indian sailors, found a way around these problems through discovering sea routes to Asia and the New World. These discoveries completely changed the geopolitical balance of power that allowed a handful of small European states perched on the western seaboard of Atlantic to dominate and control the world for four centuries through coerced trade and systematic wealth drain. By this time, the scientific project in India and the Muslim world had ended or weakened considerably, mainly due to the success of the antiscience Ottomans and other Turkish tribes and their consequent control of the land-based trade between Asia and Europe. Their political control of India, Egypt, and the Arab world devastated science in these areas, and their control of land trade between Europe and Asia began to deprive Italy and Venice the trade profits they had used to pursue science and creative endeavors, thus handing over the leadership of science for the first time in history to western Europe, a leadership initially nurtured by profits from coerced trade based on the control of high seas. While science found a shelter in Northwestern Europe for the first time in its history, these states prevented its birth or rebirth until the twentieth century elsewhere in the world. Thus, during its maturity, European historians reincarnated science as an exclusive child of the now expanded "Western" civilization.

The course of mature science, or the seventh phase, was essentially controlled by western Europe and was built on the Italian and central European synthesis. It resulted in the integration of terrestrial mechanics and heliocentric astronomy, electricity and magnetism, and electromagnetism and gravity, and today is approaching unifying electromagnetism, nuclear forces, and even gravity. This was financed by the shifting of trade pattern from land to sea derived from the discovery or rediscovery of the sea routes to India and the resulting coincidental discovery of the Americas in the process. The ensuing Industrial Revolution was financed by trade and systematic wealth drain from Asia and Africa by a smaller subset of western European states that had managed to break the hold of Christianity on science. The economic and political control of the world's civilizations by Europe effectively ended any residual science in all non-European civilizations for two centuries until the achievements of European science began to knock at their doors with undeniable force.

Thus, over the course of three millennia, the center of gravity of science moved from India/Mesopotamia to the Greek-Hellenistic world, India, Arabs, Italy and central Europe, and western Europe. We may envision these syntheses as a form of a relay race, albeit a forced one, when one civilization, due mostly to empire building, violent colonization, and systematic wealth drain, was forced to abandon the scientific project to one degree or another and handed off the project to another civilization in line. By the middle of the seventh synthesis or by about 1750, the laws of heavens and terrestrial mechanics were clearly understood, and the scientific project was ready to focus on other branches of natural science and social sciences, while continuing to develop formal sciences. Thus, by 1750, science and the scientific method were firmly established, as was the certainty of the coming hegemony of European/Western civilization. The combination of the emerging sea-based hegemony of a handful of western European states and the weakening of the Turkish land-based hegemony and control had effectively killed science or prevented its rebirth in much of the ancient centers of science, including Greece, India, West Asia, and Egypt.

Thus, the history of science moved from parallel development in multiple civilizations during the pregnancy stage to birth in a single civilization to sequential development by the leading civilization, with civilizations handing off the leadership during the development stage, to a different civilization to its monopoly by one civilization which, while nurturing it internally, effectively prevented its rise in all other civilization for nearly two centuries because of trade control and wealth drain from these civilization on a massive scale.

As a result of Turkish control of the land trade and western European control of sea trade, the march of science over the last several centuries has primarily been a western European and Western phenomenon. Because the new emerging sciences of chemistry, thermodynamics, electromagnetism, biological sciences, nuclear science, information science, and social sciences down to the twentieth century all required the breakthroughs in physics and the embedded scientific method, these sciences emerged in a rapid fire one after another. To a casual observer science would, thus, appear to be exclusively a European phenomenon not in small measure because the history of science was rewritten. This is equivalent to giving all the credit of success to the parents adopting a promising teenager at the expense of the birth parents and those who had cared for him in successive foster homes during his teenage years. Thus, from the Indian, Persian, and Arab perspectives, the Turkish land and western European sea hegemony of the last eight hundred years stands out as dark chapters, though with a critical difference. Turkish hegemony, although it did not indulge in wealth drain, excelled in religious fanaticism emanating from both their tribal roots and sharia-soaked Islam they had adopted in the tenth century. The western Europeans, though eventually becoming pro science internally and rising above religious fanaticism, killed science in civilizations they controlled because they indulged in systematic wealth drain. In other words, to oversimplify, the Turkish-Ottoman land-based empire hated science. They destroyed it internally and in civilizations they controlled through creed. Western European sea-based empires nurtured science internally and destroyed it elsewhere through greed and drain of wealth. The one civilization that bore the full and complete brunt of these two evil forces in a one-two punch, the Indian civilization, was ironically the birthplace of science.

Now let us focus on the major civilizations specifically.

Why Chinese Civilization Never Developed Science

Chinese civilization excelled in practical creativity in several phases but borrowed its religious creativity from the Indian civilization two millennia ago and its intellectual creativity from the European civilization more recently. The Chinese civilization was lucky twice in history: first in the thirteenth century when Mongols checked Muslim aggression and the second time in the eighteenth century when a strong central government slowed down European advances.

The contrast with Indian civilization could not be more dramatic. Mongol advance in India was stopped by the Delhi Sultanate and demise of the Mughal Empire in the mid-eighteenth century assured European control of India. However, despite this fortune, Chinese civilization utterly failed to create science in particular or excel in religious and intellectual creativity in general. This must be attributed to China's failure to develop and refusal to adopt abstract system-building capability, including alphabetical script, sound epistemology, and scientific method until the twentieth century. Thus, China used its linguistically static logograph to assure internal unity and create series of strong centralized states but at the expense of developing the abstract systems capacity necessary for religious and intellectual creativity. The Chinese civilization could not develop science because of its insular nature, which also determined its inability to adopt or invent alphabetical script throughout its existence. In this work, we take the position that science is not possible without alphabetical script since it is essential for creating complex abstract systems that require words and symbols with precise meaning. Despite the relative absence of both greed and intolerant creed, the failure to invent or adopt alphabetical script meant Chinese civilization contributed little to the development of science, thus channeling its enormous creative impulse into world-class practical inventions.

Why Science in Muslim Civilization Died After a Brilliant Start

The Moors in Spain initially supported the science project in the early morning of the nascent Muslim civilization. The Moors were in a new country and needed allies, Islamic law and way of life had not been worked out, and the literate Jewish community in Spain had access to Greek and Hellenistic heritage and was under attack from Christians. In addition, Indian mathematical and astronomical breakthroughs were available through the short-lived Arab beachhead in Sindh. Thus, an alliance with Jews initially sparked a synthesis of Greek and Indian achievements. This lasted for several centuries, an effort that truly expanded the frontier of science, until the implications of the Koran were worked out. By the twelfth century, Muslim civilization, under the unconscious though the then-correct assumption that the pursuit of science is not required for wealth creation, made a conscious decision that science and Islam were not compatible and walked away from science, particularly under the emerging Turkish leadership of the Muslim civilization. Religious intolerance is built into the very charter of Islam as it proclaims there is only one God: theirs, with Muslim characteristics. The later relative Turkish tolerance of religious minorities in southeastern Europe was ultimately based on practical considerations and the pressure exerted by increasingly powerful European states. It is important to remember that through political, military, and economic means, Muslims converted populations to Islam in Spain, India, West Asia, central Asia, North Africa, and Southeast Asia. They killed science in India and remained aggressive until the rise of an even more aggressive and violent Europe that successfully made an end run against their land-based empires. This process of conversion into Islam, incidentally, was quite the opposite of the European adoption of Christianity, as the latter was a bottom-up movement that actually forced the state to adopt Christianity rather than the state forcing people into a new religion in the case of Islam. However, it must be stated that the Muslim conversion process was also far more humane than the Spanish Inquisition (though it was a reaction to earlier Islamic conversions) whereby Muslims in Europe were forcibly converted back to the Christian faith.

Thus Muslim civilization advanced the cause of science dramatically until it fully internalized the teaching of Islam. Once that was complete, it consciously killed science project within the Muslim civilization, killed it in Indian civilization after it came to control Indian civilization, and refused to learn from Europe in their backyard for the next eight centuries until the twentieth century when the connection between wealth creation and science became too transparent to ignore. In the last analysis, the Muslim civilization, after a brilliant start, hurt the cause of science within itself and the Indian civilization beginning with phase VI through the adoption of the world's most intolerant creed, that of Islam. It is the only major civilization built exclusively around an intolerant creed.

Why Science in Indian Civilization Eventually Died

Until 1200 CE, the focus on science in Indian civilization (until then Indian civilization had managed to retain its sustained political independence and cultural unity by either defeating or absorbing invaders) depended on the outcome of a gentle struggle between religious impulses of monistic spirituality on the one hand and polytheism/agnosticism on the other. Periods marked by ascendant polytheism or agnosticism were periods of progress in sciences, and periods marked by monism were less so. This was not because of an inherent science-religion conflict; rather, it reflected a misplaced emphasis on spirituality as a source of absolute knowledge, liberation from the cycle of birth and death, and a dangerous devaluation of relative knowledge through science in certain periods. The anti-science Muslim invaders, though, correctly challenged the possibility of absolute knowledge through monism since it was against Islamic dogma, killed any residual scientific impulse by the fourteenth century, or drove it into pockets in South India, a place where it had never resided before. As a result, the creative energies of the Indian civilization moved away from intellectual endeavors and focused on practical creativity, religious synthesis, and arts promoted by the Muslim invaders. The civilization thus created sublime architecture and melody-based music of highest order.

The pro science European arrival in the seventeenth century hardly mourned the dying body of science in India. In their self-appointed role as exclusive creators of science, they presumed the absence of the scientific spirit to be a norm of the civilization. Their increasing control by the eighteenth century initially prevented its rebirth because of shameful wealth drain. Only toward the end of the nineteenth century, as a result of the Bengali renaissance, was the Indian science was reborn but as an offshoot of European science, disconnected from and oblivious to its own rich scientific tradition since by then science had advanced so far beyond its Indian roots that these roots became only of historic interest and were irrelevant to the state of science. Only the Indian civilization bore the full brunt of both Muslim creed and European greed.

Why Science in European Civilization Has Oscillated

We have asserted that ancient Greece was founded on achievements of Egyptian, Mesopotamian, and Phoenician civilizations and drew critical inspiration, directly or indirectly, from the Indian civilization. However, the bulk of the lasting achievements in science took place in Hellenistic states in Asia and Africa and not in Europe. The Roman Republic and Roman Empire were aggressive, insular in several arenas, and with type A internal creative balance. They not only missed out on these achievements but also destroyed both ancient Greece and the Hellenistic world in a fit of insanity that was tantamount to killing one's own best.

Though the Roman Empire destroyed Hellenistic science developed on Asian and African soil, it could not fight the onslaught of a new religion also born on Asian soil, resulting in Europeanthe masses adopting Christianity. The Roman state was forced to adopt the new religion, with Europe becoming a prisoner to monotheism, and pursued a type B2 internal creative balance for over a millennium, in effect being shut off from the science developed in their own backyard by the Muslim civilization. Only with the reconquest of the Iberian Peninsula did western and central Europe begin to show interest in science for the first time as they came in contact with Muslim achievements.

Simultaneously, trade wealth generated by the Venetian state sparked a cultural renaissance in the eastern wing of Europe, and it rediscovered Greek achievements in art and literature it had ignored for a long time. The Protestant Reformation began to loosen the shackles of religion, and it was a life-and-death necessity to make an end run against the Ottoman control of land routes after the demise of Venice trade forced Europeans out of the Mediterranean. And what a coming-out party it was. It ultimately allowed one civilization to control the resources of the entire planet through violent colonization and systematic wealth drain based on control of the high seas. Together, the loosening shackles of religion, access to Muslim achievements, and the Italian Renaissance combined to finally produce a mature science that was nourished by immense inpouring of wealth through coerced trade and systematic wealth drain from Asia and Africa, most of which was of course indeed wasted on infighting among the leading European states in the seventeenth, eighteenth, nineteenth, and twentieth centuries, including the two World Wars that were responsible for killing 100 million people.

Since the mid-twentieth century, greed has taken a different form. Control is not based on land, SGS control, or systematic wealth drain, but it is exercised through exporting technology and finance capital at electronic speed to take advantage of cheap labor and control of key commodities such as oil.

Thus, science in Greece, which was isolated from Europe, first emerged because of the openness of ancient Greece to achievements of Asia and Africa and the access to wealth of Asia through Alexander's conquests, followed by its decline because of the greed of the practical Romans, its continued decline because of the adoption of the Christian creed, and ultimately by its rise through Muslim achievements and control of the world's resources. Europe simultaneously created mature science and killed it or prevented its rebirth everywhere else through wealth drain and political and military control while loudly claiming to be chiefly responsible for the birth and development of science, a statement that is demonstrably false since western and central Europe had little interest in science until the thirteenth century, and Greek achievements of two millennia in Southeastern Europe were founded on the achievements of other civilizations and took place on foreign soil with foreign funding.

Summary

Thus, while the birth and early development of science in the Indian civilization was not funded through acquiring wealth based on greed and violence and was supported by tolerant creeds devoid of science-religion conflict, the development of science within European and Muslim civilizations occurred based on ill-gotten wealth through greed and violence and was often constrained by intolerant creed with an irrational science-religion conflict.

The European civilization helped the cause of science within itself through greed and violence (Alexander's invasion led to control of others' SGS, and violent colonization led to land grab, slavery, and wealth transfer) but hurt the cause of science in Indian, Muslim, and Chinese civilizations. The differences between the Muslim and European civilizations from the world's perspective is that Muslim civilization started out as open and became insular, and the European civilization started out as insular after the adoption of Christianity and turned open. The former sought to control the SGS of other civilizations since its leaders were of nomadic origin, while the European civilization sought to control land and slave labor and to systematically drain wealth.

We can only imagine where the state of science would be today if one civilization did not control the resources of the world precisely at a point in history when science was reaching state of maturity. Thus, we do not take the position that European civilization has advanced the cause of science; rather, the truth is that by keeping vast sections of humanity under its control, draining their wealth, and squandering a major share on internal fighting and control of others, it has enormously hurt the cause of science. It is difficult appreciate this today. However, looking back from 2100 CE, it will be obvious, even to the historians of Western civilization.

A comparison of evolution of science across civilization leads to the following significant observations:

- Intolerant monotheistic creeds with built-in science-religion conflict determined the boundaries of creative capacity of a social order and have hurt the cause of science.
- Openness to the creativity of other civilization has always helped the cause of science.
- Greed, coupled with violence, whether taking the form of SGS control through empire building, a land grab and slavery through violent colonization, or wealth transfer through a systematic wealth system based on control of territorial and trade routes, has been good for the victor and disastrous indeed for the defeated civilizations.
- The greed and aggression of civilizations that arose in temperate Europe and the arid or dry lands of West and central Asia have continually disrupted the march of science in other civilizations and periodically fed their own through wealth expropriation and knowledge acquired from others. It is noteworthy that the periods of great science in these civilizations followed periods of control of territories or trade or both. The creed of the European and Muslim civilizations destroyed or nearly destroyed the science in their own and other civilizations. We escaped by the skin of our teeth.
- The key defining difference was the development or adoption of alphabetical script, which is essential for precision in thinking and developing complex, abstract systems of thought. Thus the Chinese and Egyptian civilizations, though mightily contributing to practical creativity, remained unable to contribute significantly to religious or intellectual creativity, including science.

19.3 Lessons of History

History may not repeat itself but its lessons do because they are ignored. If one reads history with an open mind, it is screaming and saying, "Science is universal and watch out for how I am depicted!"

Science is Universal

Despite the loud claims of European historians, science is the birthright of *Homo sapiens* at a certain stage of their development, much like the birthright of *Homo sapiens* to invent fire and tools, speech, agriculture, written script, practical inventions, and religions in earlier epochs. The notions that European civilization was the first to invent science and only the European civilization could have invented science simply do not hold on scrutiny and ultimately rest on racism or presumed cultural superiority as we have hopefully demonstrated.

The Importance of Transmission of Creativity Has Been Underestimated

Throughout most of their existence, most major civilizations have transmitted and received ideas and inventions from other civilizations, directly or indirectly, consciously or unconsciously, and have learned from one another, though it is not always easy to know the specific reciprocal influences during the earliest periods of this interchange since words leave no fossils. Yet, civilizations have also shown remarkable insularity to ideas that are not their own when under religious influence or cultural isolation. However, in order to portray the European civilization as the birthplace of science, such transmission, particularly from other civilizations to European civilization, is underestimated and its influence minimized.

Creed is Not Necessarily Harmful to Science

Monotheism through direct science-religion conflict and monism through excessive spirituality have hurt the cause of science, though the former more so than the latter. However, polytheism, agnosticism and atheistic creed do not. As the linkage between science and wealth creation has become established since the Industrial Revolution, practical *Homo sapiens* everywhere, irrespective of their creed, have ostensibly become ardent supporters of science lately by either ignoring the science-religion conflict of their faiths, thus living a compartmentalized existence, or reinterpreting their faith. This effort at adopting science must be commended. Unlike in the Christian West, where critique of religion opened the path to science, in the Muslim word, adopting science will lead to critique and the reinterpretation of religion.

Victors Write History (at Least for a While)

The mainstream ethnocentric approach of *the* majority but not all European archeologists and historians over the last 250 years have consistently tried to overestimate the contributions of their own civilization and the dead civilizations of West Asia while grossly underestimating the contributions of all other living civilizations. This may be easily challenged through the following short list of intentional or unintentional lapses of judgment and emphasis and a continuing failure to acknowledge the now-questionable assumptions.

- *Homo sapiens* did not need "a hardy European climate" to invent the best stone tools.
- Agriculture was not first invented in the Fertile Crescent.
- Alphabetical script was not only invented in Mesopotamia.
- The Nordic Aryans did not invade India in 1500 BCE as Max Mueller claimed and then retracted while on his death bed.
- Indian civilization was not always ruled by foreigners. It occurred during less than 10 percent of its existence. By contrast, Britain has been ruled by foreigners for nearly half of its civilized existence.
- Greeks did not invent science; they learned it from Mesopotamians and Indians, just as they learned to write from Phoenicians. Aristotle never bothered to test his speculative physics, even through common sense.
- Greek philosophers did not excel in critical philosophy, with Plato proposing preexisting forms (!) and showing an interest in astronomy only to prove his philosophical speculations.
- West Asian religious doctrines never came close to discovering the philosophy of monism and agnosticism.
- Europeans never created any of the world's major religious doctrines.
- Calculus was not first invented in Europe.
- Northwestern Europe showed little interest in science until the Arabs left them world's scientific heritage, including the experimental method, as a gift.
- Mesopotamians probably learned mathematics, geometry, and perhaps astronomy from Indians.
- Greeks learned astronomy from Mesopotamians and that gave impetus to further developments in geometry.
- The Indian civilization invented the most scientific language of the world.
- Ptolemy set astronomy on the wrong path for a thousand years.
- Aryabhatta formulated the heliocentric solar system a thousand years before Copernicus, and even then, Copernicus did so with critical contribution from the great Persian astronomer al-Tusi, who was funded by Mongol Helagu Khan.
- The Chinese civilization made the greatest contributions in practical technology.
- The Indian civilization taught the world how to count and invented trigonometry.
- The Indians defeated the Arabs, and the Arab invasion failed in India, though it succeeded in Europe.
- Genghis Khan succeeded against all major civilizations except the Indian civilization, and that unfortunately allowed Muslim control of India to persist that ultimately led to demise of science in India.
- Turkish Muslims eventually failed to conquer the heartland of Europe but conquered India and killed science in both Muslim and Indian civilizations.
- The European civilization led in the maturation of science, funded by systematic wealth drain, but science-religion conflict and internal wars actually slowed the march of science over last several centuries, despite claims to the contrary.

- European imperialism prevented the birth and rebirth of science in all other civilizations of the world for last three centuries.
- European and now Western civilization squandered the world's resources for four centuries on infighting and controlling other civilizations and is continuing to squander it.

19.4 Summary

While the birth of science was a bloodless event, it has led a bloody existence since. Nomads harassed the peaceful Chinese civilization throughout its existence, though fortunately not by Muslim nomads or Muslim civilization. Violent Greeks, Persians, and Romans harassed the Indian and Hellenistic states. Violent and intolerant Muslim civilizations and the violent and greedy European civilizations harassed each other and just about every other civilization.

The Indian civilization was the only major civilization that bore the full brunt of Muslim creed and European greed over last eight centuries. Notwithstanding the horrible violence and greed of the last 2,500 years, science did manage to mature despite entrenched monotheism, having succeeded in killing science in the Muslim and Indian civilizations. From a "rest of the world" perspective, the maturation of science within a few European upstarts perched on the Atlantic occurred principally because of three reasons: the world's heritage of science and technology slowly fell into their laps from 1200 to 1500, CE enormous wealth drain from the Old and New Worlds from 1500 to 1750, and the linkage between science and wealth creation slowly becoming apparent after 1750 CE. The maturation of science and development of science-based technology had become necessary for continuing wealth drain from 1750 to 2000 CE.

Chapter 20 | Glimpses of the Future

20.1 Introduction

In this final chapter, we provide glimpses of the future concerning how we might meet the challenge of controlling the destructive forces arising from our instincts, aided by our unique mental gifts of observation, reason, and imagination and magnified by our institutional structures and processes while nurturing the creative, productive, and constructive powers the same unique gifts and our societal structures and processes make possible and are capable of magnifying.

We first examine the tension between capitalism, science, and religion by looking at the history and nature of capitalism. We look at ways to control institutional aggression, greed, and creed.

Capitalism, Science, and Religion

Since the USSR fell and China emerged as an effective managed economy based increasingly on free markets, fortunately capitalism once again is the economic system of choice after more than half a century of doubt in some corners. However, much like socialism, "capitalism" is not a monolithic system since it only describes the economic organization and property rights within the social order. Capitalism has historically been employed in conjunction with different political systems, differing roles of government with respect to property rights, and different degrees of freedom of the markets, a wide range of external orientations with respect to other states and civilizations, as well as internal social cohesion strategies based on a wide range of economic, religious, racial, ethnic, and gender-related policies.

20.2 A Brief History of Capitalism

The purest capitalism may be defined as an economic system where the means of wealth creation as well as the wealth created are completely privately owned and where wealth allocation to consumption, luxuries, monuments, and creative endeavors are determined through the price of labor, land, goods and services, and capital based on supply and demand in free markets. Money is the predominant mode of exchange. This definition leaves out the role of government. Therefore, this purest form of capitalism is nothing more than an economic and legal concept that has never been used in practice. Thus, contrary to conventional wisdom, capitalism came into existence with the invention of a money-based economy in those societies where slavery or feudalism was not excessive, since essential capitalism requires relatively free labor, land, and product markets, though not necessarily highly developed credit and equity markets. Advances in capitalism occurred with advances in trade and credit markets as well as advances in production technologies and is more recently based on science.

Below, we briefly review the history of capitalism, both its evolving stages throughout history and principal *reactionary* forms mostly during the twentieth century, taking into account the differing roles of government, external orientation, and internal social cohesion strategies.

Primary Stage I: Capitalism with a monarchy or an elitist "republic" with varying government control of economy, generally fair trade with other states and civilizations, social cohesion achieved through both force and religious beliefs, and a differing mix of religious, ethnic, racial, and gender equality. Stage I primary capitalism existed in several civilizations and states prior to the sixteenth century. Stage I capitalism lacked imperial ambitions.

Primary Stage II: Capitalism with monarchy and government-sponsored mercantilism and slavery with social cohesion through nationalism originated in the sixteenth- to eighteenth-century England. It was based on the North American empire created through violent colonization. Revolutions or national awakening in the North American colonies led to loss of this first English empire in the New World.

When capitalism was practiced in a low-population state that was able to successfully engage in *violent colonization* of new lands, it turned into a government and royalty-sponsored *mercantile mode* and used slavery to capture the surplus through coerced trade with new colonies and slave-based agricultural produce from new lands. Britian (together with Portugal, Spain, France, and the Netherlands) had a natural competitive advantage this process in part because of their geographical separation from the European mainland, which created *fortress Britain.*

Primary Stage III: Laissez-faire capitalism with a white male-dominated democracy and social cohesion through nationalism, slavery, and racism during the eighteenth to nineteenth centuries in the United States.

After the American Revolution, which produced the world's first white male-dominated democratic government, we witness the rise of capitalism with democratic political rights extended to all males of the dominant race, continuing slavery of as much as one-fourth of the population, and a strong sense of nationalism.

Primary Stage IV: Capitalism with expanding democracy to include women and minorities, government-sponsored systematic wealth drain from Asia and Africa, and social cohesion through nationalism and increasing gender equality from the nineteenth to twentieth centuries. National liberation movements in Asia and Africa led to the loss of these second empires of leading Western European states in the Old World by the mid-twentieth century.

As Britain, France, and the Netherlands lost their empires in the Americas, they created second empires in Asia and Africa, with the Indian subcontinent as the crown jewel of the British Empire. Here, capitalism evolved into its most insidious form yet: that of an expanding democracy with even slower expansion of gender rights and nationalism at home, coupled with a government-sponsored, ruthless, and *systematic wealth drain* of other civilizations in Asia and Africa, a slavery system, and indentured labor in the New World. It is noteworthy that Spain and Portugal were far less successful in creating second empires in Asia and Africa since their brand of capitalism remained mired in Catholicism and refused to adopt expanding political rights at home.

Primary Stage V: Capitalism with democracy managed through world institutions such as the UN, World Bank, and IMF and based on the export of finance capital and technology to exploit cheap labor abroad restricted immigration and relatively free trade in goods and services and social cohesion through nationalism and increasing gender, religious, ethnic, and racial equality.

The second empires of Britain, France, and the Netherlands also crumbled by the middle of the twentieth century, thus creating an opening for the United States to usher in a new form of capitalism, based not on political and economic control of other states but an imperialism based on unequaled military might, the export of technology, and capital in pursuit of cheap labor to all four corners of the world. It was accompanied by increasing racial, ethnic, gender, and religious equality at home because of domestic protestations and riots and because, in part, it needed to project a new face to the cheap labor states in Asia and Africa.

Thus, the evolution of capitalism in recent centuries has been led by the English-speaking Anglo-Saxons, and it will be equally clear from the remarks below that the modes of capitalism in rest of the world are indeed a reaction to the above mostly in the twentieth century.

Reactionary Type I: Capitalism with dictatorship, government-controlled economy, racism, imperial ambitions abroad, and social cohesion through nationalism. Examples include German Nazism (1914–1945), Italian Fascism (1935–1945), and Japanese empire building (1867–1945) in East Asia. They were driven by an unsuccessful ambition through two terrible world wars to duplicate what the British French, and Dutch had done in the previous three centuries.

Reactionary Type II: Capitalism mostly with military dictatorship yielding relatively quickly to democracy, social cohesion through nationalism, and an external orientation that relied on exports to states of Western civilization and fulfilling the latter's political and military objectives. It occurred in Japan (1945–), Korea (1945–), Taiwan (1949–), and Singapore (1955–).

Reactionary Type III: Capitalism with a fundamentalist religious monarchy or limited democracy, strong government intervention in the economy, and near total denial of religious, ethnic, racial, and gender equality, with often a strong alliance with Anglo-Saxon capitalism based on exploitation of oil wealth. This reactionary capitalism occurred in Muslim states of West Asia.

Reactionary Type IV: Capitalism with communist dictatorship, strong government invention in economy, social cohesion through nationalism, and increasing religious, racial, ethnic, and gender equality in China (1949–present), Vietnam (1985–present), and Russia (1989–present).

Reactionary Type V: Capitalism with democracy, strong government invention in economy, an inward-looking external orientation, social cohesion through nationalism, and religious, racial, ethnic, and gender equality in India (1947–present).

20.3 Nature of Capitalism

As noted above, capitalism is an economic system defined by free markets using money in exchange transactions and has individual property rights to wealth created. However, we must define the political system, external orientation, and nature of social cohesion in order to fully specify capitalism. In fact, these three dimensions define the differences among the primary stages of capitalism and reaction to these stages.

We believe that free markets are the greatest strength as well as the greatest potential curse for capitalism. Free markets solve the problem of wealth allocation very effectively but without managing the issue of wealth and income polarization. Clearly, governments lack the wisdom to allocate wealth to consumption and creative and productive endeavors, and they have remained the only institution to manage the wealth and income polarization. The difficulty in the role of government in a capitalist structure has been to manage the degree of wealth and income polarization through taxes; a social safety network for the poor, young, unemployed, and the elderly; and a regulatory framework, including consumer and environmental safety, while ensuring the existence of free markets. The exclusive role of government in defense and a significant role in funding science and education have also been accepted in most capitalist states.

Capitalism and science: Capitalism, with its emphasis on private wealth maximization based on free markets and competition among individual businesses is not only compatible with science but absolutely requires new technology (through development or adoption) derived from breakthroughs in science to achieve its objective. Thus, typically in capitalism, governments fund the development of science while individual businesses focus on developing specific technologies they need to survive and win in the competitive markets.

Capitalism and religion: Capitalism and religion, on the other hand, have a more complex relationship. All religions consist of metaphysical assumptions and accompanying rituals as well as practical ethics. History shows that capitalism (which in its earliest and simplest form is nothing more than the existence of product markets, property rights, and a money-based economy) is compatible with both the salvation-based metaphysics associated with monotheism, karma, and reincarnation-based metaphysics associated with the Hindu belief system and the absence of metaphysics associated with the message of Buddha and Confucius. Capitalism does not depend on beliefs concerning the other world; rather it depends on behavior in this world. It can further be shown that ethical differences associated with religions may have *potential* significance only with respect to the birth of stage II of capitalism. However, such analyses typically suffer from Eurocentrism since historically mature capitalism was born in Europe.

As an example, Max Weber's analysis of the birth of capitalism in Europe is flawed since it assumes only Christianity through the Protestant Reformation and Puritanism were capable of evolving into a form that supported the emergence of capitalism. However, any objective observer looking at Christianity even as late as the fifteenth century (let alone the thirteenth century, when St. Francis of Assisi viewed the very concept of property as antithetical to Christianity and peace in the world) would be hard-pressed to imagine that Christianity with its ties to feudalism, an acceptance of slavery, and injunctions against charging interest was consistent with a dynamic capitalism. Yet it happened. We can only do thought experiments and speculate concerning the potential of other major religions of the world to give birth to modern capitalism. It is noteworthy that the historical experience, since Weber's flawed assertions in the nineteenth century, has been that capitalism has flourished in all religions, and once capitalism is adopted, it has shown enormous power to influence the religion itself. We must, then conclude that the popularity of Weber's notions of the incompatibility of other religions (such as working actively to create wealth was looked down by Confucianism and the Hindu emphasis on liberation from the cycle and birth and death rendered Hinduism incompatible) with capitalism was based on a desire to prove the superiority of European civilization since it conveniently presumed only Christianity was capable of change and not the other religions. The reality is that the European civilization, benefitting from incoming wealth, gave birth to modern capitalism despite and not because of Christianity.

Glimpses of the Future

It is not the purpose of this work to engage in predicting the future. Our purpose has been to detail the reciprocal impact of civilizations on one another and on history of science and in particular to set the record straight concerning the contributions of major civilizations toward the development of science. Nevertheless, it is tempting to not indulge a little.

In this section, we discuss strategies to control the greed and creed (and hence aggression) that civilizations have engaged in during the violent interaction era and speculate on the path forward. The destructive greed and creeds determine who will control the surplus resulting from creative and productive powers at class, state, and civilization levels and is a struggle supported and magnified by the institutions created through the very creative and productive powers of the species. The critical difference now is that understanding the laws of social evolution is within our grasp for the first time in history, and the hold of intolerant creeds on the intelligentsia in the more advanced sections of *Homo sapiens* has dramatically weakened. Grand wars are not an option because of mutual assured destruction from nuclear weapons with awful destructive power.

With the whole universe ahead of us to explore, we do not believe that *Homo sapiens* (literally, the wise ones) are going to continue to engage in wars with one another forever in the age of awesome destructive power of weapons and the equally awesome power of productive technologies. The power of productive technologies level the difference in natural bounty and power of destructive weapons and puts real brakes on the larger-than-life worldwide conflicts, such as the two world wars of the twentieth century. It is noteworthy that the power of these weapons ended World War II and prevented the Cold War from becoming hot.

20.4 Controlling Greed

Greed can exist within a state, among states, and among civilizations. However, in the modern era under capitalism, it nearly always comes into existence within a state through power struggles among classes. Its expansion across states and civilizations is a result of greed within a state. Let us consider each of the three levels separately.

Within a State

The contradiction between productive/creative and destructive tendencies at a class level can be resolved not through the Marxist solution of eliminating classes and the utopia of a classless society but through a sociopolitical-economic system that balances compassion and justice with entrepreneurship. This is possible through direct democracy (to break the power of the lobbyists) and an economic constitution that defines the rights and obligations of different economic classes. Today, a capitalist constitution defines political rights and obligations but not economic rights and obligations, and the dominant economic class finds a thousand ways to trample over the economic rights of other classes by owning or influencing the democratically elected state.

It has been said that capitalism is the worst economic system until the alternatives are considered. Capitalism, in association with ideologies of empire building, violent colonization, systematic wealth drain, racism and Nazism, and wide range of scenarios such as national liberation movements and nation building, democracy and dictatorship, and the presence or absence of systemic corruption, has shown itself to be a system that is:

- Capable of the highest levels of wealth creation
- Incapable of stable economic output and employment both under laissez-faire and mild and strong government invention scenarios despite significant advances in economic theory
- Incapable of eliminating a permanent poor underclass

The history of capitalism since its birth proves these observations. The various ideologies and scenarios alluded to above are simply a means conceived by an ascendant class in a given period in a given state to align itself with the power of capitalism. Let us see how.

Marx was wrong because he thought the original communes that may have existed before the dawn of civilization, when the principal contradiction was between man and the beast and man and nature in the absence of sustainable growing surplus, could be duplicated in the presence of substantial, growing, and potentially limitless SGS. Marx did not realize that individual self-interest was responsible for the equality that existed in the absence of SGS. Creation of SGS through invention of agriculture changed the contradiction between man and beast and man and nature to one between man and man. *The nature of self-interest changed when surplus emerged: before surplus emerged through agriculture, self-interest created only cooperation between man and man. Now it creates both cooperation to produce wealth and conflict between man and man to control it.* But we cannot go back in a naïve or simple-minded way, appealing to the higher ideals of the species. We have to be real about it.

This natural conflict among classes can be managed through a political economy based not on laissez-faire capitalism or a capitalism mostly controlled by the dominant class and representative democracy but based on direct digital democracy and an economic contract among classes within a state.

Direct digital democracy: The current system of representative democracy is flawed: the elections are very expensive and require rich donors; large chunks of media are controlled by a dominant class; once elected, representatives cannot be held to the promises they made during elections for several years; the party in power redraws the electoral districts to its advantage; election platforms are crafted based on polls; and the dominant class exploits the ethnic, religious, and racial differences among voters and uses voter suppression techniques. The current system approaches a situation similar to the early days of the birth of democracy, when wealth determined voting rights.

In contrast, a direct digital democracy without eliminating full-time elective representatives can eliminate most of these problems through continuous feedback from the public, including the right to recall, while retaining the advantages of full-time representatives. It would no longer be a representative democracy; rather, it will be responsive direct democracy.

Economic constitution: A responsive democracy may still respond only to the majority and will naturally evolve an economic constitution to protect the minority and weak, a constitution that that parallels political constitution that is typically solely directed at how to attain political power and legislative, executive, and judicial functions of a state without regard to the outcomes the legislative and judicial process might have on different classes within the state. Today, we do not control the evolution of our social order; rather we leave it to chance, with delayed corrective action when the problems become excessive. The overarching principle embedded in the economic constitution will be to manage the wealth and income polarization within a state. Today, managing wealth and income polarization is not a stated goal. It is an outcome based on nasty infighting.

There are several reasons managing wealth and income polarization is desirable and will not lead to stagnation. First, it will substantially reduce poverty and class conflicts since the relative distribution of wealth will remain unchanged at the class level. Second, it will not affect entrepreneurial spirit, since an individual entrepreneur will still have all the freedom to create wealth and increase his absolute wealth without affecting the wealth polarization in the state as whole. Third, wealth polarization is actually managed today but inefficiently with significant and unnecessary cycling over decades, often pitting classes within a state and across different states against one another. Fourth, it will eliminate or at least significantly moderate the business cycle inherent in laissez-faire capitalism. In the broader scheme of things, this cycling in wealth and income polarization is both unnecessary and destructive.

The intellectual basis for such an economic constitution is simple: as critical as entrepreneurial energy is in creating wealth, it can hardly maximize and stabilize wealth creation without an educated population, the necessary infrastructure, government role in developing science and technology, effective monetary policy, and industrial and commercial regulations that include environmental regulations, and, most importantly, a balanced supply and demand and balanced income distribution and production. Does it make sense to have a system that leaves the degree of wealth polarization in the hands of the entrepreneurial class and the politicians it can buy and not in the hands of the society as it whole or effectively in the hands of a responsive and not a beholden government?

One can see how the forces of direct digital democracy and a well-thought-out economic constitution would reinforce one another. It is not necessary for us to speculate on the degree of desirable wealth polarization. Responsive democracy will determine it in a participative manner through trial and error. However, it is clear that if the investing class has an income share greater than what can be invested, it will create an imbalance between purchasing power and productive capacity, resulting in stagnating economic activity.

To summarize, direct digital democracy ensures that a permanent political class does not come into existence and that it cannot be bought. An economic constitution ensures the absence of excessive wealth polarization and a maximization of wealth creation. These tools are necessary to save capitalism from capitalists.

Among States

If the process of competition and cooperation among classes within a state can be effectively managed through direct digital democracy and economic constitution using the concept of federalism, it can be extended to create larger political and economic units among states, thus minimizing the possibility of conflict among states.

Across Civilizations

In today's world, only two of the four surviving major civilizations have multiple states: European/Western and Muslim. These two civilizations control the bulk of land and resources while the other two major civilizations, Chinese and Indian, are the most populous. Given the awesome power of modern weapons and the resulting mutually assured destruction, worldwide military conflict among major civilizations possessing these weapons has given way to either a war of words among the majors or localized wars between majors (mostly United States) and states lacking these awesome weapons. These local conflicts can be moderated through reforming world bodies such as the United Nations, International Monetary Fund, and World Bank, which are all controlled by European/Western civilization. The most important reforms are those of the United Nations, which is a pathetically undemocratic institution reflecting the realities of a post-colonial world in 1945. By democratizing the Security Council, direct election of the secretary general and financing the UN through a consumption tax or military hardware tax, the UN would move from being a debating body to an influential body while simultaneously promoting peace.

20.5 Controlling Creed

Intolerant creeds have been a significant direct or indirect source of conflicts in history as well as the primary source of conflict between science and religion. Some tolerant creeds, on the other hand, have often been responsible for devaluing science to one degree or another by focusing excessively on the imaginary worlds beyond death. These issues can be resolved through either atheism or agnosticism. However, atheism appears to us to be potentially intolerant and has itself led to violence and wars. It is also intellectually unattractive since it presumes to know what *Homo sapiens* cannot be certain of.

The contradiction between science and religion can and must be resolved through adopting agnosticism. Not monism, since monism devalues worldly knowledge. Not polytheism, since it belongs to the childhood of civilization. Not monotheism, with its checkered history with respect to science. The metaphysics of agnosticism or Buddhism but without post-Buddha adultrations of karma and reincarnation must replace religions of the world to address these issues. But Buddha, born in India before the era of conflict among civilizations, was unaware of civilizations with vastly differing value systems. Thus, the nonviolent and compassionate agnosticism developed by Buddha needs reinterpretation for a world where potential or actual violence exists not only within a state and among states but also among civilizations with different value systems with respect to greed, creed, and violence.

Buddhism is an ethical system that encourages a search for new knowledge based on unique mental gifts of observation, reason, and imagination. It challenges all metaphysics and insists that our problems arise from ignorance (belief in God or eternal soul), attachments (to temporary existence), and resulting suffering including ill-will and hatred. Thus, it insists that suffering originates in incorrect metaphysical assumptions and is only possible within social existence. The end of suffering therefore requires the end of imaginary otherworldly religions to be replaced by a compassionate this-worldly religion focused on humanity.

Admittedly, we are a long way from this.

20.6 Controlling Aggression and Violence

In earlier chapters, we have addressed why some civilizations turned much more violent than other civilizations and how dry, arid, and cold environments have led to violent civilizations in the absence of sufficiently developed technologies that might compensate for a less bountiful natural environment. What can be done to control violence and aggression in today's world?

If the greed within the a state can be channeled through a new political economy based on direct digital democracy and an economic constitution to manage wealth and income polarization and if agnosticism can supersede the creeds of the world, then the very existence of productive technologies of awesome power and destructive weapons of equally awesome power have the potential to nudge the world toward a new civilization based on science and agnosticism, with the proper balance between freedom and justice without violence.

20.7 The Likely Path Forward

Above, we briefly outlined the approach of how to attack the forces of greed, creed, and violence. How do we escape the vicious cycle of the rise of this class, this state, and this civilization, with each claiming it is different, their claim of exceptionalism? Is there a better balance? However, we readily acknowledge that the proposed solution is too far in the future so that it will be ridiculed today as naïve by those who claim *Homo sapiens* will always show strong tendencies toward greed, intolerant creeds, and aggression.

The history of civilization as we have constructed in the previous chapters consisted of the standalone era followed by the peaceful interaction era and the era of military conflicts among major civilizations. The inflexion points of these eras were driven by changes in transportation and weapons technologies. During the military conflicts era, often small states located in dry, arid, or cold environments succeeded in creating huge empires, establishing violent colonies, and engaging in systematic wealth drain from civilizations an order of magnitude greater and located in bountiful natural environments. The demise of colonial empires and the USSR since World War II has brought us to a point where:

- A continental-size state with a middling population (United States) is enjoying a unipolar moment of immense military, technological, and financial power with imperial ambitions based on using its technological and financial muscle to exploit cheap labor in other states
- The awesome power of modern technology has made it possible for *Homo sapiens* everywhere to achieve prosperity
- The awesome power of destructive weapons has made it impossible to engage in large-scale wars among large states or civilizations
- Deeper understanding of nature through science has destroyed the foundation of tolerant and intolerant creeds, though most humans still cling to these creeds because of existential anxiety and the momentum of past

We speculate the following scenario will occur over the next two centuries.

We envision the current stage to last for no more than twenty-five to fifty years, during which the world will transform from being unipolar to multipolar with several comparable centers of military, financial, and technological power, thus ending the unipolar world of today.

The multipolar world thus created will first perfect principles of federalism based on fiscal and monetary unions, followed by the emergence of a new political economy within each federation based progressively on concepts of direct digital democracy and economic constitution. With the establishment of the new political economy, old religious creeds will begin to lose their emotional hold.

This will be followed by a union of federations leading to a world government based on expanded direct digital democracy and agreed economic constitution on a worldwide basis. At this stage, we would have entered the planetary phase of civilization, when separate states each indiscriminately followed its perceived self-interest will become a distant memory.

The continuing development of science will have a major impact on human lifespan and quality of life. The agnostic belief system will gain momentum will keep humans focused on this world and understanding nature, and the new political economy will eliminate poverty and significantly moderate economic instability within the world civilization while continuing to value entrepreneurship.

Societal structures and processes and the creeds based on faith got *Homo sapiens* in trouble, and it will be the creation of better structures and processes while replacing creeds with agnosticism that will lead to a world civilization fulfilling the old dream.

It is indeed a great irony that era of military conflicts among civilization started about the time Buddha formulated the philosophy of agnosticism. The solution had always been there but would take nearly three millennia to implement.

20.8 Summary

The entrepreneurial energy freed from the shackles of religion though not from the shackles of greed has been responsible for the emergence of the modern world. We therefore examined the relationship between different modes of capitalism and science and religion.

We suggested that institutions and processes of *direct digital democracy* are required to move from representative democracy to responsive democracy, and of *economic constitution* to manage the inherent process of wealth polarization, of *effective federalism* to continually enlarge the size of the political units in the multipolar world of tomorrow, and of *agnosticism* to challenge the imaginary faiths of the millennia past to control greed, creed, and violence in the era of awesome creative and productive powers on the one hand and equally awesome destructive power on the other hand.

As we see it, the emerging world civilization will be based on dialectical agnosticism to continually deepen our understanding of the natural world without invoking gods and a planetwide political economy that balances entrepreneurship and wealth and income polarization. In such a civilization, *Homo sapiens* will create their own future until they come across other intelligent life forms in the universe. We have indeed no means to know what will happen then, and we don't need to know that today. The immediate task going forward is clear, generations-long, and difficult.

APPENDICES

Appendix A
Development of Social Conscience

Conscience may be defined as an inner sense of right or wrong toward other members of a socialized species within an established social order and, by extension, toward members of another social order. It arises naturally when a species finds it beneficial to cooperate based not on instincts but free will. It is a loud admission that while the individual is the apparent fountainhead of creativity, any one member is nothing without the community.

Several religions claim to explain the origin of the phenomenon of conscience in *Homo sapiens*. Hinduism sees conscience emerging within a mature soul after multiple lives of good deeds, thus basing it on free will and karma over multiple lives. Practical ethical systems stressed stoic duty and utilitarianism. Buddhism links conscience to learned compassion, not karma. The Zoroastrian faith tries to instill conscience through an after-death punishment for evil behavior. Catholicism bases conscience on the idea of free will and an after-death punishment. Islam sees Allah as the ultimate source of Taqwa, which is often translated as piety, and the Koran goes to great lengths to specify acceptable norms.

Early European psychologists saw the origin of conscience when civilization frustrated the expression of aggressive instincts. Still others see conscience as a reciprocal altruism for a socialized being. Kant's moral imperative saw conscience as based on free will, which expressed universal law. Other philosophers have linked conscience to emotions of guilt and shame. Most of these theories carry at least a grain of truth.

We believe conscience first emerged in the hunting-gathering epoch based on a struggle with instincts, generosity or harshness of MotherNature, and socialized existence. It has continued to be modified by religion, ideology, wealth and power polarization, and even law during the Neolithic or civilization epochs. Instincts are still there, no doubt, but they are no longer all-powerful; they are strong only for certain types of behavior, such as hunger and procreation. Following instincts was no longer deemed as beneficial as following the uncharted territory made possible by unique mental attributes. Experience was teaching *Homo sapiens* that applying unique mental attributes had a better payoff in the long run than relying on fixed instincts. *Homo sapiens* could see that they were capable of differentiating themselves from primates. If instincts were the fixed biological constructs to guide primate behavior, the emerging primitive conscience became a parallel and often alternate guide to the behavior of *Homo sapiens*.

Since the nature of conscience is identical to the attitudes toward fellow *Homo sapiens* in particular and other forms of life in general, it is easier to see how it emerged through a few critical attitudes, such as insularity/openness, tolerance/intolerance, greed/fairness, and aggression/peacefulness during the long period up to the birth of civilizations. However, we need to make a distinction between the roles of conscience in close personal relationships where emotional bonding is high and in social relationships where emotional investment is not so high. In any case, conscience in a close personal relationship is aided by parenting instincts, and acting with good conscience may be more natural. Our focus here is necessarily on the origin of conscience in a social, more impersonal context, but the two overlap.

Below, we analyze the possible genesis of insularity/openness, intolerance/tolerance, the extent of greed/fairness, and aggression/peacefulness spectrums that help us understand social conscience in *Homo sapiens*, whether within or across social orders.

Genesis of Insularity-Openness Spectrum

Homo sapiens have a natural openness toward others that is rooted in the instincts of sociability and curiosity. However, several natural and social factors can overpower these instincts. To start with, the geographical isolation of a social order over a prolonged period of can create apprehension about others. However, as the early experience of Europeans in North America shows, even absolute geographical isolation by itself cannot create an attitude of insularity. A persistently adverse or harmful interaction with other social orders is required to create a sense of insularity, which is nothing more than a defensive reaction to harmful experiences, such as sustained wars. However, the sense of insularity may also result from an intolerant ideology or in particular an intolerant religious doctrine.

The roots of insularity within a social order to one degree or another depend on early and continuing harmful experiences, such as coerced trade, invasions, and political, military, and economic control by other social orders. It is accentuated by geographical and linguistic isolation and the existence of an intolerant, antiscience religion—a system that unabashedly and falsely claims that it is right and all others are wrong. It claims to approval of a higher power through concepts such as a chosen people, the word of the son of God, or better yet, the word of God himself.

Yet, *Homo sapiens* are practical beings; they recognize that insularity or openness cannot be absolute, total, or undifferentiated. Thus, the attitudes of insularity/openness lie along a spectrum and vary by area. Most social orders have been open to practical creativity unless it impacts the power of those in control because practical inventions by themselves are not ideological in nature, and their effects are nearly always beneficial for the social order as a whole. The inflow of ideas and beliefs are a different matter altogether. A new religious belief system may be resisted if it conflicts with what is already believed. Similarly, intellectual creativity, in particular, philosophy (which includes critical metaphysics) and science, which abhors metaphysics and is neutral on ethics, may be in conflict with deeply held religious beliefs.

Genesis of Intolerance–Tolerance Spectrum

Intolerance is based in the instincts of intraspecies dominance and a sense of false superiority. It is mitigated by egalitarian or compassionate ideologies. Thus, a social order may develop a sense of superiority because of an assumed superior biological gift and perceived superiority of religious faith, class/caste, or ethnicity. Therefore, intolerance may be based on ideologies of racism, religious faith, class, gender, or cultural superiority. Racism, for example, is based on the assumption that a particular group with a different outward appearance also has superior inner attributes. This proposition has been claimed and disproved several times in modern history, most recently by biological sciences. Monotheism and hard atheism are more direct and believe only their versions of metaphysics are correct, which can lead to varying intolerance of all other versions—witness the claims of communism.

Intolerance from monism is more subtle. Monism claims the identity of self and God and the truth of concepts of reincarnation and karma, which lend support to a caste system and in turn leads to intolerance. Similarly, cultural superiority has been claimed directly through such concepts as middle kingdom and more subtly through historical facts of renaissance, enlightenment, and industrial revolution. In each instance, this superiority can be shown to be founded on external conditions subject to change. Intolerance toward other *Homo sapiens*, thus, is simply ignorance masquerading as superiority in one form or another. It rests on the simple fact that the time scale of social change is much larger than the average human life, thus allowing humans to confuse greater achievement in a particular era with permanent superiority.

To summarize, intolerance within a social order results when instincts of intraspecies dominance are supported by ideologies of religious, racial, or cultural superiority. These ideologies of superiority have certainly existed in the civilization epoch, but their existence in cruder, less articulate forms, though unlikely, cannot be ruled out in the hunting-gathering and Neolithic epochs. Intolerance is mitigated by egalitarian ideologies such as agnosticism, pacifism, and universal compassion. Intolerance was probably not a big issue in the civilization epoch until the rise of religion, caste systems, significant wealth polarization, and racism.

Genesis of Greed–Fairness Spectrum

Roots of greed/and the lack thereof lie in the epic struggle with the survival instinct, the possibility of power, wealth polarization within a socialized existence, and a harsh natural environment on the one hand and natural bounty and more egalitarian ideologies on the other. During the hunting-gathering period, the issue of greed arising from the polarization in wealth and power did not exist. Only during the civilization epoch did polarization in power and wealth become a major driver of greed.

Harsh or bountiful nature: The most important factor differentiating the earliest civilizations with respect to greed may well have been the geographical and climatic conditions a civilization faced during its formative period while having knowledge of the Garden of Eden. Let us examine why: a bountiful natural environment would produce a less greedy attitude, whereas a harsher arid or relatively cooler natural environment would produce the opposite. Without subscribing to the theory that geography is destiny, we emphasize that it is not what climate and natural environment do directly to the human psychology; rather, what these factors prevent a social organism from producing with relative ease explains the differing degree of greed among social orders with differing natural bounty. The history of civilizations is too short a period to induce significant biological changes.

Origin of Intraspecies Aggression

Aggression and violence in nature: There is no dearth of aggression and violence in nature. The two, however, are not equivalent. The interspecies predatory behavior, though violent, is not necessarily aggressive because it is typically triggered by hunger and must necessarily lead to killing to satisfy hunger. Thus, not all violence results from aggression, and not all aggression necessarily leads to violence. Intraspecies violence observed in nature, on the other hand, is much more benign and has the primary purpose to facilitate species perpetuation. Among primates, it entails establishing a dominance hierarchy among the male primates and optimal male-seeking behavior among the females. Because breeding requires a long gestation and nurturing period on the part of females, the males are more aggressive (though only for as long as required to establish hierarchy) than females in most species. Most non-*Homo-sapiens* intraspecies aggression and violence is purposeful and only rarely leads to killing. What is striking is that intraspecies behavior can also be "altruistic," such as when a member warns others of impending danger while putting itself in mortal danger in the process of sounding alarm. However, such "altruism" appears to be instinctual, designed by nature for species perpetuation without awareness of its consequences.

***Homo sapiens* aggression:** When we move from the animal kingdom to *Homo sapiens*, the biological instinct needed for interspecies aggression is still present, as is the instinct of intraspecies dominance. However, *Homo sapiens* aggression and violence (as opposed to dominance) is not just interspecies; it is also intraspecies as well and is highly variable across social orders. Here, what really interests us is not individual human aggression and violence (as in crimes of passion, cruelty, stealing, or a school bully establishing dominance) but the social, organized aggression and violence seen in internal wars among states of a social order and external wars among social orders. What is highly relevant and indeed curious is that while all social orders have engaged in just or unjust, lawful, or deceitful internal wars, not all civilizations have historically engaged in external wars with other civilizations. The question then may be asked why some social orders ended up becoming more aggressive and violent compared to other social orders. How is it that a mere intraspecies instinct of dominance transformed into a horrible intraspecies aggression that led to highly variable violent killing so apparent in history? The answer lies in the difference in natural bounty, degree of greed, and intolerance (particularly religious intolerance) a particular social order espoused.

Aggression and natural bounty: Imagine a newborn, simple, isolated civilization situated on relatively flat terrain, with a warm climate, multiple river systems, and fertile soil but not with the extreme warmth and moisture of the equator regions. Also imagine a nearby nomadic tribe with arid or desertlike conditions. The tendency of the civilization would be to stay put, develop, and enjoy the natural bounty. It would have little need to covet other lands and develop the needed offensive capabilities and ideologies. The tendency of the nomadic tribe may be to learn about faraway lands where life is a little better. Once it finds out about such lands, its tendency will be to put its meager surplus into military capability. When it learns that the civilization has developed a military weakness, it will want to attack and control the civilization. Thus, we may assert that the earliest roots of aggressive orientation may be found in the natural geographical and climatic differences. We believe that because these differences developed over long periods in relative isolation, they have tended to be relatively stable and became part of the soft genetic code of such civilizations and nomadic groups. It is, after all, not a coincidence that aggressive nomadic tribes developed in arid or dry regions.

The nomadic tribes were not the only ones showing extreme aggressive tendencies. Therefore, let us now imagine two civilizations in modest contact: one situated, as before, on relatively flat terrain with a warm climate, multiple year-long river systems, and fertile soil but not with the extreme warmth and moisture of the equator regions. The second is on difficult terrain, cold but not arctic climate with plenty of water during the warmer summer months and relatively far away. The tendency of the first civilization would be as described above. The tendency of the second civilization may not be the open aggression of the nomadic tribes; rather, it would be to covet, to somehow to initially benefit through coerced trade and perhaps through transfer of ideas and inventions. As it acquired means for long-distance aggression, its behavior may include land conquest and transfer of wealth through coercion.

We may conclude that bountiful natural environments tended to produce milder aggressive tendencies whereas harsher arid or relatively cold natural environments tended to produce stronger aggressive tendencies, depending on the available transport and weapons technologies in relation to the spatial distances involved. This is not because climate makes one strong or weak; rather, it is a reflection of the relationship between climate and ability to support life for a given level of available practical technology.

Aggression and greed: Natural conditions are not the only conditions that make a social order aggressive. Its elite may develop an appetite for luxuries beyond what its own surplus can support. It may develop a belief in the superiority of its economic system, leading to a desire to force others into its belief system. Or its economic system may require resources and markets it does not have. Or based on its religious beliefs, members of the elite may develop a desire for monuments it thinks it will need after death but lacks the resources to build these monuments. It may develop a belief in the superiority of its religious beliefs, leading to a desire to force others into its belief system. An overly ambitious leader may be able to force a civilization into a temporary aggressive posture to fulfill his ambition of conquest. All of these will contribute toward an aggressive orientation. In addition, marked and prolonged aggression of others may also induce aggression in a social order. If one social order develops aggressive behavior, others have four basic choices: they can destroy it, break it up, and absorb it, enslave it, or contain it. Social orders in effect make choices between a fair and peaceful existence and greed that may lead to aggression. A social order may encourage self-serving and individualistic social ethics based on its unique evolutionary history, and this will contribute to aggression. The existence of the military means—i.e., effective weapons, delivery, and transportation—will contribute to aggression as well, while an aggressive orientation also leads to developing or acquiring these weapon systems.

Aggression and creed: Intolerant creeds have played a significant supporting role in aggression throughout history as we have noted above.

Aggression and civilization antiquity: Another factor in the origin of aggression is the age of a civilization because violence has increased dramatically since the birth of civilizations. Thus, if a civilization is born in the violent era, it is liable to be more violent than otherwise. Civilizations that were intrinsically peaceful but faced a serious continuing threat from nomads that they were not able to counter effectively tended to develop an aggressive but defensive and not offensive posture

The forces affecting the genesis of intolerance, greed, and aggression are shown in figure A-1.

Figure A-1: Genesis of Greed and Creed Leading to Aggression

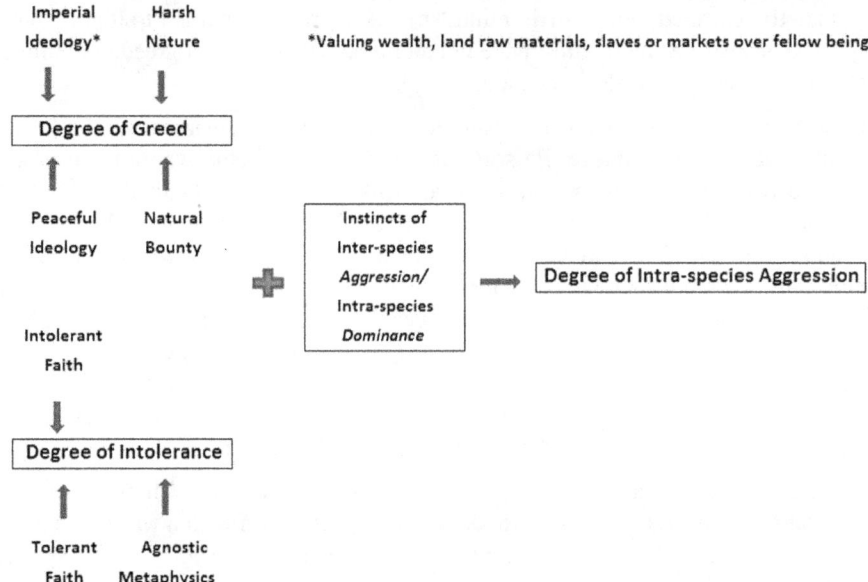

Summary

It is reasonable to conclude that during the hunting-gathering epoch, *Homo sapiens* cultures, particularly in a bountiful natural setting, had largely managed to moderate the survival, intraspecies dominance, and interspecies aggression instincts through relatively egalitarian social structures that were helped by constant struggle against nature that demanded cooperation among group members. During the Neolithic and more important during the civilization phase, as the surplus increased and became stable, particularly for civilizations and nomads situated in arid, desert, and frigid climates, social orders began to display a widely different propensity toward intolerance, greed, and aggression. Egalitarian ideologies and a mature perspective on power and wealth, on the other hand, nudged social orders toward an ethical social conscience, particularly in bountiful natural settings.

The instincts are still there, but they are no longer all-powerful in the presence of natural bounty or heightened productive powers in social orders lacking imperial and intolerant religious ideologies. When greed and intolerance are controlled within a social order, its violent behavior will naturally moderate. However, crimes of passion and individual destructive behavior may continue; that, however, is not of concern to us in this work.

Appendix B
The Development of Written Language

Next to making tools and fire, the invention of spoken language through a long trial and error process by multiple human cultures stands out as an impressive *Homo sapiens* achievement. However, impressive as this achievement was, it does have its limitations. Spoken language is based solely on memory. If human memory were perfect and unlimited, perhaps the species would have no need for a written language. In addition to perfect memory, complete trust among the members of the society would also be required to eliminate the need for a written language. Lack or loss of relatively small amount of trust would also require the need to record the important communications or transactions and have both parties verify and certify it. Additionally, as spoken communications became more complex and without the ability to record the spoken words, the learning process also becomes very cumbersome.

By about 3000 BCE or likely earlier, with the expansion of agriculture and nonagricultural sectors through the relentless march of practical technology and expanding internal and external trade, these limitations of the spoken language and the absence of an ability to record communications, transactions, or expanding practical knowledge were being acutely felt. Across the millennia, one can feel the frustration of these early humans as they must have struggled to get a handle on the expanding complexity of their societies through sheer memory and trust. The realization must have sunk in that something better was needed. They had hit a wall and they knew they needed a breakthrough.

The breakthrough they were seeking was of course a written script to record communications, transactions, or expanding practical knowledge. The full development of written language, including alphabetical script, probably spanned close to three thousand years, from crude attempts starting about 4000 BCE to about 1000 BCE. We have no direct record of this long and tortuous process. We can only construct a rough outline of this process by comparing available archeological evidence from different civilizations over these millennia. There is general agreement that the process of transition from spoken to perfect written words went through several broad stages. Some civilizations never went beyond a particular stage. Others went all the way. Because several of the emerging civilizations traded with each other, we know civilizations learned to write from one another.

It is useful to identify two broad strategies in this transition from spoken to a good enough written word over a period of more than two millennia. The first strategy was to represent an object or an idea through a picture, and the second was to analyze the spoken word into phonetic components and represent each phonetic component by a symbol. The first approach may be termed nonanalytic and the second analytic. The nonanalytic approach initially appeared like a breakthrough until it ran into difficulty based on the limits of average human memory. It was rescued by the analytical approach progressively until the emergence of the alphabetical script based completely on the analytic/phonetic approach. We may identify three broad stages in this process.

The first stage is developing pictograms or ideograms. A pictogram is a drawing to represent an object, and an ideogram is a symbol to represent an idea. A drawing of a bird is an example of a pictogram, and a face with a broad smile representing laughter is an example of an ideogram. Both pictograms and ideograms were never sufficiently developed to allow their characterization as full-blown spoken languages. Their primary importance is that they were the first attempts to represent an object or an idea using a written symbol.

As we said above, a pictogram or an ideogram soon taxed the average memory. The second stage can be characterized by development of a logo-syllabic language. In a logo-syllabic language, a spoken word may be represented each by a combination of a drawing and a phonetic syllable or even a tone in pronunciation in an attempt to reduce the total number of symbols. A logo-syllabic language typically also has a provision for specifying the temporal context and syntax, and the symbols obviously have a higher level of grammar than an ideogram or a pictogram in that symbols are not merely simplistic drawings of the ideas or objects. These elements distinguish a logo-syllabic from a pictogram or ideogram.

Modern Chinese language is basically a logo-syllabic language augmented by tones at the spoken level to limit the number of written characters.

The third stage is the development of a hieroglyphic language. Logo-syllabic languages are based on a partial phonetic analysis of the spoken word. The spoken word is analyzed into one or more syllables. A syllable is a unique combination of sounds and may consist of one or more consonants and vowels. Each syllable is represented by a unique symbol. In addition, there may be unique symbols of some of the important consonants. Written words are created by combining different images, syllables, and consonants corresponding to each spoken word. In addition, as in the case of a logo-syllabic language, there are symbols for temporal context and an agreed syntax. A purely syllabic language is useful for writing a spoken language that contains only a small number of syllables. The Japanese Kana language is an example of a purely syllabic language. By contrast, the hieroglyphic language used in ancient Egypt and was actually a composite of a logographic language, with a limited number of consonants and the determinatives used to mark certain classes of words. The latter is desirable because a hieroglyphic language lacks vowels. Determinatives were never used in the spoken version as vowel sounds were used to distinguish the words.

In figure B-1, we show these stages schematically.

We should add that many scripts, some known, some forgotten, and some still not deciphered, might be characterized as belonging to intermediate or composite stages in this long process.

The cuneiform script invented in Mesopotamia in the late fourth millennium BCE started out as pictograph and ideograph and passed through a logographic stage around 3200 BCE and a syllabic stage by 2600 BCE. Its last usage was around the first century CE, when one could discern fourteen consonant sounds and up to four vowels. Thus, in its later forms, it could be considered a protoalphabetical language. The cuneiform script was used by many other cultures, including Akkadian, Elamite, Hittite, and Persian. A distinguishing feature of cuneiform writing was the use of a blunt reed on a wet clay tablet to carve out the word, a brilliant solution before the invention of paper. This innovation may be considered one of the earliest forms of "printing" employed by humans.

The Indus script, dating back to fourth millennium BCE, seems to be a protoalphabetical script that had consonants, including composite consonants and one universal vowel. The composite consonant has continued to be a feature of later scripts arising in South Asia to this date and may be considered an important factor supporting the independent development of written scripts in South Asia. Indus script has not been fully deciphered to date.

Figure B-1: Evolution of Written Language from Spoken Language

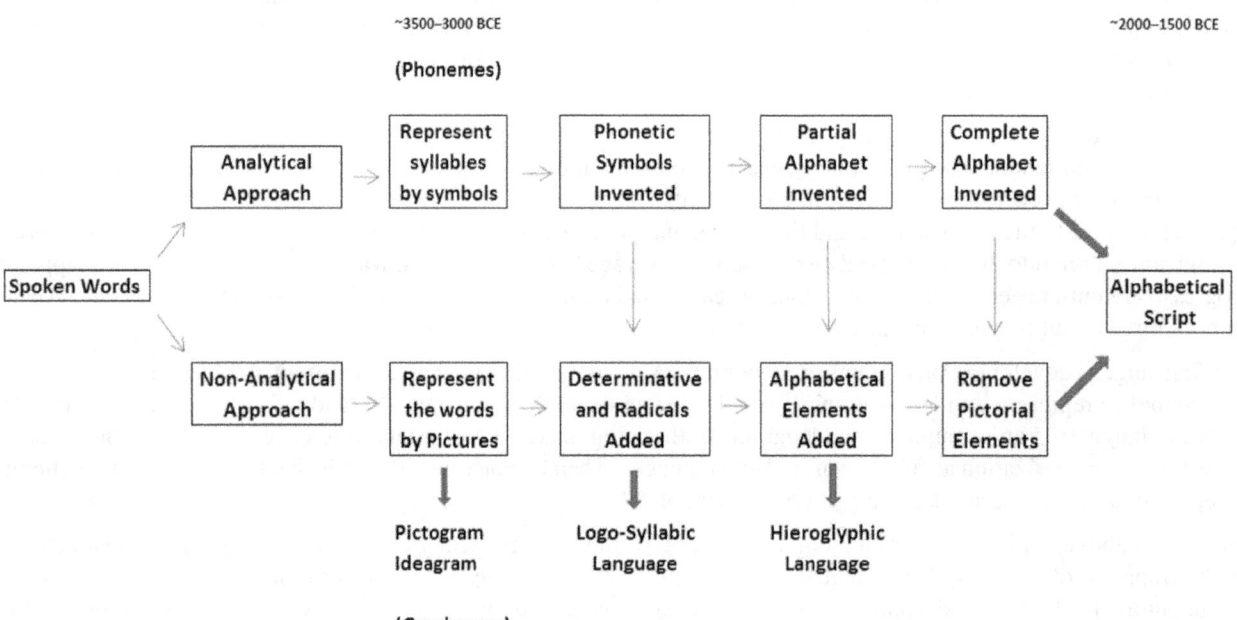

Appendix C
The Development of Alphabetical Language

We outlined the three broad stages of the evolution of written language in appendix B. The fourth and final stage in this evolution is the development of an alphabetical script. An alphabetical script is based on a partial to near perfect phonetic analysis of the spoken word. This analysis, when done right, leads to a limited number of irreducible sounds called consonants and vowels or shaping sounds that can be used to represent nearly all known or future words. Each consonant and vowel is represented by a simple abstract symbol, and the written version of each spoken word is then constructed with the help of these abstract consonant and vowel symbols. There are three variations within the alphabetical family worth mentioning.

The first is Abjad alphabets. These alphabets only have consonants, and the reader, based on his knowledge of the language, provides vowels. Arabic is an example of an Abjad alphabet.

The second family has vowels, but the battery of vowels and consonants is incomplete and does not represent the entire capability of human speech. Thus, these alphabets require combinations of vowels to create additional shaping vowels and a combination of consonants to create missing consonants. This introduces an element of ambiguity in both spelling and pronunciation in these languages. An example of this family is the modern English alphabet, where, for example, the words *but* and *put* use the same vowel but are pronounced quite differently. In addition, a consonant such as *C* can be pronounced as two different sounds, and two consonants such as *S* and *H* are combined to produce a third sound. Notwithstanding the present exalted status of English language in the world of science and commerce today, these imperfections are a reminder of humble intellectual origin of the English language.

The third family is called Abugida, but more appropriately, it should be called a fully developed alphabetical script. These languages have a full range of unique vowels as well as consonants to represent the entire anatomical capability of human speech. An example of this family is Sanskrit script. Another characteristic of many languages in this family is that vowels are represented either by a separate symbol or by a modifier or a diacritic mark placed under, over, or after a consonant. The principal reason for doing so is not conceptual but a matter of writing economy. Because Sanskrit has a full range of vowels and consonants, there is little ambiguity in how a spoken word is either spelled or pronounced. Later, Sanskrit grammar became the first context-free grammar invented by man. A context-free grammar is simply a set of finite rules that allow construction of sentences in a logical manner from the general categories of the grammar with unambiguous meaning. Sanskrit grammar is regarded by many as one of the finest intellectual achievements of man.

The full development of alphabetical script was probably completed by about 1500 BCE or earlier. It was a monumental achievement and, as we shall see below, its importance in development of complex abstract systems including science can hardly be overestimated. Below, we first look at a comparative analysis of the capabilities of various families of written languages and then move on to why a civilization using a logographic script would find it very difficult to develop complex abstract systems. This is important since of the four major ancient civilizations, two failed to develop alphabetical script, and one of these two, namely China, is a living civilization still using a logograph together with a borrowed alphabetical script. We will also look at why China did not develop an alphabetical language, how this impacted expression of creativity in ancient China, and what the continued use of logograph implies for the future of world-class science in modern China.

Comparative analysis of families of written scripts: It is important to assess the different families of languages from the standpoint of capabilities, efficiency, and effectiveness in meeting the requirements of recording communications, commercial transactions, and practical and scientific knowledge.

Pictographic and ideographic languages fail most of the dimensions of capability (ambiguous word representation, tense, syntax, punctuation, and unambiguous spelling and pronunciation), efficiency (of writing, reading, and ease of learning), and effectiveness (practically feasible vocabulary size and precision in word meanings). Logographic and syllabic languages fail on several key dimensions, while three categories of the alphabetical languages pass all of the dimensions in the table C-1.

Table C-1: Comparative Analysis of Language Families

Dimension	Non-alphabetical Scripts			Alphabetical Scripts		
	Ideograph/ Pictograph	Logograph	Syllabic	No Vowels (Abjads)	Incomplete Vowels/consonants	Complete Vowels/cons
Capability						
Word representation	yes	yes	yes	yes	yes	yes
Tense representation	no	yes	yes	yes	yes	yes
Syntax	no	yes	yes	yes	yes	yes
Punctuation						
Unambiguous spelling	no	no	yes	no	no	yes
Unambiguous pronunc.	No	no	yes	no	no	yes
Efficiency						
Of writing	low	low	low	high	high	high
Of learning	low	low	low	high	high	high
Of reading	low	low	low	high	high	high
Effectiveness						
# of symbols for full Vocabulary	100,000's	10,000's	10,000's	10's	10's	10's
Practical vocab. Size	1,000's	1,000's	1,000's	unlimited	unlimited	unlimited
Use of tonals	no	yes	yes	no	no	no
Precision of meaning	no	no	no	yes	yes	yes

The pictographic and ideographic languages were used only by prescience civilizations and are not in use today by any major civilization. Comparison with them, therefore, is more a matter of historical interest. Hieroglyphic language was used in ancient Egypt. The inherent limitations of the logographic and syllabic languages are, on the other hand, a matter of interest in understanding their abilities to support indigenous and independent scientific activity as they have been used continuously by the Chinese civilization for nearly five millennia.

Logograph and development of complex systems of thought: An alphabetical language is an amazing invention. Using less than fifty easy-to-draw symbols, it is possible to create an essentially unlimited number of words to represent concepts or objects and an effective grammar. All this is accomplished without taxing the limits of human memory for written symbols and without putting an undue burden on the time required to learn thousands of complicated word-pictures needed for an effective vocabulary without an alphabetical script. Further, this is accomplished without any loss of precision since each new word created to represent a new concept or object is unique yet uses the same familiar symbols. This capability of an alphabetical language, made possible through varying the number and order of the symbols chosen to represent a unique word precisely, is derived from the fact that an alphabet represents a sufficient number of unique sounds, and words are simply unique combinations of these unique sounds. It has been estimated that an alphabetical language using fifty symbols can create millions of unique words, each employing a limited number, about ten or less, of the unique sound symbols.

This comparison of capability of alphabetical and nonalphabetical languages is reminiscent of a comparison between the capability of the Indian and the Roman numeral systems. It is infinitely easier to do arithmetic and manipulate the numbers using the Indian numeral system compared to the Roman system. The difference, of course, being that the Muslim, Western, and Chinese civilizations adopted the Indian number system readily when they became aware of it. However, only the Chinese civilization refused to adopt the alphabetical script from Indian, Muslim, or Western civilizations. This refusal reinforced Chinese insularity. Adopting a superior numeral system has a different cultural cost/benefit equation. It was, therefore, easier for the Chinese to adopt the Indian numeral system than to switch from logographic to alphabetical language. The issue of why China failed to develop alphabetical script is discussed in more detail in appendix I.

A logographic language has a built-in need to limit the number of symbols to a few thousand because of the limitation of human memory for complex written symbols; each character must be distinguishable from all others. It thus has a tendency to use combinations of the existing characters to create new words with imprecise and overlapping meaning. Thought creates concepts and relationships among concepts, leading ultimately to the creation of the complex abstract systems encountered in science. Written words give a visible expression to these complex abstract systems and a means to communicate and preserve these abstract systems accurately. The written words also inevitably help clarify the logical relationships inherent in the abstract systems. However, if the written words do not represent the concepts unambiguously and simply, they will be unable to help create logical clarity. The iterative process outlined above, thus, consists of five steps:

1. Creation of precise abstract systems in the mind
2. Clear oral communication of these systems
3. Turning the abstract systems into a written form without loss of precision
4. Improving the precision of abstract systems through writing
5. The ability to preserve abstract systems efficiently and with precision

An abstract system in this context means complex, logical structures, such as those encountered in formal, natural, or social sciences involving relationships among precise abstract concepts.

The difficulty with a logographic language can be seen most clearly in the case of an abstract science like algebra. Here, the mathematician needs to represent and record a number with a simple meaningless symbol and be able to say it verbally for communication purposes. If one tries to represent a number with a complex logographic symbol, one can imagine what a simple equation will look like. It will be too unwieldy. It may be argued that a culture using logographic language could invent simpler symbols for use in mathematics. However, mathematicians using symbols must be able to verbally pronounce them in order to communicate them verbally to each other as well. But such symbols amount to the vowels or consonants of an alphabetical language! Therefore, a culture using logographic script would have to invent an alphabetical language to develop complex mathematics and mathematical sciences like algebra and geometry, which are prerequisites to natural sciences. We are not suggesting that mathematical thought is impossible without an alphabetical script. It clearly is possible. But communication and mature development of these ideas is not practical without an alphabetical script.

Table C-2 shows how differences in the capability of written languages affect the above five-step process.

Executing the five-step process presents serious difficulties in the absence of a written language or a written language using logographic language. Only with an alphabetical script is the entire process freed from limitations imposed by human memory.

To summarize, an alphabetical script is a critical necessity for mature philosophy, religion, and science to arise in a culture or civilization. Of course, the mere existence of an alphabetical language by no means guarantees that science will be born.

Table C-2: Language Capability and Abstract Systems

Process Step	No Written Script	Logographic Script	Alphabetical Script
Creation of precise abstract System using spoken word	limited	limited	limited
Clear oral communication Of the abstract systems	limited only by above step	limited only by above step	limited only by above step
Turning abstract systems into Written form with precision	not possible	difficult	no difficulty
Improving the precision Through writing	not possible	very difficult	no difficulty
Ability to preserve systems Efficiently and with precision	limited using oral verse form	difficult	easy

Appendix D
The Myth of the Indo-Aryan Invasion of India

The broad outline of the history of the ancient world as envisioned by Western historians is as follows. Within Eurasia, the Chinese civilization, including its nomadic neighbors, was a world unto itself. The Mesopotamian civilization in the Fertile Crescent was the birthplace of civilization, followed by the Indus and Nile episodes. All these early civilizations, except the Chinese, withered from internal or external causes. By about 2000 BCE, people from outside Indian subcontinent who called themselves Aryans (or "noble") were named Indo-Europeans by Western historians and burst upon the world scene and conquered Europe and the Middle East, including Persia; and, by 1500 BCE, they had invaded India.

The Indo-Europeans or Aryans play the role of a conquering hero in this version. But what evidence is there to prove the existence of these Indo-European conquerors?

In 1785, William Jones, an English judge in Calcutta, noted an unmistakable similarity between the languages of North India and Europe. Since then, this affinity has been extended to languages spoken by many peoples in the Middle East area, such as the Persians, Hittites, Mitanni, and Kassites. Today, the geographical area of Indo-European languages is quite vast. Jones speculated that there must be a mother language from which all these languages originated. Subsequently, it was also assumed that this linguistic affinity implied an original race and culture for these Indo-Europeans. This equating of language, race, and culture was obviously a conjecture without archeological evidence. In the absence of facts, these Indo-European people were assigned a Caucasian or even a Nordic home and a nomadic culture. The archeological establishment over the last two hundred years has been quite prolific in proposing candidates for the original home for these Indo-Europeans, anywhere from Norway to Afghanistan, based on rather thin evidence.

Although the question of the origin of Indo-Aryans, the branch that supposedly invaded India, is tied into the larger Indo-European issue, the specific Indo-Aryan issues can be stated as follows:

- Did an Indo-Aryan invasion of India take place? If yes, when?
- If no, did Indo-Aryans migrate into India? If yes, when?
- If no migration took place, how does one explain the Indo-Aryan linguistic and cultural influence outside India?

These three related issues have a history over the last two centuries that is colored by emerging evidence, ideological positioning, and even emotional attitudes.

Early nineteenth century: Abbe Dubois (1770–1848) attempted to reconcile the timing of the deluge in the bible to Indian history and conjectured that people from the Caucasus entered India not earlier than the time of biblical deluge or about 2500 BCE. In essence, this was a religious–linguistic hypothesis.

Mid-nineteenth century: Max Muller (1823–1903), a German, took the conjecture a step further and invented the theory of the Aryan invasion of India, fixing the date of the invasion at no earlier than 1500 BCE. He also arbitrarily fixed the timing of the Vedas, the Hindu scriptures. Later on his death bed, Muller conceded the purely conjectural nature of his Vedic chronology and Aryan invasion hypothesis. Muller's hypothesis of the Indo-Aryan invasion was, however, too good to not be used by the British imperialists, who had funded Muller, and, later, by the racist Nazis for political purposes.

Early twentieth century: Discovery of the Indus valley ruins by R. D. Banerjee in 1922 was initially seen as a confirmation of Muller's theory to European archeologists as it appeared that the undeciphered Indus script had no relationship to the Devnagri script used in northern Indian languages. Since the evolution of script from the Indus script to Devanagri was and is full of gaps, this conclusion was clearly hasty. The utter lack of evidence of an attack by the Indo-Aryans in the ruins did not receive the attention it deserved.

Thus, many well-known archeologists and historians, including Dubois, Muller, Childe, Marshal, and Wheeler, have contributed to this issue over the last two centuries. There are two principal shortfalls in these studies: first, the evidence was limited to linguistics and archeology, and second, more important, the linguists assumed that the hypotheses of the archeologists were correct, and the archeologists assumed the linguists' hypotheses were correct. The vested interests, Christian missionaries, the British, and the Nazis, obviously had little interest to question this hypothesis.

Evidence Contradicting the Indo-Aryan Invasion

During the last quarter of the twentieth century, a significant number of new archeological finds, literary and linguistic research, and reinterpretations have called into question the Aryan invasion theory. Below we summarize these findings briefly.

Renfrew hypothesis: In 1984, Colin Renfrew, in a controversial book titled *Archeology and Language,* convincingly argued that the original home of the Indo-European people was not Europe or the Central Asian steppes. Rather, these Indo-Europeans lived in eastern Anatolia about 7000 BCE. They spoke a proto–Indo–European language, and contrary to popular opinion, they were not nomads. They had a sedentary agricultural lifestyle. From eastern Anatolia, over time they immigrated to Europe, the Middle East, and South Asia. They mingled with local populations to create new ethnic identities. Thus, Renfrew did not equate language, race, and culture. This theory would also explain the affinity between Indo-European and a number of ancient languages in the Middle East, such as Mitanni, Hittite, and Kassite, as well as the existence of Indo-European names in Egyptian documents.

Discovery of Mehrgarh: Between 1962 and 1985, a number of French archeological teams discovered the ruins at Pirak, Mehrgarh, and Nausharo in Baluchistan near the Bolan Pass. These sites go back to 6500 BCE and present a sophisticated urban agricultural settlement. The largest site covers five hundred acres and probably supported twenty thousand people. This would make Mehrgrah about four to five times the size of the contemporaneous town of Catal Hutuk in Anatolia. This incredible discovery establishes the continuity of civilization in South Asia dating back to at least 7000 BCE. Mehrgarh would seem to provide the original basis of the Indus-Sarasvati civilization that, in turn, provided the basis of later Indian civilization in the Ganges plains.

Together, Renfrew's theory and the discovery of Mehrgarh ought to be sufficient to bury the 1500 BCE date of the Aryan invasion of India, and it pushes any plausible immigration of Indo-Aryans, who established the Mehrgarh civilization, back to 7000 BCE. There is, however, more evidence that has been accumulating from many disciplines that thoroughly expose the hypothetical nature of the Aryan invasion theory. Below, we briefly capture this evidence.

Literary evidence: The Rig Veda mentions a river named Sarasvati that flowed to the east of the Indus River. Today no such river exists. A hydrological survey done by an Italian team has conclusively shown that such a river existed and dried out around 2000 BCE, hundreds of years before the supposed invasion. The Rig Veda also mentions an ocean numerous times. It is highly unlikely that a nomadic people arriving from Central Asia would know much about an ocean. Finally, the descendants of Indo-Aryans in India, the Hindus, and other peoples outside India have no memory or record of this invasion.

Astronomical evidence: Based on the mention of the eclipses of sun and moon in another Hindu scripture called *Mahabharata*, it has been calculated that the great civil war, which the Rig Veda does not mention, between two clans took place in 3067 BCE. This would place the Rig Veda and the Indo-Aryans in the area before 3012 BCE.

Genetic evidence: Skeletons from the Indus valley ruins belong to several racial groups; all of these groups are present in India today. This contradicts the notion that a new race was introduced into South Asia around 1500 BCE.

Linguistic evidence: The undeciphered Indus-Sarasvati script bears a relationship to the later Brahmi script. In Brahmi, the letters used for individual consonants and marks used as vowel and composite consonants number about 330. The Indus-Sarasvati script has about 400 signs. Both scripts seem to use composite consonants. Many signs are modified in a way similar to Brahmi script. In addition, there are stylistic similarities between the Indus-Sarasvati glyphs and the later Brahmi script.

Cultural evidence: There is striking cultural continuity between Indus-Sarasvati ruins and the later Hindu civilization. This would be impossible if the invading Aryans destroyed this earlier civilization.

Use of horse and chariots: The Aryan invasion was thought to have used horse-driven chariots or horses. It is difficult to imagine nomads using chariots over the mountains of Afghanistan to invade India. The chariot is an invention of an urban civilization, not the nomads.

Until recently, it was believed that horse riding did not occur before the second millennium BCE, so the invasion could not have occurred any earlier. However, it has been discovered that horse riding was practiced as early as 4500 BCE in Ukraine, thus pushing the date for a hypothetical and unsubstantiated invasion by millennia.

The absence of horse images in Indus-Sarasvati seals has been taken as support for the invasion theory. Horse images in Paleolithic caves in India have been discovered. Rig Veda mentions indigenous horses with thirty-four ribs, whereas the central Asian horses that would have had to have been used in the invasion have thirty-six ribs. No horses with either thirty-four or thirty-six ribs have been found in the ruins. However, if horse-riding techniques were not fully developed, a horse could not have played a prominent role in the Indus-Sarasvati civilization, explaining absence of its images. The fact that Gita, which depicts the Mahabharata civil war of 3102 BCE, mentions horses and chariots could be explained as an addition by later authors or its limited use in chariots. Thus, it may be that horse-riding techniques and not horses themselves were imported or developed later into India sometime after the demise of Indus-Saravati cities around 2200 BCE. This would explain the absence of horse images in the Indus seals. Clearly, there are more unanswered questions than answers, and drawing a significant conclusion based on a single dimension presumed belief only serves to exposes the desperation of the Western archeological establishment.

Based on the evidence presented above, the Aryan invasion is sheer imagination. According to Renfrew's exhaustive work, migration probably occurred around 7000 BCE. Therefore, if the Indo-European people migrated to South Asia as early as 7000 BCE, they did not use horses. But there is little direct evidence of migration. In the absence of immigration, the only way one can explain the widespread nature of Indo-Aryan language, names, and gods among the many ancient peoples scattered throughout Eurasia is through a reverse migration from India in addition to a migration of Indo-Europeans into other parts of Asia and Europe from Anatolia. Thus, reverse migration is not necessarily inconsistent with the Renfrew hypothesis. Both could have occurred. This hypothesis of reverse migration, if proven correct, amounts to a major revision in ancient historiography and archeology. Renfrew did not consider the hypothesis of reverse migration, and it is obviously improper to regard Renfrew's theory as unsupportive of this hypothesis.

To conclude, the hypothesis of the Indo-Aryan invasion lies in shambles. In the absence of invasion, either the migration into India took place about 7000 BCE, a reverse migration out of India took place, or the original home of the Indo-Aryans was in fact in northwest India with a reverse migration.

It has been suggested that resolving the issue of the origin of the Indo-European peoples, including the myth of the Indo-Aryan invasion of India, is like bringing down a two-hundred-year-old oak tree with a pocketknife. It will take time, but it will happen.

Appendix E
The Roots of the Indian Civilization and Reverse Migration Theory

As we discussed in appendix D, given new data from many sources, including astronomical, hydrological, metallurgical, and DNA studies as well as a more thorough analysis of the Rig Veda, the theory of the Aryan invasion of India around 1500 BCE is essentially dead. This raises two questions: What is the true prehistory and ancient history of the Indian people, and how does one explain the presence of languages, names, and mythologies derived from India throughout central and West Asia as well as Europe? In this appendix, we will attempt to answer these two questions based on the research by a number of talented researchers, such as N. S. Rajaram, Natwar Jha, Subhash Kak, and Shrikant Talageri over the last two decades. We should keep in mind that this is a developing picture. While the research to date appears promising, it is likely to be revised in many specifics.

Prehistory of the Indian Civilization—A Mingling of Two Peoples

After the Mount Toba disaster in 74,000 BCE, which wiped out nearly all *Homo sapiens*, South Asia was repopulated from Africa around 70,000 to 65,000 BCE, particularly along the coastal areas. Based on extensive DNA studies done by Luigi LucaCavalli-Sforza, at least two groups of South Asians left the region: the first around 40,000 to 50,000 years ago to Europe and a second somewhat later to Central Asia. What precipitated these migrations is unclear at the present time. Based on these studies, however, the Europeans and West and Central Asians become descendants from these two migrations, making these populations twice removed from our African ancestors.

The ending of the last ice age around 10,000 BCE and a consequent melting of the Himalayan glaciers resulted in several mighty new rivers forming in northern and western India. This made north and northwest India suitable for agriculture because of an abundant water supply and an increasingly warmer climate, thus causing a third local migration north from the south, where they encountered Indo-Aryans that had migrated from Anatolia after 7000 BCE if one accept the Colin Renfrew hypothesis. The people mingled somewhat incompletely, forming the Indian racial type.

Mehrgarh Period

People migrating north probably established the earliest known agricultural settlement in South Asia at Mehrgarh almost certainly before 6500 BCE. This was an advanced civilization with a city of about twenty thousand people, the largest in the world at the time. It also practiced world's first dental surgery, as evidenced by teeth in the skeletal remains discovered. The Mehrgarh settlement was discovered less than twenty-five years ago. Presumably, as agricultural technology developed, population increased, and eastward migration continued in search of better agricultural lands. By about 6000 BCE, in all likelihood they established the Vedic civilization in the upper Sarasvati River area.

Vedic Civilization

Based on oral tradition transmitted by Rig Veda, it appears that around 5000 BCE or a little later (see below for a discussion of the chronology) an Indian ruler named Mandhata conducted a campaign against a people known as Druyhus, who were defeated and forced to migrate out of India. A branch of the Druhyus migrated to Europe and came to be known as Druids (Celtic priests) in ancient Europe. Druids traced their origins from Asia around 3900 BCE. It is hypothesized that these migrating Druyhus people transmitted Sanskrit language and Hindu mythologies to Europe and many other locations along the way. A thousand years later, Vedic King Sudas fought a second great war with a federation of ten kings, including the remaining Druyhus still in Northwest India. This battle is recorded in Rig Veda by the seer, Vasistha. The net result of this war was another migration out of India, including people known as Parthas, Pakthas, and Balahanas, who are known today as Parthians, Pathans, and Baluchis.

The Vedic civilization had a strong spiritual orientation with their polytheism. They believed heavenly, terrestrial, and inner psychological worlds were lawful and connected. The essence of the universe and self were not different from each other as the universe was spiritual, not material. They most certainly appear to be the first people to focus on astronomy, arithmetic, geometry, and language. This interest did not derive from a need to understand and control nature as modern science intends to do. Rather, this interest was based on a spiritual drive. They principally observed heavenly motions and the human mind. They wanted a communion with the universal spirit. As a result, they built massive altars to worship this universal spirit. The design of these altars showed their relatively sophisticated understanding of the motions of the sun, moon, and five planets. They developed geometry and arithmetic to design altars. They also embedded their astronomical observations in verse form into their scared book, the Rig Veda. Since they did not have a written language, they had to commit the Rig Veda to memory and chanted its verses during worship using the altars. It is as though the essence of the macrocosm embedded in the altars and verses would enable them to reach that macrocosm or the universal spirit. The words for them became sacred and the only means to contact the universal.

The birth of geometry, arithmetic, astronomy, and grammar began deep in the bosom of the spiritual quest of the Vedic people. These protosciences became part of Rig Veda and the Brahmanas that continued to be transmitted by memory.

Thus, the earliest birth of protoscience lies at the intersection of spirituality and intellectual confusion concerning the nature of the universe during the Vedic era. This is not too surprising once we realize that the earliest civilizations had to necessarily experience both intellectual confusion and metaphysical anxiety in equal measure. Vedic Aryans were blessed to have lived unperturbed in a Garden of Eden for millennia to ponder the nature of universe and self.

Harappa Civilization

By 4000 BCE, the Vedic civilization began to display a more practical orientation as practical technology advanced. Using the protoscience developed by the Vedic civilization, it built mighty cities and ports. The archeological discoveries at Harappa, Mohenjo-Daro, and Lotham belong to this phase. This civilization developed a close trade relationship with the emerging civilizations in Mesopotamia. Numerous seals from Harappa have been discovered in Mesopotamia. Through trade and migration, Vedic protoscience was transmitted to West Asia. Late Seidenburg's research concluded that elements of ancient geometry found in Egypt and Babylonia in the late third millennium and early second millennium stem from the Vedic protoscience. There continued more migrations to the north and northwest out of India. Ancient literature mentions the Mitanni in West Asia, who migrated from India after 2000 BCE.

The Harappa civilization consisted of two main royal families: Purus or Kurus at the northern end of the Sarasvati River and the Yadavs at the southern end. The political organization consisted of several competing states mentioned in the ancient literature. A key accomplishment of the Harappa civilization was developing a protoalphabetical script with a single universal vowel used as the first letter of the word. The Harappa civilization lasted over a thousand years when it ran into two challenges: one made by nature and a second made by man. Over a period of several centuries, the Sarasvati

River dried out, and the climate took a turn for the worse. Secondly, the great civil war of Mahabharata took place around 3102 BCE. It is noteworthy that the victors of this war renounced the kingdom and retired to the Himalayas.

The Ganges Civilization

Because of these natural and manmade destructions, the civilization declined, precipitating a move to the east along the Ganges. This migration that started before 2000 BCE initiated the Ganges civilization phase.

The migration east required a reestablishment of civilization. It required clearing the land. The discovery of iron in the middle of the second millennium eased this transition. It seems that this eastward move with resulting republican monarchies in the heartland of the Ganges plain set the stage for the epic of Ramayana, probably around 1500 BCE. A thousand years later, these republics were brought together in an empire, first by the Nanda Dynasty and a little later by the Mauryas. We thus enter the historical phase in South Asia, starting around 500 BCE or a little before.

It is noteworthy that the migration east and the resulting Ganges phase displayed a return to the spiritual orientation of the Vedic age, while the surviving civilization around the Indus River retained a practical bent. This return to the spiritual displayed by the eastern branch was clearly a reaction to ecological and political disasters. More than a thousand years later, starting about 1000 BCE, the western part would play a critical role in the birth of science.

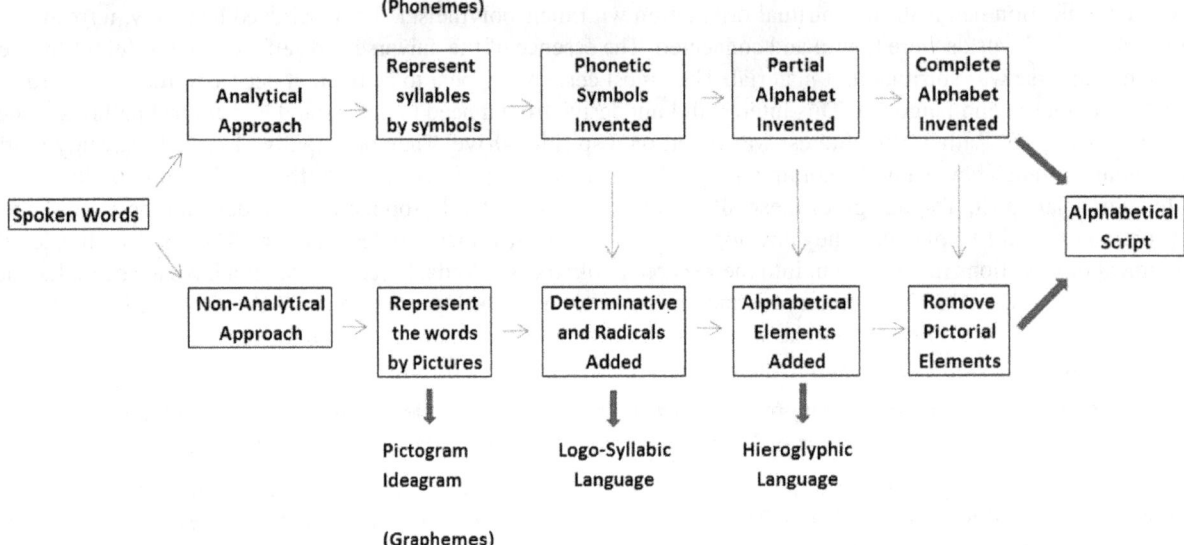

Figure E-1: Roots of Ancient Indian Civilization and Reverse Migration Theory

Where is the proof? The aforementioned sketch of South Asian ancient history is a developing picture based on recent studies. We offer the following evidence, based on the studies of N. S. Rajaram, Natwar Jha, Subhash Kak, and Shrikant Talegiri for the main chronological events in the above picture.

The first and most important and easier to establish marker is the date of *Mahabharata*:

- *Mahabharata* mentions several astronomical events, including a lunar eclipse at Pleiades followed by a solar eclipse at Antares within a month of each other just before the great civil war. It also mentions the planet Saturn at Aldebaran. Based on recent advances in planetarium software, Narahari Achar has narrowed down this combination of astronomical occurrences to two dates, 3067 BCE and 2183 BCE. The latter date may be ruled out on archeological grounds as the Harappa civilization was in decline by 2200 due to the drought from the river drying out. Thus, 3102 BCE is the likely date for the *Mahabharata*.

- Kaushitaki Brahmana mentions the winter solstice took place at the time of the *Mahabharata* on the Hindu festival Maha Shivratri or about seventy days later than today. Due to the phenomenon of the precession of the equinox, the solstice resulted in a movement of one day every 72.5 years and 70 times 72.5 is 5075, or about 3100 BCE.

- Ancient genealogical lists mention that Abhimanyu, who died in the Mahabharata war, was the thirty-first descent of the King Sudas, mentioned earlier. Using twenty to twenty-five years per generation, this would place Sudas around 4000 BCE
- A bronze head known as Vasistha's head was discovered in 1958 and has been dated to about 3800 BCE (thus questioning the invention of bronze in Mesopotamia). This head has a high silver content, suggesting it was cast before the Vedic Aryans had learned to isolate silver. At the same time, pure silver ornaments have been discovered at Kunal, which have been dated to 3300 BCE, suggesting a date between 3300 and 3800 BCE for the successful isolation of silver metal. Silver is not mentioned in the Rig Veda.
- This suggests that the composition of the Rig Veda must have started well before 4000 BCE.
- Astronomical evidence in the Rig Veda as examined by several researchers point to dates as early as 6000 BCE for Rig Veda. This would fit in with the date of 6500 BCE assigned to archeological finds at Mehrgarh, since a continuity from Mehrgarh to the Vedic civilization must be assumed in the absence of known discontinuities. An accomplishment of the magnitude of Mehrgarh cannot simply have disappeared.

Thus, using a firm marker at the time of *Mahabharata*, we may work backward to link back to the earliest known civilization in South Asia. This obviously leaves a lot of room for scholarly debate, as it should. However, when one recognizes that an achievement of the magnitude of Mehrgarh cannot disappear and gives proper weight to the Rig Vedic oral tradition, it is hard not to see a nine-thousand-year continuity in the South Asian civilization that was interrupted by the ecological disaster around 2200 BCE, from which the civilization recovered by expanding eastwards. No doubt, a million details will be added and subtracted as research continues. However, it is difficult to see how the broad picture we have laid out can materially change as future research continues.

Key Points Summary

- A series of migrations out of India easily explains the presence of Sanskrit and Sanskrit-derived languages and Vedic culture in the ancient cultural traditions of Central and West Asia and Europe.
- The Vedic culture is older than the Mesopotamian cultures by millennia.
- It appears that barbarian Europe got its culture twice: first from India through migrations and later from Mesopotamia through diffusion. Recent research is showing a strong culture in Europe before the rise of the Near Eastern civilizations in Mesopotamia, prompting Renfrew to ask, "If barbarian Europe did not acquire its important innovations from the Near East, how did they come about?" These innovations included metallurgy, language, astronomy, religion, and of course, advanced agricultural technology.
- Mesopotamia likely received its arithmetic, geometry, and astronomy from the Harappa civilization, with whom they traded extensively.
- The Vedic civilization was essentially a spiritual civilization that must be credited with discovering the principle of equivalence, the protoscience represented by arithmetic and geometry in the Sulbha Sutra, and astronomy in Rig Veda and Brahmanas. The Vedic civilization did not have a written language, and as a result, it developed an amazing oral tradition that continued long after written script was invented.
- The people of the Harappa civilization were builders and inventors as evidenced by ruins at Harappa, Lotham, and the Indus script. Harappa declined due to ecological and political reasons.
- The decline of Harappa started an eastward movement, resulting in the rise of Ganges civilization. The Ganges civilization had a spiritual orientation, though it was less than prevalent in the Vedic period.
- With the Ganges expansion, we begin to see an east–west split in South Asia. The western remnants of the Harappa phase remained more practical, and the eastern Ganges people returned to a more spiritual and philosophical orientation of the Vedic civilization, since the culture no doubt still had strong spiritual tendencies. The Western branch gave birth to science proper after 1000 BCE. One may also speculate that the ecological disaster delayed the rise of science by more than a thousand long years.

Appendix F
Researching Ancient Civilizations

The Tools of Archeology

By definition, the prehistorical phase implies an absence of written language. Written language emerged about 3000 BCE, making the entire historical phase to the present about five thousand years long. The prehistorical phase may be said to begin with the emergence of spoken word and is at least fifty thousand years long. Assuming the invention of agriculture possibly as far back as twenty thousand years ago and given its long period of diffusion and establishment, we may divide the entire period as follows:

Prebirth Era	20,000 BCE to 10,000 BCE
Birth of Civilization	10,000 BCE to 6500 BCE
Civilization Era	6500 BCE to present
Standalone Era	6500 BCE to 3000 BCE
Peaceful Era	3000 BCE to 550 BCE
Violent Era	550 BCE to present

This classification is important since each era is accessible through a different mix of research tools, with outcomes of differing uncertainties. The prebirth era is primarily accessible through the relatively new techniques of carbon 14 dating and DNA studies. There are very limited archeological records and obviously no written or oral records for this period. The birth and standalone eras are accessible through archeological finds, and of course, through carbon 14 dating, DNA, and hydrological and astronomical studies where appropriate. Significant archeological research has brilliantly uncovered the early Egyptian, Mesopotamian, Mehrgarh-Sarasvati-Indus, and Chinese civilizations over the last 175 years. In this era, the use and misuse of the linguistic studies is more likely. Over the last generation, this entire field of archeological research has been turned upside down because the reliable techniques of carbon 14 dating and hydrological, astronomical, and DNA studies are providing new data that contradict the conclusions of archeological and linguistics studies of last two hundred years, in part because these studies were tainted with intellectual, political, ideological, and cultural bias. Thus, today, we are going through a period of confusion and reassessment of the facts for this period.

With the emergence of the peaceful era, we have written records, but the issues of uneven archeological research, the destruction of older layers of civilizations through resettlement, and the preference for oral tradition by some civilizations complicate the assessment. Finally, by the beginning of the extended military conflicts era, the facts are verifiable through cross checking; however, the interpretation and ideological and cultural bias still remain important. The relative value and potential misuse of these tools for each era are summarized in table F-1.

The earliest origins of the lost Neolithic cultures in the hunting-gathering and emergence eras remain mostly hidden by necessity: there was not much from those cultures to survive to the present that could be uncovered by the tools at our disposal. We can learn more about these cultures indirectly by studying the Neolithic cultures that have survived into modern times.

Until recently, our knowledge of the civilizations and states in the standalone and peaceful eras came primarily from archeological and linguistic sources and occasionally from a reliable, but often misunderstood, oral literary tradition, such as in the case of Indo-Aryans. Archeological finds dating much before 5000 BCE are not common. This means that any exposition of a state or civilization in this era must necessarily begin in the middle, as the precise origin these earliest protocivilizations is unknown. New archeological findings pushed the prehistory back a little; however, the origin of the earliest states remains lost in the misty past. As we discussed before, archeological research is akin to a drunk looking for keys where the light is good (and for which funding is abundant).

This implies that there are significant gaps in our knowledge of the earliest cultures and civilizations because the "light" may not be equally good everywhere. Since the more complete the story, the better it sells, there is also an incentive to rush to judgment to make the story appear complete. The situation is further complicated by the inevitable political agenda and cultural prejudice in archeological and linguistic research. Over the last couple of centuries of archeology's existence as a distinct discipline, Western scholars have done most of the archeological research. Since these centuries have also been a period of Western hegemony, cultural bias must, therefore, be taken into account in any objective assessment of archeological and linguistics research. Many scholars from the Chinese, Indian, and Muslim civilizations believe that Western studies of the last two centuries are generally flawed. In addition, the depth of archeological research done to date is uneven: it is much more complete for early civilizations in West Asia and much less so for Chinese and Indian civilizations, particularly the Indian civilization. It may turn out that a historian using the tools of archeology and linguistic analysis can trace the origin of earliest civilizations borders on absurdity and leaves a lot of room for humility and open-mindedness to new data.

Past assessments are now changing dramatically with the improvements in tools like carbon 14 and newer tools like DNA, hydrological and astronomical studies, and a more unbiased study of linguistics data. However, one may expect that a new generation of researchers with no investment in the older theories, and the emergence of non-Western power centers is necessary for a scientific history of man's social evolution through uncounted cultures and civilizations to emerge.

Table F-1: Usefulness of Tools for Comparative Study of Civilizations
(All BCE, except where noted)

Tool	Hunting-Gathering Era 50 K+ to 23K	Birth Era 23K-6K	Standalone Era 6K-3K	Peaceful Era 3K-0.75K	Violent (1) Era 1K- 2K CE
Carbon-14	High/Low	High/Low	High/Low	High/Low	High/Low
DNA Studies	High/Low	High/Low	High/Low	High/Low	High/Low
Hydrological Studies	High/Low	High/Low	High/Low	High/Low	High/Low
Astronomical Studies	High/Low	High/Low	High/Low	High/Low	High/Low
Written Records	NR	NR	NR	Med/Low	High/Low
Archeological Finds	Low/Low	Low/High	Med/High	Med/High	Med/Med
Linguistic Analysis	NR	Low/High	Low/High	Low/High	Low/High
Oral Tradition	NR	NR	Low/High*	Low/High*	Low/High*

* Except Vedic Aryan Tradition (1) Extended Military Conflicts

Appendix G
Age of the Universe and Four Yugas in Ancient India

Ancient Indians estimated the age of the *present* universe to be 4.32 billion years. This number is within an order of magnitude to the modern estimate of about 14 billion years and stands in stark contrast to the age imagined by any other major civilization. The bible states the earth was created in 4004 BCE, and in late the eighteenth century, before the rise of geological sciences, Newton used science of calculus to prove it! This raises the question of how the ancient Indians estimated the age of the universe: Was it a pure guess and coincidence or was there a methodology behind it? And when was this number first estimated? In this appendix, we show one way they might have arrived at this number.

The estimate was in fact based on their understanding and speculations concerning the astronomy and cosmology, however imperfect, and their comfort with large numbers. All in all, it makes an interesting study into the working of a protoscientific mind.

The age of 4.32 billion years is first mentioned in the Brahmanas, which date back to about 1000 BCE. Surprisingly, it was based on the concept of heliocentric solar system.

- The Satpatha Brahmana states that "the sun strings these worlds—the earth, the planets, and the atmosphere—to itself on a thread." Thus, ancients had a heliocentric concept of the world, which necessary implies a rotating earth to account for the nightly rotation of the stars. They also estimated that the earth completed one circle around sun in 360 days.

- They knew of the effect, though not the cause, of the precession of the equinox. In Rig Veda, the vernal equinox was observed in the constellation Orion, and during the time of Brahmanas, it was observed in Pleiades. Thus, they were aware that the equinox moved across the zodiacs over a long period, even though they did not know that this effect was caused by the wobble of the earth's axis, with a period of about 26,000 years or one degree every seventy-two years.

- We believe that over an extended time, through observations of the location of equinox relative to fixed stars, they must have estimated this period of the sun moving across one zodiac or one-twelfth of the circle to be 2160 years. As an illustration, it was possible based on observation for them to estimate that in 360 years, the equinox moves through approximately one-sixth of a zodiac to arrive at the number 2160, by multiplying 360 and 6. They probably chose the span 360 years for two reasons: the number 360 is significant because the earth took 360 days to orbit the sun, and 360 years was long enough to see a measurable change in the position of the equinox, while 360 days was too short. The corresponding modern estimated value is 2147 years. The number 2160, thus, has an error of 0.5 percent, which seems reasonable. If the reader thinks that this was too accurate an estimate for those times, we would remind him that ancient Indians could predict the eclipses even more accurately.

- They now assumed that half of a day in a zodiac corresponds to 2,160 years, as this is the period for which one zodiac would receive sunlight, the sun being the brightest object in the universe. Therefore, a full day in the star world is double that amount or equal to 4,320 years. They saw that number as a significant or even sacred. However, they refused to believe that the length of one cycle is only movement across one zodiac. They could have multiplied this number by twelve or the number of zodiacs to arrive at the length of one cycle and a possible age of universe. However, they did not.

Thus, in the ancient heliocentric solar system, the earth rotated on its axis to explain day and night and went around the sun to correctly explain the seasons. Ancient Indians were unaware of the tilt of the earth's axis and its gravity-induced wobble. Therefore, the movement of equinoxes across the distant constellations of the Milky Way was explained through the apparent motion of the sun across the fixed stars or zodiacs. They imagined the earth paying homage to the sun, and the sun paying homage to distant stars represented by the zodiacs through Prikrima or scared orbiting, much like devotees do in Hindu temples even today.

Age of Civilization

One cycle was 4,320 years long, based on the heliocentric model above. However, they believed this number to be too small to even represent the social history of humans on earth, let alone the age of the earth or universe. This was probably because they had some memory that the history of their own civilization was longer than merely four millennia. Thus, playing it safe, they made it a thousand-fold larger and called that number one Mahayuga or a great period.

Each Mahayuga was then divided into four Yugas: Sat, Treta, Dwapar, and Kali, based on a presumed progressive moral decline from Sat Yuga to Kali Yuga. Therefore, the ages of each Yuga were 1.728, 1.296, 0.896, and 0.432 million years or exactly 40 percent, 30 percent, 20 percent, and 10 percent of the total age of the Mahayuga, respectively, as shown in table G-1. Thus, they believed that history accelerates as it experiences the moral decline from Sat Yuga to Kali Yuga, thereby serving as a theory of history and social change in the absence of knowing the age of *Homo sapiens* itself. The start of Kali Yuga was assumed to coincide with the war of Mahabharata, which took place in 3102 BCE according to the latest astronomical calculations, as well as being based on Aryabhatta's reckoning around 500 CE.

Table G-1: Highlights of the Four Yugas of Indian Culture

Yuga	Human Life, yrs	Dharma Bull legs	Human Height	Suggested Path to God Realization	Social Characteristics of the Yuga	Reason Named	Length of the Yuga, years
Satya	100,000	4	21 cubits	Vishnu Meditation	No classes or Castes	Truth	1,728,000
Treta	10,000	3	14	Yajna	Varna ashram introduced	3 legs	1,296,000
Dwaper	1,000	2	7	Temple worship	wealth polarization beginning	2 legs	864,000
Kali	100	1	3.5	Sankirtina	High Taxes!	Kali demon	432,000

Notice the desire to stay with rational fractions and decimal numbers
A cubit is approximately one and half feet

Age of the Present Earth and the Universe

Not satisfied with the length of one Mahayuga or one historical cycle of 4.32 million years as the age of the earth and universe, they increased it a thousandfold again, thus arriving at 4.32 billion years. Thus, the present earth and universe were to last a thousand historical or civilization cycles. Of course, we know today that civilization is less than ten thousand years old, and the age of *Homo sapiens* is an evolving number estimated to be 300,000 to 400,000 years.

Age of All Universes—Past, Present, and Future

Not to be satisfied with even this number, they further stated that this is just one cycle of the universe and is equal to one day in the life of Brahma (the modern equivalent being singularity at the Big Bang), the creator who lives for a hundred years, after which his creative powers are exhausted. Thus, the age of universe with all cycles was calculated to be 155.52 trillion years (4.32 billion x 100 x 360) or more than ten thousand times longer than what modern science believes without the concept of multiverses. What happens after Brahma is exhausted was, of course left unanswered, much like who created multiverses. The entire deduction is shown in Figure G-1.

In short, the age of the civilization cycle, earth, universe and all possible universes were calculated based on the best astronomy of the day and an extraordinary facility for calculation and numbers among all of the world's ancient civilizations but without reigning in the natural speculative tendencies of a protoscientific mind. In early Greece, for example, the largest number they conceived is said to be ten thousand.

Figure G-1: Highlights of the Four Yugas of Indian Culture
From Astronomy, Cosmology, Numbers Capability, and Speculation

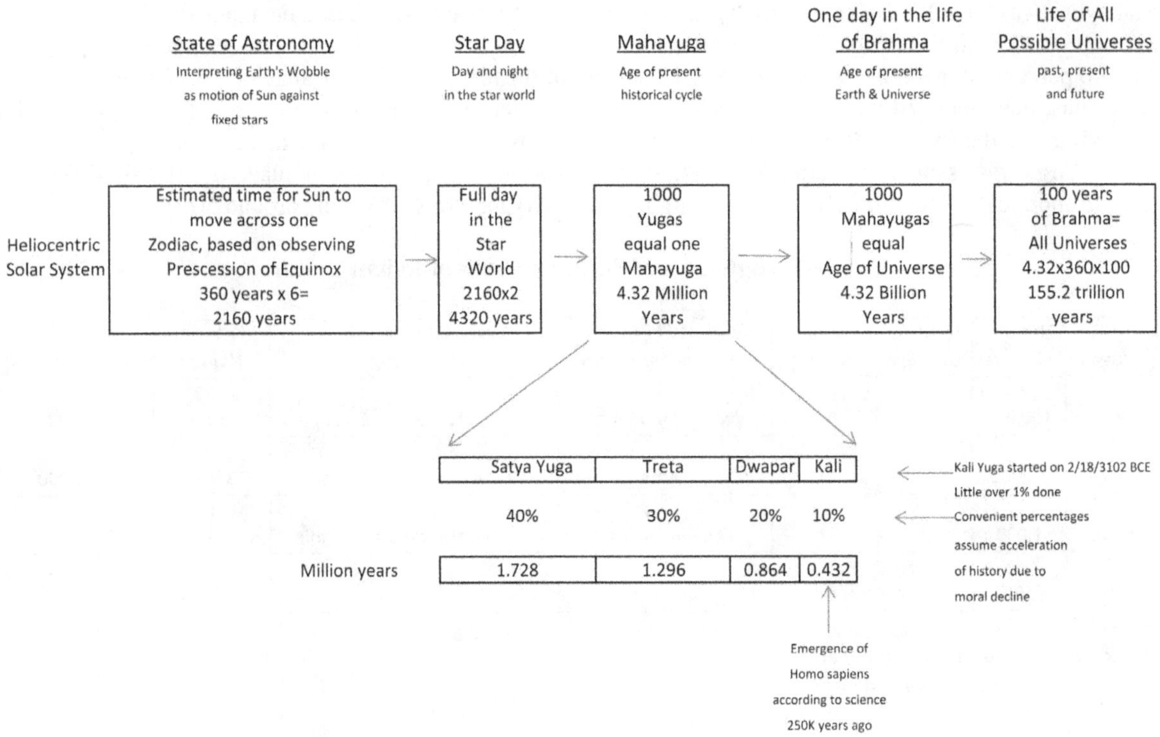

	State of Astronomy	Star Day	MahaYuga	One day in the life of Brahma	Life of All Possible Universes
	Interpreting Earth's Wobble as motion of Sun against fixed stars	Day and night in the star world	Age of present historical cycle	Age of present Earth & Universe	past, present and future
Heliocentric Solar System	Estimated time for Sun to move across one Zodiac, based on observing Prescession of Equinox 360 years x 6= 2160 years	Full day in the Star World 2160x2 4320 years	1000 Yugas equal one Mahayuga 4.32 Million Years	1000 Mahayugas equal Age of Universe 4.32 Billion Years	100 years of Brahma= All Universes 4.32x360x100 155.2 trillion years

	Satya Yuga	Treta	Dwapar	Kali
	40%	30%	20%	10%
Million years	1.728	1.296	0.864	0.432

Kali Yuga started on 2/18/3102 BCE
Little over 1% done
Convenient percentages assume acceleration of history due to moral decline

Emergence of Homo sapiens according to science 250K years ago

Appendix H
Assessment of Western Historiography

Cultural bias in history can take two forms: it can exaggerate the importance and antiquity of one's own civilization and minimize the importance and antiquity of the civilization of others. Western historiography of last two plus centuries is again a great example of both these strategies.

During the so-called Enlightenment period in the second half of the eighteenth century, northwest European historians, witnessing the world slowly but surely slipping under their domination, formulated a theory of Western civilization,

Greeks single-handedly invented science nearly 2,500 years ago. Romans brilliantly applied that science to create the Roman Empire. Around 500 AD, nomadic invaders succeeded in destroying the Roman Empire, in part because of Rome's internal weakness, thus plunging Europe into a thousand years of darkness. After the fall of Rome, Arabs, as their empire expanded in to Europe, discovered Greek science and kept it alive for a convenient handoff to the West half a millennium later, when the West woke up from its slumber to continue the scientific project through the Italian Renaissance, Reformation, scientific revolution, enlightenment, and industrial and post-industrial revolutions. This version of history glorified Alexander's adventure of "world conquest," the Roman Empire, Crusades, racism, and colonial conquest. Chinese, Indian, and other civilizations are handled as footnotes in this version of history.

Two interesting innovations are implicit in this formulation. First, southern and eastern Europe, which was historically more part of West Asia, is divorced from it. It then combines northwest and southeast Europe under the banner of a Judeo-Christian European/Western civilization. Part of the logic was that West Asia was Islamic and therefore utterly different by the eighteenth century .

Second, tearing off southern and southeastern Europe from West Asia was essential to establish that Greek science sprang out of European soil and owed little to any other civilization. It bears noting that this concept was formulated before the discovery of ancient Egyptian, Sumerian, Indus valley, and Chinese civilizations! These historians to considerable extent knew about the comparatively young Islamic civilization; however, their knowledge of ancient Middle East, Indian, and Chinese civilizations was insufficient. Perhaps these historians may be excused since no one in the eighteenth century knew the ancient history of these ancient civilizations to any significant extent. On the other hand, these historians were sophisticated thinkers and surely must have realized at some level that they were creating fiction. Because this version politically supported the forces to bring the world under the domination of northwestern Europe, it was hardly questioned. A lie repeated often enough begins to look like truth, and certainly, it began to look like truth to subsequent generations.

A powerful concept once created has a life of its own. This version of history was a powerful concept for what it explicitly claimed for the Western civilization as well as what it implicitly denied to all other civilizations. It was indeed a clever formulation. However, clever does not necessarily equal truth. As luck would have it, the ink was barely dry on this formulation when sciences of comparative linguistics and archeology were coming into existence toward the end of the eighteenth century. The next two centuries of Western historiography can be viewed as a spirited though wrong attempt to protect and defend this formulation in the light of new information from archeology, linguistics, and geology. But when truth is stretched beyond its limit, one can see right through it.

The first crack occurred in 1786 when a British Judge in Calcutta by the name of William Jones announced that several North Indian languages bore an unmistakable similarity to several European languages. He concluded that either Sanskrit or Latin were sister languages, with one of them possibly in the role of an older sister, or they had a mother–daughter relationship. Jones believed linguistic similarity necessarily implied a common group of people he called Indo-Europeans. He conceded the possibility that Indo-Europeans may have come out of India. Since this was 1786 and the British Empire was still young and growing, such an admission was not too damaging. Still, it was bothersome.

In the late eighteenth and early nineteenth centuries, the French discovered ancient Egyptian civilization with its amazing architecture and art. Fortunately, it was a dead civilization, but it was also geographically close to the Greek Islands. The Western version of history was rescued by making Egyptian civilization a heritage to the Western civilization. It was a safe thing to do since it was not a living civilization.

By the mid-nineteenth century, the British Empire was truly global. A German historian named Max Muller took up the nagging Indo-European issue again and proposed that an ancient people called Indo-European spoke an Indo-European language, lived on the steppes of central Asia, and invaded India around 1500 BC. This would be the first invasion of the subcontinent, the subsequent ones being those by Alexander, Arabs, Afghans, Mongols, and of course the British. This was a purely hypothetical construct without any analysis of the scared literature and strong oral tradition of the Indian subcontinent. However, it was presented as truth and incorporated into history books. Subsequent to Max Muller, just about every part of Europe has also been proposed as a potential home of the Indo-European people but without much success.

Near the end of the nineteenth century, another ancient civilization was discovered, this time in the modern Iraq. This civilization appeared even older than the Egyptian civilization. Fortunately, it was also a dead civilization—i.e., no continuity to the present—and by making it a heritage of Western civilization, the concept was rescued once again. It did not matter that until these civilizations were discovered, the West had no cultural memory of these civilizations. The need to preserve a hypothetical construct drove these accommodations.

As if on a cue, thirty some years later again, R. D. Bannerji discovered the Indus valley ruins in the Indian subcontinent in 1922 along the Indus River. Given the success in disposing the Egyptian and Sumerian civilizations as a post facto heritage of Western civilization, there was a need to conceive the Indus as older, dead, and divorced from the Vedic culture of Indo-Aryans preserved in the Rig Veda. This discovery was, therefore, seen as a proof of Muller's hypothesis. This was peddled despite the fact that there was not a shred of evidence of the invasion in the ruins discovered. The idea, to repeat, was that if the Indus valley civilization could be made older than and divorced from the Vedic culture of ancient India, then the Muller hypothesis could remain alive. As an aside, it may be of interest to know that in his old age, Muller, for reasons not well understood, repudiated his own hypothesis of the Aryan invasion of India. However, his denial never made it into the history books.

There were discoveries of the antiquity of the Chinese civilization over the last half a century. However, these discoveries were not perceived to be threatening to the history hypothesis for two reasons: the Chinese language never progressed beyond the syllabic stage and is totally unrelated to Indo-European languages, and Chinese civilization, though exceptionally successful in practical inventions, was unable to create science. And creation of science is what sets the West apart from everybody else in the eyes of Western historians.

To summarize, then, Western historians created a hypothetical construct in the eighteenth century to serve the political needs of the colonial establishment and have spent the last two centuries defending it in the light of new information. The issue of the Indo-Aryan invasion is most critical since if this invasion did not take place, then the home of Indo-Europeans languages could possibly be the Indian subcontinent, which means that ultimately, the roots of Western civilization grew out of the Indian subcontinent! That would clearly upset the whole apple cart.

Researchers, incidentally, face the same issue of a lack of facts when tracing the biological evolution and migration pattern of *Homo sapiens*. However, the former was confined to a much smaller geographical area in East Africa and the latter has been helped immensely by DNA tracer studies. The issue of a political agenda is also absent as both of these are far removed from both history and prehistory.

It is, therefore, important to keep in mind that the further back one goes in discussing this period, the more hypothetical one's assertions become, particularly if a cultural bias is suspected. As more research comes forth over the coming decades, perhaps we will get closer to the truth.

Appendix I
China and Alphabetical Script

Chinese civilization is the only primary civilization that did not to develop or adopt an alphabetical script. In this section, we will attempt to answer three key questions:

1. Why did the Chinese civilization not develop an alphabetical language?
2. How did logographic language impact the rise of science in ancient China?
3. How will the continued use of logographic language impact the future of independent science in China?

Why did China not develop an alphabetical language? All written languages have their origin in pictographs and ideographs to represent words and concepts. As symbols came to represent more words and concepts, a fundamental choice had to be made: break down spoken words, initially into syllables and later into consonants and shaping vowels, using unique symbols to represent words or continue to represent each word through a unique, complex symbol that utterly lacked phonetic analysis. A logograph is simply a rationalized, abstract system to represent words, with limited phonetic analysis, and relies on tonal variation. Chinese civilization chose to stay on the latter path of logograph. As long as the number of spoken words to be represented in the written form was small, the system could be made to work. However, as the number of spoken words to be represented in the written form increased, a five-tone system was imposed to keep the written characters under a few thousand characters, which is the practical upper limit for the number of complex characters that can be memorized. Using tones allowed one written character to correspond to five spoken words distinguished by the tones. As is clear, this would introduce imprecision in the written language due to an insufficient number of words, words with excessive overlapping meaning, and the inability to add new words with unique meaning.

The human mind seems to have a far greater memory for the spoken word compared to the number of unique complex written characters it can remember. We also note that the choice of the nonalphabetic path was obviously made in the absence of the unforeseeable future consequences. This, as we have noted before, is a recurring theme in history.

Chinese civilization also developed, for literally thousands of years, in relative isolation of other major civilizations. It is true that they constantly had to defend against the nomads from the north. They built the Great Wall to make this task easier. However, success in defending against the nomads, including civilizing and absorbing them, gave the Chinese civilization a sense of superiority as well as insularity. This was formalized in the political concept of the Middle Kingdom. Everybody outside the Middle Kingdom was generally believed to be uncivilized and inferior. This feeling of superiority persisted well into the modern era as hilariously captured in a letter from Chinese Emperor Chien Lung to King George III of England in 1792. In this letter, the Chinese emperor, oblivious of the realities of power, demanded of King George III a perpetual submission to the Chinese throne!

By the time the Chinese civilization learned about the alphabetical scripts perhaps toward the end of the reign of Zhous or later, too much had been invested in the highly developed logographic script. Language is the carrier of culture, and in the case of China; language was and still is an art form. It was therefore difficult, if not impossible, for China to make a switch to an alphabetical language without a pressing need. Even when a pressing need came with the rise of modern science, China adopted the approach of using English for science and continued the use of a simplified logographic script for all else. The Communist Party also resisted the switch to an alphabetical language. The party feared that it would give rise to an isolated intellectual class that would look down on the masses.

China's resistance to a switch to an alphabetical language points to a persistent pattern in history. The cultural genius of a people invents and develops an idea that is great for its time. It becomes an integral part of the culture. Times change and needs change; however, the culture is unwilling to discard the idea because it has too much physical and emotional energy invested in the idea. The same phenomenon, incidentally, occurs at the individual and organizational levels too, often with undesirable consequences. When this happens to a culture or civilization, the consequences over time can be disastrous. The only antidote against this type of cultural arthritis seems to be a belief in the inevitability of continued change and an understanding of the reasons an idea was good for its time but is no longer. In other words, a deep understanding of the history and knowledge of why the previous generations did what they did is critical to avoiding cultural arthritis through adopting change consciously. We return to this theme repeatedly in the book.

Impact on creativity in ancient China: Even a cursory look at China's long history shows an amazing outpouring of practical technology. A partial list would include, paper, the compass, the horse collar, wheelbarrows, the seismograph, matches, gunpowder, paper money, the kite, and even multistage rockets. Likewise, China developed a strong and independent tradition of art, architecture, astronomical observation, efficiency in manipulation of numbers using an abacus, and other physical artifacts. Finally, the Chinese civilization also developed remarkable concepts in practical philosophy and ethics as well as war strategy.

Innovative metaphysical systems, critical philosophy, and formal or natural sciences are missing from the above list. The principal reason for this glaring absence, in our judgment, is the lack of an alphabetical script. It should also be noted that China was able to maintain a prolonged political and cultural unity over an area far surpassing any other ancient civilization. We also find the principal reason for this to be a lack of alphabetical script. An alphabetical script is far more capable of evolution and over time leads to many differentiated but related scripts that are naturally unable to communicate with one other. In fact, both in Europe and India, the area covered by a particular alphabetical language typically does not cover an area extending around three to four hundred miles or less in all directions provided one properly takes into consideration the geographical features and imperial conquests. Without a modern means of transportation and communication, this size seems to be the limit of the reach of an alphabetical language and hence spoken language, culture, and ethnicity. In China, the size of an area under cultural unity is more than an order of magnitude higher. The spoken language in China developed hundreds of dialects, as everywhere; however, the written characters were too complex to evolve naturally except through an imperial dictates. The Chinese state was able to use a single written script to assert a central control over an area that was unheard of in the ancient world over long historical periods.

Logograph and the future of independent science in China: Some researchers recently have used the fact of ancient China's inability to develop science as a proof of racial or cultural inferiority. Claim has been made that long-term use of a nonalphabetical script impacted the Chinese culture's ability to reason abstractly, resulting in a "neurological gap" in the Chinese racial stock. Nothing could be farther from truth. One must distinguish between an ability to think abstractly and developing abstract thought systems precisely and efficiently. Clearly, the lack of an alphabetical script hinders development of abstract systems; it does not impact the racial potential. The former is merely a lingual issue, and the latter is a biological one. After all, the lack of an advanced number system did not stop Greeks from contributing to mathematical sciences or Romans from accomplishing engineering feats. One only need look at the accomplishments of Chinese foreign students overseas in the past decades to conclude that the concept of a neuro gap is bad science.

China has adopted a dual system, where English is used for mathematical sciences, and the Chinese logographic is used for all else. This certainly will not hinder the Chinese in using science. If the Chinese will have to switch to an alphabetical script and do away with logogram to develop world-class science is a question with an unclear answer today.

Finally, we note in passing that India is definitely moving in the direction of English as the written language of national unity, and it is the language used in most higher learning. But India retains use of nearly a hundred major dialects for spoken language and twenty-five plus written scripts. The change has been easier for India because the British colonizers forced English down the throats of Indians for nearly two hundred years, and native Indian languages have alphabetical script

Appendix J
Art and the Nava Rasa Theory of Aesthetics

Definition of Art

Art may be defined as something that, using an appropriate medium, evokes aesthetic pleasure in man. The aesthetic pleasure might involve a mere appreciation of likeness, experience of emotions or symbolic communication of a religious or secular theme, or simply joy of a creative form devoid of any inner meaning.

Categories of Fine Arts

Defined in the above manner, art embraces dance, music, poetry, literature, painting, sculpture, and theater. It is important to distinguish these fine arts from practical arts such as architecture and furniture design on the one hand and crafts such as engineering and farming on the other hand. Practical art combines art and utility while crafts exclusively focus on utility. Fine arts or simply art has little to do with utility.

Dimensions of Art

The dimensions of art are forms, content, and emotion. Most if not all art has elements of these three dimensions. However, their relative importance can vary to an extent that one of more of the dimensions may be practically absent. Historically, *Homo sapiens* invented art before science and philosophy but after language, practical technology, and early religion in the form of creation myths.

Types of Art

When an object of art evokes simple appreciation of likeness, it is called representational art. When the purpose of art is to evoke emotions in the spectator, it is called expressionist art. When the object of art simply presents a natural or humanly created form, it may be called formalistic art.

When art is used to convey ideas, it is called symbolic art, which may be further divided into sublime art with a religious theme or an abstract art with a secular theme. Symbolic art may be based on representational, expressionist, formalistic or symbolic art. Thus, in the final analysis, art is representational, expressionist, or formalistic.

What Does Art Require

Skill in execution is a common denominator required in every type of art. Beyond that, the requirements vary. For example, representational art requires a perceptual ability to be able to see an object as it really is. Creative imagination may be evident in the skill but is not needed by definition in representational art per se. Expressionist art requires understanding and imaginative use of emotions in the work of art. In expressionist art, the objective is to recreate the emotions experienced by the artist in a medium and to evoke a reaction to these emotions in the mind of the spectator. Formalistic art considered by some to be the only true form of art and aims at creating or appreciating interesting and pleasing forms in nature or created out of imagination. The latter, by definition, needs a highly developed imagination. Symbolic art requires a clear understanding of the idea to be conveyed. This idea may be conveyed in a straightforward representational, expressionist manner or in formalistic way.

Theories of Art

Creation and appreciation of art may involve the entire being of the artist or spectator: his perception, reason, and imagination on the one hand and his conscience, religiosity, and values, including even political values, on the other. Thus, the response to an object of art is complex and involves elements that are both subjective and objective. It is therefore not surprising that we do not have a comprehensive theory of art yet. The situation is not totally hopeless, however.

Representational art: Representational art is simply imitative. It is based on perception and skill in executing that perception in the chosen medium. Such an art is very amenable to rules based on measurements, proportion, and perspective. Representational art is also very teachable. For example, once the idea of perspective was perfected during the Italian Renaissance, it did not take too long for the entire community of artists to become good at it. One could argue that representational art is really not art, it is a skill as it does not create something new. Of course, in reality a great piece of representational art always embodies artists' imagination to varying degree since he wants to enhance what he is imitating. Plato believed that art is doubly imitative (he was referring to representational art only), since in his view existence itself was imitation of ideal forms that have existed from eternity. Thus, to the extent, a piece of art is representational, its theory is simply a theory of perception and such an art should be judged by skill of execution alone.

Expressionist art: Expressionist art is not imitative art as it aims at evoking emotions in the spectator through a unique work of art. It is a product of the artists' creative imagination and not just skill. Bharata proposed a theory of expressionist art centuries before the Common Era. It was termed the Rasa theory or theory of aesthetic pleasure. The Rasa theory viewed the artist as first subjectively experiencing the object of art being created and then objectifying that experience through a medium such as theater, sculpture, or painting, thus giving form to his formless subjective experience. The viewer then experiences similar or somewhat different emotions, depending on his own mood. Thus, art is a vehicle of self-expression for the artist, capturing that experience in the object of art, a way to communicate that experience to the viewer, and a way of reflecting on what is virtuous or meaningful in life on the part of the viewer.

The Rasa theory did not dwell on the form of the object of art; it focused on the subjective state that a work of art evokes. Thus, Rasa theory did not care to understand the perceptual or intellectual aspect of the art from a theoretical point of view. Bharata started with an analysis of the psyche (Bhava-Jagat) identifying eight inherent emotions (*sthayi bhavas*) and thirty-three transient emotions (*sanchari bhavas*) and a number of secondary emotions (*vibhavas or anubhavas*). The inherent emotions enumerated by Bharata are love (*rati*), comedy (*hasya*), tragedy (*shoka*), anger (*krodha*), valor (*utsah*), fear (*bhaya*), horror (*jugupsa*), and surprise (*vismaya*). Bharata theorized that an emotion etched into a medium is conveyed to the viewer through senses and transpired into Rasa, delighting the viewer. Rasa may be thought of as a unitary aesthetic channel through which the eight emotions express themselves through a work of art. Typically, one of these eight sentiments dominates in a particular piece of art.

A similar theory was proposed by Aristotle, and it focused primarily on the emotion of pathos or tragedy. Aristotle's main interest was to soften Plato's stand on art since Plato had banned the poets from his ideal republic. Plato believed that a focus on the emotion of tragedy (the staple of Greek drama) weakened the soul. Aristotle, on the other hand, wanted to readmit them to the ideal republic since he felt that enacting tragedy purged the soul through catharsis and made it stronger. However, Bharata's theory of expressionist art predates Aristotle and is vastly broader and positive in orientation.

Symbolic art: Until the eighteenth century, art was representational, expressive, or symbolic. However, since symbolic art uses expressionist, representational, or formalistic approach, we need not worry about a separate theory of symbolic art from an artistic point of view.

Formalistic art: Any theory of formalistic art must necessarily answer why certain forms or a combination of forms are considered beautiful or sublime even though they do not represent any known object, evoke an emotion, or convey a message. The only message is the form itself. The form may be a natural one or a creation of human imagination. Is such a judgment purely subjective or objective or both? A theory of formalistic art is only possible to the extent an aesthetic judgment is objective. There is reason to believe this is the case. Even the most primitive tribe will identify the prettiest woman in the tribe. Most people would agree on the beauty of an awe-inspiring flower or a natural scene.

Attempts by Hume and Kant in the eighteenth century to develop such a theory were not successful. Below, we summarize their views and suggest why such a theory is difficult to develop.

Hume essentially made five key points in his essay, *On Standard of Taste:* beauty in an object is not same as the emotion evoked by the object, not all art is equal, and there must be a standard of judging formalistic art, which he called taste. He said taste in art is a matter of sense perception and reason and that taste can be developed in a would-be ideal critic. He goes on to outline the characteristics of an ideal art critic. In his first observation, Hume intimates that he is chiefly concerned about formalistic art and betrays his prejudice concerning other art forms. However, his other observations do not exactly equal a theory of formalistic art, though it is hard to disagree with these rather straightforward observations. Hume's observations are simply a way to evaluate formalistic art in the *absence* of a theory of formalistic art.

Kant is more sophisticated, in part because he had the benefit of Hume's analysis, and since he respected Hume's contribution to philosophy in general, he decided to take up the issue of aesthetic judgment. Kant's theory is jargon-filled, as might be expected of a philosopher of his caliber. In simple terms, Kant's analysis showed that aesthetic judgment results from a complex interaction between perception, reason, and imagination. It is, therefore, both subjective and objective. The feeling of pleasure arises because we perceive that form of the object can be comprehended by the faculty of understanding and a belief that others who have the similar cognitive faculty can also understand the same object. It is as if Kant is saying that pleasure in art results from the anticipation of understanding that never quite fully materializes, certainly not through his theory! Kant makes an important distinction between the beautiful and sublime, the latter including a moral judgment, in addition to an aesthetic judgment. The problem with Kant's observations in the context of aesthetic theory is that one could say the same about the form of a complex, hard-to-understand object that is perceived to be ugly. Thus, Kant's analysis may be regarded as an assessment of the limitations and potential of human perception and reason in the face of complexity and no more.

Another theorist, Bell, in the twentieth century theorized that true art is formalistic art and that significant form, that is, forms and relations of forms, in a work of art evokes a uniquely aesthetic emotion. However, the existence of a unique aesthetic emotion remains a conjecture, and the definition of significant form in an object of art remained undefined. It is not clear, for example, how this uniquely aesthetic emotion is different from one that may be experienced by a mathematician after solving a historically significant, outstanding mathematical problem.

It seems that the aesthetic pleasure of formalistic art occurs when the object of art has an engaging form and has complex, higher properties such as harmony, balance, symmetry, and movement. These higher properties are noted by senses and are appreciated by reason in a general way. Formal art engages the mind without yielding to it, but reason keeps the hope of understanding alive. A theory of formal art from a mathematical point of view must be a theory of separating out a subset of infinite combination of forms with higher properties universally judged to be beautiful. An analysis of these higher properties would then constitute a theory of formalistic art. Needless to say, developing such a theory indeed is a tall order.

In summary, we have a theory of representational and expressionist art; however, a theory of formalistic art does not exist despite an effort by some of the best minds over the last several centuries, during which formal art has come into existence.

Art and Civilizations

Given the above remarks, it is clear that the orientation of ancient Greek art was primarily representational art of high skill with a focus on the human form. It has significant debt to the ancient Egyptian civilization with a similar orientation. Ancient Indian art is primarily expressionist and sublime in nature. This is hardly surprising, given the values and religiosity of ancient Indian civilization. Chinese art throughout the course of its civilization has also been representational art, but with a primary focus on nature with an early discovery of perspective, long before the Italian Renaissance. Chinese art also appears to have elements of impressionism. Italian Renaissance art is also representational with complete mastery of perspective and a dual focus on nature and human form as well as symbolic art with religious themes.

Finally, modern art over last two hundred years first went through an impressionistic phase starting about the mid-nineteenth century that was in part a reaction to the new science of photography. Photography seemed to pull the rug from under the representational art, and it reacted by going impressionistic. Following the impressionistic phase, art turned to formalistic and symbolic, with cubism as an example.

Art is one of the most doubly imitative significant creative activities of human civilization, its nature and form being determined by the deeper values of a particular civilization. Its hallmark is using powers of perception, imagination, and emotion. With formalistic art, reason begins to play an increasing role.

Appendix K
The Theory of Vaisheshika School

Many authors have commented on the Vaisheshika (which means *particularity*) school, but it is still misunderstood and underappreciated. In this appendix, we will present an analysis and interpretation of the Vaisheshika school in the following manner:

- Focus separately on metaphysics, ethics, epistemology, and speculative natural science embedded in Vaisheshika.
- Examine Vaisheshika natural science in the light of the modern science. In so doing, we hope to get a glimpse of how the Vaisheshika school could have eventually evolved over time into natural science through application of experimental method.

In so doing, we believe that the brilliant epistemology and nascent natural science embedded in this school will become clearer, and we hope this school will take its deserved position in the history of science and will be judged to be comparable in achievement to Panini's grammar. We must keep in mind that a perfect grammar could be developed without the experimental method 2,500 years ago. However, one could not develop error-free natural science without the experimental method. That is why nascent natural science must necessarily be speculative, and hence we must accord Kanada the honor of father of natural science.

Our Approach to Vaisheshika School

The Vishesha school starts by distinguishing between two different categories of objects (*patharathas*): objects that exist in the world independent of human desire for knowledge and "objects" that human beings need to create knowledge. In the former category, called substances (*dravaya*) there are three classes identified: matter, space/time, and consciousness/mind/God. Kanada then discusses the qualities and drivers or forces of change of state in each applicable class of substances. All objects in this category exist prior to any knowledge of them. Thus, Vaisheshika is a system based on philosophical realism in that while it admits nonmaterial entities, it also asserts the possibility of knowledge. In the second category, Kanada developed the key elements of his theory of epistemology, namely, generality, particularity, sensation, and inference. He then discusses his epistemology at great length, giving examples, and goes on to describe in detail the nature of these concepts.

We propose the following to separate metaphysics, speculative natural science, ethics, and epistemology in the Visheshka system:

- Classify the Vaisheshika analysis of consciousness, mind, and God as *metaphysics*
- Classify the Vaisheshika analysis of the two classes of substances, matter and space/time, as *natural science*
- Recognize Kanada's system embodying the mental categories of generality, particularity, sensation, and inference as *epistemology*
- Characterize Kanada's observations concerning moral behavior as *ethics*

We will now describe the Visheshka school along these four dimensions, demonstrating how the Vaisheshika school produced the first significant human achievement in natural science, how Vaisheshika's metaphysics contains nothing that was not already known, and how his epistemology was simply brilliant and right on the mark. We also wish to suggest that Kanada's real interest was natural science, and even his epistemology was an outgrowth of his interest in natural science. He probably felt compelled to include metaphysics and ethics in his work for two reasons: for the sake of completeness and in keeping with the norms of the period.

A. Metaphysics of Vaisheshika

The metaphysics of Vaisheshika is straightforward dualism. Vaisheshika stipulates an omniscient and omnipotent God whose intelligence, grace, and effort are eternal. He governs the universe but has no need to entangle himself in the cycle of existence. He is beyond the universe and thus transcendent. He is infinite and eternal. Consciousness and atoms are also uncreated and are eternal. While the atoms are infinitesimal, consciousness is infinite. As a result, consciousness is not movable (how do you move the infinite?). Kanada wrongly ascribes the bodily functions to consciousness, clearly not being aware of the functions of the brain. The mind, on the other hand, is infinitesimal but also eternal. It is therefore, able to move and go with the body. A key function of the consciousness is to direct the attention of the mind, leading to the possibility of knowledge of the world. The eight attributes of the consciousness are pain and pleasure, awareness of ethical and unethical, likes and dislikes, and intellect and will. The chief functions of the mind are as a tool of and a repository of knowledge generated. The existence of God, consciousness, mind, and atoms must be inferred as they are not known by senses. For example, the mind is inferred through the existence of knowledge. Consciousness may be inferred from the fact of sensation, which is different from both sense organs and the object of sensation. Awareness of objects is, thus, the proof of the existence of consciousness. Atoms are inferred from the superficial impermanence of matter. Thus, we can see that Kanada uses his theory of epistemology to establish the existence of all significant categories in his metaphysics.

Today, of course, we would consider the brain and associated mind to perform nearly all the functions Kanada attributed to consciousness and would consider the latter to be finite in space and time and unable to exist without body. Perhaps Kanada can be excused for these glaring errors in his metaphysics because of the limited knowledge of anatomy and psychology in his day.

Metaphysics is neither the most important or most original part of the Vaisheshika school.

B. Natural Science of Vaisheshika

As we said above, Kanada's analysis of the two classes of substances—matter and space/time—constitutes his natural science. Every substance Kanada defined is established through sensation or inference, and he goes on to establish their nature in detail.

Space and time: Kanada postulated space and time as infinite and eternal. The phenomenal world is a process that takes place in space and time. Reality is perceived as things moving, changing, coming into being, and as passing out of existence. This process is ordered, implying the existence of a reality that has a general relationship to the process of change. This reality is time and is considered as an independent reality pervading the entire universe. Time is responsible for the relations of simultaneity and nonsimultaneity, prior and posterior, etc. We cannot know time as such but can understand its pervasiveness through the process of change. Time is individual in character, meaning it has no lower species. Time also has the qualities of conjunction (*samayoga*) and disjunction (*vibhaga*), meaning it is continuously analyzable. Conventional units of time, such as day or hour, are derived by abstraction from concrete time and confirmed by measurement. Similarly, space is also infinite and eternal and is individual in character. Just as things move in time, they hold together in space. Space makes it possible to have a sense of direction, allowing us to understand the spatial relation of things, such as nearness and farness. The reality of space is inferred through the extension of things. Like time, space also has the qualities of conjunction and disjunction. Space and time in short are similar to the later Newtonian concept of space and time. They are conceived as real and not logical categories of existence.

Atomic theory of matter: The atomic theory of matter Kanada proposed started with the observation that material things are made up of the four observable elements (*bhutas*) of earth, fire, water, and air. These four elements are not eternal. Therefore, he wanted to understand the unchanging and eternal reality behind these changeable elements. Kanada called these eternal entities atoms (*paramanu*). In a brilliant leap of imagination, Kanada proposed the existence of molecules (*anu*). He believed that atoms by themselves are not productive. Atoms must combine with similar atoms to form dyads or triads and these dyads and triads then form the basic building blocks of ordinary matter, whose physical size depends on the number of dyads and triads. Both atoms and molecules are infinitesimal, but only atoms are eternal. The four bhutas of earth, fire, water, and air possessed their characteristic quality of touch, taste, color, and odor respectively. Although when destroyed they may lose these qualities perceived by the senses, these properties continue unperturbed at the atomic level. Clearly, Kanada's atomic theory is negated by today's science at innumerable points. However, considering the lack of experimental method, it must be regarded as simply a brilliant first attempt by man to understand the natural world based on sensual perception and subtle inferential logic.

Properties and actions: Kanada was not content to speculate about the atomic theory of matter. In fact, his interest in the atomic theory of matter resulted from his observations of ordinary perceptible matter. In addition to the four bhutas indicated above, Kanada's theory had a fifth element called *akasa* or ether. He was forced into postulating this fifth element to account for the existence of the sensation of sound. He wrongly believed that sound was carried not by air but through vacuum or ether. Thus, he has five elements at the gross matter level that correspond to the five senses. The properties (*guna*) of the ordinary matter Kanada enumerated may be classified into two broad classes: qualitative and quantitative. The former includes the five properties that correspond to the five senses, four of these have basis in properties of the bhutas and the fifth in akasa, and properties that arise from aggregate matter not atoms. This latter group includes properties such as gravity (*gurutva*), fluidity (*dravatva*), viscosity (*snigdhatva*), and inertia (*samskara*). The quantitative properties, on the other hand, are five in number, namely, number, size, individuality, farness, and nearness. While the qualitative properties are objective or based on sensation, the quantitative properties are more logical in character.

Ordinary matter not only possesses properties but is also influenced by actions (*karma*). Karma has been generally translated as action or activity. However, it is more appropriate to translate it as "effect of force or energy" on ordinary matter. Kanada did not develop the concept of force or energy. These concepts had to wait nearly two thousand years. Though not aware of these concepts, Kanada could clearly see their effects on the properties the ordinary matter exhibited. He observed and classified these effects quite clearly, as we shall see below. Thus, his concept of Karma, a word borrowed from Vedic metaphysics, may be regarded as the first precursor of the idea of force and energy. Kanada was quite clear about the relationship between ordinary matter, properties, and actions. He stated that only matter possessed properties and was affected by actions. Properties depend on matter and cannot possess other properties or matter. Properties may be destroyed in causal processes. Actions have specificity and only operate on one matter at a time. Actions do not possess qualities; they are independent causes and cannot create other causes. Basically, stated in modern terms, Kanada's world of ordinary matter consisted of matter in space/time whose properties could be changed by invisible (*adarshta*) karma or forces and energy. This was quite an achievement considering that he drew these conclusions based on gross observations and in the complete absence of controlled experiments.

Vaisheshika's natural science: The most interesting and startling aspect of the Vaisheshika school is Kanada's physics and chemistry. It is absolutely incredible that his physics have not been accorded its proper place in the history of science. Kanada basically sees two types of actions: those that occur at the ordinary matter level and those that occur at the molecular level. The former are generally "visible" while the latter are not. In the former category, Kanada identifies five actions: those of dropping (*avaksepana*), lifting (*utksepana*), contraction (*akuncana*), expansion (*prasarna*), and movement (*gamana*).

In modern language, we can identify the first action as effect of gravity (vertical force), the next three as the effects of heat or energy, and the last as the effect of a horizontal force. Through these actions, ordinary matter, more or less may retain its identity. In the second category, the actions are invisible. Therefore, Kanada postulates the existence of certain generic invisible processes to explain the change of state. He identifies the processes of conjunction (*samayoga*), disjunction (*vibhaga*), inherence (*samavaya*), and cocombination (*ekarthasamavaya*). In modern language, we may identify the first two as akin to reversible physical changes, such as evaporation and condensation, and the latter two as akin to irreversible chemical changes. Kanada also uses these generic processes to explain some of the actions at the macro level. In other words, the actions at the macro level have processes as their counterpart at the molecular level.

- Kinematics or horizontal motion: Kanada describes horizontal motion correctly by stating that action produces motion, the relationship of the motion to the object being that of samavaya or inherence meaning they cannot be separated. The motion (*vega*) continues until checked by an obstacle or gravity. In modern language, this may be stated as "a body in motion stays in the state of motion until it is acted on by a force." The property of Inertia is associated with the horizontal movement of solids and those of fluidity and viscosity to the fluid state.
- Heat: Kanada identifies effects of heat as expansion/contraction and lifting with solids and fluids respectively.
- Gravity: The property gurutva is inherent in matter and causes objects to fall.
- Physical change: The processes of conjunction and disjunction are invoked to explain physical changes, such as melting.
- Chemical change: The processes of combination and cocombination are used to explain irreversible and invisible chemical change. Kanada does not mention reversible chemical change.

In summary, the natural science imbedded in the Vaisheshika school sees a lawful universe with a Newtonian space and time pervading it. The atoms, which are indestructible, combine to create molecules, and then gross matter. The gross matter, when acted on by forces and energy, changes its properties. One can see beginnings of the theories of gravity, thermal changes, kinematics, physical chemistry, and chemical reactions in Kanada's brilliant observation based speculative science.

C. Epistemology of Vaisheshika

Kanada was not a philosopher who happened to be interested in science. Rather, he was a scientist at heart who was forced into developing a theory of knowledge needed for his science. This distinction is essential to understanding his epistemology.

Laws of casualty: Kanada saw the relationship between cause and effect as that of inherence. He identified two broad laws of casualty: from the nonexistence of the cause, we may infer the nonexistence of the effect, but from the nonexistence of the effect, we may not infer nonexistence of the cause.

Two valid means of knowledge: Two means of knowledge are possible: sensation and inference. In Vaisheshika's theory of knowledge, to know certain objects, one only needs sensation; inference is not needed. As one examines different levels of phenomenon, one needs to use inference to know.

Theory of inference: The key concepts in Kanada's theory of inference (*laingika*) are general (*samanaya*), particular (*vishesha*), sensation (*pratyaksa*), deduction, and induction.

The idea of general or universal is required to identify what is common to a group of entities. A property residing in many things is called *samanya* (or general). Generality is regarded as residing in many things belonging to the group of substance, quality, or action. Generality comes in grades. Thus, the quality *jarness* is general when it is regarded as residing in many things, and it is particular when it is used to distinguish jars from other objects.

By particularity, one can perceive things that are different from one another. If a property is regarded as distinguishing it from others, it is called particular or *vishesha*. The same property, if present in many things, could be called general. Thus, particularity is relative to thought. Individuality, on the other hand, is a uniqueness or particularity that resides in eternal substances such as space, time, matter, and mind. The particularity of these entities is thus the particularity of the individuals and not of classes.

Kanada suggests that generality and particularity are relative to thought, intellectual devices by which the variety of phenomena are classified. Yet they may be derived from real entities.

Sensation is simply what is perceived by the senses of sight, touch, taste, smell, and hearing. As mentioned above, Kanada wrongly attributed the sensation of hearing as dependent on ether.

By induction and deduction, Kanada meant a logical process by which one can establish the existence of something that cannot be established by sensation alone. Though one or more qualities or properties serve as a middle term, one can establish the presence of something else that these properties characterize, and in the absence of which that something cannot appear. Thus, inference for Kanada included both the process of induction (creation of the middle term) and a process of deduction. The process of deduction in Vaisheshika is not all that different from that of the Nyaya system. The uniqueness of Vaisheshika lies in its process of induction.

As an example of induction and deduction, Kanada gives horns, a tail with hairs at the end, and dewlap as the collection of characteristics of the Indian cattle defining the middle term. Apparently, those features are necessary together. If we see this collection of characteristics in an animal, then by virtue of the known relationship, we can infer the animal in our presence to be cattle. Note that the first part of the process is induction and the second part is deduction.

Kanada not only used the process of inference in a rather straightforward example above but also in establishing existence of less obvious entities. For example, consider the substance of air. Because air can be felt and is yet invisible—and there is no other substance like it—it must be a substance because it has property (touch) and is amenable to action (motion). Thus, the existence of air may be established through inference. Likewise, Kanada established the existence of atoms and molecules through the process of inference.

Kanada also established the existence of certain concepts also through inference. For example, the idea of inherence is established through inference. Take the example of matter in motion. Kanada noticed that motion once imparted to an object cannot be separated from it without one of them being destroyed. Similarly, the relationship of parts to whole and cause to effect is that of inherence. Inherence or *samavaya* literally means "this in that."

Invalid means of knowledge: Kanada identified four invalid sources of knowledge: errors in sensation (*andhyavasya*), errors in inference (*viparyaya*), dream (*sapna*), and doubt (*samsaya*). The latter may be regarded as an inability to draw conclusions.

Errors in induction: Mistakes are possible in induction. Kanada identifies two errors in the process of inference using induction: including a false property (*anapadesa*) and having insufficient properties. For example, including red spots as a property in the above example of Indian cattle would constitute false property, and horns alone might constitute a case of insufficient properties.

Method of exhaustion: When all other possibilities have been exhausted (*parisesa*), the remaining one may be accepted as the correct conclusion based on induction.

The crowning achievement of Kanada's epistemology was his theory of Inference, tying together the processes of induction and deduction in a brilliant manner.

D. Ethics of Vaisheshika

There is not much in Kanada's ethics that was new or revolutionary or not included in the earlier works, such as Veda and Upnishads. Vaisheshika makes a clear distinction between voluntary and involuntary actions and holds that moral distinctions only apply to the former. It also asserts that a great soul is not one that gives up the world but one that takes the vow of the welfare of others, presumably including the work of science. Vaisheshika lists thirteen universal duties of an ethical person that emphasized physical purity, psychological straightforwardness, welfare of others, and devotion to God.

We hope this presentation of Vaisheshika clearly demonstrates that Vaisheshika was a first and significant human effort to understand nature without invoking God. It obviously got most specifics wrong from the perspective of modern science. However, that can hardly be otherwise. The greatness of Vaisheshika lies in its fundamentally scientific orientation and its subtle and brilliant epistemology.

Appendix L
Who Invented Syllogism?

The reconstruction of ancient Indian science is not too dissimilar to fighting an urban guerrilla war, where a researcher is forced to conquer one city block at a time. That it is so should not come as a surprise, given the generations of outstanding and at times faulty research done by Western scholars often serving an imperialistic or racial agenda. Ancient Greek pioneers are never mentioned by ancient Indian pioneers; however, ancient Indian pioneers are often mentioned in the Greek literature as gymnosophists. Despite this well-known fact, many Western commentators on ancient Indian achievements never fail to ask if Indian achievements were influenced by the Greek work with tiresome predictability. Lack of understanding the context of Indian achievements also gives these researchers a license to belittle these achievements. The issue of precedence also looms large in these discussions, often complicated by an inability to date these materials. The development of syllogism is a case in point that we briefly wish to examine in this appendix.

Three ancient civilizations may be said to have concerned themselves with the origin and early development of the logical syllogism: Indian, Greek, and Chinese. The Arabs openly acknowledged their debt to the Greeks in general and to Aristotle in particular. Since our concern here is the origin and early development of logic, we will not focus on the substantial Arab contributions since they occurred comparatively recently and may be considered a continuation of the Greek tradition. In China, the Mohist school indeed delved into conditions of valid inference. One of the offshoots of this school was called the logicians and investigated some aspects of formal logic. This early start, however, came to an end when the Qin dynasty chose to adopt the philosophy of legalism, suppressing all others, including Confucianism and Taoism. Further development of logic had to wait until the introduction of Buddhist philosophy in China, centuries later. The Mohist work, incidentally, also includes early ideas on geometry and the atomic theory of matter.

This leaves us with the Indian and Greek traditions as far as the early development of logical syllogism is concerned.

Roots of Syllogism

There are three potential routes to the emergence of logical syllogism: number theory, linguistic theory, and geometry. It is instructive to note how these routes are different, why Indian and Greek thinkers chose different routes, and the impact of those choices on the nature of the syllogism each developed.

In both number theory and linguistic theory, the nature of inference required to develop the needed axioms or self-evident truths is quite different. In number theory and linguistic theory, the nature of inference needed is abstract and is not easily deducible from practical experience. On the other hand, the nature of inference involved in geometry is more practical and concrete and can be comprehended practically. This is because one can "see" the truth of the axioms through geometrical figures. Thus, the inference needed in linguistic theory and number theory is of a higher order compared to a relatively simple process of inference involved in axioms of geometry. As a result, ancient Indian thinkers became more familiar with the process of inference that preceded the use of deductive logic in a particular science.

That the Greek thinkers focused on geometry as an early science is not surprising because of its practical value in architecture. The Greek civilization had a more practical orientation than the Indian civilization and was spiritually immersed in shallow polytheism. Greek academies were founded to educate the elite class in charge of practical affairs. Indian thinkers, on the other hand, focused on number theory and linguistic theory early on. The developments in linguistic theory, astronomy, geometry, and number theory were linked both to their spiritual aspirations and practical needs. The perfected word was needed to communicate with the gods, arithmetic helped developed speculative theories of cosmology, geometry helped design altars for worship, and astronomy helped pinpoint the auspicious time for the elaborate ceremonies. In other words, the development of logic was intertwined with the spiritual needs, more so than in the case of Greek civilization.

The Nyaya School and Aristotle

Aristotle's syllogism was relatively straightforward, comprising of three statements:

- All men are mortal.
- Socrates is a man.
- Socrates is mortal.

It consisted, therefore, of an axiom, a fact, and a conclusion derived from the axiom and the fact.

The Nyaya "syllogism" consists of five statements:

- There is fire.
- There is smoke with the fire.
- Where there is fire, there is smoke.
- The hill is smoking.
- The hill is on fire.

The first three statements constitute the process of inference that leads to the axiom: where there is fire, there is smoke. The last three statements constitute the Aristotelian syllogism, with first statement acting as the axiom, the second as a fact, and the third being the conclusion drawn from the axiom and the fact. In other words, Nyaya logic consists of a process of inference followed by a process of deduction. It thus represents both inferential logic and a syllogism. In other words, it is an epistemological statement and not just a deductive syllogism. It represents the complete process of science and not just a process of mathematical deduction. Aristotle's syllogism is contained in the Nyaya School; however, the reverse is not true. In Aristotle, the process of inference is implicit and unconscious.

Western Critique of Aristotle and Nyaya

As the center of gravity of science began to move to western Europe in the second half of the sixteenth century, Francis Bacon, among others, began to see the limitations of Aristotle's logic with respect to the process of emerging science. He explicitly emphasized the need for observation and the process of inference based on observation and imagination. The skepticism of David Hume concerning the truth of the process of inference was still centuries away. Thus, Western European science rather unceremoniously pushed aside Aristotle as something narrow and developed the process of inference critical to science in the seventeenth and eighteenth centuries. In the nineteenth century, philosophy picked up on the critical relevance of inference, with Hegel and Mill explicitly according inference a place of honor in epistemology.

By the nineteenth century, two new developments had taken place: further development of the Neo-Nyaya school in India had long ceased because of Islam's success in controlling southern India by the early eighteenth century and later because of European control of the subcontinent in the late eighteenth century. The Nyaya school was discovered by European scholars, who initially received it enthusiastically but a generation later vilified it as such discoveries and praise did not neatly fit into the civilizing mission slogan of the British Raj in India. Let us review each of these developments briefly.

Neo-Nyaya School: The neo-Nyaya School was founded by philosopher Ganesa Upadhaya in the thirteenth century to respond to the increasing influence of Vedanta, a monist school based on Upanishad philosophy. His book, *Tattvacintimani*, examined the criticism of the Nyaya school's ontology of realism from the Vedanta perspective and placed the Nyaya epistemology on four pillars: perception, inference, deduction, and testimony or indirect perception. Obviously, the authors of neo-Nyaya never treated their system as a mere syllogism, thus continuing the Nyaya tradition. For them, it was an epistemology based on realism. As Islam gained control in the subcontinent, science died a slow death. By the time the Europeans arrived in India, the country, though wealthy, had little intellectual life left. The neo-Nyaya school too had withered, along with the general decline of science.

European discovery: H. T. Colebrooke discovered the Nyaya school and published an essay in 1824. He was chiefly responsible for its dissemination among the leading European mathematicians such as Boole, De Morgan, and Hamilton as well as English philosophers of logic. An essay written by Max Muller on the Nyaya school was included in Thompson's *Laws of Thought* for nearly thirty years in successive editions. Muller even entertained the idea that Aristotle might have learned about the syllogism from India. Similarly, John Stuart Mill, who was critical of Aristotle's syllogism from an epistemological standpoint, put forth a theory very similar to that of the Nyaya school. He made no reference to the Nyaya school despite spending most of his adult life as a colonial office in British India! Quite the contrary—he was very dismissive of Nyaya Indian logic in general. Thus, we see that within a span of half a century, European openness about the Nyaya school gave way to outright criticism. During this same period, Europe developed similar epistemology and made great strides in new types of mathematical logic, based on binary systems, set theory, and analysis of infinity.

By the end of the nineteenth century, Indian nationalism was ascendant and wanted to base itself intellectually on the spiritual/mystical heritage of Indian civilization to distinguish itself from the West, thus continuing to undervalue the scientific heritage of Indian civilization. This state of affairs has only begun to change in the last quarter century.

Vindication of Ancient Indian Position

In the last 150 years, mathematicians have thoroughly revamped the foundations of mathematical logic:

- Successful establishment of number theory as the basis of algebra and geometry and not the other way around as the ancient Greek pioneers believed.
- Development of binary logic and set theory (both concepts existed in ancient Indian systems) that has led to a convergence between mathematical logic and linguistic theory through development of Boolean and propositional logic.

Thus, we may conclude the following:

- The epistemology of the Nyaya school includes the process of inference, something absent in Aristotle's simpler syllogism.
- Research is needed to determine if Aristotle was aware of the Anviksiki (literally, "science before observation") school, a forerunner of the Nyaya school, formulated by Medhatithi Gautama in the sixth century BCE through Alexander. That would also help explain the sudden reversal of Palo's idealist position by Aristotle and successfully turning the Greek thought from pure idealism to Nyaya realism.
- The impact of European discovery of the Nyaya school and ideas about binary numbers and set theory from ancient Indian writings on the development of European logic in a completely non-Aristotelian direction in the nineteenth century was substantial and has not been given its due.

We conclude with an observation of Herman Weyl, an eminent German mathematician of the twentieth century: Occidental mathematics has in the past centuries broken away from the Greek view and followed a course that seems to have originated in India and that has been transmitted to us by the Arabs with additions; in it the concept of numbers appear logically prior to the concepts of geometry.

SELECTED BIBLIOGRAPHY

Chapter 1: Nature of Science
1. Popper, Karl R. (2002) [1959]. *The Logic of Scientific Discovery*. New York, NY: Routledge Classics.
2. Nola, Robert; Irzik, Gürol. (2005). *Philosophy, Science, Education, and Culture*. Science & Technology Education library Series Vol. 28. Springer.
3. Fara, Patricia. (2009) *Science: A Four-Thousand-Year History*. Oxford: Oxford University Press.
4. Kuhn, Thomas. (1962) *The Structure of Scientific Revolutions*.
5. Augros, Robert M.; Stanciu, George N. (1984), *The New Story of Science: Mind and the Universe*. Lake Bluff, IL: Regnery Gateway.

Chapter 2: Framing Issues—Civilizations and Evolution of Science
6. Gaukoger, Stephen. (2006) *The Emergence of a Scientific Culture: Science and the Shaping of Modernity 1210–1685*. Oxford: Oxford University Press.
7. C. Brinton, J. Christopher, and R. Wolff (1984). *A History of Civilization: Prehistory to 1715* (6th ed.). Englewood Cliffs, NJ: Prentice Hall.
8. Huntington, Samuel P. (1997) *The Clash of Civilizations and the Remaking of World Order*. London: Simon & Schuster.

Chapter 3: Emergence of *Homo sapiens*
9. Trevathan, Wenda R. (1 May 2011). *Human Birth: An Evolutionary Perspective*. Transaction Publishers. Amazon.co.uk.
10. Hill, Andrew; Ward, Steven. (1988) "Origin of the hominidae: The record of African large hominoid evolution between 14 my and 4 my." *Yearbook of Physical Anthropology*: 31.
11. Shreeve, James. (1996) *The Neanderthal Enigma: Solving the Mystery of Modern Human Origins*. Viking.
12. Roberts, Alice. (2009) *The Incredible Human Journey: The Story of How We Colonized the Planet*. Bloomsbury.
13. Stringer, Chris; McKie, Robin. (1996) *African Exodus: The Origins of Modern Humanity*. Jonathan Cape.
14. Stringer, Chris. (2011) *The Origin of Our Species*. Allen Lane.

Chapter 4: Emergence of Civilization
15. Childe, Gordon V. (1925) *Dawn of European Civilization*. London: K. Paul, Trench, Trubner & Co.
16. Sauer, Carl O. (1952) *Agricultural Origins and Dispersals*. Cambridge, MA: MIT Press.

Chapter 5: Inner Nature of *Homo sapiens*
17. Gärdenfors, Peter. (2003) *How Homo Became Sapiens: On the Evolution of Thinking*. Oxford University Press.

Chapter 6: *Homo sapiens* Creativity
18. Simonton, D. K. (1999) *Origins of Genius: Darwinian Perspectives on Creativity*. Oxford University Press.
19. Gabora, Liane. (1997) "The Origin and Evolution of Culture and Creativity." *Journal of Memetics—Evolutionary Models of Information Transmission*: 1.
20. Dacey, John. (1999) "Concepts of Creativity: A History." In Gardner, H., & Sternberg, R., Eds. *Encyclopedia of Creativity*, 3 Vols. San Francisco: Academic Press.
21. Robinson, Andrew. (2010) *Sudden Genius: The Gradual Path to Creative Breakthroughs*. Oxford: Oxford University Press.

Chapter 7: Temporal Framework
22. "Timeline of World History," Wikipedia. February 5, 2014.

Chapter 8: Driving Causes and Outcomes of Social orders

23. Mithen, Steven. (2003) *After the Ice: A Global Human History, 20,000 to 5,000 BC*. Cambridge, MA: Harvard University Press.
24. Hicks, Jim. (1974) *The Empire Builders*. New York: Time-Life Books.
25. Hobsbawm, E. J. (1989) *The Age of Empire, 1875–1914*. Boothbay Harbor, ME: Abacus Books.
26. Ferguson, Niall. (2004) *Empire: How Britain Made the Modern World*. Penguin Books.
27. Smith, Simon C. (1998) *British Imperialism 1750–1970*. Cambridge University Press.
28. Blainey, Geoffery. (2000) *A Short History of the World*. Victoria: Penguin Books, Australia.
29. *The Biosphere* (A *Scientific American* book). (1970) San Francisco: W. H. Freeman and Co.

Chapter 9: Theory of Interacting Social Orders

30. Hechter, M.; Horne, C. (2003) *Theories of Social Order. A Reader*. Stanford University Press.
31. Ukagba, George. (2013), *The KPIM of Social Order*. Xlbris Corporation.

Chapter 10: The Essential Set of Participants

Chapter 11: Birth, Development and Maturation of Protoscience

32. Bunch, Bryan; Hellemans, Alexander.(2004) *The History of Science and Technology*. Scientific Publishing.
33. Rajaram, N. S. (2006) *Saravati River and Vedic Civilization*. Aditya Prakashan.
34. Frawley, David. (2001) *The Rig Veda and History of India*. Aditya Prakashan.
35. Rajaram, N. S. (1993) Aryan Invasion of India: The myth and the truth, Voice of India.
36. Renfrew, Collin. (1973) *Before Civilization: The Radiocarbon Revolution and Prehistory of Europe*. London: Penguin Books. New York.
37. Seidenberg, A. (1978) The Origin of Mathematics, Archives for History of Exact Sciences: 18: 30–42.
38. Seidenberg, A. (1978) *The Ritual origin of Geometry*, Archives for History of Exact Sciences: 1: 488–527.
39. "History of India." Wikipedia. July 7, 2014
40. "History of Egypt." Wikipedia.June 6, 2014
41. "History of Mesopotamia." Wikipedia. June 3, 2014
42. "History of Ancient China." Wikipedia. July 3, 2014

Chapter 12: Birth of Science

43. Bunch, Bryan; Hellemans, Alexander. (2004) *The History of Science and Technology*. New York, NY: Houghton Mifflin Co.
44. History of Ancient India, Wikipedia
45. History of Ancient Greece, Wikipedia
46. History of Mesopotamia, Wikipedia
47. History of Ancient China, Wikipedia

Chapter 13: First Synthesis in Science

48. Bunch, Bryan; Hellemans, Alexander. (2004) *The History of Science and Technology*. New York, NY: Houghton Mifflin Co.
49. History of India, Wikipedia
50. History of Ancient Greece, Wikipedia
51. History of Ancient Roman Republic, Wikipedia
52. History of Roman Empire, Wikipedia
53. History of Persian Empires, Wikipedia
54. History of China, Wikipedia

55. History of Central Asian Nomads, Wikipedia
56. History of Hellenistic States, Wikipedia

Chapter 14: Second Synthesis in Science
57. Bunch, Bryan; Hellemans, Alexander. (2004) *The History of Science and Technology*. Scientific Publishing
58. History of India, Wikipedia
59. History of Roman Empire, Wikipedia
60. History of Byzantine Empire, Wikipedia
61. History of Persian Empires, Wikipedia
62. History of China, Wikipedia
63. History of Central Asian Nomads, Wikipedia
64. History of Arabs, Wikipedia

Chapter 15: Third Synthesis in Science
65. Bunch, Bryan; Hellemans, Alexander. (2004) *The History of Science and Technology*. Scientific Publishing.
66. History of India, Wikipedia
67. History of Byzantine Empire, Wikipedia
68. History of European Civilization, Wikipedia
69. History of Persian Empires, Wikipedia
70. History of China, Wikipedia
71. History of Central Asian Nomads, Wikipedia
72. History of Muslim Civilization, Wikipedia

Chapter 16: Fourth Synthesis in Science
73. Bunch, Bryan; Hellemans, Alexander. (2004) *The History of Science and Technology*. Scientific Publishing.
74. History of India, Wikipedia
75. History of China, Wikipedia
76. History of Byzantine Empire, Wikipedia
77. History of European Civilization, Wikipedia
78. History of central Asian Nomads, Wikipedia
79. History of Muslim Civilization, Wikipedia

Chapter 17: Mature Science
80. Bunch, Bryan; Hellemans, Alexander. (2004) *The History of Science and Technology*. Scientific Publishing.
81. History of India, Wikipedia
82. History of China, Wikipedia
83. History of European Civilization, Wikipedia
84. History of Muslim Civilization, Wikipedia

Chapter 18: Looking Back: Inner Nature, Civilizations and Science

Chapter 19: Conclusion and Lesson of History

Chapter 20: Glimpses of Future
85. Cornish, Edward. (2005) *Futuring: The Exploration of the Future La Vergne*, TN: Ingram

INDEX OF KEY CONCEPTS

Assessment of inner nature of social orders
    Abstract systems-building capability, 72-74, 108
    Creed, 108, 110
    Geographical isolation, 109
    Early success with nomads, 109
    Institutional greed, 110
    Linguistic isolation, 109
    Natural bounty, 108
    New technology adoption, 108
    Relative economic freedom, 108
    Social cohesion processes, 108
    Wealth allocation, 114
Classes of science, 34
Constructive outcomes
    Abstract systems-building capability, 87
    Fair trade, 87
    Peaceful migrations, 87
    Practical, religious and intellectual creativity, 87
Creative outcomes
    Intellectual, 85
    Practical, 85
    Religious, 85
    Abstract systems-building capability, 85
Destructive outcomes
    Empire building, 89
    Systematic wealth drain, 89
    Violent colonization, 89
Epochs
    Biological, 43
    Hunting-gathering, 43, 48-52
    Neolithic, 43, 52-56
    Civilization, 43, 56-57
Eras of civilization
    Peaceful interaction era, 76
    Standalone era, 75-76
    Violent interaction era, 76
Essential participants of history, 120
External peaceful perturbations
    Abstract systems-building capability, 101
    Fair trade, 101
    Institutional structures and processes creativity, 101
    Peaceful migrations, 101
    Practical, religious and intellectual creativity, 101
External violent perturbations
    Empire building, 102-103

    Systematic wealth drain, 104-106
    Violent colonization, 103-104
Fixed yet flexible inner nature of *homo sapiens*
    Conscience, 62
    Creative, productive and constructive powers, 62
    Free will, 61
    Necessity of beliefs, 63
    Self-consciousness, 61
Forms of Creativity
    Intellectual creativity, 68
    Practical creativity, 67
    Religious creativity, 67-68
High level outcomes of social orders
    Internal creative balance, 71
    Openness/insularity of social orders, 109
    Sustainable growing surplus, 91
    Sustained political independence, 112
Inner nature of social orders
    Constructive capacity of a social order, 107
    Creative capacity of a social order, 107
    Destructive capacity of a social order, 107
    External orientation, 111
    Productive capacity of a social order, 107
Instincts, 44
Internal perturbations
    Factors of knowledge replenishment, 98-100
    Factors of wealth replenishment, 98-100
Intrinsic causes
    Economic organization, 80
    Educational Institutions, 82
    Internal wars, 82
    Knowledge-creating Institutions, 81
    Legal systems, 81
    Military capability, 81
    Political system, 81
    Social cohesion processes, 82
    Social structure, 81
    Systems of religious faith, 81
    Wealth allocation processes, 82
Knowledge stock of a social order, 85
Life stages of civilization
    Literate, 74
    Mature literate, 74
    Pre-literate, 74
    Pre-scientific, 74

Rational, 74
　　　Scientific, 74
　Life stage of science
　　　Birth stage of protoscience, 74
　　　Birth stage of science, 74
　　　Development stage of protoscience, 74
　　　Development stage of science, 75
　　　Mature stage of protoscience, 74
　　　Mature stage of science, 75
　Logical stages of science, 75
　Natural causes
　　　Astronomical, 80
　　　Climatic, 80
　　　Ecological, 80
　　　Geographical, 80
　　　Geological, 80
　Phases of science
　　　Birth phase, 77
　　　First synthesis, 78
　　　Fourth synthesis, 78
　　　Mature phase, 78
　　　Protoscience phase, 77
　　　Second synthesis, 78
　　　Third synthesis, 78
　Productive outcomes
　　　Internal trade, 85
　　　New products and services, 85
　　　Wealth production, 84
　Social system as interlocking social orders, 94-95
　Unique mental attributes of *homo sapiens*
　　　Imagination, 46
　　　Observation, 46
　　　Reason, 46
　Unique physical attributes of *homo sapiens*
　　　Erect walking, 46
　　　Speech, 46
　Wealth stock of a social order, 85

www.ingramcontent.com/pod-product-compliance
Lightning Source LLC
Chambersburg PA
CBHW080526170426
43195CB00016B/2482